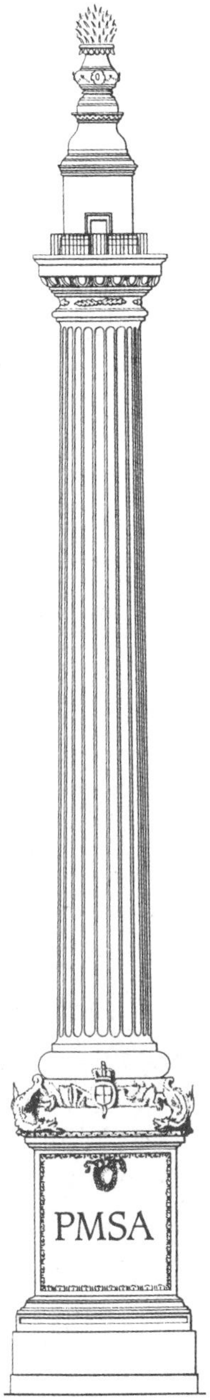

PUBLIC SCULPTURE OF BRITAIN VOLUM

Public Sculpture of Bristol

Public Monuments and Sculpture Association
National Recording Project

In grateful memory of Louis Sherwood
1941–2009

Already published in this series

PUBLIC SCULPTURE OF LIVERPOOL
by Terry Cavanagh

PUBLIC SCULPTURE OF BIRMINGHAM
by George T. Noszlopy, edited by Jeremy Beach

PUBLIC SCULPTURE OF NORTH-EAST ENGLAND
by Paul Usherwood, Jeremy Beach and Catherine Morris

PUBLIC SCULPTURE OF LEICESTERSHIRE AND RUTLAND
by Terry Cavanagh, with an Introduction by Alison Yarrington

PUBLIC SCULPTURE OF GLASGOW
by Ray McKenzie, with contributions by Gary Nisbet

PUBLIC SCULPTURE OF WARWICKSHIRE, COVENTRY AND SOLIHULL
by George T. Noszlopy

PUBLIC SCULPTURE OF THE CITY OF LONDON
by Philip Ward-Jackson

PUBLIC SCULPTURE OF GREATER MANCHESTER
by Terry Wyke with Harry Cocks

PUBLIC SCULPTURE OF STAFFORDSHIRE AND THE BLACK COUNTRY
by George T. Noszlopy and Fiona Waterhouse

PUBLIC SCULPTURE OF SOUTH LONDON
by Terry Cavanagh

PUBLIC SCULPTURE OF HEREFORDSHIRE, SHROPSHIRE AND WORCESTERSHIRE
by George T. Noszlopy and Fiona Waterhouse

In preparation

PUBLIC SCULPTURE OF OUTER SOUTH AND WEST LONDON
by Fran Lloyd, Helen Potkin and Davina Thackara

PUBLIC SCULPTURE OF CHESHIRE AND MERSEYSIDE (EXCLUDING LIVERPOOL)
by Edward Morris and Emma Roberts

PUBLIC SCULPTURE OF NOTTINGHAMSHIRE AND DERBYSHIRE
by Stuart Burch and Robert Burstow

PUBLIC SCULPTURE OF LANCASHIRE AND CUMBRIA
by David Cross

PUBLIC SCULPTURE OF EDINBURGH
by Dianne King

PUBLIC SCULPTURE OF SHEFFIELD AND SOUTH YORKSHIRE
by Darcy White, Elizabeth Norman and David Ball

PUBLIC SCULPTURE OF HERTFORDSHIRE AND BEDFORDSHIRE
by Barbara Thompson

PUBLIC SCULPTURE OF SOUTH-WEST SCOTLAND
by Ray McKenzie

PUBLIC SCULPTURE OF WESTMINSTER
by Philip Ward-Jackson

PUBLIC SCULPTURE OF BERKSHIRE, BUCKINGHAMSHIRE AND OXFORDSHIRE
by Simon Lee, Sue Malvern, Eckart Marchand and Brian O'Callaghan

PUBLIC SCULPTURE OF SUSSEX
by Peter and Jill Seddon

PUBLIC SCULPTURE OF NORFOLK AND SUFFOLK
by Richard Cocke

PMSA website: www.pmsa.org.uk
Bristol City Council public arts projects since 2000: www.aprb.co.uk

Public Sculpture of Britain Volume Twelve

PUBLIC SCULPTURE OF BRISTOL

Douglas Merritt and Francis Greenacre

with Katharine Eustace

LIVERPOOL UNIVERSITY PRESS

Front cover image: David McFall, *Unicorn*, 1950,
Bristol Council House.
Back cover image: Walter Ritchie, panel from
Creation, 1986, Lower Maudlin Street.
Cover design by Vivienne Palfreyman.

First published 2011 by LIVERPOOL UNIVERSITY PRESS,
Liverpool, L69 7ZU

HERITAGE LOTTERY FUND

The National Recording Project is supported by the
National Lottery through the Heritage Lottery Fund

British Library Cataloguing-in-Publication Data
A British Library CIP record is available

ISBN 978-184631-638-8 (paperback)
ISBN 978-184631-481-0 (hardback)

Design and production, Grant Shipcott

Typeset in 9/11pt Stempel Garamond
by XL Publishing Services, Tiverton, Devon
Originated, printed and bound in Great Britain by
Henry Ling Ltd, Dorchester

The Henry Moore Foundation

The Paul Mellon Centre *for Studies in British art*

The Society of Merchant Venturers

The Friends of Bristol Art Gallery

BCDP culture | ideas | arts and sciences

GWEBusinessWest

AlecFrench Architects

Preface

This is the twelfth volume of a series which will eventually cover the whole of Britain. The project was the initiative of the Public Monuments and Sculpture Association, which was founded in 1991 by Jo Darke. Jo died in June 2010. She was a vital member of the Editorial Board for these volumes and was always the main inspiration and principal force behind the Association. Without her this series would never have been begun and only with her continued support could it ever have reached this twelfth volume.

As with the other volumes, the catalogue excludes sculpture in art galleries and museums and for reasons of space it cannot comprehensively cover cathedral and church monuments. However, Katharine Eustace's revealing essay on Bristol's church monuments demonstrates how well ecclesiastical sculpture and monuments reveal and illustrate the history of a city. She confirms the individuality of Bristol's masons and statuaries and their comfortable interaction with the leading metropolitan sculptors of the day.

A Bristol volume was always a high priority. Rysbrack's great equestrian statue of William III, 'England's main civic icon of Whig loyalism', was once the most famous public sculpture in Britain. At a time when Bristol was commissioning major works from both the leading sculptor and the leading artist of the day, Rysbrack and Hogarth, the city was also impressively self-sufficient, with a number of local workshops and an outstanding dynasty of native sculptors and architects in the Paty family. In the nineteenth century notable Bristol sculptors were to move to London, including E. H. Baily, James Havard Thomas and C. J. Pibworth, but each returned to Bristol to execute important commissions. The tradition of rich architectural sculpture established by the Patys in the eighteenth century was to be continued to outstanding effect by Foster and Wood and well into the twentieth century by Sir George Oatley. It has been maintained for the last half-century by the Alec French Partnership.

Bristol has been quick to recognise the role of sculpture in urban renewal and regeneration. The three sculptures on Baltic Wharf, including *Atyeo* by Bristol-born Stephen Cox, are early and fine examples. More recently still, there have been works that have challenged and expanded our understanding of the medium itself. It is this continuity of interest and quality that makes the sculpture of this city of special interest. Bristol has been a major regional centre for over a thousand years and its fascinating history is reflected in its monuments, just as much of the history of British sculpture is reflected in the public sculpture within the city.

The Public Monuments and Sculpture Association is concerned not only to further the appreciation and study of public sculpture, but to encourage its conservation. The great wealth of information that this volume makes conveniently available should encourage Bristol to plan for the care of its rich heritage. In this Bristol does have one advantage. For several centuries it was Britain's second city, but by the mid-eighteenth century it was being superseded by its familiar rival, Liverpool. In the nineteenth century Bristol expanded greatly, but more slowly than the industrial cities to the north. As a result, although the quality of Bristol's monuments and architectural sculpture is exceptional, the quantity is smaller and the consequent burden should be more manageable.

It is now almost fifteen years since I asked Francis Greenacre, then Curator of Fine Art at Bristol Museum and Art Gallery, to set up a survey of Bristol's public sculpture as part of the Public Monuments and Sculpture Association's National Recording Project. He had by then been Curator of Fine Art at Bristol Museum and Art Gallery for twenty-eight years and had been closely involved with the restoration of the Edward VII Memorial Fountain and of the mediaeval sculptures within St Mary Redcliffe. Douglas Merritt, Honorary Visiting Professor of Graphic Design at the University of the West of England, bravely undertook the research. The project was initially generously supported by the trusts of two Bristolians, the late Richard Lalonde and Sir James Tidmarsh. Their encouragement proved to be vital evidence of local support and a crucial component of the Association's successful application to the Heritage Lottery Fund for a nation-wide survey of public sculpture. The Faculty of Art, Media and Design of the University of the West of England subsequently supported the project and now holds the archive of the recording project for the South West Region, which itself was largely the creation of Douglas Merritt and Janet Margrie.

In 2002 Douglas Merritt's book *Sculpture in Bristol* was published by Redcliffe Press with the financial assistance of Bristol City Council, Arts Council England and, most generously, of the late Louis Sherwood. The present volume considers three times as many works in very much greater depth. Francis Greenacre had been assisting Douglas Merritt since 2006. Following Douglas's illness in 2007 he undertook to bring the volume to completion. The two authors have undertaken both the research and photography and have borne all the associated costs. Most of the photographs were taken very recently by Francis Greenacre. Generous grants towards the costs of the production of this book have come from the Henry Moore Foundation and the Paul Mellon Centre for Studies in British Art. Crucial local sponsorship is most gratefully acknowledged by the authors below.

Edward Morris, Chairman of the Editorial Board

Authors' Acknowledgements

We have enjoyed the assistance of sculptors, artists and architects, librarians and archivists, curators, wardens, custodians, conservators and historians, both professional and amateur. Their ready and sympathetic response to our enquiries and requests has ensured that research has always been a pleasure and we are very grateful for much help over many years.

There must be exceptions to such necessarily impersonal acknowledgements. Dr Pat Prior kindly made her unpublished study on the statue of *Neptune* available and Dr Sarah Whittingham generously supplied important information from her book on Sir George Oatley before it was published. Anthony Beeson, who retired last year after 38 years as the Fine Art Librarian, created the Bristol Central Library's sculpture files, which have been a vital source of information. The assistance of the staff at Bristol Record Office and of Andy King, Sheena Stoddard and Karin Walton at Bristol Museum and Art Gallery has been exemplary. Chris Bertram and Gerry Nichols have readily supplied photographs, when the authors were defeated.

We are especially grateful to Katharine Eustace, now editor of the *Sculpture Journal*. In 1982, when at Bristol Art Gallery, she organised the outstanding Michael Rysbrack exhibition. Her essay on Bristol's church monuments greatly broadens the scope of this volume and confirms the importance of Bristol's own sculptors.

In the early days of the PMSA survey in the later 1990s two professors at the University of the West of England, Dr Paul van der Lem and Dr Paul Gough, arranged additional funding for the Bristol survey and enabled its extension to cover the South West Region until mid-1999. Michael Liversidge, lecturer in the History of Art at the University of Bristol and later Dean of the Arts Faculty, was also of great assistance to the project and, more recently, the Professor of the History of Art, Dr Elizabeth Prettejohn, has been a helpful advocate for the publication of this volume. Edward Morris, as Chairman of the Editorial Board, has a title calculated to disguise the importance of his role as the manager of this most demanding series of publications. The publication of this, the twelfth volume, is a special tribute to his encouragement and determination as well as to the continued commitment of the Liverpool University Press. Grant Shipcott is now both designer and typesetter for the series and he has done an outstanding job.

Bristol has itself given most important financial support towards the publication costs of this volume. The late Louis Sherwood, to whose memory this volume is most gratefully dedicated, was very closely involved with the Bristol Cultural Development Partnership and GWE Business West and both of these organisations have contributed generously. The Society of Merchant Venturers and the Friends of Bristol Art Gallery have also helped to make publication possible. The Alec French Partnership, architects with a long tradition of commissioning sculpture for their buildings (to Bristol's considerable benefit), have given us vital assistance.

Our personal debts go deeper than we can properly express. Janet Margrie, Douglas's partner of the past twenty-two years, agreed in 1995 to work with him on the project. Janet, an artist and architectural historian, has done much more than that and, when Douglas fell ill, she gave all possible assistance to ensuring that work continued. Mary, my wife, has generously shared my enthusiasm. And both Douglas and I have proudly enjoyed the privilege of taking due advantage of the particular skills of our respective children.

Francis Greenacre and Douglas Merritt
March 2010

Contents

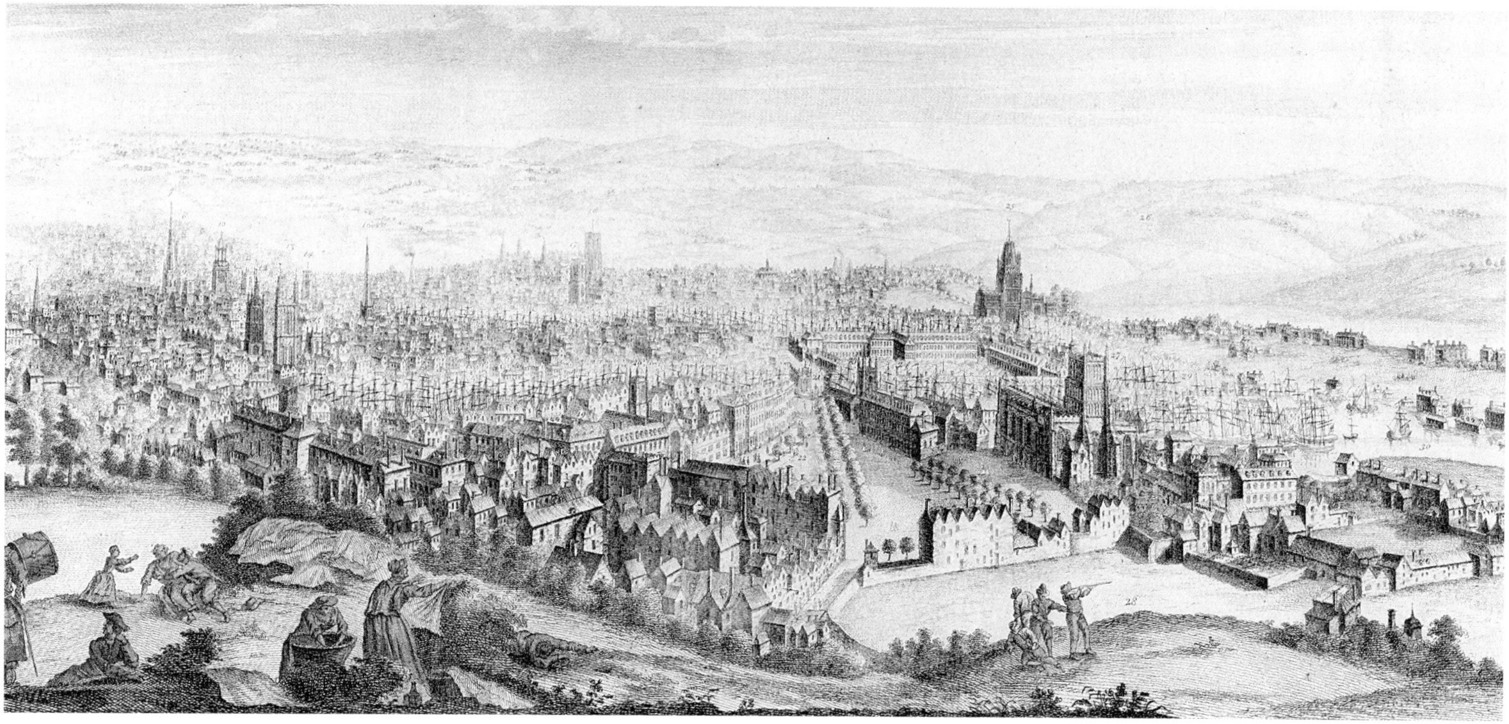

Fig. 1 *The north-west prospect of the City of Bristol* (detail), engraving by Samuel and Nathaniel Buck, 1734 (Society of Merchant Venturers)

Map A

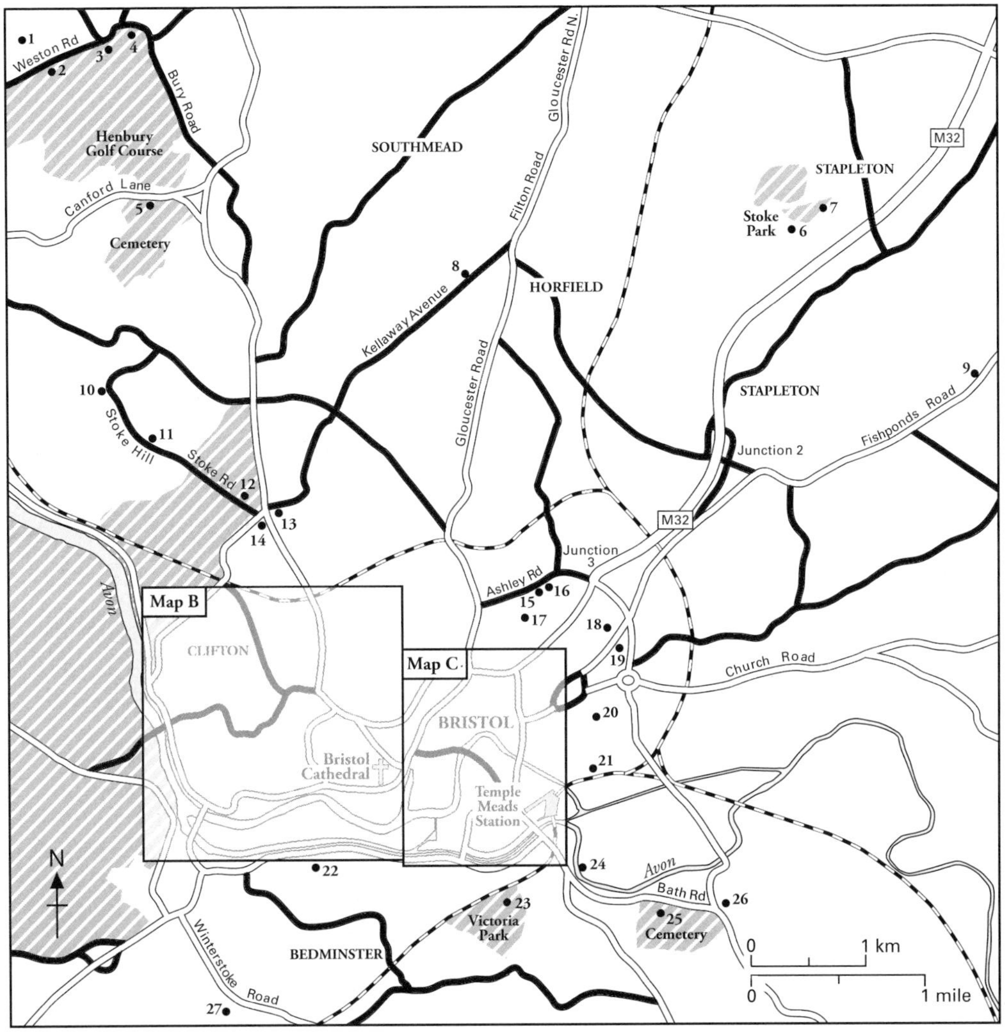

A1 Blaise Hamlet – *Pump and sundial*
A2 Blaise Castle Estate – *Guard Dog*
A3 Blaise Castle House – *Urn*
A4 Rectory Gardens – *Neptune*
A5 Canford Cemetery – *Christ the King*
A6 Stoke Park – *Obelisk*
A7 Stoke Park – *Sarcophagus*
A8 Horfield Common – *Drinking Fountain*
A9 Fishponds Road – *War Memorial*
A10 Stoke Hill – *Jubilee Fountain*
A11 Stoke Hill – *Trinity College portico*
A12 Stoke Road – *Drinking Fountain*
A13 Redland Hill – *Obelisk*
A14 Blackboy Hill – *Drinking Fountain*
A15 Ashley Road – *Alfred Fagon*
A16 Ashley Road – *Greater Crested Plunger*
A17 Grosvenor Road – *All our tomorrows*
A18 Armoury Square – *Edward Colston*
A19 Stapleton Road – *Caterpillar*
A20 St Philips Road – *Twisted Arch*
A21 Oxford Street – *D of the Dings*
A22 Beauley Road – *Roundel*
A23 Victoria Park – *Maze*
A24 Albert Road – *Basset Hounds*
A25 Arno's Vale Cemetery – *Raja's tomb*
A26 Bath Road – *Gateway statues*
A27 Winterstoke Road – *Four Bristol scenes*

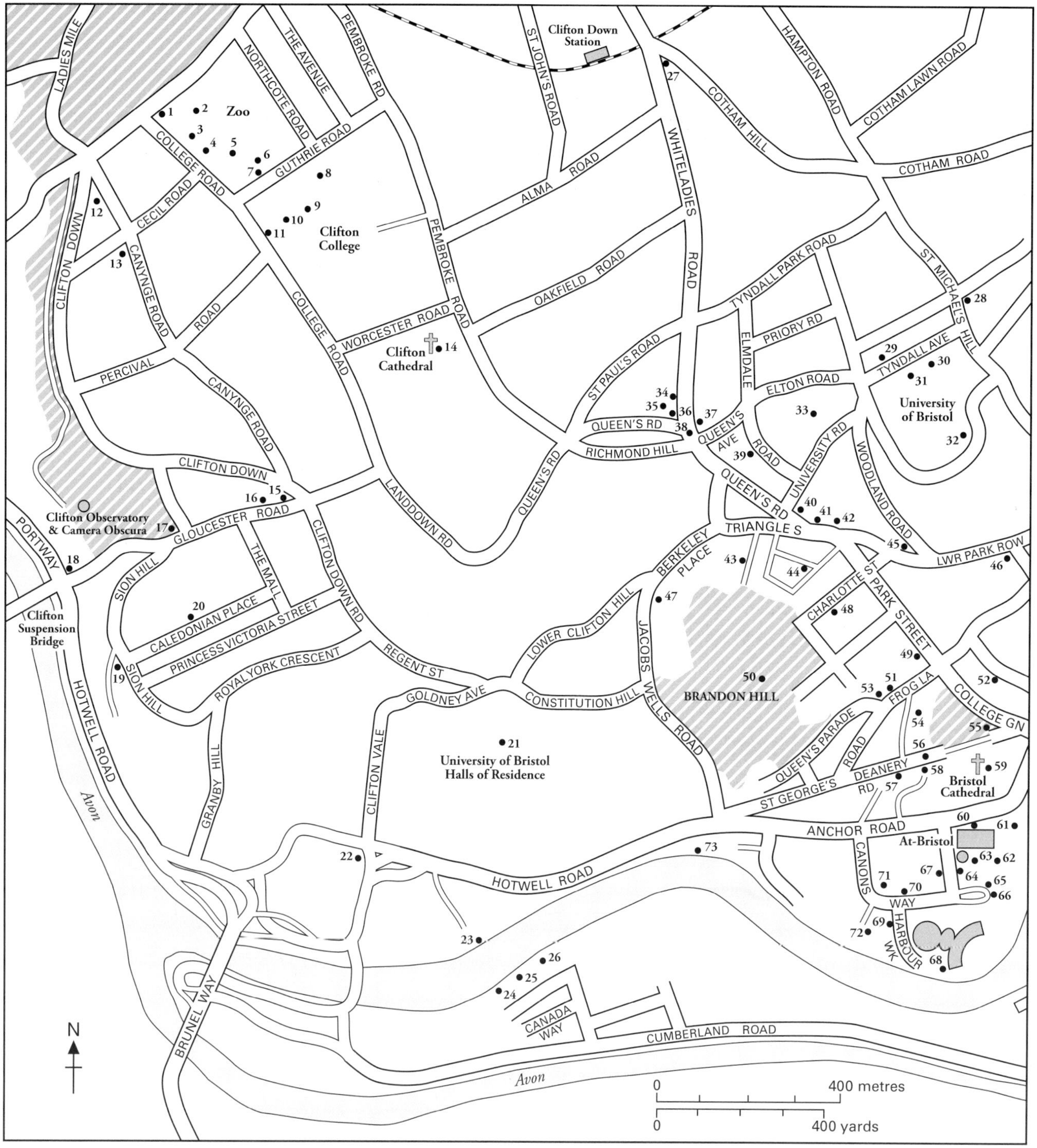

Clifton Down Station
LADIES MILE
NORTHCOTE ROAD
THE AVENUE
PEMBROKE RD
ST JOHN'S ROAD
HAMPTON ROAD
COTHAM LAWN ROAD
Zoo
COTHAM HILL
COLLEGE ROAD
GUTHRIE ROAD
ALMA ROAD
WHITELADIES ROAD
COTHAM ROAD
CECIL ROAD
Clifton College
PEMBROKE ROAD
CLIFTON DOWN
CANYNGE ROAD
OAKFIELD ROAD
TYNDALL PARK ROAD
ST MICHAELS HILL
ROAD
COLLEGE ROAD
WORCESTER ROAD
Clifton Cathedral
ELMDALE
PRIORY RD
TYNDALL AVE
PERCIVAL
ST PAUL'S ROAD
ELTON ROAD
University of Bristol
CANYNGE ROAD
QUEEN'S RD
QUEEN'S AVE
ROAD
RICHMOND HILL
UNIVERSITY RD
QUEEN'S RD
CLIFTON DOWN
WOODLAND ROAD
QUEEN'S RD
Clifton Observatory & Camera Obscura
GLOUCESTER ROAD
LANDDOWN RD
CLIFTON DOWN RD
TRIANGLE S
PORTWAY
LWR PARK ROW
BERKELEY PLACE
SION HILL
THE MALL
CHARLOTTE ST
PARK STREET
Clifton Suspension Bridge
CALEDONIAN PLACE
PRINCESS VICTORIA STREET
LOWER CLIFTON HILL
JACOBS WELLS ROAD
REGENT ST
ROYAL YORK CRESCENT
SION HILL
GOLDNEY AVE
CONSTITUTION HILL
BRANDON HILL
FROG LA
COLLEGE GN
HOTWELL ROAD
University of Bristol Halls of Residence
QUEEN'S PARADE
ROAD
GRANBY HILL
CLIFTON VALE
ST GEORGE'S
DEANERY RD
Bristol Cathedral
Avon
ANCHOR ROAD
At-Bristol
HOTWELL ROAD
CANONS WAY
HARBOUR WK
BRUNEL WAY
CANADA WAY
CUMBERLAND ROAD
Avon
N
0
400 metres
0
400 yards
1 2 3 4 5 6 7 8 9 10 11 12 13 14 15 16 17 18 19 20 21 22 23 24 25 26 27 28 29 30 31 32 33 34 35 36 37 38 39 40 41 42 43 44 45 46 47 48 49 50 51 52 53 54 55 56 57 58 59 60 61 62 63 64 65 66 67 68 69 70 71 72 73

Map B

B1 Clifton Down – *Lodge frieze*
B2 Clifton Down – *Tree of Life*
B3 Clifton Down – *Girl and Kid*
B4 Clifton Down – *Mute Swan*
B5 Clifton Down – *Elephant Tower*
B6 Clifton Down – *Alfred*
B7 Clifton Down – *Ying and Yang*
B8 College Road – *John Percival*
B9 College Road – *S. African War Mem.*
B10 College Road – *Earl Haig*
B11 College Road – *Memorial gateway*
B12 Clifton Down – *Proctor's Fountain*
B13 Clifton Down – *Thomas Proctor*
B14 Worcester Road – *Katyn memorial*
B15 Clifton Down – *79th Regiment of Foot*
B16 Clifton Down – *William Pitt*
B17 Susp. Bridge Road – *Drinking Fountain*
B18 Susp. Bridge Road – *Brunel plaque*
B19 Princes Lane – *Caryatids*
B20 Mall Gardens – *Shooting Star*
B21 Clifton Hill – *Hercules, River God etc.*
B22 Trinity Place – *Simon Short fountain*
B23 Poole's Wharf Court – *Untitled*
B24 Baltic Wharf – *Topsail*
B25 Baltic Wharf – *Atyeo*
B26 Baltic Wharf – *Hand of the River God*
B27 Whiteladies Road – *Kings and Queens*
B28 Myrtle Road – *Microscopic Observations*
B29 Tyndall Avenue – *Flat Out*
B30 Tyndall Ave. – *Stretching a Point*
B31 Tyndall Ave. – *Entrance surround etc.*
B32 Royal Fort Gardens – *Classic Flight*
B33 University Road – *Dr J. W. Caldicott*
B34 Whiteladies Road – *Four Atlantes*
B35 Queen's Road – *Goddess of Wisdom*
B36 Queen's Road – *Edward VII, fountain*
B37 Queen's Road – *Reynolds, Flaxman etc.*
B38 Queen's Road – *Glos. Regimental Mem.*
B39 Elmdale Road – *Aesop's Fables*
B40 Queen's Road – *Capitals*
B41 Queen's Road – *Arts, Atlantes, Lions*
B42 Queen's Road – *Nine muses etc.*
B43 Upper Byron Place – *Virgin and Child*
B44 Berkeley Square – *Bristol High Cross*
B45 Park Row – *Nipper*
B46 Park Row – *Sir Charles Wetherell*
B47 Jacob's Wells Road – *Q. E. H. Schoolboy*
B48 Great George St. – *Girl into reed...*
B49 Park St. – *Bristol, Minerva and Apollo*
B50 Brandon Hill – *Cabot Tower*
B51 St George's Road – *Horse and Man*
B52 Denmark St. – *Gaunt's House reliefs*
B53 St George's Road – *I.K. Brunel*
B54 College Green – *John Cabot, Twinned Cities, Unicorns, Seahorses and Riders and Raja Rammohun Roy bust*
B55 College Green – *Queen Victoria*
B56 College Green – *Raja Rammohun Roy*
B57 College Green – *Library reliefs etc.*
B58 College Green – *Gatehouse figures*
B59 College Green (churchyd.) – *Refugee*
B60 Anchor Road – *Small Worlds*
B61 Millennium Sq. – *Beetle*
B62 Millennium Sq. – *Aquarena*
B63 Millennium Sq. – *Zenith*
B64 Millennium Sq. – *Tyndale, Penn, Chatterton* and *Movie Star*
B65 Millennium Sq. *Bill and Bob*
B66 Millennium Sq. *Telespine*
B67 Harbourside – *Field of Play*
B68 Harbourside – *The Pavilion*
B69 Harbourside – *Weathervane*
B70 Harbourside – *Secret Industry*
B71 Harbourside – *Parallax*
B72 Harbourside – *Domain*
B73 Hotwell Road – *Samuel Plimsoll*

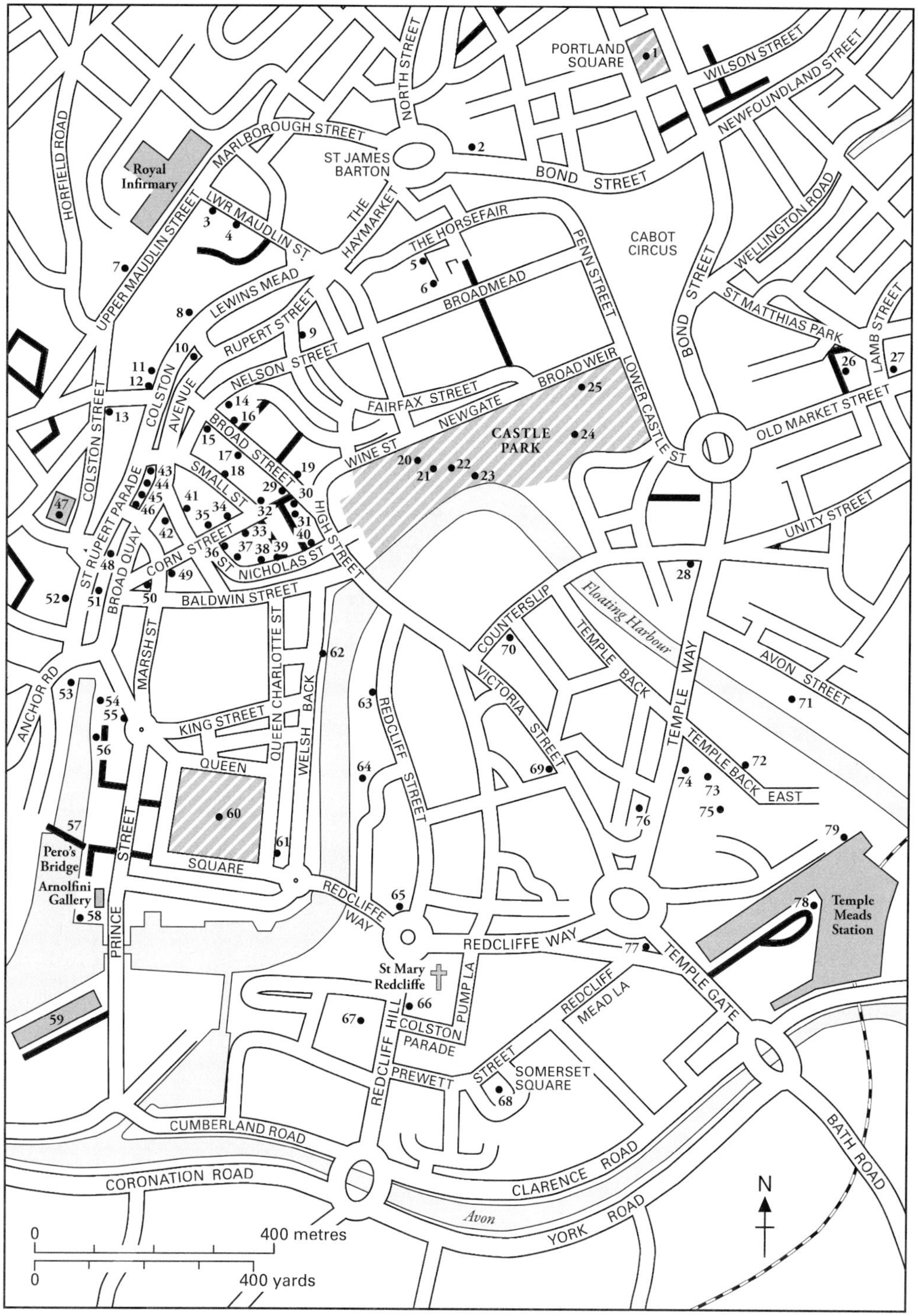

Map C

C1 Portland Sq. – *George III (formerly)*
C2 St James's Barton – *Spirit of Bristol*
C4 Lower Maudlin St. – *Creation*
C5 Horsefair – *Charles Wesley*
C6 Horsefair – *John Wesley*
C7 Upper Maudlin St. – *Lollypop Be-bop*
C8 Lewins Mead – *St Francis of Assisi*
C9 Bridewell Street – *Justice*
C10 Lewins Mead – *Samuel Morley*
C11 Lewins Mead – *Cloaked Horseman*
C12 Christmas St. – *Virgin and Child*
C13 Colston St. – *John Foster etc.*
C14 Nelson Street – *St John's Conduit*
C15 Broad Street – *Brennus and Bellinus*
C16 Broad Street – *Edward Everard*
C17 Broad Street – *Guildhall figures*
C18 Small Street – *Victoria and Albert*
C19 Broad Street – *Quarter Jacks*
C20 Castle Park – *Line from Within*
C21 Castle Park – *Throne*
C22 Castle Park – *Beside the still waters*
C23 Castle Park – *Drinking Fountain*
C24 Castle Park – *Play sculpture*
C25 Castle Park – *Only dead fish...*
C26 Old Market St. – *Ald. John Barnstaple*
C27 West Street – *Telamones*
C28 Narrow Plain – *Oracle*
C29 Corn Street – *Justice*
C30 Corn Street – *The Bristol Nails*
C31 Corn Street – *Exchange decoration*
C32 Corn Street – *LloydsTSB decoration*
C33 42 Corn Street – *Figures etc.*
C34 43 Corn Street – *Figures and relief*
C35 37–39 Corn St. – *Peace and Plenty etc.*
C36 36 Corn St. – *Caryatids and keystones*
C37 42 St Nicholas St. – *Putti, relief*
C38 20 St Nicholas St. – *Elephant*
C39 18 St Nicholas St. – *Four busts*
C40 St Nicholas St. – *Queen Victoria fount.*

C41 13 St Stephen's St. – *Three busts*
C42 55 St Stephen's St. – *Two figures*
C43 Centre – *Cenotaph*
C44 Centre – *Drinking Fountain*
C45 Centre – *Fourteenth Army plaque*
C46 Centre – *Edward Colston*
C47 Colston St. – *Donor portrait reliefs*
C48 Centre – *Edmund Burke*
C49 32 Corn St. – *The Queen and the...*
C50 28 Clare St. – *Decorative sculpture*
C51 Centre – N*eptune*
C52 St Augustine's Parade – *Demerara*
C53 St Augustine's Parade – *Pediment*
C54 Broad Quay – *George V fountain*
C55 Broad Quay – *Bristol's History*
C56 Narrow Quay – *Fountain of Sabrina*
C57 Narrow Quay – *Pero's Bridge*
C58 Narrow Quay – *John Cabot*
C59 Princes Wharf – *Robinson frieze*
C60 Queen Square – *William III*
C61 19–21 Queen Sq. – *Four Continents*
C62 Welsh Back – *Merch. Seafarers' Mem.*
C63 Redcliffe Street – *Exploration*
C64 Ferry St. – *Grain chute*
C65 Redcliffe Way – *Phoenix*
C66 Redcliff Hill – *Redcliffe Pipe*
C67 Redcliff Hill – *Phoenix relief*
C68 Somerset Square – *Fountain*
C69 Victoria St. – *Three naked males*
C70 Counterslip – *Fireman*
C71 Avon Street – *Time and Tide*
C72 Temple Quay – *Pelorus*
C73 Temple Back East – *I.K. Brunel*
C74 Temple Quay – *Templar Stone*
C75 Temple Quay – *Six Portwall Markers*
C76 Temple Way – *Rotating Columns*
C77 Temple Gate – *Queen Victoria*
C78 Temple Meads Station – *E. Saunders*
C79 Temple Meads Station – *Brunel mural*

Chronological List

Chronological list of public sculpture in Bristol before 2009

Date	*Artist*	*Subject*	*Street*	*map ref.*
1240	unknown	Virgin and Child enthroned	Christmas Street	C12
1400	unknown	Figures, north side	College Green, Abbey Gatehouse	B58
1560, 1866	unknown	St John's Conduit	Nelson Street	C14
1595–1631	Thomas Hobson and unknown	The Bristol Nails	Corn Street	C30
1669	unknown	Portico	Stoke Hill, Trinity College	A11
1700	unknown	Neptune	Rectory Gardens, Henbury	A4
1700	unknown	Brennus and Bellinus	Broad Street, St John's Gate	C15
1705	John Nost	Hercules	Clifton Hill, Goldney House	B21
1706	unknown	Queen Elizabeth's Hospital schoolboy	Jacob's Wells Road	B47
1721	John Randall	Neptune	Centre, The, St Augustine's Pde.	C51
1728	James Paty I, attributed to	Quarter Jacks	Broad Street, Christ Church	C19
1736	Michael Rysbrack	William III	Queen Square	C60
1739	Daniel Millard	Alderman John Barstaple	Old Market Street	C26
1742–3	Thomas Paty	Festoons and coats-of-arms	Corn Street, Exchange	C31
1743	C. Boni and J. Griffin	Interior plaster reiefs	Corn Street, Exchange	C31
1742–4	Thomas Paty	Keystones	Corn Street, Exchange	C31
1750	Thomas Paty, attributed to	River God, lion and lioness and lion	Clifton Hill, Goldney House	B21
1756	Thomas Wright	Sarcophagus: Charles, Duke of Beaufort	Stoke Park	A6
1760	Thomas Wright	Obelisk: Lady Elizabeth Somerset	Stoke Park	A7
1767	Thomas Paty, attributed to	79th Regiment of Foot	Clifton Down	B15
1768	James Paty II, attributed to	Monument to William Pitt	Clifton Down	B16
1806	Coade & Sealy	Coade stone urn after the Medici Vase	Blaise Castle House	A3
1810	Joseph Panzetta of Coade & Sealy	George III	Portland Square (formerly)	C1
1811	James George Bubb	Commerce, City of Bristol, Navigation etc.	Corn Street (Commercial Rooms)	C34
1815	unknown	Memorial pump and sundial	Blaise Hamlet	A1
1818	unknown	Princess Charlotte obelisk	Redland Hill	A13
1824	Edward Hodges Baily	Bristol with Minerva and Apollo	Park Street	B49
1827	Edward Hodges Baily	Justice	Corn Street, Old Council House	C29
1839	Thomas Tyley the Younger	Sir Charles Wetherell	Park Row, Red Lodge	B46
1841	M. L. Watson and Jabez Tyley	Pediment, Goddess of Wisdom	Queen's Road, Victoria Rooms	B35
1843–4	William Prinsep	Tomb of Raja Rammohun Roy	Arno's Vale Cemetery	A25
1843–6	John Thomas	Six figures	Broad Street, Guildhall	C17
1849	unknown	Fountain	Somerset Square	C68
1849–1956	John Thomas, H. Hems and E. Pascoe	High Cross; remnants of replica	Berkeley Square	B44
1851	unknown	Demerara's figurehead, replica	St Augustine's Parade	C52
1854–7	John Thomas	LloydsTSB façade decoration	Corn Street, Lloyds TSB	C32
1857	John Thomas	Painting, Architecture and Sculpture	Queen's Road, R. W. A.	B37
1857	John Thomas	Decorative Arts	Queen's Road, R. W. A.	B37
1857	John Thomas	Sir Joshua Reynolds	Queen's Road, R. W. A.	B37

Date	*Artist*	*Subject*	*Street*	*map ref.*
1857	John Thomas	John Flaxman	Queen's Road, R. W. A.	B37
1859	W. & T. Wills	Queen Victoria drinking fountain	St Nicholas Street	C40
1866	Walter MacFarlane & Co.	Drinking fountain	Suspension Bridge Road	B17
1867	Thomas Colley	Caryatids and keystones	Corn Street, 36	C36
1867	Mr Porter	Elephant	St Nicholas Street	C38
1868	unknown	Four busts	St Nicholas Street	C39
1868	unknown	Queen Victoria and Prince Albert	Small Street, Assize Courts	C18
1869	unknown	Telemones	West Street, Palace Hotel	C27
1870	unknown	Queen Victoria	Temple Gate	C77
1872	George and Henry Godwin	Proctor's Fountain	Clifton Down	B12
1872	unknown	John Foster	Colston Street (Foster's Almshouse)	C13
1872	unknown	Model of the almshouse	Colston Street (Foster's Almshouse)	C13
1872	Edward William Wyon	Caryatids	Corn Street, Exchange	C31
1866–72	unknown	Capitals	Queen's Road, former Bristol Museum	B40
1873	Joseph William King	Kings and Queens	Whiteladies Rd., 1–3 Whiteladies Gt.	B27
1875	unknown	Samuel Plimsoll	Hotwell Road, Capricorn Quay	B73
1876	George Gamon Adams	Thomas Proctor	Clifton Down, Mansion House	B13
1877	unknown	E. S. & A. Robinson frieze	Princes Wharf, Bristol Industrial Mus.	C59
1877	John Henry Hirst	Drinking fountain	Stoke Road, Durdham Down	A12
1878	unknown	Milton, Raleigh and Shakespeare	13 St Stephen's St.	C41
1879	Edward Sheppard	Justice	Bridewell Street	C9
1880	Thomas Woolner	John Percival	College Road, Clifton College	B8
1883	unknown	Aesop's Fables	Elmdale Road, 8, 9, 10 and 11	B39
1885	unknown	Grain chute	Ferry Street	C64
1887	James Harvard Thomas	Samuel Morley	Lewins Mead	C10
1888	Sir Joseph Edgar Boehm	Queen Victoria	College Green	B55
1890	unknown	Roundel	Beauley Road	A22
1894	James Harvard Thomas	Edmund Burke	Centre, The, St Augustine's Pde.	C48
1894	Edward Gabriel	Pediment and weathervane	St Augustine's Parade, Watershed	C53
1895	John Cassidy	Edward Colston	Centre, The, Colston Avenue	C46
1896	George James Frampton	Dr John William Caldicott	University Rd. Bristol Grammar Sch.	B33
1894, 1897	unknown	Caryatids and spandrels	Prince's Lane, Sion Hill	B19
1897	unknown	Jubilee fountain	Stoke Hill	A10
1898	William Venn Gough	Cabot Tower	Brandon Hill	B50
1899	Timpthy Butler, after	Christopher James Thomas	Colston Street, Colston Hall	C47
1899	unknown	Alfred Price	Colston Street, Colston Hall	C47
1899	unknown	Joseph Storrs Fry	Colston Street, Colston Hall	C47
1899	unknown	Herbert Thomas	Colston Street, Colston Hall	C47
1900	unknown	Lewis Fry MP	Colston Street, Colston Hall	C47
1900	Walter MacFarlane & Co.	Drinking fountain	Horfield Common	A8
1900–1	William James Neatby	Edward Everard	Broad Street	C16
1901	unknown	Drinking fountain	Centre, The, Colston Avenue	C44
1901	Henry Richard Hope-Pinker	Sir William Henry Wills	Colston Street, Colston Hall	C47
1901	Henry Richard Hope-Pinker	Elisha Smith Robinson	Colston Street, Colston Hall	C47
1902	Tom E. Dove	Simon Short	Trinity Place, Hotwells	B22

Date	*Artist*	*Subject*	*Street*	*map ref.*
1903	unknown	Putti: Justice and Enterprise	42 St Nicholas Street	C37
1903	Benjamin Creswick	Spirit of Commerce	43 St Nicholas Street	C37
1904	J. Whitehead & Sons	Urijah Thomas memorial fountain	Blackboy Hill	A14
1904	Alfred Drury	South African War Memorial	College Road, Clifton College	B9
1904	Gilbert Seale, attributed to	Figures and decorative carving	42 Corn Street	C33
1904	Onslow Whiting	Gloucestershire Regimental Memorial	Queen's Road	B38
1904	William John Smith	Architecture, Painting and Sculpture	Queen's Rd. Bristol Mus. and Art Gallery	B41
1905	Charles J. Pibworth	Three reliefs	College Green, Bristol Central Library	B57
1905	William Aumonier	Decorative sculpture	College Green, Bristol Central Library	B57
1905	William John Smith	Atlantes	Queen's Rd. Bristol Mus. and Art Gallery	B41
1905–6	Gilbert Seale	Sculpture and decoration	28 Clare Street	C50
1913	Henry Poole	Edward VII	Queen's Road, Victoria Rooms	B36
1913	Henry Poole	Edward VII fountain	Queen's Road, Victoria Rooms	B36
1914	Charles J. Pibworth	Figures, south side	College Green, Abbey Gatehouse	B58
1915–17	Henry Poole	Edward VII lions	Queen's Road, Victoria Rooms	B36
1915	John William Smith	Four Atlantes	Whiteladies Road	B34
1920	Humphries and Oakes	War memorial	Fishponds Road	A9
1922	C. Holden, Eric Gill & L. Cribb	Memorial Gateway	College Rd., Clifton Coll.	B11
1922–5	Jean Hahn and others	Figures, decoration, grotesques	Queen's Rd., Wills Memorial Bdg.	B42
1923–5	E. F. Fabian and others	Nine Muses	Queen's Rd., Wills Memorial Bdg.	B42
1921–7	Jean Hahn and others	Entrance surround, lions' heads etc	Tyndall Ave., H. H. Wills Phys. Bdg.	B31
1928	E. E. Faithfull of H Tyley	Emma Saunders	Temple Meads Station	C78
1929	Edgar Thomas Earp	Entrance lodge frieze	Clifton Down, Bristol Zoo	B1
1929	William John Smith	Lions	Queen's Rd. Bristol Mus. and Art Gallery	B41
1931	William McMillan	Earl Haig	College Road, Clifton College	B10
1932	H.Heathman, Miss E.Blacker	Cenotaph	Centre, The, Colston Avenue	C43
1932	Hermon Cawthra	Peace and Plenty etc.	37–39 Corn Street	C35
1932	A. Compton-Roberts, R. P. Roberts	Wisdom	37–39 Corn Street	C35
1932	Arthur George Walker	John Wesley	Horsefair, John Wesley's Chapel	C6
1932	Sir George Oatley	Redcliffe Pipe	Redcliff Hill	C66
1933	Eric Gill	Christ the King	Canford Cemetery	A5
1933	William John Smith	Virgin and Child enthroned	Upper Byron Place	B43
1935	unknown	Two figures	St Stephen's Street	C42
1939	Frederick Brook Hitch	Charles Wesley	Horsefair, John Wesley's Chapel	C5
1949	Roy Smith	Alfred	Clifton Down, Bristol Zoo	B6
1950	Paul Vincze	Charles Holden	College Green, Bristol Central Library	B57
1950	David McFall	Unicorns	College Green, Council House	B54
1951	Charles Wheeler	John Cabot	College Green, Council House	B54
1951	Esmond Burton, attrib. to	Gaunt's House reliefs	Denmark Street, Chantry Court	B52
1953	David McFall	Seahorses and Riders	College Green, Council House	B54
1959	A. W. Banks	Brunel centenary plaque	Suspension Bridge Road	B18
1959	unknown	Three naked male figures	Victoria Street, Transport House	C69
1960	Ernest Pascoe and students	Reliefs	Colston Street, Colston Hall	C47
1962	Ernest Pascoe	Three King's of Cologne	Colston Street (Foster's Almshouse)	C13
1968	Jerry and Anne Hicks	Microscopic Observations	Myrtle Road	B28

Date	*Artist*	*Subject*	*Street*	*map ref.*
1968–70	Paul Mount	Spirit of Bristol	St James's Barton	C2
1971	David Wynne	Mute Swan	Clifton Down, Bristol Zoo	B4
1974	Judith Bluck	Life of St Francis of Assisi	Lewins Mead, Greyfriars	C8
1974	Frants Belsky	Oracle	Narrow Plain	C28
1974	Ernest Pascoe	Phoenix	Redcliff Hill	C67
1975	Roy Clapp	Girl and Kid	Clifton Down, Bristol Zoo	B3
1979	John Huggins	Classic Flight	Royal Fort Gdns, Bristol University	B32
1980	Naomi Blake	Refugee	College Green, Cathedral churchyard	B59
1980	Walter Ritchie	The Queen and the Washerwomen	32 Corn Street	C49
1980	Gerald Laing	Fountain of Sabrina	Narrow Quay	C56
1978–81	Michael Rysbrack, after	Edward Colston	Armoury Square	A18
1981	Philippa Threlfall, Kennedy Collings	Aspects of Bristol's history	Broad Quay	C55
1905, 1982	Derek Carr	King George V memorial fountain	Broad Quay	C54
1982	John Doubleday	Isambard Kingdom Brunel	Temple Back East	C73
1984	Vincent Woropay	Hand of the River God	Baltic Wharf	B26
1984	David Backhouse	Cloaked Horseman	Lewins Mead	C11
1984	Stephen Joyce	Horse and Man	St George's Road, Brunel House	B51
1984	Peter Milner, Jane Norbury	St Mary Redcliffe Maze	Victoria Park	A23
1985	Stephen Joyce	St Odilia and the Bird	Lower Maudlin Street	C3
1985	John Doubleday	Phoenix	Redcliffe Way	C65
1985	Alexander Paul Klecki	Katyn Massacre memorial	Worcester Rd. Clifton Cathedral	B14
1885–86	unknown	Four Continents	19–21 Queen Square	C61
1986	Stephen Cox	Atyeo	Baltic Wharf	B25
1986–7	Keir Smith	Topsail	Baltic Wharf	B24
1986	Walter Ritchie	The Creation	Lower Maudlin Street	C4
1986	Stephen Joyce	John Cabot	Narrow Quay	C58
1986	Stephen Joyce	IsambardKingdom Brunel	St George's Road, Brunel House	B53
1987	David Mutasa	Alfred Fagon	Ashley Road	A15
1991	Rodney Harris	Basset Hounds and Basenjis	Albert Rd. Bristol Dogs' Home	A24
1991	Andy Frost	Play sculpture	Castle Park	C24
1991	Philippa Threlfall, K. Collings & J. Blunt	Exploration	Redcliffe St.	C63
1992	Barbara Ash	Four Bristol scenes	Winterstoke Road, Sainsbury's	A27
1993	Ann Christopher	Line from within	Castle Park	C20
1993	Rachel Fenner	Throne	Castle Park	C21
1993	Peter Randall-Page	Beside the still waters	Castle Park	C22
1993	Kate Malone	Drinking Fountain	Castle Park	C23
1993	Victor Moreton	Only dead fish go with the flow	Castle Park	C25
1994	Georgina Redfern	Time and Tide	Avon Street, Trinity Quay	C71
1994	Susan Dring	Four statues	Bath Road, Arno's Court Gateway	A26
1984–95	Niranjan Pradhan	Raja Rammohun Roy, bust	College Green, Council House	B54
1997	Niranjan Pradhan	Raja Rammohun Roy, statue	College Green	B56
1997	Simon Thomas	Stretching a point	Tyndall Ave. Physics Extension Bldg.	B30
1999	Sue Webster, Tim Noble	Arewehappynow?, Everythingwas…	Millennium Square	B62
1993–9	Eilis O'Connell	Pero's Bridge	Narrow Quay	C57
1999	unknown	Untitled	Poole's Wharf Court	B23

Date	*Artist*	*Subject*	*Street*	*map ref.*
2000	William Pye	Aquarena	Millennium Square	B62
2000	Cathie Pilkington	Bill and Bob; Jasmine	Millennium Square	B65
2000	Lawrence Holofcener	William Tyndale	Millennium Square	B64
2000	Lawrence Holofcener	William Penn	Millennium Square	B64
2000	Lawrence Holofcener	Thomas Chattterton	Millennium Square	B64
2000	Nicola Hicks	Beetle	Millennium Square	B61
2000	unknown	Nipper	Park Row	B45
2000	Pat Daw	Pelorus	Temple Quay, 1 Temple Back East	C72
2001	Simon Thomas	Small Worlds	Anchor Road	B60
2001	Philip Bews	Tree of Life	Clifton Down, Bristol Zoo	B2
2001	Julian Warren	Ying and Yang	Clifton Down, Bristol Zoo	B7
2001	David Ward	Zenith	Millennium Square	B63
2001	Graham Ibbeson	Movie Star	Millennium Square	B64
2001	Chee Horng Chang	Telespine	Millennium Square	B66
2001	David Backhouse	Merchant Navy Memorial	Welsh Back	C62
2002	Andrew Smith	Lollypop Be-bop	Upper Maudlin St. Children's Hospital	C7
2003	Philip Bews	Elephant Tower	Clifton Down, Bristol Zoo	B5
2003	Stephen Joyce	Fireman	Counterslip	C70
2004	Jason Lane	Guard Dog	Blaise Castle Estate	A2
2001–4	Ian Hamilton Finlay	Girl into reed...and other works	Great George Street	B48
2004	Philip Bews	Shooting Star	Mall Gardens, Clifton	B20
2004	Jane L. Richards	Templar Stone	Temple Quay	C74
2004	John Aiken	Six Portwall Markers	Temple Quay	C75
2004	Jon Buck	Flat Out	Tyndall Avenue	B29
2005	Valda Jackson	All our tomorrows	Grosvenor Road, St Paul's	A17
2005	Rodney Harris	Caterpillar and Woodlouse	Stapleton Road	A19
2006	Jim Butler	Twinned cities plaques	College Green, Council House	B54
2006	Tim Knowles	Field of Play	Harbourside	B67
2006	Dail Behennah	The Pavilion	Harbourside	B68
2006	Janice Kerbel	Weathervane	Harbourside	B69
2006	John Pym	Secret Industry	Harbourside	B70
2006	Langland and Bell	Domain	Harbourside	B72
2006	Walter Jack	D of the Dings	Oxford Street, The Dings	A21
2006	Stephen Joyce	Brunel mural	Temple Meads Station	C79
2006–7	Richard Box	Parallax	Harbourside	B71
2006–7	Walter Jack	Rotating Columns	Temple Way	C76
2007	Louise Vergette of Codsteaks	Twisted Arch	St Philips Road	A20
2008	Mike Baker	Fourteenth Army memorial	Centre, The, Colston Avenue	C45
2008	Jason Lane	Greater Crested Plunger	Ashley Road	A16

Introduction by FRANCIS GREENACRE

Bristol's Sculpture before 1700

Rysbrack's statue of William III in Queen Square was erected in 1736. Bristol may justly claim that it is the finest equestrian monument in northern Europe and that it is altogether fitting that the largest square outside London should have been adorned by the masterpiece of the leading metropolitan sculptor of the day (Fig. 2).

Just two years earlier, Samuel and Nathan Buck had inscribed one of their two engraved panoramas of Bristol with the words: 'This City is the most valuable for its extensive Trade, to all Parts of the World; in which it exceeds all other Cities and Towns in Great Britain, except London....' (Fig. 1). Ironically, just as that second-city status was being so openly claimed, it was also being threatened for the first time in four hundred years by the great industrial cities to the north, and especially by the rival city and port of Liverpool. Surviving sculpture pre-dating the eighteenth century, bearing witness to that status, is, however, remarkably rare. And where it survives, it often deserves very much more care and attention than it is receiving.

In comparison to London, Bristol's history is short; indeed, it is only a little longer than Liverpool's. Evidence of Bristol's existence is almost non-existent before the second millennium. Coins minted in Bristol in 1009 or 1010 imply that it was already a market town. It is probably to around 1050 that the seven-foot-high relief of the *Harrowing of Hell* in Bristol Cathedral may be dated (Fig. 3).[1] It is 'one of the finest carvings of its day in Britain, or indeed in western Europe' and it is well and proudly displayed in the South Transept. With his right hand Christ both blesses Adam and Eve and holds a staff topped by a cross. With his left hand he raises Eve from the jaws of hell, whilst his feet trample upon Satan. This powerful image of salvation was discovered under the floor of the

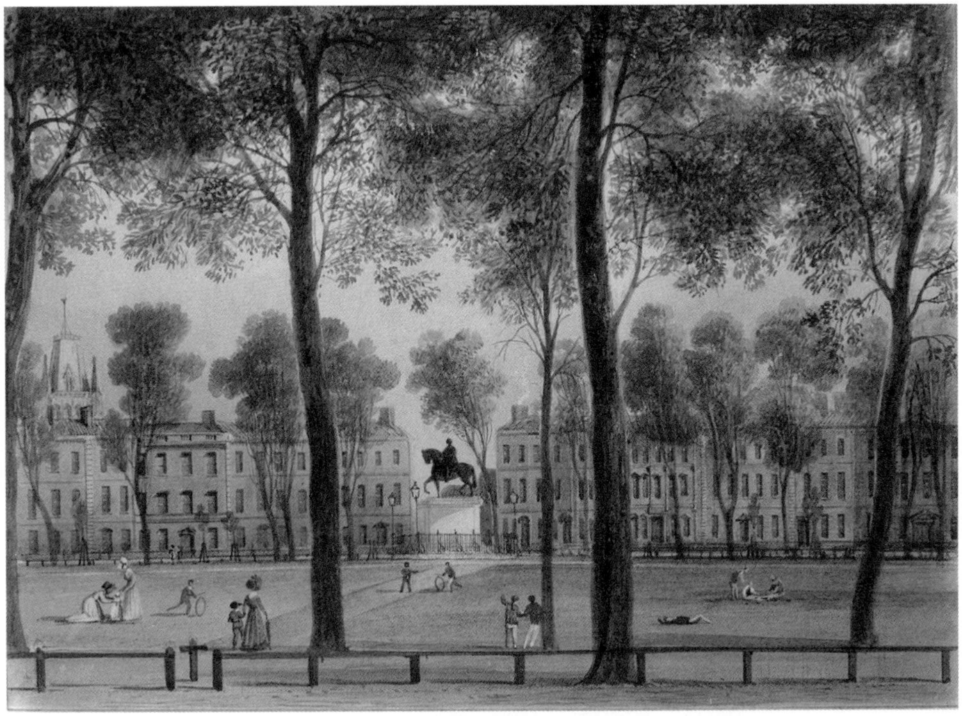

Fig. 2 ***Queen Square, looking south-east with Rysbrack's equestrian statue of William III*, watercolour by T. L. Rowbotham, 1827 (Bristol Museum and Art Gallery, M2206)**

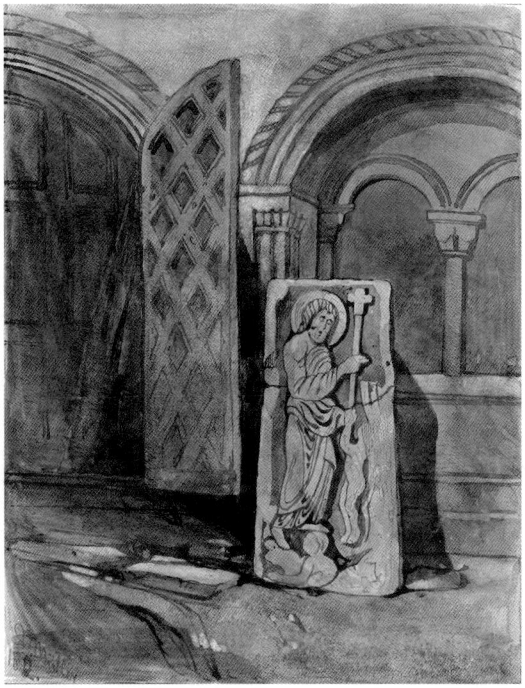

Fig. 3 ***The discovery of the 'The Harrowing of Hell' in 1832 in the Chapter House, Bristol Cathedral*, watercolour by W. J. Müller, 1832 (private collection)**

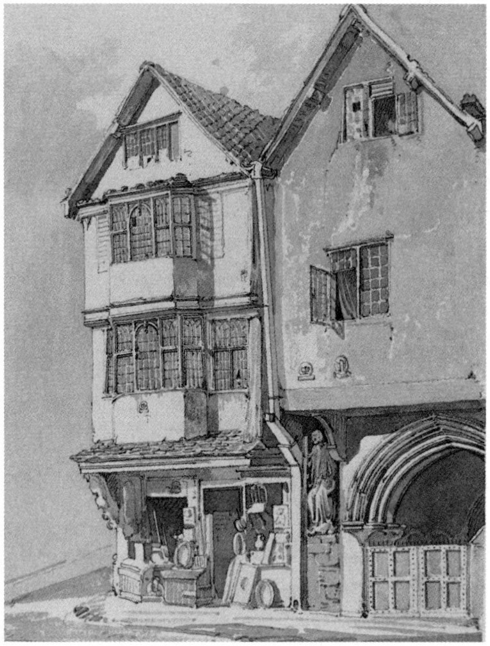

Fig. 4 *'Virgin and Child Enthroned' beside the entrance to St Bartholomew's Hospital, Christmas Street, c.1240*, **watercolour by Hugh O'Neill, 1820 (Bristol Museum and Art Gallery, M2572)**

Norman Chapter House during the restoration that followed the Bristol Riots of 1831. It was being used as a tomb cover and it is possible that this was the sculpture's original function. The stylised and linear treatment of the drapery owes much to contemporary manuscript illustration.

Church sculpture and church monuments are not included in the core catalogue section of this volume. Thus the earliest sculpture recorded here, the *Virgin and Child Enthroned* (see Christmas Street), has long been separated from its original ecclesiastical context (Fig. 4). It is a severely damaged work of great sophistication that may have adorned a gateway or chapel entrance within St Bartholomew's Hospital. It was recently moved a few metres to its present location for preservation's sake, but it is still at risk and now almost invisible to the general public. Its approximate date on stylistic grounds of around 1240 represents a moment of enormous importance in Bristol's history.

Bristol was built on a small rise at the conjunction of the tidal Avon and the un-navigable Frome. The Frome circled much of this hill, running below the town wall along the approximate line of today's Baldwin Street, probably entering the Avon just below Bristol Bridge. Beginning in 1240, a great trench was dug, nearly half a mile in length, five-and-a-half metres deep and thirty-six metres wide, running from well to the north of St Stephen's Church to the Avon below the bend at Redcliffe by today's Arnolfini. In 1247 this became both the new course of the Frome, and a much extended harbour with a rock-free ground of soft mud for vessels to lie on at low tide. At the same time the wooden bridge across the Avon was replaced by a stone bridge of four arches. It was soon to have thirty wooden four- or five-storey houses built upon it, much in the manner of Old London Bridge, which had been completed earlier in the same century. New town walls were also built at this time. The largest of the six *Portwall markers*, completed in 2004, by John Aiken (see Temple Quay), combines art and archaeology with considerable success. Conserved beneath it and visible through it are the foundations of one of the mid-thirteenth century watergates to the town, a rare reminder of Bristol's medieval past.

It was in the early fourteenth century that the great choir of St Augustine's Abbey (Bristol Cathedral) was built. Pevsner thought it 'superior to anything else built in England and indeed in Europe at the same time', and it is certainly one of the most stimulating and inventive of all architectural interiors.[2] The cathedral contains much medieval architectural and decorative stone carving, but it is St Mary Redcliffe, built a little later in the same century, that holds some of the very finest English sculpture of the period. Scattered, somewhat haphazardly, along the side of the north aisle are the original figures from the north porch dating from about 1340 (Fig. 5).These battered figures, contorted and compressed, suggest a wry and moving sympathy for the human predicament. The figures struggle to support the vestiges of the pedestals

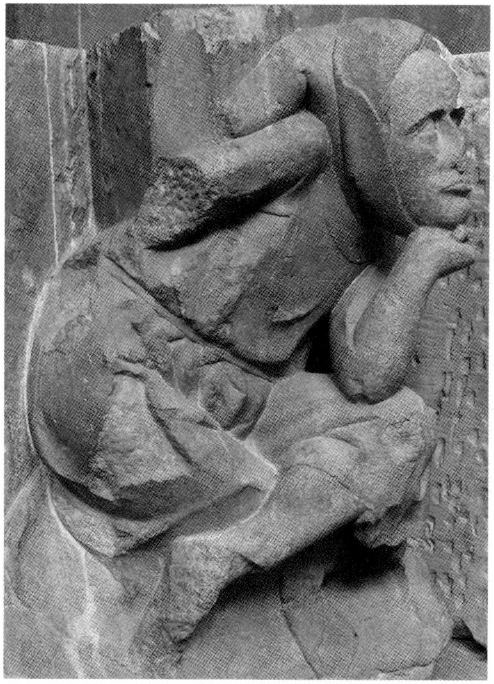

Fig. 5 *Figure from the north porch of St Mary Redcliffe, c.1340*, **now in the north aisle**

or plinths above them, on which statues of the sanctified fathers of the church once stood.

The magnificent church of St Mary Redcliffe proudly proclaimed both the wealth and the relative independence of Redcliffe. It was in 1373 that Edward III granted, or perhaps more accurately sold, a charter to Bristol, conferring county status on the town and thus unifying Bristol with its own prosperous suburbs of Redcliffe and Temple and freeing the citizens from the previous jurisdiction of Gloucestershire and Somerset. The new boundaries acknowledged Bristol's need to protect its growing trade. They extended down the seven miles of the Avon and far into the Bristol Channel to include the islands of Steep Holm and Flat Holm. Bristol was now the wealthiest provincial town in England.

Not surprisingly, Bristol had two substantial medieval statues of Edward III. Both survive, not as a result of the same civic pride that led to their creation, but thanks to the interests of the antiquarian collectors of the eighteenth century.

When Bristol's medieval gateways of Newgate and Lawford's Gate were demolished in 1766 and 1769, it was William Reeve of Arno's Court, Quaker merchant and copper smelter, who rescued them and built a handsome new gateway (Fig. 6) on which to place them (see Bath Road). The statues of Edward I and Edward III from Lawford's Gate and the two from Newgate remained on the gateway until 1898. They are today in St Nicholas Church Museum, now closed to the public. Modern versions did not replace them on the gateway until 1994. William Reeve also incorporated medieval sculptural fragments, some from Bristol buildings, into the entrance to his tunnel under the Bath Road and into his surviving stable and office building, the Black Castle, where they can still be seen.[3]

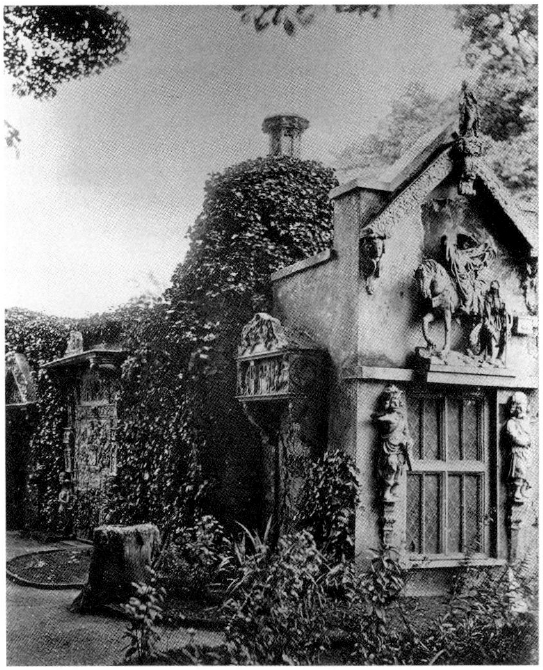

Fig. 7 ***Three doorways and sculpture in the garden of G. W. Braikenridge's residence, Broomwell House, Brislington*****, photograph, c.1860 (Bristol Museums and Art Gallery, K4951)**

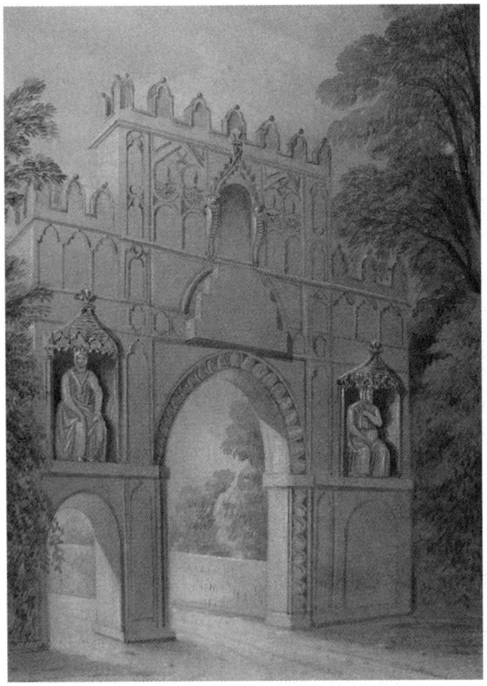

Fig. 6 ***Arno's Court Gateway from the north with the medieval statues of Edward III and Edward I*****, watercolour by T. L. Rowbotham, 1826 (Bristol Museums and Art Gallery, M3493)**

Some of these fragments are recorded in the collection of Bristol's most remarkable antiquarian collector, George Weare Braikenridge (1775–1856). His famous collection of drawings and watercolours of Bristol, mostly executed in the 1820s and now in Bristol Museum and Art Gallery, has ensured that Bristol's record of its past appearance is richer than that of any other English city. He was also a collector of sculpture, not only saving the *Christ Church Quarter Jacks* (see Broad Street), but also purchasing substantial pieces, often foreign, for his extraordinary garden buildings (Fig. 7).[4]

The second of the two statues of Edward III was on Bristol's High Cross. The High Cross deserves particular attention, for its very survival in Stourhead Gardens, 'a pretty conceit among the Classical Temples of a

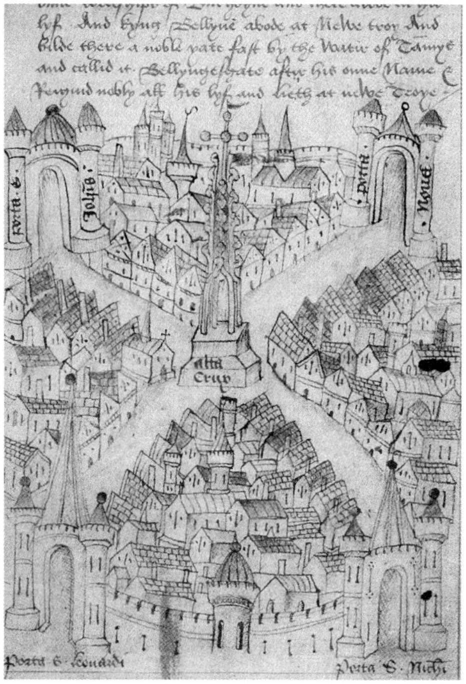

Fig. 8 *Plan of Bristol with the High Cross*, from the Mayor's Calendar compiled by Robert Ricart, c.1480 (Bristol Record Office)

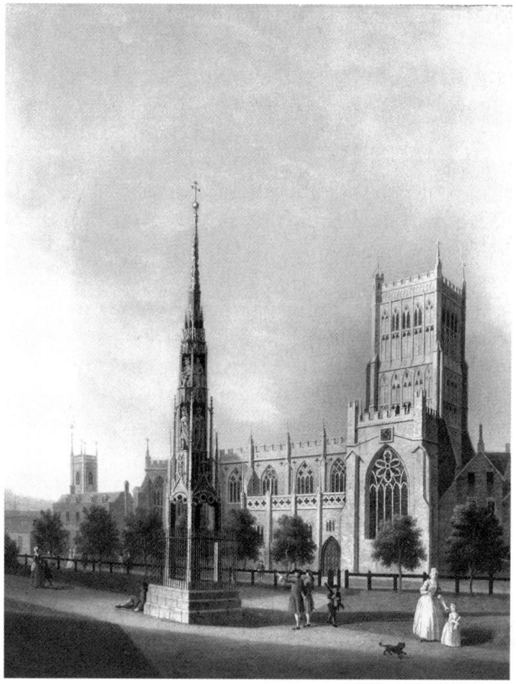

Fig. 9 *High Cross on College Green with the Cathedral*, oil on canvas by Samuel Scott, c.1755 (Bristol Museum and Art Gallery, K4177)

Georgian antiquary's domain', has come to represent the loss – almost total – of the visual reminders of Bristol's rich medieval past.[5]

The High Cross stood at the junction of High Street, Corn Street, Broad Street and Wine Street. Until the Blitz, this was the very heart of Bristol, as is so graphically, if symbolically, expressed in the illustration to *Ricart's Calendar*, a chronicle of Bristol begun in 1479 (Fig. 8). It is often said that the High Cross was specifically erected to celebrate the granting of county status in 1373. More probably, it was put up closer to the end of the century, replacing an earlier market cross. It was later to be much altered, most substantially in 1633–4, when another storey with statues of four additional monarchs was added. There were also new armorial shields, baroque cherubs and an elaborate finial, all of which John Norton so deliberately expurgated from his purified mid-nineteenth-century replica (see Berkeley Square).

In 1733 the corporation received a petition arguing that the cross was 'a ruinous and superstitious Relick, which is at present a public nuisance'.[6] The Common Council voted overwhelmingly for demolition and this was promptly carried out. Three years later, Alderman Price and 'some gentlemen living near College Green' raised a subscription to re-erect the cross near the Cathedral with the consent of the dean and chapter, the owners of the land (Fig. 9). By the late 1750s, there were moves, again funded by local subscriptions, to raise and widen the walks on College Green, where the cross 'interrupted gentlemen and ladies from walking eight or ten abreast'.[7] The cross, 'rudely torn down and much injured by the workmen employed, was thrown by in a corner of the Cathedral, where it lay for a long time neglected'.[8]

In 1763 Henry Hoare, the merchant banker who was then creating a classical Arcadian landscape at Stourhead in Wiltshire, visited Horace Walpole's new Gothic villa, Strawberry Hill House, at Twickenham. There he would have seen Samuel Scott's painting of the High Cross on College Green.[9] It hung in the Long Gallery and was almost certainly commissioned by Walpole.[10] In the same year Henry Hoare's close friend, the Reverend Cutts Barton, was appointed Dean of Bristol Cathedral. It was in the following year, on 2 October 1764, that the dean was 'so obliging as to write me word I may send for the Cross directly'.[11] Mr Hoare's words have since been unjustly used to condemn the dean, without whose initiative the cross would certainly not have survived. The letter was to Thomas Paty and it discussed the carriage of the cross to Stourhead, 'safely and carefully packed and well padded with hay or straw' in six wagons.

Thomas Paty oversaw the re-erection of the cross in 1765, when he rightly renewed the lower piers, on which the cross stands, but unwisely introduced iron rods, dowels and ties whose corrosion was to cause serious problems later in the century (Fig. 10). It was the later fragility of

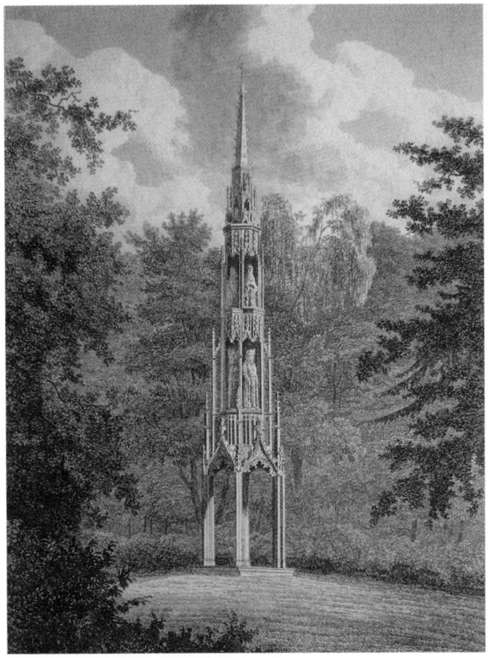

Fig. 10 *Bristol High Cross at Stourhead*, engraving by J. Skelton after John Willis, c.1825 (Bristol Museum and Art Gallery)

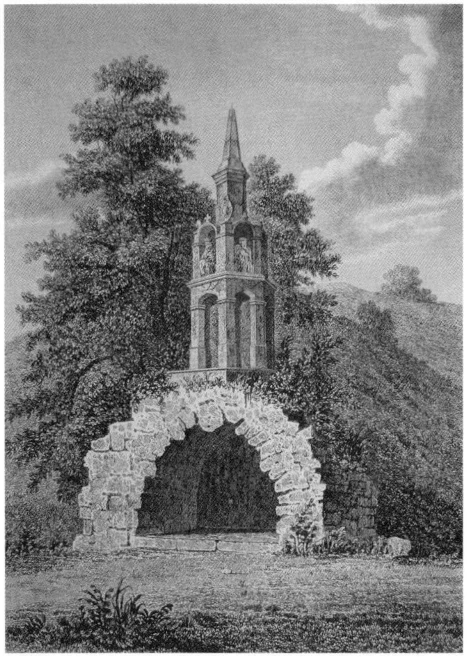

Fig. 11 *St Peter's Pump at Stourhead*, drawn and engraving by J. Skelton, c.1825 (Bristol Museum and Art Gallery)

the cross that stymied negotiations for its return to Bristol in both 1848 and 1888 (see Berkeley Square).

In 1980 a final opportunity occurred for Bristol to retrieve a portion of its heritage. The Bristol Museum and Art Gallery was offered the opportunity to take on long-term loan the four late-fourteenth century statues of kings from the original lower tier of the cross, if the cost of replicas (£12,000) was met. The National Trust, now owners of Stourhead, had resolved to replace the four original statues with the replicas. The necessary demolition of the High Cross prior to its conservation and the move of the statues to the Victoria and Albert Museum for examination led to scandalised headlines in the Bristol press, and to a bitter spat between the head of Bristol's Museum and Art Gallery and the Director of the V & A, Sir Roy Strong.[12] In April 1981 the National Trust was finally informed that there was no chance of Bristol raising the necessary funds, a paltry sum. The originals remain in London.[13]

It is often forgotten that a second cross containing just six statues of British monarchs, rather than the eight upon the High Cross, also left Bristol in the 1760s. Only a year after Thomas Paty had set up the High Cross at Stourhead, he was rebuilding Bristol Bridge to the designs of James Bridges. On 7 July 1766 the bridge trustees, who were responsible also for improving the approaches to the new bridge, resolved 'that St Peter's Cross and Pump should be removed "with all expedition", and that a new pump should be erected nearby'.[14] Through the agency of Thomas Tyndall of the Royal Fort, where the Patys had recently done so much work, Henry Hoare promptly offered to take down the edifice at his own expense. His offer was accepted 'with alacrity'. It was re-erected in 1768, raised high upon a grotto-like mound in the gentle valley of Six Wells Bottom at the source of the Stour and on the fringes of Stourhead Gardens (Fig. 11).

Until the fifteenth century it was known as St Edith's Well, implying a Saxon origin. Its site, just to the north of St Peter's Church, may have been at the heart of pre-Conquest Bristol.[15] The well head was first rebuilt by the greatest of Bristol's merchant princes, William Canynge, and completed by his executor, William Spenser, following Canynge's death in 1474. In 1633 both the High Cross and St Peter's Cross were taken down and substantially rebuilt. We know that in 1660 a mason, almost too fortuitously named Henry Hoare, was paid to set up a statue of Charles II, doubtless filling the vacated niche once occupied by the figure of his father. The mechanics of the pump were a repeated cost to the parish and, like the High Cross, it was a growing encumbrance to carriages and sleds. One account testifies in 1680: 'putting a stoane to keep drays from ye pump 00.00.04.'

The rebuilding of St Peter's Cross in 1633 was almost certainly at the expense of Robert Aldworth, who died the following year. Above the six very weathered statues of monarchs are panels, one of which bears

Aldworth's merchant's mark and others that bear devices which were are also featured on his magnificent tomb in St Peter's Church (Fig. 12). Today, only the shell of the church remains. The monument was almost totally destroyed in the Blitz, as was Aldworth's house, which is still remembered as St Peter's Hospital.[16] That building, which bore the date 1612, was as richly ornamented as a Victorian bank and probably just as deliberately demonstrative of the owner's wealth and security (Fig. 13). Carved wooden corbels of grotesque figures, richly carved cornices and barge boards and extensive strap work covered the façade. In contrast to the finesse of Aldworth's sophisticated tomb, the effect was vigorous, even vulgar. The building was not only Aldworth's residence, but housed his sugar refinery, Bristol's earliest. It was later to be a pioneering workhouse, hospital and asylum.

Robert Aldworth is a poignant reminder that 'Elizabethan and early Stuart Bristol has all but disappeared'.[17] So much of Bristol's medieval and late medieval past that was not subsumed in the continued expansion and rebuilding of the city in the eighteenth and nineteenth centuries was obliterated in the Blitz. Aldworth deserves to be better remembered, but so too do other leading merchants of the late sixteenth and early seventeenth centuries, such as Sir John Young (d. 1589), Robert Kitchin (d. 1594) and John Whitson (d. 1629). Fortunately, church memorials and other tangible reminders of these great men have survived. John Whitson, like William Canynge, is recorded by two effigies, both in St Nicholas Church (see 'Bread and Sermons', Figs 46 and 47), but it is the happy continuation of the school that he founded, Red Maids School, that does most to keep his memory alive. By contrast, Robert Kitchen has a surprisingly modest memorial in St Stephen's. An ornamental frame encloses an image of his family and a long inscription incised on what may be gilded plaster over wood in imitation of brass.[18] It tells us that that the 'ALDERMAN & HIS WIEF... TO THE POORE GAVE ALL THEIR GOODES AWAY LEAVING IN TRUST SUCH MEN TO ACT THE SAME AS MIGHT WITH TRUTH PERFOR[M] THEIR GOOD ENTEN[T]...'. One of the so-called Bristol 'nails' (see Corn Street) was installed as a result of those worthy trustees. But it is also possible that the earliest of the pillars, together with the concept behind all of them, was due to Robert Kitchen himself. These complex baluster-shaped bronze columns date from around 1595 to 1631 and have no obvious parallels. Although this book discusses their history and function at some length, the stylistic origins of the pillars' distinctive shapes remain unexplained. Recently the city council responded promptly to vandalism with some careful conservation work, but this unique group continues to be casually subjected to unjustifiable risks (Fig. 14).

The artistic legacy of the third of those three merchant magnates, Sir John Young, is still more remarkable. He has a grand tomb now in pole position at the west door of the cathedral (see 'Bread and Sermons', Fig. 51), but it is the Great Oak Room in the Red Lodge on Park Row that is

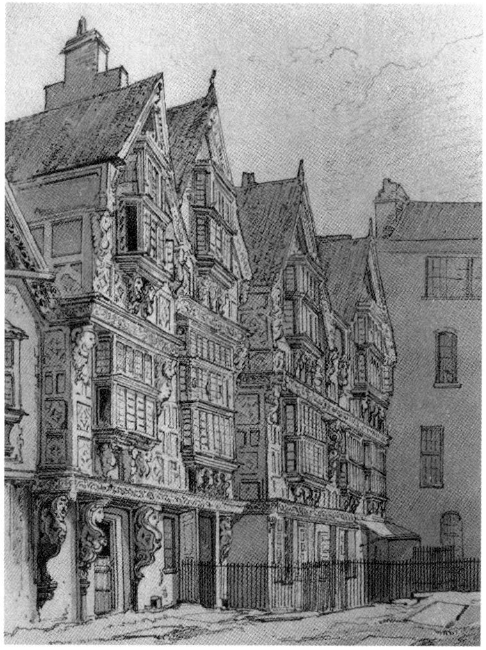

Fig. 13 ***Residence of Robert Aldworth, later known as St Peter's Hospital, 1612*****, (detail) drawing by James Johnson, 1821 (Bristol Museum and Art Gallery, M2681)**

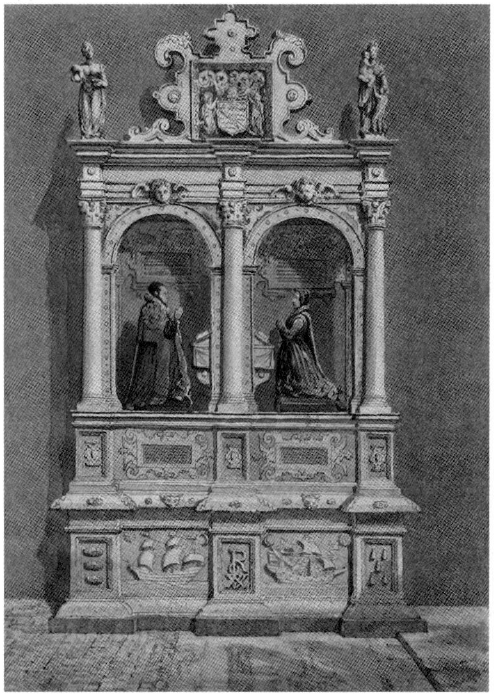

Fig. 12 ***Tomb of Robert Aldworth, died 1634, and his wife, Martha, in St Peter's Church*****, watercolour by Edward Cashin, 1825 (Bristol Museums and Art Gallery, M2667)**

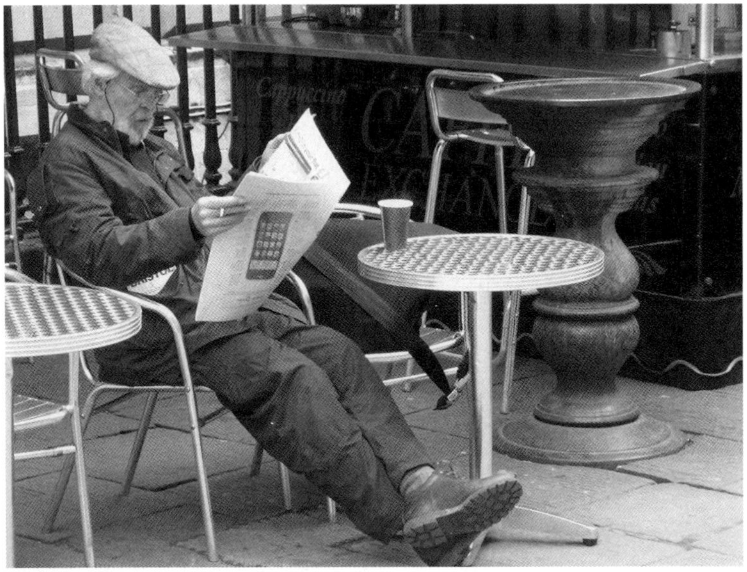

Fig. 14 ***The earliest of the Bristol 'nails', Corn Street, c.1595*, photographed February 2009**

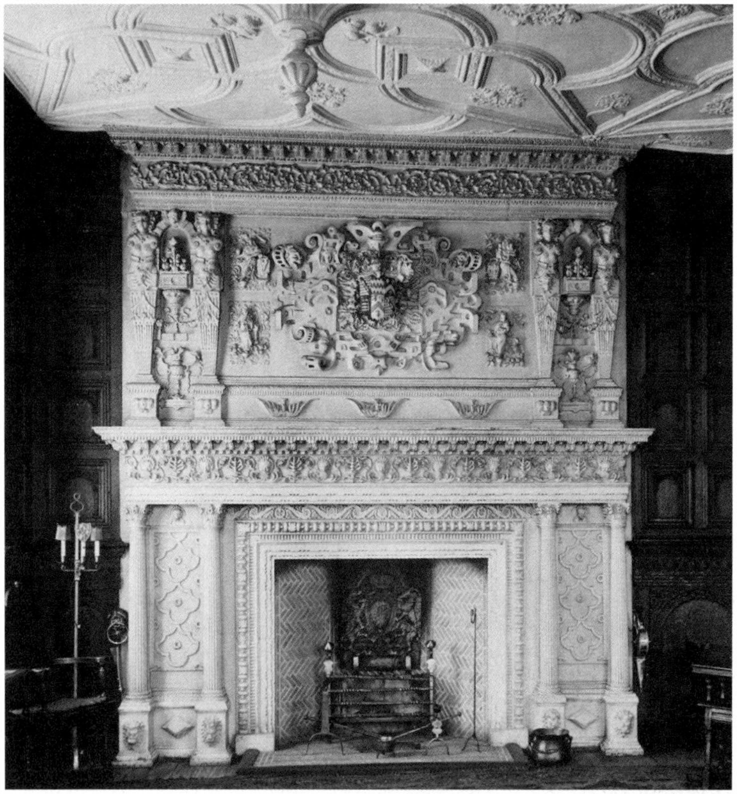

Fig. 15 ***The fireplace surround in the Great Oak Room of the Red Lodge, Park Row, c.1585*, photographed c.1960 (Bristol Museum and Art Gallery)**

his principal legacy (Figs 15, 16). It is one of the finest – perhaps the finest – of late-Elizabethan interiors to survive in England. Bristol once had many similarly ornate interiors and innumerable sculptural fireplace surrounds, but probably none of such extravagance or refinement. We are peculiarly fortunate that a period of such prosperity in Bristol should still be represented by an interior of such exceptional quality, and that the only fireplace surround to remain *in situ* in the city should also have been the very best of its kind. Sir John Young lived in the Great House further down the hill on the site of today's Colston Hall. Here Queen Elizabeth stayed in state during her visit to Bristol in 1574. Over the following decade Young built the Red Lodge 'to accommodate guests, or as a pleasant retreat for meals and entertainment'.[19] Both the elaborate carved timber porch and the limestone and alabaster fireplace and overmantel include relatively pure classical or Renaissance forms in such as arches, columns and cornices, together with complex strapwork cartouches and exotic pilaster figures that are said to 'derive from two mid-C16 suites of engravings by Jan Vredeman de Vries'.[20] The mixture is impressively rich, calm and comfortable.

Queen Elizabeth knighted John Young for his troubles. But when Charles II made a decidedly hurried visit to Bristol while taking the waters at Bath in 1662, Sir Robert Cann was mayor and already a knight. A few days later he was made a baronet. His residence, Stoke Lodge (now Trinity College, see Stoke Hill), was then outside Bristol in Stoke Bishop,

Fig. 16 ***The porch to the Great Oak Room, Red Lodge, c.1585*** **(detail)**

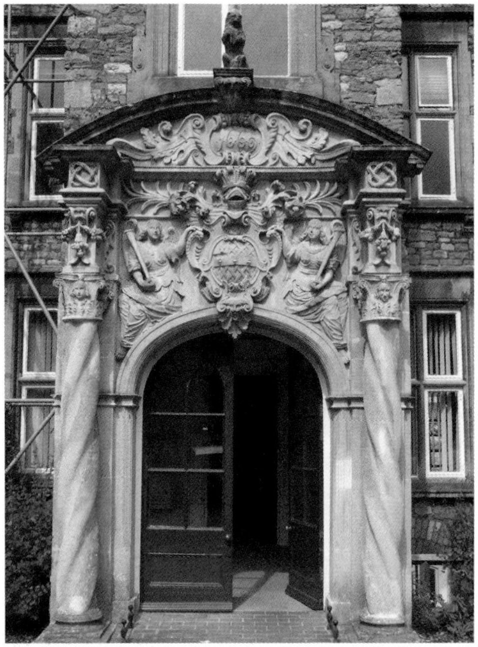

Fig. 17 *Porch of Stoke Lodge, now Trinity College, Stoke Hill, 1669*

Gloucestershire. The flamboyant baroque porch is dated 1669, and the sculpture and decorative detailing upon it may also be the product of somewhat haphazard plundering of foreign engravings, both mannerist and baroque (Fig. 17). It has a splendid – or ridiculous – exuberance, and its lack of coherence may be distinctly provincial or a just reflection of its time. Only a year earlier Samuel Pepys, then Secretary of the Admiralty, had had a thoroughly enjoyable visit to Bristol and described the city as 'in every respect another London'(Fig. 18).[21]

Bristol Sculpture after 1700

The earliest engraved view of Queen Square dates from about 1730 and it portrays the square as a vast, barren and gravelled space, as if desperately in need of Rysbrack's equestrian statue of William III, which was to be commissioned in 1731.[22] But this print after William Halfpenny was produced for inclusion in the architect's treatise on perspective, and he deliberately omitted the lines of lime trees that had been planted as early as 1710, when the earliest of the houses were barely finished.[23] The last houses were completed in 1727[24] and it was for a completed square that the statue was to be commissioned (Fig. 2). Politics and civic pride, especially, but also the self-interest of the residents and the particular initiative of one man, John Elbridge, were behind the project (see Queen Square). Similar politics may also have been behind the garden statues of Hercules and Neptune. Images of 'Hercules, the strong-but-just leader'

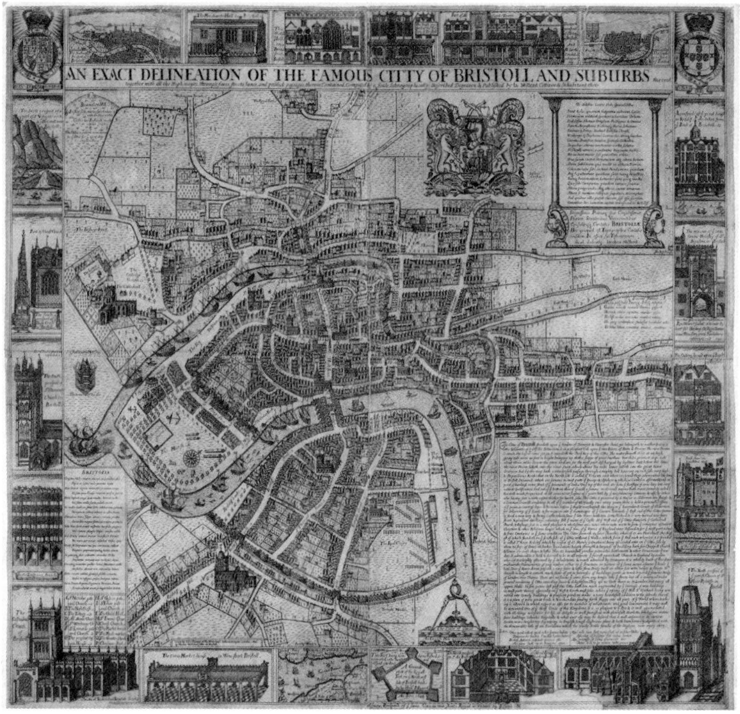

Fig. 18 ***An exact delineation of the famous citty of Bristoll and suburbs*, engraving by James Millerd, 1673 (Bristol Museum and Art Gallery)**

(with whom William III had long wanted to be identified) and of Neptune (who represented 'the saviour beyond the seas') were often overt statements from supporters of William III, the Protestant succession and the ideals of the Whig party (see Rectory Gardens, Henbury Awdlett; Clifton Hill, Goldney House).[25]

There is no reason to suspect that the evident success of the Queen Square statue affected future town planning and commissions in Bristol. An obelisk was later to grace St James's Square (Fig. 19), originally laid out in 1707, and a short-lived Coade stone statue of George III was erected in Portland Square in 1810 (see Portland Square). It was not until the first stage of the filling in of the Floating Harbour at St Augustine's Reach in the early 1890s that free-standing statues were perceived as the means to enhance a new urban open space (see The Centre). The statues of Edmund Burke and Edward Colston of 1894 and 1895, and the Industrial and Fine Art Drinking Fountain of 1901, were almost certainly part of a concerted programme led by J. W. Arrowsmith, printer and publisher, to dignify this large new space, named Colston Avenue (Fig. 20).

Instead, the sculpture of eighteenth century Bristol was largely

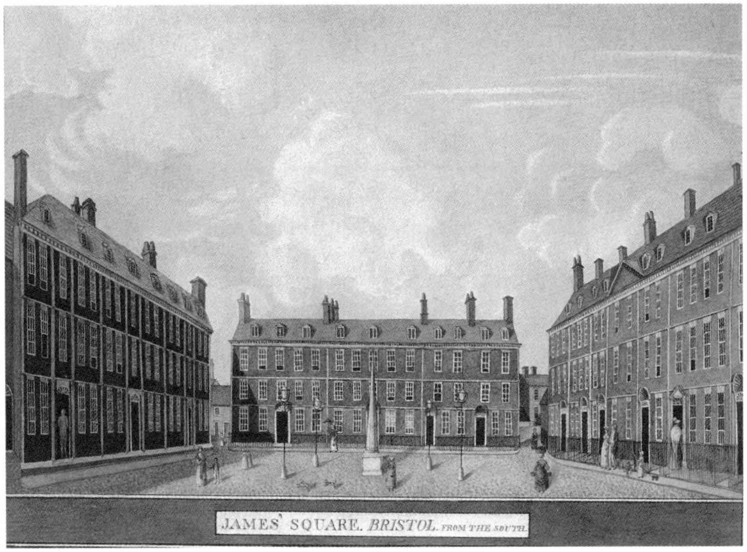

Fig. 19 *Obelisk in St James's Square*, watercolour attributed to Dr Thomas Pole, c.1810 (Bristol Museums and Art Gallery, K4352)

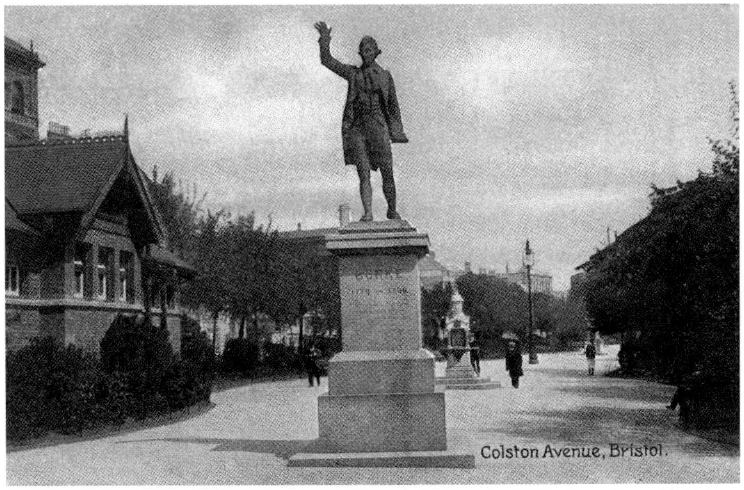

Fig. 20 *Postcard of Colston Avenue, now known as 'The Centre', c.1904 with the statue of Edmund Burke, the drinking fountain and the base of the statue of Edward Colston*

commissioned to ornament the gardens and landscapes of its most successful citizens or to enliven its public buildings. The exception is the lead statue of Neptune erected in 1721 to embellish the rebuilt water outlet of the Temple Conduit (see The Centre). Like the structure built around St John's Conduit (see Nelson Street) in about 1560, the statue was more probably a celebration of the continuing importance of these vital medieval water sources, rather than a political statement (Fig. 21). Endlessly moved, the soft lead figure has become distorted, the detail has blurred (Fig. 22) and the figure is now regarded with amused affection

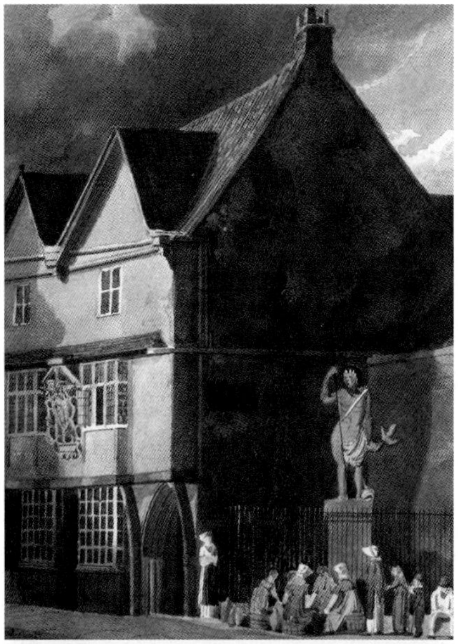

Fig. 21 *The statue of Neptune, painted, beside Alderman White's Almshouses*, detail of watercolour by Samuel Jackson, 1822 (Bristol Museums and Art Gallery, M2127)

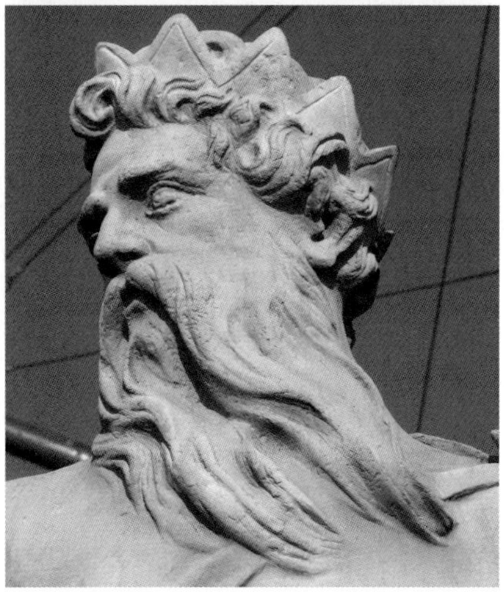

Fig. 22 *The head of Neptune*, by John Randall, 1721, 'The Centre'

and as a symbol of Bristol's maritime past. Despite its local maker, it deserves comparison with John Nost's earlier and equally baroque statue of Hercules, which was moved to Thomas Goldney's garden in Clifton in the mid-eighteenth century (see Clifton Hill, Goldney House).

A member of the Paty family can be linked to the statue of Neptune. The 'James Patty' who supplied the Portland stone surround is almost certainly James Paty I. He was the first of the dynasty of Patys, 'makers of eighteenth-century Bristol', as the subtitle of the recent book about them states.[26] Builders, masons, carvers, statuaries and architects, sometimes competent in each discipline, they dominated architecture and sculpture in eighteenth-century Bristol. James Paty's Quarter Jacks on Christ Church are probably deliberately archaic, imitating the earlier jacks that they replaced, but the sophistication of his early monument to Reverend Richard Sandford of 1721 in St Mary Redcliffe is not in doubt (see 'Bread and Sermons', Fig. 61). He was the builder of the City Library in King Street, and the carver of the industrious children reading books above the windows and of the coat-of-arms within the pediment (Fig. 23).[27] He may also have been the architect. Sadly, around 1960 all the decorative carving and projecting stonework was brutally shaved from this important but decrepit building, owned by the city council.

We have already met Thomas Paty, James's probable nephew, the diligent carrier and re-erector of the High Cross at Stourhead. His first major work, begun in 1740, was the fine carving in stone and wood for Redland Chapel, now the parish church, where the impressive restoration of the interior limewood carving has just been completed. In 1762 John Innys, the brother-in-law of the chapel's patron, wrote that Thomas Paty was now 'generally esteemed one of the Best Carvers in England', and Mr Innys's evident pride in the growth of that reputation was entirely justified. Subsequently, the carving was quite erroneously attributed to Rysbrack, and not without reason, for the church contains four marble busts by him.[28] In 1742 Thomas became the 'Ornament carver to the Exchange', Bristol's finest eighteenth-century building by John Wood (see Corn Street). The Exchange desperately needs a comprehensive programme of conservation. Indeed, much of Paty's work on individual houses in Bristol – such as Clifton Hill House, Arno's Court and Royal Fort House (Figs 24 and 25), none of which has an entry in this volume – has survived in very much better condition than the spectacular coats-of-arms, festoons and keystones on the Exchange. Inside the Royal Fort are 'incomparably the best C18 interiors in Bristol'.[29] The elegant and fanciful stucco work is by Thomas Stocking, and of such quality that it has overshadowed appreciation of the range of Thomas Paty's decorative carving both at the Royal Fort and elsewhere in Bristol. A drawing, reasonably attributed to Thomas Paty, well represents the remarkable standard of rococo craftsmanship in Bristol (Fig. 26).[30]

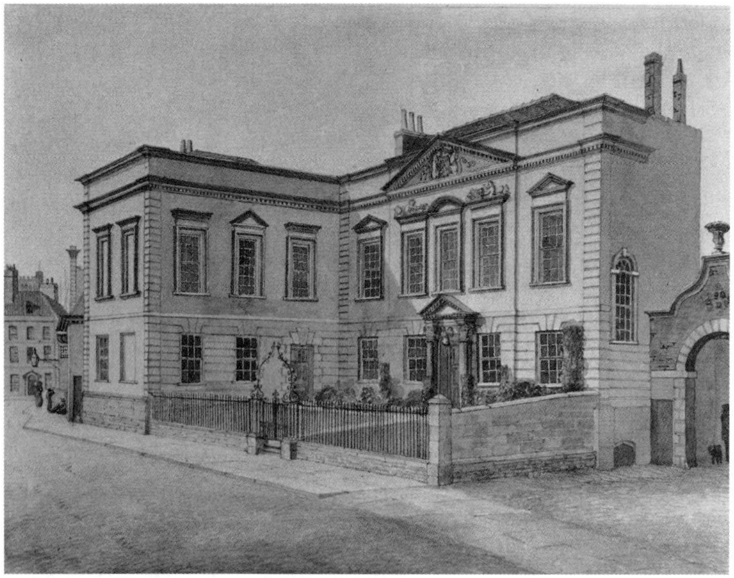

Fig. 23 ***Former City Library, King Street, carving by James Paty I, 1739,*** **watercolour by Edward Cashin, 1823 (Braikenridge Collection, Bristol Museum and Art Gallery, K216)**

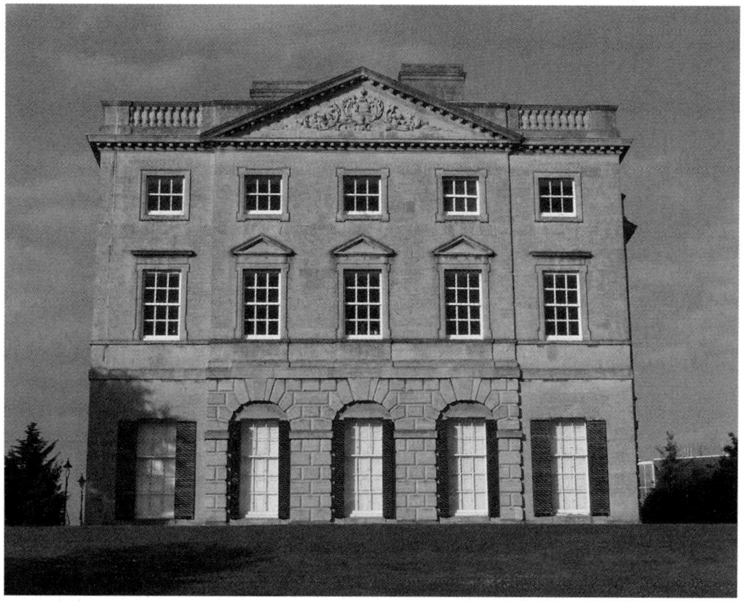

Fig. 24 ***Royal Fort House,*** **by James Bridges, 1758–61, external carving by Thomas Paty**

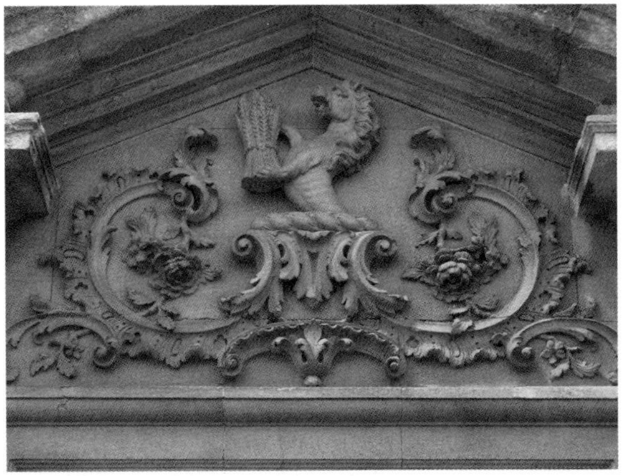

Fig. 25 ***Royal Fort House tympanum carving*****, by Thomas Paty, c.1760**

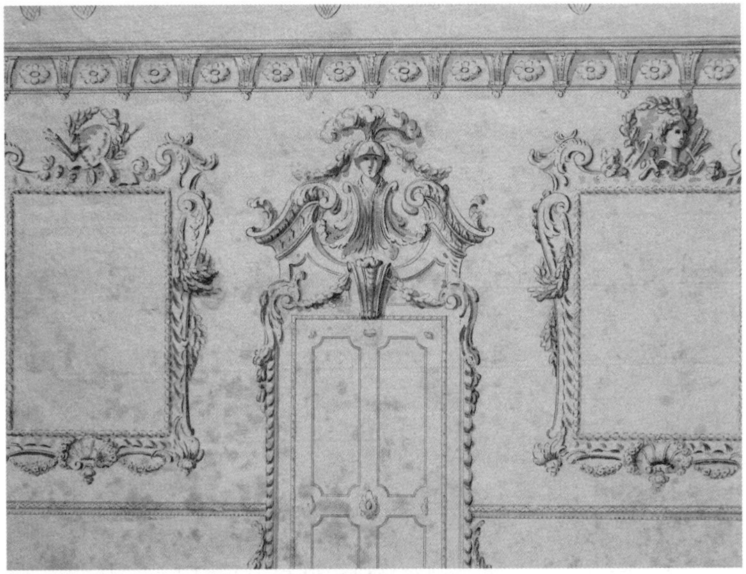

Fig. 26 ***Design for an interior*** **(detail), pen, ink and wash drawing attributed to Thomas Paty, c.1760 (Bristol Museum and Art Gallery, K5026)**

Thomas Paty was also both a builder and an architect and responsible in particular for many of the Georgian terraces and squares in Bristol and Clifton. Before his death in 1789, his son William, who had studied architecture at the Royal Academy Schools in London, had probably been the firm's lead architect for some years. William was the architect of Blaise Castle House and is associated with the great terraces of Royal York Crescent and Cornwallis Crescent, finally completed long after his early death in 1800. He was also a statuary, and there are many monuments by him in the West Country and as far afield as the West Indies.

'Bristol has long had a tradition of decorative craftsmanship that, for all its Paladian elegance, Bath never developed'.[31] Extensive decorative architectural detail had been a striking feature of Bristol's architecture in the seventeenth century. In the following century the Patys, as masons, carvers and architects, brought an increasing sophistication and coherence to this characteristic. In the nineteenth century the first of the equally important dynasty of Fosters was James Foster, grandfather of John Foster of Foster and Wood. James had been a pupil and apprentice of Thomas Paty, setting up on his own as both architect and statuary in 1800 and evidently enjoying the same combination of skills.[32] Later in the century this commitment to carved embellishment was to be most obviously maintained by Foster and Wood, whose exceptionally productive partnership lasted from 1849 to 1906. The former Bristol Museum and Library by John Foster (see Queen's Road) is still, despite its losses, the outstanding example (Fig. 27).

The tradition was continued by Sir George Oatley, 'the doyen of Bristol architects', for the next half-century. Indeed, had we not restricted selection to just two of Oatley's buildings for this volume, the sculptural details that so enliven his architecture, most especially the innumerable

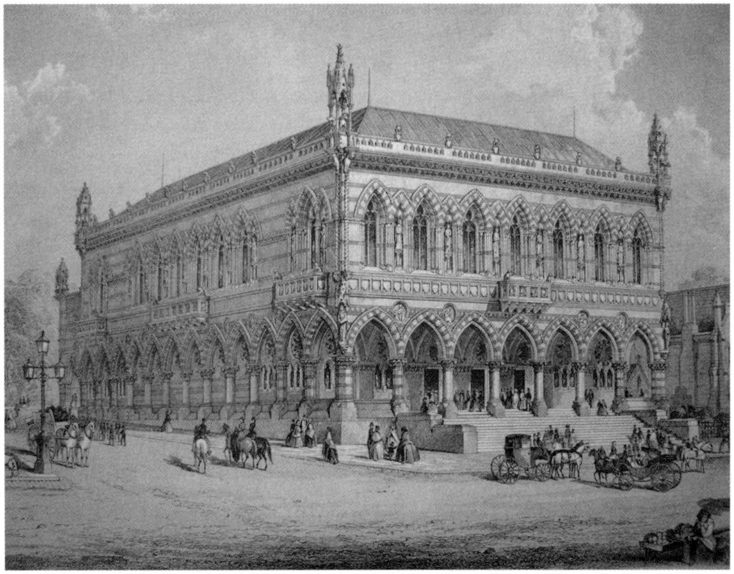

Fig. 27 ***Design for Bristol Museum and Library, Queen's Road by 'Messrs Foster & Wood & A. C. Ponton'*** **(detail), lithograph by J. R. Robbins, c.1867 (Bristol Museum and Art Gallery)**

heads, would have dominated it (see Queen's Road and Tyndall Avenue). More recently, decorative and freestanding sculpture has also been a commendable feature of the Alec French Partnership (see Broad Quay, Denmark St, Lewins Mead, Narrow Quay, Redcliffe St and St George's Rd).

The relationship between the architect and the sculptor has varied considerably. At the Exchange in Corn Street Thomas Paty was employed, in effect, as a decorative sculptor. Early in the following century, the young sculptor J. G. Bubb was chosen by his former fellow student at the Royal Academy, the architect C. A. Busby, to design and carve the more independent classical figures and the bas-relief that adorn the façade of the Commercial Rooms in the same street (see Corn Street). A few years later, in 1824, E. H. Baily – Bristol-born and now a full member of the Royal Academy – was adding a curving relief beneath the portico of the Bristol Institution (see Park Street) a year after the building had opened. It was not part of Robert Cockerell's original design. Its purpose was to promote the sculptor's reputation in his native city.

The prestige that individual sculptors were enjoying was both maintained and eroded by the building boom of the Victorian era. In the middle of the century John Thomas, supervising sculptor of hundreds of figures for the new Palace of Westminster, and indefatigable organiser of a very large workshop, produced six statues for the Guildhall (see Broad Street), the first of the statues for John Norton's replica High Cross (see Berkeley Square), the statues and lunettes for the façade of the future Royal West of England Academy (see Queen's Road) and the most richly sculpted bank façade (Fig. 28) in the country (see Corn Street). Thereafter, in Bristol, a considerable amount of the architectural sculpture is anonymous. We know of Thomas Colley working on two banks by W. B. Gingell in Corn Street in the 1860s. He had settled in Bristol by 1870, when he calls himself 'Sculptor etc.', as if to emphasise that he is also available as a mason and carver. But we do not know the names of the sculptors who worked for Foster and Wood, for example, nor for Ponton and Gough. The latter's façade in Broad Street of 1868, the Avon Insurance building, which is not included here, exemplifies the necessarily arbitrary nature of selection for inclusion in this book. One spandrel containing a sleeping lion is of such quality that any distinction between mason and sculptor or decoration and sculpture becomes perverse (Fig. 29).[33] John Ruskin, who had such faith in the genius of the medieval craftsman and who believed that all decoration should be executed by the man who designed it, would have been impressed.

It might be expected that Sir George Oatley, architect of the great tower of the Wills Memorial Building (see Queen's Road) and an architect much affected by the Arts and Crafts movement, would have matched Ruskin's ideals. Perhaps, in a complicated way, he did. He employed a designer, Jean Hahn, who in turn employed several modellers to work up the designs for sculpture and decoration in clay, which were

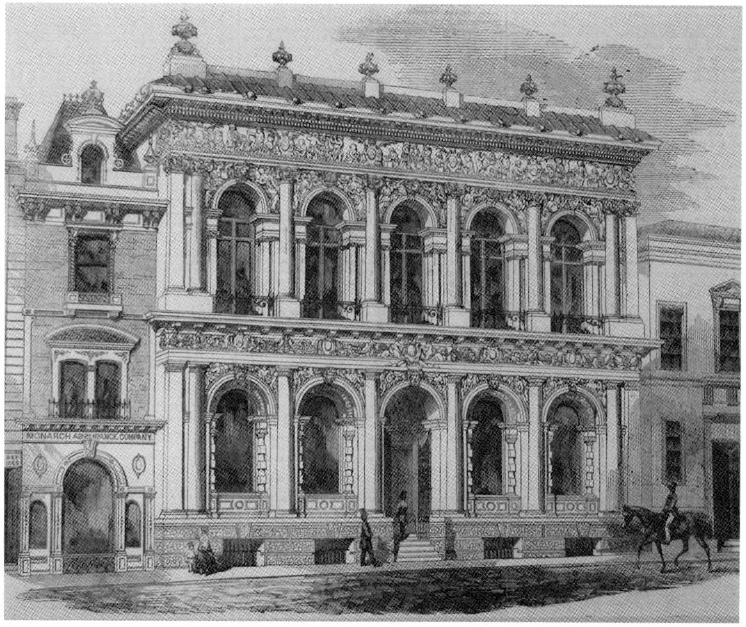

Fig. 28 ***West of England and South Wales Bank, Corn Street*****, sculpture by John Thomas, 1854–7, engraving (Bristol Museum and Art Gallery, Mb7074)**

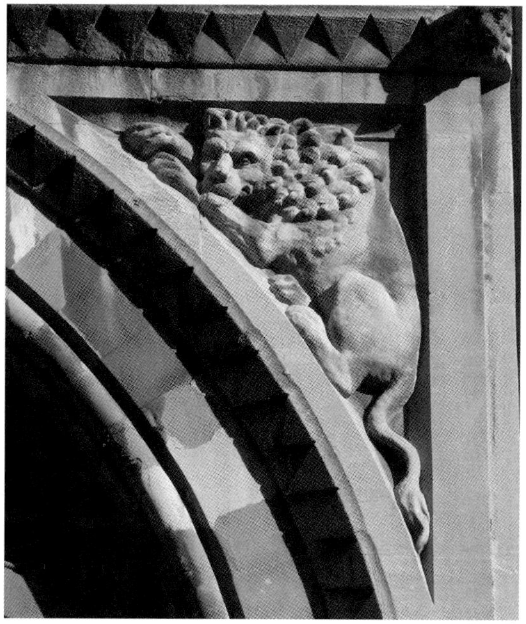

Fig. 29 ***Sleeping Lion, 51 Broad Street*** **by Ponton and Gough, 1868**

then carved in situ or sent out to be carved by individual masons or sculptors. Oatley's standards were high and his controls tight. After failing to get an artist to model some gryphons for the H. H. Wills Physics Building (see Tyndall Avenue) to his taste, he abandoned them. 'Better no ornament than execrable ornament!' [34] And yet the very quantity of carving on his buildings meant that Oatley was also actively seeking ideas from the craftsmen around him. The variety and so often the humour of the works make it clear that individual craftsmen exercised considerable independence, despite the lengthy process.

The role of the architect in the commissioning of independent sculpture can be crucial, neutral or even destructive. Sir George Oatley's largely advisory role in the two major commissions at John Wesley's Chapel (see the Horsefair) was constant and sensitive, involving every aspect from selection and siting to the design of the plinths and the surroundings. When advising the patron on his own personal recommendation of sculptor, he introduced A. G. Walker with the words: 'I have no fancy for any of the modern men, some of whom are unpleasantly "modern" in their ideas and in their outlook and line of life.'

The architect's personal choice of sculptor was not necessarily undermined by a subsequent competition, as the well-documented and fascinating saga of the competition for the statue of Edward VII demonstrates (see Queen's Road, Victoria Rooms).[35] E. A. Rickards had been appointed 'architect of the laying of the ground' in 1910, and he almost immediately presented an ambitious complex of statues, fountains and framing masts on an awkwardly sloping site that perfectly complemented the classical façade of the Victoria Rooms. His brilliant proposals were published in *The Builder* before the competition was even begun, but certainly after he had himself determined upon his chosen sculptor (Fig. 30). The discreet manipulation of the competition apparently went unnoticed, and his preferred sculptor was duly selected. Rickard's partner later trumpeted the importance of the 'domination of the designer', justly citing the Bristol project as 'an excellent example of virility in design and grandeur of conception'.[36]

There were no competitions to hinder Vincent Harris. Determined upon the importance of the setting of his Council House, he successfully demanded the lowering and redesign of College Green as if it was the council's front garden rather than the property of the cathedral's dean and chapter. For him, the removal of the statue of Queen Victoria and of the Victorian High Cross was but 'a minor detail'.[37] Public demand was to lead to Queen Victoria's return, but the High Cross was all but destroyed in storage (see Berkeley Square). Harris was only to be thwarted in his choice of F. H. Hardiman for the thirty-foot-high bronze statues of *Night* and *Day* that were to go in the centre of the two flanking fountains in front of the Council House. *Night* was exhibited in plaster in 1945 at the Royal Academy, and the caption revealed the destination of the finished work. News of her nakedness was reported to the council, and

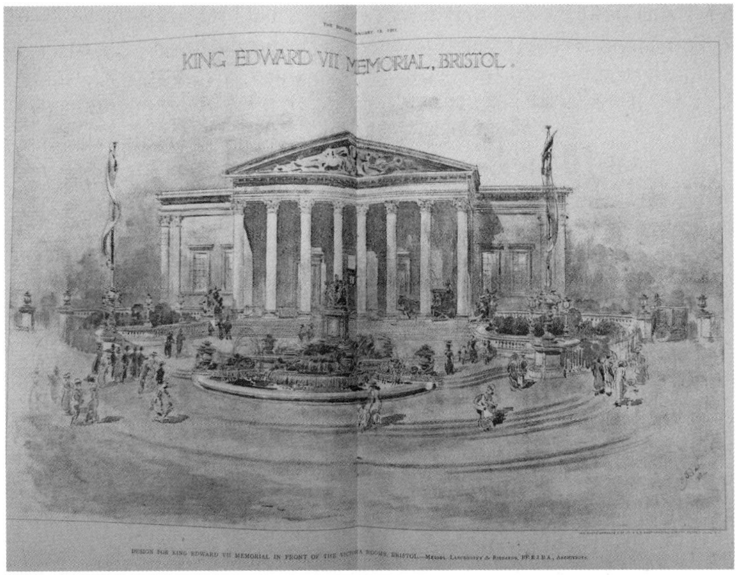

Fig. 30 ***Design for the Edward VII Memorial, Victoria Rooms, Queen's Road,*** **by E. A. Rickards, 1910, illustrated in *The Builder*, 13 January 1911**

the commission was shelved.[38] David McFall's sprightly *Unicorns* and later Charles Wheeler's *Cabot* arrived in Bristol to the bewilderment of the council's officers and to the cheerful contempt of the press. Charles Wheeler, who often enjoyed the company of Vincent Harris at the Chelsea Arts Club, made the mischievous understatement: 'Mr Harris sometimes does things which the City Fathers do not know about'.[39] We are now the fortunate beneficiaries of his arrogant lack of consultation. The quality and success of his commissions for the Council House, inside as well as outside, were exceptional. Within are the frescoed ceiling by Thomas Monnington, the painted murals by John Armstrong and the coats-of-arms by the outstanding designer and calligrapher, Reynolds Stone.

Bristol Sculpture after 1968

The sculpture at the Council House was directly linked to the building itself. Until surprisingly recently, all sculpture in Bristol and almost all sculpture elsewhere in Britain was either architectural, in the sense of being applied or linked to a building, or it was a commemorative statue or monument, a fountain or a water source. There had been intermittent but pioneering open-air exhibitions of contemporary free-standing sculpture in Battersea Park since 1948, organised by London's county council and the Arts Council of Great Britain. The challenge was slowly taken up by a few municipal parks and university campuses and by Harlow New Town.[40] In 1968 three exhibitions marked an abrupt change. The Arts Council organised a travelling exhibition entitled 'Sculpture in a City'; Camden Arts Centre put 130 works onto the streets and into buildings within the City of London in an exhibition of the same title; and Jeremy Rees of Bristol's own contemporary arts centre, Arnolfini, organised a substantial exhibition entitled: 'New British Sculpture/Bristol' (Fig. 31).

Jennie Lee, the minister responsible for the arts, opened the Bristol exhibition. Coloured sculptures, mostly in welded steel, by such artists as Anthony Caro, Garth Evans, William Tucker and William Turnbull were shown on College Green, Queen Square and elsewhere in the city. Most of the works were utterly unsuited to permanent outdoor display, and Jeremy Rees acknowledged that 'we hope to attract those who are shy and inexperienced at walking around galleries'.[41] Four years later, Rees organised a major travelling exhibition for the Arts Council, 'City Sculpture', supported as before by the Peter Stuyvesant Foundation, which now had the declared intention of encouraging the commissioning of sculpture for city centres.

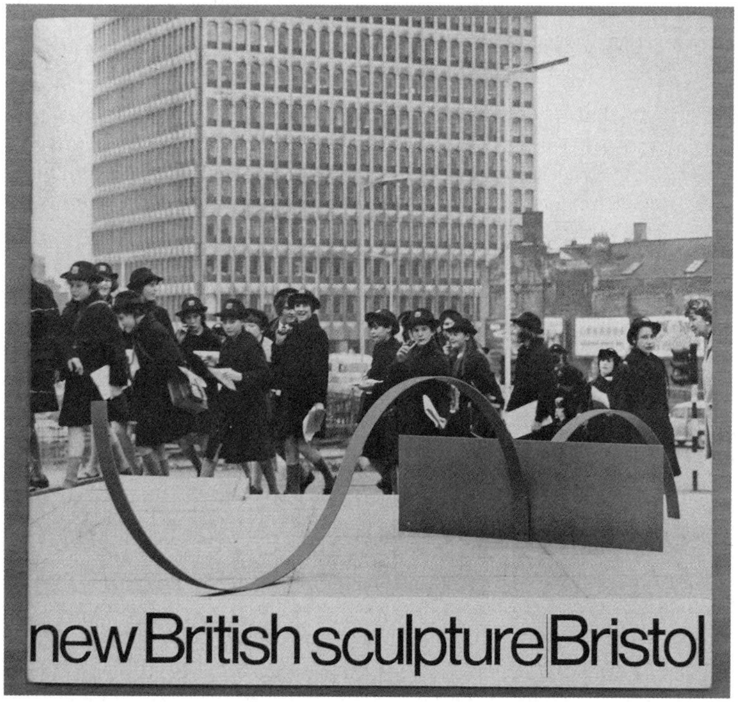

Fig. 31 ***Exhibition catalogue cover for*** **New British Sculpture/Bristol,** ***1968, illustrating*** **Tundra,** ***1967, by Ron Robertson-Swann*** **(Arnolfini archive, BRO)**

Bristol's first art-for-art's-sake free-standing sculpture was probably commissioned in 1968, the year of the 'New British Sculpture/Bristol' exhibition.[42] *Spirit of Bristol* makes an inspired connection between Bristol's maritime past and Concorde, whose very first flight was from Bristol in 1969 (see St James's Barton). It is now largely hidden by trees and very awkwardly squashed against railings, but it has survived very much better than other modern sculptures in the city. In 1980, just one hundred and fifty metres away, two important abstract sculptures were unveiled. With the advice of the Arts Council, the insurance company Sun Life had staged a competition assessed by the company's chairman, the architect of their new building (Sun Life Court) and the directors of the Tate Gallery and Arnolfini, Alan Bowness and Jeremy Rees.[43] The architect, Richard Towning Hill, boycotted the ceremony in protest, presumably at the committee's descision.[44] Initially, Nicholas Pope's *Five Amorphous Shapes* gave the courtyard and the main entrance area the enviable calm of a Japanese garden.[45] There were, however, problems with drainage and the load-bearing capacity of the floor. Once Pope's large Forest of Dean stones became known as 'the elephant droppings', their fate was sealed and they were banished to the company's sports fields. Their whereabouts is now unknown. John Maine's ten-ton block of Carrara marble, *Monolith II* (Fig. 32), dignified the approach to the courtyard for twenty-one years until the company, now AXA SunLife, moved to Stoke Gifford in South Gloucestershire and resited *Monolith II* in the gardens of the new offices.

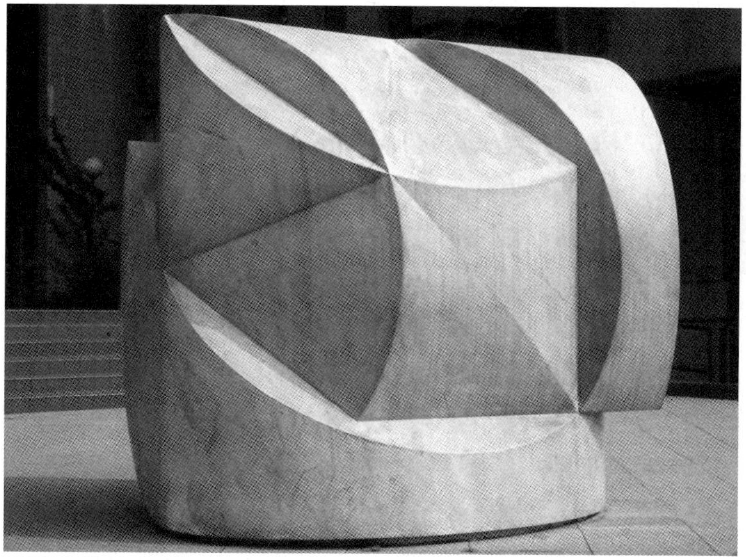

Fig. 32 ***Monolith II,*** **by John Maine, 1980 (when at Sun Life Court, St James's Barton)**

Other contemporary sculpture designed to complement the new office blocks of the 1970s has also suffered from changes of ownership and redevelopment. Judith Bluck's nine reliefs on Greyfriars (see Lewins Mead) were destroyed in 2008, and Franta Belsky's *Oracle* was removed and sold, and its integral artist-designed base was destroyed in the same year (see Narrow Plain). Paul Mount's welded steel sculpture, *Skysails*, on the façade of Brigstowe House on Welsh Back was removed when the building became a hotel in 1988, reappearing to advantage on the Streatham Campus of Exeter University (see St James's Barton, *Spirit of Bristol*). All three works were first erected in 1974.

Paintings and sculpture within the entrance halls of new office blocks can suffer a similar fate. An enormous painting by Patrick Caulfield was erected in the foyer of London Life Association's new offices in Temple Street in 1983 to mark the company's move from London. Fourteen years later, KPMG replaced the insurance company and the painting now languishes in bits in a Clifton basement.

The earnest approach to the competition and commission of the Sun Life Court sculptures by Nicholas Pope and John Maine was to be repeated five years later at Baltic Wharf in 1984. This time, wisely, the management of the selection and the commissioning of the three free-standing works were entrusted to Lesley Greene, director of the Public Art Development Trust, which she had, in effect, founded the previous year. The archive of this trust was acquired by the Henry Moore Institute in 2005, an indication of the national significance of this trust in the history of British sculpture over the next twenty years. In Bristol, Lesley Greene was herself involved in four further projects, both through the PADT and as a private consultant, and the city is much indebted to her.

At Castle Park from 1991 to 1993, Lesley Greene managed the largest of all public art commissioning programmes in the south-west. She took the fullest possible advantage of Peter Randall-Page's preliminary report recommending the integration of 'art and craft work into the fabric of the place, as it is attention to detail, not grand gestures, which will have the most profound effect'. There were to be over twenty separate commissions, from seating, litter bins and bridges to free-standing sculptures. Only six of the of the more traditionally sculptural commissions are included in this book, but all, as Randall-Page anticipated, were vital to the success of the project (Fig. 33). Of these six works, only Peter Randall-Page's *Beside the Still Waters* (see Castle Park) does not directly reflect an aspect of the history of the site. There were also collaborative projects, the involvement of school children, the commissioning of a poem, a video installation and other temporary art works. The pattern and process of future commissions in Bristol was being set.

Lesley Greene was next involved in the selection of an artist to work with the engineers Ove Arup & Partners on the new footbridge over St Augustine's Reach (see Narrow Quay). It was a commission that

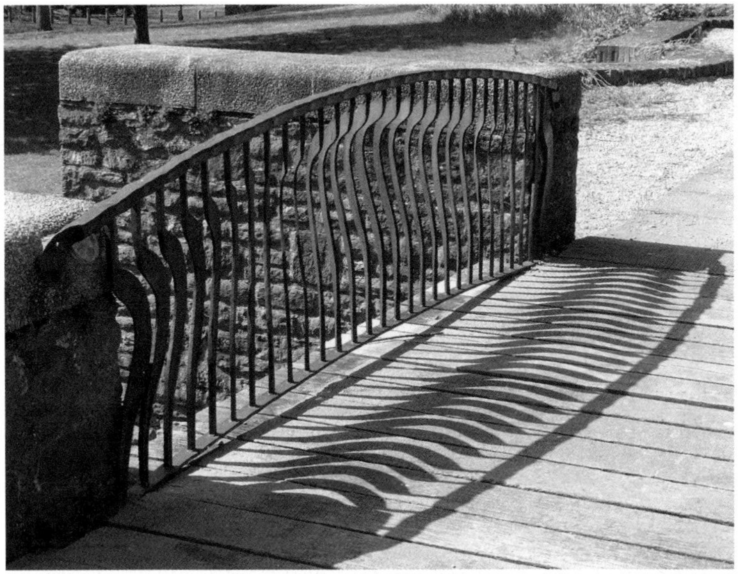

Fig. 33 *Bridge in Castle Park*, by James McCullogh, 1991–3

perfectly matched her repeated arguments for the early appointment and involvement of an artist in architectural and engineering projects. Delays that continued long after she had ceased to be involved were to diminish the success of this project, but her arguments certainly ultimately triumphed at Jack's Brasserie (see Harbourside, the Pavilion). There Dail Behennah, who had woven metal waste baskets for summer use at Castle Park, collaborated with the architect Nick Childs to great effect. Whether the resulting rhythms of the metal work and its shadows are considered as sculpture or as craft, as design or as architecture, is irrelevant. It is outstanding public art.

In the winter of 1996–7, Lesley Greene developed an arts strategy for the nascent Bristol Royal Hospital for Children, ultimately managing a commissioning budget of £1.3 million and involving over twenty artists. Most of the works are within the hospital, but *Lollypop Be-bop* (see Upper Maudlin Street) is not only by far Bristol's tallest[46] and most colourful sculpture, it is also the most public and cheerful demonstration of the confidence of the hospital authorities in the relevance of the arts to the healing process (Fig. 34). In 2009, just a hundred metres away, the new Bristol Heart Institute opened, with seven completed art works ranging from special lighting to an atrium mobile, and internal and external wall decoration. The commitment has also come from family doctors within the community, and in 2004 Lesley Greene provided initial advice that led to seven artworks within the new Bedminster Family Practice, a doctors' surgery. In 2006 a new campus-style mental

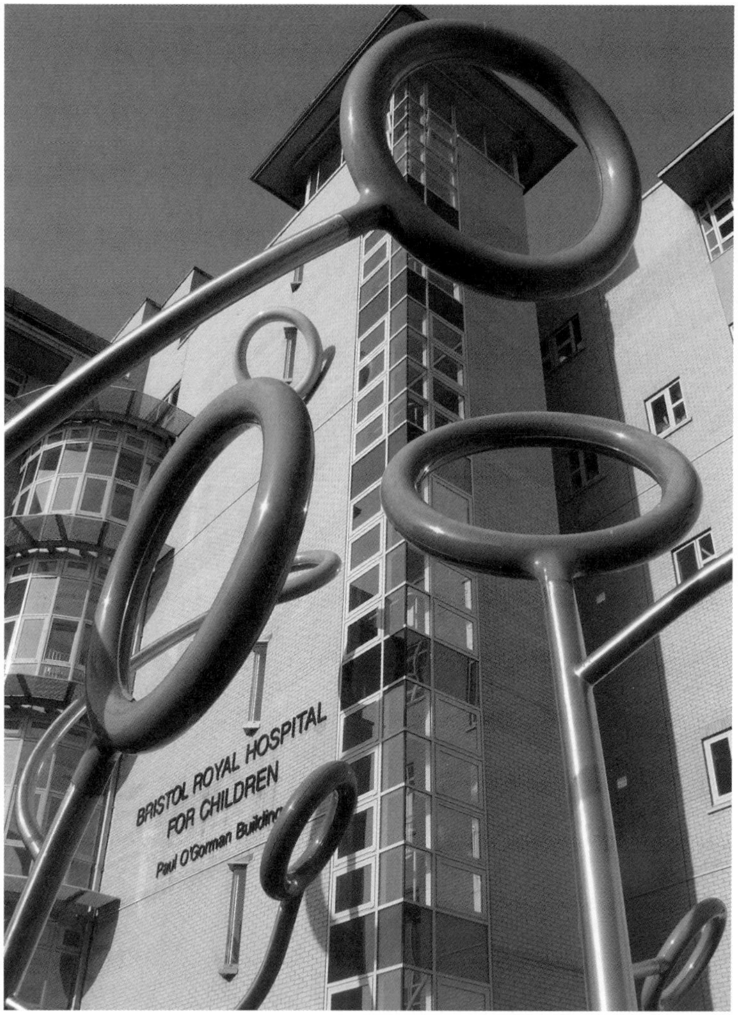

Fig. 34 *Lollypop Be-bop*, by Andrew Smith, 1999–2002 (Bristol Royal Hospital for Children, Upper Maudlin Street)

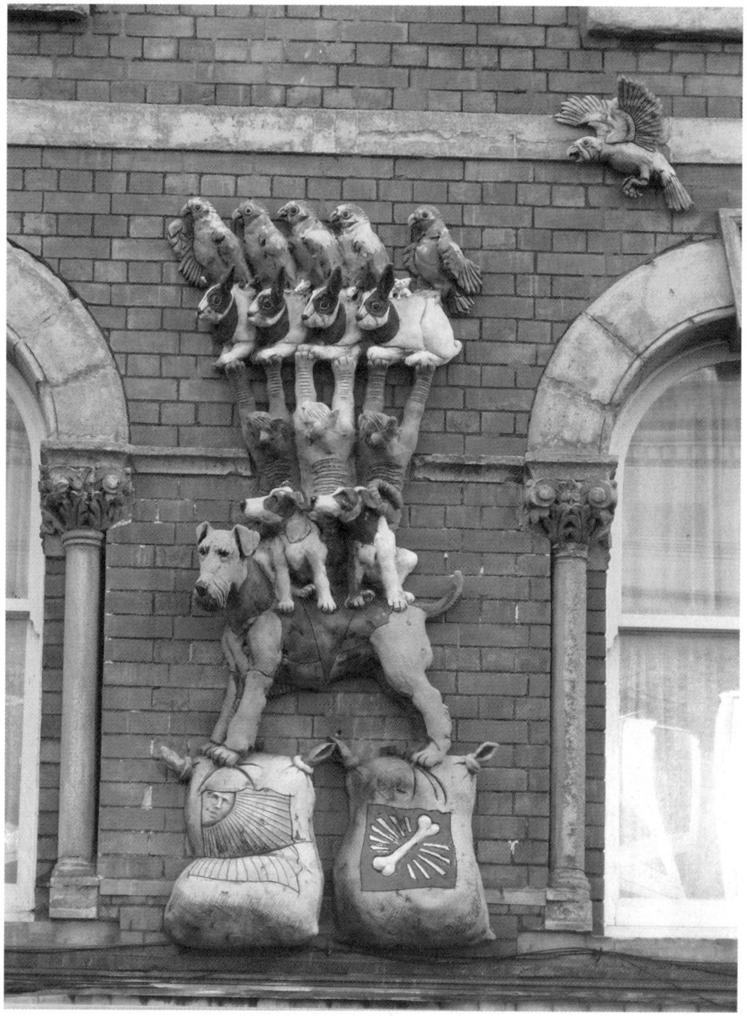

Fig. 35 *Pet shop sign*, by Steven Joyce, 1992/3 (East Street, Bedminster)

health hospital, Callington Road Hospital in Brislington, opened, with seventeen site-specific art works. *Blueskyfence*, at Callington Road, *Endless Ring* at the Bristol Heart Institute and *Staircase* at the Wellspring Healthy Living Centre, Barton Hill, are the principal features of substantial public art projects, and all are from the Walter Jack Studio. This successful Bristol workshop was set up over a decade ago by Walter Jack as the furniture designer responded to the demand for 'public realm improvements' (see Temple Way and Oxford Street, The Dings).[47]

Health and regeneration were successfully combined at the Wellspring Healthy Living Centre at Barton Hill, but not at Knowle West Health Park, where the project *Art of Wellbeing* sought to 'develop the physical fabric of the park'.[48] The major commission was a disaster. Not a trace remains of *Life Cycle*, two trees – one living, and one both dead and upside down – by Elpida Hadzi-Vasileva, installed in 2004. The artist's website bitterly observes that the 'public art programme has left a legacy of vandalism, disappointment and disagreement'.[49]

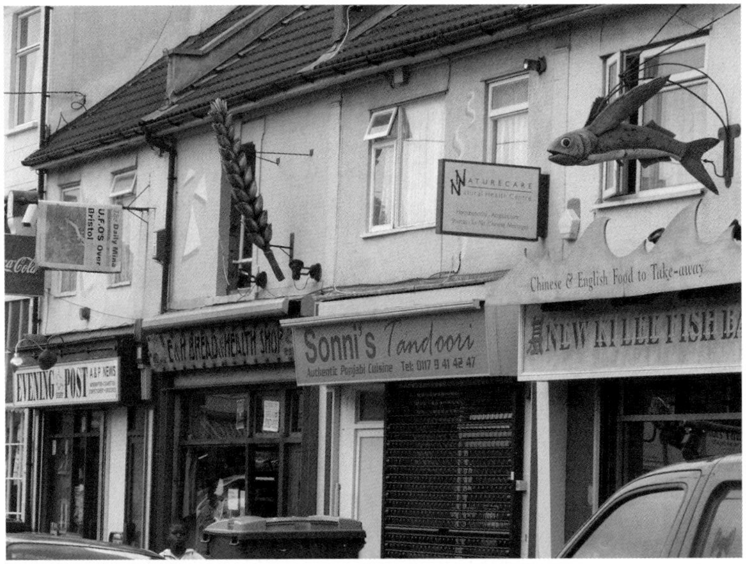

Fig. 36 *Shop signs*, by Jon Bentley (far left) and Steven Joyce, c.1997, Mina Rd, St Paul's

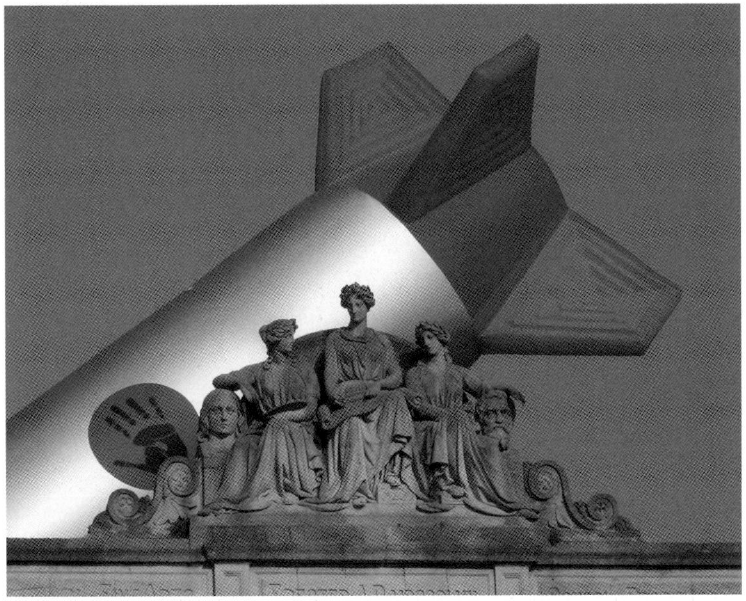

Fig. 37 'Crimes of Passion' exhibition, 2009, *Bomb* by FilthyLuker, behind *Painting, Architecture and Sculpture* by John Thomas, on the roof of the Royal West of England Academy, Queen's Road

Elsewhere, however, the deliberate involvement of public art as one arm of regeneration has had considerable success in Bristol. Such works as those of Walter Jack and others at The Dings (see Oxford St) and of Rod Harris at a small community garden (see Stapleton Rd) are included in this volume, but much has gone unrecorded, most notably the shop signs by Bristol's most familiar sculptor, Steven Joyce. Six of his works are noted here, but not one of the eighteen shop signs that he has undertaken for urban renewal schemes is included. Shops may close and move on and their signs go with them, but there remain excellent examples of this ancient and revitalised genre in Mina Rd (St Pauls), St Mark's Rd (Easton), Stapleton Rd and East St (Bedminster) (Figs 35 and 36).

Street art, in its more usual role and meaning, has just entered the hallowed halls of the Royal West of England Academy. In the spring of 2009 the RWA held an exhibition entitled: 'Crimes of Passion – Street Artists in Bristol', with a subtitle that carefully avoided the word 'graffiti': 'Bristol's celebrated street artists invade the city's grandest gallery for six weeks' (Fig. 37). Here, several years ago, there was a major exhibition of the work of Richard Long, incomparably the most important of all artists, sculptors or land artists to have been born and educated in Bristol, who, incidentally, still lives nearby.

The gulf between the two shows may not be quite the chasm that it appears to be. In 2006 the Arts Council's 'British Art Show 6' was held in Bristol at several venues, but also with some specially commissioned external works. At the entrance to the Harbourside development site were two giant billboards by Mark Titchner. One had a powerful abstract design, and the other was a striking text piece produced with the active participation of young people. The text might be a manifesto for contemporary public art artists, official and unofficial:

> ART YOU DON'T HAVE TO PAY FOR.
> ART THAT YOU CAN WALK OVER.
> ART WHERE THE PUBLIC IS.
> ART THAT IS AVAILABLE TO EVERYONE.
> IS IT FOR THE PEOPLE?
> IS IT BY THE PEOPLE?
> SOMETHING, SOMEWHERE THAT ALTERS
> EVERYTHING AROUND IT.
> ART IS BETTER THAN BUILDINGS.

Notes

[1] L.V. Grinsell, *The History and Coinage of Bristol Mint* (Bristol, 1986), p.25; M. Q. Smith, 'The Harrowing of Hell relief in Bristol Cathedral', *Transactions of the Bristol and Glos. Arch. Soc.*, 1976, vol. 94, pp.101–6. [2] N. Pevsner, *North Somerset and Bristol, Buildings of England* (Harmondsworth, 1958), p.372. [3] S. Stoddard, *Mr Braikenridge's Brislington* (Bristol, 1981), pp.44, 47. [4] No traces remain at Brislington, but decorative sculpture survives at Braikenridge's later home, Claremont Villa, Clevedon, both inside and outside; S. Stoddard, 'George Weare Braikenridge 1775–1856: a Bristol antiquarian and his collection', M.Litt thesis, University of Bristol, 1983. [5] B. Little, *The City and County of Bristol: A Study of Atlantic Civilisation* (London, 1954), p.73. [6] M. Liversidge, *The Bristol High Cross*, BBHA, no. 42, 1978. [7] W. Barrett, *History and Antiquities of the City of Bristol* (2 vols, Bristol, 1789), pp.474, 475. [8] Op. cit., p.475. [9] Samuel Scott's painting is based largely on an engraving, *The North-West view of Bristol High Cross…*, by W.H. Toms after a drawing by R. West, 1737, published 1743. [10] *The Works of Horace Walpole, Earl of Oxford*, ed. R. Walpole and M. Berry (London, 1798), vol. II, pp.464, 465; an engraving of the Long Gallery showing the painting, fp. 461. [11] Three letters between Henry Hoare and Thomas Paty were given by Henry Wood, sculptor and mason, to G.W. Braikenridge in 1827 and are part of a substantial collection of High Cross material in the Bristol Reference Library's Braikenridge Collection, vol. XV. [12] *Bristol Evening Post*, 15 June 1980; *Western Daily Press*, 12 and 13 June 1980. [13] BRO 38544/1/ [14] J. Latimer, *Annals of Bristol in the Eighteenth Century* (Bristol, 1893 (1970)), p.377. [15] C.E. Boucher, *Transactions of the Bristol and Gloucestershire Archaeological Society*, vol. 61, 1939, pp.95–6, 'St Edith's Well and St Peter's Cross, Bristol', from which most information has been drawn. [16] Weathered fragments that survived within the gutted ruins of the church until 1958 are now in Bristol Museum: S. Stoddard, *Bristol before the Camera: The City in 1820–30: Watercolours and Drawings from the Braikenridge Collection* (Bristol, 2001), p.35. [17] A. Gomme, M. Jenner and B. Little, *Bristol, An Architectural History* (London, 1979), p.11. [18] H.S. Cowper, *Robert Kitchen, Mayor of Bristol; A Native of Kendal* (Kendal, 1928), p.193, states that the engraving is on stone; N. Pevsner, *North Somerset and Bristol; Buildings of England* (Harmondsworth, 1958), p.409, states that it is on brass. [19] S. Levitt, *The Red Lodge* (Bristol, 1986), p.3; the Red Lodge is in the care of the curator of applied art, City Museum and Art Gallery. [20] A. Foyle and B. Cherry, *Bristol* (New Haven, CT and London, 2004), p.231. [21] Quoted in J.H. Bettey, *Bristol Observed* (Bristol, 1986), p.54. [22] Illus. K. Eustace, *Michael Rysbrack, Sculptor 1694–1770* (Bristol, 1982), p.23, fig. 6. [23] BRL Braikenridge Collection, vol. XV, p.265. [24] Foyle and Cherry, as note 20, p.162. [25] T. Richardson, 'Political hotbeds', *Financial Times*, 23 June 2007; see also T. Richardson, *The Arcadian Friends: Inventing the English Landscape Garden* (London, 2007). [26] G. Priest, *The Paty Family: Makers of Eighteenth Century Bristol* (Bristol, 2003). [27] Foyle and Cherry, as note 20, p.160, state that the stone figure now in a niche on St Michael on the Mount Primary School may come from the library; this is correct but it was a Victorian addition to the library, being placed in the alcove formed when the staircase window on the east side was blocked up; see A. Beeson, *Bristol Central Library and Charles Holden* (Bristol 2006), illus. fp. 32. [28] K. Eustace, 'A place full of rich and industrious people' ,*The British Art Journal*, vol. VII, no. 1, pp.3–16. [29] Foyle and Cherry, note 20, p.244. [30] See M. Snodin, *Rococo: Art and Design in Hogarth's England* (exib. cat., London, 1984), M20, p.205; M. Liversidge, 'The poetry is in the Paty', *Bristol University Newsletter*, 18 March 1982, p.18. [31] T. Mowl and N. Menneer, *Bristol, City on the Edge* (London, 2006), p.51. [32] Gomme, Jenner and Little, as note 17, p.433. [33] T. Mowl, *Bristol: Last Age of the Merchant Princes* (Bath, 1991), pl.43. [34] Quoted in S. Whittingham, *Sir George Herbert Oatley: Architect of Bristol* (Bristol, 2009). [35] See King Edward VII Memorial, n.7. [36] Op. cit., n.1. [37] See College Green, Queen Victoria, n.20. [38] See College Green, Council House, Unicorns, n.7. [39] See College Green, Council House, Cabot, n.7. [40] W.J. Strachan, *Open Air Sculpture in Britain* (London, 1984). [41] *Guardian*, May 1968, uncat. cutting in BRO Arnolfini archives. [42] The date is uncertain; see St James's Barton, *Spirit of Bristol*, n. 7. [43] *Bristol and West Country Illustrated*, May 1980; Rees's own files concerning this commission are in the Arnolfini archives in the BRO. [44] *Western Daily Press*, 29 October 1980. [45] Strachan, as at note 40, illus. p.96. [46] No longer: Ackroyd and Harvey's imposing, elegant and rather grim sculpture, *Twist*, erected December 2008, at the end of the M32 at the apex of Cabot Circus, is 20 metres high. [47] www.walterjack.co.uk. [48] BCC, *Creative Bristol, A Sketchpad*, 2005, p.9. [49] www.elpihv.co.uk/work/commissions/life-cycle/.

Bread and Sermons by KATHARINE EUSTACE

Bread and Sermons: History in the Public Acknowledgement of Individual Lives

This essay does not propose to be a complete survey of the many church monuments that survive in Bristol churches. Rather, it will look at a number of outstanding monuments in a more or less chronological progression, as they reflect and contribute to the history of the city of Bristol. It will also attempt to give flesh to some of the masons who made them.

In the early 1730s, a letter in the *Free Briton* argued that 'perpetuating the memory of Great Events by Trophies, Statues, etc.... has proved the most powerful Method to cultivate Virtue and Publick Spirit'.[1] Taking up the same theme a hundred years later, John Evans pointed out when discussing the Colston monument, 'it is thus that the productions of the chisel may become monuments of historical reference'.[2] Margaret Whinney wrote in 1964, in the introduction to her survey of British sculpture, that post-Reformation, 'for the next two hundred years the history of English sculpture is very largely a question of tombs and monuments'.[3]

Before the nineteenth century, commemorative public sculpture in this country was confined almost exclusively to the monarchy, but dynastic imperatives and spreading social identity encouraged the use of the funerary monument as an expression of a need to record for posterity the great and the good. But it must be acknowledged from the outset that while church monuments as material evidence convey much information, they represent the well-to-do establishment, and in a city like Bristol – with a long history of iconomachic puritanism and later non-conformity – only a part of that establishment. Thus there is no monument to the city Maecenas and early industrialist, the Quaker ironmaster Thomas Goldney (1696–1768), for Quakers specifically rejected funerary identification. Furthermore, many plantation owners preferred (as did the Pinney family) to set up memorials in the country parishes where they identified their roots,[4] and whose epitaphs provide no hint of where and how they made the money that paid for such memorials.

In a city such as Bristol, it was the *civis bonum* that was at stake. Bristol was heavily industrialised well before the Industrial Revolution. There had been shipbuilding since time immemorial; the smelting of ores in this European centre for the production of high quality copper and brass; and, from the late seventeenth century, sugar refining (as the fruits of the slave trade were imported from the West Indies), and glass and ceramics exported to Europe. It was a port, with all the social disadvantages that follow: problems of social migration, where people came from all over Europe to take ship to the New World; of the transport of felons to the penal settlements in the Americas, and their return; of alcoholism associated with the trade in wines and spirits, considered to affect all classes; and of vagrancy, child abduction and child exploitation. City fathers and benefactors, the founders of hospitals, almshouses and schools, were acknowledged on their tombs for their *pro bono* activities. Their monuments survived the religious iconoclasm of the sixteenth and seventeenth centuries and the Low Church sentiments of many Bristolians in the eighteenth and early nineteenth centuries, precisely because their benefactions continued to play an important part in the social cohesion and identity of their native city. The message was 'Go, and Do Thou Likewise', the motto of Edward Colston, one of Bristol's best known benefactors.

A recurring theme in benefactions to the city of Bristol was one of anti-Catholic and anti-Dissenting prejudice. The language of the times was full of phrases such as 'polluted with Superstition and Idolatory', and 'Popery and Slavery' (slavery, that is, to Rome). It was William III, 'who freed this Nation from being manacled in the Chains of Romish Slavery and Superstition',[5] who was commemorated by the equestrian bronze in Queen Square in 1736.[6] Ridley's almshouses, founded in 1716 by the will of Sarah Ridley, was for five old men and five old women 'as were not nor ever have been Roman Catholics, or inclinable to such, but who shall have been educated in and always professed the Protestant religion'.[7] Ridley's bequest included money for bread for the poor, as did many other benefactors, and when Joseph Leech attended Sunday service at St Mary Redcliffe in 1843, he found that:

> Redcliff Church, for a building so old, does not abound in monuments; the most remarkable I noticed was a heap of quartern loaves, which partially blocked up one of the windows of the north aisle. Whoever the ancient worthy may have been by whose munificence this Sunday supply is distributed, his descendants seem determined to make his works so shine forth before men that they shall not forget them.

Leech adds in his usual dry and mildly cynical way: 'nor have I any serious objection, only that it gives that part of the church the appearance of a baker's shop'.[8]

Monuments may have been purposefully removed in the mid-sixteenth century, and again in the mid-seventeenth century, for reasons of religious prejudice, practice and belief. In 1577, Sir John Young contributed a 'massive tomb' from the former Carmelite church to the repair of the quay wall, and tomb stones were removed from St Lawrence

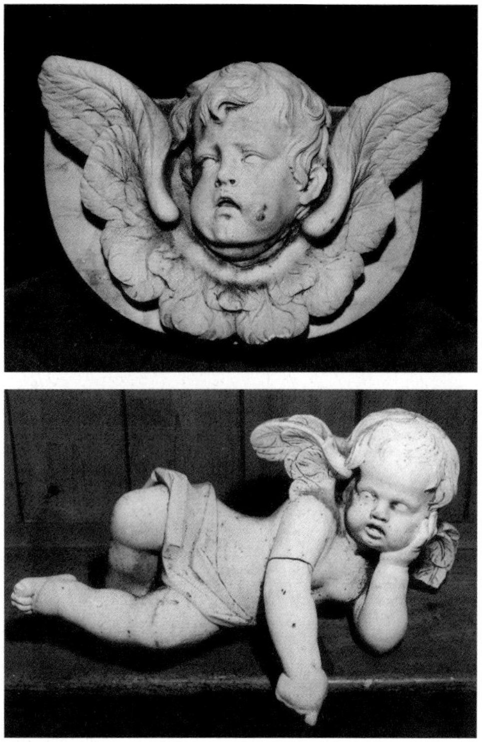

Figs 38 a & b *Fragments of ornamental detail from eighteenth-century monuments,* **photographed in the churchyard of St James in 1981**

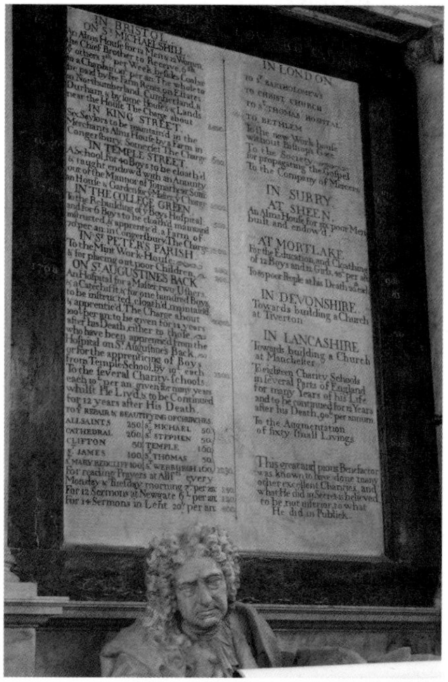

Fig. 39 *Detail of the inscription tablet, listing benefactions, from the monument to Edward Colston (d. 1721),* **All Saints**

for the same purpose.[9] Much must have decayed and been tidied up in the early eighteenth century in the reordering of medieval interiors, again in the mid-nineteenth century when the Gothic was once again a taste to be admired, and finally in the years after the Second World War (Figs 38a and b).

In the aftermath of the Reformation, Bristol became very Low Church, and visual stimulus to the senses was not encouraged. This might also be said of Bristol's politics, which was largely Whig[10] and loyal to a constitutional monarchy only so long as it was seen to be an upholder and defender of the Protestant faith. A latent iconomachism would appear to have informed the religious devotions of Bristolians for large stretches of time. As late as 1876, a group of figures by James Redfern (1838–76), designed for niches in G. E. Street's north porch in Bristol Cathedral, were summarily removed by Dean Elliott amid an outcry of anti-popery.[11] Non-conformism was a powerful force among the population of Bristol, and non-conformity characterised its attitude to politics. Quakers prospered despite, or perhaps because of, being denied the freedom of the city with its civic responsibilities and local politics.[12] Huguenots found a home here, became pillars of the establishment, and were leading figures in the 'Africa trade' in slaves.[13] Bristol became the cradle for John Wesley and the Bristolian George Whitfield's Methodism, which flourished and grew into a worldwide movement.[14]

Memorials are a public way of reminding executors of the generosity of the dead, and of their duties. The small wall memorial in St James to Henry Dighton (d. 1673) states in the epitaph that he left £5 for ten coats for the poor of the parish, while that to Edward Colston (d. 1723) in All Saints lists every pound left by the deceased in every corner of the country, including money for sermons (Fig. 39). It is marked that the monuments that survive the repeated urges to tidy up in the reordering of interiors, to conform to changes in liturgical practice and custom (Fig. 40), or the need for restoration of the fabric, are, by and large, those to figures who are remembered in Bristol as much for their benefactions to the city as for their fine memorials. Hence William Canynges, Alderman Whitson and Edward Colston are remembered as part of the fabric of the city and its history largely through their monuments, which became public memorials to civic pride and gratitude.[15] They were preserved, restored and imitated as such, and even publicised; the contemporary engraving of the monument to Edward Colston has on the one hand a traditional figure of Charity, and on the other grateful recipients acknowledging their gratitude (Fig. 41). The energy behind the foundation of the Bristol Infirmary in the 1730s came from John Elbridge (c.1682–1738).[16] His draft will specifically required that he be interred 'in the vault where my late devoted friend Thomas Moore Esqr. lies' in St

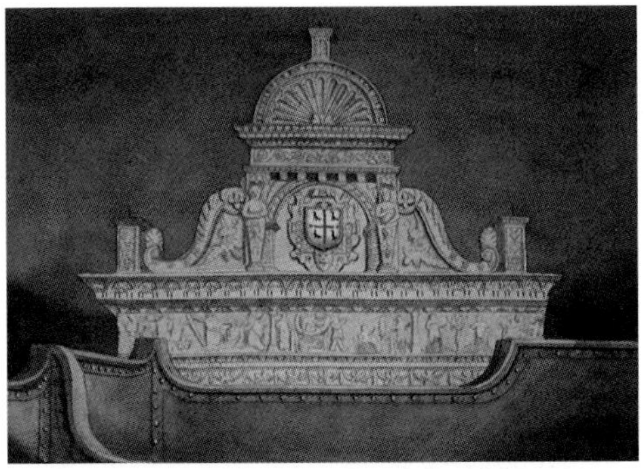

Fig. 40 ***Box pews obscuring a monument in the Lord Mayor's Chapel*****, detail of a watercolour by Joseph Manning, 1827 (Bristol Museums and Art Gallery, M2618)**

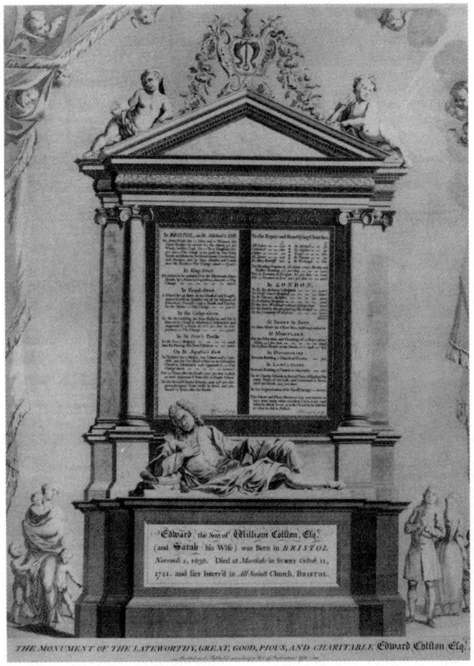

Fig. 41 ***'The monument of the late worthy, great, good, pious and charitable Edward Colston Esqr.' in St Stephen's*****, engraving by G. Scotin, 1751 (Bristol Museums and Art Gallery, Mb 423)**

Peter's, and 'a suitable monument be there sett up in Remembrance of my Death'.[17] However, as the historian of the Bristol Royal Infirmary puts it: 'Few men who have spent so much on the poor and uneducated have received so little acknowledgement after death',[18] and the name of Elbridge no longer rings a bell in the historical collective memory of Bristol.

St Mary Redcliffe, in the diocese of Bath and Wells until 1542 when Bristol became one of the six new dioceses, was the most important parish church in Bristol. It is to this day the centre of civic ritual and tradition. Within it lie two effigies of William Canynges, 'ye Richest Marchant of ye towne of Bristow', MP and five times mayor of Bristol, who died 7 November 1474.[19] This led to confusion as to who was who, but the married merchant and the priest are one and the same.[20] It is probable that William Canynges had a monument erected to his wife Joan or Johanna on her death in 1467, and included himself in mayoral robes in effigy, a not uncommon practice; and here, by his wish, he was later to be buried (Fig. 42).[21] After his wife's death, Canynges retired to a monastic foundation, the College at Westbury-on-Trym.[22] There, according to the inscription above the second effigy (Fig. 43), he employed eight hundred 'handy craftsmen, besides Carpenters & masons' over eight years, from the profit of his ships; the inscription ends: 'to shrine his Bones, deserves a tomb^e^ of gold'.[23] The re-presentation of Canynges as dean and monk at

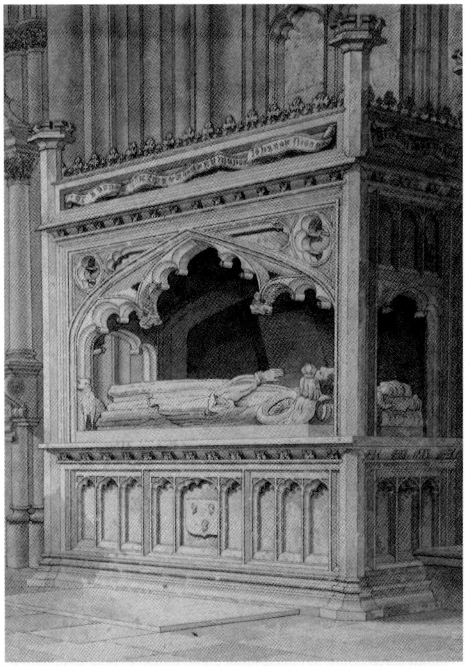

Fig. 42 ***Tomb of William and Joan Canynge*****, south transept, St Mary Redcliffe, watercolour by W. H. Bartlett, 1825 (Bristol Museums and Art Gallery, M1973)**

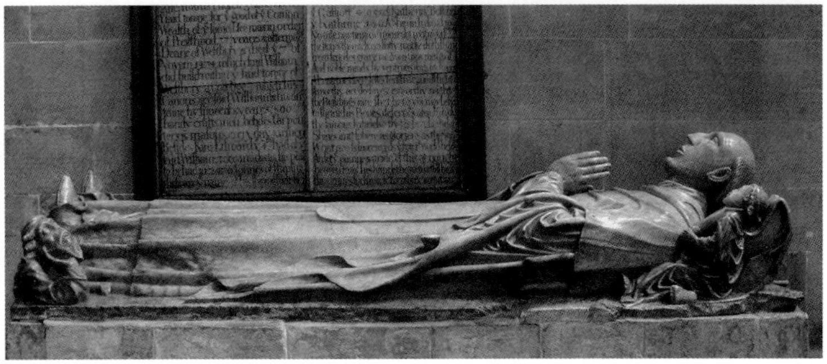

Fig. 43 ***Effigy of William Canynges (d. 1474)*****, alabaster, north transept, St Mary Redcliffe**

Westbury may have been organised by John Carpenter, Bishop of Worcester. At the dissolution of the college in 1544 it is probable that the effigy, and possibly the entire monument, was brought to Bristol from Westbury for safekeeping, to the chantry in the church to which he had been such a spectacularly generous benefactor. In what must be one of the finest alabaster figure sculptures of the period,[24] the dean appears in quire vestments, cassock, surplice and rochet, and over that the almuce and hood, his well-shod feet resting on a fine turbaned beadsman.[25] Canynges's tonsured head is supported on a cushion supported by a pair of angels, and lying on a great clasped book. John Latimer, Bristol's historian, provides an account of the effigies of 'so worthy a benefactor' being saved from destruction by Dr Yonge when he was bishop in the early 1760s.[26] More questionably, Latimer also noted that the restoration work, begun with the encouragement of the antiquarian John Britton in the 1840s, revealed 'the original tombs of William Canynges and his wife' in the ornate recesses of the south aisle, but 'the face of these beautifully canopied recesses had been ruthlessly cut away and wainscoted over in the reign of Queen Anne.' The 'effigies then lying in the south transept... were replaced in their original position' in 1852, but they were later returned to the south transept.[27]

In 1542 Bristol became a city, and the former Augustinian abbey became its cathedral.[28] The monument to the first Bishop of Bristol, Paul Bush (1489/90–1558) is an important early example of Northern European humanist classicism fused with a late medieval iconography of death. The tomb and the man it commemorates are typical of the religious, social and cultural transitions of the mid-sixteenth century. The typical product of an age of self-made men, Bishop Bush came from a farm belonging to the Augustinian priory at Edington in Wiltshire,[29] where he was probably educated and went from there to the Augustinian St Mary's Hall, Oxford. A theologian with an interest in medicine and Latin poetry, Bush was ordained priest and became a royal chaplain. One of his many theological and devotional works in English and Latin was dedicated to the Princess Mary in 1526. He appears to have been a successful trimmer throughout his career. In 1538 he oversaw the dissolution of Edington priory, of which he had become rector, and whereby his elder brother gained stewardship of lands in Wiltshire, reinforcing the yeoman base for the reformed religion. He must have impressed Thomas Cromwell for, in spite his conservatism, or perhaps because of it, he was appointed the first bishop of Bristol in June 1542. He married under Edward VI's dispensation of 1549, and, on Mary's succession in 1553, despite his apparent willingness to resume the old worship in the diocese, and despite his being by then a widower, he was forced to resign. Again he survived the inquisitions of men like Edmund Bonner, bishop of London, and retired to the rectory of Winterbourne just outside Bristol. There he lived well and wrote a defence of the mass and the doctrine of the real presence, published in London in 1554. He died in the year of Elizabeth's succession and was buried in the cathedral, as his wife had been before him.[30]

The siting of his tomb is indicative (Fig. 44), isolated between the north choir aisle and the Lady Chapel, with its resplendent series of former abbots, and not occupying the security of a magnificent stellate recess like them. The tomb itself is a vivid expression of the tensions exemplified by the times and by his life. Like the main feature of the tomb, a symbol of transience, it is in transition. Gothic ornament and structure have disappeared, to be replaced by simple classical detail introduced in the form of six curiously composite Ionic columns supporting a plain canopy. The escutcheons carved and painted with his coat of arms are typical of the dynastic awareness of the new self-made men of the period. The Latin inscriptions, too, prevaricate. One set runs around the tomb-chest, painted or stencilled in traditional Gothic script, while that around the canopy is in incised Roman lettering, knowingly picked out in black and red. The effigy however is a late medieval conceit, a rude reminder of mortality. It lies beneath the canopy, a *transi* or cadaver on a rush mat, with its tonsured head, finely observed hands and a rudimentarily carved ribcage. There is little of the panoply of office other than the mitre that the effigy's head rests on, and the remains of his staff or crozier lying beside him. There are no intercessors in the way of angels or saints, and the mortal remains lie naked before God.[31] From the residual colour of the mitre's jewelled ornament and its crimson lining, it is likely that the figure would have been gessoed and painted, so that the

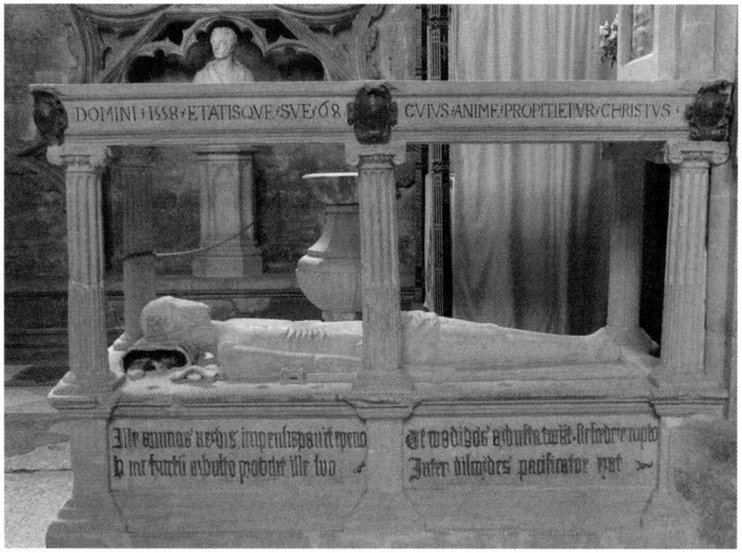

Fig. 44 ***Monument to Bishop Bush (d. 1558)*****, free stone, eastern Lady Chapel, Bristol Cathedral**

whole would have been more naturalistic, and thus more exemplary, in its decay.[32]

A near contemporary source was possibly the monument to Dean Colet in Old St Paul's (c.1520), with its scholar-type demi-effigy portrait of the great humanist in a shell niche above the canopy under which lay a *gisant* or skeleton.[33] Another possibility is that Bush intended to have his figure lie resplendent in bishop's robes, mitre and crozier above the canopy, as Henry Chichele's does above a cadaver at Canterbury (1443).[34] Closer to home, a source could be the monument to Richard Bekynton or Beckington at Wells (1465).[35] Perhaps it did have an effigy as in life, resplendent in robes, which was removed subsequently as too episcopalian, or too damaged.[36] It may be no coincidence that Bush used a prototype current a hundred years earlier. Chichele's career in particular paralleled Bush's own in navigating a mean way in matters of church and state, while Bekynton was at the centre of a literary circle that advocated moderation and toleration. Both men had been actively engaged in the refutation of Lollardy, the populist reform movement with its tendency to iconoclasm, which had begun in the Bristol region.[37]

John Whitson (1553/5–1629) was a merchant venturer who provided the backing for a number of expeditions, including Martin Pring's voyage to North America in 1603. He appears to have been constantly at odds with the Exchequer over customs at a time of numerous royal incursions into the city's privileges. He held all civic posts including mayor, was master of the Society of Merchant Venturers in 1606 and 1611, and from 1605 five times an elected MP for Bristol.[38] The biographer John Aubrey (1626–97) was Whitson's step-grandson, the latter having married the widowed grandmother, Rachel Aubrey, as his third or fourth wife in 1617. Much of what we know about him comes from the typically highly coloured, even bawdily anecdotal, account in Aubrey's *Brief Lives*,[39] from which we learn he lived in St Nicholas Street where he 'lived nobly and kept a plentiful table' in 'the stateliest dining room in the city'.[40] He had no direct heirs, and, already generous in his lifetime, left his entire estate to the city of Bristol 'for pious uses'.[41] This included the foundation of the Whitson almshouses and the Red Maids' School in 1634, both of which still exist.[42] Whitson's funeral was characteristically magnificent in the Bristol way, the overall cost being £418. Latimer provides some of the expenses at random:

Epitaph, 10s
Mustard, 1d
Making 75 gowns for the poor, 75s
Wine from the Bull, £5 17s 6d
Making a coffin, 14s
Baking of pies, 7s 6d
To Mr Palmer for making the verses on the Monument, 20s

It is likely that his monument in St Nicholas would not have survived the many vicissitudes to come if it had not been so clearly associated with the anniversary rituals of his benefactions.[43] It was moved on several occasions within the upper church, and then at the beginning of the nineteenth century into the lower chapel or crypt, where it is today. The effigy, in its eternally uncomfortable semi-recumbent pose, wears alderman's robes,[44] sits in a 'shallow standing monument with arched canopy on pilasters topped by pinnacles' (Fig. 45).[45] These might better be described as starved obelisks, a ubiquitous detail of Netherlandish, humanist-orientated decoration. The now overly-clean monument, the canopy and pinnacles scrubbed down to the local freestone, would originally have been gessoed, marbled, coloured and no doubt gilded.

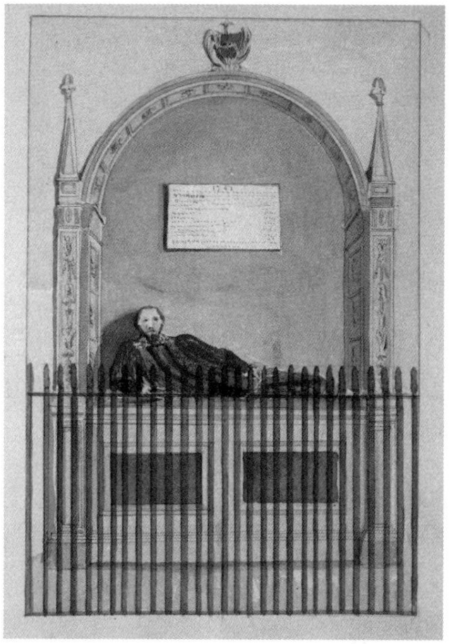

Fig. 45 ***Monument to Alderman Whitson (d. 1629)*, St Nicholas, watercolour by T. L. Rowbotham, 1827 (Bristol Museums and Art Gallery, M2204)**

In 1822 or 1823, an entirely new effigy and canopy by the mason-sculptor Thomas Clark (1764–1829) was set up under the tower in the entrance to the upper church, a forceful reminder as one entered of Whitson's charity and civic pride (Fig. 46). Clark had been an assistant to Sir Richard Westmacott, notably at Eaton Hall in Cheshire, and on ornamental work in the new Council House on Corn Street.[46] At the time he was engaged in restoration work in the Mayor's Chapel under the supervision of Thomas Garrard, the city chamberlain, 'a well-meaning collector of antique curiosities'.[47] The design for the canopy, in which Garrard must have had a hand, was a superb if anachronistic interpretation of the Bristol floriated style. Of this later version, only the stiff reclining effigy survives. The 'very elegant canopy in the perpendicular style' has gone, no doubt as the result of bomb damage.[48]

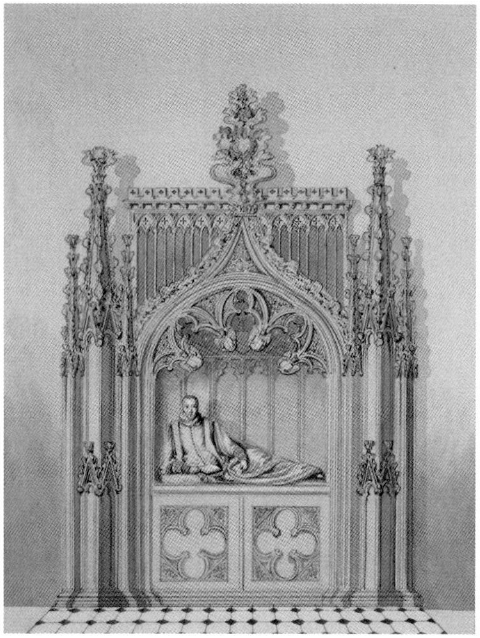

Fig. 46 ***Monument to Alderman Whitson (d. 1629), by Thomas Clarke, 1822–3, St Nicholas;*** **pencil and wash drawing by Hugh O'Neill, 1821 (Bristol Museums and Art Gallery, M2202)**

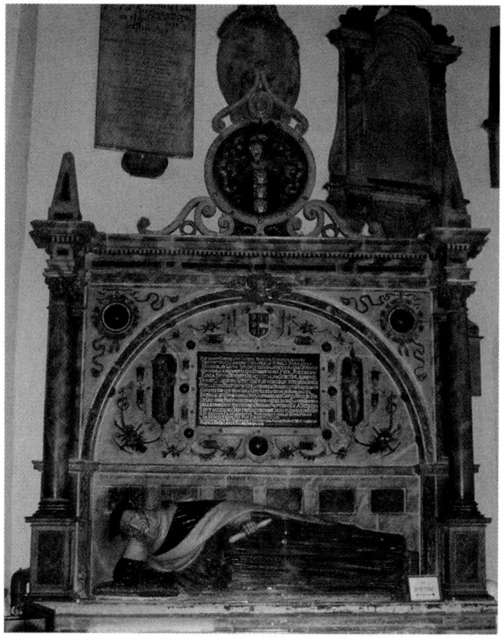

Fig. 47 ***Monument to Sir George Snygge (d. 1617),*** **St Stephen's**

Clark's effigy was restored and set up in the crypt in 1984, with an archaisingly cut dedicatory plaque, with the lines: A worthie patterne / to all that come/ after him. In line with the original, it creates a rather curious double image and poses the question: why was the original replaced? This was undoubtedly about the city's politics and its charitable resources. The city fathers, in renewing and even aggrandising the memorial to Whitson, were making a public demonstration of the importance of benefactors. In the 1820s, a time of political and social unrest, this was a further reminder of the city's independence.

Another hero of the resistance to the fiduciary injustices of the early Stuart period was one of Whitson's co-evals, Sir George Snygge (d. 1617), who had been recorder of Bristol and an MP. He resigned both on becoming a baron of the Exchequer in 1604, to be replaced by Alderman Whitson as Bristol's representative in parliament. Snygge found in favour of a Bristolian petition against a royal prisage on wine, and was, like Whitson, regarded as an upholder of the city's rights and liberties.[49]. His monument in St Stephen's has the hallmarks of a metropolitan piece sent from London (Fig. 47). It is a late Flemish two-tiered type on which the semi-recumbent effigy resides in judge's robes, between paired Corinthian columns and typical Southwark strapwork.

Two monuments that survive in good if gaudy condition from the first and last quarters of the seventeenth century are to mariners whose claim to fame is their role in extending the first British empire in the Americas. The first of these is to Martin Pring (d. 1626) (Fig. 48), described on the

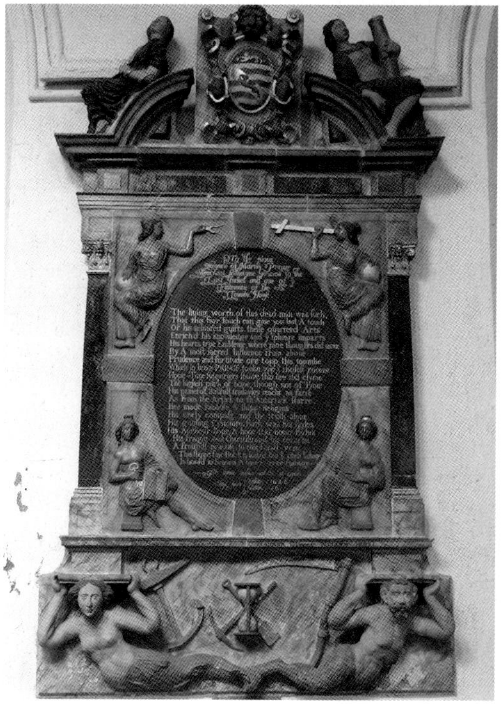

Fig. 48 ***Monument to Martin Pring (d. 1626),*** **possibly by the Baldwin workshop, St Stephen's**

inscription tablet as 'Merchant, sometime Generall to the East Indies and one of ye Fraternitie of the Trinitie House'. The verse epitaph includes the lines:

> His painefull, skillfull trauvayles reach't as farr
> As from the Arctick to th' Antarktick Starr

With the encouragement of a prebendary of the cathedral, Richard Hakluyt, and the financial backing of the aldermen Aldworth and Whitson, he set out in March 1603, aged 23, in the ship *Speedwell* with a crew of 35. Accompanying them was a bark, the *Discoverer*, with a crew of 13. They reached land in early June, and gave the name Whitson to the harbour in the Bay of Massachusetts, from which Pring conducted several months surveying. Seventeen years later it would be renamed Plymouth by the pilgrims on the *Mayflower*. A further expedition was undertaken in 1606 under the patronage of Sir Fernando Gorges, founder of the Virginia Company. Pring's account of these expeditions provided much of the source for Hakluyt's writings, published posthumously in 1625, edited by Samuel Purchas and entitled *Hakluytus Post-humus, or Purchas his Pilgrims*. In 1610 and 1611 Pring surveyed the Bristol Channel for the city corporation, and in the 1620s was a successful privateer, bringing a series of prizes into Bristol.[50]

Pring's hanging wall monument in St Stephen's, the parish of mariners and sail- and block-makers, was considered by Esdaile to be a good example of a local school of 'peculiar exuberance'.[51] More recently, the Pevsner guide described the figure work as a 'naïve figured surround'.[52] The type is that of a Flemish wall hanging tablet, ornamented with Mannerist virtues, the four central figures in low relief alabaster deriving from the engravings of Cornelis Floris. It is a less exalted version of a type best exemplified by Nicholas Stone the Elder's monument for Sir Thomas Bodley (d. 1613, erected 1615, Merton College, Oxford).[53] Pring's monument rests on a label supported by two caryatid-like creatures in a robust vernacular idiom, such as one might associate with ships' carvers and their figureheads, but which, as a mermaid and Time, are also the supporters for the Merchant Venturers' coat of arms.[54] An inscription informs us that it was 'Beautified by Mrs Hannah Oliver Widdow 1733'. Misleadingly, there is a later mason's inscription label inscribed: WM. PUGH, which has lead to confusion.[55] William Pugh was a monumental mason responsible for a number of signed wall tablets in Bristol in the early nineteenth century, such as that to William Delpratt (d. 1826), also in St Stephen's,[56] and that in the cathedral cloister to Charles McNish 'of the Island of Jamaica', who died at Clifton in 1829. It is here suggested that he merely acted as the restorer of the Pring monument, a hundred years after Hannah Oliver's intervention. Further, comparison with the four virtues (Faith, Hope, Charity and Peace) in low relief on the monument to Richard Delabere (d. 1636) at Bishop's Cleeve in Gloucestershire prompts a tentative attribution to the Baldwin workshop of Stroud and Gloucester.[57] The Baldwins provided monuments for the region within a fifty mile radius of Gloucester in the first half of the seventeenth century. The evidence of the well-endowed harpies in the lower storey of another monument in the cathedral suggests a kinship with the Pring figures of the mermaid and Time. This mutilated but now heavily restored monument (Fig. 49), which contains the effigy of Joan Wadham (d. 1603), wife of Sir Giles Strangways (1) and Sir John Young (2), has been attributed to Samuel Baldwin.[58] Sir John Young (d. 1589), an example of the new men who made good in the period following the Reformation, had built the 'Great House' on the site of the Carmelite friary, which he had purchased in 1568. He received Queen Elizabeth there in 1574, and was knighted for his hospitality.[59]

The hanging wall monument to Admiral Sir William Penn Kt. (1621–70) was erected by his widow, Margaret Jasper of Rotterdam (d. 1682) (Fig. 50).[60] Penn, the son of a sea captain with court connections, was baptised in St Thomas's Church, Bristol. A career naval officer whose loyalty to the regime of the moment was often questioned, Penn played an active part in the parliamentary navy during the civil war, and thereafter for Cromwell, notably in the Caribbean, where he took Jamaica from the Spaniards. He was, however, among those who sailed with the fleet to bring Charles II back from exile, and he served under the Duke of York in the Second Anglo–Dutch War. Although he died at Wanstead in Surrey, he was buried in the south aisle of St Mary Redcliffe. The inscription on the memorial written by his more famous son – the

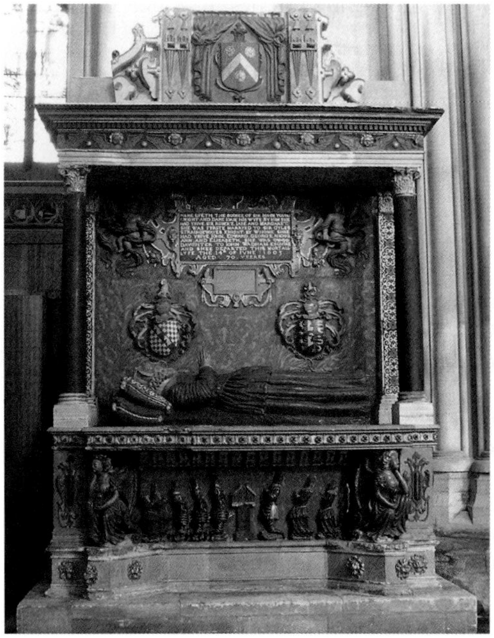

Fig. 49 ***Monument to Sir John Young (d. 1589) and his widow, Joan Wadham (d. 1603)*, west end of nave, Bristol Cathedral (by permission of the Dean and Chapter)**

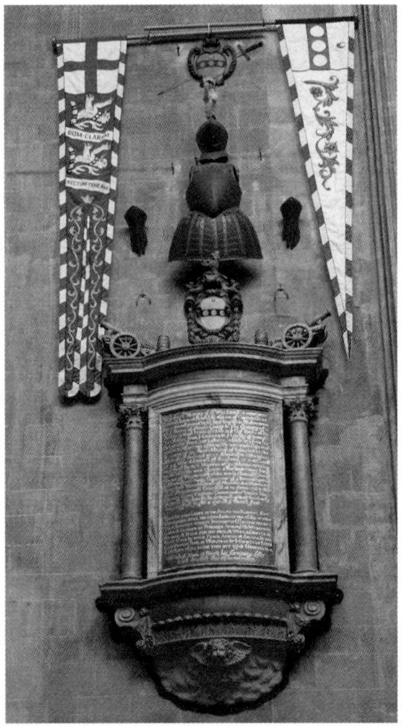

Fig. 50 ***Monument to Admiral Sir William Penn (d. 1670)*****, west end of nave, St Mary Redcliffe**

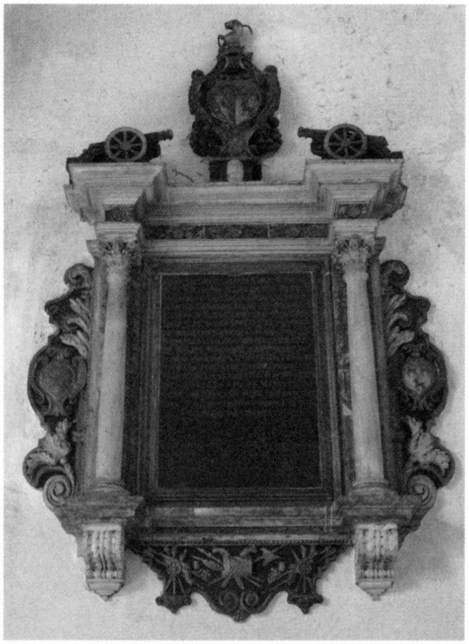

Fig. 51 ***Monument to Colonel Sir James Russell (d. 1674)*****, St James**

Quaker founder of Pennsylvania, William Penn (1644–1718) – gives a concise account of his successful career.[61] In 1843, Joseph Leech commented on it as the monument 'to some ferocious defunct, who has surmounted his tablet with a brace of ten-pounders, a tattered banner, and a battered helmet'. At that time, the monument and funerary achievements were very prominently displayed on two separate piers of the south transept.[62] When the Victorians purged the church of innumerable wall memorials, the monument and the achievements were brought together and hung needlessly high at the west end of the nave. Recently, the few decayed remnants of the funerary pennants were taken down and conserved. In 2006, two pennants were replaced by smaller replicas with the deliberate intention of drawing attention to this important but skied monument.

Penn's monument is a variant on the hanging wall monument to Colonel Sir James Russell (d. 1674) in St James, whose martial motifs include a similar pair of cannon and a powder keg on the upper frame, and an inscription tablet set between two slender Corinthian columns. The Russell monument differs in having lateral subordinate low relief ornament of coats of arms, and military trophies (Fig. 51).[63] Russell had been one of the first settlers on Nevis in the Windward Islands, and its first governor, appointed by Charles II. In 1666 he had successfully defended the island from the French and the Dutch, returning to Bristol to die aged 74.

St Mark's, or the Gaunt's, Chapel is particularly rich in early to mid-seventeenth century monuments, probably because it has always been in essence a private chapel, and thus removed from the whims of individual incumbents. That so many survive from this period is perhaps because it was first almost a family mausoleum for the Berkeley family, the powerful landlords just to the north of Bristol. As a non-parochial chapel outside the city on the farther side of the Frome and St Augustine's Reach, it appears to have been a refuge in death for non-Bristolians and possibly High Church royalists.[64] From 1687 until 1722 it was Bristol's Huguenot chapel. As tenuous tenants, the Huguenots were unlikely to take down existing monuments. In 1722 it was 'beautified' and the bells recast 'for the Grandeur of the City and it was their private chappell', the Mayor's Chapel.[65] As a civic chapel it escaped the interference of the diocesan authorities,[66] and became the last resting place for a few out-of-towners and civic dignitaries such as Henry Blake, steward of the Sheriffs Court from 1722 until his death in 1731. Blake's fine Augustan bust was identified in the1980s as by Michael Rysbrack (Fig. 52).[67]

The first quarter of the eighteenth century is marked in Bristol by an urge to rectify years of neglect in the unsettled period of the previous fifty years. At St John's in 1716, Jeremy Innys, senior churchwarden, was instructed by the vestry to 'forthwith beautify y[e] Church by new painting, whitelimeing, glazeing windows, and carpenters worke',[68] and to provide 'Three handsom Irons for the Branches and to have one new Branch for the Body of the Church… and to provide a good new pulpit and sounding Board and to raise the pews'.[69] In 1717, Edward Colston

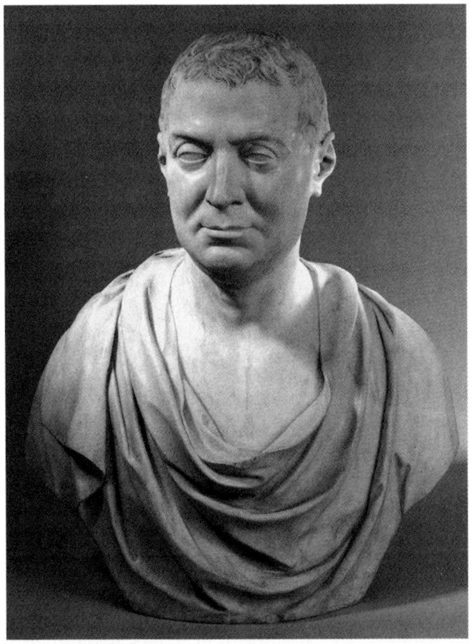

Fig. 52 ***Bust of Henry Blake (d. 1731)*, by Michael Rysbrack, marble, St Mark (Lord Mayor's Chapel)**

contributed £250 to the building of the new tower of All Saints,[70] and, as the inscription on his monument makes clear, to the 'Repair & Beautifying' of places of worship.[71] The refurbishment of church interiors, the addition of pews against the cold and damp, the installation of organs, and the commissioning of paintings were all part of a concerted effort to encourage people into church as part of an Anglican revival at a time of demographic expansion, and in the face of the increasing success of populist Methodism under the Wesleys and others.[72]

The baroque is conspicuously missing from monuments in Bristol and, as the style most associated with Rome and the Counter-Reformation, it would no doubt have been anathema. However, the church of All Saints houses without doubt the finest monument erected in Bristol in the eighteenth century,[73] the 'noble lofty Monument of marble'[74] to Edward Colston (1636–1721), merchant and philanthropist (Fig. 53).[75] The reputation of Colston, who never lived in the city, had been chequered from the start. A century ago it was his exemplary philanthropy that was still being repeatedly celebrated. The south-west tower of the cathedral was constructed in his name, and the north transept window dedicated to his memory in 1890. In 1899, Bishop Percival of Hereford, the former headmaster of Clifton College, presided over the University College Colston Society, founded with the intention of endowing Colston Chairs in the college, now the University of Bristol.[76] Today, it is his association with the slave trade through his close involvement with the Royal African Company that is most often recalled.

Colston was a member of a powerful merchant family that had been engaged in Bristol business and politics since the Reformation, and actively engaged in the early explorations of the North American coast. His father, William Colston, had been denied office during the Commonwealth, and the family had retired to London. Colston maintained business interests and shipping in Bristol. He was a partner in the Elbridge sugar refinery at St Peter's Churchyard, importing muscovado from the Caribbean between 1661 and 1679, and an active member of the Royal African Company from 1680.[77] In the eighteenth century he was the nearest thing to a saint in the Church of England, being virtually canonised by his native city:

> He was one of the best and most religious men that ever existed; his universal benevolence and extended charity, like the sun in the firmament, diffused blessings on all around; he was eyes to the blind, feet to the lame, a father to the fatherless, and the widow's tears he wiped away… and thousands that are yet unborn shall celebrate with thankfulness and festive joy, the annual return of that auspicious day, which gave him birth.[78]

Colston's birthday became a public holiday in Bristol, marked by processions, bells and feasting.[79] In 1727, *Farley's Bristol Newspaper* recorded:

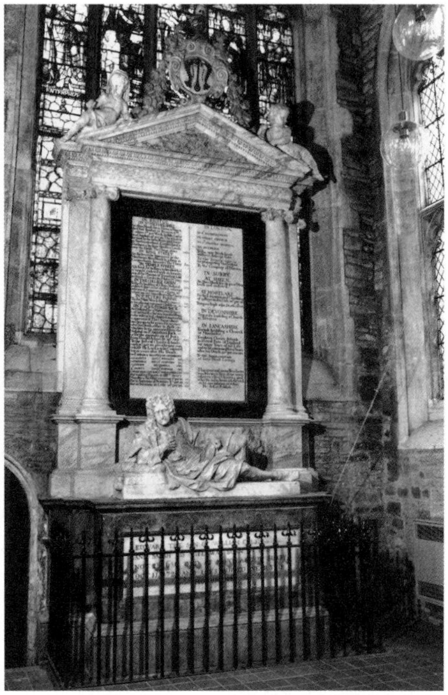

Fig. 53 ***Monument to Edward Colston (d. 1721)*, by James Gibbs, Michael Rysbrack and Michael Sidnell, 1728–9, All Saints**

Thursday being the nativity of that late Glorious Benefactor Edward Colston Esq., the Bells from each steeple began about 5 in the morning to proclaim his immortal memory; and at Night were several Private Entertainments in Commemoration of him, as Tokens to perpetuate his Memory to latest posterity.[80]

Colston retired from business in London to live at Mortlake in 1689, and the rest of his life was devoted to works of charity. Largely concerned with education and the aged,[81] his charities included Colston's Almshouses on St Michael's Hill (1690) and Colston's School (1706). A high church Tory, Colston was a hard line opponent of Catholicism, Dissenters and Whiggism, and his motive appears to have been a desire to re-establish the Church of England in Bristol. The boys in his school were to be 'bred up in the Doctrine of our present Established Church of England'. Indeed, all Colston's benefactions had the strictest conditions attached to them concerning the religious practice and beliefs of their inmates and staff: no books of a Whiggish persuasion were allowed, the children of Dissenters were excluded, and he refused to allow schoolboys to be placed out or apprenticed to 'any Men that are Dissenters'.[82] As the city was four-fifths Whig, this led to opposition, accusations of bigotry and even a smear campaign. The corporation refused his offer of a school for boys because of the uncompromising conditions attached to it. Subsequently, the Merchant Venturers undertook its administration.

Colston's monument was commissioned by his executors, his nephew Francis Colston and the charities' lawyer, Thomas Edwards Senior.[83] They were strong Tories in a Whig climate. In September 1714, on the death of Queen Anne, at the accession of George I and the initiation of the Hanoverian dynasty, Francis Colston was charged with dispersing a Jacobite pamphlet. Thomas Edwards Jr, who was married to Colston's niece Mary Hayman,[84] had stood as Tory candidate in Colston's stead in 1713, and again in 1715. In much the grandest monument of the period in Bristol, much grander than the comparatively simple shield tablets to other members of the Colston family in All Saints,[85] one may detect more than family piety and pride. This should be set in the context of the active interest of the city, or at least a faction within it, in commemorating its most distinguished benefactor, and city politics must have played a part.[86] Indeed, despite Colston's will, which had requested that he be buried 'without any manner of Pomp or Ostentation',[87] his body was brought back to Bristol in great state to be interred in the family vault.[88]

That tensions in the city could and did manifest themselves in funerary obsequies is evident from the account Latimer gives of Colston's funeral in 1723, and that of Thomas Day five years later. Alderman Day died at Brentford in 1728, 'leaving instructions as to his interment which shocked the sentiments of the age', requesting that his remains be buried by daylight, no monument was to be erected, his coffin was to be without 'gimcracks, or what some people call ornaments', and nothing was to be given at the funeral, 'no, not wine (which was always given)'.[89] It may be no coincidence that this was at the time that Colston's monument was being set up in All Saints, for monuments such as these were political and religious statements.[90]

The choices of Colston's executors were significant: the leading metropolitan architect of the day, James Gibbs (1682–1754) as designer; his protégé Michael Rysbrack (1694–1770), a rising star in the metropolitan sculptural firmament, as the sculptor of the effigy and the pair of *putti* on the entablature.[91] As has been pointed out, it 'provides a particularly complete picture of the complicated activities in designing, carving and erecting a major monument in the early Georgian period'.[92] A thoroughly metropolitan piece, it was designed by James Gibbs, the effigy carved with that immediacy and attention to personal characteristics that was to make Rysbrack's name as a portraitist.[93] The whole was assembled and finished by the Bristolian mason architect Michael Sidnell, who signed it.[94]

Gibbs illustrated the monument in his *Book of Architecture* (1728) (Fig. 54).[95] This publication,[96] the first of its kind produced by a British architect,[97] provided patterns for architects, masons and layman, and included monuments and chimneypieces. It was indeed Gibbs's intention that it should be 'of use to such Gentlemen as might be concerned in Building, especially in the remote parts of the Country, where little or no

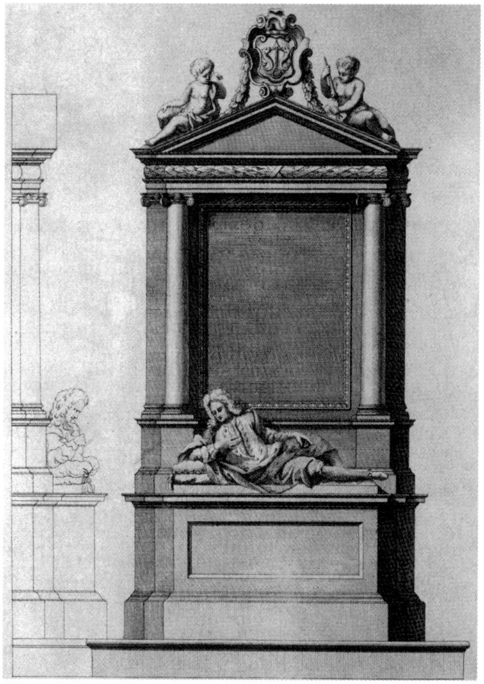

Fig. 54 ***Monument to Edward Colston*****, engraving from *A Book of Architecture* by J. Harris after James Gibbs, 1728, plate 113 (Bristol Museums and Art Gallery, M1646)**

assistance for Designs can be procured which may be executed by any Workman who understands Lines'.[98] If, in calling on James Gibbs, Bristolians were for the first time using a metropolitan architect,[99] in Michael Sidnell – one of the four guinea subscribers to the *Book of Architecture*, which in itself suggests a man of substance and of a non-parochial outlook – the local 'workman' was more than one who understood lines.

Sidnell is the first independent freemason of any individuality to emerge from the many employed in Bristol. Like the Paty family, he had pretensions to being an architect. He is thought to have been working in the city from as early as 1714,[100] and was 'made free', or freeman or burgess, of the city on a fine of £10 on 2 July 1718, the day that John Patty was deferred.[101] It seems that in the 1720s and 1730s, it was Sidnell who held a premier position in the building trade in Bristol. On 29 September 1727, 'Michael Sidnell Freemason' was paid by the corporation for rebuilding Cornmarket in Mary le Port Street, and, in 1729, for pulling down and rebuilding Redcliffe Gate.[102] In 1733, he was being paid for work on the City Gate at Temple Street.[103] He appears in the poll books for the first time in 1739 as 'Michael Sydnell, Stone Cutter' in the parish of St James.[104] However, he was bankrupted in 1742,[105] and was then found assisting Thomas Paty at Redland Chapel. In the 1740s, Michael Sidnell, 'Freemason and Stone Cutter' was a vestrymen at St James, signing vestry meeting minutes until, in 1746, he resigned on becoming sexton.[106] Thereafter there are recorded numerous payments to him for maintenance work.[107]

Under its vicars Benjamin Baily and Dean Creswicke, the parish of St James appears to have been a centre for the revival of the established church.[108] From it stemmed the benefactions to the Royal Infirmary which opened in Maudlin Street in 1735, and for which the parish church was subsequently the centre of anniversary ceremonials and celebrations.[109] Members of the Edwards family were benefactors of the parish of St James: Jane Edwards (d. 1733) left money to the poor of St James for bread and sermons, and so did Walter Edwards (d. 1758), as well as £20 for the repair of two monuments, one to the memory of his father and mother (Thomas (d. 1727) and Jane), and one to his wife Mary (d. 1736) (Figs 55 and 56). In 1759, the vestry paid out the interest to repair the monuments, 'which are now in a state of good repair, and intended to be so kept',[110] and no doubt to add to the inscription the name of this benefactor.[111] Walter Edwards, one of the four sons of Thomas Edwards Sr, commissioned both monuments. He was also a lawyer, living in Lincolns Inn Fields, London. The design of the monument to Thomas and Jane Edwards is clearly influenced by Rysbrack's wall tablet to Andrew Innys of 1726 in St John's (Fig. 57).[112] The broken pediment supported on a pair of Ionic columns, themselves resting on a pair of

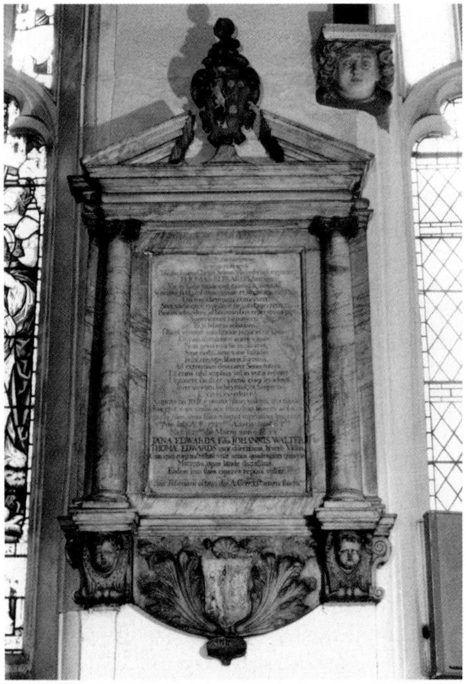

Fig. 55 ***Monument to Thomas and Jane Edwards, 1733,*** **by Michael Sidnell, St James**

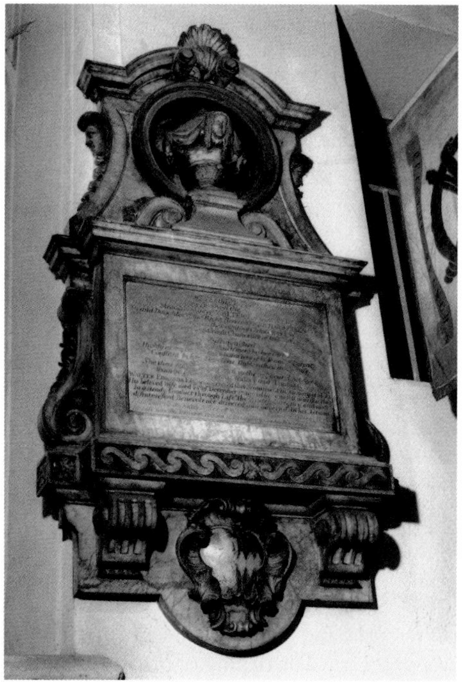

Fig. 56 ***Monument to Mary Edwards (d. 1736),*** **attributed to Michael Rysbrack, St James**

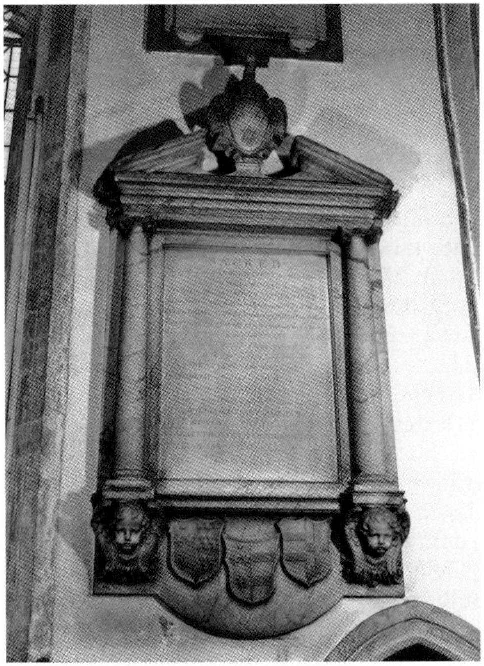

Fig. 57 ***Monument to Andrew Innys*****, signed by Michael Rysbrack, 1726, St John**

cherub-head soffits, is identical in composition if not in execution. It is signed by Michael Sidnell. The design for the hanging wall monument to Walter's wife Mary (d. 1736), the daughter of Richard Freeman of Batsford Court, Gloucestershire, is taken straight from Gibbs's *Book of Architecture*, plate 123.[113] Although unsigned and sometimes attributed to Sidnell,[114] it has all the metropolitan hallmarks of the work of Michael Rysbrack.

Sidnell's residence in the parish is indicative. The parish of St James, a former priory outside the city walls, was a rapidly expanding suburb in the first half of the eighteenth century, with a large number of freeholders.[115] St James's Square was completed in red brick in 1709, and King's Square was finished in 1741. It is noteworthy that in the poll books for elections throughout the eighteenth century, whereas the city-bound parishes might have up to three masons each, St James had upwards of twenty in 1722, rising in the building boom to upwards of thirty in 1739 and 1754.[116] There are obvious reasons for this, among them the fact that, but for its churches, the city centre was largely timber, and so crowded that yards would have been expensive, inaccessible and noisy. The returns throughout the period refer largely to 'masons', with only three 'freemasons' recorded for 1722.[117] This lack of differentiation is unhelpful in distinguishing the type of work carried on by named individuals, and is in marked contrast to other trades where specialisation was apparent. The baking of bread, for example, was distinct from confectionery or gingerbread-making, while rope-makers, cordwainers and twine-spinners were clearly not to be confused. In 1734 the word 'Carver' is recorded; there were six of them, but as three were in St Stephen's parish it is possible that they were woodworkers or ships' figurehead carvers. An interesting specialisation appears uniquely in the person of Thomas Gough, 'Marble Sawier' or 'Sawyer', in St Peter's parish in 1734, 1739 and 1754. A degree of differentiation is indicated in descriptive phrases such as 'Rough Mason' and 'Freestone Cutter' in the 1739 returns. To this is added in 1754 'Stone Cutter'.

By and large, 'Mason' remained a generic, and gives little indication of the status in the trade of individuals who may have been quite simply builders, or worked stone for such simple architectural detail as lintels or architraves, or for ornament, internal and external, such as the fine oak-leaf-adorned door jambs to Wood's Exchange or Thomas Paty's Christ Church. In 1750, Thomas Paty 'Carver' was being given a voucher by the corporation for the coat of arms over the Exchange,[118] but by then he was operating a very large business with several yards, and one might question how much of the work attributed to him is by him and not by an employee, or whether indeed he still did any of the hands-on work himself.

There were two branches of the Paty family, and up to four family firms, the ramifications and complexities of which have recently been considered by the Bristol architectural historian Gordon Priest.[119] Their near monopoly of the expansion in domestic buildings (and of ecclesiastical building works and participation in civic building programmes) does not concern us here, but a few details can be added to what is already known about them; as monumental masons, they dominate the eighteenth-century funerary records of Bristol. One of the earliest documented works by a member of the Paty family was the payment of 'Sundry expenses to Mr Pattey' in 1710–11 for laying out the chancel, marbling and paving in St John's as part of the revivalist restoration work already discussed.[120] On 2 July 1718, John Patty 'Carver' petitioned to become a free burgess, but was deferred.[121] On 31 October that year, James Patty 'Carver' was made free on a fine of fifteen shillings.[122] The fine suggests that he was not a native of Bristol, nor yet married to one.

One might call this the minor branch, where the name 'James' appears dynastic and distinguishing, for it does not seem to have played a major part in the entrepreneurial development of the city and its suburbs. 'Pattee, James Carver' appears in the parish of St James in the poll book returns for 1739.[123] In 1738 on 22 September, James Paty was paid for cleaning 'the pedestall of King W^{m}. in Queen's Square', which took three men six days at a cost of 16 shillings, in preparation for the visit of the Prince of Wales.[124] There are numerous monuments signed by two generations of James Patys: for example, that to Richard Sandford (d. 1721) signed by the elder James (d. 1748), under the tower in St Mary

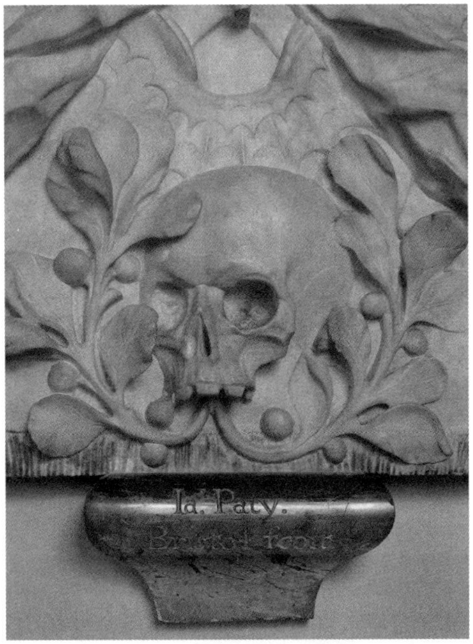

Fig. 58 ***Detail of the monument to Richard Sandford (d. 1721)*, signed by James Paty I, Chapel of St John the Baptist, St Mary Redcliffe**

Redcliffe (Fig. 58); or that to John Foy (d. 1771) by the younger James (1748–1807), in SS Philip and Jacob. This is a fine portrait medallion set upon an obelisk with a low relief of a mourning woman and children.[125] By 1774, 'Patty James, Carver' was in St Augustine's, along with his kinsmen 'Patty Thomas, Carver, Fr',[126] whose yards were in Limekiln Lane below Brandon Hill.[127]

The major branch of the Paty family under Thomas Paty (1713–89) had at one time a virtual monopoly of ecclesiastic building works in Bristol. This must have given him an advantage when it came to memorials and monuments, but not an unfair one, for his reputation was already considerable. John Innys, in his 'Chronological account of the most material accurances of or relating to Redland Chapel' (written in 1762), described the font and cover as 'designed and made by Mr Thomas Paty of Bristol who is generally esteemed one of the Best Carvers in England either in wood or Stone by whom all the rest of the Ornaments in the Chapel was designed and carved'.[128]

The monument to William Hilliard (d. 1735)[129] in the Lord Mayor's Chapel is considered Thomas Paty's most impressive work (Fig. 59). Hilliard had left instructions in his will of 28 March 1713 to be buried in the chancel of St Augustine's, to which parish he bequeathed £100.[130] However, when he died in 1735 aged 72, he was buried in what was the south aisle of the Lord Mayor's Chapel. His widow died ten years later, aged 77, in 1745, having left £200 for a monument to her late husband.[131] The monument, which is likely to date from 1745, was designed by Thomas Paty, and is the most considerable if awkward monument by him. The source must be Gibbs's design for the monument to the poet Matthew Prior in Westminster Abbey (1721). This had been engraved as plate 112 in the *Book of Architecture*.[132] The bust is the *en négligé* or indoor dress type made fashionable by Coysevox's portrait of Prior (1714), and possibly familiar to some Bristolians in Rysbrack's busts of the Innys brothers, William and John.[133] The rope-tasselled swag of bunched drapery and the fine naturalistic wreath that surrounds the coat of arms pinned to the obelisk are entirely characteristic of Paty's own invention.

It appears that both Thomas's sons went to London to attend the Royal Academy Schools; John was admitted aged 17 on '10th Decr last' (1771). The entry does not give his designation, though Thomas Ride, the only other admittee on that same day, was an architect.[134] Ten years later, John was registering a vote in the elections of 1781 in St Augustine's parish, as 'Paty John, Carver'.[135] His younger brother William was admitted as an architect, aged 18, in 1775.[136] William signs numerous monuments, whereas John does not. If the older Paty was influenced in the second quarter of the eighteenth century by the metropolitan style of Michael Rysbrack, the younger, William (1758–1800), was indebted to John Bacon in the last quarter of the century, and 'was inevitably

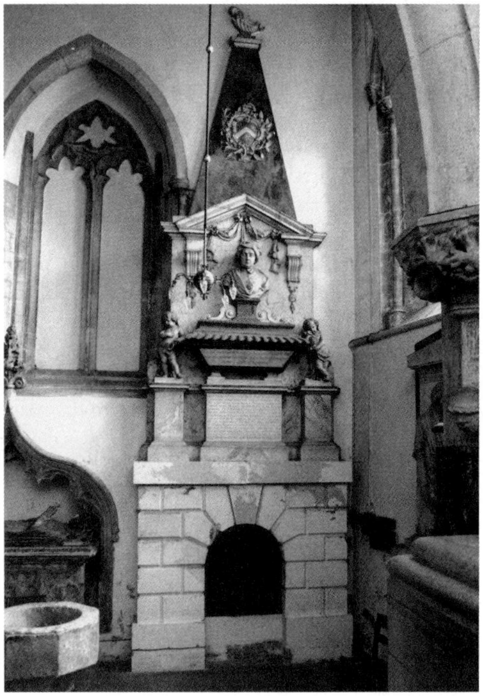

Fig. 59 ***Monument to John Hilliard by Thomas Paty*, 1745, St Mark (Lord Mayor's Chapel)**

attracted by the current popular theme of mourning ladies with an urn',[137] as in the monument to Mary Stretton (d. 1794) in St Michael's, which he signed. Both Patys favoured polychromatic marbles, and while Thomas's designs were solid, three-dimensional and on occasion ponderous, William's were light, filigree and elegant. Much of their work was exported to the West Indies, particularly Barbados.[138]

William Paty's death at the comparatively early age of 43 in 1800 brought to an end the dominance of the Paty dynasty in Bristol. The yard and business was sold to Henry Wood in 1801. An 'architect and statuary of London',[139] Wood almost certainly acquired the stock patterns of the Paty business. These survive in two groups: one now in the Bristol University Library and one in the Henry Moore Institute, Leeds. The Bristol volume has been collated comparatively recently and remounted, probably with a connoisseurship intended to identify the Paty workshop designs. However, it also includes designs attributable to later Wood productions, just as the so-called Wood album at Leeds includes designs by William Paty. This is not the place for an in-depth analysis of the designs, but the albums do provide insights into working practices. The Leeds album is set up as a pattern book with an identifying catalogue code number, measurements and prices according to size. Wood modified the Paty designs, often carefully blacking out the polychromatic marbles (Figs 60 and 61), perhaps in response to changes in fashion or economy. There is also evidence that Wood cut up and reused the backs of sheets of Paty designs for (Fig. 62) chimney pieces, which suggests that he did not work in that business, and was a specialist funerary mason. Generally speaking, Woods designs, as executed, are of the simplest type and often not more than an inscription tablet, with – as Leech put it – 'a sprinkling of weeping willows, smoking torches, and tea urns'.[140] Wood must have had entrepreneurial instincts, for the company under his name came to monopolise the region over the next thirty years in the production of a routine supply of simple wall plaques or tablets. Invariably in monochrome sheets of black touch or grey marble with white marble low relief inscription tablets superimposed, their uniformity and repetitiveness can only be described as dull. The sheer numbers reflect the demographic explosion at the end of the eighteenth century and the beginning of the nineteenth, and their lack of ostentation was in accord with both the neo-classicism of the period and a Bristolian disinclination towards iconographic excess. Wood's business was clearly highly successful in a period of unostentatious but widespread commemorative practice. His work is found throughout the hinterland of Bristol and South Wales, and was exported to the colonies, India and the West Indies, Barbados in particular. St James has numerous examples of what might be termed Wood's stock output, which can be matched with the designs in these pattern books: so much so that the east wall of the south aisle might almost be a page from the Leeds volume of designs.[141] They are often so unaffected and simple that only the dates provide possible insights. From

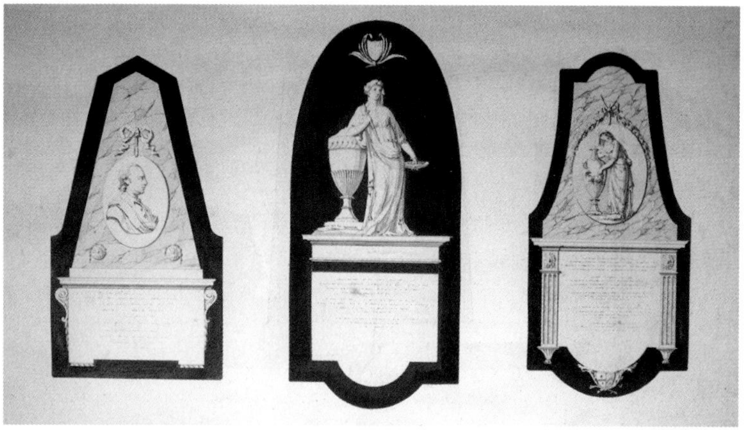

(above) Fig. 60 ***Designs for three monuments attributed to William Paty, with alterations by Henry Wood*****, watercolour from the Wood Album, Leeds Museums and Galleries (Henry Moore Institute Archive)**

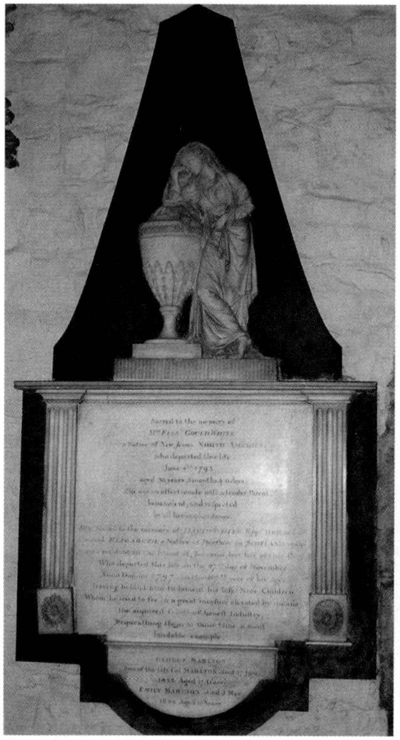

Fig. 61 ***Monument to Elizabeth Gould White (d. 1793), with additional members of the family in 1797, 1823 and 1824*****, probably by William Paty or Henry Wood, cloister, East Walk, Bristol Cathedral**

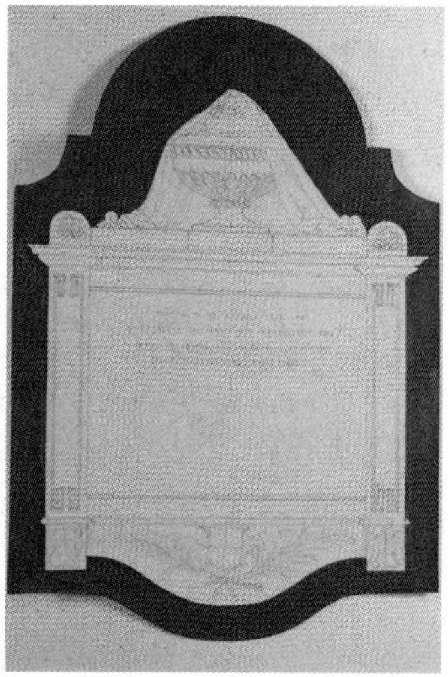

Fig. 62 ***Unfinished design for a wall monument by Henry Wood*****, pencil, pen and ink, from the Wood Album, Leeds Museums and Galleries (Henry Moore Institute Archive)**

the wall tablet to the wife and children of Major William Ledlie (Fig. 63), which can be matched with a design in the Leeds volume,[142] we learn that his daughter Isabella Bridget was four and a half when she died in 1838. The following year her mother, Isabella, died aged 27, less than a month after her two-year-old son William Robert. The tablet is signed on a separate block: H.WOOD BRISTOL. One of his sons, whom Gunnis designates as Henry Wood the Younger,[143] continued the business. His most distinguished memorial is to the Unitarian minister Lant Carpenter (d. 1840) in Lewins Mead Chapel (Fig. 64). With its fine portrait medallion, it is a rare example of an iconographic memorial to a non-conformist. As such it is in the long tradition of recognition of achievements that are more than personal.

The family of Tyley were active in Bristol for a hundred years between 1792 and as late as 1891, when H. Tyley signed the monument to Dean Elliott in the north transept of the cathedral. In the Tyleys, Bristol would appear to have developed a local school of distinction which, like the Patys and the Woods, also conducted a thriving export trade to the colonies. They appear to have had a virtual monopoly of the cathedral, where tablet after tablet is signed by them. This sort of monopolisation was common in cathedrals, where the dean and chapter clearly preferred the devil they knew, whose style and manner of working conformed to the collective; permissions for monuments or stained glass were often granted on condition that a preferred name was employed. It is difficult to distinguish between the work of different members of the family, for there appear to have been two Thomases and two Jameses in two generations, and most monuments were signed simply: TYLEY / BRISTOL, and occasionally T.TYLEY.[144] Much of their production was of a routine sort, on a par with that of their rivals the Woods, so much so that the thought occurs that they must both have had access to the same set of patterns, or that their respective patterns were collated at a later stage into the compilations to be found in the two 'Paty' and 'Wood' albums.

Evidence that they were rivals in a flourishing market is to be found in a design in the Wood album for a memorial plaque to Lord Henry Somerset, fifth son of the Duke of Beaufort. The design, a very plain draped tablet, is inscribed: 'WOOD: Sculptor: Bristol'.[145] The commission went, however, to the Tyleys, perhaps because of the advantage alluded to here, and a pair of identical plaques to two Somerset brothers were set up in the cathedral cloister. Yet the inventiveness and variety of design and the quality of carving as executed by the Tyleys was far in excess of that of the Woods. The scale of the soldier figures on the monument to Major William Gore (d. 1814) is something that neither the Patys nor the Woods attempted. The finely carved relief figure of a woman seated as though in a sea breeze at the end of the north choir aisle by the Lady Chapel in the cathedral successfully captures the spirit of romanticism in the wall monument erected by his widow to John Campbell (d. 1817, aged 61), 'of the Gibraltar Estate in the Parish of Trelawny... Jamaica' (Fig. 65). The sleeping child on the small wall relief to Georgiana Lucy Worrall, aged four when she died in 1832, owes something to examples by Flaxman and Chantrey. One is tempted to suggest that these neat, crisply confident carvings are the work of Thomas Tyley the Younger, who had won a

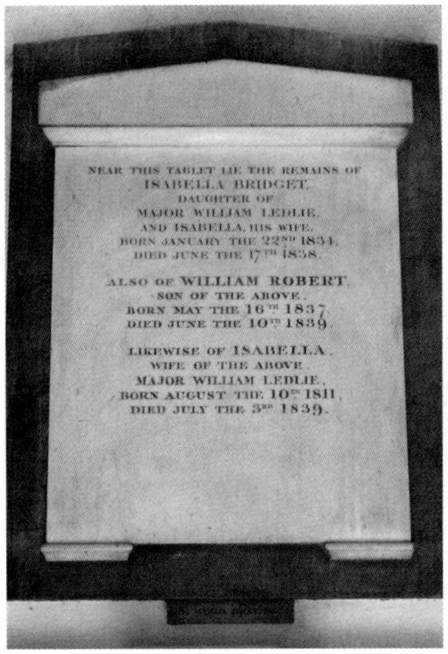

Fig. 63 *Wall tablet to the wife and children of Major William Ledlie (d. 1828)*, **signed** H.WOOD *BRISTOL*, **St James**

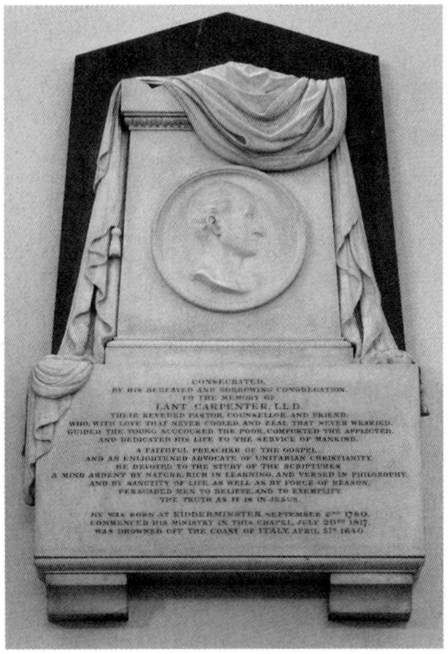

Fig. 64 *Monument to Dr Lant Carpenter (d. 1840)*, **by John Wood the Younger, Lewins Mead Chapel**

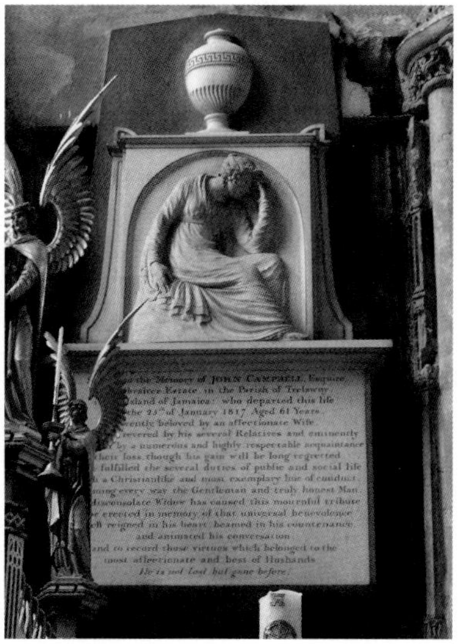

Fig. 65 *Wall tablet to John Campbell (d. 1817)*, **signed** TYLEY.BRISTOL, **north choir aisle, Bristol Cathedral**

silver medal from the Society of Arts in 1811 for a group entitled *Christ Healing the Sick.*[146] However, a more mawkish low relief (whose subject implies the title *Suffer the Little Children*) on the tablet to Enura Josephine, Charles Roper and Laura Henrietta Malwyn (d. 1843, 1850 and 1850 respectively), is signed: 'T.TYLEY / Sc. / BRISTOL' (Fig. 66).

Towards the end of the eighteenth century, College Green had become the geographical epicentre of the expanding city as the outlying pockets of fashionable settlement at the Hotwells and Clifton coalesced. Those who came to take the waters, and who failed to find remedy or return home, found an earthly rest in the cathedral, which became the repository of fashion and fame. With this trend came an inevitable use of metropolitan sculptors. The first of these was John Bacon RA. Born at Southwark in 1740, he came from a strong Dissenting background,[147] as did Mrs Coade for whom he worked as the designer at the factory in Lambeth that made artificial stone statuary. Bacon never went to Rome, and this and his Dissenting background may have had something to do with his later employment in Bristol. Bacon developed a pointing machine which, in an age when the fashion for memorials burgeoned, allowed the mass production of memorials by a large workshop of between fifteen and twenty assistants.[148] He was considered by contemporaries to have developed a near-monopoly of the army and navy commissions that resulted from the Napoleonic Wars.

One of Bacon's earliest monuments in Westminster Abbey was to the poet Thomas Gray (1716–71), which had been paid for by the Reverend William Mason (1725–97),[149] himself the subject of one of Bacon's last memorials, set up in Poet's Corner, Westmister Abbey in 1799.[150] In his lifetime, Mason's considerable reputation rested on his poetry and on his promotion of the better known Gray. He was Gray's executor, edited his poems and letters, and wrote his life. Today, unread as a poet,[151] Mason may be remembered as a designer of gardens for his many friends and patrons, notably those at Nuneham Courtney for the second Earl Harcourt. He combined both these claims to fame in the blank verse poem *The English Garden*, published in four volumes between 1771 and 1781, and in the epitaph for Capability Brown's tomb at Fenstanton, Suffolk. Mason was a champion and innovator in church music, and actively concerned for the lunatic and the criminal in the diocese of York. He was a friend of Wilberforce, and an early abolitionist and vociferous opponent of the slave trade. In 1777 he baptised Benjamin Moor, a young black American, in York Minster. A Yorkshire prelate of a Whiggish disposition like Lawrence Sterne, Mason was born and brought up at Hull, and became the often absentee incumbent of Aston-cum-Aughton, south-east of Rotherham, a benefice he held for 43 years. Mason married Mary Sherman (c.1738–67), the daughter of the garrison quartermaster at Hull in 1765. She died eighteen months later of consumption, having gone to Bristol to take the waters at the Hot Wells. She was buried in the cathedral, and Mason wrote and signed her epitaph, which begins: 'Take, Holy earth, all that my soul holds dear', on the monument he set up there. It includes a medallion depicting Mary expiring in the arms of William, both in classical dress, with a river goddess and a cliff face in the background, and was executed by Bacon to a design by James 'Athenian' Stuart.[152]

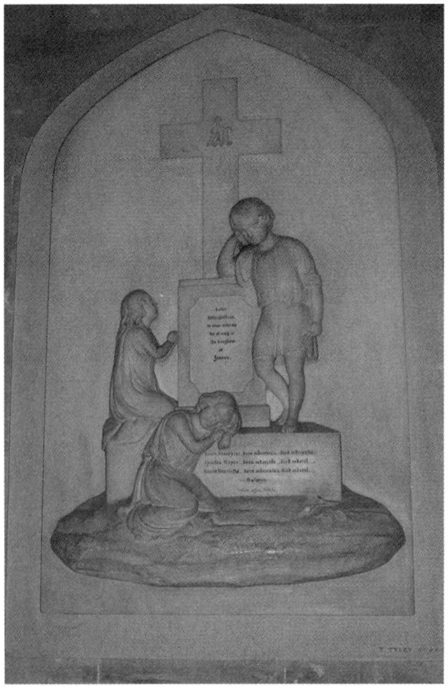

Fig. 66 *Wall tablet to the Malwyn children*, signed: T. TYLEY. Sc. *BRISTOL*, c.1850, south transept, Bristol Cathedral

The Masons might well have seen the actor-manager William Powell (1735/6–69) while in Bristol.[153] Powell became David Garrick's understudy at Drury Lane in 1763. From 1764 he appeared regularly in the summer season at the Jacob's Well Theatre, midway between the Hotwells and the cathedral. So popular was he that after a benefit performance in 1765, he had to publish an apology in the local newspapers addressed to those who had been turned away for lack of seats.[154] In 1766 he became a partner in the new Theatre Royal, recently built by Thomas Paty in King Street, which rapidly became a fashionable venue, attracting visitors, among them Garrick himself, to Bristol. Powell's two summer seasons there were beset by ill-health, and he died of pneumonia at his lodgings in King Street on 3 July 1769; the play *Richard III* went on, but the farce was cancelled that night with the audience's agreement.[155] His body was carried in procession, preceded by a choir, and the dean, before a large crowd of spectators, conducted the funeral in the cathedral. Powell's wife Elizabeth erected the monument in the cathedral in 1771 (Fig. 67). Signed by James Paine Jr. (1745–1829), the son of the architect James Paine Sr, it was set up in the period when Paine

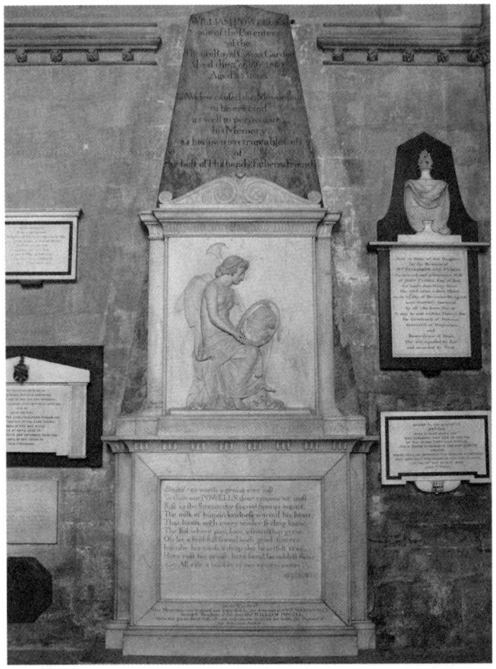

Fig. 67 *Monument to William Powell (d. 1769)*, by James Paine, 1771, north choir aisle, Bristol Cathedral

was in London in between two long periods in Rome. With an obelisk almost seventeen feet high, and a figure of Fame holding a portrait medallion, it has been regarded as the most important of Paine's monuments.[156] The epitaph was written by Powell's erstwhile partner in the Covent Garden Theatre, and 'faithful friend', George Colman.

The most outstanding example of this trend, however, must be John Bacon's monument to Elizabeth Draper, *née* Sclater (1744–78), who had died at Bristol aged 35 and was buried in the cathedral.[157] Here indeed is celebrity as it is understood today in the early twenty-first century: fame by association, with the prurient ingredients of a vicar and a married woman. The vicar wrote two of the most salacious and successful satires of the time. Elizabeth had been born in India and married, at the age of fourteen, Daniel Draper, a member of the East India Company and a government official in Bombay. This must have given her a certain exotic cache when she met, at the age of 22, on a visit to London in January 1767, the 54-year-old Laurence Sterne (1713–68). He clearly conceived a passion for her, which continued after she left England in April until letters from her in July appear to have extinguished it.[158] She returned to England in 1776, eight years after the death of Sterne, and capitalised on her position as his muse in Sterne's best known, most read, final work, *A Sentimental Journey* (1768). Sterne invokes her personally in the first paragraph when we learn that he carries a miniature of her in a locket, a 'little picture' about his neck.[159] He speaks of her 'pure taper', and places her on an emotional level with the heroine Maria.[160]

As Sterne's biographer in the *Oxford Dictionary of National Biography* put it, she 'attracted far more attention in the century following her death than was called for'.[161] Such fame was the catalyst for one of Bacon's most elegant works, a successful design that he was to use again and again (Figs 68 and 69),[162] although Bacon used it for other virtues and poses: Genius with her torch,[163] Benevolence carrying the pelican and her young in a nest; the latter detail so ubiquitous in Bacon's monuments as to have been described as his trademark.[164] In their turn, Bacon's figures would prove an inspiration to others, including the Patys, even though his classical baroque style was not informed by a genuine interest in the antique.

The introduction of a purer form of antique-inspired monument was the work of John Flaxman (1775–1826). He had been admitted to the Royal Academy Schools in the same year as Bacon in 1769, and was awarded a Silver Medal in that year.[165] He trained, like Bacon, and like his favourite pupil E. H. Baily after him, as a modeller. As a modeller, Flaxman was responsible for the adaptation of Etruscan or Greek vase-painting to the jasperware products of Bentley and Wedgwood's Etruria factory, while his illustrations to Homer received a European acclaim for their purity of line.[166] From 1810 to his death, Flaxman was the first professor of sculpture at the Royal Academy Schools, where he promoted the work of Antonio Canova and encouraged the appreciation of the Elgin Marbles.

His earliest work in Bristol was the small high-relief wall monument to Troth Blisset in All Saints in 1805 (Fig. 70). Troth Blisset, who had died the previous year, was the widow of Joseph Blisset of Chancery Lane and the daughter of John Freeman. This connection explains her presence among the extended Colston family, for her great-aunt was married, as we have seen, to Walter Edwards,[167] and Colston's niece, married to Thomas Edwards Jr, was Walter's sister-in-law. Her son, described by Flaxman as 'Joseph Blisset Esqr Clifton near Bristol', commissioned the monument. Flaxman records in his account book for 8 March 1805 that he had received on account £35 for a £100 monument, 'affixing exclusive' the expenses, which were set out as follows:

Coach hire & expences to & from Bristol 5 5
Board and lodging 1 4
7 days work 1 15
Cramps 1 7
Case 2 13 9½

As Flaxman records, the account was paid.

The monument is the earliest of a type used by Flaxman for a number of memorials, notably that to Sarah Udny (1812) in Chichester Cathedral,[168] its gothic canopy or frame a very early example of a renewed sympathy for the Gothic.[169] The Blisset tablet is signed on the right hand

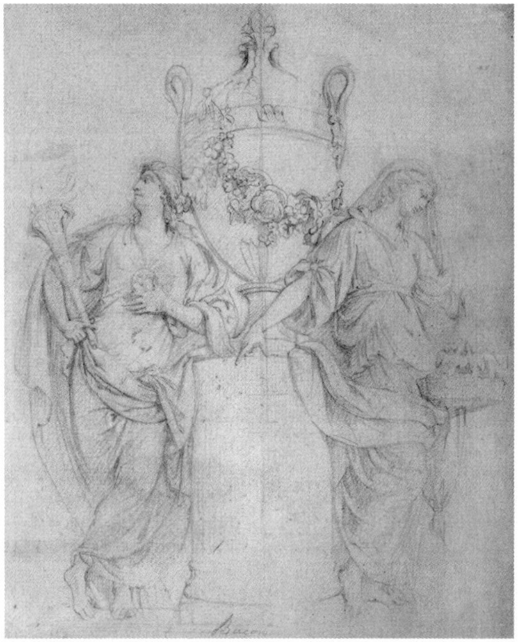

Fig. 68 *Design for the monument in Bristol Cathedral to Elizabeth Draper*, by John Bacon RA, c.1780, pencil (Royal Academy of Arts, JU/1/17)

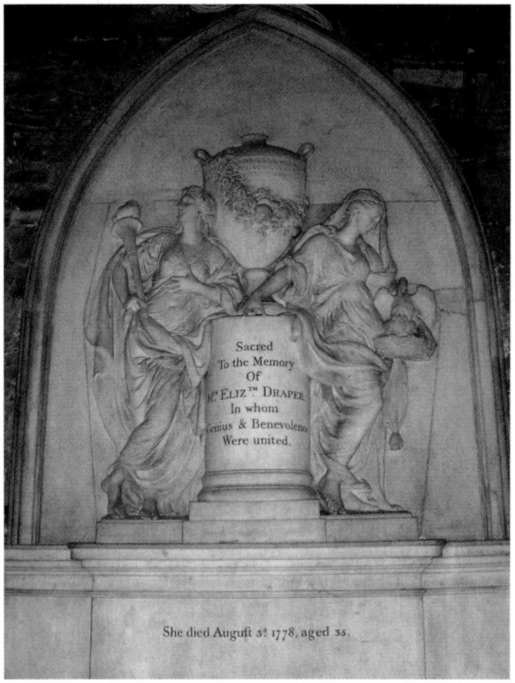

Fig. 69 *Monument to Elizabeth Draper (d. 1778)*, by John Bacon RA, 1780, cloister, East Walk, Bristol Cathedral

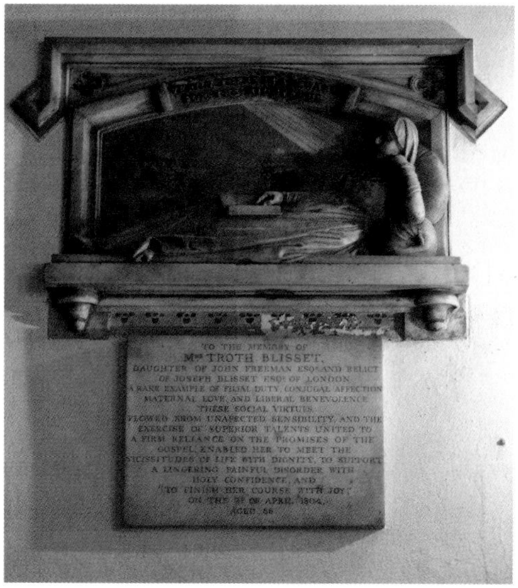

Fig. 70 *Monument to Troth Blisset (d. 1804)*, by John Flaxman RA, 1805, All Saints

Fig. 71 *Monuments (above) to William Brame Elwyn (d. 1841) by E. H. Baily RA, and (below) to Mary Brame Elwyn (d. 1818), by Francis Chantrey RA*, 1822, south choir aisle, Bristol Cathedral

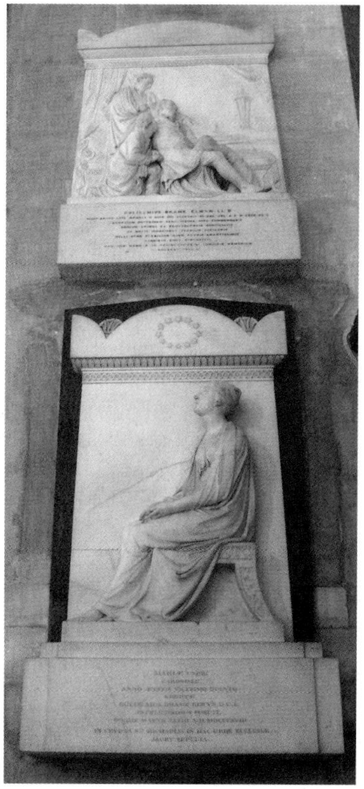

side of the plinth below the relief: 'FLAXMAN R.A. SCULPTOR'.[170]

Flaxman's entry tells us a lot about the business of delivering and setting up the monument, but not who did the installation. Many of the other entries mention the assistance of masons, their time and expenses. A coach 'hire' suggests that whoever went from London was not travelling by stagecoach. Did Flaxman go himself on this occasion? If he did, did he in the seven days spent in Bristol meet the young Edward Hodges Baily, or did his workman?

Sir Francis Chantrey's monuments for Bristol are all to be found on College Green, and are all from the early 1820s. Two are in the cathedral. The earlier is to Mary, the wife of William Brame Elwyn, who had died in 1818.[171] Chantrey's ledger records: 'Mr Elwin' ordering a monument 'pursuant to an approved design' in the same year. The 'Sitting figure in Relief the size of life'[172] is signed and dated 1822 (Fig. 71). As a type, the seated female figure looking heavenwards in high relief before a Greek stele with acroteria derives from Flaxman's *Resignation*, which he had exhibited at the Royal Academy in 1809; he used variations of this for several monuments.[173] Mrs Elwyn's monument is positioned so that she looks up to her husband (d. 1841) (Fig. 71), the scene of whose death is described in a narrative relief tablet by E. H. Baily. The moment of Elwyn's death appears more immediate than was usual in other such representations of the period.

Chantrey found that despite their agreement, he was to be paid £42 less than the final £315, because Elwyn, 'a sharp clever man ... managed to make me pay Church fees'.[174] This clearly rankled, and when next working for a Bristolian commission, he ensured that the church fees were paid separately. This was the monument to Dr Walter Kennedy Craufuird (d. 1817) and his wife Emma, with its very fine double portrait in profile (Fig. 72). Craufuird had been a physician at the Bristol Infirmary, which had become the centre of Bristol's civic conscience and its pride,[175] and its physicians in some sense replaced the individual benefactors of the seventeenth century. In the early twentieth century the infirmary would commission one of the earliest and finest modernist buildings in Europe, Charles Holden's Babylonian edifice, now much mutilated. It remains at the heart of the life of Bristol and its hinterland.

Craufuird's names and the archaic form of his surname suggest that he had come, like many other doctors, from Scotland. An entry for August 1821 in Chantrey's ledger records an order from Dr Bernard, a fellow infirmary physician, 'to execute a monument according to an approved design in memory of the late Dr Craufuird and his wife, the price fixed by the will'.[176] The monument is signed and dated 1823, and it appears from the ledger that Chantrey sent in his invoice for £210 'including expenses of erection and carriage and excluding Church fees' on 19 July 1824.[177] He was paid on 7 February 1826, 'by a Bill on Barclay & Co.'.[178] The 'Mr King' who paid the church fees[179] may have been the mason builder employed to set the monument up in the cathedral, possibly a member of the family of Bath statuary masons connected by marriage to the Patys.

The third monument by Chantrey is in St Mark's, in the Lord Mayor's Chapel. Signed and dated 1823, it commemorates Henry Bengough (1738–1818),[180] alderman and mayor of Bristol (Fig. 73). He had been a partner of Bristol City Bank, a solicitor, and leader of the Whig party in Bristol. More importantly in this context, he had endowed an almshouse, which still bears his name, 'for poor men and women of all religious denominations'. As the inscription on the monument declares, 'he took a zealous and active interest in the welfare of the city'.[181] Chantrey recorded the commission on 27 May 1819 from 'Arthur Palmer Esqr. of Bristol', a fellow solicitor, judge and local politician, who represented the city corporation. It was to cost £700, according to the will, and that sum was 'By 3 PCt. consols transferred by Mr Palmer and Mr Cave of Bristol' in January 1824.[182] The 'all-powerful'[183] subject is seated in high relief, and,

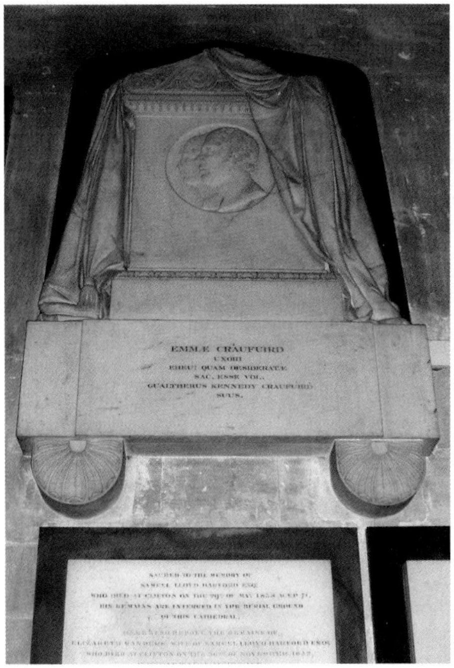

Fig. 72 ***Monument to Walter (d. 1817) and Emma Craufuird*, by Francis Chantrey RA, 1823, south transept, Bristol Cathedral.**

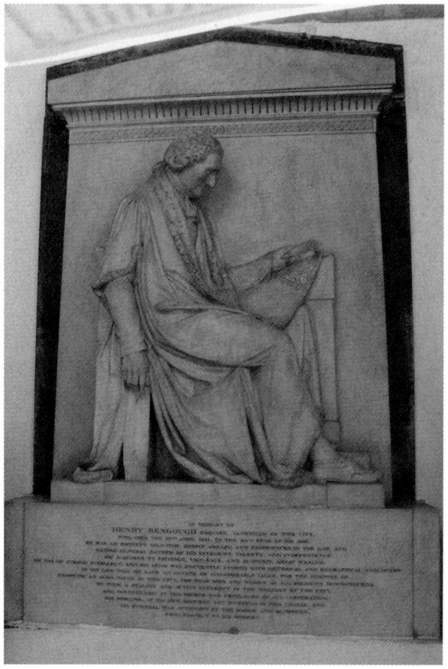

Fig. 73 ***Monument to Henry Bengough (d. 1818)*, by Francis Chantry RA, 1819, St Mark (Lord Mayor's Chapel)**

like his predecessor Whitson, in his furred alderman's gown. He wears his legal but otherwise outdated bag-wig.[184] As a type, it owes a lot to Flaxman's monument to the poet William Collins (1792) in Chichester Cathedral,[185] and was used several times by Chantrey, as in the monument to John Phelips at Wells Cathedral in 1835, which was paid for by a member of the Bristol family of Hobhouse.[186]

These are metropolitan interventions at the top of the market. But at this juncture Bristol, which was also the birthplace of the future president of the Royal Academy, Sir Thomas Lawrence, produced a native sculptor of national, even international standing. Edward Hodges Baily (1788–1867) was from a low church nonconformist background, the son of a carver of ship's figureheads.[187] Tradition has it that he was introduced by a Dr Leigh of Bristol to John Flaxman, thereby beginning an association that lasted until the death of the older sculptor, whose mantle Baily may be said to have assumed. He was admitted as a sculptor to the Royal Academy Schools on 18 March 1809, aged 21, and proceeded to be awarded a Silver Medal in 1809 and a Gold Medal in 1811.[188] He was elected full RA in 1817. A distinguished modeller for the major silversmiths of the early to mid-nineteenth century,[189] Baily was responsible for many fine portrait busts of the leading scientists, politicians, poets and painters of the time, and the executor of some of the best known public figure sculpture of the day.[190] He was the author of numerous poetic ideal subject groups, which achieved European fame and emulation.[191] Despite this evident success he was bankrupted several times like many sculptors, whose overheads (including the cost of materials, premises and assistance) were always high. Baily sought the support of his fellow citizens of Bristol in various ways,[192] and appealed to the Royal Academy's Artists' Benevolent Fund on several occasions.

It is difficult to imagine the esteem in which he was held contemporaneously. In 1857, the year Baily designed the Turner Medal for the Royal Academy, the *Art Journal* described him as the most distinguished sculptor among those elected to the Royal Academy.[193] In the same year, the *Athenaeum* called him 'our Marble Poet'.[194] Ten years later, however, the *Illustrated Times* described him in an obituary as 'a modeller of soup tureens and tea-pots', albeit 'the very head of his profession'.[195] Baily had in a long working life gone full circle, but at the end was reduced to the ranks of the artisan by mid-nineteenth century artistic and social snobbery, his reputation wiped out by the vanguard of a new wave of aesthetic sensibility. His pupils were many, and some are better known than he is today.[196]

Baily designed distinguished monuments for a distinguished clientele across the entire country,[197] and it is not surprising that his work should be in demand in his native city. One of the earliest is to a non-Bristolian, Harriet Isabella Middleton (d. 1826). It is in the cathedral, and was set up by her husband, John Middleton of Clifton, who survived her by 42 years, dying at the age of 96 in 1868.[198] The almost life-size kneeling female figure type in three dimensions has an interesting iconographical history, and is clearly indebted to Flaxman (Fig. 74).[199] Baily was to use it again several times, [200] and as a type it had been used by Chantrey.[201] Baily's is the sparest, purest example, and must have been something of a sensational innovation in Bristol, where life-size kneeling figures had not been seen on monuments since the early seventeenth century, and then largely in the special conditions prevailing in the Lord Mayor's Chapel. In a heavy, greyish marble it is almost all drapery and bereft of detail, save the right foot. Feet were a speciality of Baily's, and the nicely articulated toes clearly invite, like St Peter's, a tangible response. The drapery has a proto-modern quality in its simplified forms, and perhaps for this reason appears at odds with the Gothic chest on which the figure kneels.

One monument by Baily that is closely identified with one of the most violent and destructive events in Bristol's history is that to Bishop Robert Gray (1762–1834).[202] He had a traditional education and career in the Anglican hierarchy in the diocese of Durham. There he had a reputation for philanthropy, and established several schools and a local infirmary and dispensary at Bishopwearmouth. He encouraged Humphry Davy's work on the safety lamp for the use of his miner parishioners. He had married Elizabeth, daughter of the Reverend John Camplin (the precentor

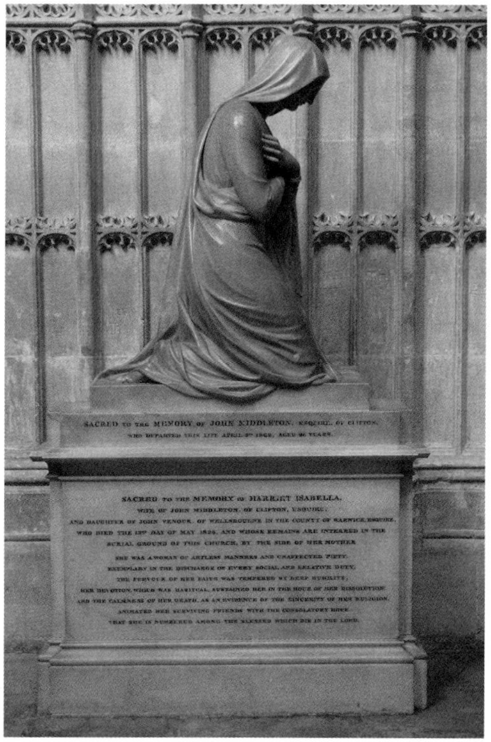

Fig. 74 *Monument to Harriet Middleton (d. 1826)*, signed and dated by E. H. Baily RA, south choir aisle, Bristol Cathedral

of Bristol Cathedral in 1794 and a mayor of the city), but he was not elevated to the bishopric of Bristol until 1827. As an opponent of Catholic emancipation he was able to express the traditional anti-Catholic views of Bristolians in the House of Lords in the debates about the proposed bill. However, he was also doggedly anti-parliamentary reform, and reaped a whirlwind, having voted against it, when the Reform Bill failed in October 1831. The people of Bristol rioted over the weekend of 29–31 October, and the Bishop's Palace was, like other buildings, set on fire and burnt to the ground, including a library of 6,000 books. It was one of the incidents dramatically recorded by the painter William Müller.[203] Throughout the anarchy, Gray refused to cancel services, and he himself preached at one. He died at Rodney House, Clifton, whence he had removed after the Riots, due to ill-health probably brought on by the shock. He was buried in the churchyard adjacent to the cathedral and his monument inside was erected by the clergy and laity of the city, perhaps in a spirit of remorse. As a design it is reminiscent of John Bacon's for the Draper monument of almost half a century earlier. Indeed it may be in homage to that influence, for Baily is reputed to have said that it was on seeing Eliza Draper's monument that he resolved to become a sculptor. The monument is skied and the resulting foreshortening of the figures does it no credit (Fig. 75).

It was not, however, Baily's monuments in the manner of Flaxman or Bacon that were in demand in Bristol, but his portrait heads. This introduced a new element into funerary commemoration in Bristol: the presentation of a portrait – the subject as in life – as the dominant feature of the memorial. The stark simplicity of this type of presentation suits the character and importance of Thomas Biddulph, by Baily in St James's (Fig. 76).[204]

Thomas Tregenna Biddulph (1763–1838) was at the centre of evangelicalism in the late eighteenth and early nineteenth century, and the controversies which raged around the doctrine of regenerative baptism in the west country.[205] A child, on both sides, of the rectory, Biddulph went to Queen's College, Oxford, after grammar school in Truro, and was ordained in the diocese of Exeter in 1785. He was twice curate of St Mary-le-Port, Bristol, becoming perpetual curate of St James's in 1799 until his death in 1838. He lived in St James's Square. A strict Calvinist, Biddulph's appointment was an odd choice for the parish of St James, which had been markedly high Anglican throughout the eighteenth century,[206] and he was unpopular at first. It may have been strategically intended to counter the success of the Baptist movement, which since the mid-seventeenth century was a powerful sect in Bristol, particularly among the artisan communities.[207] His reputation as a preacher and his devotion to his calling won the respect of his parishioners and others. He was a prolific writer in the evangelical cause, in the face of rising Tractarianism, and active in evangelical societies such as the Church Missionary Society, the British and Foreign Bible Society, the Protestant

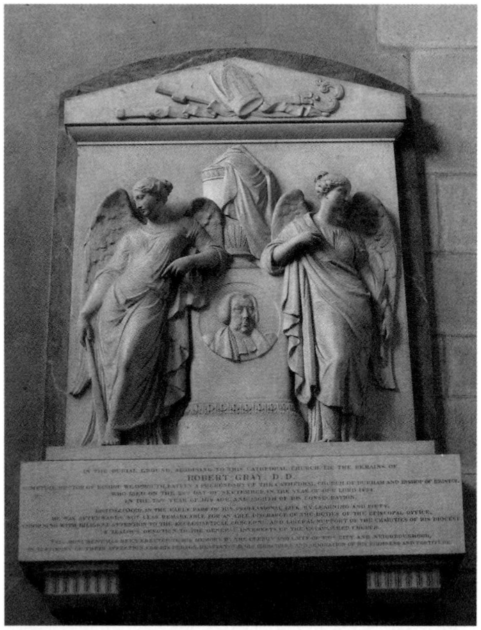

Fig. 75 ***Monument to Bishop Robert Gray by E. H. Baily RA*, south transept, Bristol Cathedral (by permission of the dean and chapter, P3010060)**

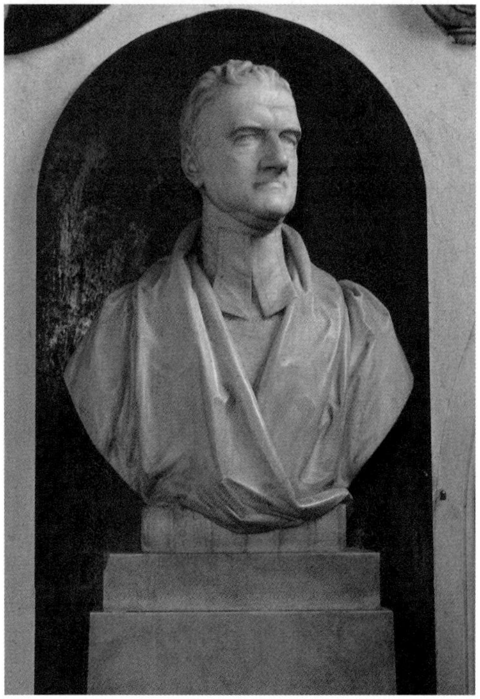

Fig. 76 ***Memorial portrait bust of the Rev. Thomas Biddulph (d. 1838) by E. H. Baily RA*, 1842, St James**

Reformation Society and the Church Pastoral Aid Society. He was the first secretary and treasurer of the Bristol Clerical Education Society, which supported would-be evangelical ordinands at university. He founded *Zion's Trumpet* in 1789, which later became the *Christian Guardian*, and in 1835 he had St Matthew's, Kingsdown built to designs by Thomas Rickman. The full-length torso in contemorary clerical dress is signed and dated 1842, and rests on a book, inscribed 'HOLY BIBLE', with lively drapery. The divine's collar stands up in a virtuoso touch, while the eyeballs are incised so that the sitter is not being presented in a purely Classical manner

In the following year (1843), the poet and political and religious commentator Robert Southey, Poet Laureate, died.[208] He had been born in the centre of old Bristol, in Wine Street in 1774. A precocious and prodigious writer from an early age, Southey espoused the republican fervour of the end of the century. He was expelled from Westminster School for writing an attack on corporal punishment, for which the school had been famous since the late seventeenth century. While at Oxford in 1794 he met Samuel Taylor Coleridge, and there began a friendship that has become enshrined in literature as a cornerstone of English romanticism. Their first Pantisocractic commune was in a cramped flat at 25 College Green.[209] They married the Bristolian sisters Edith and Sara Fricker in St Mary Redcliffe, and shared the support of the Bristol publisher Joseph Cottle. Together they settled with their wives at Greta Hall in Keswick, Cumbria, and there Southey remained for the next forty years. He was buried at Crosthwaite, Keswick.[210]

Southey's prolific journalistic writings kept him afloat. Politically he went from radicalism to centre right in matters of foreign policy. He became Poet Laureate in 1813, a role he took very seriously, seeing it as an opportunity to influence ideas and politics. It could be argued that Southey's views reflected the ambivalence of his native city in matters of religion and trade. His fierce denunciations of Catholicism and wariness towards the 'enthusiasms' of nonconformity found his cenotaph well placed at the centre of Bristol's establishment in the cathedral.

The original intention had been to set up a memorial to the poet on College Green, but a meeting presided over by the mayor failed to raise more than £50, £20 of which was advanced by the designated sculptor, E. H. Baily.[211] The committee settled for a bust to be set up in the cathedral (Fig. 77). Baily's bust, with a long draped torso, the drapery in cushiony plump folds, is a dramatic portrait likeness, presenting the poet bare-chested in a classical manner, the eyeballs blank. The plinth however, in dove-grey marble, is Gothic, the sculptor being sensible of its intended context.[212] It is entirely appropriate that Southey's memorial in the cathedral should have been executed by Baily, his fellow Bristolian. It is unlikely that many could claim to have read any of Southey's innumerable and interminably long epic poems, or to have heard of the sculptor. Yet in their lifetimes, Baily and Southey attained a national, not

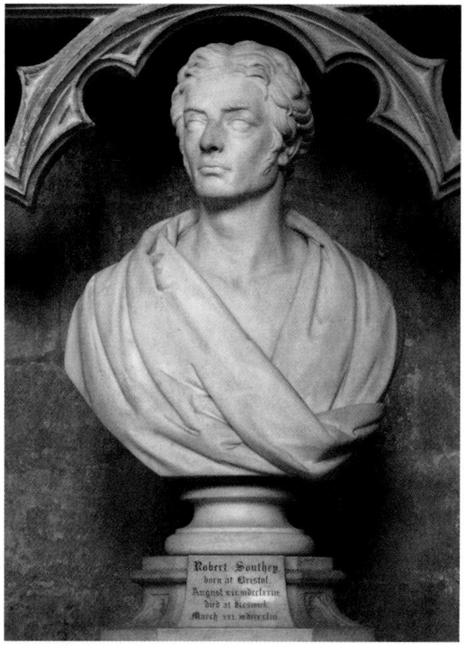

Fig. 77 ***Memorial portrait bust of Robert Southey, Poet Laureate (d. 1843) by E. H. Baily RA*, 1844, north choir aisle, Bristol Cathedral**

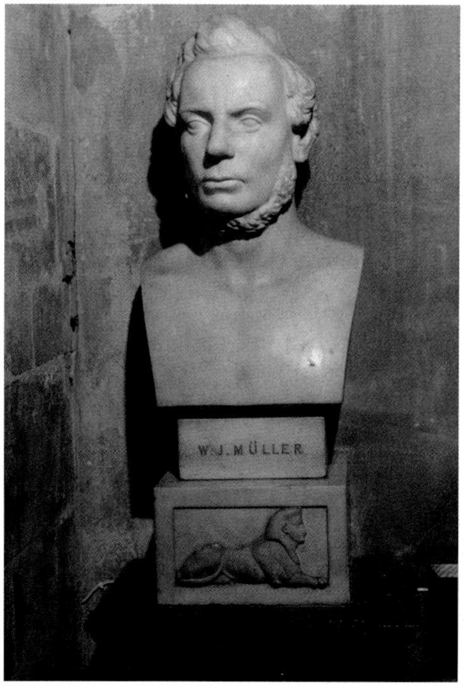

Fig. 78 ***Memorial portrait bust of William Müller (d. 1845) by Nathan Branwhite*, c.1846, erected 1893, south transept, Bristol Cathedral**

to say European, status.

Another of Bristol's distinguished sons, the painter William Müller (1812–45), was described by Latimer as 'the greatest painter to which Bristol has given birth'.[213] His presence in the cathedral was effected by the presentation by his sister-in-law, Rosa Müller in 1892, of a bust by Nathan Branwhite (1813–94), not otherwise known as a sculptor.[214] A subscription was raised 'to defray the cost of a pedestal', and it was set up the following December.[215] The bust, with a tame Egyptian sphinx on the socle and its pedestal, are squeezed uncomfortably in behind the door to the cloister (Fig. 78). It is possible that any plans for a grander monument in commemoration of Müller's life and work coincided with the mid-century national movement against more monuments in churches, which in some quarters amounted to a revulsion against memorials of all kinds. One might, however, speculate about a connection with a series of preparatory designs for a large monument in a distinctly Egyptian manner by a hand other than Wood's in the Leeds Wood album (Fig. 79). Bristol was in the vanguard of the taste for the Egyptian. Giuseppe Belzoni (1778–1823), the explorer of Egypt, was married to Sarah Banne, a Bristolian who published his drawings of the royal tombs at Thebes in 1829, while Brunel's winning design for the Clifton Suspension Bridge in 1831 was in the Egyptian style. Müller, who died just as his reputation achieved national recognition, had travelled for six months in Egypt in 1838, and the work that was inspired by that experience contributed to his success, but perhaps it was too exotic a location for a church monument for the persistently visually cautious citizens of Bristol.

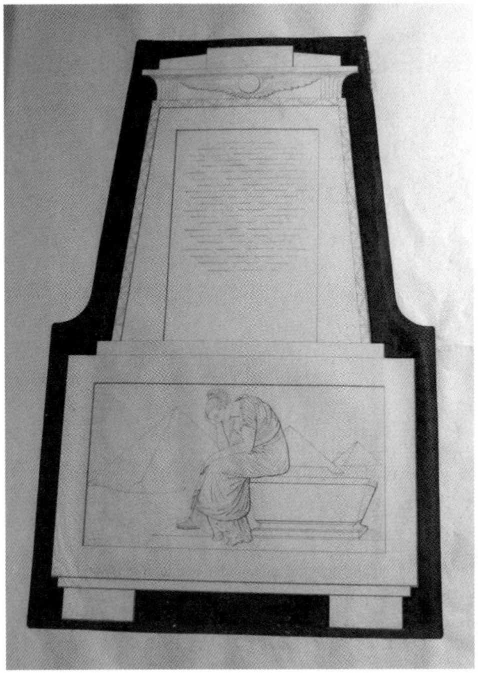

Fig. 79 ***Design for a monument in the Egyptian style*****, pencil, pen and ink, Wood album, Leeds Museums and Galleries (Henry Moore Institute Archive)**

The latter part of the nineteenth century saw few memorials erected in the churches of Bristol. The Burial Act of 1852 (which made burial in church impossible), and the increasing use of cemeteries such as Arno's Vale, coalesced with the Gothic revival, a reaction in taste against the classical of which Barry's Houses of Parliament were an early manifestation. The debate took off with A. W. N. Pugin's writings in the early 1840s, accompanied by the campaign in the *Ecclesiologist,* and an increasing sensitivity to the medieval fabric created a climate hostile to monuments in churches. One of the leaders of the reaction, A. J. B. Beresford Hope, writing in the *Christian Remembrancer* in 1855, described 'mural tablets of a wholly incongruous character… allowed to blister the walls of the nave' at Canterbury.[216] This must have struck a chord, and as elsewhere, funds that might have gone to sculptors for marble memorials were channelled into restoration projects or memorial windows. But the cathedral continued to act as a place of public memorial, and a number of historical personalities were commemorated by inscription tablets. The chroniclers of Bristol are there, including Richard Hakluyt (1586–1616), in a posthumous tablet signed by Tyley and dated in what must be a letter-cutter's mistake MDCCCCX, which is wreathed in oak leaves. In Bristol, oak leaves had a particular significance and were associated with royalist Jacobite sympathies. John Latimer also found a place. He was editor of the *Bristol Mercury* from 1858 to 1883, and in his retirement he researched (with the thoroughness of late nineteenth-century historiography) four centuries of Bristol's history, and wrote it up with equal vividness in four volumes published between 1887 and 1908. More unlikely is the bicentenary memorial of 1888 recalling the part played by Sir Jonathon Trelawny (1650–1721) in the suppression of the Monmouth Rebellion. A rather unsympathetic portrait is drawn by Latimer of this 'hunting parson' and Cornish hero. He was one of the seven bishops imprisoned under James II, and was immortalised in *The Song of the Western Men*, now the Cornish anthem:

> And shall Trelawny die!
> And shall Trelawny die!
> There's twenty thousand Cornish lads
> Will know the reason why.

He raised an army against the Duke of Monmouth, fought in the field, and was rewarded by William of Orange with the bishopric of Bristol. This being a poor see, he ensured his translation soon after to Exeter, and thence to Winchester.[217] The memorial in the Newton Chapel, a bronze relief by Alfred Drury RA (1856–1944) (Fig. 80) commissioned by the Bristol and District Cornish Association, must be one of the last manifestations of this type of Protestant historical collective memory. It is also one of the first inspired by local national pride, for Trelawny (as the

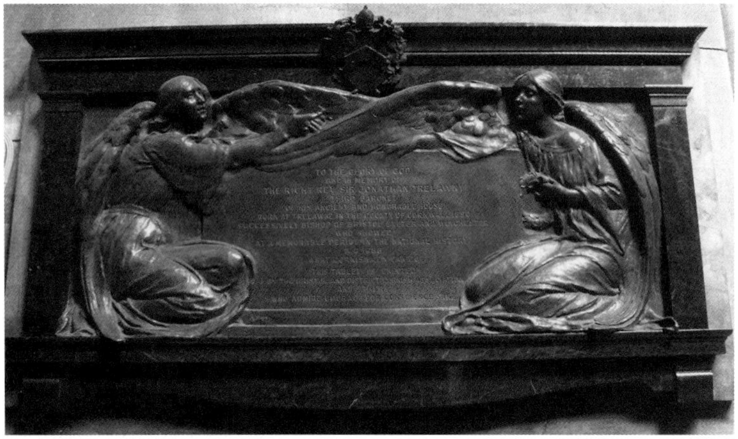

Fig. 80 ***Memorial to Bishop Trelawny by Alfred Drury RA*****, 1888, bronze, Newton Chapel, Bristol Cathedral**

inscription informs us) 'showed/ at a memorable period in the National history / A.D. 1688 / What Cornishmen can do'. The style chosen suggests that the sculptor either had little knowledge of the subject, or deliberately preferred to ignore it, for the design of a pair of female figures supporting the inscription derives not from the seventeenth century, but from a type of Flaxman design. The design, in the plastic medium of bronze, has a distinct style associated with the New Sculpture, and was later adapted by the sculptor for the inaugural plaque to the Blackwall Tunnel's northern approach (1897).[218]

Mary Carpenter (1807–77)[219] was one of those remarkable women of the mid-nineteenth century who – like the better known Florence Nightingale – overcame inimical social conventions and changed the social landscape of their times. She was the daughter of the minister of Lewin's Mead Unitarian Chapel, Lant Carpenter (1780–1840), and his wife Anna Penn. Like all Unitarian women she was educated on a par with boys; in her case in her father's school, where among her fellow pupils was James Martineau, who later wrote her epitaph. She began a traditional life as a governess, but was influenced by the great Indian religious and educational reformer Raja Rammohun Roy (1772–1833), who was visiting Bristol in 1833 when he died.[220] In 1835 she founded the Working and Visiting Society, based on Joseph Tuckerman's work in Boston.[221] With the help of John Bishop Estlin,[222] a surgeon at the Bristol Royal Infirmary, Carpenter established the first ragged school in Bristol in the slums around Lewin's Mead, just below the infirmary, in 1846. Here she gained the experience that informed her tolerant, Unitarian-inspired theories of child-centred education. In 1851 she published the influential *Reformatory Schools for the Children of the Perishing and Dangerous Classes, and for Juvenile Offenders*, whose basic principle was the inculcation of self-worth. It has a contemporary ring to it; Carpenter's thesis was that the retribution and punishment of children was not constructive, but that encouragement and security were. She founded a mixed school at Kingswood, outside Bristol. This soon closed because of the 'wild and violent' girls. However, in 1854 Lady Byron, the poet's widow, bought the Red Lodge for Carpenter, and this became the first reform school for girls in this country. In the early years there were riots, pregnancies, runaways and fire-raisers, but it continued for sixty years, until, in a war-changed world, it closed in 1917.[223]

Her *Juvenile Delinquents, their Condition and Treatment* (1853) had a direct bearing on the Youthful Offenders Act of 1854, and her published work and active lobbying continued to influence reforming government policy. In spite of continuous ill-health, Carpenter travelled to India in 1866, 1868, 1869–70 and finally 1875–6. Her views on the education of women and penal reform were sought and acted upon on the subcontinent, and Queen Victoria, interested in Indian education and having read *Six Months in India* (1868), gave her an audience. In 1869 she set up girls' schools in Bombay and Ahmadabad. She founded the National Indian Association as a disseminator of ideas on education and reform, first in Bristol, and later at Bombay, Calcutta and Dacca. In 1873 she was touring North America, lecturing on prison reform and learning about the condition of Native Americans. She was a signatory to the memorial at the Senate of the University of London, calling for degrees for women; late in life, she identified with the women's suffrage movement. She was buried in the cemetery at Arnos Grove, and her memorial in the cathedral was paid for by a cross-section of the city. As Latimer remarked, there was no hint of sectarianism attached to the response for subscriptions.[224]

Mary Carpenter's memorial of 1878 (Fig. 81) is in the manner of the time, a large inscription panel listing her many virtues, relieved by a profile portrait medallion by James Havard Thomas (1854–1921), rather awkwardly placed on the top. Havard Thomas was born and trained in Bristol, attended the Bristol Art School, and went on to do work of national importance,[225] including the lions on the Menai Straits Bridge, and the entrance piers to the gates to Buckingham Palace. There is a nice synchronicity here, as Baily had worked at Buckingham House at the beginning of the century.

Immediately above the Carpenter memorial is another fine relief portrait by Havard Thomas, in which portrait and text are comfortably united, and the window image owes little to the tradition of the cameo relief. The memorial was erected by public subscription to commemorate Frederick John Fargus (1847–85), the author of *Called Back.* First published in 1883, this early thriller, said to be a gripping tale of blindness, amnesia, political assassination and exile to Siberia, became a sensational best-seller, and is certainly the most popular novel ever written and published in Bristol. Fargus was an accountant and auctioneer

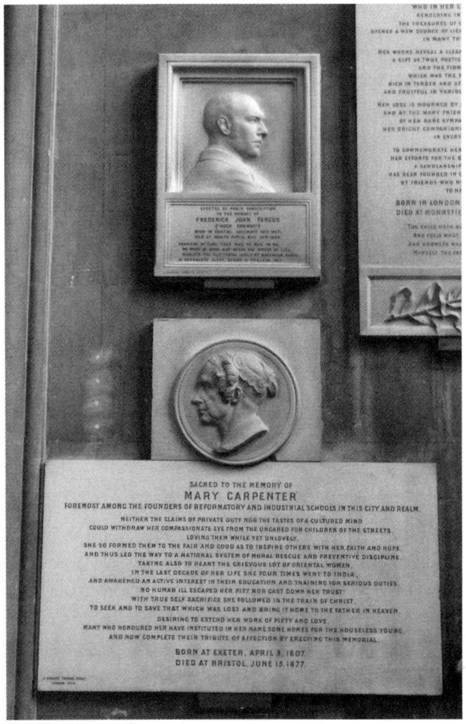

Fig. 81 ***Memorials by James Havard Thomas to (below) Mary Carpenter (d. 1877), dated 1878, and (above) Frederick John Fargus (d. 1885),*** **erected 1886, north transept, Bristol Cathedral**

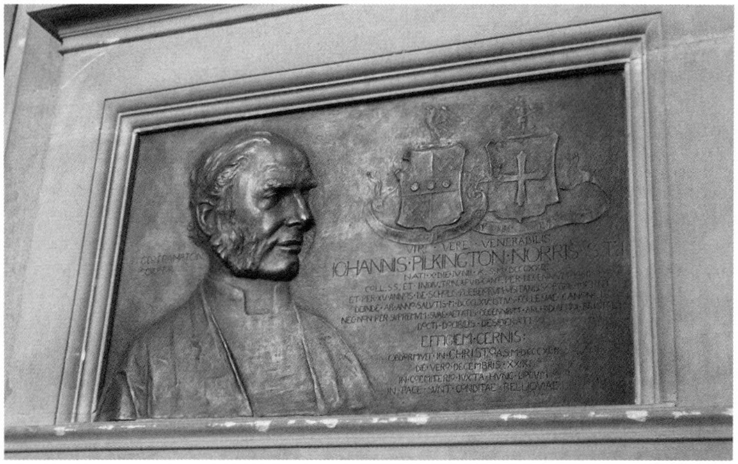

Fig. 82 ***Memorial to Canon John Pilkington Norris (d. 1891),*** **by George Frampton RA, bronze, north-west crossing pier, nave, Bristol Cathedral**

in Bristol, as well as a poet and novelist. He became master of the Antient Society of St Stephen's Ringers at the early age of 27, and played a major part in the de-Georgianisation and restoration of St Stephen's church. He died of typhoid in Monte Carlo.[226]

At the end of the nineteenth century, a creeping revival in monuments occurred in the cathedral, if not elsewhere. Under the High Church Dean Francis Pigou (1832–1916), commemoration was once again in order,[227] at least for the members of chapter, among them Dr John Pilkington Norris (d. 1891), canon of the cathedral. He had been archdeacon since 1881, and his 'untiring work' of restoration and his determination to raise funds and see the nave rebuilt is recorded by a bronze relief portrait and inscription by Sir George Frampton RA (1860–1928, best known for his *Peter Pan* (1912) in Kensington Gardens and the memorial to Edith Cavell in St Martin's Place (1917–20)) (Fig. 82).[228] A very late example is the portrait bust by Kathleen Scott (1878–1947) to George Forrest Browne (1833-1930), the 48th bishop of Bristol (1897–1914) (Fig. 83). Scott, who had trained at the Slade and worked in Rodin's studio, was married first to the polar explorer Robert Falcon Scott and then to the Labour politician Edward Young, later Lord Kennet, and maintained an independent career as a successful portrait sculptor.

It is surely no coincidence that the nineteenth century should see the near extinction of the funerary or sepulchral monument as memorial, as these began to leave the security of the established church and take their places on streets and squares as part of a wider urban cultural identity and landscape. Previously, if one wanted to be reminded of an historic individual or admire some of the finest examples of sculpture in the country, a visit to church was undoubtedly as good or better than a book or gallery, when churches were public spaces accessible to all.

St Augustine's, St Mary-le-Port, St Nicholas, St Peter's, Temple or Holy Cross and St Andrew's, Clifton were all destroyed on the night of 24 November 1940. The first and last of these were demolished; St Augustine's went in 1962, and was finally replaced by an extension to the Royal Hotel in the 1990s. St Nicholas became Bristol's Church Museum for a brief period in the 1970s and 1980s, and still has custody of a number of boxed and crated monuments.[229] A monument to the Reverend Dr Bridge in St Nicholas by E. H. Baily must be one of the many

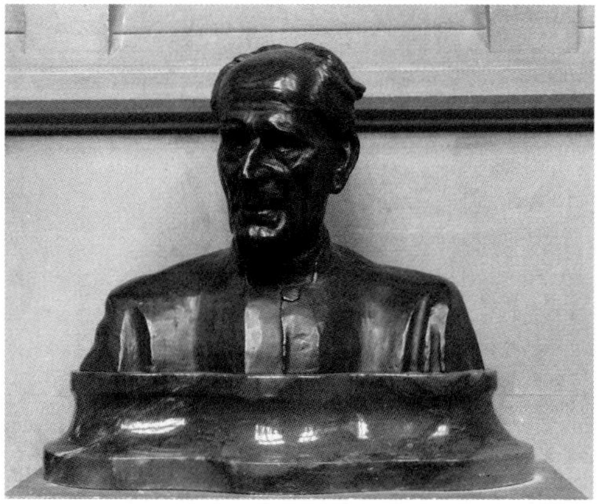

Fig. 83 ***Memorial portrait bust of Bishop Browne (d. 1914),*** **by Kathleen Scott, north choir aisle, Bristol Cathedral**

destroyed by the Blitz.[230] Another loss was the monument to the Aldworth family in St Peter's.[231] The other three churches remain as shells and towers, stripped of their ornament and furnishings, stained glass, and carving in wood and stone. They are memorials to an earlier age, almost an earlier civilisation: St Peter's, once the centre of a thriving timber-built city, is now the main axis of Castle Park, a landscaped and planted public space, originally designed by Sir Hugh Casson (later president of the Royal Academy) as a memorial to the civilians of Bristol who died in the Second World War.

Bristol took the decision in the 1950s, as did Coventry, not to rebuild but to leave the ruins, albeit shored up and maintained. This is in the spirit of the founding principles of the Commonwealth War Graves Commission, 'an enduring record and seemly sculpture';[232] 'sculpture' is here used in its most generous sense of three-dimensional form, to provide a sense of place and an equality in death. This has been the mark of most monuments and memorials of the twentieth century; all are individuals and all are heroes, there are no individual heroes.

I would like to thank John Bryant of the Bristol Rescue Archaeological Unit, St Nicholas; Anthony Beeson and the staff of the Central Reference Library; Dawn Dyer and the staff of Bristol Record Ofice; Sheena Stoddard, Julia Carver and Karin Walton of the City Art Gallery, Bristol; Victoria Worsley and Ian Kaye at the Henry Moore Institute, Leeds; and Mark Pomeroy, archivist at the Royal Academy, for their assistance and unfailing help and advice. To Susan Jotcham at St James' Priory, Tara Cale-Morgan (administrator of St Stephen's), and the staff of the Diocesan Education Centre, All Saints, my thanks for allowing me access to the churches for which they had responsibility; and to my family James and Marie Hamilton, thanks for their help in the business of recording inscriptions.

Notes

[1] 6 April 1733, No. 113. [2] J. Evans, *New Guide, or Picture of Bristol with Historical and Biographical Notices* (3rd edition, Bristol, c.1820–3). [3] M. Whinney, *Sculpture in Britain 1530–1830* (Harmondswoth: Penguin, 1964), p.1. Whinney acknowledges the importance of the great two-tier chimney-pieces that were such a feature of domestic architecture in the sixteenth century, particularly in Bristol. There are examples in the Red Lodge, the Savages' Wigwam at the Red Lodge, and the City Art Gallery Café. [4] J. Coutu, 'Carving histories: British sculpture in the West Indies', *Church Monuments*, vol. XII, 1997, pp.77–85. Azariah (d.1760) and his brother John Frederick (d.1762) at Wayford, both attributable to Thomas Paty on grounds of style, and their nephew John Pinney (d.1818) at Somerton. None of the inscriptions make any reference to their presence in Jamaica. I am grateful to Karin Walton for providing me with the details and images of these monuments. [5] *Bristol Weekly Intelligencer,* 11 November 1749. [6] See K. Eustace, 'William III, Queen Square, Bristol 1731–1736', in K. Eustace et al., *Michael Rysbrack Sculptor 1694–1770* (exhib. cat., Bristol: 1982). [7] T.J. Manchee, *The Bristol Charities, being the Report of the Commissioners for enquiring concerning Charities in England and Wales, so far as relates to the Charitable Institutions in Bristol* (2 vols, Bristol, 1831), vol. I, p.196; in fact not built until 1733 when the city surveyor was 'to view lands in Milk Street for building Mrs Ridley's Hospital'; BRO Common Council Proceedings, fol. 346. [8] J. Leech, *Rural Rides of the Bristol Churchgoer* (first published in the *Bristol Times*, 1843–5), (ed. A. Sutton, Stroud, 2004), p.40. [9] J. Latimer, *Sixteenth Century Bristol* (Bristol, 1908), p.66 [10] From 1689 to 1812 the Whigs controlled the Corporation; E. Ralph, *Government of Bristol 1373–1873* (Bristol, 1973), p.25 [11] For a full account see J. Bettey, 'Bristol Cathedral: the rebuilding of the nave' (Bristol: Bristol Branch of the Historical Association, 1993), pp.14–16; the figures – St Gregory in a papal diadem, St Jerome considered at the time to have a passing likeness to John Henry Newman – are illustrated in J. Rogan (ed.), *Bristol Cathedral History and Architecture* (Stroud, 2000), fig. 22 [12] The Friends Meeting House built at Quakers' Friars by George Tully in 1747, 'the most ambitious of its type and date in England', while Wesley's New Room, begun in 1739, was enlarged in 1748, probably also by George Tully; A. Foyle with B. Cherry, *Bristol* (New Haven and London, 2004), p.21, pp.174–5. [13] In the 1720s and 1730s the names Dampier, Peloquin and Laroche appear as aldermen, mayors, and sheriffs; see for example the 'List of the Gentlemen of the Corporation' in the Poll Book for 1739, Bristol Central Reference Library (B8769); see also H. Thomas, *The History of the Atlantic Slave Trade 1440–1870* (New York, 1997), p.245 [14] In 1739 John Wesley and George Whitfield were excluded, and barred from preaching in the established church by the Bishop of Bristol. [15] M. Baker and D. Bindman, *Roubiliac and the Eighteenth-Century Monument: Sculpture as Theatre* (New Haven and London, 1995), pp.44–5, illus. [16] K. Eustace, '"A Place full of Rich and Industrious People": art and patronage in Bristol in the first half of the 18th century', *British Art Journal*, vol. VII, no. 1, 2006, pp.3–16. [17] BROAC/WO/10(14)a). But the will, as proved in London in 1739, does not refer to a monument; BRO AC/WO/10 (14)b, c) and d). [18] G. Munro Smith, *History of the Bristol Royal Infirmary* (Bristol, 1917), p.44. [19] An eighteenth-century inscription painted on panel, and a version in Latin, which may themselves replace tomb inscriptions, provide these details. This may be part of the restoration work instigated by Dr Yonge. [20] See J. Sherborne, 'William Canynges 1402–1474' (Bristol Branch of the Historical Association, 1985); F.H. Crossley, *English Church Monuments A.D.1150–1550* (London, 1921), p.182, illus. 193; B. Kemp, *English Church Monuments* (London, 1980), p.23. [21] Sherborne, op. cit., p.27, and note 60. [22] Crossley, as at note 20, p.183, illus. 198 and 200; M.Q. Smith, *St Mary Redcliffe: An Architectural History* (Bristol, 1995), p.97. [23] As at note 19. [24] It would appear to be of the same school, even the same hand, as the effigy to John Camel (d.1487), lay treasurer of Glastonbury Abbey, in St John the Baptist, Glastonbury. [25] The Canynges coat of arms was a turbaned moor in triplicate. The dowel hole for the now missing hand of the beadsman is indicative of the customary fixing technique of the alabaster men; see F. Cannan, 'Alabaster representation of the Holy Spirit and allegations of Lollard vandalism', *Sculpture Journal*, vol. 15.1, 2006, pp.92–7. [26] J. Latimer, *Annals of Bristol in the Eighteenth Century* (Bristol: 1893, p.345). [27] The Canynges Society was founded in 1848 to support the restoration work; J. Latimer, *Annals of Bristol in the Nineteenth Century* (Bristol: 1887), p.260. [28] The half-built nave begun by Abbot Newland (d.1515) was pulled down and houses built in its stead; Crossley, as at note 20, illus. p.190, p.183; Foyle and Cherry as at note 12, p.51. [29] For the biographical details that follow see J.H. Bettey, *Oxford Dictionary of National Biography* (Oxford, 2004, hereafter *ODNB*). [30] It is noteworthy that though celibacy was not a requirement of the reformed church, rather the reverse, post-Reformation bishops and clergy do not at any period appear on their tombs or monuments with their wives, whereas for secular tomb-making society it was the norm. [31] Cadavers were not an innovation of the sixteenth century; they had been prevalent throughout the fifteenth century (Crossley, as at note 20, p.79, and n.3, p.183). For the intellectual context of the phenomenon in the fifteenth century, see P. King, 'The cadaver tomb in England', *Journal of the Church Monuments Society* (hereafter *Church Monuments*), vol. V, 1990, pp.26–38. That Thomist ideas were still current in the mid-sixteenth century is evident in private devotions and public monuments; see N. Llewellyn, *The Art of Death: Visual Culture in the English Death Ritual c.1500 – c.1800* (London, 1992), illus. 2, 65; and for a skeleton upon a

mat on a wall monument whose second storey is flanked by a pair of Corinthian columns, see the Blount monument (St John the Baptist, Mamble, Hereford and Worcester) of about 1561; Llewellyn, illus. 86. [32] See S. Oosterwijk, 'Food for worms, food for thought: the appearance and interpretation of the "verminous" cadaver in Britain and Europe', *Church Monuments*, vol. XX, 2005, pp.40–80, col.pls 1a and b. [33] Destroyed in the Great Fire of 1666, it survives as an illustration to William Dugdale's *History of St Pauls* (1658) in an engraving by Wenceslaus Hollar; Llewellyn as at note 31, illus. 99. [34] See C. Wilson, 'The medieval monuments', in P. Collinson, N. Ramsay and M. Sparks (eds), *A History of Canterbury Cathedral* (Oxford, 1995), pp.476–81, illus. 103. [35] See King, as at note 31. [36] Chichele's effigies were vandalised during the Commonwealth, and later restored; see Wilson, as at note 34, n.127. The very weathered remains of Bush's coat of arms, three boars or forest pigs have been set up at the end of the canopy in a later ashlar frame. [37] John Wycliffe was a prebendary of Aust, just to the north of Bristol, and his translation of the Bible, the first in English, was disseminated by John Purvey in Bristol in the 1380s. [38] A. Thrush, *ODNB*. [39] J. Aubrey, *Brief Lives*, (ed. R. Barber, Chippenham, 2004), pp.322–4. But for accuracy see Thrush, op. cit. [40] Aubrey, op. cit., p.323. [41] Ibid. [42] Whitson's almshouses were sold in 1999 with other similar charities and reconstituted as Bristol and Anchor Almshouse Charity, which is engaged in the provision of housing. [43] The annual Red Maids' School remembrance service is still held in the crypt. Whitson is included with Edward III, who granted Bristol's privileges in 1373, and Colston among others figures by John Thomas on the façade of the Guildhall (1843–6); B. Read, *Victorian Sculpture* (New Haven, CT and London, 1982), p.235, illus. [44] It is not unlike that to the 1st Lord Coventry (d.1639), Croome D'Abitot, Worcs. [45] Foyle and Cherry, as at note 12, pp.104–6. [46] R. Gunnis, *Dictionary of British Sculptors, 1660–1851* (London, n.d.). [47] J. Latimer, *Annals of Bristol 1600–1900* (7 vols, Bristol, 1893 (1906)), vol. V, pp.101–3. [48] I.M. Roper, *The Monumental Effigies of Gloucestershire and Bristol* (Gloucester, 1931), p.134. [49] See J. Latimer, *Annals of Bristol in the Seventeenth Century* (Bristol, 1900), passim. [50] Op. cit., pp.19–20, 27, 94. [51] See K. Esdaile, *English Church Monuments 1510–1840* (London, 1946), p.45, illus. 88; for a complete transcription of the inscription and an interesting analysis of the allegorical figures, see J. Wilson, 'Ethics girls: the personification of moral systems on Early Modern English monuments', *Church Monuments*, vol. XIII, 1998, pp.87–105. [52] Foyle and Cherry, as at note 12, p.109. [53] A. White, 'Biographical dictionary of London tomb sculptors, c.1560–1660', *Walpole Society*, vol. LX1, 1999, pp.1–162, figs 24, 25; and J. Wilson, 'The memorial by Nicholas Stone to Sir Thomas Bodley', *Church Monuments*, vol. III, 1993, pp.57–62, illus. [54] For a fine rendition of this coat of arms, see J. Latimer, *History of the Society of Merchant Venturers of the City of Bristol* (Bristol, 1903). [55] Foyle and Cherry, as at note 12, p.109. [56] Signed: W^M PUGH / BRISTOL. Another, signed in the same way, in the Cathedral cloister is 'sacred to the memory of Charles McNish of the Island of Jamaica' who had died after a long illness at Clifton in 1829, and whose son (aged six weeks) had died in 1826. [57] See J. Broome, 'Samuel Baldwin: carver of Gloucester', *Church Monuments,* vol. X, 1995, pp.37–49. [58] Ibid. [59] J. Latimer, *Sixteenth Century Bristol* (Bristol, 1908), p.119. Young is recorded as the first man to keep a 'black moore' as a gardener; C. Eickelmann and D. Small, *Pero, the Life of a Slave in Eighteenth-Century Bristol* (Bristol, 2004), p.47. [60] C.S. Knighton, *ODNB*; illustrated in Llewellyn, as at note 31, p.68, illus. 47; see also M. Craske, *The Silent Rhetoric of the Body, A History of Monumental Sculpture and Commemorative Art in England, 1720–1770* (Yale and London, 2007), p.73, fig. 42. [61] William Penn married Hannah Callowhill at the Quakers' meeting house in the Friars in 1696. Her mother Hannah Hollister was the daughter of Dennis Hollister MP from the Barebones Parliament, who had introduced George Fox and Quakerism to Bristol; see Latimer, as at note 49, passim. [62] Leech, as at note 8, p.40 [63] A drawing in the Braikenridge Collection of Bristol Museum and Art Gallery from the 1820s by M.H. Holmes (M1954) confirms that Penn's monument already had no flanking ornament that could have been lost in its subsequent move. [64] Such as the Throkmortons. Sir Baynham Throkmorton (d.1664) had been granted the rights to the royal chase at Kingswood, and whose administration was notoriously incompetent and grasping; Latimer, as at note 48, passim. His wife Margaret had died thirty years earlier, presumably in childbirth as she is presented in a reclining effigy cradling a baby, and the monument has been altered to accommodate the effigy of Throkmorton himself; Foyle and Cherry, as at note 12, p.102. [65] BRO CCP 1704-22, fol. 609. Since 1899 it has been the Lord Mayor's Chapel. [66] Leech, as at note 8, pp.60–5. [67] See Eustace, as at note 6, cat no. 32. [68] 14 June 1716 Vestry Minutes 1676–1726 P/St JB. [69] 31 August 1716, ibid. [70] Latimer, as at note 47, vol. III, pp.91–2. [71] All Saints, the Cathedral, Clifton, St James, St Mary Redcliffe, St Michael, St Stephen, Temple, St Thomas and St Werburgh's were all beneficiaries under his will, and recorded as such on the monument; See Roper, as at note 48, pp.87–92. [72] Organs for Christ Church in 1708 by Renatus Harris, St Thomas Martyr in 1728 by John Harris of London, and St Mary Redcliffe in 1728 by Harris and Byfield; Foyle and Cherry, as at note 12, p.95, pp.110–11, and Eustace, as at note 16, pp. 3-16 [73] All Saints is now the Diocesan Education Centre; an appointment has to be made to view the monuments. [74] J. Matthews, *Bristol Guide; By Bristoliensis* (third edition, Bristol, 1815), p.156. [75] K. Morgan, *ODNB*. [76] J. Latimer, *Annals of Bristol in the Nineteenth Century (Concluded) 1887–1900* (Bristol, 1902), pp.19, 89. [77] D. Jones, 'Bristol's sugar trade and refining industry', *Bristol Branch of the Historical Association*, no. 89, 2003, p.6. [78] Shiercliff's *Guide to Bristol and the Hotwells* (Bristol, 1793), p.43. [79] See St John's Parish Accounts 1710–52 for annual disbursements for bell ringers on 2 and 5 November, from 5, 8 or 16 shillings, for example 'it being Mr Colston's Birthday of pious memory', 2 November 1734. In the 1750s, 5 November is spelt out as 'being Popish Plott'; the custom appears to have stopped in 1753. [80] Saturday, 4 November 1727. [81] *Chilcott's Descriptive History of Bristol, Ancient and Modern; or a Guide to Bristol, Clifton and the Hotwells* (sixth edition, 1844). [82] Copies of Mr Colston's Settlements; Central Reference Library, L36.3, p.69. [83] BRO, Merchants' Hall, Books of Proceedings, Book 4 (Microfilm). Thomas Edwards Senior was MP for Wells in 1714, 1722 and 1727. He appears as a guardian, an assistant and later an hon. guardian and governor, and as a benefactor of the Bristol Corporation of the Poor; Bristol Record Society, vol. III, 1932. It was he or his son Edward junior who owned the *Betty*, a gally cleared for Africa in 1722, 1723 and 1724; W.E. Minchinton, 'The trade of Bristol in the eighteenth century', *Bristol Record Society*, 1957. Thomas Sr and Jr were executors for Arabella Astry, Countess of Suffolk, and partners with Sir John Smyth in coal mining in the 1720s; BRO AC/AS 70/2 87. [84] For further connections see S. Rudder, *A New History of Gloucestershire* (1779, repub. 1977), pp.800, 802 [85] Colston had erected a hanging wall monument to his mother Sarah Colston (d.1701), with its Corinthian frame on scrolled brackets, swan-neck pediment and putti opening a draped canopy, to reveal the inscription; Foyle and Cherry, as at note 4, pp.92–94. [86] Matthew's guides, from the first edition in 1794, repeatedly suggested that 'a statue of brass, on a pedestal of marble' might be set up in the city centre by St Augustine's Parade, 'opposite the school he founded'; W. Matthews, *New History, Survey and Description of the City and Suburbs of Bristol* (Bristol, n.d.), p.218. The statue by John Cassidy was erected in the centre (Colston Avenue) in 1895 many years after the school had moved out to Stapleton. [87] Quoted in T.F. Friedman, 'Rysbrack and Gibbs', in Eustace, as at note 6, p.18 and n.10. [88] J. Latimer, *Annals of Bristol in the Eighteenth Century* (Bristol, 1893), pp.8–9. [89] Op. cit., p.159. [90] For the most recent commentary see Craske, as at note 60, pp.377–9, fig. 179, and p.489, n.94. [91] A common link was probably St Bartholomew's Hospital, London's hospital for the poor. James Gibbs was the architect of the new buildings at Bart's, of which Colston had been a governor, and to which he left £500. Francis Colston became a governor in the same year as Gibbs, 1723. [92] Friedman, as at note 87, p.18. [93] In 1702 the corporation had commissioned a portrait of Colston from Jonathon Richardson, and a version was acquired by the Merchant Venturers at the same time. It was from the Merchant Venturers' version that Rysbrack modelled the likeness of Colston for the effigy; see Eustace, as at note 6, cat. no. 5; BCMAG (K4753). It was engraved by George Vertue in folio and octavo, in 1722, the year after Colston died; Bristol Museums and Art Gallery, (M3002); H. Walpole, *Anecdotes of Painting in England* (three vols, London, n.d.), 'List of Vertue's Works', p.10 (bound in with vol. III). [94] Bottom right-hand corner of the superstructure: SIDNELL Bristol / Fecit 1729. For a full account of the commission see Eustace, as at note 6, cat. nos 5–9. Sidnell was paid sums by the Vestry Committee of All Saints on 4 May 1728 and 11 August 1729; BRO P/AS/ChW/3(b). [95] James Gibbs, *A Book of Architecture* (London, 1728), p.113. [96] A number of wall monuments derived from the plates in Gibbs's *Book of Architecture* are to be found in Bristol and in its hinterland; see Eustace, as at note 6, cat. no. 11, and figs 31, 36. [97] T.F. Friedman, *James Gibbs* (New Haven and London, 1984), passim and p.265. [98] Gibbs, as at note 95, p.i. [99] Foyle and Cherry, as at note 12. [100] See Gunnis, as at note 46; H. Colvin, *Biographical Dictionary of British Architects 1600–1840* (third ed., New Haven and London, 1995); J. Physick, *Designs for English Sculpture 1680–1860* (London, 1969, p.22, n.1. [101] BRO CCP 1704–22, fols 504 and 506. [102] BRO Audits 04026 (99), no. 22 and no. 82, fols. 80 and 84. [103] £50 and £40: BRO Audit 1733, fol. 85. Other unidentified payments include: note and order no. 49, £9:10:0; Audits Sept. 1735, fol. 58 and note and order no. 71 £4:18:0; Audits 29 Sept. 1736. [104] He is described as 'Neuter', so probably did not exercise his vote; BCRL (B8769), Poll Book 1739, p.133. In the same return and the same parish a 'Daniel Sidnell, Freestone Cutter', voted for the successful Whig candidate, the Hon. Edward Southwell; op. cit., p.129. Daniell was paid for work on the Mayor's Chapel; BRO, CCP Accounts Voucher Box 37/38, 29 Sept. 1739. A 'James Sidnell' was also being paid for Corporation work in the 1730s; BRO, CCP Vouchers 1733 box no. 110, Sept. 29 1737. [105] See Gunnis, as at note 46 and Colvin, as at note 100. [106] BRO, P/StJ/V/4 December 29 1746. [107] BRO, P/StJ/ChW/Ic) etc, Accounts. [108] Eustace, as at note 16, n.49. [109] See BRO, R. Smith, *Bristol Infirmary BiographicalMemoirs* (3 vols), vol. III, p.114. [110] Manchee, as at note 7, vol. I, pp.449, 451. [111] For a transcription see Eustace, as at note 6, p.196. [112] Andrew Innys who practised law at Clements Inn, London was a considerable property holder in Bristol from as early as 1665; BRO 30631 14 and b, 3801 (8–9), 08767; see Eustace, as at note 6, figs 28 and 30. [113] Eustace, as at note 6, cat no. 11. [114] See B. Little, *The Life and Work of James Gibbs*, London 1955, p.107, and most recently in Foyle and Cherry, as at note 12, pp.110–11. [115] St Mary Redcliffe and St Philip and Jacob, both outside the city, had larger numbers but never as many as St James. Between 1712 and 1735, 1,390 new houses had been added to Bristol as a whole; P.T. Marcy, 'Eighteenth Century views of Bristol and Bristolians', in P. McGrath (ed.), *Bristol in the Eighteenth Century* (Newton Abbot, 1972), p.17; see also the Poll Books. [116] Bristol Poll Books 1722, 1734, 1739, 1754; BCRL (B8766-9). [117] Esdaile pointed out that in the seventeenth century, 'sculptor' and 'mason' were synonymous. K. Esdaile in A.S. Turberville, *Johnson's England* (Oxford, 1933), 2 vols, p.72. [118] BRO, CCPVoucher Box 1750 no. 36. [119] G. Priest, *The Paty Family, Makers of Eighteenth-century Bristol* (Bristol, 2003). [120] BRO St J Parish Accounts 1710–1752. [121] BRO, CCP 1704-1722, fol. 506. [122] Ibid., fol. 518. [123] Poll Book 1739, p.128; BCRL (B8769). [124] BRO, CCP Voucher Box 37/38. [125] Foyle and Cherry, as at note 12, p.107. [126] 'Fr' stands for 'freeholder'; Poll Book 1774; BCRL (B8772). [127] A photograph of a mason's yard taken c.1878 in the parish of St Augustine's, is illustrated in J. Bettey, as at note 11, p.17. [128] 18 October 1754, Redland BRO P/RG/R/3b). 'The Monument in the Chapel Vestry to the memory of the Founder John Cossins Esq[r] and of Martha his wife… was this day finished it was designed and Executed by Mr Thomas Paty of Bristol'; 15 July 1762, ibid. [129] He was probably the son of William Hilliard Esq., of Sea, Somerset. He married (c.1696) Mary, younger daughter and co-heiress of Gabriel Goodman, of Kilmersdon, where she was buried; Roper, as at note 48, p.83. [130] Manchee, as at note 7, vol. I, p.355. [131] W. Barrett, *History and Antiquities of the City of Bristol* (2 vols, Bristol, 1789), p.347. [132] Friedman, as at note 87, p.17, fig. 3; Whinney as at note 3, p.131. [133] See Eustace, as at note 6, cat. nos. 19, 20. [134] 11 June 1772; S.C. Hutchinson, 'The Royal Academy Schools, 1768–1830', *Walpole Society*, XXXVIII, 1960–62, p.138. [135] Poll Book 1781; BCRL (B10980). [136] 4 December 1775, for '26 Feby next', the orthography has him as 'Poty' in the Royal Academy lists, and as 'Paty' in the council minutes; ibid, p. 141. [137] Whinney, as at note 3, p.131. [138] Many were subsequently destroyed by earthquakes and hurricanes; Coutu argues that monuments gave planters in the West Indies what they might otherwise lack in the way of dynastic roots, and that many set up monuments 'at home' for the same reason; Coutu, as at note 4. [139] Quoted in Colvin, as at note 100. Rupert Gunnis conjectured that he might be a son of Henry Wood the Elder, who was a London-based decorative sculptor of means in the last three decades of the eighteenth century; Gunnis, as at note 46, p.439. [140] Leech, as at note 8. [141] University of Bristol Library (Special Collections) and the Woods Album of Monumental Masonry, Henry Moore Institute, Leeds; (Woo 13), 214 designs on 104 leaves. Hereafter UBL and HMI. [142] The type appears on the left-hand middle row of nine vertical tablets with no inscriptions, lettering or prices, in the Leeds volume; HMI (Woo 13), fol. 113. [143] Many of the designs for memorial tablets are signed 'J' Wood, which suggests there was another son in the business, but Gunnis, who was not aware of the two volumes of designs, does not record this. [144] Thomas appears to have had a brother, Jabez, to whom the memorial to 'Jane' Campbell in the Cathedral is attributed; see Rogan, as at note 11, p.117. [145] HMI (Woo 13), fol. 73. [146] Gunnis, as at note 46. [147] He was a member of the Congregation of Protestant Dissenters, Bury Street, and his children were baptised by dissenting ministers; he was buried at Whitfield's Tabernacle, Tottenham Court Road; A. Cox-Johnson, *John Bacon RA 1740–1799*, St Marylebone Society, no. 4, 1961, pp.6–7, 43. [148] R. Cecil, *Memoirs of John Bacon, Esq. RA* (London, 1801), pp.6–7; A. Cox-Johnson, ibid. [149] J. Smith, *ODNB*. [150] With the poet's portrait in profile, it redeploys a leaning figure of the type established in the Bristol monument to Elizabeth Draper; see J. Physick, as at note 100, pp.162–3, figs 125, 126. [151] Not a single line is recorded in the *Oxford Dictionary of Quotations*. [152] Cox Johnson, as at note 147, p.42, n. 12. [153] LduS. Read, *ODNB*. [154] See K. Barker, 'The Theatre Royal Bristol: the first seventy years', in McGrath, as at note 115, p.66. [155] Op. cit., p.69. [156] Gunnis, as at note 46; see also Colvin, as at note 100. [157] Signed and dated *J.Bacon fecit*/London 1780. [158] M. New, *ODNB*. [159] L. Sterne, *A Sentimental Journey* (London, 1768; Penguin Illustrated Classics, 1938), pp.13–14. [160] Op. cit., pp.69, 170. [161] New, as at note 158. [162] The model was exhibited at the Royal Academy in 1780; Whinney as at note 3, p.168, and p.270, n. 17. Variants on the type to a grander or lesser extent are the monuments to John and Jane Ashley (c.1784, Ashby-de-la-Zouch, Leics), Samuel Egerton (1792, Rostherne, Cheshire) and Ann Whytell (1791, Westminster Abbey); illustrated in Esdaile, as at note 50, pl. 34, and Whinney, as at note 3, p.168, Pls 129a and 130a, revised J. Physick (London, 1988), figs 223 and 224; in single form for Rosa Palmer (d.1790, St James, Montego Bay, Jamaica); see Coutu as at note 4 , fig. 5. [163] M. Whinney points out that Mrs Draper was a poetess, as at note 3. She is not recorded as such in M. Drabble, *Oxford Companion to English Literature* (London, 1985). *Journal to Eliza* was first published in 1904. [164] Coutu, as at note 4, p.82. [165] Hutchinson, as at note 134, p.134. [166] D. Irwin, *John Flaxman 1755–1826: Sculptor Illustrator Designer* (London, 1979), pp.67–92. [167] The inscription on Mary Edwards's *née* Freeman's monument in St James informs us that she was the daughter of Richard Freeman of

Batsford, Gloucestershire, 'Sometime Lord High Chancellor of Ireland'; for a complete transcription see Eustace, as at note 6, p.196. [168] Illustrated in Irwin, as at note 166, pl. 209. [169] For a design type see D. Bindman (ed.), *John Flaxman R.A.*, (exhib. cat., Royal Academy of Arts, London, 1979), cat. no. 138. [170] There is a related drawing in the British Museum (BM 1882-3-8-27), and the original plaster is in the University College, London, Collection. An inscription in bronze letters reads *Verily there is a Reward for the Righteous*; E. Croft-Murray, 'An account book of John Flaxman, RA', *Walpole Society*, vol. XXVIII, 1939–40, p.84. [171] Inscription: MARIAE UXORI / CARISSIMAE, / ANNO AETATIS VICESIMO QUINTO/ EREPTAE / GULIELMUS BRAME ELWYN, D.C.L. / INFELICISSIMUS POSUIT, / OB: DIE MARTII XXVIII A.D. MDCCCXVIII./ / IN CRYPTA Sti. MICHAELIS IN HAC URBE ECCLESIAE JACET SEPULTA.; M. Baker, I. Lieberman, A. Potts and A. Yarrington, ' An edition of the ledger of Sir Francis Chantrey, RA, at the Royal Academy, 1809–1841', *Walpole Society*, vol. LVI, 1991–2, ledger no. 90a, p.108 and pl. 65. [172] Ibid. [173] Notably the Baring monument, Micheldever, Hants; and the Bromely-Davenport monument, Baginton, Warks; Bindman, as at note 169, cat. nos 124, 125 and 134. [174] Yarrington, as at note 171. [175] The proceeds of the opening night of the Theatre Royal in 1765, sixty guineas, had gone to the Infirmary, to placate those of a puritanical turn of mind; see Barker, as at note 154, p. 68. [176] Inscription: EMMAE CRAUFUIRD/ UXORI / EHEU! QUAM DESIDERATAE/ SAC/ ESSE VOL/ GUALTHERUS KENNEDY CRAUFUIRD/ SUUS; Yarrington, as at note 171, ledger no. 140a, p.163 and p.l94. [177] Ibid. [178] Ibid. Chantrey was to use the same design for the monument to the parents of his friend and patron, the painter David Wilkie, at Cults in Fife in 1832, and again for a monument to members of the Acland family at Selworthy in Somerset in 1837; op. cit., pp.273–4, 316–7. [179] Op. cit., p.163. It is not clear from the entry whether at a later stage, 25 July 1834, Chantrey was finally reimbursed for the Elwyn monument fees. [180] Whinney, as at note 3, p.223, illus. 184, revised J. Physick, fig. 306. [181] For the full inscription see Ledger 107a; Yarrington as at note 171, p.125. [182] Ibid., and pl. 83. [183] See J. Latimer, *Annals of Bristol in the Nineteenth Century* (Bristol, 1887), pp.80 and 37. [184] Illustrated in Whinney, as at note 3, Pl.184A. [185] See Bindman, as at note 169, cat. no. 132, pp.113–5. [186] Yarrington, as at note 171, p.300, pl. 16. [187] K. Eustace, *ODNB*. There is a portrait bust of E.H. Baily by his grandson, Edgar George Papworth Jnr. (b.1832) in the Bristol City Art Gallery (K4486). [188] Hutchinson, as at note 134, p.165. Spelled there with an 'e', council minutes spell it 'Baily'. With, among others, Peter de Wint and Lewis Vuillamy, and Henry Wyatt Jr. [189] On the death of Flaxman, Baily became chief modeller and designer at Rundell and Bridges Manufactury in Dean Street. From 1848 to 1857 he was designing race cups for Godward and Doncaster, for the Royal Thames Yacht Club, and Presentation and Memorial plate such as the Tweedale testimonial and the testimonial to Jenny Lind (1847) for the silversmiths Hunt and Roskell, and Storr and Mortimer. These were routinely published with wood-engraved illustration in the *Art Union Journal*, *The Builder* and the *Illustrated London News*. [190] The seventeen-foot high Admiral Lord Nelson, made in two pieces from Grampian granite for Railton's column in Trafalgar Square, and finally completed 1844; Earl Grey on a similar column in Newcastle upon Tyne (1838), Sir Robert Peel (1852, Bury, Lancs), and the figures of William Murray, Earl of Mansfield (1855) and Charles James Fox (1856), for St Stephen's Hall, Westminster. [191] *Eve* (1821 and 1849), *Maternal Affection* (1837?) and *The Tired Hunter* (1851). Minton bought the right to reproduce *Eve Listening to the Voice* in ceramic, of which 5000 were said to have been sold in the USA. *Eve at the Fountain* was reproduced in bronze by Barbedienne in Paris 1886, and may be a source for Edvard Eriksen's *Little Mermaid* (1913) in the harbour at Copenhagen. [192] See C. Jordan, 'The very spirit of purity and chastity: *Eve at the Fountain*, by Edward Hodges Baily', *Sculpture Journal*, vol. 15.1, 2006, pp.19–35. [193] 1 July 1857, p.261. [194] 19 December 1857, p.593. [195] 8 June 1867, reprinted in the *Builder*; R. Riddell, Collections Concerning E.H. Baily RA; British Library, ADD. 38678 cat. no. 19-1911-1915, fol. 33. [196] For a list see Read, as at note 43, p.68. [197] Among them the seated figure of the third Earl of Egremont (d.1837, Petworth Parish Church); Eliza Mortimer (d.1826, St Martin's Exeter) in which the 'soul' bursts out of the grave, in the idiom of his master John Flaxman; the recumbent effigy of Charles James Mann, Viscount Brome (d.1835, Linton, Kent); and Dean Dawson (d.1840, St Patrick's Cathedral, Dublin). See N. Penny, *Church Monuments in Romantic England* (New Haven and London, 1977). [198] It is signed, as always: E.H. Baily R.A. Sculp. / London. [199] David Irwin traces it to Masaccio's donor figure in the *Trinità* fresco in St Maria Novella, Florence; Irwin, as at note 166, pl.175. [200] Penny, as at note 197, p.73, illus. 52; also the monument to Bishop Pelham (d.1827, Buckden, Huntingdonshire) and Mrs Vernon (d.1830, Ardington, Oxfordshire). [201] Monuments to Martha, Countess St Vincent (1818), Frances Puleston Cook (1820) and Lady Charlotte Finch (1824); see Yarrington, as at note 171, pls 50, 51 and 64. [202] B.H. Blacker and M.E. Clayton, *ODNB*. [203] *Bristol Riots, the Burning of the Bishop's Palace*, oil on card, c.1831; BCAG (M4122); see F. Greenacre and S. Stoddard, *W.J. Muller 1812–1845* (Bristol, 1991), cat. no. 32, col. pl. 5. [204] Signed and dated: E.H. BAILY, R.A. Sculp./ LONDON 1842. [205] G. Carter, *ODNB*. [206] See Eustace, as at note 16, ns 49, 50. [207] See S. Sloman, 'An eighteenth-century stonecarver's diary identified; eight months in the life of Thomas Parsons (1744–1813) of Bath', *British Art Journal*, vol. VII, no. 3, 2006–7, pp.4–13. [208] G. Carnall, *ODNB*. [209] See R. Holmes, *Coleridge Early Visions* (London, 1989), p.88. [210] There is a monument by J.G. Lough (1845), at Crosthwaite, Keswick. [211] Latimer, as at note 183, pp.277–8. [212] The bust is signed: E.H.BAILY / Sculp./ 1845; the plinth: E.H.BAILY R.A. / Sculp. London. [213] Latimer, as at note 183, p.292. [214] The plaster original was purchased from the Bristol Fine Arts Academy in 1915: BCMAG (L9). It was based on a death mask, and published in the *Art Journal* in 1850 (p.344); see Greenacre and Stoddard, as at note 203, cat. no.183. [215] Latimer, as at note 76, p.28. [216] Quoted in K. Eustace, 'The post-Reformation monuments', in Collinson etc., as at note 33, p.533. [217] Latimer as at note 47, pp.428–9. [218] S. Beattie, *The New Sculpture* (New Haven and London, 1983), p.111, pl. 90. [219] F. Prochaska, *ODNB*. [220] He was buried in Arnos Grove Cemetery. There is a bravura portrait of him by H.P. Briggs in the City Art Gallery. [221] M. Carpenter, *A Life of Joseph Tuckerman* (Bristol, 1848). [222] A bust of Estlin, signed and dated E.H. Baily 1856, is in the Bristol City Museum and Art Gallery (K4734). [223] K. Walton, *The Red Lodge* (Bristol, 1986), pp.5 and 26. [224] There is a portrait bust of Mary Carpenter signed and dated R. Price Bristol MDCCCLXI (1820–65); Bristol City Museum and Art Gallery (K4731). Price was born in Bristol, a student at Bristol School of Art, where he won the Bronze Medal in 1857; Local Artist Index, Department of Fine Art, BCMAG. [225] For J.H. Thomas's statues of Edmund Burke (the Centre) and Samuel Morley (Lewins Mead) see this volume, and Read as at note 43, pp.317–18 [226] C. Kent, Rev. G. Law, *ODNB*. [227] His first move was to put a brass crucifix, candlesticks and flowers on the High Altar; P. Barrett, *ODNB*. [228] See A. Jezzard, '"An all-round craftsman": George Frampton's church monuments', *Journal of the Church Monuments Society*, vol. XI, 1996, pp.61–70, fig. 3. [229] These wall monuments in the crypt, some of them re-sited from the main church after the war, were taken down in the 1980s; I am grateful to John Bryant of Bristol and Regional Archaeology Services, based currently at St Nicholas, for help with this. An inventory list and contact sheets exist in the City Museum and Art Gallery. [230] Riddell, as at note 195, fol. 60. [231] It was 'beautified' or restored by a descendant, the philanthropist John Elbridge in 1732. D. Jones, 'The Elbridge, Woolnough, and Smyth families of Bristol in the eighteenth century, with special reference to the Spring Plantation, Jamaica', MA dissertation, University of Bristol, 1971; copy BRO 34328(a). [232] Sir Edward Lutyens, quoted in J. Summers, *Remembered. The History of the Commonwealth War Graves Commission* (London and New York, 2007), p.7.

Public Sculpture of Bristol

Albert Road

On the footpath beside the River Avon at the rear of the Bristol Dogs Home

Basset Hounds and Basenjis A24

Sculptor: Rodney Harris

Date: 1991
Materials: Ibstock bricks
Dimensions: left panel, 180cm high; right panel, 200cm
Signed: RODNEY / HARRIS / 1991
Inscription: on slate plaque, presently obscured – BRISTOL DOGS HOME / AND / BRISTOL / DEVELOPMENT / CORPORATION / 1991
—: around the circumference – JOINTLY FUNDED BY / ENVIRONMENTAL IMPROVEMENT
Status: not listed
Owned by Trustees of the Bristol & District RSPCA Branch
Condition: poor; obscured by extensive graffiti and ivy

The two reliefs, one of three basset hound puppies and their mother and the other of three young basenjis, were commissioned by the RSPCA and the Bristol Development Corporation as part of the environmental improvements to the River Avon Walkway (today called the River Avon Trail), which runs along the back of the Bristol Dogs Home.

The path is well used by commuting cyclists and by dog walkers during the day. At night these enticing reliefs are unlit and unseen, and this large brick wall has become another tempting canvas for vandals. Today, ivy and undergrowth have begun to engulf the graffiti.

This was Rod Harris's first major commission and it followed from the display of some his degree-show work at the Ibstock Brick Design Centre in Queen Square, Bristol.[1] The brief suggested that the relief should encourage 'family feeling', a reference, no doubt, to the 'good home' that is sought for the many dogs on the other side of the wall. Harris chose to depict two families of dogs, one of which, the basenjis, does not bark, a point of gentle irony and some significance at this otherwise peaceful riverside spot.

Four hundred solid but unfired 'green' bricks were supplied by Ibstock Bricks. The wall was built up with spacers in place of mortar and the relief was carved. The wall was then dismantled with each brick being numbered. The bricks were returned for firing and the wall subsequently securely rebuilt. The carving itself took six months to complete.

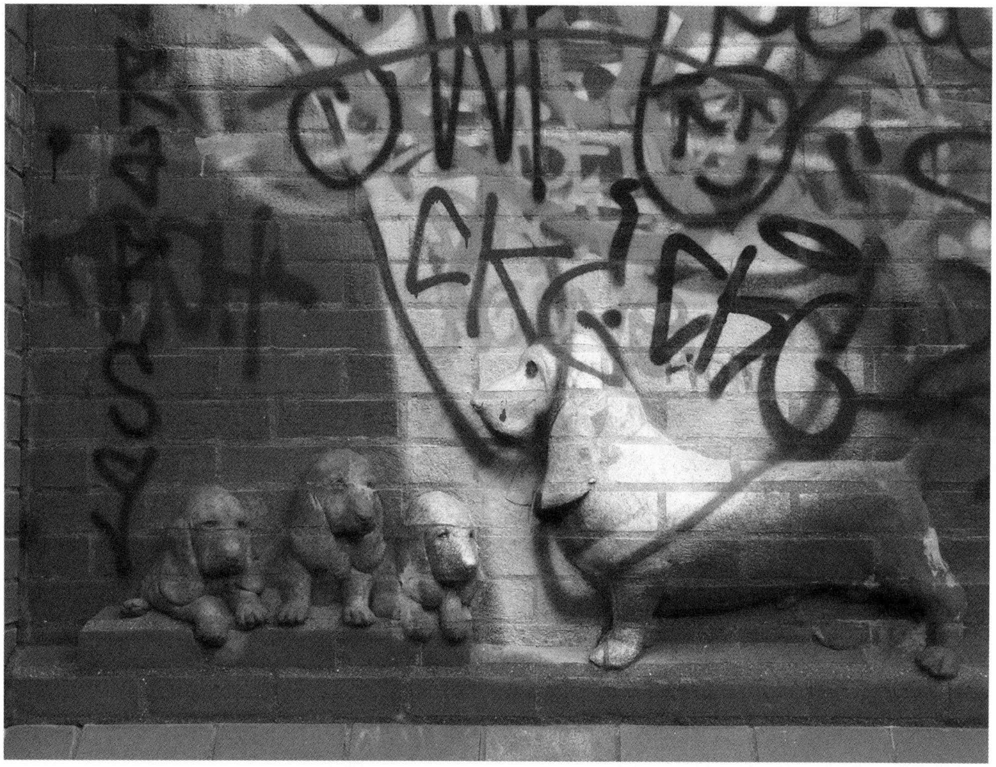

Rodney Harris, *Basset Hounds*

Note

[1] Information from the artist, May 2008, and www.jacksonharris.co.uk.

Anchor Road

Outside the Explore building on Anchor Road opposite Bristol Cathedral

Small Worlds B60

Sculptor: Simon Thomas

Date: 2001
Materials: 'Fibrocem', a cement with alkali-resistant chopped strand glass fibre
Dimensions: 550cm high, 160cm diameter at the base
Inscription: on a bronze plaque set in pavement – 'Small Worlds' / by Simon Thomas / Fibre Cement / 2000AD / Supported by the Institute of Physics / in commemoration of Paul Dirac / Bristol born physicist Paul Dirac (1902–1984) was one of the greatest / scientists of the 20th Century. By the age of 31 he had received / the Nobel Prize for Physics for his work on quantum mechanics / – the theory that describes the world at the level of atoms / and molecules. He also predicted the existence of anti-matter. / Simon Thomas's sculpture of concentric cones / creates a scaled path through space, pointing / towards the ever smaller worlds / studied by Dirac. / At-Bristol
Status: not listed
Owned by At-Bristol
Condition: good

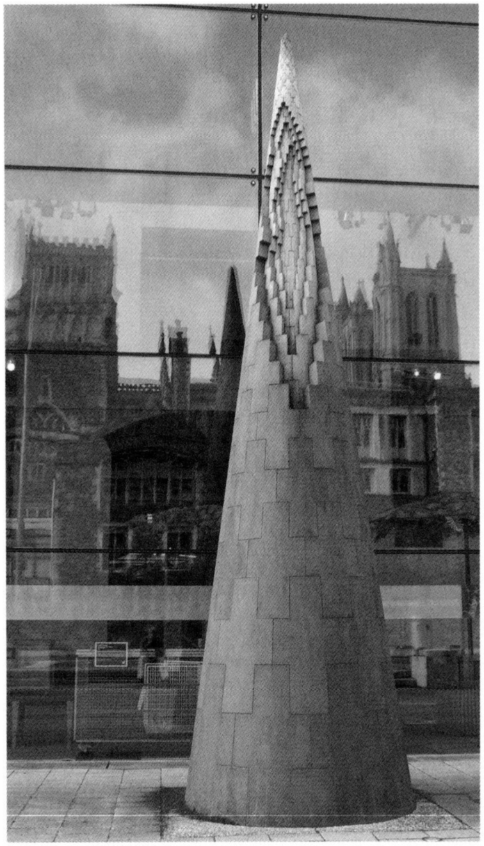

Simon Thomas, *Small Worlds*

The bronze plaque, transcribed above, justly states that *Small Worlds* commemorates one of the greatest scientists of the twentieth century.

Paul Adrien Maurice Dirac, OM, FRS (1902–84), was born at 15 Monk Road, Bishopston, Bristol and educated in the city.[1] His Swiss-born father taught French at the Merchant Venturers' Technical College, which Paul attended before entering the University of Bristol in 1918. There he took his degree in electrical engineering before staying on to study applied mathematics. In 1923 he became a research student in mathematics at St John's College, Cambridge, under the theoretical physicist Ralph Fowler.[2] In 1926 he wrote 'On the theory of quantum mechanics', one of the most influential scientific papers of the twentieth century. In 1931 he predicted the existence of anti-matter, one of the most famous of his contributions to physics. Dirac shared the Nobel Prize for Physics with the Austrian scientist Erwin Schrödinger in 1933. His seminal textbook, *The Principles of Quantum Mechanics*, had first been published in 1930. Dirac taught at Cambridge, where he was made Lucasian Professor of Mathematics, a post held by Isaac Newton. He died in Tallahassee, Florida, USA, on 20 October 1984.

The tall and slender cone appears to be built of layers of cross-shaped interlocking bricks that decrease proportionately in size as the cone narrows. Half way up the cone the brick layers begin to fall away, emphasising the decreasing size of the component parts. The cone is both sturdy and fragile, rising to a delicate point.

Quantum mechanics is 'the theory that describes the world at the level of atoms and molecules',[3] and this sculpture, *Small Worlds*, suggests the search on an ever-decreasing scale for the complex structures of matter. Simon Thomas has explained that he 'decided to point towards the depth of scale present in the universe. *Small Worlds* is a clustering of conic shells, whose wall thicknesses are proportional to their given radii. The sculpture expresses an energised (colours) conic graph of 3-D space; its diminishing forms suggest a journey towards infinitely smaller sub-divisions of space'.[4]

Simon Thomas's long-term interest in science and mathematics has permeated much of his sculptural work. He was artist-in-residence in the Physics Department of the University of Bristol, under Professor Mike Springford, when in 1997–8 he made *Stretching a Point* for a stairwell in the Physics Building in Tyndall Avenue. At the end of 1997 Thomas became aware that no sculptor working in Bristol was contributing to the Millennium Square project, and he approached staff of the At-Bristol project with proposals for a memorial to Paul Dirac. He discussed his ideas and Dirac's work with Professor Michael Berry of the university, who suggested that he should contact the Institute of Physics publishing house, based in Bristol at Dirac House. They were supportive and just under £30,000 was raised, to include design, construction and delivery. The model was approved and Thomas began to fabricate the finished structure, using his own innovative techniques. Casting was not possible. A full-size cone was coated with two layers of cement render, reinforced with alkali-resistant chopped strand glass fibre. This surface, the thickness of a tile, was built up by hand. The size and colour of each block is governed by its proximity to the axis of the structure. Dragging a steel edge across the curved surface produced the required texture. Pigments were added to produce the colours.[5]

This tribute to Paul Dirac was unveiled by Sir Michael Berry, Royal Society Research Professor at the H. H. Wills Physics Laboratory, in December 2001.[6]

Notes
[1] Professor Sir Michael Berry, 'Paul Dirac: the purest soul in physics', *Nonesuch*, autumn, 2002, pp.22–5; there is a plaque on the house. Professor John Steeds made generous amendments to an earlier draft of this entry; the very recent biography (G. Farmelo, *The Strangest Man, The Hidden Life of Paul Dirac, Quantum Genius* (London, 2008), was not consulted. [2] H. Kragh, *Dirac, Paul Adrien Maurice*, *ODNB*. [3] From the bronze plaque. [4] The artist's website: simonthomas-sculpture.com. [5] Notes from the sculptor. [6] *Nonesuch*, letters, winter, 2002.

Armoury Square

On the façade of 1 & 2 Colston Villas, Armoury Square, St Paul's

Edward Colston A18

Replica of the terracotta bust by Michael Rysbrack
Date: 1978–81
Material: pigmented fibreglass resin
Dimension: 57cm high
Status: Grade II
Owned by Bristol City Council
Condition: fair

Early in 1976, an architect brought an unidentified life-size bust of a bewigged gentleman to Bristol Museum and Art Gallery.[1] But for a worn terracotta-coloured patch on the top of the sitter's head, the bust was entirely covered in layers of peeling black and white paint, a negative of the make-up of the music-hall's black and white minstrel. The architect explained that the bust had been removed from the central niche of the façade of 1 and 2 Colston Villas, a part of Armoury Square, off Stapleton Road, Bristol. These houses were being rebuilt or renovated by Bristol Council as part of the regeneration of an area much affected by the building of the M32.

The similarity of the bust to the head of Edward Colston on the monument by Michael Rysbrack in All Saints Church in Corn Street was immediately recognised. There was much suppressed excitement, together with the hope that this might be Rysbrack's own preparatory terracotta model for the monument. And such it quickly proved to be, after being taken in and examined in the art gallery's conservation laboratory.

In March 1976, the Housing Department agreed to allow ownership to pass to the City Art Gallery subject to various conditions that included the provision of a painted replica and base.[2] This was made by the Archaeological Conservator for the Area Museum Council for the South West, and installed in 1981. The following year a gunmetal plaque inscribed '1837 / COLSTON / VILLAS / REBUILT 1976' was made at the City Art Gallery's expense and placed on the building high above the niche. In 1982, the Museum and Art Gallery celebrated this remarkable discovery with a large and scholarly exhibition devoted to Michael Rysbrack's sculpture in Bristol and the West Country.[3]

How or when the terracotta bust came to be placed in the niche in Armoury Square is still uncertain. The building of the armoury itself had begun in 1805. It had an impressive classical façade, contained 20,000 arms, and was protected by a wall that was three metres high and a garrison of 24 soldiers. It was bought by the Guardians of the Poor in 1831 to become an asylum, but was first used as a barracks for troops following the Bristol Riots later in the same year. In 1837 it was put up for sale by the

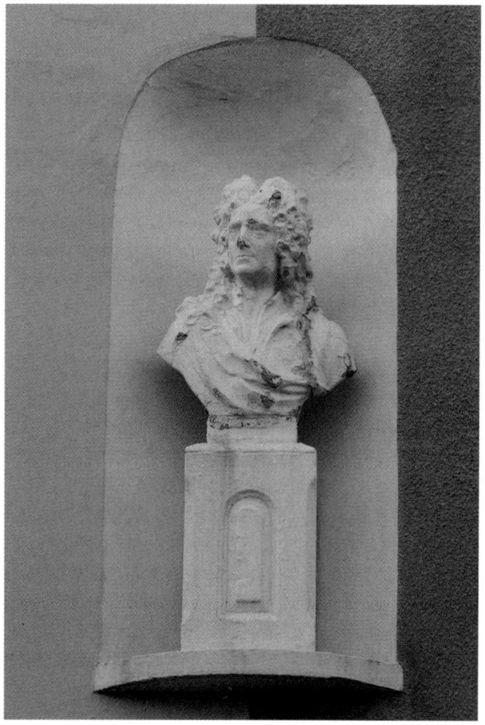

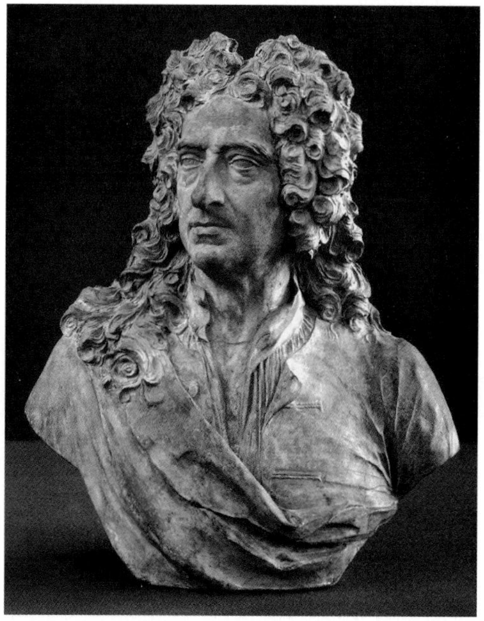

(left) After Michael Rysbrack, *Edward Colston*
(above) Michael Rysbrack, *Edward Colston*
(Bristol Museum and Art Gallery)

Guardians of the Poor, although completion was not to take place until 1840.[4] By 1848 only three houses had been erected; two of the later houses, Colston Villas, built after the 1851 census, presumably took their name from the bust that had already been placed upon them.[5]

In 1698, the Guardians of the Bristol Corporation of the Poor had purchased a building known then as the Mint, but soon to be re-named St Peter's Hospital.[6] One of the joint owners of the Mint was Edward Colston. But the connection with the terracotta bust is more likely to lie with the ornate and grand Court Room of the Hospital, dating from the early seventeenth century. Here, meetings of the many charitable concerns that had benefited from Edward Colston's gifts, and which were concerned with his memorial, may well have been held. And here, once approved for translation into marble, the bust may have remained, perhaps until the Guardians of the Poor became indirectly involved with the development of the armoury site.

'The vivid character of the bust has led to speculation that it might have been modelled from the life.'[7] However, although it is of a man in middle age, it was 'almost certainly made in preparation for the monument in All Saints', and is based upon a portrait by Jonathan Richardson in the Merchants' Hall.[8]

The cast of the original terracotta bust, from which the fibreglass resin copy was to be made, was made before the small cracks and damages to the terracotta were filled. The filling of some of these same cracks and damages, which were replicated in the cast, appears to be deteriorating. The replica has been repeatedly over-painted.

Notes

[1] The architects for the reconstruction of Colston Villas were Tranter, Britton and Cornish. [2] Letter from the director of housing to the director of the City Art Gallery, 11 March 1976, Bristol Museum and Art Gallery. [3] K. Eustace, *Michael Rysbrack, Sculptor, 1694–1770*, (exhib. cat., Bristol Museum and Art Gallery, Bristol, 1982). [4] Op. cit., p.70; J. Bartlett and J. Penny, 'Bristol's vanished Georgian armoury' (Fishponds History Group, 2001); D. Harrison, *Bristol Times Revisited* (Bristol, 2003), pp.125–7. [5] See Bartlett and Penny, as note 4. [6] E.E. Butcher, *Bristol Corporation of the Poor, 1696–1898* (Bristol, 1972), p.5; St Peter's Hospital was destroyed in the Blitz. [7] Eustace, as note 5, p.70. [8] Op. cit., p.68.

Arno's Vale Cemetery

Approximately 60 metres from the main entrance on the right

Tomb of Raja Rammohun Roy A25

Designer: William Prinsep

Date: 1843–4
Material: limestone masonry
Dimensions: approximately 6m high, excluding base; 4m square at the base
Mason: John N. Brown of Stokes Croft
Inscriptions: on the north-west face of a stone block set centrally under the chattri – RAJAH / RAM MOHUN ROY. / DIED / 27 SEPTEMBER 1833
—: on the south-east face of the same block – BENEATH THIS STONE REST THE REMAINS OF/RAJA RAMMOHUN ROY BAHADOOR,[1] / A CONSCIENTIOUS AND STEADFAST BELIEVER IN THE UNITY OF THE GODHEAD, / HE CONSECREATED HIS LIFE WITH ENTIRE DEVOTION TO THE WORSHIP OF THE DIVINE SPIRIT ALONE, / TO GREAT NATURAL TALENTS, HE UNITED THOROUGH MASTERY OF MANY LANGUAGES / AND EARLY DISTINGUISHED HIMSELF AS ONE OF THE GREATEST SCHOLARS OF HIS DAY. / HIS UNWEARIED LABOURS TO PROMOTE THE SOCIAL, MORAL AND PHYSICAL CONDITION OF THE / PEOPLE OF INDIA, HIS EARNEST ENDEAVOURS TO SUPPRESS IDOLATRY, AND THE RITE OF SUTTEE / AND HIS CONSTANT ZEALOUS ADVOCACY OF WHATEVER TENDED TO ADVANCE THE GLORY OF / GOD AND THE WELFARE OF MAN LIVE IN THE GRATEFUL REMEMBRANCE OF HIS COUNTRYMEN. / THIS TABLET / RECORDS THE SORROW AND PRIDE WITH WHICH HIS MEMORY IS CHERISHED BY HIS DESCENDANTS. / HE WAS BORN AT RADHANAGARE IN BENGAL IN 1774,[2] / AND DIED AT BRISTOL SEPTEMBER 27TH 1833.
Status: Grade II*
Owned by Bristol City Council and managed by the Arno's Vale Cemetery Trust
Condition: good; conserved 2008

Raja Rammohun Roy's tomb is the most elaborate and exotic edifice in this remarkable cemetery. The cemetery's future is now assured, thanks to a long and persistent campaign by the local community. Conservation work, funded in large part by the Heritage Lottery Fund, began in April 2008 and is due for completion in the autumn of 2009.

A brief biography of Raja Rammohun Roy (1772–1833), the great reformer, accompanies the account of his statue adjoining College Green.

The open-sided Hindu shrine is cruciform in plan. The plinth is ashlar and there are twelve decorated columns, three rising from each corner of the plinth. These support a flat roof that has four pendentives about each capital. On the roof are eight small pinnacles and a central square-sided and tall pointed dome with three leaves to each side. A rectangular block of stone set in the centre of the *chattri* has the inscriptions recorded above on two sides. About twenty years ago, pale mauve paint was applied to the capitals and central details of each column. No trace remains following the diligent conservation in 2008.

Raja Rammohun Roy died on 27 September 1833 while staying in Beech House, a villa at Stapleton Grove, Bristol.[3] He was buried there in a 'picturesque tomb' in the grounds adjoining the house.[4] Revered by the family, his remains stayed there until 1843. In that year Dwarkanauth Tagore, grandfather of the Indian poet Rabindranath Tagore, a friend and executor of Rammohun Roy, came to Bristol to visit the tomb and a decision was made to move the remains to a more conspicuous resting

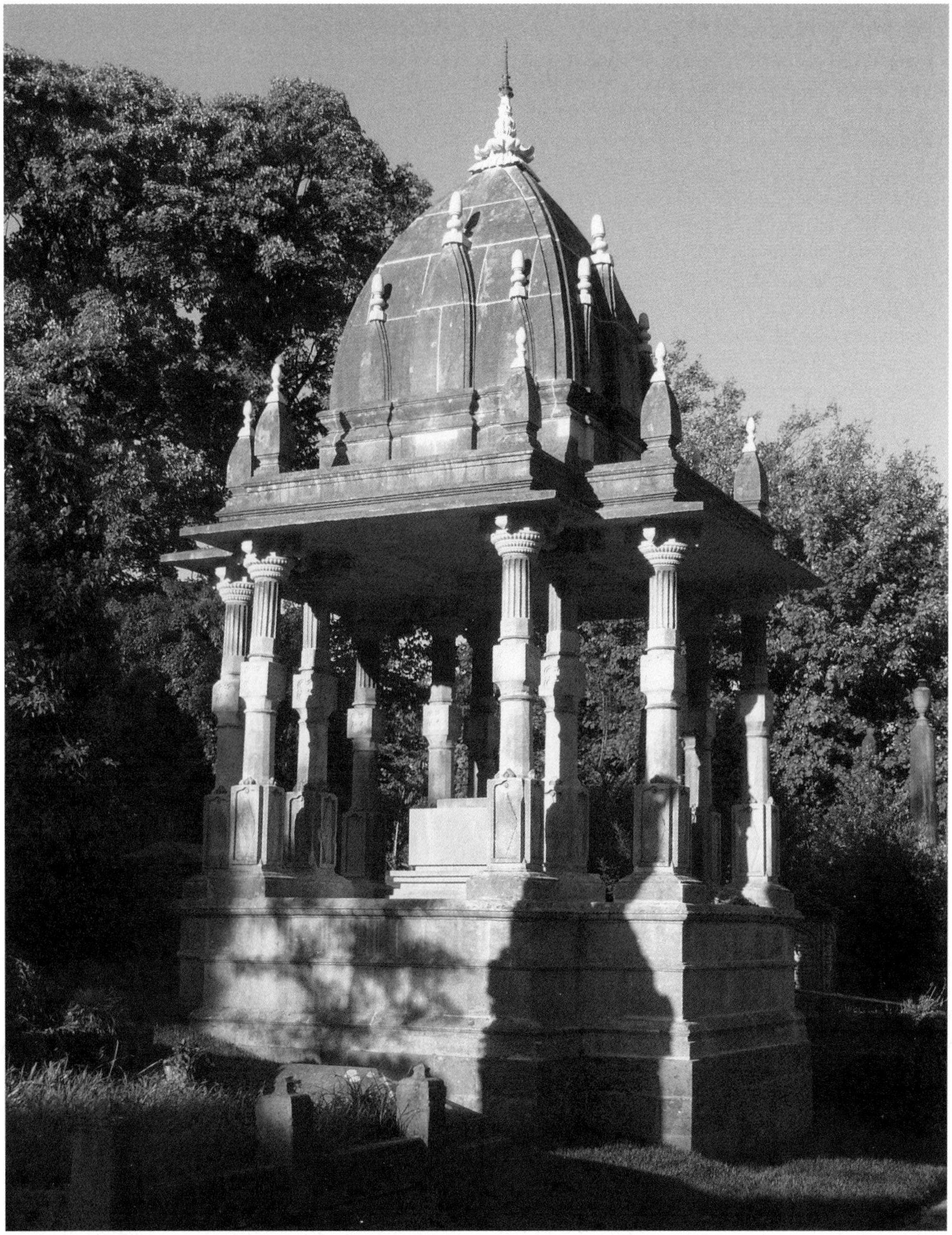

William Prinsep, *Tomb of Rajah Rammohun Roy*

place.[5] In July 1843 a Bristol newspaper reported: 'Raja Ramah (sic) Roy – The remains of this individual, who, it may be in the recollection of our readers, died at Stapleton Grove, in the residence of Michael Hinton Castle, Esq., about eleven years since, and was buried in the grounds adjoining the house, were removed on Monday last to the Cemetery, at Arno's Vale, and interred in that portion appropriated to the use of the dissenters. We understand that a sum of money has been forwarded from India, for the purpose of erecting a stately monument on the spot. It will be in the Hindu style of architecture, and upwards of thirty feet in height.'[6] On 29 May 1843 the coffin had been removed and reburied without ceremony in an unconsecrated section (Square L No. 4) of Arno's Vale Cemetery, which had been opened only four years earlier in 1839.[7] This had been purchased only three days previously by 'William Carr Esqr. of St Mary Church, Devon, and of London'.[8]

The elaborate memorial was designed by William Prinsep (1794–1874), a member of a famous family of which at least three generations lived and worked mainly in India.[9] Prinsep was a talented amateur artist, and the pen and ink drawings of his design for Rammohun's memorial are in the Victoria and Albert Museum.[10] One drawing is inscribed: 'My design for monument executed by a Bristol mason in Arno's Vale Cemetery'.[11] The work was started after 29 May 1843 and completed by 11 February 1844.[12] The mason was probably John N. Brown, for Brown's trade card has a line drawing of the tomb. His address is given as Backfields, Stokes Croft, and Brown is described as 'Building Contractor & Mason in general'. The card also says he is 'Mason to the Bristol General Cemetery'.[13]

In the mid-1990s, Anthony Towner, then the private owner of Arno's Vale Cemetery, closed the cemetery on the anniversary day of Rammohun Roy's death when Indian diplomats and others wished to visit the site. This was during a dispute with the Indian High

Commission over a £25,000 repair estimate and concerns over its deterioration. Towner, a solicitor, claimed that his action was taken because the 'pilgrims' had refused to keep a safe distance from the 150-year-old monument. In 1997, Chris Smith, the Culture Secretary, was asked to intervene.[14] In the same year, Dr. Laxmi Mal Singhvi, the High Commissioner, when unveiling the statue of Rammohun Roy near College Green, offered to pay for tomb's repair.[15] By the end of 2003 no work had been carried out and much of the stone and paintwork was in an advanced state of erosion. On 12 June 2007, £50,000 was presented to the Trustees of Arno's Vale Cemetery by the Indian High Commission for the tomb's restoration.[16]

In the late 1980s, a group of local enthusiasts campaigned vigorously against the owner's plans to develop part of the cemetery. In 2003, after a long legal battle, Bristol City Council acquired the cemetery by compulsory purchase order, and in December 2005 the Arno's Vale Cemetery Trust was successful in its bid for £4.8 million from the Heritage Lottery Fund.

Notes

[1] This word describes Rammohun Roy's status in The East India Company and is similar to 'Hon.' or 'Esq.'. [2] This should be 1772. [3] *Bristol Gazette*, 8 July 1843, p.3, column 4. [4] *Bristol Mercury*, 10 July 1843, p.6, column 1. [5] Ibid. [6] *Bristol Gazette*, as note 3. [7] Caption to plate 3: 'Register of Burials, Bristol General Cemetery Company Records', an exhibit in the exhibition on Rajah Rammohum Roy held at Bristol Museums and Art Gallery in 1983. [8] Ibid. [9] Op. cit., caption to plate 1. [10] Copies are in the PMSA files. [11] As note 7, caption to plate 8. [12] Ibid. [13] Trade card, Blaise Castle Museum, TA5330. [14] 'Indians ask for help to save hero's tomb', *The Times*, 24 November 1997. [15] *Western Daily Press*, 21 November 1997, p.5. [16] http://news.oneindia.in/2007/06/12. Aditya Poddar, a Kolkata businessman, was the principal donor; Carla Contractor, a trustee of Arno's Vale Cemetery, led the campaign.

Ashley Road, St Paul's

In the small park at the junction of Ashley Road and Grosvenor Road

Alfred Fagon A15

Sculptor: David Mutasa

Date: 1987
Materials: bust, bronze; pedestal, black marble
Dimensions: bust, 70cm high; pedestal, 131cm high, 65cm square
Signed: DAVID MUSTASA / 1987
Inscription: on front of the pedestal – ALFRED FAGON / 1937–1986 / POET PLAYWRIGHT ACTOR / "THROUGH GRIEF TO HAPPINESS" ERECTED / ON THE FIRST ANNIVERSARY / OF HIS DEATH / 29 AUGUST 1987. / BY THE FRIENDS OF FAGON /
Status: not listed
Owned by the Friends of Fagon Committee; maintenance by Bristol City Council
Condition: good

Alfred Fagon (1937–86) was an actor, playwright and poet who was 'greatly loved and won respect as well as renown'.[1] He lived in St Paul's, Bristol, during the 1960s and 1970s.

Fagon was born in Clarendon, Jamaica in 1937. He left school at the age of twelve to work on his father's orange plantation and then, aged eighteen, came to England in 1955. Fourteen years passed before he turned to writing. Fagon worked on the railways in Nottingham and, while serving for four years in the British army, became middleweight boxing champion of the Royal Corps of Signals. On leaving the army he travelled in England as a singer of calypsos, and later settled in Bristol. From amateur theatrical appearances at Bristol's King's Square Arts Centre, he progressed to a six-year acting career in live theatre, film and television, including work with HTV. He subsequently established himself as a writer. He worked with the ICA in London and, as a playwright, he worked with the BBC, the Royal Court and Foco Novo. His plays included *No Soldiers in St Pauls* (1974) and *Death of a Black Man.* [2] After moving to London, Fagon lived alone. At the time of his death he was the only black British playwright to have had work broadcast on national television.[3]

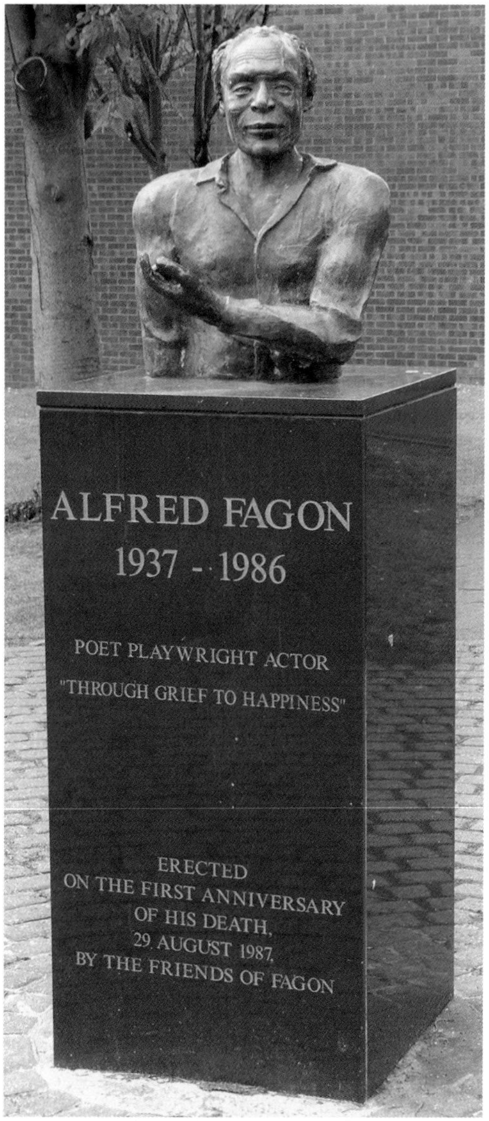

David Mutasa, *Alfred Fagon*

The circumstances of his sudden death were the subject of a documentary made by HTV.[4] He was a fitness fanatic, a habitual jogger, and well-known to his Brixton neighbours as 'the smartly track-suited Alfie' and 'the coloured man who ran'. One morning in early August 1986 the Metropolitan Police found a black man, collapsed in a Brixton street, wearing a tracksuit without any identification. He was dead on arrival at hospital.[5] 'None of the authorities followed any of the leads which could have established his identity', and he was cremated not under a name, but under the number T91.[6] Three weeks later, police enquiries linked Fagon's disappearance with the cremation of 'T91', and they contacted his friends in Bristol and his sister, Bevie St John, an actress living in Los Angeles.[7]

Their shock on hearing the circumstances of his death led to a memorial service attended by several hundred people at the Parkway Methodist Church in November 1986. Many of those present felt that there should be a permanent memorial to the playwright, and the Friends of Fagon Committee was subsequently formed for this purpose.[8]

The committee selected David Mutasa, a Zimbabwean sculptor who at this time had an exhibition in St David's Hall, Cardiff, and who had been working in the UK for several months. The committee also 'discussed the idea with businesses and residents who surround the triangle', and they requested the council's 'assistance in provision of a sculpture'.[9] The council was able to link the proposal to an environmental improvement scheme for the open space at the junction of Ashley Road and Grosvenor Road, St Pauls. The Planning and Traffic Committee resolved to 'support in principle the proposal for a memorial to Alfred Fagon' and requested that 'a sum of £1,000 be made available… to establish a fund and enable design work on the memorial to be commissioned.' The Race Equality Committee gave further support for the proposals on 16 March 1987.[10]

A report of the Public Works Committee stated: 'The request for a statue representative of the black community in Bristol was an early aspiration for this site on the part of the local people. There is strong support for a memorial to Alfred Fagon because of his local links, his achievements and the tragic circumstances of his death. There are no public monuments presenting black people in Bristol and this memorial is seen as a very appropriate subject and a means of communicating to all members of the public.' The meeting commended the site and the contribution of £1,000 from its own budget, and agreed that 'ongoing maintenance of the memorial will be the responsibility of the Committee'.[11]

Within five months, further money was raised and the bronze bust was cast and ready by late August. Bevie St John flew from Los Angeles to England to unveil the memorial on 26 August 1987, the first anniversary of Alfred's death. Among the 200 people present were the sculptor David Mutasa, Rudolf Walker (the star of the television programme *Love thy Neighbour*), Jim Williams (Bristol's first black councillor) and Joan Jones, the Deputy Lord Mayor.[12]

The original clay modelling is broad and loose with signs of tool marks. The free-standing bronze is mounted on a highly polished and disproportionately large rectangular black marble pedestal, composed of five thin slabs. Attempts were made to remove the bust in August 2008. The bust was subsequently re-secured and the base repaired and strengthened.

Notes

[1] *Venue*, 24 April – 7 May, 1987. [2] *Ibid.* [3] *Venue*, 11–24 September, 1987. [4] *Alfred Fagon*, HTV documentary, 1987. [5] Ibid. [6] Ibid. [7] Ibid. [8] BCC, *City Planning Officer's Report*, 24 March 1987. [9] Ibid. [10] Ibid. [11] Ibid. [12] *Venue*, as note 3.

At the apex of the small park at the junction of Ashley Road and Grosvenor Road, at the centre of St Paul's

The Greater Crested Plunger, the Crested Columbus Plunger and the Hooked Beaked Bantom A16

Sculptor: Jason Lane

Date: 2008
Materials: recycled steel on steel columns
Dimensions: approximately 1m on 4m supports
Inscribed: in solder on the columns – CRESTED / COLUMBUS / PLUNGER / LANE / 2008 – GREATER / CRESTED / PLUNGER / LANE / 2008 – HOOKED BEAKED BANTOM / LANE / 2008
Status: not listed
Owned by Bristol City Council
Condition: good

So recent is the appearance of these friendly scavengers that we must rely on information thoughtfully attached to the railings below them.

> 'Information about this art work
>
> This is a sculptural gateway sign welcoming people into the centre of St Pauls.
>
> The work was commissioned by people living in St Pauls, who in consultation with the community wanted something a bit different and cutting-edge.
>
> The work was built by Jason Lane, a local artist with a studio in Ashley; we liked the fact that his sculptures are made from recycled materials.
>
> He has a fascination for birds due their strong individual characters. These are some less commonly known birds, *The Hooked Beaked Bantom* and *The Plinger*, and they display some fantastic characteristics.
>
> The Hooked Beaked Bantom
> It is unusual to see one of these birds so high up, as they spend most of their time on the ground running through the undergrowth.

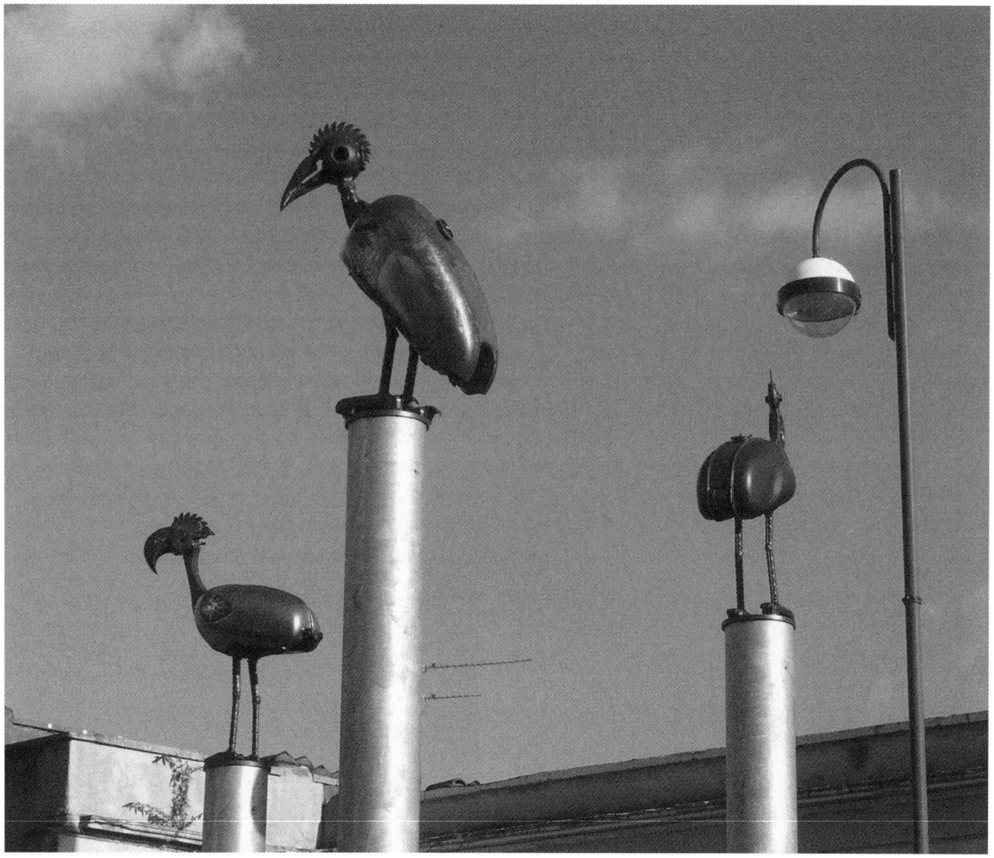

Jason Lane, *The Great Crested Plunger…*

They are vegetarian, and their hooked beaks are incredibly powerful, enabling them to crack open some of the most challenging nut shells. They are a much-loved bird due to their sociable, playful and gentle nature.

The Plunger
These birds rarely fly, but instead they mostly fluff up their wings to scare off predators. They are reliant on looking fiercer than they actually are, as their hunting skills are very limited. They sit for many hours on a high perch and then launch themselves in a very haphazard manner onto prey passing below. This rarely results in them catching anything and so they rely more on foraging and pooling their resources. Their family life is strong, and they are always on the look out for one another and will often share their food.'

There was a time when the notices on zoo cages would tell you only the name of the beast, its country of origin and, always, the length of pregnancy. Understandably enough, this helpful notice is not concerned with the long and fraught gestation of these particular birds. That is revealed in the minutes of the St Paul's External Environment Task Group, which met on 10 April 2007.

'Gateway Sign
A steering group was set up and they commissioned a sign from a local artist, Jason Lane. It was a 15ft-high metal tree with creatures hanging in it, but had not been universally well received so the artist is now reworking his ideas.
There was general concern that this had happened without the involvement of the group members as previously agreed, and did not follow the principles in the public art strategy. This was the 3rd year that this money had been available and rushed decisions had been made... advised that such a large structure would need planning permission and structural checks.'[1]

The substantial polished steel columns are broad enough to support storks' nests, and are far harder to climb than the recycled scaffolding poles that might have been expected. Jason Lane's earlier public work recorded here, *Guard Dog*, is at Blaise Castle (see Blaise Castle Estate), where vandalism had long bedevilled the council's improvements. Both works are robust and humorous, the wisest response to the threat of casual malice. And besides their wit, they also combine imagination with the most accomplished craftsmanship.

Note
[1] www.stpaulsunlimited.org.uk/taskgroups/documents/Minutes_April-07.doc.

Avon Street

On Trinity Quay, within the eastern courtyard of NatWest Life Headquarters

Time and Tide C71

Sculptor: Georgina Redfern

Date: 1994
Materials: painted metal and stainless steel
Dimensions: 340cm high, 360cm wide, 130cm deep
Made by Planet Fabrication, Northampton

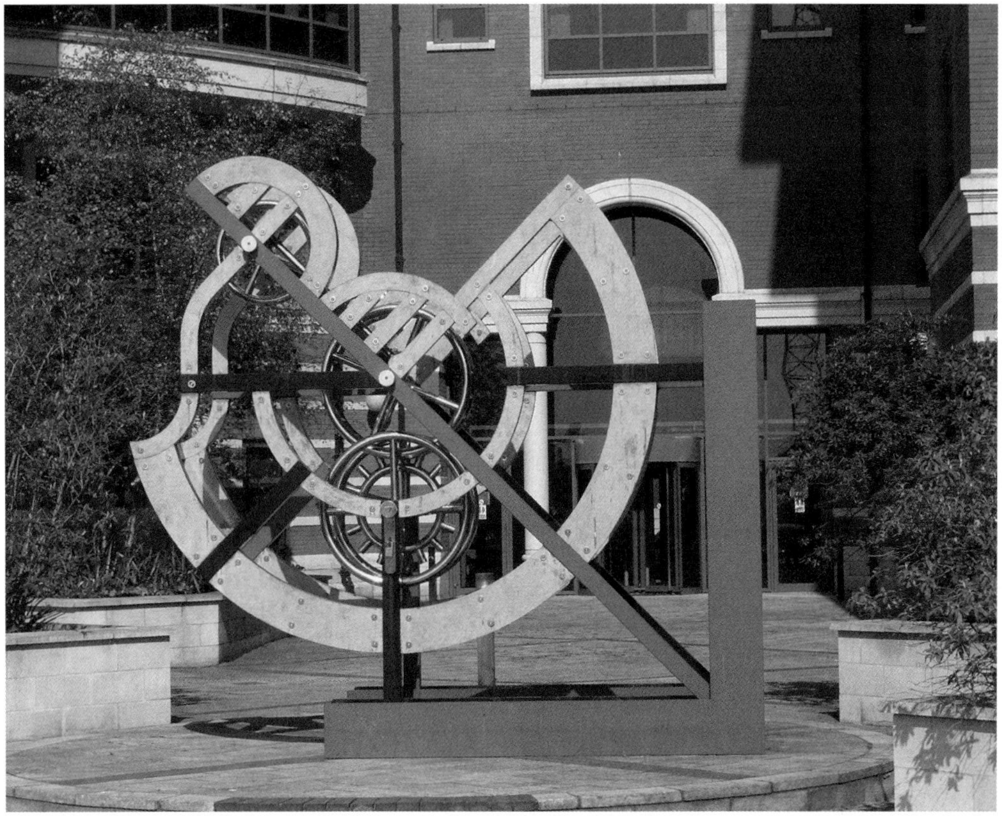

Metal plaque inscribed: "Time and Tide....." / by / Georgina Redfern / January 1994 / Winner of The NatWest Life Student Sculpture Commission
Status: not listed
Owned by Norwich Union
Condition: good; some rusting

Georgina Redfern, *Time and Tide*

Two twin right-angled brackets support large semi-circular rings, within which are three chrome wheels that can be moved. A padlock must first be removed and some lubricating oil may also be required. All the parts, except the chrome elements, are painted or patinated either bright red, black or copper-green.

The Royal Society of British Sculptors organised a nationwide competition for art students on behalf of National Westminster Life Assurance for a work of art for their new headquarters in Bristol. The winning entry was *Time and Tide* designed by Georgina Redfern. A company brochure stated:

> The sculpture was designed with NatWest Life and its life assurance products in mind. Based on the circle, details of the kinetic piece include three interlinked rings which can be set in motion by turning a key... Time equates with life and the form of the sculpture suggests a clock. Tide reflects the maritime traditions of Bristol, and the overall design suggests nautical instruments such as a compass, sextant and a ship's wheel.

Georgina Redfern graduated with a first class degree in fine art and sculpture from Loughborough College of Art and Design in 1993.

Baltic Wharf

Three sculptures, *Atyeo*, *Hand of the River God* and *Topsail*, were commissioned by the three developers of the Baltic Wharf private housing estate: Bristol and West Housing Association, the Nationwide Housing Trust and Rendell Partnership Developments Limited. The commission was made in 1985 as a consequence of the government's 'Percentage for Art' policy. That policy enabled local authorities to require developers to spend a small percentage of building costs on public art.

The project was overseen by John Sansom, who had been the Bristol and West Building Society's public relations officer, but who was then, as he is now, a publisher of books.[1] He advised on the appointment of the Public Art Development Trust for the selection of the sculptures. The trust's director, Lesley Greene, who was later to direct the art commissions at Castle Park and at the Bristol Royal Hospital for Children, managed the project. Sansom has said that although:

> maritime themes were encouraged this was not made a prerequisite. We were looking for works of real quality, challenging perhaps, but something Bristol could be proud of. The city has been given too much mediocre public 'art' in recent years.[2]

The total budget was set at £30,000, with £24,000 provided by the three developers and the balance from South West Arts. Four works were originally proposed, but this was later reduced to three. The sculptors were selected through a limited competition in which up to six artists were to be paid £500, inclusive of expenses, to produce maquettes as well as provide budget proposals for making, transporting and erecting their work on site.

The brief was for sculpture for the newly opened public promenade at Baltic Wharf, and the artists were asked to 'consider the maritime occupations, which have traditionally been a way of life in this area of the city'. It was also suggested that each work 'might be figurative, or contain figurative elements'. Any durable medium could be chosen, and the sculptures should be 'approximately life-size'. The artists were also asked to prepare a maintenance programme for the city council, into whose care and ownership the works would pass.

The selection jury was composed of the chairman of the Bristol & West Housing Association, the general manager of Rendell Partnership Developments Limited and the director of the Nationwide Housing Trust Limited, balanced by Tony Foster, the visual arts officer of the South West Arts Association, Rupert Martin of Arnolfini and Lesley Greene. The judges met on 3 December 1985. Vincent Woropay was one of two sculptors chosen for the two main sites. Woropay's estimated cost was £12,000. Stephen Cox was the other sculptor present. Keir Smith, the third sculptor selected, was invited to produce a smaller version of his submitted design, to be sited at 'one (or preferably both) ends' of the promenade, at a cost of £5,000. Planning permission for the whole scheme was then sought from Ian Patterson, Bristol's chief planning officer.[3] The creation of a public walkway around the entire Floating Harbour had been his initiative, and the new promenade at Baltic Wharf made this long stretch of the waterside accessible to the public for the first time.

On the Baltic Wharf quayside between Westbrooke Court and John Cabot Court

Hand of the River God B26

Sculptor: Vincent Woropay

Date: 1984
Materials: bronze on a limestone pedestal

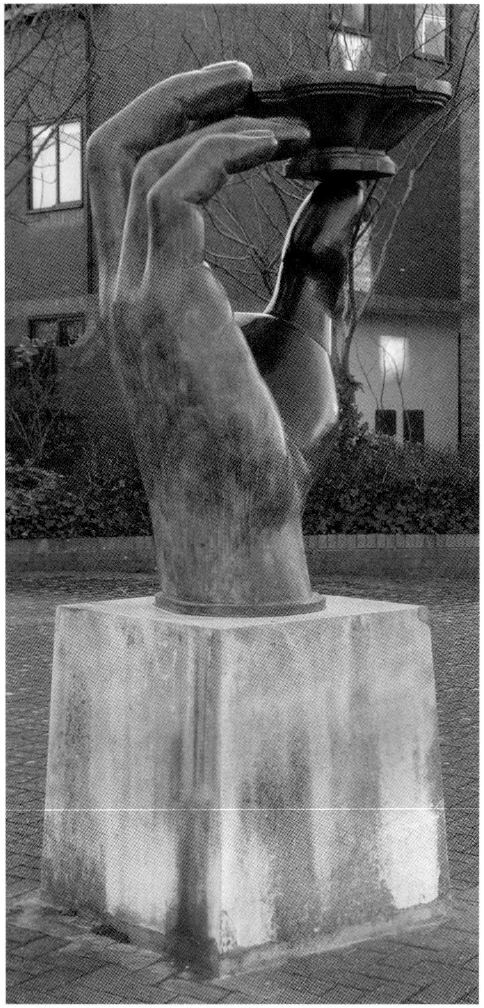

Vincent Woropay, *Hand of the River God*

Dimensions: sculpture, 235cm high; pedestal, 80cm high, 89cm square at base
Inscription: on the rim at the base of the bronze casting – A & A SCULPTURE CASTINGS LONDON VINCENT WOROPAY 1984
Status: not listed
Owned by Bristol City Council
Condition: poor; the stolen figure of Hercules carrying the obelisk has not been replaced

This is an impressive but sadly truncated work. Within his outline proposals, the artist wrote:

> The sculpture consists of a colossal hand holding up a fountain between fingers and thumb, as though to display it to public gaze. Both hand and fountain were patinated in deep green. The scale of the fountain is minute when compared to that of the hand. The fountain is composed of a male figure supporting an obelisk, in the centre of a basin with scalloped sides… Four jets of water rise from points around the rocky base on which the figure stands; the water is then drained back into the bottom of the basin and re-circulated. The figure grasps the obelisk from below, and is clearly exerting all his strength in order to maintain a near upright position.[4]

Vincent Woropay saw his design as a symbolic allusion to the waters of the Avon. His figure of Hercules, carrying an obelisk, was inspired by a preliminary sketch made by the Italian architect and sculptor Gianlorenzo Bernini (1598–1680); the sketch is now in the Vatican Library. This drawing was an early proposal for Bernini's surviving monument of an elephant supporting an ancient Egyptian obelisk in the Piazza della Minerva near the Pantheon in Rome.[5]

Woropay's submission stated that his sculpture:

> dramatises the action of proposing a monument for the city of Bristol, and setting that monument in place. The hand holding the fountain aloft indicates that the monument is something to be offered to the view of the people of Bristol as a source of delight, whilst the Herculean figure… alludes to the toil and effort which must necessarily be expended in order to produce a monument worthy of the city. The figure also refers… to the heroic labours which have in the past been expended on Bristol's many striking sculptural and architectural features.[6]

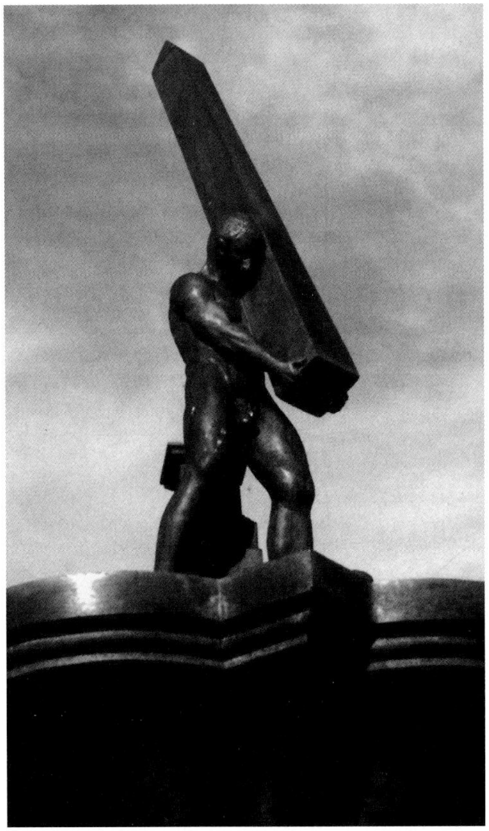

Vincent Woropay, *Stolen figure from Hand of the River God*

The fountain has not operated since it was installed, and the small figure of Hercules with the obelisk was stolen in 1998, leaving the sculpture's message still more ambiguous.[7]

Woropay's name appears in capital letters less than one centimetre high on the casting, but the evocative title is not displayed. We are deprived of any clue of the artist's concept, in this case a symbol of 'a river god directing attention to the beauty of the river under his protection'.[8]

On the Baltic Wharf quayside opposite Westbrooke Court

Atyeo B25

Sculptor: Stephen Cox

Date: 1986
Material: red Verona marble
Dimensions: 178cm high, 85cm wide, 108cm deep
Status: not listed
Owned by Bristol City Council
Condition: fair

This piece was carved by the sculptor from a single block of red Verona marble, weighing about three-quarters of a ton. Stephen Cox, who was born in Bristol in 1946, submitted a simple line drawing, and later a maquette, to the judging panel. The maquette was to give an indication of the shape intended, but not to represent the variations of colour and texture of the final work.[9] In his proposal he wrote:

> The sculpture would be in red Verona marble and the selected stone would determine to large extent the final 'look' of the sculpture, as my approach is to enter into a 'dialogue' with my material rather than override it completely with a predetermined form, which would be derived from ideas embracing the globe, the river, the sea and castellation symbolising the city.[10]

He wished the sculpture and the pedestal to be taller than an adult figure, and he recommended the pedestal should be rough-surfaced to deter climbing, while the smooth globe 'should remain accessible as hand contact would serve to polish the form'. This polishing continues. He also suggested that a harbour-side object, for example an old capstan, might serve as a base.

Cox's agent, Nigel Greenwood, presented an estimate. This gave the approximate cost of the marble as £4,000, including the quarrying in Italy, plus £1,500 for the transport and £6,000 for the artist's fee and expenses. The plinth was

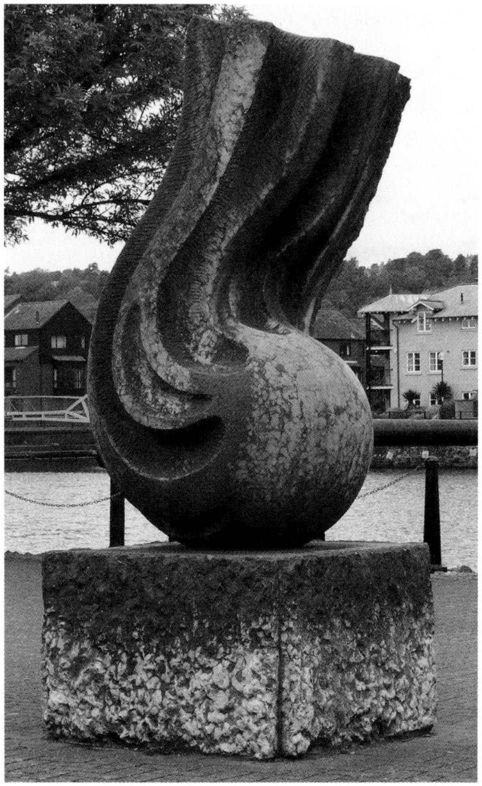

Stephen Cox, *Atyeo*

estimated at £750.[11]

In a paper to the judges, commenting on Stephen Cox's proposals, Lesley Greene said 'Red Verona marble is the most compact stone outside of the porphyries and, unlike the white or Carrara marbles, is *not* porous.'[12] This marble was selected partly because its colours would complement the tones and colours of the materials used in the buildings of the Baltic Wharf development. It was also easy to clean with solvents if sprayed with graffiti.

The environment minister, then William Waldegrave, unveiled the sculpture on 13 August 1986 in the presence of Joan Jones, the lord mayor of Bristol.[13] A local press report on the ceremony was headed: 'Is it a fishtail? Is it a shoe? No, it's a – well it's symbolic'.

Cox named his work *Atyeo* in homage to the former Bristol City centre-forward, John Atyeo, his teenage hero.

On the Baltic Wharf quayside to the right of Westbrooke Court

Topsail B24

Sculptor: Keir Smith

Date: 1986–7
Material: Portland stone
Dimensions: 142cm high, 244cm long, 100cm wide
Status: not listed
Owned by Bristol City Council
Condition: good, with developing lichens

Topsail was carved from a single block of Portland stone. A smooth-surfaced mast, spar and sail emerge from more roughly chiselled shapes that suggest cumulus clouds and the powerful winds that accompany them.

In his submission to the competition judges, the sculptor stated that he wished to carve as much as possible of the design on site, although the roughing out would have to be carried out with power tools. He had found that local communities reacted very positively when they saw a sculpture being made, and he wrote that if 'deemed appropriate I would be willing to work on site with limited public access'. This would take between four to six weeks, and slightly longer if the public were allowed access.[14]

Kier Smith's presentation drawing showed more detail than finally appeared in the carving, in which there are minimum overhangs and undercuts to lessen the risk of damage.[15] Much work went into the selection of the right stone. The sculptor sought a weather-resistant, durable and easily maintained local stone, which could be easily cleaned if vandalised. However, 'he could find nothing to fulfil all those criteria'.[16] He finally selected a seven-ton block of base-bed Portland stone, from the renowned quarry on Portland Bill. Its extreme hardness and weather-resistance makes it ideal for architectural sculpture. His detailed estimate listed the price of the stone at £504; transporting the block from the quarry to the studio and then to the Bristol site, £280; the hire of the crane, £264; hire of tools, £500; his own fee, £3,600, including accommodation while carving on site; plus £500 for his assistants.

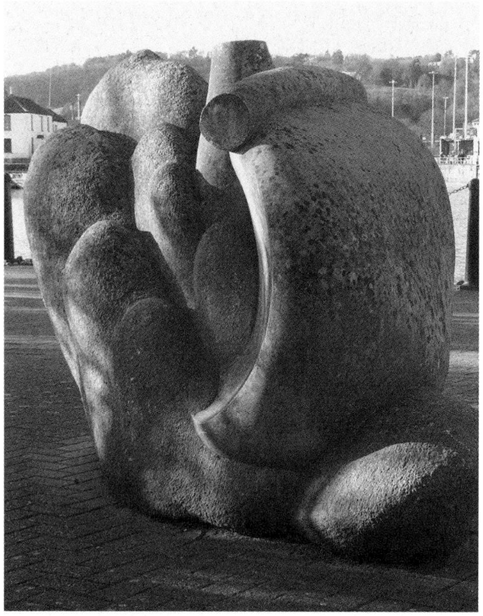

Keir Smith, *Topsail*

Notes

[1] Amongst books on many Bristol subjects, John Sansom published: D. Merritt, *Sculpture in Bristol* (Bristol, 2002). [2] 'Bristol's waterfront sculpture', *Art South West* (September/October 1986). [3] Minutes of the Judges' meeting on 3 December 1985. [4] V. Woropay, 'A proposed sculpture for Baltic Wharf, Bristol', submission to the Art Development Trust Limited (1983); see Public Art Development Trust. [5] C. Avery, *Bernini, Genius of the Baroque* (London, 1997), p.192. [6] Woropay, as note 4. [7] *Bristol Evening Post*, 26 January 1999, p.7. [8] Ibid. [9] Report by Lesley Greene, 'Stephen Cox: a sculpture for Baltic Wharf', 4 March 1986. PMSA (Bristol) BRO. [10] Stephen Cox, 'Proposals to the jury' (1985), Public Art Development Trust. [11] 27 November 1985. [12] Woropay, as note 4. [13] Quita Morgan, 'The whatsit on our wharf', *Evening Post*, 14 August 1986. [14] Kier Smith, 'Submission to the judges of the Baltic Wharf Competition', 1985. See Public Art Development Trust. [15] Ibid. The preliminary drawing is illustrated in Merritt, as note 1, p.121. [16] Report by Lesley Greene, 'A sculpture for Baltic Wharf: Topsail', 4 March 1986. PMSA (Bristol) BRO.

Bath Road

At the junction of Spine Road, on Arno's Vale gateway

Four Statues on Arno's Court Gateway: Edward I, Edward III, Geoffrey, Bishop of Coutances and Robert, Earl of Gloucester A26

Sculptor: Susan Dring

Date: 1994
Material: Bath stone
Inscription: BUILT IN THE 1760S TO SERVE AS A GATEWAY TO THE / STABLES AT ARNOS COURT, MOVED TO ITS / PRESENT POSITION IN 1912 AND RESTORED IN 1995 / WITH REPLICA FIGURES OF EDWARD I, EDWARD III, / GEOFFREY, BISHOP OF COUTANCES IN NORMANDY AND / ROBERT, EARL OF GLOUCESTER / BRISTOL DEVELOPMENT CORPORATION / WILSON CONNOLLY
Status: Grade II*
Owned by Bristol City Council
Condition: good but at risk; ivy is already encircling two of the figures and has reached the top of the gateway

These four modern versions of surviving medieval statues were commissioned by Bristol Development Corporation in 1994. Mike Jenner, the BDC's architectural advisor, oversaw the restoration of the rococo Gothic gateway as part of the substantial redevelopment of the area.[1] It was as a result of his initiative that the statues were installed.

William Reeve, a Quaker copper-smelter and the owner of Arno's Court, built the gateway in

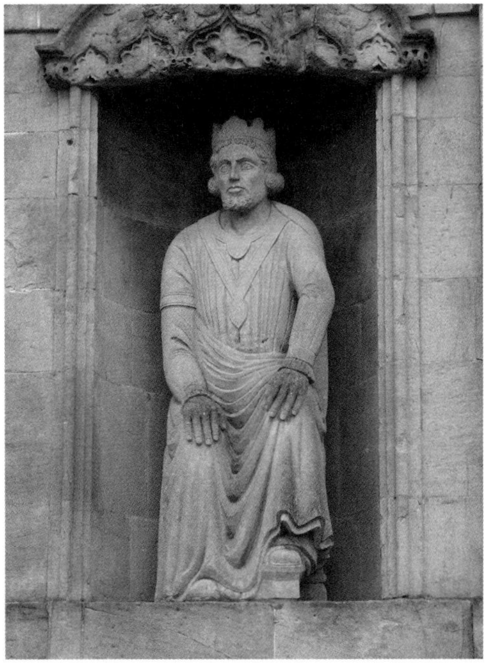

Susan Dring, *Edward I*

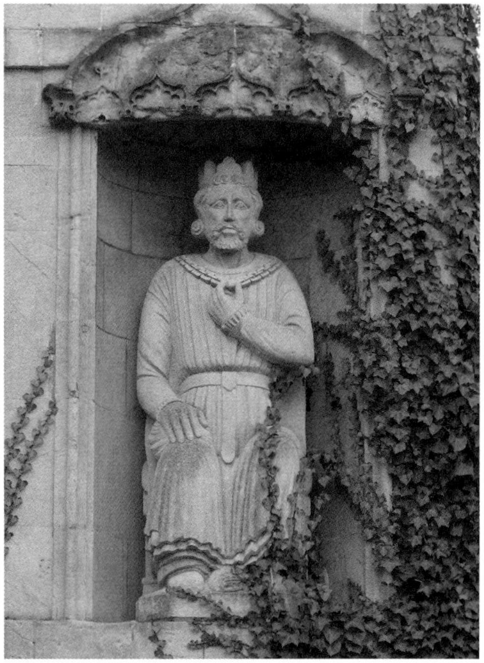

Susan Dring, *Edward III*

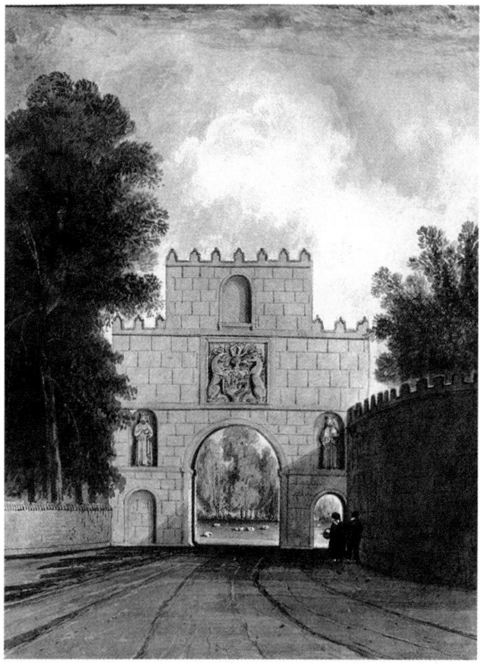

***Arno's Court Gateway from the south with the original medieval statues of Bishop Geoffrey of Coutances and Robert Fitzroy, Earl of Gloucester,* watercolour by T.L. Rowbotham, 1826 (Bristol Museum and Art Gallery, M3494)**

the 1760s as an entrance to his stables and offices, now called the Black Castle. James Bridges may have been the architect.[2] The medieval figures were acquired by Reeve when two of Bristol's ancient gateways, Newgate and Lawford's Gate, were demolished in 1766 and 1769. 1766 was also the year in which the Bristol Bridge Trustees were disposing of St Peter's Pump to Henry Hoare, who had already erected the Bristol High Cross at Stourhead. Reeve, himself, was also rescuing sculptural fragments from alterations to St Werburgh's church, then in Corn Street, and incorporating them into the walls of the Black Castle, where they can still be seen.[3] The statues were removed from the Arno's Court gateway in 1898 due to their deteriorating condition, and they are now in the collection of Bristol Museums and Art Gallery.[4] In 1912 the gate had to be moved a short distance to its present position, facing up the Bath Road.[5] Today, it is isolated by a complex road system and the archway leads nowhere.

The original sculptures of the two kings came from Lawford's Gate at the end of Old Market.[6] Both Edward I (1239–1307) and Edward III (1312–77) were important to the city. When Edward I was only fifteen his father gave him Bristol as part of a generous wedding settlement. He also received parts of France, Ireland, much of Wales and the Channel Islands. Edward III granted Bristol a royal charter, conferring upon it the status of a county in 1373. The originals of the other two statues came from the Newgate. These have long been thought to represent Bishop Geoffrey of Coutances and Robert Fitzroy, Earl of Gloucester. Bishop Geoffrey was rewarded for his part in William the Conqueror's successful invasion of England, and he was the first builder of Bristol Castle. Robert Fitzroy, who built the castle's Great Keep, was an illegitimate son of Henry II and is buried at St James's Priory, Bristol, which he founded. It is also possible that these two statues are instead two of the three kings of Cologne, the wise men of the nativity, and it is certainly likely that each of these four medieval statues predates the gateways from which William Reeve rescued them. The original statues, now around six centuries old, are eroded and damaged and they have been badly restored in the past. They are presently in St Nicholas Church Museum, now closed to the public.

The modern versions of Edward I and Edward III are on the north side of the gateway. Bishop Geoffrey of Coutances and Robert Fitzroy, Earl of Gloucester are on the south side. They are not precise copies. On the north side a blank ziggurat of stones from the 1760s still awaits a coat of arms. Bristol's coat of arms was carved on the opposite side.

In June 1994, Mike Jenner applied for planning permission to put up new carved figures, which were at first intended to be painted and gilded, and for permission to carve the city's coat of arms on the uncarved blocks.[7] Susan Dring was later commissioned to make clay mock-ups based on the originals.[8] When these were approved she carved the 1.8m figures from stone quarried for the purpose from a deep seam found at Limpley Stoke, south-east of Bath.[9] The uncarved blocks were not touched.

Notes
[1] Michael Jenner, 'The Arnos Gateway, Brislington', *Follies, the International Magazine for Follies Grottoes and Garden Buildings*, Summer, 1998. [2] English Heritage listed description, 901-1/56/428. [3] J. Latimer, *Annals of Bristol in the Eighteenth Century* (Bristol, 1893), p.377. [4] As note 1. [5] Ibid. [6] A drawing of the gateway and the statues by James Stewart, 1745, is in the Bodleian Library. [7] Correspondence relating to this application is in Fine Art Dept. Bristol Museums and Art Gallery. [8] As note 1. [9] Ibid.

Beauley Road

On 12 Beauley Road at the corner of Raleigh Road, Southville

Terracotta roundel A22

Sculptor: unknown

Date: c.1890
Material: terracotta
Dimensions: approx. 100cm diameter
Status: not listed
Condition: good

This high-relief terracotta roundel, dating from about 1890, depicts a youngish man in a wig and apparel from about 1800. It has been inserted at first-floor level into the side of a former shop at the corner of two Victorian terraces. It is smaller than the roundels in St

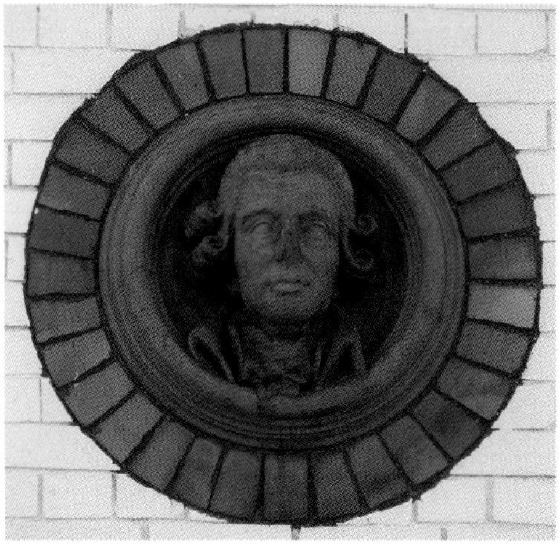

Terracotta roundel

Stephen's Street, and the surround is more like a frame than the portholes through which those historical figures peer. It seems likely that this terracotta comes from a demolished W. D. & H. O.Wills tobacco factory building in Bedminster or Southville, and perhaps from one designed by Henry Williams, who used terracotta extensively. If so, it could be an imaginary portrait of the first Henry Overton Wills (1761–1826), who in 1786 became a partner in a small tobacco business in Castle Street, Bristol.

Berkeley Square

In the north-east corner of the gardens

Bristol High Cross; Remnants of the Replica B44

Sculptors: John Thomas, 1849–51; Harry Hems, 1889; Ernest Pascoe, 1956

Architect: John Norton

Dates: 1851, 1889, 1956
Materials: oolitic limestone from Combe Down[1]
Dimensions: 655cm high, 140cm square at the base
Inscription: on plaque, no longer present – THE BRISTOL HIGH CROSS / Bristol's first High Cross was set up at the central cross / roads of the old town to commemorate Edward III's / Charter of 1373 which made Bristol a separate county. / In 1633 it was enlarged. In 1733 it was moved to / College Green. In 1765 it was re-erected at Stourhead / in Wiltshire. / In1851 a new cross, reproducing the design of 1373 / was set up in College Green. A century later, / when the Green was lowered, it was taken down. / In 1956 to save it from destruction, the stonework / of this second Cross was bought by a Son of Bristol, / and given by him to the Berkeley Square Association. / Part of it has been re-erected here for the enjoyment of / residents and visitors. /
—: eroded and damaged lettering below the figures; on the north side – HENRY VI /
—: on the west side – CHARLES I /
—: on the south side – ELIZA**** /
—: on the east side – JAMES *
Status: Grade II
Owned by the Berkeley Square Association
Condition: poor but secure

A brief history of Bristol's medieval High Cross, removed from the city in 1764 and erected the following year at Stourhead, Wiltshire, is given in the inscription recorded above and discussed in the Introduction. Lord mayors of Bristol, who still periodically seek the 'return' of the High Cross, may justly feel that the High Cross should mean almost as much to Bristol as the Elgin marbles do to Greece. However, they forget the less flattering parallels, and they certainly ignore the history of this sadly truncated substitute.

The remnants of the new High Cross, re-erected in Berkeley Square in 1956, consist only of the upper tier and spire of the monument erected in 1851 on College Green, and of four of the eight statues added to it in 1855 and 1889.

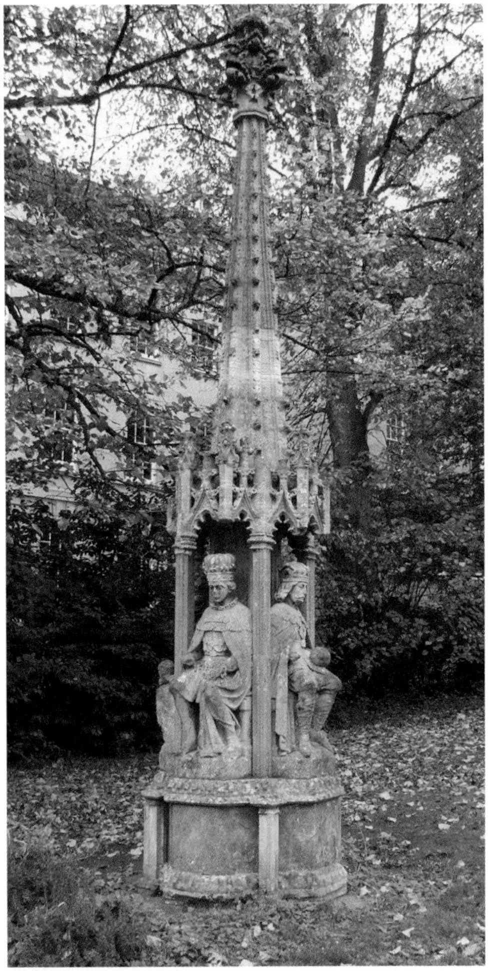

John Thomas, Harry Hems and Ernest Pascoe,
Remains of the replica of the High Cross

The seated monarchs are Henry VI, Elizabeth I, James I and Charles I, each of whom is credited with presenting a charter to Bristol.[2]

Proposals for a replica of the High Cross were confirmed at a public meeting on 22 September 1848, the costs to be met by public subscription. There had been earlier initiatives, especially in 1821 and 1840.[3] The catalyst may have been the euphoria following the council's purchase of the Bristol Dock Company in 1848 and the prospect of an end to crippling port dues. One correspondent writing in support of the new High Cross foresaw it coming 'at a singularly auspicious epoch in the annals of our city, when the institution of Bristol as a Free Port promises to open up new paths of enterprise to her industrious population'.[4] A year later, 'on 8 August 1849, the foundation stone of the civic High Cross in College Green was laid, with full Masonic rites, by the mayor, Mr J. K. Haberfield; the architect was Mr Norton and the ground was given by the dean and chapter'.[5]

The commission is one of the earliest works undertaken by the Bristol-born architect John Norton (1823–1904), who had been a pupil in the London office of Benjamin Ferrey, A. W. N. Pugin's friend and biographer.[6] Norton is now best known as the architect of Tyntesfield, near Bristol. Before commencing his design, Norton studied the original High Cross at Stourhead and in 1849 he read a paper to the Bristol and West of England Architectural Society, in which he observed that the old Cross was constructed of:

> coarse-grained oolite, the ova being large and distinct, and hence liable to absorb moisture, and become injured by frost. This fault was remedied, as we have seen, for many centuries by the application of polychromatic colouring, which evidently formed an effectual preservative against the weather.[7]

More significantly, Norton noted the 'debased and discordant' seventeenth century additions to the medieval Cross and recorded that he had made an attempt 'not only to preserve the beautiful outline, but to embody one uniformly harmonious feeling throughout, being that period of its earliest foundation'. A similarly zealous purification was already bedevilling the restoration of St Mary Redcliffe, but we should remember that, here, the intention was to create a new High Cross for Bristol rather than to simply reproduce the original.

At the end of 1851, Norton reported to *The Builder* that the architectural work was now complete and only awaited the statues. The project was £170 overspent. Against costs of £450, only £280 had been raised. Among the detailed accounts that include no fee for the architect, the largest sum went to John Thomas, the sculptor and mason, who was paid £300. Thomas himself told *The Builder* that he would search for the best material from:

> Caen, Painswick, or Box-hill stone, model and execute four standing figures, 6 feet high, and four sitting figures, 4 feet 6 inches high, to fill the eight niches in the new cross at Bristol, fixed complete, for the sum of £480.[8]

John Norton had argued forcibly, but vainly, for 'the public duty' of adding the statues. 'I know of no work of architecture so specifically needing the aid of the sister art of sculpture.' It was as yet just 'a tame and insipid work'.[9]

In 1855, the Freemasons paid for the first statue, that of Edward III, and in 1889 the remaining seven statues by Harry Hems of Exeter were added.[10]

In May and June 1888, there had been negotiations between John Fuller Eberle (a former mayor of Bristol, the patron of the Bristol Savages and the saviour of the Red Lodge) and Sir Henry Hoare over the return of the original High Cross from Stourhead 'before, as is so highly probable – the Wind or the Weather Completes its destruction'.[11] Surprisingly, Sir Henry was ready to sell, but the project foundered on the purchase price, the expenses of removal and the high cost of restoration.[12] The initiative may have been prompted by the decision to move the Victorian High Cross to make way for Boehm's Golden Jubilee statue of Queen Victoria (see College Green), and it is possible that Eberle was subsequently the leading contributor to the cost of the new statues for the High Cross. The Cross was moved closer to the medieval Cross's

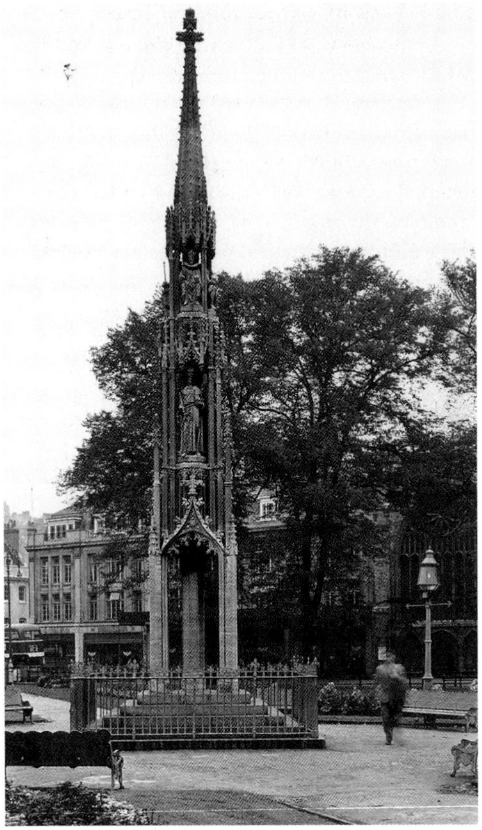

Replica of the High Cross, **College Green, September 1950, shortly before demolition**

old site near the centre of College Green. The addition of the figures and the reconstruction were supervised by the joint architects Walter S. Paul and H. C. M. Hirst.[13]

John Norton's High Cross remained on College Green until 1950, when Vincent Harris's Council House was at last nearing completion. Harris regarded the re-landscaping of College Green as an integral part of his design. He argued that the removal of both the statue of Queen Victoria and of the High Cross would be a 'minor detail'.[14] With the same commitment to renewal and modernity that was to mark the great Festival of Britain exhibition of 1951, the two monuments were removed late in 1950 and College Green was soon lowered and levelled after the felling of all its trees.

It was public demand that led to the return of the statue of Queen Victoria in 1953. The High Cross, however, was in a seriously dilapidated state and the statues had been further damaged by vandals while supposedly in protective storage in a city yard near the Central Library. Repair was estimated at £7,000.[15] A photograph shows three of the statues in an appalling condition: James I is headless and all three are without forearms.[16]

An appeal for the costs of restoration, backed by the Civic Society, failed, and the council offered to sell the remnants. The 'son of Bristol' referred to in the inscription quoted above was Donald Hughes, a former estate agent, Berkeley Square resident, chairman and later president of Clifton Arts Club and the saviour of Blaise Hamlet. He purchased the remains for £50 and formed a committee composed of the Civic Society, the Park Street Traders and the Berkeley Square Association. They raised £300, enabling the upper portion of the cross and the four seated figures to be erected in Berkeley Square.[17]

The complex restoration work was carried out under the direction of Ernest Pascoe, then a lecturer at the West of England College of Art, in the beautiful summer of 1956. He was assisted by Stuart Jennings, RWA, a student at the college and then in his final year.[18] The Cross was unveiled by the Duke of Beaufort in Berkeley Square on 5 October 1956, followed by luncheon at the Royal Hotel to celebrate the completion of the project.[19]

Reece Winstone, Bristol photographer and historian and at that time chairman of Bristol's Civic Society, was able to preserve the statue of King John 'left over from the restoration', and that statue, carved by Harry Hems of Exeter in 1889, was set up in Winstone's garden in Bristol.[20]

Notes

[1] E. Stonebridge, *Bristol: Heritage in Stone* (Bristol, undated). [2] R. Winstone, *Bristol Today* (Bristol, 1963), captions 82–84. [3] Braikenridge Collection, BRCL vol. XV, p.245, newspaper cuttings April 1821 and 1840. In 1821, R.C. Hoare of Stourhead offered to help with replication; he recommended George Ashley of Bath, who had done much work for him, to do the job; and he wrote: 'my original is in such a tottering state no time should be lost.' [4] Braikenridge Collection, BRCL, vol. XV, p.181, newspaper cutting, December 1848; the writer also stated that the 'delapidated state [of the Stourhead High Cross] renders removal impossible'. [5] J.F. Nicholls and J. Taylor, *Bristol Past and Present* (3 vols, Bristol, 1881–2), vol. III, p.346. [6] *ODNB*. [7] Quoted by C. Pooley, *Notes on the Old Crosses of Gloucestershire* (London, 1868); see also Michael Liversidge, *The Bristol High Cross*, BBHA, no. 42, 1978. [8] *The Builder*, 27 December 1851, p.816. [9] Quoted by Pooley, op. cit. and by Liversidge, op cit. f.n.36. [10] Liversidge, op. cit. [11] BRO 28049 (102)c, Eberle to Stourton Estate Office, 28 May 1888. [12] Ibid (102)a–f; the medieval High Cross was to be rebuilt and restored in 1894. [13] R. Winstone, *Bristol in the 1880s* (Bristol, 1962), illus. 4; caption within the original photograph identifies the joint architects. [14] Winstone, *Bristol 1950–1953* (Bristol, 1964). [15] Winstone, *Bristol As It Was, 1950–1953* (Bristol, 1980), p.115. [16] Ibid. [17] Ibid. [18] S. Jennings, 'Bristol High Cross', *RWA Friends' Newsletter*, Spring, 2000, p.22. [19] Ibid. [20] Winstone, *Bristol Today*, illus. 82–4; Winstone, *Bristol in the 1880s*, introduction.

Blackboy Hill

On a traffic island at the top of Blackboy Hill

Memorial Fountain and Clock Tower to Urijah Thomas A14

Designers: J. Whitehead and Sons

Date: 1904
Materials: stone structure with tiled roof
Dimensions: approximately 18ft in diameter at base
Contractors: J.Whitehead and Sons, London and Aberdeen
Inscription: THIS FOUNTAIN / WAS SET UP IN MEMORY OF/ THE REV. URIJAH REES THOMAS

/ BY HIS FELLOW CITIZENS OF ALL PARTIES AND BELIEFS / IN GRATEFUL RECOGNITION / OF THE CATHOLIC SPIRIT AND GENEROUS ARDOUR / WITH WHICH HE GAVE HIMSELF TO THE PUBLIC SERVICE / AND ESPECIALLY OF HIS WISE AND TENDER CARE / FOR THE CHILDREN OF THE CITY / AND FOR ALL THE FRIENDLESS AND UNHAPPY / THE DEFENCELESS AND THE POOR / (DASH) THIS COMMANDMENT WE HAVE FROM HIM, THAT HE WHO / LOVETH GOD LOVE HIS BROTHER ALSO / 1 JOHN IV: 21 / BORN 16TH FEBRUARY 1839 / DIED 8TH MARCH 1901

Status: Grade II
Owned by Bristol City Council
Condition: good, but no longer functions as a drinking fountain or as a timekeeper

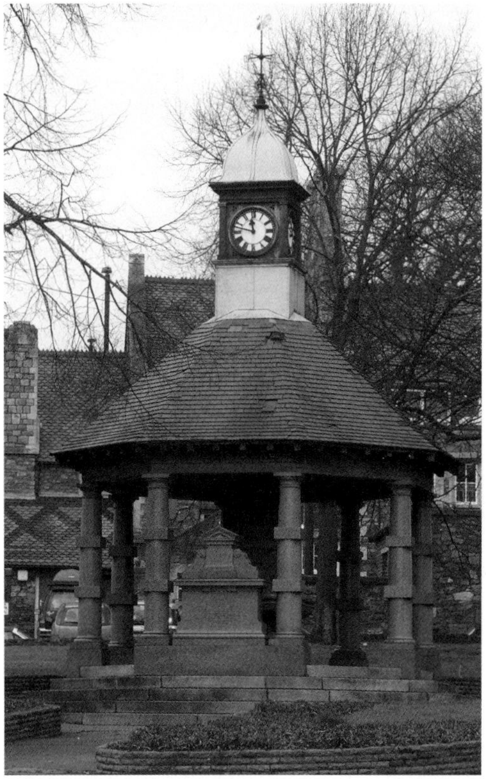

Memorial to Urijah Thomas

Rev Urijah Rees Thomas (1839–1901) was the first minister of Redland Park Church, now the United Reformed Church.[1] He was appointed in 1862, direct from college, aged 23, and this was his only ministry.[2] He died 'in harness, 39 years later'.[3] 'Urijah Thomas loved the city of his adoption and gave of himself unreservedly, not alone to its multifarious religious activities, but to its varied social and political life as well.'[4] He supported the temperance movement and women's suffrage. Science and religion, he believed, were not in conflict if properly understood.[5] In his dedication to education he was elected for 27 successive years as vice-chairman and chairman to the Bristol School Board, from 1874 until his death. 'No greater or kindlier personality ever presided over its deliberations, and the deep interest he took in the child life of our city earned for him the title "the children's friend"'.[6] Thomas worked to establish non-sectarian education in state schools and did much to alleviate poverty in the Dings area of St Philips.[7] He established the Bristol Children's Help Society, providing 'free breakfasts, halfpenny dinners, winter playrooms, and holidays in the countryside'.[8] Thomas never married and was buried in Arno's Vale Cemetery next to the family of Wilberforce Tribe, with whom he had lived in Westfield Park for many years.[9]

This large structure, incorporating fountain, clock and weathervane, was designed and erected by J. Whitehead and Sons of London and Aberdeen. The pavilion enclosing the fountain is octagonal and stands on a grey granite platform of five steps. On this are eight highly polished Aberdeenshire red granite columns, with moulded bases and Doric capitals, each carved from a single stone. These, and the huge central column of red Mansfield stone, support the octagonal entablature and roof of pitch pine and Broseley tiles. Around the central column are four circular red granite drinking basins. All the visible woodwork on the roof and the surmounting clock turret is oak. The turret roof is covered with copper and surmounted by a vane. The long inscription is on a red granite tablet on a moulded granite plinth.

There were memorials to Reverend Urijah Thomas in Redland Park Church, where a memorial window and a plaque were destroyed in the last war. This substantial memorial is, however, unusual, for it was a relatively prompt civic tribute to a private citizen. The council was 'unanimous in appropriating and laying out a site for the Fountain, which it was resolved to erect by general subscriptions'.[10] 'Small amounts only were asked for, that all might have an opportunity of engaging in the work.'[11] The land was provided by Bristol City Council for a small sum. In October 1903, under the heading 'Civic Memorial', the church magazine said: 'At last a start has been made… the foundation stone is being put in, but it will be some time before the work will be visible'.[12] On 6 February 1904, Sir Herbert Ashman, a former lord mayor, presided over the unveiling. Canon Prideaux, from Bristol Cathedral, and Reverend Arthur Furner, Urijah's successor, were present. Reverend Arnold Thomas unveiled the tablet and read the inscription.[13] The lord mayor, Sir Robert Symes, 'set the clock going'.[14]

Notes

[1] Stanley Hutton, *Bristol and its Famous Associations* (Bristol, 1907), p.383. [2] Redland Park; United Reformed Church website; based on P. Thomas, *A History of Redland Park Church* (Bristol, n.d.). [3] Ibid. [4] 'Bristol Civic Memorial to the late Rev. Urijah Rees Thomas', *Redland Park Recorder*, Vol. IV, No. 1, 1 February 1904. [5] As note 2. [6] As note 1. [7] As note 2. [8] Ibid. [9] Ibid. [10] As note 4. [11] *Bristol Times and Mirror*, 8 February 1904. [12] As note 4; October 1903, Vol. III, No. 10. [13] *Bristol Times and Mirror*, 8 February 1904. [14] Ibid.

Blaise Castle Estate

By the Blaise Castle Estate café next to the car park off King's Weston Road.

Guard Dog A2

Sculptor: Jason Lane

Date: 2004
Material: metal, recycled mechanical parts
Dimensions: 1m high; base approx. 1.2m high
Owned by Bristol City Council
Condition: good

Jason Lane's hound sits on a traditional stone plinth with its own permanent water bowl on the hard-standing below. He guards the park's new cafe, toilet and offices, opened in 2005. The award-winning building, designed by CODA

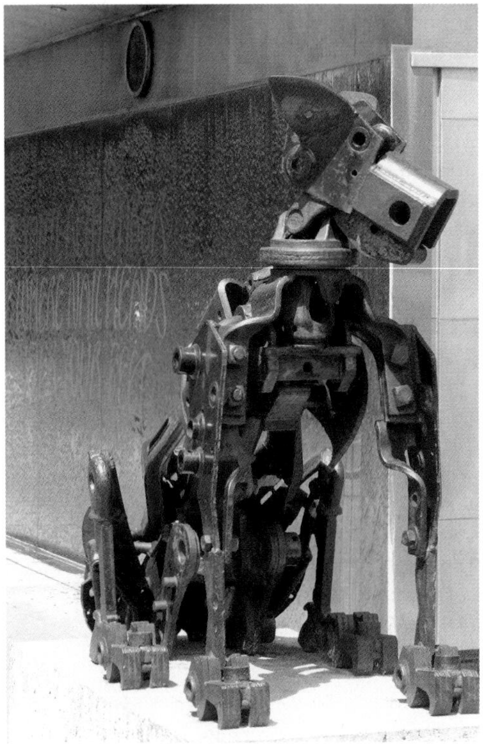

Jason Lane, *Guard Dog*

Architects, needed to be 'open and friendly during the day yet robust and secure at night', a reference to the problems of vandalism that have plagued the Blaise Castle Estate for many decades.[1] The lovable guard dog is in light-hearted contrast to the poetry engraved on Alan Wilson's steel-faced Water Wall and to the poem by Fiona Hamilton on the glass walls of the cafe. The words on the Water Wall are from a poem by Alicia Stubbersfield and all the excellent calligraphy is by Pip Hall.

The cafe was developed from former football changing rooms, originally built as a cow byre. The conversion was one aspect of the £5.6m project supported by the Heritage Lottery Fund to restore the historic landscape and public park at Blaise.

Note
[1] Blaise Castle Estate newsletter, No. 4, 2005.

Blaise Castle House

In the Dairy Garden of Blaise Castle House Museum, King's Weston Road, Henbury

Coade Stone Urn after the Medici Vase A3

Sculptors: Eleanor Coade and John Sealy

Date: 1806
Material: Coade stone
Dimensions: 128cm high; base of vase, 455mm square
Stamped: COADE & SEALY. LONDON. 1806
Owned by Bristol City Council
Condition: fair; conserved

This fine Coade stone urn is the only original and complete survivor of the many early nineteenth-century urns and vases that once surrounded Blaise Castle House.

In May 2008 it was re-erected on a modern base in the relative security of the locked garden close to John Nash's thatched dairy to the east

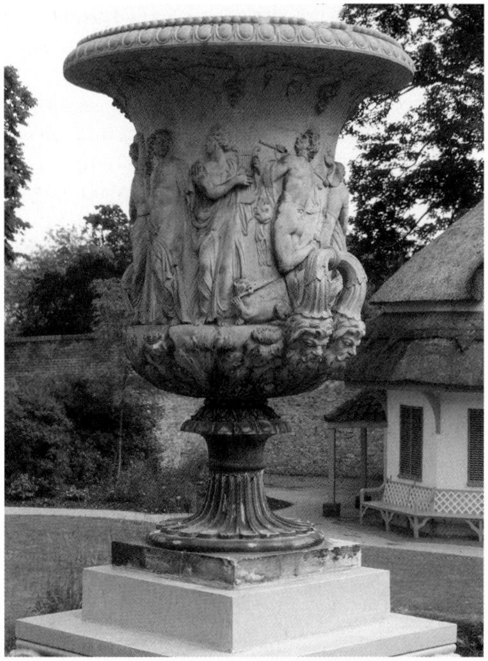

Coade and Sealy, *Coade stone urn after the Medici Vase*

of the house. Photographs from about 1906 and 1930 show a similar urn in approximately the same position. This would not have been the original site.[1]

The Medici Vase upon which this Coade stone urn was based is likely to date from the second century AD and to have been made in Greece for the Roman market. It is known to have been in the Villa Medici in the later sixteenth century and it is now in the Uffizi Gallery in Florence. In the eighteenth and early nineteenth centuries copies of the Medici Vase, whether in alabaster, bronze, cast iron, silver or Coade stone, were often paired with versions of the equally famous Borghese Vase, a similar if slightly earlier and larger Greek vase, now in the Louvre. 'The originals were revered by Georgian connoisseurs who believed, mistakenly, that they had been carved by Phidias.'[2] The Coade stone copies, at two-thirds of the size of the originals, were the grandest of the many vases made by the Coade firm. Examples survive at Buckingham Palace, Coleorton Hall, Kedleston, Sezincote, Stourhead and Uppark; a role call of some of the most imposing Georgian stately homes. Of the pair ordered for George IV by John Nash for Royal Lodge, Windsor, in 1825, one is now at Kew and the other at Wrest Park, Bedfordshire.[3] At Blaise Castle House there were three pairs of these Medici and Borghese vases, an unrivalled concentration with but one original survivor.[4]

The identity of the subject matter and the figures remains uncertain. Iphigenia may be seated below a statue of Diana with Agamemnon and either Achilles or Odysseus on either side. Mrs Coade's own catalogue titled this item 'the Sacrifice of Iphigenia'.

It has been assumed that the vase and its former companions were acquired soon after 1832, when the architect, Charles Robert Cockerell, had begun substantial additions to William Paty's dignified square block of 1796–7, which had succeeded the old manor house at Blaise.[5] Cockerell's alterations included the addition of the picture gallery and its grand Ionic colonnade, the entrance portico and the encircling balustrade. The balustrade enabled the house to rise less abruptly from the small knoll upon which Humphry Repton had recommended that it should be built. Early photographs show that this balustrade was ornamented with three pairs of large Coade stone urns based upon the Medici and Borghese vases as well as two pairs of smaller vases.[6] The purchase of the Blaise Castle estate by Bristol Corporation in 1926 was followed by the growth of suburban estates around the park and the military use of the house and park during the last war. Since the war, repeated vandalism has led to the destruction of most of the urns and of the entire balustrade and to the deliberate, but belated, removal of the remnants in the late 1980s.

At Blaise, C. R. Cockerell was employed by John Scandrett Harford the younger (1787–1866). Harford was to use an image of the Medici Vase as the frontispiece to his translation of *Agamemnon of Aeschylus*, published by John Murray in 1831. The publication and its date, a year before the commission, confirm the sympathy he would have felt for Cockerell, the finest of the later neo-classical architects and a visitor to Greece some twenty years earlier. Harford's better known literary works are his *Life of Michel Angelo* (published in 1857) and his *Recollections of W[illiam] Wilberforce*, his friend (which appeared in 1864). His fine collection of paintings has been dispersed, but within the house and the orangery and on the stable block there are still works from his collection of plaster casts. These include casts after the Elgin Marbles and after works by Bertel Thorvaldsen and Michelangelo, including the latter's statue of Lorenzo de Medici in the Medici Chapel in Florence.

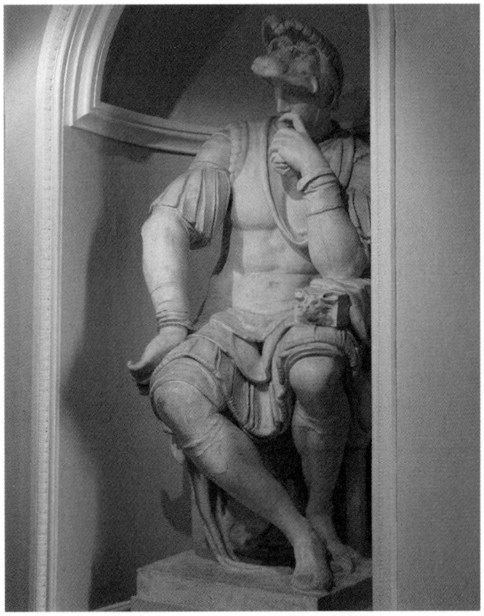

Blaise Castle House, ***Plaster after Michelangelo's statue of Lorenzo de Medici, Medici Chapel, Florence***

The Harford family was 'the chief among several interrelated Quaker families in Bristol'.[7] John Scandrett Harford the younger left the Society of Friends in 1809, but he was to continue his active opposition to the continuance of the slave trade abroad. Of relevance to this volume is his influential role as the first chairman of the Clifton Suspension Bridge committee, set up in 1829. The bridge was ultimately completed thirty-five years later as a memorial and monument to the great engineer. Despite many changes in the design, the bridge still retains elements of the Egyptian design that the committee selected in 1831. It was intended that it should be covered in sculpted reliefs and Harford supported the plan with particular enthusiasm.

Eleanor Coade had set up her manufactory in Lambeth in 1769, producing an exceptionally durable, ceramic, artificial stone. She was later to take into partnership her cousin, John Sealy. The surviving Medici Vase at Blaise is stamped 'COADE & SEALY 1806'. After Mrs Coade's death in 1821, her former manager, William Croggan, carried on the business.[8] It is recorded that one of the other Coade stone urns formerly at Blaise was stamped 'CROGGAN LAMBETH 1823'.[9] The presence of three pairs at Blaise was apparently a unique extravagance. They may have been acquired 'second hand' from separate estates, although it is possible that the later pair was acquired directly from the Coade firm by John Scandrett Harford and perhaps some years before Cockerell's alterations.

Very recently, the balustrade, the vases and urns and even the two copies of the British Museum's Molossian hound, which were once on either side of the entrance portico, have all been replaced by artificial stone replicas made by the decorative plasterers, now of international renown, Hayles and Howe of Templegate, Bristol.[10] This dramatic improvement, which included the conservation of the surviving Coade stone urn and its re-erection in the Dairy Garden, was part of the restoration and enhancement of Humphry

Repton's surrounding parkland. With the exception of the one original Coade stone urn in the Dairy Garden, the scheme was completed in 2007 with the substantial support of the Heritage Lottery Fund.

Notes
[1] Bristol City Council, Blaise Castle Dairy Garden design brief, August 2002, figs. 4, 13; the surviving fragments from the other vases are now stored in the Orangery at Blaise. [2] A. Kelly, 'Coade stone in Georgian gardens', *Garden History*, vol. 16, no. 2, 1988, p. 111; see also F. Haskell and E. Penny, *Taste and the Antique: The Lure of Classical Sculpture 1500–1900* (New Haven, CT and London, 1981), pp.314–6. [3] Ibid; the Borghese vase is illustrated p.110. [4] As note 1. [5] D. Eveleigh, *'A Popular Retreat': Blaise Castle House and Estate* (Bristol, 1987), p.14. [6] Ibid, pp.19, 21. [7] P. Wakelin, *ODNB, Harford Family*. [8] As note 2, p.109. [9] Bristol Museum and Art Gallery, Fine Art files, Blaise urns. [10] The Molossian hound, a Roman copy of a Hellenistic original, was purchased in Rome by Henry Jennings in the 1750s; he brought it to England where many copies were made; see Blaise Castle Dairy Garden design brief, fig. 1.

Blaise Hamlet

On the green surrounded by the cottages of Blaise Hamlet

Memorial Pump and Sundial A1

Designer: unknown

Date: 1815
Material: Bath stone and metal
Dimensions: approximately 425cm high; base, 85cm square
Inscriptions: base – THESE COTTAGES / DESIGNED BY JOHN NASH ESQ / WERE ERECTED BY THE LATE / JOHN S HARFORD ESQ / IN THE YEAR 1811 / HIS SON JOHN S HARFORD ESQ / THE PRESENT OWNER / GRATEFULLY RECORDS / IN TESTIMONY OF FILIAL AFFECTION / THIS ACT OF HIS / BENEVOLENT PARENT / AUGUST 1815[1]
—: sundial – WATKINS BRISTOL
Status: Grade I
Owned by the National Trust
Condition: good

Nikolaus Pevsner called Blaise Hamlet 'the *nec plus ultra* of picturesque layout and design'.[2] Today, it not only continues to define a movement and to encapsulate dreams of a rural retreat, but it is also again influencing town planning. Designed by John Nash, assisted by Humphry Repton's son, George, it was commissioned by John Scandrett Harford for his retired estate workers. Harford, a Quaker banker and industrialist, died in 1815, just four years later. It was his son, John Scandrett Harford the younger, who appears to have erected the pump as a memorial to his father's benevolence. It is just possible that he may have only added the dedicatory inscription.

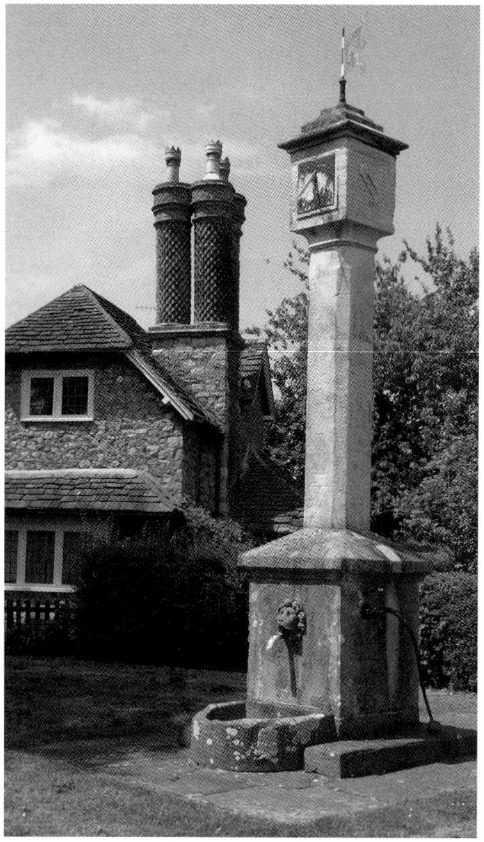

Blaise Hamlet Memorial Pump and Sundial

The general form of this combined pump and sundial are strikingly close to the early eighteenth century sundial, known as the Dial, which stood on Broad Quay and which was certainly still standing when John Scandrett Harford commissioned the pump.[3] The column at Blaise Hamlet is square with chamfered edges rather than round, and the square base that holds the pump mechanism is considerably larger. A lion's head, from which the water spouts, is on the south face of the base, and on the north face is the worn dedicatory inscription recorded above. Above the sun dial at Blaise is a gilded weathervane incised with the family initial 'H'. Below, on the south face, is the metal sundial signed by W. Watkins of St Augustine's Back, a shop that would have looked toward Broad Quay and the Dial itself. A relief of the Harford coat of arms is on each of the other three faces.

Notes
[1] As recorded 1982 on architect's drawing in NT files; date and some words now illegible. [2] Quoted by A. Foyle and B. Cherry, *Bristol* (New Haven and London, 2004), p.289. [3] The best visual record of the dial is a watercolour by H. O'Neill, 1824, BCMAG M2917, illus: F. Greenacre and S. Stoddard, *From Bristol to the Sea: Artists, the Avon Gorge and Bristol Harbour* (Bristol, 2005), p.86; the earliest image of the memorial pump at Blaise Hamlet may be Francis Danby's watercolour of c.1822, illus. Eveleigh, *'A Popular Retreat'*, p.18.

Brandon Hill

At top of the hill, best approached from the south-east corner of Berkeley Square

Cabot Tower B50

Designer: William Venn Gough

Contractors: Love and Waite of Backfields, St Paul's, Bristol
Date: 1898
Materials: red rubble Sherwood sandstone from Mansfield with limestone dressings
Dimensions: approx. 32m high

Inscriptions: on a bronze plaque on the east side – THIS TOWER / WAS ERECTED BY PUBLIC SUBSCRIPTION / IN THE 61ST YEAR OF THE REIGN OF QUEEN VICTORIA / TO COMMEMORATE THE FOURTH CENTENARY OF / THE DISCOVERY OF THE CONTINENT OF / NORTH AMERICA / ON THE 24TH OF JUNE, 1497, BY / JOHN CABOT / WHO SAILED FROM THIS PORT IN THE / BRISTOL SHIP MATTHEW, WITH A BRISTOL CREW / UNDER LETTERS PATENT GRANTED BY KING HENRY VII / TO THAT NAVIGATOR AND HIS SONS / LEWIS, SEBASTIAN AND SANCTUS.

—: on a bronze plaque on the south side, underneath a relief of a dove surrounded by a garland of olive leaves – THIS TABLET IS PLACED HERE BY THE / BRISTOL BRANCH OF THE PEACE SOCIETY / IN THE EARNEST HOPE THAT PEACE AND / FRIENDSHIP MAY EVER CONTINUE BETWEEN / THE KINDRED PEOPLES OF THIS COUNTRY / AND AMERICA. / "GLORY TO GOD IN THE HIGHEST AND ON / EARTH PEACE, AND GOODWILL TOWARDS MEN." / LUKE 2.14

—: on a bronze plaque on the west side – THE FOUNDATION STONE OF THIS TOWER / WAS LAID BY / THE MARQUESS OF DUFFERIN & AVA / ON THE 24TH JUNE, 1897, / AND THE COMPLETED TOWER WAS OPENED / BY THE SAME NOBLEMAN / ON THE 6TH SEPTEMBER, 1898. / W. HOWELL DAVIES, CHAIRMAN OF THE EXECUTIVE COMMITTEE / E. G. CLARKE, / J. W. ARROWSMITH, / HON. SECRETARIES. /

Status: Grade II

Owned by Bristol City Council

Condition: poor; the coats of arms are damaged, and columns and side spirelets are missing from the aedicules; public access currently forbidden for safety reasons (July 2010).

Cabot Tower was built to celebrate the 400th anniversary of John Cabot's departure from the Bristol in 1497 in the small ship *The Matthew* with a crew of eighteen, and his 'discovery' of Newfoundland, the mainland of North America.

The tower commanding this prominent site is one of Bristol's most conspicuous landmarks. 'As a piece of stage scenery it is highly effective and one always expects to hear a muezzin crying from its lofty curved balconies.'[1] Or Rapunzel, perhaps, letting down her hair. The architecture has been described by English Heritage as 'Tudor Gothic revival'. [2] At ground level, on each of the four sides, is a large white stone aedicule, one of which forms the entrance surround. Inside those are deeply-carved stone reliefs. Over the entrance is Bristol's coat of arms. The other reliefs are the arms of Henry VII, the Society of Merchant Venturers and Venice, of which Cabot was a citizen. Four letter 'C's are cut in the stonework, beneath the reliefs. These signify the four centuries since Cabot's epic voyage. Below these are the three large bronze inscription plates. At the very top of the tower is a ball finial on which stands the carved figure of an angel with folded wings. One description of this figure, too high to be seen clearly from the ground, is 'a gilded, winged figure representing the spirit of commerce mounted on a globe of the world'.[3] The right hand is raised as if giving a blessing, and in the left is a model of a ship. The viewing gallery is open on all four sides and there are three engraved brass panels (the fourth is missing) on which various sites within the 360° panorama are pinpointed.

The design of the foundations for the tower allowed for the placing of four Russian guns, captured during the Crimean War, at the four corners of the platform. These had been placed on the site in 1857, but were to be removed soon after the outbreak of the Second World War.[4]

A beacon was installed at the top of the tower in the 1920s as a navigational aid for aircraft. It flashed BRISTOL in Morse code. A computer-controlled programme now enables the sending of different messages, which an ever-increasing number of people cannot read.[5]

The mayor's (R. H. Symes) announcement to the Bristol Council in 1897 that the Royal

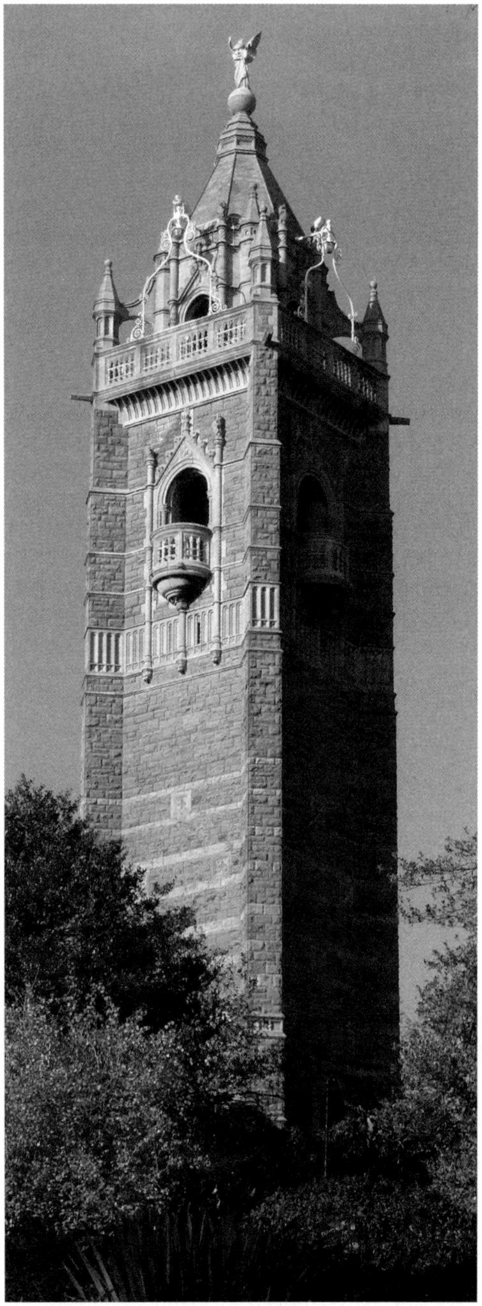

William Venn Gough, *Cabot Tower*

Society of Canada had invited the corporation to send two representatives to its next meeting to celebrate the anniversary may have acted as a spur to Bristol. Two former mayors were present when a memorial tablet was placed in the Province Building in Halifax.[6] A Cabot celebration committee was subsequently formed in Bristol.

The cost of the tower was £3,300. This sum was raised with some difficulty by public subscription, and the total was not achieved until February 1899.[7] An appeal brochure inadvertently admits to the fundraising problems:

> To loyal citizens a further inducement to help will be the fact that up to the present time no steps have been taken to indicate in any public place that the year 1897 is the 60th of her Majesty's glorious reign; and on the tablet specifying the object of the Tower an inscription will be added recording that fact, so the Cabot Tower will really serve the two purposes.[8]

The main panel does record that the tower was 'erected in the 61st year of her reign'.

A competition was held, and the designs of William Venn Gough and George Oatley were shortlisted. The other entrants were J. Hart, J. H. Hirst and E. P. Warren, all Bristol architects, although Warren was practising in London.[9] Other proposals for the memorial were presented in the Bristol press before William Venn Gough's design was chosen.[10] One design suggestion was for a statue of Cabot together with one of his sons. John Fisher of the Berkeley Square branch of the Kensington School of Art was the designer, and the proposed site was on Clifton Down, in place of the Observatory.[11] Several Clifton residents then petitioned the Merchant Venturers, the owners of both the land and the former windmill, and its society duly rejected the proposal.[12] After further discussion, Brandon Hill emerged as the most suitable site. Even here, objections were made on the grounds that 'persons who climbed the tower might possibly, with the aid of a telescope see in to the back gardens of some of the surrounding houses.' [13] Another proposal, drawn by Samuel Loxton, the prolific Bristol newspaper illustrator, shows a vast domed building, one hundred feet high. Set on a huge square promenade, with flights of steps on four sides and a winged Victory at the summit of the cupola, this was also to serve as a museum or an art gallery.

A crowd of 50,000 people are said to have gathered when the Marquess of Dufferin and Ava came to lay the foundation stone on 24 June 1897.[14] He had been a governor-general of Canada and:

> he was conducted in state from Temple Meads to the Council House [then in Corn Street] where he was presented with the Freedom of the City, and then to the Victoria Rooms where he addressed a brilliant luncheon gathering on the qualities of Cabot and the virtues of the Bristolians who sent him forth.[15]

Only fifteen months later, the marquess returned to open the tower on 6 September 1898.

Recently, Professor Paul Gough has suggested that the raising of the Cabot Tower was part of a battle between two ruling elites for control of the commemorative landscape of Bristol.[16] On Brandon Hill, he argues, the Tory-based Merchant Venturers were in command. Later, a higher tower, the Wills Memorial Building for Bristol University (1925), was the creation of non-conformist and liberal industrialists, especially the Wills family. However, the plaque on the Cabot Tower records that J. W. Arrowsmith, head of the Bristol printing firm, was one of the two honorary secretaries to the memorial committee. This demolishes a thin thesis, but usefully draws attention to the importance of this distinctly liberal figure. He was already playing a crucial role in the foundation of the university and had been an honorary secretary for the Industrial and Fine Art Exhibition in 1893, and was the initiator of the statue to Edward Colston and perhaps also of that to Edmund Burke (see Colston Avenue and St Augustine's Parade).

Notes

[1] T. Edwards, *British Cities: Bristol* (London, 1951), p.75. [2] English Heritage, 901-1/41/18, p.130. [3] J. Belsey, 'Towering discoveries', *Offbeat Bristol* (Bristol, 1992), p.50. [4] A. King, *The Centenary of the Cabot Memorial Tower 1897–1997* (Bristol, 1997); R. Winstone, *Bristol As It Was 1937–1939* (Bristol, 1987) pl. 142. [5] Ibid. [6] Ibid. [7] Bristol Central Library, *Minute Book of Cabot Celebration Committee*, Acc. No. B4398. [8] 'Cabot 1897 Appeal for £5,000'; B. Buchanan, 'How Cabot got his tower', *Bristol Evening Post*, 6 September 1974. [9] King op. cit.; Warren's entry was illustrated in *The Builder*, 6 October 1898, p.308. [10] Two of Gough's drawings for the tower are in the BRO, Acc. No. 4312(29). [11] Patrick McGrath, *The Merchant Venturers of Bristol* (Bristol, 1975), pp.432–3. [12] Ibid. [13] *Bristol Observer*, 17 April 1897, quoted by Andy King; see note 4. [14] Ibid. [15] As note 4. [16] P. Gough and S. Morgan, 'Manipulating the metonymic', *Journal of Historical Geography*, 30, 2004, p.668.

Bridewell Street

Above the main entrance of the Old Magistrates' Court on Bridewell St.

Justice C9

Sculptor: Edward Sheppard

Architect: Josiah Thomas

Date: 1879
Material: Portland stone
Dimensions: approx. 3m high
Inscribed on the base: E SHEPPARD SCULPTOR / BRISTOL....
Status: Grade II
Owned by Bristol City Council
Condition: poor

Justice sits uneasily on the curved pediment. Her right hand rests on a broadsword, but the scales are missing from her left hand. Like

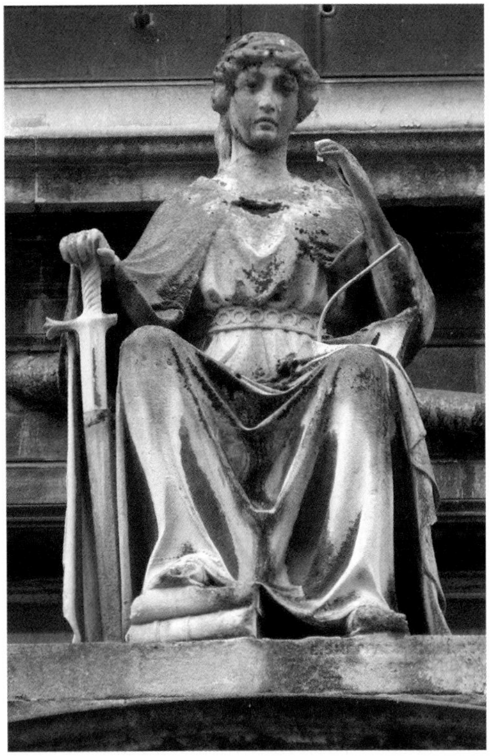

Edward Sheppard, *Justice*

Justice on the Old Council House in Corn Street, she is not blindfolded. And she seems similarly superfluous to the design of the façade.

The Old Magistrates' Court is presently impressively black and empty. It is distinguished by its extensive and excellent terracotta panels and perhaps the finest nineteenth century iron railings and gates to have survived in Bristol. They are replete with the motifs of the aesthetic movement. The architect, Josiah Thomas, was the city surveyor.[1]

The sculptor, Edward Sheppard, is for the moment otherwise unknown. He is recorded in Bristol directories from 1871 (when he was listed as a carver of York Street, St Paul's) until 1887 (when he is described as a sculptor and as a stone and wood carver of Wilson Street, St Paul's).[2]

Notes
[1] A. Gomme, M. Jenner and B. Little, *Bristol, an Architectural History*(London, 1979), pp.393, 442. [2] Wright & Co. Bristol Directories; in 1881 he was at 7 Paul St and in 1884 at 22 Paul St.

Broad Quay

At the junction of Broad Quay and Narrow Quay near Broad Quay House

King George V Memorial Fountain

C54

Sculptor: Derek Carr and unknown
Architects: Alec French Partnership

Dates: 1905 and 1982
Materials and dimensions: Portland stone figures, 170cm high, 135cm wide, 75cm deep; red brick arch, 275cm high; pool, 720cm diameter; cast aluminium lion's head spout, 95cm diameter
Inscription: on the east side of the brick arch – IN MEMORY OF KING GEORGE V 1910 – 1936
Status: not listed
Owned by Bristol City Council
Condition: good; fountain works intermittently

This is a distinctly two-faced fountain. On one side is a lion's head that occasionally spouts water and an inscription that is easily overlooked. The inscription tells us that the fountain, erected in 1982, commemorates King George V, who had died nearly half a century earlier. On the other side are two of the six large sculptures that were once on the nearby Co-operative Society headquarters, designed in 1908 and replaced by Broad Quay House in 1981. The royal memorial was a simple matter of expediency; a mere convenience to enable a long-unused fund, made up of public donations for a memorial to the king, to be used in part for a very different purpose. The fountain's principal function, and the impetus behind its creation, was the preservation of two of the Co-operative sculptures. So back to back with the regal lion's head commemorating the king are the two figures that once so well represented the egalitarian principles of the Co-operative Society.

The two salvaged statues are set within a semi-circular red brick and concrete arch. One represents a farm worker, with rolled-up sleeves, kneeling and about to lift two sheaves of corn. The other figure is a coal miner. Stripped to the waist, he crouches under the arch, supporting his weight on the rocks around him. A pickaxe and a miner's lamp are nearby. Two pools, one higher than the other, are contained within a circular wall approximately sixty centimetres high. Water should pour from the mouth of a lion's head spout on the Broad Quay House side. The head is centred below the inscription that dedicates the memorial to George V. It was designed and cast in aluminium by Derek Carr of Timsbury.[1] A spotlight is directed onto the head.

The Bristol headquarters of the Co-operative Wholesale Society, known as the CWS Western Depot, was opened in May 1906 on the site of what is now Broad Quay House.[2] Old photographs show that it dominated the centre for nearly eighty years .

When the depot was about to be demolished in 1973 and its sculptures removed, there was 'an outcry'.[3] The Bristol trades council and amenity groups protested about the loss of a landmark. Six statues, including those of the farm worker and miner – idealised representations of the trades of many of the members of the society – were donated in that year to the city by the CWS.[4] The sculptor is unknown, but the architect was F. E. L. Harris, ARIBA.[5] Two figures appear on an elevation drawn by the architect in 1902 for the premises between Broad Quay and Thunderbolt Street. Four other statues were said to have been placed in storage, but they are not now in any Bristol Museum store.[6]

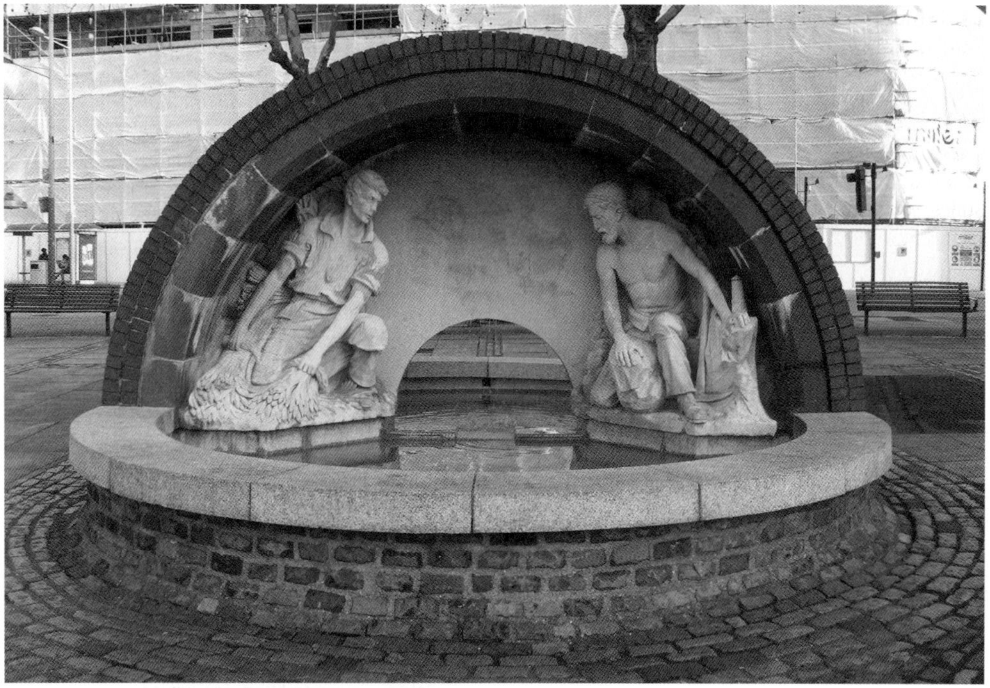

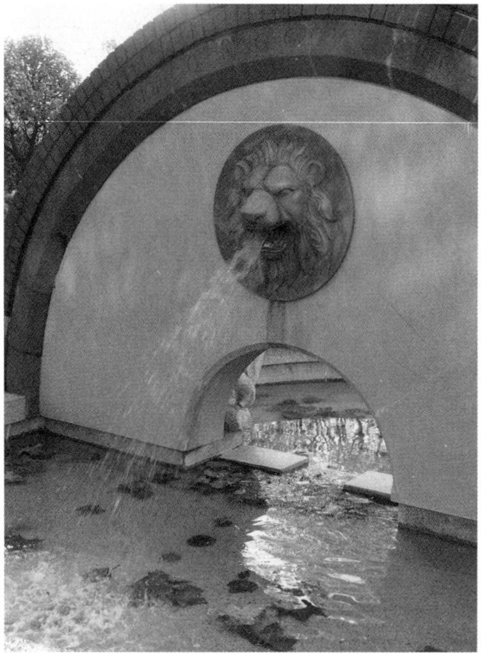

(above) *Figures from the Co-operative Society building on King George V Memorial Fountain*
(left) **Derek Carr**, *King George V Memorial Fountain*

The complex history of this memorial began with the death of George V in 1936. 'In 1937 an appeal was launched to build a memorial to King George… Bristol responded quickly and generously.'[7] However, no agreement could be reached on what form the memorial should take. Suggestions included: a pillar topped by a beacon, an old sailing ship, a sunken pool and fountains, and a 68ft metal monument to resemble Cleopatra's Needle. By the late 1960s the fund, which was in the care of the city council, had reached about £8,000, and a former lord mayor was quoted as stating that 'something should have been done long ago… the money cannot be used for anything else'.[8] No progress was made until Broad Quay House was being constructed and its architects, the Alec French Partnership, were working on the landscaping of the surrounding area in 1981. Pressure to preserve the figures from the demolished Co-operative building led to the idea of an architectural feature that would incorporate them. It was suggested that the King George V Memorial Trust could provide much of the funding if a memorial was also included. 'Rather than let these sculptures gather dust in the museum warehouse we incorporated them into a sculptural arch of the same dimensions' as the original arch over the CWS entrance, from which the miner and the farm worker came.[9] Council minutes from 7 July 1981 show that the cost of the fountain, £25,000, was met by the King George V Memorial Fund Trustees. The Standard Life Assurance Company, owners of Broad Quay House, would pay £30,000 for landscaping the area facing 'the centre' and the costs of landscaping the area facing Narrow Quay – £28,000 – would be met by Bristol city council. The monument itself was fastidiously integrated into the landscaping of the quayside. The cobblestones run up the side walls of the fountain and the surface bricks of the arch match those of Broad Quay House. Sadly, it is no less anomalous, because of the care that went into its design.

The Lord Mayor of Bristol, George Maggs, officially opened the memorial on 27 May 1982.

Notes

[1] Richard Lee, 'A Spell of History', *Evening Post*, 15 March 1983. [2] Co-operative Group, Manchester, *The CWS in Bristol* (Manchester, 1933), p.8. [3] Julie Hendy, 'Statues are set to return', *Bristol Evening Post*, 19 September 1980. [4] BCC Engineers' Department, 'Memorials, fountains and statues', December 1982, p.35. [5] F.E.L. Harris, ARIBA, architect, 1 Balloon Street, Manchester; scale drawing 1902, BRO. [6] As note 4; a search made by the curator of the Industrial Museum in 2005 was unable to trace them. [7] Q. Morgan, 'Cash in "forgotten fund" sleeps on', *Evening Post*, c.1966. [8] Ibid. [9] Richard Lee, Alec French Partnership.

Broad Quay

Panels on the Redcliffe Way façade of Broad Quay House

Aspects of Bristol's History C55

Sculptors: Philippa Threlfall and Kennedy Collings

Architects: Alec French Partnership

Date: 1981
Materials: fifteen ceramic plaques made in terracotta and buff clays with manganese and copper oxides and copper lustre glazes
Dimensions: each plaque 100cm high, 150cm wide
Inscriptions: the texts on the panels are set out in the descriptions given below
Status: not listed
Owned by Standard Life Assurance
Condition: good

The theme was described by the architects of the project as a 'depiction of aspects of Bristol's history through eight centuries, from the city's Royal Charter in the 13th century, to the building of Concorde'.[1]

There are fifteen rectangular, glazed ceramic panels set into the brickwork approximately four metres above the pavement. They are all at the same level and placed at equal intervals from each other. Every panel has the same cartouche 'based on the dolphins and anchor of the eighteenth century arms of Edward Colston'.[2] The central circular images are all different. From the left they are:

1 The reverse of the thirteenth-century common seal of the burgesses of Bristol showing a tower of Bristol Castle's Watergate approached by a single-masted merchant ship with a sail. The Latin text around the edge of the seal is: '† SECRETIC CLAVIS SVPORT NAVITANAVIS PORTA' CVSTODIT PORT' VIGILINDI CEPDIT'

(right) Philippa Threlfall and Kennedy Collins, *Obverse of the common seal of Bristol*

2 A fourteenth-century roof boss with two intertwining dragons from the church of St Thomas the Martyr.

3 The great stone keep of Bristol Castle, with a trumpeter in one tower, taken from the obverse of the thirteenth century common seal of the burgesses of Bristol. Text around the rim: '† SIGILLVM: COMMVNE: BURGENSIVM BRISTOLLIE:'.

4 St Katherine's wheel from a badge of the Bristol Guild of Weavers.

5 Cabot's ship *The Matthew* based on a fifteenth century admiralty court seal and contemporary drawings. Text around the circumference: 'ON THE MATTHEW JOHN CABOT 1497'.

6 A view of St Mary Redcliffe, based on Millerd's plan of Bristol from 1673. The truncated quotation has long been optimistically attributed to Queen Elizabeth I. Text: 'ye parrifh Church of St Marie Redcliffe – The faireft goodlieft and most famous parrifh church in England'.

7 Sixteenth-century Common Seal of the Mayor & Commonalty of the City of Bristol, showing the city shield and unicorn supporters; granted by Elizabeth I and in used in the sixteenth and seventeenth centuries. Text: 'SIGILLUM · COMMUNE · MAIORIS · ET · COMMUNITATIS · CIVITATIS ·BRISTOLLIAE · A^{O} · DOMINI 1569'.

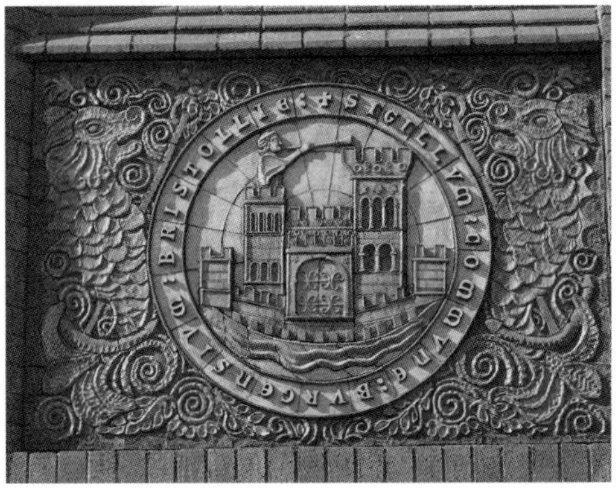

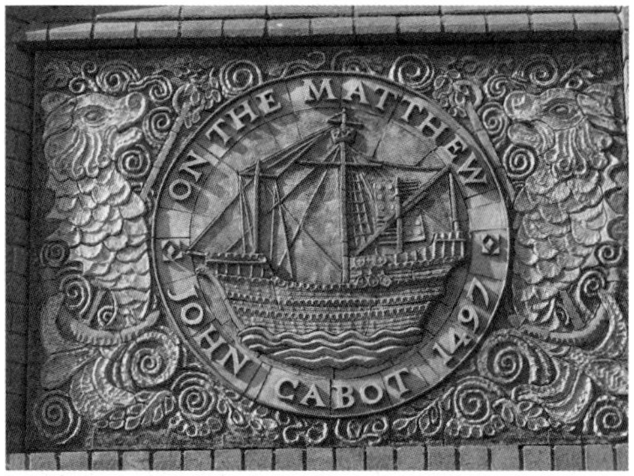

Philippa Threlfall and Kennedy Collins, *The Matthew*

8 A medal, struck to mark the fall of Bristol to the Royalists in 1643, has a view of Bristol from the south. Text around the circumference: 'CIVITATIS · BRISTOLL · REDUCTA · 1643 ·'.

9 Seventeenth-century halfpenny trade token issued by the Mermaid Inn. Text around the image of a mermaid holding what looks like a large spoon: 'MREMAYD · ON THE · BACKE'.

10 Eighteenth-century penny token, issued in 1796, showing the façade of John Wood's Exchange. Text: 'EXCHANGE / 1796 / BRISTOL'.

11 An eighteenth-century tobacconist's sign depicting a North American native smoking a pipe against a background of tobacco leaves. Text around circumference: 'FINE SHAGG TOBACCO'. 12 An eighteenth-century penny token displaying a glass kiln. The outer text reads: 'SUCCCESS TO THE GLASS MANUFACTORY'.

13 The *Great Britain* appears in profile above the flying swan taken from the stern of the ship. Text: 'GREAT BRITAIN / 1843 / BRISTOL / SCREW STEAMSHIP'.

14 The wheat-sheaf symbol of the Co-operative Wholesale Society that built the nineteenth-century building on this site. Text on a cartouche: 'LABOUR AND WAIT'.

15 Representing the twentieth century: an air

intake from a Concorde engine.

The source material for the images and texts was drawn from the Bristol Record Office, St Nicholas Church Museum (now closed), Bristol City Museums and Art Gallery, W. D. & H. O. Wills Archives, *SS Great Britain* and the CWS archives in Manchester.[3] The commission was one of two ceramic-based works that Philippa Threlfall and her husband and partner, Kennedy Collings, undertook for the Alec French Partnership. The other is *Exploration* off Redcliff Street. They were also responsible for the fine ceramic panels for the Friendly Society in Colston Street opposite Colston Hall.

Notes
[1] Notes from Alec French Partnership, the architects. [2] Ibid. [3] From a broadsheet: 'Description of mural panels at Broad Quay House', BRL sculpture files.

Broad Street, Christ Church

On the entrance façade of Christ Church

Quarter Jacks C19

Sculptor: attributed to James Paty I

Architect: Thomas Paty

Date: 1728
Material: painted wood (oak)
Dimensions: 1.6m high
Status: not listed
Owned by Bristol Museums and Art Gallery[1]
Condition: poor

Bristol Museums and Art Gallery is the owner of these ancient quarter jacks and it is surely time that they were taken into care, once again. It is a long and intriguing story.

James Paty I is presumed to have been their carver in 1728.[2] Then, they were on the Wine Street façade of Christ Church and looked down on Bristol's High Cross at the very centre of the city.[3] There had been quarter jacks on Christ Church over a century before James

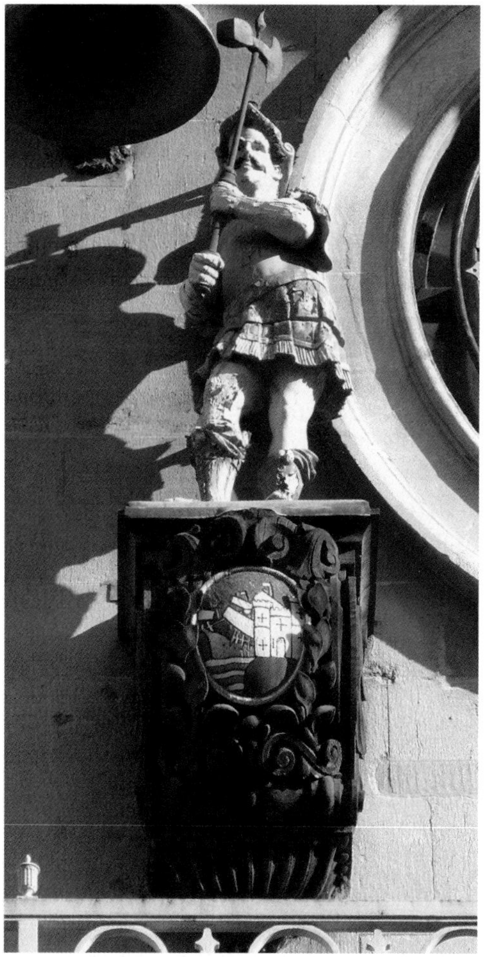

James Paty I (attributed to), ***Christ Church Quarter Jack***

Paty's were erected. William Tyson recorded references among the church wardens' papers to 'Jackes' in 1608 and to 'Quarter Jackes' in 1616 and to the tiling, sealing and plastering of the 'Jack-house' in the same year.[4] Thus, it is likely that the present figures were commissioned as replacements for much earlier figures. They do not so much belong 'to a folk tradition rather than a sculptural one', as has recently been rather patronisingly suggested,[5] but instead almost certainly deliberately echo the early seventeenth-century style of their predecessors.

A carver and mason, Paty was admitted a free burgess of Bristol in 1721 on payment of a fine, suggesting that he was not a native of Bristol, but the earliest of that remarkable dynasty of Patys, 'Makers of Eighteenth-century Bristol'.[6] It was his nephew, Thomas Paty, whose business declared the medieval church ruinous in 1783, and who designed the new building, begun in 1786. It was completed in 1790/1 by his great nephew, William Paty.

The quarter jacks were removed from the old building and subsequently stored in the new tower.[7] The poet Robert Southey was baptised in Christ Church in 1774 and he recalled the statues with affection in a letter of 1806. 'I have many a time stopt with my satchel on my back to see them strike. My father had a great love for these poor quarter-boys, who had regulated all his movements for about twenty years; and when the church was rebuilt, offered to subscribe largely to their reestablishment; but the Wine streeters had no taste for the arts, and no feeling for old friends, and God knows what became of the poor fellows.' [8] Southey also remembered seeing them represented on the stage: 'only stage quarter-boys, and not the real ones'. This was in a pantomime at the Theatre Royal, entitled *Brystowe, or Harlequin Marmer*, when their appearance was greeted 'with unbounded applause'.[9] In 1813 there seems to have been an early attempt at their erection on the new church, but the expenses at £300 were too high.[10] Some time thereafter, 'Mr Oldham, a Haberdasher of Wine Street' purchased them from the vestry.[11] He evidently lent them out for special occasions.

> In the procession which was formed on the 19th July 1821 in Bristol in honour of the Coronation of George IV these two figures were placed on a Platform decorated with laurel & accompanied by a banner and preceded the Gentlemen of Christ Church… These Quarter Boys… were recognized by

many persons & afforded no small degree of pleasure.[12]

In 1824 the figures were sold to a bookseller, Charles Frost of Broad Street, who sold them on to George Weare Braikenridge of Brislington, the great antiquarian collector.[13] In 1908 one of his sons bequeathed them, and much of his remarkable collection, to Bristol Art Gallery. On 9 July of that year, King Edward VII and Queen Alexandra visited Bristol Art Gallery before opening the Royal Edward Dock at Avonmouth. A newspaper cutting from a day or two earlier reports that the statues:

> now stand over a doorway in the room in which the King is expected to lunch, so the boys will have the honour of attending the civic feast given to Edward VII and his greatly beloved Queen… it seems a pity that they cannot be recovered and re-erected on Christchurch.[14]

Four years later, in 1912, the Bristol Art Gallery committee agreed to the conditional loan of the quarter jacks to Christ Church. The clock mechanism to operate the figures was presented in memory of the former rector, and carved wooden corbels were made to support them.

The quarter jacks are jointed at the waist, and the upper torsos turn on pivots. They still work, but only as a result of repeated conservation work. As well as repainting, there is evidence of extensive repairs in 1933, 1974, 1986 and more recently. They again need attention, and it is time to consider their retirement. Good replicas made of more durable materials should succeed them.

Notes

[1] BCMAG, Accession No. 224, 28 August 1912, General Register, p.169. [2] W. Ison, *The Georgian Buildings of Bristol* (London, 1952 (1978)), p.39. [3] For an engraving of the High Cross and Christ Church and the Quarter Jacks beyond, see W. Barrett, *History and Antiquities of the City of Bristol* (Bristol, 1789), illus. f.p.464. [4] BCRL 24411 (BL2H), unnumbered MS papers of William Tyson FSA concerning clocks and bells of Bristol, transcript from *Bristol Mercury*, 8 January 1810. [5] G. Priest and P. Cobb, *The Paty Family: Makers of Eighteenth-Century Bristol* (Bristol, 2003), p.16. [6] The subtitle of Priest's book. [7] As note 4. [8] Quoted by Nicholls and Taylor, *Bristol Past and Present*, vol. II, p.172; from C.C. Southey, *The Life and Correspondence of Robert Southey* (London, 1849–51), vol. III, p.32. [9] As note 4. [10] Ibid, undated folio. [11] BCMAG, G.W. Braikenridge's catalogue entries to M2345 & M2346. [12] Ibid. [13] BCMAG Fine Art Files, Quarter Jacks loans out, report to committee 1981. [14] Ibid.

Broad Street, Guildhall

On the Guildhall façade in Broad Street

Guildhall Figures C17

Sculptors: John Thomas

Architect: Richard Shackleton Pope

Date: c.1843–6
Material: Bath stone
Status: Grade II*
Owned by Bristol City Council
Condition: fair; the Guildhall's Broad Street façade and sculptures were cleaned in 2006–7 and the figures were netted

The Guildhall and the Assize Courts are in different streets and of different dates, but they back onto one another, and, after a brutal internal reorganisation in 1961, now function as one building.

The Guildhall, Broad Street, was designed by Bristol Corporation's surveyor, Richard Shackleton Pope, in 1843 and it is 'historically noteworthy as the first town hall in England to adopt the national, i.e. Gothic style'.[1] His building was influenced by Sir Charles Barry's Houses of Parliament, begun in 1839, and the six figures on the Guildhall's façade are by the

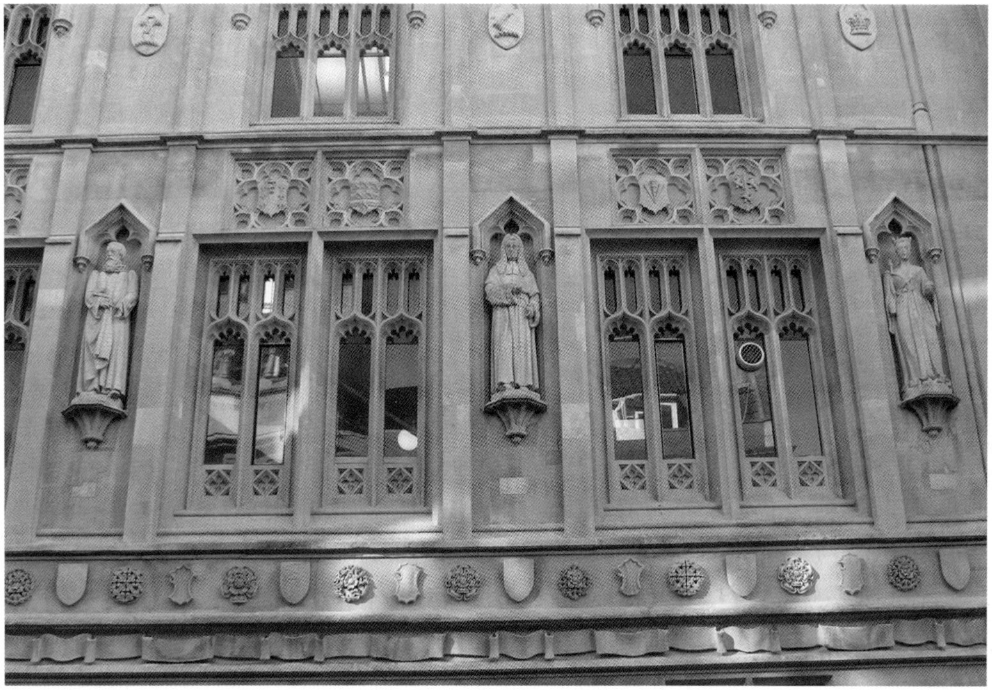

John Thomas, *Guildhall statues of Alderman Whitson, John Dunning and Queen Victoria*

young sculptor, John Thomas, whom Barry had chosen to superintend the stone carving on the new parliament buildings.[2] The foundation stone for the Guildhall was laid on 30 October 1843 by the mayor, James Gibbs, 'with great Masonic ceremony'.[3]

The six figures on the Guildhall façade are all in narrow niches between the windows on the first floor. From left to right, facing the building, they are: alderman Thomas Whitson, the Right Honourable John Dunning and Queen Victoria. To the right of the central tower are King Edward III (who granted Bristol county status in 1373), Sir Michael Foster and Edward Colston. John Whitson (c.1553–1629) was twice mayor and twice master of the Merchant Venturers, an MP and, like Edward Colston, a great philanthropist. Sir Michael Foster (1689–1763) was a recorder of Bristol and an outstanding judge. John Dunning, first Baron Ashburton (1731–83), was also a recorder of Bristol and an exceptional barrister and distinguished politician.

The initials 'JT' appear on one side of the octagonal corbels of three of the statues: Whitson, Edward III and Victoria. Directly above each statue, between the windows of the second floor, are heraldic emblems. These emblems relate to each figure and are carved on shields held on cords by cuffed hands. There are also 'Shields in the coupled quatrefoils over the windows [which] bear the arms of eminent men connected with Bristol's history, such as Cabot, Penn, Camden and Southey'.[4]

The face of Edward Colston and the two judges are much eroded, and Queen Victoria's sceptre and the cross of her orb have broken away. Fingers and hands are missing or damaged on most of the six statues.

There are said to be full-sized casts of all six figures inside the building. Certainly Queen Victoria and the two recorders are in the lobby above the entrance to the building. These were either cast when the originals were in better condition, or they were 'improved' on being cast, possibly in 1961, when the interior was altered. On Pope's rather mean central staircase is a heavily painted stone figure, approximately 2.5m high, of King Alfred, which almost certainly dates from the 1840s.

Notes

[1] A. Gomme, M. Jenner and B. Little, *Bristol: An Architectural History* (London, 1979), p.229. [2] R. Gunnis, *Dictionary of British Sculptors, 1660–1851* (revised edition, London, 1951), pp.388, 389. [3] J. Latimer, *Annals of Bristol in the Nineteenth Century* (Bristol, 1887), p.345; R. Winstone, *Bristol As It Was, 1960–62* (Bristol, 1981) pl. 24, has photo of King Charles I, very eroded, being removed from the Guildhall on 4 March 1960. [4] C. Crick, *Victorian Buildings in Bristol* (Bristol, 1975), p.17.

Broad Street

Façade of 37 & 38 Broad Street and drainpipe hopper in John Street

The Edward Everard Façade and Drainpipe Hopper Dragons C16

Decoration: Willam James Neatby

Architect: Henry Williams

Date: 1900–1
Materials: glazed ceramic tiles and terracotta
Inscription: in letterforms designed by Everard Everard – GUTENBURG [sic] / MORRIS / EDWARD EVERARD.
—: also two complete alphabets, one in Gutenberg-style capitals and one in William Morris's first typeface, Golden
Tiles by Doulton and Company
Status: Grade II*
Owned by The Royal Bank of Scotland Group
Condition: good

Edward Everard 'saw himself as a craftsman printer in the tradition of Gutenberg as the father of printing, and Morris, as the renewer of craftwork'.[1] He commissioned this extravagant façade to his printing works from the architect, sculptor and designer William James Neatby (1860–1910), one of Doulton & Co.'s 'principal artists'.[2] Everard himself described the

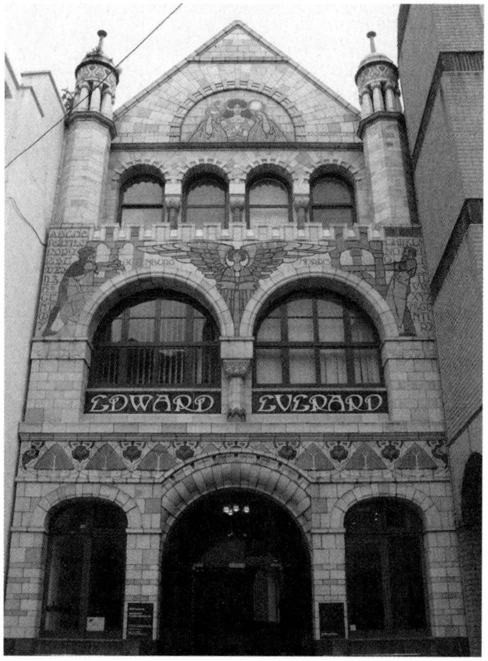

William James Neatby, *Edward Everard façade*

completed decorations as uncompromisingly Celtic, but Andor Gomme suggests that in 'place of Everard's original idea of combining Celtic and Byzantine forms, Neatby went for a kind of Art Nouveau in the largest decorative façade of its kind in Britain'.[3] It was Everard who requested that the building should 'repeat the salient features of St John's Gateway'.[4]

The façade's bright polychrome tiles are set against a background of creamy-white tiles that Doulton & Co., Lambeth, called Carrara-ware because of their resemblance to marble.[5] The figure in the pediment holds a lamp and mirror, representing light and truth. Some way below her is the winged Spirit of Literature holding an open book. On either side of this figure are Gutenberg, who introduced moveable metal type into Europe, and William Morris, the leader of the late-Victorian renaissance in fine printing. Both are toiling at their presses, and

William James Neatby, ***Edward Everard entrance gate*** **(detail)**

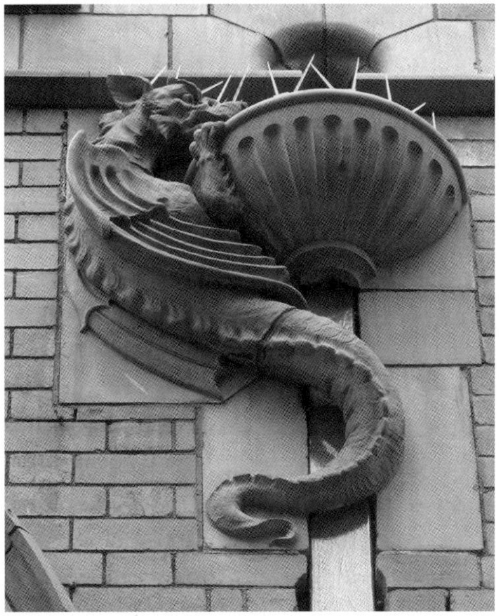

William James Neatby, ***Edward Everard hopper dragon in John Street***

around them are their own respective alphabets. Below the two first-floor arches is Edward Everard's name in the typeface that he designed. 'EE', surrounded by a wreath of oak and mistletoe in repoussé copper, decorates the heavy wrought iron gates below.

A Bristol newspaper reported that the 'idea of an illuminated building originated with Mr. Everard' and that the use of Carrara-ware on this scale had never been attempted before.[6] The building was welcomed as:

> one of the most courageous attempts to get colour and interest into our streets... Bristol is a very dull sort of city and not easily aroused but when the scaffolding was removed... the Police had to regulate the traffic [for two days].[7]

Another Neatby commission, using ceramic tiles, is the Harrods Food Hall in Knightsbridge, London.

The interior and rear of the building were demolished and developed by the Legal and General Assurance Society for National Westminster Court. The project was completed in 1972. Outside in John Street, only one spectacular terracotta dragon, clinging to a drainpipe hopper, survives to suggest the richness of the side elevations in Cattybrook brick with much terracotta detailing. A double dragon-hopper is now preserved in the foyer.

A plaque in the foyer, unveiled by Mrs Lilian Nicol on 17 October 1990, recognises the craftmanship of this lady's father, Walter Thomas Yoxall, who first worked on the façade at the age of 18 and went on to be a master tiler in Bristol.

Notes

[1] Gomme et al., *An Architectural History*, p.409. [2] E. Everard, *A Bristol Printing House, Spoken of in Several Fragments by Edward Everard* (London, 1902). [3] As note 1, p.411. [4] As note 2. [5] As note 2. [6] *Western Daily Press*, 15 November 1902. [7] J. Miller Carr of Doulton's, *The Stone Trades Journal*, May 1903.

Broad Street, St John's Gate

The city gateway beneath St John's church tower and spire facing Broad Street

Brennus and Bellinus C15

Sculptor: unknown

Date: c.1700
Material: stone
Dimensions: approx. 2m high
Status: not listed
Vested in the Churches Conservation Trust
Condition: fair, conserved 2006

Brennus and Belinus were the legendary founders of Bristol. Robert Ricart, Bristol's town clerk, popularised this ancient myth in his history, *The Maire of Bristowe, is Kalendar* (known as the Mayor's Calendar) in the late fifteenth century.[1] The two brothers were supposedly the sons of the first king of England, and following their father's death they led an army of Gauls and Britons into Italy, where they sacked much of Rome in 391 BC. On this occasion, it was only the alertness of geese that saved the Capitol itself. Ricart continues the story:

> After they had this doon, the said two brethern retorned home into this land of grete Bretaigne, with their Bretonnes, and dwelled here togeder in grete joye. And then Brynne first founded and billed this worshypfull towne of Bristut, that now is Bristowe, and set it upon a little hill; that is to say, betweene Seinte Nicholas Yate, Seint Johnes Yate, Seint Leonardes Yate, and the Newe Yate.[2]

Bristol, of course, is remarkable not for its age, but for its youth. There was probably a millennium to pass between that early sacking of Rome and the presence of a settlement of any significant size at the junction of the Avon and the Frome.

'Seint Johnes Yate', the old North Gate, is below the tower and spire of the church of St

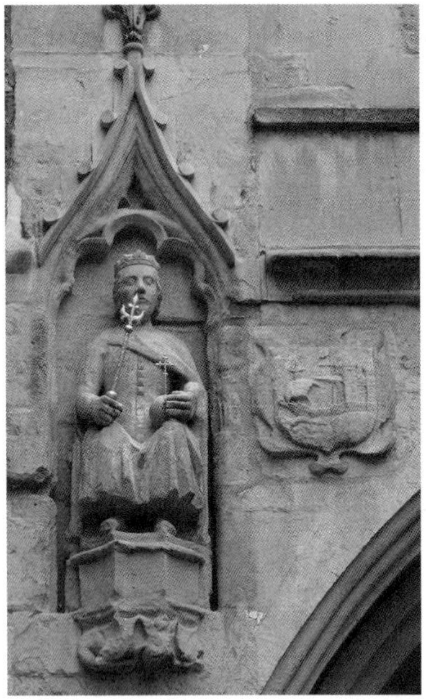

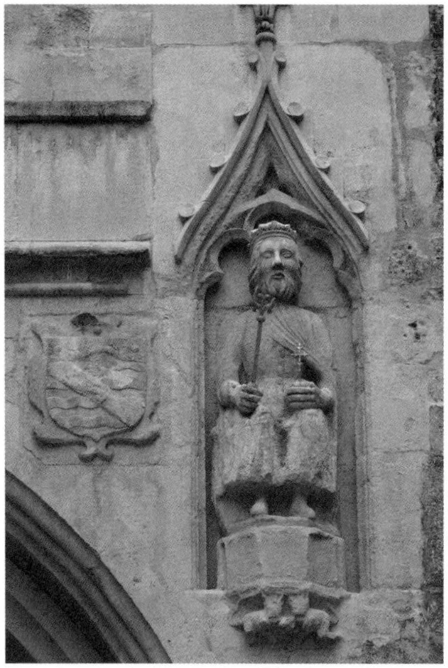

(left) St John's Gate, *Brennus* (right) St John's Gate, *Bellinus*

John the Baptist, and it is the only medieval Bristol gateway that survives. Founded in the twelfth century, the present building dates from 1350 to 1500.

When the figures were repainted in 1935, Professor Tristram of Bristol University dated them to the fourteenth century. Professor Pevsner wisely gave no date in 1958, but Andrew Foyle in the revised *Pevsner Architectural Guide* for Bristol in 2004 bravely suggests 'possibly seventeenth century'.

Neither the Stuart coat of arms above the arch nor the arms of the City of Bristol and of the Merchant Venturers, which are uncomfortably close to the two niches, are likely to be a secure indication of the date of the two statues. The worn ornamental cartouches upon which the two lower shields are laid may be early seventeenth century, and the Stuart coat of arms was once surrounded by elaborate architectural details of columns, cornice, buttresses and base, all also of the very early seventeenth century. These are very clearly depicted in O'Neill's watercolour of 1821.[3] The niches themselves could predate the figures by several centuries, although their canopies are modern restorations.[4] The two figures are seated, as are the larger medieval statues of Edward I and Edward III, which were once on Lawford's Gate (see Bath Road), which may have inspired these two later additions to St John's Gate. The High Cross was at the opposite end of the same street, Broad Street. It was extended in 1633, with similar seated figures being added. Brennus and Bellinus may have been added to the gateway some time thereafter.

The gateway and tower were restored in 2006–7 by Strachey and Strachey Conservation with Paul Richold of Architecton at the cost of £268,000.[5] The paint was removed from the statues and the right forearm of the figure on the left was replaced.[6] That arm was already missing in O'Neill's drawing of 1821.[7] The hands and forearms of both figures, together with the orbs and sceptres, are not original.

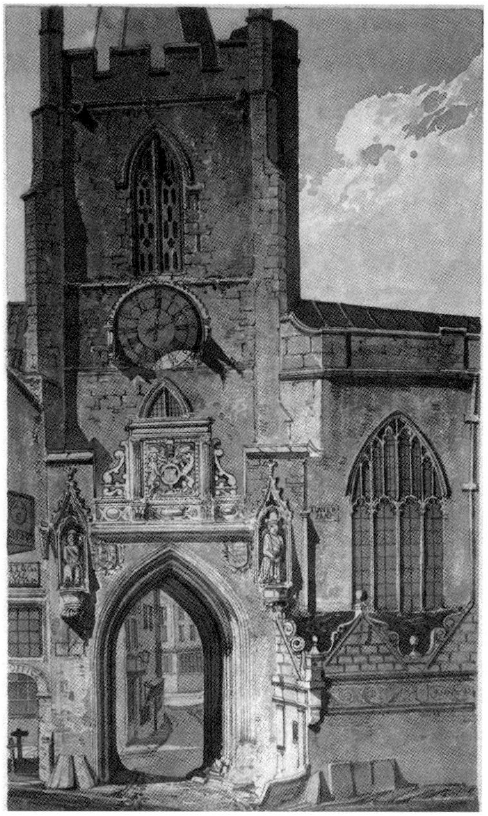

St John's Church and Gate with *Brennus and Bellinus and St John's Conduit*, watercolour by Hugh O'Neill, 1821 (Bristol Museum and Art Gallery, M2394)

Notes

[1] C. Burgess, *ODNB*, *Robert Ricart*. [2] Quoted by Nicholls and Taylor, *Bristol Past and Present*, vol. I, p.5. [3] BCMAG M2394, watercolour by H. O'Neill of St John's Gateway, 1821; the royal arms were taken down in 1849, when they were in danger of falling. Braikenridge Collection, BRL, vol XVII, p.23; newspaper cutting, 10 November 1849. [4] BCMAG M2765, pencil and wash by H. O'Neill of the statues on St John's Gateway, 1820. [5] The Churches Conservation Trust website, St John the Baptist, Bristol, 31 July 2008, which refers to the statues as fourteenth century. [6] J. Lea-Jones, *Bristol Curiosities* (Edinburgh, 2007), p.108. [7] As note 4.

Canford Cemetery

In Canford Cemetery, Westbury on Trym, against the north wall; approximately 50m along the first path on the right from the main gate

Christ the King A5

Sculptor: Eric Gill

Lettering cut by Lawrence Cribb

Date: 1933 (1931–62)
Material: Portland stone
Dimensions: central headstone, 215cm high, 70cm wide, 25cm deep
Inscription: beneath the sculpture on the central headstone, in Roman caps – ABIGAIL / PHILOMENA / CHUTE / NÉE HENNESSY / WIDOW OF JAS. / MACREADY / CHUTE / ON WHOSE SOULS/ SWEET JESU / MERCY
Status: not listed
Owned by trustees of the Chute family
Condition: fair

Three headstones commemorate Abigail Chute, her sister Annie Oates, and her son Desmond Chute, one of Eric Gill's closest friends. Above the central headstone commemorating Abigail Chute is the sculpture *Christ the King.*

Abigail Philomena Chute (1855–1931) was the matriarchal figure in a family of actor-managers that guided the theatrical world of Bristol for several generations. When she married James Macready Chute in 1886 she became the daughter-in-law of James Henry Chute, who had built the Prince's Theatre in Park Row, Bristol, in 1867.[1] Later he leased both the Theatre Royal in King Street, Bristol, and the Theatre Royal in Bath. The Prince's was one of the biggest theatres ever built in the provinces; it could hold 2,800 people, with some of the audience standing.[2] Abigail's husband was a descendant of the nineteenth-century actor-manager William Charles Macready (1793–1873). When her husband died in 1912, Abigail took over both the artistic and

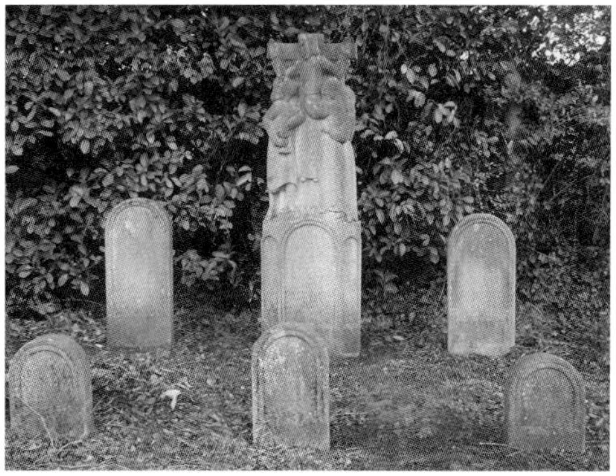

Eric Gill, *Chute family graves*

the day-to-day management of the Prince's Theatre, which she ran with great authority until her death in 1931.[3]

Abigail Chute was the daughter of Joseph Henessy, a prominent Bristol liberal and businessman in the cattle trade. The Henessys were Irish and Roman Catholics. Desmond, Abigail's son, was ordained as a Roman Catholic priest in 1927. He had met Eric Gill when Gill was carving the *Stations of the Cross* in Westminster Cathedral. Desmond attended the Slade School and then became an 'apprentice' to Gill at Ditchling, where in April 1918 Chute started stone carving.[4] Through that relationship, Gill, one of the most influential English sculptors of the first half of the twentieth century, became deeply involved with the Chute family. Gill wrote that Desmond was 'the only man with whom he had been able to talk without shame and without reserve'.[5] He saw him as a substitute son.[6] Gill found Mrs Chute to be a prima donna and 'rather difficult to cope with'.[7]

German bombing destroyed the Prince's Theatre on Sunday 24 November 1940.[8] It was never rebuilt. On the site, now a petrol station, a mere trace remains: a single pilaster on a shop front in Park Row.

The three headstones form a single coherent unit. Each has a small footstone. All have

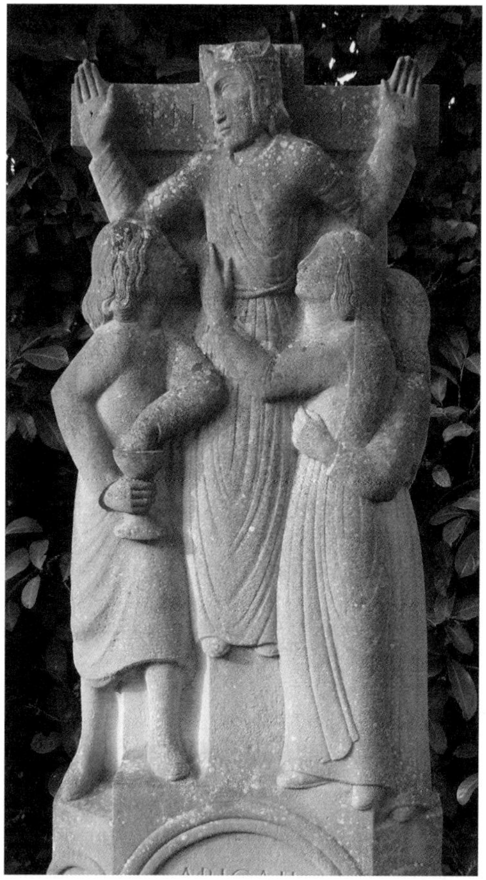

Eric Gill, *Christ the King, Abigail Chute's headstone*

rounded tops, double-rolled moulding on the main panels and a single moulding on the others. The central headstone commemorates Abigail Chute, and this has an alto-relief carving in Portland stone with three standing figures. They mourn a crowned and robed figure of the risen Christ before the cross. Between Christ's head and his pierced hands is carved: *I.N / I.R.*. St John, on the left, holds a chalice, and on the right Mary embraces her son and Mary Magdalene clasps Mary, her face touchingly hidden. The headstone to the right commemorates Mrs Oates, Mrs Chute's sister, who died only eight months after her. The headstone to the left records the death of Desmond Chute, Abigail's son, and the Latin inscription shows that he died in Rapallo in 1962 and was buried there: *Pulvis attamen sacerdos* (Dust yet a priest), *Ecce ego servus tuus et filius ancillae tuae Rapalli mortuus et ibi sepultus* (Behold, I thy servant and son of thy handmaid, died at Rapallo and was there buried).[9] The first six lines of this inscription, down to the uncompleted date, would have been carved by Gill's assistant, Laurie Cribb. The last three lines, possibly the last six, would have been cut following Desmond Chute's death.

Abigail Chute did not die until 5 October 1931, but Desmond had commissioned Gill to carve a memorial during her final illness. Gill had produced a scale drawing by 31 July.[10] When he wrote to console Desmond, he said: 'so she is gone – praise to God and thanks, joy submerges sorrow. A good life and a long life'.[11] Not until November 1931 did Desmond Chute purchase the cemetery plot.[12]

On 22 November, Gill wrote:

> Herewith sketches for the gravestones. I hope you will approve. They are very rough... As to the figure of Christ: I hope you'll approve the robed and crowned version. I'd rather carve the naked figure but it seems to me: 1. Christ the King is what is wanted today – more than Christ the victim. 2. The risen Christ is more the thing for a Christian's grave than the dying or the dead Christ. But I'll bow to your wishes in this matter.[13]

A week later Gill made further drawings.[14]

No references to carving the figures appear in Gill's diary until July 1933.[15] Then, throughout August, there are eleven days when carving work is recorded. Gill's accounts show that the decision to create a headstone for Desmond, as an integral part of his mother's and his aunt's memorial, was taken as early as 1932. Portland stone for three headstones was purchased in the summer of 1933.[16] The large headstone cost £150 and the two smaller stones £25 each. Gill's accounts record that he worked for 30 days, between November 1931 and 1934, designing and carving the memorial. Lawrence (Laurie) Cribb, Gill's long-term assistant, carved the lettering for Mrs Chute's and Mrs Oates's stones, and his work and expenses were charged. By 21 August 1932 Cribb had already been paid £30.

Judith Collins says there is a footstone with a Madonna and Child.[17] That feature may have been on some drawings, now lost, but it is not on the site. Gill's sketches for the commission were listed by the William Andrews Clark Memorial Library at UCLA, but cannot now be traced. Gill's accounts show that Cribb was sent to Canford Cemetery in 1934 to cut the inscription, *Beati pacifici* (Blessed are the peacemakers), for the footstone of Mrs Chute's grave.[18]

On the evidence of the accounts, Gill appears not to have charged a fee for his own work, although he recorded the time he spent designing and carving the sculpture: approximately 40 days. The total bill for the whole commission was £200. 4. 0. Gill made a visit to Bristol on 2 October 1933, after the headstones were erected. His rail fare of £1. 15. 0. was charged.

Gill had other links with Bristol. In 1926 he painted the fascia above Douglas Cleverdon's bookshop at 18 Charlotte Street in his sans serif lettering, and 'it does seem certain that the idea of commissioning a new sans serif typeface occurred to Stanley Morrison at the time of his own visit to Bristol in 1927.'[19] Like Mrs Chute's theatre, Cleverdon's bookshop was destroyed by a bomb during the Second World War.

There is another fine memorial sculpture by Eric Gill in Bristol: *The Good Shepherd* in Cotham Parish Church. Gill also carved an inscription in 1929 in All Saint's Church at Compton Greenfield near Bristol, for Kossuth Robinson and his three sons, all killed in action in 1915. He also inscribed a plaque to the memory of Douglas Cleverdon's parents for Zion Chapel, Bedminster.[20] This plaque is now on loan to Bristol Museums and Art Gallery.

Notes

[1] D. Carleton, *The Princes of Park Row* (Bristol, 1983), p.1. [2] Op. cit., p.2. [3] F. MacCarthy, *Eric Gill* (London and Boston, CT, 1989), p.136. [4] Ibid., p.137. [5] Ibid., p.138. [6] Ibid., p.135. [7] Ibid., p.136. [8] As note 1. [9] Translations: Professor Alan Ryder, University of Bristol. [10] J. Collins, *Eric Gill: The Sculpture* (London, 1998), p.173. [11] Ibid. Letter from Gill to Chute, 8 October 1931. [12] Register at Canford Cemetery, 'Grave No. 368 Pink N'. [13] As note 10, letter from Gill to Desmond Chute, 22 November 1931. [14] Gill's diary, William Andrews Clark Memorial Library, UCLA. 27 November 1931. [15] Ibid. 6 July 1933: 'Desmond C. Headst. in m& ev', and on the 7 July: 'Desmond C. carving all day'. [16] Ibid. Gill's accounts. 'Rev. Desmond Chute, 1162, Gravestones at Bristol. DC, Mrs. C., Mrs. O.' [17] As note 10. [18] As note 14. [19] D. Peace, *Eric Gill: The Inscriptions* (London, 1994). Entry 484, p.117. 'Painted by EG Oct 30–Nov. 1, 1926... from letters used on this board the type design Gill Sans was developed in 1927'; Cleverdon became a BBC radio producer and was responsible for the first broadcast of Dylan Thomas's *Under Milk Wood*.

Castle Park

1991–3

This thirteen-acre park covers the former heart of medieval Bristol. The park was, in effect, created in November 1940 by the Blitz. Some post-war development took place at the western end of the site along High Street and Wine Street, and there was to be some landscaping of the largely derelict park, but it was nearly fifty years before the future of the park was resolved.

In the late 1980s, Norwich Union's development on the opposite side of Newgate of the adjoining shopping mall, The Galleries, was permitted with a conditional 'planning gain', which involved a contribution of around £1.5 million towards the landscaping and enhancement of Castle Park. Most of the money was used for engineering, landscaping, planting and archaeological excavations to improve the semi-neglected park.[1] About

£50,000 was allocated to begin a programme of sculpture and artist's installations. Further contributions were acquired, including £20,000 from South West Arts and £25,000 from the Foundation for Sports & Arts. Much of the funding for the involvement of artists and craftsmen in the design of such functional items as railings, bridges and paving came from the landscaping budget.

The Castle Park art programme is the largest public landscape and art commissioning project in the south-west. It is a good example of a collaborative approach which brought together commissioned artists with landscape designers and other professionals. A public art consultant guided the project with the support of the Castle Park Steering Group.[2]

Lesley Greene, formerly the director of London's Public Art Development Trust, was appointed by Bristol City Council as its freelance public art commissioner from March 1991 to May 1993.[3] She later reported:

> when the project began there were no recent precedents... in the summer the park is used by 2,000 people a day... the keep of the original castle, dating from 1120, remains... the pieces we commissioned had to be sensitive to the park's history, landscape and public use.

Lesley Greene had the advantage of following upon a report by the sculptor, Peter Randall-Page, who was later to produce the major artwork for the park. In July 1990 he not only recommended the appointment of a specialist 'art/craft work coordinator/advisor', but argued that 'the main thrust of effort should be to integrate art and craft work into the fabric of the place, as it is attention to detail, not grand gestures, which will have the most profound effect'.[4] He emphasised the potential railings and fences, bridges, litter bins, signage, paving, stone walls, seating and tables, and play equipment, in all of which artists and craftspeople were to be involved. There were to be over twenty separate commissions, from seating to freestanding sculptures. Six of these commissions are included in the main entries of this book. However, the benches in oak and steel by Alan Tilbury and in peat bog oak by Alan Peters, the railings by the herb garden by Alan Evans and by the sallyport by James Horrobin, the waste bins by Dail Behennah (see also Harbourside), the bridge balustrade by Matthew Fedden and other commissions are omitted from this book, although, as Randall-Page anticipated, they are no less important to the success of the project.

Detailed briefs were prepared and sent to selected artists and architects, or to teams who wished to make collaborative submissions. These were returned with estimates, 1:20 scale models, drawings and/or and photomontages to the public art consultant's office in December 1992. The selection panel consisted of Richard Burton (RWA council member), Tessa Jackson (director of the Arnolfini Gallery) and Sir Roger de Grey (president of the Royal Academy). Lesley Greene's role remained of paramount importance.

In Castle Park, facing Union Street and north of the ruins of St Mary le Port

Line From Within C20

Sculptor: Ann Christopher

Date: 1993
Material: sand-cast and patinated bronze
Dimensions: 460cm high, 160cm wide, 15cm thick
Foundry: Pangolin, Stroud
Status: not listed
Owned by the Royal West of England Academy, on permanent loan to Bristol City Council
Condition: good

This tall free-standing bronze sculpture is made up of two flattened pillars, each topped with an irregular off-centre rectangle. Along the upper edge are five small semi-circular cut-outs or bites. The surface detail is textured to reveal the sand-casting process created by Ken Cook at the foundry. There is no visible base, as the bronze is fixed by an integral underground plate.

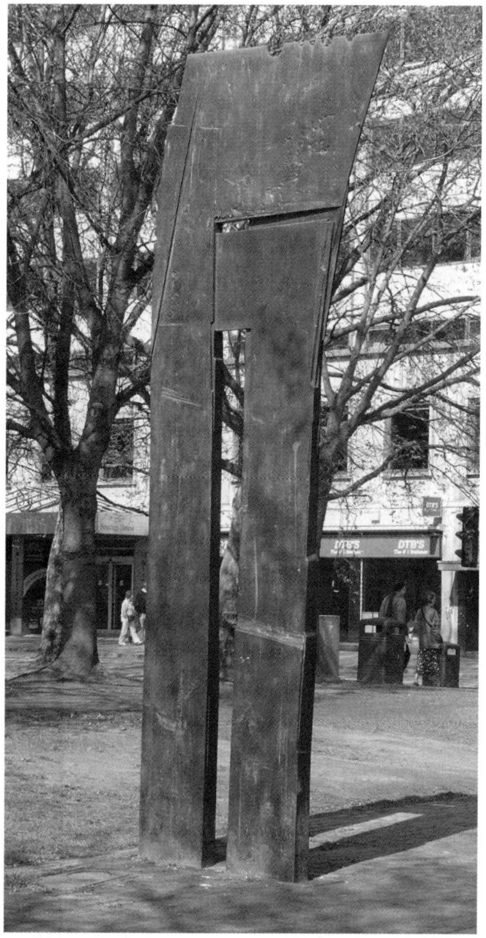

Ann Christopher, *Line From Within*

This work was commissioned as part of the redevelopment of Castle Park, and was the last of the artworks to be completed. It was funded through the Talboys bequest, a trust set up to allow the Royal West of England Academy to buy works from its own members.[5] The work is now on permanent loan to Bristol City Council from the RWA.[6] At the unveiling ceremony on 25 October 1993 it was officially handed over to the lord mayor of Bristol, councillor John Channon, by the president of the Royal West of England Academy, Leonard Manasseh, OBE, RA, PRWA, FRIBA, who said 'it symbolised a threshold to the park'. [7]

An interviewer, speaking with Ann Christopher, said: 'It's like a window – you look through it and it frames the view and helps to redefine the whole space.' To which the sculptor replied 'Yes, *Line From Within* is very much about doing that. I've actually used that cut through for quite a long time.' [8]

The brief for all the sculpture commissioned for the park was to reflect the history of the site.[9] Ann Christopher chose a site that is one of the busiest entrances to the park, and marked this with flat shapes suggesting a castle gate rising from the hidden foundations of the ancient city beneath.[10] *Line From Within* marks the site of one of the ancient gateways to one of the earliest Norman castles in England.

Notes

[1] N. Swengley, 'Castle Park', *Crafts*, November 1993, p.14. [2] BCC, Director of Leisure Services, 'Public Art Development Plan' (October 1995), p.1. [3] As note 1. [4] BCC, Leisure Services Committee, P. Randall-Page, 'Castle Park Project, a strategy for arts and crafts', 1990, Appendix A. [5] 'High profile art makes a mark on city park', *Evening Post*, 26 October 1993. [6] J. Lane, *Ann Christopher, Sculpture 1989–1984* (London, 1994), p.22. [7] As note 5. [8] As note 6. [9] D. Price, M. Rieser and S. Swingler, *Castle Park: Public Art in Practice* (1996), CD, UWE. [10] Ann Christopher, notes, July 1996.

In Castle Park, to the north of St. Peter's Church

Throne C21

Sculptor: Rachel Fenner

Date: 1993
Material: Normandy limestone
Dimensions: 105cm high, 115cm wide, 125cm deep
Status: not listed
Owned by Bristol City Council
Condition: good

A rectangular block of stone is minimally carved to suggest a vacated throne with a once-soft seat, the impression of an absent hand on the right arm and two ghostly footprints. The folds of a robe shape the seat and the outline of a leg is pressed into the lower part, while a discarded robe is draped over the left side. The viewer is invited to usurp the throne of the absent ruler, and many younger visitors do so.

'The "Throne" embodies a sense of the past and acts as an unseen presence – that of the Norman kings, for whom the castle was a seat for so long.'[1] A discussion paper written in the early stages of planning the Castle Park project proclaimed: 'Castle Park is where Bristol began.'[2] Rachel Fenner has carved her sculpture in stone from a Normandy quarry, recalling the invaders who determined much of Bristol's early history.

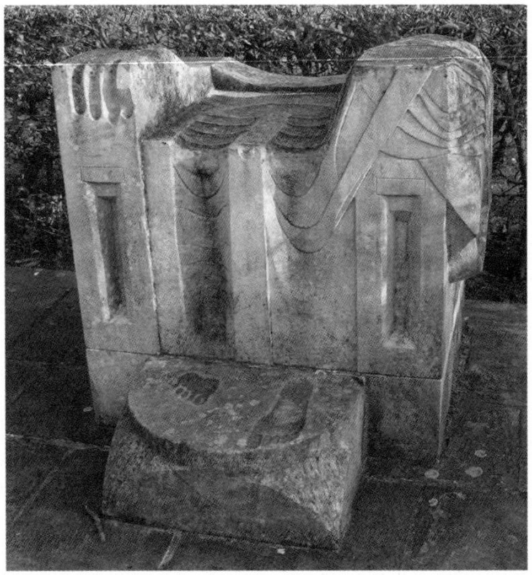

Rachel Fenner, *Throne*

The best known of the potential ghostly occupants of the throne is Robert, Earl of Gloucester, illegitimate son of Henry I and builder of the Great Keep of Bristol. The park takes its name from this early twelfth-century castle, of which vestiges remain. Robert also built the Priory of St James in Bristol and was buried there in 1147.

Bristol city council commissioned work from over 20 artists when Castle Park was being landscaped in the early 1990s. Two landscape architects, Martin Deaville and Alex Frazer, were appointed 'to create an outdoor space that could be used for events', and they collaborated with Rachel Fenner, a landscape designer.[3] They worked together to develop the forms of the arena on a five-day consultancy in the summer of 1991.[4] Her proposals were more radical than the realisation.[5] Later, she took part in a competition for the sculptural feature. Her original intention was for a throne to be placed on the top of a 'motte' that had evolved in the landscaping. Unfortunately the weight of the stone was too great and there were also archaeological problems.[6]

The present site, close – arguably much too close – to Peter Randall-Page's work, was selected as an alternative to the 'motte'. This decision was later criticised for causing overcrowding, and the landscape architect on the project was to regret that insufficient time had prevented the satisfactory resolution of this area of the park.[7]

Notes

[1] BCC, *Castle Park: Public Art Programme* (Bristol, C.1993). [2] BCC, 'Castle Park Project', Appendix I, July 1990. [3] As note 1. [4] L. Greene, List of proposed commissions/sites of Castle Park, 20 November 1991. [5] Price et al.,*Castle Park.* [6] Ibid. [7] Ibid.

In Castle Park, to the east of the ruined church of St Peter's

Beside the Still Waters C22

Sculptor: Peter Randall-Page

Date: 1993
Material: Kilkenny limestone
Dimensions: pine cone, 200cm high, 100cm diameter; fountain, 80cm high, 115cm diameter
Inscription: cut in a slate rectangle set in the pavement by the eastern carving – BESIDE THE STILL WATERS / 1993 / PETER RANDALL-PAGE
Status: not listed
Owned by Bristol City Council
Condition: good

Two stone forms of approximately equal volume are carved into organic forms. The taller one, the farthest from St Peter's Church, has the appearance of a closed pine cone. The other is a cinquefoil form, cut horizontally with five hollows at the top from which the water flows. Each carving is set in a circular pond at opposite ends of a narrow channel of water. Both sides of this channel are paved and bordered by an avenue of lime trees. The flowing water is precisely aligned with the east–west line of the nave of the bombed church.

The installation was part of a joint initiative between Bristol City Council and Arnolfini for the improvement of Castle Park. Peter Randall-Page was awarded one of the major, and arguably most successful, commissions. He had earlier been consulted as an advisor by the city council in the very early stages of the project.[1] That was before Lesley Greene, the public art coordinator, was appointed and before he knew he would be contributing to the scheme. Subsequently, his brief was simply 'to provide a key work for the park'.[2]

The council's landscape architects and water-engineering consultants were closely involved in the design.[3] In summarising the scheme to researchers from the University of the West of England in 1995, Peter Randall-Page said:

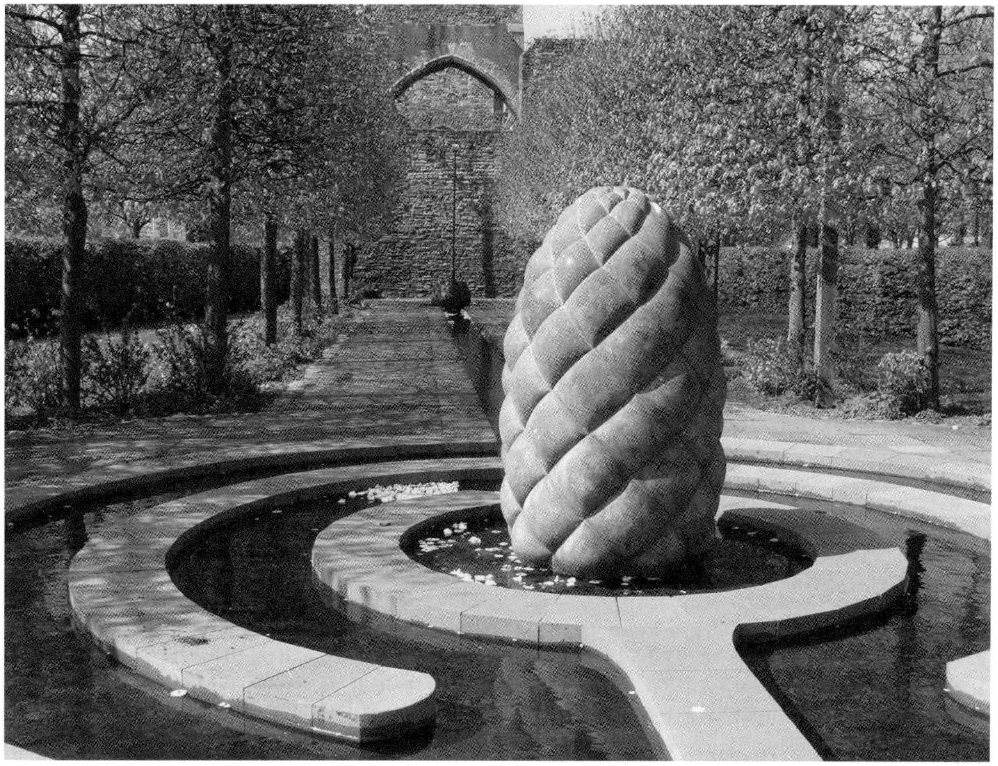

Peter Randall-Page, *Beside the Still Waters*

> The first decision to be made about the site is should it be formal or informal. In a city and with the church [as part of this site], I liked the idea of making something rather formal and the idea of water flowing in a very gentle way, down the avenue of trees.[4]

The sensual elements of the design were emphasised, but the sculptor has said that there was no intentional symbolism and that he did not consider the history of the site on this occasion.

Much of the sculptor's inspiration comes from the observation of natural forms. Coils and knots are also frequent themes. In this instance, approximately half-size wax maquettes were made first. Of the construction of the final pieces, Randall-Page said: 'Carving on a large scale is always a collaborative process unless one is going to make very few works in one's lifetime.'

The two carvings cost £22,000, while the total cost (including integral landscaping and the water features) was approximately £50,000.[5] Norwich Union, the developers of the Galleries shopping centre, paid £35,000 towards this, and in November 1992 there was an appeal to Bristolians to raise the remaining £15,000 required for this commission.[6] The local press described *Beside the Still Waters* as 'an oasis in the heart of the city', and the article was illustrated with an 'artist's impression of the new sculpture'. An exhibition of Randall-Page's work was held at Arnolfini in September and October 1992, coinciding with the appeal.[7]

A pencil-and-wash preliminary drawing, showing the sculpture in its setting, and a measured drawing (1:100), both made by the sculptor for the Castle Park Project, were presented to the Bristol Museum and Art Gallery in 1993.[8]

Notes
[1] Swengley, 'Castle Park', p.17 [2] Price et al.,*Castle Park.* [3] T. Jackson and L. Greene, 'Castle Park, Bristol: a commission for Peter Randall-Page', press release, 1992. [4] As note 2. [5] Ibid. [6] *Bristol Evening Post*, V. Moss, 'Sculpture showpiece for park revamp', 5 September 1992. [7] Arnolfini broadsheet, 'Peter Randall-Page: sculpture and drawings 1980–1992', September 1992. [8] Bristol Museum and Art Gallery, *Beside the Still Waters,* K5798, 1992, and *Lime Avenue*, K5799, c.1992.

In Castle Park, close to the cycle path by the edge of the river

Drinking Fountain C23

Sculptor: Kate Malone

Date: 1993
Materials: bronze fountain, 110cm high, 105cm diameter at top; brick and terracotta tiled base, 340cm diameter
Cast by Pangolin Foundry, Stroud
Status: not listed
Owned by Bristol City Council
Condition: good

Orange juice and red wine spurted from the fish's mouths on the day this drinking fountain was unveiled by Jerry Hicks, the chairman of the Bristol Civic Society.[1] That expansive gesture was short-lived but, unlike so many other drinking fountains and fountains in Bristol, Kate Malone's drinking fountain does still work. At the ceremony she was reported as saying: 'I grew up in Bristol and was delighted to have been able to create something which commemorates its heritage', as well as to refresh exhausted walkers and cyclists. The fountain fulfilled Bristol City Council's commitment to implement Sustrans' policy of providing drinking fountains every few miles for travellers on the Bristol–Bath cyclepath, which runs through Castle Park.[2]

There are two elements to Kate Malone's work: the bronze drinking fountain, which weighs a quarter of a ton, and the brick paving on which it stands. Water spouts from the open mouths of two fish in the central basin. They emerge from a pattern of waves forming six curves at the upper rim. A button, concealed as the eye of a fish on the side of the fountain, releases the water. Relief decoration covers the central form and this divides into three sections. At ground level is the hull of a wooden boat with three tobacco leaves above the prow. A castle tower, with battlements, emerges from the boat and there are two doors, one to port and one to starboard. A ship, castle and fish are the essential components of Bristol's thirteenth-century seal and modern coat of arms. However, above these, in a mass of fish and sea wrack, the head and wings of black angels appear at six points just below the rim. These are derived from the little eighteenth-century baroque angels, painted brown in recent times, on the headstone to the grave of Scipio Africanus, a slave, in Henbury churchyard.

The circular pavement is made up of eight rows of bricks in the form of a compass. The outer two rows contain cream-coloured bricks impressed with lettering to indicate places of interest, abroad and in the city, that were of significance to Bristol's trading history, such as Bordeaux for wine and Scandinavia for timber. Rows four and six contain terracotta bricks impressed with a mass of child-like images ranging from eighteenth-century wine decanters to modern balloon flights. Several refer to slavery, the Clifton Suspension Bridge and the Blitz. The remaining rows are plain black engineering bricks.

The sculptor gained this commission, as did other artists in the Castle Park scheme, through a limited competition.[3] Malone has said that she was one of four artists invited to the Council House to make presentations for this project.

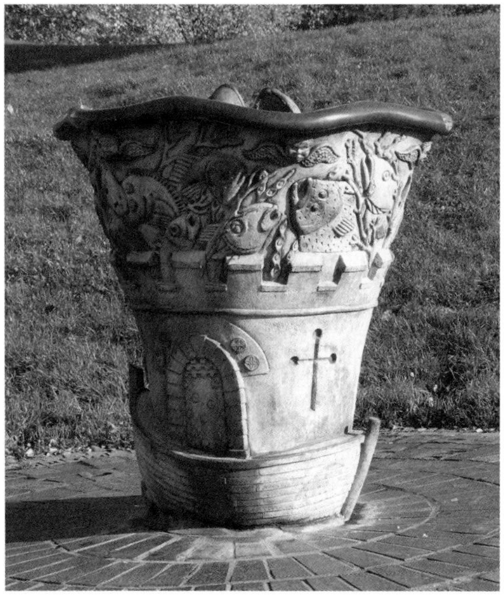

Kate Malone, *Drinking Fountain*

She recollected that the total budget was £15,000 and the casting costs were around £5,000. The bricks were decorated at Brimsham Green School, Yate, where Kate Malone and Mike Hughes (a lecturer at the University of the West of England) involved the children in decorating them. Ibstock Bricks provided the soft bricks. After they were impressed with images they were fired and delivered to the site.

Kate Malone works in ceramics, and on this occasion she used coiled clay to make the main vessel. Cast clay reliefs were applied before firing. Brightly coloured glazes evoked the sea. The Pangolin Foundry in Stroud then cast the bronze version for the park from the pottery version, using the lost wax (*cire perdue*) process.[4] The artist donated her original ceramic version to the Bristol Museum and Art Gallery, where it has been on almost constant display.[5]

Notes
[1] *Bristol Evening Post,* 'That's cool! Fountain is on stream', 17 August 1993. [2] BCC, 'Castle Park public art programme', c. 1993. [3] Swengley, 'Castle Park',

pp.14–15. [4] Ibid. [5] Malone's own working file and drawings are held at the Bristol Museum and Art Gallery; the fountain was featured in L. Jackson and K. Malone, *A Book of Pots: Kate Malone* (London, 2003).

At the north eastern end of Castle Park near the children's playground

Only the Dead Fish Go With the Flow C25

Sculptor: Victor Moreton

Date: 1993
Materials: glazed ceramic moulded fish and tiles
Dimensions: floor area, approx. 750cm by 650cm; tiles, 38cm by 19cm; fish, 35cm x 18cm
Inscription: 'ONLY THE DEAD FISH GO WITH THE FLOW' / PORCELAIN PAVEMENT / BY VICTOR MORETON WITH CERAMICA DO DOURO / 1992–93 / WITH FINANCIAL ASSISTANCE FROM / THE EUROPEAN FESTIVAL OF ARTS / PORTUGAL 600, BRISTOL–OPORTO / ASSOCIATION AND CERAMICA DO DOURO / NEAR THIS SITE STOOD RICHARD CHAMPION'S PORCELAIN WORKS 1768–1782. / HAND PAINTED BY / 1993-05-15 CERAMICA DO DOURO / PORTUGAL
Status: not listed
Owned by Bristol City Council
Condition: poor

The long inscription begins with the title given by the artist, Victor Moreton. He has said that the words are a quotation from the famous actor, W. C. Fields, a man who, reputedly, knew very little about water.[1]

Only a minority of installations in Castle Park display the title, the name of the sculptor and details of the sponsors, as does this piece. The inscription, now illegible, is hand-painted in blue on a panel of twelve white tiles within a patterned border. These are covered by a glazed wooden frame, now in a very dilapidated state. So too is the work itself. There has never been a reliable supply of water, and the source is now deliberately blocked. There seems to be little purpose in restoration; better to start afresh.

The work is within four low, rebuilt walls above the early medieval foundations of Bristol Castle and consists of a floor, approximately seven meters square, of white ceramic tiles. On the southern wall, a vertical panel of three tiles marks the outlet of a source of water that once flowed across the floor. Flat ceramic fish skeletons are fixed in a pattern that gives the impression that they are following the flow of water from that point.

Victor Moreton was awarded this commission through a limited competition as part of the Castle Park project. He decided to commemorate the nearby site of an eighteenth-century Bristol porcelain factory by creating a large ceramic installation.[2] Moreton had wanted the tiles to be black with white fish, but this

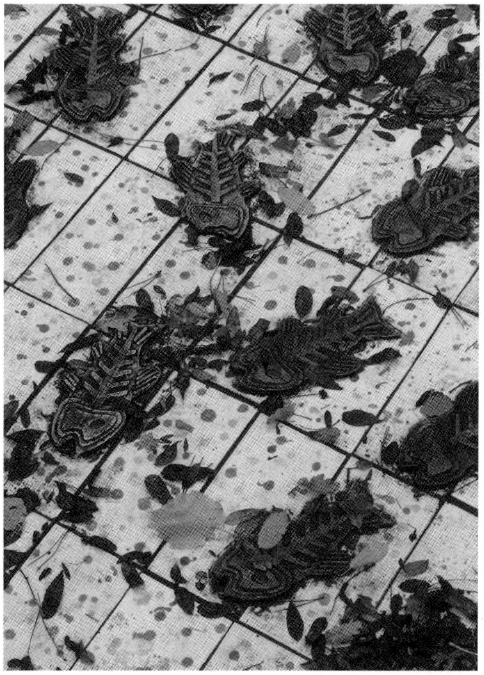

Victor Moreton, *Only the Dead Fish Go With the Flow*

proved impractical. He then selected blue and white as the predominant colours used in eighteenth-century porcelain. The tiles were made by the Oporto factory of Ceramica do Douro in Portugal. Oporto is twinned with Bristol, and Moreton has said that the 'design for the fish fossils is reminiscent of the medieval salt cod trade, which Bristol and Oporto had in common and which Oporto still has'.[3]

The Castle Green porcelain factory that the artist sought to commemorate was set up by Richard Champion in 1768 in partnership with William Cookworthy.[4] Until 1782, china of the very highest quality was produced to rival the royal factories of Sèvres and Dresden. Champion boasted that had his factory survived longer it would have become 'the greatest ever known in England'.[5] Commercial depression caused by the outbreak of the American War of Independence lead to the collapse of one of Champion's best markets. This, and the hostile actions of Josiah Wedgwood, ended the business, and the works were closed.

Notes
[1] Swengley, 'Castle Park', pp.14–15. [2] Ibid. [3] BCC, 'The Castle Park public art programme', pamphlet, c.1993. [4] Hutton, *Bristol and its Famous Associations*, p.227. [5] Ibid, p.228.

In the children's play area on the eastern side of Castle Park

Play Sculpture C24

Sculptor: Andy Frost

Date: 1991
Material: painted wood
Dimensions: human figures and animals approximately life-size, castles and other buildings at a scale to form climbing frames
Status: not listed
Owned by Bristol City Council
Condition: poor; repainting and some restoration required

The fenced-off play area for young children has climbing frames and other equipment

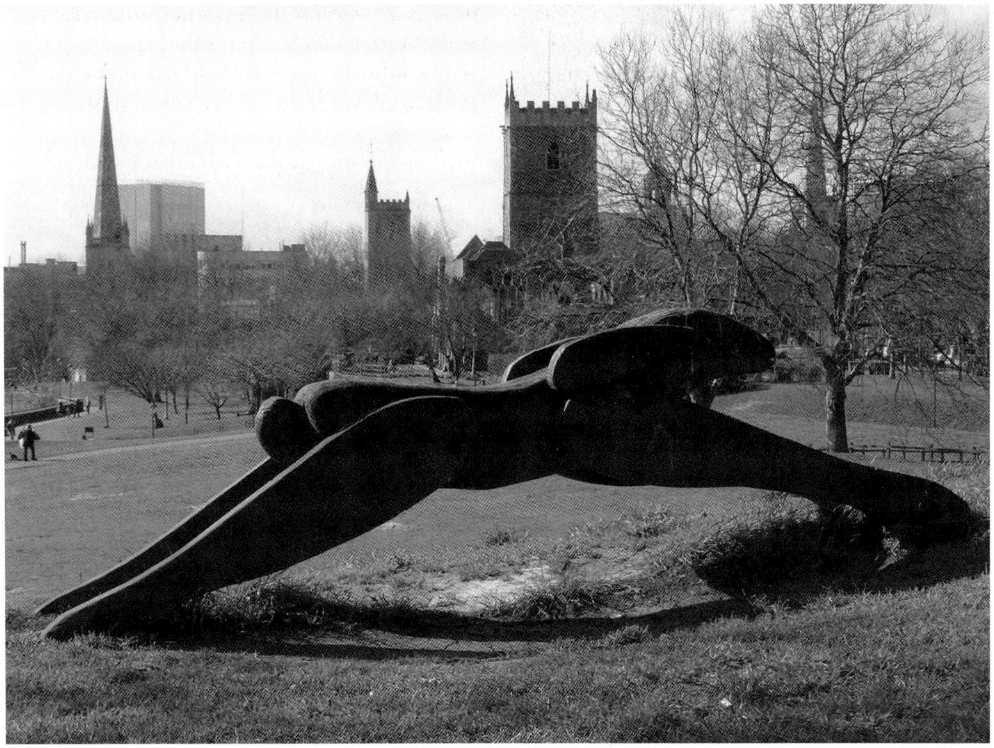

Andy Frost, *Running Hare Play Sculpture*

representing medieval buildings and human figures. Outside the enclosed area there are running hares, about three times life-size, set on hilly ground to the west. There are also sheep to the east and a fox to the north.

Softwood and marine plywood are the only materials, and these, bolted together in a simple manner, were painted with bright colours. After ten years they need to be refreshed. Deep silver sand was used throughout the area to form a safe surface in case of falls.

Andy Frost was one of about twenty artists to be involved in the Castle Park project that started in 1991.[1] He submitted a portfolio of work, including designs for children's play areas. After discussions, the proposal for a permanent playground emerged and Frost submitted ideas connected to the story of Bristol Castle and the early community on the site. He was concerned not to make the objects, or the surroundings, too warlike. The result is a medieval settlement where, among castle-like climbing frames and market stalls, sheep may safely graze, where dogs run and wooden men are at work; two can be seen carrying a large beam.

Safety was a vital factor. This affected the design by inhibiting pointed edges, demanding thick components for arms and legs and the avoidance of sharp upright shapes. However, rather than feeling constrained, the sculptor noted: 'Collaboration between artists, play officers and landscape designers can provide more imaginative and site-specific play equipment'.[2]

Drug-users' syringes and needles were found in the sand in 2001 and the playground was temporarily closed.[3] The remarkable expansion of Broadmead with the addition of Cabot Circus and the completion of residential buildings nearby in 2008–9 should cause much greater use of this end of Castle Park. It should also prompt the restoration of the playground and the surrounding animals.

Notes

[1] Price et al., *Castle Park.* [2] Ibid. [3]'Area open again for play', *Evening Post,* 9 June 2001.

'The Centre'

Colston Avenue, opposite St Stephen's Street

Edward Colston C46

Sculptor: John Cassidy

Date: 1895
Materials: bronze; pedestal, Hoptonwood stone
Dimensions: 260cm; 80cm square at base; pedestal, 315cm high; four relief plaques, 95cm high, 65cm wide
Foundry: Coalbrookdale
Inscriptions: metal letters applied to the front of the pedestal: –EDWARD / COLSTON / BORN 1636 / DIED: 1721
—: bronze panel – ERECTED : BY : / CITIZENS of BRISTOL / AS A MEMORIAL/ OF ONE OF THE MOST / VIRTUOUS : AND / WISE : SONS OF / THEIR : CITY / A.D. 1895 / JOHN CASSIDY / FECIT
Signature, base below left foot: John Cassidy
—: below the right foot: Coalbrookdale
Status: Grade II
Owned by Bristol City Council
Condition: good

Edward Colston (1636–1721), merchant of Bristol and London, continues to be celebrated as one of Bristol's most generous philanthropists. At the unveiling of this statue in 1895, the mayor of Bristol had no doubts that Colston was the most 'noble' and the most 'bountiful' of all the city's great benefactors.[1] Many of the charities he set up or supported still flourish, as do a number of societies that perpetuate his name and his memory, and continue to raise funds for charitable purposes. By the mid-nineteenth century there was criticism of Colston's religious views: 'his antipathy to dissent, it must be acknowledged, approached the confines of bigotry'.[2] Today, it is for the presumed source of some of his wealth that he is most often remembered.

> This statue of Edward Colston... idealises him as a revered Bristol benefactor and is silent about his role as a member of the Court of Assistants to the Royal African Company, which had official monopoly on the slave trade until 1698.[3]

Edward Colston was born on 2 November 1636 in Temple parish, the son of a wealthy Bristol merchant. He was to be a member of the Society of Merchant Venturers, an alderman of Bristol and in his old age an MP for the city, but he lived almost all his life in London, dying in Mortlake in 1721. The sums he gave to charities are vast in modern terms. He established Colston's Almshouse on St Michael's Hill (1691), enabled the enlargement of Merchants' Almshouse in King Street, and founded Colston's Hospital boys school in 1710. There were to be further substantial charitable donations in Bristol and elsewhere. Several important and continuing Bristol charities were founded in his memory, particularly the Dolphin, Grateful and Anchor Societies.[4]

The almost hunched, contemplative figure represents Colston in his maturity. For a likeness, the sculptor may have turned to Jonathan Richardson's portrait of 1702, a version of which hangs in the Council House.[5] The reclining figure by Rysbrack on Colston's tomb in All Saints, Corn Street, may also have been useful. The monument shows a younger, more vigorous man, although Rysbrack may well have used the same source. Cassidy's statue depicts Colston in early eighteenth century clothes.

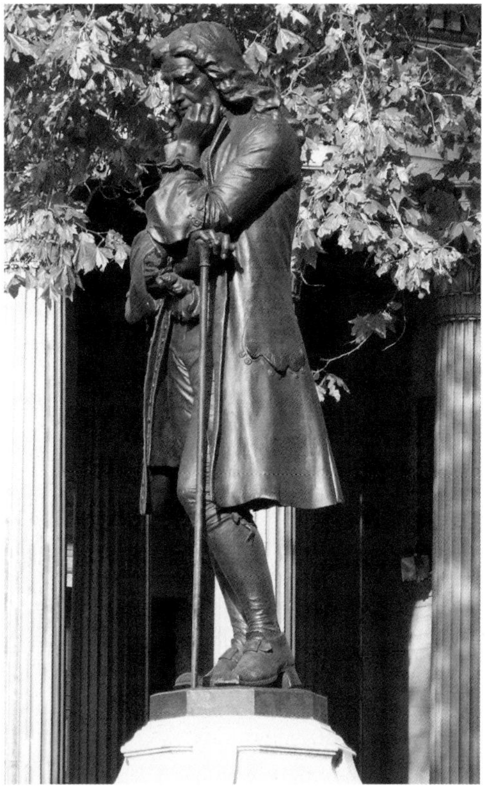

John Cassidy, *Edward Colston*

> Undue ornamentation in the matter of dress has been avoided. At the same time there is nothing heavy in the treatment of the figure, the pose of which is easy and graceful. The features denote deep thought.[6]

The elaborate pedestal is described as 'a good neo-Baroque type... of considerable dignity and fine detail'.[7] *The Bristol Mercury and Daily Post* stated that the pedestal is made of Hoptonwood stone, 'a hard material which takes a good polish and appears like a fine grey marble'.[8]

Three of the side reliefs show apocryphal or symbolic scenes from Colston's life. One shows Colston distributing alms in the street; another depicts mythical seahorses and tritons pulling an anchor; the third depicts the legend – 'told with considerable power' – of a dolphin plugging a leak in one of Colston's ships.[9]

> The head of a dolphin appears through the aperture, completely filling it, and keeping out the water, and while two sailors with a cord are making fast the creature which prevents them foundering. The ship's officer looks on astonished and two others behind him are evidently amused at the peculiarity of the situation.

It was this 'incident' that is said to have caused Colston to adopt the dolphin as his emblem. Stylised dolphins, with writhing tails and looking more like animated catfish, are at each corner of the pedestal. The fourth panel bears an inscription and the sculptor's name.

The statue is one of this Manchester-based sculptor's more important public works. A Bristol newspaper was complimentary: 'It is an excellent piece of work, and will fittingly preserve the features and the memory of one to whom Bristol owes so much'.[10]

The unveiling on 13 November 1895 was undertaken by W. Howell Davies, Mayor of Bristol. It was the 259th anniversary of Colston's birth, and *The Times* reported, under the heading 'Colston's Day at Bristol', that

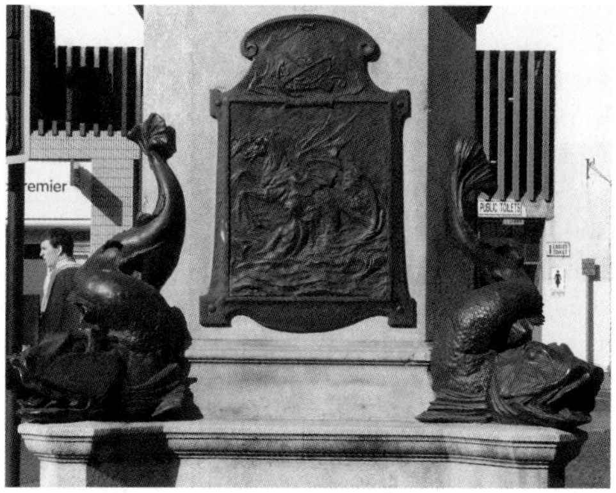

John Cassidy, *Edward Colston, plinth with dolphins*

members of the Dolphin Society went first to Bristol Cathedral and then to 'St Augustine's-parade, where a statue of Edward Colston, the cost of which has been partly defrayed by public subscription, was unveiled by the Mayor'. A long description of the statue followed. The foundry is credited but there is no mention of the sculptor.[11] After the unveiling, a local newspaper said the statue would testify 'to strangers and posterity that in 1895 there were to be found those who regarded Edward Colston as one of the first of Bristol's citizens'.[12]

Recently, historians have endeavoured to politicise the commissioning of this statue.

> [The] Tory and Anglican merchant class were memorialising themselves and their own values, their favourite son was being represented as an embodiment of benign paternalism.[13]

This casual thesis ignores the liberal politics of the statue's principal proponent, who was also president of the Anchor Society, the Whig-affiliated Colston society. It was J. W. Arrowsmith, head of a large printing company in the city, who first made a proposal for the statue.[14] The *Daily Press* had reported a Colston Fraternal Society dinner, held on 31 October 1893, when Arrowsmith said it was a shame that after 200 years there was no statue in Bristol to honour a man who had done so much for the city's charities and schools. 'One ought to be erected at the earliest opportunity'.[15] Arrowsmith also commented that Bristol had few statues, and the generosity of a citizen was about to give the city a statue of Burke (see 'The Centre'). 'It would be well to place, upon the open space near St Augustine's Bridge, a statue of one of the greatest men who had ever lived in Bristol.' This speech was made after the city had decided not to erect municipal buildings on the space created by the covering over of the Frome up to the Drawbridge. Arrowsmith set up a committee of officers of the various Colston societies and, on 8 March 1894, it was resolved to raise funds for a statue of the great man.

Although 1,500 circulars were distributed, the response was poor. The first subscription list produced only £201. A second appeal raised the total to £407. By June the committee decided that 'citizens generally' should be invited to subscribe. 'The promoters had no idea of turning back because they were not so enthusiastically supported as they might have been.' Even this did not raise the sum required, but the competition went ahead. Models from 23 sculptors from Edinburgh, Manchester, Birkenhead, London and Bristol were received, and the 'commission was placed in the hands of Mr John Cassidy, of Manchester'.[16] Fundraising continued in 1895 when, encouraged by the success of the Industrial Exhibition of 1893, a Handicraft Exhibition was held in the Rifle Drill Hall. The result was poor. Although 96,510 visitors attended, only £170 was raised for the Colston statue fund. By the unveiling the £800 required had still not been fully subscribed. An Anchor Society banquet raised £12, and the Dolphin Society contributed £1. 10s and the balance, 'about £150, was given by an anonymous citizen who had already subscribed liberally'.[17] This was almost certainly Arrowsmith himself.

In a report on the statue, Andrew Naylor notes that there were long-term links between Coalbrookdale and Bristol. Abraham Darby came from Bristol, and Thomas Goldney and other Bristolians had shares in the company, but this monument is the last remaining evidence of the connection.[18] The statue and its setting were prepared by Messrs W. Cowlin and Sons of Bristol.[19] Cowlins also erected *Queen Victoria*, 1888 (see College Green) and *Edmund Burke*, 1894 (see 'The Centre').

A full-length painted plaster statue of Edward Colston , just under two metres high, is at Colston's Collegiate School. Evidently made for a niche, it may date from soon after the move of the school to the former Bishop's Palace at Stapleton in 1857.

Notes

[1] *Bristol Mercury and Daily Post,* 'Colston anniversary', 14 November 1895. [2] T. Garrard, *E. Colston, The Philanthropist* (Bristol, 1852); quoted in S.D. Major, *New Illustrated Handbook to Bristol, Clifton and Neighbour hood* (Bristol, 1872), p.205. [3] BMAG, *Slave Trade Trail Around Central Bristol* (Bristol, c.2007), p.21. [4] H.J. Wilkins, *Edward Colston (1636–1721): A Chronological Account of his Life and Work Together with an Account of the Colston Societies and Memorials in Bristol* (Bristol, 1920). [5] The painting is in the Lord Mayor's Parlour. [6] As note 1. [7] B. Little, *Bristol: The Public View* (Bristol, 1982), pp.72–3. [8] As note 1; Andrew Naylor and English Heritage say it is Portland stone. [9] As note 1. [10] As note 1. [11] *The Times,* 14 November 1895, p.10. [12] As note 1. [13] Gough and Morgan, 'Manipulating the metonymic', p.668. [14] Arrowsmith had published Jerome K. Jerome's *Three Men in a Boat* in 1889. [15] As note 1. [16] One of a short list of four was 'a local sculptor', but his name is not given. [17] As note 1. [18] As note 9. [19] *The Builder,* 23 November 1895, p.385.

'The Centre', Colston Avenue, between the Cenotaph and Edward Colston

Industrial and Fine Art Exhibition Drinking Fountain C44

Designer: unknown

Date: 1901
Dimensions: 290cm high, 90cm square at base
Materials: fountain, grey and red granite; brass plaque and spout
Inscription: THIS FOUNTAIN / WAS ERECTED / TO COMMMEMORATE THE / SUCCESSFUL INDUSTRIAL / AND / FINE-ART EXHIBITION / HELD ON THIS SITE IN 1893 / AS THE RESULT OF WHICH A SUM / OF £2,200 WAS DISTRIBUTED / AMONGST FIVE BRISTOL / MEDICAL CHARITIES. / W.R. BARKER CHAIRMAN, / (MAYOR) / J.W. ARROWSMITH / E.G. CLARKE / HON. SEC[S] / OF THE EXHIBITION COMMITTEE. /
Status: Grade II
Owned by Bristol City Council
Condition: fair, but not functioning

Bristol's thirteenth-century harbour, a remarkable feat of medieval engineering, was developed from the River Frome and stretched the full length of today's open space, now so misleadingly known as 'the Centre'. Six centuries later, the first part of the harbour and river to be filled in and culverted ran from St Augustine's Bridge, opposite Clare Street, to the Stone Bridge well to the north of St Mary-on-the-Quay. The work was completed in 1893. The nearby statues of Edmund Burke and Edward Colston were erected in 1894 and 1895 on this new land (see Fig. 23). The area was landscaped and named Colston Avenue, although it was quickly became known as Magpie Park after a scurrilous magazine printed nearby.[1]

But first, this new open space at the heart of Bristol was almost immediately used for the Bristol Industrial and Fine Art Exhibition from August 1893 to January 1894.[2] This proved the

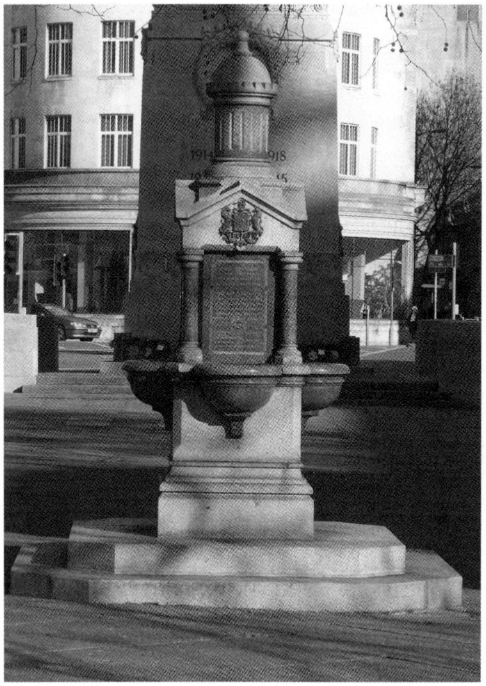

Industrial and Fine Art Exhibition Drinking Fountain

most successful venture of the kind ever held in the city. [3] More than half a million people attended, and the receipts totalled nearly £25,000.[4] The profit was distributed among five Bristol medical charities. To commemorate this triumph, this fountain was erected in 1901 at a cost of £220.[5]

The drinking-water fountain is set on two square granite steps, above which this compact and complex fountain is made up of three stages in grey and red granite. On the face of the south side of the central stage is the inscription. The other three sides are decorated with an incised pattern that was probably once inlaid with a different stone or material. Only the west side, facing St Mary on the Quay, retains its lion's head spout.

One of the secretaries to the Exhibition Committee in 1892 and 1893 was J. W. Arrowsmith, head of the printing and publishing firm. He was a lifelong liberal, and closely involved with the future University of Bristol. It was Arrowsmith who proposed and organised the statue of Edward Colston, and it may well be through his initiative that Sir William Henry Wills presented the statue of Edmund Burke. These two statues, together with this fountain, quickly brought a certain dignity to this new park in the midst of the city (see Fig. 21).[6]

This 'attractive drinking-water fountain' was suffering from 'too much care' when inspected by a conservator in 1982. Regular cleaning with brass polish was wearing away detail and spoiling the stonework.[7]

Notes

[1] P. Elkin, *Images of Bristol* (Bristol, 1995), pp.23–5. [2] Ibid, illus. p.24. [3] *Bristol Times and Mirror*, 11 June 1925, caption to a drawing of Colston Avenue by Herbert Helps. [4] Ibid. [5] BCC Engineers' Department, *Memorials, Fountains and Statues* (Bristol, 1982), p.31. [6] See Merritt, *Sculpture in Bristol*, p.28. [7] A. Naylor, 'Survey of Bristol's public monuments and fountains in bronze' (unpublished, 1983).

'The Centre', Colston Avenue, between the Drinking Fountain and Edward Colston

Commemorative Plaque to the Fourteenth Army 1942–45 C45

Sculptor: Mike Baker

Date: 2008
Dimensions: 29in diameter
Materials: bronze set in Bath stone
Inscription around the rim: FOURTEENTH ARMY * FIELD MARSHAL "BILL" SLIM 1891–1970 * KOHIMA EPITAPH "WHEN YOU GO HOME, TELL THEM OF US AND SAY – FOR YOUR TOMORROW WE GAVE OUR TODAY"
—: explanatory plaque on the bronze relief – THE FOURTEENTH ARMY 1942–45/ THIS PLAQUE COMMEMORATES THE MEN AND WOMEN OF THE FOURTEENTH ARMY, 1942–1945, LED BY BRISTOL-BORN FIELD MARSHAL SIR WILLIAM ("UNCLE BILL") SLIM, THE 1ST VISCOUNT SLIM OF BISHOPSTON AND JARAMULLA, KG, GCB, GCMG, GCVO, CBE, DSO, MC, (1891–1970), KNOWN AS "THE FORGOTTEN", THEY DEFEATED THE JAPANESE INVASION OF INDIA IN 1944 AND LIBERATED BURMA IN 1945. THIS WAS BRITAIN'S LARGEST AND MOST DIVERSE ARMY COMPRISING MANY NATIONALITIES AND FAITHS, THEY FOUGHT FOR THE CAUSE OF FREEDOM. This plaque was commissioned and supported by the Burma Plaque Commemorative Appeal Committee, The Cultural Palace, Ray King and the Burma Star Association, Friendship Global, TocH, Gurkha Veterans Foundation, Sikh Resource Centre, the John James Bristol Foundation, Veterans donations, Bristol City Council, the Bristol Commonwealth Society and Living Easton.
Status: not listed
Owned by Bristol City Council
Condition: good

The so-called Kohima epitaph quoted on the rim of the plaque may have been first inscribed on the war memorial at Kohima in November

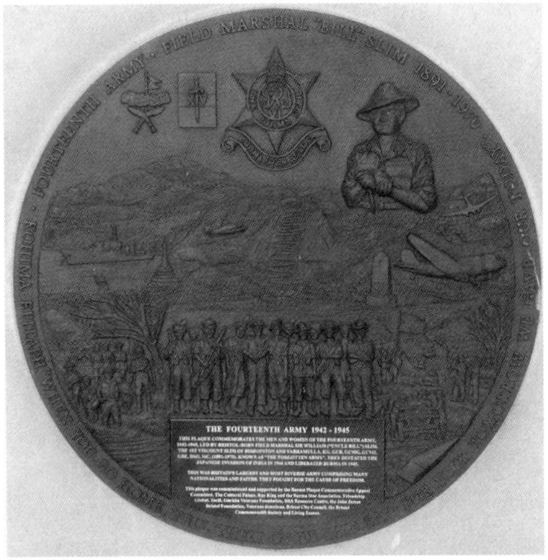

Miles Baker, *Commemorative Plaque to the Fourteenth Army 1942–1945*

1944. Major John Etry-Leal, a classical scholar, was movingly adapting or perhaps misremembering an epitaph by another classical scholar, J. M. Edmonds, who had earlier written: 'When you go home, tell them of us and say / "For your to-morrows, these gave their today"'.[1] It was at Kohima that the Fourteenth Army first halted the invasion of India by the Japanese.

Viscount Slim was born in Bishopston, Bristol, in 1891, the son of a hardware merchant. He attended St Brendan's Catholic School, then in Berkeley Square. In 1903 the family moved to Birmingham, where he later went to King Edward's School. In 1914 he was commissioned in the Royal Warwickshire regiment. He was wounded at Gallipoli, and he was later at the capture of Baghdad. In 1919 he was transferred to the Indian army, ultimately taking command of the 2nd battalion, 7th Gurkha rifles in 1938. Slim was to see much action in the Middle East before taking command of 1st Burma corps and brilliantly managing its retreat from Burma. He then took over the so-called Fourteenth Army, successfully repulsing the Japanese invasion of India. His bold and superbly managed pursuit of the Japanese through Burma was to be the Indian army's last great campaign. He enjoyed the affection and trust of his troops to an almost unprecedented extent.[2] Slim was to be Chief of the Imperial General Staff, succeeding Montgomery, and whilst governor-general of Australia, he wrote *Defeat into Victory*, perhaps the finest of all military memoirs.

Slim was raised to the peerage in 1960 and it was his son, Lord Slim, who unveiled this memorial on 7 September 2008.

> If my father was here, he would say this plaque was a memorial to his soldiers. They came from every culture and creed you can think of: Indians, Gurkhas, Nepalese, Chinese, West African, Burmese, Australians and Canadians as well as Britons… it was a lesson in multi-culturalism. Bring your children to this plaque and learn about integration.[3]

Some Bristol members of the Burma Star Association are reported to have boycotted the occasion, believing that the Field Marshal should have been commemorated with a statue rather than a plaque.[4]

Notes

[1] www.perkins-smart.com/burmacampaignsociety/archive/news_pdf/2003Mar.pdf. [2] *ODNB*, *Raymond Callahan*. [3] Bristol Evening Post, 8 November 2008. [4] Ibid.

'The Centre', Colston Avenue, opposite St Stephen's Street

Cenotaph C43

Architects: Heathman and Blacker

Date: 1932
Materials: Portland stone ashlar with bronze reliefs, swords and coats of arms
Dimensions: approx. 630cm high; 380cm wide and 250cm deep at the base
Inscriptions: on the north side, facing away from the city centre, in cast numerals – 1914/1918 1939/1945
—: in raised roman capitals on a bronze plaque – SACRED TO THE MEMORY / OF BRISTOL'S SONS AND / DAUGHTERS WHO MADE / THE SUPREME SACRIFICE
—: below, in smaller caps – THEY DIED THAT MANKIND MIGHT LEARN TO LIVE IN PEACE
—: on the south side, facing the city centre, in cast numerals – 1914/1919 1939/1945
—: in raised roman capitals on a bronze plaque – "O VALIANT HEARTS WHO TO YOUR GLORY CAME, / THROUGH DUST OF CONFLICT AND THROUGH BATTLE-FLAME; / TRANQUIL YOU LIE, YOUR KNIGHTLY VIRTUE PROVED, / YOUR MEMORY HALLOWED IN THE LAND YOU LOVED. / SPLENDID YOU PASSED THE GREAT SURRENDER MADE, / INTO THE LIGHT THAT NEVERMORE SHALL FADE; / ALL YOU HAD HOPED FOR, ALL YOU HAD, YOU GAVE / TO SAVE MANKIND, YOURSELVES YOU SCORNED TO SAVE." On this plaque are two downward-pointing torches, a Roman funerary symbol
Status: Grade II
Owned by Bristol City Council
Condition: fair; conserved 2008

Bristol's cenotaph was designed to commemorate the 6,000 men and women of Bristol who died in the First World War. Around 55,000 citizens had been on active service, and the crowd that assembled when the Cenotaph was finally unveiled in 1932 was estimated at about that number.[1] Later, the dates '1939' and '1945', in cast metal, were added to match those of the earlier war.

The memorial follows the general form of Lutyen's cenotaph in Whitehall. It is quite properly much smaller, while having more decorative detail. The committee's selection of this design by an otherwise obscure architectural practice after long delays and controversy, detailed below, is understandable. The finished work, however, appears rather busy in outline and has the dignity but not the monumentality of Lutyens's masterpiece.

The cenotaph is faced with Portland stone.

The most prominent features on both the main sides of the memorial are large relief laurel-wreaths with ribbons, with a bronze sword set in the centre. When unveiled the swords were described as golden.[2] Below the large wreaths a frieze runs round all four sides. This contains circular reliefs of regimental insignia, four on each long side and two on each short side. There is an inscribed bronze plaque on the two longer sides. Both of the shorter sides have bronze casts of Bristol's coat of arms. On the top is a symbolic sarcophagus with consoles at each end. Below this are *fasces* (a bundle of rods tied together) as a symbol of strength through unity. The fascist associations of this symbol, which are also over the entrance to Bridewell Police Station (1928), were not of significance in Britain in the early 1930s. The cenotaph stands on a single step. There is then a wide base of three low steps. At the extreme corners of this are four rectangular stone blocks. The four corners of the wider paved area are marked by four fine lamp standards, which were part of the original design.

In 1930, when the site for the memorial was still undecided, a local newspaper quoted an 'old sailor' as saying that 'Bristol responded very well to the war but very badly to the War Memorial'.[3] The initial response was certainly prompt. 'Shortly after the termination of the 1914–18 War the then Lord Mayor, Ald. Twiggs, consulted a number of leading citizens. A committee was set up… but nothing concrete emerged.'[4] These are the words of the Alderman R. F. Lyne, who served as one of the chairmen of the War Memorial Committee that was formed some ten years later. Lyne also said:

> there had never been anything but a desire and willingness in the House [Bristol City Council] to recognise the services of the men killed in the war. The only difficulty had been as to what form the memorial should take.[5]

Throughout the 1920s, opinions were divided as to whether a memorial should be reverential

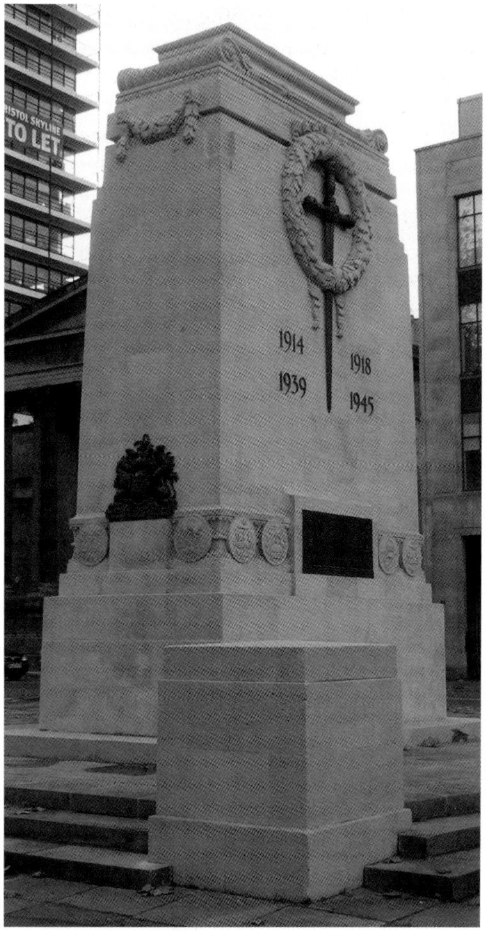

Heathman and Blacker, *Cenotaph*

or utilitarian, providing survivors with material needs, especially those who were wounded.

> It soon became clear there was no chance of raising anything like enough money to provide special homes or hospital treatment… they therefore concentrated on a memorial of the reverential type and sought a site.[6]

The Bristol branch of the British Legion had been reconstructed around 1925, and it provided the initiative for the establishment of a working committee under the chairmanship of the lord mayor, which campaigned for funds and a suitable site. Bitter arguments over alternative sites also caused much delay. Among those contemplated by the committee were: the corner below St Augustine's Church Yard; College Green; Old Market; The Horsefair; the Downs; and Colston Avenue, which was said to be 'in rather a mess'. The committee recommended that the statue of Queen Victoria on College Green should be removed to make way for the tribute to the city's war dead. The local press decided to conduct a ballot. A majority of 4,926 voted for her to remain, while 4,280 voted for her removal. The proposal was dropped. The British Legion did not give up. On 8 January 1929 a member of the city council moved a motion that Bristol should have a war memorial and that an appropriate committee of the city council should recommend a site. Another councillor moved an amendment that the memorial must be in the form of some sort of provision for the survivors. This was carried by a large majority. By November of 1929 the new committee was obliged to accept that there was no chance of the public subscribing sufficient funds and the project again stalled.

In October 1930, a petition signed by 3,552 citizens, over half of whom were ex-servicemen, was presented to the dean of Bristol Cathedral.[7] This requested that College Green should be the site for Bristol's war memorial. The dean and chapter said they could not grant the request because 'from many quarters we have evidence that there is a marked division of opinion among those actively interested in the scheme'.[8] Then, through more activity by the British Legion, money was collected. Alderman R. F. Lyne was later to write: 'I am quite certain that no memorial of the kind in the kingdom was more truly built by the efforts of small people who gave their services and their mites with great willingness'.[9]

The debate continued until the *Evening Times* and its rival, *The Bristol Times and Mirror*, cooperated in an appeal and raised just under £17,000.[10]

In announcing a competition in January 1930, the *Evening Times* acknowledged that through the 'tireless energies of Colonel [E. T.] Knox, the chairman of the Bristol ex-Services War Memorial Committee', the Colston Avenue site had been accepted. Both newspapers sponsored a competition to enable a Bristol architect to design the memorial.[11] Headed 'Chance for local architects', the rules were set out. A short list would be chosen from the entries by G. C. Lawrence, FRIBA, an assessor selected by the president of the RIBA. The architect whose design was voted best by the newspaper's readers was to be 'awarded a cheque for ten guineas whether this design be finally approved by the assessor or not'. The design favoured by the readers would, after approval by the assessor, be presented to the Bristol War Memorial Committee for adoption.

Eighteen designs were submitted, from which the assessor selected three. They were by C. R. Beecroft (third place), Adrian E. Powell (second place) and Heathman and Blacker.[12] All three designs selected by the assessor were illustrated in *The Builder*.[13] The Heathman and Blacker sketch confirms that the memorial was constructed to their competition design with the exception of the four excellent lamp standards, which are a considerable improvement on the rather prosaic examples in the background of the illustration in *The Builder*.

The Builder describes the architects as 'of Clifton'. They have not been identified, although Heathman and Blacker submitted applications to a Scottish competition for housing in 1921.[14] Plans of 1936 and 1938 by 'Heathman and Blacker' for factory extensions in St Paul's, Bristol, are in the Bristol Record Office.

The Cenotaph was unveiled on 25 June 1932 by Field-Marshall Sir William Birdwood. This was 'a momentous occasion, a rare moment of civic unity given the chequered history of the memorial scheme'.[15] The dedication was by the Bishop of Bristol and among those present were the Duke and Duchess of Beaufort and the Lord Mayor and Lady Mayoress.[16]

When defending the creation of the memorial against accusation of glorifying of war, Alderman Lyne had written 'the men who died and who were to be remembered… had died that mankind might learn to live at peace'.[17] When the project was completed, Lyne was asked by the British Legion to compress his sentiment for use on the Cenotaph. He did so, and his words 'THEY DIED THAT MANKIND MIGHT LIVE IN PEACE' are included on one of the bronze plaques. Lyne hoped these words 'may live after me'.[18] Under a joint headline: 'We will remember them', the *Western Daily Press* published a long report on the unveiling ceremony of the Cenotaph. It began 'Bristol has at last honoured her Dead'.[19] Beside this was an account of the unveiling of the statue of Earl Haig at Clifton College, which took place on the same day.

In 1998, a project to clean, repair and apply a 'shelter coat' to the Cenotaph was given listed building consent and funded by Bristol City Council.[20] This was carried out in the autumn of 2003. The shelter coat may have caused yellowing of the stone. The Cenotaph was conserved again in 2008 by Nimbus Conservation.

Notes

[1] *Bristol Evening Post*, 'Tens of thousands see Cenotaph unveiled', 27 June 1932. [2] As note 1. 'The memorial was disclosed with the golden sword gleaming.' [3] Press cutting file, April 1930, Bristol Central Library; quoted in *National Inventory of War Memorials*, 7324, p.154. [4] Alderman R.F. Lyne, *Bristol Evening Post*, 'How the Cenotaph came'. 8 November, 1946. [5] *Bristol Evening Post*, 'War memorial site approved', 18 June 1930. [6] As note 4. [7] As note 1. [8] Ibid. Letter signed by Dean H.L. Candole of Bristol Cathedral (1 December 1930). [9] As note 4. [10] *Evening Times*, 'City of Bristol War Memorial', 20 January 1931. [11] Ibid. [12] As note 3. [13] *The Builder*, 19 June 1931, pp.1092, 1100. [14] http://www.scottisharchitects.org.uk/architect_list.php?alpha=b. [15] As note 3. [16] *Bristol Evening Post*, 27 June 1932, p.7. [17] As note 3. [18] As note 4. [19] *Western Daily Press*, 27 June 1932, p.8. [20] Garry Reeder, senior surveyor, Bristol City Council, 14 October 1998; see also *Bristol Evening Post*, 9 October 1998.

'The Centre', St Augustine's Parade, on the central promenade

Neptune C51

Maker: John Randall

Date: 1721
Materials: lead; Dartmoor granite pedestal
Dimensions: statue, 225cm high; trident, 330cm long; pedestal, 220cm high; metal plaque, 48cm high
Inscription on a bronze plaque in raised Roman capitals: NEPTUNE / GOD OF THE SEA / ACCORDING TO ANCIENT MYTHOLOGY / THIS LEAD-COVERED STATUE WAS / PRODUCED BY JOSEPH RENDALL / FOUNDER. BRISTOL. 1723 / AND ERECTED ON THE SITE OF / THE OLD RESERVOIR OF TEMPLE / CONDUIT IN TEMPLE STREET / RE-ERECTED IN BEAR LANE. / TEMPLE. 1787 – REMOVED TO / CHURCH LANE. TEMPLE. 1794 – / REMOVED TO THE JUNCTION OF / TEMPLE STREET AND VICTORIA / STREET 1872. / ERECTED ON THIS SITE. / LATITUDE 51 27' 06" NORTH / LONGITUDE 2 35' 47" WEST / 10TH MAY 1949 /
Status: Grade II*
Owned by Bristol City Council
Condition: fair, after much conservation

Neptune is an impressively baroque statue, windswept and full of movement. The vigorous *contraposto* pose, the movement of the drapery and the flow of his beard, suggest that this could be the work of a sophisticated sculptor of the early eighteenth century. An historian of architecture and another of sculpture have been less generous, referring to 'a somewhat pot-bellied deity' [1] and 'a flabby Neptune'.[2] Such criticisms may be unjust. The statue's former concrete core, perhaps added in the nineteenth century, may have filled him out and seriously distorted his appearance. The figure is cast in lead, which lacks the rigidity of bronze and which can soften and lose surface detail. There could also have been problems early in the statue's life, exacerbated by its numerous moves. Such considerations were not made by the most recent conservator to work on the statue. Andrew Naylor wrote that *Neptune*:

> was obviously not the work of a formally trained sculptor as the modelling is naïve and simple... it is not inconceivable that the actual sculptor was a shipyard carpenter/carver who had been trained in the tradition of ship decoration and figurehead carving.[3]

The old and possibly original plinth was replaced by two blocks of rough-hewn Dartmoor granite when the statue moved to the end of St Augustine's Reach in 1949. On the upper block is an inscription listing earlier locations, before 1949, and the precise latitude and longitude of St Augustine's Reach. The figure has recently been painted matt grey to simulate lead, but the council's property services manager has acknowledged that the tone is too light. At the present site, selected in late 1999, the pedestal rests on the pavement with no additional steps and *Neptune* now faces the river.

Evidence that this statue was made in the year 1721 comes from the parish records of the Temple District for the accounts relating to St Paul's Fair, dated January 1722.[4] The following entries appear on the same page: 'To John Randall for the Figure Neptune & Peddistoll £32.10.' and 'To Widow Maddox for Paynting Neptune & Irons.£2. 12.', an entry that confirms that the statue was originally coloured. Simon Edney was paid £35.18.9 for the 'Iron Pallisades' around it and 'James Patty' was paid £11.4 for the Portland stone surround. Randall was also paid for 'for freestone for coping of New Cistern £2.9.', for the building of which John Noads received £22. 8. 8. Randall's comparatively modest payments confirm that he was the founder or maker of the

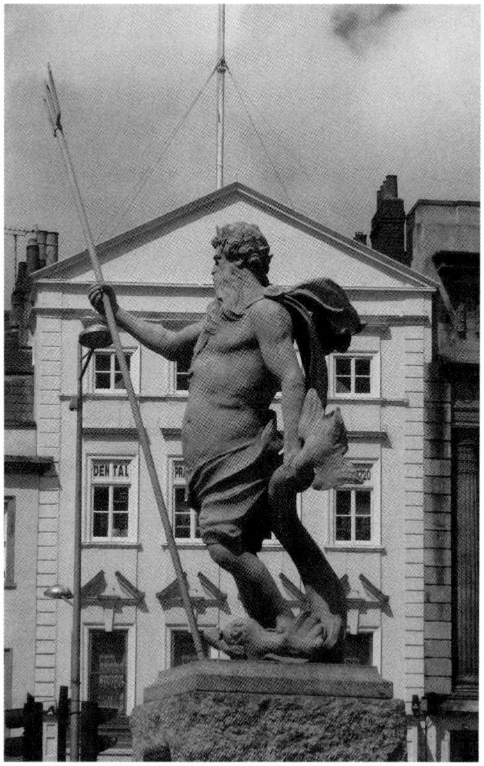

John Randall, *Neptune*

statue. The sculptor remains unidentified.[5] Simon Edney is likely to be related to William Edney, maker of magnificent wrought-iron gates within St Mary Redcliffe and other Bristol churches at this time. James Patty is likely to be James Paty I, the earliest of that remarkable dynasty of Bristol masons, carvers and architects.

In the late nineteenth century, the historian John Latimer recorded that when the 'old reservoir of Temple Conduit was taken down and a new one constructed, chiefly of the old materials... the statue of Neptune, cast by a person named Randall, made its first appearance on the renovated structure'.[6] He stated that two dates appeared on the 'front stone' of the reservoir – '1586 and 1723' – the first denoting the year when the old conduit was erected, the second when the rebuilding was completed. Temple Conduit was one of the city's most important sources of fresh water, and was fed from a spring below Totterdown.

An inscribed plaque, added to the new pedestal when the statue was moved in 1872, asserted that 'the figure was set in the reign of Elizabeth to commemorate the defeat of the Spanish Armada.' Latimer dismissively called this 'a remarkable illustration of the rapid development of local legends'.[7] Latimer also pointed out that a Joseph Rendle, founder, appears in a Bristol poll book for 1734. It is this name, rather than John Randle, that appears on the present 1949 plaque, transcribed above.[8]

The earliest known printed account of *Neptune* is a newspaper advertisement of 1728; a dealer announced that his goods would be on sale 'at the Barber's Pole and Sign of the Looking Glass, a little below the *Neptune* in Temple Street'.[9] An image of Neptune that was quite possibly inspired by the statue appears on a Bristol-made flower brick in tin-glazed earthenware of about 1740.[10]

The statue has had six separate sites, involving more moves than any other sculpture in the city. The precise position of the first site of the statue at a conduit in Temple Street is still uncertain;[11] it was probably at the corner of Water Lane. After 64 years, *Neptune* moved to its second site in 1787, to the end of Beer Lane, near Dr White's Almshouses. Only seven years later, in 1794, the third move was to a site in Church Lane. It remained there for its longest stay, 78 years, until November 1872 when the building of Victoria Street from Bristol Bridge to Temple Meads prompted its fourth move, to the junction of Temple Lane and Victoria Street. There it was set on a pedestal with animal troughs outside the King's Head, by the tower of Temple Church.[12] These four sites were each on the course of the water conduit. *Neptune* was next moved in May 1949, when the statue received a new granite pedestal for a fifth setting at the Bridgehead at St Augustine's

Quay. It no longer marked a water source, although the River Frome now flows beneath it. At the end of 1999 the statue was moved a short distance to overlook rows of spouting fountains in the newly-designed traffic island known as 'the Centre', a shortening of 'tramway centre'.

In 1981, the Conservation Department of the Bristol Museum and Art Gallery inspected the statue and noted the urgent need for major repairs and conservation. Their report stated that the cracks in the statue were so severe that they 'threaten the stability of the statue in the immediate future'.[13] An approach to Andrew Naylor for his views was supported by Dr Jonathon Ashley-Smith, keeper of conservation at the Victoria and Albert Museum. *Neptune* was transported to Naylor's workshops in Telford in 1982. The conservation work revealed a supporting iron armature in the concrete core that had been added during an earlier repair, and deep corrosion of the inner lead surfaces.[14] On removing the armature the lead fell into more than 19 pieces. These were re-formed around a stainless steel armature and other internal reinforcing. The cost of this work was estimated at £5,500.[15] Naylor's company spent over 1,000 hours on the conservation, and the final cost approached £10,000. Naylor and his company were to conserve the statue again in 1987 when it was damaged by falling scaffolding after a gale.[16]

Evidence that *Neptune* was painted comes both from the original payment to Widow Maddox and particularly from a watercolour of 1825 by George Delamotte, when the statue stood in Church Lane.[17] In this work, Neptune is distinctly flesh coloured, his hair, beard and drapery are grey and the serpent is a dark colour with a gilded mouth and tail. Neptune's crown is also gilded. A few years earlier, the future poet laureate, Robert Southey, who was born and married in Bristol, had humorously described this statue as if he were a first-time visitor to the city: 'I saw something like a public fountain, with a painted statue of Neptune above it, which is as little creditable to the decency of the magistrates as to the state of the arts in the city'.[18] In the later nineteenth century, the statue was given a bronze finish and this approach was repeated at the 1982 restoration. It was then argued that the effect 'was aesthetically unpleasing and resulted in the sculpture appearing as a large dark blob'.[19] The present lead-coloured acrylic masonry paint, now acknowledged as too light, was sprayed on in 1987.[20] The late Gervase Jackson-Stops argued persuasively in the same year that most eighteenth century lead statues were gilded, painted to imitate stone or bronze or given a life-like appearance.[21]

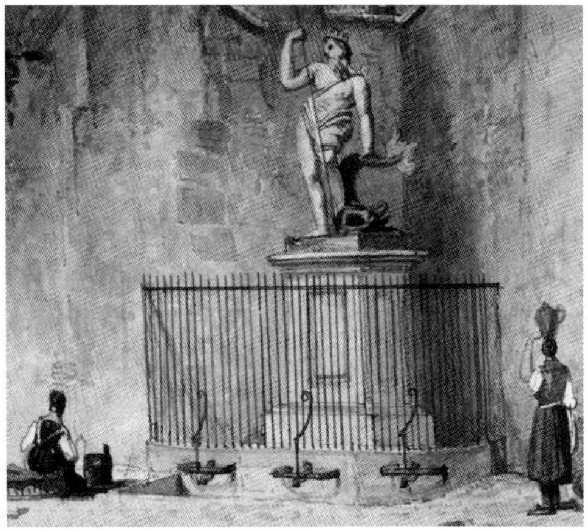

***Neptune in Church Lane, near Temple Church*, detail of a watercolour by George Delamotte, 1825 (Bristol Museum and Art Gallery, M2170)**

The Romans identified their own ancient deity of fresh water, Neptune, with Poseidon, the Greek god of the sea. Thus Neptune became directly linked to the Greek myth and has since been known as a sea god. However, his ancient festival, Neptunalia, was on 23 July in the heat of the summer, when streams dry up and water is most wanted.[22] The appearance of a statue of Neptune at a source of fresh water, the Temple Conduit in this instance, would have had greater resonance in the eighteenth century. Modern accounts are inclined to assume, erroneously, that Neptune was chosen for this early public sculpture because of Bristol's seafaring associations.

A suggestion that the cast-lead dolphins on either side of the entrance to Edward Colston's school in the Great House may have come from Randall's foundry has led to a theory that the philanthropist, whose emblem was a dolphin, may have been responsible for the conduit and for *Neptune*.[23] Colston died in 1721, the year the statue was being made, and the provision of fountains and water conduits was often the result of charity. However, there is no documentary evidence to connect Edward Colston with this statue.

Notes

[1] B. Little, *Bristol: the Public View* (Bristol, 1981), pp.70, 71. [2] J. Darke, *The Monument Guide to England and Wales* (London and Sydney, 1991), p.101. [3] A. Naylor, 'Bridgehead Neptune', press release, 24 August 1983. [4] 'St Paul's Fair for charges attending it and then Parish Water which the Profits of the Fair are to defray', BRO, Access number BRO/CA27. [5] Gunnis, *Dictionary of British Sculptors*, has an entry for John Randle of Gloucester, stone-cutter, commissioned to build a six-foot monument at Newent in 1709. [6] John Latimer, *Annals of Bristol in the Eighteenth Century* (Bristol, 1893), vol. III, pp.135–6; Latimer stated that his information came from 'Mr Tyson' notes preserved in the Jefferies MSS. [7] Ibid. p.135; this plaque was given to the Bristol Museum and Art Gallery. [8] Ibid. [9] Latimer, *Bristol in the Eighteenth Century*, vol. II, p.136: *Sarah Farley's Bristol Journal*, 22 December 1787. [10] A.E. Lange, *Delftware at Historic Deerfield 1600–1800* (Deerfield, MA, c.2001), p.116. [11] BCC Engineers' Department, *Memorials, Fountains and Statues.* [12] A late nineteenth-century watercolour in a private collection by E. Parkman shows this site. [13] Report by conservation assistant, Bristol Museum and Art Gallery, 20 July 1981. [14] As note 3. [15] 'Why poor old Neptune is cracking up', *Western Daily Press*, 12 January 1982. [16] 'Tide is turning for city statue', *Evening Post*, 16 April 1987. [17] George Delamotte, *The Neptune, Church Lane, near Temple Church,* M2170, (1825), Braikenridge Bequest, Bristol City Museum and Art Gallery. [18] R. Southey, *Letters from England, 1807* (ed. A. Sutton, Bristol, 1984), p.475. Southey's book was satirical and 'tongue in cheek'. [19] A. Beeson, *Evening Post*, BRL file of press cuttings etc. [20] G. Jackson-Stops, 'New deities for old parterres; the painting of lead statues', *Country Life*, 29 January

1987, pp.92–4. [21] Ibid., a photograph of Bristol's *Neptune* being painted is on p.94. [22] J. Herrman and C. Kondoleon, 'The poetry of water in Roman Imperial art', *Apollo*, May 2003, p.14. [23] Note from A. Beeson, BRL.

'The Centre', St Augustine's Parade, on the central promenade opposite Baldwin Street

Edmund Burke C48

Sculptor: James Havard Thomas

Date: 1894
Materials: bronze; pedestal, Aberdeen granite
Dimensions: statue, 284cm high, 150cm wide, 162cm deep; pedestal, 280cm high, 137cm square
Foundry: Sommer, Naples
Inscription: on the front of the pedestal – BURKE / 1774–1780 / 'I WISH TO BE A MEMBER / OF PARLIAMENT TO HAVE MY / SHARE OF DOING GOOD AND / RESISTING EVIL' / SPEECH AT BRISTOL 1780
—: on the rear of the pedestal – TO / HIS FELLOW CITIZENS. / FROM / WILLIAM HENRY WILLS. / BART. / 1894.
—: signed and dated on the base of the bronze cast – I Havard Thomas / MDCCCXVIV CAST CIRE PERDVE / SOMMER NAPLES
Status: Grade II
Owned by Bristol City Council
Condition: good; some shrapnel damage

The dates '1774–1780', inscribed directly under the single name 'Burke', record the six years when Edmund Burke (1729–97) represented Bristol in Parliament. He is the most distinguished politician ever to have done so. He gained the seat when he was 45 and 'at the height of his powers'.[1] Always noted for his eloquence and brilliance as an orator, he was rarely in the city.

Born in Dublin, his father, an attorney, was a Protestant, and his mother a Catholic. He entered Trinity College, Dublin in 1743 and later came to London to follow a legal career.[2] Poor health from early childhood, possibly consumption, continued and he first came to the West Country to take the waters of Bath and the Hotwells in Bristol.[3] He was first elected to Parliament in 1765, representing the pocket borough of Wendover. In 1774 the longstanding Tory interest at Bristol was in some disarray, and the Whigs were short of a convincing candidate to run alongside Henry Cruger, an American-born merchant of radical views and little political experience. Richard Champion, the Quaker merchant and porcelain manufacturer, acted as campaign manager. He presented Burke to his friends as 'indisputably the first literary Character in the Kingdom' and 'a perfect Master of its commercial Interests'. The new MP was elected with startling ease and at little expense to himself.[4]

Cruger and Burke's success was partly due to their sympathy for the American colonists. Burke supported the repeal of the unpopular Stamp Act, and this was the subject of his maiden speech. However, Burke also made a speech in Bristol on the day of his election in which he asserted:

> Parliament is not a congress of Ambassadors from different and hostile interests… but… a deliberative assembly of one nation, with one interest, that of the whole; where, not local purposes, not local prejudices ought to guide, but the general good… you choose a member indeed: but when you have chosen him, he is not a member of Bristol, he is a member of parliament.[5]

This did not endear him to Bristol, and towards the end of his term Burke realised that his constituents would not accept his support of the lifting of trade restrictions with Ireland and of toleration of both Catholics and dissenters. He argued for the reform of the slave trade and its ultimate abolition. Furthermore, as the nation's enemies increased, so too did loyalist support. On the first day of the 1780 election he polled so badly that 'with the unanimous advice of his friends, he decided to withdraw'.[6] He later remarked that 'If I had followed the humours of this town, which are called opinions, I should have been more frequently wrong, than even if I had been guided by the Court'.[7]

The statue is larger than life-size. The figure is clothed in the style of the 1780s: an unfastened knee-length coat, a waistcoat, a stock tied at the neck, breeches, stockings and low-heeled shoes. Burke steps forward with the

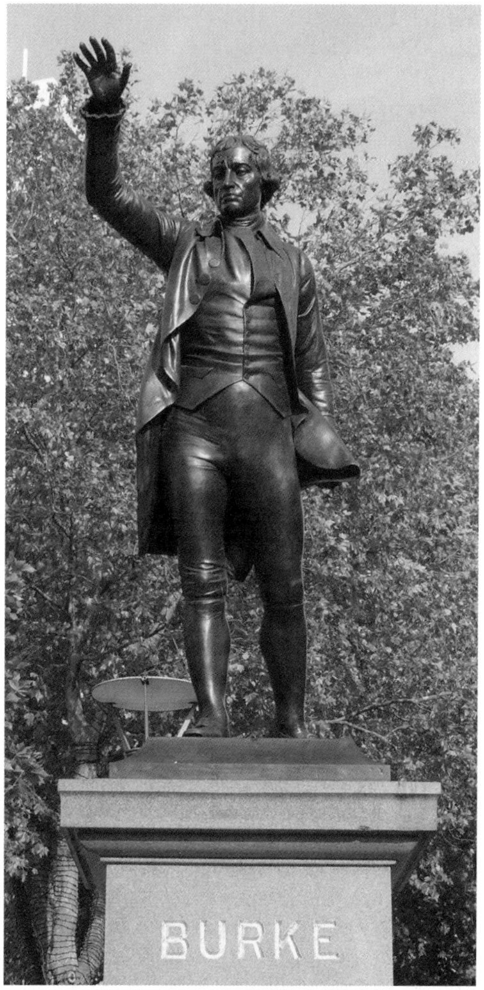

James Havard Thomas, *Edmund Burke*

weight on the right foot and faces the quay head to the south. His right hand, open with palm down, is raised in a dramatic declamatory gesture. His left hand holds a wide-brimmed tricorn. His short hair forms a fringe over his forehead and finishes in curls, above the collar. The strongly featured face has an intense expression and most clearly resembles the portrait by Sir Joshua Reynolds.[8] The pose may owe something to a painting of Charles James Fox and Burke in the National Gallery of Ireland, and perhaps also to a figure in Jacques Louis David's *Oath in the Tennis Court* at Versailles.[9]

This statue was a gift, as the pedestal inscription proclaims, to 'his fellow citizens' from the tobacco magnate William Henry Wills (1830–1911), later Lord Winterstoke. He first entered parliament as the Liberal MP for East Bristol in 1894.

Burke was broadly considered a 'liberal', and the Liberal Party had powerful supporters in Bristol at the end of the nineteenth century among the non-conformist and manufacturing families such as the Wills and the Frys. There was, in the 1880s, growing goodwill between Bristol, the United States and Canada. Burke's pro-American views were again in favour.

Although prominently signed by the sculptor, James Havard Thomas, the statue has previously been repeatedly described as a bronze replica of the marble statue by William Theed the Younger made for the Palace of Westminster in 1858. This misattribution may be partly due to Latimer's *Annals of Bristol*, which states that a letter from 'Mr W. H. Wills' was read at a Council meeting on 14 June 1892. This offered 'to erect… a replica in bronze of the marble statue of Edmund Burke standing in St Stephen's Hall, Westminster'.[10]

There is no resemblance between the two statues.[11] Another source of the incorrect attribution was a book published to celebrate the fiftieth anniversary of *The Western Daily Press* in 1908: 'On Oct. 30th 1894, Lord Rosebery, the Premier, unveiled a bronze statue of Edmund Burke in Colston Avenue. It was a replica of one in the Houses of Parliament'.[12] A reprint of this book published in 1909 contains the following erratum:

> The reference to the Burke statue on page 311 of this section needs correction. Sir William Henry Wills, (now Lord Winterstoke) in his communication to the City Council in 1892, offered to present a bronze replica of the marble statue in Westminster Abbey [sic]. The success of the Bristol sculptor, Mr J. Havard Thomas, however, led to the commission being entrusted to him, and the statue in Colston Avenue is his work.[13]

As the inscription implies, the bronze was cast at the Fonderia Sommer in Naples. Havard Thomas:

> lived in Naples, Pompeii and Capri, [1889 and 1906] studying the old work, particularly the Greek bronzes: in Naples he made the fine bronze statue of Burke, which is now in Bristol, working at the foundry and making himself a thorough master of the art of bronze founding.[14]

A poignant link between sculptor and subject comes from Sir George Clausen. As a fellow student at the South Kensington Schools he recalled Havard Thomas in the 1870s:[15]

> I remember him bringing an atmosphere of the eighteenth century classicists into the school; he would quote Burke on the Sublime and Beautiful, and would discourse on Hamilton's Greek vases… it is evident that from those early days to the end of his career, he held consistently to the same ideal to follow the classic tradition of fine sculpture. His life was an unceasing effort to find out how.[16]

A small bronze of Burke (75cm high), thought to be Havard Thomas's model on which the full-scale statue was based, was auctioned in Bristol in July 1977. The newspaper photograph of the statuette shows that Burke's raised right hand is not in the same position as that in the Bristol statue.[17]

Lord Rosebery came to Bristol to unveil the statue in October 1894.[18] He had become the Prime Minister in March, when he took over from the 85-year-old Gladstone. Due to heavy rain, Roseberry delivered his address on the life and character of Burke and his connections with Bristol in the Colston Hall:

> It is about 114 years since Bristol dismissed Edmund Burke from her service. She has long since repented that dismissal… she repents it today… in the nobler and more significant form of that effigy that has been unveiled outside. (Applause.)

The site for the statue had only recently been formed when in 1892–3 the River Frome between St Augustine's Bridge, opposite Clare Street, and the Stone Bridge above St Mary on the Quay, was covered over.[19] The setting and the erection were prepared by the firm of Messrs Cowlin and Sons, which also erected the statues of Queen Victoria in 1888 and the adjacent Colston in 1895. The council paid for the statue's erection, and the accounts record that £250.17.4 was expended 'in connection with the Burke statue'.[20]

Burke has since been moved three times, but it is now close to its first site, although on a different traffic island. J. W. Arrowsmith, a close friend of William Henry Wills, was behind the statue of Edward Colston, 1894, and the fountain, 1901, and it is possible that Arrowsmith may also have played a part in this commission also.

The bronze was taken down on 25 January 1922 for a copy to be made, and was re-erected on 19 February.[21] Havard Thomas had died the previous year. The statue was re-cast in bronze by H. H. Martyn & Co. of Cheltenham, and the copy now stands on a granite pedestal at the junction of Massachusetts Avenue and 11th and 12th St, NW in Washington, DC. The inscription differs from the Bristol version.

Under 'BURKE' are the dates of his birth and death, and the quotation: 'MAGNANIMITY / IN POLITICS IS / NOT SELDOM THE / TRVEST WISDOM'.

A government guide to statues in Washington says that Burke 'advocated liberal treatment of the American colonies' and that the statue was 'donated to the people of America by Sir Charles Cheers Wakefield through the Sulgrave Institution under an Act of Congress, approved on April 25, 1922 (42 Statue.499) without expense to US. Dedicated November 12, 1922'.[22] Lord Wakefield had been chairman of Wakefield Lubricants, a former Lord Mayor of London and the honorary treasurer of the Anglo-American Society.[23]

In 1983, the Bristol statue was the subject of a professional conservation report.[24] The surface was then covered with thick black paint, but the metal was exposed in places. Some holes appeared to be shrapnel damage. These were above the right elbow, on both sides of the forearm, above the eyebrow and below the mouth. The chest had punctures on both sides. There were patches of corrosion on the left leg. Further holes were found in the left inner ankle, the left side and the right leg. The core was still inside the casting and water penetration was causing internal corrosion. Major conservation was recommended, but not carried out. In January 1999 a further report was prepared and in 2003 the statue and the pedestal were fully conserved.[25] The name 'Burke' was re-gilded and the statue moved some 60 metres south and aligned with the statue of *Neptune*.

Notes

[1] P.T. Underdown, *Bristol and Burke* (Bristol, 1961), p.3. [2] A bronze by J.H. Foley RA (1868) stands near the entrance of Trinity College. [3] G.E. Weare, *Edmund Burke's Connection with Bristol, from 1774 Till 1780* (Bristol, 1894), p.vii. [4] *ODNB, Paul Langford* [5] As note 3, p.89; Burke's speech to the electors of Bristol, 3 November 1774. [6] As note 1, p.17. [7] As note 4. [8] Sir Joshua Reynolds, *Edmund Burke* (1771) oil on canvas, National Portrait Gallery, London. [9] T. Hickey, *Charles James Fox and Edmund Burke*, National Gallery of Ireland, Dublin. [10] J. Latimer, *Annals of Bristol in the Nineteenth Century Concluded, 1887–1900* (Bristol, 1902), p.27. [11] Letter and photograph of William Theed the Younger's statue from Jacqueline Riding, assistant curator at Palace of Westminster, 3 June 1998: 'The statue (in St Stephen's Hall) is indeed by William Theed. Commissioned in 1856 by the Fine Arts Commission. It was the last of the set to be completed and was put up into position in 1858.' [12] G.F. Stone, *Bristol: As It Was and As It Is – A Record of Fifty Years of Progress* (Bristol, 1909), p.311. [13] As note 12, addendum from *Bristol Evening News*, p.314. [14] Beaux Arts Gallery, *J. Havard Thomas (1854–21), Commemorative Exhibition of Sculpture and Drawings* (exhib. cat., London, 1936). [15] Ibid. A memoir by Sir George Clausen, RA, published by the Leicester Galleries. [16] Edmund Burke, *A Philosophical Inquiry into the Origin of our Ideas of the Sublime and Beautiful* (London, 1757). [17] 'Model statue for auction', *Evening Post*, 21 May 1977; private coll., Bristol. [18] 'Lord Rosebery in Bristol', *The Western Daily Press*, 31 October 1894. [19] *Ordnance Survey Map Bristol (NW) and Clifton 1901*, (Newcastle upon Tyne); a photographic card of 1909 and line drawings of Colston Avenue by Samuel Loxton, *Bristol Times and Mirror*, 1905. [20] City of Bristol, 'Abstract of accounts (1894–1895) General Disbursements', BRO. [21] BCC Engineers' Department, report, December 1982, p.21. [22] *Statues, Monuments and Memorials in the Parks of the National Capital* (Washington, DC, 1973), p.5. [23] *Kelly's Handbook to the Titled, Landed and Official Classes* (London, 1931). [24] Naylor, 'Bristol's public monuments'. [25] Garry Reeder, senior surveyor, Bristol City Council, 1999; Bristol Evening Post, 31 July 2001 announced a £5000 'facelift'.

Christmas Street

Within St Bartholomew's Gateway at the bottom of Christmas Steps off Host Street

Virgin and Child Enthroned C12

Sculptor unknown

Date: c.1240
Material: limestone, possibly from Dundry
Dimensions: 120cm high, 50cm wide at the base
Inscription on a bronze plaque: The restoration of St Bartholomew's Hospital was / carried out for the Trustees of Bristol Municipal / Charities with the aid of grants from the Historic / Buildings Council and Bristol City Council by / Moxley Jenner and Partners Architects and / Quantity Surveyors and C. H. Pearce & Sons Ltd. / Contractors. The completed works were opened / by Lord Montague of Beaulieu Chairman of the / Historic Buildings and Monuments Commission / for England on 4 July 1984 / Charles N. Clarke Chairman of the Trustees / Richard S. Hawkins Secretary General
Status: Grade II
Owned by Bristol Charities
Condition: poor; very damaged and black, at risk

This headless and much damaged statue is a precious fragment of exceptional quality. The restored remains of St Bartholomew's Hospital, established sometime before 1207, are of considerable interest, but when Nikolaus Pevsner visited the site in the mid-1950s, he found this medieval statue on a wall at the entrance, 'disgracefully squeezed in by a waste-pipe'.[1] He described it as 'very defaced, but evidently once of very high quality and in the style of the Wells [Cathedral] façade'.[2]

A drawing of 1820 shows the statue wedged in-between the gateway archway and the drainpipe, and resting on an infill of unevenly shaped stones (Fig. 4). The statue is clearly headless, but the drawing shows a separate head, now lost, lodged between the Virgin's right shoulder and the wall.

After the restoration and development of the Hospital site in 1984, the statue was moved to within the shelter and relative security of the medieval entrance-way. It is now set on a modern stone column against the wall, approximately 160cm from the ground.

A well-informed correspondent writing to the *Evening Post* suggested that the statue was carved from Dundry stone.[3] The Virgin's forearms are missing, as is the upper torso of the Christ Child. The Virgin's knees are also

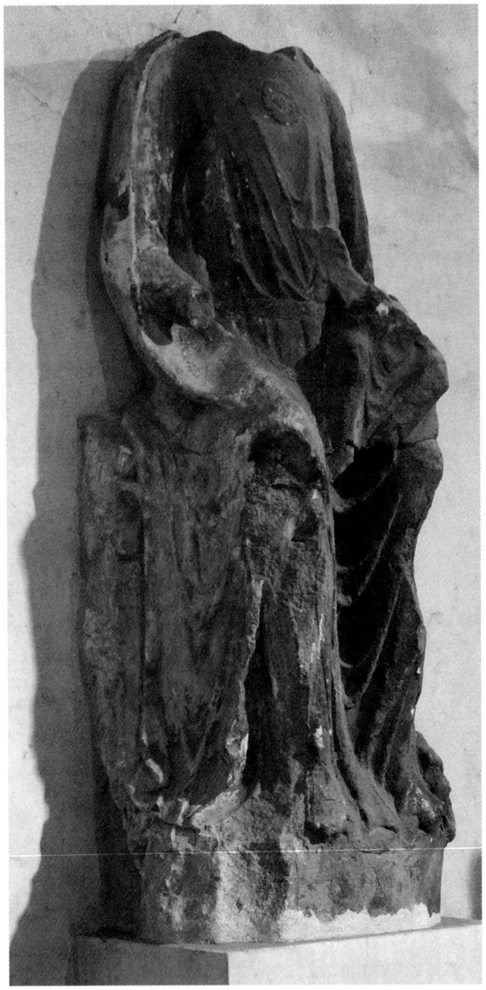

Virgin and Child Enthroned

missing, but the adjoining parts have large conical dowel holes, as does the lower part of the Christ Child's body.

A report on St Bartholomew's Court published by the National Health Service, which in the 1980s occupied part of the building, stated that St Bartholomew's was one of about a dozen ecclesiastical foundations in Bristol that cared for the sick, the old, the destitute and travellers.[4] The report states that the figure is stylistically 'similar to the sculptures on the west front of Wells Cathedral, so it was probably made either in the workshops there, or in Bristol, by a Wells mason. As that gives it a date exactly contemporary with the founding of St Bartholomew's it seems reasonable to assume the Madonna was made for the hospital chapel and has been in the building ever since'.[5] The elongation of the figure and the perspective of the seat or throne, together with the folds of the drapery at the sides of the figure of the Virgin, suggest that the statue was originally contained within an architectural setting. It could have been the central feature of a tympanum above the entrance to a church or chapel.

The statue, previously half sunk into plaster, was found to have traces of paint, similar to the colours on the statues at Wells, when it was removed from the outer wall.[6] The relocation of this rare and graceful statue to within the relative the shelter of the porch followed the redevelopment of much of the St Bartholomew's Hospital site. Bristol council contributed £1000 towards the costs of the statue's relocation, in support of which a councilor ambitiously stated: 'This will be a landmark of interest and a tourist attraction for the city'.[7]

The statue is continuing to suffer damage, perhaps from passing scaffolding poles and such like. Although safer than before, it is now unnoticed by passers-by. It deserves both full and expert conservation and a museum environment.

Notes

[1] N. Pevsner, *North Somerset and Bristol, Buildings of England* (Harmondsworth, 1958), pp.438–9. [2] Ibid, p.439. [3] Stephen Barrow, *Evening Post,* 26 October 2004. [4] National Health Service Training Directorate, *History of St Bartholomew's Court* (c.1986), p.1. [5] Ibid, p.2 [6] Ibid. [7] Ibid, Councillor Claude Draper.

Clare Street

Clare Street House, now Halifax, on the corner of St Stephen's Street and Clare Street

Sculpture and Decorative Detail to 28 Clare Street C50

Sculptor: Gilbert Seale

Architect: George Oatley

Date: 1905–6
Material: stone
Status: Grade II*
Condition: good

28 Clare Street brings together an outstanding late Victorian decorative carver from London, one of Bristol's greatest architects and her most important businessman and entrepreneur at the beginning of the twentieth century.

The headquarters of George White's numerous and ever-expanding transport companies had been on the upper floors of 28 Clare Street on the corner with St Stephen's Street.[1] On the opposite corner was – and still is – the domed, columned and distinctly Baroque Scottish Provident Institution by George Oatley of 1903–5. Another nearby and equally striking corner building is Alfred Waterhouse's former Prudential building of 1899, a hot terracotta Flemish-Renaissance concoction. Oatley had been remodelling Cotham House for the Whites between 1902 and 1904, and he was then commissioned to remodel the corner block of 28 Clare Street, Clare Street House, into the whole of which George White's companies were moving. There had previously been shops on the ground floor and it had been built only twenty or so years earlier, the architect being Henry Crisp, a future partner of Oatley's.

The transformation of the exterior:

> was achieved mainly through the carving of practically every previously plain surface in an early French Renaissance style. Oatley

sent the carver, Gilbert Seale, a drawing of part of the façade of L'Hôtel de Bourgtheroulde at Rouen to show him what he had in mind. This was probably a drawing of a wing of the building called the Galerie d'Aumale, constructed between 1520 and 1530. It is the most famous part of the building – the arches are decorated with deep sumptuous carving – and Oatley would have seen it when he visited Rouen in 1882. The Bureau des Finances on the Place de la Cathédrale, Rouen, begun in 1509, is similarly decorated. Oatley was obviously looking to princely early-Renaissance buildings such as these to fulfil White's aspirations.[2]

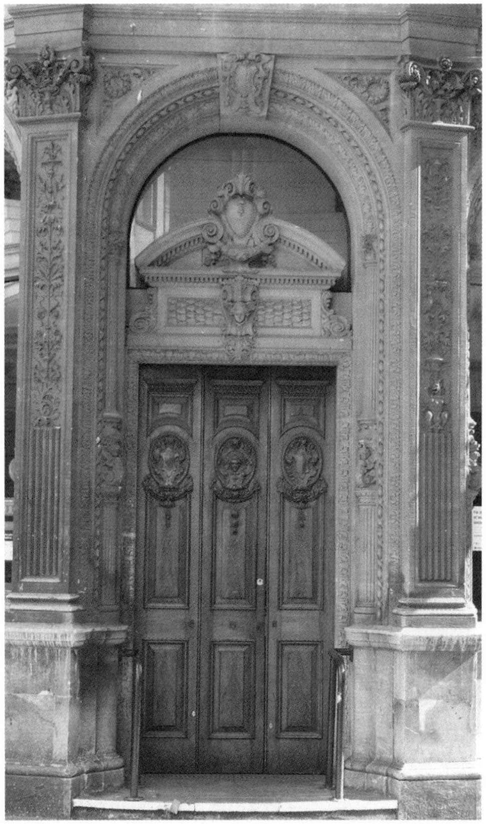

Gilbert Seale, ***28 Clare Street entrance***

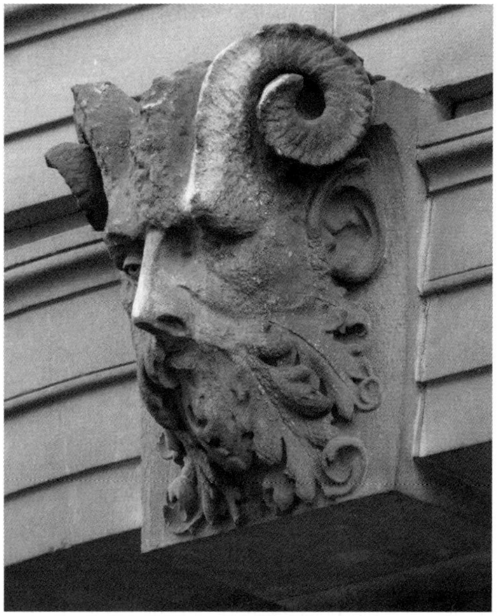

Gilbert Seale, ***28 Clare Street keystone head***

Gilbert Seale's caryatids and decorated pilasters and the original carved wooden doors are particularly noteworthy. 'Through a misunderstanding, Seale carved male as well as female figures for the façade, when it was intended that they all be female but varied slightly. To avoid delay the carvings were fixed on the building and the client must have approved them.'[3] In a letter of 1920, Oatley was to refer to Cotham House's 'over-elaborate finishings'.[4] Clare Street House may more accurately reflect the taste of the client than of the architect.

Notes
[1] This entry is most gratefully based upon Dr Sarah Whittingham's book *Sir George Herbert Oatley: Architect of Bristol* (Bristol, 2009) [2] Ibid. George White also knew Rouen well and the recommendation may well have come first from him; information from Sir George White Bt. FSA, 2008. [3] Ibid. [4] Ibid.

Clifton Down: Sir William Draper and his monuments

Lieutenant-General Sir William Draper (1721–87) erected two monuments, a cenotaph and an obelisk, in the garden of his house, Manilla Hall, where Manilla Road now stands. The cenotaph commemorates the 22 officers, ensigns and surgeons who died fighting with him, and the obelisk records his profound admiration for William Pitt, Earl of Chatham.[1] The survival of the memorials may, in part, be credited to the 'public spirit' of Dr John Beddoe FRS (1826–1914).[2] Following the purchase of Manilla Hall by an order of French nuns, he organised a public subscription and persuaded the Downs Committee and the Society of Merchant Venturers to permit and contribute to the careful removal of the two monuments. They were re-erected just a hundred metres or so away near the edge of Clifton Down in 1883.[3]

Draper was a descendant of a family of minor gentry from Oxfordshire. His father had come to Bristol, where he was found a 'place' in Customs and Excise. He died, aged only 25, a month or two before William was born in 1721, leaving his wife with four children below the age of eight. William was educated at the Cathedral School, Bristol, and as a King's Scholar at Eton College.[4] In 1749 he was elected Fellow of King's College, Cambridge, but chose a military rather than an academic career.[5] As an ensign he fought at Culloden in 1746 and later raised his own regiment, the 79th Regiment of Foot in 1757.[6] While an officer in the East India Company, Draper visited the Philippines and 'with the keen eye of a military man, saw the importance of their acquisition and their utter defencelessness against a possible enemy'.[7] In 1762 his expedition against the Spanish base at Manila was successful. The city was to be ransomed for a million pounds, but the Spanish court in Madrid declared the seizure to be piracy, and refused. Manila was later restored to Spain without compensation.[8]

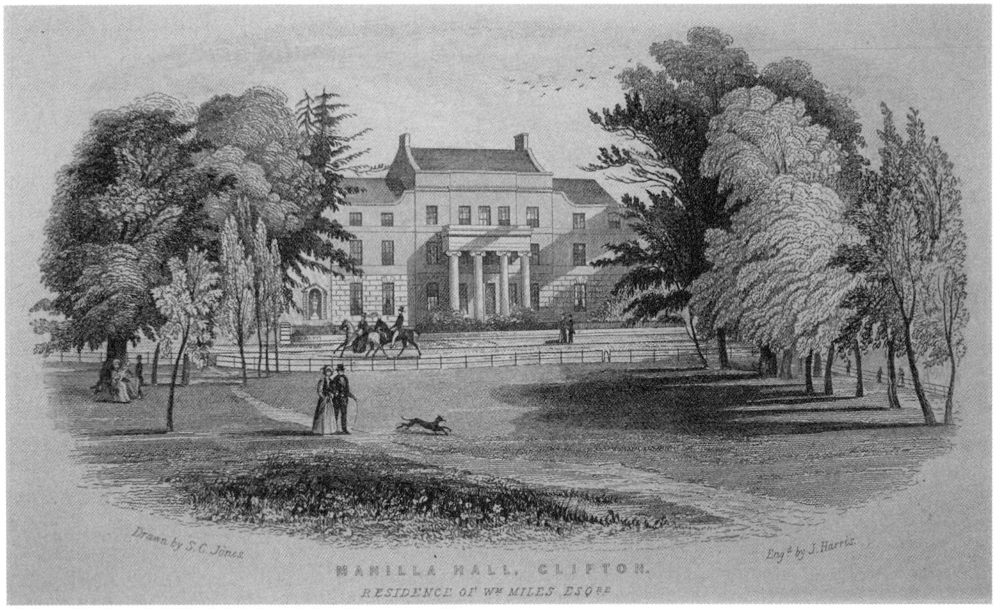

Manilla Hall, Clifton, **engraving after S.C. Jones, c.1830**

When Draper returned to England in April 1763, his 'achievement' was already a political embarrassment.[9] He received only £5,000 of an anticipated 'putative fortune of the victors', but this enabled him to build Manilla Hall.

> Although Sir William Draper came under the lash of that master of invective, Junius, [by foolishly involving himself in a public correspondence with him] he must have been as admirable a man as he was a distinguished soldier, or Pitt would never, in his speech on American taxation in January 1766, have described him as 'a gentleman whose noble and generous spirit would do credit to the proudest grandee of the country'. [10]

Draper was attacked by another contemporary, Nathaniel Wraxall, a diplomat, politician and adventurer, in his memoirs:

> Sir William's vanity, which led him to call his house at Clifton near Bristol 'Manilla Hall' and there to erect a cenotaph to his fellow soldiers who fell before the city during the siege, exposed him to invidious comments.[11]

Draper died at Bath in January 1787. There is a tablet in Bath Abbey with a long Latin inscription, composed by his friend, the poet Christopher Anstey, describing him as a 'splendid man, gifted in mind and body' and 'an energetic leader and a gently noble man'.[12] In 1766 the Merchant Venturers gladly accepted an offer from Sir William 'to act as Conservator of Clifton Down'.[13] In 1774 Sir William chaired a committee that laid down the rules of cricket, the foundation of the modern game.[14]

Clifton Down

At the junction of Suspension Bridge Road and Clifton Down Road, Clifton

79th Regiment of Foot Memorial B15

Sculptor: attributed to Thomas Paty

Date: 1767
Materials: limestone with slate and copper inscription panels
Dimensions: approx. 360cm high; 295cm long; 180cm wide
Inscriptions: on a slate panel on the east side of the pedestal, on the left – SACRED / To the Memory of thofe departed Warriors / of the feventy ninth Regiment / By whofe Valour Diferpline and Perfeverance / The French Land Forces in Afia were firft withftood and repulfed / The Commerce of Great Britain preferved / Her Settlements refcued from unpending Deftruction. / The memorable Defence of MADRAS / The decifive Battle of WANDEWASH / Twelve ftrong and important fortreffes. / Three fuperb Capitals / ARCOT PONDICHERRY MANILLA / And the PHILIPPINE ISLANDS / Are lafting Monuments of their Military Glory – on the right of the panel: Their generous Treatment / of a vanquifhed Enemy / Exhibits an illuftrious Example / of true Fortitude and Moderation / worthy of being tranfmitted / To lateft Poferity / That future Generations may know / HUMANITY if the Characteriftic / of BRITISH CONQUERORS.
—: on a copper plate on the west side of the cenotaph, added after the memorial was moved to the present site in 1883, in Roman capitals – THESE TWO MONUMENTS WERE ERECTED BY LIEUT GENERAL / SIR WILLIAM DRAPER K.B. IN THE GARDEN OF HIS HOUSE MANILLA / HALL ON THE SITE OF WHICH MANILLA ROAD NOW STANDS / BORN IN BRISTOL IN 1721 HE WAS IN 1744 ELECTED A FELLOW OF / KING'S COLLEGE CAMBRIDGE,

BUT CHOSE A MILITARY RATHER THAN /AN ACADEMIC CAREER. THE CENOTAPH COMMEMORATES THE 79TH. / REGIMENT OF FOOT. A CORPS WHICH HE HIMSELF RAISED IN 1757 FOR / SERVICE IN THE EAST DURING THE SEVEN YEARS' WAR.THIS REGIMENT / WAS LATER DISBANDED / IN 1762, DRAPER COMMANDED A FORCE WHICH CAPTURED THE / SPANISH COLONY OF MANILA (sic) IN THE PHILIPPINE ISLANDS. BY THE / TREATY OF PARIS (1763) THIS CONQUEST WAS RETURNED TO SPAIN / WITHOUT RANSOM OR INDEMNITY. / THE OBELISK IS A TRIBUTE TO WILLIAM PITT EARL OF CHATHAM/ WHO, AS PRIME MINISTER, PLANNED AND INSPIRED THE VICTORIOUS / CAMPAIGNS OF THE SEVEN YEARS' WAR. AS A RESULT OF THESE THE / BRITISH REPLACED THE FRENCH AS THE RULERS OF INDIA AND CANADA / IN 1766 THE SOCIETY OF MERCHANT VENTURERS DEPUTED TO / SIR WILLIAM DRAPER AUTHORITY FOR THE KEEPING OF ORDER OF / CLIFTON DOWN.THE OLDER TREES ON THIS SPOT MAY HAVE BEEN / PLANTED BY HIM. HE DIED AT BATH IN 1787 AND LIES BURIED / IN THE /ABBEY THERE.

—: on the east-facing side, cut into the sarcophagus in Roman capitals, each line centred – SISTE GRADUM SI QUAE EST BRITONUM TIBI CURA VIATOR / SISTE GRADUM VACUO RECOLAS INSCRIPTA SEPULCHRO / TRISTIA FATA VIRUM QUOS BELLICUS ARDOR EORUM / PROH DOLOR HAUD UNQUAM REDITUROS MISIT AD ORBEM / NEC TIBI SIT LUGERE PUDOR SI FORTE TUORUM / NOMINA NOTA LEGAS SED CUM TERRAQ MARIQ/ INVICTOS HEROUM ANIMOS ET FACTA REVOLVAS / SI PATRIAE TE TANGIT AMOR SI FAMA BRITANNUM / PARCE TRUMPHALES LACHRYMIS ASPERGERE LAUROS / QUIN SI ASIAE PENETRARE SINUS ATQ ULIMA GANGIS / PANDERE CLAUSTRA PARES INDOSQ LACESSERE BELLO / EX HIS VIRTUTEM DISCAS VERUMQ LABOREM / FORTUNAM EX ALIIS / *[Stay your step, O, Wayfarer, if for Britons you have any care. Stay your step that you may consider inscribed upon the empty monument the melancholy fate of men whom their own warlike ardour sent to the East never again, alas, to return. Nor should you be ashamed to mourn if perchance you read the familiar names of your own, but by land and sea reflect upon the invincible spirits and the deeds of heroes if love of Country, if Britain's fame moves you. Forbear to scatter tears upon triumphal laurels rather, if you are prepared to penetrate the deepest parts of Asia, uncover Ganges' inmost bounds and smite Indus with war, then from these you may learn valour and true toil – from others luck.]* [15]

—: on five raised ovals, on the left buttress on the north-side – CONJEVERAM [Conjeeveram] / taken by Storm/April 13/1759

—: on centre of the pedestal, to the left – The Lines / of PONDICHERRY / Stormed Sep 10/1760

—: to the right – PONDICHERRY / furrender'd / Jan 16/1761

Centred beneath these: MANILLA / taken by Storm / Oct 6/1762

—: on buttress to the right – CARICAL/ taken April /1760

—: on three raised ovals on the south side; to the top left – Siege of / MADRASS / raif'd Feb: 17:/1759. – to the top right: Battle of / WANDEWASH / Gained Jan: 22:/1760 – centred beneath these: ARCOT / recovered / Feb 10/1760

—: on lower buttress to the north-east – LIEU[TS]. / WHALEY / G : BROWNE / HOPKINS / ROBINSON / T BROWNE / LE GRAND / WINCHELSEA / ROSTON / CAMPBELL / FRYER / TURNER / RICHBELL / BOUCHIER / BUSTEED / HARDWICK

—: on the other side of the same buttress – ENSIGNS; COLLINS / VASLETTE / LA TOUR / HORLER / MAC MAHON / SURGEONS / SMITH / ATHERTON

Status: Grade II*
Owned by Bristol City Council
Condition: good; conserved 2003 [16]

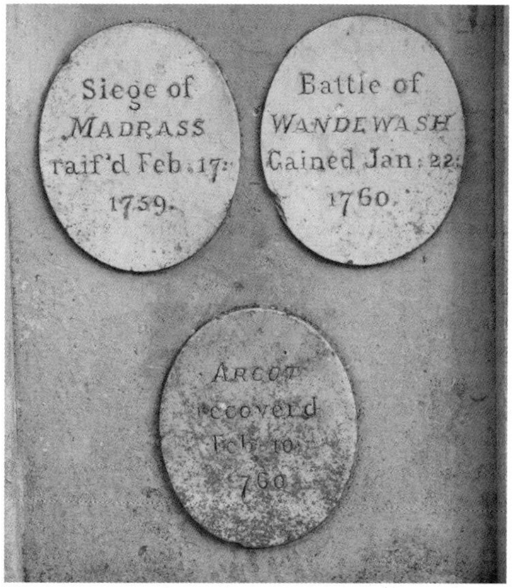

Thomas Paty (attributed to), *Memorial to the 79th Regiment of Foot* (detail)

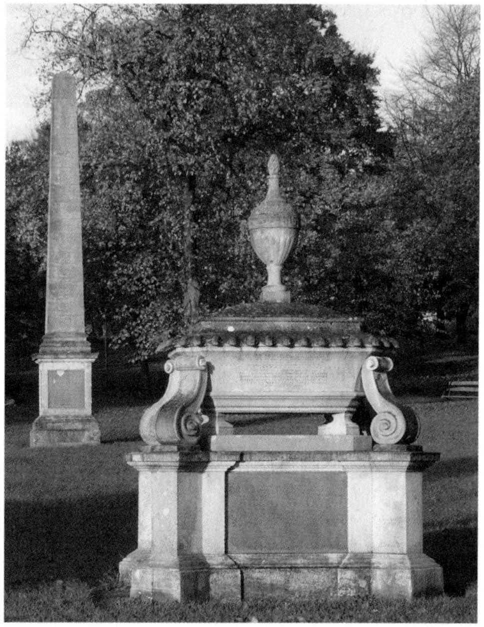

Thomas Paty (attributed to), *Memorial to the 79th Regiment of Foot* and *Monument to William Pitt, Earl of Chatham*

An account of this monument's creation is engraved on the copper panel on the west side of the pedestal, and the full text is quoted above. Lieutenant-General Sir William Draper, whose life is summarised in the preceding paragraphs, commissioned the memorial in memory of the officers and men who had died in the regiment that he had raised, the 79th Regiment of Foot.

An urn surmounts a classical stone sarcophagus, supported by four diagonal volutes. The heavy volutes rest on the buttresses at each corner of the rectangular pedestal. The two long sides of the pedestal contain panels bearing inscriptions; the panel to the west is copper and to the east slate. The ends of the pedestal, and some the faces of the buttresses, have raised ovoid plaques and these also have inscriptions. The similarity of the design to many of the drawings in the so-called *Paty Copybook* suggests that the memorial was designed by Thomas Paty or possibly by his son, William.[17]

The general shape of the monument, in particular the diagonal buttresses at the corners of both the sarcophagus and the plinth, echoes the shape of the larger and very much more rustic monument within Stoke Park, near Bristol (see Stoke Park). That sarcophagus may have been designed by Thomas Wright in the earlier 1760s for Norbonne Berkeley and built by James Paty the Second. Thomas Paty remains the more likely designer and builder of the Clifton sarcophagus.

The Latin inscription was drafted by Draper's lifelong friend from Eton and King's College, Cambridge, the poet Christopher Anstey.[18] Anstey had achieved literary celebrity in 1766 as author of the *New Bath Guide*, a satire on the social life of the city. Anstey also helped in 1768 in drafting another Latin text for the Chatham obelisk. His long inscription is unusual in containing the words 'BRITISH CONQUERORS'. These conquerors are praised for their 'generous treatment of a vanquished enemy' and their 'moderation' and 'humanity' are commended to future generations.

The sarcophagus was pitted by shrapnel during bombing in the Second World War, and had deteriorated badly by 1951 when it was restored. The cost, £200, was shared equally between the War Damage Commission and the Bristol City Council.[19]

Notes

[1] J. Dreaper, *Bristol's Forgotten Victor, Lt. Gen. Sir William Draper K.B. (1721–1787)*, BBHA no. 94 (1998), p.1. [2] Obituary in Bristol Naturalists' Society, *Proceedings*, 4th series, vol. III, 1914, p.8; Beddoe was honorary professor of anthropology in the University of Bristol. [3] McGrath, *Merchant Venturers of Bristol*, p.433. [4] As note 1, pp.2–3. [5] Op. cit, pp.3–4. [6] Op. cit, fn. 14, p.27. [7] Hutton, *Bristol and its Famous Associations*, p.308. [8] From the inscription on copper panel on the nearby cenotaph. [9] As note 1, p.9. [10] As note 7, pp.308–9. The Junius Letters were the work of a political insider intent on bringing down the government. [11]As note 1, p.9, quoting N.W. Wraxall, *Historical Memoirs of My Own Time* (London, 1904). [12] Op. cit., pp.23–4. [13] Op. cit., p.14. [14] Op. cit., pp.18–19. [15] Translation: Professor Alan Ryder, School of History, University of Bristol, March 1999. [16] The Clifton and Hotwells Improvement Society wrote to compliment Bristol City Council on the high standard of the conservation work carried out in 2003 by Sue and Lawrence Kelland. [17] Priest and Cobb, *The Paty Family*; designs for 125 funerary monuments by the Patys are reproduced. [18] As note 1, p.15. [19] National Building Commission, caption to photograph 25759, 19 November 1951.

Clifton Down, at the junction of Suspension Bridge Road and Clifton Down Road

Monument to William Pitt, Earl of Chatham B16

Sculptor: attributed to James Paty II

Date: 1768
Materials: limestone ashlar and slate
Dimensions: approx. 8m high, 145cm square at base; four slate panels each 80cm square
Inscriptions: cut in Roman lettering; in slate, on the west face, is the full text that Sir William Draper intended to display; it was not inscribed in this form until 1883, 115 years after its composition – VIRO MEMORABILI INVICTO / QUI IN DUBIIS TREPIDISQ REBUS / PATRIAE LABORANTI / VINDICEM SE IMPAVIDUM OBTULIT / RUENTIS IMPERII STATOR / CONSILII EXEMPLI SINGULARIS AUCTOR / ET AUSUS ET GRANDIA ASSECUTUS / NOMINIS BRITANNICI / REIQ MILITARIS GLORIAM / JAM PROPE INTERMORTUAM / RESUSCITAVIT ADAUXIT / QUI ORBEM FERE UNIVERSUM ANIMO COMPLEXUS / HOSTIBUS TERRA MARIQ PROFLIGATIS / EUROPAM ASIAM AFRICAM AMERICAM / VICTORIIS PERAGRAVIT / TRUMPHIS ILLUSTRAVIT / GULIELMO PITT COMITI DE CHATHAM / HOC AMICITIAE PRIVATAE TESTIMONIUM / SIMUL ET HONORIS PUBLICI MONUMENTUM / POSUIT GULIELMUS DRAPER
[To a renowned and invincible man who in uncertain and troubled times came forward as the fearless avenger of his afflicted country, the sustainer of a falling empire, the matchless author of wise counsel. He dared and accomplished mighty deeds; the glory of Britain's name and its military reputation, so far decayed, he resurrected and increased; encompassing almost the whole world in his mind, he overthrew the enemy on land and sea; victoriously he traversed Europe, Asia, Africa, America and brightened them with his triumphs. To William Pitt, Earl of Chatham, William Draper has erected this monument both as a testimony of private friendship and public honour.][1]
—: inscribed on the slate panel on the east face is the original dedication, as requested by Pitt, being the last four lines of the longer inscription – Gulielmo Pitt Comiti de Chatham / Hoc Amicitiae Privatae Testimonium / Simul et Honoris Publici Monumentum / Posuit Gulielmus Draper.
—: on the north face – The entire Dedication / composed by Sir WILLIAM DRAPER / in 1768 / is now / in accordance with his original intention / inscribed on this monument / on its removal hither / from the Grounds of

Manilla Hall / 1883. / JOSEPH D WESTON MAYOR.

Status: Grade II*
Owned by Bristol City Council
Condition: good; conserved 2003

William Pitt the Elder, 1st Earl of Chatham (1708–78), was greatly admired by General Sir William Draper. Pitt had planned and inspired the victorious campaigns in which Draper had triumphed. The general's tribute to Pitt as a 'great war leader was not mere flattery; it was recognition of the fact that Pitt had chosen him for his first major command in India and thereafter assisted him in his ascent up the military ladder'.[2] William Pitt's family had strong links with India through his grandfather, Thomas Pitt (known as 'Diamond Pitt'), who had become immensely wealthy as the governor of the East India Company at Madras, the city that Draper was later to win for his country.[3]

William Pitt's commanding presence – tall and lean with a Roman nose – and his powerful voice added considerably to his authority as an exceptional orator and statesman.[4] He became paymaster general in 1746, but behaved honourably, avoiding the corruption of past incumbents, and introducing many administrative reforms. After many gifts, £10,000 from the Duchess of Marlborough and £3,000 a year from Sir William Pynsent, plus the estate of Burton-Pynsent in Somerset, and much preferment, Pitt became secretary of state and, in effect, prime minister in 1756.[5] He started a war against France, raised the militia and increased the navy. After a brief period of resignation, his vigorous war policies continued and the French armies were defeated by Britain and her allies in India, Africa, Canada and Germany. This succession of victories held until 1761, when he was forced to resign after a majority of the cabinet refused to declare war on Spain. Pitt was pensioned off until 1766. He then formed a new ministry while holding office as Lord Privy Seal and sitting in the House of Lords as Viscount Pitt, Earl of Chatham.[6] By then he was ill and played little part in a weak administration that ended when he resigned in 1768. It was in that year that Draper sought to honour him with the Bristol obelisk.

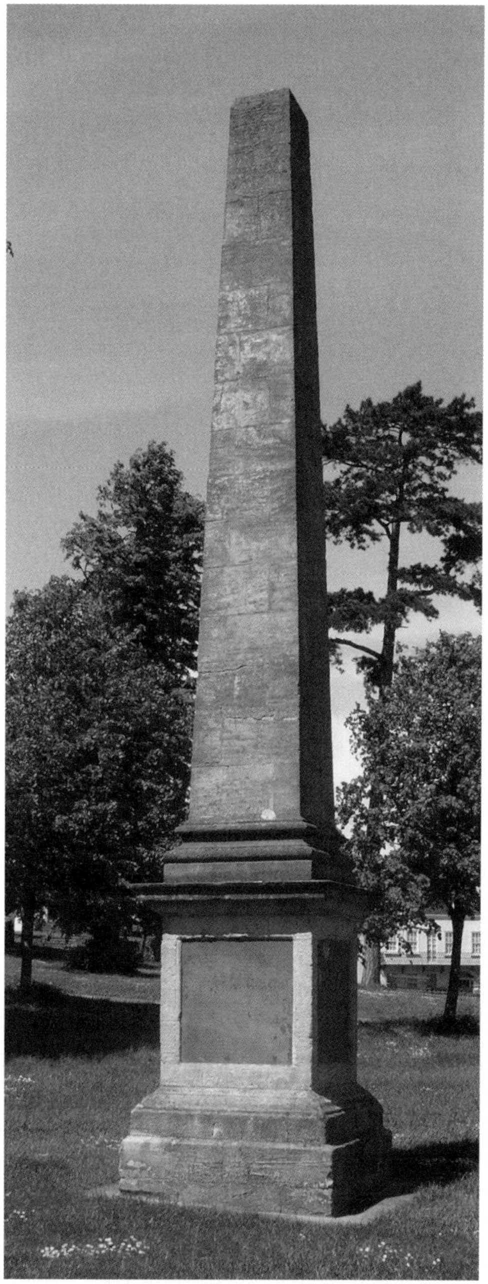

Thomas Paty (attributed to), *Monument to William Pitt, Earl of Chatham*

The obelisk and pedestal are traditional in design and built of ashlar limestone. There are four slate panels, each inset on the sides of the pedestal. Two have Latin inscriptions and one has an English text. The fourth is blank.

In 1768, Draper sought the Earl of Chatham's approval of a long dedicatory inscription. Pitt's permission was elegantly refused in a reply from his wife, Hester, Countess of Chatham. On 16 June 1768, she wrote:

> My lord… desires to say that he is most truly touched with the too favourable and partial sentiments of one who is himself so justly the admiration of his country and so distinguished an instrument of its glory. He begs to add, as nothing can or ought to make him so proud as the testimony of Sir William's private friendship that he hopes Sir William will give him leave earnestly to entreat that of an Inscription so infinitely partial the last four lines alone may remain.[7]

Pitt's command was respected and the monument was thus inscribed. The full dedication was not to be added until 1883.

The Latin inscription, revealing Draper's devotion to the Earl of Chatham, was composed by Christopher Anstey, Draper's long-term friend from Eton and Cambridge.[8] Anstey was an accomplished Latin scholar and he had written the satirical poem *The New Bath Guide* in 1766. In his otherwise humorous poem, *An Election Ball* (1776), Anstey inserted fifteen lines to record 'the success of his friend Sir William Draper in defeating the Spanish and capturing Manila', a victory that had occurred almost fifteen years earlier.[9] By praising Draper for his compassion in sparing the defeated, Anstey differentiates him from other British officers who returned and in many cases settled in Bath 'to live comfortably upon the plunder and gain'.[10]

James Paty II was the site architect and main contractor working on the house when the much larger obelisk was made for Norbonne Berkeley at Stoke Park in 1762 (see Stoke Park). Draper may have also have commissioned his obelisk from James Paty or from his brother, Thomas. The plinth to the Stoke Park obelisk has icicle panels and a certain rustic grandeur, well suited to its spectacular site above the Frome valley. Draper's obelisk is more elegant and better suited to its original garden setting.[11]

During the Second World War the obelisk was pitted with shrapnel, and the War Damage Commission spent £50 on repairs in 1951.[12] Both the obelisk and the sarcophagus were conserved by Lawrence and Sue Kelland in 2003.

Notes

[1] Translated by Professor Alan Ryder, University of Bristol. [2] Dreaper, *Bristol's Forgotten Victor,* p.15; although Dreaper's name is not spelled the same way, he is a descendant of Sir William. [3] *Chambers' Biographical Dictionary*, ed. J.O. Thorne (London, 1961), pp. 263, 264. [4] Ibid. [5] Ibid. [6] Ibid. [7] As note 2, p.15. [8] Ibid, p.15. [9] G. Turner, *The New Bath Guide by Christopher Anstey: An Introduction with Notes on the Text* (Bristol, 1994), p.11. [10] Ibid. [11] Priest and Cobb, *The Paty Family*, p.33. [12] National Building Commission, caption to photograph 25759.

Clifton Down, on The Triangle between The Promenade and Clifton Down Road

Alderman Proctor's Fountain B12

Designers: George and Henry Godwin

Builders: Broad and Tucker of Bristol.[1]
Date: 1872
Material: Box limestone, Mansfield stone, Rouge Royal marble and Pennant stone [2]
Dimensions: approx. 750cm high; each side 325cm at base
Inscriptions: on an inset stone panel on the north side in lead Gothic capitals – ERECTED BY ALDERMAN THOMAS PROCTOR, OF BRISTOL, TO / RECORD THE LIBERAL GIFT OF CERTAIN RIGHTS OVER CLIFTON DOWN / MADE TO THE CITIZENS BY THE SOCIETY OF MERCHANT VENTURERS / UNDER THE PROVISIONS OF THE CLIFTON AND DURDHAM DOWNS ACTS / OF PARLIAMENT, 1861, WHEREBY THE ENJOYMENT OF THESE DOWNS / IS PRESERVED TO THE CITIZENS OF BRISTOL FOREVER
—: on a bronze plaque, in raised Roman capitals and upper and lower case, each line centred – CITY OF BRISTOL . SOCIETY OF MERCHANT VENTURERS . COUNTY OF AVON / *Re-siting and refurbishment* / *of* / ALDERMAN PROCOTOR'S DRINKING FOUNTAIN / *To commemorate its re-opening* / *by* / THE Rt. Hon. THE LORD MAYOR OF BRISTOL /COUNCILLOR C. D. M. B. ALDERSON / *and* / THE CHAIRMAN OF AVON COUNTY COUNCIL / COUNCILLOR W. FOWLER / *1st May 1988* / ENGINEER FOR THE WORKS N. W. LEE B.Sc. C. ENG. FICE COUNTY ENGINEER AND SURVEYOR / CONTRACTOR H. MEALING AND SON
Status: Grade II
Owned by Bristol City Council
Condition: good

This large Gothic fountain was presented to the city by Alderman Thomas Proctor, as the inscription says: 'to record the Liberal gift of certain rights over Clifton Down... by the Society of Merchant Venturers to the citizens of Bristol forever'. That gift had been made in 1861. Alderman Proctor had first proposed the fountain in 1867 and it was completed in 1872.[3] The function of the monument was, however, more important than its role as a memorial. Alderman Proctor himself stated that it provided sufficient water for the 'thousands who avail themselves of the downs on the Sunday afternoon and evening... but to meet any extra demand, my man takes out a number of half-pint mugs'.[4] Proctor was also to contribute to the costs of the other large fountain on the Downs completed in 1877 (see Stoke Road, Durdham Down).

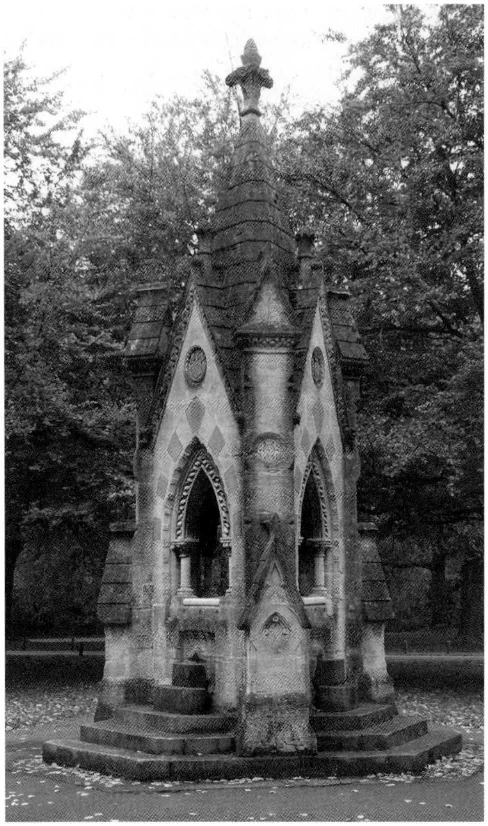

George and Henry Godwin, *Alderman Proctor's Fountain*

Triangular in plan, the fountain is mainly of Box limestone with red Mansfield voussoirs.[5] Each face is pierced by a pointed arch supported on Rouge Royal marble columns. Cut roundels over each of the three arched-openings contain the arms and mottoes, now invisible, of the Merchant Venturers, Thomas Proctor and the City of Bristol. There are three drinking troughs for dogs. Three pennant stone steps on each of the three sides 'make you climb as to an altar to quench your thirst'.[6] Additional steps have been added for children. Fresh water is still available from two of the three taps.

The fountain originally stood at the top of Bridge Valley Road on the levelled site of the demolished Clifton Turnpike tollhouse and beside the first public road to use John McAdam's method.[7] The fountain remained there until 1988 when it was found to be a hazard to traffic and moved to the present site at a cost of £15,000.[8] A further £1,500 was required for stone cleaning and refurbishment.[9] The new site is now closer to the Mansion House on the Promenade. This was formerly Elmdale, Thomas Proctor's private home, which was also designed by George and Henry Godwin. George Godwin was the editor of the architectural magazine, *The Builder*, in which both the future Mansion House and the fountain were reviewed and illustrated.[10]

One observer has described the fountain as 'shrine-like' and 'one of Bristol's most fanciful Gothic monuments'.[11] Another assessment is less approving: 'its grotesquely disproportionate masses of masonry and comically innocent display of all the tricks in the Gothicist's copybook might be a church steeple shrunken into ten per cent of itself'.[12] But here Andor Gomme was perhaps taking revenge for the severity of Godwin's restoration of St Mary Redcliffe, so much of which had been funded by Alderman Proctor. The fountain does have a certain earnestness in the complexity of its design, but it also has charm, confidence and a generous extravagance in its material and details.

Notes

[1] *The Builder*, 3 August 1872, p.604. [2] Ibid. [3] McGrath, *Merchant Venturers of Bristol*, p.432. [4] As note 1. [5] Ibid. [6] T. Mowl, *Bristol: Last Age of the Merchant Princes* (Bath, 1991), pl. 51. [7] W.J. Reader, *Macadam: The McAdam Family and the Turnpike Roads, 1798–1861* (London, 1980), p.156. [8] 'Two deaths at junction', *Evening Post*, 18 April 1984. The move was paid for by Avon County Council. [9]Ibid. Bristol City Council met this cost. [10] Crick, *Victorian Buildings*, pp.31, 54. [11] Op. cit., p.32. [12] Gomme, Jenner and Little, *An Architectural History*, p.333.

Clifton Down, Bristol Zoo

On the façade of the entrance to Bristol Zoological Gardens

Entrance Lodge Frieze B1

Sculptor: Edgar Thomas Earp

Date: c.1929
Material: relief panels, cast concrete
Dimensions: 50cm deep, 420cm wide
Status: Grade II
Owned by Bristol Zoo Trustees
Condition: fair

Bristol Zoo was founded by the Bristol, Clifton and West of England Zoological Society in 1835 and first opened to the public on 11 July 1836.[1] Perhaps two or three years later, the two elegant and detached neo-Greek entrance lodges were built to the designs of William Harris.[2] Around 1929 the two lodges were linked by a shallow central building and the relief above the entrance was commissioned at that time or soon after.

The frieze shows a delightful procession of 23 animals. They were modelled and cast in four concrete blocks.[3] They are presently painted a gloss black on a white background and from a distance they look like silhouettes, but there is considerable detail modelled in the surfaces.

After frustrating searches, the identity of the sculptor of the frieze was finally revealed through the vigilance of Anthony Beeson of Bristol Central Library. During conversations with the authors of a book on Thomas Earp, published in 2002, he learnt that the frieze was the work of Earp's son, Edgar Thomas.[4] Earp, Son and Hobbs continued after Earp Senior died in 1893. Edgar became a partner and he did work inscribing First World War memorials throughout the West Country.

Appropriately, Earp's lively animals may well have been inspired by the lines of animals in black and white silhouette at the top and

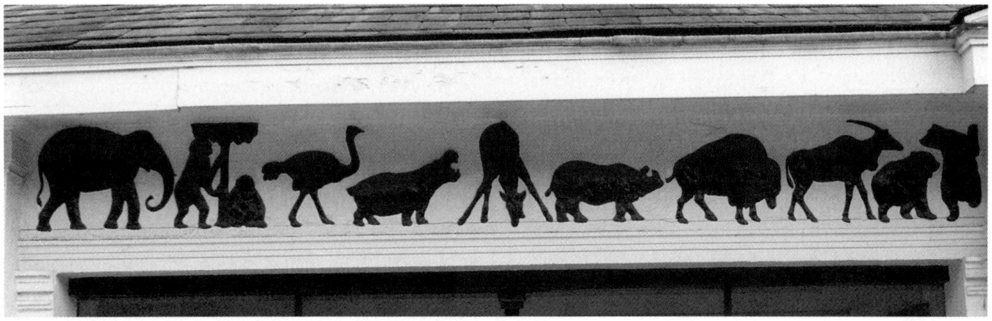

Edgar Thomas Earp, *Entrance Lodge frieze* (left and right)

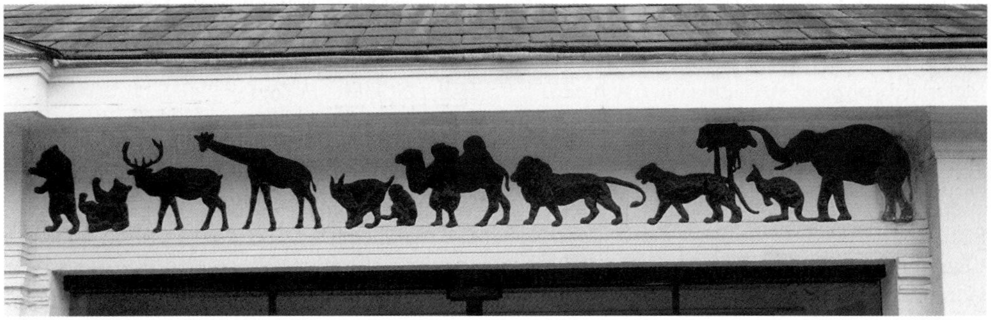

bottom of the covers of early editions of Rudyard Kipling's *Jungle Book* and *Just So Stories*. These memorable covers were developed from Kipling's own drawings of animals in silhouette that illustrated his extremely popular books. This link with Kipling is confirmed by the building of the zoo's Monkey Temple in 1929, the same year as Earp's frieze. The inspiration for the Monkey Temple was Kipling's Cold Lairs in the *Jungle Book* and it 'represents an Indian temple abandoned by human beings and occupied by the Bandar log or Monkey folk'.[5]

The relief is now encrusted with many layers of paint and it deserves careful conservation.

Notes

[1] R. and A. Warin, *Portrait of a Zoo: Bristol Zoological Gardens 1835–1985* (Bristol, 1985). [2] The two lodges do not appear on Richard Forrest's original plan for the layout of the gardens, lithographed 1835, but are clearly visible in George Ashmead's map of Clifton, 1849. The architect of the two lodges was William Harris, as revealed by an engraving in Bristol Museum and Art Gallery (Mb 3719), 'Entrance to the Bristol & Clifton Zoological Gardens from a design by Mr Wm. Harris Arch, drawn and engraved by Wm Hunt, dedicated to the Subscribers'. [3] Olive Mitchell, Edgar Earp's niece, in a letter, 29 January 2004. SWRA files/UWE/BR131. [4] A. and O. Mitchell, *Thomas Earp: Eminent Victorian Sculptor* (Buckingham, 2002). [5] *Bristol Zoo Book and Official Guide* (1948), p.11.

On the lawn before the curved herbaceous border at Bristol Zoo

Mute Swan B4

Sculptor: David Wynne OBE

Date: 1971
Material: bronze on steel and concrete base
Dimensions: 3.5m wingspan
Steel plaque: MUTE SWAN / DAVID WYNNE (SCULPTOR) /1971 / PRESENTED BY / M.V.B HILL ESQ D.S.O. M.C.
Status: not listed
Owned by Bristol Zoo Trustees
Condition: good

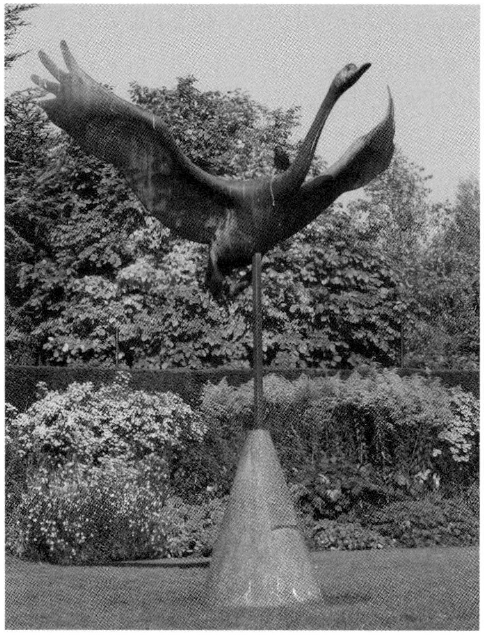

David Wynn, *Mute Swan*

This bronze *Mute Swan* is a version of the third of the five swans in *Swans in Flight*, a sculpture completed in 1968 for the new Civic Centre at Barras Bridge, Newcastle upon Tyne. There, the swan is discreetly supported by the two of the other swans, whose wings just touch a pool of water that also disguises further upright supports. Here, at the zoo, a steel support rises from a concrete cone and stakes the swan, arresting the movement common to many of David Wynne's most successful works, of which the best known may be *Boy with a Dolphin* on Cheyne Walk, Chelsea. The sculpture was presented by Lt. Col. M. V. B. Hill, DSO, MC in 1971.

By the playground in the centre of Bristol Zoo

Elephant Tower B5

Sculptor: Philip Bews

Date: 2003
Material: cedar of Lebanon
Dimensions: 5m high
Inscription on bronze plaque: ELEPHANT / TOWER / Wendy, the Asian elephant, died / on 12th September 2002, aged 42. / She lived at Bristol Zoo for over / 40 years, and was much loved. / This sculpture was created by Philip Bews in 2003 from / a cedar of Lebanon, and is modelled on Wendy.
Status: not listed
Owned by Bristol Zoo Trustees
Condition: good

The exemplary bronze plaque tells almost all. This is a memorial to both a beloved elephant

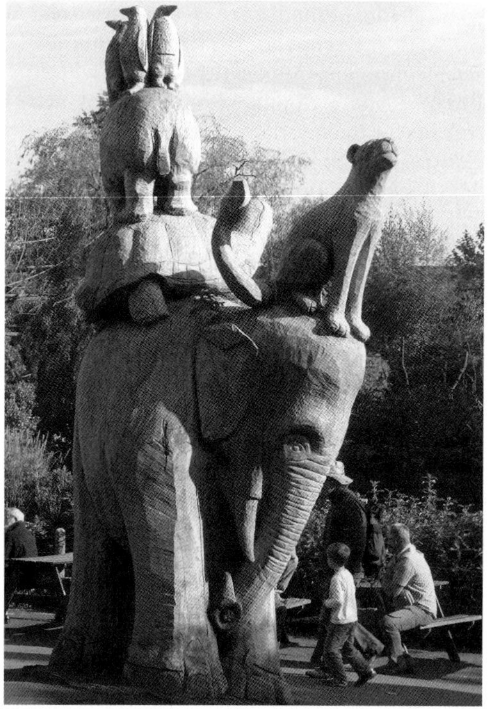

Philip Bews, *Elephant Tower*

and a fine cedar of Lebanon planted approximately one hundred and seventy years earlier. Gentle Wendy now carries a giant tortoise, a baby or pygmy hippopotamus, a troop of precariously perched penguins and a lioness. Wendy did not actually carry children on her back as did her predecessors at the zoo, but she wandered among the public with apparent affection and was stroked by innumerable children.

Both this cedar and the *Tree of Life*, below, were planted according to Richard Forrest's plan for the layout of the zoological gardens, which opened in 1836. They would have been planted by John Miller of Miller and Sweet's enormous nursery off Whiteladies Road, the last vestiges of which, Garraways, were closed in 2008. Nursery Villas, where Miller lived, can still be seen in Chantry Road. John Miller was himself an exhibiter of exotic animals at the nursery and laid out eight acres of short-lived zoological gardens at Arnos Vale early in 1835.[1]

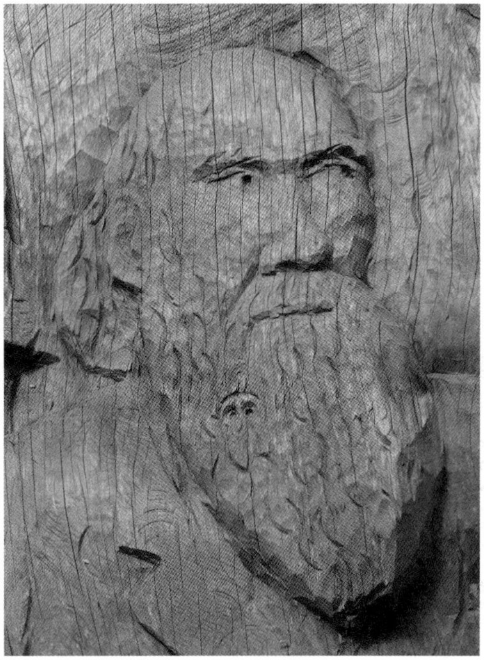

Near the Clifton Down entrance to Bristol Zoo

Tree of Life B2

Sculptor: Philip Bews

Date: 2001
Material: cedar
Dimensions: 6m high
Status: not listed
Owned by Bristol Zoo Trustees
Condition: good

A largely unnoticed relief portrait of Charles Darwin is carved into the trunk of the remains of a cedar tree. A baby monkey looks out from within his beard, as if to advise us not to take the sculpture's title too seriously. Above, on the old central trunk of the tree, is a chimpanzee with young. At the end of the three branches are fishes exploding into the air, an eagle landing and a giant Galapagos iguana basking in the sun, perhaps to remind us of the genesis of Darwin's revolutionary ideas. Despite Bristol Zoo's profound commitment to conservation, which will certainly embrace theories that have their origin in Darwinism, the invention here is entirely the sculptor's.

Bristol Zoo possesses other works of art that are not presently on public display. These include Michael Bizley's *Maternal Love*, purchased with the support of South West Arts in the 1980s and, until very recently, an early replica of E. H. Bailey's *Eve at the Fountain* in Bristol Museum and Art Gallery. This was at the edge of the lake. It may yet be there, hidden by the lemurs' appropriate jungle setting.

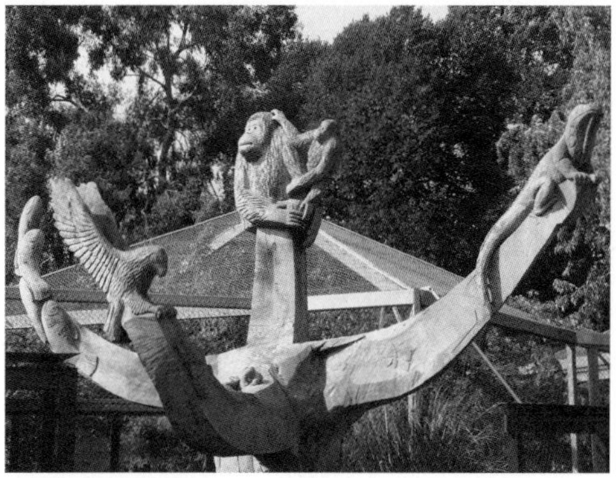

(above) Philip Bews, *Tree of Life*

Philip Bews, *Tree of Life, Darwin* (detail)

Opposite the Guthrie Road entrance to Bristol Zoo

Ying and Yang B7

Sculptor: Julian P. Warren

Date: 2001
Material: black painted metal
Dimensions: 3.3m long
Status: not listed
Owned by Bristol Zoo Trustees
Condition: good

Two giant metal stag beetles, set in a large

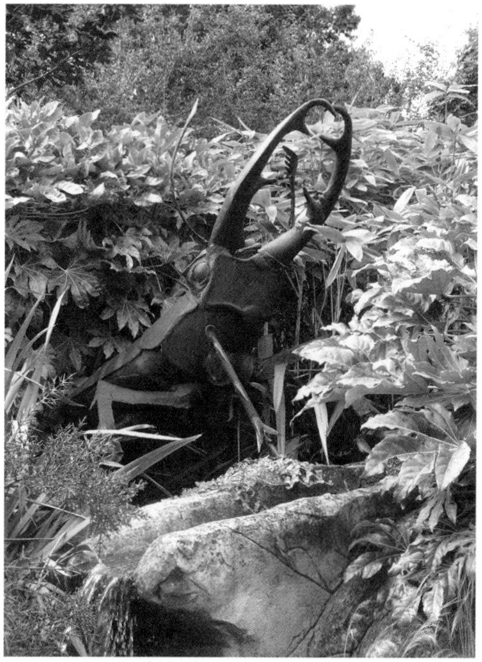

Julian P. Warren, *Ying*

raised bed of plants, greet visitors entering the zoo by the Guthrie Road entrance. Commissioned in 2001 by the retiring director Geoffrey Greed, it was hoped that they would draw attention to the zoo's own Bug World as well as to the declining numbers of this harmless but spectacular British insect.

Julian Warren lives in Burlington Road off Whiteladies Road, and on the corner of the street are two banks. When visiting one of them, Geoffrey Greed parked in Burlington Road and admired the animal sculptures on the railings of No. 18, where there is still a permanent display of Julian Warren's work. The commission followed.

At the edge of the Pavilion restaurant rose garden, Bristol Zoo

Girl and Kid B3

Sculptor: Roy Clapp

Date: c.1975
Material: alabaster
Dimensions: approx. 1m high
Presented by Professor and Mrs Bruce Perry
Status: not listed
Owned by Bristol Zoo Trustees
Condition: fair

The sculpture movingly depicts the joy that a blind girl has in handling a live animal, in this instance a young goat. The work is by the son-in-law of the donors.

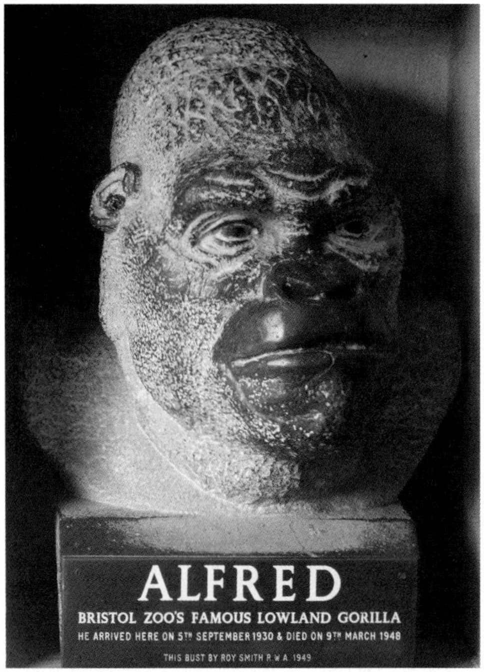

Roy Smith, *Alfred*

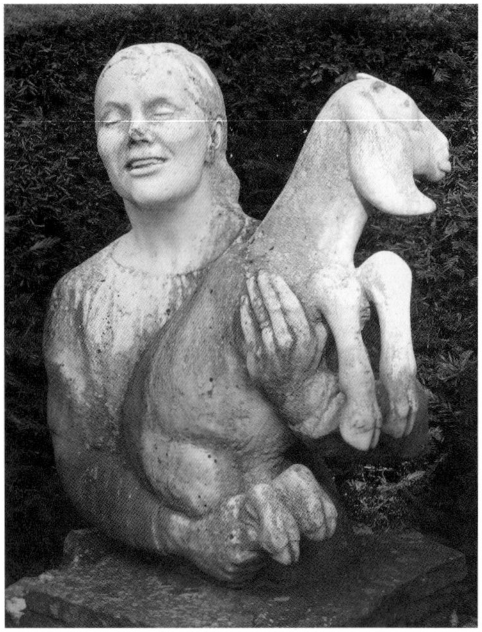

Roy Clapp, *Girl and Kid*

Set into the wall of the former Elephant House, Bristol Zoo

Alfred B6

Sculptor: Roy Smith RWA

Date: 1949
Material: bronze
Dimensions: 18in x 12in
Bronze caption: ALFRED / BRISTOL ZOO'S FAMOUS LOWLAND GORILLA / HE ARRIVED HERE ON 5TH SEPTEMBER 1930 & DIED ON 9TH MARCH 1948 / THIS BUST BY ROY SMITH R.W.A. 1949
Status: not listed
Owned by Bristol Zoo Trustees
Condition: good

Bristol Zoo's 1948 guidebook could confidently claim that Alfred had been 'undoubtedly the best known and most popular animal in any Zoo in the world'.[2] He had died suddenly in March of that year after never having been 'sick or sorry' but 'extremely happy and contented'. Born in the Kivu Mountains, he had been captured when very young and brought up by a native woman. He was purchased by the zoo in September 1930, when he was about two years old and weighed 25 pounds. No gorilla had previously survived in captivity in England for any length of time. However, Alfred was given a large open air cage, carefully protected from human infections and given a liberal supply of vitamins, particularly vitamin D. He grew to weigh over 35 stones (220 kilograms).[3]

Alfred was to be given another life in a glass case in Bristol Museum and Art Gallery. There he has been on constant display for sixty years. Only recently has his long lead in the museum's popularity stakes begun to shorten.

Notes

[1] D. Jones, *A History of Clifton* (Chichester, 2002), p.120; A. Beeson, *Bristol in 1807* (Bristol, 2009), p.42; correspondence with Geoffrey Greed, 2009
[2] Bristol Zoo Book and Official Guide (1948), p.17.
[3] R. and A. Warin, *Portrait of a Zoo*, p.29; the 1948 guidebook, above, says over 400lbs.

Clifton Down, Mansion House

In the entrance hall of the Mansion House, The Promenade

Thomas Proctor B13

Sculptor: George Gamon Adams

Date: 1876
Material: marble bust and plinth
Dimensions: 77cm high
Inscription: thomas proctor. j.p. / Alderman 1853 / 1811 NIL DESPERANDUM 1876
Status: not listed
Owned by Bristol City Council
Condition: good

Alderman Thomas Proctor (1812–76) self-effacingly described himself as a 'bone merchant, dealer in portable manure, agricultural implements and the like'.[1] He was well trained in 'agricultural sciences' and an 'influential pioneer of chemical fertilisers' in which the family had traded, as H. & T. Proctor, from 1812. In 1850 he purchased over six hundred acres of reputedly poor land at Wall Court Farm, (known locally as 'Starve-All Farm') at Stoke Gifford, near Bristol.[2] There he tested his farming methods. He may also have been the major property developer of much of High Victorian Clifton and Redland.

In April 1874 Proctor made a gift of his own house, Elmdale, to the city for use as the Mansion House.[3] The architects George and Henry Godwin had designed this for him in 1867 with this future function specifically but secretly in mind. He also commissioned the same architects to design the fountain, known as Proctor's Fountain, to commemorate the preservation of the Downs for the people of Bristol.

As a churchwarden of St Mary Redcliffe, Thomas Proctor signed the first appeal for funds for the restoration of the church. He was, in effect, the founder and first chairman of the Canynges Society in 1848, which, today, continues to raise funds for the care and

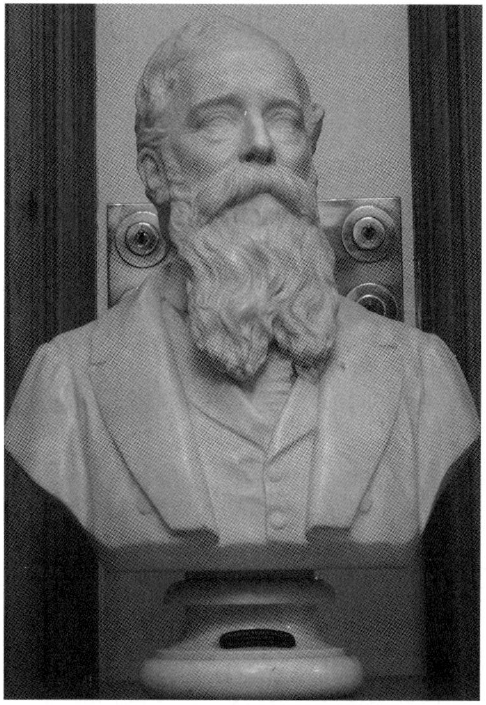

George Gamon Adams, *Thomas Proctor*

restoration of the fabric. Proctor was to invent an anonymous donor known as 'Nil Desperandum' whose crucial gifts paid for the restoration of the North Porch and much more. Only on his death was the inevitable identity of the donor revealed. He also ensured the preservation of the great Hogarth altarpiece from St Mary Redcliffe, now stored so ignominiously in St Nicholas Church.[4]

Among innumerable charitable works, Proctor gave land and a playground and 'playshed' at Fishponds, and 'he converted, at his sole cost, the dusty highway of Coronation Road, by the New Cut, into a bright and refreshing boulevard on the riverside, accommodated with seats and shaded with trees, the changing verdure of which is at this moment a most fitting monument of his kindly thoughtfulness'.[5]

In his will, Proctor requested that the bells of St Mary Redcliffe should be rung annually on 21 April in commemoration of the laying of the first stone of the long restoration of the church from 1846 to 1872.[6]

The conventional white marble bust was presented to the city by Thomas Proctor's widow.[7] The date inscribed on the bust is 1876, the year of the sitter's death, and the bust may well be a posthumous commission.

Notes

[1] M.E. Williams, *Civic Treasures of Bristol* (Bristol, 1984), p.76. [2] *Temple Local History Group Newsletter*, No. 3. 1987, pp.23–30. [3] Latimer, *Annals of Bristol in the Nineteenth Century*, p.478; John Hudson, *The Mansion House, Clifton* (Bristol, 1993); *The Builder*, 2 May 1874, p.367. [4] E. Ralph, '"Nil Desperandum": Thomas Proctor 1812–1876', *Canynges Society Annual Gazette*, 1990, pp.10–12. [5] Obituary, *Bristol Times and Mirror*, 16 May 1876. [6] R.F. Cartwright, *Pictorial History of St Mary Redcliffe, Bristol* (London, 1971), p.22; 'Proctor's Day', as it became, is no longer observed. [7] As note 1.

Clifton Hill, Goldney House

The site of the present house first came into the possession of the Goldneys, a Quaker family, when Thomas Goldney II took a lease on the property in April 1694.[1] He was to be the principle investor in Captain Woodes Rogers's highly profitable privateering voyage around the world in the *Duke* and the *Duchess.* It was during this voyage that Alexander Selkirk, on whom Defoe's Robinson Crusoe was based, was rescued. Of more importance was his vital support for Abraham Darby and Coalbrookdale. His son, Thomas Goldney III, was born in Goldney House in 1696.[2] Thomas Goldney III was to be still more closely involved in both the development and the management of Coalbrookdale, stretching his Quaker conscience by selling cast-iron guns in the 1740s. He was a major shareholder in the Warmley Brass Works and the Bristol Lead Company, and an important Bristol banker.

Thomas Goldney III inherited his father's estates in 1731 and he was soon making significant changes to the gardens. He began the grotto – 'the finest surviving early eighteenth-century garden grotto in Britain' – in 1737, and the basic structure was completed by August 1739.[3] The extraordinarily rich decoration of shells, corals, fossils and such local minerals as Bristol diamonds was to take some 27 years to complete. The last payment to Thomas Paty, the Bristol mason, statuary and architect, was in 1765 for the completion of the cutting and laying of the grotto's beautiful ceramic floor tiles.[4]

Other major developments in the gardens undertaken by Goldney included the elevated bastion, the great terrace, the colonnaded rotunda, the canal and the tower, within which was the fire engine or beam engine that powered the fountain in the canal and the flow of water through the grotto.

The house and grounds, together with the grotto, are now owned and well cared for by the University of Bristol.

Clifton Hill, Goldney House

On the garden terrace of Goldney House, approximately 100 metres south of the house

Hercules B21

John Nost, attributed to

Date: c.1705
Material: lead statue on a limestone pedestal
Foundry: probably John Nost in London
Dimensions: statue, approx. 165cm high, 120cm wide, 150cm deep; pedestal, approx. 140cm high, 115cm wide, 48cm deep
Status: Grade II*
Owned by the University of Bristol
Condition: good after major conservation work in 1995

Statues of Hercules were a familiar feature in eighteenth century ornamental gardens. Many were derived from the famous Roman statue, then in the Palazzo Farnese, of a heroic Hercules in repose, leaning on his club.[5] The sculptor of this very much more active Hercules was probably John Nost, an influential figure in the history of garden sculpture.

At Goldney, Hercules wears a lion's pelt with its head and upper jaw as a helmet. It is may be the pelt of the Nemean lion, whose killing was the first of the twelve labours of Hercules, but it may also refer to Hercules's destruction at the age of eighteen of the lion of Cithaeron, which had attacked herds of cattle belonging to the Athenian king. Hercules 'dressed himself in its pelt and wore the gaping jaws for a helmet'.[6]

Hercules leans forward with all his weight on his left leg. A large rough wooden club, held with both hands, rests on the back of his neck and is about to be swung forward in a manner that has been described as a superbly executed late cut, but which now has more in common with the posture of a baseball batter. The pedestal is panelled with bowed ends.

It is very likely that the statue of Hercules was commissioned for King's Weston house within the first decade of the eighteenth century. It would have been moved to Goldney half a century or so later at the time that Edward Southwell III first commissioned Lancelot 'Capability' Brown to re-landscape King's Weston. Brown was to obliterate much of the formal gardens. King's Weston house, designed in 1710 by Sir John Vanbrugh, is three miles to the west of Bristol. Although this 'is one of the smallest houses which Vanburgh designed… it excited the greatest admiration for the setting was superbly chosen on rising ground, with a view over the Bristol Channel'.[7]

The earliest documentary record of the statue's presence at Goldney appears in a retrospective inventory of Goldney garden in December 1768, the year Thomas Goldney III died, but written some time later: '1 Large Leaden figure of a Hercules'.[8] The same account reveals that there were at least fifteen figures in the garden at this time. Goldney had commenced the great terrace at the southern end of the garden, where the *Hercules* is sited, in 1753.[9]

Three items of evidence link the Goldney *Hercules* to King's Weston. There is Kip's engraving of the Tudor mansion that preceded Vanbrugh's great house. Published in 1712, it shows an unidentifiable statue amidst the parterres.[10] It is possibly the same statue that is next seen in a drawing by James Stewart inscribed 'The Front View of Edw. Southwell Esq's Seat at Kings Weston, James Stewart, 1746'.[11] The image is too small to identify the statue for certain, but it shows a single male figure on a very similar pedestal. The statue is again before the south front of the house, now rebuilt, but in the midst of the Great Court, created some thirty years earlier but soon to be

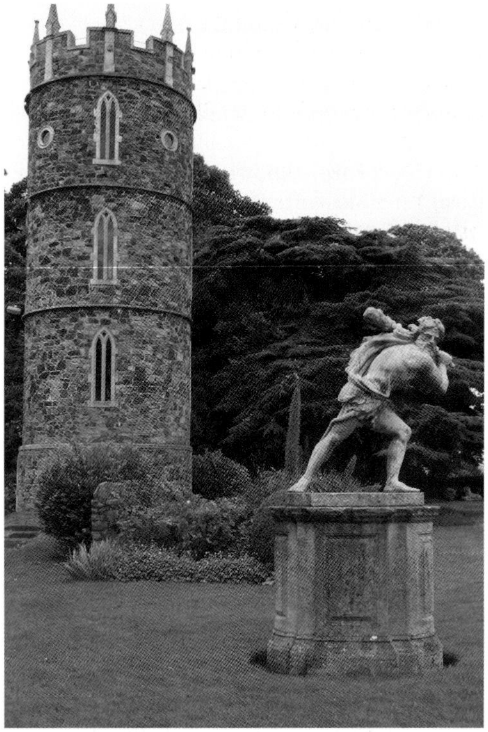

John Nost (attributed to), *Hercules*

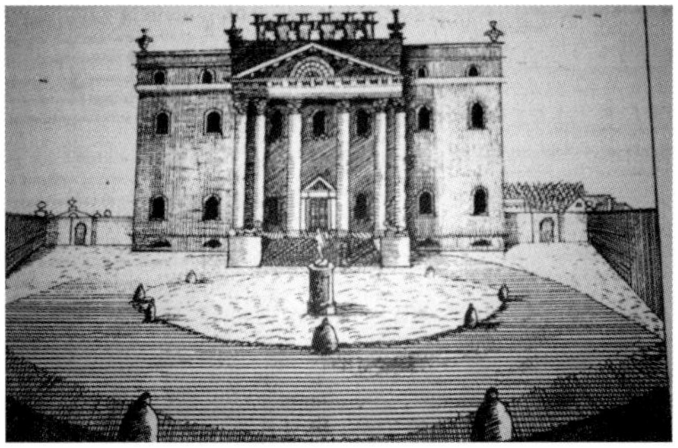

James Stewart, *Pen and ink drawing of King's Weston*, 1746 (Bodleian Library, Oxford)

obliterated by Capability Brown.[12] Finally, there is an early eighteenth-century scaled drawing in the Vanburgh Album in Bristol Record Office of the 'Pedestal of Hercules at Kingsweston'.[13] The design and the measurements are close, although not an exact match, to those of the Goldney House pedestal.

The once tentative attribution of this sculpture to John Nost was recently strengthened by estimates and contracts in the archives of Hopetoun House, near Edinburgh. They show that Nost presented details of various statues of classical subjects to Charles Hope, First Earl of Hopetoun in 1709 and 1718.[14] Included in the 1718 papers is an 'Artikle of Agreement between John Nost... and John Gordon of Edinbourough Marchant' to make 'four Mettle statues'.[15] One of these is described as 'Hercules with a club'. Another measured drawing was found with the description 'A Pedestal for Baccus & Ceres'. The style of this pedestal, the form of its lettered title and the size of the drawing are identical to the King's Weston drawing of the Goldney pedestal in the Vanburgh album. It is this drawing that supports the attribution of the Goldney statue to John Nost, rather than to such contemporary sculptors as John Cheere or Andrew Carpenter.[16]

The statue was conserved by Andrew Naylor in 1995, assisted by funds from the Alumni Foundation.[17] The lead figure was also made a little more erect, but not yet as upright as it probably once was.

Within the grotto in the centre of Goldney House's garden; the stone lion is at the eastern end of the Great Terrace

A Stone River God and a Plaster Lion and Lioness; A Stone Lion B21

Sculptor: attributed to Thomas Paty

Designer: Thomas Goldney III

Date: c.1750
Material: Bath stone and plaster of Paris
Dimensions: river god, approx. 55in; lion, 53 x 37in
Status: Grade I
Owner: University of Bristol
Condition: fair

In 1756, Mrs Delany described Thomas Goldney's grotto as 'much the finest thing of the kind I ever saw'.[18] It had been begun in 1737 and was completed 27 years later.

In the early 1760s, the Duchess of Northumberland wrote: 'There is at one end of the Terrace a Lyon carv'd in Stone as large as the Life'.[19] That is where the stone lion is today. There is a plaster replica of this lion in the central hall of the grotto. He guards a cave or lion's den in which there is a truncated stone lioness. She has no hind quarters, which are unseen, obscured by the den's entrance. It is just possible that the duchess's visit coincided with the laying of the fine tiled floor and that the stone lion had been temporarily removed. But why or when the replica was made, and for how long the stone lion has been on the terrace we do not know.

The date of the carving of both the lion and the river god is also uncertain. In 1749 a local diarist, Reverend Alexander Catcott of Temple Church, mentions that the water is to fall from 'out of an urn of a Sea-God, seated (reclined on his Elbow)' and that 'A Gloomy den in which there is to be a lion' was ready, but 'the Lion not yet made'.[20] This could imply that the river god was both made and seen by Reverend Catcott, but not yet in place. Not until Mrs Delaney's visit in 1756 is there unequivocal evidence of the river god's presence inside the grotto. Surprisingly, neither she nor the Duchess of Northumberland in the early 1760s make mention of the lions within the grotto, and it is not until 1776 that there is an account of them in the position in which we see them today.[21]

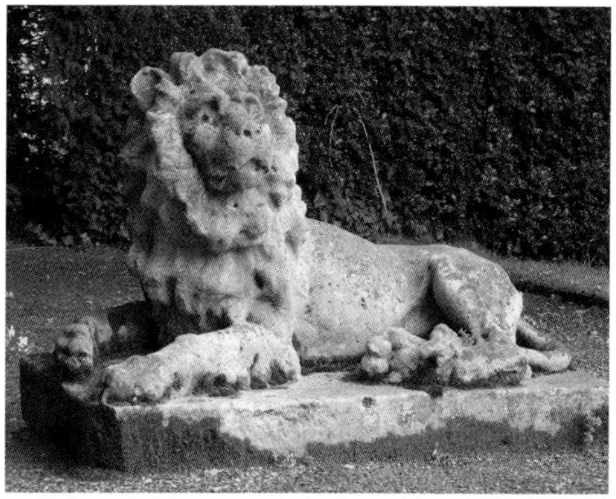

Thomas Paty (attributed to), *Stone lion on the terrace at Goldney*

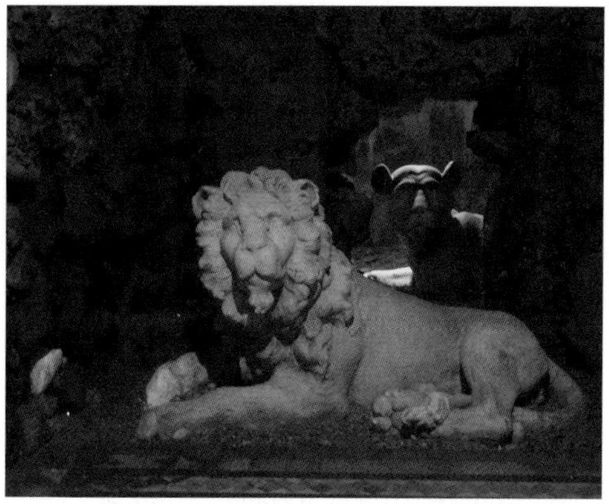

Thomas Paty (attributed to), *Plaster lion and lioness in the grotto at Goldney*

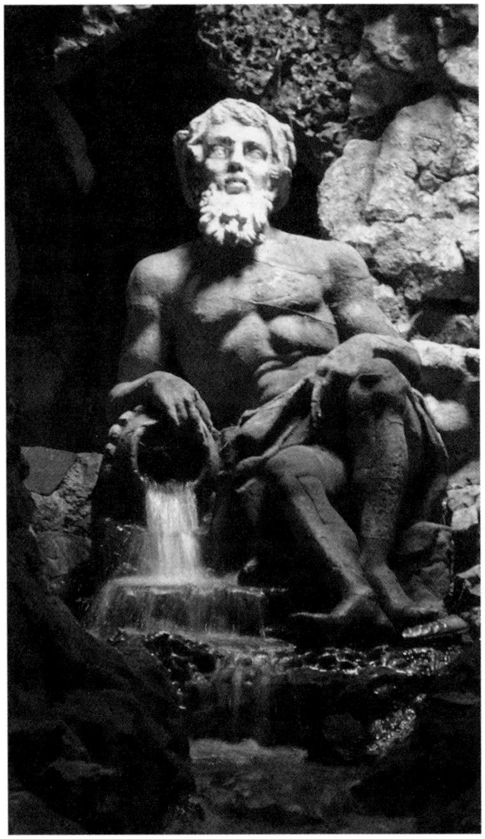

Thomas Paty (attributed to), *River god in the grotto at Goldney*

The river god reclines in a relaxed and suitably everlasting pose at the head of the cascade. He is slightly less than life size, deliberately so, in order to support the narrowing perspective of the 20ft tunnel, which appears considerably longer. He is bearded and is said to wear a garland of oak leaves.[22] One arm rests on the urn and the other on his knee. There appear to be substantial stone insets to both legs, but the condition of the figure as a whole cannot be established from the viewpoint of the central hall. The head looks upward rather than along the cascade, as one might expect, and this could be a mistake of restoration.

The modelling of the torso of the river god and of the stone lion is impressively naturalistic and of considerable quality. It is possible that Thomas Goldney employed Thomas Paty to carve these figures or, at the very least, to oversee their production. Between 1746 and 1750 Paty had been very closely involved with the building and decoration of Clifton Hill House, just 50 yards from Goldney House, to the designs of Isaac Ware.[23] And he was to be paid for the tiling of the grotto's floor between 1862 and 1865.[24]

The plaster version of the lion lacks the sensitivity of the original stone figure, but reveals some details now lost to weathering, most notably the goatee beard. The quality of the carving of the stone lion is still easily appreciated, but the deterioration is not going to slow down and consideration should be given to the long-term preservation of this fine mid-eighteenth century sculpture.

Notes

[1] P.K. Stembridge, *Goldney, A House and a Family* (Bristol, 1969) p.7. [2] Ibid, p.8. [3] R.J.G. Savage, 'Natural history of the Goldney Garden Grotto, Clifton, Bristol', *Journal of the Garden History Society*, vol. 17, no. 1. [4] As note 1, p.19. [5] The sale catalogue of 'Mr Van Nost's Collection' after his death lists two lead statues by him after the Farnese Hercules (52 and 61) photocopy, Conway Library, Courtauld Institute of Art. [6] R. Graves, *Greek Myths* (London, 1958), pp.164, 169. [7] M. Bingham, *Masks and Façades: Sir John Vanburgh, the Man in his Setting* (London, 1974), p. 216. [8] Inventory for Goldney garden, University of Bristol Library, information from Peggy Stembridge; English Heritage Listed Buildings, PRN:901-1/14/785. [9] As note 1, p.19. [10] Johannes Kip, King's Weston the seat of Sir Edward Southwell, from Sir R. Atkyns, *Ancient and Present State of Gloucestershire* (London, 1712). [11] Bodleian Library, Oxford. Ms Gough, Somerset 7 numbered 36. [12] J. Russell, 'The "Great Court" at Kings Weston', *Avon Gardens Trust Journal*, no. 2, summer, 2007, pp.29–37. [13] *Vanburgh Album*, BRO 33746, vol. 131, 1996; Merritt, *Sculpture in Bristol*, illus. p.68. [14] Marquess of Linlithgow Archives NRA(S) 888 Bundle 630, Estimate from John Nost I, 1709, Hopetoun House, Edinburgh. Hopetoun's archivist, Pat Crichton, greatly assisted in this investigation. [15] Op. cit., contract 1718, bundle 2694. [16] The date of Nost's death is uncertain and may be as early as 1710, but his London workshop continued under Nost's nephew, Gerard Nost. [17] University of Bristol, *Convocation* (1996), p.10. [18] Robert J. G. Savage, *op. cit.* p.34 [19] quoted in part: P. K. Stembridge, *Thomas Goldney's Garden*, 1996 p.8; transcript of Duke of Northumberland MS 121/177, Alnwick Castle, kindly supplied by Miss Stembridge [20] *ibid.*; differently, but more fully quoted by Robert J. G. Savage, *op cit*, p.33 [21] As note 1, p.22 [22] As note 3, p.3. [23] Priest and Cobb, *The Paty Family*, p.51. [24] As note 20.

College Green

On College Green, opposite the Marriott Royal Hotel

Queen Victoria B55

Sculptor: Sir Joseph Edgar Boehm

Architect: W. S. Paul

Contractor: William Cowlin and Sons
Date: 1888
Materials: Carrara marble; pedestal, Portland stone, partly encased in bronze
Foundry: Thames Ditton Foundry, Surrey
Masons for pedestal and paving: H. Tyley of St Augustine's Back
Dimensions: statue 260cm high, 100cm wide at base; pedestal, 185cm high overall, 210cm wide at base; bronze casing, 85cm deep
Inscriptions: on the front of the bronze casing to the pedestal – VICTORIA, / QUEEN AND EMPRESS.
—: on the rear – THIS STATUE / ERECTED TO / COMMEMORATE THE / COMPLETION ON 20TH OF JUNE / 1887 OF THE FIFTIETH YEAR / OF THE REIGN OF / QUEEN VICTORIA / WAS UNVEILED BY / PRINCE ALBERT VICTOR / ON 25TH JULY 1888 / CHARLES WATHEN MAYOR / R. H. SYMES, SHERIFF / J. E. BOEHM. SC
Status: Grade II
Owned by Bristol City Council
Condition: fair; parts of the crown and fingers from the right hand are missing

Bristol proudly celebrated the golden jubilee of Queen Victoria's reign in 1887, although she had had few associations with the city. In the early years of her childhood she stayed, with her mother, for a brief time in Clifton at what are now the Assembly Rooms in The Mall, now the Clifton Club. In 1856 the queen's train had waited briefly at Temple Meads Station when she travelled from Plymouth to Osborne, on the Isle of Wight. Thereafter she was to visit the city only once, in 1899. She was 80 when she opened the Queen Victoria Jubilee Convalescent Home in Redland in November of that year (see Redland Hill).

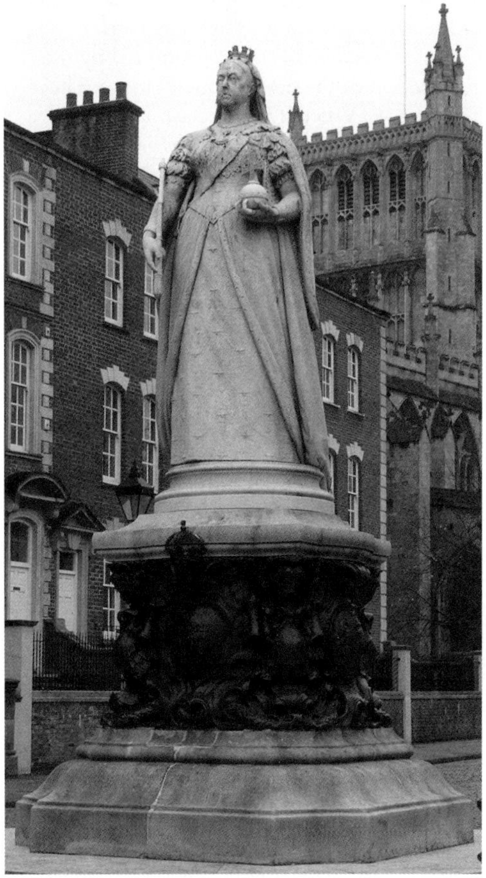

Joseph Edgar Boehm, *Queen Victoria*

Sir Joseph Edgar Boehm carved this over life-size statue from 'one block of the finest white Carrara marble'.[1] It portrays Queen Victoria in her maturity. She wears flowing robes and stands without a hint of movement looking out imperiously over the city of Bristol. She is crowned and carries both the sceptre and orb, which are based on studies of the originals in the Tower of London.[2] The robes are copied from those she wore at the wedding of her youngest daughter, Princess Beatrice, on 23 July 1885. They appear in photographs of the queen taken in 1887 when she was 68 years old.[3] Her decorations are the Order of the Garter, worn with the ribbon across her left breast; the Order of the Star of India; and the Saxe-Coburg Order with the double cameo of the Queen and Prince Albert. She also wears two bracelets, as well as the necklace, consisting of large octagonal diamonds, the Koh-i-noor in front.

The tiny crown is perched precariously on her head, over an elaborate lace veil. It was based on one especially made for her by Messrs Garrard and Company. This crown had been ridiculed when Boehm used it on his designs for the Jubilee coinage in the same year. 'The prime target was Boehm's new effigy of Queen Victoria, which showed her wearing a tiny crown apparently in danger of slipping from the back of her head.'[4] There were cartoons and adverse comments on these coins in the press. One *Punch* cartoon was entitled 'Mint Sauce'.[5] The Bristol statue was given the same crown but no adverse remarks have been found in the local press.

The detail of the carving reflects the praise paid to the sculptor:

> In contrast to his rivals in the Royal Academy…[Boehm] possessed the overwhelming advantage of having the technical training to suggest in marble the differences in texture between flesh and fabric, fur, jewels and metal.[6]

Further praise of Boehm's realism has come from Sir David Piper, who described him as 'a brilliant master of the three dimensional facsimile in marble'.[7]

The circular plinth on which the queen stands is an integral part of the sculpture, and it is carved from the same piece of marble. Her robes drape over the plinth at the rear. The statue rests on a highly decorated square pedestal of 'the very best selected stone from Portland Island', and its core is 'encased with richly ornamented bronze scroll work, with one

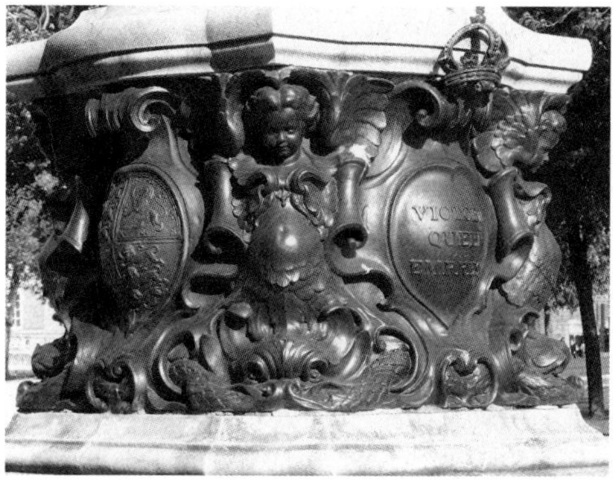

Joseph Edgar Boehm, *Queen Victoria* (detail of bronze plinth)

oval-shaped shield on each quarter'.[8] This casing is in 'a neo-Baroque idiom, with lush corner compositions of the heads of putti, the masks of dolphins, grotesque bodies and foliage'.[9] The front shield is surmounted by a crown and bears the inscription: 'Victoria, Queen and Empress'. On the south-side shield are the royal arms, on the north are the arms of Bristol and on the back is the inscription recording the details of the unveiling as well as the sculptor's name.

The statue and plinth have remained unaltered since the unveiling, but the settings have changed on each of the three moves within College Green. The original setting, with the statue inside a rectangle of railings and wide steps, was the most elaborate. There were two ornamental lamps on pedestals and around the base of the pedestal was a wide pavement of Portland stone. On the most recent move (1994), the statue and pedestal were placed on a small circular surround of Portland stone steps and granite setts.

We would know more about the commissioning of this statue if Boehm's executors had not burnt 'every private paper apart from a few token items' within days of his sudden death in The Avenue Studios, South Kensington in 1890.[10] The papers 'would have provided an incomparable record of the comings and goings in one of the busiest and most important sculptor's studios in Victorian London'.[11]

It was Princess Louise, the Marchioness of Lorne (1848–1939), Queen Victoria's fourth daughter, who discovered the sculptor's body. She was alone and was inevitably compromised. A cover-up ensued. The princess had been a pupil of Boehm's and a long friendship had developed. Boehm probably died of a heart attack and no inquest was held.

Boehm's biographer, Mark Stocker, makes no reference to the commissioning or making of the Bristol statue. Lengthy newspaper reports of the 1880s provide much of the following information.

The proposal for a Bristol statue to celebrate the fiftieth year of Queen Victoria's reign came from group of influential citizens, but it was not made until 20 December 1886. With this late start the unveiling did not take place until the year after the jubilee.

The group, known as 'The Statue Committee', recommended that not more than £5,000 should be raised. The committee was led by Sir George William Edwards, who had previously launched the project privately and subscribed £100 towards the cost.[12] He was a tobacco manufacturer who had served as mayor for several years. A sub-committee was formed and Edwards, James Dole (a provision merchant), F. Joseph Storrs Fry (a member of the Society of Friends and of the chocolate manufacturing dynasty and chairman of Bristol General Hospital Committee), together with the architect, Walter S. Paul, visited Boehm's studio in November 1887.[13]

No evidence of the Statue Committee's decisions regarding the appointment of the sculptor has been traced, but it seems highly probable that the queen herself was consulted. The choice was not surprising; Boehm was said to be her favourite. Mark Stoker quotes the queen's frequent references to Boehm from her journal; Boehm's monument to Prince Leopold, she felt, was 'lovely' and 'touching and beautiful'. Stoker describes Boehm as the 'the perfect sculptor' for the royal family, saying that:

> he combined a consistent ability to convey likeness – and thus stir fond memories – with a tactful readiness to design memorials according to the queen's wishes.[14]

The queen had appointed him Sculptor in Ordinary in 1881. 'In May 1889 [a year after the unveiling of the Bristol statue] he was made a baronet, the first sculptor to be so honoured since Henry Cheere in 1766.'[15]

The architect W. S. Paul, a member of the Statue Committee, supervised the setting and all the operations carried out in Bristol.[16] The local masons, Tyley, supplied the original Portland stone paving and grey granite kerbing from the Penryn quarries in Cornwall.[17] W. H Cowlin, under the direction of 'Mr. Tyley', did the masonry and placed the statue in position. Messrs Edbrooke of College Place later fixed the ornamental wrought iron railings.

Queen Victoria's grandson, Prince Albert Victor (1864–92), performed the unveiling on 25 July 1888. Two years later he became Duke of Clarence and Avondale, and heir presumptive to the throne until his death less than four years after this ceremony. The prince was presented with the honorary freedom of the city of Bristol at the Council House during his visit. The newspaper reported the ceremony 'was performed during a heavy shower' and a photograph of the event shows Boehm as one of the very few present not sheltering under an umbrella.[18] The mayor, Charles Wathen, later Sir Charles, a wholesale clothier, represented the city.

In 1926, only 38 years after the unveiling, a committee endeavouring to erect a memorial to the city's dead from the First World War proposed to remove the queen's statue from the College Green.[19] This suggestion was taken so seriously that a local paper conducted a public ballot. There were 4,926 against its removal – a majority of only 646 – and the suggestion was dropped.

The removal of Queen Victoria's statue and of the Victorian replica High Cross from College Green in 1951 was prompted by the completion of the new Council House. The architect, E. Vincent Harris, considered the re-landscaping of College Green as an integral part of his design: 'I hope very much that the Green will be lowered. It is going to "make" my building. The removal of the statue of Queen Victoria and the Cross would be a minor detail'.[20]

The last photograph of the statue on its original site, where she had reigned for 62 years, was taken on 19 November 1950.[21] Many alternatives were proposed: the site of a drinking fountain in Victoria Park, Bedminster, Temple Meads station incline, the Blackboy Hill roundabout and the Prince Street roundabout.[22] All these were abandoned and the statue was taken into temporary exile for three years at Redcliffe Wharf in February 1951.[23] A capsule containing the full range of Victorian coins, from a gold sovereign to a farthing, was found under the statue at this time. When finally re-erected on the south-eastern point of College Green on 17 March 1953, a set of nine coronation coins – the first of the reign of Queen Elizabeth II – and contemporary newspapers were added to the 1888 capsule.[24]

There the statue remained until a new design was imposed upon College Green, involving the closure of the road running close to the north side of the Cathedral. The project was funded and carried out through a partnership between Bristol City Council, Avon County Council, the European Commission, English Heritage and the Dean and Chapter of Bristol Cathedral. It was completed in September 1993.[25] Queen Victoria's statue was moved a short distance to the new forecourt of the re-furbished Swallow Royal Hotel, now the Marriot Royal Hotel. The statue was restored and the work funded by Swallow Hotels and Avon County Council in a project coordinated by Bristol City Council and carried out by Bristol Contract Services and Naylor Conservation. The date of the dedication was 24 May 1994, the 175th anniversary of Victoria's birthday.[26]

Fragile parts of the marble statue have often suffered from vandalism. When the cross on the orb was broken off in 1888 a local paper reported this as 'slight damage' by a 'gang of about a dozen hobbledehoys'.[27] No one had seen a stone thrown, but two ladies found pieces of marble and some passing gentlemen took possession of them. It was at first hoped that a reward would lead to the detection of the miscreants, but the newspaper later admitted that there was no evidence against the so-called 'hobbledehoys'.

Vandalism occurred early in 1999, and the orb and fingers 'were found in a school ground outside Bristol'. They were discovered to be made of cast concrete and were evidently earlier replacements.[28] In 2002 the council carried out conservation work to repair damages using marble. There have since been further breaks and repairs.

Notes

[1] 'The Royal Visit to Bristol', *Bristol Times and Mirror*, 26 July 1888. [2] Ibid. [3] These were the Jubilee Cabinet albumen photographs by Alexander Bassano, National Portrait Gallery, acquisition no. X8753. [4] M. Stocker, *Royalist and Realist: The Life and Work of Sir Joseph Edgar Boehm*' (New York, 1988). [5] Op. cit., illus. 290. [6] R. Dorment, 'Mourning glories', *Times Literary Supplement*, 11 November 1988. [7] D. Piper, 'The National Portrait Gallery: some recent acquisitions', *The Connoisseur*, 1954, no. 54, p.183. [8] As note 1. [9] Little, *The Public View*, p.73. [10] As note 4. [11] Dorment, 'Mourning glories'. [12] B. Little, 'Victoriana', *Bristol Illustrated*, July 1988, p.41. [13] A studio and foundry in Fulham Road once owned by Baron Carlo Marochetti. [14] As note 4. [15] Ibid. The honour was given to acknowledge the Queen's 'high appreciation of artistic eminence, and the beauty of great works … produced'. Lord Salisbury to Boehm, 22 May 1889, note 64, p.327. [16] As note 12; W.S. Paul was an Old Cliftonian; he designed the setting for the South African War memorial at Clifton College. [17] Ibid; the Tyley family were Bristol masons and sculptors involved in many of the city's monuments. [18] Winstone, *Bristol in the 1880s*, photograph 66; Boehm can be seen, wearing a bowler hat, to the right of the statue. [19] R.F. Lyne, 'How the Cenotaph came', *Bristol Evening Post*, 8 November 1940. [20] R. Winstone, *Bristol 1950–1953*, photographs 45 and 46, 'The Rape of College Green'. [21] Op. cit., photograph 52. [22] 'Queen Victoria sets a problem', *Bristol Evening Post*, 11 October 1950. [23] Winstone, *Bristol As It Was 1950–53*, pls. 73 and 74 show the statue in Redcliffe wharf yard with large chips to the circular marble footing of the statue block. [24] 'Queen Victoria is back in College Green', *Bristol Evening World*, 17 March 1953. [25] A plaque on College Green, approximately 60m from the north door of the cathedral, records that the College Green Enhancement Scheme was inaugurated by the Lord Mayor of Bristol, Councillor John Channon, 27 September 1993. [26] An inscription about the statue is on the wall at the entrance to the Marriot Royal Hotel. [27] *Bristol Times and Mirror*, 26 November 1888. [28] Letter from Garry Reeder, senior building surveyor, Bristol City Council, 1 November 1999.

On an island site outside the entrance to Bristol Central Library, College Green

Raja Rammohun Roy B56

Sculptor: Niranjan Pradhan

Date: 1997

Material: bronze; Portland stone pedestal by W. R. Bedford, Bedminster, Bristol; bronze plaque by Ward and Company, Barton Hill

Dimensions: 850cm high; base, 80cm square; pedestal, 75cm high

Inscription: cast in raised roman capitals on bronze plaque – RAJAH RAMMOHUN ROY / BORN ON 22 MAY 1772 IN RADHANAGAR BENGAL / DIED ON 27 SEPTEMBER 1833 IN BRISTOL / PHILOSOPHER, REFORMER, PATRIOT, SCHOLAR / A FOUNDING FATHER OF INDIAN RENAISSANCE / UNVEILED BY HIS EXCELLENCY DR. L. M. SINGHVI / THE HIGH COMMISSIONER FOR INDIA IN THE UK, / IN THE PRESENCE OF THE RIGHT HONORABLE / THE LORD MAYOR OF BRISTOL, COUNCILLOR JACK FISK, / TO MARK THE GOLDEN JUBILEE OF INDIA'S INDEPENDENCE / ON 20 NOVEMBER 1997. / SCULPTED BY MR. NIRANJAN PRADHAN / GIFT OF RPG ENTERPRISES

—: cast in the base, close to the left foot, in hand-written sans serif capitals – SCULPTOR / NIRANJAN PRADHAN / CALCUTTA / 1997 / INDIA

Status: Grade II*

Owned by Bristol City Council

Condition: good

Rammohun Roy was born in 1772 at Radhanagar in Bengal, and was of the Brahmin caste or class. He was one of the first Hindus to visit Britain. Fluent in Persian, Arabic, Sanskrit and English, he had already published extensively and contributed to the banning of *suttee*, both on humanitarian grounds and with arguments that it represented a false interpretation of Hindu texts. He argued:

> all religious traditions are true in that they teach belief in God as revealed in the design of the universe, but that they are false in that they add unnecessary and conflicting beliefs to this common core.[1]

This led to close friendship with leading Unitarians, notably Dr Lant Carpenter of Bristol. Rammohan Roy had left India for Britain in 1830 as the ambassador of the Mughal Emperor Akbar II of Delhi, who had conferred on him the title of raja. He died of meningitis while staying at Beech House, Stapleton Grove in September 1833, and was buried in the garden of that house. Ten years later his coffin was taken to Arno's Vale Cemetery, where his unusual *chattri* (funeral monument), based on

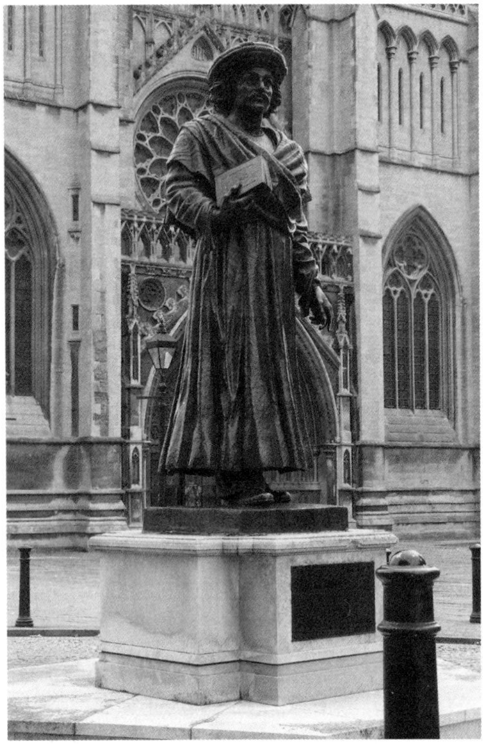

Niranjan Pradhan, *Raja Rammohun Roy*

Hindu temple architecture, still stands. His achievement was to change 'the attitudes of a sub-continent and its relation to others, in ways wholly beneficial to all concerned.'[2]

The sculptor, Niranjan Pradhan, turned to the large oil painting in the Bristol Museum and Art Gallery by H. P. Briggs RA for both the likeness and the costume. That portrait was made from life only a year before Rammohun Roy's sudden death. In both the portrait and the statue, the raja holds an unidentified book. On its cover is a distinctive flame motif, a symbol of a god or of God in many religions, including the Hindu religion, and of the Holy Ghost in Christianity.[3] His Persian shawl and his other clothes are those worn by him when he travelled as an ambassador.

'It took fifteen years from concept to achievement, 1982–97' to erect this statue.[4] The process commenced when a committee, chaired by Bhupinder Luther (Chairman of Bristol Indian Association), was established in anticipation of the 150th anniversary of Rammohun Roy's death.[5] This included representatives of Avon County Council, Bristol Cathedral, Bristol Council for Racial Equality, the City Museum, Carla Contractor and many other Bristolians with Indian origins or commitments. At this stage Carla Contractor proposed that there should be a permanent memorial, or a new building or a road named after the raja.[6] 'Rammohun Roy' events were organised over many years by various Bristol committees. In 1991 the City Planning Department agreed to support proposals for a major statue as part of the re-landscaping of College Green following the closure of the road across it. £1,500 was required, but this was not raised until Dr L. M. Singhvi, the Indian High Commissioner, was approached as a friend and supporter in 1992.[7] Dr Singhvi was to be crucial to the success of the project. It was he who conceived the annual Pravasi Bharatiya Divas, the event now organised every January by the Indian government to engage with the nation's 25 million-strong diaspora in 130 countries. In 1993, when the Bristol Hindu Temple joined the Congregations Organised for Greater Bristol, it was suggested that the Royal Society of British Sculptors should organise a competition open to British sculptors of Indian origin. A short list was drawn up, but funding from both the Cadbury Foundation and South West Arts proved insufficient. At this point Carla Contractor advised Dr Singhvi that there was a one-and-a-half life-size bust of Rammohun Roy in Calcutta. He made contacts, and a copy of this bronze by Niranjan Pradhan was presented to the City of Bristol as a gift from Jyoti Basu and the people of West Bengal in 1995 (Council House).[8] A large public statue was still the aim, and this was kept alive by reserving the site by College Green. By 1996 Dr Singhvi was nearing the end of his long posting, and he renewed efforts to raise funds from sources in India. The bronze casting was to cost 650,000 rupees, approximately £13,000.[9] Planners in Bristol agreed to Pradhan being granted the commission, and he and his wife were invited to Bristol to view the site in October 1996.[10] A maquette was made and approved. The statue was cast in his own studio at Salt Lake in Calcutta. It was flown to Heathrow, via diplomatic bag, where it was mislaid. Forwarded to Bristol by the High Commission, the statue arrived on its plinth only 24 hours before it was unveiled. Jack Fisk, Bristol's lord mayor, and the sculptor and his wife were present when Dr Laxmall Singhvi unveiled the statue on the evening of 20 November 1997, in heavy rain, on the golden jubilee of the independence of India.[11]

The statue of Rammohun Roy is at one of the most prestigious sites in the city, set between Bristol Cathedral, the Council House and Bristol Central Library. Rammohun Roy died four years before Queen Victoria came to the throne, and his statue and that of the Empress of India now stand, back to back, at opposite ends of College Green. It was the brave closure of the road along the north side of the cathedral that created a dead-end and the opportunity for a statue in the centre of the turning circle. The actual site was just outside the boundaries of College Green, a part of the ancient Augustinian abbey, and still the property of the dean and chapter of the Cathedral. But the backdrop to the statue is unquestionably the Cathedral rather than the Council House, the Abbey gateway or the library. The conjunction of this most eminent Hindu reformer and the imposing Victorian façade of Bristol Cathedral continues to mystify most visitors.[12]

Notes

[1] *ODNB*, *Dermot Killingley*. [2] R. Barot, *Bristol and the Indian Independence Movement* (Bristol, 1988), p.4. [3] J. Hall, *Illustrated History of Symbolism in Eastern and Western Art* (London, 1997), pp.100, 101. [4] Notes from Carla Contractor. [5] For an account of Bhupinder Luther's

contribution to race relations in Bristol, see *Evening Post*, 26 April 2008, p.18. [6] Letter from Frederick Apperley, Lord Mayor of Bristol, 1983; he hoped the city would honour Rammohun Roy by naming a road after him. [7] As note 4. [8] Niranjan Pradhan is an assistant professor at the Government College of Art and Craft in Nehru Road, Kolkata. [9] A. Sen, 'Linking Bristol to Calcutta', *Nonesuch*, spring 1998, p.24. [10] Ibid. [11] 'A great man is remembered', *Bristol Evening Post*, 21 November 1997. [12] In 1997 there were inevitable letters to the *Bristol Evening Post* : 'Why put a statue to a Hindu there he was not even a Christian ... put Muller (of the Muller Orphanage) there'; and 'What has Roy ever done for Bristol?'.

College Green, Abbey Gatehouse

Between the west front of the Cathedral and Bristol Central Library

The Abbey Gatehouse was originally built between 1140 and 1170 as the main entrance to St Augustine's Abbey's precincts.[1] Both sides contain statues. Those on the north side, facing College Green, are largely medieval. Those on the south side are replacements added in 1914.

The only remaining part of the Norman building is the ground floor, a deep archway with zigzag geometric decoration on both sides. The form of the upper part of the twelfth-century gatehouse 'is not currently known'.[2] The two storeys above the Norman structure, now much restored, were constructed between 1481 and 1526 in a Perpendicular Gothic style.[3] These were built by two abbots, Newland (alias Nailheart) and Elyot.[4] The long oriel windows were removed in the Georgian period and changed to sash windows. Early in Victoria's reign, the whole gatehouse was dilapidated and the poor condition of the statues is shown in a calotype of 1853.[5] It was not until 1888 that restoration by John Loughborough Pearson created much of the present appearance and the double-height oriel windows were restored.[6] Pevsner describes this as 'drastically restored in the nineteenth century'.[7] J. L. Pearson had worked on the adjacent west front of Bristol Cathedral after G. E. Street, the architect of the nave, died in 1888.[8] Charles Holden's design for the adjoining Bristol Central Library façade (1902–6) took careful account of the gateway and it was Charles Pibworth, sculptor of the Library reliefs, who later made the statues for the south side of the gatehouse.

Four Figures on the North Side B58

Sculptor: unknown

Date: fourteenth or fifteenth century
Material: limestone
Status: Grade I
Owned by the Dean and Chapter of Bristol Cathedral
Condition: fair; recent conservation work

The four statues in the niches 'appear to date to the fourteenth or fifteenth century'.[9] All are eroded, and the subjects are difficult to identify. The two crowned statues on the left are clearly kings. A 1942 edition of the *Historical and Descriptive Handbook* on Bristol Cathedral merely says 'two of the statues on the north side represent Henry II and Robert Fitzhardinge'.[10] William Barrett, a Bristol doctor, attempted to identify all four statues in 1789.[11] His book has 'an engraved plate but an imperfect one.' He states that the top statue on the left-hand side is Edward the Confessor and the king below is Henry II, but he is uncertain about the statues on the right. He describes the lower one, placed there by Abbot Newland, as a 'compliment to the founder of the

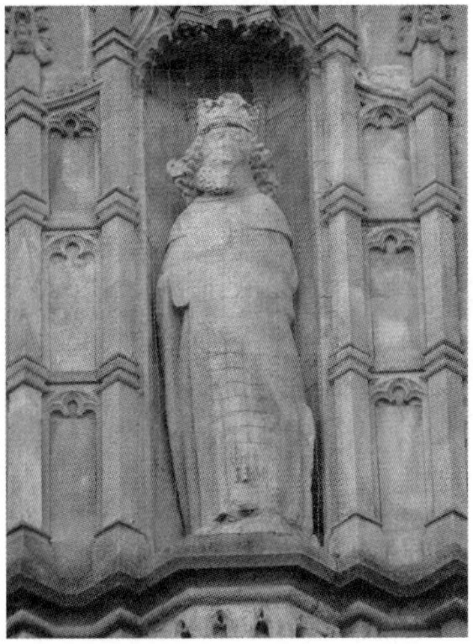

Edward the Confessor

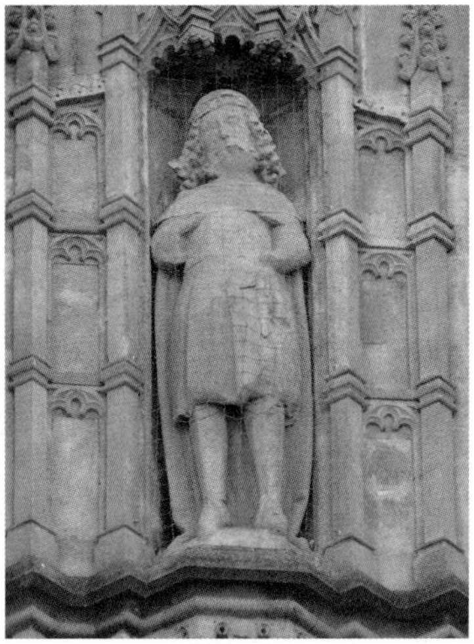

Robert Fitzharding

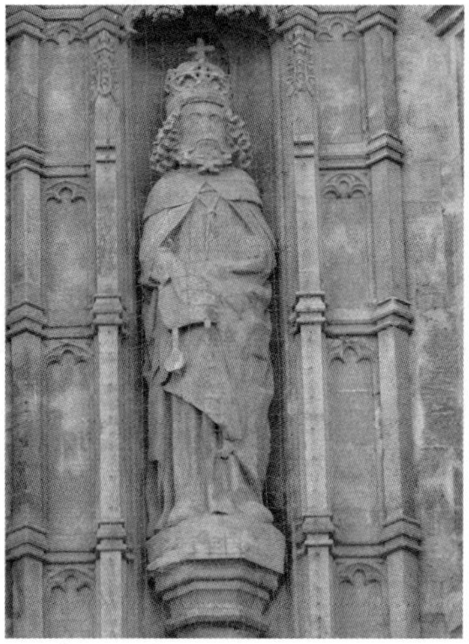

Henry II

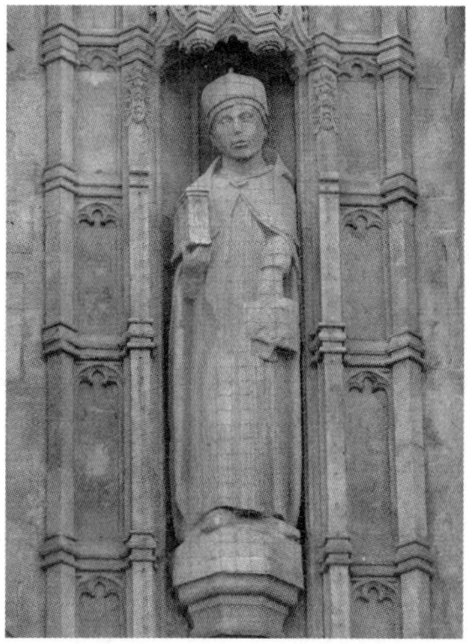

Abbot John Newland

monastery… with a model of the conventual church in one hand and the foundation charter in his other'. He concludes that it must represent the founder of the abbey, Robert Fitzharding. Barrett adds that he had not found the name of the other figure. It is more probable that it is the upper statue, the only figure not in ecclesiastical dress, which represents Robert Fitzharding and it is possible that the lower represents Abbot Newland.

In the engraving of 1788 in William Barrett's *A History of Bristol*, all but the upper right-hand figure hold charters or seals. The heads of the statues have probably been recut or, possibly, replaced. In 2004 the sculptures and the whole gateway were part of a major conservation programme.

Four Figures on the South Side B58

Sculptor: Charles James Pibworth

Date: 1914
Material: Portland stone
Status: Grade I
Owned by the Dean and Chapter of Bristol Cathedral
Condition: good after recent conservation work

Barrett named three of the subjects that were on the south side when he wrote in 1789: 'Abbots Newland and Elliot' [sic] and 'besides the abbots in effigy… are the Virgin Mary and Child', but he does not identify the fourth.[12] These severely eroded figures were replaced in 1914 by Portland stone statues of four abbots.[13] They were carved by the Bristol-born sculptor Charles Pibworth, eight years after he was commissioned to make the three large reliefs on the adjacent Bristol Central Library. The statue of the *Virgin and Child* mentioned by Barrett was not replaced. The two upper figures represent Abbot Knowle (1306–32), holding a model of his church, and on the right Abbot Snow (1332–41), the first mitred abbot, holding a scroll to which a seal is attached. The lower figures are Abbot Elyot (1515–26), with a crozier holding a model of the Gatehouse, and on the right Abbot Newland (1481–1515), chronicler of the abbey and of the Berkeley family, holding a crozier and a book.[14] Elyot and Newland were responsible for adding the upper part of the gatehouse.

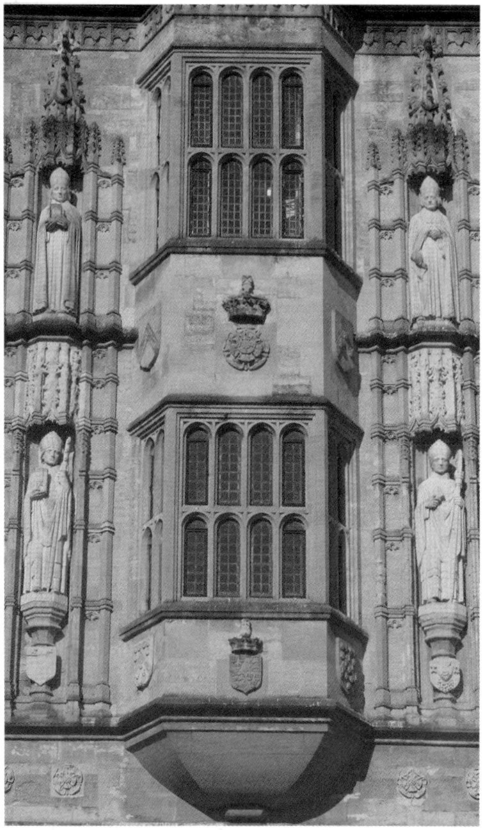

Abbey Gatehouse, south side

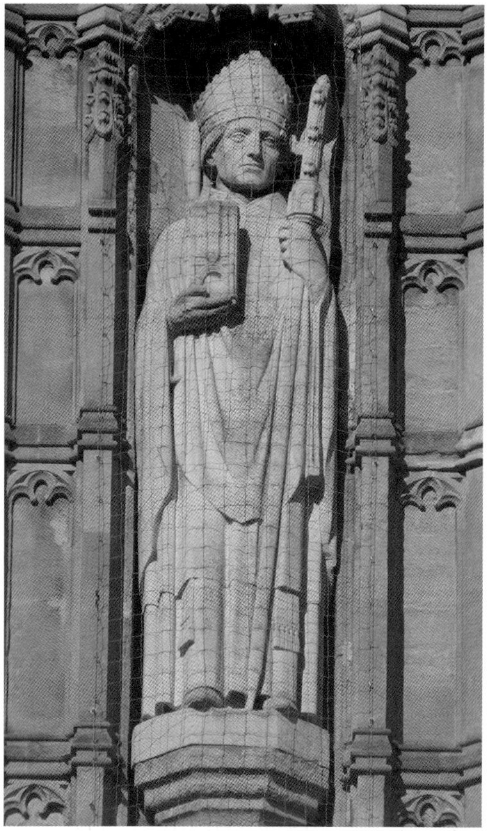

Charles James Pibworth, *Abbot Elyot*

Notes
[1] Bristol Urban Archaeological Database, Monument Record, No. 517M. [2] Ibid. [3] J. Ross, *The Cathedral Church of Bristol, Historical and Descriptive Handbook* (Gloucester, 1935), p.58. [4] Ibid. [5] Winstone, *Bristol in the 1850s* (Bristol, 1978), pl. 5, a calotype of the arch from College Square, 1854. [6] Foyle and Cherry, *Bristol*, p.62. [7] Pevsner, *North Somerset*, p.386. [8] Op. cit., p.380. [9] As note 1. [10] As note 3, pp.58, 60. [11] Barrett, *A History of Bristol*, p.287. [12] As note 11. [13] The engraving by John Carter, 1788 in Barrett's *A History of Bristol* shows one statue on the south side headless and a second faceless; a watercolour by M.K. Moore (1882) in Bristol Museum and Art Gallery, K380, shows three of the statues to be headless; see also note 5. [14] As note 3, p.60.

College Green, Bristol Central Library

On the Deanery Road façade

Chaucer and the Canterbury Pilgrims; The Venerable Bede and Early Literary Saints; King Alfred and the Medieval Chroniclers B57

Sculptor: Charles James Pibworth

Architect: Charles Holden

Date: 1905
Material: Portland stone
Dimensions: each approximately 190cm high, 370cm wide
Signed on right-hand reveal of the central relief: C. PIBWORTH, SCULPTOR. 1905
Status: Grade I
Owned by Bristol City Council
Condition: good; conservation work by Bristol City Council, 2003

Bristol's first free public library, one of the earliest in England, opened in 1615.[1] Towards the end of the nineteenth century, plans for its direct descendant, a new central library, foundered for lack of funds. Then in 1899 Vincent Stuckey Lean, a bachelor barrister born in Clifton but residing in Clevedon, bequeathed £50,000 to Bristol for the purposes of a new reference library.

The architectural practice in which Charles Holden worked won a limited competition for the new library in 1902, and it was built between 1903 and 1906. The competition rules had specified that 'simplicity and breadth of effect are most desirable' and that 'the lavish use of ornament is to be avoided'.[2] In fact, Holden introduced more decoration into his façade than he showed on his early plans. As well as Charles Pibworth's large lunettes, there are many floral devices and vines, grapes and figs and other natural ornamentation by William Aumonier.

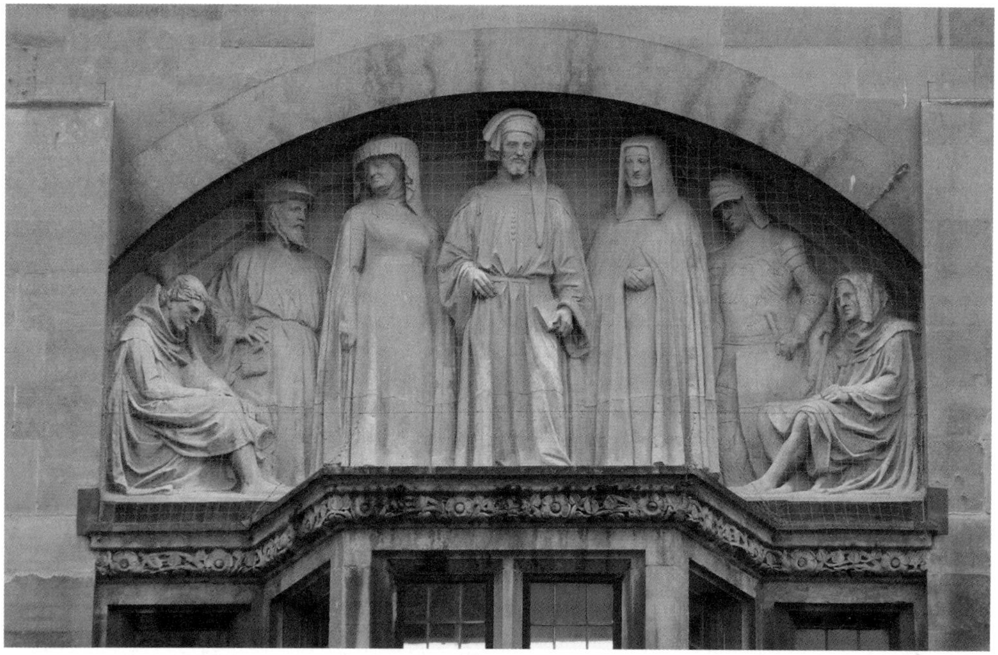

Charles James Pibworth, ***Chaucer and the Canterbury Pilgrims***

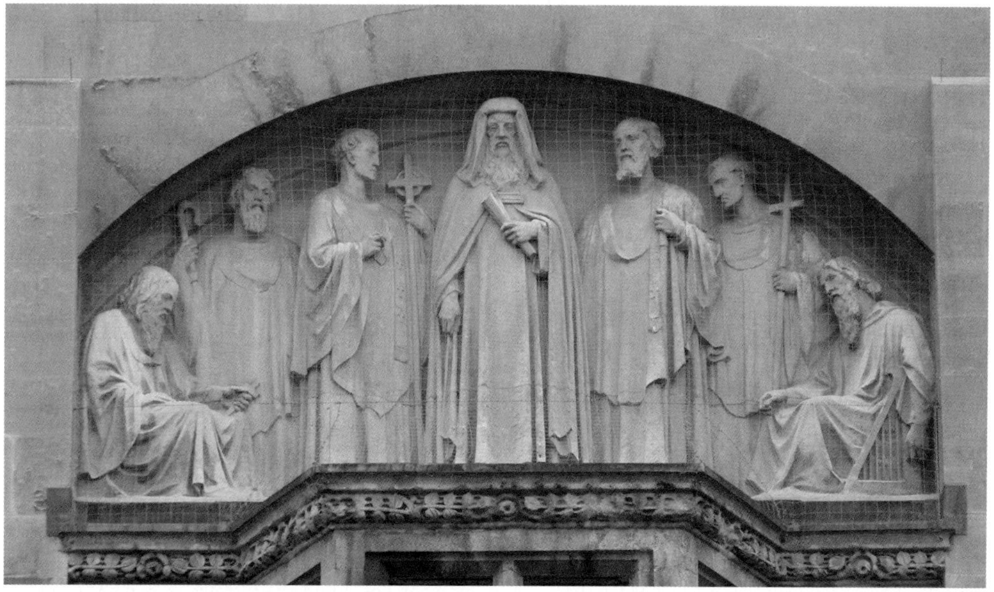

Charles James Pibworth, ***The Venerable Bede and Early Literary Saints***

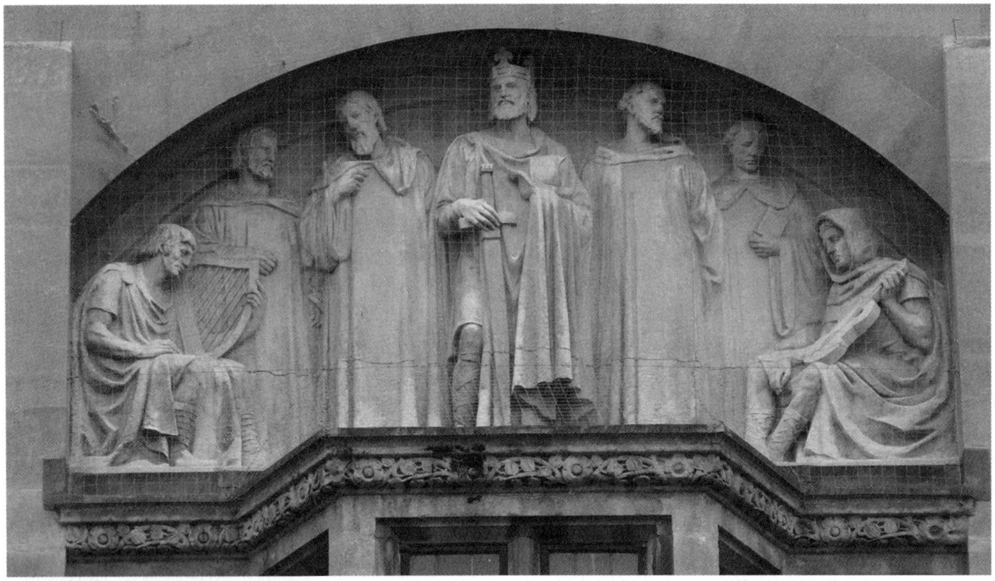

Charles James Pibworth, ***King Alfred and the Medieval Chroniclers***

The three bas-reliefs were later described by the sculptor as being 'carved in Portland Stone' and as 'Gothic panels... containing twenty-one life-size figures almost in the round'.[3] They represent early English writers from Bede to Chaucer, together with some of the characters they created. They are contained in three segmental-arched recesses set above the oriel windows of the first floor. Each figure was identified by the sculptor. The panel on the right contains Chaucer, at the centre, and pilgrims from *The Canterbury Tales*. The three characters to Chaucer's right are the Miller, the Merchant and the Wife of Bath; to his left are the Prioress, the Knight and the Man of Law. The central panel has the Venerable Bede surrounded by other English writers. St Aidan, St Chad, and St Augustine are to Bede's right and St Cuthbert, St Paulinus and Caedmon, the earliest poet whose name has survived, are to his left. The central figure in the right-hand panel is King Alfred. On his right are a minstrel, Cynewulf the travelling bard, and St Gildas. On his left are William of Malmesbury, Florence of Worcester, and Wace the Norman minstrel.[4] Line drawings of the work were reproduced when a Bristol newspaper reported in 1905:

> The public have now an opportunity of admiring the finely-sculptured panels at the new Central and Reference Library in Deanery Road. They are the work of Mr Charles Pibworth, who was formerly a student at the Bristol School of Art in Queen's Road...[5]

Holden's design of the library is a masterpiece of the early modern movement. The rear elevations have often been compared with Charles Rennie Mackintosh's work in Glasgow at the same period. English Heritage praise Holden's building as 'a supreme example of Edwardian free style, which in its bold rationalist design was to have great influence in shaping the work of other architects in the vanguard of architectural development.'[6] Pevsner described the library as 'perhaps Charles Holden's most remarkable work before he started his chain of underground stations in 1932'.[7] He also said that 'friezes of figures' were 'a favourite motif of progressive architects of c.1895–1905'. However, in her book *The New Sculpture*, Susan Beattie is critical:

> The work of Pibworth contains, moreover, a threat to the standards of the New Sculpture more serious than either neo-classicism or historical anecdote: his harsh simplifications and concern to echo the geometry of the masonry block, particularly evident in the sculptures on Holden's library extension to the Law Society in Chancery Lane, do much to explain why he was succeeded in the architect's favour by Jacob Epstein and Eric Gill.[8]

The Bristol Library was a vital commission for Pibworth; he was 24 and Holden was only three years older. He was to use this early Bristol success to impress the lord mayor when attempting unsuccessfully to gain the commission to design the statue for Bristol's Edward VII Memorial in 1910.[9] He emphasised: 'I write to you hoping that, as I am a Bristolian, I may have the honour of being chosen as your Sculptor'.

We do not know how Holden came to choose this young sculptor, but Pibworth was born in Bristol and he had first studied there. When he left the Royal Academy Schools in 1902 he was awarded a prize and Holden's practice won the competition in that same year.

Photographs of the three panels, taken by Pibworth, are reproduced in *Bristol and its Famous Associations*.[10] These show slight differences from the final carved work and were probably views of his clay models. A Bristol woman, Harriet Fricker, has been identified as the model for the prioress. She was Pibworth's sister-in-law and was born in Frog Lane, Bristol in 1872.[11] Pibworth was to be paid £425 for the lunettes, but he successfully petitioned for an increase of £50.[12]

Decorative Sculpture B57

Sculptor: William Aumonier

Architect: Charles Holden

Date: 1905
Material: Bath stone

Over the main entrance to the Central Library, Aumonier carved Bristol's coat-of-arms surrounded by unusually deeply cut acanthus leaves through which there are glimpses of the leaves' curving stalks. At the foot of the staircase are the arms of Vincent Stuckey Lean, presented in a similar manner. Outside Aumonier was responsible for the panels of vines and grapes and branches loaded with figs, symbolic of the Tree of Knowledge, below the two large oriel windows on the façade. Above the three smaller oriel windows immediately under Pibworth's panels is a frieze of rambling roses, an allusion to the Tudor roses of the Abbey Gateway.[13] On the outside of the staircase tower are three rebus shields reminiscent of the work of mischievous medieval masons. Raised bands, half-calf and quarto are illustrated by visual puns. Much of the remaining decorative detail, inside and outside, is likely also to be by Aumonier.

William Aumonier had already worked with Charles Holden on an extension to the Law Society's building in Chancery Lane, 1902–4, where Charles Pibworth had also carved large allegorical figures.

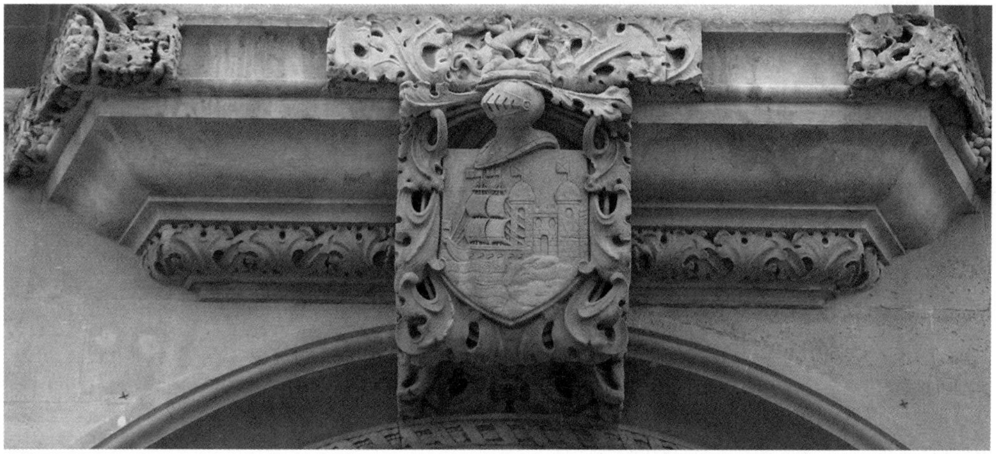

William Aumonier, ***Decorative details above the entrance to Bristol Central Library***

Inside Bristol Central Library on the first floor of the old building

Relief Portrait of Charles Holden B57

Sculptor: Paul Vincze

Date: 1950
Material: circular bronze medallion
Dimensions: 17cm diameter
Inscription: around the rim in Roman capitals – CHARLES H. HOLDEN D.LIT. LITT. D. F.R.I.B.A. M.T.P.I.
—: signature – P.VINCZE / 1950
Status: Grade I
Owned by Bristol City Council
Condition: fair; the surface of the medallion is worn, due to destructive polishing.

Charles Henry Holden (1875–1960) was one of the outstanding British architects of the twentieth century, and it was for Bristol that he designed his most important early works. Through his partnership with H. Percy Adams, who specialised in hospitals, he designed the Bristol Central Library at the age of 27 and, four years later, the Bristol Royal Infirmary, King Edward VII Wing. The library was 'perhaps Charles Holden's most remarkable work', displaying 'a freedom instigated by Mackintosh's Glasgow School of Art'.[14] Holden

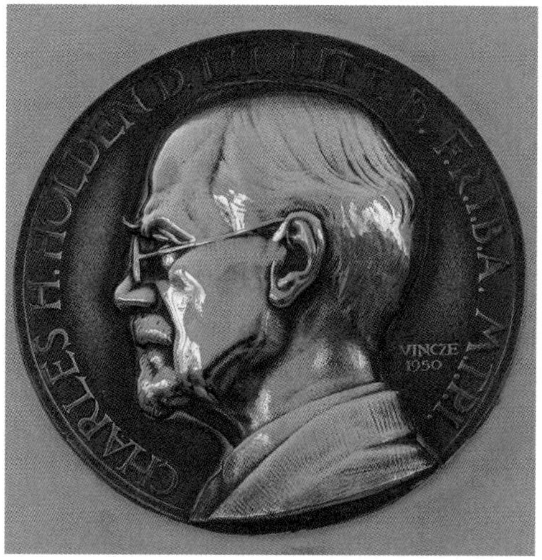

Paul Vinze, ***Charles Holden, architect of Bristol Central Library***

was later to design several London Underground stations in the 1930s in an interpretation of the Bauhaus style that 'did so much to establish the modern idiom in Britain'.[15] London University's towering and austere Senate House is perhaps his best known building.

Holden, born in Bolton and one of six children, was a Quaker. His father's business failed and his mother died, leaving him to be brought up by a sister. He was to build up one of the largest architectural practices of his generation in a very long career and he twice refused a knighthood, saying that it would 'alienate him from the people'.[16]

The bronze bas-relief medallion is set flush with the plaster wall in the first floor corridor leading to the main Reference Library. The inscription does not say he was the architect of the library, but there is now printed information in a frame beneath the medallion. This is headed: ' "With his genius and modesty he compels admiration." C H Reilly 1938.'

This discreet tribute was erected ten years before Holden died and nearly half a century after he had won the competition to design Bristol's highly praised public library in 1902. No record of the commission has been traced, but Anthony Beeson of Bristol Central Library has suggested that it may have been arranged through the Royal Institute of British Architects to mark Holden's seventy-fifth birthday in 1950, the date recorded on the medallion.

Notes
[1] A. Beeson, *Bristol Central library and Charles Holden* (Bristol, 2006), p.4. [2] Ibid, p.12. [3] Letter from Charles Pibworth to Alderman Swaish, 12 October 1910, BRO 03919 10a. [4] Hutton, *Bristol and its Famous Associations*. [5] *The Western Daily Press*, 'New Central and Reference Library, the sculptured panels', 21 December 1905. [6] English Heritage Listed Building Database. PRN: 901-1/15/70. [7] Pevsner, *North Somerset*, p.417. [8] S. Beattie, *The New Sculpture* (New Haven, CT and London, 1983), pp.131–3. [9] Letter from Charles Pibworth to the Lord Mayor of Bristol, 7 September 1910, from 14A Cheyne Row, Chelsea, but inscribed 'Till Sept 12th next 64 Beauley Rd, Southville, Bristol'. BRO 03919 (6) a & b. [10] Hutton, *Bristol and its Famous Associations*, f.p.228. [11] See note 1, p.13. [12] Ibid. [13] As note 1, pp.13, 14. [14] Pevsner, *North Somerset*, p.417. [15] Ibid, p.26. [16] As note 1, p.9.

In the churchyard of Bristol Cathedral, College Green; visible from Trinity Street

Refugee B59

Sculptor: Naomi Blake

Date: 1980
Material: resin bronze
Foundry: Dunton
Dimensions: 210cm high
Inscriptions: cut in roman capitals on a stone slab at the base of the sculpture – SURVIVOR OF AUSCHWITZ
—: on a bronze plate mounted on this stone – REFUGEE / BY / NAOMI BLAKE A.R.B.S. / 1980 / TO THE VICTIMS OF ALL RACIAL PERSECUTIONS
Status: not listed
Owned by the Dean and Chapter of Bristol Cathedral
Condition: good

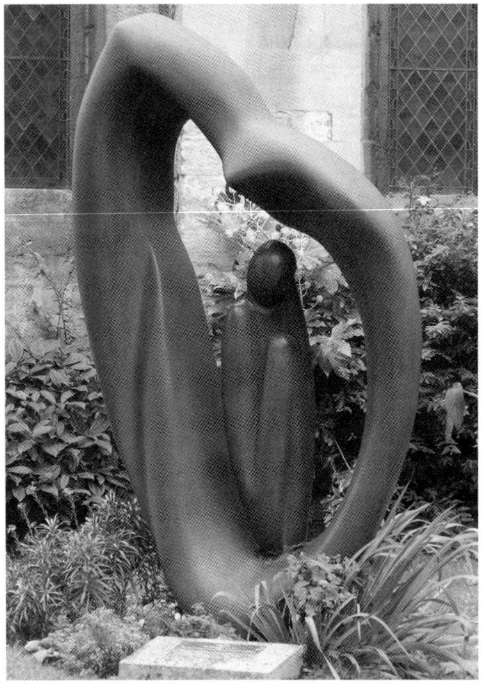

Naomi Blake, *Refugee*

The sculptor, born in Czechoslovakia, survived Auschwitz and came to London after the war.[1] She presented this work to Bristol Cathedral after a smaller version was shown there in an Amnesty International exhibition. It was made in 1979 and unveiled by Cosmo Desmond, the director of Amnesty, on 14 December 1980.[2] In welcoming the gift, the Dean, the Very Reverend Horace Dammers, said that he was delighted that the sculpture, 'dedicated to the victims of all racial persecution, has found sanctuary outside Bristol Cathedral'.[3]

Refugee was first sited on the lawn outside the West Door and mounted on a rough-hewn piece of rock about 50cm high. On 31 March 1992, when preliminary work for a visitor centre began, it was moved to a secluded part of the graveyard garden, where it could only be seen by those who had first entered the cathedral. By 2000 it had been moved to its present site, where it can be seen from the public pathway.

An exhibition of Naomi Blake's work was held in the Chapter House in July 1981, a year after the unveiling.[4] The artist has stated that her work expresses her personal experience of the Holocaust and her hope for a better future.[5] When commenting on a recent Holocaust Memorial Day, Valerie Davey, MP for Bristol West, said:

> One of the survivors, Naomi Blake, is a distinguished sculptor and one of her pieces of work, *The Refugee*, is in the garden of Bristol Cathedral… go and see it and stop to remember. Here is the evidence of the human spirit overcoming evil.[6]

Notes
[1] 'Artist survived death camp', *Western Daily Press*, 15 December 1980. [2] Notes from Naomi Blake, 24 July 1996. [3] As note 2. [4] N. Blake, *Sculpture by Naomi Blake* (private view leaflet, 1981). [5] 'Statue of the Week', *Evening Post*, 29 March 2005. [6] Ibid.

Under the central porch of Bristol Council House, College Green

John Cabot B54

Sculptor: Charles Wheeler

Architect: E. Vincent Harris

Date: 1951
Material: Portland stone
Dimensions: statue, 260cm high, 85cm wide, 70cm deep; pedestal, 150cm high
Contractors: W. Cowlin & Sons
Status: Grade II*
Owned by Bristol City Council
Condition: good

Since this statue was erected, Bristol City Council has usually, but not always, referred to it as 'An Elizabethan Seaman'.[1] It was set up only ten months after the furore prompted by the sudden and unexpected arrival of the *Unicorns* for the roof of the same building. The precise subject of the statue was apparently unknown until the day it was delivered to the city. The newspapers then reported that the sculptor himself had declared that the statue was of John Cabot.[2]

When Charles Wheeler (1892–1974) undertook the commission he was 59, a leading sculptor and a Royal Academician. In 1956 he became the first sculptor to be elected president of the Royal Academy, and he served in that role for ten years.

The statue gives no specific clue to the figure's identity. Wearing the sixteenth-century costume of a wealthy merchant, the bearded figure sways a little sideways, his weight on his left leg. In an attitude of contemplation, his right hand fingering his small beard, he holds a scroll of parchment with a suspended seal, suggesting a royal charter. His deeply pleated knee-length coat has a large collar and it is fur-trimmed, and the sleeves are slashed. From his belt hangs an astrolabe (an instrument for measuring the altitude of the sun and stars and a navigational aid). Turned-down boots and a supporting dolphin reinforce the figure's seafaring role. The city's arms are in low relief on his coat.

The statue was not formally unveiled and the Council House not officially opened until the queen came to Bristol in April 1956. A brochure produced on that occasion said the decision to build had been taken in 1934.[3] 'Mr. E. Vincent Harris RA was appointed architect' in June 1933, but only the shell of his building had been completed when war was declared in 1939.[4]

A week before the statue arrived from the sculptor's South Kensington studio on 28 August 1951, a Bristol newspaper remarked: 'As yet no one, other than the architect and the sculptor, knows its design and shape.' The city architect said he thought the figure will be 'Cabot'.[5]

The day after it was erected, *The Western Daily Press* declared:

> The mystery of the identity of Bristol's 'sailor statue' for the new Council House is ended. Shortly after the statue, wrapped in sackcloth, had been delivered by lorry at College Green, Mr Charles Wheeler, the sculptor, speaking from London, said: 'The statue is of John Cabot.'[6]

Wheeler went to inspect his three-ton statue on 31 August. In interviews he stated that he was 'pleased with Cabot' and with regard to the inscription on the pedestal, he said: 'Mr Harris or the council will decide. Perhaps just one word – "Cabot". But I don't know. Mr Harris sometimes does things which the City Fathers do not know about'.[7] *The Western Daily Press* said Wheeler had been working on the carving for two years. The same report said: 'The official Corporation answer remained, "It's a statue symbolic of the Elizabethan seamen".'

The imbroglio over the statue's title became so ingrained that over a decade later, a Bristol councillor corrected a contributor to an article in *Country Life*. He wrote that the author had made a slight error. 'The statue in the front of

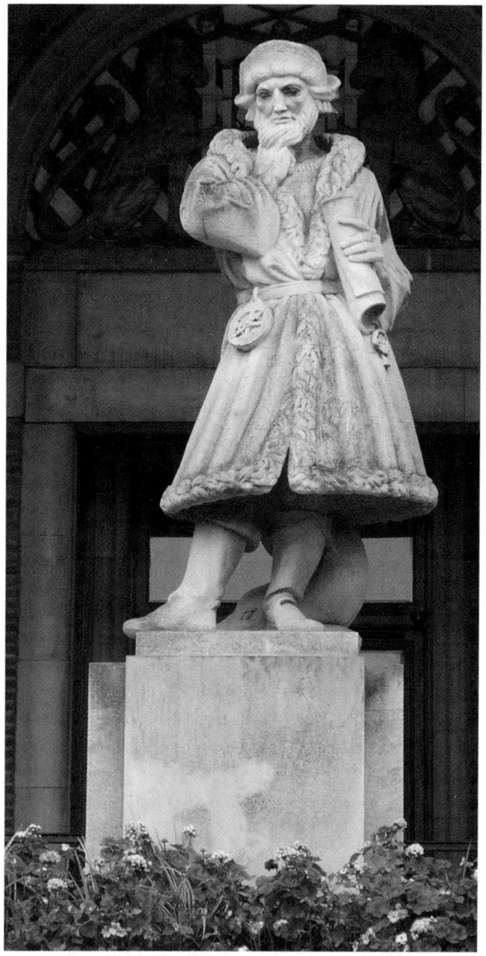

Charles Wheeler, *John Cabot*

the Council House… is not the Cabot Statue, but in fact merely "An Elizabethan Seaman".' He referred to the Cabot Tower as Bristol's only monument to the explorer.[8] The city's archivist determinedly maintained the official line in 1984, describing the figure as 'symbolic of an Elizabethan seaman'.[9]

Most commentators have followed the sculptor. In 1952, Margueritte Fedden reported that the statue cost £2,000 and 'Charles Wheeler of London says he is meant to be Cabot'.[10]

Pevsner agreed,[11] and Mike Jenner, a Bristol architect and architectural historian, also referred to the statue as of John Cabot in 1985, when comparing Joyce's new statue of the explorer outside Arnolfini.[12]

The minutes of the Municipal Buildings Committee suggest some reasons for the muddle. When Vincent Harris proposed this statue he had recently been criticised for commissioning the *Unicorns* for the roof without permission. With this work he was more cautious. He asked for authority 'to provide an 8ft stone figure of Cabot to stand inside the porte-cochère'. It would be, he said, 'a symbolic figure of Cabot, not purporting to represent either John or Sebastian Cabot'.[13] The sculptor was to be 'Mr Wheeler' and 'provision for the cost had been included in his estimate for the completion of the building'. Challenged by a committee member, Alderman Lyne, Vincent Harris said 'he was not proposing to provide any other statues or embellishments to the building'.[14] Permission for the statue was granted.

In 1952, Wheeler exhibited his study for this statue at the Royal Academy as: 'Number 1423. John Cabot – sketch model for the statue on the New Council House, Bristol'.[15]

Immediately after the statue was erected, a Bristol brewery requested permission from the council to use a picture of the statue in advertisements for Cabot Ale, their 'strong beer'. The minute refusing the request contradictorily called it the 'Cabot Statue'.[16] When the statue was daubed with red paint in 1953, another council minute called it the Cabot statue.[17] Dye was also poured over the statue during university rag week in March 1955, and once again the slip occurred.[18]

Wheeler does not mention the Bristol commission in his autobiography.[19] There was no competition, and Wheeler was appointed directly by Vincent Harris. Their relationship is revealed in the autobiography, in which Wheeler names those with whom he frequently lunched and drank at the Chelsea Arts Club: 'It is still a club of character where I have found many friends… within walking distance of my studio'.[20] One of them was 'Vincent Harris, the classical architect, who has built many town halls… [and] helps us to put the modern world into its proper place'.

Notes

[1] G. Reeder, senior building surveyor, Bristol City Council, letter, 19 May 2000. [2] *Bristol Evening Post,* 'Statue is John Cabot', 29 August 1951. [3] BCC, *The Council House Bristol 1956* (Bristol, 1956), p.5. [4] Municipal Buildings Committee, Minute No. 38, 16 November 1950. [5] Ibid. E. Nelson Meredith was the city architect . [6] *The Western Daily Press,* 'Statue is Cabot – sculptor says so', 29 August 1951. [7] *Bristol Evening World,* 'Taxi driver had a shock for the secret statue's sculptor', 31 August 1951; he told Wheeler, 'They ought to have put Queen Victoria there'. [8] J. Lavery Crook, letter to *Country Life,* 25 July 1963. [9] Williams, *Civic Treasures of Bristol,* p.32. [10] M. Fedden, *Bristol Vignettes* (Bristol, 1952), p.15. [11] Pevsner, *North Somerset,* p.413. [12] M. Jenner, 'Works of art the reveal waste', *Evening Post,* 1985; Jenner, compares the Cabot on Narrow Quay with 'the figure of Cabot in the middle of the ramp outside the Council House which is by the late Sir Charles Wheeler, RA, the head of his profession'. [13] Bristol City Council, Minute 38, 16 November 1950. [14] Ibid. Lyne took a leading role in the creation of Bristol's War Memorial. [15] Royal Academy summer exhibition catalogue (1952), p.262. [16] Bristol Municipal Buildings Committee, Minute No. 52, 18 October, 1951; the brewery was Georges and Co. Ltd. [17] Bristol City Council, Minute 101 'Cabot (sic) statue', 15 January 1953. [18] Bristol City Council, Minute 90, 17 March 1955. [19] C. Wheeler, *High Relief: The Autobiography of Sir Charles Wheeler, Sculptor* (Feltham, 1968). [20] Op. cit., p.121.

Set in the paving in front of Bristol Council House moat, College Green

Twinned Cities B54

Modelled by Jim Butler

Date: completed 2006
Material: eight bronze plaques
Dimensions: 60cm deep, 75cm wide
Foundry: cast by Ward and Company (Letters), Barton Hill, Bristol
Inscriptions: centre plaque – Bristol has played an important historical / role in promoting world peace, / reconciliation and development. / Through seven twinning partnerships, / the people of Bristol continue to support / educational, cultural, social and / commercial initiatives around the world. / These plaques commemorate those / international links.
—: from left to right – BEIRA, MOZAMBIQUE. 1990 – TBILISI, GEORGIA. 1988 – BORDEAUX, FRANCE. 1947 / LILIA SOLA REGVNT LVNAM VNDA CASTRA LEONEM – HANNOVER, GERMANY. 1947 – MORAZÁN-TONALA, NICARAGUA. 1989 – ANTIGA, MUI NOBRE, SEMPRE LEALE INVICTA CIDADEDOPORTO / PORTO, PORTUGAL, 1984 [This plaque was designed and cast in Oporto] – GUANGZHOU, CHINA, 2001
Status: not listed

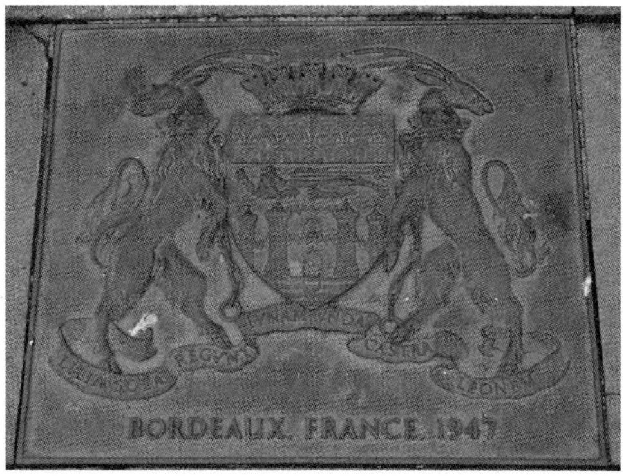

Jim Butler, *Twinned Cities – Bordeaux*

Owned by Bristol City Council
Condition: good

The eight reliefs in front of the Council House commemorate seven international partnerships set up by Bristol City Council and the Bristol International Twinnings Association between 1947 and 2001. BITA is an umbrella group core-funded by Bristol City Council. It also receives support from the University of the West of England. The day-to-day work of 'twinning' covers a broad range of activities: economic activity, education and cultural exchanges.

The Bordeaux and Hanover twinnings were among the first in Britain to be established after the Second World War. The Bristol–Bordeaux Association is considered to be among the most active of all twinning organisations. The friendship between Bristol and Hanover was the earliest to be formalised with a German city. The Bristol–Tbilisi Association, a non-political organisation, was formed before the Berlin Wall came down. In 1985, initiatives were made to encourage local authorities to build relationships between the northern and southern hemispheres. Bristol responded and formed a link with Puerto Morazán, a fishing community of about 2000 people in Nicaragua. The association with Beira – the second largest city in Mozambique – was made by a Declaration of Friendship in 1990. This twinning has raised funds for health and education projects and has financed self-help projects. The seventh and most recent link, with Guangzhou (Canton), was set up to enhance trade, the environment and technology, through a 'sister city' agreement made in 2001.

All the plaques are rectangular and the same size. The Oporto version was designed and cast in Oporto, but the others, based on designs supplied by each city, using their coats of arms and other emblems, were modelled and cast in Bristol. The late Jim Butler was employed by Ward and Company of Bristol.

On the roof of Bristol Council House

Two Unicorns B54

Sculptor: David McFall RA
Architect: E. Vincent Harris

Date: 1950
Material: cast bronze and gold leaf
Foundry: Morris Singer, Lambeth, London[1]
Dimensions: 3.6m high
Status: Grade II*
Owned by Bristol City Council
Condition: possible serious corrosion

These two unicorns are among the most successful and enduring sculptures from the sparse post-war years in Britain. They deserve much wider recognition for their exceptional quality rather than for the oft-repeated story of their unexpected arrival in Bristol in 1950.

The unicorns adorn the ridge of the pavilion roofs at each end of the long curve of the Council House. They are identical. Their pose suggests the heraldic form *passant*. The thin spiral horn is very long, longer than the neck. The mane consists of three groups of flying plumes. The front right leg is raised and the hooves of the left legs are set close together. On the neck is a collar or heraldic belt decorated with two small symbols: alternately a Greek cross and a *fleur de lys*. The long tail rises in three decreasing curves. On the upper part of the unicorn's flanks, the gilding is patterned or mottled, perhaps a stylised interpretation of the markings on fallow deer.

Two unicorns have been an essential part of Bristol's coat-of-arms since the grant of crest and supporters in 1569, when the chamberlain of the city recorded payment for making a new common seal. The attributes of unicorns are many, but the city chose them 'to represent beasts of homage to those who are virtuous', complementing the city's motto, *Virtute et Industria*. Unicorns had come into heraldry through the crusaders, who, when fighting in the Middle East, had seen wild antelopes with

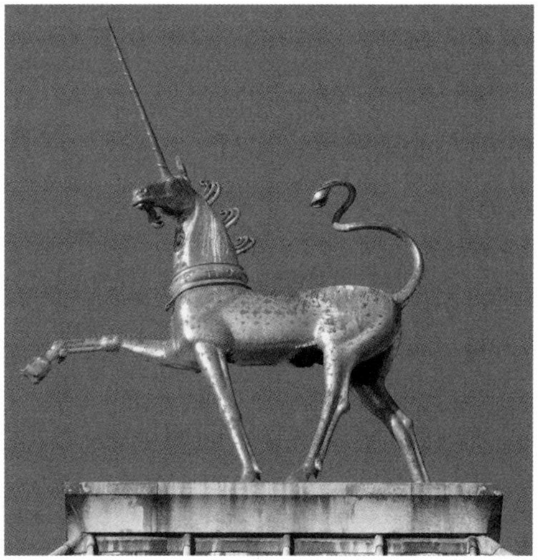

David McFall, *Unicorn* (north)

long, straight horns.[2] Traditionally, unicorns have the head and body of a horse, the tail of a lion, and the legs and hooves of a stag.

Early in October 1950, the two gilded sculptures arrived in Bristol without apparent warning. A storm broke in the press. One national newspaper had the front-page headline: 'Well, who ordered unicorns anyway?' [3] A Bristol paper had no answers: 'No one knows, or at any rate no one will say, who ordered the unicorns and why their erection was stopped'.[4] The city architect, J. Nelson Meredith, told the press: 'the whole thing is a complete mystery to me. Unicorns have never been mentioned for the Council House. I do not know who ordered them'.[5] It was soon acknowledged at a Council Meeting that unicorns *had* been considered in the early planning stages, but the Municipal Buildings Committee then issued a misleading statement saying that another sculptor, Alfred F. Hardiman RA, had been invited to make unicorns for the entrance. This idea had been shelved in 1948 and Hardiman had died in 1949.[6] In fact, it seems that Vincent Harris had first planned for two very substantial statues in the midst of the fountains at either end of the curving stretch of water in front of the Council House. Hardiman was evidently well advanced with preparations for two thirty-foot bronze statues of *Night* and *Day* when *Night* was exhibited in plaster at the Royal Academy in 1945. Subsequently this full frontal nude was 'jilted for her brazen symmetry which might have shocked the piety – or prudery – of the public!' [7]

The situation in October 1950 was inevitably aggravated by the absence of the architect, Vincent Harris, who was on holiday in Italy.[8] He had been working on the project since 1938, and the Second World War and ensuing austerity had delayed progress. Contact with David McFall in his Glebe Place studio in Chelsea 'threw no light' on enquiries by the *Western Daily Press*: 'Nothing further can be done until Mr Vincent Harris… returns'.[9] In due course Vincent Harris, then aged 71, was called before the council. The minutes state:

> Mr V. H. intended the roof should be decorated by 600ft of ornamental lead ridging but he subsequently decided to dispense with this and erect two unicorns modelled in lead. Later he arranged for two unicorns in bronze. The cost of the unicorns, £2,400, would fall within the estimate of the building and he claimed that as the architect he was entitled to alter any detail that did not infringe the terms of the contract.[10]

The council wisely, if reluctantly, accepted Vincent Harris's explanation. On 24 October 1950, in bright sunshine, the 'gleaming, lantern-jawed, wild-eyed, stiff-legged… gilt-painted one-ton unicorns' were hoisted into place. [11] 'Hundreds Cheer as the Unicorns Go Up' was the local headline.[12]

Stiff-legged and stylised these mythical beasts may be, but they are also spirited, proud and independent, worthy supporters of the city they survey. And they bring vital relief to the otherwise monotonous outline of the Council House.

David McFall exhibited his preliminary bronze model of 'The Bristol Unicorn' at the 1951 Royal Academy Summer Exhibition.[13] It is now in the Lord Mayor's Parlour in the Council House. The model lacks the substantial collar of the finished versions. There are other differences of great subtlety that ensured that the monumental statues managed the change of scale and gained a sense of forward movement as well as an even sprightlier step.

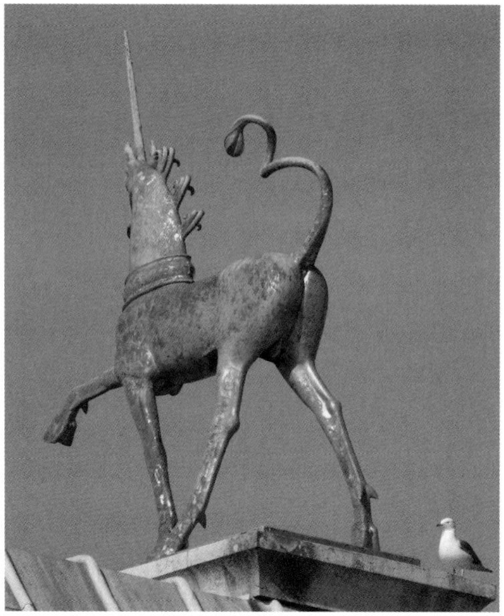

David McFall, *Unicorn* (south)

Notes

[1] Press release, David McFall Sculpture. [2] A.C. Fox-Davies, *A Complete Guide to Heraldry* (London, 1909), p.219. [3] *Daily Express*, 7 October 1950. [4] *Bristol Evening Post*, 7 October 1950. [5] *Western Daily Press*, 7 October 1950. [6] *Bristol Evening World*, 11 October 1950. [7] *Western Daily Press*, 28 August 1951 and other cuttings, Local Sculpture Files, BRL. [8] *Western Daily Press*, 7 October 1950. [9] *Western Daily Press*, 11 October 1950. [10] BCC Minutes, 'Bronze unicorns', 24 October 1950, BRO. [11] *Bristol Evening Post*, 25 October 1950. [12] Ibid. [13] *Royal Academy Exhibitors, 1905–1970: A Dictionary of Artists and their Work in the Summer Exhibitions of the Royal Academy of Arts* (Wakefield, 1973–1982); for an illustration of the bronze model, see Williams, *Civic Treasures of Bristol*, p.37.

On the roof of the two rear extensions of Bristol Council House

Seahorses and Riders B54

Sculptor: David McFall, RA

Architect: E. Vincent Harris, RA

Date: 1953
Material: Portland stone
Dimensions: 244cm high
Status: Grade II*
Owned by Bristol City Council
Condition: good

Two adventurous children ride seahorses on the Council House roofs. The two groups are carved from single blocks of Portland stone. From ground level they appear identical, but a very young boy rides the giant seahorse on the southern finial and to the north the figure is of a young girl. Straight-backed, their arms grasp the manes as they stand on the bulbous curl of the seahorses' tails. The top of each integral pedestal is shaped to suggest the crest of a wave. Notes from the sculptor give the date of the works as 1950–3, and confirm that they were made of Portland stone.

The architect, E. Vincent Harris, had already been working on the building for nearly twenty years when he reported to the Municipal Building Committee in January 1953.[1] He informed the committee that he had commissioned a young sculptor, David McFall, to design and carve seahorse finials for the rear roofs of the Council House. They had been commenced around 1950 and a council meeting minute states:

> By March 1953 the stone finials would be complete and fixed. These would take the form of seahorses, 8ft high, carved in stone and each would cost £600. That expenditure was included in the construction of the roof.[2]

By making this announcement Harris wished to avoid the storm of adverse publicity that had greeted the arrival of the same sculptor's

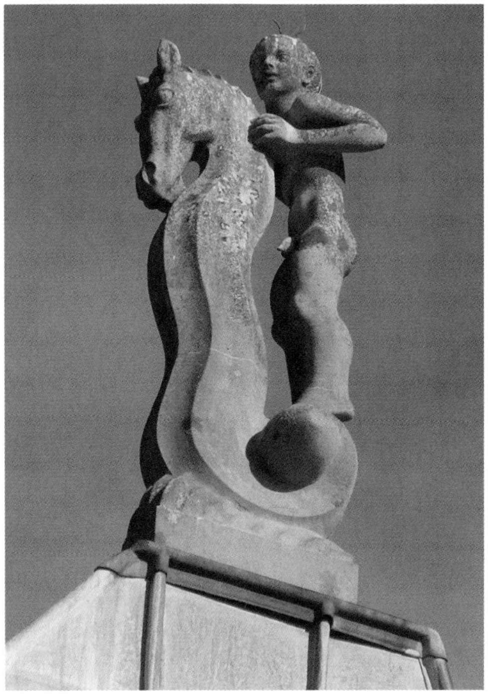

David McFall, *Seahorse and Rider* (south)

unicorns in 1950.

At the formal opening of the Council House by the queen in 1956, a booklet described the finials as 'consisting of a seahorse and figures of a boy and a girl… The representation portrays "the spirit of the Avon as a symbol of belief in the future of Bristol".' [3]

English Heritage's lists mistakenly state that 'the rear elevation has… flanking towers with Epstein sculptures on top'.[4] McFall had worked as an assistant to Epstein when he left the Royal College of Art and, as an accomplished letter cutter, he had carved inscriptions for the more famous sculptor.

Notes

[1] The building itself bears the dates 1935–1955. [2] Municipal Building Committee, Minute no. 75, 17 January 1953. [3] BCC, *Council House Bristol 1956*, p.7. [4] English Heritage, 901-1/15/72, p.425.

In the main foyer of the Council House to the right of the entrance

Raja Rammohun Roy B54
Sculptor: Niranjan Pradhan

Date: 1984–95
Materials: bronze; pedestal, wood, green marble and formica
Dimensions: 84cm high, 65cm wide, 53cm deep
Inscription: on brass plate fixed to front of pedestal – RAJAH RAMMOHUN ROY / 1772–1833 / Scholar, Reformer, Patriot, Pioneer / Visionary of Inter faith Harmony, / Harbinger of the Indian Renaissance / THIS BRONZE BUST GIFTED BY THE / HON'BLE CHIEF MINISTER SHIRI JYOTI BASU / ON BEHALF OF THE / GOVERNMENT OF WEST BENGAL, INDIA / Unveiled by / H. E. DR L. M. SINGHVI / HIGH COMMISSIONER FOR INDIA / In the presence of / THE RT. HON. LORD MAYOR OF BRISTOL, / COUNCILLOR MRS C.M. WARREN / 27 APRIL 1995 / SCULPTED BY SHRI NIRANJAN PRADHAN
—: inscribed in the cast on the rear of the bust – Gov. Calcutta College of Art and Craft/N PRADHAN/1984
Status: Grade II*
Owned by Bristol City Council
Condition: good

Raja Rammohun Roy (1772–1833) was an Indian religious reformer who died on a visit to Bristol. Details of his life, and his connections with the city, are included in the entry relating to his full-length statue near College Green. The fervent inscription on the plinth to this bust, detailed above, demonstrates the respect in which he continues to be held by many, particularly in Bengal, where he was born.

The bust is sited inconspicuously to the right of the main entrance. Its likeness and costume are based on the oil portrait by H. P. Briggs RA, in the Bristol Museum and Art Gallery, painted from life in 1832.

This bronze was presented to Bristol City Council in the course of a fifteen-year campaign to commemorate Rammohun Roy, a campaign that culminated in the statue that was to be erected just outside College Green in 1997.

A committee was first established in Bristol to organise various celebrations for the 150th anniversary of his death in September 1983.[1] The committee included Carla Contractor, a local historian with a special interest in Rammohun Roy, and it was she who first proposed to the Lord Mayor that some permanent memorial should be created.[2] For several years various committees composed of members of the Bristol Hindu Temple (The Deevya Santan Mandal) and a group called Congregations Organised for Greater Bristol arranged celebrations every year on 29 September, the day of Rammohun Roy's death. When in 1993 Carla Contractor learnt of a bust that had recently been erected in Calcutta, she informed the Indian High Commissioner in

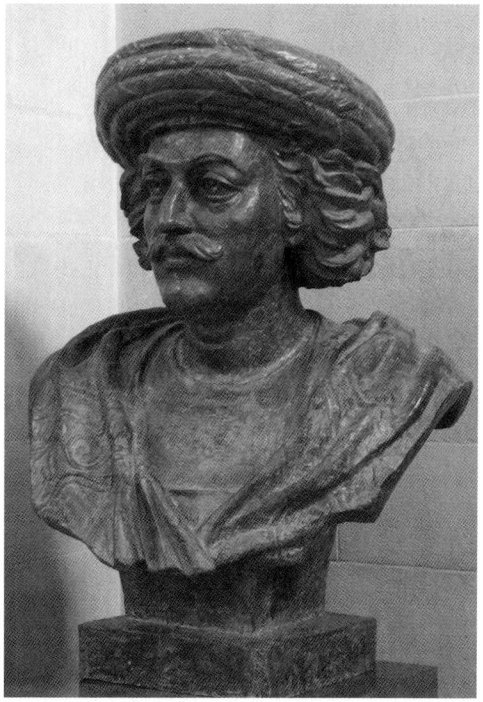

Niranjan Pradhan, *Raja Rammohun Roy*

Britain, Dr L. M. Singhvi. By the following year he had negotiated the delivery of this bust, a gift from Jyoti Basu (the communist Chief Minister of West Bengal) and the peoples of West Bengal state to the city of Bristol. The bronze, which is clearly dated 1984, must be a version or cast of the Calcutta bust. The bronze was unveiled by Dr Singhvi on 27 April 1995.

Notes
[1] Carla Contractor, letter and notes, 5 June 1998, p.2. [2] Ibid.

College Road

Clifton College, within a niche at the end of the main corridor leading to the chapel

Dr John Percival B8

Sculptor: Thomas Woolner RA

Date: 1880
Material: white marble
Dimensions: 75cm high, 30cm wide
Status: Grade II*
Owned by Clifton College Council
Condition: good

When the outstanding Victorian painter, George Frederick Watts, first saw Dr Percival, he asked 'Who is that man? I must paint his portrait.'[1] This suggests something of 'the powerful impact Percival seems to have made on those who encountered him'. In the apt opinion of the poet and old Cliftonian, Sir Henry Newbolt, Percival had 'the grace of a marble statue'.

The bust is in a surprisingly severe classical style, perhaps the sculptor's deliberate response to the manner and character of the sitter. Percival looks directly ahead. He is unclothed and only the shoulder-less upper torso is shown. 'In Woolner's masterly work Percival's face, seen from one side, smiles grimly: yet on the other side the same smile appears entirely benign.'[2] The bust now sits in a shallow niche and has been mistakenly backlit.

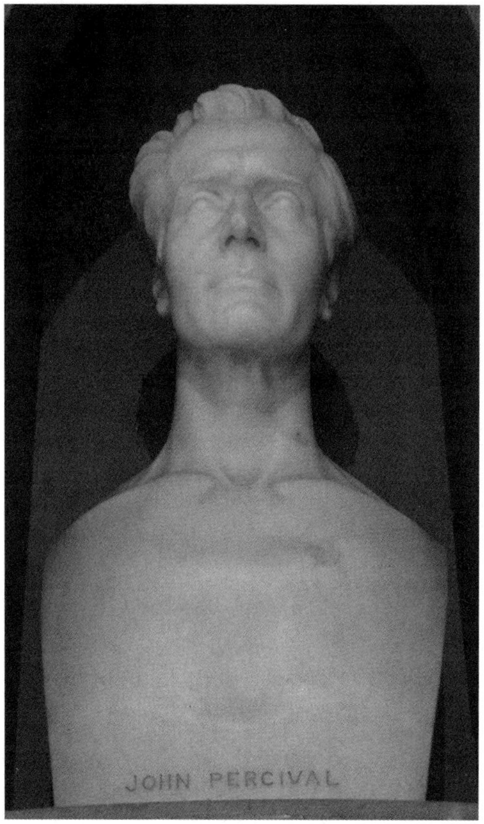

Thomas Woolner, *Dr John Percival*

Dr John Percival (1834–1918) was the founding headmaster of Clifton College, Bristol, headmaster at Rugby, president of Trinity College, Oxford, and finally Bishop of Hereford. His father was a Westmorland farmer of modest means and his mother died when he was only four, leaving him to be fostered by an uncle's family. After village schools he attended Appleby Grammar School, where he gained an excellent grounding in mathematics, Latin and Greek. In 1855, when he was 21, he won an open scholarship to Queen's College, Oxford, where he gained a double first in Classics and Maths that led to his election as a fellow of the college. Overwork left him in ill-health and while on a rest-cure in the south of France he met a young English woman, Louisa Holland, whom he later married. On returning to England he took holy orders, serving at Queen's College for two years before teaching at Rugby. At the age of only 27 he was appointed the first headmaster of Clifton College, taking up the post a few weeks before the new school opened on 30 September 1862. Once again he suffered from overwork, but his success is recognised as having few 'parallels in the history of the public schools'. When he left after sixteen years in 1879, the college had grown from 76 to 680 pupils. Percival is said to have been 'even as a young man… unquestionably formidable' and is described as not 'an entirely loveable figure'. His influence on education in Bristol, however, was immense. Lewis Fry, son of the chocolate magnate, said that the creation of a university in Bristol should be credited to him, and he played a vital role in the establishment of both Clifton High School and Redland High School, as well as a 'ragged school' in the Dings, one of the poorest areas in the city. He was made president of Trinity College, Oxford, before his lasting ambition was fulfilled in 1886 when he accepted the headmastership of Rugby, a post for which he had applied on two earlier occasions. In 1895 through the influence of the Liberal prime minister, Lord Rosebery, he was created Bishop of Hereford. He died in 1918, and at his request he was not buried in Hereford Cathedral, but in a tomb beneath the high altar of Clifton College Chapel.

Notes
[1] Quoted from W. Temple, *Life of Bishop Percival* (London, 1921), p.42 by D. Winterbottom, *John Percival; The Great Educator* (Bristol, 1993), from which both the biographical information and all quotations are taken [2] The bust is illustrated in four photographs from different angles in J. Potter, *Headmaster: The Life of John Percival, Radical Autocrat* (London, 1998).

South side of Clifton College Quadrangle, overlooking the Close, College Road

South African War Memorial B9

Sculptor: Alfred Drury

Architects: W. S. Paul and R. C. James

Date: 1904–5[1]
Materials: statue and four plaques in bronze; pedestal, Portland stone
Foundry: J. W. Singer and Sons, Frome
Dimensions: statue, 245cm high; pedestal, 370cm high
Signed: A. DRURY. A.R.A. Sc
Inscription on front of the pedestal: SOUTH AFRICA / 1899–1902 / CLIFTON / REMEMBER THESE / THY SONS WHO FELL / FIGHTING / FAR OVER THE SEA / FOR THEY / IN A DARK HOUR / REMEMBERED WELL / THEIR WARFARE / LEARNED OF THEE /
Status: Grade II*
Owned by Clifton College Council
Condition: good; deteriorating brown protective paint

The figure of St George commemorates 43 Old Cliftonians of all ranks who died in the South African War (1899–1902). Few statues fit so perfectly into their architectural setting or so movingly express the ethos of their time.

The memorial has been described as a 'exemplifying the patriotic and chivalric spirit of the nineteenth century public school movement'.[2] Mark Girouard has written that it 'epitomises everything that Clifton of those years stood for'.[3]

The sculptor wrote:

> The armour is of the period of the late fourteenth century; the shield is Gothic, with the cross of St George on it; the handle of the sword is surmounted with a figure emblematical of Love; the figure of Christ is surmounted by a symbol of the Holy Ghost, intended to represent the descent of the Spirit of God or the Word of God; the hilt takes the form of an anchor representing the anchor of Hope. In the head of St George I have endeavoured to express his character of Fortitude and Virtue without effeminacy.[4]

The bareheaded standing figure supports a massive sword of almost his own height in his right hand.

The intricate Gothic Revival pedestal – designed by two Old Cliftonian architects, W. S. Paul and R. C. James – was carved by H. H. Martyn and Co. of Cheltenham. Messrs Davey and Bushell carved the balustrade pillars. The steps and balustrade were erected by Edwin Clarke of Fishponds.[5]

Bronze plaques are on each of the four sides of the pedestal. Three contain the names of those who died in the war. The names are not in alphabetical order, but in the chronological order in which the men died. In contrast to the long lists of names on the nearby Memorial Gateway, the rank of each of the fallen is recorded. 347 former pupils of the college served in the war. The fourth plaque has the dedication. This quatrain, quoted above, was composed by Sir Henry Newbolt (1862–1938), Clifton College's famous poet.

Even before the full extent of the losses in the South African War was known, the decision to create a memorial to the dead had been made. A meeting of the Old Cliftonian Society, presided over by the Bishop of Hereford, was held in London in May 1901. It resolved to set up a committee led by the bishop. On it were

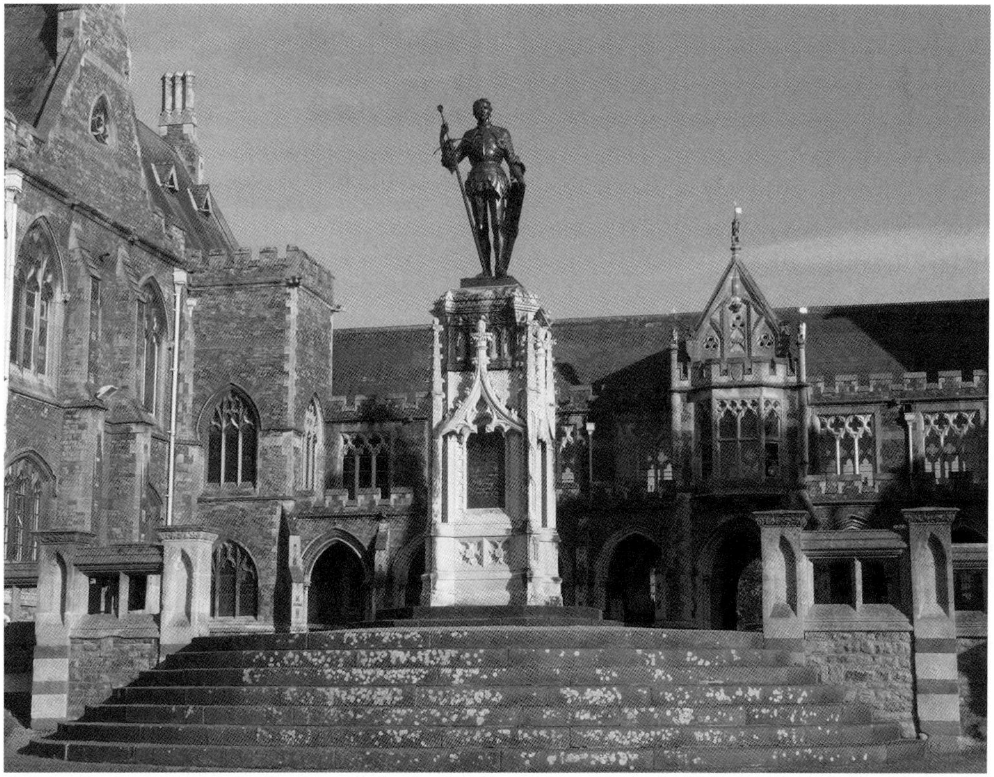

Alfred Drury, *South African War Memorial*

ten Old Cliftonians, including Henry Newbolt, Rowland Whitehead and the philosopher John McTaggart.[6] Later, at a general meeting of the Old Cliftonian Society, the committee's proposal to erect an architectural monument on the terrace overlooking the Close was approved.[7] 'A Gate-house or gateway at the entrance in College Road' and a logia along the west front of the chapel were also considered.[8]

Designs for the setting and for the pedestal were invited from architects, all Old Cliftonians, and these were sent to the Royal Institute of British Architects for adjudication. The institute recommended R. Selden Wornum FRIBA as assessor and adviser.[9] Wornum awarded 'first premium' to two Bristol-based architects, W. S. Paul and R. C. James.[10] A drawing of their design was reproduced in *The Cliftonian*.[11] It shows a balustrade, a pedestal and a knight in medieval armour. At the architects' suggestion, 'the committee then approached the well-known sculptor Mr Alfred Drury, ARA'.[12]

At the committee's request, Drury submitted two sketch models for his design of the statue for their decision, one a modern soldier in khaki and the other St George in armour. The committee continued to be divided on whether the statue should depict a soldier or a saint, and a further meeting of subscribers had to be called before the choice finally fell on St George.[13]

Drury exhibited a bronze version of his study for the head of St George at the Royal Academy in 1905 and showed a full-length plaster study for the bronze the following year.[14] It seems likely that Drury began with a study from the life, very possibly a carefully chosen sitter: an individual, rather than an idealised head. By combining actuality with ethos – the Clifton spirit embodied in the armour of St George – Drury had provided the committee with both a powerful compromise and a moving image that, in view of the willingness with which so many Old Cliftonians were soon to go again to war and to

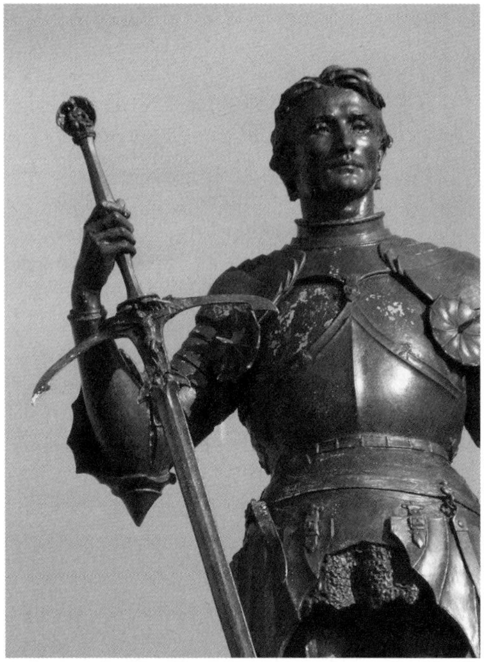

Alfred Drury, *South African War Memorial, St George* (detail)

slaughter, now seems so full of foreboding.

Lord Methuen, an Old Cliftonian, unveiled the statue on 25 June 1905.[15] Four wreaths of bay leaves were laid at the base of the pedestal on behalf of college masters, ladies of the college, Old Cliftonians and the present members of the school. The inscribed tablet was covered by 'a Union Jack attached at half-mast to a flag-pole, at the head of which hung a wreath of laurel leaves, intertwined with South African war ribbons'.[16] The service was conducted by the Bishop of Hereford, Dr John Percival, Clifton College's first headmaster. It was Dr Percival who formally handed over the memorial to the Council of the College, thanking the architects and sculptor 'for enriching the lives of generations to come by the influence which that monument would exercise over… an untold number of boys'.[17]

In his address, General Lord Methuen referred to another Old Cliftonian, Colonel Haig, who had served in the South African campaign and of whom the 'British Army was proud, as a man who had zeal, ability, and a charm of manner'.[18] Methuen made a plea for those privileged to be at the public schools of England to be an example by joining their volunteer corps to do their utmost to be prepared in peace, if they were to be successful in war. Millions of lives, he said, would be thrown away when war broke out, unless they set to work day-by-day to make their system of defence perfect.[19]

The memorial was then unveiled, and buglers played 'The Last Post'. Canon Glazebrook, the headmaster, expressed his gratitude to those who had helped to realise the monument: to Mr. Rowland Whitehead, who had led and inspired the Old Cliftonian Society; to the architects, who had designed the pedestal; and to 'Mr Drury for producing that grand embodiment of patriotism, the figure of St George, which they trusted would be an inspiration for many years to come'. The headmaster 'did not think it was possible to imagine a figure more suitable for the purpose, which was that the school should have before it a continual reminder that chivalry was one of the first duties of life'.[20]

The names of those inscribed on the memorial are given in more detail (rank, regiment, circumstances, place and date of death) in *Clifton College Annals and Register*. An enlarged photograph of the unveiling ceremony, 'taken by Mr Moberly', was later presented to the school.[21] 'The total cost of the memorial was £1,985; the sum raised by subscriptions etc., was £2,103.' The balance was used to set up a school prize.[22]

Notes

[1] D.S. James, *A Century of Statues* (Basingstoke, 1984). [2] English Heritage Bristol, Listed Buildings Database, 901-1/2/831, p.436. [3] M. Girouard, *The Return to Camelot* (New Haven, CT and London, 1981), p.174. [4] *The Cliftonian*, June 1904, p.194. [5] Op. cit., p.192; J. Gildea, *For Remembrance and in*

Honour of those who Lost their Lives in the South African War (London, 1911), p.64. [6] D. Winterbottom, letter, 22 May 2004. [7] F. Borwick (ed.), *Clifton College Annals and Register, 1862–1925* (Bristol, 1925), p.6. [8] As note 4, p.191. [9] As note 1. [10] W.S. Paul had designed the setting for Queen Victoria's Jubilee statue on College Green; a classical design by W.L. Lucas for this memorial is illustrated in *The Clifton Magazine*, 2007 p.25, from *The Builder*, 5 March 1904. [11] *The Cliftonian*, March 1903, opp. p.356. [12] *The Cliftonian*, June 1904, p.191; the Bristol-based Old Cliftonians, Paul and James, may have been aware of Alfred Drury's twelve surviving busts for Henry Martin Gibbs's garden at Barrow Court, near Bristol, c.1898. [13] Ibid. [14] 'Study for St George for statue erected at Clifton College – bust, bronze' (1807) 1906; the full length study is illustrated in A. Koch, *Sculptures from 'Academy Architecture' 1904–1908* (London, 1908), pl. 80. [15] 'The Memorial', photocopied pages from *The Cliftonian*, c.1905. [16] As note 7, p.7. [17] As note 15, p.10. [18] Ibid. [19] Op. cit., p.12. [20] Op. cit., pp.12–13. [21] Moberly was a senior master; information from Derek Winterbottom. The photograph is illustrated in Merritt's *Sculpture in Bristol*, p.32; the sculptor can be seen at the far right of the photograph below the balustrade, next to a policeman. [22] As note 15, p.13.

At the entrance to Clifton College, on College Road

Memorial Gateway B11

Architect: Charles Holden

Lettering: Eric Gill, carved by Laurie Cribb

Date: 1922
Materials: red sandstone and Bath stone ashlar; oak doors
Dimensions: approx. 7m high, 11.6m wide, 5m deep
Inscriptions: the same texts, high on the inner sides of both side walls, in Roman capitals – TO THE MEMORY OF / THE 853 CLIFTONIANS / WHO FELL IN THE WARS / 1914–1919 1939–1946
—: in italic – From the great Marshal to the last recruit / These, Clifton, were thy Self, thy Spirit in Deed, / Thy flower of Chivalry, thy fallen fruit, / And thine immortal Seed.[1]
—: the initials and surnames of the men (without their rank), who died in both wars, are cut in Roman capitals on the inner walls in the order of the year in which they died. The name and rank of one Old Cliftonian, who died in the Korean War, has been added to the outside of the north wall.
Status: Grade II
Owned by Clifton College Council
Condition: good

The gateway discreetly and sensitively echoes the college's own collegiate Gothic style, with pointed arches and a small amount of matching local red sandstone. However, Charles Holden did not compromise his own modernism. Modest in size, the gateway is massive in its form and there is an evident delight in smooth flat surfaces. A recent criticism, 'crushingly mundane after the glory of his Central Library', makes no allowance for the sombre purpose of the memorial, nor that it is so purposefully linked to the college buildings by both design and materials as well as by the long balustrade, the first part of which was to Holden's design.[2]

The gateway was constructed of red sandstone, excavated from two quarries in the bank bounding the Close, and Bath stone.[3] The large central gothic archway has a quadripartite vault, and there are smaller pedestrian archways on either side. Above the smaller archways are two-light, stained-glass windows which illuminate the names higher up on the side walls. The centre of each parapet has a relief of the college crest on both façades. These are

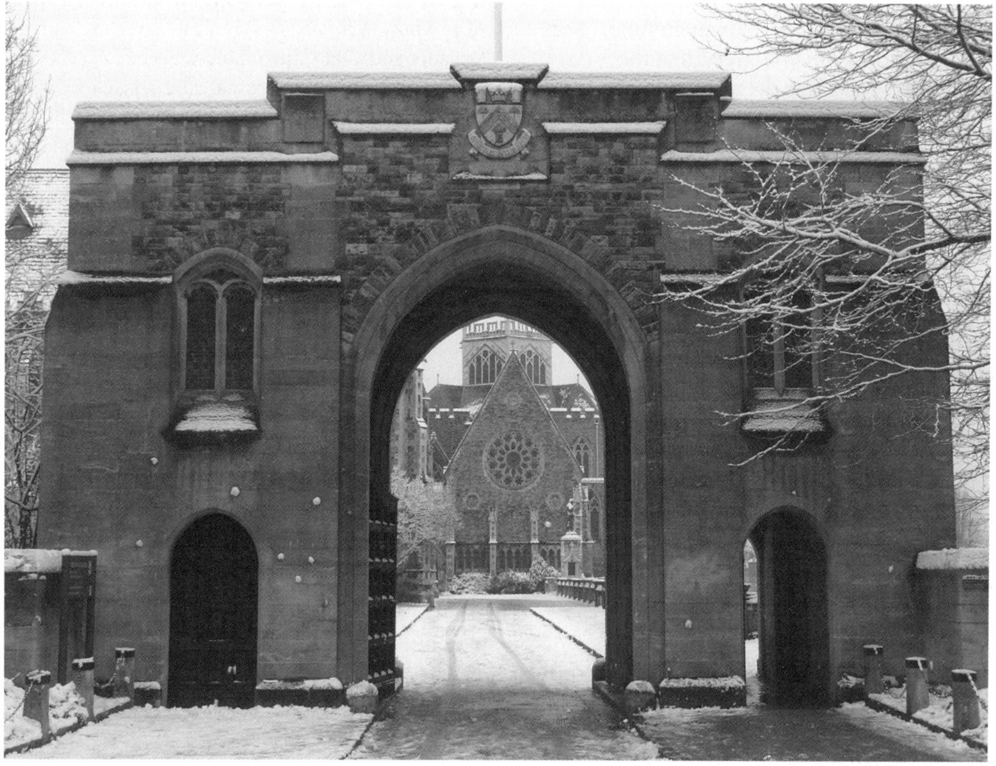

Charles Holden (and Eric Gill), *Clifton College Memorial Gateway*

coloured and gilded and they display the motto 'Spiritus intus alit' ('the spirit moves within').[4]

The names of the 578 Cliftonians who died in the First World War are carved on the two inner side walls, and those of the 275 Cliftonians who fell in the Second World War are carved on the inner walls above the side entrances and below the windows. High on one side wall is a coloured stone relief of the college's coat of arms and Sir Henry Newbolt's dedication to Clifton's 'fallen fruit'.

On 22 November 1917, a year before the Armistice brought the war to an end, the Old Cliftonians' Society held a meeting in London. They resolved that a total of £5,000 should be spent both on a permanent memorial and on a scholarship fund for the sons of Old Cliftonians who had been killed or incapacitated. Any balance from the funds raised would go to an endowment fund.[5] The Old Cliftonians finally agreed that the memorial would take the form of a gateway, and designs were submitted by Major Holden, architect to the Imperial War Graves Commission, and by two Old Cliftonian architects whose identity is uncertain.[6] Holden had by then designed the Bristol Central Library (1902–6) and the Bristol Royal Infirmary (1911–2).

The president of the Royal Academy, the architect Sir Aston Webb, adjudicated the competition and selected Charles Holden's design. In spite of the early decision to create the memorial, work did not start until August 1921.[7] At the time of the planning application the building company, Henry Willcocks, estimated costs at £7,000 to £8,000.[8] 'The Memorial Gateway and balustrade [built at the same time] cost £10,056' and more than £50,000 was collected.[9]

Holden, who was later to employ Eric Gill as a sculptor on several of his buildings, asked Gill to undertake the carving of the names. Gill travelled to Clifton College in May 1921 to discuss the commission.[10] The work was carried out from April to June, a year later, by Gill's assistants. His accounts show that Laurie Cribb, his 'virtuoso letter cutter, more skilful than Gill and even better than his brother', worked for nine weeks[11]. Then in mid-April 1922, as time was running out, two other assistants, Joseph Cribb and Albert Leany, were sent to Bristol to help.[12] The inscriptions were completed only days before the unveiling. Gill's total charge for cutting and colouring the lettering and carving the crest, including lodging, was £257.5.0.

The unveiling ceremony was held on 30 June 1922 and nearly 600 Old Cliftonians were present, approximately the number of dead they were commemorating.[13] The College Council gave a luncheon at which Earl Haig presided, and the lord mayor and the sheriff of Bristol were present.[14] The Officer Training Corps was drawn up in the Close facing the South African War Memorial. Visitors, relatives of the dead, masters and Old Cliftonians who had served in the war were on the terrace. The service was conducted by the dean of Gloucester, and Sir Francis Younghusband presented a golden key to Earl Haig. The procession then moved to the Memorial Gateway, where the Earl unlocked the gate and unveiled the names. The flag was lowered to half-mast, the OTC presented arms, and 'The Last Post' was sounded and later 'Reveille' from the roof. In his address, delivered in front of the South African War Memorial, Haig said:

> Courage, manliness and truth, clean living and honest dealing are the qualities that have made our nation great, and must be preserved if that greatness is to last. Nothing can take their place. Cleverness and skill in arts and sciences are much, but they are not enough, if the other qualities are absent.[15]

A statue of Haig, standing approximately 25m east of this gateway, was unveiled in 1931.

Notes

[1] Sir Henry Newbolt (1862–1938). An Old Cliftonian, he wrote a similar poetic dedication for the college's South African War Memorial in 1904. [2] Foyle and Cherry, *Bristol*, p.236. [3] Borwick, *Clifton College Annals*, Chapter XVIII, p.cxxiv. [4] 'Spiritus intus alit, totamque infusa per artus Mens agitat molem, et mango se corpore miscet.' Virgil, *Aeneid*, Book 6, line 726. 'The spirit within nourishes, and mind instilled throughout the living parts activates the whole mass and mingles with the vast frame.' [5] O.F. Christie, *A History of Clifton College, 1860–1934* (Bristol, 1935), p.193. [6] It is likely they were the brothers W.S. and A.J. Paul, who were in partnership in Bristol. They designed the South African Memorial at Clifton College and the pedestal for Bristol's statue of Queen Victoria on College Green. [7] Op. cit., p.194; Holden was in the London practice of Adams, Holden and Pearson. [8] BRO, planning application. [9] *The Cliftonian*, June 1922, p.1. [10] Gill's diary, 8 May 1921, William Andrews Clark Memorial, UCLA. [11] MacCarthy, *Eric Gill*, p.199. [12] As note 10. 'Chas. Holden p.805, Clifton Coll. Inscripts', Gill's account sheet. [13] As note 5, p.194. [14] Ibid. [15] Ibid.

Outside School House, Clifton College, overlooking the Close, College Road

Earl Haig B10

Sculptor: William McMillan

Date: 1931
Materials: statue, bronze; pedestal, limestone
Foundry: A. B. Burton of Thames Ditton, Surrey
Dimensions: statue, 245cm high, 75cm wide at the base; pedestal, 100cm high, 95cm wide
Inscription: on the front of the pedestal – HAIG —: signed on right-hand side of bronze base – W. MCMILLAN. 1931
Status: Grade II*
Owned by Clifton College Council
Condition: good

The statue of Field Marshal Earl Haig (1861–1928) overlooks the college playing fields and stands outside School House, in which he resided when a pupil at the college. It is just a few metres from the Memorial Gateway on which the names of so many of his fellow pupils, who lost their lives in the First World War, are inscribed. Haig had, himself, ceremonially 'unlocked' the gateway on 30 June 1922.

The field marshal is shown wearing a regulation army greatcoat, not the full dress uniform of his rank. The unbuttoned coat has deep cuffs and is belted at the rear. His cavalry boots are spurred. He holds a partially opened map, which he has evidently been studying and looks thoughtfully into the distance, as if across his own lines to enemy positions and beyond. At the unveiling ceremony, the bishop of Coventry was to say that Haig had carried the burden of the First World War more than any other single person.[1] That dreadful responsibility is expressed in the statue with impressive candour and sympathy. McMillan himself had seen active service in France as a young officer with the 5th Oxfordshire and Buckinghamshire light infantry.[2]

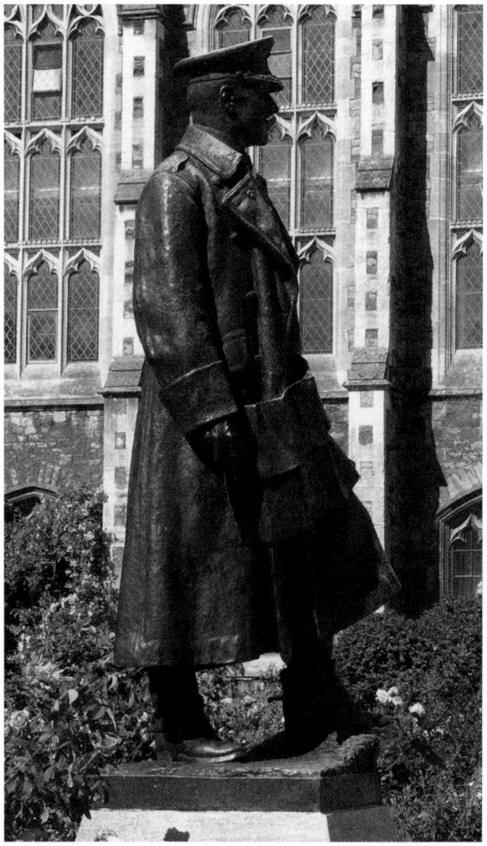

William McMillan, *Field Marshall Earl Haig*

Throughout most of the First World War, Haig was the commander-in-chief of the British forces in France and in Belgium. Late in 1917 he was promoted to field marshal. In 1919 he was created Earl Haig, Viscount Dawick and Baron Haig of Bemersyde.

Assessments of his leadership still arouse controversy. As recently as 1998, one national newspaper campaigned for the removal of his bronze equestrian statue in Whitehall.[3] More recently, a military historian has written: 'It is difficult to remain objective about the Battle of the Somme… its immediate aim of breaking through the German lines failed, but without it the Allies would have undoubtedly failed to win the war in November 1918.' The offensive was based on attrition, and:

> attrition won the First World War, not the taking of ground… however, the uninitiated look at the limited ground taken and the massive casualties incurred and come to the conclusion that the battle was a failure – it was not… the Somme was Haig's grand plan to win the war.[4]

A college history records that the decision to commission a statue, as a gift from the Old Cliftonian Society, was made in 1930.

> There had been some debate… as to what should be the proper memorial of Earl Haig, but in the end it was decided to erect his statue in the School House garden, standing and looking over the Close; Mr W. McMillan, CVO, ARA, was chosen as the sculptor.[5]

McMillan exhibited his model at the Royal Academy in 1932.[6]

Countess Haig was prevented by illness from unveiling the statue on the morning of 25 June 1932, Clifton College's Commemoration Day. Her daughter, Lady Alexandra, 'took her place and made her first public speech' and said the statue 'is not only a memorial to one man, but is a symbol of the part played by Clifton and all our public schools in the Great War'.[7] The figure was revealed from beneath a Union Jack, and the headmaster thanked the Old Cliftonian Society. Wreaths of poppies from the Haig family, the Old Cliftonians and the school were laid, and the pupils then filed past.

Bristol's belated cenotaph (Colston Avenue) in the centre of the city was unveiled the same morning. The *Western Daily Press* reported both events under a single headline: 'We will remember them', and noted that simply 'Haig' was inscribed on the Clifton College pedestal.[8] Field-Marshal Sir William Birdwood unveiled the cenotaph and, as president of the Old Cliftonians' Society, he was also present at the College unveiling. *The Times* carried a long report on the Clifton unveiling with similar information.[9]

Notes

[1] *The Cliftonian*, July 1932, p.307. [2] *ODNB*. [3] 'Why do we let this man cast a shadow over our war dead?', *The Express*, 6 November 1998. [4] Lloyd Clark, Department of War Studies, the Royal Military Academy, Sandhurst. [5] Borwick, *Clifton College Annals*. [6] *Royal Academy Exhibitors*, p.95. 'William McMillan, CVO, RA, Sculptor and Painter, 6, Alexandra Mansions, Chelsea, SW3. 1932, No.1525, F-M, the late Earl Haig, KT, GCB, OM. Model of statue to be erected at Clifton College, Bristol.' [7] *The Cliftonian*, July 1932, p.310. [8] *Western Daily Press Bristol and Bristol Mirror*, 27 June 1932. [9] 'Haig Memorial at Clifton', *The Times*, 27 June 1932.

Colston Street, Foster's Almshouse (now The Kings' Court) and the Chapel of the Three Kings of Cologne

The original Almshouse and Chapel were founded by John Foster (d.1492), a Bristol merchant, between 1481 and 1484. Foster was a shipbuilder and a salt merchant.[1] He traded in Icelandic waters until he and other Bristol merchants were 'eased out by the German Hanseatic League in the 1480s'. However, when

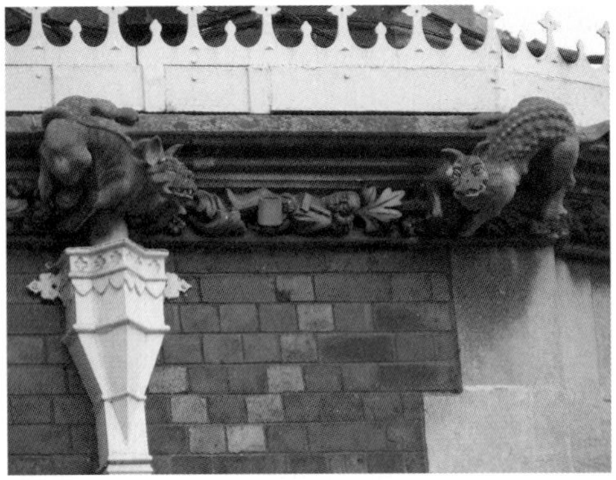

John Foster, architect, *Foster's Almshouse, drunken mason* (decorative details)

he died there were 200 tons of salt in his cellars.[2] He lived with his wife, Elizabeth, a son and daughter in Small Street, now occupied by Foster's Chambers and Foster's Rooms, perhaps the oldest non-ecclesiastical buildings in Bristol.[3]

The Chapel was built 'in honour of God and the three Kings of Cologne', and an indenture of 12 April 1484 reveals that Foster held the land on a 99-year lease from the abbot of Tewkesbury. The dedication is believed to be unique in the British Isles.[4] Foster's trade with the Rhineland may have led him to visit Cologne, where the supposed relics of the three kings had been brought from Milan by Archbishop Reinald von Dassel in 1164. Cologne's massive cathedral was commenced in 1248 to house the shrine.

In 1708, Foster's Almshouse was rebuilt and it was again rebuilt in three phases between 1861 and 1883.[5] A drawing of the elevation of the east wing of the Almshouse dated 1872, by Foster and Wood, is in Bristol Record Office.[6] The completion date of 1883 is recorded above the ornate oriel window, where the date of Ralph Edwards' diligent restoration of 1965 has been discreetly added. Foster's Almhouse was sold by Bristol Charities, formerly Bristol Municipal Charities, in 2006 and it has recently been converted to small apartments.

The decorative work in stone, lead and wood throughout the exterior of the building is exceptionally extensive and of very fine quality. Although evidently inspired by Burgundian Gothic architecture and particularly the Hotel de Dieu in Beaune – perhaps the most famous of all hospices or almshouses – there is no question of imitation. This is original High Victorian architecture, designed with both wit and imagination.

Under a Gothic canopy on the wall of Foster's Almshouse, Colston Street

John Foster C13

Sculptor unknown

Date: c.1872
Material: Bath stone
Dimensions: approx. 115cm high, 50cm wide
Status: Grade II*
Owned by Queenwood Group
Condition: fair, with signs of conservation, possibly carried out at the time of the 1962 work.

This delicately carved figure was certainly an

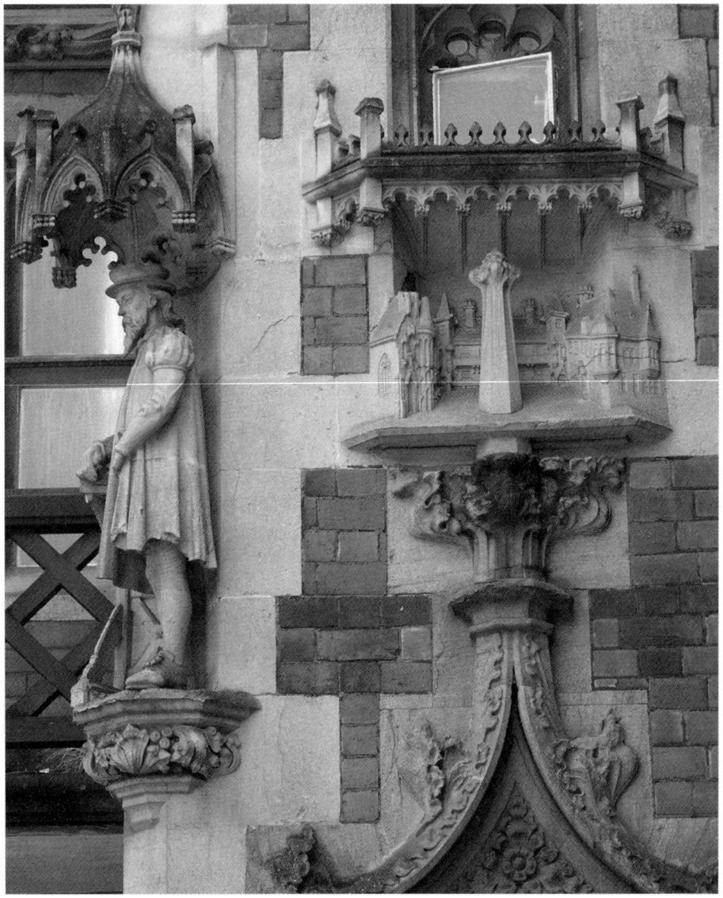

John Foster, architect, *John Foster and the model of Foster's Almshouse*

integral part of the rebuilding of the Almshouse to the designs of Foster and Wood between 1862 and 1883. The surviving architect's drawing of the east wing dated 1872 has prompted the approximate date given above.

Set at first floor level in the south-eastern corner of the forecourt, the bearded figure rests his right forearm on a lectern and holds a paper scroll. He wears a soft circular hat, an outer coat with puffed sleeves, a short tunic of the same length, breeches and hose. On his shoes are large rosettes.

An identical niche at the north-east corner of the forecourt is empty. A Bristol newspaper of 1964 referred to the missing figure and suggested that it may have held a statue of John Foster's wife, Elizabeth. However, there is as yet no evidence, beyond the depiction of a figure in the model discussed below, that the niche was ever filled.[7]

On the wall of Foster's Almshouse, Colston Street, to the right of the statue of John Foster

Relief Model of Foster's Almshouse C13

Sculptor unknown

Date: c.1872
Material: Bath stone
Dimensions: 50cm high, 80cm wide
Status: Grade II*
Owned by Queenwood Group
Condition: good

This most imaginative relief depicts the whole of the almshouse building in perspective, viewed from Colston Street. The deeply cut relief reproduces Foster and Wood's Victorian design in great detail: the façade of the chapel, the spiral staircase tower, the many roof turrets, the statue of John Foster, a tiny reproduction of the statue of a woman (now sadly missing or maybe never carried out), and even an indication of this 'model view' itself. A decorated finial, from elaborate tracery on the wall below, protrudes in an eccentric manner in the centre of the forecourt, to form something like a decorated obelisk.

There is a deep horizontal crack in the centre of the relief. It is in a protected position and was probably cleaned and restored at the time of the 1962 conservation work.

On the courtyard façade of the Chapel of the Three Kings of Cologne, Foster's Almshouse, Colston Street

Three Kings of Cologne C13

Sculptor: Ernest Pascoe assisted by John Huggins

Architects: John Foster and Joseph Wood, 1872–83
Architect of 1962 restoration: Ralph Edwards
Date: 1962
Material: Clipsham stone[8]
Dimensions: approx. 135cm high, 35cm wide
Status: Grade II*
Owned by Queenwood Group
Condition: good

There were no statues of the three kings on the Chapel until these were made in the early 1960s. Three empty niches appear on the architects' elevation in their design of 1872.[9] When changes were made in 1883, a Bristol newspaper account said that a large tracery window was removed from the front of the Chapel in order to insert three niches that were 'probably destined for

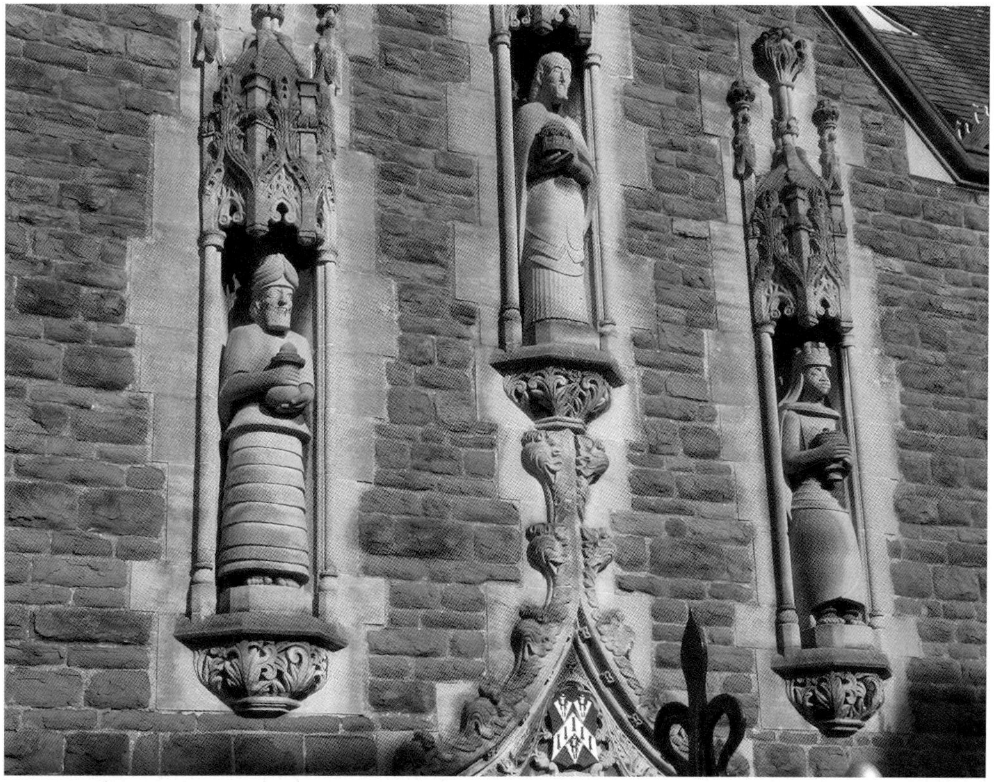

Ernest Pascoe, *Three Kings of Cologne, Foster's Almshouse*

the reception of three figures representing the Kings of Cologne'.[10] In 1907 the *Transactions of the Bristol and Gloucestershire Archaeological Society* reported:

> Its front is beautified by three important canopied niches… no doubt intended to receive the figures of three kings, though how much of this is original or how much is the creation of the restoring architect it is difficult to say.[11]

A photograph of the Chapel published in 1957 shows that the niches were still empty.[12]

The three kings were commissioned when the buildings were restored by the architect Ralph Edwards from 1962 to 1967 for the Trustees of Bristol Municipal Charities. Ernest Pascoe, the versatile Bristol sculptor and teacher, designed and carved the statues.[13] He was assisted by the sculptor, John Huggins, newly appointed lecturer at what was then the Royal West of England College of Art, where the figures were carved during the summer vacation.[14]

Pascoe's stylised figures have the appearance of rigid chessmen and fit tightly into the three narrow niches. Each holds an attribute suggesting the traditional nativity gifts. The head of the left-hand figure has Assyrian characteristics, the central figure may be based on a French medieval saint and the third has the features, somewhat exaggerated, of a Benin bronze head. John Huggins remembers the figures as representations of Asia, Europe and Africa.[15] At the top of the tracery above the central figure is a single star.

In the New Testament, St Matthew's gospel refers to a number of 'wise men', and specifies the three gifts that were offered: gold, frankincense and myrrh.[16] The names of the Magi – Caspar, Balthazar (generally shown as an African or Moor) and Melchior (often light-skinned and dressed as a king) – are apocryphal.

Notes

[1] D. Jones, *John Foster's Almshouse and the Chapel of the Three Kings of Cologne* (Bristol, n.d.), p.2; this booklet refers to Bristol Customs Records that show John Foster received salt cod from Iceland in September 1471. [2] Op. cit., p.3. [3] As note 1, p.3. [4] Op. cit., p.4. [5] Op. cit., p.5. [6] Crick, *Victorian Buildings*, illus. p.28. [7] *Evening Post*, 'A face-lift for the Almshouses', 4 February 1964. [8] Letter from John Huggins to FWG, 3 July 2008. [9] BRO, John Foster and John Wood, 'Elevation for Foster's Almshouse, Colston Street'. [10] As note 1. [11] C.E. Boucher, *Transactions of the Bristol and Gloucestershire Archaeological Society* (Bristol, 1907), p.201. [12] *The Rumsey Record*, 'Brights of Bristol' advertisement, September 1957. [13] As note 1, p.7. [14] Letter from John Huggins to FWG, 3 July 2008. [15] Ibid. [16] St Matthew II, verses 1–12.

Colston Street, Colston Hall

Since it was first opened in 1867, Colston Hall, has, in effect, been rebuilt four times. Planning for a fifth Colston Hall, which began in 2004, is presently in abeyance.[1]

By the mid-nineteenth century, 'the want of a commodious hall for public meetings, entertainments, etc., had long been painfully felt'.[2] This 'want' was heightened after St George's Hall, Liverpool, was completed in 1854. Finally, in 1861 the opportunity was seized when the boys' school, Colston's Hospital, which had stood in Colston Street for 160 years, moved out to Stapleton. A large central space was now available. The Colston Hall Company was founded and a 'few public-spirited gentlemen' purchased the land for £3000. The architects were the Bristol partnership of John Foster and Joseph Wood.[3] Building started in May 1863 for a 2500-seater hall at an estimated cost of £17,000. However, only the main hall was opened on 20 September 1867, and at a cost of £45,000. The first Colston Hall 'had a classical interior, after St George's Liverpool with aisles, columns to an entablature, and a coffered barrel-vaulted ceiling'.[4] In 1869 a further £15,000 was raised 'through the zeal and liberality of some ten or twelve of the original promoters'.[5] That allowed a second and much smaller hall, a grand staircase, an entrance hall and today's surviving

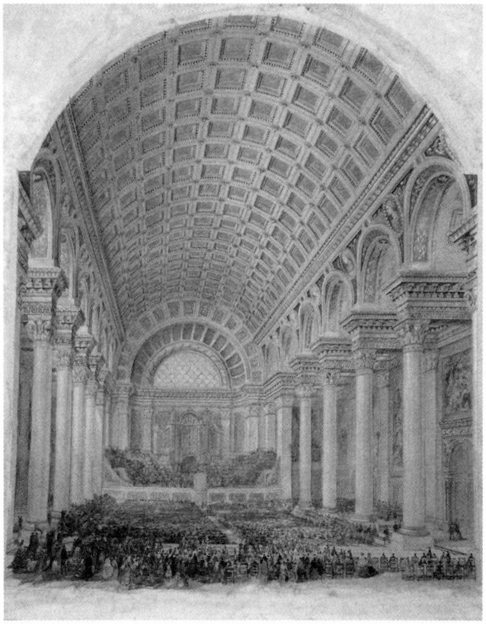

Colston Hall interior, watercolour of the 1863 design by John Foster (Bristol Museum and Art Gallery)

entrance façade to be completed by 1873 at a cost of £40,000.

After a fire in 1898, the Colston Hall Company had largely rebuilt the hall by 1900.[6] Bristol Corporation did not contribute, but in 1919 the City Council purchased the hall from the company. The interior was subsequently modernised and largely rebuilt, re-opening on 11 December 1936. After surviving the Blitz, the interior was destroyed by a second fire in 1945. The city architect, J. Nelson Meredith, redesigned the hall to seat 2,180, and a tablet in the upper foyer records that the Duke of Gloucester opened this fourth hall in 1951, the year of the Festival of Britain.[7]

When St George's Hall had opened in 1854, the *Illustrated London News* could trumpet that Liverpool was now surpassed only by London, but that 'in the quick yet solid growth of its commercial greatness [Liverpool] surpasses even the metropolis itself'.[8] By this date the speed of Bristol's commercial growth was far, far behind that of its old rival, Liverpool. And yet a small number of private citizens were ready to be inspired by Liverpool's daunting example. Today's Colston Hall, which enjoys a continuity of purpose and function that Liverpool must now envy, remains as a legacy of the pride and public-spirited zeal of these impressive Bristol benefactors.

Most of the sculpture associated with Colston Hall commemorates those benefactors. The list is modest; indeed, it pales into insignificance beside St George's Hall. A report, probably written in 1900 when the second hall opened, mentions the seven relief portraits that have survived on the once-grand staircase and upper vestibule.

> The architectural effect of the vestibule has been much admired. In bas-relief are portraits of Mr Herbert Thomas (for 34 years Chairman of the Company), Mr Joseph Storrs Fry, Mr Christopher J. Thomas, the Rt. Hon. Lewis Fry, and Mr Alfred Price, the Originator and first Secretary of the Company; whilst two sculptures by Mr Hope Pinker arrest the attention, a striking likeness of Mr Elisha S. Robinson, and an equally life-like presentment of Sir William Henry Wills, Bart., to whose generosity the Company is indebted not only for the gift of the Grand Organ, but also for his munificent subscription for debenture stock.[9]

Two further reliefs of William Butcher and Henry Riseley, mentioned in the report, are missing.

Around 1960, when there were changes to the entrance areas, the first floor's deeply-recessed arched windows of the 1873 façade were filled in and the three external reliefs were installed.[10] However, these modern works failed to disguise or excuse the loss of Foster and Wood's dramatic arcade of windows.

On the first landing of the main staircase in Colston Hall

Sir William Henry Wills C47

Sculptor: Henry Richard Hope-Pinker

Date: 1901
Material: white marble relief with grey-green marble frame
Dimensions: 85cm high, 60cm wide
Signed: H. R. Hope Pinker Sc 1901
Inscription: SIR WILLIAM HENRY WILLS BAR^{T} / DIRECTOR 1865 –
Status: Grade II
Owned by Bristol City Council
Condition: good

William Henry Wills (1830–1911), created Baron Winterstoke in 1906, was the most eminent member of the Wills family.[11] He was Chairman of W. D. & H. O. Wills and, among many other directorships, on the boards of GWR and Phoenix Assurance.[12] As well as being an early director of the Colston Hall Company, he presented the grand organ and a 'munificent subscription for debenture stock'.[13] His philanthropic and cultural gifts to Bristol included the Bristol Museum and Art Gallery; donations to the Royal West of England Academy, where he served as president; and towards the foundation of Bristol University. The Wills Memorial Tower was built as a tribute to him by his sons. He paid for the statue of Edmund Burke designed by his 'favourite' sculptor, James Havard Thomas. At his death he left £2.5 million.

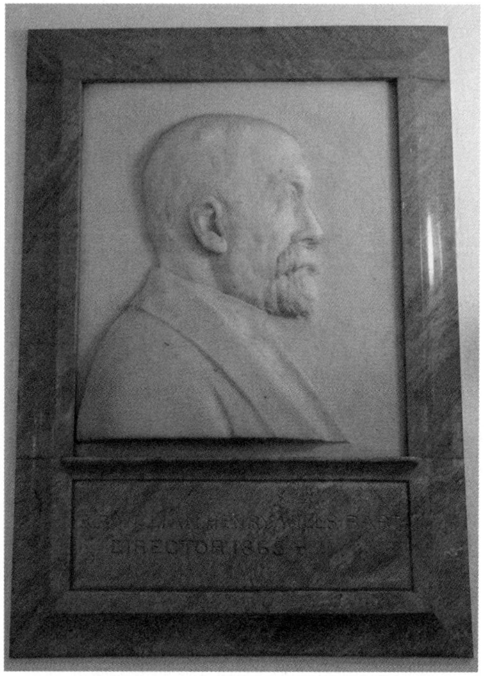

Henry Richard Hope-Pinker, *Sir William Henry Wills*

The relief is set side-by-side with that of Elisha Smith Robinson. An art critic wrote of Hope-Pinker in 1901:

> It is a feature of Mr Pinker's work that it has life, and that it is distinguished besides by a quality which, for want of a better word, I may term 'roughness', whereby the artist avoids that close resemblance to actual clothing which, whether in marble or bronze, is so distressing a quality in many statues.[14]

The breadth of the surface treatment of the hair and the clothes in these two reliefs confirm this observation.

On the first landing of the main staircase in Colston Hall

Elisha Smith Robinson C47

Sculptor: Henry Richard Hope-Pinker

Date: c.1901
Materials: white marble relief with grey-green marble frame
Dimensions: 85cm high, 60cm wide
Inscription: ELISHA SMITH ROBINSON. / ONE OF

THE FOUNDERS OF / THIS HALL. / BORN MARCH 12TH. 1817 / DIED AUGUST 29TH 1885. / HRHP SCULPT
Status: Grade II
Owned by Bristol City Council
Condition: good

Elisha Smith Robinson (1817–85) was a founder and director of the Colston Hall Company and, no doubt, a considerable benefactor. In 1844 he had arrived in Bristol with '£90 of his own and £100 borrowed from a friend'. He was the son of a paper-maker from Overbury in Worcestershire and had served an apprenticeship with an uncle who kept a grocer's shop at Blockley, near Chipping Campden. Elisha's knowledge of grocery and the paper trade were the foundation of his success. He first set up in Baldwin Street as a supplier of wrapping paper and paper bags, mainly to grocers and drapers. By 1846 the company had moved to 2 Redcliffe Street. Joined by his younger brother, Alfred, in 1848, letterpress printing was installed, followed by lithography.[15] Robinson built up one of the largest printing companies of the Victorian era, and his company, E. S. & A. Robinson, made Bristol the centre of the packaging industry. By 1900 there was a work force of 1,450. As a result of a merger of Robinsons and John Dickinson and Company in 1966, the Dickinson Robinson Group was formed, manufacturing paper, board, envelopes and stationery.

E. S. Robinson had died in 1885 and this relief, the finest of these portraits, would have been based upon photographs.

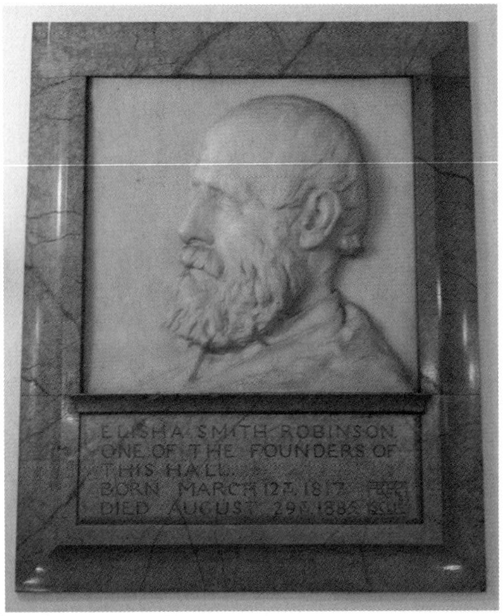

Henry Richard Hope-Pinker, *Elisha Smith Robinson*

On the wall of the first floor lobby of Colston Hall

Alfred Newell Price C47

Sculptor: unknown

Date: probably installed before 1900
Materials: painted plaster
Dimensions: 75cm high, 65cm wide
Inscription: ALFRED N. PRICE. J.P.
Status: Grade II
Owned by Bristol City Council
Condition: fair

Alfred Newell Price (1834–1928) was the 'originator and first secretary' of the Colston Hall Company.[16] He was a partner in the family business making stoneware pottery that had begun in Bristol in 1796 and continued until 1961.

> From the age of 15 he entered the family business, and in the later part of the nineteenth century he was mainly responsible for its expansion. He represented the Bristol Stoneware Potters at meetings of the London Potters' Association. He was a Trustee of Bristol Municipal Charities and for many years a magistrate. In 1875 he became a Governor and Trustee of his old school, Bristol Grammar School.[17]

Joseph Storrs Fry C47

Sculptor: unknown

Date: probably installed before 1900
Materials: painted plaster
Dimensions: 75cm high, 65cm wide
Inscription: JOSEPH STORRS FRY.
Status: Grade II
Owned by Bristol City Council
Condition: fair

Joseph Storrs Fry (1826–1913) was a great-grandson of the great Joseph Fry (1728–87), whom biographers praise for his enterprise, business acumen and scientific abilities.[18] Joseph Fry built a worldwide chocolate manufacturing company whose name has continued into the present century. The verdicts on his great-grandson's business skills are not so flattering and he is said to have lacked vigorous leadership.[19] Other companies outstripped J. S. Fry & Sons, and only six years after his death the company was merged with Cadburys. His brothers, Sir Edward and Lewis Fry (the subject of a similar relief in Colston Hall), took little interest in the manufacture of chocolate.

Joseph Storrs Fry served the city generously in many ways, through charities, through his devout membership of the Society of Friends, by his work at Colston Hall and in his support for temperance societies and Sunday schools. He was a governor of the Queen Victoria Jubilee Convalescent Home, Redland, and chairman of Bristol General Hospital, where he visited every patient on Christmas Eve.

Christopher James Thomas C47

Sculptor: after Timothy Butler

Date: probably installed before 1900
Materials: painted plaster
Dimensions: 75cm high, 65cm wide
Inscription: CHRISTOPHER J. THOMAS.
Status: Grade II
Owned by Bristol City Council

Condition: fair

Christopher James Thomas (1807–94) was one of the first directors of the Colston Hall Company in the early 1860s.[20] His prosperity was based on the manufacture of soap.[21] Bristol had been a pioneering centre of this industry in the medieval period, and in the nineteenth century Christopher Thomas & Bros. became one of Britain's largest manufacturers, being finally taken over by Lever Brothers in 1913.[22]

He was a Unitarian with family links to the Bristol reformer and philanthropist Mary Carpenter. He entered local politics, representing St Philip's ward as a Liberal from 1845 to 1887, and became one of the longest serving members of the city council. For thirty years he was a member of the Bristol City Docks committee and he was mayor in 1874–5.[23] In 1863 Thomas was chairman of the Bristol and South Wales Union Railway and Steam Ferry, and his appointment is recorded in a huge cast plaque still to be seen at Temple Meads Station. A journey to Florence in 1881 was to lead to the distinctive towers on his company's factory at Broad Plain (now the Gardiner of Bristol building), which were inspired by the Palazzo Vecchio.[24]

The high quality marble relief on Christopher Thomas's memorial in the Unitarian Chapel, Lewins Mead, was the model for this work. It is signed 'T. BUTLER, Sc' and the surround is inscribed 'F D BELL, Sc BRISTOL'. The monument is inscribed: 'Wise in judgement, firm in faith, and of gracious generosity'.[25]

Herbert Thomas C47

Sculptor: unknown

Date: probably installed before 1900
Materials: painted plaster
Dimensions: 75cm high, 65cm wide
Inscription: HERBERT THOMAS
Status: Grade II
Owned by Bristol City Council
Condition: fair

Herbert Thomas (1810–1903) was chairman of the Colston Hall Company for 34 years.[26] He was a director of the Bristol soap manufacturers developed by his elder brother, Christopher James Thomas. In 1848 he married Anna Carpenter. She was 11 years his senior and the daughter of the Bristol philanthropist, Dr Lant Carpenter, co-pastor of Lewins Mead Unitarian Chapel.[27] Her sister, Mary Carpenter, was the founder of the Red Lodge School for Girls in 1854, and Herbert became a great supporter of Mary's causes. When Mary died in 1877 Herbert ceded 4 Broad Plain to the Mary Carpenter Memorial Trust as a boys' home. The Thomas family was mostly Unitarian, and Herbert's links with the Lewins Mead Chapel were especially strong. As chairman of the governors of Bristol Grammar School, he laid the foundation stone for the new building in Tyndall's Park in February 1879.

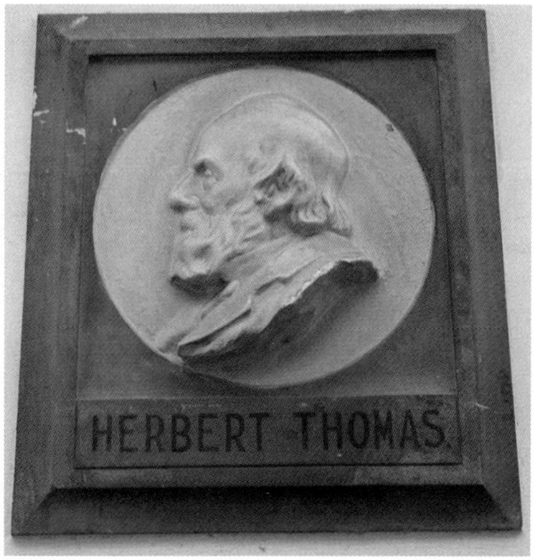

Timothy Butler, after, *Herbert Thomas*

On the first landing of the main staircase of Colston Hall, centred above the reliefs of W. H. Wills and E. S. Robinson

Lewis Fry MP C47

Sculptor: unknown

Date: c.1900
Materials: plaster
Dimenions: 95cm high, 70cm wide
Inscriptions: beneath the relief – LEWIS FRY —: on a circular scroll around the portrait – LEWIS FRY MP 1878–1885 1895–1900
Owned by Bristol City Council
Condition: fair

Lewis Fry PC, JP, DL, LLD (1832–1921), was a great-grandson of Joseph Fry, the Bristol-based founder of the chocolate empire. Lewis Fry owned and lived in Goldney House, Clifton. Trained as a lawyer, he practised as a solicitor and was a Liberal Unionist MP for Bristol and later for North Bristol.

He was an associate of the Bristol Liberal MP, Samuel Morley. On retiring from the House of Commons in 1900 he was made a privy councillor. At various times he served in Bristol as a member of the city council, chairman of the school board, a governor of Clifton College, pro-chancellor of the University of Bristol and president of Clifton High School for Girls.[28]

This plaque was erected in Fry's lifetime. It does not relate in style to the other reliefs on the staircase. Covered in thick cream paint, it has the appearance of a plaster copy rather than an original.

Notes

[1] *Bristol News*, Spring 2004, p.2. [2] J. Latimer, *Annals of Bristol in the Nineteenth Century* (Bristol, 1887), pp.389–90. [3] English Heritage Bristol, Listed Buildings Database, The Colston Hall, PRN:901-1/11/86. [4] As note 2; Foster and Wood's spectacular watercolour design for the interior is illustrated in Crick, *Victorian Buildings*, pl. 44, p.45. [5] As note 1. [6] As note 3. [7] *The Builder*, vol. CLXXXI, October 1951, pp.482–6. [8] *Illustrated London News*, vol. XXV, no. 703, 23 September 1854. [9] Extract from a

description of the second hall, c.1900, obtained from the administrator of Colston Hall. [10] As note 3. [11] D. Milner, *The Royal West of England Academy Bristol* (Bristol, 1985), p.21. [12] B.W.E. Alford, *W.D. & H.O. Wills and the Development of the UK Tobacco Industry, 1786–1965* (London, 1973), pp.327–8. [13] Extract from a description of the second hall, c.1900, obtained from the administrator of Colston Hall. [14] D. Bilbey, *British Sculpture 1470–2000: A Concise Catalogue of the Collection at the Victoria and Albert Museum* (London, 2002), p.306. [15] M. Turner and D. Vaisey, *Art for Commerce: Illustrations and Designs in Stock at E.S.&A. Robinson, Printers* (Menston, 1973), pp.viii. [16] Extract from a description of the second hall, c.1900, obtained from the administrator of Colston Hall. [17] Barney Price, postscript to his grandfather's recollections, Bristol Central Library Local Collections. [18] *ODNB*. [19] Op. cit., p.100. [20] Stone, *Bristol*, p.200. [21] J. Somerville, *Christopher Thomas: Soapmaker of Bristol* (Bristol, 1991), p.31. [22] Op. cit., p.31. [23] Op. cit., pp.37, 51. [24] Op. cit., pp.112, 113, photograph. [25] Op. cit., p.65, photograph of memorial to Christopher James Thomas; Gunnis, *Dictionary of British Sculptors* records a bust of 'Mr Thomas', 1865, for Bristol General Hospital, with which Charles Thomas was much involved, by the London sculptor Timothy Butler. [26] Extract from a description of the second hall, c.1900, obtained from the administrator of Colston Hall. [27] As note 21. [28] *Who Was Who, a Companion to Who's Who, 1916–1928*, ed. G. Blakemore Evans (London, 1934), p.384.

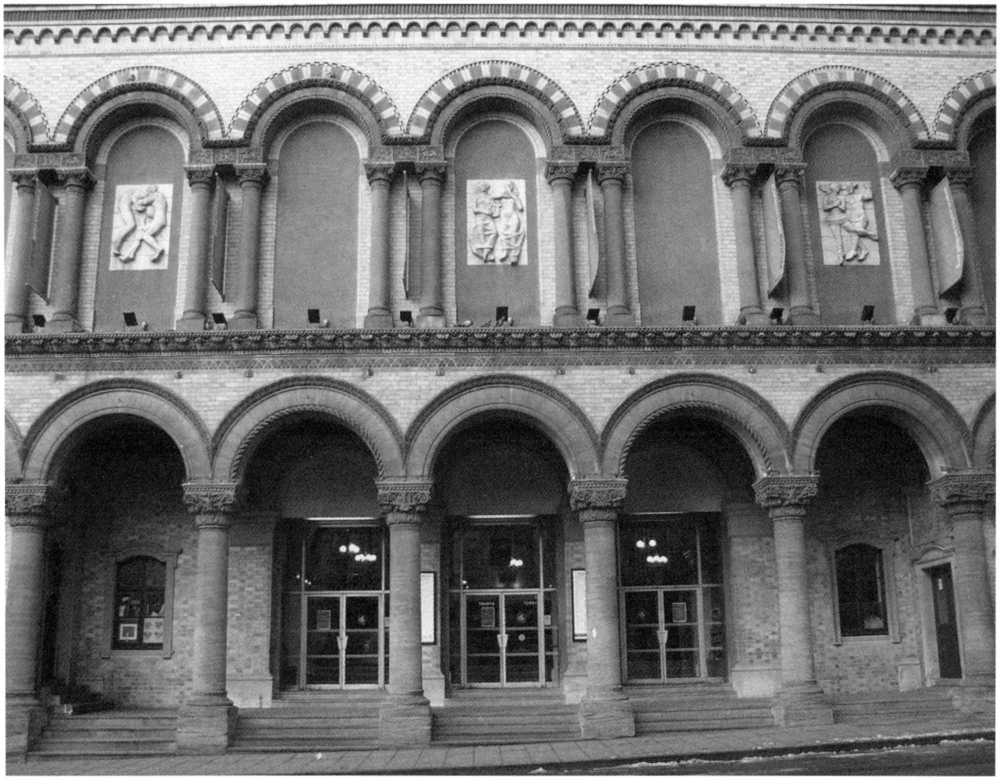

Colston Hall façade

On the façade of Colston Hall

Wrestling, Music and Ballet C47

Sculptors: Ernest Pascoe and staff and students of the West of England College of Art

Architect: J. Nelson Meredith
Date: c.1960
Material: Portland stone[1]
Dimensions: each approx. 160cm high
Status: Grade II
Owned by Bristol City Council
Condition: fair

In about 1960 the fine Foster and Wood façade of Colston Hall (1869–73), which had survived two fires and much modernisation, suffered from the addition of a 'crassly intrusive' glass canopy and from the blanking out of the deeply-recessed arched windows on the upper floor.[2] In an attempt to enliven the newly in-filled arches, these three rectangular reliefs were inserted into three of the seven spaces. It was an unhappy marriage.

When plans for the redevelopment of next-door Colston House as a foyer to Colston Hall were announced early in 2004, it was stated that the architects would 'work closely… to ensure the new building complements the Grade II-listed nineteenth-century façade' and the exterior of Colston Hall would be cleaned and restored.[3] It must be hoped that the wretched canopy will go, the upper windows will be restored, the façade will be cleaned and that its especially rich variety of colour, materials and carving will again be revealed. A new home or use should be found for these three self-consciously modern reliefs representing wrestling, music and ballet. Today, May 2009, the vast and spectacular foyer is complete but the work on Colston Hall's Victorian façade has yet to begin.

The panel in the second arch from the left contains two naked male wrestlers. The central arch has two diaphanously-draped female figures holding musical instruments. The woman to the left holds a lyre; the other plays panpipes. In the sixth arch there are two ballet dancers.

The works are unsigned and undated, and their origin was only recently established following an appeal for information in a local

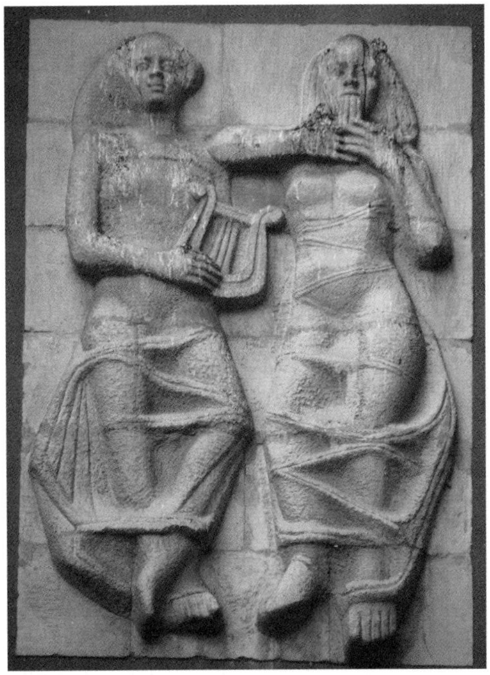

Ernest Pascoe and others, *Music*

newspaper. Michael Dymond, a former Bristol art teacher, who had attended the West of England College of Art as a student in 1960, responded:

> The College [now part of the University of the West of England] was then situated in Queen's Road. There was great excitement at the time, as the Sculpture Department had been chosen or commissioned to design and create the relief panels to depict the various events displayed at the Colston Hall – wrestling, dance and music. The Head of Sculpture was then Ernest Pascoe, himself a well-known sculptor. Although the work was in progress when I arrived at the college, I got the impression that the project was a cooperative enterprise, carried out under the supervision of Ernest. I think the designs were arrived at 'by committee' and carried out by the students. I have recollections of seeing the large preliminary drawings around the walls of the studio and later full-size clay versions of the designs.[4]

Two other members of staff, Gerald Scott and Roger Baker, and some of the students were involved in making the finished work, carved in Bath stone blocks. Ernest Pascoe had already designed applied reliefs for the front of the 'boxes' inside the modernised Colston Hall when it re-opened in 1951. J. Nelson Meredith, the city architect who designed the new interior, may have invited Pascoe and his students to undertake the three large reliefs as part of subsequent alterations made to the façade.

The sculptor, John Huggins, was one of seven or so students who worked on the project. He has written recently that the reliefs were designed by the students under Pascoe's guidance.[5] They were carved in the garden of the art school at the back of the Royal West of England Academy. The students were not paid.

> It was not a pleasant job, the stone chipped at the joints and whenever the blocks were moved. Quite a lot of filling was required when they were erected. No one on the team had much experience and it shows. It is not a job anyone could be proud of and if they are moved I would confine them to hardcore.

Notes

[1] Letter from John Huggins to FWG, 3 July 2008. [2] Gomme et al., *An Architectural History*, p.370. [3] *Bristol News*, Spring 2004, issue 48, p.2. The architects were Levitt Bernstein Associates. [4] Mike Dymond, *Evening Post*, 15 June 2004. [5] As note 1.

Corn Street

On the pavement in front of the Corn Exchange

The Bristol Nails C30

Makers: unknown, excepting the third pillar of 1625 by Thomas Hobson

Dates: the first undated, c.1595; the others, 1630, 1625 and 1631

Dimensions: each approx. 100cm high; circular tops, approx. 65cm diameter; the pillars approx. 8m apart

Material: bronze

Inscriptions: most are cast as raised letters; words underlined have either eccentrically ligatured or reversed characters; the sign '♦' indicates diamond-shaped marks

—: first pillar (c.1595) on the left when facing the Exchange; no inscription but a shield bearing a chevron, identical to that on Robert Kitchen's coat of arms, is on the top face of the pillar

—: second pillar (1630) around the vertical rim – THIS POST IS THE GIFT OF MASTER ROBERT KITCHIN MERCHANT SOMETIME MAIOR AND ALDERMAN OF THIS CITY WHO DEC ♦ 1♦ SEPTEMB ♦ 1594

—: around the circumference of the face – HIS EXECVTORS WERE FOWER OF HIS SERRVANTS IOHN BARKER MATHEW HAVILAND ABELL KITCHIN ALDERMEN OF THIS CITY AND IOHN ROWBOROW SHERIF 1630

—: on the circular top of the nail – COMMEMORAVERVNT · INCOMMEMORABILIORA / PRÆTERMISERVNT · COMMEMORABILIA (these four words are in Roman characters and, unlike the older inscriptions, sharply defined. They were re-cut in 1937 but the recorded words 'NEMO SIBI NASCITUR' and 'HILAREM DATOREM DELIGIT DEUS' have been lost)[1]

—: third pillar (1625) around the circumference of the face – THOMAS HOBSON OF BRISTOL MADE ME ♦ NICHOLAS CRISP OF LONDON GAVE ME ♦ TO THIS HONORABLE CITTY ♦ IN REMEMBRANCE OF GODS MERCY ♦ IN ANNO DOMINI ♦ ♦ 1625♦ N. C. [Nicholas Crisp]

—: around the vertical rim – PRAISE THE LORD O MY SOVLE AND FORGET NOT ALL HIS BENEFITS ♦ ♦ ♦ ♦ HE SAVED MY LIFE FROM DESCRVCTION AND ♦ ♦ TO HIS MERCY AND LOVING KINDNESS ♦ PRAISE ♦ ♦ ♦ ♦ (the top

face of this pillar is blank)
—: fourth pillar (1631) around the circumference of the face – THIS IS THE GVIFT OF MR GEORGE WHITE OF BRISTOLL MERCHANNT BROTHER VNTO DOCTOR THOMAS WHITE A FAMOVS BENEFACTOR TO THIS CITIE AD 1631
—: around the rim – ♦ SO WAS THE WORKE OF THE PILLARS FINISHED : THE CHVRCH OF THE LIVINGE GOD IS THE PILLAR : AND GROUND OF THE TRVETH (the top face of this pillar is blank)
Status: Grade I
Owned by Bristol City Council
Condition: fair, but at risk

A wine merchant visiting Bristol in 1665 described the so-called Bristol Nails as 'brass pillars, about an elle high for peoppell to leane uppon, and to talke, tell money, sign anie writings or the like'.[2] Today they are employed much as they were in 1807, when Robert Southey noted in *Letters from England* that newspapers were being sold from one pillar and a cage of goldfinches from another. Although the section of Corn Street in front of the Exchange was pedestrianised in September 1976, the risk of serious damage to the pillars from the manoeuvring of heavy market carts, vending machines and hot-food stands increases. They have already been abraded, dented and scarred by corrosive liquids. The occasional blocking of drainage holes will be causing internal damage, and the pillars are often obscured from view. Their survival through four centuries is remarkable and the risk, to which they continue to be subjected, is inexcusable. The market is, however, crucial to the continued vitality of Corn Street during the day and there is no doubt of the concern of the city council's staff. Following recent vandalism to the top of the fourth pillar, all were conserved and given a wax coating by Eura Conservation.[3]

The *British Archaeological Association's Proceedings* of 1859 stated:

> It seems an extraordinary fact that these columns, and the custom connected with them, should have been passed over by most writers on Bristol; and it would be of interest to ascertain if anything like them, or the curious practice alluded to, exists in any other part of the country.[4]

Other metal-topped pillars existed for the same purpose in Limerick and Liverpool and elsewhere, but Bristol's have always been unrivalled in number and quality.

The phrase 'on the nail' cannot be exclusively associated with Bristol. It may also have misled us in our understanding of the function of the pillars. The flat tops of the pillars have raised rims, which would prevent coins sliding over the edge, but it is argued below that they were originally more often used for the binding of deals rather than for the final completion of commercial transactions and the actual exchange of money.

The second and third pillars have similar baluster profiles, but the first and fourth are very different. Only the first pillar has extensive engraved decoration. The pillars were cast at separate times over nearly forty years from about 1595 to 1631. Three are inscribed and dated.

The first pillar, furthest to the left, 'appears to be somewhat older than the rest, and bears on its face a shield charged with a chevron… all traces of an inscription are entirely removed'.[5] An outline of this shield is still just visible. This baluster 'is un-inscribed, but is enriched in some parts with designs which seem to fix its date to the reign of Elizabeth or James I'.[6] Small circles on the upper band contain, alternatively, flying birds and six-rayed stars. Another band consists of scrolls terminating with acorns and dragons' heads with forked tongues. On the bowl are acanthus leaves and acorns. Many sources have dated this pillar to 1594. That was the year in which Robert Kitchin died and the chevron on the shield relates to his arms.

The next three pillars are not in chronological order. The second commemorates its donor, Robert Kitchin (variously Kechen and Kitchen), 36 years after his death. He was born in Kendal, Westmoreland. He came to Bristol as a young man in 1548 and became a very wealthy merchant, trading largely with Spain and Portugal. The Earl of Leicester, Elizabeth I's favourite, and the Earl of Warwick were entertained in great state in his house in Small Street. A surprisingly modest wall memorial in St Stephen's depicts Robert and his first wife, Joan, at prayer, 'WHO TO THE POORE GAVE ALL THEIR GOODES AWAY', as one line in the verse below the image states.

An enigmatic inscription, in Latin, was later added to the circular face of the second pillar some time before 1859. This inscription was to be re-cut, for the letters are sharply defined in intaglio Roman capitals, unlike the raised seventeenth-century letters of the other inscriptions. In 1859 George Pryce FSA, of the British Archaeological Association, tried to read a 'much worn' inscription. It was, he said, 'as near as I can decipher it "COMMEMORAVERVNT INCOMMEMORABILIORA PRAETERMISERVNT COMMEMORABILIA / NEMO SIBI NASCITVR"' [7] (They have commemorated things more unmemorable but omitted the memorable things… No one is born for himself). The last three words are no longer visible. In between these inscriptions appears a large Roman capital 'P', extending its entire depth. Under that appears 'HILARLI DATORE D… CLI' [probably part of a date] 'DEVS'.[8] There may have been some other words below, but only a few straggling letters can now be made out.[9]

This and another Latin quotation, both long erased from the surface, are recorded in *Robert Kitchen, Mayor of Bristol*. In full they were: NEMO SIBI NASCITUR ('None of us lives to himself', from Romans, xiv, 7) and HILAREM DATOREM DEGLIT DEUS ('God loves the giver who gives cheerfully', from Corinthians, ix, 7).[10] Brass rubbings of the inscriptions on the pillar were made by 'Mr. Ponting, one of the City's Valuers', in July 1925.[11] The outline of

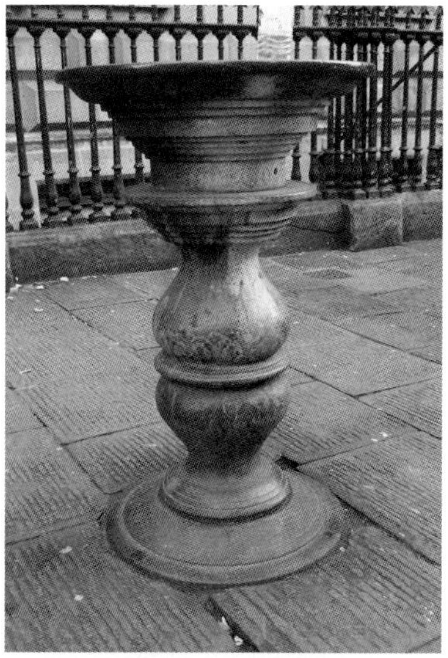

First pillar, c.1595

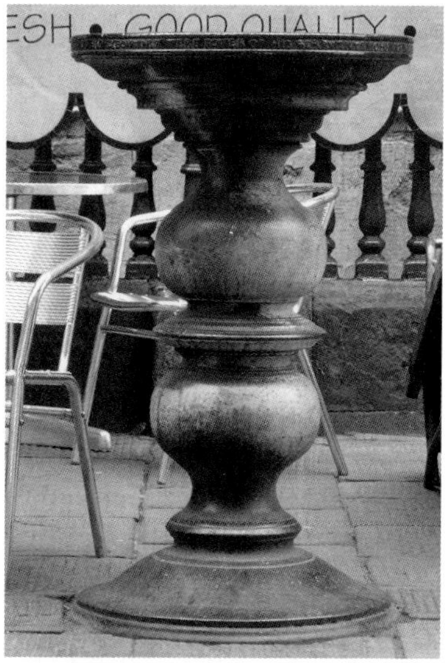

Thomas Hobson (attributed to), *Second pillar*, gift of Robert Kitchen, 1630

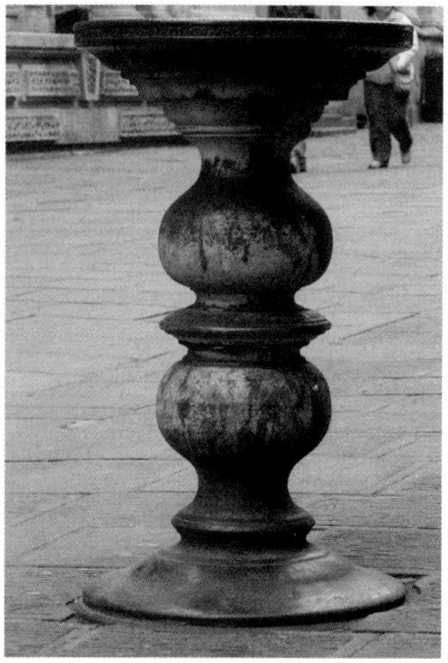

Thomas Hobson, *Third pillar*, gift of Nicholas Crisp, 1625

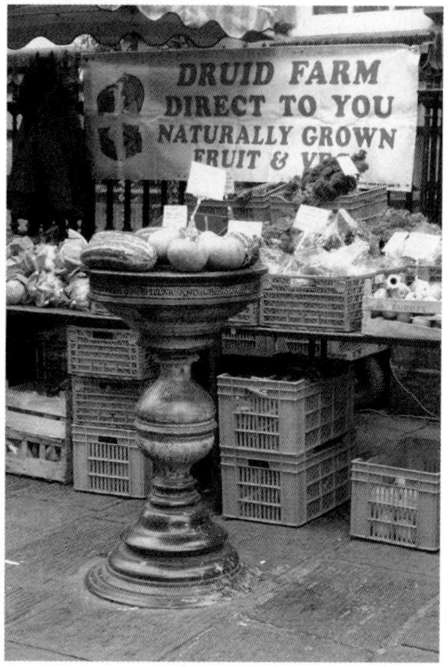

***Fourth pillar*, gift of George White, 1631**

the second pillar is so close to that of the third and earlier pillar that it may reasonably be attributed to Thomas Hobson.

The third pillar is the only one to be attributed to a maker, 'Thomas Hobson', and the donor is recorded as 'Nicholas Crisp of London'. This may be Sir Nicholas Crispe, a member of the London Company of Salters, who was 'cultivating madder extensively at Deptford in 1660'.[12] This pillar's two inscriptions suggest that the gift was a thanks-offering for escape from London's fearful epidemic of bubonic plague in 1625. The inscription on the upper edge of the rim was 'reinscribed' by Mr James Barr Street in 1937.[13]

The fourth pillar, given by a Bristol merchant George White, commemorates the donor's brother, Thomas White (1550–1624), a doctor of theology. This reverend gentleman amassed a considerable fortune from benefices in London, Oxford and Salisbury. A renowned preacher of patriotic Protestantism, he spoke against usury and covetousness, 'especially such excessive indulgence as the use of down beds and the payment of cooks to produce elaborate meals'.[14] Born in Temple parish, Bristol, he founded and endowed an almshouse there in 1613. Many substantial bequests included the founding of Sion College in London and money for the improvement of Bristol's roads.

There is evidence that there were more than four pillars erected at the Tolzey in Corn Street, close to the High Cross at the very heart of Bristol, although it is likely that the surviving four pillars were the only ones to be made entirely of bronze. At the Tolzey, they had all stood beneath an open-air but covered colonnade, a place of business for Bristol's merchants as well as for the adjudication of commercial disputes. All four pillars have drain holes to allow rainwater to run off easily, confirming that they were designed to stand outside.

Millerd's 1673 map of Bristol implies that the Tolzey consisted of two separate colonnades on opposite sides of Corn Street. The map clearly shows the Tolzey and its colonnade on the north side of Corn Street at the corner with Broad Street, the site of successive Council Houses.[15] The same buildings and colonnade are depicted in the border of the map in one of two vignettes that show the Tolzey. One is inscribed 'The south prospect of ye Tolzey of Bristoll' and it shows part of the colonnade with three of the four Nails beneath it. The other vignette shows 'Part of All Saints Tower' and 'The north prospect of ye Tolzey of Bristoll And All Saints Conduit adioyneing'. Here the colonnade has seven columns and there are six pillars. John Latimer implies that these were wooden pillars with brass tops. He records that they were repaired in 1732: 'The Corporation... paid £6 to one John Mason, for "turning six large posts for the brass heads to be put on at the Tolzey, near All Saints' Church."'[16]

Latimer also implies that the four pillars were moved to their present position in 1732–3 rather than in 1771, when the 'first [stone] flagging in the City... a space seven feet in width' was created.[17] This new and superior pavement was recorded in a letter to the *Bristol Journal* appreciating the 'smooth paved stones'.[18] The obsolete Tolzey was not to be demolished until 1782.[19] To complicate matters, the engraving in William Barrett's history of Bristol shows the four pillars beneath a four-columned colonnade against All Saints Church.[20] By the date of the book's publication, 1789, they had of course been moved to today's positions. It is possible that the pillars were first erected on the north side of the street and then moved across to the Tolzey colonnade by All Saints Church, perhaps when the first purpose-built Council House was erected in the 1720s.

The inscription on the 1631 pillar, the last to be made, includes the words: 'so was the work of the pillars finished', indicating that the Nails were part of a finite plan that had taken nearly four decades to complete. The next phrase on the same pillar emphasises their religious significance: 'the church of the living God is the pillar and the ground of the truth'. The number four also has particular religious significance. Reference to 'pillars' in *Cruden's Concordance* reveals two verses, from *Exodus*, in which Moses receives commands from God to construct a shrine, or tabernacle, and to erect four bronze pillars: 'There shall be four pillars' and 'their pillars are to be bronze'.[21] The Bristol Nails were far more than utilitarian posts on which merchants completed their deals. These four costly bronze columns proclaimed the merchants' shared Christian faith and the deeply religious nature of the oaths that bound their transactions.

A note in the *Gentleman's Magazine* in 1858 referred to Bristol's 'four brazen columns... on which, by the laying on of hands, bargains are concluded'.[22] A year later, a related paragraph in the *British Archaeological Association's Proceedings* went further still and referred to the 'brazen columns... upon the tops of which persons were wont to lay their hands in token of the conclusion of a bargain – a practice apparently derived from the ancient custom of touching the altar to render an oath inviolable, as was done by Harold when he swore fealty to duke William'.[23] Like an oath upon a bible, a deal struck over a pillar was eternally binding.

Notes

[1] These are quoted in H.S. Cowper, *Robert Kitchen, Mayor of Bristol; A Native of Kendal* (Kendal, 1928), p.193. [2] Quoted in B. Little, *The City and County of Bristol: A Study of Atlantic Civilisation* (London, 1954), p.144. [3] Bristol Evening Post, 14 April 2009. [4] *The Journal of the British Archaeological Association*, 'Proceedings, 12 January', 1859, p.341; plate 27 is an engraving of the profiles of three of the 'Brass Tables at Exchange, Bristol' to the scale of one inch to the foot. [5] As note 4, p.275; Robert Kitchin's heraldic shield bore the same chevron. [6] Op. cit., pp.340–1. [7] Ibid. As note 4, p.275: 'They have commemorated things more unmemorable but omitted the memorable things... No one is born for himself. They have related that which is unworthy of note. What is worthy of praise they have omitted. No man lives to himself.' 'They' refers to the executors; translations Professor Alan Ryder. [8] HILARLI DATORE means 'cheerful donor' or 'glad giver'. [9] As note 1. [10] Ibid. [11] The Latin text was recorded by George Pryce FSA in *The Journal of the British Archaeological Association*, 1859, p.275. Brass rubbings of the inscriptions are in the BRO. 'The inscriptions were re-cut by Mr James, 26 Bath Street, Bristol.' BRO 2179(1-5). [12] See J. Thirsk, *Alternative Agriculture: A History from the Black Death to the Present Day* (Oxford, 1997), p.112. Dyeing was an important Bristol trade. I am grateful to Jayne Semple of Bath for tracing this information. [13] BRO III/68 typescript; copy in PMSA files. [14] *Stephen Wright, ODNB*. [15] J. Millerd, *An Exact Delineation of the Famous City of Bristol and Suburbs* (Bristol, 1673). [16] J. Latimer, *Annals of Bristol in the Eighteenth Century* (Bristol, 1893), p.183. [[17] Ibid. 'The Common Council of Bristol resolved, on the 28 September, that a paved way, seven feet wide, should be made before the Exchange, to which it was also determined to move the four brass pillars that had long stood before the Council House.' [18] C.F.W. Denning, *The Eighteenth-Century Architecture of Bristol* (Bristol, 1926), p.95. [19] Op. cit., p.276. [20] Barrett, *History and Antiquities*, opp. p.437. [21] A. Cruden, *Cruden's Complete Concordance to the Bible* (London and Guildford, 1933), p.495; Exodus, 27:16. [22] *Gentleman's Magazine*, June 1858, p.650. [23] *British Archaeological Association's Proceedings*, 1859, p.340.

The Exchange, Corn Street

Decorations on and inside the Exchange C31

Sculptors: Thomas Paty, Edward William Wyon and others

Architect: John Wood the Elder and Edward Middleton Barry
Date: c.1741–3 and 1870–2
Status: Grade I
Owned by Bristol City Council

John Wood's small but elegant monograph on his own building, *A Description of the Exchange of Bristol*, published in 1745, confirms the attribution of the stone carvings to Thomas Paty, 'Ornament Carver to the Exchange'.[1] The Exchange account books call Paty 'Carver and Freemason' and 'Freestone carver', titles given to no other craftsman recorded in the books.[2]

Wood had already established a reputation as an architect in Bath, when, on 4 February 1741, he attended an interview with Bristol Corporation to discuss the replacement of Bristol's ancient exchange building, known as the Tolzey. He was immediately 'given proper instructions' and asked 'to form designs'.[3] His proposals were presented to the Bristol committee less than a week later. This was to be 'Wood's outstanding public building, a Palladian design of great distinction'.[4]

Ralph Allen, who had been approached by the committee before John Wood, supplied the stone, and William Biggs of Comb near Bath won the freemason's contract, underbidding the separate bids of Thomas Paty, James Paty and

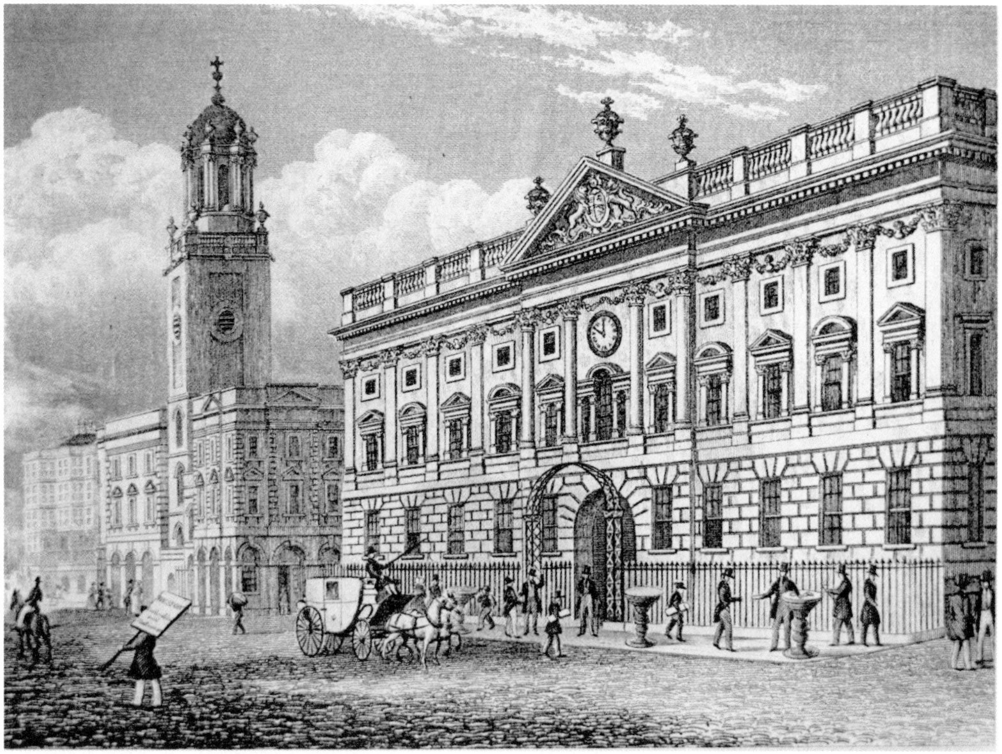

***The Exchange, Corn Street*, engraving by W. Lander, c.1825**

others.[5] The principal mason and sculptor was Thomas Paty, 'a brilliant sculptor and… the most successful of the Bristol monumental masons of the time'.[6]

John Wood originally proposed a covered courtyard, and it was the corporation that preferred the more traditional open-air space for trading. A hundred years later, in 1848, the building was being restored 'in consequence of the softness of the stone' and a correspondent to a local newspaper proposed the covering over of the inner courtyard.[7] It was not until 1869, however, that the merchants finally sought protection from the elements, and in 1870–2 Edward Middleton Barry added a storey to Wood's colonnade with a domed iron and glass roof above. This iron roof was replaced in 1949 by a glass roof at the lower level of Wood's colonnade, condemning E. W. Wyon's 24 stone caryatids to the elements.

On the Corn Street façade and within the courtyard of the Exchange

Festoons and Coats of Arms C31

Sculptor: Thomas Paty

Date: 1742–3
Material: Bath stone
Condition: fair

On the Exchange's Corn Street façade are eleven festoons with human and animal heads, the very large coat of arms of George II, and three urns or acroterial vases. The architect, John Wood, described this façade:

> in the Tympan of which the King's Arms are carved in stone… the Spaces between the Capitals of the Columns and Pilasters in this Front, are filled with Festoons, which represent Great-Britain and the four Quarters of the World, with the chief Products and Manufactures of every Country.[8]

Similar carvings of exotic animals and fruit appear on Wood's Exchange building (1778–55) in Liverpool.[9]

The sculptural elements on Bristol's Exchange have been patronisingly described as:

> a blowsy bucolic free-for-all that still cleverly manages to be correct in the Palladian sense… the overall spirit is that of a cheerful West Country baroque. Turks' heads, elephants, camels, rum barrels, bales and pineapples riot symbolically.[10]

Tim Mowl, joint author of those words, later relented. 'Bucolic in the very best sense of the word, it reflected the city's prosperity with authority and originality.'[11] The careful symbolism confidently puts Britain and Bristol at the very centre of an expanding world.

Thomas Paty's own drawings of these festoons survive in a volume in the Royal Academy's library.[12] They may well have been drawn for the benefit of the architect John Wood in order to inform the illustrations to his book on the Exchange, and were thus drawn after the carvings were completed. The drawings are of some assistance in the identification of the carvings.

The first three festoons from the left represent Asia. In the centre of the first is a camel's head with exotic fruits and bound boxes, perhaps containing silks and possibly a jar of frankincense. The first head is of a turbaned and moustachioed figure with fruits, bales of cloth and more distinctive bound boxes. Next is the head of a lion or leopard, with rolls of cloth and various fruits. The next two festoons represent Europe. Europe herself has a headdress that could represent a market house or a temple of learning. On her festoon are books, a crown and flags, a globe and an artist's palette. Next is a horse with shells and cornucopia spilling fruits. In the centre bay beneath the pediment is the head of Britannia with a compass, pickaxe and sledgehammer, some strange bricks, perhaps, and presumably other significant objects of trade and manufacture. The following two festoons represent America. First is a bear surrounded by sugar cane and tobacco and other possible fruits from Bristol's West India trade. Then comes an Indian in a short feathered head-dress with a quiver full of arrows. On the festoon are rolls of tobacco and some unfamiliar fruits, including tubers, perhaps oca. The last three festoons represent Africa. First is a lion's head together with tusks, barrels and exotic fruits; then a bejewelled and moustachioed prince surrounded by pineapples, and, surprisingly, cocoa pods and perhaps ground nuts. Finally there is an elephant's head with tusks, bunches of dates and other fruits.

Within the pediment or tympanum of the façade is the spectacular coat of arms of George II with splendid rococo flourishes beyond the lion and unicorn.[13]

On the rear of the frontage, within the equivalent pediment looking down on the original open courtyard or market, is Bristol's coat of arms.[14] It is now invisible to visitors, hidden above the roof installed in 1949 and severely eroded.[15] Nonetheless it is probably one of the biggest and finest of the City of Bristol's carved coats of arms. Set against a magnificent double seashell, the unicorns are almost headless, but the motto 'Virtute et Industria' is as crisp as ever and clearly visible to the city council's auditors, presently in the offices above the market.

Thomas Paty's third coat of arms is in the south pediment facing onto the general market.[16] Here, in a virtuoso carving that remains in a remarkably fine state, the city's unicorns are replaced by fruits and flowers

Thomas Paty, ***Asia, second festoon***

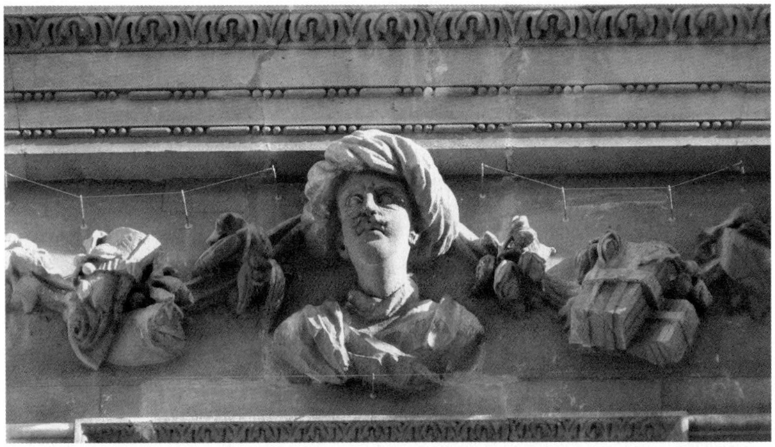

Thomas Paty, ***America, eighth festoon***

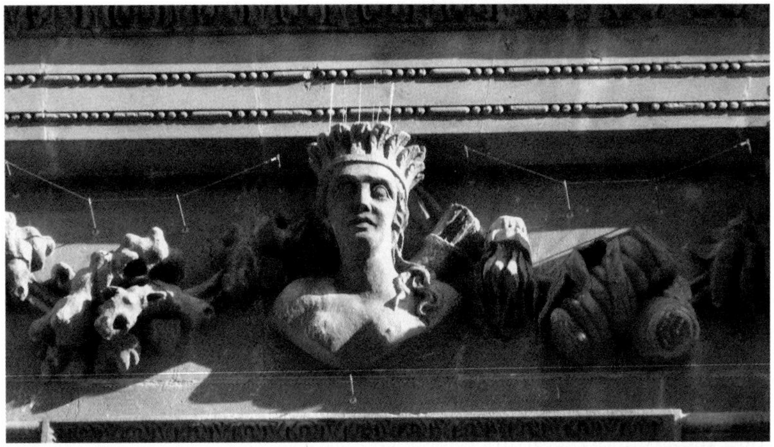

Thomas Paty, ***Africa, tenth festoon***

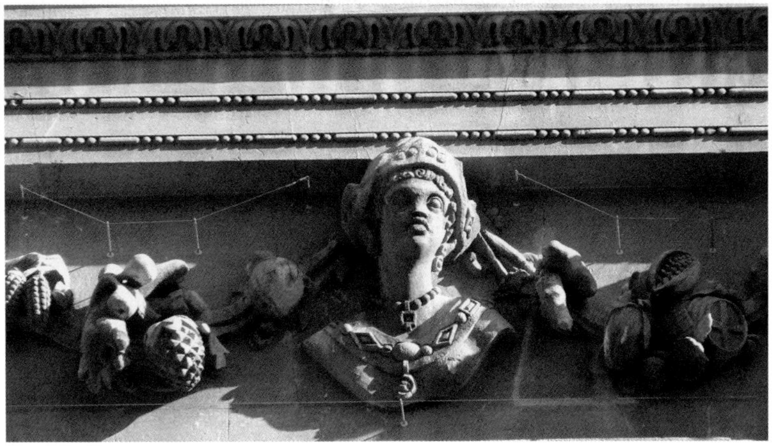

Thomas Paty,
George II's coat-of-arms, Corn Street façade **(after cleaning in 2009)**

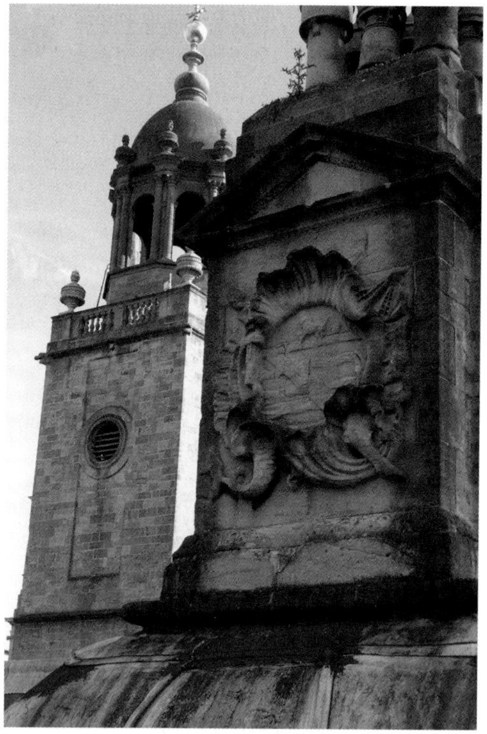

Thomas Paty,
Merchant Venturers' coat-of-arms (and All Saints' Tower)

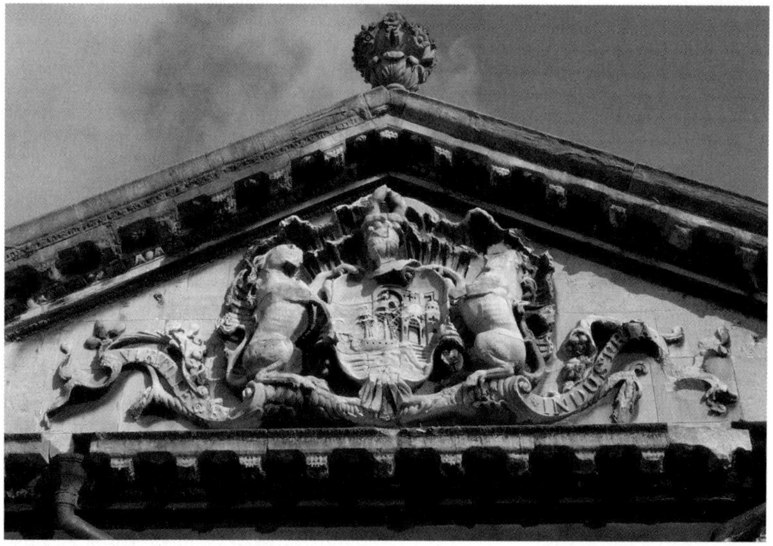

Thomas Paty,
Bristol's coat-of-arms, courtyard pediment

against an especially ornate seashell.[17] Unfortunately this pediment is both protected and obscured by especially heavy netting.

Two further coats of arms are on the inner breasts of the east and west chimneys. Now unseen by visitors, they would originally have been visible from the open courtyard, as an engraving after Edward Bird of 1808 demonstrates. The eastern coat of arms is that of the Society of Merchant Venturers. John Wood records that the 'Merchants Arms adorn the West Front of the Turret, on the East side of the PERISTYLE, as a Complement for their Benefaction of two thousand Pounds towards the Work'.[18] The arms are within a particularly ornate rococo cartouche, with, for example, the satyr's leg of 'Time' protruding like a lean haunch of venison from the shell surround. Sadly, it is very worn, but it is still a deliciously informal interpretation, possibly suggesting that it was designed by the rococo engraver William Milton of Bristol. We know from the exchange accounts that Milton was paid a guinea for drawing the city's coat of arms in March 1742.[19] There is unusual whimsy and asymmetry in Milton's surrounding shells and cartouches in his surviving designs for trade cards and coats of arms in an album of his drawings.[20] Thomas Paty may well have been influenced by him or perhaps employed him as a draughtsman.

The coat of arms on the opposite turret or chimney was described by John Wood as being 'the most antient Arms of the CITY'.[21] However, the present shield, containing three lions *passant*, and the surrounding cartouche are probably a nineteenth century replacement.

In the main foyer from Corn Street of the Exchange

Keystones C31

Sculptor: Thomas Paty

Date: 1742–3
Material: Bath stone
Condition: fair

John Wood describes the three keystone heads in the vestibule entrance to the Exchange:

> The Arch of every Corinthian Gate in this Room has a Key Stone, carved with a Head, to denote the Business of the Place to which the Aperture under each of those Arches makes an Entrance: Mercury's Head is next the Coffee-House; [to the left of the entrance] Bacchus's Head is next the Tavern; [to the right] and the Head of Dea Pecunia of the Antients is next the Place of Exchange.[22]

Bacchus is an obvious subject for the tavern entrance. *Mercury*, in his role as a messenger, decorates the entrance to the coffeehouse, in which reading newspapers was a major activity.[23] *Dea Pecunia* was the Roman goddess of wealth, or as John Wood also called her, 'the Goddess of Money'.[24] On one side of this head is a cornucopia and on the other are scales, which are barely visible today, but which are identified in a memorandum initialled by the architect himself.[25]

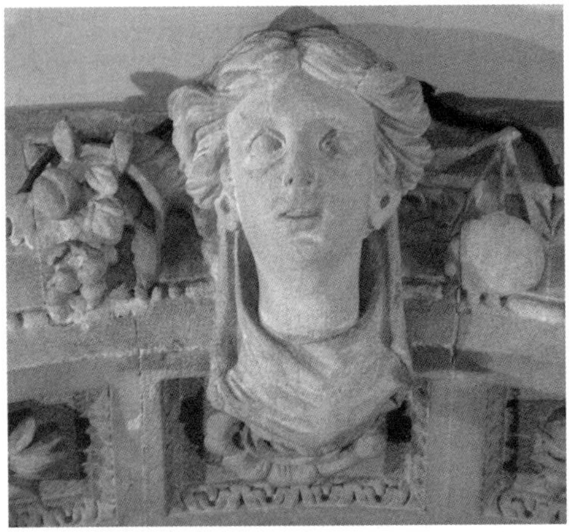

Thomas Paty, *Dea Pecunia, goddess of wealth*

In his book, published in 1926, C. F. W. Dening reproduced a photograph of the superb gates that were beneath the head of *Dea Pecunia* and described them as 'admirable in design and execution'.[26] In 1982 Bryan Little noted that the 'wrought-iron gates, with rich scrollwork, which once led into the central piazza have been taken down'.[27] Their present whereabouts are unknown. Within the vestibule, the railings beside the steps up to the tavern and coffee house entrances may be original. In front of the façade are the original 'Palisades before the Front of the Exchange', for which James Hilhouse & Co was paid £85 10s on 4 August 1744.[28] These dignified railings were restored in 2008 and it is to be hoped that this was a first stage in the restoration and rehabilitation of this magnificent building.

On the ground-floor walls of the central quadrangle of the Exchange

Interior Plaster Reliefs C31

Attributed to Charles Boni and John Griffin

Date: 1743
Material: painted plaster
Dimensions: 150cm high, 300cm wide
Condition: fair

Within the once-open peristyle or piazza, the decorative sculpture at ground floor level is in plaster with the apparent exception of the stone head over the entrance from the outer hall. There was, and possibly still is, some confusion over what was done in stucco or in stone within the courtyard. Wood himself records that one of the heads was in stone and that it was his intention that the reliefs, 'those ornaments in the Portico', should be in stone, 'which, by meer Accident, were performed in Stucco'.[29] This refers to the three semi-circular spandrels above the doors. It is possible that these were designed by Thomas Paty but made by Charles Boni and Co., and maybe John Griffin, as a result of the confusion referred to by John Wood.

The surviving documents compound the confusion. There is a memorandum signed by Thomas Paty and dated 21 April 1743 which states that 'Mr Patty Proposes to Carve festoons between the Capitals round the Inside of the Exchange for Forty five pounds'.[30] Cha: Boni and Co. were paid for 'stucco work' and 'festoon work' in July and August 1743, with the final payment being received in London.[31] There is also John Griffin to consider. He is listed as a subscriber to Wood's book as 'Mr. John Griffin, of Bristol, one of the ornament plasterers of the Exchange'.[32] He and his partner, Thomas North, appear repeatedly in the account books as tilers and plasterers throughout the Exchange, and were responsible for most of the architectural plasterwork, architraves, cornices and 'flowers'. However, they also worked on 'the festoons in stucco, between the pilasters round the Walks of the Exchange, as also all ye spandrels'.[33] They were paid for the festoons, 'after deducting for one in stone'. Their work in the spandrels may possibly have been limited to the floral work within them.[34]

Each of the semi-circular spandrels above the central doors on three sides of the hall has a centred female head where a keystone would be set. The hair and dress of each head is different. The three spandrels have a central roundel with the head and shoulders of figures representing Asia, Africa and America, together with appropriate fruits and animals. John Wood wrote:

> The Spaces between the Capitals of the Pilasters in the Porticos of the Peristyle are adorned with Heads and Festoons, one space in Stone, [this is above the door from the

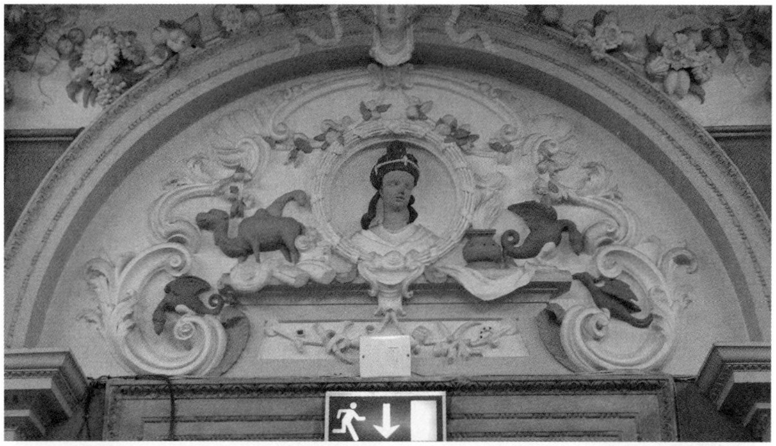

Charles Boni (attributed to),
Asia

Charles Boni (attributed to),
Africa

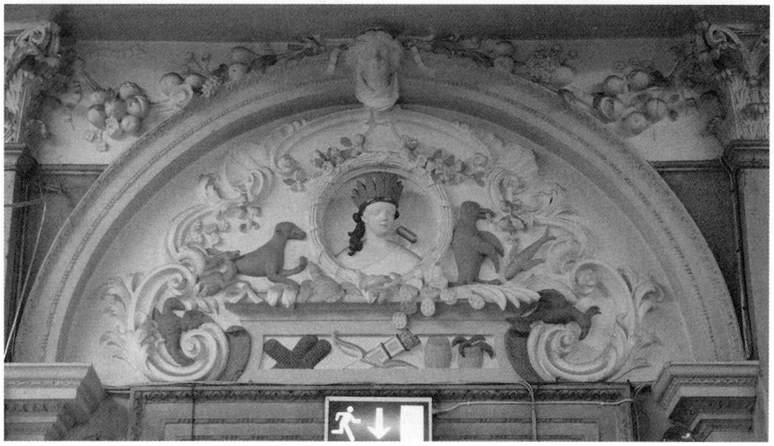

Charles Boni (attributed to),
America

> entrance hall] the rest in Stucco, the three Quarters of the World, Asia, Africa, and America.[35]

Asia is represented by a turbaned bust, a camel, a giraffe, an incense burner and three exotic gryphons or dragons, now sadly painted blue. The negro head representing Africa is encircled by a horse, an ostrich, an elephant, a lion and a crocodile. For the Americas there is again a female head in the short-feathered head-dress usually associated with South America. She is accompanied by a moose (perhaps), a possible seal, a turtle, a penguin, a flying fish, two cockatoos and cacti.

Every one of the 32 bays has a shallow rectangular plaster relief forming a continuous frieze filled with a similar array of fruit and leaves. All the reliefs were garishly painted around 1990.

Considering they were partially open to the weather for over one hundred years, the plaster is in remarkably good condition. The building was completed in 1743, but the piazza was not first roofed until 1872.

John Wood had hoped that 24 'Statues of Eminent men for Trade and Navigation' might go in the niches of the peristyle 'since such Statues would not only contribute to the Ornament of that COURT but, perhaps, excite an Emulation in Youth to Business'.[36]

In the upper storey of the courtyard of the Exchange

Caryatids C31

Sculptor: Edward Willam Wyon
Architect: Edward Middleton Barry

Date: 1872
Materials: Bath stone
Dimensions: arches, 270cm wide; caryatids, approximately 150cm high
Condition: fair; open to the weather for over half a century, eroded, but complete and very well worth conserving

In 1872, E. M. Barry added a floor to the Wood's inner colonnade and roofed over the courtyard. The 24 caryatids rose at first floor level above the eighteenth-century columns, with the intended illusion that they were supporting the ornate iron and glass clerestory and roof above them. These substantial sculptures have been hidden from view since 1949, when 'a coarse utilitarian glass roof' replaced much of Barry's work.[37] This 1949 roof is itself failing, and it is to be hoped that a lighter version of Barry's original roof above the caryatids will soon be the most practical solution.

John Wood's original desire had been to build an 'Egyptian Hall' to cover the

Edward William Wyon, *Caryatids and keystones*

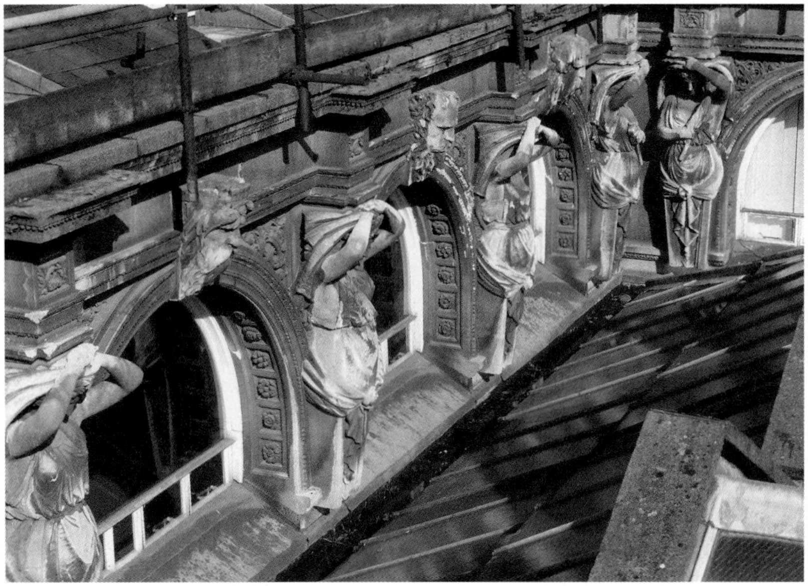

***E. M. Barry's design for the upper storey and glass roof of the Exchange*, watercolour, c.1870 (Bristol Museum and Art Gallery, K419)**

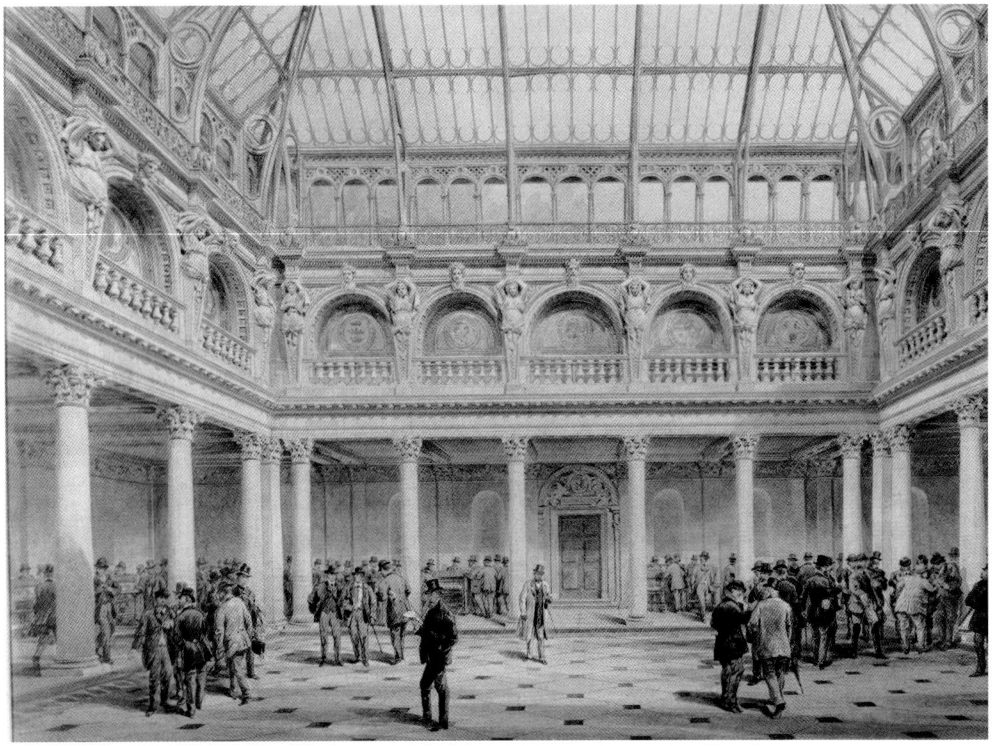

colonnaded central piazza of his Exchange, but the Bristol merchants disagreed.[38] Their 'wish to trade in the open – as they had in the Tolsey' prevailed.[39]

A contemporary report in *The Builder* noted that between:

> the arched windows, and over each column, are carved figures, or caryatides, well executed by Mr E. W. Wynn [sic], sculptor. From these figures start the arched principals of the roof, which is of wrought-iron and glass, and rises to a height of 66ft.[40]

Barry's work of 1872:

> gave the court of the Exchange itself a thumping upper storey with rows of overdressed caryatids whose job was to carry lumps of stone entablature from which incongruously sprang the principals of an iron-framed conservatory roof.[41]

Six caryatids separate the five arches on each side. Each arch has a keystone head. The 24 caryatids and 20 keystone heads are impressively various, but only 'earth', which is inscribed TERRA, and 'air', which is distinctly windswept, are immediately identifiable amongst the key stones. Originally the arches were set back about 60cm and filled with decorative panels. They are now windows to offices.

Edward Middleton Barry, the son of Sir Charles Barry – architect of the Houses of Parliament – had been invited to design large-scale alterations to include additional offices as well as the roof over the courtyard. His choice of Edward William Wyon (1811–85) as his sculptor could have been influenced by Wyon's statue of *Britomart* for the Egyptian Hall of London's Mansion House. That commission had provided Wyon, then in his mid-forties, with his first experience of monumental sculpture. There were serious delays, and Wyon was to write plaintively: 'All my life has been devoted to small works, and I have laboured with peculiar anxiety, looking to this statue as a means of earning a reputation for larger and nobler works'.[42]

Notes

[1] J. Wood, *A Description of the Exchange of Bristol* (Bath, 1745), reprinted in facsimile 1969; the 'List of Subscribers' shows Thomas Paty bought seven copies. [2] BRO 04223 f28 f36; BRO 04221 f10, f13, f30, f33, f40, f49, f51,f57; BRO 01125 f55. [3] Minutes of the Committee of Bristol Corporation, 1741, quoted by Ison, *Georgian Buildings of Bristol*, p.97. [4] D. Jones and A. Gomme, 'A Bristol street index of buildings of architectural or historic interest', BCRL, p.19. [5] Ison, *Georgian Buildings of Bristol*, pp.96, 98; Priest and Cobb, *The Paty Family*, p.123. [6] Op. cit., p.37. [7] Braikenridge College, Bristol Reference Library, newspaper cutting, March 1848, vol. XIV, p.329. [8] As note 1, p.22. [9] T. Cavanagh, *Public Sculpture of Liverpool* (Liverpool, 1997), p.74. [10] T. Mowl and B. Earnshaw, *John Wood, Architect of Obsession* (Bath, 1988), pp.163–4. [11] T. Mowl, *To Build the Second City; Architects and Craftsmen of Georgian Bristol* (Bristol, 1991), p.45. [12] Royal Academy Library 8516/51A f9-12. [13] Op. cit., f20. [14] Op. cit., f28; Paty's drawing of this pediment is accompanied by a letter to John Wood Jnr, dated May 1744–5, and stating that the drawing of the carving was 'as executed'. [15] Wood's illustration of this elevation is illustrated by Ison, *Georgian Buildings of Bristol*, p.104. [16] Op. cit., p.102. [17] Priest and Cobb, *The Paty Family*, p.37, refers to the background as a 'flourish of acanthus leaves'. [18] As note 1, p.25. [19] BRO 04221 pp.22, 33. [20] BRL B10124, 'Milton's Drawings and Engravings'. [21] As note 1, p.25. [22] Dea Pecunia was a Roman goddess of wealth. [23] Little, *The Public View*, p.26. [24] As note 12, f48. [25] Ibid. [26] Denning, *Eighteenth Century Architecture of Bristol*, p.93, photograph p.94. [27] As note 23. [28] BRO 04221 f10, f55. [29] As note 1, pp.25–7. [30] RA Library 8516/51A f29. [31] BRO 04221, 1/C30, f40, 88 and BRO 04223, f37; we are grateful to Katharine Eustace for drawing our attention to these records. [32] As note 1. [33] BRO 04221 f88, 6 May 1743. [34] BRO 04223 f53; here their much larger payments are for 'Corinthian architrave' and 'Sophites with Flowers'. [35] As note 1. [36] As note 1, pp.26, 27. [37] Jones and Gomme, 'Bristol street index'. [38] Ison, *Georgian Buildings of Bristol*, p.97. [39] Op. cit., p.98; the Tolsey was the lean-to structure traders had used in Corn Street for centuries. [40] *The Builder*, 24 August 1872, vol. XXX, no. 1542. [41] As note 37, p.336. [42] P. Ward Jackson, *Public Sculpture of the City of London* (Liverpool, 2003), p.252; letter from Wyon, 27 January 1860.

Old Council House, Corn Street, now the Registry Office

Justice C29

Sculptor: Edward Hodges Baily, RA
Architect: Sir Robert Smirke, RA

Date: 1827
Material: Portland stone
Dimensions: over life-size figure
Signed on base: E H BAILY RA
Status: Grade II*
Owner: Bristol City Council
Condition: poor

Robert Smirke's Greek Revival Council House was erected between 1824 and 1827. The Bristol historian John Latimer implies that E. H. Baily's statue was installed early in 1827. He records that it was soon the subject of ridicule at the corporation's expense.

The aldermanic body was not held in much esteem, and a joke, to the effect that the

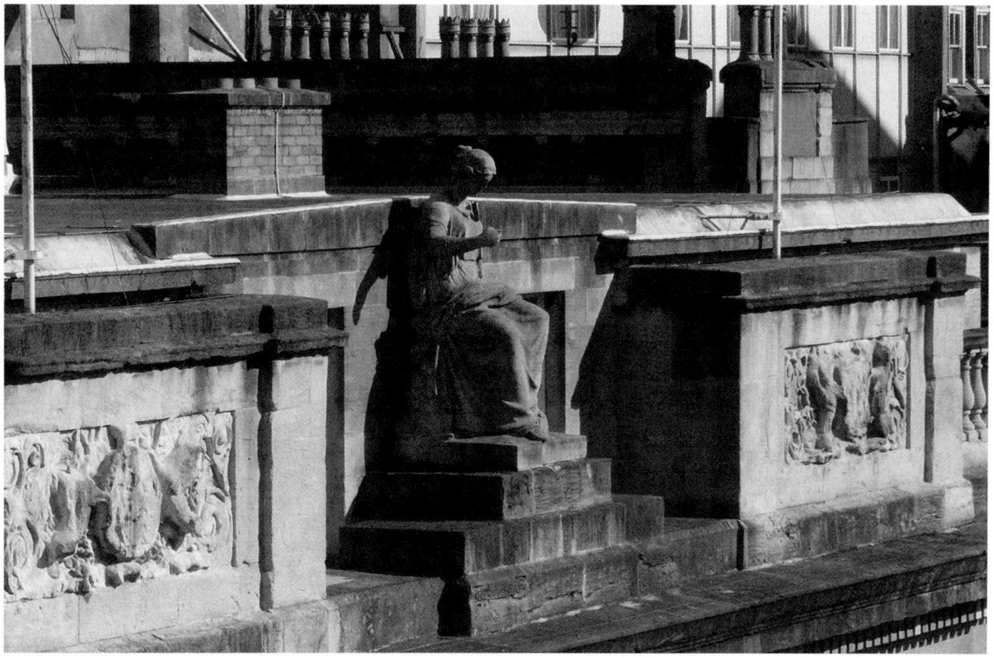

Edward Hodges Baily, *Justice*

statue was only too faithfully symbolic of the bench, inasmuch as it was armed with a sword but was destitute of a balance, had widespread success.[1]

Today, the sword is also missing.

The statue sits in the centre of the recessed bay at attic level between two panels carved with the arms of the City of Bristol and of King George IV. The panels are now hopelessly weathered, but photographs suggest that they were once of considerable quality, although quite out of sympathy with the crisp and deeply cut decorative details of the rest of the façade.[2] They are the work of the Bristol sculptor, Thomas Clark, who was paid £160. 6s. 4p. Baily received only £210, a modest figure compared to the £650 that the Bristol Institution had agreed to pay Baily for his statue of *Eve at the Fountain* in 1825.[3] That offer had been made in generous response to Baily's pleas of near penury following his gift of the frieze over the entrance to the Bristol Institution in Park Street.

Baily's statue of *Justice* does not command attention, because of its modest size and the dominance of the grand cornice below it. Comparison with other works by Smirke suggests that he would have designed the balustrade above the cornice to be similar to that on the Broad Street façade, with no central emphasis. Both the panels with the coats of arms and Baily's statue are likely to have been an afterthought, perhaps the result of the sculptor's initiative or that of his Bristol supporters. The council itself may have failed to appreciate the refined dignity of Smirke's design, and demanded more pomp. The absence of a blindfold and scales on Baily's statue could be the result of the recycling of the statue from a different and cancelled commission; or was it intended to represent Britannia, as the shield could imply?

Notes

[1] J. Latimer, *Annals of Bristol in the Nineteenth Century* (Bristol, 1887), p.109. [2] Ison, *The Georgian Buildings of Bristol*, pl. 21a; this photograph predates the regrettable heightening of the roof line and the insertion of windows to the attic floor in the mid-twentieth century. [3] Op. cit., p.138.

The façade of Lloyds TSB, 53 and 55 Corn Street, opposite the Exchange

Lloyds TSB, formerly West of England and South Wales District Bank C32

Sculptor: John Thomas

Architects: William Bruce Gingell and T. R. Lysaght

Date: 1854–7
Materials: Bath stone and Portland stone
Status: Grade II*
Owned by LloydsTSB
Condition: good; recently conserved

The decision to form the West of England and South Wales District Bank was taken at a meeting held in the Bush Inn, Corn Street, in October 1834. The bank was duly formed four months later, operating in John Wood's Exchange on the opposite side of the street until this extraordinary façade arose on the site of a demolished inn 23 years later.[1]

> The new bank was to be built in the surroundings of many other banks, and opposite the Exchange. The proposed building had not only to compete, but also to stand out as a symbol of the bank's integrity and character. In other words it had to be the best.[2]

Despite the profusion of sculptural decoration, every figure and object represents an aspect of banking or of the trade and industry of Bristol. Before the addition of an entrance bay on the ground floor in the 1920s, there were only five large keystones, each depicting a specific river god, on the ground floor.[3] From the left, the god of the Taff represented Cardiff, the Exe (Exeter), the Bristol Channel (Bristol), the Avon (Bath) and the Usk (Newport). Above each head is the relevant coats of arms. In the ground floor spandrels are semi-nude, muscular male figures 'emblematical of the chief products of the city, town, and country in which the company have establishments'. On the first floor, draped females proclaim 'Justice, Charity, Integrity, Education, Art and Science', with references to everything from music to motherhood. The upper frieze illustrates the history and process of banking as undertaken by baroque children in a variety of exotic headdresses. They are die-sinking coins, printing money, and book-keeping, and are as busy as the elves in Santa's workshop.

The whiter sculpture in the twenty spandrels and the upper frieze is carved from Portland stone. The remainder of the sculpture is in Bath stone from quarries at Hampton Down, Coombe Down and Box.[4]

The West of England and South Wales District Bank had been incorporated in 1834 with unlimited liability. When they decided to create their head office and the finest bank in Bristol, they set up a public competition and 'over 50 designs were submitted and unsuccessful contenders included E. M. Barry and John Gibson. Both these architects were rewarded with "premiums".'[5] The result was announced in May 1854 when 'the directors decided to carry out the design prepared jointly by Mr W. B. Gingell and Mr T. R. Lysaght, architects, of London.' The bank was completed in a little over two years.

The architects based their design on the Library of St Mark, a mid-sixteenth century Renaissance building designed by Venice's leading architect, Jacopo Sansovino. The architectural historian Tim Mowl recently praised the architects for giving the sculptor 'licence to carve even more richly and more robustly than his Venetian precursors'.[6] And with reference to Robert Smirke's next-door Council House and to the accompaniment of a rare exclamation mark, Professor Pevsner declared: 'How the architect must have enjoyed

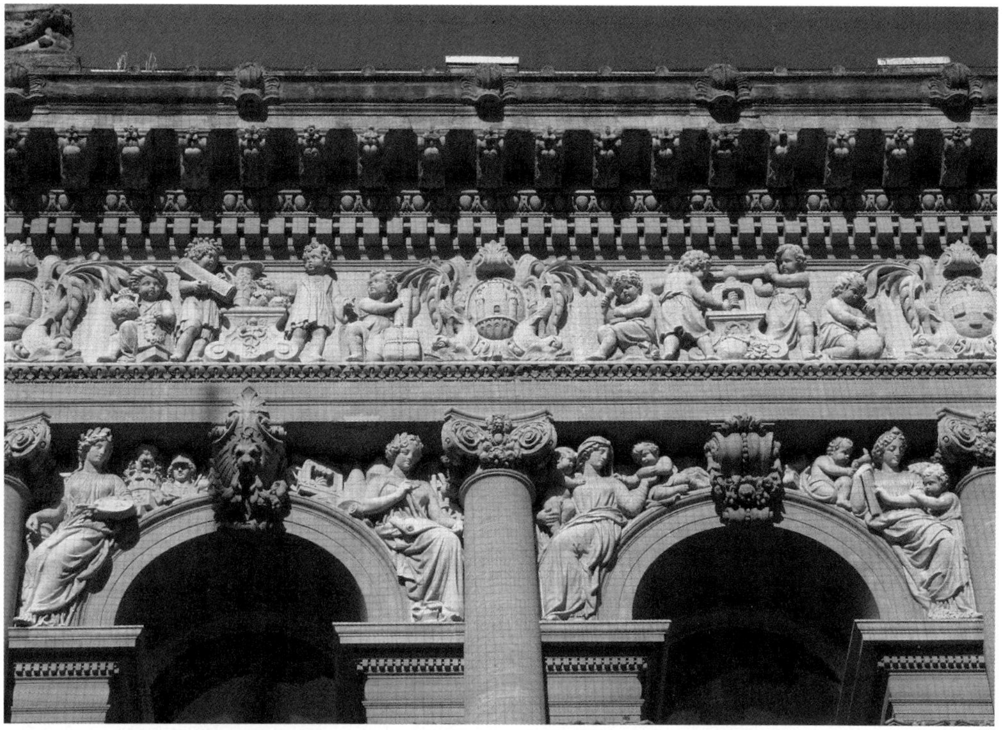

John Thomas, *Art and Science, Charity and Education, and Banking*

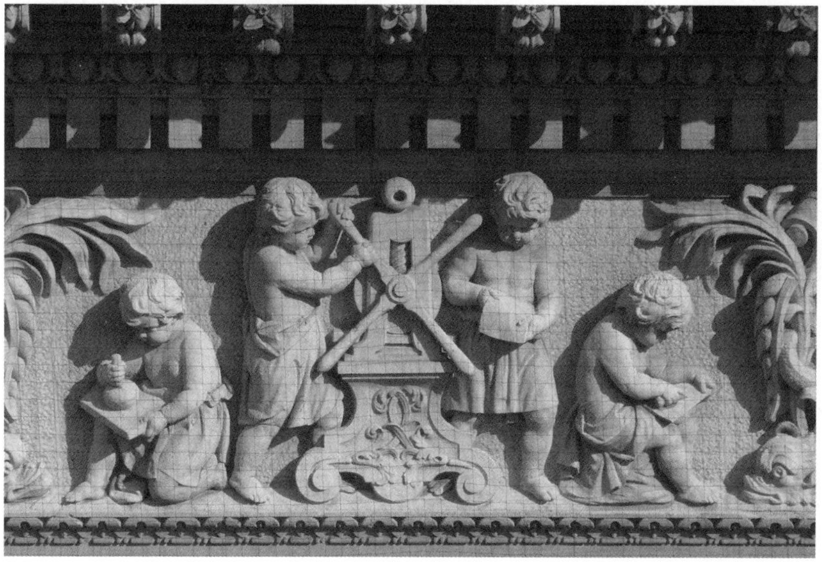

John Thomas,
Printing money

knocking out his Grecian neighbour!' with this 'unbelievably rich façade… in a glorious Venetian Cinquecento'.[7]

The Builder reported: 'The whole of the carved and sculptured work was executed by Mr. John Thomas'.[8] Thomas had been engaged by Charles Barry to superintend the stone carving of the new Houses of Parliament, much of which Thomas himself carved. He is also credited with the sculpture of an earlier and similarly 'opulent Venetian *palazzo*-style' building, the National Bank of Scotland (by the bank architect John Gibson) in Langside Avenue, Glasgow.[9] There, the keystones symbolised five great British rivers: the Clyde, the Thames, the Tweed, the Severn and the Humber. Other works by John Thomas in Bristol are on the Guildhall in Broad Street and the Royal West of England Academy in Queen's Road.

The sumptuous design of the West of England and South Wales District Bank 'was immediately interpreted as a sign of the real solidity of the funds'.[10] When it opened for business in February 1857, *The Builder* commented: 'if any architectural attraction could reconcile a man to any rate of discount, no customer should ever go away dissatisfied'.[11] But over-optimism led to disaster. After only twenty years the bank crashed 'with liabilities amounting to upwards of £3,000,000'. The directors were put on trial in 1880, but found not guilty.[12]

Notes

[1] Lloyds Bank, *Dark Horse*, March 1957, p.205. Lloyds Bank magazine; the celebrated Bush Inn appears in Dickens's *Pickwick Papers*. [2] Documents supplied by Natasha Cole-Jones, Lloyds Bank Group Archives, January 2002. [3] *The Builder*, 15 May 1858, p.337. [4] Ibid. [5] J. Booker, *Temples of Mammon: The Architecture of Banking* (Edinburgh, 1990), p.84. [6] Mowl, *Last Age of the Merchant Princes*, pl. 28. [7] Pevsner, *North Somerset*, p. 424. [8] As note 3. [9] R. Mackenzie, *Public Sculpture of Glasgow* (Liverpool, 2002), pp.273–4. [10] Gomme et al., *An Architectural History*, p.351. [11] Ibid, quoted from *The Builder*, vol. XIX, p.629. [12] Nicholls and Taylor, *Bristol Past and Present*, p.354.

Commercial Rooms, Corn Street

A coffee room already existed in Corn Street inside John Wood's Exchange, but in 1808, 'perhaps because of an optimistic mood brought on by the impending completion of the Floating Harbour, plans were made for something more ambitious'.[1] Furthermore, as Walter Ison has argued, the Exchange had never really found favour with Bristol's merchants, who carried on their transactions elsewhere.[2] A 'purpose-built edifice, of club-like character, a gathering place for Bristol businessmen' was to be welcomed.[3]

The result was to be 'a charming Græco-Roman' building.[4] In 1809, the committee had advertised for designs. Eight submissions were considered, and Charles Augustus Busby (1788–1834) was selected. He was a London architect, aged only 21, and an admirer of Sir John Soane.[5] It was his first important commission.[6]

Busby invited James George Bubb (1782–1853), a fellow student from the Royal Academy Schools, to design and make the 'three figures that grace the Corn Street front'.[7] Bubb also designed the large bas-relief for the portico, and the twelve Coade Stone caryatids for the lantern.[8]

The inscription on the foundation plate, now lost, recorded:

> The Bristol Commercial Coffee Rooms. This building was erected by the subscriptions of the most eminent merchants and inhabitants of the city of Bristol, and the foundation stone was laid on 19th day of March, 1810, in the fiftieth year of the reign of our beloved sovereign, King George the Third, by the hands of George Dyer, esq., Chairman and Treasurer, in the presence of the Right Worshipful John Hilhouse Wilcox esq., Mayor; Mr W. L. Clarke, Secretary; C. A. Busby, Architect, London.[9]

A long poem by Dr Busby (perhaps the architect's father, a musician and writer) praising Bristol, and her enterprise was recited at the foundation stone ceremony.

The rooms opened in October 1811, at a cost of a little over £20,000, and were considered a rival to Lloyd's Coffee House in London.[10] The first president was John Loudon McAdam, later the administrator and builder of roads in Bristol and, later still, throughout England.[11]

When the first telegraph line from London was installed, the Bristol office was set up in the Commercial Rooms in 1852. It continued to function as a private club until 1994, when there were only 100 members. After an emergency meeting, the building was sold to a London developer who has spent approximately £1 million refurbishing it as a public house and restaurant.[12]

Three stone statues on the parapet of the former Commercial Rooms

Commerce, the City of Bristol and Navigation C34

Sculptor: James George Bubb

Architect: Charles Augustus Busby

Date: 1811
Material: limestone
Dimensions: approximately one-and-a-quarter life-size
Status: Grade II*
Owned by Cedar House Investments Limited, Nottingham
Condition: poor

An early engraving depicts the three statues

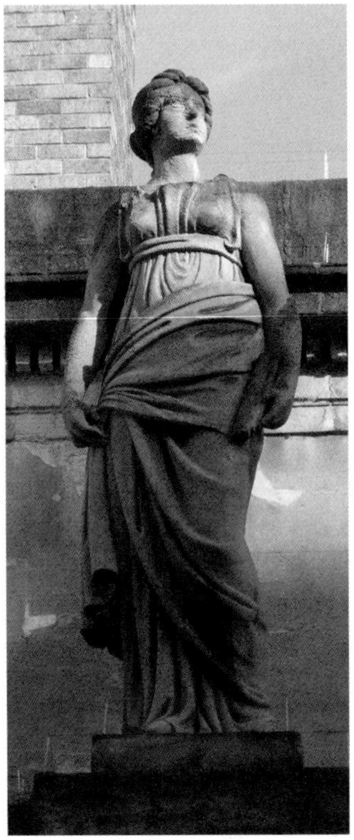

James George Bubb, *Commerce*

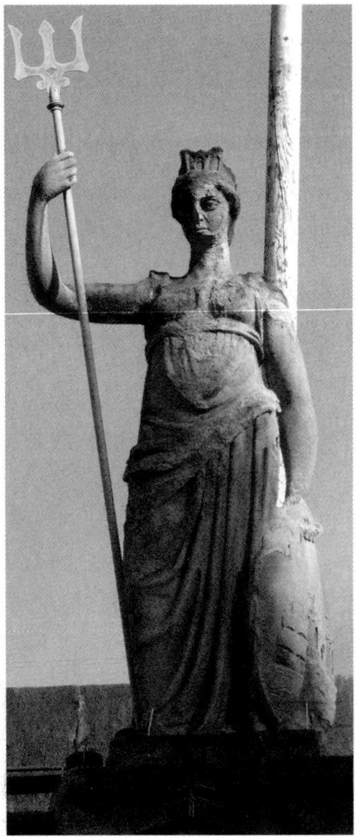

James George Bubb, *City of Bristol*

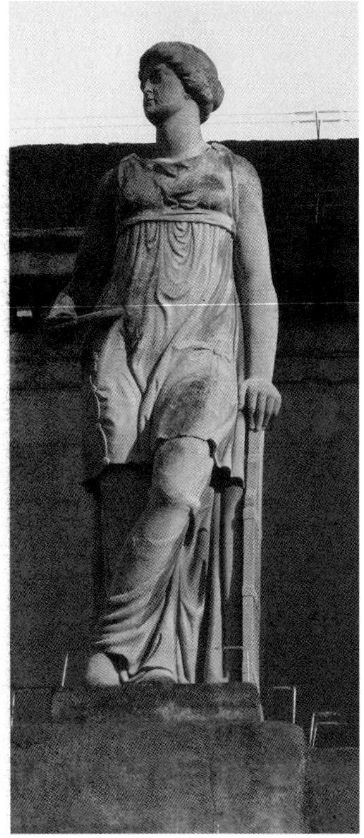

James George Bubb, *Navigation*

with the caption: 'Commercial Coffee Rooms. Statues *now* executing in Stone by Mr J. G. Bubb. Sculptor. London.' The engraving is inscribed: 'C. A. Busby, Arch^{t}. London'.[13] This image identifies the three figures as Commerce, the City of Bristol and Navigation, and it shows the attributes that they were first intended to display. It also confirms the order in which they are placed.

The central figure, the City of Bristol, is crowned, and in her raised right hand she now holds a bronze trident, although the original engraving showed a spear. Her stone shield bears the ship and castle from of the city's coat of arms. Her right arm has been replaced and there is serious crumbling in progress. To her right, Commerce grasps a small scroll in her left hand. In the engraving she is shown holding a caduceus, the winged staff entwined with two serpents usually carried by Hermes, messenger of the gods. To her left, Navigation leans on a ship's rudder.[14] A small disc in her right hand may represent the sun and its importance in navigation.

A bas-relief inside the portico of the former Commercial Rooms

Britannia, Attended by Neptune and Minerva C34

Sculptor: James George Bubb

Date: 1810
Material: painted stone
Dimensions: 550cm long; 90cm deep
Status: Grade II*
Owned by Cedar House Investments, Nottingham
Condition: good

The full title of this relief appears on a contemporary engraving: 'Subject – Britannia, attended by Neptune & Minerva receiving tributes from the four Quarters of the World.' The print also bears the words: 'Commercial Coffee Rooms, Bristol. Basso-relievo now

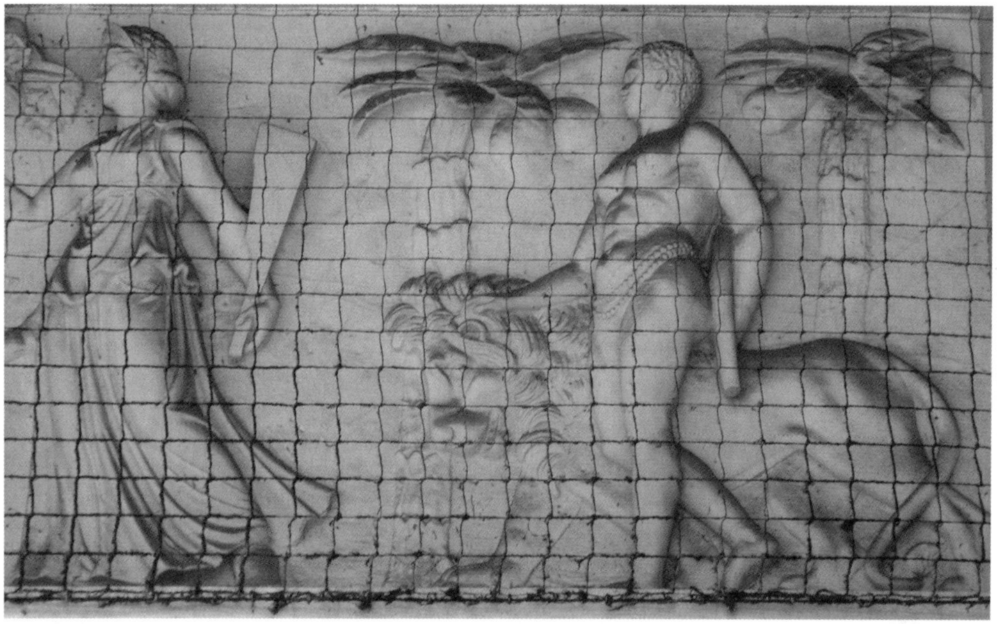

James George Bubb, *Portico relief* (detail of *Africa*)

executing in Stone by Mr J. G. Bubb. Sculptor. London.'[15]

The deeply modelled panel is high above the doorways and beneath the deep portico. This has protected the work, but it has also made it difficult to see and still harder to photograph. A large lamp masks the central figure, and the relief is now covered with many layers of paint and heavy protective netting.

The composition is symmetrical. In the centre, Britannia is seated in a huge scalloped shell resting her right hand on a shield. The trident she originally held in her left hand is missing. A naked Neptune stands to the left of Britannia, with his own right foot encircled by the fishtail of one of the two web-footed seahorses that accompany him. A winged cupid flies by, close to the horses' heads. At the far left a llama, beside a palm tree, follows a near-naked woman who personifies the Americas. She wears a feathered headdress. The bow, which she may have held in her right hand, has been lost. On her back is a quiver. The bunch of leaves in her left hand may be tobacco. Next, a camel follows Asia, who wears a flowing costume and carries a vase. She is led towards the central group by two winged cherubs. To the right of Britannia, a helmeted Minerva holds a shield. Her short spear is missing. Two more horses rise from the sea and a cherub flies near

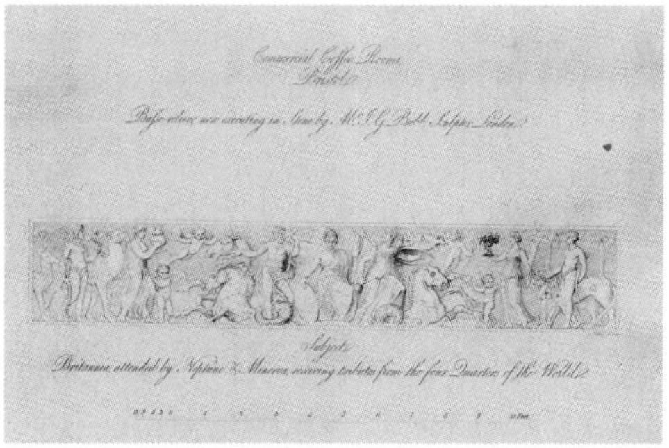

Engraving of proposed portico relief by J. G. Bubb, 'Britannia, attended by Neptune and Minerva receiving tributes from the four Quarters of the World'

them. Another female figure, representing Europe, is escorted by a standing cherub. She offers a basket of fruit and holds a rudder, symbols of abundance and prosperity. Finally, a near-naked Africa walks in front of palm trees. She has an elephant tusk under her left arm and a lion to her side.

Supporting the lantern dome of the Great Room of the former Commercial Rooms

Twelve Caryatids C34

Sculptor: James George Bubb

Date: 1810
Material: Coade Stone
Dimensions: approx. 3 metres high
Status: Grade II*
Owned by Cedar House Investments, Nottingham
Condition: good

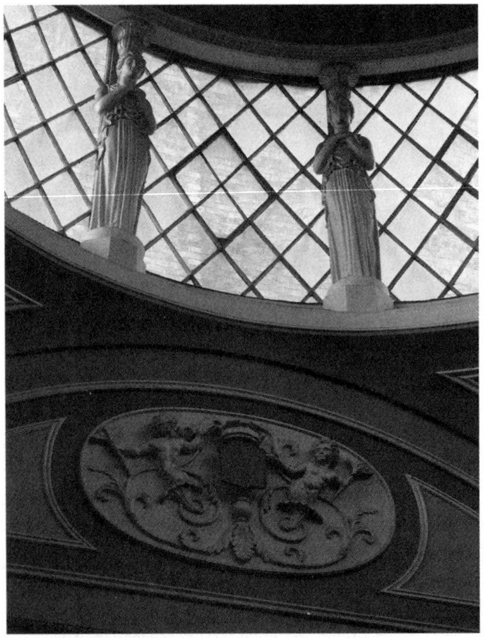

James George Bubb (attributed to), ***Caryatids in the Grand Room***

The historian of the Coade Stone factory, Alison Kelly, states that J. G. Bubb 'paid £378 for the caryatids, £1388 for all the statuary' on the Commercial Rooms.[16] As the cost of the four Coade Stone figures once on Sir John Soane's Lothbury Arch was over £500, it is likely that £1388 represents the cost of just the twelve caryatids.[17] They were necessarily made in a lighter material than stone, which would have been too heavy for the pendentive dome. Both the dome and the caryatids were probably derived from the Soane's Consuls Transfer Office at the Bank of England.[18]

Notes
[1] B. Little, 'Restoring a Grecian masterpiece', *Country Life*, 23 September 1976, p.831. [2] Ison, *The Georgian Buildings of Bristol*, p.134. [3] As note 1. [4] As note 2. [5] Ibid. [6] N.R. Bingham, *C.A. Busby – the Regency Architect of Brighton and Hove* (London, 1991), p.32. [7] As note 6. [8] As note 1. [9] J. Latimer, *Annals of Bristol in the Nineteenth Century* (Bristol, 1887), p.32; the inscription was, until 1994, preserved in a massive frame in the conference room. [10] As note 1; Ison and Latimer, see notes 2 and 9, say £17,000 and that the opening was in September. [11] *ODNB, Brenda J. Buchanon*; M. Fells, 'Rooms at the heart of Bristol business', *Evening Post*, 6 April 2004, p.40. [12] Ibid. [13] Braikenridge Collection, Bristol Central Library; illus. Merritt, *Sculpture in Bristol*, p.71. [14] The rudder is an emblem of Tyche, who presided over a city's prosperity. [15] Braikenridge Collection, Bristol Reference Library. [16] A. Kelly, *Mrs Coade's Stone* (Upton-upon-Severn, 1990), p.372. [17] P. Ward-Jackson, *Public Sculpture of the City of London* (Liverpool, 2003), p.24. [18] Pevsner, *North Somerset*, p.424.

42 Corn Street, built for the London and Lancashire Insurance Company

Figures on the Pediment and Other Decorative Carving C33

Sculptor: attributed to Gilbert Seale
Architect: Edward Gabriel

Date: 1904
Material: limestone
Dimensions: approximately one-and-a-half times life-size
Status: Grade II
Owned by Galliard Developments
Condition: fair

The façade is a late work, completed in 1904, by the Bristol architect Edward Gabriel for the

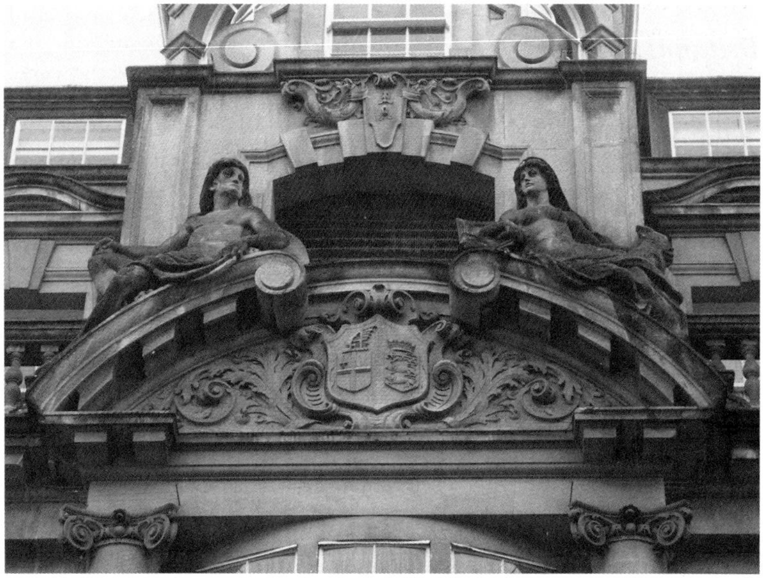

Gilbert Seale, ***Pediment figures and decorative carving***

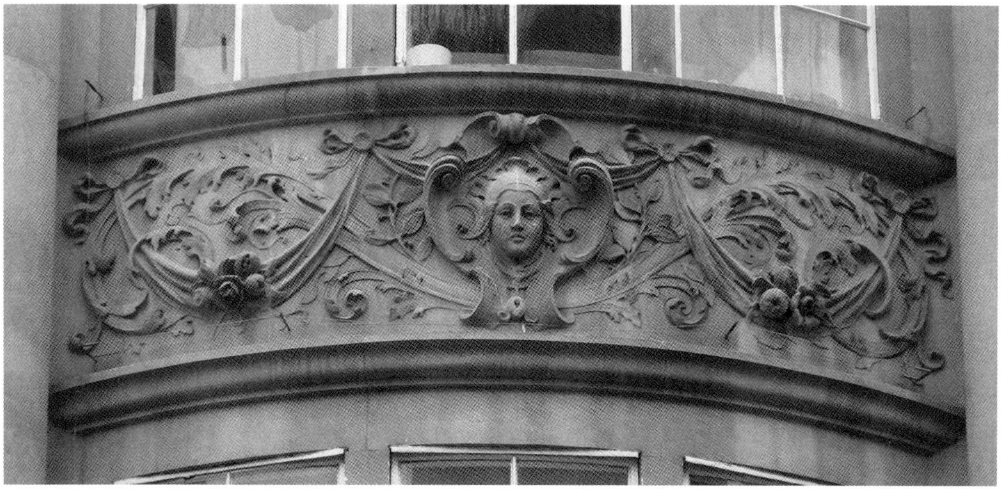

Gilbert Seale, ***Decorative carving***

London and Lancashire Insurance Company.[1] The building replaced the company's earlier offices on the same site built in 1864 to the designs of Gabriel's father, S. B. Gabriel.[2] The premises are presently used as apartments, with an Italian restaurant on the ground floor.

It is likely that all the sculpture and decorative detail of the façade is by the London sculptor and decorative carver and plasterer, Gilbert Seale.[3]

The two figures surmount the sides of a broken pediment on a complex façade that Andor Gomme described as 'exuberant Arts-and-Crafts baroque'. [4] On the left is a bearded nude male. He holds drapery across his loins with his left hand. His female companion is also naked but her legs are fully draped and a scarf trails from her heavily braided hair. In her right hand is a key and her left arm supports a large pitcher. The symbolism is uncertain.

The lively floral garlands and cartouches in the three reliefs between the first and second floors, and the flourishes of acanthus leaves surrounding the coats of arms within the central pediment, may better represent the sculptor (Gilbert Seale) than these two rather ponderous, even incongruous, figures. It is possible that the company's directors succumbed to the pressure of Corn Street's earlier and still grander banks and insurance companies, and demanded the addition of these figures.

Notes
[1] Gomme et al., *An Architectural History*, p.434. [2] Ibid, p.435. [3] A. Stuart Gray, *Edwardian Architecture, A Biographical Dictionary* (London, 1985). [4] Gomme, 'Bristol street index', p.19, BRL.

On the façade of 37–39 Corn Street

Peace and Plenty, Benevolence and Prudence C35

Sculptor: Hermon Cawthra

Architects: A. W. Roques FRIBA; façade by Sir Giles Gilbert Scott RA, PRIBA
Date: c.1932
General contractors: Messrs. W. Cowlin
Materials: two Portland stone relief carvings
Dimensions: approx. 170cm high
Status: Grade II
Condition: fair

This 'lean art deco interpretation of neo-classicism',[1] so brilliantly enlivened by sculpture and by excellent cast-metal detailing in the windows, doors and grilles, was opened in 1933. This was also the year when the façade's designer, Giles Gilbert Scott, was president of the Royal Institute of British Architects and when his work on Battersea Power Station was nearing completion.[2] 37–39 Corn Street may seem comparatively restrained among so many impressive façades in this street, but it has a particular vitality and sophistication, and even an optimism arguably at odds with the period of economic depression in which it was conceived.

The figure of Peace and Plenty is on the pilaster to the left of the central window on the first floor. She gazes at a pair of doves on her shoulder and steadies her right hand on a large cornucopia, spilling the contents at her feet. Benevolence and Prudence is to the right. She holds an olive branch and, with her head bent,

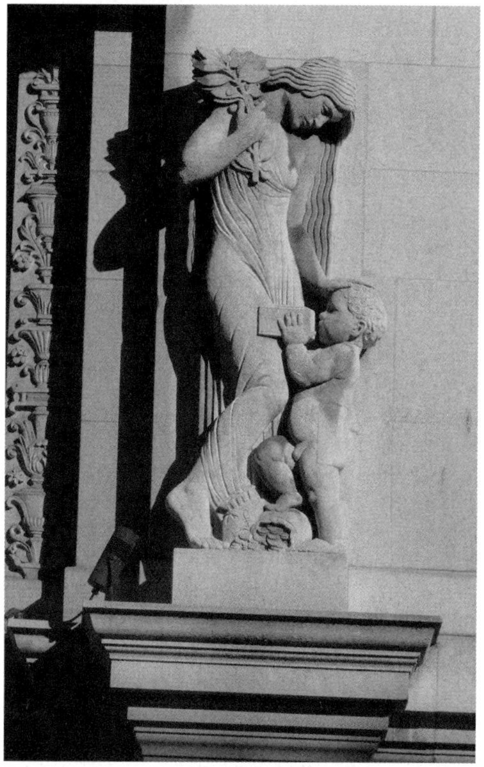

Hermon Cawthra, ***Peace and Plenty***

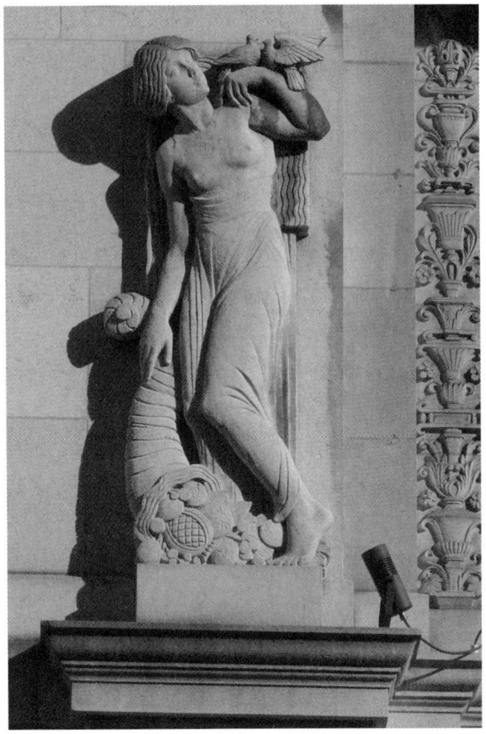

Hermon Caethra, *Benevolence and Prudence*

she places her hand lovingly on the head of a naked putto. Standing on a bag of coins, he proffers what seems to be a moneybox. Both figures appear as if gently draped in fine diaphanous cloth. The building is of steel construction and it is faced with Portland stone. The two deep-relief sculptures by Hermon Cawthra (1886–1971) are carved from similar stone.[3]

Two dilapidated Georgian buildings were demolished for this project, one of the very last major changes to Corn Street. The new building was the Friends Provident and Century Life Office.

In recent years, the ground floor has been a restaurant and successive occupants, following the conversion of so many banks to beer palaces, have had to join the battle for custom that now bedevils Corn Street. In August 2008 three large glazed menu-holders, two illuminated hanging signs and six large 'to let' signs, brutally and illegally screwed to the façade, illustrate the failure of planning legislation and controls, as well as the sad decline of this distinguished street.

Also on the façade of 37–39 Corn Street

Wisdom C35

Sculptors: A. Crompton-Roberts and R. Pryce Roberts

Date: c.1932
Materials: Birmabright casting
Dimensions: approx. 260cm wide; 70cm deep
Status: Grade II
Condition: fair

Above the main door is a shiny cast-metal grille with a chorus-line of six naked art deco maidens. They are dancing before the central female figure, representing Wisdom. They each step in an identical pose, with their arms splayed, supporting circular discs on which are various symbols. The robed Wisdom holds an owl in her right hand and a mirror in her left.

The design of the grille was drawn in detail on the elevation issued by Giles Gilbert Scott in July 1931.[4] *The Builder* gives us the name of the designer and maker of this impressive period piece. It is a Birmabright casting 'designed by Messrs A. Crompton-Roberts and R. Pryse Roberts (of the Forge Ltd)'.[5] Andrew Foyle calls the material of the metal work 'white anodium metal'.[6]

Notes

[1] Foyle and Cherry, *Bristol*, p.137. [2] BRO has the plans by the architect A.W. Roques, and the façade elevation design by Giles Gilbert Scott, vol. III, f.27–8; the plans were approved on July 30 1931. Giles Gilbert Scott is also well known for Liverpool's Anglican Cathedral, the red telephone kiosk designs and Bankside Power Station, now Tate Modern. [3] The sculptor and the designer of the metalwork are named in *The Builder*, vol. 149, 25 October 1933, pp.721,734, and in *The Architects' Journal*, 1 June 1933. [4] As note 2. [5] As note 3. [6] As note 1.

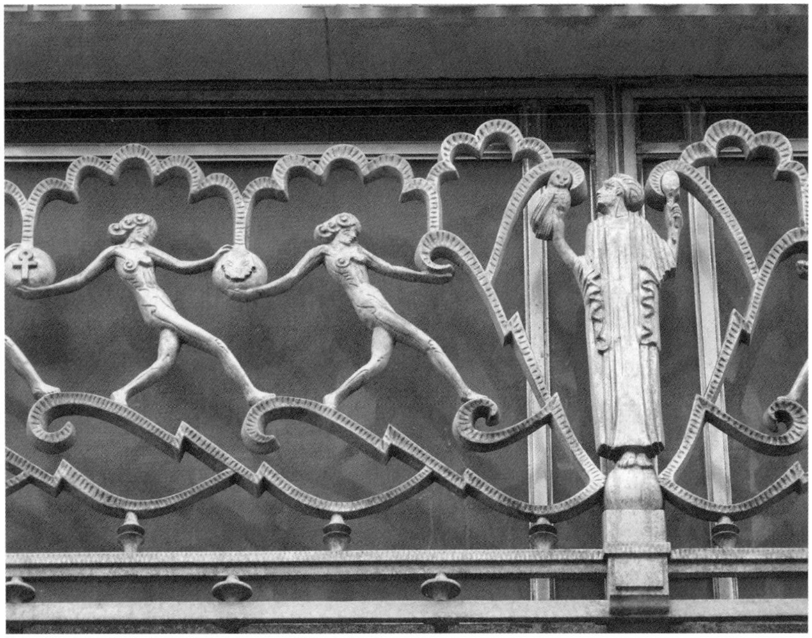

A. Crompton-Roberts and R. Pryce Roberts, *Wisdom* (detail)

Façade of 36 Corn Street, built for Liverpool, London and Globe Insurance

Caryatids and Keystones C36

Sculptor: carved by Thomas Colley; design attributed to William Bruce Gingell

Architect: William Bruce Gingell

Date: 1864–7
Material: limestone
Dimensions: over life-size figures
Status: Grade II
Owner: The Royal Bank of Scotland Group
Condition: good

36 Corn Street was built for Liverpool, London and Globe Insurance. Only the façade of the original building now remains. English Heritage has recorded this façade as being in a 'baroque revival style',[1] which Andor Gomme describes more robustly as 'full-blooded baroque'.[2] In fact, it has a rigid, even stiff, vertical emphasis, offset by projecting cornices of almost vicious angularity, but the overall richness of effect is exceptional. As Andrew Foyle writes: 'the joy is in Thomas Colley's sculptured details'.[3]

Today, a major part of the original sculpture is missing, although so much remains that the loss goes unnoticed. All the figures in the pediment were probably removed when the interior was rebuilt in 1977. *The Builder* described the contents of the pediment in 1870:

> A figure of Minerva occupies the central position, and with outstretched arms is directing her attendants to dispense gladness and aid to the widows and orphans, the aged and the unfortunate, who, by some prudential steps, have been brought under her protection.[4]

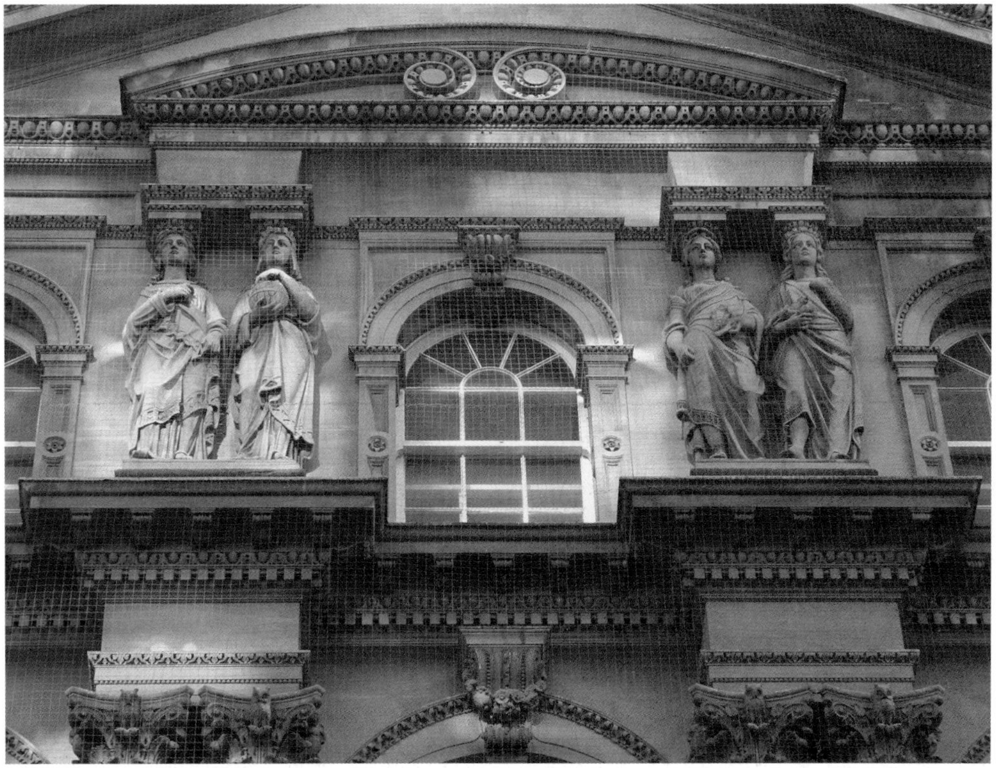

Thomas Colley, *Fire, Air, Water and Earth*

Below the now empty pediment are the giant caryatids of the fourth storey, well above the cornices of the two neighbouring buildings. *The Builder* described these as:

> eight sculptured female figures, arranged in pairs to correspond with the coupled columns below, and representing the elements and the seasons – the four central ones being Fire, Air, Earth, and Water; and the others, Spring, Summer, Autumn and Winter. Each figure is nearly 8ft. high [2.4m], and has suitable emblems and decorations.[5]

These are impossible to identify from below in 'the too-narrow street'.[6] On the capitals on the ground floor 'the fabulous bird known as the "liver", which is the crest in the arms of Liverpool… has been introduced in a central position among the foliage'.[7]

There are five fine keystones, all male heads, in the ground floor arches. The central keystone head, 'symbolising Time',[8] has a long wild beard and above his flowing hair are two bat's wings. His head appears to be crowned, but closer examination reveals an hourglass, a sickle and a serpent. The two outer keystones over the entrances have the appearance of ancient river gods. They have ships' prows on their heads, one representing the Mersey, the other the Thames. The remaining two keystones are firemen, 'classically treated'[9] but reminiscent of helmeted Prussian soldiers. They have axes behind their headgear and both are excellent portraits, alert and individual.

The two oval plaques of white marble at ground floor level, inscribed 'Old Bank', came from Bristol's earliest bank, founded in 1750

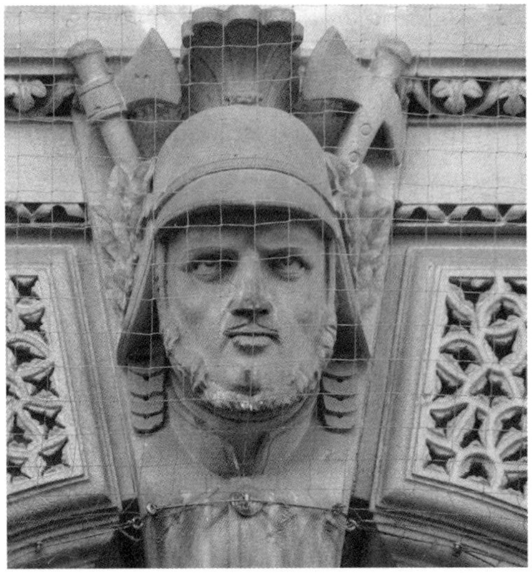

Thomas Colley, ***Fireman***

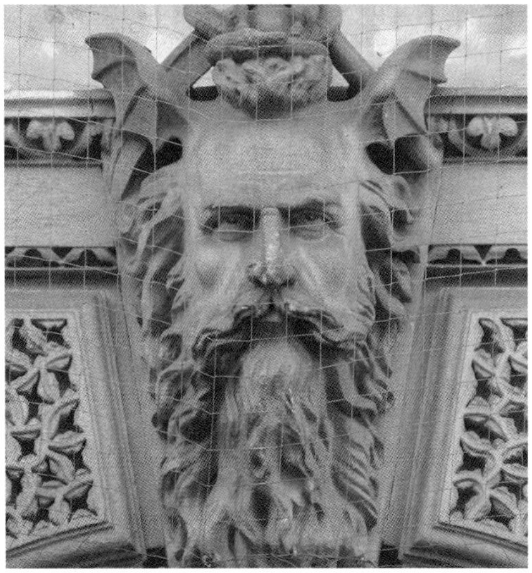

Thomas Colley, ***Time***

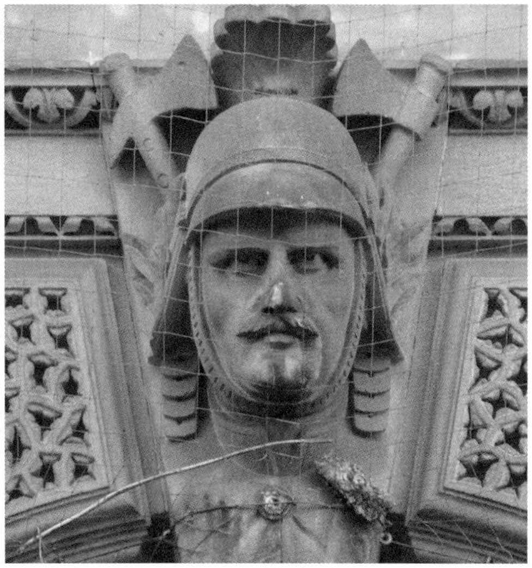

Thomas Colley, ***Fireman***

and formerly at No. 35, on the opposite side of the street.[10]

In the mid-1850s, the same architect had presented another sculptor, John Thomas, with a similarly generous commission for Corn Street's most sumptuous bank façade, opposite the Exchange. However, at 36 Corn Street the sculpture is more strictly architectural: keystones, capitals and caryatids. 36 Corn Street is more disciplined than the earlier work, but no less striking. The *Bristol Almanac and Companion* of 1871 described it as 'one of the most remarkable examples of exuberant ornament in provincial street architecture',[11] and John Latimer, writing in the 1880s, thought that the façade 'surpassed all others in the city as regards the richness of its front'.[12]

Andor Gomme has written that 'all the sculpture and carving was designed by Gingell and executed by T. Colley'.[13] This is presumably based on the wording of the two accounts in *The Builder* of 1867 and 1870, in which Mr T. Colley, the sculptor, is first described as being responsible for the 'execution' of the sculpture, and secondly as having 'executed' it.[14] In this later review, Colley is described as of 'Stoke's-croft, Bristol, late of London'. He had earlier worked for the same architect on the National Provincial Bank at 33 Corn Street in 1864,[15] when he was referred to as 'Mr T. Colley, of London'.[16] The earliest Bristol directory to confirm his move from London to Bristol is that of 1870.[17]

The cost of the external carving and sculpture and of the rich internal plaster decoration, all by Thomas Colley, was £1,780 against a total building cost, not including the purchase of the site or the architect's commission of almost £11,000.[18]

Notes

[1] English Heritage, Listed Buildings of Bristol, 901-1/16/563, p.472. [2] Gomme, 'Bristol street index', p.352. [3] Foyle and Cherry, *Bristol*, p.136. [4] *The Builder*, 4 June 1870, p.445. [5] Ibid. [6] *The Builder*, 19 October 1867, p.757. [7] As note 4. [8] Ibid. [9] Ibid. [10] As note 2. [11] *Bristol Almanac and Companion*, 1871, p.37. [12] J. Latimer, *Annals of Bristol in the Nineteenth Century* (Bristol, 1887), p.421, quoted by Gomme, 'Bristol street index', p.352, fn8. [13] Gomme, 'Bristol street index', p.352. [14] As notes 6 and 4. [15] The original façade has been replaced. [16] *The Builder*, 6 August 1864, p.585. [17] *Matthew's Directory*, 1870: 'Thomas Colley, sculptor etc. 10 Stoke's-croft' [Stokes Croft]. [18] As note 4.

32 Corn Street, NatWest Bank, on a wall inside the banking hall

The Queen and the Washerwomen

C49

Sculptor: Walter Ritchie

Date: 1980
Materials: intaglio carving in brown-veined Napoleon marble
Dimensions: approx. 480cm high; 390cm wide
Inscription on an anodised aluminium plaque:
Tradition has it that when Queen Elizabeth I rode / down Corn Street in August 1574, she was in an ill/ humour because her fine ruffs had suffered on the / journey over the bad roads. The mayor gave the / ruffs to the loyal wives of Bristol who laundered / them with such skill that they were returned to the / Queen next day in an immaculate condition. / Her Majesty was delighted and asked what favour / she could bestow. They replied that it was their / custom to wash their linen in the pure water of / Jacobs Well and hang it to dry on the southern slopes of

/ Brandon Hill but of late Her Majesty's Ranger had / encouraged his dogs to pull down their washing. / The Queen graciously decreed that the wives of / Bristol should henceforth enjoy the right to hang out / their washing on Brandon Hill without hindrance / and this right exists to this day. / This scene was carved by Walter Ritchie in / Napoleon marble for the opening of Bristol City / Office in 1980. The unusual and exacting concave / technique is known as Intaglio and white / colour is produced naturally by the chisel crushing / the marble.

Status: not listed
Owned by the Royal Bank of Scotland Group
Condition: good

In 1980, the National Provincial Bank, the Westminster Bank and the District Bank merged to form the NatWest Bank, and the opportunity arose to commission a sculpture for the refurbished banking hall.

Hugh Duckett, the bank's regional architect, suggested that the sculptor should interpret some incident from Bristol's history, and he offered a number of options. From these, Walter Ritchie chose the story of Queen Elizabeth and the washerwomen, which is well summarised on the inscribed plaque, transcribed above.

The large surface of the relief is made up of eight rectangles of highly polished marble. The images are shallowly tooled to form light matt areas against the dark polished surface of the grey marble.

> Ritchie gives the story a lyrical, fairy-tale atmosphere: beautiful young women proffer the laundered goffered frills to the Queen; Leicester is there, and the Mayor, too; savage hounds are seen tearing the washing; and the lines of washing become the brave flags of the vindicated women of Bristol.[1]

The author of those words optimistically claims that the relief gives 'the historically true anecdote of the "Queen and the Washerwomen of Brandon Hill"', and states that Queen Elizabeth I was responsible for a local by-law permitting Brandon Hill to be used for the drying of clothes.[2] This story of royal privilege is said to be confirmed by James Millerd's map of 1673. However, the precise words on Millerd's map are less specific: 'This Hill is a publick convenienc to ye Cittie for ye use drying Cloaths'.[3] Bristol Corporation did not acquire Brandon Hill until 1625, half a century after the Queen Elizabeth's visit. Under the terms of the purchase, the corporation agreed to permit 'the drying of clothes by townsmen and townswomen as had anciently been accustomed'.[4]

Whatever the facts, the legend is as pleasing as the relief and the members of the Antient Society of St Stephen's Ringers will continue, once a year, to sing this verse of the ballad *The Golden Days of Good Queen Bess* at their annual dinner:

> Bristol maids, aye, and widows, too, by royal decree, sir,
> From that time made their spouses of this ancient city free, sir;
> With privilege beside, which they all inherit still, sir,
> Of hanging out their smikets white to dry on Brandon Hill, sir.[5]

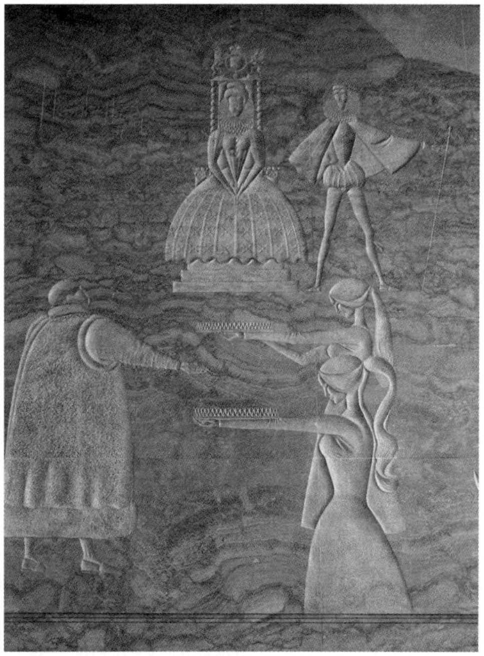

Walter Ritchie, *The Queen and the Washerwomen* (detail)

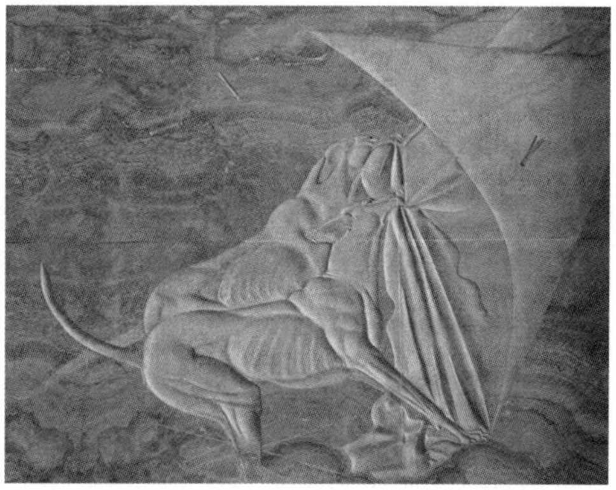

Walter Ritchie, *The Queen and the Washerwomen* (detail)

Notes

[1] Sue Roseveare, 'Sculpture in the high street', Whitsun, 1983, p.32. [2] Op. cit., p.33. [3] Four lines of Latin appear on Millerd's plan, under the heading 'Brandon Hill'. Translated, they read: 'Like sun upon snow I rise, a bright beholder. As night falls the hill is wont to come alive'; translated by Professor Alan Ryder. [4] Nicholls and Taylor, *Bristol Past and Present*, vol. I, p.284. [5] *Arrowsmith's Dictionary of Bristol*, pp.391–2; the ballad was composed in 1788 by J. Collins.

Counterslip C70

Outside the Avon Fire Brigade headquarters, at the corner of Counterslip and Temple Back

Fireman

Sculptor: Stephen Joyce

Date: 2003
Material: bronze
Foundry: Fine Fettle art foundry, Frome
Dimensions: 190cm high
Signed on back of lower left leg: steve joyce '03
Inscription: on plaque on the plinth – GREATER LOVE HATH / NO MAN THAN THIS, / THAT HE LAY DOWN HIS LIFE / FOR HIS FRIENDS
—: inscribed on plaque on the building – The statue in this vicinity / was officially unveiled / by the / Chair of the Fire Authority, / Councillor Terry Walker / on 23rd May 2003 / Chief Fire Officer Kevin Pearson / MA MCGI MIFireE /
Status: not listed
Owners: Avon Fire Brigade
Condition: good

A fireman gazes upwards, shading his eyes from the heat or brightness of a fire. He holds his helmet in readiness for immediate action and is depicted assessing the narrow boundary between safety and danger, risk and sacrifice.[1] He is deliberately placed at the very edge, the forward edge, of the plinth.

Substantial improvements to the headquarters of the Avon Fire Brigade led to this commission. There was a desire to provide a more prominent focus for the wreaths laid annually on Remembrance Day, and to bring greater emphasis to the modest corner entrance of the building.

The commission was the particular initiative of the chief fire officer, Kevin Pearson. Following an enquiry to the Royal West of England Academy, Steve Joyce was approached as a result of his statue of Cabot on Narrow Quay. At his suggestion, he first made several

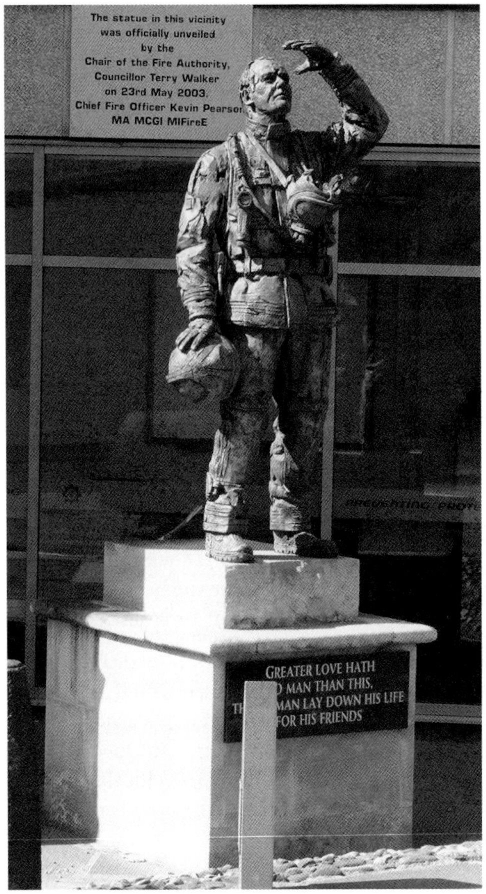

Stephen Joyce, *Fireman*

drawings with alternative proposals from which the preferred choice was made. A maquette was subsequently prepared. The sculptor's request for a model in 'combat gear' was met, and Dave Pole 'sat' for four hours a day for several weeks. As this officer was a little below the average height of the brigade, Joyce was discreetly asked to increase his stature.

Private individuals and organisations within the service, and many suppliers of goods and equipment to the fire services, contributed to the Memorial Fund set up to support the project.[2] Joyce found that he was under considerable pressure to be accurate in the detail, and the statue is consequently an impressive record of the clothes and equipment of a British fireman at the start of the third millennium.

Notes
[1] Conversation with the artist, 17 August 2008, from which this entry is largely drawn. [2] A list of donors is displayed in the entrance area.

Denmark Street

Denmark Street façade of Chantry Court, formerly Gaunt's House

Ten Reliefs B52

Sculptor: attributed to Esmond Burton[1]

Architects: Alec F. French & Partners
Date: 1950–2
Material: Bath stone
Dimensions: each approx. 180cm high, 150cm wide
Status: not listed
Owned by Unite Group
Condition: good

Ten substantial reliefs enliven the façade of this nine-storey office block rising above a narrow medieval street. These excellent panels go almost entirely unnoticed, and understandably so. The architect seems to have worked as if the tall auditorium of the Bristol Hippodrome, which the building overlooks, did not exist. As if to confirm this, the artist's watercolour of 1950 of Alec F. French's proposed design omits the theatre altogether.[2]

Gaunt's House was built for Pearl Assurance. In 2001 it became Chantry Court, after being converted by Unite from offices to affordable housing for students and key workers.[3]

The fascinating history of the site on which this building stands is graphically told by eight of the ten panels, all of which are impressively

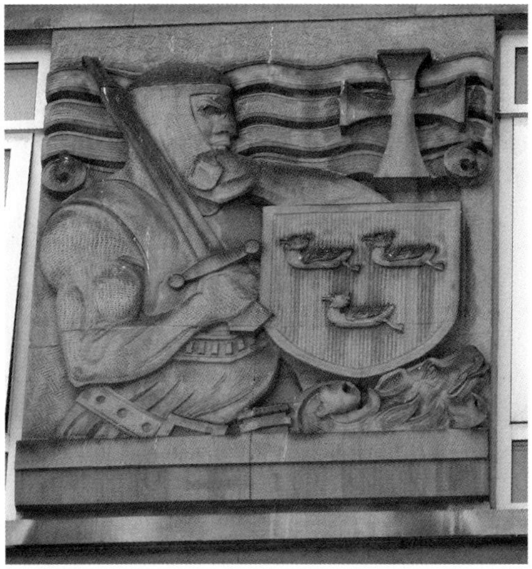

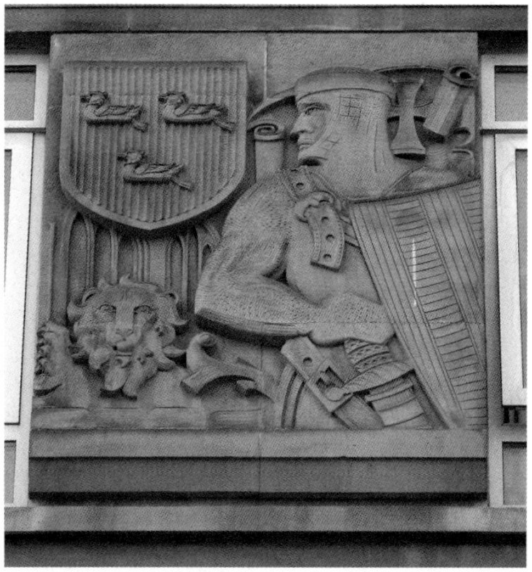

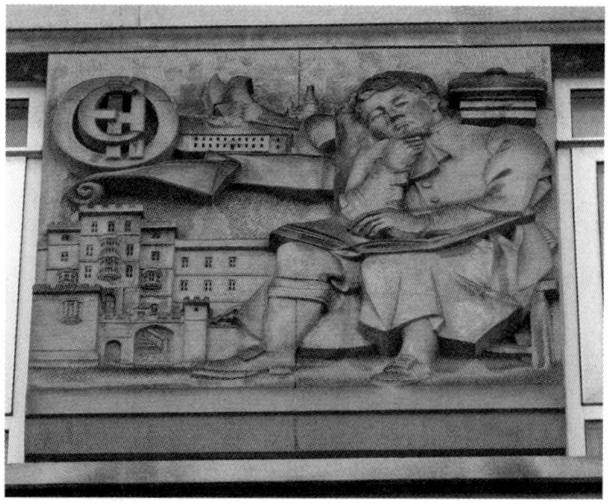

Esmond Burton (attributed to), from left: ***Maurice de Gaunt, co-founder of the Hospital of the Gaunts; Robert de Gournay, co-founder of the Hospital of the Gaunts; Queen Elizabeth's Hospital***

legible from the ground. The two panels on the second floor depict the fully armed co-founders of the Hospital of the Gaunts.[4] Maurice de Gaunt (on the left), grandson of Robert Fitzhardinge and the founder of St Augustine's Abbey (Bristol Cathedral), founded the hospital in 1230. His nephew and heir, Robert de Gournay, made it independent of the abbey and further endowed it to take twelve scholars. The next two panels record the surrender of the hospital at the Dissolution of the Monasteries in 1539, and the subsequent acquisition by the City of Bristol of the hospital buildings, including the Chapel of St Mark, now the Lord Mayor's Chapel, in 1541. The panels on the fourth floor record the two schools so closely associated with the site, whose pupils still worship in the chapel. On the left are a Red Maid in her bonnet and cap, and John Whitson, whose will led to the foundation of the Red Maids School in 1634. On the right is a boy from Queen Elizabeth's Hospital, together with an image of today's school buildings on Brandon Hill. The school was founded in 1590 and first occupied the master's lodge at Gaunt's Hospital. The fifth-floor panels illustrate the destruction during the Blitz of the former school buildings on the site and the survival of the chapel tower; the right-hand relief depicts the ancient craft of printing, which was still being carried out on a part of the site until its demolition in 1950. The two sixth-floor panels are identical. They consist of a monogram in a Gothic script, made up of a capital 'G' and a lowercase 'h', representing 'Gaunt's House'. Both are intertwined with acanthus leaves, very much in the manner of medieval illuminated initials.

Panels were indicated on the architect's early plans.[5] However, as one should expect, their rough indications bear no resemblance to the images on the final reliefs.

Notes

[1] Richard Lee of today's Alec French Partnership has photographs of all the reliefs, but no record of the sculptor; the reliefs have considerable similarities to Esmond Burton's figures on the Cheapside front of New Change Buildings in the City of London. See Ward-Jackson, *Public Sculpture of London*, p.288. [2] The perspective watercolour is illustrated as the frontispiece to the presentation book prepared for Pearl Assurance of which a copy is held by the Alec French Partnership. [3] Information from Tabitha Burchell, Unite, Temple Street, Bristol. [4] See W.R. Barker, *St Mark's or the Mayor's Chapel* (Bristol, 1892). [[5] Bristol City Council Planning Office, Drawing 1477/57-April 1950.

Elmdale Road

Panels on four private houses in Elmdale Road, Nos 8, 9, 10 and 11

Aesop's Fables B39

Sculptor: unknown

Architect: attributed to Charles F. Hansom

Date: 1883
Material: twelve Bath stone panels
Dimensions: nos 8 and 9, approximate measurements: four outside panels, 55cm wide; two centre panels, 90cm wide; nos 10 and 11, all six panels, 90cm wide
Status: not listed
Owned by various private companies
Condition: fair

There is much fine decorative carving on Bristol houses of the 1870s and 1880s, but the ambition and charm of this group is exceptional. The architect has set three panels on each projecting bay between the ground and first floor windows. The subjects are taken from Aesop's fables, or perhaps from Jean de la Fontaine's later versions and additions.[1]

There are twelve separate, deeply cut reliefs. The small panel on the left of No. 8 shows a large alert rabbit, with a young one hiding among ferns. This is similar to the small panel on the right at No. 9, where a rabbit stands guard above three young. These two panels portray La Fontaine's fable of *The Rabbits*, where the moral is about the risk of forgetting danger as soon as it has passed.[2] The large central panel on No. 8 is based on *The Wolf Accusing the Fox Before the Monkey*.[3] A monkey, holding a pair of scales, finds both the thief and the accuser guilty, while the wolf and the fox, not easily distinguishable one from the other, protest wildly. The dishonest, even if they tell the truth, will not be believed. The panel to the right of No. 8 shows a squirrel eating acorns. It is possible that no specific fable is being illustrated here, although numerous morals are associated with both the forward planning and the forgetfulness of squirrels. In the panel based on *Heron Among the Rushes*, on the left of No. 9, the bird – spoilt for choice – cannot decide which fish to spear and ends up hungry, catching nothing.[4] The central panel illustrates *The Monkey and the Cat*, in which the monkey flatters the cat into singeing its paws to steal roasted chestnuts from a fire on the monkey's behalf.[5]

The small left-hand panel on No. 10 shows *The Crow and the Pitcher*. Here, the crow, dying of thirst, drops pebbles into a jug surrounded by ornamental poppy leaves and pods, in order to raise the level of the water so that he can drink.[6] The central panel shows the first scene from the famous fable of *The Tortoise and the Hare*, with the hare racing ahead of the tortoise.[7] *The Raven and the Snake* are on the right-hand side. Here, the bird lands upon a sleeping snake to take it as a meal, but the snake twists round and fatally bites it: easily found riches can be disastrous.[8] The two side panels on No. 11 illustrate *The Fox and the Stork*.[9] On the left, a fox invites a stork to

Wolf Accusing the Fox Before the Monkey

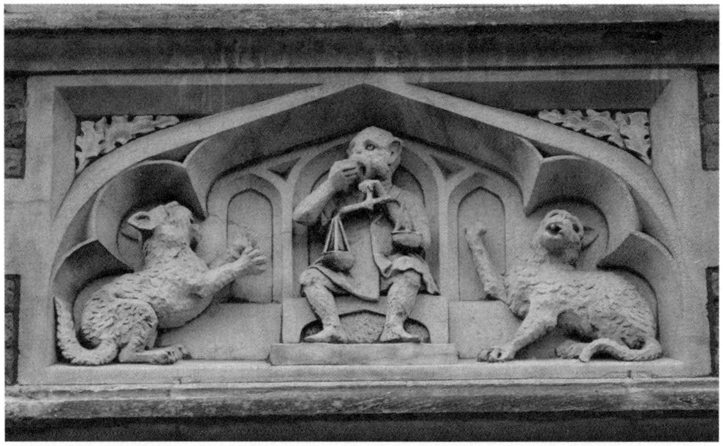

Monkey and the Cat

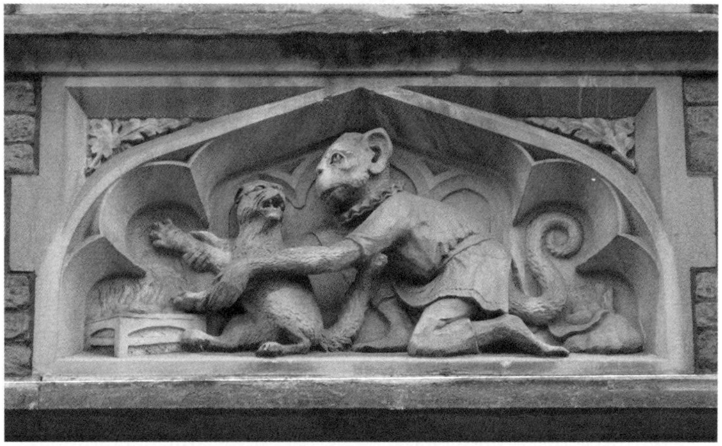

Crow and the Pitcher

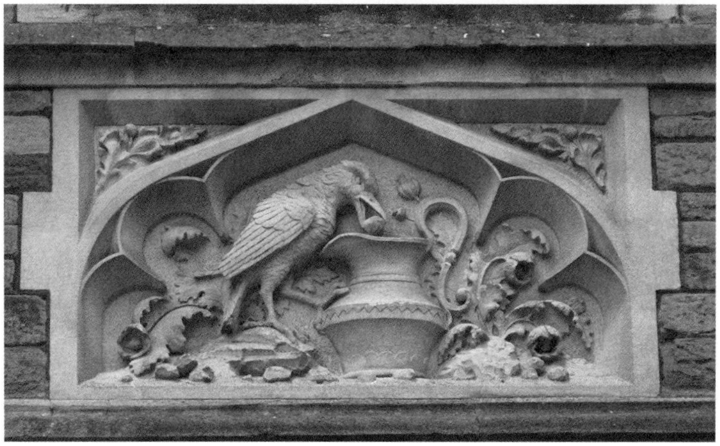

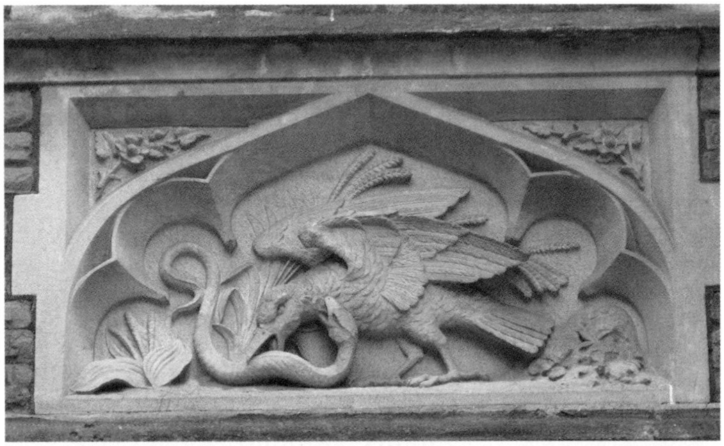

Raven and the Snake

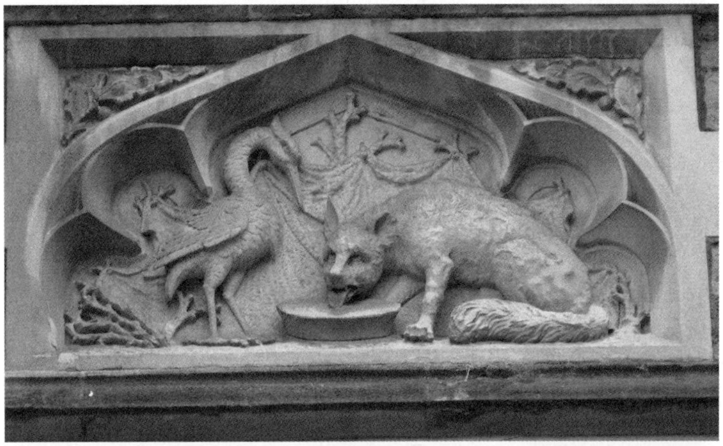

Fox and the Stork (I)

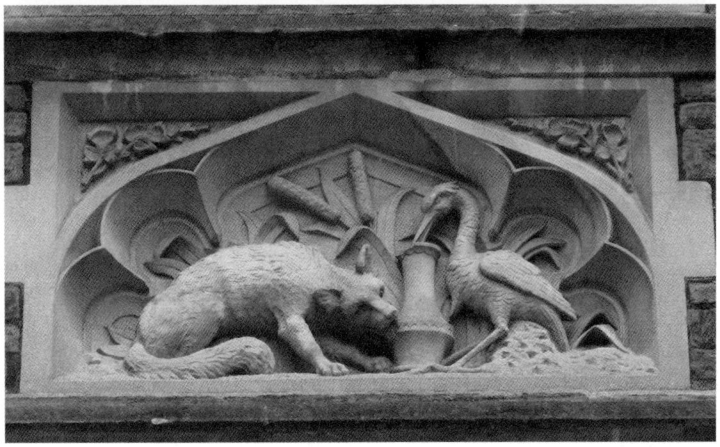

Fox and the Stork (II)

dinner and serves soup in a shallow platter. The stork goes hungry. In the right-hand panel, the stork entertains the fox, and in revenge puts morsels of meat in a long-necked jar. The fox can only dribble and drool. Between these two carvings, the central panel completes the story of *The Tortoise and the Hare*, with the over-confident hare sound asleep as the tortoise wins the race.

These carvings are not signed or marked in any way, and the identity of the sculptor or mason is unknown. The sculptor seems more at home with ferns and stylised birds, and struggles a little with the form of the animals. The fables do not appear to have been selected other than for ease of translation into these relatively small panels, and the sequence and pairing is arbitrary. It is tempting to conclude that the scheme as a whole is the result of the initiative of a practised decorative carver, who has persuaded the builder or developer to let him be very much more ambitious than usual. The lively and naturalistic carving on the former Bristol Museum and Library by Foster and Wood, 1866–71, just fifty metres away at the end of the street, was celebrating John Ruskin's belief in the genius of medieval craftsmen. Here, in Elmdale Road, it is evident that Ruskin's conviction that ornamentation should be both designed and executed by the same craftsman is now affecting suburban housing.

The date of the buildings, 1883, is recorded on the two central drainpipe hoppers. Charles Hansom's boarding houses at 32–34 College Road for Clifton College, datable to 1884, are very much larger and more austere, but similar in style. Hansom's University College buildings of 1880 in University Road at the end of Elmdale Road also have similarities.[10]

Notes

[1] Aesop: sixth century BC, Greece; Jean de la Fontaine: 1621–95. [2] E. Wright, *Masterpieces of Foreign Literature* (London, 1866), p.257. [3] Op. cit., p.188. [4] Op. cit., p.221. [5] Op. cit., p.247. [6] B.E. Perry, *Babrius and Phaedrus* (Cambridge, Mass.,

1965), pp.493, 494. [7] *Aesop Fables*, trans. Sir Roger L'Estrange (Everyman Library) (London, undated, c.1960), pp.224, 225. [8] As note 7, pp.276, 277. [9] As note 7, pp.90, 91. [10] Foyle and Cherry, *Bristol*, p.241.

Ferry Street, off Redcliffe Street

Near the quayside between Buchanan's Wharf North and Buchanan's Wharf South, off Ferry Street

Grain Chute C64

Maker: unknown

Date: c.1885; erected 1989
Material: sheet metal, painted
Dimensions: 6m high
Status: not listed
Managed by the Buchanans Wharf Management Company
Condition: good

This is an original nineteenth-century double-spiral sack chute. At Buchanan's Wharf, the bagged grain would have been craned from the vessel below up the outside of the building in sling nets to the upper floors, and then fed down shutes to wherever it was needed for processing and transport. The two brick buildings on either side of this *objet trouvé* were a granary and a flour mill, built in 1884. They were converted into flats in 1988–9, when the elevator was erected, painted dark blue and a seat placed around it.[1]

Buchanan's warehouses were built as Baker's Mill and Granary by Alderman William Proctor Baker, who, as chairman of the Docks Committee in the early 1880s, fought hard for the development of the City Docks in the face of competition from the new and initially privately-owned docks at Portishead and Avonmouth.[2]

In 1881, Alderman Baker successfully proposed that the wharfage dues for grain cargoes shipped into Bristol should be suspended, and that the expense of discharging

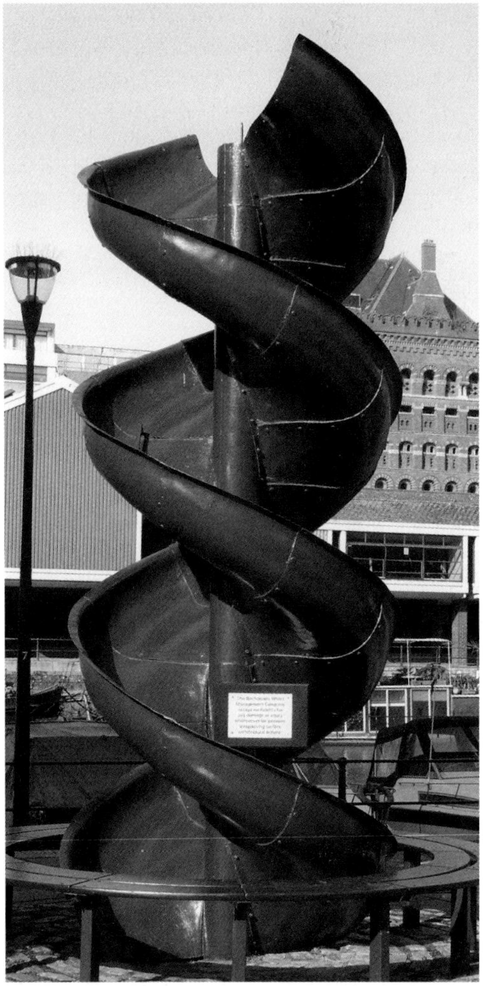

Grain Chute

grain should be 'defrayed out of the dock estate, so as to encourage corn merchants to bring vessels to Bristol'.[3] Dues on other cargoes were also subsequently reduced, but, not surprisingly, Alderman Baker had to endure 'insinuations which he indignantly repudiated'.[4] By May 1884, when the High Court finally determined that these self-serving subsidies were illegal, the city was already planning the seven-storey Corporation Granary on the site of today's Museum of Bristol, and was about to purchase the river-mouth docks. Still larger grain and flour mills were to be built at Avonmouth.

Notes
[1] Foyle and Cherry, *Bristol*, p.188. [2] Elkin, *Images of Bristol*, p.29. [3] Latimer, vol. III, p.496. [4] Ibid.

Fishponds Road A9

In the centre of Fishponds Park

War Memorial

Sculptors: Humphries and Oakes

Date: 1920
Materials: statue, bronze; pedestal, granite
Dimensions: statue, 220cm high; pedestal, 230cm high, 140cm wide, 120cm deep
Inscriptions: on a bronze plaque beneath the figure – '1914 Victory 1918'
—: four bronze plaques, one on each side of the pedestal, display the names of those who died, their rank and regiments; a small later plaque records – FREDERICK G. ROOM V.C. / 2nd Bn. The Royal Irish Regiment / 1895–1932
Signed on the base of the statue, at the rear near the right foot: Humphries & Oakes
Status: not listed
Owned by Bristol City Council
Condition: fair

A private soldier in First World War battle dress carries a rifle in his right hand. Bareheaded and gaunt, he waves his steel helmet in his left hand, perhaps in a gesture of victory, for VICTORY is spelt out in bronze letters just below his feet. There is little sense of triumph, however, perhaps more a sense of relief at the prospect of a welcome home.

The soldier has puttees on his legs; a large bag is slung on his left hip, a water bottle on his right. There are ammunition pouches on his chest. Where the rifle has been broken, it has

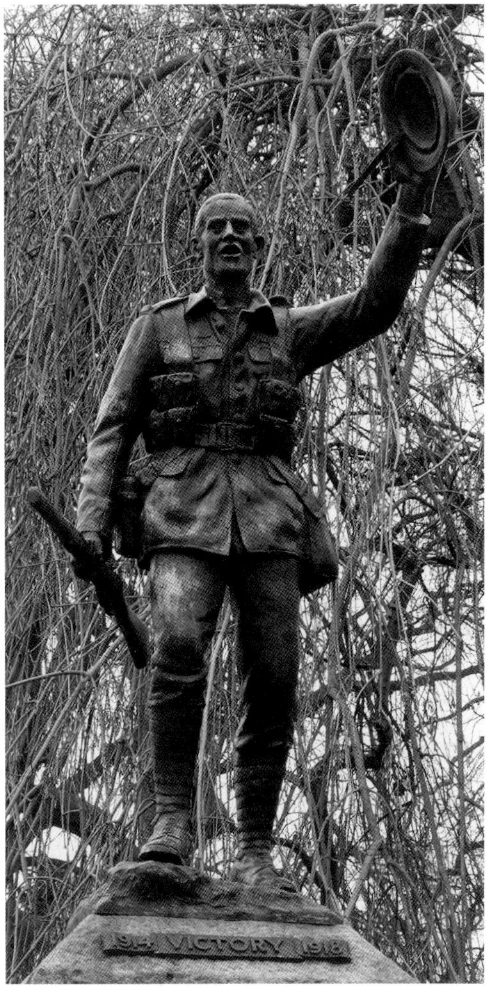

Humphries and Oakes, *War Memorial*

been repaired with an iron collar and a section of the rifle harshly ground off with an angle-grinder.[1] The bayonet is missing, and when inspected by a conservator in 1983 it was said to be in store due to repeated vandalism.[2]

This First World War memorial was unveiled in the centre of this small park in June 1920, having been commissioned by the residents of Fishponds at a cost of £600.[3]

Among the 213 names there are only twelve officers. The ranks of NCOs are not recorded. Among the officers is Lt W. S. Yalland, certainly a close relation and probably a grandson of John Yalland JP, who in 1893 had presented the nearby fountain to commemorate the 'laying out of this pleasure ground for the public use in 1888'.[4] In the adjoining churchyard just outside the south porch is the monument of the Yalland family of Manor House, Fishponds.[5]

Notes

[1] Naylor, 'Bristol's public monuments', 1983. [2] Ibid. [3] BCC Engineers' Department, 'Memorials, fountains and statues'. [4] The fountain is inscribed: THIS FOUNTAIN / PRESENTED BY / JOHN YALLAND ESQURE. J.P. [/ THE FIRST CHAIRMAN OF THE / LOCAL BOARD / TO COMMEMORATE / THE LAYING [OUT OF THIS / PLEASURE GROUND / FOR THE PUBLIC USE IN 1888. / ERECTED 1893 [5] John Yalland JP died in 1897 aged 84, and William Stanley Yalland was killed at Ypres on 23 October 1914, aged 25.

Great George Street

Works in the garden of St George's Brandon Hill, Great George Street

Girl Into Reed… and Other Works

B48

Sculptor: Ian Hamilton Finlay

Lettering by Caroline Webb and Andrew Whittle

Date: 2001–4
Status: Grade II*
Owned by the Trustees of St George's Bristol
Condition: good

Oval plaque set in the ground set in the ground of the forecourt at the west end
Materials: stainless steel letters set into Caithness stone
Dimensions: 345cm by 300cm
Inscription around the circumference: GIRL INTO REED · REED INTO AIR · AIR INTO MUSIC
[Ovid, *Metamorphoses*, Book I]

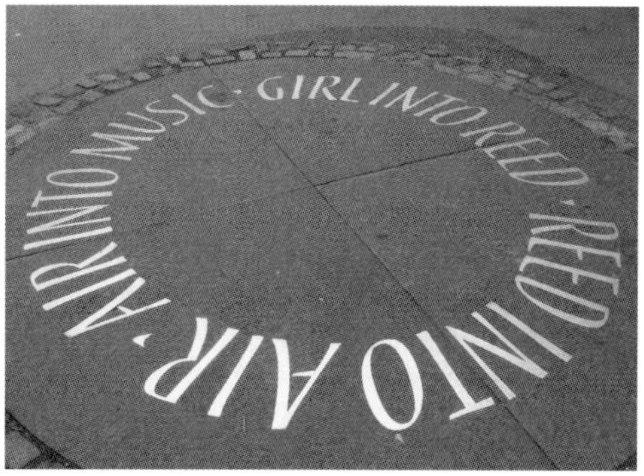

Ian Hamilton Finlay and Andrew Whittle, *Girl into reed…*

Free-standing post on the upper terrace to the south of the hall
Materials: teak
Dimensions: 1000cm high, 15cm diameter
Inscription: HOC MIHI CONLOQUIUM TECUM MANEBIT
[Then will you and I speak together in unison; Ovid, *Metamorphoses*, Book I]

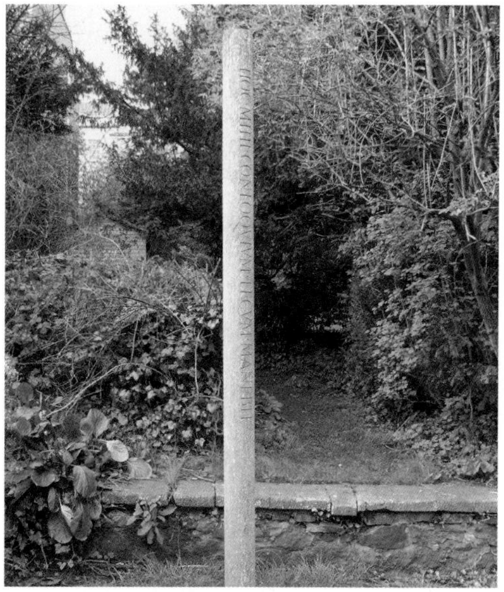

Ian Hamilton Finlay and Caroline Webb, *Hoc mihi conloquium…*

Pair of benches in the upper Memorial Garden to the north-west of the hall
Materials: riven Caithness stone
Dimensions: 135cm long, 35cm wide and 40cm high
Inscriptions: to the right of the cross – LIKE A HEAVY BEAUTIFUL DREAM / IN WHICH I AM BEWITCHED / JANÁČEK· LETTER TO KAMILA
—: to the left of the cross – JANÁČEK· LETTERS TO KAMILA I KNOW THAT / I'D BE CONSUMED IN THAT HEAT / WHICH CANNOT CATCH FIRE

Plaque on the wall of the lower terrace to the north of the hall by the crypt entrance
Materials: Burlington slate
Dimensions: 25cm by 45cm
Inscription: ON THE PATHS I'D PLANT OAKS / WHICH WOULD ENDURE FOR / CENTURIES, AND INTO THEIR / TRUNKS I'D CARVE THE WORDS / I SHOUTED IN THE AIR / JANÁČEK

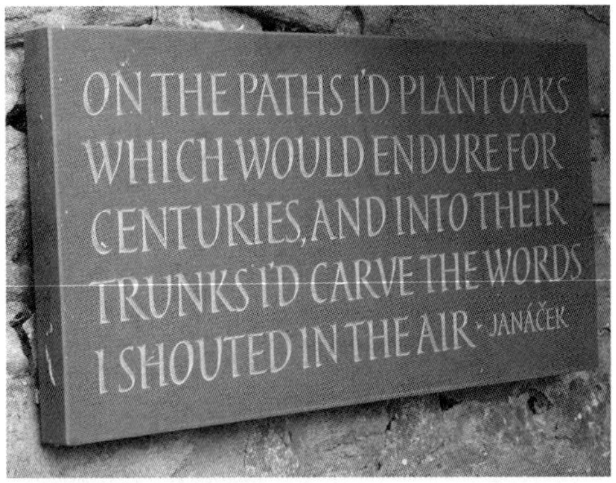

Ian Hamilton Finlay and Caroline Webb, *On the paths I'd plant oaks…*

Two benches side by side, on the lower terrace to the north-east
Materials: riven Caithness stone
Dimensions: 85cm long, 35cm wide, 40cm high
Inscriptions: on the bench to the left – CARMINIBUS CIRCE / SOCIOS MUTAVIT ULIXI / VIRG. ECL. VIII
—: on the bench to the right – CIRCE WITH SONGS / TRANSFORMED / ODYSSEUS' MEN / VIRG. ECL. VIII

Two benches side by side on the lower terrace, south of the hall
Materials: riven Caithness stone
Dimensions: 85cm long, 35cm wide, 40cm high
Inscriptions: on the bench to the left – CARMINA VEL CAELO / POSSUNT DEDUCERE / LUNAM / VIRG. ECL. VIII
—: on the bench to the right – SONGS ARE EVEN ABLE TO / DRAW DOWN THE MOON / FROM HEAVEN / VIRG. ECL. VIII

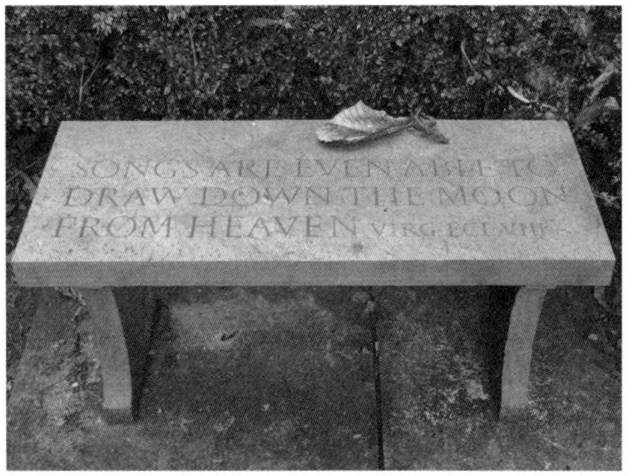

Ian Hamilton Finlay and Caroline Webb, *Songs are even able…*

St George's, Brandon Hill, was a commissioners' church built between 1821 and 1823 to the designs of Sir Robert Smirke, architect of the Royal Opera House, Covent Garden, Bristol's Old Council House in Corn Street and the British Museum. A few years after the death of the last incumbent in 1976, the church became the home of the St George's Music Trust. In 1999, after a major refurbishment, it reopened as St George's Bristol with its exceptional acoustics unimpaired. It continues as a venue for a wide range of musical performance: orchestral concerts, international soloists and opera. The churchyard, apart from the moving of the memorial garden and the opening up of the forecourt at the west end of the church, has remained largely unaltered. Ian Hamilton Finlay's work, commissioned in 2001 with the assistance of the Arts Council, quietly secularised the churchyard, most subtly affirming the relationship between the garden and the new concert hall.

> The commission consists of three pairs of benches, a large oval floor piece, a wall plaque and a teak post. Apart from the post, the material used is Caithness stone, and all works bear poetic inscriptions concerned with the transformational power of music and nature.[1]

One pair of benches is sited in the recently formed Memorial Garden on the upper terrace to the north of the forecourt. The other two pairs are on each of the two lowest terraces in front of the retaining walls.

Jonathan Stracey, the former director of St George's, Bristol, visited the garden of the 'landscape sculptor and poet' Ian Hamilton Finlay some time before 2001.[2] This garden, developed over forty years at Little Sparta, near Biggar in Lanarkshire, holds many examples of Finlay's inscribed stones, benches and tree plaques. These 'make use of quotations about the power of sound, and the effects of music from sources as diverse as Virgil and Janáček'. Stracey was deeply impressed by the combination of classical allusions and landscape, and from his visit came an agreement to commission works for St George's.

The most prominent feature of the commission is the large oval floor-piece at the forecourt entrance, composed of four equal segments of Caithness stone. This is surrounded by two rows of pennant stone setts. The inscription 'Girl into reed, reed into air, air into music' encapsulates Ovid's story of the nymph Syrinx. Pursued by Pan, she requests the gods to turn her into reeds, which Pan grasps. The wind blows across the reeds and they make a plaintive sound, and Pan fashions them into a pipe. In Finlay's Scottish garden, the same text also appears on a tree plaque alongside a bubbling burn. Here, in Bristol, the emphasis shifts to the music, through which Pan realises he can still commune with Syrinx. It is Pan's final words in Ovid's account that are inscribed on the post in a different part of the garden: Hoc mihi conloquium tecum manebit, *Then will you and I speak together in unison*.[3]

Two of the pairs of benches have texts from Virgil about the seductive power of song. The third pair of stone benches and the slate plaque have texts taken from a letter from Leoš Janáček (1854–1928) to his much younger muse, Kamila Stösslová, written on 25 April 1927.[4] Janáček was to die a year later at the age of 74. These texts, quoted above, remind us of the deep passions that can both inspire music and be so movingly expressed through it.

Ian Hamilton Finlay's sculptural or constructed works were always carried out in collaboration with carefully selected craftsmen, who not only undertook all the practical work, but, as in this instance, designed the lettering themselves. Andrew Whittle designed and made the steel letters for the forecourt floor-piece, and Caroline Webb designed and carved all the other inscriptions. Both artists, outstanding specialists in the art of lettering, had collaborated with Ian Hamilton Finlay over many years.

Notes

[1] Press release, St George's, Bristol, August 2004. [2] Notes from Jonathan Stracey, November 2001. [3] From unpublished notes to a lecture by Graeme Moore at the Architecture Centre, Bristol, on the occasion of Ian Hamilton Finlay's 80th birthday, 28 October 2005. [4] See L. Janáček, *Intimate Letters: Leoš Janáček to Kamila Stösslová* (London, 1994), pp.103–4.

Grosvenor Road

St Paul's Learning and Family Centre, Grosvenor Road, St Paul's

All Our Tomorrows A17

Sculptor: Valda Jackson

Date: 2003–5
Materials: Ibstock bricks
Dimensions: 770cm wide, approx. 250cm high
Status: not listed
Owned by Bristol City Council
Condition: good

In 2002, Gloria Ojulari Sule was appointed artist researcher to advise Bristol City Council's Building Design Team on the incorporation of art and arts facilities at the new St Paul's Learning and Family Centre. Sule painted portraits of local residents for the library; Chris Trow created stained glass windows for the café; Barbara Disney undertook mosaics for the entrance; and in 2005 Valda Jackson completed one of the largest and possibly the most enduring and trouble-free of all recent works of public sculpture in Bristol.[1]

This ambitious work is at first-floor level and covers the full width of the west end of the building. The whole commission, including meetings with the architects, public consultation and workshops, took more than two years. The creation of the work itself took about thirteen months. The technique was similar to that employed by the sculptor, Rodney Harris – with Valda Jackson's help – on *Basset Hounds and Basenjis* at Albert Road. The wall was first built in unfired bricks and carved. It was then dismantled, the bricks were fired and the wall was finally rebuilt.

Valda Jackson described the subject of the relief for an audio tour of Easton and St Paul's.[2] Her own edited transcription reads:

> *All our tomorrows*: I have used flight as a metaphor for learning and achievement. The narrative or theme is presented in three parts, in the form of a triptych. On the left are the father and child where the child floats within the protective arms of the father. I wanted to create a positive image of black fatherhood – inspired by some of the black fathers I know. The central figure, a Madonna figure, features an Asian mother and baby flanked by an older child who flies low, within her reach. On the right hand side I include an elder and a teenage boy ready to take flight; while at the top centre of the image is a high-flying figure which is what

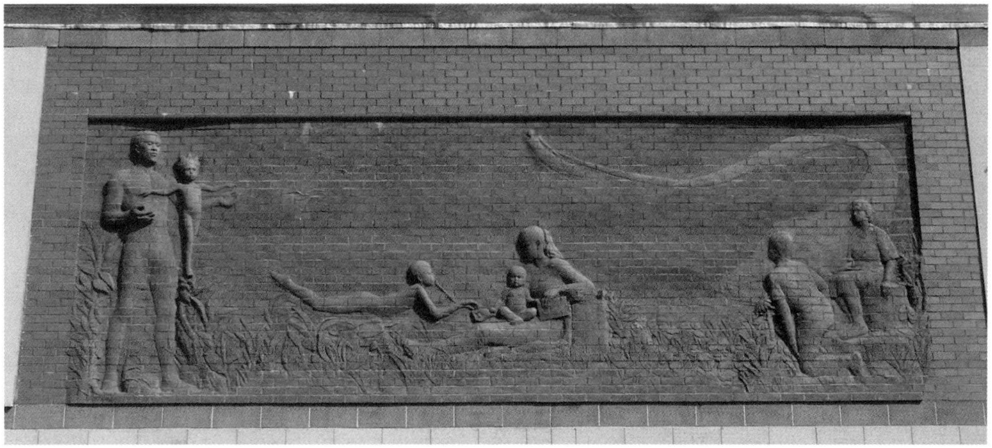

Valda Jackson, *All Our Tomorrows*

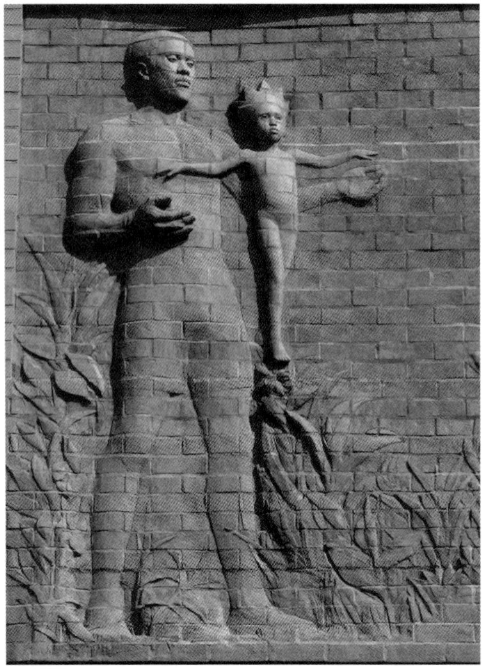

Valda Jackson, *All Our Tomorrows* (detail)

> all of the children in the piece would be aspiring to. My hope… is that people feel comfortable with the imagery and they recognise themselves in it. This is why it is important that this work is not a painted mural, which is temporary, but that the images are carved into the fabric of the building and therefore remain permanent.[3]

Valda's mother-in-law, Bristolian-born, sat for the figure of the 'elder' on the far right: an affectionate tribute from her daughter-in-law.[4] The relief has an inspiring optimism, and its subject could hardly be more closely related to the ideals of the Learning and Family Centre.

The commissions, as a whole, were supported by the Arts Council of England, Objective 2, Neighbourhood Renewal and the Learning and Skills Council.[5] The unveiling ceremony in the presence of Lord Mayor Councillor Peter Abraham, was on 27 May 2005, and the ceremony was linked to the launch of the city council's Neighbourhood Arts Strategy.[6] The relief is unsigned and there is no longer any explanatory plaque inside or outside the building.

Notes
[1] BCC, 'Bristol Creative Neighbourhoods: Neighbourhood Arts Strategy' (Bristol, 2005), pp.10, 11. [2] http://www.visiteastside.co.uk/walk/download_mp3s.html. [3] Letter to the author, 20 June 2008. [4] Information from the sculptor's husband, Rodney Harris, May 2008. [5] As note 1, p.11. [6] *Bristol Evening Post*, 31 May 2005.

Harbourside

The first six public artworks, 2003–7

In November 2003, Tim Knowles was appointed by the developers Crest Nicholson to be lead artist in the first phase of the housing, office and commercial development of the western section of Harbourside. Knowles had played a major role in the relocation of Artspace to Spike Island in the 1990s, when he had also chaired Open City, an artists' initiative funded by South West Arts and Bristol City Council, which presented site-specific artworks for a month per year for four years. At Harbourside, as the developers proudly stated:

> He has been responsible for a budget of well over £1 million to curate and deliver temporary and permanent public art. Working closely with master planners Edward Cullinan Architects and landscape architects Grant Associates, the objective was to develop an arts vision for one of the largest regeneration projects in Europe.[1]

The near completion of the first six works was celebrated in Crest Nicholson's marketing suite on 16 November 2006. The names of other artists to receive commissions for the forthcoming second phase were announced, and included Simon Faithfull, Julie Verhoeven, Sans Façon, Daphne Wright and Matt Calderwood. Mariele Neudecker's commission 'to create a flagship piece of public art right on the waterfront at Harbourside' was made public in July 2008.[2] The recession has since caused inevitable delays, but Tim Knowles continues to gather together a fascinating anthology of public art of the first decade of this century.

On the entire façade of the building overlooking the west side of Millenium Square, Harbourside

Field of Play B67

Artist: Tim Knowles

Lighting architects: Speirs and Major Associates

Date: 2006
Status: not listed
Condition: fair, continuing technical problems

Field of Play is a live, interactive light drawing generated by the public as they move within Millennium Square. Individuals either knowingly interact with or unwittingly create the work. Surveillance cameras look down onto the square, and video processing software uses this footage to track people's movements. These tracks are mapped onto The Lightwall, which is made up of thousands of LED nodes and coloured LED backwash floodlights. Individuals appear as a blob of light moving around the screen and leaving a slowly diminishing 'vapour trail' behind them.[3]

Tim Knowles has successfully managed commissions and exhibitions of the work of other artists. His own work is also, in part, that of an enabler or stage manager. The completed works are generated by processes beyond his immediate control. For example, in 2005 he attached pens to the tips of branches of trees and, after placing paper on an easel in front of them, allowed the chance movement of the wind to dictate the composition of the final drawings.

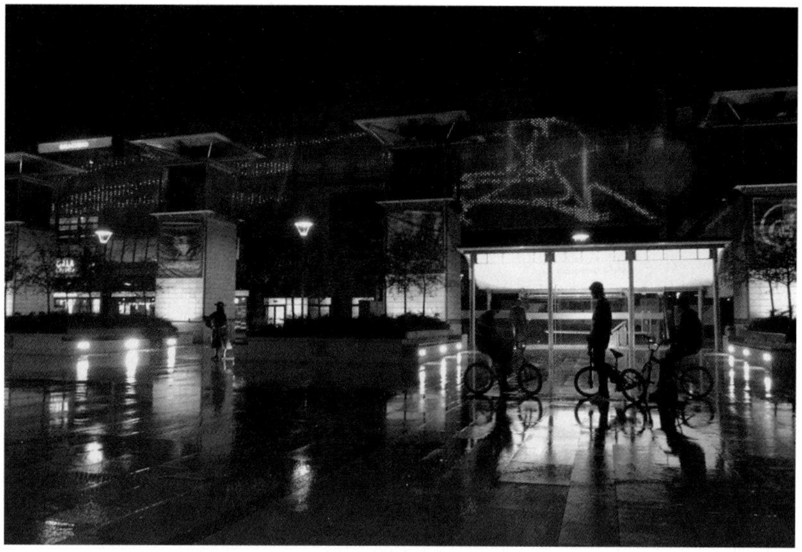

Tim Knowles, ***Field of Play***

Tim Knowles creates drawings independent of his own hand, using elaborate apparatus or time-consuming practices. Interested in the process of drawing, Knowles invents experimental and playful procedures to introduce chance and unpredictability into his work… The artist surrenders final control of the work, questioning the authority of the artist whilst allowing the fundamental and primordial characteristics associated with drawing to be communicated.[4]

During the day, Millenium Square's lightwall – the artist's canvas – is blank and grim. Visitors may wonder if they are looking at an unfamiliar form of covered scaffolding. At night, *Field of Play* delights all who interact with it.

On top the HBOS building on Canons Way, east of Cathedral Walk, Harbourside

Weathervane B69

Artist: Janice Kerbel

Date: 2006
Material: stainless steel
Status: not listed
Condition: good

'Designed in stainless steel to complement the galvanised steel plant room on [the top of] the HBOS plc building, Janice Kerbel's artwork is a deceptively simple structure'.[5] The immediacy and unfamiliar speed with which the arrow responds to the slightest change in the wind's direction compels attention, and overshadows 'the symbolic links to the world of finance'. The developer's brochure suggests that the weathervane 'displays mankind's ability to predict changes in weather conditions alongside the forecasting of market conditions within the business world'.[6] Alternatively, the banker in the building below, who observes the constant and seemingly anarchic movement of the arrow, may have his own confidence in the predictability of the market utterly undermined. All the more so if he knows that in 2001, Alice Kerbel published an artist's book, *15 Lombard Street*, a rigorously researched plan on how to rob the Lombard Street branch of Coutts & Co.[7]

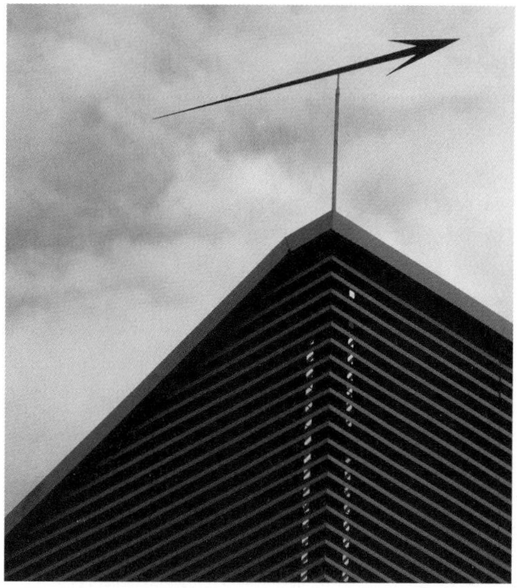

Janice Kerbel, ***Weathervane***

Jack's Brasserie on the quayside between Cathedral Walk and LloydsTSB, Harbourside

The Pavilion B68

Artist: Dail Behennah

Architect: Nick Childs of Childs & Sulzmann

Date: 2006
Material: stainless steel, wood and glass
Status: not listed
Condition: good

Dail Behennah determinedly calls herself a basket maker. However, her work is concerned with form and structure, and with light and shade, and of all the artists so far involved with the Harbourside development, she may most comfortably be described as a sculptor. If her work at The Pavilion was described simply as good craftsmanship imaginatively applied to good architecture, Dail Behennah would take no offence. But there is greater purpose in acknowledging that, in this instance, exemplary collaboration between artist and architect has led to outstanding public art.

One of the conditions of the planning permission granted in November 2003 was that Bristol Council's Public Art Policy should be followed, and that a professional artist should be appointed to work with the architect's design team. Six local artists were considered, and two were interviewed in their studios before Dail Behennah was selected.

The artist quickly identified three areas in which she might influence the design and construction of the south-facing façade of The Pavilion: the balustrade and stairs, the security screens and the glazing.[8] Both artist and architect have spoken of their collaboration to Public Art South West.[9]

> I really enjoyed this project. I had never undertaken anything like it before and I learnt a lot. As the building was going to be very small in comparison with other buildings around it, we knew that ours had to be interesting if it was not to be dwarfed by the rest. I became involved in the project very early on and from the start stated that I wanted my contribution to be integral to the building rather than something added on. My own work is about line, light and shadow, and as the site is south-facing I had the opportunity to develop these ideas on a large scale. I wanted to introduce lines and shadows which would move and animate the space.
>
> I began working with my usual grid structure and was excited by the idea of using mixed metals to add colour, until the structural engineer pointed out that different metals can set up electrolytic currents and eat each other. Further constraints were that no gap must be wider than 10 cm, and that you shouldn't be able to climb the railings.
>
> Nick was brilliant throughout the project. He fought battles with the planners and developers to ensure that my ideas were not watered down and above all he listened. This was a true collaboration. I learnt that on any

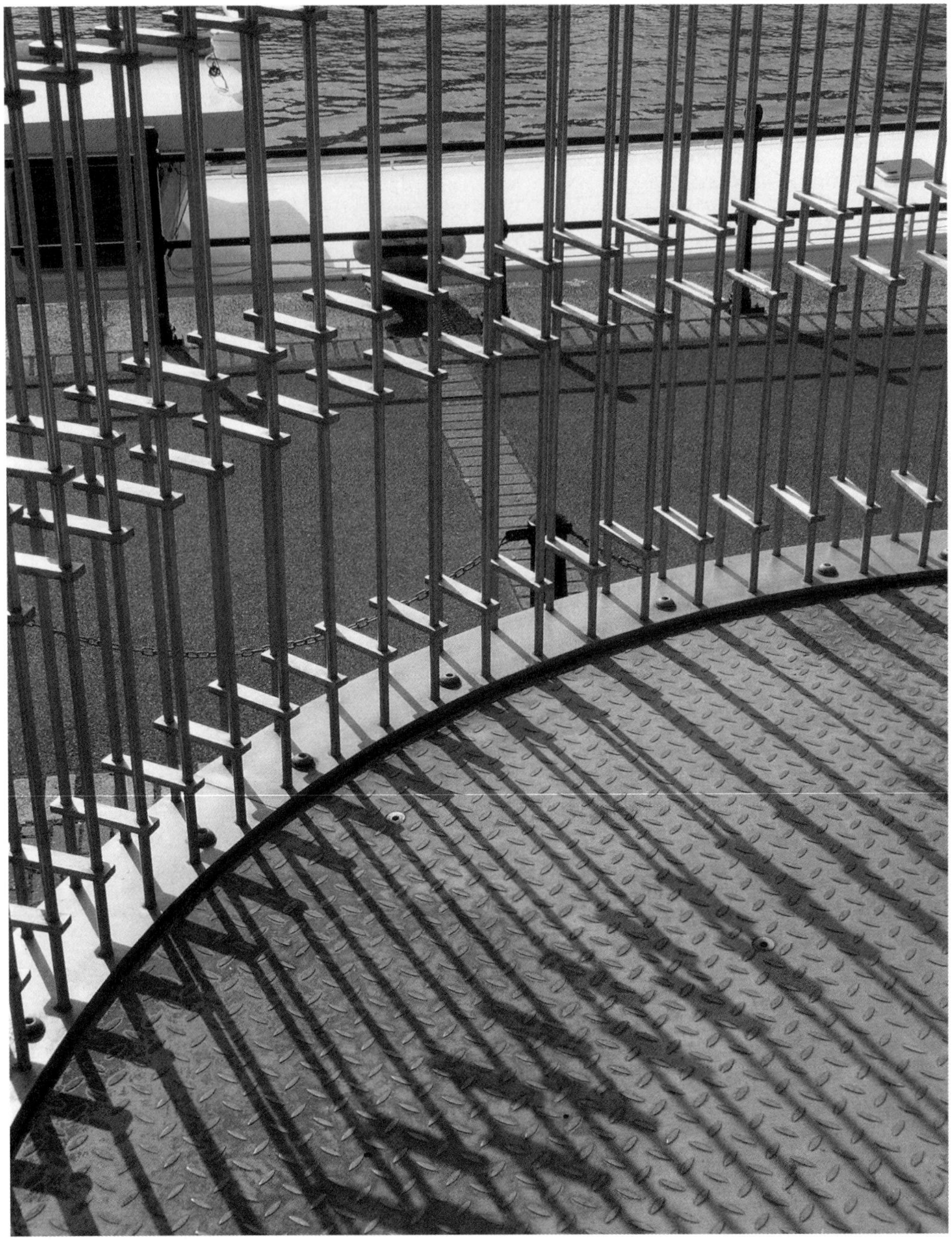

Dail Behennah, *The Pavilion* (detail)

big building project, there are long periods when nothing seems to happen and then there is suddenly a flurry of activity and everything needs to be finalised tomorrow. I was grateful that he steered me though everything and periodically said 'stop working now', otherwise I would have spent every day of the three years changing and refining my ideas. As usual, the first idea was the best.

I think that one thing that has been lost in a lot of modern architecture is good detailing, because of cost constraints, and that this is an area where the percent for art can be used. I went to several planning meetings to present my ideas about light and shadow and kept on saying that we wanted the building to be beautiful, but that it should work as a whole. I didn't want it to be obvious which elements I had been involved in. I think that we have achieved the beautiful building and I am very pleased with the result. The balustrade is a double layer of steel rods and as you walk along it, the lines at the front and the back come into and out of focus and flicker. Although it is made of tons of stainless steel, the overall effect is light and almost filigree, and it is calm.

It has been beautifully crafted by Grail from the Forest of Dean, who took great pains to work out a way of countersinking all the welds to get the effect I wanted. And the shadows work exactly as I had hoped, moving and lengthening and shortening throughout the day. (Dail Behennah)

The collaboration with Dail Behennah was particularly successful due to the mutual respect between the two parties. We were not forced together but willing participants in the project. The artist's contribution to the building was not, and was never intended to be, an addition to the architecture. The ambition was always to work together throughout the process and to integrate the artwork into the fabric of the building.

The results speak for themselves. The whole of the building has benefited from another pair of eyes and a more astute aesthetic judgement. But the evidence is most tangible in the elegance of the balustrade and the design of the security doors. The balustrading is reminiscent of basket work and references Dail Behennah's interests in weaving and woven structures. It takes advantage of the southerly aspect of the site to cast complex patterns of light and shadow.

Dail was very keen that we avoided the ubiquitous solution of intermediate supports with infill panels. The result is a continuous glistening ribbon of metalwork which wraps round the front of the building and down the stair.

The whole experience of working with Dail was a delight and the finished building [was] the result of true collaboration. (Nick Childs of Childs & Sulzmann Architects)

On the lawn of Cathedral Walk, south of Canons Way, Harbourside

Domain B72

Artist: Langlands and Bell

Date: 2006
Material: Portland stone
Status: not listed
Condition: good

Created from Portland stone, Domain serves as a sculpture and tranquil seating area. Carved on to the surface of the stone is a circle of 45 top-level domain codes. These evoke thoughts unique to each person's experience: global communication and circulation; collaboration and exchange; journeys of discovery; expectation; space, time and change. As a non-fiction abstraction, the codes are landing points offering departures into the imaginary,

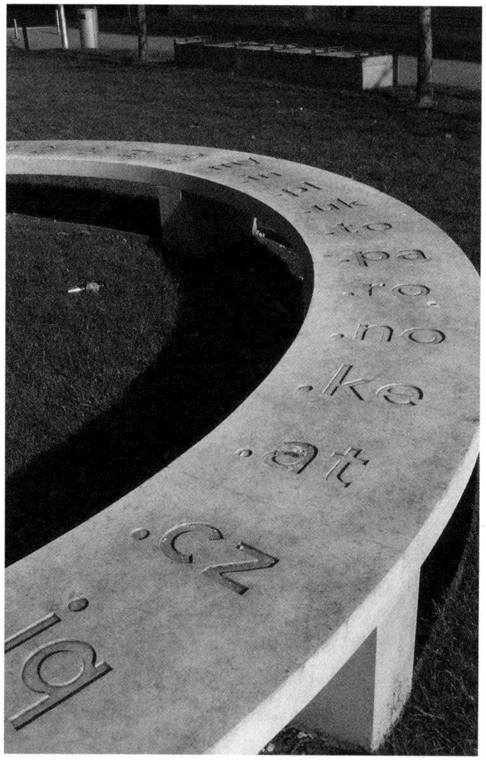

Langlands and Bell, *Domain* (detail)

where human activity may be explored through the places and structures we inhabit, and the routes which link them.[10]

Ben Langlands and Nikki Bell are perhaps the best known of the Harbourside development artists. Shortlisted for the Turner Prize in 2004, they have recently completed two major exterior art works for Heathrow's Terminal 5.

Cathedral Walk, north of Canons Way

Parallax B71

Artist: Richard Box

Date: 2006–7
Material: over 200m of catenary side-glow fibre-optic cord

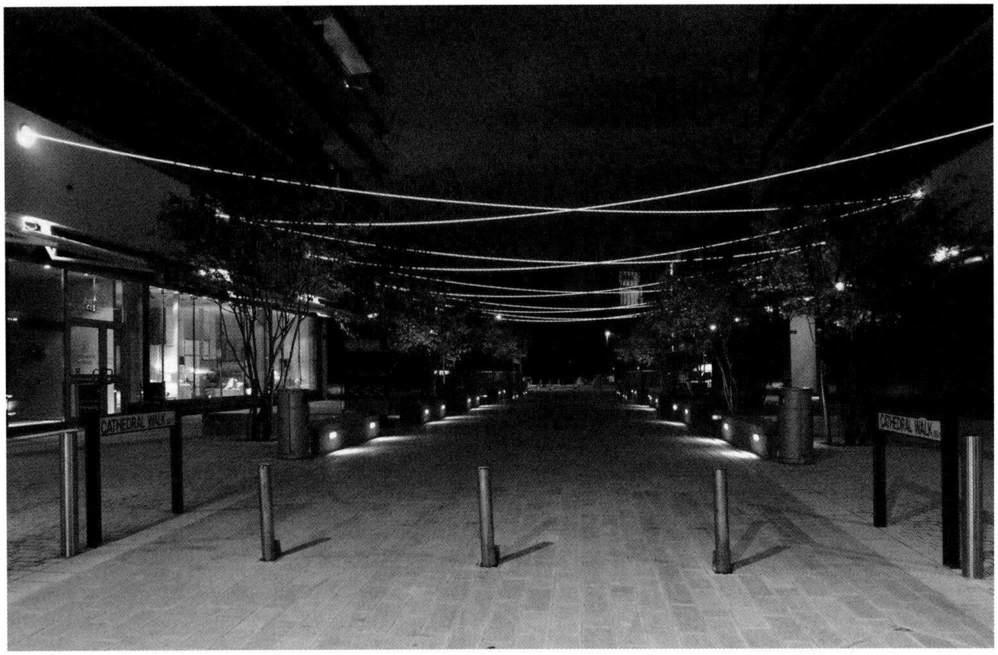

Richard Box, ***Parallax***

Status: not listed
Condition: good

Five pairs of criss-crossing, side-emitting, fibre-optic cables link the first floor balconies on either side of Cathedral Walk. Barely noticed during the day, they emit a distinctive yellow glow at night. 'Soaring through the air, their bright swooping arcs create a carnival feeling, inviting people into the space they outline.'[11] The cables were originally intended to change colour, but this proved impractical on site.

Parallax is just a touch higher than the lines of trees on Cathedral Walk, and there is certainly the suggestion of a boulevard *en fête.* For the moment, however, with much of the development halted and some of the completed blocks discreetly mothballed, *Parallax* can only bring some heart to a setting that is, as yet, more reminiscent of Eastern Europe.

Richard Box has had a studio at Spike Island, Bristol, since 1995, and was the third artist-in-residence at Bristol University's department of physics. He is best known for *Field*, an image of 1301 glowing fluorescent tubes powered by the electromagnetic field surrounding overhead power lines.

Within the multi-storey car park east of Cathedral Walk off Cathedral Walk, north of Canons Way, Harbourside

Secret Industry B70

Artist: John Pym

Date: 2006
Materials: various
Status: not listed
Condition: good

The stairways and lift lobbies of multi-storey car parks are not usually areas where people pause to admire the architecture, so John Pym used this to his advantage. The model walkways and ladders replicate their

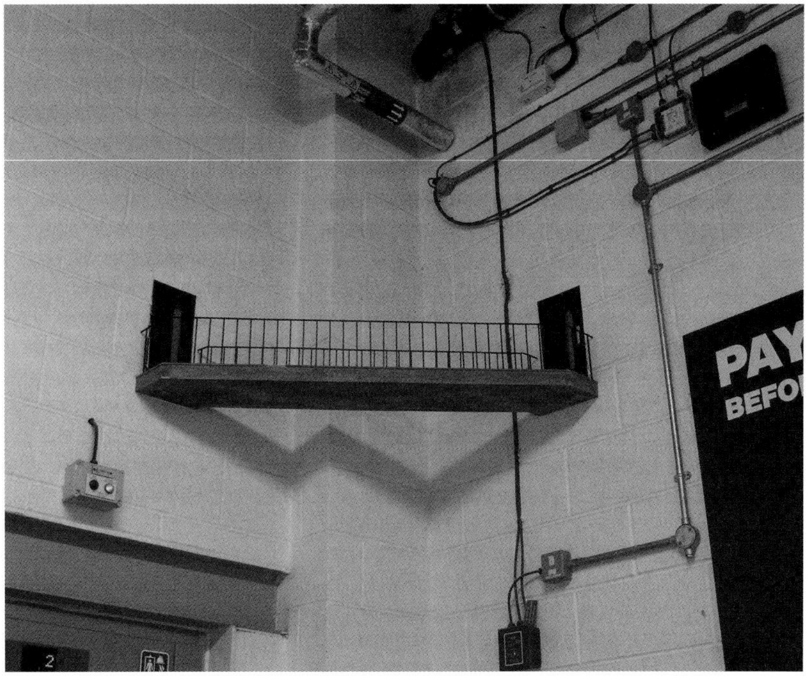

John Pym, ***Secret Industry***

full-scale counterparts and are a playful way of suggesting an alternative, unseen service industry at work within the building. Superficially mundane, some people may use the car park for years without being aware of their presence, while others will notice straight away. The artist sees it as a reward for those who look more closely at their surroundings.[12]

The artist has brought humour and imagination to the bleak and utilitarian breeze-block interior approaches to a car park. Unfortunately, despite the anticipation of the artist, the architect and Justin Knowles, much has happened since the artworks were first installed. Wires, conduits, junction boxes, alarms and cameras have subsequently been added, crowding the installations.

Notes
[1] Crest Nicholson, *Harbourside's Hidden Gems, a Public Trail* (Bristol, 1977); the HBOS banking group bought Crest Nicholson in 2007 through Uberior Investments, its private equity arm, in partnership with West Coast Capital; *The Times*, 11 August 2008, p.44. [2] *The Bristol Magazine*, August 2008, p.6. [3] As note 1. [4] B. Greenacre, *Tim Knowles and Catherine Moorland* (London, 2006). [5] As note 1. [6] Ibid. [7] J Higgie, 'Get it while you can', *Frieze Magazine*, 77, September 2003. [8] BRO, Childs and Sulzmann, proposal, Public Art at Building 12A, ref 03/02420/F. [9] www.publicartonline.org.uk/current/collaboration/craft.html. [10] As note 1. [11] Ibid. [12] Ibid.

Horfield Common

Near the junction of Kellaway Avenue and Wellington Hill West

Memorial Drinking Fountain and Street Lamp A8

Designers: Walter MacFarlane & Co.

Date: 1900
Dimensions: approx. 5m high
Materials: cast iron on a circular pennant stone plinth
Foundry: Walter MacFarlane & Co., Saracen Foundry, Possilpark, Glasgow
Inscriptions: lettering, raised on a cast plaque – ERECTED BY PUBLIC SUBSRIPTION / TO THE MEMORY OF / W. D.WATTS, / LATE MEMBER OF THE GLO'STER / COUNTY COUNCIL FOR THIS DISTRICT. / 1900
—: stamped in the casting – WALTER MACFARLANE & CO GLASGOW
Status: Grade II
Owned by Bristol City Council
Condition: good

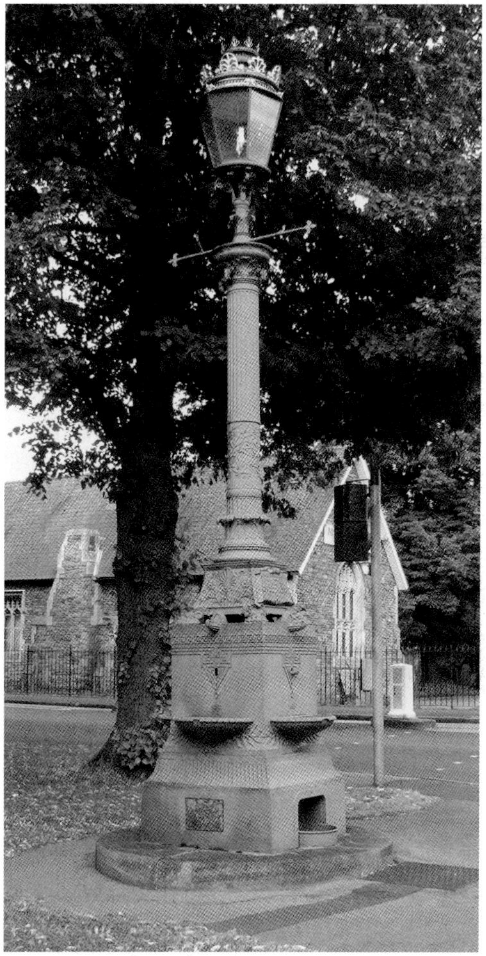

This unusual combination of drinking fountain and street lamp is made up of two standard parts produced by the prolific Glasgow foundry of Walter Macfarlane & Co. The base of the lamp section rests on lions' feet that stand on the corners of the simpler drinking fountain. The same gas lamps can still be seen outside Aberdeen's Central Library, and there are twelve similar lamps outside Glasgow's Mitchell Theatre.[1] That theatre dates from 1877, which may provide an approximate date for the design of the lamp, although it is 23 years earlier than this Bristol memorial.[2] The design involves an eclectic but impressively contemporary mixture of decorative motifs: the stylised Grecian honeysuckle motif, the Aesthetic sunflower, the classical and naturalistic acanthus leaf, and a willow pattern further up the lamp column that is surprisingly

Walter MacFarlane & Co., *Memorial Drinking Fountain and Street Lamp*
(below) Walter MacFarlane & Co., *Memorial Drinking Fountain* (detail)

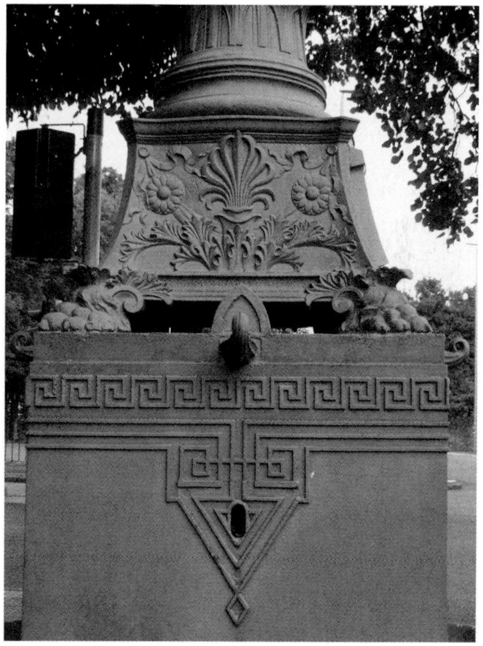

close to William Morris. On the drinking fountain section there is the ancient key motif, and below it is the kind of abstract design favoured by Christopher Dresser.

At the top, the cross bar for the gas lamplighter's ladder survives. The lamp, now electric, works, but the internal drinking fountain apparatus has long been defunct.

The combined lamp and drinking fountain is a memorial to a local solicitor and councillor, William Day Watts. It originally stood at the junction of Gloucester Road and Egerton Road, close to his former home. It is now a few yards from his grave in the churchyard of Horfield's parish church. There, it is recorded that he 'served the parish in various capacities first as chairman of its local Board (1869–76) and lastly as its representative on the Gloucestershire County Council from the creation of that body in 1889 until the extinction of the office in 1897 on the extension of the City of Bristol'. He died in 1899 in his 62nd year.

Notes

[1] Mackenzie, *Public Sculpture of Glasgow*, pp.190–2. [2] The base of the lamp section has a registration mark, made illegible by layers of paint, but which could provide a date.

The Horsefair

John Wesley's Chapel, The New Room

The New Room has become 'to Methodists the equivalent of Jerusalem's holy places'.[1] Nonetheless, the survival of the New Room and of the surrounding land, on which the statues of John and Charles Wesley were to be erected, is impressive.[2] In over 270 years there have been numerous changes of ownership and, following the total destruction of the adjacent buildings in the Second World War, Bristol's main shopping area now surrounds the site.

John Wesley arrived in Bristol in 1739, and his open-air preaching attracted large crowds. Two congregations formed very quickly. By 9 May, Wesley described in his journal how he had purchased 'a piece of ground, near St James churchyard, in the Horsefair, where it was designed to build a room large enough to contain both the societies'. Three days later he reported: 'the first stone was laid, with the voice of praise and thanksgiving.' The New Room was not intended primarily for worship, but to support Wesley's work and as a meeting room.[3] The chapel was enlarged and registered for public worship in 1748.[4] After Wesley's death his congregations declined. Welsh Calvinistic Methodists bought the premises in 1808.[5] They used it until 1929 and it was 'providential that the Welsh Calvinistic Methodists never found it necessary to pull down and enlarge the original building as might have been the case had it belonged to a numerous people in Bristol'.[6]

Edmund Sykes Lamplough (1860–1940), deputy chairman of Lloyd's of London and long-term benefactor of Methodism in Bristol, bought the New Room in 1929 and presented it to the Wesleyan Methodist Conference in the following year.[7] He invited the doyen of Bristol architects, Sir George Oatley, to undertake a 'faithful restoration'.[8] By 1930, dilapidated shops on the Horsefair side had been purchased to improve and open up the site.[9]

George Oatley was to work closely with Lamplough in the commissioning of the John Wesley statue, and most of the correspondence between Oatley, Lamplough and Dr Ferrier Hulme, a leading Bristol Methodist, is in the New Room Library. These letters reveal the extreme care that they took in the commissioning of the statues of both John and Charles Wesley.

The following inscription is on the west wall of the New Room:

> This plaque commemorates those who made possible and carried out the re-purchase, restoration and re-opening of John Wesley's Chapel, especially: Rev. T. Fenner Hulme, Chairman of Bristol and Bath District of the Wesleyan Church, Rev. John A. Broadbent, Supervisor of Bristol Mission, Mr Edward S. Lamplough who generously paid the whole cost, and Sir George Oatley, Architect. Dedicated on the 50th Anniversary of the re-opening February 13th 1980 by the Vice President of the Conference of Welsh Methodists.

In the north courtyard of John Wesley's Chapel, The New Room, 36 The Horsefair

Charles Wesley C5

Sculptor: Frederick Brook Hitch

Date: 1939
Materials: bronze, on a Horton stone pedestal
Foundry: not known
Dimensions: 200cm high; base, 60cm x 60cm; plinth, 115cm high
Inscription on the front of the plinth: CHARLES WESLEY / 1707 – 1788 / O LET ME COMMEND / MY SAVIOUR TO YOU
Signed by the left foot: F. Brook Hitch / 1938
Status: Grade II
Owned by the Wesleyan Methodist Church
Condition: good

Charles Wesley (1707–88), one of the world's outstanding hymn-writers, was born, as was his brother, John, at the rectory at Epworth, Lincolnshire.[10] He died at Marylebone, London but the most important and productive twenty years of his life were passed in Bristol. The inspiration for many of his hymns came while he was taking his favourite walks in Redland and on the Downs, or riding to preaching sites.[11] Charles had first lived in the New Room after it was enlarged in 1748, but the following year he married. The couple were to live in various houses in Bristol over the next 22 years, including 4 Charles Street, now preserved as a memorial to the Wesleys. Charles and his family moved to London in 1771. He died on 20 March 1788 and was buried in Marylebone Old Churchyard.[12]

The bronze 'shows Charles as a sturdy,

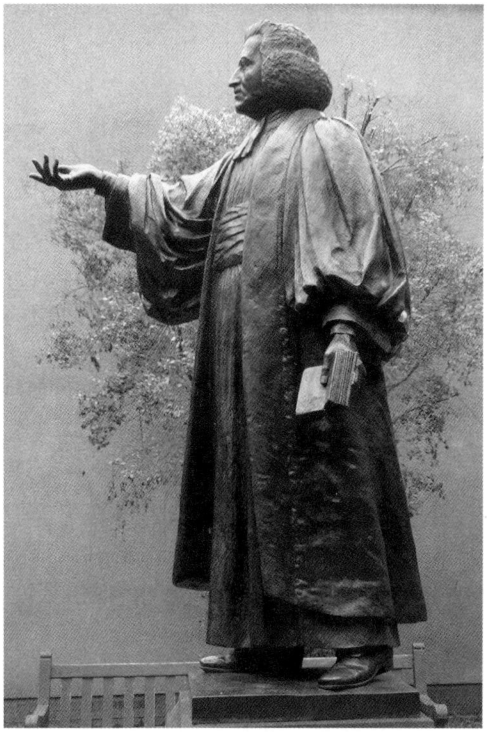

Frederick Brook Hitch, *Charles Wesley*

combative figure, holding a Bible and wearing the cassock, preaching bands and gown of an Anglican clergyman of his time'.[13] The statue is of a standing figure in late middle age, straight-backed and commanding. The face is deeply lined. He wears a wig and gown and plain buckled shoes. The square limestone pedestal consists of three blocks. Inscribed on the front top section are the subject's name and dates and the quotation given above. Many images of Charles Wesley would have been available to the sculptor, including engraved portraits and an oil painting in the collections of the New Room.[14]

Proposals for statues had emerged in the autumn of 1930 as the restoration of the New Room neared completion. The first to be erected, in 1933, was the equestrian statue of John Wesley. It was in the same year that enough freehold land was donated by a local benefactor to create a north forecourt. This enabled the New Room Trustees to fulfil their dream of a statue of Charles Wesley. First, some dilapidated shops had to be acquired, or the forecourt and the statue would be hidden from public view and inaccessible from the Horsefair. Edmund S. Lamplough (1860–1940), deputy chairman of Lloyd's of London, who had played the vital role in the commissioning of the statue of John Wesley, now continued his 'unquenched generosity', and in the autumn of 1933 purchased the two shops. However, it was not until 1936 that the trustees decided to go ahead and commission a statue of Charles Wesley.[15]

At one stage there had been a suggestion that the equestrian statue of John Wesley should be moved to the new forecourt, but Sir George Oatley, architect to the New Room restoration, advised that the Broadmead-side site was larger, sunnier, and was more appropriate because of its proximity to Wesley's stable.[16]

Through the influence of the Rev. Dr. T. Ferrier Hulme, Sir Arthur Munro Sutherland, of Newcastle-on-Tyne, agreed to fund the commission.[17] By 1938 the London-based sculptor Frederick Brook Hitch (1887–1957) had been engaged. Oatley records that on 16 February in that year he met the sculptor at 'Temple Meads at 11.17 and took him to the New Room. He had brought his sketch statuette of Charles Wesley and that was exhibited in the Long Room upstairs. The Trustees saw it and generally approved of it'.[18]

The trustees made three criticisms: 'that the book would be better in the left hand with the right hand raised as now in gesticulation… that the cassock is somewhat long – more Rome than Anglican', and, as mentioned to Oatley in a private aside by Dr Church, 'the feet are a little large'.[19] Brook Hitch was praised for achieving the animation which had been suggested at an earlier meeting at City Road, London, when Wesley's great-great-grandsons had been present. Oatley also told Brook Hitch that he felt the moulding of the plinth on the pedestal should be less heavy. The sculptor agreed to send a full-size drawing that Oatley could amend, but he would now proceed to make the full-sized model. The deadline for the unveiling, 3 June 1939 – chosen to mark the two hundredth anniversary of the opening of the chapel when John Wesley had been the preacher – was confirmed. Final preparations for the forecourt were begun in March 1939.[20]

The donor, Sir Arthur M. Sutherland, was present when the statue was unveiled on the allotted day by his sister, Miss Florence Sutherland.[21] The president of the Methodist Conference, Dr W. L. Wardle, many church representatives and civic dignitaries attended. Edmund Lamplough, who had contributed to the project, was unwell and did not attend. He died in his 81st year in October 1940.

In 1954, a Bristol newspaper observed:

> The statue of Charles, executed by Mr Brook Hitch, was an important step towards the perfection of this Methodist shrine visited by adherents of the faith from all over the world.[22]

It was not until the post-war development of Broadmead shopping area that the arched entrance from the Horsefair, the present layout of the garden and the setting for the statue were brought to their present state.

In the southern courtyard of John Wesley's Chapel, The New Room, 36 The Horsefair

John Wesley C6

Sculptor: Arthur George Walker

Date: 1932
Materials: bronze statue on a limestone pedestal
Foundry: A. B. Burton of Thames Ditton
Dimensions: statue, 240cm high, 240cm long, 70cm wide; pedestal, 22cm high, 250cm long, 140cm wide
Signed: A. G. WALKER. SC. /1932

Inscription: A. B. BURTON / FOUNDER
—: related tablet on the entrance arch – THIS CHAPEL WAS BUILT BY / JOHN WESLEY / A.D. 1739 / AND KNOWN AS THE / NEW ROOM / IN THE HORSEFAIR. / HE REBUILT AND ENLARGED IT / A.D. 1748 / IT WAS ACQUIRED FOR THE USE OF / THE WELSH CALVINISTIC / METHODIST CHURCH / A.D. 1808: / REPURCHASED AND RESTORED / BY PRIVATE BENEFACTION / A.D. 1929 / GIVEN TO THE / WESLEYAN METHODIST CHURCH/ AND RE-OPENED / 13TH FEBRUARY 1930. /
Status: Grade II
Owned by the British Methodist Conference
Condition: good

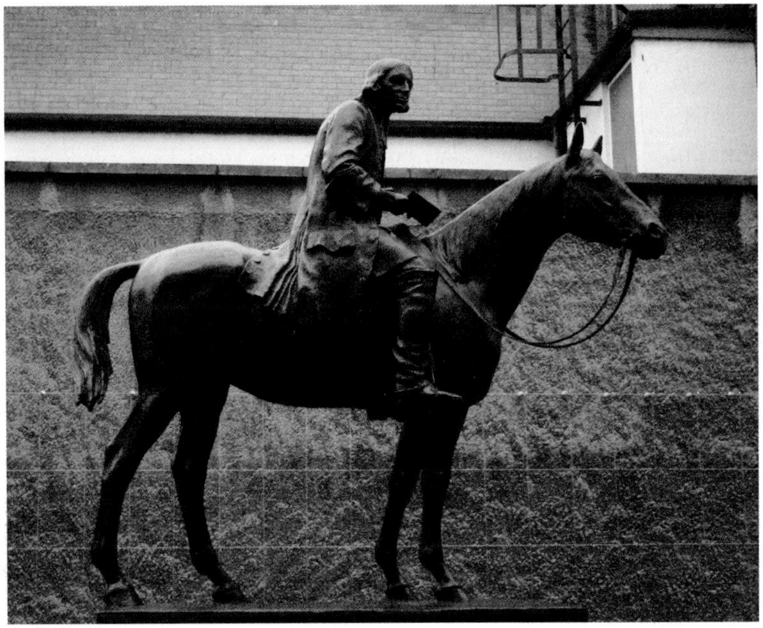

Arthur George Walker, *John Wesley*

John Wesley (1703–91) was the founder of Methodism. Born on 17 June 1703 at Epworth, Lincolnshire, he was four-and-a-half-years older than his brother Charles, upon whom he exerted a strong influence throughout his life.[23] John attended Charterhouse and in 1720 entered Christ Church, Oxford.[24] He was made a deacon in 1725 and the following year elected a Fellow of Lincoln College. He was ordained in 1728.[25] Returning to Oxford, he joined Charles and other undergraduates who had formed the Holy Club to read the Bible and pray together.[26] Their activities among the poor and in prisons made them conspicuous and had earned them, before John arrived, various derisive nicknames, including 'Methodists'. John took over the leadership of the new group.

Late in 1735, the brothers went to America to the new colony of Georgia, where John Wesley remained for two years.[27] One factor that brought John Wesley to Bristol was the radical open-air preaching of George Whitefield (1714–70), and his encouragement to Wesley to do the same. John first preached to a crowd of about 3000 at St Philip's Marsh, Bristol, on 2 April 1739. The following month he laid the foundation stone of the New Room, the oldest Methodist building in the world. For half a century thereafter, London and Bristol (and later Newcastle) were to be the focal points of John Wesley's evangelism as he travelled Britain on horseback, preaching and fostering Methodism.

Wesley and his horse became part of Methodist folklore, and it is this traditional image which this equestrian statue so successfully perpetuates.[28] He sits astride his alert horse, and the heads of both horse and rider are turned slightly to the right. He holds a book in one hand and his tricorne hat in the other; the reins are untouched. His full-length boots are in the stirrups and he wears spurs. The sculptor must surely have read Wesley's journal:

> How is it that no horse stumbles while I am reading… No account can possibly be given except this: because when I throw the reins on his neck, I then set myself to observe; and I aver that in reading above a hundred thousand miles, I scarce ever remember any horse… to fall or make a considerable stumble, while I rode with a slack rein.[29]

The opportunity to commission the statue arose when an extensive and faithful restoration was carried out on the New Room in 1929–30. The two men involved were Edmund Sykes Lamplough (1860–1940) and Sir George Herbert Oatley (1863–1950). Lamplough was a devoted Wesleyan, the deputy chairman of Lloyd's of London, vice-president of the Methodist Conference in 1935 and president of the Wesley Historical Society. The eminent Bristol architect, George Oatley, was also deeply religious and 'a Congregationalist but ecumenical in his outlook'.[30] Lamplough, who in 1929 had purchased the New Room, presenting it in the following year to the Wesleyan Methodist Conference, paid for both the restoration of the building and for the statue.

George Oatley first proposed a statue of Wesley to Lamplough in October 1930 and, at that early stage, even named the sculptor he had in mind, Arthur George Walker (1861–1939):

> Dr Ferrier Hulme has an idea the American people might be willing to present an

equestrian statue of Francis Asbury. Be that as it may, I am strongly of the opinion that it would be an immense attraction if we could have a statue of John Wesley himself. There is nothing of the kind in this part of England, and of all places there could scarcely be one more suitable. The sculptor would want careful selection. I have no fancy for any of the modern men, some of whom are unpleasantly 'modern' in their ideas and in their outlook and line of life, so that I should be sorry to have them associated with so sacred a subject. Do you happen to know A. G. Walker, A.R.A.? He is an extraordinarily nice man, and a very able sculptor – more after the Old School.[31]

Lamplough replied the following day saying he liked the idea of 'a statue of John Wesley rather than, or perhaps in addition to an equestrian statue of Francis Asbury'.[32] He said he had little knowledge of sculptors but he knew Mr Maurice Webb, a son of Sir Aston Webb, had a very good opinion of the London-based sculptor, E. S. Frith, although he was evidently impressed by Walker's credentials.

Sir George next revealed that the idea of a statue of John Wesley was not his own. It had originally come from 'Mr E. F.[?] Jones'.[33] Oatley then doubted that the space in front of the New Room could contain two statues, supposing two were desirable, but if 'the Americans offer a statue of Asbury it can scarcely be declined'. It might arouse the interest of people in England who knew little about him. Lamplough then proposed a conference between himself, Dr Ferrier Hulme, the local chairman of the Wesleyan District, and Oatley in order to resolve such questions as 'is the space large enough for the two statues?' and 'American help or none'. He made it clear that he would insist on 'a Wesley statue for the adornment of the ground'.[34]

Oatley began to plan the site. 'I suggest placing the statue of Wesley, looking towards the present Entrance Roadway. Then the statue would then be seen in profile from the street.'[35] An ashlar wall to about 15 feet would be built as a dignified background. 'It is essential that everything should be absolutely simple to accord with the Chapel.'

By November, Lamplough had given Oatley permission to contact Walker, hoping 'he would make a plaster model… if he could get away from the conventional and give us a really inspirational figure, it would immensely please'.[36] Oatley undertook to guide Walker to the best portraits of Wesley, and proposed the sculptor should read Wesley's journal and some of his sermons, and become saturated with his character and purpose. Walker 'has no sympathy with the trend of the Modern School, which, in my opinion, has in it an element of moral perversion – sign of general decadence'.[37] Lamplough sent Oatley a copy of Telford's *Sayings and Portraits of John Wesley*, and reminded him there were two paintings of Wesley in the National Portrait Gallery.[38] Walker reported that although they were of little value as works of art – they were bad portraits – they would be of assistance.[39] Among the possible references for the likeness was the black plaster bust of Wesley held in the New Room. This bust is attributed to Enoch Wood (b. 1759), a master modeller in the Potteries. Wesley is said to have sat for Wood on five occasions between 1781 and 1784, and the bust has been described as 'the most faithful likeness of that eminent person ever produced'.[40]

At this early stage, only a statue of a standing figure was envisaged. Should he be preaching? Did he preach in the open air without a gown or surplice? Much discussion on the form of dress ensued. Oatley suggested that Lamplough should meet Walker to answer these questions, and gave him the address of the sculptor's Chelsea studio.

It was not until the beginning of December that Oatley raised the question of costs.

I do not know what you may be willing to spend upon a statue? I fear that by the time it is cast in bronze it may come to more than you contemplate. Upon sounding Mr Walker about this the other day he said that the cost would be something like £1000 to £1200 including the bronze. This would be exclusive of the pedestal which we should provide locally, but that would be a comparatively small matter.[41]

Replying the following day, Lamplough was shocked: 'Regarding the cost, I had not any idea that it would amount to so much.' He had information that the bronze of John Wesley in City Road, London, had cost £1000.[42] Stone or marble had been suggested as less expensive, but he did not think these would be 'suitable to the neighbourhood in which the statue is to stand'. After Sir George had reminded him that the City Road statue had been erected forty years previously, Lamplough replied: 'I am hopeful, however, that as Mr Walker regards £1200 as the maximum, he has good ground for this figure.'[43]

On 24 February 1931, Lamplough, Ferrier Hulme and Mr Broadbelt (the minister at the New Room) went to Walker's London studio. The following day Lamplough wrote to say that they were all pleased by the meeting, but:

the Sculptor asks for the unmounted statue £1250, and for the equestrian £2500. I must say I am staggered by these figures. Though I am not suggesting for a moment that Mr Walker is asking a sum that would not amply be represented by the eventual statue…[44] If it were desired to place, say, in Hyde Park, a worthy statue of John Wesley as the greatest figure of the eighteenth century, where countless people could see a worthy representation of our great Founder, and get inspiration from the sight, that would be one thing, but in situ in Broadmead, I fear that apart from newspaper men and a small number of Bristolians, the statue would be hidden away and its permanent witness largely nullified.

He would 'have to consider the matter carefully'. There is no confirmation within the correspondence of what Lamplough agreed to pay. One recent account does say that the £2500 Walker had sought was paid.[45]

Two sketch statuettes were prepared for comparison. One was an equestrian version; the other was of Wesley preaching. For nearly six months, Oatley was by-passed. By August 1931 he had to ask Lamplough what had been decided:

> I understand from Mr Walker that you have placed with him the commission for the equestrian figure, but I am wondering if this is for London or Bristol! As soon as I know… I can proceed with the scheme for the layout.[46]

In January 1932, Walker became ill. This delayed the modelling and casting, and he was still suffering from bronchial pneumonia a year later when he needed to inspect the final bronze.[47]

The unveiling by Edmund Lamplough was arranged to coincide with the third anniversary of the re-opening of John Wesley's Chapel, and took place at 2.30pm on the 16 February 1933. The statue was floodlit in the evening.[48] Walker exhibited a bronze statuette of this work at the Royal Academy's summer exhibition in 1934, two years before he was elected R A.[49] This was Walker's last public work. He died in 1939.

The frontispiece of Dr T. Ferrier Hulme's book, *John Wesley and his Horse,* published in 1933, is a photograph of Walker's full-size plaster cast.

Notes

[1] R. Hattersley, *A Brand from the Burning: The Life of John Wesley* (London, 2002), p.369. [2] Wesley avoided 'chapel' or 'church' to escape the accusation of starting a separate denomination. [3] M. Edwards, *The New Room* (Bristol, 1972), p.2. [4] Ibid, p.3. [5] F.F. Bretherton, 'The Welsh Congregation at the "New Room"', *Proceedings of the Wesley Historical Society*, vol. XXIII, 1941–2, p.90. [6] Op. cit., pp.90–1. [7] Letter from Mark Topping, warden of The New Room Library, Horsefair, Bristol, 12 December 2001. [8] T.H.B. Burrough, 'Bristol', *Studio Vista*, 1970, p.28. [9] Letter from Lamplough to Oatley, 15 October 1930; New Room Library, Horsefair, Bristol. [10] J.A. Vickers, *Charles Wesley* (Peterborough, 1990), p.20. [11] 'The writer of 1,000 hymns', *Evening Post*, 22 July 1954. [12] As note 10, p.34. [13] Little, *The Public View*, p.73. [14] The painting is dated 1735. [15] W.J. Little, *John Wesley's Chapel: A Short History* (Bristol, 1981), p.12. [16] Notes by Sir George Oatley, headed 'New Room Garden and Charles Wesley Statue', 16 February 1938, New Room Library. [17] Rev. Dr T. Ferrier Hulme, MA LL.D, was the chairman of the Wesley Methodist District. He lived at Durham Park, Bristol; 'Sir Arthur Sutherland met the cost of the statue – £709.16.6: the laying of the foundations and the Horton stone pedestal – £60.11.3: the stone pavement surround – £21.19.0: and expenses relating to the unveiling – £4.14.10.' (Letter from Mark Topping, warden of the New Room, 12 December 2001.) [18] As note 17. [19] Ibid; Brook Hitch was to confer with Dr Church over the length of the cassock and to look at illustrations at City Road, while Oatley resolved to write to the sculptor on the delicate matter of the feet. [20] 'There by hangs a tale: The writer of 1,000 hymns', *Evening Post*, 22 July 1954. [21] As note 5, p.91. [22] As note 11. [23] G.S. Wakefield, *John Wesley* (Peterborough, 1990), p.4. [24] Op. cit., p.8. [25] Op. cit., p.10. [26] As note 1, pp.71–3. [27] Op. cit., Chapter 6. [28] As note 24, p.148. [29] N. Curnock (ed.), *The Journal of the Rev. John Wesley* (London, 1938), vol. 5, pp.360–1. [30] S. Whittingham, 'Sir George Herbert Oatley: a Nonconformist architect', PhD diss. (University of Bristol, 2005). [31] Francis Asbury, described as 'the apostle of American Methodism', left Bristol in 1771. Dr T. Ferrier Hulme, MA, LL.D, was the chairman of the Wesley Methodist District in Bristol and the author of *John Wesley and his Horse* (London, 1933); Oatley to Lamplough, 20 November 1930. [32] Lamplough to Oatley, 15 October 1930. [33] Oatley to Lamplough, 16 October 1936. Oatley suggests that Edwin Jones of 54 Clarendon Road, Bristol, a Methodist sympathiser, was the first to propose the Wesley statue. [34] Lamplough to Oatley, 17 October 1930. [35] Oatley to Lamplough, 18 November 1930. [36] Lamplough to Oatley, 19 November 1930. [37] Oatley to Lamplough, 20 November 1930; a probable reference to Jacob Epstein. [38] Lamplough to Oatley, 21 November 1930. There were three portraits of Wesley in the NPG at that time: They were by William Hamilton (1788), George Romney (1789) and Nathaniel Hone. [39] Oatley to Lamplough, 29 November 1930. [40] R. Lee, *Wesleyana and Methodist Pottery* (London, 1988), p.11. [41] Oatley to Lamplough, 3 December 1930. [42] Lamplough to Oatley, 4 December 1930. The statue was *John Wesley*, 1891, by J. Adams Acton, at Wesley's Chapel, 47 City Road, EC1. [43] Lamplough to Oatley, 9 December 1930. [44] Lamplough to Oatley, 25 February 1931. [45] Little, *John Wesley's Chapel*, p.11. [46] Oatley to Lamplough, 11 August 1931. [47] Oatley to Lamplough, 29 January 1932 and 20 January 1933. [48] New Room Library, draft text of the programme for the unveiling. [49] A.G. Walker, '1586 John Wesley – equestrian statuette, bronze', RA Exhibitors (1934).

Hotwell Road

Capricorn Quay opposite SS Great Britain

Samuel Plimsoll B73

Sculptor unknown

Date: circa 1875
Materials: Servezza marble; pedestal, polished Cornish granite; base, York stone
Dimensions: bust, 95cm high, 85cm wide, 55cm deep; pedestal: 160cm high, 60cm square at base
Inscription: cut on the front of the pedestal – SAMUEL / PLIMSOLL / M.P. / 1824–1898 [centred beneath this wording is a Plimsoll mark]
—: cast in a bronze plate on the right side of the pedestal – SAMUEL PLIMSOLL, M.P. / BORN IN THIS / CITY AND PORT OF BRISTOL / 1824 / DIED IN / 1898 / HIS UNTIRING EFFORTS LED TO THE / MERCHANT SHIPPING ACTS OF 1875 / AND 1876 WHICH FIRST MADE LOAD / LINES COMPULSORY FOR THE SAFETY/ OF SHIPS
Status: Grade II
Owned by Bristol City Council
Condition: poor

Samuel Plimsoll MP (1824–98), renowned shipping reformer and politician, was known as 'the sailors' friend'. Uncertainty as to whether or not he was born in Bristol initially delayed proposals for a memorial. In 1940 the hurried acquisition of a marble bust, now of questionable identity, ultimately resulted in the setting up of the statue beside the tidal waters of the Avon in 1962. The weathered and irreversibly damaged bust was successfully erected on Capricorn Quay in 2010.

Samuel Plimsoll was the eighth of thirteen children of Thomas Plimsoll, of Huguenot descent, and of his wife Priscilla Willing. A biography published in 1975 finally confirmed that he was born in Bristol on 10 February 1824, when his family lived in a rented house at 3 Colston Parade.[1] He was baptised at Bridge Street Congregational Church on 30 January 1825.[2] His father was a clerk in the Customs House and Excise Office in Queen Square. Samuel was only four-and-a-half when his father's promotion took the family to Penrith, Cumbria. They moved to Sheffield in 1838 and never returned to Bristol.

Plimsoll left his Sheffield school at fifteen, when his father died, and he helped support his mother and five young children by working as a solicitor's clerk and later for a brewery.[3] He then became involved with his brother in developing the transport of coal from Yorkshire by railway to London. In 1851, Henry Cole appointed him as secretary of the Sheffield Great Exhibition committee. Two years later, when south Yorkshire mine owners agreed to support his coal transport plans, Plimsoll moved to London. His 'naïve enthusiasm' led to bankruptcy, but after his marriage in 1857 his coal merchant business at 32 Hatton Garden prospered and he patented a 'sliding tip', which avoided coal being broken when being emptied into wagons.

His wide experience had given him a sense of social justice and a particular concern for those in dangerous trades. He decided to enter Parliament. Described as an 'advanced liberal', he was defeated when he stood for Derby in 1865, but he won the seat in 1868. He became interested in the welfare of seamen, and launched a campaign against insurers and shipowners and their infamous 'coffin-ships'. 'By the 1870s more than 3000 merchant seamen were lost each year, their families condemned to fatherless poverty.'[4]

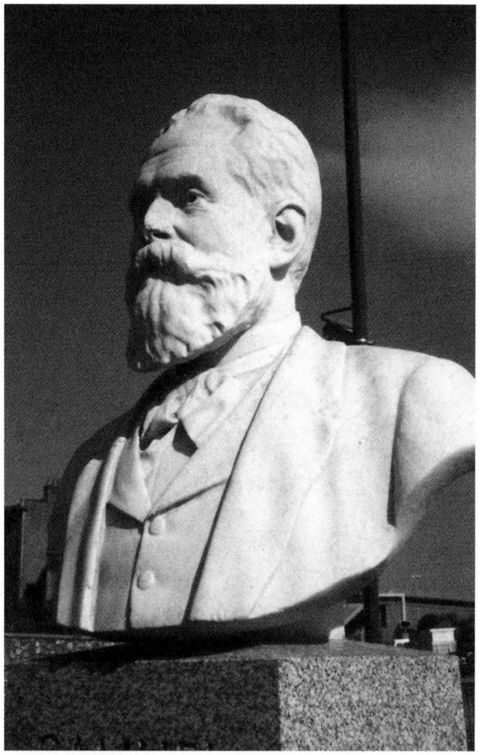

Samuel Plimsoll

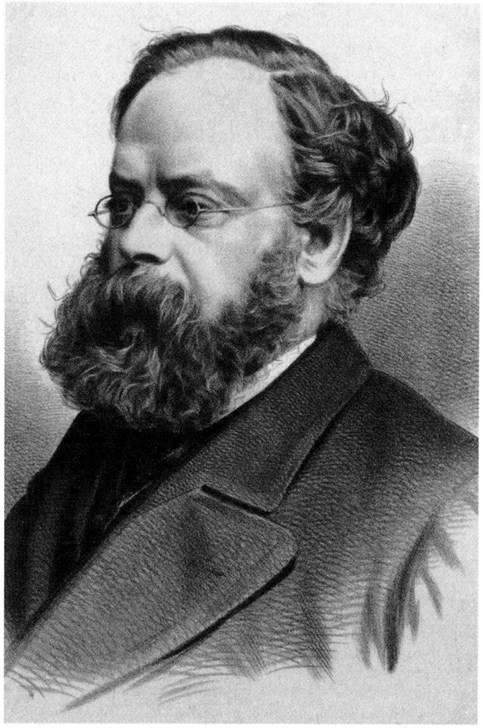

***Samuel Plimsoll*, colour lithograph by Cassell, Petter and Galpin, c.1890 (detail)**

To support his views, Plimsoll published *Our Seamen: An Appeal* in 1873. Through Parliament, he called for and gained a Royal Commission to examine the high loss of merchant ships between 1856 and 1872. A proposal to amend the Merchant Shipping Act did not satisfy him, and he moved his own Shipping Survey Bill. On its narrow defeat the government strengthened its own bill, but in July 1875 Disraeli allowed this bill to run out of time. Plimsoll was incensed. He accused shippers and some members of being 'villains who sent sailors to their death' and stormed from the House shouting 'villains' and 'scoundrels'.

A year later, the Merchant Shipping Act was passed. It obliged shipowners to mark foreign-going vessels with a maximum load-line with a circle and a horizontal bar. Plimsoll himself was not finally satisfied until 1890, when another act required the Board of Trade rather than the shipowner to fix the 'Plimsoll line'.[5]

The earliest recorded attempt to set up a memorial in Bristol was in 1919.[6] The Lord Mayor T. J. Francombe presided at a meeting at the old Council House and 'the proposal was greeted with much enthusiasm until someone got up to ask if there was any evidence that Plimsoll really was born in Bristol'. Sheffield claimed him and so did a town in Scotland, and 'the meeting was adjourned until evidence of Plimsoll's birth in Bristol had been found'.

There was a revival of interest in the project in 1928, prompted by the news that 'there is a movement on foot to erect a permanent memorial on the banks of the Thames to the sailors' friend'.[7] A spate of correspondence and editorials followed :'Bristol Born', 'Plimsoll's Birthplace' and 'Mr Plimsoll and Bristol'.[8] Another item was headed 'Sheffield Claims Plimsoll'.[9] In due course, there were accounts in the *Western Daily Press* of the unveiling of an impressive memorial commissioned by the National Union of Seamen on the Victoria Embankment in August 1929.[10] The report lamented: 'It would have been appropriate if this had been set up in Bristol.' Mistakenly, it added: 'As a young man… when walking round our quays, he constantly had evidence of dangerous conditions in which some ships put to sea.' In February of the following year, an ex-lord mayor, W. H. Eyles, and an ex-sheriff published an invitation to the citizens of Bristol to meet at the Council House on 12 March 1930 'to consider the desirability of a Bristol Memorial… and if approved, what suitable form it should take'.[11] Those present included the Bristol architect Sir George Oatley, and J. A. Short, a local philanthropist and long-term campaigner for a Plimsoll memorial. F. V. Blundstone, sculptor of the London memorial, also attended with the apparent hope that a replica of his memorial would be commissioned for Bristol.[12] The meeting's verdict was clear. This was 'an inopportune moment to launch an appeal' – there were too many other appeals – but a committee was duly set up.[13] No progress was made. In July 1939, the *Western Daily Press* reported on 'a stone bust' of Plimsoll that had 'turned up' in Nottingham. It was 'a good piece of work' and could be 'acquired for about £25'.[14] The Museum and Art Gallery might consider purchasing this bust for the city if a 'suitable site could be found'. Teasingly, the news item ended: 'By the way, is it known where Plimsoll was born?' The museum's records confirm that a bust was purchased in May 1940.[15]

It was this bust, 'in Servezza marble', that was unveiled by Lord Mayor L. K. Stevenson on 24 July 1962. The mayor proudly claimed that it had been 'left to a Bristolian to set about improving the staggering loss of life at sea'.[16] The Bristol Port Authority had prepared the site at Hotwells between the Portway and the river, and it had also supplied the pedestal and a York stone base for £575.[17] There the bust remained, gazing down the Avon Gorge and weathering away in the salt-laden air and exhaust fumes, until 2005. In that year, Wessex Water began work close to the site and Bristol Council commissioned Cliveden Conservation Workshop to prepare a report on the memorial's condition and its possible relocation. The report recommended an area close to the Floating Harbour but well away from the polluting Portway in order to slow down the erosion of the marble and to be more accessible.[18] It noted that the 'surface damage is irreversible'.[19] The bust was re-erected on Capricorn Quay opposite SS *Great Britain* in March 2010.

There is a bronze replica of this bust in the USA.[20] After members of the Plimsoll Club of New Orleans visited Bristol in 1968, they commissioned a replica through the Port of Bristol Authority. The late Ernest Pascoe, then head of sculpture at the West of England College of Art, made a plaster cast. The final bust, made by the Art Bronze Foundry, cost £500.[21]

With the exception of the beard, the bust does not bear a close resemblance to any other image of Plimsoll. There is no documentary evidence to support the identity of the subject, to name the sculptor, or to suggest a date for the carving of the work.

Notes

[1] G.H. Peters, *The Plimsoll Line:The Story of Samuel Plimsoll* (Chichester, 1975). [2] Ibid. [3] Anita McConnell, *Samuel Plimsoll, ODNB*. [4] Ibid. [5] Ibid. [6] *Evening Post*, 'A Plimsoll memorial meeting of 1919', 14 November 1952. [7] *Western Daily Press,* 'Mr Plimsoll and Bristol', 14 February 1928. [8] Cross heads from *Western Daily Press*, 14 to 22 August 1929. [9] *Western Daily Press*, 18 September 1929. [10] *Western Daily Press*, 'The Plimsoll Memorial', 22 August 1929; a large photograph of the London unveiling accompanied the report; the memorial, by Ferdinand Victor Blundstone, is still on the same site. [11] Leaflet headed 'The Council House, Bristol', 20 February 1930. [12] *Western Daily Press*, 12 March 1930. [13] *Western Daily Press*, 13 March 1930. [14] *Western Daily Press*, 'Bust of Plimsoll', 3 July 1939. [15] Bristol Museum and Art Gallery, historical file No. 2554. There is no inscription, the sculptor is not named and the source is given as 'a dealer in Stratford-on-Avon'. [16] *Evening Post*, 'Hotwells statue is Bristol's mark for Sam Plimsoll', 12 May 1962. [17] *Evening Post*, 'Bristol's bust of Plimsoll unveiled', 24 July 1962. [18] Cliveden ConservationWorkshop, report, November 2005. [19] As note 18. [20] *Evening Post*, 'Bust of Plimsoll to US', 10 September 1969. [21] 'Tideway Topics', *Shipshape*, vol. 18, 1969–70.

Jacob's Wells Road, Clifton

Within an alcove in the entrance hall of Queen Elizabeth's Hospital school

Queen Elizabeth's Hospital Schoolboy B47

Sculptor: unknown

Date: c.1706
Material: stone, painted
Dimensions: 165cm high
Status: not listed
Owned by Queen Elizabeth's Hospital
Condition: good

This statue may be one of the earliest and best preserved of the many statues of children that once adorned the façades of Blue Coat schools, charity schools and orphanages in the early eighteenth century.

Queen Elizabeth's Hospital opened in 1590 with twelve boys. It was founded by John Carr, 'a wealthy soap boiler of our city', in imitation of Christ's Hospital, London.[1] Bristol's mayor and members of the common council were the governors. The school occupied the Hospital of the Gaunts, a thirteenth century foundation on College Green. This, together with today's Lord Mayor's Chapel, had been purchased by the Corporation of Bristol in 1541, following the dissolution of the monasteries.

At the beginning of the eighteenth century, the medieval school buildings between the chapel and Unity Street were rebuilt following a public subscription that was headed by Edward Colston, who contributed approximately one-fifth of the total costs and who had already endowed six places.[2] The date of the ambitious rebuilding of the school is uncertain. It was certainly complete by 1706.[3] The statue may well date from this time and was probably placed in a niche above the main entrance.

In 1767 the school was obliged by the Corporation of Bristol to exchange premises with Bristol Grammar School and to occupy, once again, the premises of a medieval 'hospital', this time St Bartholomew's at the bottom of Christmas Steps. The statue will have accompanied the move.

A drawing of the school's previous Unity Street premises in 1821, when occupied by the Grammar School, clearly shows an empty niche above a plaque over the entrance.[4] There is no visual evidence that it was displayed externally, either at St Bartholomew's or when the school moved to its third and present site on Brandon Hill in 1847. Thus, it may have been exposed to the elements for only a little over half a century.

The unusually good condition of this stone statue, exemplified by the crisp detail of the bow at the boy's waist, ensures that the figure is an impressive record of the school's uniform, aspects of which could well reflect the school's sixteenth-century foundation.

Excepting the shoe buckles, the black shoes, yellow stockings, breeches and clerical tabs or bands are still worn. However, in place of today's long and buttoned blue coat, the statue shows three separate garments. The boy wears a doublet with capped shoulders. A century earlier the sleeves would have been detachable. Here they are buttoned at the cuffs and may be attached to an undergarment at the shoulder. The doublet is hooked rather than buttoned at the front. The long separate skirt is open at the front from the waist downwards, as it is today, but here it is tied with a bow at the waist, where it is rucked or pleated in a manner that suggests it is of a lighter woollen material than the stiffer blue coat that followed. The belt already looks superfluous, although it is still worn today. On the statue it is perhaps more obviously a descendant of the later medieval belt from which hung a leather purse or, when the wearer was older, a dagger or a sword.

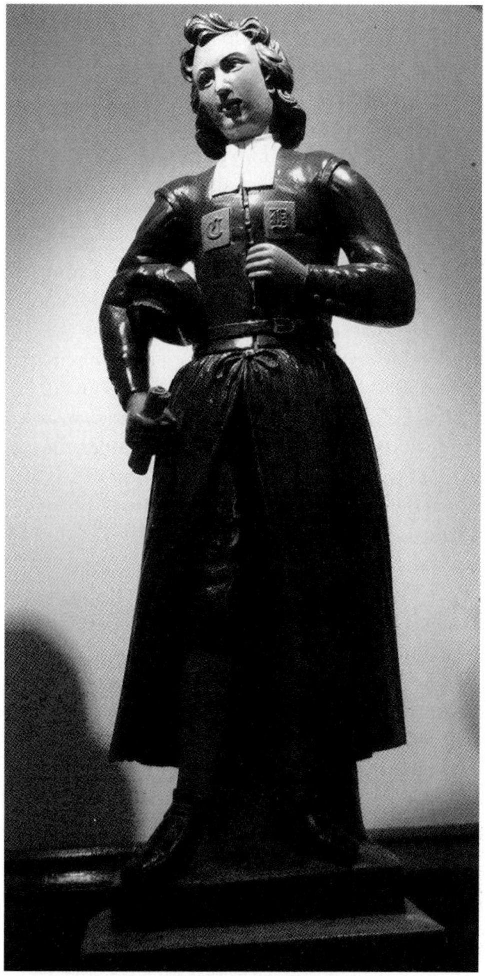

Queen Elizabeth's Hospital schoolboy

From the early seventeenth century, each boy had flannel letters sewn onto their coats or jackets 'for a special remembrance of the particular benefactor' who had enabled their presence in the school.[5] Here the letters are C and B for City of Bristol. Although John Carr had endowed eight places to Bristol's six and there were several other benefactors similarly commemorated by initials, it was the Corporation of Bristol that effectively – and later most appallingly ineffectually – ran the school and managed the rebuilding at the beginning of the eighteenth century. Today, initialled brass badges have replaced the flannel letters and the school is fully independent and coeducational.

Notes

[1] Hutton, *Bristol and its Famous Associations*, p.392. [2] F.W.E. Bowen, *Queen Elizabeth's Hospital* (Bristol, 1971), p.32. [3] Nicholls and Taylor, *Bristol Past and Present*, vol. 3, p.263; a model of the new building is illustrated in C.P. Hill, *History of Bristol Grammar School* (London, 1951), pl. IV; see also: W.A. Sampson, *History of Queen Elizabeth's Hospital* (Bristol, undated); J.R. Avery, *'While We Have Time', 1590–1990* (Bristol, 1990). [4] BCMAG M2542, watercolour by M.H. Holmes, *Grammar School from Unity Street*, 1821. [5] As note 2, p.21.

Lewins Mead

On the forecourt of St Bartholomew's office block, Narrow Lewins Mead

Cloaked Horseman C11

Sculptor: David Backhouse

Architects: Alec French Partnership
Date: 1984
Material: bronze
Foundry: Burghleighfield Studios, High Wycombe, Bucks
Dimensions: 230cm high, 200cm long
Inscription on a metal plaque: CLOAKED HORSEMAN / by / David Backhouse / Commissioned by Haslemere Estates / and presented by them / to the City of Bristol in 1984

Signature on the horse's rear right leg:
Backhouse / 1 / 3 / 1984
Status: not listed
Owned by Bristol City Council
Condition: good

This free-standing equestrian statue is placed in the centre of a slight circular mound, paved with granite setts. The bareheaded horseman is without stirrups, bridle or saddle and he gazes towards St John's Gate at the bottom of Broad Street. This fine archway is Bristol's only surviving medieval gateway, and the statue is carefully aligned to suggest that the traveller is about to enter the city.

The work was commissioned for the office block known as St Bartholomew's. The site had been sold to Haslemere Estates in 1981, and the building was finished in 1984.[1] The sculptor had previously completed a work for the developers for an office block in London.[2] Images of the statue were used prominently in the prospectuses and advertising when the building was first in the hands of letting agents.

Before the Lewins Mead site was developed, an archaeological investigation revealed part of a thirteenth-century bridge that once crossed the River Frome outside the city walls.[3] The sculpture stands over a culvert made in the early 1890s and the river still flows beneath the site. This information guided the sculptor in his choice of subject: a traveller arriving outside a fortified city in medieval times.

St Bartholomew's Hospital, founded about 1220, cared for travellers and possibly lepers for over three hundred years.[4] After the Reformation, Bristol Grammar School and later Queen Elizabeth Hospital were here.[5] From the mid-nineteenth century onwards, the site was used by various industries, including the Burleigh Press from 1900 to 1976. Some remains of the ancient hospital may be seen about fifty metres south of the *Cloaked Horseman*, near the foot of Christmas Steps. Here, under the arch, at the entrance to St Bartholomew's, is a much defaced early thirteenth-century carving, *Virgin and Child Enthroned*, said by Pevsner to be in the style of the statuary on the façade of Wells Cathedral (see Christmas Street).[6] Backhouse has said that this work influenced him during his study of the site.

The sculptor made four maquettes of the horse and rider before one was selected and enlarged to a full-size plaster model in the artist's studio at Bradford on Avon.[7]

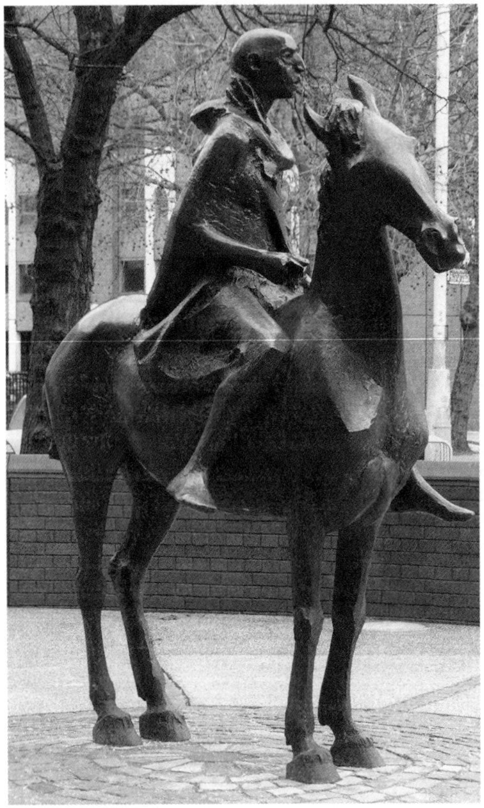

David Backhouse, *Cloaked Horseman*

Notes
[1] Office development prospectus, Haslemere Estates (c.1984). [2] A sculpture called *Aspiration,* at Bury Court House, City of London; notes supplied by David Backhouse, February 1994. [3] David Backhouse, notes written February 1994. [4] National Health Service Training Directorate, *History of St Bartholomew's Court*, p.1. [5] Op. cit., pp.2–3. [6] Pevsner, *North Somerset*, pp.438–9. [7] As note 3.

Lewins Mead, Greyfriars

FORMERLY on a wall to the left of the main entrance of Greyfriars, an office block, and in the interior at ground and first-floor levels

The Life of St Francis of Assisi C8

Sculptor: Judith Bluck

Architects: Kenneth Wakeford, Jerram & Harris
Senior architect: Jack Fraser
Date: 1974; **destroyed 2008**
Material: six exterior and three interior reliefs in cement fondu, suspended in polyester resin reinforced with fibre, GRP
Cast by the artist
Dimensions: all six exterior reliefs: 150cm high, 65cm wide, 20cm deep
Three interior reliefs: behind reception desk: 155cm high, 195cm wide, 20cm deep; opposite reception desk: 155cm high, 63cm wide, 20cm deep; on second floor: 140cm high, 280cm wide, 20cm deep
Push plates in bronze on the entrance doors designed by the artist: 39cm high, 16cm wide, 5cm thick.
Signed: most of the reliefs are signed: bluck – the third exterior relief and that opposite the reception desk are signed: bluck 74
Inscriptions: beneath each relief is a title – Francesco young knight of Assisi – Francesco kisses the hand of a leper – Francesco dreams of his fair bride poverty – Francesco renounces his worldly possessions – Francesco takes Clare into the Order – Francesco tames the wolf Agolio
–: beneath the reception hall reliefs and the second floor relief – FRANCESCO GREETS CARDINAL UGOLINO AT THE CHAPEL OF THE MATSE – FRANCESCO PREACHES TO THE BIRDS – FRANCESCO DEDICATES HIS CANTICLE TO THE SUN
Owned by GE Capital Corporation (Investment Properties) and Opus Land

Condition: the reliefs and door furniture were destroyed in September 2008 by Midas Construction with the agreement of the architects, Stride Treglown, and the owners, Arlington Property Investors on behalf of South Tyneside Council's Tyne and Wear Pension Fund. 'A key part of the proposal to re-image the external appearance is to construct a new glazed entrance to the building from Lewins Mead that would provide a greater sense of arrival for visitors and enhance the relationship between the entrance of the building and the public realm.'[1] The works were first offered to the artist and to Bristol Museums and Art Gallery.

(Description as of May 2008) Six large exterior panels and three still larger interior panels are modelled in very deep relief. Their subjects are described by their titles, recorded above. The thick bronze push plates on the entrance doors have images of St Francis on the outside and of St Clare on the inside. St Francis has a rabbit at his bare feet and he holds a bird with open wings. Beside St Clare, similarly bare-footed, is a squirrel.

A large and long inscription on two white marble slabs is set in the pavement outside the entrance. It begins with the words of St Francis and then outlines the history of the Franciscan friary on this site:

> GREYFRIARS
> "My sisters the swallows you have chattered enough" / he said "It is my turn to speak now, and / I pray you to keep silence and listen to what I have to say to the people." St Francis of Assisi / Greyfriars of the Franciscan community / founded by St Francis of Assisi built a friary / on this site circa 1250, about 30 years after / the order first came to England. / Additional land given by five Bristol citizens / in 1386 enabled expansion of the friary. / It included a more elaborate church with a / vestry, choir, buttery, hall and kitchen. / A feature was a water supply, piped from / Kingsdown./ In addition to a cloistered walk, records / indicate that there are gardens, dovecotes, / orchards, pools and a lime kiln. / The preaching and teaching of the friars / continued until the Reformation / when the friary was surrendered to / Henry VIII's Commissioners. / The deed was signed by six friars on / September 10th, 1538

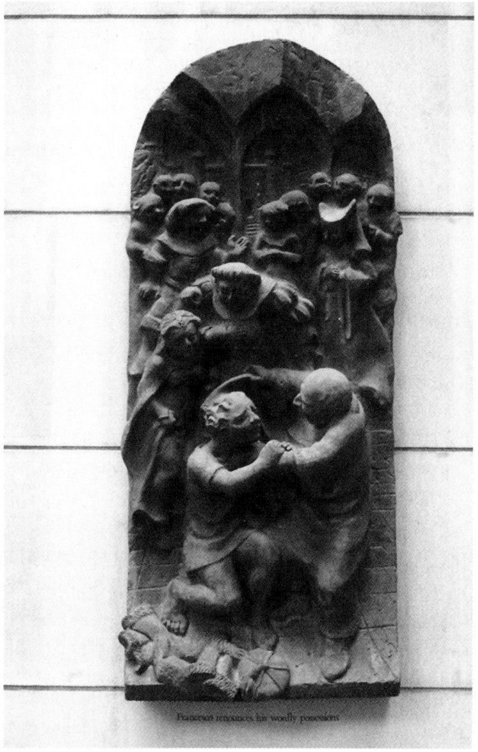

Judith Bluck, *Francesco renounces his worldly possessions*

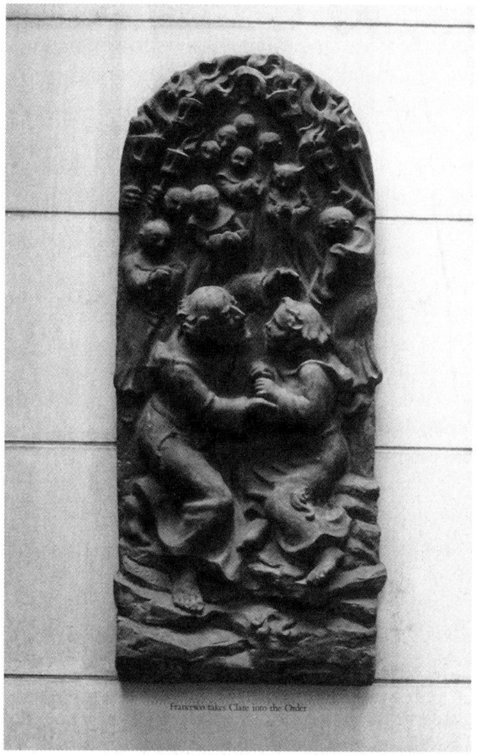

Judith Bluck, *Francesco takes Clare into the Order*

St Francis, Francesco Bernadone (1181/2–1226) was the son of a wealthy merchant of Assisi, and he appears to have lived well in his youth. After a serious illness in 1202 he devoted himself to solitude and prayer. He went on pilgrimage to Rome and gave profusely to the poor. Francis then spent many years in absolute poverty, often among lepers. He was a mystic with an extraordinary capacity for prayer, and his love of animals led to one of the most popular images in Western art: St Francis preaching to the birds. His order of Franciscan friars had been founded in 1209, and three years later he established the Franciscan order of the Poor Clares. He was canonised within two years of his death, at age 44 in 1226. By 1230 a Franciscan friary had been founded within Bristol's city walls. In the middle of the century it moved to this new site on the banks of the Frome, where it flourished until the dissolution of the monasteries in 1538. Excavations in 1974 revealed the foundations of the church.

This £4 million office development was

carried out by Howard Farrow in conjunction with the Church Commissioners for England.[2] The unusual dominance of religious imagery is striking. Even the glass entrance doors and windows are engraved with the image of a kneeling friar. The *Estates Times* saw irony in the presence of actual 'modern monks' as guests at 'a celebration in the modern temple of capitalism – a speculative office block' now associated with a saint who lived by the ideal of absolute poverty.[3] Sadly, in January 2008 the owners of the building asked the artist to recommend a new home for the reliefs and this unusual group, which so purposefully reveals Bristol's early medieval history, must be considered to be at serious risk.[4]

No competition was held for this substantial commission. Judith Bluck was recommended to Jack Frazer, the architect in charge of the project, by someone who knew her work.[5] Father Norman, a Franciscan scholar, provided notes on the history of the order. All the reliefs were modelled in clay, moulded in plaster and cast in *cement fondu* suspended in resin with fibre and some metal. With the exception of the bronze push plates, all this work was done by the sculptor in her own workshop. The works were 'unveiled' by Gervas Walker, Chairman of Avon County Council, in March 1975, when the sculptor was present.

Notes

[1] http://www.stridetreglown.co.uk/index.php?option=com_content&task=view&id=504&Itemid=233&limit=1&limitstart=1. [2] *Bristol Evening Post*, 30 January 1975. [3] *Estates Times*, 13 February 1975. [4] FG in conversation with artist, 28 January 2008. [5] Information from the artist.

Lewins Mead

On a triangular traffic island between Lewins Mead and Rupert Street

Samuel Morley C10

Sculptor: James Havard Thomas

Date: 1887
Materials: white marble; pedestal, red granite; base, grey granite
Dimensions: statue, 255cm; pedestal, 255 cm high, 140cm wide; circular base, 310cm diameter
Signed: J HAVARD THOMAS / SCULP. 1887[1]
Inscriptions: on front of pedestal cut into the granite in sans serif letters – SAMUEL MORLEY / MEMBER OF PARLIAMENT FOR THIS CITY / FROM 1868 TO 1885 / TO PRESERVE FOR THEIR CHILDREN / THE MEMORY OF THE FACE AND FORM / OF ONE WHO WAS AN EXAMPLE / OF JUSTICE, GENEROSITY AND PUBLIC SPIRIT / THIS STATUE WAS GIVEN / BY MORE THAN 5000 CITIZENS OF BRISTOL.
–: cut in the same style on the rear of the pedestal – "I BELIEVE THAT THE POWER / OF ENGLAND IS TO BE RECKONED / NOT BY HER WEALTH OR / ARMIES, BUT BY THE PURITY / AND VIRTUE OF THE GREAT / MASS OF HER POPULATION". / SAMUEL MORLEY
Status: Grade II
Owned by Bristol City Council
Condition: fair; surrounded by trees; a green coating has formed on the surface of the statue

Samuel Morley (1809–86) was the youngest son of a Nottingham manufacturer of hosiery. He was born in Hackney, London, and by 1860 was sole owner of what had grown into the largest company of its kind in the world. 'Morley was recognised as one of the most significant entrepreneurs in the country – and as one of the most dependable, steady, and honourable.'[2] He had been urged by Richard Cobden to stand for Parliament as early as 1857, but he declined for a decade due to his heavy workload. He was returned as the Liberal MP for Bristol on four occasions from 1868 to 1885.[3] Like the earlier members of the Wills family, he was 'a keen, though un-bigoted Congregationalist' and very active in various religious, philanthropic and temperance movements.[4] He contributed much to the completion of Bristol Cathedral.[5] He died on 5 September 1886.

> In some of the notices of his career which appeared in the newspapers it was stated that Mr. Morley had for many years dispensed between £20,000 and £30,000 of his large income annually in the support of pious and philanthropic objects.[6]

When he became one of the proprietors of the national *Daily News*, the main Liberal paper of period, he reduced its price to one penny and turned its loss to gain and greater influence.[7] Although a loyal supporter of William Gladstone, Morley disapproved of the House of Lords and declined a peerage.[8] He was buried in Abney Park Cemetery, Stoke Newington, where his funeral was attended by representatives of nearly a hundred associations. Morley's social concerns live on. He supported Emma Cons, the London-based evangelist and philanthropist, who developed an imaginative adult education centre in south London with Morley's assistance. In 1889, three years after his death, Morley College was founded as Morley Memorial College for Working Men and Women.

The statue depicts Morley in the formal dress of a man of the late 1880s: narrow trousers, frock coat, high collar and cravat. Bryan Little described the statue as 'somewhat stiff and pompous', but it is possible that Havard Thomas portrays Morley's character accurately.[9]

> Firm, frank, and somewhat severe in manner, Morley disliked laziness, time-wasting, and hesitancy and was impatient and irritable on encountering them… Immensely shrewd and

diligent in business, he devoted what was left of his time to serving his religion, in politics and philanthropy, and died a Victorian hero.[10]

There are two known maquettes, and Little noted that the one in the Bristol Art Gallery, inscribed 'James Havard Thomas. Sc. 1888', was better than the actual monument.[11] The other, a plaster cast, is in the National Portrait Gallery; the pose is different and there is a book on a pedestal to Morley's left. There is also a white marble relief portrait of Morley, again by Havard Thomas, on a memorial tablet dated 1887, in the nave of Bristol Cathedral.

Samuel Morley was greatly admired and deeply mourned by persons of every political and religious persuasion. 'Some months before his decease, a movement had been started among the Liberals of Bristol with a view to erecting some permanent memorial of his connection with the city.'[12] Within only few weeks of his death in 1886, a meeting was held at the Guildhall on 1 October to discuss the erection of a 'worthy memorial', and it was resolved to commission a marble statue.[13] 'Within six months of his death the statue was sculpted, money collected, site chosen, erected and unveiled!' [14]

The inscription on the pedestal records that '5000 citizens of Bristol' subscribed to the cost. The Bristol-born sculptor James Havard Thomas gained the commission, and *The Builder* reported 'a competition in which his model was successful'.[15] Bryan Little hints that Havard Thomas may have been selected by his admirer William Henry Wills, who 'would have been prominent among those who pressed for the statue's erection'.[16] On 27 October 1887 the statue was 'unveiled by Sir Joseph Weston in the presence of the Lord-Lieutenant, the Earl of Ducie and a crowd of several thousand'.[17]

The statue has been moved four times. Photographs show the statue on its original site in Baldwin Street, by the eastern end of St Nicholas Church, near Bristol Bridge.[18] This site became so busy that in September 1921 the statue made its first short move to allow a tramline to be laid closer to the church.[19] In the same year the statue went to its third site at Horsefair.[20] In 1954 the statue moved to a large grassed area that became known as the 'Morley Roundabout'.[21] Here the statue remained for 42 years, with minor road changes, until the Broadmead Gateway Project led to the fourth move in 1996. As the monument was listed Grade II, listed building consent was required. 'Samuel was lifted on 23 July 1997 and reset on his relocated plinth on 1 August 1997, having received a light clean in the interim period.'[22]

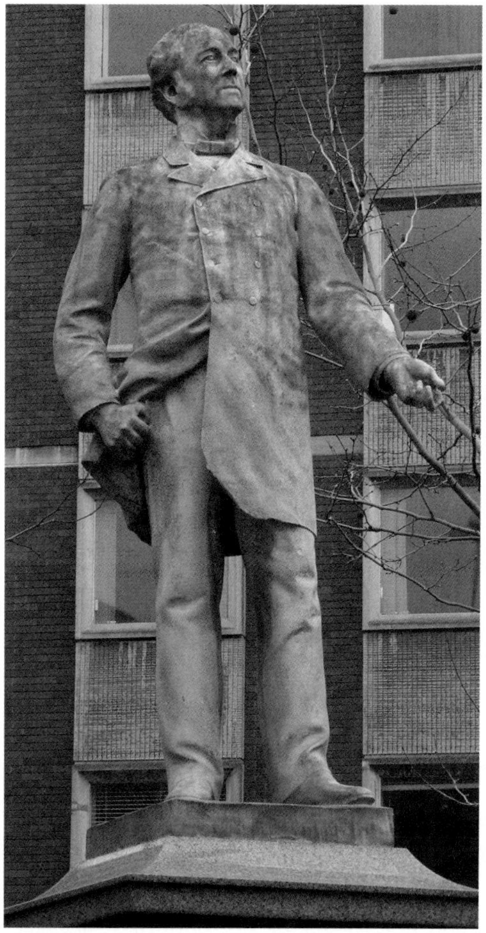

James Havard Thomas, *Samuel Morley*

The position of Morley's left arm in the statue was the subject of a letter from an elderly woman in a Bristol newspaper in 1964.[23] As a small child in the late 1890s her grandfather took her in a horse and cart once a week past the statues of Queen Victoria and Morley. He amused her by telling her that, on a full moon on the stroke of midnight from St Nicholas Church, Samuel Morley would hold out his hand to see if it was raining. If the weather was good he would make a dash to College Green to try to kiss the queen.

There is a version of the Bristol statue of Samuel Morley at the top of Market Street, Nottingham.

Notes

[1] Most unusually, the date is marked by preparatory drill holes only and was never completed. [2] J. Parry, *Samuel Morley*, *ODNB*. [3] Latimer, vol. III, p.233. [4] Little, *The Public View*, p.48. [5] R. Winstone, *Bristol in the 1920s*, caption 22. [6] As note 2, p.534. [7] Ibid. [8] As note 2. [9] As note 4. [10] As note 2. [11] As note 4; L28, inscribed: JHT Sculptor 1888. [12] Latimer, vol. III, p.534. [13] Ibid. [14] As note 4. [15] *The Builder*, 1886. [16] As note 4. [17] As note 12. [18] As note 5. [19] Ibid. [20] Ibid. [21] R. Winstone, *Bristol in the 1950s*, caption 56. [22] Garry Reeder, for the director of Corporate Resources, Bristol, letter to SWRA. [23] A. Palmer, *Evening Post*, 10 October 1964.

Lower Maudlin Street

On the outside wall of ground floor of the Bristol Eye Hospital

Creation C4

Sculptor: Walter Ritchie

Architects: Kendall Kingscott Partnership
Date: 1986
Material: Ibstock brick
Dimensions: approx. 18.50m long; each panel 210cm x 360cm
Inscription: on the panel on the far right (the letters were formed by the sculptor, using

clay from the same quarry as was used for the bricks) in sans serif – DISASTER AND CRISIS WERE ALWAYS ADVERTISED, / SETTLEMENT AND TRANQUILLITY SELDOM. / ONLY IN RETROSPECT COULD WE SEE THINGS IN THEIR / RELATIONS. WHEN WE PASSED FROM THE YEARS TO THE / CENTURIES, AND FROM THE CENTURIES TO THE WHOLE / EXPANSE OF MAN'S STORY – OUT OF CHAOS INTO LIFE, / FROM ANIMAL LIFE INTO HUMANITY, AND ON / INTO CIVILISATION; WHEN WE SAW MAN IN HIS COSMIC / SETTING, THE LATEST CHILD OF THE UNIVERSE WEDDED TO / AN ETERNITY, HIS THOUGHT TRANSCENDING MATTER / AND SEEKING DEITY – THERE WAS NO ROOM FOR IGNOBLE / DESPAIR: RATHER WOULD OUR MINDS BE FILLED WITH / WONDER AND OUR HEARTS WITH THANKFULNESS.

–: in an ellipse beneath this, in roman lettering – 1st Viscount Samuel /Commissioned by South West Regional Hospital Authority

Status: not listed

Owned by the United Bristol Healthcare NHS Trust

Condition: good

The Bristol Eye Hospital has been in Lower Maudlin Street since its foundation in 1810, when Dr William Goldwyer, a surgeon with skill in cataract operations, persuaded eminent people in Bristol to join him in founding 'an Institution for the cure of diseases of the eye amongst the poor'.[1] In 1839 the institution purchased 12 Lower Maudlin Street from the Blind Asylum. The façade of this house has survived.[2] A later hospital, designed by Sir George Oatley, was opened in 1935 by the Duchess of Beaufort. It was demolished in 1982, and the present building, a 78-bed hospital designed by the Kendall Kingscott partnership, opened in 1986 (the year of the 175th anniversary of the institution).[3] Kendall Kingscott and the South West Regional Health Authority commissioned Ritchie to enliven the blank street-level façade.

The themes of the five panels, reading from the left, were described in press information prepared at the time of the unveiling as: 'The origins of the earth, Seeds and flowers, Fish and birds, Animal life and Humanity'. The images present these concepts in a clear and immediately understandable manner. In the right upper corner of the fifth panel is an inscription taken from Viscount Samuel's 1947 Romanes lecture at Oxford, 'Creative man', which was broadcast on the BBC Third Programme to wide acclaim.

At the time of this sculpture commission, Kendall Kingscott's leading architect was Alan Beattie. His brief specified a range of consulting rooms with the privacy of limited windows. For easy access by patients these had to be close to the main entrance at street level. This might have resulted in a vast blank wall, but the solution produced one of the most admired sculptural commissions in Bristol. 'Plain brick on its own was considered too dull.'[4] Mosaic, ceramics and other materials were considered but, by chance, Beattie saw an article that prompted him to visit Ritchie's *The Queen and the Washerwomen* relief in the NatWest Bank, Corn Street. He was impressed, and contacted the South West Regional Health Authority for their agreement to commission Ritchie. 'At that time few clients, particularly public bodies, were prepared to spend money on "art" on the exterior of a building. To my everlasting surprise, they gave permission to allocate about £10,000.'[5]

When first approached, Ritchie gave a guarded 'yes' and Beattie and a colleague visited his studio and workshop at Kenilworth, Warwickshire.

> He was shy and rather reclusive and he lived simply and alone, looked after by his house-keeper. He had small, tortured looking hands with bent, possibly arthritic fingers, which seemed anything but those of a sculptor capable of the most delicate work. But evidence to the contrary was all around us.

Ritchie was slow to respond, but when he

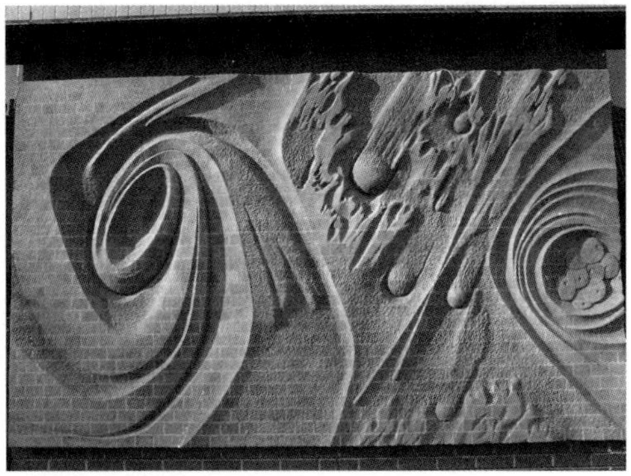

Walter Ritchie, *The origins of the earth*

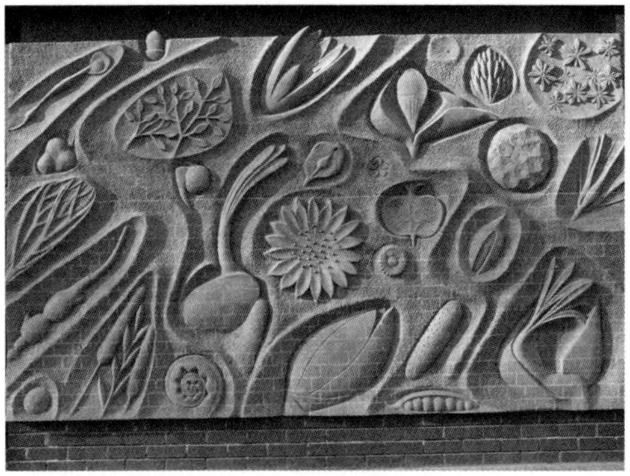

Walter Ritchie, *Seeds and flowers*

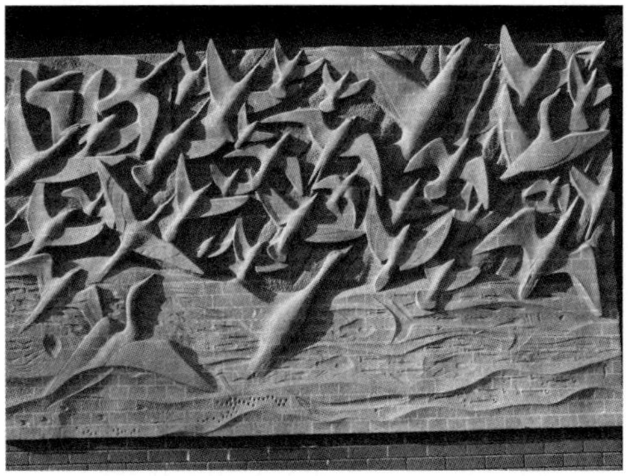

Walter Ritchie, *Fish and birds*

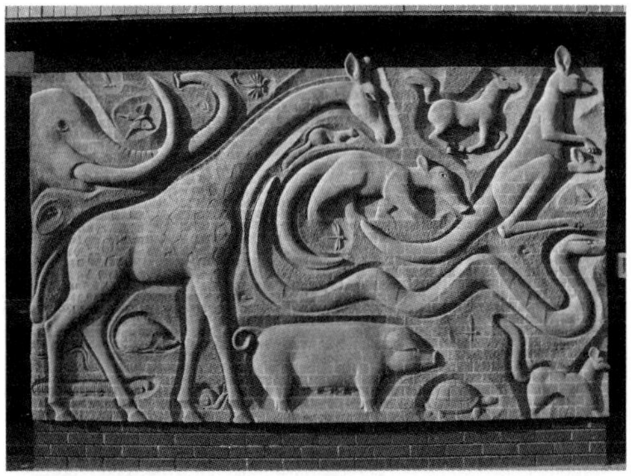

Walter Ritchie, *Animal life*

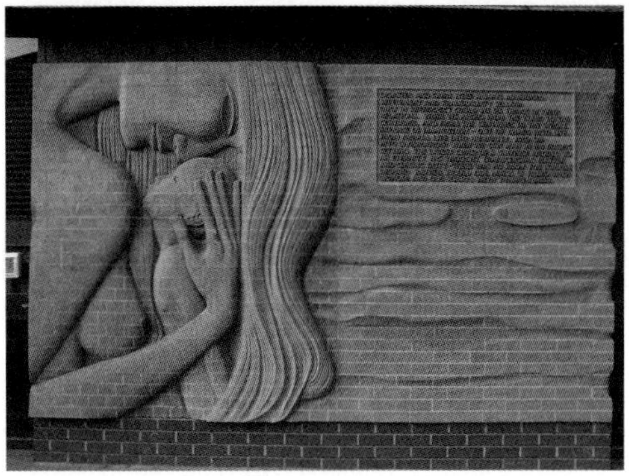

Walter Ritchie, *Humanity*

wrote to offer to take on the commission he wanted 'a completely free hand with the subject matter and design detail'.[6] Alan Beattie persuaded the chairman of the commissioning committee to visit Ritchie, and subsequently the decision to proceed was made.

> Walter asked for a fee of £25,000 but the best we could do was around £13,000. He obviously wanted to do it, as he agreed to the lower figure. I'm sure he saw it as one of his greatest challenges.

Ritchie had earlier written that his first brick sculpture 'was carved into the wall of a school and done primarily to economise in material, but brick attracted me for several reasons'.[7] He cited the ease of carving and superior weathering compared to many other types of material. 'In thirty years practice, however, despite attempts to popularise the medium with architects, I made only four sculptures in brick against several hundreds in other materials.' George Armitage and Sons commissioned his first work in this medium when he made a sculpture for their brick factory at Wakefield.[8]

Creation took three years to carve and the three bas-reliefs constitute the largest public sculptural work in the city. Bricklayers constructed the panels to precise specifications, and Ritchie carved them in Kenilworth. They were transported in sections by lorry to the site. The first two panels were set up in 1984, to be refined by the sculptor on site.[9] All the bricklaying was by Len Aiken.[10] Ritchie said the quality of the final result was as dependent upon him, 'a trusted friend and craftsman', as on his own design and carving. This modest remark recalls Eric Gill's confidence in his own assistants and pupils. When working on *Creation*, Ritchie would have been Gill's oldest-surviving former pupil.

Notes

[1] V.J. Marmion, *The Bristol Eye Hospital: A Monograph* (Bristol, 1985), p.6. [2] Caption to a drawing by A.C. Fare, ARIBA, of Oatley's 1935 hospital, from a card published by United Bristol Healthcare NHS Trust. [3] Press release from the Kendall Kingscott Partnership. [4] A. Beattie. Letters written in November 2005. [5] Ibid. [6] Ibid. [7] W. Ritchie, *Sculpture in Brick and Other Materials* (Kenilworth, 1978). [8] Ibid. [9] D. Harrison, 'Walter goes up the wall for his art', *Evening Post*, 31 May 1986, p.5. [10] As note 3.

In the inner courtyard of Bristol Eye Hospital, Lower Maudlin Street

St Odilia and the Bird C3

Sculptor: Stephen Joyce

Date: 1985
Materials: figure, bronze; bird, bronze resin
Dimensions: 160cm high; suspended bird, 240cm wingspan
Cast by Morris Singer, Basingstoke (the bronze figure only)
Inscription on a bronze plaque on the wall of the reception area: ST ODELIA, THE PATRON SAINT OF EYESIGHT LIVED / IN THE 9TH CENTURY: BLIND AT BIRTH SHE WAS / CAST OUT BY HER FAMILY AND ADOPTED BY NUNS. / AT THE CONVENT SHE /MIRACULOUSLY / REGAINED HER SIGHT AND LATER BECAME THE / ABBESS. THE SCULPTURE SHOWS HER SEEING / A BIRD FLYING OVERHEAD AT THE MOMENT IN / WHICH HER SIGHT RETURNS. / THIS STATUE WAS FUNDED BY THE TRUSTEES / FOR THE UNITED BRISTOL HOSPITALS AND / CREATED BY STEVE JOYCE IN 1985.
Status: not listed
Owned by the United Bristol Healthcare NHS Trust
Condition: good

Saint Odilia is said to have been the daughter of an eighth-century nobleman of Alsace, who rejected her at birth because of her blindness. She miraculously recovered her sight when she was baptised at the age of twelve. Ultimately she was to found two Benedictine convents and to become an abbess. Her shrine at Odilienburg is still a place of pilgrimage, and she is the patron saint of opticians.[1]

The life-size figure stands in the middle of a raised flowerbed in the centre of an inner courtyard of Bristol Eye Hospital. The woman looks skyward, her arms are raised and her hands shield her eyes. Her ankle-length dress is plain and coarse. She wears simple short, soft boots and stares at the bird suspended on wires from the surrounding buildings, approximately 15 metres above the ground. The wings are fully extended and it is loosely based on an Arctic Tern, made much over life-size for this sculpture.[2] Since the work was installed, health and safety regulations have led the hospital to lower the bird and to use cumbersome wires that are far too obvious.[3]

There was no competition for this project.[4] By the time Stephen Joyce was approached by

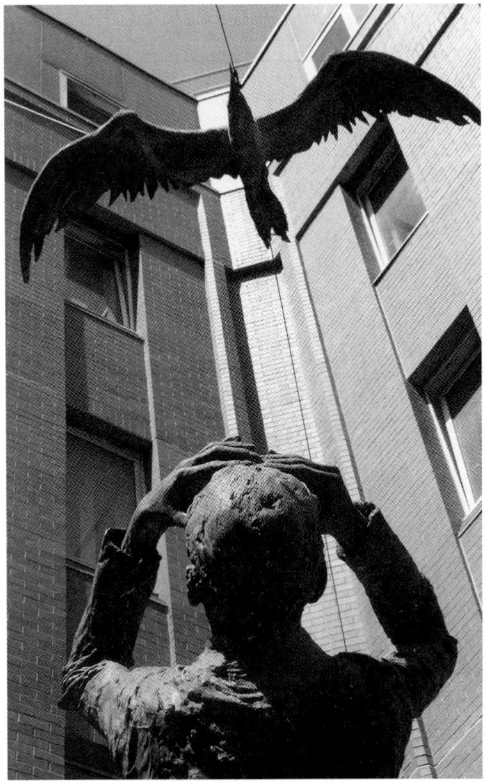

Stephen Joyce, *St Odilia and the Bird*

the United Bristol Healthcare NHS Trust, he was well known in Bristol for his sculpture of John Cabot (Narrow Quay) and for *Horse and Man* (St George's Road). The work, funded by the Special Trustees of the Hospital, was first discussed when the large brick relief was being made for the neighbouring façade of the newly-built Eye Hospital by Walter Ritchie.[5] Joyce's brief was simply to make something to fill the tall, enclosed courtyard.[6] Unfortunately the budget was small, barely adequate for materials. For his first meeting Joyce produced a drawing of a standing figure shielding its head, much in the attitude of the finished sculpture. To make use of the height of the courtyard, he proposed that the raised head would be looking at a suspended bird. The hospital committee liked the concept but asked whom the figure was meant to represent. Joyce then did some research and discovered the story of St Odilia. New drawings of a female figure and of a bird in flight were made. At a second presentation his proposals were immediately accepted and the sculptor made the full-size clay version before the figure was approved and cast in bronze. As the bird needed to be lighter in weight, it was made in bronze resin in the sculptor's workshop.

Notes

[1] D. Attwater, *Penguin Dictionary of Saints' Names* (Harmondsworth, 1995), p.249. [2] Information from Stephen Joyce. [3] As note 2. [4] As note 2. [5] Evelyn Mooney, general manager's secretary. [6] Discussions with the sculptor.

Mall Gardens, Clifton

Within the western public garden between West Mall and Caledonia Place, Clifton

Shooting Star and *Planet Bench* B20

Sculptor: Philip Bews

Date: 2004
Material: horse chestnut and holm oak
Dimensions: 2.4m high
Status: not listed
Owned by Bristol City Council
Condition: good

The example of Philip Bews's two cedar-tree sculptures in Bristol Zoo encouraged a resident of West Mall gardens, Toni Brown, to arrange for the existence of a condemned horse chestnut to be prolonged. It was fully understood that, unlike cedar wood, horse chestnut will decay. This is an ephemeral work with the bonus of an increasingly various and abundant growth of fungi.

Toni Brown enjoyed the active support of the council's Parks Department and the agreement of the Mall Gardens residents' association. The sculptor submitted two alternative proposals, and *Shooting Star* was chosen. The bench is made from the wood of a holm oak from Ashton Court. Its pilaster supports are made of reinforced concrete and local residents were much involved in its construction.

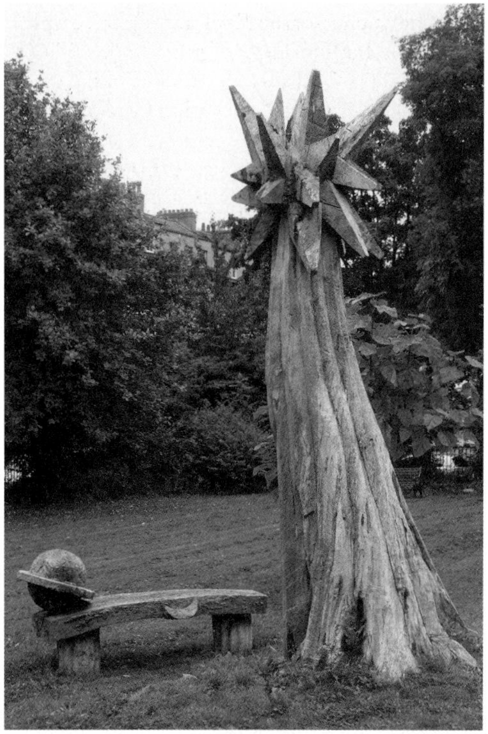

Philip Bews, *Shooting Star* and *Planet Bench*

Millennium Square

In November 1994, a consortium, initially called Bristol 2000 and later At-Bristol, was formed. It bid successfully to redevelop an eleven-acre portion of Canons' Marsh, now renamed Harbourside. Funding came from the Millennium Commission, English Partnerships, Bristol City Council and private sources. Building work started in 1997. Three new learning and leisure ventures were constructed: 'Explore' (now called At-Bristol), developed from the science-based Exploratory at Temple Meads and built inside the 1903 Canons' Marsh Goods Shed; 'Wildscreen', which told the story of life on earth and the evolution of plants from single-cell life to complex creatures; and a giant-screen Imax cinema. The whole project was officially opened by HRH the Prince of Wales on 14 June 2000. Together with the nearby Watershed Media Centre and Arnolfini, which was deliberately linked to Harbourside by the building of Pero's Bridge (Narrow Quay), At-Bristol was a major part of what was now perceived as Bristol's cultural quarter. Both *Wildscreen* and the Imax cinema closed in 2008.

A commissioning programme for public sculpture began in 1998. At-Bristol appointed Helen Carey to direct the process. She was advised and supported by the Concept Planning Group, a team of Bristol-based architects that included George Ferguson, Richard Lee and David Mellor. The trustees of At-Bristol were also closely involved, and it is to the personal initiative of the chairman, Nick Hood CBE, that we are indebted for William Pye's *Aquarena*.

Reflection and exploration were the common themes of the commissions, which were awarded to invited artists, after briefs had been made and the artist's proposals had been agreed.

A case study on the Millennium Square project on Public Art South West's admirable website labours the consequences of the commissioning of art by non-art organisations.[1] It argues that the technical team at At-Bristol, which now has responsibility for day-to-day maintenance, should have been involved in these technically complex and impressively various commissions from their inception. Certainly, there were problems. *Jasmine*, the painted-bronze Jack Russell, was too successful, too tempting. It was stolen, and after repeated attacks on its replacement, it was moved inside. The statue of William Penn, whose liberal principles were so far ahead of his time, but who, nonetheless, was a slave owner, was subjected to 'energetic interaction by the public' and had to be temporarily removed. Nicola Hicks's bronze *Beetle* proved to be irresponsibly fragile. Fortunately, all its more dangerous spikes had been broken off before inflicting serious damage on any clambering child. The two light works in the underground car park electrocuted staff who were replacing failed bulbs and both had to be removed within a year. The computer-driven stage-lighting system for the large floor piece *Zenith* started to fail early on. It was working again in 2008 for the first time in many years. Against this apparent catalogue of woes, all potentially temporary, is the triumph of William Pye's *Aquarena* and the successful – if very demanding and costly – maintenance of its complex hydraulics and computer systems, which run the waterfalls and water jets. There is now a new contract with Almeda for the mechanical and electrical maintenance of the buildings and site, and a determination to see all the problems resolved.[2] Simon Thomas's *Small Worlds* is supported by an annual maintenance grant from the Institute of Physics for the sculpture's first ten years. *Telespine* is now also the responsibility of At-Bristol, not of its previous owners, Orange. It is just outside Millennium Square, and although it was a joint initiative with At-Bristol, it was not originally seen as a part of the project. Public Art South West studiously ignores it altogether.

On the east side of Millennium Square

Aquarena B62

Sculptor: William Pye

Date: 2000
Materials: stainless steel, Welsh and green slate, bronze, limestone and water
Dimensions: approx. 52.5m long, 15m wide
Status: not listed
Owned by At-Bristol

Aquarena is the presiding presence within Millennium Square. It is an independent work of art of great refinement, a remarkably successful piece of landscape architecture and a paddling pool.

There are five elements covering approximately 70m², in which water is managed to various effects, from comparative tranquillity to fairly strong movements. The largest is the *Terraces*, a platform of four levels in black slate, about 60cm high, covered with about 2.5cm of constantly flowing shallow water. This terrace area can be drained to become 'a highly original performance space', giving the water sculpture its title, *Aquarena*.[3] At the northern end is a curved *Water Wall* made of polished stainless steel over which water flows in wave patterns. It is through a gap in this wall that many visitors make their first dramatic entrance into Millennium Square. The *Waterfall* is a low-level trough at the foot of the curved wall. At the southern end of the *Terraces* is the *Canyon*, two large vertical prism-shaped monoliths of highly polished stainless steel about 3m high. The *Vault*, covering nearly the whole length of the *Terraces*, is created by two rows of jetted water. The jets are rarely operated, but it is a measure of the success of the sculpture that, even without them, it remains an elegant and complete work of art.

Millennium Square was designed with a large and long rectangular pool beside the Explore building, together with the polished steel sphere of the planetarium at the north-east corner. William Pye, who had by then established a worldwide reputation for water sculpture, was chosen to create an additional 'fountain' feature to enhance this public space.[4] The original brief was for a water sculpture in the centre of the square, and William Pye's proposal gained the commission on this understanding. The client team then decided that this first design would prevent the use of the square for events 'involving large numbers of people and the feature was re-designed for the east side'.[5]

'The character of this feature will be monumental and dramatic when the hydraulics are fully employed; there will be periods when

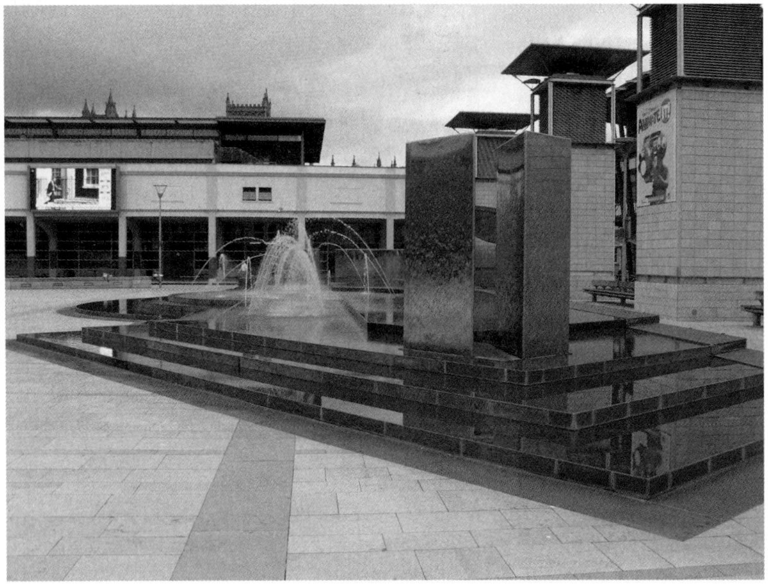

William Pye, *Aquarena*

the serene nature of water will be evident and lend the visitor somewhere calm and contemplative.'[6] William Pye's initial conception for the redesigned sculpture was very much as we usually see it today: that is, constant, calm and contemplative, and without water jets. Pye was encouraged to consider water jets and, after initial reluctance, he took up the idea with some enthusiasm.

At the opening, the sculptor described the work to *The Times*:

> There are some stepped terraces of shallow water, I've used dark surfaces for these so we can enjoy a bit of geometry here. And there's a curved wall of water flowing over mirror-polished stainless steel; and the centrepiece is a dome of water, a circle of 16 lamina jets directed and valved to create a skeletal dome structure of water. On either side of that, two rows of jets are directed up towards each other to create vaults of jetted water. These and the dome will be something quite special because there is a light in each nozzle so that at night it will create a wonderful skeletal structure that's lit from within.[7]

The jets were programmed to perform on the hour for a sequence of 15 minutes, but there were soon problems with the hydraulics, the internal lighting and the computer system. The computer system was updated in 2007 and the lights have been successfully replaced by LEDs.[8] After several years, the slate flooring of the pools had to be re-bedded, a nine-month project undertaken at the expense of the installers of the work, Carillion.

There was an estimate of £250,000 for artist's fees, materials and hydraulics, but additional costs were covered in a construction budget.[9]

William Pye has said:

> For me, water shapes the concept, directing the form and determining the fabric of the sculpture. It is often the smallest and most timeless of means by which water can be controlled that hold the greatest fascination, utilising those natural laws that govern the way water behaves.[10]

The sculptor's discreet and exact management of those laws demanded the firmest foundations and much precision engineering, or the water would have followed its own seemingly anarchic tendencies. Instead, the cascades continue to flow evenly over long walls of steel and the timeless repetition of complex moving patterns is mesmerisingly calming and reassuring. That the formality and dignity of the overall design is actually enhanced by the interaction of the public – by children paddling – is a further triumph. The children paddle as happily here as they once did above the weirs on the Frome at Stapleton. In summer, the innocence of childhood, so perfectly portrayed by Francis Danby in his paintings of those scenes in the 1820s, also becomes an inherent feature of this impressive sculpture.

Across the central surface area of Millennium Square

Zenith B63

Artist: David Ward

Lighting designer: Chris Baldwin of ACT Consultant Services
Date: 2000
Materials: 52 airport runway landing-lights, set flush with the surface of the square
Dimensions: approx. 46m long, 7.5m wide
Inscription on a bronze plaque: 'Zenith' / by David Ward / 2000 AD / Lighting Designer Chris Baldwin / Supported by AXA / Zenith is based on an analemma – the line / traced by the sun recorded at noon over a / year. An analemma was used by navigators, explorers and astronomers to determine / where they were. The 52 lights are / programmed to reflect the constantly / changing position of the sun as / it appears from earth / At-Bristol
Status: not listed
Owned by At-Bristol
Condition: good

Zenith recreates on the ground the sun's analemma in the sky as seen from earth. An analemma is the line or curve traced by the sun (or other celestial body) over the course of a year, when recorded from a fixed point at the same time every day or, as in this instance, every week. The figure-of-eight shape, like the changing seasons of the year, results from the tilt of the earth's axis in its relation to the orbit of the sun and from the elliptical rather than circular passage of the earth around the sun. The tilt or declination of the analemma across the square, as in the sky, is a reflection of Bristol's geographical latitude.

David Ward has said:

> *Zenith*'s visual formation and its performance as a light work relate to the source image of the analemma on a poetic level, as an analogue rather than a literal, mechanical model, allowing broader associations of astronomy, observation, movement, time and dynamics to come to mind.[11]

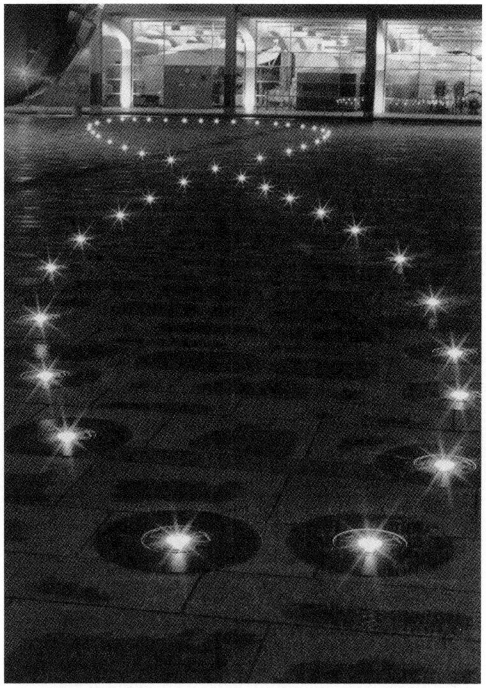

David Ward, *Zenith* (photo. Jack Tait)

The artist's aim was to suggest broad associations with astronomy and time, fitting well with the themes behind the commissions for Millennium Square, which were 'reflection' and 'exploration'.

The work consists of 52 runway landing-lights, one point for every week of the year. They are set into the surface of Millennium Square and form an elongated figure-of-eight, the sign for infinity. The lighting units are of the type used in heliports to produce an intense beam for long-distance visibility. The top point of the figure-of-eight (furthest from Explore) marks the highest position of the sun in midsummer. Each light is connected to a separate dimmer in a 72-way Strand EC90sv dimmer rack. They are 'programmed to trace a constantly changing orbital path across the square'.[12] The remaining 20 channels, with three remote Strand LD90 24-way dimmer racks, switch the Millennium Square lighting, thereby providing a total and coherent lighting control system for the entire space. Or so it was intended.

Zenith's computer-driven stage-lighting system started to fail soon after installation. It was eventually established that the cables had corroded because the correct type of waterproof armoured cable had not been selected. The square was dug up in two stages over two years and restoration was completed in 2008.

In the foyer of At-Bristol, Millennium Square

Jasmine
Sculptor: Cathie Pilkington

Date: 2000
Materials: bronze, painted in naturalistic colours
Dimensions: 35cm high, 80cm long, 15cm wide
Royal College of Art Foundry, London
Status: not listed
Owned by At-Bristol
Condition: good

The life-size Jack Russell terrier is in painted

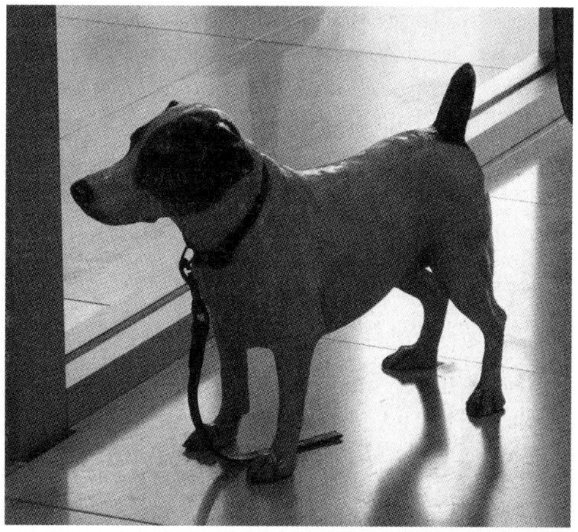

Cathie Pilkington, *Jasmine*

bronze and there is a trailing lead. The pose is of an alert animal that appears to have been abandoned or is perhaps waiting for its owner. Originally there was a circular bronze plaque in the pavement, giving details of the sculptor and the title of the work, but the sculptor asked that this be placed some distance from *Jasmine* to avoid giving the game away.

This was Cathie Pilkington's first public commission and she approached it with a determined independence:

> When I was invited to make some work for the space, I was interested in making something small which may easily get overlooked. The antithesis of much public art. I wanted to make something very ordinary. Using a small dog which was permanently sited drew on the content of my current work whilst throwing up some new thoughts. I used to live in Edinburgh, so I am very familiar with the story and monument of Greyfriars Bobby, who over the years has gained mythic status as a sentimental hero. Taking this as my cue I am particularly interested in the public response to *Jasmine*.[13]

That response was to be so strong that *Jasmine* was twice stolen. She was first placed near the bus stop on the Anchor Road side of the At-

Bristol building. Steel bolts were broken off and her paws left in the concrete.[14] When recovered, she was repaired and re-painted. Later she was placed inside the entrance to *Wildwalk*, where she guarded the reception desk and could be locked in at night. Following the closure of *Wildwalk* in 2008, she went into store, before reappearing in the summer of 2010 in the foyer of At-Bristol.

> The dog itself was modelled in clay over a wooden armature. The completed model was moulded and cast into bronze at the Royal College of Art Foundry. The two swimming dogs are made from the same mould and cut down at the wax stage of the casting process. The finished bronzes are painted with oil paint and sealed with lacquer.[15]

It was accepted that the dogs would have to be re-painted at intervals, and advice on that point was sought from the Tate Gallery. The total cost of designing, modelling and casting all three dogs was approximately £6000.

South-east corner of Millennium Square

Bill and Bob B65

Sculptor: Cathie Pilkington

Date: 2000
Materials: bronze and rubber painted in naturalistic colours
Dimensions: 17cm high, 60cm long
Royal College of Art Foundry, London
Status: not listed
Owned by At-Bristol
Condition: good

To the delight of children and most adults, the Jack Russell terriers, *Bill and Bob*, wallow half-submerged in a deep and irregularly shaped 'puddle'. The puddle is beside a ventilation shaft for Millennium Square's underground car park and it is surfaced with blue rubber granules.

Millennium Square's underground car park, outside the central southern staircase on levels -1 and -2

Arewehappynow? and *Everythingwaswonderful* B62

Sculptors: Sue Webster and Tim Noble

Date: 1999
Materials; steel, glass and light bulbs`
Status: not listed
Owned by At-Bristol
Condition: restored and redisplayed, 2010; not illustrated

These two installations, which greeted all those using the underground car park, were removed from display within a year. The bulbs were set in series, as once were Christmas tree lights. When one went, they all went. Furthermore, the bulbs were in un-insulated holders, and At-Bristol's estates director, valiantly battling to maintain so many recalcitrant works of art, received an electric shock. That same director was determined that the electrical components of these two pieces should be redesigned and the two works were finally reinstalled in July 2010.

At-Bristol's own press release describes the two works:

> Made of stainless steel and carnival bulbs sequenced to shimmer continuously, these art works appear to be, from a distance, just a beautiful glow floating above the exit from At-Bristol's car park to the lift area. Both pieces comprise handwritten text with individual words running into one another, forcing the viewer to examine them closely, in order to realise that they are letters which say something, while enjoying the beauty of the overall effect that the art work creates.

For Noble and Webster, perhaps these words hint at a perfect moment. Perhaps the viewer will pause to look at them on their way out of the car park, or they might not notice them until returning. Optimism and curiosity are at the core of the art work, as well as the leap into the unknown that optimism brings – what will the next step bring if everything was wonderful. If it was wonderful, what's next? Are you happy now, and if so, why, and if not, why not? Noble and Webster's interest in controlled environments – such as an underground car park – evokes parallels with Las Vegas and its human-made timelessness, the subject of earlier work by Noble and Webster. Light and power fuel these environments on many levels.

> This is the first permanent commission of Tim Noble and Sue Webster's work for the outdoors, extending the art gallery outside and increasing access to their work. It also encourages the idea that car parks – and in particular, underground car parks – need not be threatening, dark or forbidding spaces.

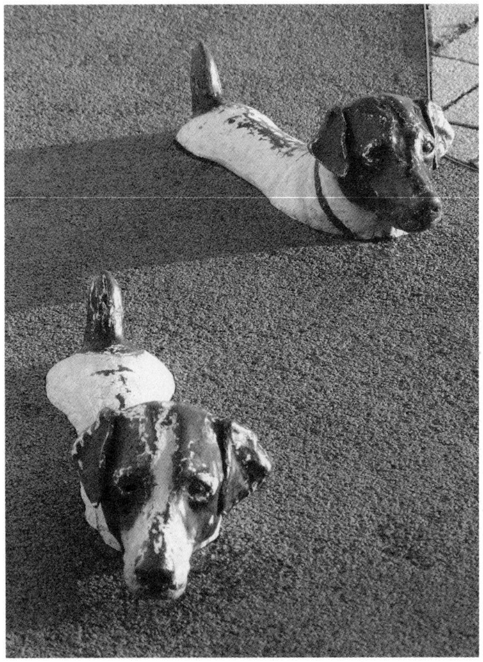

Cathie Pilkington, *Bill and Bob*

At-Bristol's car park is a superb space, reassuring, beautifully designed and easy to use – its art works also make it unusual and provocative.[16]

Tim Noble and Sue Webster have had considerable international acclaim since 1999, and these two cheerful if provocative works were an apt complement to a welcoming and impressively user-friendly car park that was intended to serve the Centre for the Performing Arts on the harbour's edge. That has yet to be built, but the site remains.

On the west side of Millennium Square

William Tyndale, William Penn and Thomas Chatterton

Sculptor: Lawrence Holofcener

Three related bronze figures were commissioned for Millennium Square in 1999. Tyndale, Penn and Chatterton are presented as eminent Bristolians, as their plaques proclaim, although neither Tyndale nor the younger William Penn was a Bristolian by birth or adoption. All were commissioned from Lawrence Holofcener. He came to attention when his bronze sculpture *Allies* was unveiled in Bond Street, London, in 1995. The work depicted Franklin D. Roosevelt and Sir Winston Churchill seated on a bench, with a space large enough for any passer-by to sit between them. This created a photo-opportunity that few visitors miss. In the later 1990s, anyone commissioning public sculpture with the aim of directly engaging the audience was likely to be aware of Holofcener's Bond Street sculpture. He was approached by Helen Carey, who led those responsible for the Millennium Square sculptures, but the selection of the sculptor and of the subjects was largely made by Nicholas Hood, the chairman of At-Bristol. To his far greater credit, the chairman was also responsible for the choice of William Pye for the sculpture on the opposite side of the square, a bold commitment and a most successful commission.

At the end of June 1999, Holofcener sent images of a number of small clay maquettes to demonstrate various poses, and in July he received a contract for all three statues. He presented a paper to the At-Bristol commissioning team explaining that he had arranged the three sculptures in a way that placed them in a 'surreal' meeting and suggested that they were communicating and observing each other. This interrelationship was not to be achieved.

Fixed to a bench at the centre of the south-west side of Millennium Square

William Tyndale B64

Sculptor: Lawrence Holofcener

Date: 2000
Material: bronze
Foundry: Bronze Age, London
Dimensions: 125cm high
Inscription on a circular bronze plaque set in paving close to the statue: An eminent Bristolian / William Tyndale / 1492–1536 / Translator of the Bible into English / – Martyred 1536 / by Lawrence Holofcener / 2000 AD / Bronze / Supported by / The Bristol Evening Post and Press / The Bristol Cancer Help Centre / Bristol Cathedral / At-Bristol
Status: not listed
Owned by At-Bristol
Condition: good

William Tyndale (c.1490–1536) 'gave us our English Bible':[17]

> The great change that came over England from 1526, the ability of every ordinary man, woman, and child to read and hear the whole New Testament in English, accurately rendered, was Tyndale's work, and its importance cannot be overstressed.[18]

There is little documentary evidence for Tyndale's early years, but 'the church at North Nibley is still thought… to be where the translator was baptised'.[19] There is a memorial tower at North Nibley, near Stinchcombe, and no doubt he was brought up in the wool-rich countryside of Gloucestershire and the Cotswold hills.[20] He was educated at Magdalen Hall, Oxford, from about 1506 to 1516, where he was influenced by a group of humanist scholars.[21] Tyndale was ordained aged 29, around 1521. For two years he became chaplain and tutor to Sir John Walsh's children at Old Sodbury, near Bristol.[22] His duties were light and allowed him time to preach in Bristol, and there is evidence that he did so on College Green, Bristol, and in neighbouring villages. This is his only direct link with Bristol.

Early in his life his views caused him to be summoned by the Bishop of Worcester and accused of heresy. He became determined that the Bible alone should be the basis of the doctrines and practices of the church: 'If God spare my life, ere many years I will cause a boy that driveth the plough shall know more of the Scripture than thou dost.'[23] When the English church authorities pursued him in 1524 he fled to Germany. There he made his first translation of the New Testament from Greek into English. This was printed in Cologne by July 1525. He then commenced a translation of the Old Testament but was arrested in Antwerp. For his great endeavour Tyndale was tried and later strangled and burnt at Vilvorde, near Brussels.

In 1784 Dr Andrew Gifford bequeathed the most complete surviving copy, lacking only the title page, of Tyndale's Bible's first print run (probably 3000 copies) to Bristol Baptist College.[24] This remained in its possession until 1996, when it was sold to the British Library for over £1 million when 'safety, preservation and availability to scholars was not satisfactory at the College'. Only two other copies are known: one in St Paul's Cathedral and the only complete copy, discovered after the sale of the

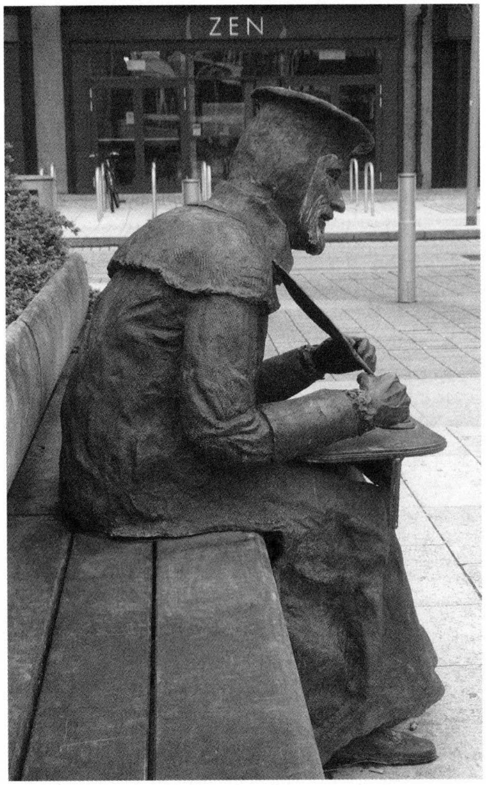

Lawrence Holofcener, *William Tyndale*

Bristol version, in Stuttgart's Landesbibliothek.

> Tyndale's gift to the English language is unmeasurable. He translated into a register just above common speech, allied in its clarity to proverbs. It is a language which still speaks directly to the heart. His aims were always accuracy and clarity. King James's revisers adopted his style, and his words, for much of the Authorized Version.[25]

The bronze figure of Tyndale is seated on a public bench where people can sit beside him. The portable wooden desk on his lap has an inkwell. A sixteenth-century English version of the Lord's Prayer is written on a 'sheet of paper' in his hand. He wears a circular cap and full-length clerical gown with a cape. A small satchel hangs at his side. No reliable contemporary portrait of Tyndale exists and his appearance, here, is based on later portrait engravings.

Standing in the south-west corner of Millennium Square

William Penn B64

Sculptor: Lawrence Holofcener

Date: 2000
Material: standing bronze figure, fixed to pavement
Dimensions: 180cm high
Foundry: Bronze Age, London
Inscription: on a circular bronze plaque formerly set in paving beside the statue – An eminent Bristolian / William Penn / 1644–1718 / Quaker – First Governor of Pennsylvania / – Essayist / by Lawrence Holofcener / 2000 AD / Bronze / Supported by / The Society of Merchant Venturers / of the City of Bristol / At-Bristol
–: inscribed on the 'paper' held in Penn's hands: Death is but crossing / the world / as friends do the seas, / they live in / one another still / William Penn / Quaker / Governor / Essayist / Egalitarian
Status: not listed
Owned by At-Bristol
Condition: good; plaque missing

A plaque, presently missing, described William Penn (1644–1718) as an 'eminent Bristolian'. His eminence is certainly unassailable. As a zealous and outstanding leader of the Quaker faith and as the founder and governor of Pennsylvania, he is justly revered. However, his links with Bristol are slight. His father, Admiral Sir William Penn (1621–70), was born in Bristol and he was buried with great pomp in St Mary Redcliffe, although he never lived in Bristol beyond his infancy. William Penn was born at Tower Hill, London. He was to visit Bristol on several occasions and his second marriage took place at the old Quaker Meeting House in Broadmead in 1696.

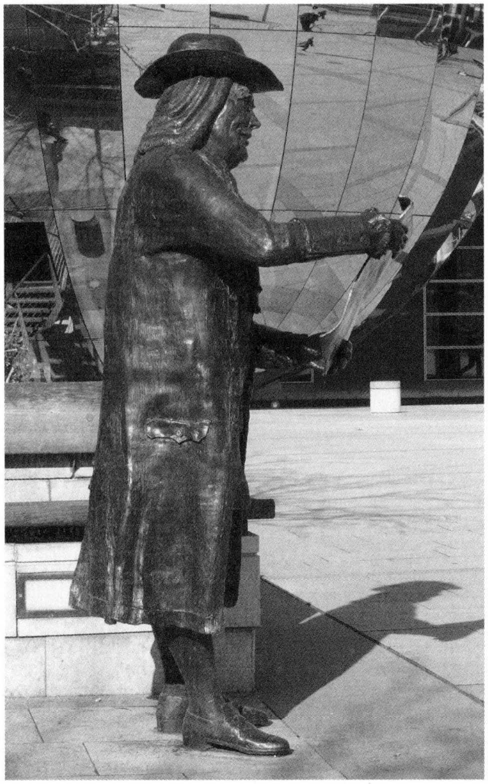

Lawrence Holofcener, *William Penn*

The free-standing figure is in seventeenth-century clothes: a domed broad-brimmed hat, cravat, coat, waistcoat, breeches, stockings and shoes with buckles. Penn is depicted reading from his own essays, and the words inscribed in the bronze, recorded above, are apt and moving, this work's one redeeming feature. His appearance is based on the many engravings that show him in Quaker dress of the period. The life-size bronze has no pedestal and, in its original position, it surprised passers-by as they entered or left the underground car park. It was originally fixed to paving stones by pinning with steel rods. This made the sculpture easy to push over and attempts began soon after it was erected in 2001.[26] It has recently been reinstated in a different position and without the separate explanatory plaque.

Details of this commission, one of three works by Holofcener, are given above.

Fixed to a bench on the south-west side of Millennium Square

Thomas Chatterton B64

Sculptor: Lawrence Holofcener

Date: 2000
Materials: bronze
Dimensions: approximately 125cm high
Foundry: Bronze Age, London
Inscription: on a circular bronze plaque set in paving beside the statue – An eminent Bristolian / THOMAS CHATTERTON / 1752–1770 / Poet – 'a marvellous boy' / by Lawrence Holofcener / 2000 AD / Bronze / Supported by / Winterthur Life UK / At-Bristol
:– a note once held in the poet's left hand read: 'To the memory of / Thomas Chatterton / Reader Judge not / if thou art a Christian, / believe that he shall / be judged by a superior / power. To that power / only is he now answerable – the same text is on two sheets, fallen by his feet.
On the book on his lap: ROWLEY / PAPERS /THOMAS / CHATTERTON
Status: not listed
Owned by At-Bristol Limited
Condition: fair

Thomas Chatterton, poet, was born in Bristol in 1752. He died in London only seventeen years later in 1770 in his room above a brothel. The coroner's verdict stated that he had 'swallowed arsenic in water' and he was declared a *non compos mentis* suicide.[27] William Wordsworth was soon to immortalise his memory as 'the marvelous boy / The sleepless soul that perished in his prime'[28] and the enthusiasm of Coleridge, Shelley, Keats,

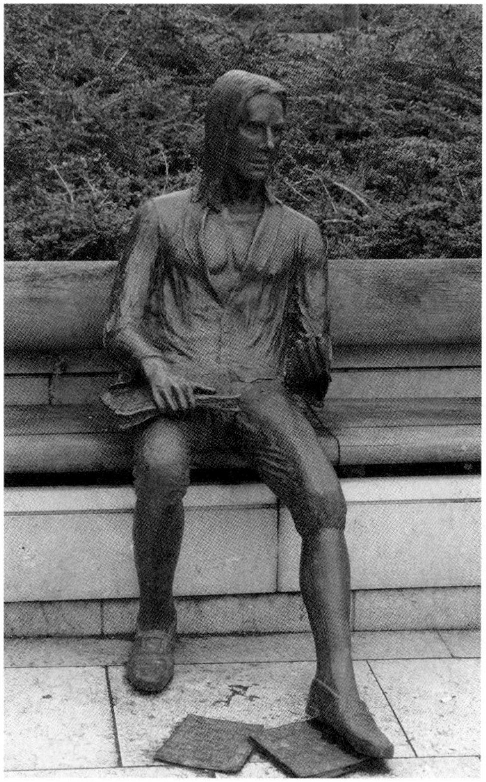

Lawrence Holofcener, *Thomas Chatterton*

Crabbe, Scott and Byron ensured his fame. However, pity and sensationalism, and especially Henry Wallis's painting of the *Death of Chatterton* (1856, in the Tate Gallery), have 'immortalised the pathos of the juvenile suicide in purple and puce' and disguised his considerable genius and his role as the 'loudest herald of the Gothic Revival'.[29] The suicide verdict itself has now been convincingly challenged. It is very possible, indeed more likely, that Chatterton 'was treating himself with arsenic for the pox, and either deadening its pain with opium or simultaneously taking opium recreationally'.[30]

Chatterton was the son of the master of the Pile Street school close to St Mary Redcliffe. At the age of seven he went to Colston's Hospital, then in the Great House on St Augustine's Back, where Colston Hall now stands. At fourteen he was apprenticed to an attorney in Corn Street and in April 1770 he moved to London, where he lived for four months before his death.

It was probably Chatterton's father, who died before the boy was born, who first brought home ancient deeds and manuscripts from chests in the muniment room above the North Porch of St Mary Redcliffe. Thomas's mother may have used the parchment for dressmaking patterns. For the precocious poet they were to be a gateway to a medieval world of fantasy centred on the real William Canynges and on Chatterton's own invention, the fictitious priest and secretary Thomas Rowley. At the age of eleven he passed off a work on parchment as an original. Thereafter much of his best work was composed in a mock medieval style and, if not always composed in order to deceive, it was certainly later promoted as medieval by Chatterton himself. In 1769 Horace Walpole was briefly duped, and controversy about the authenticity of other medieval manuscripts that Chatterton claimed to have discovered lasted far into the following century.

The bronze figure of Chatterton sits informally on a public bench. He was originally reading a 'sheet of paper', now detached and in store, in his raised left hand. His clothes – a loose shirt, close fitting breeches, stockings and plain shoes – are based on those in Henry Wallis's painting depicting his suicide.[31] Much of the surface of the bronze is textured. The inscription, detailed above, on the papers at his feet is from 'a mock suicide note he wrote to shock his employer into releasing him from his indentures' when he was still in Bristol.[32]

Bristol's monuments and memorials to Chatterton have had a chequered history into which Holofcener's boneless figure fits all too well. Although a Bristol monument to Chatterton's memory was first proposed in 1792, it was not until 1838 that John Britton

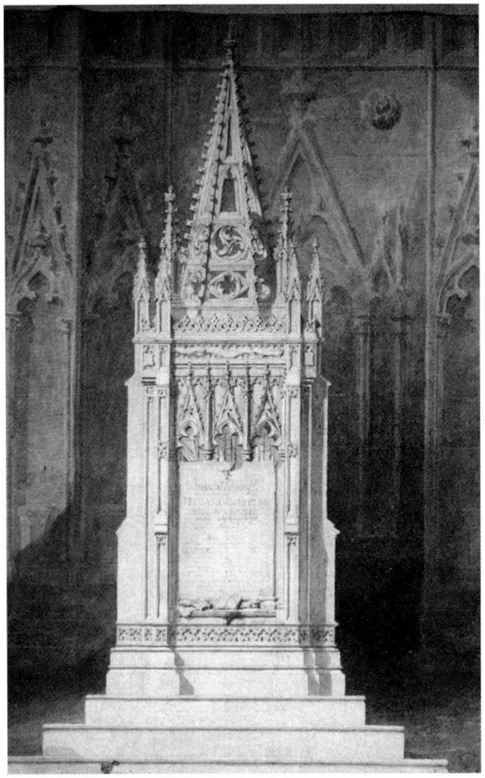

John Britton, *watercolour design for a memorial to Chatterton*, December 1838 (Bristol Museum and Art Gallery, M1102)

designed a fine early Gothic Revival cenotaph.[33] It was not taken up. Instead, a rather diminutive statue of Chatterton in the uniform of a Colston's Hospital schoolboy, paid for by public subscription, was erected on a tall Gothic column in 1839.[34] It was designed by the architect S. C. Fripp, a former pupil of Thomas Rickman and one of Bristol's three city surveyors. The monument was awkwardly sited, wedged between the north porch and the tower, possibly because this site was at the time believed to be unconsecrated ground, befitting a suicide, but also because it elevated the image of the poet to within a few feet of the muniment room above the porch.

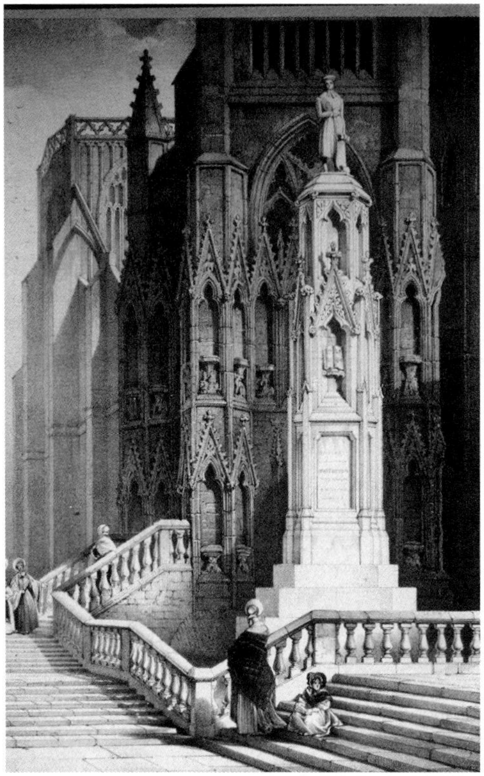

S. C. Fripp, *Chatterton's monument at St Mary Redcliffe*, lithograph, 1839, after S. C. Jones (Bristol Museum and Art Gallery, Ma4157)

In January 1846 the statue and its column were taken down, just a few months before the long and radical restoration of the church was begun.[35] It was re-erected over a decade later on 31 July 1857 on unconsecrated ground about 15 yards to the north of the transepts, opposite the Pile Street school that Chatterton had attended and close to his birthplace.[36] This was just a year after Henry Wallis's famous painting had been a sensation at the Royal Academy's summer exhibition. A photograph from about 1890 shows the statue behind ten-foot railings that possibly marked the front edge of the south side of Pile Street, whose demolition in the 1840s had so suddenly opened up unfamiliar vistas of the north side of the church.[37]

The monument survived until 1967, when, badly weathered and seriously damaged, it was demolished.[38] The footless and hopelessly eroded statue of Chatterton was rescued by museum staff and moved across the road to the little Georgian house that is now so inconveniently marooned beside Redcliffe Way.[39] The building is now called Chatterton House, but the original plaque upon it proclaims: 'This House was erected by GILES MALPAS of St Thomas Parish Gent for the use of the Master of this School AD 1749'. It was here that Chatterton was born in 1752, soon after the death of his father, the master of the Pile Street school.

In 1938–9, when Redcliffe Way was constructed as part of the new inner ring road, the north side of Pile Street was demolished, together with the school. In a questionable act of preservation, the school's facade was then re-erected as a screen against the highway side of Chatterton House. Within the pediment of that façade is a plaque, installed in 1897 by the Clifton Antiquarian Club, which somewhat misleadingly states that Chatterton attended the school. It could only have been a forerunner of this school at which Chatterton was briefly taught, for the façade dates from 1779, a decade after his death. At the age of seven he had gone on to Colston's Hospital, then in the Great House on St Augustine's Back, where Colston Hall now stands.

The earliest recorded memorial to Chatterton was erected in 1783 in Bath by Philip Thickness (1719–92), a wealthy and much maligned eccentric, in his garden at Sion Hill. 'A copper engraving of 1784 portrays a romantic grotto of tufa stone with commemorative urn and subscription'.[40]

Holofcener's bronze is the most recent memorial, and it perpetuates the suicide story. When last examined in March 2008, the fingernails of Chatterton's raised index and forefingers had been painted with an oddly appropriate purple nail varnish. Chatterton appeared to be making a V sign, once again expressing his bitter contempt for the Bristolians around him.

On the west side of Millennium Square

Movie Star B64

Sculptor: Graham Ibbeson

Date: 2001
Materials: bronze
Foundry: A B Fine Art
Inscription: An Eminent Bristolian / Archibald Leach / also known as / Cary Grant / 1904 – 1986 / 'Movie Star' / by Graham Ibbeson / Bronze / Unveiled by Gary's widow / Barbara Jaynes / 7 December 2001 /Supported by Gary's/ family, friends and fans
:– on the script: TO/ CATCH/ A / THIEF/ DIRECTOR / ALFRED / HITCHCOCK
Status: not listed
Owned by At-Bristol
Condition : good

'Today, as his contemporaries fade, Cary Grant remains indestructible, the all-time greatest male movie star'.[41] He was born at 15 Hughenden Road, Horfield, Bristol on 18 January 1904. His father was a tailor's presser, his mother was the daughter of a shipwright and his name was Archibald Alec Leach. He died in Iowa in 1986.

Archie's early years were unhappy. His father left home, and when he returned in 1913 his mother's mental state collapsed and she was committed to an institution. Nobody told the boy. Not until the 1930s when he returned to Bristol for his father's funeral did the Hollywood star, now called Cary Grant, establish that she had not died as he had for so long believed, but was still alive. He arranged for her release from hospital and settled her in a house of her own in Bristol. Cary Grant was to visit his mother many times until her death in 1973.

He left school at the age of fourteen and joined a troupe of boy acrobats, stilt walkers and slapstick comics called Bob Pender's Knockabout Comedians. In 1920 the company toured the USA, where he and some of the younger members stayed on. He acted in his first film in New York in 1931, before moving to Hollywood and a five-year contract with Paramount. In 1936 he bravely refused to renew his contract, insisting on a share of the box office returns as well as a fee.

> A dark, handsome man well over 6 feet tall with thick, wavy hair and an attractively cleft chin, he was a romantic comedian, suave and well dressed, ironic, jaunty, and a touch caustic, but very, very funny. The world accepted this relaxed figure as the real person, and to his many friends he was an amusing and generous individual. But the image was carefully cultivated, and behind it was a complex and troubled man.[42]

In 1974, Cary Grant unveiled a plaque in New York recording the thousands of tons of rubble from blitzed Bristol that was taken as ballast and used as foundations for the East River Drive highway. There is a replica of this plaque in the city centre, close to the Hippodrome where Archibald Leach had performed as a teenager.

As with the Holofcener works, the statue has no plinth. The life-size figure, dressed in a single-breasted dinner jacket with wide and long lapels, a bow tie and a handkerchief in the breast pocket, appears to stroll casually across the square. His right hand is in his trouser pocket and in his left he holds the script of a Hitchcock film, *To Catch a Thief*, in which he starred.

Four Bristol businessmen – Simon Cook, Peter Gifford, David Long and David Showler – campaigned for over two years to raise funds to commission this statue. They cited the statues of other media stars that had been erected in English cities – Charlie Chaplin in London, Gracie Fields in Rochdale and Tony

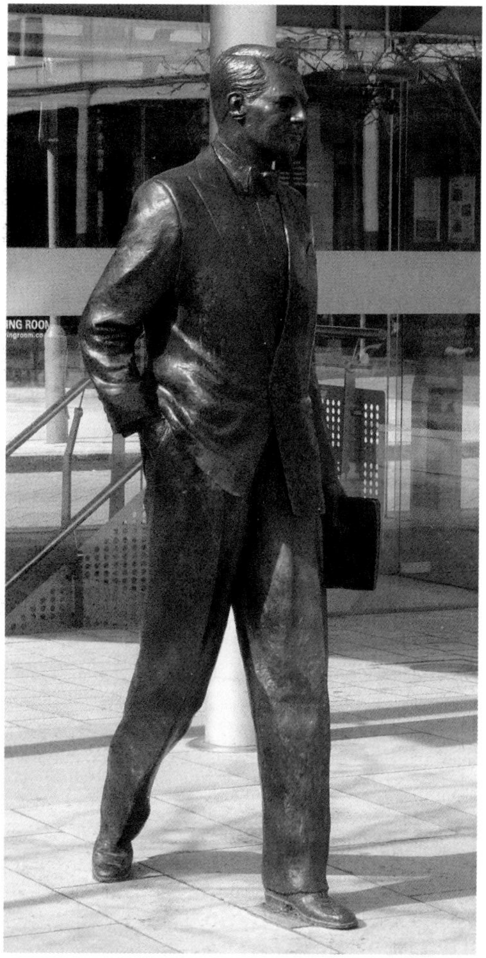

Graham Ibbeson, *Movie Star*

Hancock in Birmingham – and they looked upon Millennium Square with due optimism. Early patrons enlisted were Grant's widow Barbara Jaynes, Peter Cadbury, John Cleese, Lord Puttnam and Sydney Sheldon.[43] The organisers were determined that funds should be raised from public and corporate sponsorship, and within a relatively short time they were successful. A large crowd was present on 7 December 2001, when Grant's widow made a short speech and unveiled the bronze.

The sculptor said that he had found this statue the most challenging of all his commissions in thirty years.

In Anchor Square between the Leadworks and At-Bristol, north-east of Millennium Square

Beetle B61

Sculptor: Nicola Hicks

Date: 2000
Materials: bronze, painted black, on a limestone pedestal
Dimensions: 90cm high, 265cm long, 120cm wide; pedestal: 80cm high, 340 long, 175cm wide
Foundry: Bronze Age, London
Inscribed on a circular bronze plaque set in paving beside the sculpture: 'Beetle' / by Nicola Hicks / 2000 AD / Bronze / At-Bristol
Status: not listed
Owned by At-Bristol
Condition: fair

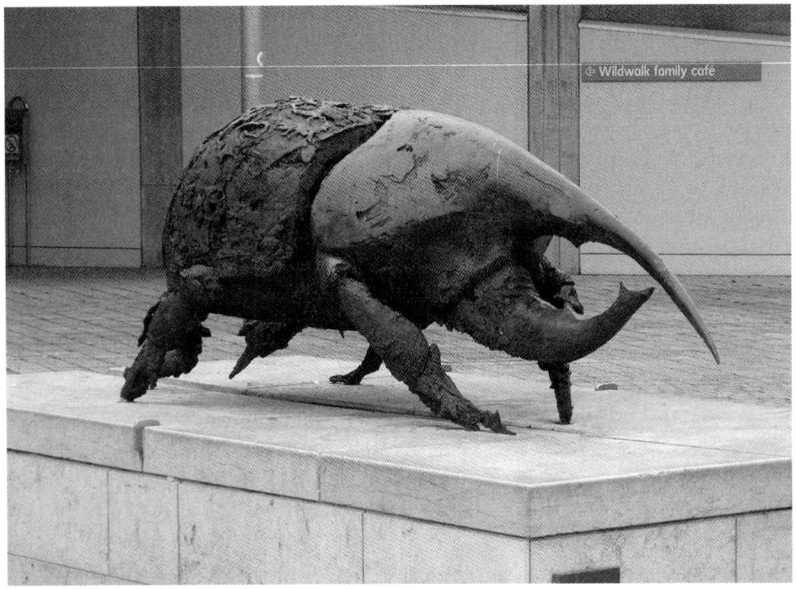

Nicola Hicks, ***Beetle***

This vastly oversized bronze beetle, nearly two metres long, is painted black and placed on a low rectangular stone pedestal. The form was based on the Rhinoceros beetle, one of various scarabaeid beetles that have one or more horns on their heads. The Rhinoceros is 'one of the world's strongest creatures that can support up to 850 times its own weight'.[44]

This work is sited near the industrial Leadworks building, now a restaurant and offices, but close to the former entrance to Wildscreen, At-Bristol's second major science project, which was obliged to close in 2008.

Much of the fine detail of this bronze sculpture was broken off within weeks of installation, although only the antenna can be considered a serious loss. The damage was a consequence of the method of construction and a necessary stage in making the work safe: in effect, in turning it into a public sculpture.

The sculptor's dealer, Flowers East, has stated:

> Hicks' primary media are plaster and straw, and huge sheets of brown paper on which she works up her dynamic charcoal drawings. Many of the sculptures have subsequently been cast in bronze, often with such subtlety that every fragile detail of plaster and straw is reproduced.[45]

Such fragility is, of course, utterly unsuited to public sculpture, a fact that a long-established London dealer of 'one of the foremost sculptors of her generation' should surely have acknowledged. As At-Bristol's own website states, this work has 'a sense of immediacy and a tactile quality which invites interaction from the viewer'. Fortunately no one was hurt in the brief, inevitable and, in this instance, necessary process of vandalism, some of it official, that removed the fragile but potentially vicious protuberances.

Canon's Road, to the south of Millennium Square, above the vehicular entrance to the underground car park

Telespine B66

Designer: Chee Horng Chang

Engineers and urban designers: Alan Baxter and Associates
Date: 2001
Dimensions: 20m high
Materials: painted steel and stainless steel
Inscription on a bronze plaque set in the pavement: Orange TM / Millennium Landmark structure/ 2000 AD / The Orange Millennium Landmark initiative is a national / design competition developed to strike a balance between / the technical requirements for a transmitter site while at the / same time providing an environmentally sensitive structure. / Designed by Chee Horng Chang and developed by / London based designers, Alan Baxter and Associates / the winner of the 1999 competition is not only an / example of innovative design but also provides / additional coverage within the Orange/ wirefree village At-Bristol/ At-Bristol

Status: not listed
Owned by Orange P.C.S.
Condition: good

Consisting of eleven steel sections around a gently curving circular central pipe, the tapering tower is initially reminiscent of a human spine, perhaps deformed. The whole structure is coated in a white high-gloss finish. Two unashamedly functional transmitters or aerials interrupt the outlines at the fourth joint from the top. The tower ends abruptly at the top. It rises from within a disproportionately large polished steel base, introduced to deter climbers.

This Orange transmitter mast is the outcome of a competition, a worthy initiative that ultimately only confirmed the pitfalls of employing art as camouflage, rather than relying on good design.

In order 'to find a new way of thinking about mobile telephone masts in our environment', the Orange Millennium Landmark Initiative was developed in conjunction with the Prince of Wales's Institute of Architecture.[46]

> Designers, artists, architects, sculptors, students and children as well as other members of the public were invited to design an aesthetically pleasing and environmentally sound telecommunications mast. Entrants had to ensure that their design fulfilled the technical requirements of a mobile transmitter while being a fitting millennium landmark. In other words, entries had to balance technical necessity with artistic and environmental concerns. Entrants were encouraged to create positive celebrations of place and they were advised against making masts invisible or disguising them.[47]

The overall winner and the winner of the student category was a student of architecture at Nottingham University, Chee Horng Chang. 'I based my design on a sound wave, creating a physical representation of the fundamental element of any communication.'[48] Whether or not there is an intended analogy between sound wave and spine, it is of a spine that the viewer first thinks, and with some confusion, for the component parts are not based on any animal structure. The confusion is compounded when the viewer spots the aerials or reads the plaque's explanatory inscription.

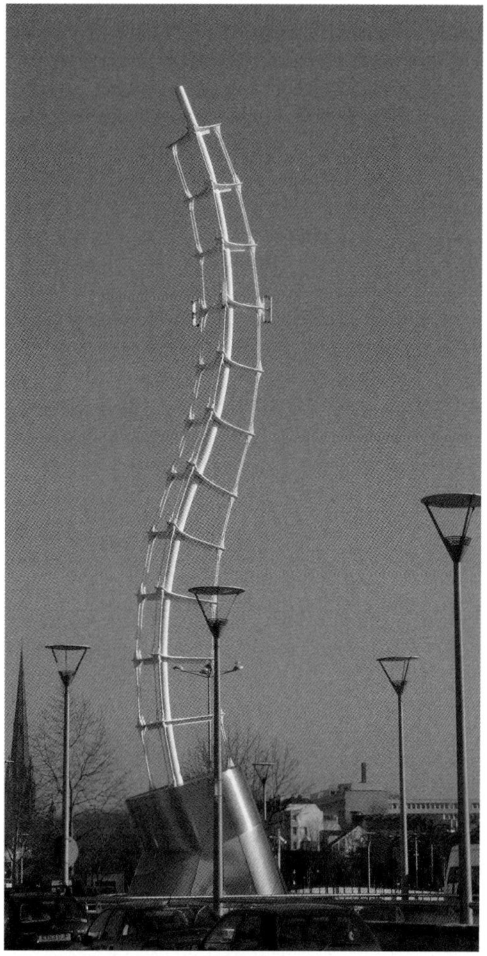

Chee Horng Chang, *Telespine*

The mast has recently been decommissioned, superseded by nearby aerials. Orange, who were major sponsors of At-Bristol and whose support enabled the building of the planetarium, offered the mast to At-Bristol. Faced with the possibility of losing a now familiar landmark, At-Bristol, perhaps mistakenly, elected to take it on. Formal ownership has yet to be transferred.[49]

Notes

[1] Joanna Morland, www.publicartonline.org.uk/archive/casestudies/atbristol/description.php. [2] Mike Rippon, estates director at At-Bristol, has had only a normal building maintenance team to manage the sculpture and does not have access to the specialist staff maintaining *Explore's* exhibits, as implied by Joanna Morland, above. [3] www.at-Bristol.org.uk/open/Aquarena.htm. [4] Undated press release, 'Aquarena, Millennium Square', p.1. [5] As note 4. [6] Undated press release, 'Water & art At-Bristol', p.1. [7] *The Times*, 7 July 2000, p.16. [8] Mike Rippon, estates director at At-Bristol, has maintained *Aquarena* with enormous determination, effort and expertise. [9] As note 6. [10] As note 6. [11] At-Bristol press release; www.at-bristol.org.uk/open/Zenith.htm. [12] As note 11. [13] Cathie Pilkington, information for public art at Bristol, sent to the At-Bristol project; *Greyfriars Bobby*, set up by Baronesss Burdett Coutts in 1873, commemorates a dog who visited the churchyard grave of his master for fourteen years. [14] *Evening Post*, 'Thieves have carried off Jasmin', 4 May 2000, p.2. [15] Cathie Pilkington, as note 13. [16] www.at-bristol.org.uk/open/everything.htm. [17] D. Daniell, *William Tyndale, A Biography* (New Haven, CT and London, 1994), p.i. [18] *ODNB*. [19] As note 1, p.10. [20] As note 1, p.13. [21] *Encyclopedia Britannica*, fourteenth edition, vol. 22, p.643. [22] Hutton, *Bristol and its Famous Associations*, p.348. [23] *ODNB*. [24] Mary Barker, college librarian, Bristol Baptist College, letter dated 14 September 2000. Source: A.S. Herbert, *Historical Catalogue of Printed Bibles: English 1525–1961* (London, 1968). [25] *ODNB*. [26] Mike Rippon, estates director, At-Bristol, November 2005. [27] A. Heys (ed.), *From Gothic to Romantic: Thomas Chatterton's Bristol* (Bristol, 2005). [28] The lines come from the poem *Resolution and Independence* (initially entitled *The Leech-Gatherer*), first published in 1807 in *Poems in Two Volumes.* [29] B. Cottle, *Thomas Chatterton* (Bristol, 1965). [30] As note 27, chap. 7; Groom, *The Death of Chatterton*, pp.116–25. [31] Henry Wallis, *The Death of Chatterton,* 1856, Tate Gallery. This was painted in the room where he died. [32] G. Young, *Bristol Civic Society Newsletter*, January 2005, p.8. [33] John Britton's watercolour is in Bristol Museums and Art

Gallery, (M1102); John Britton F.S.A. (1771–1857), antiquarian and topographer, was the author of a pioneering architectural history of St Mary Redcliffe, published in 1813, which included an essay on Thomas Chatterton. [34] A lithograph by Day and Hague after S.C. Jones depicts the monument in 1839, Bristol Museums and Art Gallery (M818). [35] Nicholls and Taylor, *Bristol Past and Present*, vol. III, p.345. [36] Op. cit., p.348. [37] Bristol Museums and Art Gallery (Ma4157). [38] For photographs, see Winstone, *Bristol As It Was 1937–1939*, pl. 83–6 and *Bristol As It Was 1953–1956*, pl. 217. [39] Bristol Museums and Art Gallery, in store at L Shed. [40] J. Lees Milne and D. Ford, *Images of Bath* (Richmond-upon-Thames, 1982), p.64; the engraving appeared in *The Lady's Magazine*, February 1784; see also Heys, op. cit., chap. 4; K. Turner, 'Dr Viper's Monkey: Philip Thicknesse and the 'Chatterton Momument" in Heys (ed.), *From Gothic to Romantic*, pp. 64–79 (illus. p.67). [41] Mark Steyn, *The Spectator,* 1 September 2001, p.43. [42] *Rachel Low, ODNB*, from which much of the biographical information is drawn. [43] D. Long, *West Country Life*, 18 May 1999. [44] Letter from Flowers East, Nicola Hicks's agent. [45] www.flowerseast.com/FE/Artists_Originals.asp?Artist=HICKS. [46] Orange UK environment report (1999), pp.29–32. [47] Op. cit., p.29. [48] Op. cit., p.30; the title 'Telespine' is also recorded on p.30 of this report. [49] Mike Rippon, estates director at At-Bristol, 2008.

Myrtle Road

At the main entrance to the Public Health Laboratories

Microscopic Observations B28

Sculptors: Jerry and Anne Hicks

Date: 1968
Materials: cast concrete with glass and optical items inset
Dimensions: 190cm high, 360cm wide; each hexagon, 60cm wide
Status: not listed
Owned by Public Health Laboratories
Condition: fair

This work is outside the main entrance to the Public Health Laboratories. Thirteen cast-concrete hexagons, of which seven are threaded onto vertical scaffolding poles and six are mounted onto a wall, form a screen. The main surfaces of the hexagons have varied relief patterns and some have glazed insets containing laboratory equipment.[1] The hexagons that are fixed to the steel poles are double-sided. Another, on the wall, was originally backlit.

The purpose of the screen was to give prominence to the entrance to the laboratories as visitors approached through a courtyard from Myrtle Road. The artists were asked to create images based on discoveries made when a new electron microscope revealed the hexagonal forms of viruses in random distribution. Many examples of the new images were shown to the artists, and the screen is an unusual reference to a significant turning point in microscopic observation.[2]

The entrance to this building is now a sorry sight. An air-conditioning unit, cycle shed, security camera and bright blue paint, and usually a motor scooter, surround the screen; this is a form of urban decay with which the artists are familiar. Jerry and Anne Hicks, who were both at the Slade School of Art, are better known for their paintings, but both have been actively and most effectively concerned with Bristol's architectural environment for over 50 years. Jerry continues to be responsible for Bristol Civic Society's urban development portfolio.

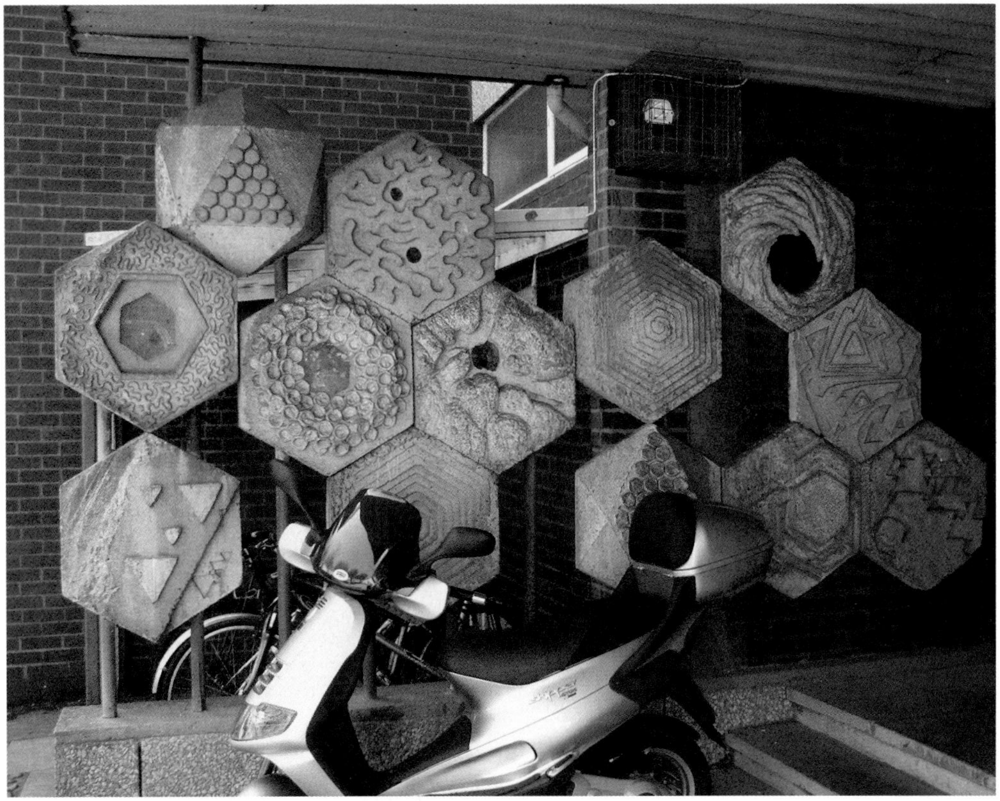

Jerry and Anne Hicks, *Microscopic Observations*

Notes
[1] Jerry Hicks, letter, 24 September 2005. [2] Ibid.

Narrow Plain

Outside Temple Way House, formerly the offices of Clerical Medical; ***REMOVED JUNE 2008*** *when the building and sculpture base were demolished*

Oracle C28

Sculptor: Franta Belsky

Architects: Steward Edwards
Date: 1973–4
Dimension: 640cm high
Material: aluminium-filled polyester resin on concrete columns
Signed: Fr. BELSKY '73–4
Status: not listed
Owned by Clerical Medical Assurance
Condition: good, before destruction of the base and removal of the sculpture in June 2008

Oracle was commissioned to celebrate the opening of Temple Way House, the new headquarters of Clerical Medical Assurance, in 1974.

Two identical abstract forms, with a winged appearance, are cast in 'aluminium, filled with polyester resin gel coat'.[1] These were set beside each other and not opposite and in a line, as in the recent auction house catalogue illustration shown here. They rested on two separate but adjoining pillars that were designed by the sculptor.

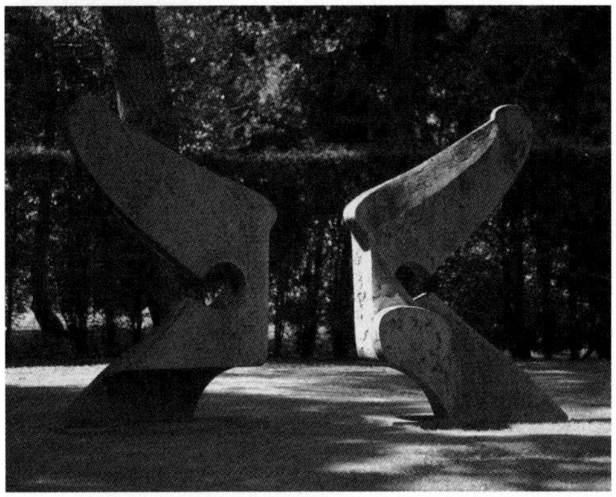

Franta Belsky, *Oracle* (after removal, Summers Place Auctions)

In 1974 the sculpture was awarded the Royal Society of British Sculptors' Sir Otto Beit Medal. A cast plaque recording the award is fixed to the face of one of the supporting pillars.[2]

Oracle has been described as 'two balancing forms of delphic inspiration'.[3] Franta Belsky himself said that the commissioning brief asked for 'a temple guardian', and he wrote that the work was 'originally conceived as a fountain – with water running on the inside of the shaped pillars into a pool'.[4]

A recent local commentary on the public art of nearby Castle Park dismissively described this work 'as a simple piece of brutalism'.[5] Although this substantial sculpture did blend too well with the background of the textured concrete panels of the Clerical Medical building, its forms successfully allude to the winged victories of classical sculpture and to the concept of a guardian angel. It may also anticipate the work of Peter Randall Page, sculptor of Castle Park's nearby masterpiece, by taking inspiration from natural forms, in this instance the distinctive shape of a sycamore seed.

The main forms were cast by Belsky in his own studio, while the concrete pillars were made by a contractor following a model provided by the sculptor. Belsky had pioneered the use of lightweight resins, a technique that enables sculptors to cast their own work and to bypass the traditional bronze foundry. His first sculpture to use this material was *Triga*, three massive horses made in 1958 for Caltex House, Knightsbridge, opposite Harrods.[6]

Reporting on *Oracle*, the *Architectural Review* said: 'Unlike America or France large-scale sculpture in public places is still a rarity in England.' Belsky was praised as one of the few sculptors in this country to have consistently accepted major public commissions.[7]

The two concrete pillars, designed by the artist, that supported *Oracle* were demolished

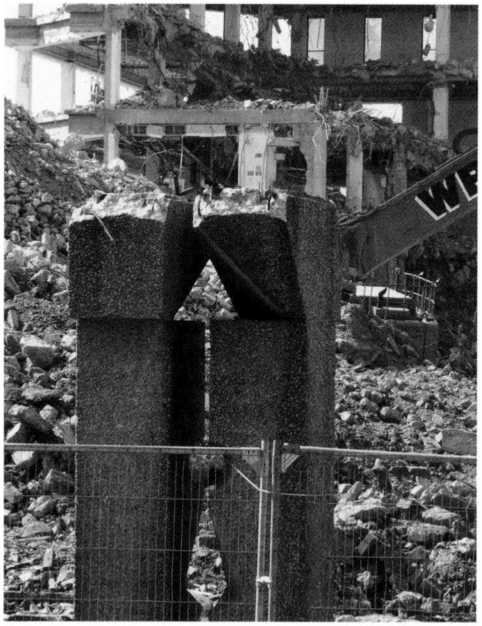

Franta Belsky, *Oracle* (plinth shortly before demolition, 2008)

in June 2008, but the two abstract forms were removed and subsequently sold at auction by Summers Place Auctions on 21 October 2008 for £9500 (lot 127).

Notes

[1] 'Sculpture in the city', *Architectural Review*, April 1978, p.192. [2] Ibid. [3] Ibid. [4] Franta Belsky, notes sent to SWRA, 24 July 1996. [5] Price et al., *Castle Park.* [6] *Architectural Review*, February 1959, p.192. [7] Ibid; the Belsky archive (2001.94) of over 4500 documents at the Henry Moore Institute has not been consulted; see *Henry Moore Institute Newsletter*, April/May 2006, no. 65.

Narrow Quay

At the southern end of Narrow Quay outside Arnolfini

John Cabot C58

Sculptor: Stephen Joyce

Date: 1986
Material: bronze
Foundry: Morris Singer, Basingstoke
Dimensions:185cm high
Inscriptions: cast on a bronze 'timber' set in the pavement, in the top recess – IN MAY 1497 JOHN CABOT / SAILED FROM THIS HARBOUR / IN THE MATTHEW AND / DISCOVERED NORTH AMERICA
–: in the lower recess – THIS STATUE WAS CREATED BY / STEPHEN JOYCE AND FINANCED / BY BRISTOL CITY COUNCIL / AND ACCES. (MSC).
Status: not listed
Owned by Bristol City Council
Condition: good

John Cabot (Giovanni or Zuan Caboto) may have been born in the Italian port of Genoa in about 1451. He became a citizen of Venice in 1476 and is reported to have first moved there in the early 1460s. The Cabot family settled in Bristol in 1495, and on 5 March 1496 John Cabot successfully petitioned Henry VIII for the right to sail in search of new lands to the east, west and north, excluding Spanish lands to the south.[1]

Cabot's first voyage from Bristol in that year was aborted, but in May 1497 he left the city in the ship *The Matthew* and first sighted land on 24 June. Landings on Newfoundland were made. Cabot may have assumed that he had found the north-east coast of Asia. He described the land as excellent and the climate as temperate, with an abundance of fish. He is presumed to have been lost at sea on a second voyage to America in 1498.[2]

This sculpture is set directly on the cobbled quayside. Cabot sits on a weathered piece of wood, cast in bronze from timber found by the sculptor in the Avon. He gazes westward across the Floating Harbour, with his shoulder-length hair covered by a scarf. He wears a coarse open-necked shirt and his hands are crossed on his lap. Hanging from his waist on his right hip is a buckled bag.

Stephen Joyce worked for ACCES (Avon Community Environmental Service) from 1984 to 1986 supervising unemployed artists, and was based in a disused chapel at Fishponds.[3] Towards the end of that period one of the projects, suggested by an architect working for Bristol City Council, was a proposal to make a statue of John Cabot to be sited on Welsh Back, near the Llandoger Trow. The council, encouraged by the Lord Mayor of Bristol, gave their full support. However, Joyce decided to leave ACCES before the project was completed. He had already made the first clay model, which was to be close to the finished work. He then worked on a freelance basis and advised the council that it would cost £1,000 to make moulds and a fibreglass version in his own workshop. It was then decided to site the statue on Narrow Quay, outside Arnolfini. There was pressure from some council advisors for a more traditional approach: Cabot wearing a large coat, standing on a pedestal, holding an astrolabe and looking towards the heavens. Joyce resisted, responding that 'Bristol did not need another old geezer on a pedestal'.[4] He experimented with the request for the long coat but, on the seated figure, this looked ridiculous. The short tunic was retained.

There is no contemporary image of John Cabot, so Joyce sought guidance from a number of sources. Bryan Little, a Bristol historian, advised that there were records to say there was a barber on board *The Matthew* and it was decided to present Cabot as clean-shaven. Little also gave advice about the kind of boots he may have worn. The first fibreglass model to be made was only life-size. When a fibreglass cast of this was taken to Narrow Quay and viewed by those involved, including the director of Arnolfini, the unanimous decision was to increase the statue to one-and-half-times

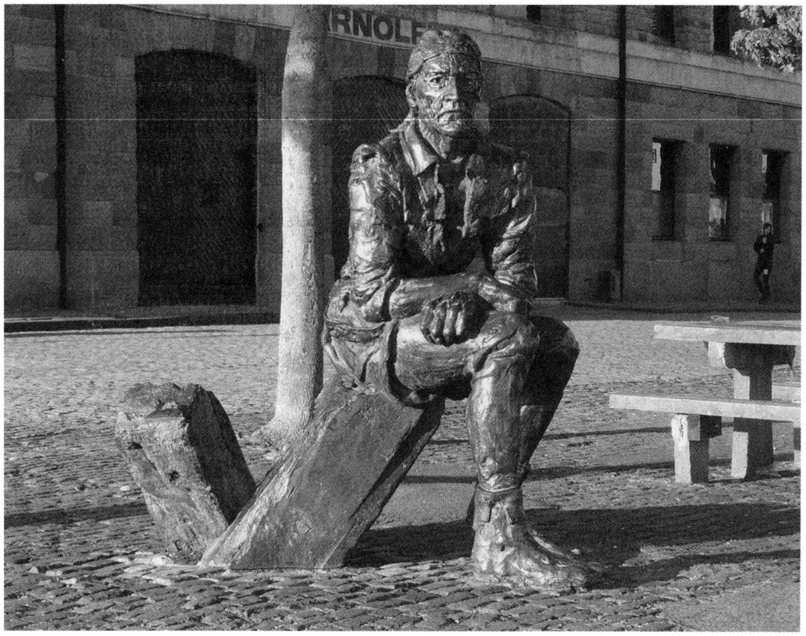

Stephen Joyce, *John Cabot*

life-size. Joyce made a new clay model before the second fibreglass version was moulded and taken to the site. On approval, this larger version was presented to the founders for casting in bronze. The total cost had reached approximately £13,000.[5]

There was no unveiling ceremony and hence little press comment on this statue of Bristol's most famous explorer. However, soon after the statue was erected, Reece Winstone, a local historian and photographer of the city for many years, sent the following invective to the *Evening Post*:

> Approaching it from Prince Street Bridge and the corner of Narrow Quay, I spotted what looked like the back view of a large frog, just the right dirty colour. The front view of the monstrosity gave me a portrait of Neanderthal Man, or Piltdown Man, not our famous explorer.[6]

No doubt, Reece Winstone would have preferred Ernest Board's skilful but theatrical painting of *The Departure of John and Sebastian Cabot* in Bristol Museum and Art Gallery, whose figures might be taken from a maritime musical at the Hippodrome, all tights and heraldry.[7] In response, the Bristol architect Michael Jenner praised the statue in the same newspaper for its accessibility and the delightful effect it had on children.

The sculpture may have been inspired by memories, perhaps from the artist's own childhood, of Sir John Everett Millais's painting *The Boyhood of Raleigh*. In this famous work a weather-beaten sailor sits on a broken spar, gesturing towards the sea, as he tells tales to the young and enthralled Walter Raleigh.[8]

Notes

[1] David B. Quinn, *Cabot, John*, *ODNB*. [2] As note 1. [3] Stephen Joyce in conversation with the author, 9 July 2003. [4] Ibid. [5] Ibid. [6] R. Winstone, *Evening Post*, 24 April 1986, p.54. [7] Merritt, *Sculpture of Bristol*, p.55. Ernest Board's painting dates from 1906. [8] Tate Gallery, London, 1870; in a recent conversation, the sculptor had no memory of this painting.

Across the River Frome at St Augustine's Reach between Millennium Square and Narrow Quay

Pero's Bridge C57

Sculptor: Eilís O'Connell

Date: 1993–9
Materials: stainless steel, painted stainless steel and cast iron
Inscription on a bronze plaque set in a granite block on Narrow Quay: PERO'S BRIDGE / THIS BRIDGE IS DEDICATED TO / THE MEMORY OF PERO, AN / ENSLAVED MAN OF AFRICAN / ORIGIN WHO WAS BROUGHT / FROM THE CARIBBEAN ISLAND OF / NEVIS TO BRISTOL IN 1783. HE WAS / A SERVANT OF THE PINNEY FAMILY / WHO LIVED IN WHAT IS NOW THE / GEORGIAN HOUSE MUSEUM / IN GREAT GEORGE STREET. / HE DIED IN THE CITY IN 1798. / March 1999
Contractor: Dew Construction
Builder: David Abels Boatbuilders
Engineeers: Ove Arup & Partners
Status: not listed
Owned by Bristol City Council
Condition: good

The bridge is named after Pero, a servant in the ownership of John Pinney, a Bristol merchant and plantation owner. In July 1765, Pinney had purchased a boy, his two sisters and a 25-year-old enslaved woman on Nevis, one of the Leeward Islands. The four Creoles cost Pinney £115 sterling, calculated as £5,750 in 2004.[1] The boy, known only as Pero (although one reference calls him 'Pero Jones', the surname of the woman who sold him), was said to be twelve years old and his sisters eight and six.[2] When he arrived in England in August 1783 as Pinney's personal servant, he was thirty. Pinney had returned to Bristol where a new house – now the Georgian House Museum, 7 Great George Street – was being built for him.

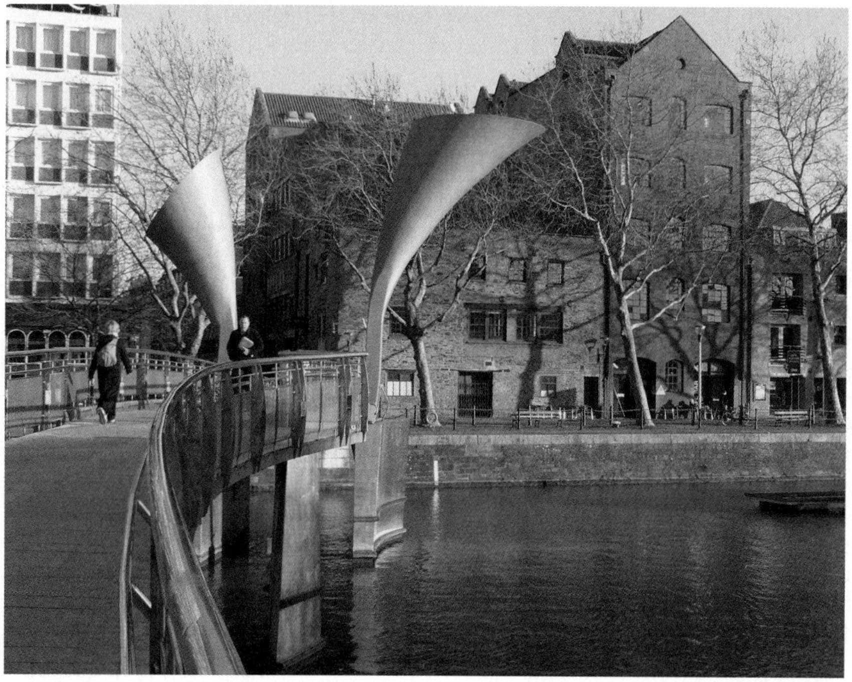

Eilís O'Connell, ***Pero's Bridge***

During his long service Pero returned to Nevis on at least two occasions, in 1790 and 1793.[3] In 1794 Pinney wrote:

> almost ever since we left… his conduct has been very reprehensible – insomuch, that his Mistress and every branch of my Family have urged me to discharge him back to Nevis with an annual allowance.[4]

At the end of May 1798 Pero was ill. Pinney did not expect him to recover, and wrote: 'he has waited on my person upwards of thirty two years, and I cannot help feeling much for him'.[5] When Pero died at the end of 1798, a letter from Pinney said he had become 'almost useless, caused by drunkenness and dissipation'.[6]

The bridge is raised by a hydraulic ram and the horns of the counterweights are the most distinctive aspect of the sculptor's design. The opposing curves of the footpath successfully suggest movement, and there is much thought and subtlety in the design of the supporting steelwork and railings.

> The inclusion of an artist in the scheme for a proposed bridge was championed jointly by Arnolfini in its support for contemporary artists and by Lesley Greene, public art consultant and formerly director of the pioneering Public Art Development Trust.[7]

An artist's brief for a footbridge with a central lifting span, to allow tall vessels to pass, was prepared by the J. T. Group, Bristol City Council and Ove Arup & Partners.[8] The aim was to design an 'appropriate and memorable cultural standard and symbol for Bristol'. Twelve artists were invited to submit examples of their work for possible entry in a limited competition. Five were selected for interview: Lilian Lijn, Ray Smith, Mark Dunhill, Eilís O'Connell and Richard La Trobe Bateman. The last two were chosen to meet Ove Arup & Partners before presenting initial ideas for the bridge. Eilís O'Connell was commissioned on 6 October 1993 to collaborate with the structural engineers. The overall budget for site preparation, construction and design fees was fixed at £350,000.[9] O'Connell was impressed with the site and admired the old cast iron elements of the harbour-side. For that reason she used cast iron for the deck plates, 'using a linear pattern similar to ripples on water which refer to the river flowing underneath'.[10] She made a 1:25 scale model in steel and cast iron in her studio.

The sculptor was to write that the 'counterweights were the most difficult; each one had to weigh five tons'.[11] O'Connell wanted them to be cast in bronze, but the constraints of the budget made that impossible. Construction of the counterweights was ultimately to be undertaken in haste, and the fabricator, David Abels, was not able to follow the forms the sculptor required, 'particularly the transition between the box section and the curved plates'.[12] Despite her 'disappointment about the level of craftsmanship', O'Connell said 'I am still very proud of it'.[13]

The director of Arnolfini, Tessa Jackson, was very supportive of the sculptor throughout the project and arranged a major exhibition of her work.[14] Some of the works in that show revealed a similar failure to resolve conflicts between design, craftsmanship and technology. When the sculptor blamed the fabricator for the crude transition from circle to square at the base of the horns, she was surely improperly shifting the responsibilities of her own chosen craft and profession. And where were the engineers?

In response to these charges Nick Childs has written a spirited defence, involving a very full and reasoned, if partisan, account of the commission.[15] He was design director of the Consultancy Division of the J. T. Group until November 1994. He was, in effect, the project manager. He points out that all parties 'understood that the bridge had to work physically as well as aesthetically' and that the artist 'was wonderfully accommodating'. By the spring of 1994 the design was complete, all planning permissions had been granted and a contract for fabrication was the next stage. This, Childs explains, was then delayed for three years because of a depression in the property market. In 1997 a new project manager was appointed who 'had little interest in the aesthetic qualities of the design and did not understand the artist'. A new engineer at Ove Arups was involved, costs had risen and continuity had been lost. Eilís O'Connell was not initially reappointed, but planning permission was conditional on the resolution of some outstanding details to the satisfaction of the artist. Nick Childs was commissioned to resolve these problems and the artist was duly reappointed. The contract was placed and as construction progressed amendments and refinements were agreed with the sculptor. However,

> it became increasingly clear that the whole job was a little more complicated and time-consuming than originally anticipated. The contractor checked his obligations to the developer and discovered that he was not required to satisfy the Artist at every point – and stopped asking.

Deadlines for completion were set and pressures on the fabricator mounted. 'There was nothing we could do about the twisted "horn", or the decision to paint the cast iron deckplates that should have been left to glitter with embedded carborundum.' But, continues Nick Childs, 'the bridge was a great success… Only the artist was disillusioned and disappointed.'

The bridge enabled direct pedestrian access between Queen Square, Narrow Quay and Arnolfini and the newly developed Millennium Square. Paul Boateng, then the Home Office Minister, carried out the dedication ceremony on 16 March 1999. Paul Smith, chairman of Bristol City Council leisure services, had declared that it was 'a symbolic bridge across the centuries' and added 'we have a large number of streets, buildings and statues in Bristol dedicated to people who benefited from the slave trade and we felt there was a need to start redressing the balance'.[16]

Notes
[1] C. Eickelmann and D. Small, *Pero: The Life of a Slave in Eighteenth-Century Bristol* (Bristol, 2004), p.20. [2] Ibid. [3] Op. cit., pp.42, 51. [4] Op. cit., p.55. [5] Op. cit., p.58. [6] Ibid. [7] Arnolfini Galleries Information, undated press release, p.1. [8] Op. cit., p.2. [9] Op. cit., p.3; notes by Eilis O'Connell (July 2004) say that this increased to 'around £400,000, but it was widely reported the project cost£900,000' and O'Connell considered her fee was 'miniscule'. [10] Eilis O'Connell's report on the project to Douglas Merritt, July 2004. [11] Ibid. [12] Ibid. [13] Ibid. [14] *Eilís O'Connell: A Decade of Sculpture*, 13 November 1999 to 30 January 2000. [15] Public Art South West's web site: www.publicartonline.org.uk/current/collaboration/collaboration_architect.html [16] G. Gibbs, *The Guardian*, 15 March 1999, p.20.

Courtyard of Broad Quay House, Narrow Quay

Fountain of Sabrina C56

Sculptor: Gerald Laing

Architects: Alec French Partnership
Date: 1980
Materials: four bronze figures; a basin of granite sections and granite setts
Dimensions: 318cm high, 190cm wide
Foundry: Kinkell Castle and AI Welders, Inverness
Inscription on a metal plaque fixed to the stone basin: A metaphor for the triumph of life over death / and a subject for contemplation. / 1980/1981 / GERALD LAING
Status: not listed
Owned by Standard Life Assurance
Condition: poor; painted 2008, not working 2009

Sabrina, the Roman name of the River Severn, appears in Milton's poem *Comus*, a masque first performed at Ludlow Castle in 1634:

> There is a gentle nymph not farr from hence,
> That with moist curb sways the Severn stream,
> Sabrina is her name, a virgin pure.

In British legend she was a Romano-British

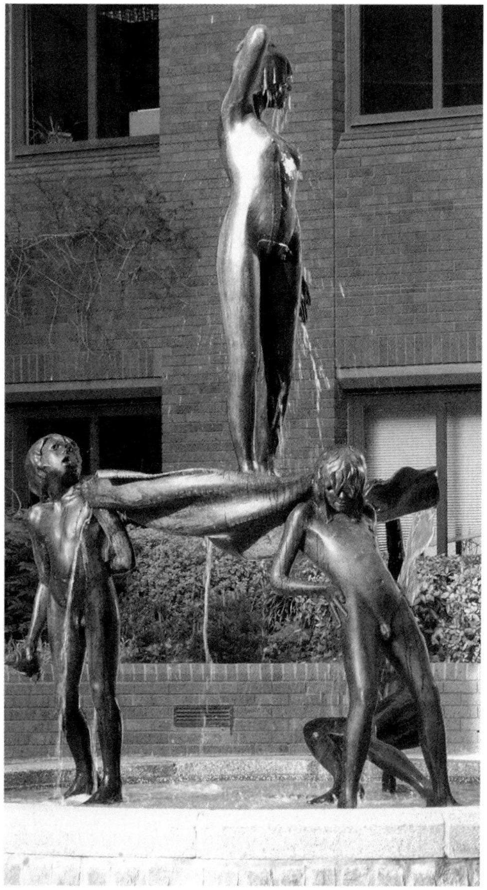

Gerald Laing, *Fountain of Sabrina*

princess who was the daughter of Locrine and his mistress Estrildis. Locrine's queen vowed vengeance and overthrew her husband in battle. 'Sabrina fled and jumped into the Severn; Nereus took pity on her, and made her goddess of the river, which is hence poetically called Sabrina.'[1]

The fountain depicts Sabrina and three naked boys at the moment of her rebirth from the depths of the river and her transformation into a goddess. She rides on a seashell in the manner of Botticelli's *Birth of Venus*.[2] Her left hand is held in a position 'derived from Nijinsky's choreography for *L'apres midi d'un Faun*'.[3] Sabrina:

> has just ascended from the riverbed. Therefore the points of contact between the boys and the shell have been kept to a minimum, consonant with good engineering, in order to suggest the idea of flight and forward movement.[4]

The figures are one-and-a-quarter life-size. A closed system with a circulating pump runs the fountain. Two pipes enter through the legs of the front boy and one goes to the head of the female figure. Water runs out from top of her head at the point covered by her right hand and runs over her body into the shell. Another pipe, at the back of the head of the central boy, allows more water into the shell to ensure a plentiful 'shedding' from six low points on its edge to fall on, and around, the boys. All the water is re-circulated from the shallow lower basin.

Gerald Laing completed a large frieze, *The Wise and Foolish Virgins*, for a Standard Life Assurance Company office in Edinburgh in 1978. Peter Henwood, the property development manager, then asked him to discuss making a sculpture for Broad Quay House in Bristol, which was under construction.[5]

Henwood believed that 'sculpture could enhance a building out of all proportion to its relevant cost'.[6] The first request from Henwood to the sculptor about this commission was to consider a 'problem wall' – a gable in the adjacent Co-op building – and to create a relief similar to the Edinburgh commission. Laing did not agree to this and was able to persuade the client that the courtyard, a focal point between two buildings, was the preferable site for sculpture.[7]

Gerald Laing wrote:

> With the assistance of George Mancini, who had retired after sixty years as a bronze caster a couple of years previously, I had

established my own foundry at Kinkell Castle in 1975. George, whose skill was legendary (he was called out of retirement just before his death in order to restore and make further casts of Eros[8]) continued to give me technical advice and practical assistance and he supervised the final installation of the fountain, at Broad Quay House.

All the figures were cast by the sculptor, using the lost wax method, at Kinkell Castle in Ross and Cromarty, but the shell was sand-cast at AI Welders in Inverness. The whole project took almost a year.

The historian Bryan Little took a personal dislike to this fountain:

> A recent, none too attractive addition to Bristol's publicly displayed sculpture… is in the open courtyard of the new Standard Life Building. Its inspiration, with some strange freedom of interpretation, comes from Milton's *Comus*, for the unattractive nude figure, standing on a scallop shell more fitting for the seashore than a river, is that of Sabrina, nymph of the river Severn.[9]

He made the comment that Sabrina,

> dwelling as she did under the 'glassy, cool, translucent wave' rather than in the tidal, turgid waters near Avonmouth, would more probably have had her haunts in the clear upper waters of the Severn.[10]

It is not surprising that the elderly historian was unsettled by this sculpture. Despite the artist's admission of his debt to Botticelli, the fountain has none of the enticing discretion of *The Birth of Venus*. Instead, Sabrina is not a goddess but a moist nymph, who, like the boys beneath her, positively revels in her nakedness. Mr Little's alarm was countered by the project architect, Richard Lee, in the *Evening Post*:

> The sculptor, Gerald Laing, has produced here work of great beauty and meaning and should not be lightly dismissed by the public, let alone local historians… May Bristol long continue to embellish its buildings and public places with fine works of art such as these.[11]

Regrettably, the courtyard in which the sculpture stands cannot any longer be described as a public space. It is only just visible from Narrow Quay, along which thousands walk every day, and it is usually obscured and inaccessible behind high black railings and gates.[12]

Notes

[1] Rev. E. Cobham Brewer, *A Dictionary of Phrase and Fable* (London, new edition, undated, c.1920), p.949; there are numerous variations to the legend. [2] G. Laing, specification and technical notes, June 1981. [3] Ibid. [4] Ibid. [5] Laing, letter to Peter Henwood, Standard Life Assurance, 5 April 1979. [6] Notes from Gerald Laing, Kinkell Castle, 1996. [7] As note 6, 5 April 1997. [8] Alfred Gilbert's *Eros*, Piccadilly Circus. [9] Little, *The Public View*, pp.76–7. [10] Ibid. [11] Richard Lee, Alec French Partnership, letter, *Evening Post*, 10 March 1983. [12] The addition of the gates and railings, regretted by the architect in conversation, give the impression that the sculpture is at the back of the building rather than at its core, as Lee and the sculptor intended.

Nelson Street

Adjoining the east end of St John's Church on Nelson Street

St John's Conduit C14

Sculptor: unknown

Date: c.1560 and 1866
Material: stone
Status: Grade I
Owned by Bristol City Council
Condition: poor

A drawing of 1821 by Hugh O'Neill shows St John's Conduit in its original position (see Broad Street, *Brennus* and *Bellinus*).[1] The substantial structure was just within the walled city on the inside of St John's Gateway at the very beginning of Broad Street. The water came

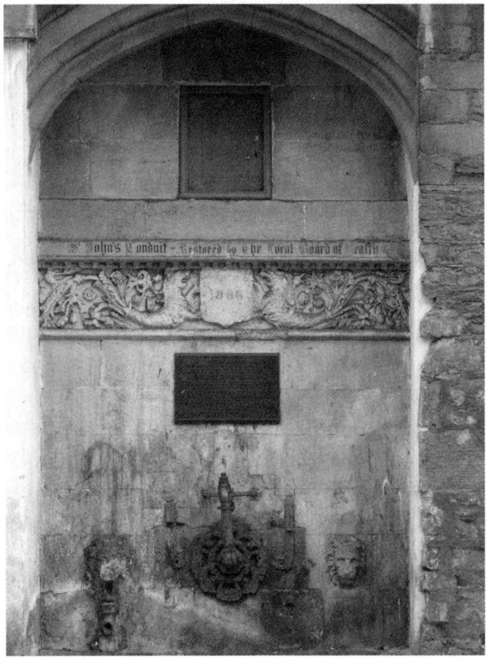

St John's Conduit

from the Carmelite Priory, founded in the thirteenth century on the other side of the Frome on the site of Colston Hall. Beginning in 1267, the Carmelite friars had piped the water from a spring on Brandon Hill at the top of Park Street.[2] A century later they gave permission to the parishioners of St John's on the Wall to install a small branch pipe, or 'feather'.[3] Following the dissolution of the monasteries, the entire cost of maintaining this vital water supply fell to the church of St John the Baptist.[4]

It may have been later in the sixteenth century, some time after the dissolution of the monasteries, that the ornamental structure protecting the cistern was built. This structure was taken down in 1827 when the church tower was restored and the opportunity was taken to build a new entrance to the church, which had previously been under the tower and from within the narrow and dangerous archway.[5] A

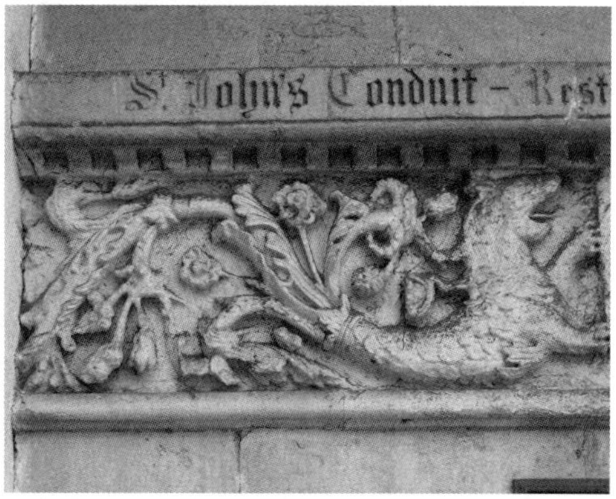

St John's Conduit, sixteenth-century fragment

new passageway for pedestrians was also created to match that on the opposite side, which had been built a few years earlier in 1805 at the expense of the corporation.[6]

The outlet for the conduit was then moved to the north side of the church on Nelson Street (adjoining Quay Street), where it is today. In the summer of 1864 there was a severe drought, and in the following year the corporation took on the responsibility for the conduit and evidently soon made alterations to the outlet's architectural surround. A shield supported by exotic scaled beasts, from whose tails sprout flowers and foliage, bears the date 1866. Surprisingly, the shield and all the stone carving to its left, and some of that to the right, may well be sixteenth century and have been carefully transferred from the earlier structure. Some of the carving to the right is certainly nineteenth century, but the relief as a whole is close to that recorded in O'Neill's watercolour and closer still to that seen in George Delamotte's watercolour of 1825.[7] Although this may be but a small fragment of the original sixteenth-century cistern, its survival is impressive.[8]

In 1984, the Temple Local History Group could congratulate the city engineer's department on having one of the very few medieval conduits in the country that was still

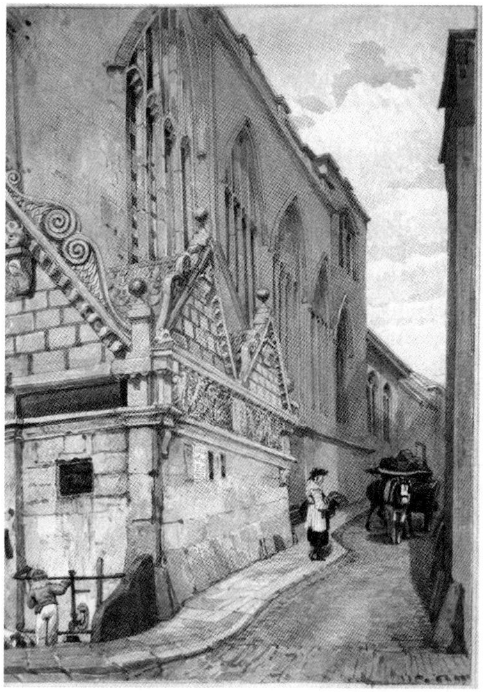

***St John's Conduit*, watercolour by G. Delamotte, 1825 (Bristol Museum and Art Gallery, M2393)**

in working order, after 717 years.[9] Today it no longer functions, perhaps partly a consequence of the redundancy of the church beneath which is the conduit's cistern. The church was vested in the Churches Conservation Trust in 1985.

Notes

[1] BCMAG M2394, watercolour by H. O'Neill of St John's Gateway, 1821. [2] J. Lea-Jones (ed.), 'An account of St John's Conduit, Bristol's medieval water system', *Temple Local History Group Report*, 1984, p.2. [3] Ibid. [4] Nicholls and Taylor, *Bristol Past and Present*, p.157. [5] Braikenridge Collection, BRL, vol. XVII, p.23, newspaper cutting, 17 March 1827. [6] J. Latimer, *Annals of Bristol in the Nineteenth Century* (Bristol, 1887), p.24. [7] BCMAG M2393 G. Delamotte, *St John's Conduit*, watercolour, 1825. [8] Mike Jenner states that the ornament repeats exactly that on a mid-sixteenth century fireplace at Bisham Abbey, Berkshire: Gomme et al., *An Architectural History*, p.75. [9] As note 2, p.22.

Old Market

Trinity Hospital North, on the north side of Old Market, viewable from Albion Place

Statue of Alderman John Barstaple C26

Sculptor: Daniel Millard

Architect: Frank Wills and Sons (1913)
Date: 1739
Materials: stone, painted
Dimensions: approximately 250cm high
Bronze plaque inscribed: TRINITY HOSPITAL NORTH / THIS ALMSHOUSE (WITH TRINITY HOSPITAL SOUTH) / WAS FOUNDED BY / JOHN BARSTABLE / UNDER LETTERS PATENT OF KING RICHARD II / 10 DECEMBER 1396 / THE ENDOWMENT WAS AUGMENTED BY ISABELLA BARNSTABLE, 1411, / JOHN MATTHEWS 1531, FRANCIS CODRINGTON 1572 & RICHARD REYNOLDS. / REBUILT 1672–76, EXTENDED 1739–40, / AND REBUILT BY / FENWICK RICHARDS / (CHAIRMAN OF THE TRUSTEES BRISTOL MUNICIPAL CHARITIES) 1913 / RENOVATED BY KNIGHTSTONE HOUSING ASSOCIATION LIMITED. 1984
Status: not listed
Owned by Knightstone Housing Association
Condition: poor

John Barstaple's Almshouse, Trinity Hospital South, founded at the end of the fourteenth century, is on the south side of Old Market at the corner of Midland Road. That fine Victorian building, largely of the 1860s and 1870s, by Foster and Wood is still an almshouse, and in the chapel are the medieval memorial brasses bearing the effigies of John Barstaple and his wife Isabella. John was three times mayor of Bristol, an office that Isabella's father, Walter Derby, held five times.[1]

Isabella Barstaple has often been proposed as the founder of Trinity Hospital North on the north side of the street. However, Wilfred Leighton convincingly established that both

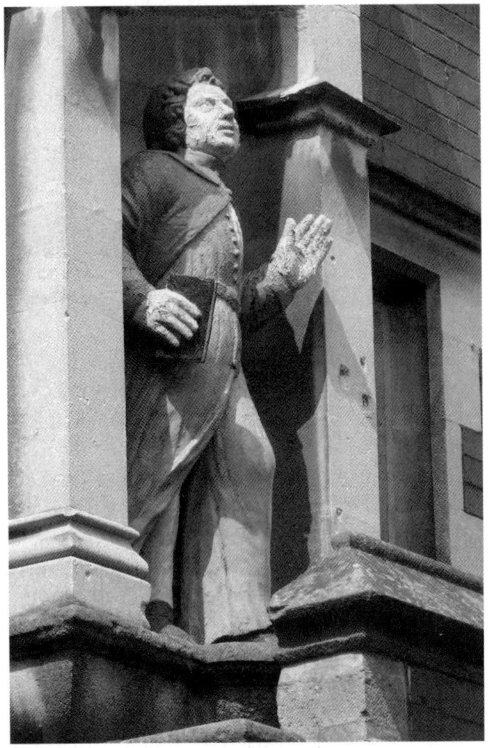

Daniel Millard, *Alderman John Barstaple*

almshouses were founded by John Barstaple in 1395.[2] He suggested that Trinity Hospital North was initially 'a place of temporary rest for poor travellers', and noted that the earliest clear reference to its use as an almshouse is in 1512. On the evidence of documents in the care of Bristol Municipal Charities (now Bristol Charities), he recorded that 'in 1739 the buildings on the north side were extended at a cost of £753 14s. 10d., including a sum of £10 paid to Daniel Millard, the builder, for an effigy of the founder, which was placed in a niche in the centre of the new portion'.[3] The almshouse was rebuilt in 1913 and the statue transferred.

Were it not for the sword, the statue is today painted in such a manner that it might depict a Colston Hospital or Queen Elizabeth Hospital schoolboy in traditional buttoned blue coat with yellow stockings. The clothing is eighteenth century and there is no reference whatsoever to the medieval image of John Barstaple recorded in the memorial brass. However, the main garment is of cassock length and the cloak has both a high collar and lapels. A drawing of this statue dated 1821 states clearly that the statue depicts the founder.[4] Another drawing by the same artist from 1822 shows the statue in a niche at first floor level on the eighteenth-century forerunner to the present building.[5] This drawing appears to depict the head of a man rather than a schoolboy. The statue's head is turned to the left and looks upwards, presumably heavenwards, and in the right hand is a book, presumably a Bible. The paint is peeling. Much of the original detail may be disguised under many layers of paint or, more probably, it has been lost through the weathering of the stone.

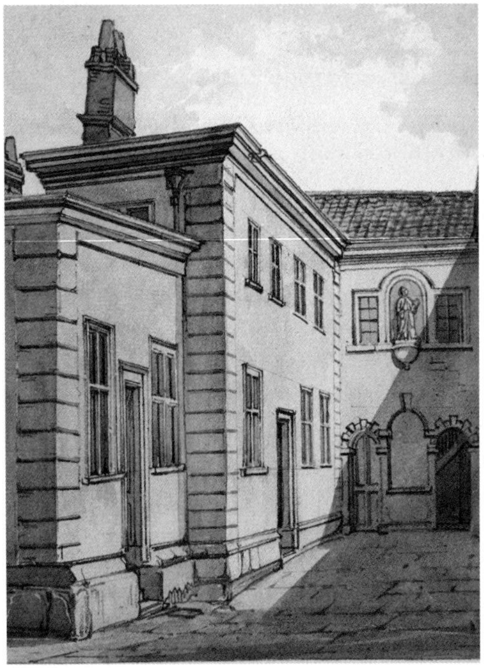

***Trinity Hospital North with statue of John Barstaple*, watercolour by H. O'Neill, 1822 (Bristol Museum and Art Gallery, M2763)**

Bristol Municipal Charities took over the two Trinity Hospital almshouses in 1836. Trinity Hospital North was sold to the Knightstone Housing Association in the early 1980s.

Also in Old Market, almost next door to Trinity Hospital North, was Alderman Thomas Steven's almshouse, built in 1686. This was similarly arranged around an oblong court and it, too, had a statue of the founder in a first floor niche at the far end of the court. This half-length statue is recorded in another drawing by the same artist, Hugh O'Neill, also from 1821.[6] Beneath the statue were the initials T. S., and the date 1725 or possibly 1721.[7] The date is likely to record the elaborate classical niche rather than the statue itself, which was almost certainly earlier in date, but its erection may well have been a stimulus to the commissioning of the supposed statue of John Barstaple. Alderman Thomas Steven's almshouse was destroyed in the Blitz, with the presumed loss of the statue.

Notes

[1] www.bristolcharities.co.uk/history_almshouses_barstaple.asp [2] W. Leighton, 'Trinity Hospital, Bristol', *Transactions of Bristol and Gloucestershire Archaeological Society*, vol. XXXVI, 1913, pp.251–87. [3] Payments by Bristol Corporation to Daniel Millard as a carpenter are recorded in BRO F/AC/Box/47/1 in 1739 and 1740. [4] BCMAG M2765 (a38) by Hugh O'Neill. [5] BCMAG M2763 (A2++) by Hugh O'Neill; the statue is also shown in a photograph of 1906: K. Costello and R. Burley, *Charity on camera in Edwardian Bristol* (Derby, 1997), pl. 5. [6] BCMAG M2766; see also photograph of 1906, Costello and Burley, as note 5, pl. 9, p.45. [7] Nicholls and Taylor, *Bristol Past and Present*, vol. II p.116, reads it as 1725 but O'Neill records it as 1725 in BCMAG M2766 and 1721 in BCMAG M2767.

Oxford Street, the Dings

Oxford Street, the Dings, and the streets within Barton Road, Kingsland Road and Oxford Street

D of the Dings and Memoirs of the Dings A21

Sculptor: Walter Jack

Artists: Claire Williamson, Beth Trimmer and Teucar Wilson
Date: 2006
Material: cast metal; stone
Dimensions: approx. 4m high
Foundry: D. M. Foundry, Stroud
'D' inscribed in raised lettering: DESIGNED BY WALTER JACK STUDIO / CAST BY D M FOUNDRIES / WHY DO WE CALL 'THE DINGS'? / ....[etc., and] OLD NAMES FROM THE DINGS....[etc.]
Status: not listed
Owned by Bristol City Council
Condition: good

The commissioning of art in order to encourage a renewed sense of ownership and community coherence and, in this instance, to assist in traffic calming, can seldom have been better demonstrated.

Two of three giant cast metal 'D's are at either end of a street which used to be a commuter's rat run and which borders on a recently rejuvenated playground and a small park. At the eastern end of the street, Oxford Street, the 'D' is followed by bollards in the form of a lower-case 'i', 'n' and 'g'. Then comes a large recumbent wooden 'S' lying on its side: a community bench. It is reminiscent of a Victorian love seat, but without a back, a comparison with which Walter Jack, the sculptor and furniture designer, would have been very much aware. Cars can still use the street, but they are now guests in an area where resurfacing has blurred the distinctions between pavement and road. The 'D's and the bollard

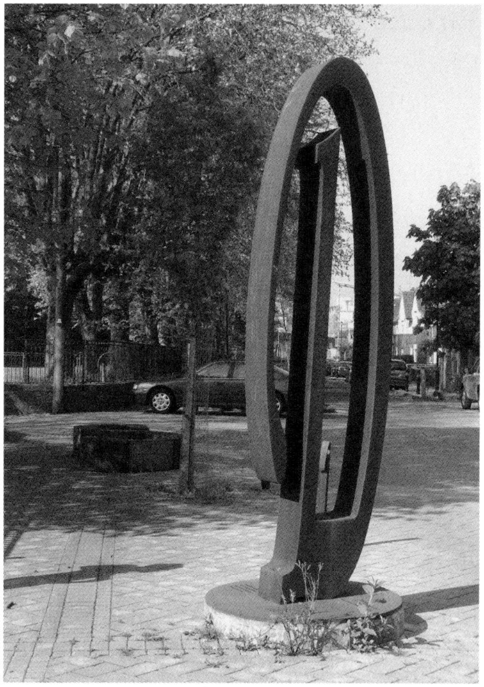

Walter Jack, ***D of the Dings***

letters assist other measures in narrowing Oxford Street's two entrances. A third 'D', together with four bollard letters including an upright 's', is in Barton Road, closing off vehicular access to a side street.

The project sought to create 'a better balance of road space use for pedestrians and to create a high quality urban space'. Trees were planted, car parking layouts and signage were radically altered, and 'the inclusion of public art to enhance aesthetics and a renewed sense of ownership was a key element'.[1] Community involvement came, in part, through historical research and consultation regarding the texts of the stone and metal plaques placed on walls and roads throughout the seven streets of this

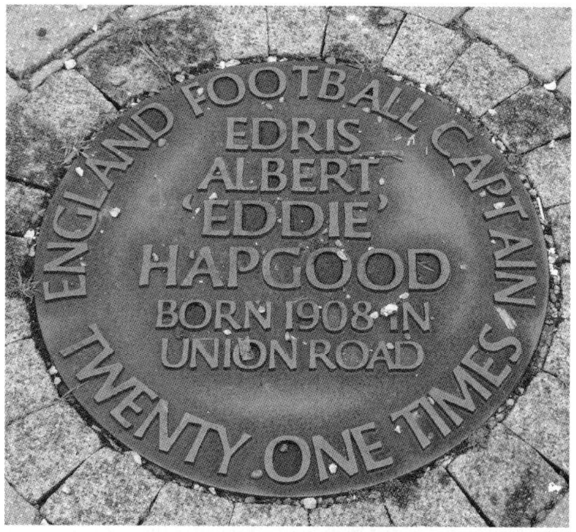

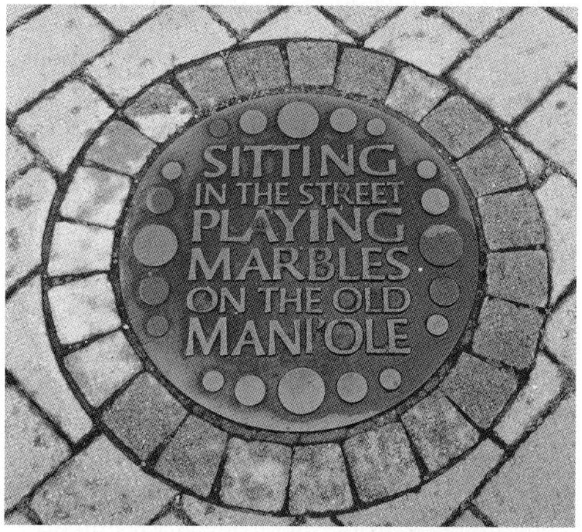

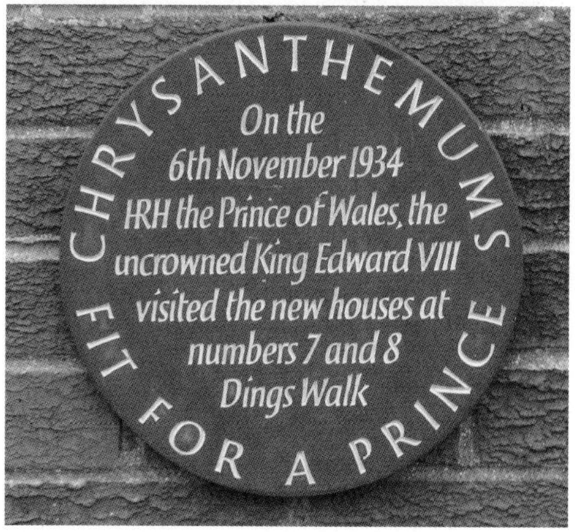

(right) Teucar Wilson, ***Memoirs of the Dings:*** **from top,** ***'Eddie' Hapgood; Playing marbles; Visit of the Prince of Wales***

triangular area behind Temple Meads Station, long known as the Dings.

The texts as a whole are by Claire Williamson, poet, performer, writer and counsellor, and Beth Trimmer, local historian and broadcaster. Both artists allowed the residents to speak through the artists' chosen words. Teucar Wilson, stone carver and lettering designer, carved the stone roundels or plaques and designed the lettering for the cast iron plaques. Discreetly and proudly, they express a little of the history of the Dings with considerable subtlety: 'The DINGS / LITTLE ISLAND / SURROUNDED BY INDUSTRY AND FORGOTTEN BUT / ALWAYS BURSTING WITH LIFE'. The landscape architects were Reckless Orchard.

Behind the project is a new approach to traffic management pioneered in the Netherlands, thanks to a complex series of European Union funding initiatives and the admirable opportunism of Sustrans, the Bristol-based sustainable transport charity. Sustrans assisted Bristol City Council in becoming one of only five European city authorities to make a successful bid to the European Commission's CIVITAS programme in order to be a part of the VIVALDI project, demonstrations of innovative transport projects that would be studiously evaluated and help to determine future policy. The four-year project, which in Bristol involved initiatives beyond the 'Dings Home Zone', began in 2002. The capital budget for the entire Dings Home Zone project was £390,000, but substantial additional funding was secured from Community at Heart, the organisation managing Bristol's New Deal for Communities in this area.[2] VIVALDI in Bristol was managed by Sustrans' Liveable Neighbourhoods team.

Notes

[1] www.sustrans.org. [2] Sustrans information sheet FF41.

Park Row

On the corner of Merchant Venturers Building at the junction of Park Row and Woodland Road

Nipper B45

Sculptor unknown

Date: 2000
Materials: cast metal
Dimensions: approx. 35cm high
Inscription in white lettering on a circular metal plaque, painted blue: HMV symbol / "His Masters Voice" / Mark Barraud 1848–1887 /owner and master of / Bristol born dog / Nipper 1884–1895 / was employed as a scenic / designer in the Prince's / Theatre in Park Row
Status: not listed
Owned by University of Bristol
Condition: good

'Nipper' achieved worldwide fame, posthumously, as the dog depicted on HMV gramophone record labels, one of the most successful of all trademarks. He was born in Bristol in 1883 or 1884.[1] His owner, Mark Barraud, was a scenic artist at the Prince's Theatre, which until its destruction in the Blitz stood in Park Row opposite the site of this memorial. On his owner's death, Nipper went to Barraud's brother, Francis, in Liverpool. Both Nipper – who was part bull terrier, part fox terrier – and his new owner later moved to London, when Francis became the manager of Mayell's photographic studio in Piccadilly. Francis was an accomplished painter. He had studied at Heatherley's School of Art and the Royal Academy schools. His painting of Nipper listening to a phonograph was not completed until 1899, four years after Nipper's death. He submitted this painting to the Royal Academy's summer exhibition but it was rejected. He subsequently re-titled the work *His Master's Voice*.[2] In June 1899, realising the potential commercial value of his painting,

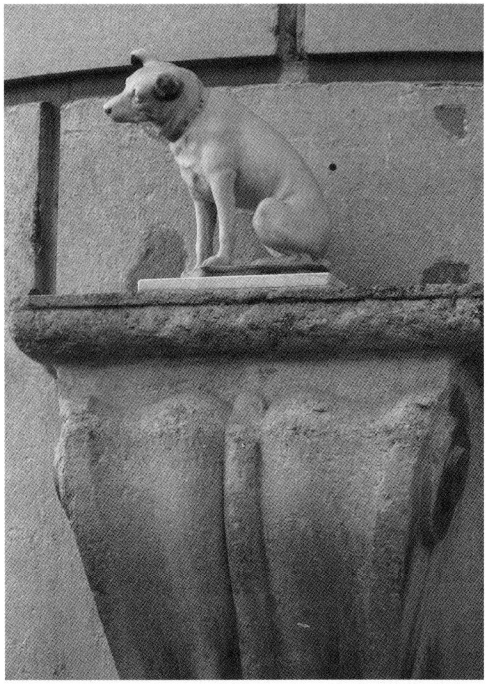

After Francis Barraud, *Nipper*

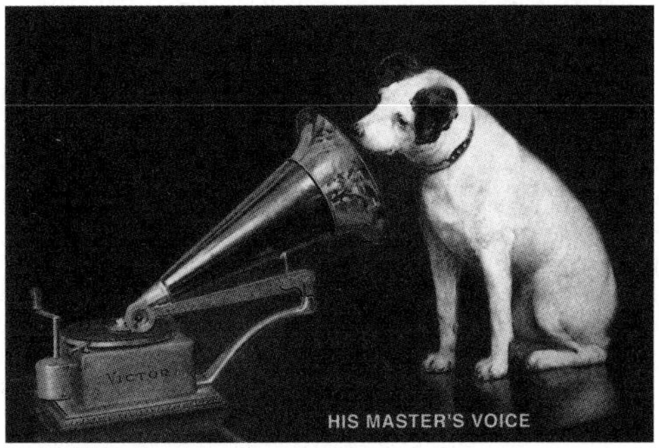

***His Master's Voice*, after the painting by Frank Barraud, trademark of EMI Records (Robert Opie Collection)**

Francis Barraud approached the US firm Gramophone Company, which had opened an office in London. By September the company had agreed to purchase the picture and the copyright for £50. Barraud had also undertaken to re-paint the phonograph as a gramophone, with a brass horn, which the company provided. HMV was first registered as a trademark in the USA by Emile Berliner in 1900. Nipper did not appear in Britain on the most expensive range of records until February 1909, and it was a year before the words 'His Master's Voice' were used on all products.

During the 1990s, EMI decided that the HMV trademark dog should go. As might have been expected, 'putting down' a small dog, after nearly a century of service, proved to be poor PR. The decision was reversed, and a man's best friend was restored to EMI's products and advertising.

Many metal sculptures of Nipper were made by HMV for sale and for display. They varied from only 4cm high – sold as paperweights, pen-trays and ashtrays – to giant versions of approximately 1.5m.[3] These were anatomically correct and painted in naturalistic colours. The 35cm bronze on this site was not especially commissioned, but cast from moulds made from one of the commercially produced models. The setting up of the plaque and the making of the bronze sculpture was the result of a campaign by Anthony Mitchell, a collector of gramophones who lives in Bristol.[4] He paid for the costs of the bronze casting. The memorial was unveiled by the Lord Mayor of Bristol, Councillor Graham Robertson, on 24 January 2001.[5]

The small bronze dog is set on one of the disproportionately large and original corbel-shaped keystones at the corner of the building, about 3m above the ground. Few people notice Nipper, but those that do are delighted. An explanatory plaque is equally high on the wall to the left of the dog.

The building itself opened as the Coliseum cinema in 1910, later becoming a dance hall, an ice skating rink, an aeroplane factory during the First World War, and later the university's School of Veterinary Science.

Notes

[1] L. Petts, *The story of 'Nipper' and the 'His Master's Voice' Picture Painted by Francis Barraud* (Bournemouth, 1973), from which most of the details below are taken. [2] Op. cit., p.18. Letter from Francis Barraud, 6 June 1899. The phonograph, which was used to record and replay the human voice, pre-dated the gramophone. [3] As note 1, p.52; a photograph shows a sculptor working on a 'giant' plaster cast of Nipper. [4] Press release, University of Bristol Public Relations Office, 22 January 2001. [5] Ibid.

Park Row, Red Lodge

In an alcove on the east side of the rear garden of the Red Lodge

Sir Charles Wetherell B46

Sculptor: Thomas Tyley the Younger

Date: 1839
Material: limestone
Dimensions: 220cm high, 90cm wide
Status: Grade I
Owned by Bristol City Council
Condition: conserved 2009

Sir Charles Wetherell (1771–1846) served twice as attorney general in the reign of King George IV.[1] He is now mostly remembered as the man whose arrival in Bristol as the recorder for the opening of the assizes on 29 October 1831 prompted the disturbances that developed into the Bristol Riots, the bloodiest riots of the nineteenth century.[2]

The riots were a symptom of the general unrest in Britain preceding the great Reform Act of 1832. Wetherell, an MP for a Yorkshire pocket borough, had unwisely declared in the House of Commons that the people of Bristol were largely indifferent to reform. The House of Lords had recently rejected the Reform Bill, and in anticipation of trouble the mayor and Corporation of Bristol brought in troops and swore in three hundred special constables, ultimately to no avail. For two days following Wetherell's arrival, the city was in the hands of a riotous and drunken mob. Prisons, tollhouses, the Custom House and two sides of Queen Square were destroyed.

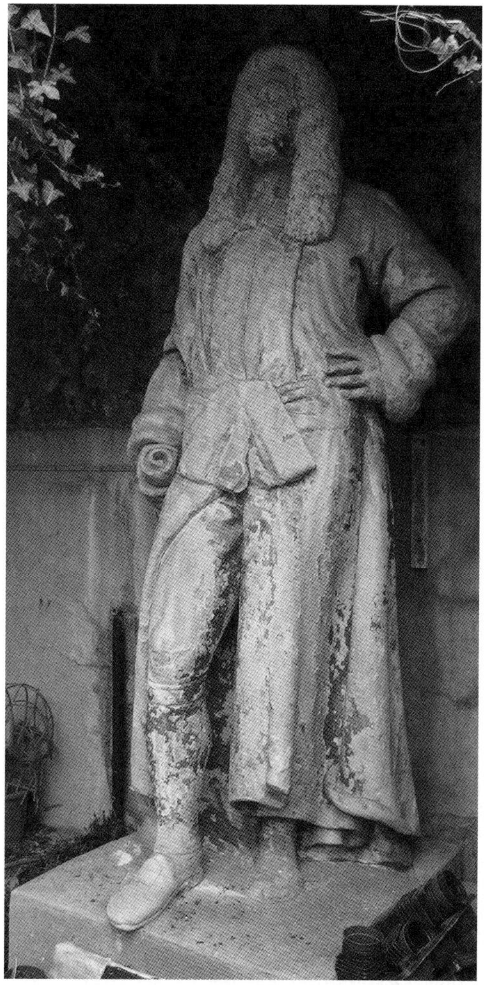

Thomas Tyley the Younger, *Sir Charles Wetherell*, before restoration in 2009

In a caption to a newspaper photograph published when this statue was craned into its present position in the Red Lodge garden in 1983, Wetherell was described as 'one of the nineteenth century's most hated travelling judges'.[3] The statue, itself, however, is a reminder that after the riots there were some who regarded Wetherell as a redoubtable defender of the state's security in the face of dangerous revolutionary forces, and a defender, also, of the country's established religion, for he had strenuously opposed the Catholic Emancipation Act.

The figure is now extremely weathered and eroded. The face has almost disappeared. However, the standing male figure is clearly a judge in robes, wearing a full-bottomed wig. He looks directly forward with his left hand resting on his hip. The right arm hangs at his side holding a rolled paper. He wears breeches, stockings and buckled shoes.

Although members of the Tyley family made many monumental sculptures, this is the only free-standing statue known to be by any of them. The provenance and the attribution are dependant on Wetherell's obituary in the *Gentleman's Magazine*: 'A statue of Sir Charles Wetherell, by Mr Tyley, was erected, in 1839, on the premises of Mr Milsom, builder, near Meridian-place, Clifton.'[4] Whether Milsom paid for the statue on his own or through public subscription is not known. Gunnis's entry on the Tyley family says: 'A younger Thomas Tyley… made a statue for Clifton of Sir Charles Wetherell.'[5] The statue was set up in the garden of 4 Wetherell Place, Clifton, in 1839.[6] Sometime later it was removed to 'a monumental mason's yard in St George's Road, whence it was rescued by the Savages'.[7] The rescuer is likely to have been J. Fuller Eberle. He was a founding member of the artists' society the Bristol Savages, and an avid collector of art and antiques, whose business premises, the Fuller coachworks, were also in St George's Road. In 1907, soon after the Savages were formed, Eberle had encouraged the artists to meet at Brandon Cottage, an office he owned on Brandon Hill.[8] A photographic postcard dating from between 1907 and 1920 shows Tyley's statue in the main studio.[9] The statue moved again when the Savages came to their present headquarters, known as the Wigwam (adjoining the Red Lodge), in December 1920. In that year J. Fuller Eberle had purchased the Red Lodge and presented the building to the city. The statue remained within the Wigwam until moved into the garden, where it deteriorated still further. During improvements to the garden in September 1983, it was moved from the end wall and placed in its present position under an alcove. The Museum and Art Gallery's ownership of the statue was confirmed in the same year.[10]

The statue was conserved by Cliveden Conservation in September 2009 with the financial assistance of the Friends of Bristol Art Gallery, the Society of Merchant Venturers, the Bristol Savages and Rosemary Furber (née Wetherell).

Notes

[1] S. Urban, Sir Charles Wetherell obituary, *The Gentleman's Magazine*, vol. XXVI, October 1846, pp.426–30. [2] For a short account and illustrations of the riots, see F. Greenacre and S. Stoddard, *W.J. Muller 1812–1845* (Bristol, 1991), pp,70–82. [3] C. Wells, *Grouse: The Savages' Journal*, December 1929, p.6. [4] As note 1, p.430; the identity of Mr Milsom is, as yet, a mystery. [5] Gunnis, *Dictionary of British Sculptors*, p.404. [6] Letter from G. Langley, County Reference Librarian, to Mrs Wetherell, 14 September 1982. [7] M. Fedden, *Bristol Bypaths* (Bristol, 1954), p.77. [8] W. C. Broome, *Notes and Records of Bristol Savages 1904–1977* (Bristol, 1979) Session 1919–20. [9] C. Waite, *The Story of the Bristol Savages* (Bristol, 1971), illus. p15; a copy of a later photograph belonging to Rosemary Furber, a descendant of the Wetherell family, was presented to the PMSA archive in 2005. [10] John Bedford, former honorary secretary, Bristol Savages, letter to Karin Walton, assistant curator, Bristol Museums and Art Gallery, 16 September 1983.

Park Street

17 Park Street; in the portico of the Masonic Hall, at the junction with St George's Road

Bristol with Minerva and Apollo B49

Sculptor: Edward Hodges Baily

Architect: Charles Robert Cockerell RA
Date: 1824
Material: Carrara marble
Dimensions: approximately 820cm long, 80cm high
Signature: E. H. BAILY. RA *Sculp^t. London.*
Status: Grade II*
Owned by Provincial Grand Lodge of Bristol
Condition: good

The building, once the Bristol Institution and now a masonic hall, has a convex colonnaded portico over its corner entrance. E. H. Baily's frieze of Carrara marble is recessed high up on the curved wall of Bath stone ashlar.[1]

In 1824, the Bristol Institution's original share certificates, which Baily himself designed, reproduced the frieze on the heading of their share certificate with the following description:

> he Arts and Sciences and Literature are introduced by Apollo and Minerva to the City of Bristol; who, seated on the Avon receives them under her maternal protection and dispenses to them encouragement and rewards, whilst Plenty unveils herself to Peace, since under their happy influence, those explanations of the human intellect flourish and improve.[2]

Recently, Bristol's Fine Art Librarian has given a fuller account:

> The seated figure of Bristol turns her face to the left. She wears a castellated crown, representing the city, and holds laurel wreaths in both hands. The wreath in her left hand is above a circular shield of the city

arms. The sculptor's name is very prominently incised in the rock upon which she sits. To her right stands Apollo, holding the hand of the first of six of the nine muses. Each holds their appropriate attribute representing the arts and sciences. The order of procession of the muses is: Calliope, Muse of Heroic Song and Epic Poetry, holds a writing tablet; Terpsichore, Muse of Choral Dance and Song, holds a lyre; Thalia, Muse of Comedy, holds a theatrical mask; Melpomene, Muse of Tragedy, holds a tragic mask and the club of Hercules; Polyhymnia, Muse of Sacred Hymns, has no attribute and Urania, Muse of Astronomy carries a celestial globe. Minerva stands in the right hand section with a circular shield and spear in her left hand. The wreath in Bristol's right hand is proffered above the head of a bearded figure, resting on a pitcher from which water pours, representing the Avon. Beside Minerva stand the four Graces. The four Graces are without attributes. In the far-left corner of the frieze Abundance and Peace sit in attendance with a cornucopia.[3]

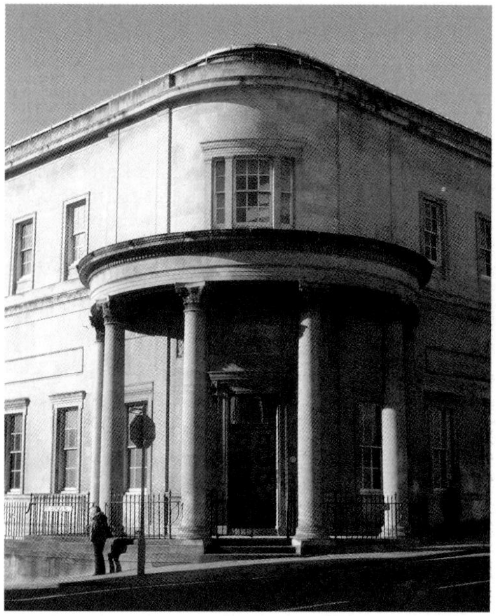

The foundation stone of the Bristol Institution was laid on 2 February 1820.[4] It was to house both the Bristol Institution of Science and Art and the Philosophical and Literary Society, a society founded in 1808 and the initiator of the building project. The architect was Charles Robert Cockerell and the building opened in 1823. Within a decade, significant collections of geological and Egyptian material were on display. Lectures on scientific, literary and art subjects were held. There were exhibitions of Old Masters, and in the winter of 1824–5 there was the first substantial exhibition of works by artists of the Bristol School.

In 1821, the Bristol-born sculptor E. H. Baily had been elected a full member of the Royal Academy, where, the following year, he exhibited the life-size statue of *Eve at the Fountain*.[5] In 1823 the statue was shown at the British Institution, winning a major prize of 100 guineas, but again not finding a buyer. It was in the same year that Baily offered to carve the portico frieze for free, an offer that was enthusiastically accepted, with the prompt reward of honorary membership.[6] There is no reason to believe that Cockerell had planned any decoration for the convex wall.

E. H. Baily was then in his mid-thirties and the inclusion of 'London' after his incised signature on the frieze may have been a proud statement of the progress of the son of a Bristol carver of ships' figureheads to the metropolis. The lettering of the signature and inscription is arguably disproportionately large. It is on the outward-sloping underside of a rock, ideally and perhaps deliberately angled towards anyone entering the building.

Unfortunately, the substantial overheads incurred through the costs of materials and premises for work on both *Eve* and the portico frieze drove Baily towards bankruptcy. In order to assist him, one Bristol Institution committee proposed in August 1825 that the profits of the

Charles Robert Cockerell, architect, *The Bristol Institution* (now the Masonic Hall)

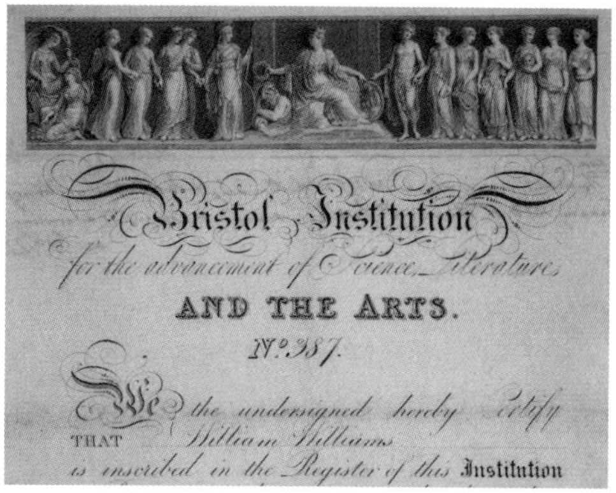

***Detail of the engraved share certificate for the Bristol Institution for the Advancement of Science, Literature and the Arts*, designed by E. H. Baily, 1824, with Baily's relief (Bristol Museum and Art Gallery, Mb 6793)**

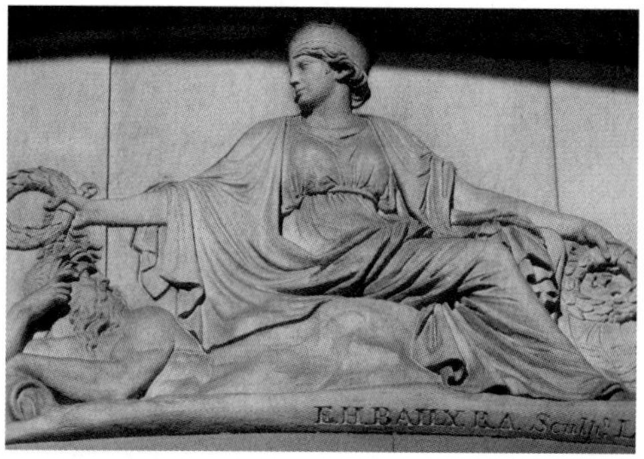

E. H. Baily, *Bristol*

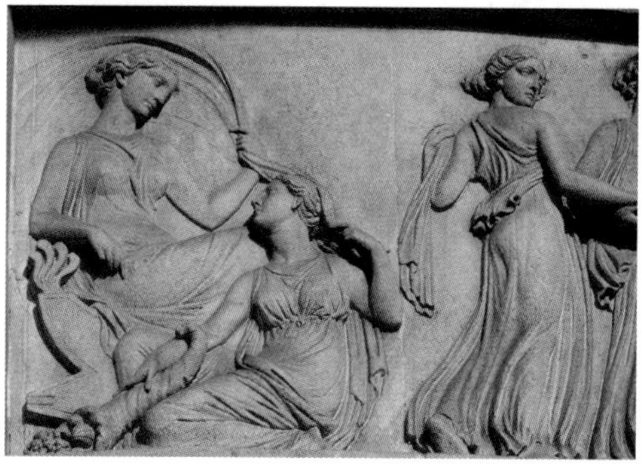

E. H. Baily, *Peace and Abundance and two of the four Graces*

Old Master exhibition of over £300 should go to towards the commissioning of 'a bust of Sir Humphrey Davy or some other distinguished character connected to Bristol'.[7] In February of the following year it was reported to another committee 'that Mr Bayly's circumstances are in a very embarrassed situation owing to misplaced confidence' and it was resolved to recommend that the Bristol Institution purchase 'his celebrated statue of Eve'.[8] A figure of £630 was subsequently agreed and substantial private subscriptions supplemented the exhibition profits.[9] *Eve* went on display in May 1826.[10]

In April 1872, the contents of the Bristol Institution were moved to the newly opened Bristol Museum and Library Association building in Queen's Road (now Browns restaurant). In 1905, *Eve at the Fountain* was transferred to the new Bristol Art Gallery next door, where she remains on display.

The Bristol Institution building was reopened in 1872 as the Freemasons' Hall. Sir Ernest Henry's Cook's history of the hall proudly reminds us that both Brother Cockerell and Brother Baily were masons. The hall was gutted in the Blitz, but the frieze was fortunately undamaged.[11]

Notes
[1] Roger Clark, curator of geology, Bristol Museum and Art Gallery, confirmed in a letter, 21 August 2000, that the stone is Carrara marble. [2] This share certificate, of which there is an example in Bristol Museum and Art Gallery, was also produced by E.H. Baily himself; Bristol Institution, 'Committee Book for General Purposes, 1822–7', BRO, 6 October 1823, 18 December 1824, 7 April 1825, no pagination. [3] Anthony Beeson, librarian of fine art, Bristol Central Library provided this description in May 1998. [4] K.-M. Walton, *75 Years of Bristol Art Gallery* (Bristol, 1980). [5] See C. Jordan, 'The very spirit of purity and chastity: *Eve at the Fountain* by Edward Hodges Baily', *The Sculpture Journal*, vol. 5.1, 2006. [6] Bristol Institution, book of letters from honorary members, p.6, BRO. [7] Bristol Institution, 'Proceedings of the subcommittee for the regulation of the exhibition rooms', 31 August 1825, BRO. [8] Bristol Institution, special subcommittee book 1824–, 7 February 1826, BRO. [9] As note 7, 3 November 1825. [10] As note 7, 3 May 1826. [11] E.H. Cook, *The Freemasons' Hall, Bristol* (Bristol, 1939).

Poole's Wharf Court

In the garden of Poole's Wharf Court, Hotwells, visible from the Floating Harbour quayside

Untitled B23

Sculptor: unknown

Date: 1999
Material: polished stainless steel
Dimensions: 2.8m tall, 1.2m wide
Engineering: David Abel's Boatyard
Status: not listed
Owned by Crest Homes
Condition: good

The polished stainless steel 'door' stands in a garden at the radial apex of a crescent of houses. It is close to the public quayside walkway, which was built by the developers at the behest of the planners.[1] The housing development of 93 units by Crest Homes was very close to completion early in 1999. The site was the old Sand Wharf, the last working dockside site to bring in regular commercial shipping to Bristol. Sand dredgers were unloading here until the 1990s.

Many residents had already moved in when a wooden mock-up of the sculpture was erected early in March 1999. They had not been consulted and, under a newspaper headline 'ART? WE'LL TEAR IT DOWN', they duly expressed their contempt.[2] Today, a decade later, 'Some residents have grown to like it, others tolerate it and others would like something "nicer".'[3]

Crest Homes had approached the University of the West of England's School of Art at nearby Bower Ashton and the students submitted several proposals. The name of the artist of the selected work has already been forgotten. Only the artist's gender is remembered. He may well prefer it thus. The work is carefully sited, rather bland and oddly out of date.

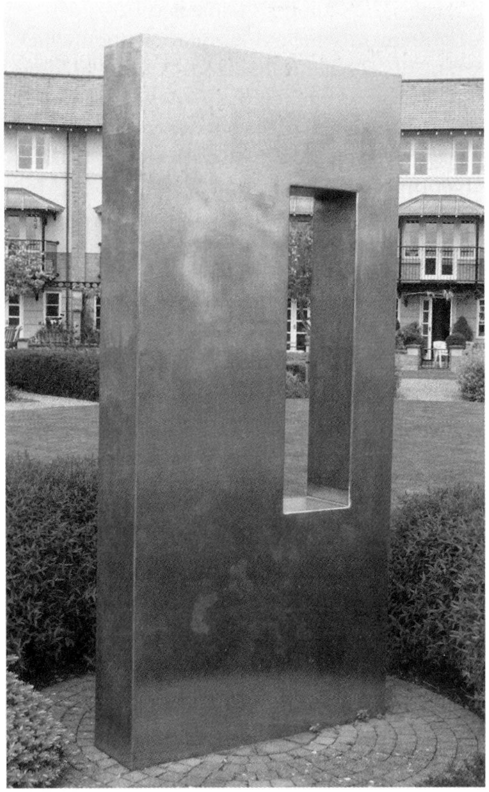

Untitled **(Poole's Wharf Court)**

Notes
[1] The walkway was handed over to Bristol City Council in November 1999; Bristol City Council, Finance and Property Services Subcommittee, 9 November 1999, no. 18. [2] *Bristol Evening Post*, 9 March 1999. [3] Correspondence with a local resident, 27 April 2008.

Portland Square

***FORMERLY** in the centre of Portland Square*

George III C1

Sculptor: attributed to Joseph Panzetta of Coade and Sealy

Date: 1810; destroyed April 1813
Materials: Coade stone statue
Dimensions: probably 4.5m high
Inscription on the front of the pedestal: GEORGE THE THIRD / the Father of his People / having on 25th of October, 1809, / through the Favour of DIVINE PROVIDENCE, / attained the 50th Year of his Reign, – to commemorate that happy event, / and in testimony of their Gratitude / for the Blessings enjoyed / under the mild Government / of the best of Kings, / the loyal Inhabitants of St. Paul's Parish / erected this Statue / A.D. 1810[1]
Owned by the original subscribers in the Parish of St Paul's

This full-length Coade stone statue of George III (1738–1820) was one of many monuments erected throughout the kingdom in celebration of the fiftieth year of the king's reign. It was destroyed within three years.

No illustration has been found. Fortunately, various Bristol newspapers quoted the inscription when reporting the unveiling. One newspaper added:

> the costume, the likeness, the ornaments and the whole detail do the artists Messrs. Coade and Sealy great credit. It is quite as well done, as clean and as minute in its finishings as the chissel [sic] of Flaxman or of Nollekens could have made it.[2]

Walter Ison described the square as 'once the finest and most uniform of Bristol's eighteenth-century building ensembles'.[3] It had been laid out and the buildings designed by Daniel Hague in 1789–90. As in Clifton, the builder-speculators went bankrupt in 1793 and several of the houses were not to be completed until well into the second decade of the nineteenth century.

An obelisk was first erected in Portland Square on 28 October 1809, just three days after the fiftieth anniversary of George III's accession. Six months later, in April 1810, the obelisk was replaced by this Coade stone statue. When the statue was destroyed in March 1813, *The Bristol Mirror* reported:

> We are sorry to state that on Tuesday evening, the Statue of His Majesty in Portland Square, was pulled down, and broken to pieces. The noise of its fall alarmed the neighbourhood, and two gentlemen, who repaired to the spot, observed three men within the railing, one of whom they took into custody; but he has since obtained bail. A reward of 50 guineas has been offered for the apprehension of his accomplices in the disgraceful outrage.[4]

Another newspaper said that Henry 'Orator' Hunt, a radical agitator who was later a principal speaker on the day of the Peterloo Massacre in 1819, had made a speech outside The Exchange in Corn Street, Bristol, in favour of the Princess of Wales, Princess Charlotte, (see Redland Hill) and against her father, the Prince of Wales. By nine o'clock in the evening of the same day, a group of 'eight or nine in number, entered the inclosed [sic] plantation in Portland-Square in this city, and by throwing a rope it is supposed around the statue of the king erected there at the Jubilee, displaced it from the pediment, and it fell with a tremendous crash.' One of the men arrested, John Harris, was later found guilty as an accessory at the Quarter Sessions in May 1813 and sentenced to a year's imprisonment in Newgate and fined 40 shillings.

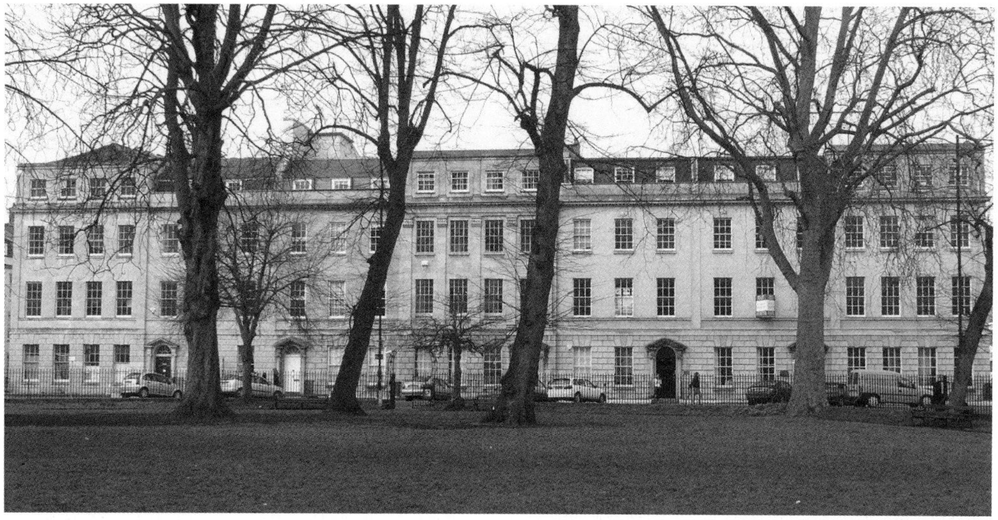

Portland Square, site of the destroyed statue of George III

The Portland Square statue was one of four Coade stone statues erected to commemorate the king's jubilee.[5] The others were at Weymouth, Southampton and Dunston, near Lincoln. The sculptor of the Dunston figure (made in 1809 and originally 4.5m high) is known to be Joseph Panzetta, the chief sculptor for Coade and Sealy in the early nineteenth century. Alison Kelly assumes that the other three were editions of the same work. Only the bust section of the Dunston figure remains.

This is in the Museum of Lincolnshire Life at Lincoln Castle, where it is known as 'George One-Third'. A photograph of the Dunston fragment shows that the statue fits the descriptions in the Bristol newspapers.

Nearby, there was an obelisk in St James's Square, perhaps erected at the same time as the obelisk that preceded the statue in Portland Square.[6] Or, it is possible that the two obelisks are one and the same and that St James's Square was the subsequent site of the Portland Square obelisk. The St James's Square obelisk is depicted in a watercolour in Bristol Museum and Art Gallery, attributed to Dr Thomas Pole and previously dated to about 1805 (see Introduction, Fig. 19).[7] Half of the square was destroyed during the Second World War, and the remainder was lost to post-war planning, which obliterated this small uniform square of red brick houses laid out in 1707. A series of photographs taken in October 1930 suggests that the obelisk had already been demolished.[8]

Notes

[1] *The Mirror*, 28 April 1810. [2] *Felix Farley's Bristol Journal*, 28 April 1810. [3] Ison, *The Georgian Buildings of Bristol*, pp.220–3. [4] Information from G. Langley, former reference librarian, Bristol Central Library. [5] Kelly, *Mrs Coade's Stone*. [6] As note 3, pp.149–52, pl. 24a, which also shows the obelisk. [7] K. Eustace, 'Drawings of a neo-classical town garden in Bristol', *The Connoisseur*, CCI, June 1979, p.95. [8] Winstone, *Bristol As It Was 1928–1933*, p.122–4.

Prince's Lane, Sion Hill

Rear façade of the Grand Pump Room and Baths, part of the Avon Gorge Hotel, at the top of Princes Lane

Grand Pump Room Caryatids and Spandrels; Entrance Portico to the Clifton Grand Spa Hydro Hotel Baths B19

Sculptor: unknown

Architect: Philip Munro

Date: 1894 and 1897
Materials: Bath stone
Status: Grade II
Owned by Swire Properties
Condition: poor

Muscular putti pose amongst acanthus leaves which evolve into dragons. Winged cherubs hold a jug and a chalice-like cup, and the two rather florid caryatids are a little careless with their towels. The initials on the armorial cartouche of this grandiose and decrepit structure are GN.

The publisher and MP Sir George Newnes persuaded the Society of Merchant Venturers in 1890 to permit the building of a hydraulic railway inside the hillside from Hotwells up to Clifton. The Merchant Venturers, who had originally developed the Hotwells Spa at the very end of the seventeenth century, gave their permission for the railway on condition that a hydropathic institution, including a pump room, was also built at the top of the hill. Both the new spa and the railway were opened in 1894.[1] The Grand Pump Room was advertised as 'second to none in point of grandeur and completeness for its purpose of any health resort in the World'.[2]

The Clifton Rocks Railway's tunnel still emerges next to the Grand Pump Room at the junction of Prince's Lane and Sion Hill. It linked Clifton to the Bristol Port and Pier Railway from Avonmouth. Opened in 1865, this line terminated just downriver from the Clifton Suspension Bridge. The once fashionable Hotwells Spa at the river's edge immediately below today's hotel had been sold by the Merchant Venturers in 1867 and was subsequently demolished. The spa had, in effect, already moved up to Clifton, where the Sion Spring or New Hot Well had become the St Vincent's Rocks Hotel and Baths by the 1870s.[3]

After the building of the Grand Pump Room, three of the houses at the top end of Prince's Buildings were reconstructed to make the Clifton Grand Spa Hydro Hotel (now the Avon Gorge Hotel), which opened in 1898. The

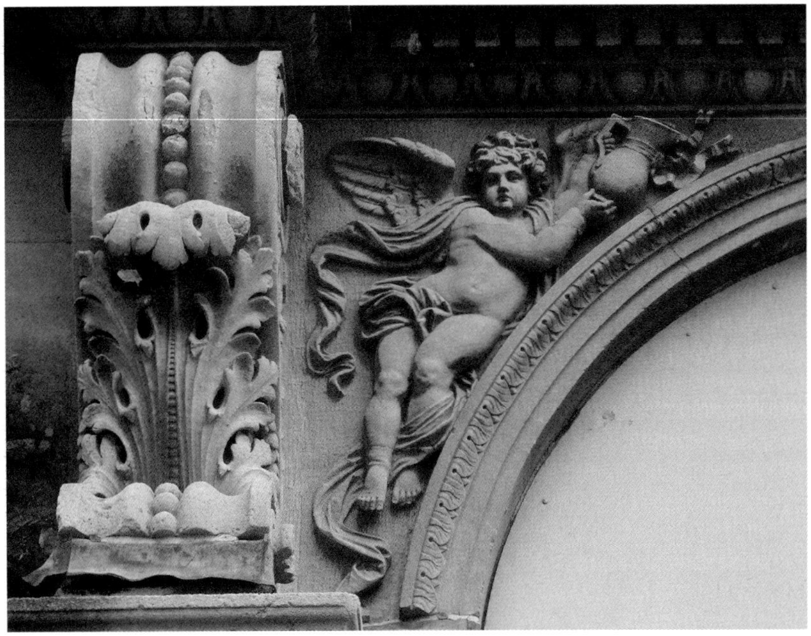

Spandrel on the Grand Pump Room

entrance to the baths, which is close to the entrance to the earlier pump room, is dated 1897. The architect was again Philip Munro, and the carver of the similar beasts and foliage over the entrance was almost certainly the same unknown sculptor.

'The Grand Pump Room's marble fountain dispensed its healing waters for barely twenty years.'[4] By 1920 it had become a cinema and it was later a dance hall and disco until the 1970s.

Successive plans to redevelop the site have failed. The most notorious attempt came very early in 1971, when plans were submitted for a 'monstrous' (Sir John Betjeman's description) hotel extension involving 126 additional double rooms above a car park for 203 cars, together with banqueting facilities for 250 people. Passed by the council's planning committee, it led to a novel and successful alliance between local protesters and Whitehall, and a public inquiry that was superbly stage-managed by the objectors' lawyers, notably Paul Chadd QC.[5]

Notes
[1] McGrath, *Merchant Venturers of Bristol*, p.334. [2] S. Watson, *Secret Underground Bristol* (Bristol, 1991), pp.40–3. [3] Greenacre and Stoddard, *From Bristol to the Sea*, p.127; the St Vincent's Rocks Hotel at the corner of Sion Hill and Caledonia Place continued as a hotel until 1999. [4] Op. cit., p.43. [5] G. Priest and P. Cobb, *The Fight for Bristol: Planning and the Growth of Public Protest* (Bristol, 1980), pp.62–7.

Prince's Wharf

Bristol Industrial Museum (in store)

E. S. & A. Robinson's Factory Frieze C59

Sculptor: unknown

Architect: William Bruce Gingell
Date: 1876–7
Materials: Bath stone
Dimensions: approx. 24m in length
Status: not listed
Owned by Bristol Museums and Art Gallery

This very long, deeply carved relief decorated the façade of Robinson's factory and offices at the corner of Victoria Street and Redcliffe Street from 1877. Gingell's surviving design for the building shows that the frieze was an agreed part of the original design of 1876.[1] It was on the semi-circular corner tower above the first floor, unusually high up.

The 22 blocks of carved stone, each 50cm in height, were salvaged when the building was demolished in 1960. Colin Beales, job architect for Group Architects DRG, proposed to the Directors that the frieze, forming a section of a circle approximately 24m in circumference, should be displayed at the rear of the new offices. That was discounted, and the carvings were stored in the basement of the new building for 28 years before being presented to Bristol Industrial Museum, where they are now held.

E.S. & A. Robinson specialised in printing and packaging, and for three-quarters of a century was one of the largest employers in Bristol. The activities of the workers on the frieze – men, women and children – are all related to printing and packaging.

The heads may be deliberately large because of the considerable height of the frieze. The impressive representational skills of the unknown sculptor have been confirmed by experts identifying the many different pieces of machinery, but the lack of sophistication is undisguised.[2] This must surprise us, for ten and twenty years earlier Gingel was the architect of

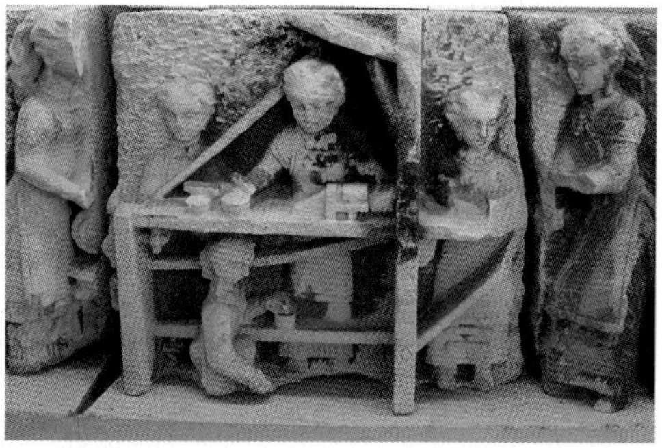

E. S. and A. Robinson's Factory Frieze **(detail)**

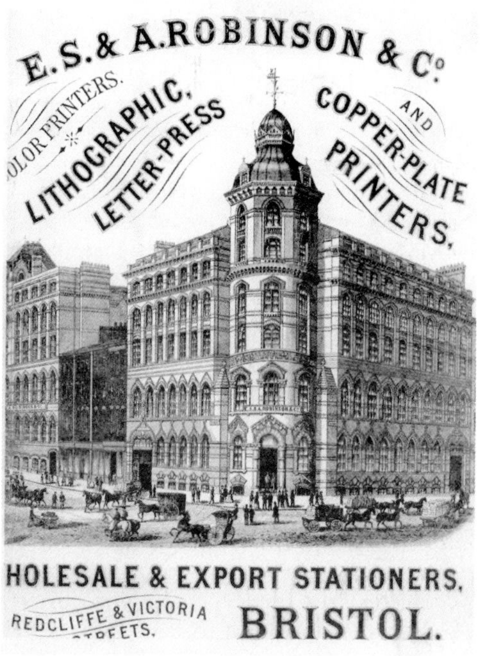

E. S. and A. Robinson Building, Victoria Street, **detail from a lithograph, c.1885**

the two most richly ornamented buildings in Corn Street: No. 36, an insurance office; and No. 55, the former West of England and South Wales Bank, where John Thomas's frieze of putti, at a similar height, demonstrates the various processes of banking. In comparison, the Robinsons frieze is crude and lacking in sophistication. Instead, it has an immediate and personal relevance to the employees within the building, rather than to the potential customers outside. Social historians may also be intrigued by the number of female workers apparently employed at Robinsons, as well as by the preponderance of layered petticoats and drop earrings.

Notes
[1] Crick, *Victorian Buildings*, pl. 41. [2] Andy King, curator, Bristol Industrial Museum; for a photograph see D.J. Eveleigh, *Bristol 1920–1969* (Stroud, 1998), p.167.

Queen Square

William III C60

Sculptor: Michael Rysbrack

Date: 1736
Materials: bronze; pedestal, Portland stone
Foundry: unknown, perhaps Nost foundry, London
Dimensions: approx. 285cm high, 1050cm long, 250cm wide
Inscriptions: cut on the front of the original pedestal – WILLIAM III / BY / RYSBRACH [sic] / ERECTED 1736
–: in the Portland stone paving cut by Peter McLennan of Bath on the perimeter of an ellipse – THIS INSCRIPTION COMMEMORATES THE RETURN OF THIS HISTORIC SPACE TO THE CITIZENS OF BRISTOL. THE WORK WAS COMPLETED IN THE YEAR 2000 THROUGH THE SUPPORT OF THE HERITAGE LOTTERY FUND, BRISTOL CITY COUNCIL & THE QUEEN SQUARE ASSOCIATION.
Status: Grade I
Owned by Bristol City Council
Condition: good; recent damage and loss to the reins and bit

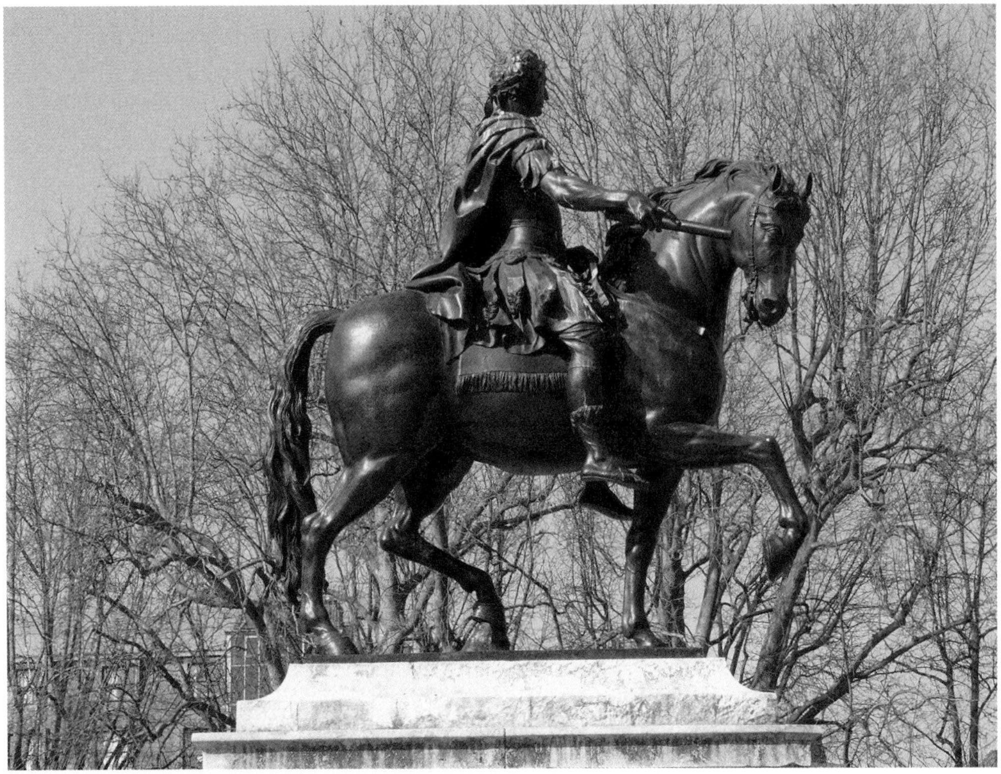

Michael Rysbrack, *William III*

Of the many fine monuments to William III (1650–1702) 'the one in Queen Square is surely the finest'.[1] 'If it were in a provincial town on the Continent sightseers would go a long way to see it.'[2] A still bolder claim that this is 'Western Europe's finest eighteenth century equestrian monument' has gone unchallenged.[3]

The over life-size equestrian statue is set on a pedestal with a moulded plinth and cornice. The king's hair is tied with a loose ribbon. A windswept cloak covers his short Roman tunic. Beneath that is a skirt of hanging leather straps (pteruges) and he is seated on a fringed saddlecloth. Unarmed, and without body armour (a cuirass), he carries a baton in his extended right hand and the reins in his left hand. He wears sandals and there are no stirrups. The horse is set on three legs with the front right leg raised. 'Altogether there is an appearance of naturalness and free movement about William III which compares very favourably with the models of the equestrian statues of Louis XIV by Girardon and others.'[4] The rider has a relaxed authority and there is a controlled liveliness, tension and elegance about the horse. There is an easy bond between the two and a unity about the whole, all qualities expected in the winner of an international dressage competition. This is an idealised commander-in-chief presiding over peace, not war, and it is the stability and prosperity of William III's reign that is being celebrated.

The pose and dress of the king were evidently also inspired by the statue of the Roman Emperor Marcus Aurelius, erected around 180 AD.[5] Rysbrack did not visit Rome, but he owned a book by François Perrier (1590–1650) that has two engravings, a front and a rear view of the famous Roman statue.[6]

William III had the briefest contact with Bristol. He passed hurriedly through the city on 7 September 1690. His fleet had anchored at King's Road, at the mouth of the Avon, on the return from Ireland following the defeat of James II at the Battle of the Boyne. He stayed overnight at King's Weston with the new owner of the house, Sir Robert Southwell, his secretary of state for Ireland.

The earliest reference to the commissioning of the statue is in the Proceedings of the Bristol Common Council for 8 December 1731, nearly thirty years after William III's death. A commitment was made to 'erect a public Statue to the memory of our Great and Glorious Deliverer'.[7]

'The Chamber agreed to allow the statue to be erected in Queen Square, and contribute to "so agreeable a Design", though not the thousand pounds at first suggested.'[8] On 25 August 1733 the Bristol Chamberlain was instructed to pay John Elbridge £500 to erect the statue.

Queen Square had recently been developed on a reclaimed marsh. Laid out in 1699 and completed in 1727, it was the corporation's most ambitious project of aggrandisement before the building of the Exchange in Corn Street. It was the first substantial residential square to be built outside London. Only Lincoln's Inn Fields is larger.

Evidence about the competition comes solely from notes by George Vertue, Rysbrack's contemporary. These confirm that Rysbrack's only rival was another émigré, Peter Scheemakers, also from Antwerp. They both submitted models in 1732.[9] Hull adopted Scheemaker's design, and this is still gilded and in the Market Place where it was first erected.[10]

Rysbrack had been in England since 1720 and his reputation in Bristol was well established when the competition arose. His earliest work in the city is the monument of 1726 to Andrew Innys in St John the Baptist, Broad Street.[11] In 1729 he made his reclining figure for the Edward Colston monument in All Saints, Corn Street.[12] The portrait bust in the Lord Mayor's Chapel of Bristol's town clerk, Henry Blake, who died in 1731, could be posthumous but it almost certainly dates from before the commissioning of the equestrian monument.[13]

As early as August 1732, Vertue wrote:

> The Moddels of King William on horseback being some time in hand & partys animating the Artists to out vie each other. one was made being the larger by M^r^. Rysbrack. and an other by M^r^. Schemaker – both the Moddels or casts guilt with Gold, being first Viewd by judges of Art & horses was sent to Bristol. where the Subscribers for erecting this Equestrian Statue. had collected about 2,000 pounds to pay the expence of it... They returnd their resolutions on that accompt & approbation of M^r^. Rysbracks Moddel desireing that the brass Statue bigger than nature, being about, or near 12 foot high, from the ground to the top of the Kings head. & agreed to pay to M^r^. Rysbrack 18 hundred pounds for his whole trouble & charge of Materials[14]

There is an early reference to Rysbrack's casting of the statue. Sir John Clerk and John Scrope[15] visited Rysbrack, 'a very great sculptor', and saw:

> many bustos and bas-reliefs in marble and clay, done with exceeding delicacy. Amongst other things we found a model of King William III on horseback which is to serve for a cast in copper for the town of Bristol. We saw the furnaces &a. for melting the metal and the rest of the apparatus which is very great.'

This reference also confirms the cost of the statue at £1,800.[16]

Recently, it has been argued that Rysbrack managed every 'phase of the commission as a public event from the initial competition to the commission, to the casting and ceremonious erection'. The writer quotes a newspaper report for August 1735 that 'the nobility and lovers of statuary resort daily to that Gentleman's House in Hyde-Park-Corner to view the finished bronze.'[17] In June 1735, Queen Caroline made a special visit to Rysbrack's studio to see the statue. On 7 July it was taken on board a vessel in the Thames to be shipped to Bristol and its departure was duly noted by the national press.[18]

George Vertue recorded that Rysbrack had begun the full-size clay model in May 1733 and that it was in plaster by August. Even at this early stage, he reports: 'the Criticks skilfull in that Art thought it to be the best statue ever made in England.'[19] Of the casting process, Vertue says:

> the brass horse Cast all at once. that is. all the horse (excepting the tail) and the leggs of the figure on each side of the horse. the statue it Self being cast before as far as the middle down to the thighs. By Mr. Rysbrack. Aug. first.

When it was finished in mid-July 1735, Vertue recorded:

> it was expected on account of his extraordinary care. & skill. and several losses. by casting – the Bristolians would have made him a voluntary present. over and above the contract. but no such thing was done.

We do not know who cast the statue and there is no record of Rysbrack having his own foundry. The majority of his work was modelled in clay and then carved in stone and marble or fired as terracotta. An unconfirmed account, written in 1872, says:

> The bronzed equestrian statue of King William III, was erected in 1735, after a model presented by Rysbach [sic]. It was executed by Van Oost, a teacher of flower painting and cost £18,000 [sic].[20]

If this is correct it might have been cast in the foundry owned by the Nost family.[21]

On 25 September 1736, Lyonel Lyde, the Mayor of Bristol, told the chamber that the statue had been erected in Queen Square and was 'now entirely completed in the handsomest manner & he believed to everybodie's satisfaction'.[22] Soon after the statue was in place, the council spent money on trees to improve the setting and by 1738 there were almost certainly 'railings' with lamps at the four corners around the king.[23] These railings and the lamps survived until 1937.

In February 1749, the Bristol Common

Council discovered 'defects' in the statue and instructed a committee that had inspected King William 'to employ such Person or Persons as they shall think proper to repair the Defects in the said Statue at the expence of this House and Mr Chamberlain is to issue for that purpose moneys for that purpose agreeable to their order'.[24] In April, the council asked the mayor to write to Rysbrack and:

> acquaint him with the Defects in that Statue are of such a kind as if not soon remedyed will absolutely ruin a Statue which well deserves to be as lasting as it is elegant and beautiful: that it is expected some care be taken about this affair because the present condition of the Statue is a Standing Reflection not only upon the Gentlemen who were at considerable Expence in paying for Erecting this Statue but also upon the Statuary himself that the work is not Substantially executed.[25]

There is no evidence about the nature of these defects or that Rysbrack ever visited Bristol.

Until recently, this masterpiece has suffered little from either protest or celebration. In July 1807 the Lancastrian Militia, which had distinguished itself at the Battle of the Boyne, was quartered in Bristol. King William was duly decorated with orange and purple ribbons on the anniversary of the battle.[26] In October 1831 Rysbrack's statue, still protected by surrounding railings, survived the bloodiest disturbances of the nineteenth-century when rioters burnt two sides of Queen Square. During the Second World War the statue was removed to Badminton and not returned until 1945.

Just before the war the direction of the statue was changed when Redcliffe Way, part of an inner ring road scheme, was extended to cut diagonally through the square to improve traffic flow. William III remained in the centre of the square, but isolated on a narrow traffic island and now without surrounding railings.

In the later 1990s, Queen Square was impressively restored to its eighteenth-century layout. The statue was returned to its original alignment and the brutal diagonal carriageway and attendant cherry trees were removed. Discreet floodlighting was installed within an unnecessarily complex oval design in the pavement around the statue. The council refused to replace the railings, despite the absence of any conflict between the longer-term conservation interests of the statue and the historical restoration of the square. The reins and the ornate curved bit were soon damaged and some parts subsequently lost. They have not been replaced.

The National Heritage Lottery Fund joined Bristol City Council and the Queen Square Association to fund this major restoration project, and English Heritage paid for the work on the statue, which was carried out by Cliveden Conservation.[27] The Queen Square enhancement project was officially opened on 19 September 2000.[28]

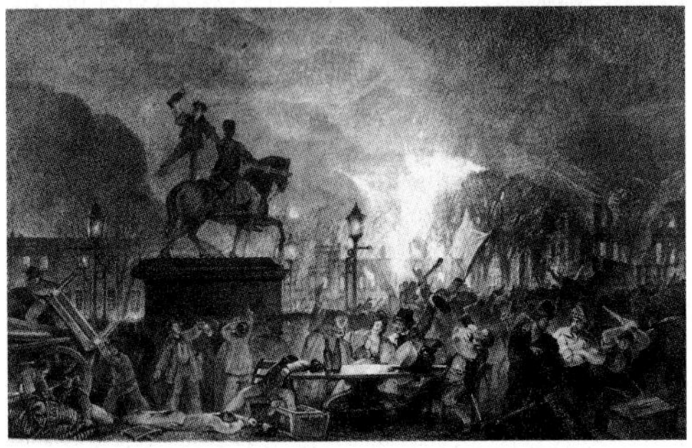

***Queen Square on the night of 30 October 1831*, lithograph by W J Müller (Bristol Museum and Art Gallery, M269)**

Notes

[1] Eustace, *Michael Rysbrack*, p.23; see also Eustace, 'A place full of rich and industrious people', *The Bristish Art Journal*, vol. VII, no. 1, 2006. [2] M.I. Webb, *Michael Rysbrack, Sculptor* (London, 1954), p.140. [3] As note 1, p.6. [4] As note 2, p.141; Rysbrack had a plaster model of Giradon's Louis XIV statue; the original statue was destroyed in the Revolution. [5] The statue, now in the Piazza del Campidogli, is a copy made in early the 1990s; the

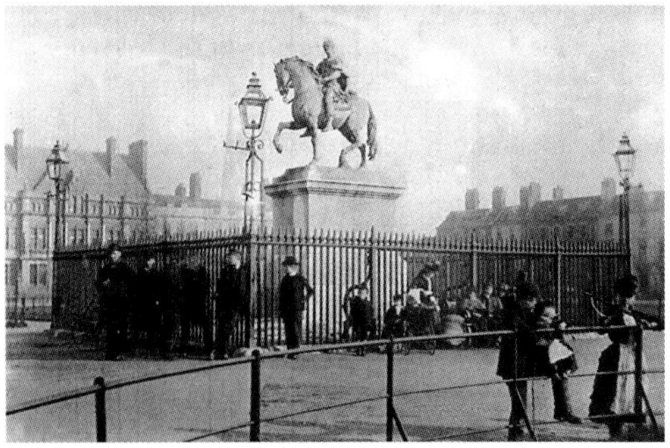

***Rysbrack's statue of William III surrounded by railings c.1890*, Bristol Docks Offices to the left (Bristol Evening Post)**

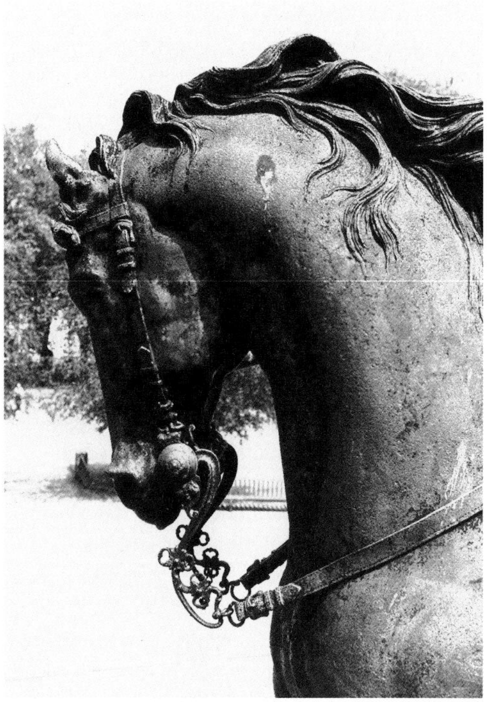

Michael Rysbrack, *William III*, detail showing the ornate bit, now missing (Bristol Museum and Art Gallery, photographed 1981)

conserved original is inside the Capitoline Museum. [6] As note 1, illus. p.99; F. Perrier, *Segenta nobilium signorum et statuarii* (Paris, 1638). [7] As note 2, p.141. [8] As note 1, p.27. [9] In 1994, Bristol Museum and Art Gallery purchased a gilded plaster model (692mm high, K5705), which may well be Rysbrack's 1732 submission; the final casting has a victor's wreath on William's head but the maquette has a simple headband. [10] N. Smith, 'Great Nassau's' image, Royal George's' test', *The Georgian Group Journal*, vol. 6, 1996, p.16. [11] As note 1, p.27. [12] N. Pevsner, *North Somerset and Bristol*: 'figure outstandingly good in its characterisation, urbane and easy yet of great dignity', p.387. [13] As note 1, pp.104–6. [14] As note 2, p.142. [15] Scrope was a Whig MP for Bristol; as a close ally of Walpole he supported the proposal for the William III statue. [16] Clerk mss., quoted in J. Fleming, *Robert Adam and his Circle in Edinburgh and Rome* (London, 1962), fn. p.329. [17] M. Craske, *The Silent Rhetoric of the Body* (New Haven and London, 2007), p.119. [18] As note 2, p.32. *General Evening Post,* a London newspaper, 8 July 1735. [19] As note 2, p.142. [20] J. Taylor, *A Book about Bristol, Historical, Ecclesiastical, and Biographical* (Bristol, 1872), p.323; the title page says that the author worked from original research but no sources are given. [21] Dr John Physick's notes, prepared for the revised Gunnis dictionary: 'The Nost yard remained with the family until it was taken over by John Cheere from Anthony Nost in 1739.' John Nost was also known as Van Ost; the foundry was in Portugal Row. [22] As note 3, p.145. [23] BCC and English Heritage, 'Aspects of the Square', *Queen Square*, 1996, p.24. [24] Bristol Common Council, 24 February 1749, BRO, p.116a. [25] As note 1, pp.32–3;. Bristol Common Council, 20 April 1749, p.100. [26] *Felix Farley's Bristol Journal*, 18 July 1807, quoted in Beeson, *Bristol in 1807*, p.169. [27] A. Kelly, *Queen Square Bristol* (Bristol, 2003), p.55. [28] Ibid, p.32.

19–21 Queen Square, Queen Square House, formerly Bristol Docks Office, later called Port of Bristol Authority

Four Female Figures: Europe, Asia, Africa and America C61

Sculptor: unknown

Architect: William Venn Gough
Date: 1885–6
Material: Portland stone
Dimensions: approx. 3m high
Inscriptions: on the bases [Europe and Asia illegible] – AFRICA – AMERICA
Status: Grade II
Owned by Mnopf Trustees
Condition: fair

This proud Victorian office block in red brick and buff terracotta, with its strikingly white columns and four large statues, has been consistently condemned for the arrogant insensitivity with which it intrudes upon the Georgian decorum of Queen Square. Pevsner called it a calamity, 'higher and bigger and with more motifs than any house of the eighteenth century would bear to display'.[1] But William Venn Gough, the 'rogue architect',[2] unwittingly brought an illusory unity to the rest of Queen Square, more than half of whose houses had to be rebuilt after the Bristol Riots of 1831. Gough 'on occasion could bring off a remarkable theatrical *tour de force*, whose very brashness was persuasive', and he has done so here.[3] The architect should also be judged by the delicious whimsy of the red terracotta panels just above the floor of the entrance porch and hall, depicting winged cherubs playing with dolphins and sea horses.

The grandeur of these offices deserves some explanation. Deep-water docks were developed privately in the 1870s at Avonmouth and at Portishead. Bristol Corporation bought them both in 1884. Bristol's inland harbour, the Floating Harbour, was also advancing with the completion of a railway line along the south side of the harbour, involving a tunnel under St Mary Redcliffe's churchyard, in the early 1870s. When, in 1885, the chairman of the docks committee proposed a raft of further improvements costing £340,000 (which, as Latimer wrote, 'would have taken away the breath of any previous generation of civic senators'), there was hardly any opposition.[4] Thus, these grandiose new offices in Queen Square for the staff of Bristol Docks at a cost of only £9200 must have seemed a trifle in

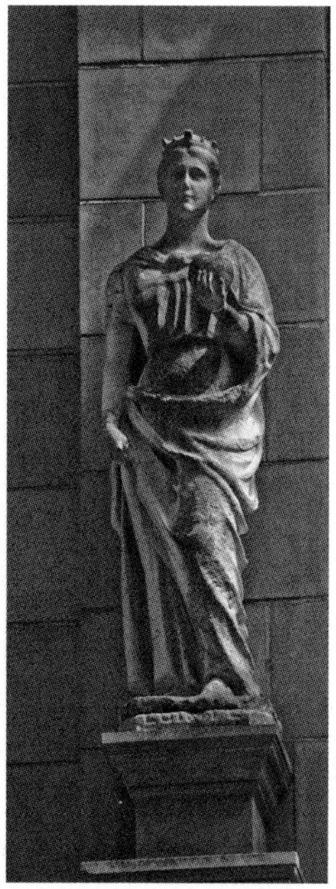
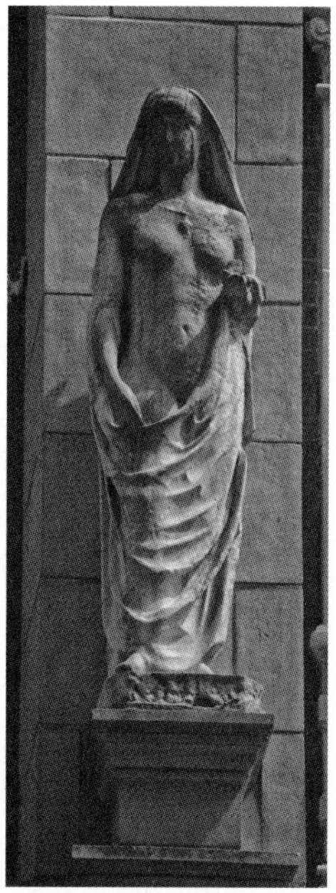

William Venn Gough, architect; clockwise from top left: *Europe*; *Asia*; *America*; *Africa* (photos: Chris Bertram)

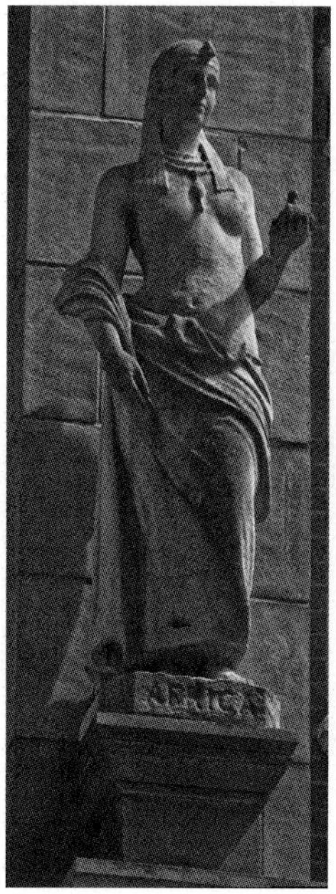
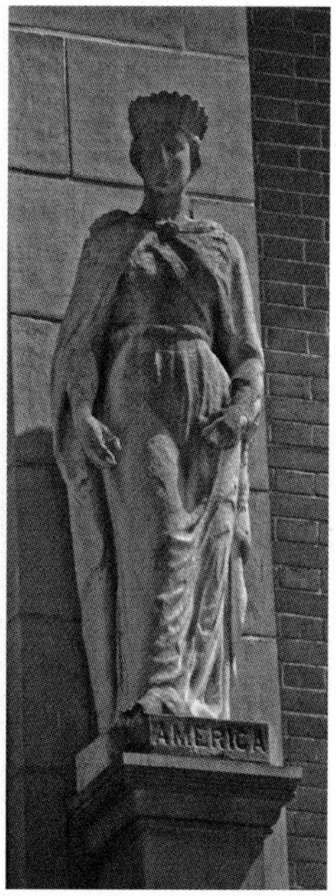

comparison.[5] The building bears the date 1885 and was opened on 10 May 1886.

The confident members of the docks committee may have seen themselves as carrying out the former responsibilities of the Society of Merchant Venturers, which had managed Bristol's port until the early years of the nineteenth century and whose splendid Merchants' Hall was just outside Queen Square at the end of King Street. Docks committee members now met in a grand committee room beneath a splendid Tudor-style ceiling, behind a façade decorated with statues representing Europe, Asia, Africa and America – the continents with which they facilitated trade.

Notes

[1] Pevsner, *North Somerset*, p.431. [2] Gomme et al., *An Architectural History*, p.436. [3] Ibid. [4] J. Latimer, J., *Annals of Bristol in the Nineteenth Century* (Bristol, 1887), p.529. [5] Op. cit., p.532.

Queen's Road

On the traffic island in front of the Victoria Rooms

Gloucestershire Regimental Memorial B38

Sculptor: Onslow Whiting

Date: 1904
Materials: bronze; pedestal, Cornish granite
Dimensions: statue, 250cm high; pedestal, 230cm high, 170cm wide
Signed in the bronze: ONSLOW.WHITING / 1904
Inscription cut in Roman caps on the front of the pedestal beneath the regimental badge: IN MEMORY OF / THE OFFICERS, NON COMMISSIONED OFFICERS / AND MEN OF THE GLOUCESTERSHIRE REGIMENT / WHO GAVE THEIR LIVES FOR THEIR SOVEREIGN / AND COUNTRY IN THE SOUTH AFRICAN CAMPAIGN / 1899–1902 / ERECTED BY ALL RANKS / OF THE SEVEN BATTALIONS OF THE REGIMENT /
Status: Grade II
Owned by Bristol City Council
Condition: good; statue and pedestal recently conserved

The inscription on the memorial refers to the 'South African Campaign' with the dates 1899–1902. This was the second of the South African wars between the British and the descendants of the Dutch settlers, the Boers. Now familiarly known as the Boer War, it ended in the defeat of the Afrikaners and the absorption of the Boer republics of the Transvaal and the Orange Free State.

The infantryman is in the battledress worn in South Africa: pith helmet, desert jacket, and breeches bound with puttees from below the knee. He looks ahead, 'alert and manly'.[1] He is advancing and in the process of reloading. The bolt of his rifle has been drawn and a bullet in his right hand is about to be inserted. There were claims that the soldier is putting the wrong foot forward,[2] but the regiment confirms that the pose is correct.[3] Across his chest is an ammunition belt. A water bottle and a bayonet hang at his waist, and on his back is a bedroll. In 1983 the tip of the rifle-barrel was reported to be loose and the rifle-strap was missing. The rough-hewn granite pedestal is original. On the front is a gilded bronze representation of the Gloucestershire Regimental badge, a sphinx above the word 'EGYPT' and a festoon of palm leaves tied with a ribbon. The badge was re-gilded and the names were re-cut during conservation in 2002.

The earliest reference to this commission is a letter from the most efficient organiser of the project, Major A. C. Lovett.[4] Seven months after the war had ended, Lovett presented his plans for a Bristol memorial to honour 249 officers and men.[5] Nearly seventy of the dead were Bristol citizens, and the regiment's headquarters were in the city. The lord mayor 'offered a very good site on Blackboy Hill, near Durdham Downs, which was accepted'.[6]

The memorial was to be 'a bronze figure standing on a roughly-hewn block of granite upon which would be fixed a bronze panel inscribed with the roll of names of the fallen'.[7] 'The services of Mr Onslow Whiting, an eminent sculptor whose work is frequently exhibited at the Royal Academy, have been secured, and he estimates the work to cost about £500.' Subscriptions were to be restricted to 'officers and men, past and present, of the seven Battalions, as it is intended to be a Memorial or Tribute from soldiers to their fallen comrades'. Lovett added, 'The men have shewn their enthusiasm for the scheme by contributing in small donations more than £20 at Horfield Depot alone.' He also reported that the the Earl of Ducie (colonel of the Volunteer Battalion) and 'other senior officers of the Regiment have made most generous contributions to the Fund', and Field-Marshall Rt. Hon. Earl Roberts, VC, KG, 'heartily approves' and 'it will afford his Lordship much pleasure to subscribe to this very worthy movement.'

During the next two years the proposed site was changed to the more prestigious area in front of the Victoria Rooms, close to the future site of the statue of King Edward VII and of the fountain. On 4 March 1905 it was Lord Roberts who unveiled the statue of an infantryman in action. This was just four months before the completion of Clifton College's memorial to the South African War (see College Road). That was also to be a statue of a single figure, but rather than representing the fortitude of the common soldier, it depicts a knight in shining armour, evoking the heroic chivalry of a bygone age.

The Bristol Times and Mirror gave a detailed report of the unveiling of the Gloucester Regiment memorial, stating that the £700 cost of the statue had been borne by 'the officers and men, past and present, of the seven battalions'.[8] In his speech, the lord mayor said that Bristol and her neighbours had raised £21,000 for the wounded, widows and orphans. Lieutenant Colonel Vines, the officer deputising for Lord Ducie, said that he 'handed over our memorial statue… knowing full well that you and your successors in years to come will guard and

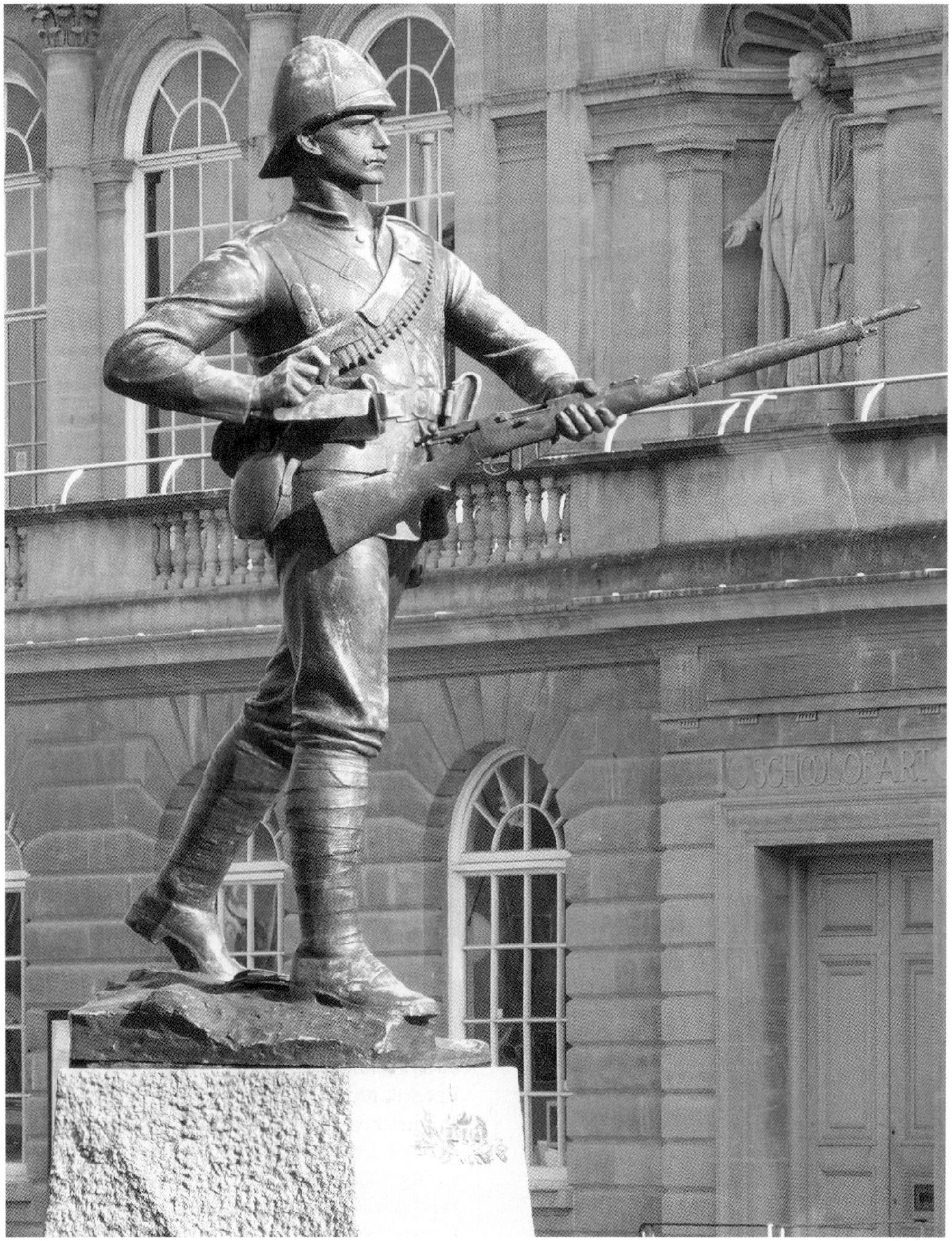

Onslow Whiting, *Gloucestershire Regiment Memorial*

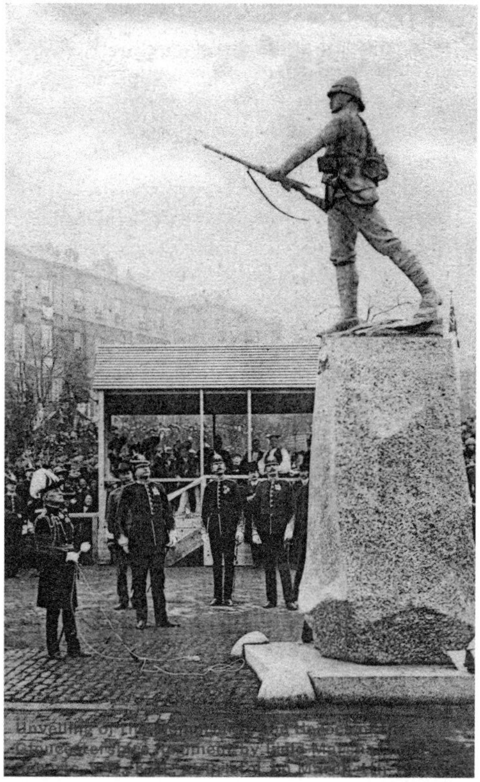

The unveiling of the Gloucestershire Regiment Memorial by Field Marshall Lord Roberts V.C., K.G., 4 March 1905

preserve… an inspiring and lasting token of courage and devotion'.

The sculptor, Onslow Whiting, had exhibited his model of the memorial at the Royal Academy in 1905.[9] Two of his other earlier works, listed in the RA catalogues, were also of military subjects and they may reveal why he gained the Bristol commission. One, a relief on the *Prince Christian Victor Memorial* (1903) outside The Citadel, Plymouth Hoe, is of the Glosters in action in the South African War. This was being made while Major Lovett was organising the Bristol work. Another relief shows that Whiting had a specialised knowledge of military equipment.[10]

Barely five years after the unveiling, Major Lovett wrote to Thomas Yabbicom, the Bristol city engineer, to say that 'a rumour has reached us of a contemplated removal of the Gloucester Regiment South African Memorial'.[11] Yabbicom had given 'great assistance' to Lovett when the statue was commissioned and Lovett now reminded his friend, a retired colonel, that 'after Lord Roberts's stirring speech on 4 March 1905 the Lord Mayor, on behalf of the Council, undertook the charge and preservation of the Statue'.[12]

Only months after King Edward VII had died in 1910, the newly formed memorial committee commandeered the front of the Victoria Rooms for a statue to the king. With staggering insensitivity, the committee did not approach the Glosters. Lovett was incensed. Yabbicom was sympathetic, but deeply embarrassed. He said the architect, E. A. Rickards, had decided to remove the statue.[13] Lovett met the lord mayor, but the only offer was to 'shift' the statue to the site at the top of Blackboy Hill that had been first proposed, or to a space known as 'Parkers Nursery Ground', south of the Victoria Rooms.[14] The major was horrified.[15]

Rancorous discussions about alternative sites continued until January 1912. These involved the council, the regiment, the King Edward VII memorial committee, the Society of Merchant Venturers, who owned some of the land, and their respective solicitors.[16]

Compromise prevailed and the honour of the regiment was preserved. The road layout was changed and the Society of Merchant Venturers sold the land. The infantryman advanced some 70m to his present position at a cost of £70. Yabbicom had obtained an estimate to move the statue.[17] Just before the move – as late as March 1913 – the sculptor warned that the original 12-ton granite pedestal had split before it reached Bristol.[18] Presumably all went well. The statue may well have gained by the move, for the Victoria Rooms were no longer an overwhelming backdrop.

Notes

[1] Little, *The Public View*, p.76. [2] Fred Little Collection, photo-caption: 'People say that he is a disgrace to his Regiment as he is placing the wrong foot forward.' p.39. [3] G.C. Streatfield, curator, Soldiers of Gloucestershire Museum, Gloucester Docks, 2001. [4] Soldiers of Gloucestershire Museum, open letter headed 'Royal Military College Sandhurst', from Major A.C. Lovett requesting subscriptions, December 1902; the last paragraph says: 'I beg to ask if you will participate in assisting to raise this Regimental Memorial, which will be a dignified and distinctive tribute'; Lovett signs himself 'Hon. Sec. Gloucestershire Regimental Memorial Fund'. [5] Soldiers of Gloucestershire Museum: a halftone of a watercolour by Onslow Whiting, entitled 'Preliminary sketch model of the memorial statue', was probably sent with the above letter. [6] C. Newbould and C. Beresford, *The Glosters: An Illustrated History of a County Regiment* (Stroud, 1992), p.23; Major Lovett was an excellent watercolour artist, specialising in Indian Army uniforms. [7] Ibid; the bronze inscription panel was not made and the names are cut in the stone face of the pedestal. [8] *The Bristol Times and Mirror*, 'The Gloucesters in South Africa: tributes to fallen heroes', 6 March 1905, p.7. [9] *Royal Academy Exhibitors*, p.273, 'No.1747. A soldier – sketch model etc. statue etc. Clifton'. [10] Ibid. '1901. No. 1730 Field guns going into action – Colenso: relief.' [11] Major Lovett to T.H. Yabbicom, Bristol City engineer, 10 October 1911, BRO 02919. [12] Ibid, 'The custody of the memorial'. [13] Yabbicom to Lovett, 12 October 1911, BRO, 02919. [14] Undated report by Yabbicom, written between November and December 1911, BRO, 02919(45)a-f. [15] Lovett to Yabbicom, 22 November 1911; the major visited Blackboy Hill and found it 'quite impossible owing to great electric light and tram masts'. BRO, 02919. [16] Yabbicom to Lord Mayor of Bristol, 25 April 1913, BRO, 02919. [17] Yabbicom to Messrs. Cullis & Co. Contractors, 8 January 1913, BRO, 02919. [18] Soldiers of Gloucestershire Museum, Lord Roberts to a Colonel of the Glosters, quoting Onslow Whiting, 19 March 1913; the unveiling of the King Edward Memorial had been scheduled for 4 July 1913.

In the pediment of the Victoria Rooms

Goddess of Wisdom B35

Design: attributed to Musgrave Lewthwaite Watson

Carving: attributed to Jabez Tyley

Architect: Charles Dyer
Date: 1841
Material: Bath stone
Dimensions: approx. 22m long
Status: Grade II*
Owned by University of Bristol
Condition: good

A year before Queen Victoria came to the throne, 'a body of Conservative gentlemen' felt that the various assembly rooms in Bristol were no longer adequate for the expanding and fashionable population.[1] They may have been spurred on by a meeting held in the autumn of 1836 by the mayor of Liverpool 'to suggest that a concert hall could be funded by public subscription' in Bristol's rival city.[2] By May 1837, a triangular site at the bottom of Whiteladies Road had been purchased for a building called merely 'the Undertaking' on the deed of settlement.[3] Charles Dyer, who had practices in both London and Bristol, was appointed architect. Site work started in 1837, and by the end of that year the young queen was crowned and her name was given to the new suite of rooms.[4]

The foundation stone was laid on Queen Victoria's twenty-third birthday, 24 May 1838. The building is clearly 'signed' by the architect and dated 1840 on the left of the facade architrave, but it was not until the corresponding day in 1842 that the rooms were opened, unfinished. A lavish public dinner for 350 local worthies was held, at which orchestral excerpts from two operas by Bellini and from one by Donizetti were performed.[5] Local maps then marked the site as the 'Victoria Conservative Rooms'. Queen's Road was not named until 1854, when the Queen's Hotel

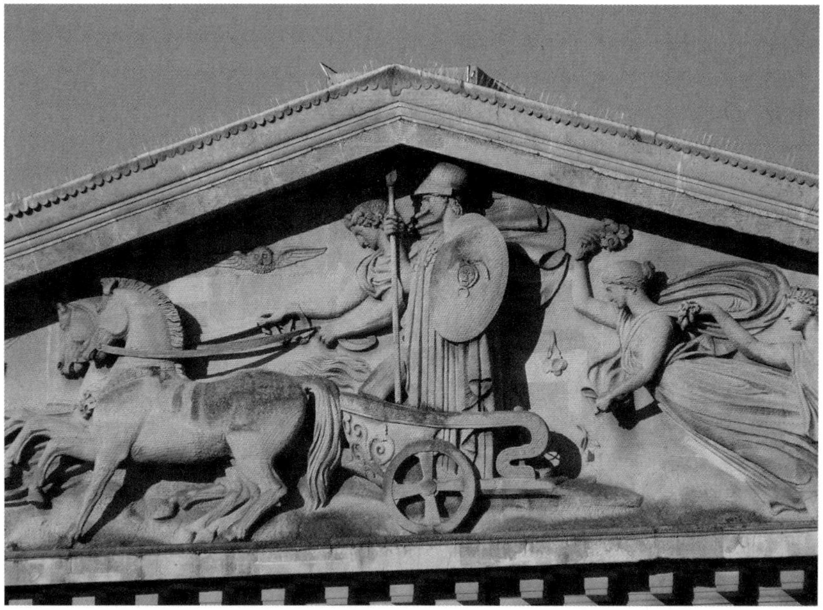

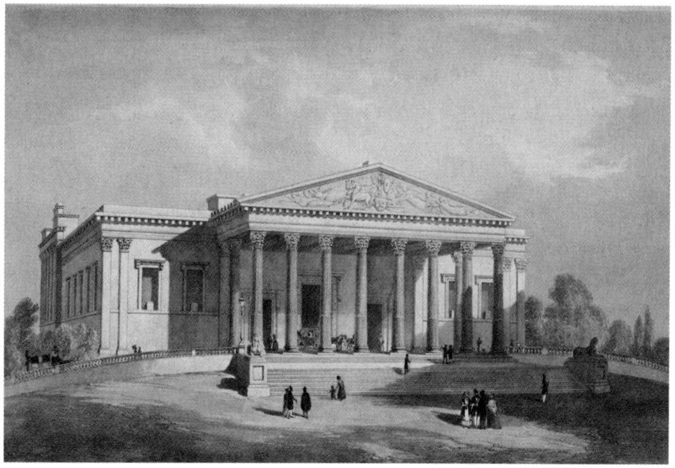

(left) Musgrave Lewthwaite Watson, *Goddess of Wisdom*

(above) *Victoria Rooms, architect Charles Dyer*; **lithograph published 1841 after S. G. Tovey (Bristol Museum and Art Gallery, M5219)**

(now occupied by Habitat) was opened.[6] The building's cost, around £28,000, was raised by the sponsors, not by a public appeal.[7]

Among those who were to appear in the Victoria Rooms were Jenny Lind, Charles Dickens (who gave readings before he went to the USA), Sarah Bernhardt, Oscar Wilde, Sir Arthur Sullivan and Ellen Terry. The scheme, however, never made money. In 1857 the rooms were conveyed to the 'Proprietors', which in 1886 became a private company and by 1891 a limited company.[8] The company was in financial difficulties when Sir George Wills purchased the building, subsequently arranging for the trustees of the rooms to convey ownership to the University of Bristol in July 1920.[9] In 1934 a fire destroyed the interior but the exterior sculpture survived unharmed.[10] The Victoria Rooms were used by the university's student union from 1925 until the 1970s, and they are now occupied by the university's department of music.

Following the death of Edward VII, the forecourt of the Victoria Rooms became the site of Bristol's memorial to the king. It was probably at this time that the two sphinxes on either side of the steps leading up to the façade were removed.

The pediment's deeply cut relief has been given many titles: *Advent of Morning*, *Dawn* and *Athena driven by Apollo* – all have been found in descriptions of the work. *Goddess of Wisdom* was the invention of the biographer of the sculptor, Musgrave Lewthwaite Watson:

> The Goddess of Wisdom is represented in a car drawn by horses – a model somewhat similar to the horses and chariot group of the Vatican Gallery. Music, Poesy, and Light, attended by her emblematic bird, guide the Goddess of Wisdom while following in her path are the Graces, strewing flowers. Two flying figures precede the car – Night, clasping an owl to her bosom with her right hand, and holding drooping poppies in her left, while Morning, following in her wake, has an hour-glass in her hand extended towards the horses of Aurora, and opening flowers in her right.[11]

The influence of John Flaxman and particularly of his illustrations to Homer's *Iliad*, published in 1805, is evident. Musgrave Lewthwaite Watson had been one of Flaxman's assistants.[12]

The work has been praised as 'the most convincing neo-classical group in Bristol',[13] and it has been argued that 'the quality of the carving is superb in depth and purity.'[14] However, there has long been uncertainty about the identity of the sculptor of this impressive frieze. It has repeatedly been attributed to Jabez Tyley, the probable carver of the work, rather than to Musgrave Lewthwaite Watson, its likely designer. In 1982 Benedict Read wrote that the frieze 'is normally attributed to the Bristol sculptor, Jabez Tyley, member of a local family of sculptors who flourished from 1792 to 1864'.[15] That, for example, was the attribution given by Pevsner in 1958.[16] However, Read observed that the 'quality of the design is perhaps rather beyond the capacities of a Bristol statuary family (Jabez or Thomas Tyley) more accustomed to bust and funerary monuments'.[17] He added: 'in fact there is reason to believe this is a rare surviving relief by Musgrave Lewthwaite Watson.' He then summarised an account written by Watson's biographer, Henry Lonsdale.[18] Lonsdale visited Bristol in February 1865 and, standing near the Queen's Hotel, he studied the pediment sculpture. The work reminded him strongly of the Cumbrian artist, M. L. Watson. He said the 'conservator' of the rooms could give him no information, but an 'obliging secretary' said that Dyer had commissioned Watson to make a classical group in plaster of Paris. That model had been in the building until the 1860s. Some weeks later, Lonsdale returned to Bristol to confront 'T. Tyley', whose name he had seen on the relief using a field glass.[19] At first Tyley 'spoke of the work as his own', but then admitted it was based on a model made by Watson. He confessed that the design he had submitted was not accepted and he was contracted to copy Watson's design in Bath stone, inscribing his name.[20] Lonsdale concluded that:

> [the] writer would have failed in his trust if he had omitted to notice this local chiselling by the Bristol burgher… it is to be hoped that Mr Dyer, whose name appears as the architect, or those who represent him, or the institution, will endeavour to see justice done to Watson as the designer of a highly decorative work that gives character to one of the best edifices in Bristol.

Lonsdale's encounter occurred twenty-five years after the sculpture was completed. No signature is now visible on the relief. Musgrave Lewthwaite Watson lived until 1847, five years after the building was opened. He did not exhibit either his drawings or the maquette for this important commission at the Royal Academy, although he did exhibit his drawing for the Royal Exchange competition, which he lost to Richard Westmacott.[21]

A large wood engraving of the Victoria Rooms façade appeared in *The Bristol Mirror* on 5 May 1838, but the image in the pediment shows only a seated Britannia with a lion and two meagre fronds. It may record Jabez Tyley's rejected design.

A prominent public work by Watson is the large bronze relief on the west face of the pedestal of Nelson's column in Trafalgar Square.

Notes

[1] *Bristol Evening Post*, 'Bristol landmarks – 10', 3 July 1954; in *Victorian Buildings in Bristol,* p.6, Clare Crick says Charles Dyer's drawings for the Victoria Rooms were exhibited at the Royal Academy as early as 1832. However, *The RA Exhibitors* gives '1838 and 1839'. [2] T. Cavanagh, *Public Sculpture of Liverpool* (Liverpool, 1997), p.253. [3] B. Little, 'The Story of the Victoria Rooms, 1836–1990', foreword to an unpublished paper in Bristol Central Library, p.1, BCL/L79.22/19. [4] As note 3, p.2. [5] Op. cit., p.4; the portico had been finished by 1840, when Dyer's name and the year were so prominently cut in the architrave. [6] Ibid. [7] Ibid. [8] Op. cit., p.6. [9] Op. cit., p.10. [10] Op. cit., p.11. [11] H. Lonsdale, *The Life and Works of Musgrave Lewthwaite Watson, Sculptor* (London, 1866), p.132. Londsdale (1816-76) was born in Carlisle; he practised in Edinburgh then returned to Carlisle in 1844 to publish widely on medicine; in 1851 he abandoned this to pursue his interest in art. He wrote *Worthies of Cumberland* (1873) and was a political radical, having Mazzini and Garibaldi as his friends. [12] R. Essick and J. La Belle, *The Iliad of Homer Engraved from the Compositions of John Flaxman* (New York and London, 1997). [13] Gomme et al., *An Architectural History*, p.245. [14] Mowl, *Last Age of the Merchant Princes*, caption to Figure 9. [15] As note 13. [16] Pevsner, *North Somerset*, p.418. [17] B. Read, *Victorian Sculpture* (New Haven, CT and London, 1982), p.220. [18] As note 11. [19] Ibid, pp.130–1; Gunnis refers to 'James and Thomas Tyley and Sons, of Bristol. Firm *fl.* 1792–1864'. [20] Op. cit., p.131. [21] The Royal Academy exhibitors' '1847 (1078) competition drawing for the pediment of the Royal Exchange', p.170.

Victoria Rooms, Queen's Road

King Edward VII Memorial

All the sculptural elements of this impressive memorial are inextricably linked. Although it began with a competition solely for the statue of the king, and although the other sculpture, the fountain, the two lions and the Venetian masts came later, the entire complex was the creation of a single architect and of just one sculptor.

Soon after the architect's early death in 1929, his partner made a plea for closer collaboration between sculptors and architects in the design of public monuments. H. V. Lanchester argued that:

> greater unity would be achieved by the domination of the designer, and that this is possible is demonstrated by Rickards's memorial to King Edward VII at Bristol – an excellent example of virility in design and grandeur of conception.[1]

Earlier, and with peculiar awkwardness, E. A. Rickards himself had commended the organising committee for having courage:

> practically without precedent in this country, at least as far as the provinces are concerned. It is an effort which can rank with many a continental attempt at street decoration and time will verify, it is hoped, the confidence of the committee on their own judgement in the conduct of the trust imposed on them by the subscribers to the fund.[2]

That the architect possessed exceptional qualities is confirmed by the author, Arnold Bennett, who shared a close friendship with both Rickards and the sculptor, Henry Poole. The three men travelled together on the continent, and soon after Rickards's death aged 48, Bennett wrote: 'The two most interesting, provocative and stimulating men I have yet encountered are H. G. Wells and E. A. Rickards'.[3]

The success of Rickards's ambitious conception has been readily acknowledged. For example, the architectural historian, Brian Little, has stated that the statue was part of a 'superlative plan' with 'swirling baroque steps and fountain basins that would seem quite inappropriate to go in front of the restrained neo-classicism of the Victoria Rooms… but in fact each provide a perfect foil to the other'.[4]

After a long period as the heir apparent, Edward VII had a comparatively short reign,

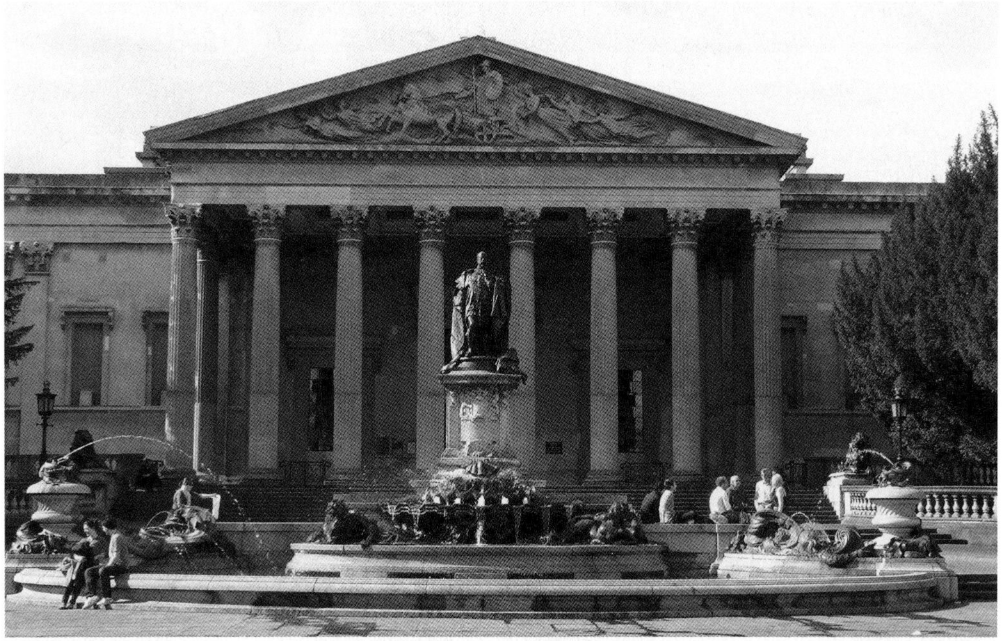

Victoria Rooms and forecourt with statue of Edward VII, fountain and lions

but he was broadly popular and considered a peacemaker. When he died on 6 May 1910, 'the effect on the nation was all the more crushing because it had been unexpected'.[5] Although Bristol acted promptly and the King Edward VII Memorial Committee was formed, it was to be seven years before the lions were in place and the memorial was complete. The work was hampered by indecision, delays and the First World War.

The final balance sheet for the whole memorial shows that the total receipts from subscriptions, including £2,450 from Royal Visit Funds, amounted to £13,638. The sculptor received £2,270 over the seven years. That included his foundry costs for the statue, the fountain and the lions. Lanchester and Rickards were paid £570. A balance of £184 was retained by the council 'towards the upkeep of the Memorial'.

The committee minutes, together with most of the correspondence received by those who planned the memorial, survive in the Bristol Record Office. They provide the fullest account of any public sculpture scheme in the city.

In front of the Victoria Rooms, Queen's Road

King Edward VII B36

Sculptor: Henry Poole

Architect: Edwin Alfred Rickards
Date of casting: 1913
Materials: statue, bronze; pedestal, Bath stone with granite base
Foundry: Singer and Son, Frome
Contractor: George Humphreys and Sons
Dimensions: statue, 260cm high; pedestal, 250cm high, 225cm wide, 235cm deep
Inscription: on the front of the pedestal – EDWARD VII / 1901–1910
–: on the coat of arms: DIEU ET MON DROIT
–: on the rear: VIRTUTE ET INDUSTRIA
Status: Grade II*
Owned by Bristol City Council
Condition: statue good, pedestal showing signs of erosion

King Edward VII (1841–1910) is portrayed in the robes of the Order of the Garter, as the competition rules required, creating a profusion of ribbons, tassels, chains and a lace cravat. The front and back of the pedestal are similar, with two pilasters at each side, each headed with a dolphin. The front displays the royal arms while the Bristol arms are on the rear. Below each coat of arms is a large scallop shell. At the beginning of 2000, the statue was conserved by Bristol City Council and the patina, described as 'an extremely beautiful varied green', was covered with a preservative blue/black paint.[6]

The correspondence preserved in Bristol Record Office encourages the conclusion that the architect manipulated the outcome of the competition (set up only for the design and making of the statue) to ensure that his own preferred sculptor gained the commission.

Within six weeks of the king's death, the Lord Mayor of Bristol, Alderman Christopher S. Hayes, convened 'a Meeting of leading Citizens' at the Victoria Rooms on 21 June, at which the King Edward VII Memorial Committee was formed.[7] At a meeting of a sub-committee on 4 July 1910, the lord mayor was asked to write to the Victoria Rooms Committee, as the space in front of that building had already become the preferred site.[8] The lord mayor's well-laid proposals were seconded by the sheriff, and supported by Sir George White (the Bristol tramways and aircraft entrepreneur) and Joseph Storrs Fry(of the chocolate-making dynasty). The lord mayor agreed to contact 'the Presidents of the Royal Academy and the Society of Architects' to suggest names of those 'thoroughly competent to carry out the work'.

The next meeting was open to the public, and was held on 4 October 1910 at the Guildhall, 'to consider the form of a proposed memorial to the late King Edward'.[9] The lord mayor was supported by about eighty named citizens, including the sheriff, the master of the Society of Merchant Venturers, the archdeacon of Bristol, and the president of the Chamber of Commerce. As the *Bristol Times and Mirror* reported, the lord mayor had already asked the president of the Royal Academy to recommend 'the best sculptor in England or in the world'. The mayor made clear his wish that the memorial should be more than a lone statue. A bronze statue on a suitable pedestal should be 'surrounded by groups of figures and emblems illustrating some of the chief characteristics of the late king and incidents in his reign, and, if possible, fountains and flowerbeds should be included in the design'. The Bristol audience saw two virtues in the lord mayor's scheme: 'The addition of a fine statue to the existing rather meagre attractions of this kind which our city can boast' and the 'long-desired improvement' of the space in front of 'the fine façade of the Victoria Rooms'. The mayor had already gained the agreement of the owners to sell the triangle of land in front of the rooms if this site was chosen.

A note of warning came from the audience at the Guildhall meeting when Mr James Baker said:

> In the Victoria Rooms we have one of the finest pieces of classical architecture to be found in the Kingdom. It is necessary we should be careful what kind of statue we erect in front of it.

The statue would be equestrian in form and of bronze, the lord mayor replied. He insisted nothing would be done to injure the appearance of the Victoria Rooms, but there was a problem; the memorial statue to the Gloucestershire Regiment (erected only four years earlier) was not 'in harmony with the surrounding buildings'. The newspaper reported that 'the statue of the man in khaki' was to be moved, deeply offending the regiment (see Queen's Road).

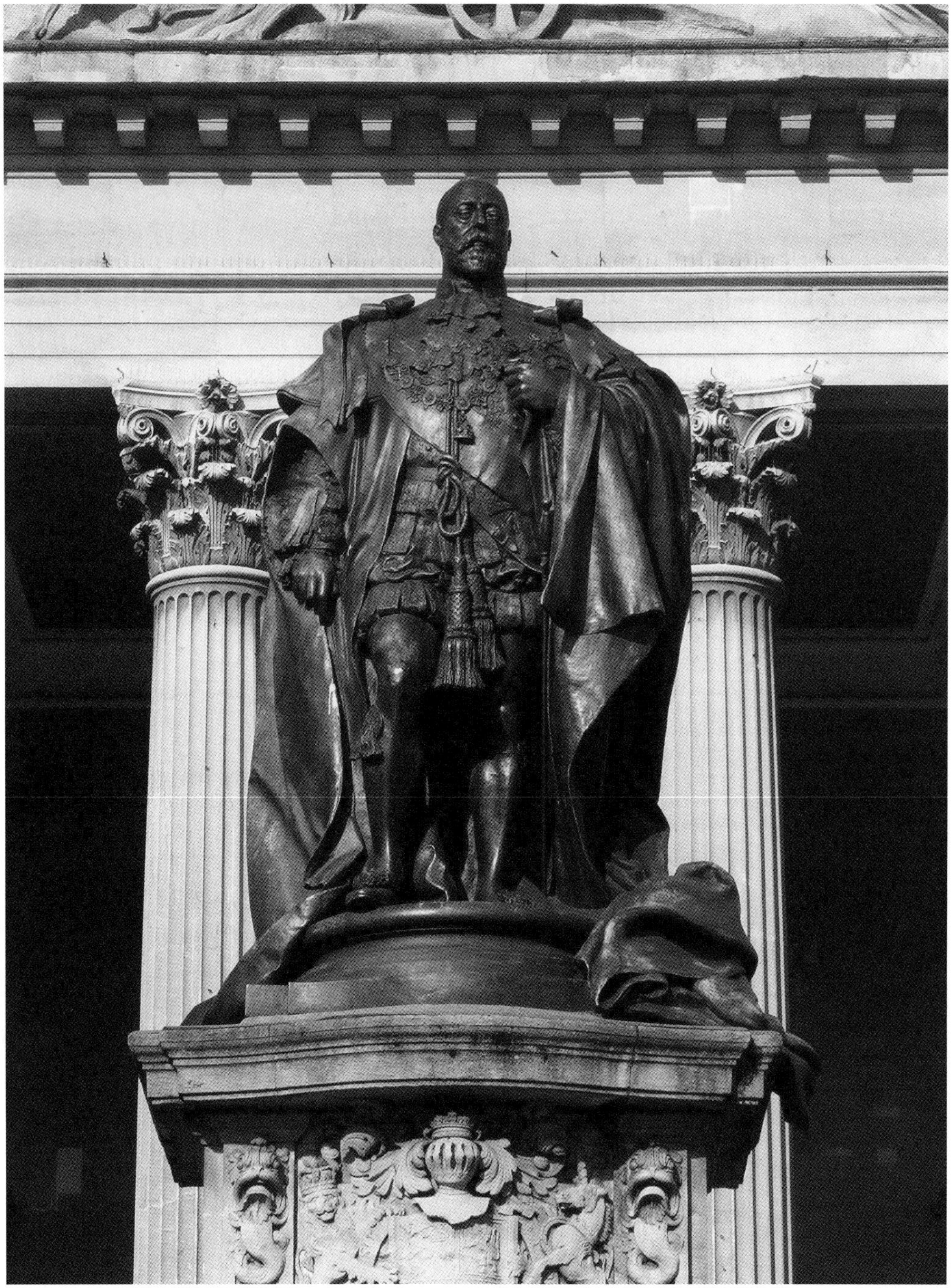

Henry Poole, *King Edward VII*

The dean and chapter of Bristol Cathedral had offered a site without cost, on College Green, but this was rejected and the meeting agreed that the space in front of the Victoria Rooms, a 'beautiful building', would be 'superior'. The lord mayor told his audience of his approach to the president of the Royal Academy. He did not reveal that the names of five sculptors had already been given to him. The city would need to raise about £10,000. Unusually, this estimate proved to be accurate. The meeting was told that £1,700 had already been committed.

At first, 'a number of generous subscriptions were given', but delays depressed interest. At the end of the year the total was still well below requirements. The new lord mayor, Alderman C. J. Lowe, then made a fresh public appeal and, following its success, the site was purchased. By July 1911, George Humphreys and Sons had won the contract to lay out the grounds. No. 2 Whiteladies Road was purchased and demolished. The Royal Colonial Institute was to be built on part of the site in 1916 (see Whiteladies Road). A sketch showing an aerial view of the Lord Mayor's proposals for the memorial was printed in *Bristol Times and Mirror* on 5 October 1910.

On the recommendation of the president of the Royal Institute of British Architects, E. A. Rickards of Lanchester & Rickards was appointed in October 1910 as the architect 'to advise the committee during the preliminary stages'.[10] Rickards first visited the site later that month. Lanchester & Rickards had already designed Cardiff City Hall and Law Courts and the Methodist Central Hall, Westminster.[11] An executive committee meeting held on 17 December 1910 adopted Resolution 2: 'That Mr E. A. Rickards be appointed architect of the laying of the ground'. Shortly afterwards:

> Mr Rickards submitted and explained in Models and read out a list of prices of the various items of his scheme... He left the room and after discourses the committee approved Rickards' general scheme and layout.

The terms were to be: 'All preliminary work to be merged in 5% of commission of work executed and the extra amount for travelling expenses shall not exceed 40 guineas'.[12]

Rickards had proposed a stepped and terraced concourse as the setting of the statue. Only weeks later, in January 1911, a double-page perspective drawing by Rickards appeared in *The Builder* with the comment: 'The citizens of Bristol are fortunate in having secured an exceptionally suitable site for their memorial to King Edward VII'.[13] The comprehensive nature of the plan is striking (see Fig. 30). It showed the statue (seated at this stage), the fountain and the two groups of figures where the lions were to go. It also includes the 'two Venetian masts', the terraces, and the new gates and posts at either end of the carriage drive, all of which were later built. Today, the University of Bristol should take note of the drawing in which long curving banners hang down from the masts. Rather than persisting with the banners that so often disfigure the columns of the Victoria Rooms, the university could advertise events by utilising the masts as originally intended, allowing them to frame this spectacular composition.

An accompanying report in *The Builder* praised the choice of the site, but made no mention of whether or not a competition would be held for the sculptor. Six months earlier, in July 1910, the lord mayor had written to Sir Edward Poynter, president of the Royal Academy. In his reply, Poynter made it clear that the lord mayor had asked him only for 'the names of two Sculptors'.[14] Poynter had been instructed that the statue was to be an equestrian one. His long and detailed letter shows that this became the focus of his thoughts. He said he had delayed writing in order to examine the sculpture in the RA Summer Exhibition; 'Mr Thomas Brock, RA, was of course the first name that occurred to me, but he is engaged on the great Memorial in front of Buckingham Palace.' There was no example of an equestrian statue in the exhibition, but 'of the younger men' Poynter suggested W. R. Colton, ARA.

> On my recommendation a few years ago he made an equestrian portrait of one of the Maharajahs (to replace a very poor work by Onslow Ford)... another very good Sculptor is W. Goscombe John, RA.

John had exhibited a frieze of the charge of Balaclava 'in which the horses appear to me to be excellent'. Poynter ended by listing Goscombe John RA and four ARA members (Colton, Drury, Pomeroy and Pegram) 'who have all done good work'. Pegram was to be the only one of these artists to enter the Bristol competition.

Poynter assumed that the sculptor would be chosen from those he had recommended. Four months after his first letter, he wrote again asking if there was to be a competition and, if not, could he offer further assistance.[15]

The crucial decision to hold a limited competition was made the following month, on 17 December 1910. Rickards must have proposed or agreed to the idea, for it was the day on which his plans were approved.[16] In mid-February 1911, Rickards sent his drafts for an invitation and specification for the sculptors and the rules of the competition.[17] Although he was a judge, Rickards's letter named nine sculptors he had selected to compete. His close friend and colleague Henry Poole (1873–1928) was one of them. The other eight were: 'E. Fabian (Municipal School of Art, Clifton), J. Havard Thomas, A. Turner, Basil Gotto, E. A. [sic] Walker, Leonard Jennings, Mr Fisher and H. C. Fehr'. George Frampton, L. S. Merrifield and John Cassidy were added later.

Bristol Record Office files contain another handwritten note with the names and addresses of seventeen sculptors: 'Colton / Goscombe John / Drury / Pomeroy / Pegram / Bruce Joy / Adrian Jones / Wade / Pibworth / Williamson / Lynn Jenkins / Farran(?)/ Merrett / Taubman

/Roselieb /Hampton / W. C. H. King'.[18]

The lord mayor reported to the executive committee that he had received a letter from Rickards informing him that he had heard via Lord Knollys (equerry to George V) that the new king was 'averse to an equestrian statue at least as far as the proposed London memorial to his father', on the grounds that it would be too militant. To make sure of this, the lord mayor sent an official enquiry to Knollys and he replied: 'His Majesty thinks a non-equestrian statue of King Edward, either standing or sitting, in uniform or in robes would be most suitable'.[19] This led to another resolution. The statue was to be presented in robes, standing on a pedestal with 'four panels' showing designs in bronze, 'emblematic of the peaceful reign of the late king'.

The sculptor Francis Derwent Wood wrote in March 1911 to accept his appointment as an assessor, alongside Rickards, and to thank the committee for 'the Handsome fee of Twenty-five Guineas'.[20] This delayed acceptance was a formality, for his name was already in the competition rules, which accompanied the invitation to the sculptors to submit their designs. These were sent out on 20 February 1910. Derwent Wood and Rickards alone were to judge the competition.

The competition rules were for the statue only. No reference to the fountain, or to the other sculptural groups that Rickards intended to include, was made at this stage:

> 1. The height of the full-size statue is to be 8 feet 6 inches – head to foot. It should show the King standing in robes. 2. The model submitted for the Competition to be the scale of $1^{1/2}$ inches to the foot. 3. The Sculptor competing may, or may not, show the model with a pedestal. What is suggested by the Architect of the scheme for the Memorial is shown in the general view now enclosed. To each Sculptor taking part in the Competition a drawing of this to be 1½ inches in scale will be sent. 4. The statue to be Bronze and to contain 90% copper.[21] 5. The sketch models are to be sent to the Lord Mayor, packed at the sender's risk and expense, not later than April 6th, with a sealed envelope enclosed in the case, giving name and address of the artist. 6. The price of the Bronze statue to be £1,200, delivered and fixed in situ. 7. The Committee have appointed Mr F. Derwent Wood ARA and Mr E. A. Rickards ARIBA to act as assessors and advisers to the Memorial Committee. The Sculptor selected will be commissioned to undertake the work on the following conditions, viz. The client shall pay the Sculptor the remuneration agreed upon by the following instalments. Two hundred pounds on approval by the client of the design submitted by the Sculptor. Five hundred pounds on completion of the full-sized model. Balance on completion of the work.[22]

Many of the responses were amazingly fast. Some were dated the following day. The total number of sculptors invited reached 29, and finally 20 maquettes were submitted. There were several refusals, some of which were disdainful and contentious.

When the sculptor George Frampton replied to the invitation, he wrote: 'I beg to say that I do not compete for commissions.' He congratulated the Bristol committee for appointing 'such a distinguished artist as Mr Derwent Wood to act as one of the assessors'. He added: 'As the result of competitions is very doubtful and often disappointing I would like to suggest that the commission be given to the Artist I have mentioned. I feel sure he would do a fine work of art.' Frampton concluded, 'May I ask your Committee, as well as yourself to treat this communication as private and confidential?' [23]

When Wood wrote to accept his appointment, he referred to Frampton's 'very flattering' letter that had been passed to him, and rejected Frampton's suggestion that a competition would not produce a satisfactory result. Nor, Wood protested, should Frampton's nominee (Derwent Wood) be directly appointed. This, Wood said, was 'out of the question'. 'I feel convinced The Bristol Memorial Committee will be satisfied with the result of this competition.'[24]

Among those who refused to take part was James Havard Thomas. He already had two statues in Bristol: *Samuel Morley* (1887, Lewins Mead) and *Edmund Burke* (1894, The Centre). He wrote:

> To make such a model in the way I should do it would take me a considerable time, in fact quite a large proportion of the time necessary to make the full-sized model. In view of this and the fact that my work is well known at Bristol I much regret that I do not see my way to enter into the proposed competition. Needless to say I am cognisant of your good wishes in asking me to compete.[25]

Bruce-Joy replied swiftly. He had importuned Poynter to be given the commission, but said:

> I have for many years past declined all invitations to compete in fact ever since the time when I was successful in the Harvey Tercentenary Memorial Colossal Statue competition when two of the best sculptors were against me. In the present case, I could – even if asked to make the statue – not have undertaken it for the price available.[26]

Captain Adrian Jones was just completing a five-year task – the 38-ton bronze *Quadriga of Peace* at Hyde Park Corner– and his refusal bore the telegraphic address 'Equisculp, London'. He wrote:

> unfortunately the form you have decided upon precludes me doing so. I cannot bring myself to portray a King, such as Edward was, in a standing figure such as is normal to commemorate a Politician. This with all due defference [sic] to King George who appears

to have allowed you to have your wish.[27]

Robert Colton probably did not know that the president of the RA had recommended him, and he gave an aloof response: 'Sir, I must decline your invitation to compete for the Statue of King Edward as it is not the custom of members of the Royal Academy to do so'.[28] Frederick William Pomeroy did not accept or refuse. He argued that the terms of the competition would make assessing the work almost impossible:

> The terms of payment and the sum allowed for the bronze statue of the late King is satisfactory but I must point out that the scale model asked for i.e. 1½ to foot, will be so small that it will be impossible for anyone to really judge the ability of the Sculptor or the quality of his design for the full size work when completed.

Pomeroy then suggested, like Frampton: 'It would surely be safer to give the work at once to some sculptor of known ability and repute'.[29] Quarter-scale was the most satisfactory size for a sketch model for him.

A Bristol-born sculptor, Charles Pibworth, had written a letter to the lord mayor before the decision to hold a competition was made in December 1910.[30] His Bristol address was written boldly over his printed Cheyne Row letterhead. Proclaiming he was a Bristolian, Pibworth hoped the honour of being chosen would be his, and added: 'Should the work be entrusted to me I feel confident of designing a monument of worth.' He listed his successes, the relief panels for Bristol Central Library (1906, Deanery Road) being the most prestigious. He noted other towns that had favoured their own sons: Cardiff had employed Goscombe John, Newcastle-upon-Tyne had commissioned a fellow citizen to do a war memorial commission, and Bury had used Albert Toft for two statues, including that of the late king. Pibworth was duly invited to compete.

John Cassidy accepted the invitation. He had written earlier to say that his bronze of Edward Colston was already in the centre of Bristol (Colston Avenue): 'If you have not already decided upon the sculptor for the statue of His late Majesty King Edward VII will you do me the honour of placing my name on the list?'[31]

Not surprisingly, Henry Poole, who had been introduced to the competition by his associate Rickards, accepted immediately and graciously.

After the submission of the competition entries by the due date, 6 April, the models were judged. A hand-written 'Report of the Assessors on the Competition for the Central Statue' states that the works had been arranged in three sections:

> 1. The possible models of outstanding merit. 2. The Mass who are much the same in quality. 3. The Models that are incompetent in design. In all 20 Sketch models have been submitted & the committee may be congratulated on the responses the competition has met with, as the cost to the unsuccessful sculptors has been considerable. The conditions stipulated by the committee have been observed by the competitors. After careful deliberation we have no hesitation in awarding the 1st place to the Model marked E which contains the fine elements of composition and craftsmanship together with a marked evidence of harmony of Statue and Pedestal. The Statue has a truly regal appearance and when the likeness of his Late Majesty is properly carried out in the full size model, this work will be worthy of the site selected, and of the City of Bristol. Though his model is strictly in accordance with the height imposed it has an effect of size and Majesty fitting to the subject, which is not approached by any other model, while the handling of the detail shows indubitably the capacity of the Sculptor to carry out this work successfully. 3. The assessors are confirmed in their previous opinion that the scale of one inch and a half to the foot is amply sufficient to show the artistic capacity of the competitors. F. DERWENT WOOD, E. A. RICKARDS.[32]

With this report is a separate note:

> On the motion of the Lord Mayor, Mr. Hy. Poole 1 Wentworth Place whose Model marked E was awarded the 1st place in the Competition and unanimously appointed the Sculptor of the King Edward Statue. A very cordial vote of thanks was awarded to the Assessors. C. C. Hayes.'

It has been argued that 'Rickards must have been pleased when the winning sculptor turned out to be Henry Poole'.[33] Rickards would certainly have been pleased, but he could not have been surprised. He had had every opportunity to contrive the result. He was one of only two judges and he had appointed the other. They both knew the names of all the competitors. Rickards had written to ensure that Poole was included. Both the architect and the sculptor were working on Westminster Central Hall at the time and Rickards would surely have recognised Poole's maquette from a hundred yards. Derwent Wood and Henry Poole also knew each other well; they lived in adjacent roads in Chelsea.

The modelling of the full-size statue of the king began in Poole's studio. Visits by the current and previous lord mayors and members of the memorial committee were made in the autumn and in the spring of 1912.[34] In the middle of June 1913, a deputation from the council visited the foundry at Frome. They reported: 'the work had been admirably carried out, and the likeness of the King was an excellent one'.[35] 'Bristol will possess a memorial worthy of its reputation, and worthy of a great monarch, whose labours for the good of his people Bristol desires to record for future generations.' *The Clifton Chronicle* of 9 July 1913 described the work as 'a perfect casting'.

King George V was in Bristol for five hours

to visit the Royal Agricultural Show on the Downs on 4 July 1913.[36] 'At the Victoria Rooms a halt was made to enable his Majesty to view the statue, just previously unveiled by the Lord Mayor with appropriate ceremony.' He did not alight.[37] 'A few persons had the honour of being presented individually, and the Corporation's loyal address was handed to the king, who handed his reply to the Lord Mayor.' It said, 'I have viewed with admiration the fine statue of my father which you have erected... and I appreciate deeply the affection for his memory which the statue represents.'

In front of the Victoria Rooms and the statue of Edward VII, Queen's Road

King Edward VII Fountain B36

Sculptor: Henry Poole

Architect: Edwin Arthur Rickards
Date: 1913
Materials: fountain, bronze; walls, granite; urns, polished grey granite
Foundry: J. W. Singer & Sons, Frome, Somerset
Masonry: Whitehead of London
Overall dimensions: approx. 240cm high, 20m long, 8m wide Status: Grade II*
Owned by Bristol City Council
Condition: fair; not fully functioning

> The sculpture of the fountains is magnificent fun, a tangled profusion of water nymphs, fishes, sea lions and seaweed, sporting in jets of water which cascade and spurt in every direction. The exuberance and richness of invention is without any rival in the city... The fountain and steps is one of our most precious possessions, and yet scarcely given more than a mention in any of the book on Bristol or nineteenth century architecture or sculpture.[38]

A small, high, basin is centred above a large main semi-circular basin. All the retaining walls are in granite. To the left and right of the central feature are two similar decorative groups. Both groups culminate in granite urns encircled with bronze seaweed. This giant seaweed disguises two opposing waterspouts, which, if they were brought back into operation, would send opposing arcs of water across the lower basin, bringing coherence and vitality to the fountain as a whole. Much of the side-sections are surmounted with bronze sculptures that have 'a hint of Art Nouveau sinuosity'.[39] The highest part of the centrepiece is a cascade, a huge formalised shell. Beneath is a seahorse between two spiky shells. In the first basin, to the left, is a triton holding a large fish under his right arm. To his right, with a small bunch of seaweed in her right hand, is a mermaid. Around are crustaceans, seaweed, shells, fish, and a seal eating a fish. Hidden at the back of the left-hand side, behind two exotically-finned fish, is an octopus. In the section on the far right, a turtle emerges from the waves. There are at least ten jets and today the fountain flows impressively, if not yet to full effect, after many years of intermittent operation.

After a detailed inspection, Andrew Naylor declared in 1983 that the fountain was:

> a monument to bad workmanship... the splendour of the concept, which transforms an otherwise formal, barren, concourse into an animated, pleasant, oasis has not been equalled in technical or professional expertise. There are countless examples of bad workmanship, blow-holes... poor fitting joints...[40]

Naylor may not have been aware of the chaos and delays that brought the sculptor and the

Henry Poole, *King Edward VII fountain, triton*

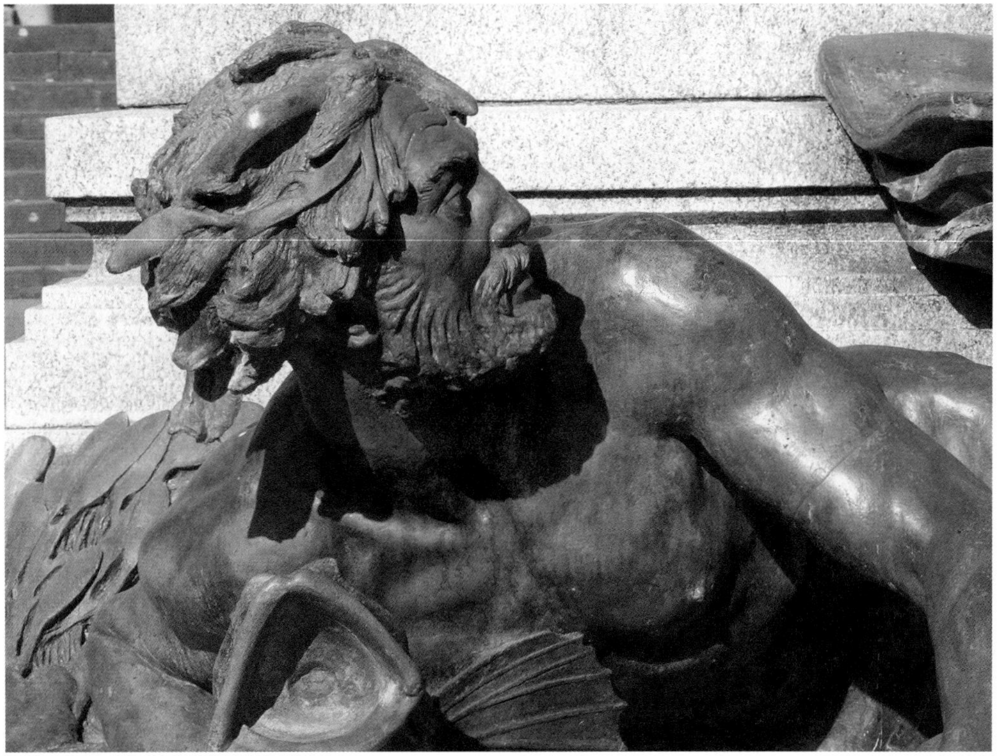

foundry he used, Alexander Parlanti of Albion Works, Fulham, so close to financial ruin.

The architect for the memorial, E. A. Rickards, determined that Henry Poole, who had previously won the competition for the statue of Edward VII, should design and make all the remaining sculpture for the memorial. The large fountain and two other sculptural groups, which were not to be completed, were all to Poole's design. Twenty-six separate bronze castings would be needed for the fountain.

Rickards later wrote: 'So satisfied were they with Mr Poole's abilities that all the other decorative bronzework of the fountain was entrusted to his execution, so that the same spirit is evident all through the details of the memorial'.[41] On Rickards's instructions, Poole began work on clay models in 1911, and in January 1912 members of the committee, including Christopher Hayes, went to Poole's Chelsea studio to inspect the statue of Edward VII and they saw the early models for the fountain.[42]

The trouble began here. By the middle of March, Rickards sent a demanding letter to Mr Hayes, who had initiated the statue of the king but was no longer the lord mayor, saying:

> I want you now to authorise me to give an order for £2,115... to enable Mr Poole to proceed with the work. The expenses to him are of course considerable and he will require money from time to time like any other sub-contractor...[43] He has done a great deal of the full-size models in addition to the small-scale model which you have already inspected and approved.

Henry Poole, ***King Edward VII fountain, mermaid***

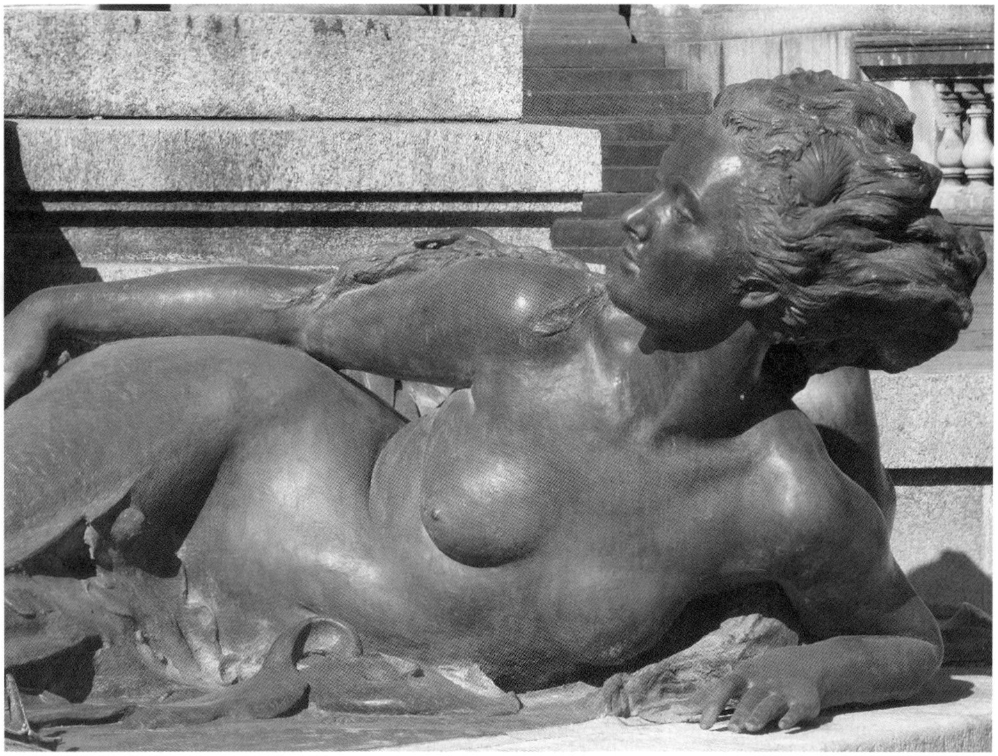

A timetable for the completion of the clay models, the plaster casts and the final bronzes for eight main elements was given, concluding with the vases by 31 March 1913. Five days later Reed, then secretary to the new lord mayor, wrote from the Council House refusing to do anything until the committee had met, the design was approved, and an estimate had been agreed. 'I do not see my way clear to sign any cheque without authority.'[44] The following day Rickards replied saying that Hayes had already told him to give an order to the main contractor. He sounded his first warning. 'Mr Hayes knows that this must be proceeded with or we shall never get the memorial finished.'[45] Rickards prevailed and the cheques were soon cleared.

With the help of assistants, Poole modelled frantically for a year. The next sign of anxiety was a letter from Parlanti to Poole: 'We note the date of the King's visit & shall have to keep hard at it in order to finish all in time'.[46] They then had to soothe the lord mayor: 'We are sorry you have received the impression that the Bronzes should be in a more advanced stage than they are... by the end of May we hope to have all in Bronze'.[47]

Parlanti's hopes were not fulfilled. At the end of May they wrote to say the bronzes could not be cleared until the end of June. This was for the 4 July unveiling. The engineers needed at least three weeks on site after delivery of the castings to fix the piping.[48]

All appeared complete at the unveiling, but in the last few days Poole was obliged to cast a plaster version of one of the larger figures and to paint it to look like bronze.[49] Corrective work went on until October 1913.[50] Poole blamed Parlanti for grossly underestimating their fee and the time required to meet the deadline; 'their idea of approximation appears to be one and a half times... their original estimate'.[51] That had been £940, while their final charge was £1,389.

Poole, not Rickards, had negotiated with the foundry and he was out of pocket on the deal.

He managed the situation with exemplary courtesy and patience and went on to make the two bronze lions.

Rickards and Poole made a final inspection in October 1913 when the jets:

> were exactly as designed… the water takes the lines which from most points of view most happily contrast with the lines of the fountain and any alteration in this respect will be a departure from the original intention for which I am personally responsible…[52] We have obtained the best results from everyone employed and I am afraid in certain instances at a figure which has allowed very little margin for profit.

Forty years ago, a headline below a photograph of the fountain said: 'Bristol landmark a rubbish dump'.[53] By the mid-1970s the fountain was flowing again as a result of pressure from the Clifton and Hotwells Improvement Society, together with the determination and expertise of John Grimshaw.[54] In the summer of 1999, Bristol City Council announced its intention to commence the 'repair and renovation' of the King Edward VII Memorial for the millennium.[55] That work was carried out by Rupert Harris Conservation, and the bronze of the fountain temporarily lost its 'extremely beautiful varied green'.[56] They reported: 'Compared to the lions and the statue… the fountain was in a very poor condition'.[57] Surface limescale caused by the calcium in the Bristol water was the main problem. Low-pressure steam was used to clean off the old wax and pollution and then the limescale was removed. After thorough drying with gas torches, three coats of micro-crystalline wax were applied and a final coat, with colour tints, hid areas where the patination was thin or discoloured.

On either side of the steps below the Victoria Rooms, Queen's Road

King Edward VII Lions

Sculptor: Henry Poole

Architect: Edwin Arthur Rickards
Date: cast 1915, erected 1917
Foundry: J. W. Singer & Sons, Frome, Somerset
Materials: lions, bronze; plinths, dark grey polished granite
Dimensions: lions, 120cm high, 10cm long, 115cm wide; plinths, 40cm high, 200cm long, 145cm wide
Status: Grade II*
Owned by Bristol City Council
Condition: good; right lion has lost the end of his tail

The two lions are set at either end of the steps. They are not identical. The lion to the left is snarling and his right paw grasps the edge of the base while his left paw is curled. His companion on the right is calm and imperious, his paws resting on the granite plinth.

By January 1913, the statue and fountain were in production with only five months to the unveiling. However, no decision on the spaces either side of the steps had been made, and the empty plinths, which had previously held sphinxes, became a matter of serious concern.[58]

Rickards's original scheme for the plinth areas was for two life-size groups based on Bristol's history. He pressed for decisions to be made by the Bristol committee, and wrote to John Reed, secretary to the King Edward memorial committee:

> I am delighted to learn that we are likely to get the memorial completed at last as I have the work very much at heart & have been so disappointed with what I consider the mutilation of the scheme entailed by the leaving out of the accessory features of the design… if in addition Mr Poole can be commissioned to carry out his two groups of the Merchant Venturers & the Bristol Industries, the memorial will have a further story to tell & a much greater interest to the public.[59]

Poole must have been advised that he could proceed. On 20 January he wrote:

> My design for the Cabot group [Rickards called this the 'Merchant Venturers group'] is still in the clay, and before I forward it to the Council House for inspection of the Committee I should like to carry it a little further. It must then be cast in plaster. This will take a little while, but I will proceed with it as quickly as possible.[60]

This must have been a small model and it was duly submitted for approval. Whether on grounds of time, cost or aesthetics, the ledger records: 'A suggestion was made that instead of the flying groups there might be a single animal on either side, such as a lion. The architect and Poole agreed to consider this.'[61]

No further mention of the plinths was made until the end of the year, when Poole sent an estimate to Bristol for 'two lions cast in bronze from two models, together with their two granite super-pedestals according to the sketch models at a sum of £830'.[62]

On the next day, Poole sent two models in plasticine, commenting: 'The heads of the lions look inwards towards the statue of the King'.[63] These and the estimate were approved on the condition they were to be in position in eight months.[64]

They were not. The first full-size model was not approved until November 1914. That was done by the past lord mayor, who had initiated the memorial scheme, and by Ernest Cook, chairman of the Municipal School of Art.[65] Poole asked for permission to cast the first lion a few days later.

Perhaps because of the First World War, Poole was still working on them in 1915. By August of that year he advised Bristol that 'one bronze lion is quite ready and the other nearly

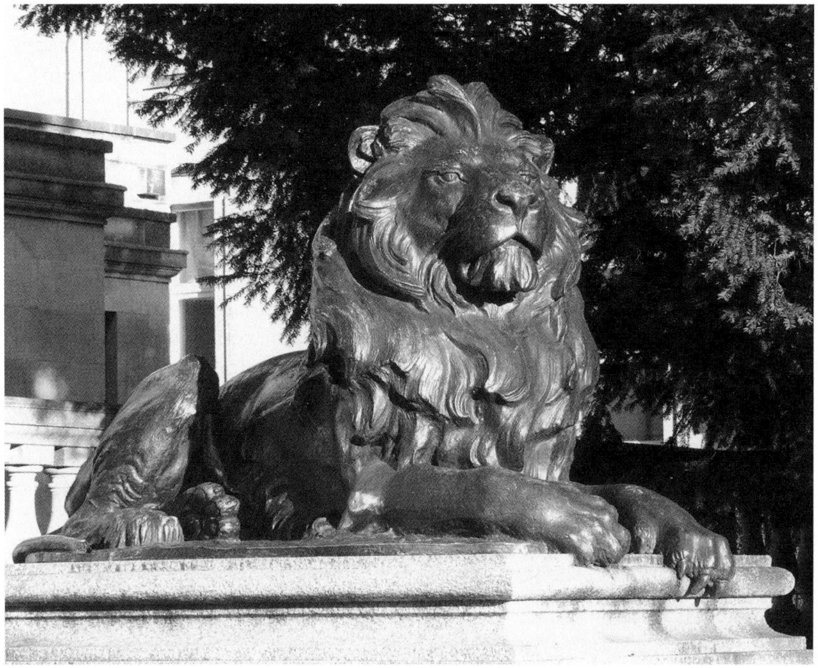

Henry Poole, *King Edward VII monument; lion*

so'.[66] The granite monoliths for the new plinths were put in position.

After the completion of the casting, the Singer foundry reluctantly held the lions captive until early in 1917. They then wrote to Poole in exasperation because the clients, Bristol City Council, had been unable to take delivery. The foundry needed space for its munitions' work, and Singer had also not been paid.[67] Poole took action, and by April the lions were in position after the Great Western Railway had finally given permission for a train to be used, bringing the King Edward VII Memorial to its conclusion.[68]

An undated and unattributable paper in the Bristol Record Office, headed 'Mr. Tryon's Note', says the Victoria Rooms committee and the memorial committee 'mutually agreed' that the lions would remain the property of the city. The Victoria Rooms committee undertook not to cancel the agreed 'annual tenancy' unless the building was reconstructed and the steps were removed. In those circumstances, the Victoria Rooms would 'do their best to arrange for an alternative site for the said Lions'.[69] The Victoria Rooms has since become the property of the University of Bristol.

Notes

[1] An undated statement on Lanchester and Rickards' letterheaded paper, probably written by Richards as a press-release for the unveiling in 1913, BRO 03919. [2] Ibid, p.6. [3] A. Bennett, H.V. Lanchester and A. Fenn, *The Art of E.A. Rickards* (London, 1920), p.57. [4] Little, *The Public View*, p.74. [5] K. Middlemas, *The Life and Times of Edward VII* (London, 1972), p.211. [6] M. Jenner, 'The grand finale', *Bristol Illustrated*, March 1985, pp.43–6. [7] King Edward VII Memorial Ledger, BRO/03919(87)a; this contains the minutes of meetings and pasted-in documents and press cuttings; the access number for all documents relating to the memorial is BRO/03919. [8] The Victoria Rooms were then owned by a private company. [9] 'Bristol's memorial to King Edward', *Bristol Times and Mirror*, 5 October 1910. [10] An undated statement by Lanchester and Rickards, probably written by Rickards as a press release for the unveiling in 1913. The RIBA president at the time was Leonard Stokes (1910–12). [11] Stuart Gray, *Edwardian Architecture*, pp.308–10. [12] As note 7; minutes of meeting are pasted into the ledger. [13] *The Builder*, 13 January 1911, p.44. [14] Poynter to Lord Mayor, letter from the RA, 17 July 1910, (12)a. [15] Poynter to Lord Mayor, letter from 70 Addison Road, Kensington, 22 November 1910, (10)c. [16] Minutes of the King Edward VII Memorial Executive Committee, Resolution 4, 17 December 1910, BRO/039919. [17] Lanchester and Rickards to Lord Mayor, letter, 13 February 1911, (12)b. [18] Handwritten list, BRO/071199(2)e. [19] King Edward VII Memorial Ledger. This account appears, with an undated press cutting, in the minutes of 17 November 1911 pasted in the ledger. (87)a. [20] Derwent Wood, letter to J.H. Reed, 9 March 1911,(20)a. [21] To produce bronze the remaining 10 per cent would be zinc. [22] The competition rules and a covering letter, dated 20 February 1911, from J.H. Reed (secretary to various lord mayors of Bristol) are pasted into the ledger. (87)a; the pages are not numbered. [23] George Frampton to J.H. Reed, 22 February 1911, (20)b. [24] As note 20; Wood had been one of Frampton's assistants. [25] James Havard Thomas, 24 February 1911, (10)j. [26] A. Bruce-Joy, 21 February 1911, (10) g. [27] Adrian Jones, 21 February 1911, (10)b. [28] Robert Colton, 21 February 1911, (10)e. [29] F.W. Pomeroy, 21 February 1911, (13)b. [30] Charles Pibworth, 7 September 1910, (6)a & b. [31] John Cassidy, 22 January 1911, (10)d. *The Builder*, 13 October 1911, noted Cassidy was appointed as the sculptor of Manchester's massive King Edward VII statue. [32] King Edward VII Memorial Ledger. (87)a; undated, but soon after 6 April 1911. [33] Little, *The Public View*, p.74. [34] Various letters: 8 November 1911, 5 January 1912, etc. [35] As note 7. [36] *The Times*, 5 July 1913, p.8; no assessment of the statue was given. [37] Winstone, *Bristol As It Was 1913–1921*, pl. 3–6, which suggest that the king did alight. [38] As note 5, p.46. [39] Mowl, *Last Age of the Merchant Princes*, illus. p.89. [40] A. Naylor, conservation report for Bristol City Council, 1983. [41] Statement by Rickards at the time of the unveiling. BRO 03919 (77) a, b, c. [42] BRO/03919 letter, 5 January 1912. [43] Rickards to Hayes, 13 March 1912, (40) h.1–2. [44] J.H. Reed, secretary of King Edward Memorial Fund to Rickards, 20 March 1912, 40, 2. [45] Rickards to Reed, 21 March 1912, BRO 3919 (40) i ½. [46] Parlanti to Poole, 15 April 1913, (43). [47] Parlanti to the Lord Mayor, 21 April 1913. [48] Parlanti to the Lord Mayor, 27 May 1913. [49] Rickards to Reed, 28 February 1914. [50] Rickards to Reed, 14 November 1913. [51] Poole to Reed, 18 December 1913. [52] Rickards to Reed, 14 November 1913. [53] *Evening Post*, 3 November 1969. [54] Francis Greenacre was then chairman of CHIS and John Grimshaw was a water engineer; he

was soon to found the cycling pressure group Sustrans, which has since proved to be the most prolific patron of public sculpture in Britain's history. [55] 'Millennium hat-trick', *Bristol News*, No. 32, July 1999. [56] As note 5, pp.43–6. [57] M. Rodda, senior conservator, Rupert Harris Conservation, 2001. [58] Rickards to Reed, 11 January 1913, BRO 03919(40) 2.1-2; for an illustration of the sphinxes *in situ*, see Crick, *Victorian Buildings of Bristol*, pl. 5. [59] Ibid. [60] Poole to Reed, 20 January 1913, BRO 03919(75d). [61] Ledger minutes, 9 February 1913, BRO 03919. [62] Poole to Reed, 8 December 1913, BRO 03919. [63] Poole to Reed, 9 December 1913, BRO 03919; Plasticine was a fairly new material invented by William Harbutt of Bath in 1897. [64] Ledger minutes, 19 June 1914, BRO 03919. [65] Alderman C.C. Hayes to Alderman Lowe, 12 November 1914, BRO 03919(75h); and Ernest Cook to Alderman Lowe, 13 November 1914, BRO 03919(75i). [66] Poole to Read, 25 August 1915, BRO 039919(75)k. [67] Singer of Frome to Poole, 24 February 1917, BRO 03919(75)l. [68] Poole to Reed, 9 April 1917, BRO 03919(75)n. [69] Typed sheet, headed 'Mr. Tryon's Note'. BRO 03919(87)f.

The Royal West of England Academy

The Royal West of England Academy opened in 1858 as the Bristol Academy of Fine Art. Its façade was designed by John Henry Hirst and the block behind it, together with the interiors, was by Charles Underwood. This apparently amiable compromise succeeded a long and courteous battle of styles between the two architects.[1]

In December 1854, the council of the Bristol Society of Architects proposed that 'the designs prepared by Mr Underwood in the Classic style of Architecture and that by Mr Hirst in the Italian style be recommended to the Society of Artists'.[2] Underwood's crisp neo-classicism was well represented in Clifton by Worcester Terrace, begun in 1851, whose 'Greek Doric purity [was] so ruthless and repetitive that the houses were not selling well'.[3] Hirst, who had recently visited the continent's most advanced art galleries in Berlin, Dresden, Munich and Vienna, had submitted an Italianate or Victorian Rennaissance[4] design that ultimately triumphed.

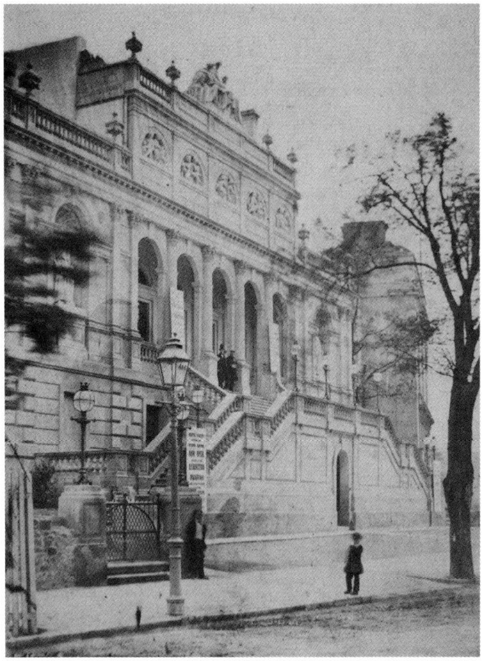

Photograph of the Bristol Fine Arts Academy (Royal West of England Academy) in 1858 **(Bristol Museum and Art Gallery, K2969/130)**

Tim Mowl points out that this decision was being made in 1854, when Gingell's design for the West of England and South Wales District Bank in Corn Street, inspired by Sansovino's library façade in St Mark's Square, Venice, was already known. He sees Hirst's academy design as an amalgam of Gingell's bank, Munich's Alte Pinakothek and Rome's Palazzo Barberini, together with 'a Ruskinian profusion of sculptural invention'.[5]

By December 1855 John Thomas had already prepared a design for a group of figures for the new academy, and at the AGM the following May 'much was made of Thomas's connection with the sculpture on the Palace of Westminster'. An additional £230 was duly requested for sculpture.[6] Thomas was probably simultaneously at work on the wealth of decorative sculpture for Gingell's Corn Street bank, and he had earlier completed the six figures for the Guildhall façade in Broad Street and been closely involved with John Norton's replica High Cross for College Green.

John Thomas's work for the bank involved the luxurious decoration of friezes, spandrels and corbels. There, his sculpture is integrated, even subsumed, into the architecture, but vital to its overall character. At the Academy, Hirst compartmentalised the sculpture into niches and lunettes, but it is no less vital to the design as a whole. Indeed, the completion of the composition of the façade, with its original external double staircase, was dependent on the group of figures at its summit.

The replacement of the staircase in 1912–13 by today's covered entrance hall and offices has fundamentally altered the façade and our relationship with the sculpture. No longer do we climb a grand open staircase, overlooked by the muses of painting, architecture and sculpture. We are unlikely to notice the five lunettes, in which cherubs are busily engaged in various decorative arts, and we no longer pass between the statues of Flaxman and Reynolds that flanked the open loggia.

The statues are of considerable historical importance. Conservation work undertaken in 2002 revealed that they were cast, not carved, as all the sculpture on the façade had been presumed to be.[7] They were hollow cast in a cement/concrete aggregate with china chippings and 'finished with a shelter coating that gave a smooth stone-like appearance'.[8] That coating had weathered away. Drill samples show that a brick support was made first and the gap between that and the exterior castings were filled with loose rubble and mortar.[9]

When Ellen Sharples had first proposed the bequest that was to lead to the building of the academy, she had written pointedly: 'If the Bristolians are only now liberal, all preceding neglect of Art will be forgotten: an elegant edifice will arise an ornament and honour to the city'.[10] Bristolians had long been aware of their wretched reputation and the desire to redress the balance was well expressed by the academy's president, John Scandrett Harford, in the year before the building was opened. He was determined that the new edifice would remove 'for ever from Bristol the stigma of neglecting the Arts which are the result and the evidence of a high state of civilisation'. The façade of the academy was a proud declaration of progress.

Above the parapet wall on the Royal West of England Academy, Queen's Road

The Arts: Painting, Architecture and Sculpture B37

Sculptor: John Thomas

Architect: John Henry Hirst
Date: 1857
Materials: cast concrete with brick, rubble and mortar core
Status: Grade II*
Owned by the Council of the Royal West of England Academy
Condition: good; yellow fumitory grows profusely between the figures

All three laurel-crowned figures are seated and wearing Greek tunics drawn with girdles at the waist. The attributes of the central figure, a scroll across her lap and dividers in her right hand, imply that she represents Architecture. To her right, Painting holds a brush and palette, and on the left, Sculpture has a mallet. Painting casually rests her right arm on a bust of Raphael, and Sculpture leans on a bearded classical bust, perhaps the head of Zeus by Phidias.

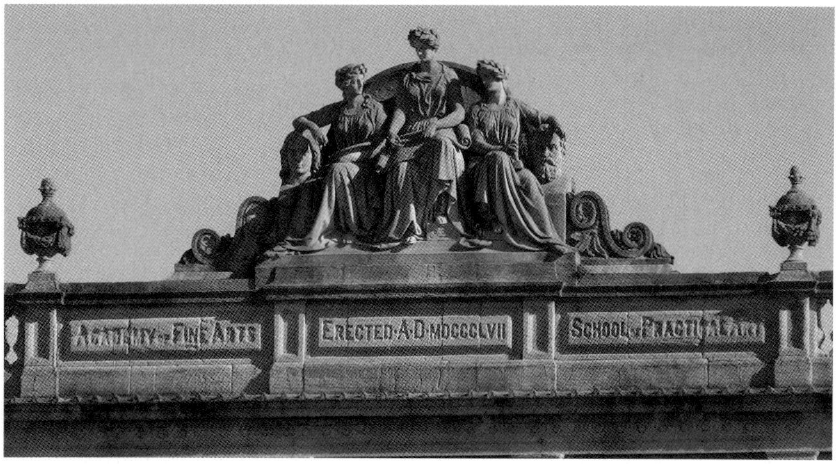

John Thomas, ***Painting, Architecture and Sculpture***

Five lunettes below the parapet of the Royal West of England Academy

Decorative Arts B37

Sculptor: John Thomas

Architects: John Henry Hirst
Date: 1857
Material: cast and partly modelled in concrete[11]
Status: Grade II*
Owned by the Council of the Royal West of England Academy
Condition: good

All five lunettes contain putti in very high relief, projecting well beyond the vertical plane of the semi-circular surrounds. They are engaged in activities connected with the so-called decorative or applied arts, determinedly illustrating the academy's inclusion of an art school in the new building. Above them on the frieze are the words: ACADEMY OF FINE ART / ERECTED AD MDCCCLVII / SCHOOL OF PRACTICAL ART. Under the chairmanship of Philip Miles, vice-president of the academy, the Bristol School of Practical Art had been founded in 1853. Its curriculum was based on

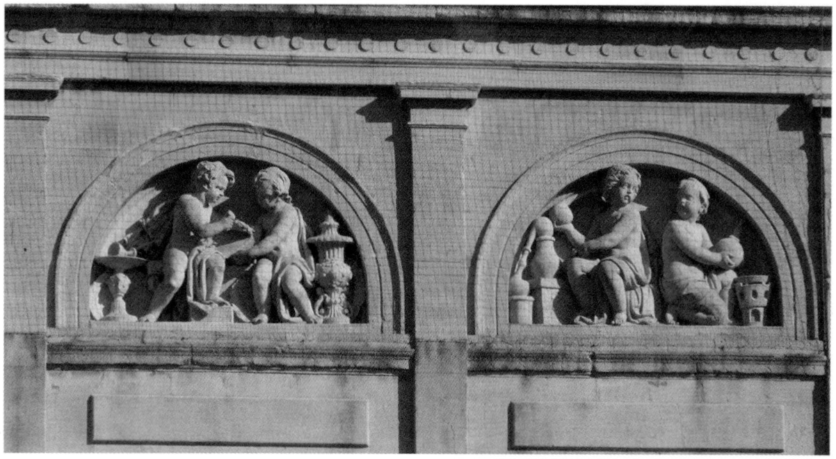

John Thomas, ***'Practical Arts'***

the government's pioneering South Kensington model and it was to become the Bristol Municipal School of Art in 1904.[12]

The first lunette, on the far left, has two figures surrounded with scrolls with a pot to the right, suggesting ink or paint. The child on the right has a pad in his left hand and appears to be drawing. In the second arch are two figures involved with ceramics: one is drawing, the other holds an ornate vase. The middle arch represents sculpture and modelling. One putto works on a large vase in the centre. A classical bust of a female is set beside a mallet in the left-hand corner. The second figure is engaged with pottery. The fourth arch depicts metalwork, with the figure on the left using a hammer and a punch on a plate that is held by his companion. The last lunette, to the far right, includes retorts and a burner and may represent the complex technical processes involved in many crafts: science in the service of the arts. Beneath each of the five arches is a raised panel, which may have been intended for inscriptions to denote the activities.

On the right side of the façade of the Royal West of England Academy at first floor level

Sir Joshua Reynolds B37

Sculptor: John Thomas

Architect: John Henry Hirst
Date: 1857
Materials: cast concrete with brick, rubble and mortar core
Dimensions: statue, 260cm high; pedestal, 160cm high, 155cm wide
Status: Grade II*
Owned by the Council of the Royal West of England Academy
Condition: fair, after conservation in 2002; chipped, probably by scaffolding poles, with damaged foot and fingers

Sir Joshua Reynolds (1723–92) was born in the west country at Plympton, Devon. He gained a great reputation as a portrait painter and as a teacher. When the Royal Academy was founded, in London in 1768, he became its first president and he was knighted the following year.

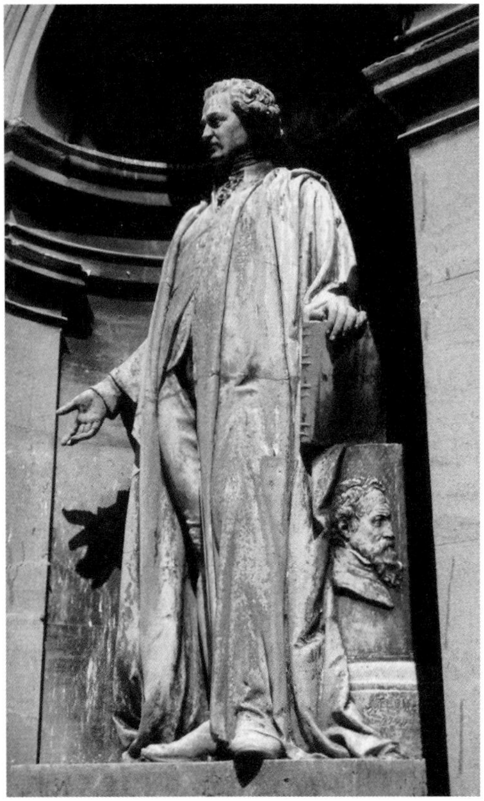

John Thomas, *Sir Joshua Reynolds* (before conservation)

The statue of Reynolds is in a shell-head niche, identical to that containing the figure of Flaxman. He rests a copy of his *Discourses*, held in his left hand, on a broken column on which there is a profile portrait of Michelangelo in relief. Here, John Thomas makes subtle reference to Reynolds's own self-portrait painted for the Royal Academy, 1779–80, to celebrate the move of the academy to prestigious new premises at Somerset House. In both the painting and the sculpture Reynolds wears an academic gown, for he was an Oxford doctor of civil law. Both works also include an image 'of his beloved Michaelangelo – "that truly divine man", as he called him in his last *Discourse*', delivered to students of the Royal Academy in December 1790.[13]

The statue was clearly cast in two main sections and joined horizontally below the waist.

On the left side of the façade of the Royal West of England Academy at first-floor level

John Flaxman B37

Sculptor: John Thomas

Architect: John Henry Hirst
Date: 1857
Materials: cast concrete with brick, rubble and mortar core
Dimensions: statue, 245cm high; pedestal, 125cm high
Status: Grade II*
Owned by the Council of the Royal West of England Academy
Condition: good, after conservation in 2002

After attending the Royal Academy Schools, John Flaxman (1755–1826) worked alongside his father for Josiah Wedgwood, designing cameos, classical friezes and medallions, gradually taking on an increasing number of private commissions.[14] He spent seven years in Italy from 1787. He was elected an associate of the Royal Academy in 1797 and a full member in 1800, and he became the academy's first professor of sculpture in 1810.[15] On his death his pupil, the Bristol-born sculptor E. H. Baily, completed his unfinished works.[16] In a lecture given on Flaxman's death, the sculptor Sir Richard Westmacott said that he was the greatest of modern sculptors who 'not only had all the fine feelings of the ancient Greeks but united to it a readiness of invention and a simplicity of design truly astonishing'.[17]

A shell-head niche to the left of the façade contains the figure of Flaxman, standing beside a pedestal. He looks towards a model of one of his own marble groups on the top of the pedestal: *St. Michael Overcoming Satan.* This was made for Lord Egremont and remains on display at Petworth, Sussex. Flaxman wears a loose-fitting gown, tied at the waist with lapels, perhaps a working smock. The portrait relief on the side of the pedestal may represent the Greek sculptor of the Parthenon, Phidias.

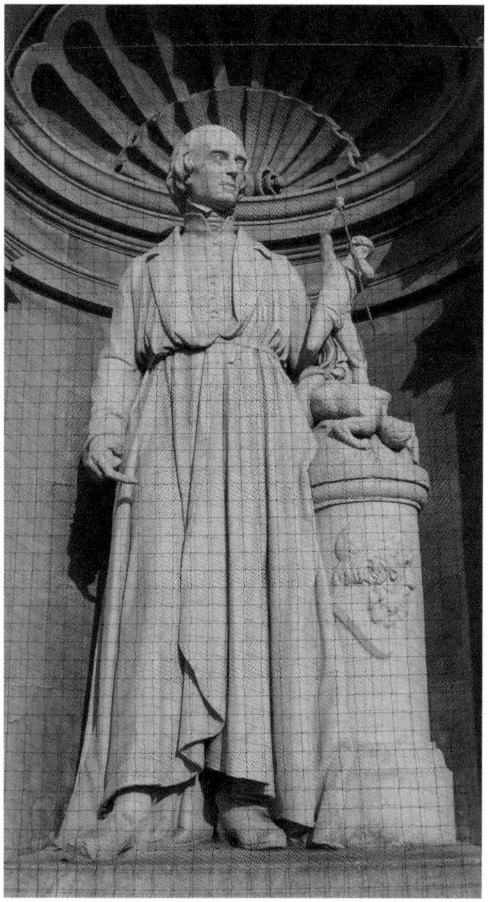

John Thomas, *John Flaxman* (after conservation)

The figures of Flaxman and Reynolds were commissioned in addition to the decorative sculpture on the façade and special 'subscriptions were invited to cover the cost of these two statues'.[18]

Thomas's name is boldly incised on the statue of Reynolds but not on this one, and it has been suggested that Thomas may not have made these figures himself as he was still superintending the stone-carving for the entire Houses of Parliament at the time.[19] However, the relative novelty of the technique employed for all the façade's sculpture, discussed above, makes it very much more likely that Thomas gave this project his particular attention. The model of *St Michael Overcoming Satan* may have been a deliberate demonstration of the virtues of the process. It would have been readily recognised that a stone version would have weathered and fractured within a few decades.

Notes

[1] T. Mowl, 'Battle of the Styles', chap. 4 in J. Sansom (ed.), *Public View: A Profile of the Royal West of England Academy* (Bristol, 2002). [2] Op. cit., p 67. [3] Op. cit., p 63. [4] Foyle and Cherry, *Bristol*, p.229. [5] Sansom, as note 1, p.67. [6] Op. cit., p.71. [7] English Heritage Bristol, Listed Buildings Database, PRN:901-1/9/957. [8] Jo Hibbert, letter from Acanthus Ferguson Mann, Architects, 19 December 2001. [9] Rene Rice, conservator working on the RWA façade. Letters to SWRA. [10] Sansom, as note 1; S. Stoddard, 'The Sharples Family' (see Sansom, as note 1), p.41. [11] I am grateful to Rene Rice, the conservator, who worked on the RWA facade in 2002 for this advice. [12] Sansom, as note 1, p.75. [13] I. McIntyre, *Joshua Reynolds, The Life and Times of the First President of the Royal Academy* (London, 2003), caption to portrait facing p.113. [14] Gunnis, *Dictionary of British Sculptors*, p.147. [15] Op. cit., p.148. [16] Ibid. [17] Op. cit., p.149. [18] D. Milner, *The Royal West of England Academy Bristol*, p.7. [19] E. Beresford Chancellor, *Lives of the British Sculptors* (London, 1911), p.236.

Former Bristol Museum and Library, on the façade of Brown's Restaurant at the corner of Queen's Road and University Road

Capitals B40

Sculptor: unknown

Architect: John Foster
Date: 1866–72
Material: Bath stone
Status: Grade II*
Owned by Browns Restaurant and Bar, Mitchells and Butlers
Condition: poor

Had John Foster's museum and library building been completed as originally conceived, there would be no better or richer example of the influence of John Ruskin and his celebration of Venetian Gothic art and architecture. The comfortable integration of polychromatic materials, ornament and sculpture into an architectural whole would have been demonstrated to perfection.

The Blitz removed much of the completed external decoration, such as the pinnacled corner shrines and grotesques at the top of the building, but the ornate niches and canopies for

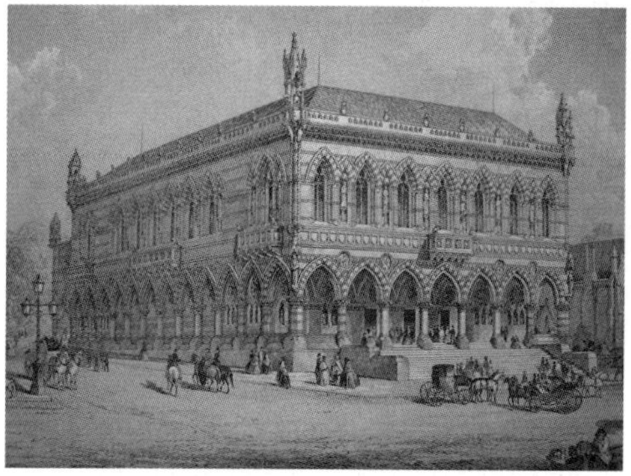

***Design for Bristol Museum and Library, Queen's Road, by Messrs Foster & Wood & A. C. Ponton,* lithograph by J. R. Robbins, c.1867 (Bristol Museum and Art Gallery)**

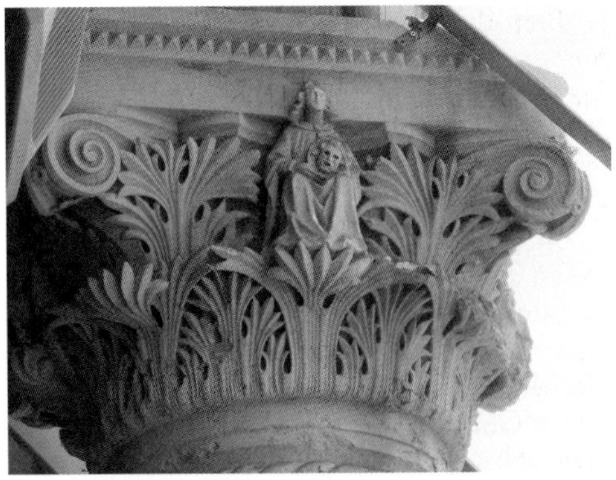

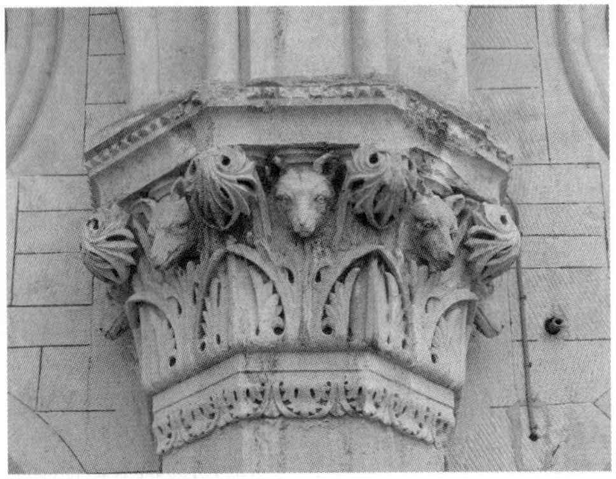

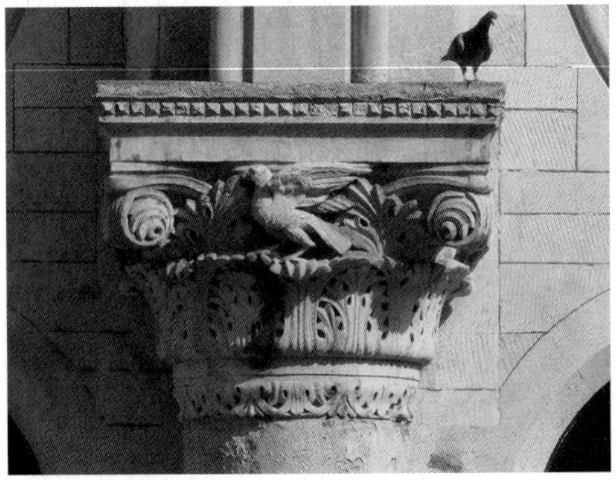

(top) *Capital with Tragedy*, façade of former Bristol Museum and Library

(middle) *Capital*, University Road elevation of the former Bristol Museum and Library

(bottom) *Capital*, University Road elevation of the former Bristol Museum and Library

the statues, the barley-sugar twists and much surface ornamentation were shaved away in the post-war 'restoration'.[1] Much more, still, was never built, as John Foster's original watercolour design confirms.[2] The polychromatic design was quietened, the balconies were omitted and the many roundels and twenty full-length statues were never executed. But the building remains a remarkable tribute, not only to John Ruskin but also to John Foster, perhaps the most versatile, inventive and eclectic of all Bristol's architects.

The remaining decorative sculpture is limited to the capitals on the façade and the University Road side of the building. Their design is a free and sophisticated interpretation of Venetian Gothic carving that makes due reference to the original function of the building.

It was built to house the Bristol Library Society and the combined Philosophical and Literary Society and the Bristol Institution for the Advancement of Science and Art, whose Park Street premises had been sold in 1870 (see Park Street). The new Bristol Museum and Library opened on 1 April 1872.[3] It was taken over by Bristol Corporation in 1893, and in 1895 changes to the band of shields and to the four central entrance capitals were made.[4]

The capitals to the entrance façade have figures representative of the arts and sciences that sit, like diminutive fairies, on the broad acanthus foliage. In the capitals of the side elevation, now called University Road, animal heads emerge from the variously stylised acanthus leaves and represent the museum's emphasis on the natural sciences. Naturalism was associated with Ruskinian Gothic and, as Clare Crick observed, 'the "modern" style of Gothic, as opposed to the classicism of the British Museum, for example, reflected a new attitude towards an investigation of the natural sciences'.[5]

Following the Second World War, when incendiary bombs gutted the building, the natural history and geology sections were squeezed into Bristol Art Gallery next door and the building was acquired by Bristol University. In 1949, after the rebuilding of the interior, John Foster's building became the university's refectory. It became known familiarly as the Doge's Palace. After the sale of the premises, the building reopened as Brown's Bar and Restaurant in 1992. The cavalier cleaning of the exterior that ensued and the subsequent damage to the capitals for the sake of awnings and light fittings remain a perpetual indictment of Bristol's ineffectual enforcement of planning regulations. The façade was cleaned again in 2008.

Notes

[1] A barley-sugar twist survives on the rear, north-western corner, together with an indication of the amount of surface decoration erased in 1949; for a photograph of the building in 1898 see Anon., *Bristol in 1898: Contemporary Biographies* (2 vols, Bristol, 1898), p.36. [2] Bristol City Museums and Art Gallery, K105, 20ins x 32ins, attributed to John Foster; illustrated in colour on the cover of Crick, *Victorian Buildings in Bristol*. [3] K.M. Walton, *75 Years of Bristol Art Gallery* (Bristol, 1980), p.4. [4] Little, *The Public View*, p.44; Bryan Little had access to Foster and Wood's papers and drawings, then in the care of Eustace Button FRIBA and now lost; Little implies that the entrance capitals date from 1895, but it is possible that changes were limited to the re-carving or replacement of the weathered heads of the small figures. [5] Crick, *Victorian Buildings in Bristol*, p.32.

Bristol Museum and Art Gallery, Queen's Road; on the parapet

Architecture, Painting and Sculpture B41

Modeller: Edward George Bramwell

Carver: William John Smith

Architect: Sir Frank Wills
Date: 1904
Material: Bath stone from Hartham Park quarries
Dimensions: approximately 2.5m high
Status: Grade II*

Owned by Bristol City Council
Condition: fair

Built between 1901 and 1904, the 'Bristol Art Gallery' was 'the gift of Sir Henry Wills to his fellow citizens', as the words on the façade proclaim. It was designed by Sir Frank Wills, a cousin of the donor. Members of the public were first admitted on 22 February 1905.[1] Within the building were collections of fine and decorative arts and of antiquities and anthropology. The seated muses that preside above the entrance front thus represent only architecture, painting and sculpture. The natural sciences were already represented in John Foster's Venetian palace next door, opened in 1872 as Bristol Museum and Library. It was only after that building was badly hit during the Blitz that the surviving natural history and geology collections were concertinaed into the renamed Bristol Museum and Art Gallery.

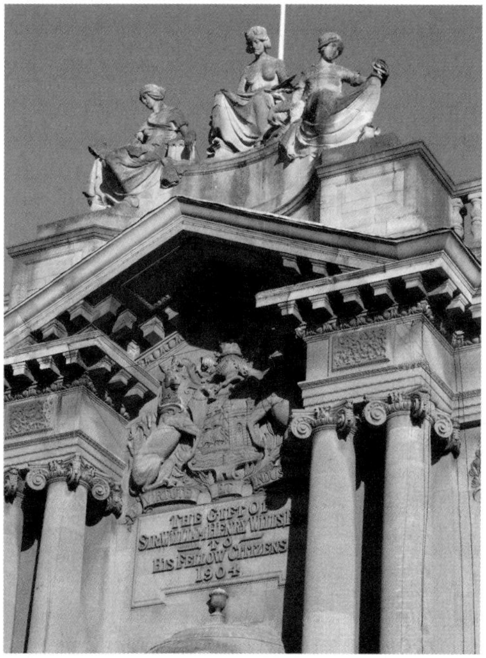

William John Smith after E. G. Bramwell, *Architecture, Painting and Sculpture and Bristol's coat of arms*

The three seated female figures have been referred to as *The Three Arts* and the objects they hold – so far above the ground that they are almost impossible to see – identify their roles. To the left, *Architecture* studies a plan while resting her left arm on the model of a classical temple. The central figure, *Painting*, has a palette and once held a paint brush. On the right, *Sculpture* has a mallet in one hand while gazing at a damaged statuette, which was once a model of a *Slave* by Michelangelo. Only the legs remain.[2] *Architecture* and *Sculpture* are fully draped while *Painting* is bare-breasted. After a century of weathering the trio is much eroded, but 'W. SMITH. S^c' is well defined beneath the muse on the right.

The Builder magazine states clearly that the sculpture on Bristol Art Gallery 'was modelled by Mr E. G. Bramwell of London, and executed on the spot by Mr W. Smith of Bristol'.[3] This is certainly confirmed by the close stylistic similarities between Bramwell's statue of *Literature* on the façade of Glasgow Art Gallery, Kelvingrove (1898) and the Bristol figures. Bramwell taught modelling at Westminster School of Art and specialised in statuettes and small groups.[4] Whether Bramwell also modelled the other art gallery sculpture, notably the Atlantes described below, is uncertain.

William Smith's great-grandson, Timothy Bradshaw, has written that the façade figures were carved *in situ* and that Smith was seriously injured by a fall during the work and became deaf as a result.[5] Bath stone from Hartham Park quarry, Corsham, Wiltshire, was used for the façade and, as the group is so well integrated into the surrounding fabric and design of the building, it seems likely that the stone for the figures may have come from the same quarry.[6] Bradshaw also attributes the vast and spectacular coat of arms on the façade below the pediment to Smith, together with the later lions in the back hall.[7]

In Bristol Museum and Art Gallery's front hall, known as the Winterstoke Hall, above the main entrance doors

Atlantes B41

Sculptor: William John Smith

Architect: Frank W. Wills
Date: 1905
Materials: Bath stone from Hartham Park quarry [8]
Status: Grade II*
Owned by Bristol City Council
Condition: good

The two near-naked atlantes are crouched in apparent support of the balcony above them. They are anatomically sound with prominent veins and naturalistic muscle structure.

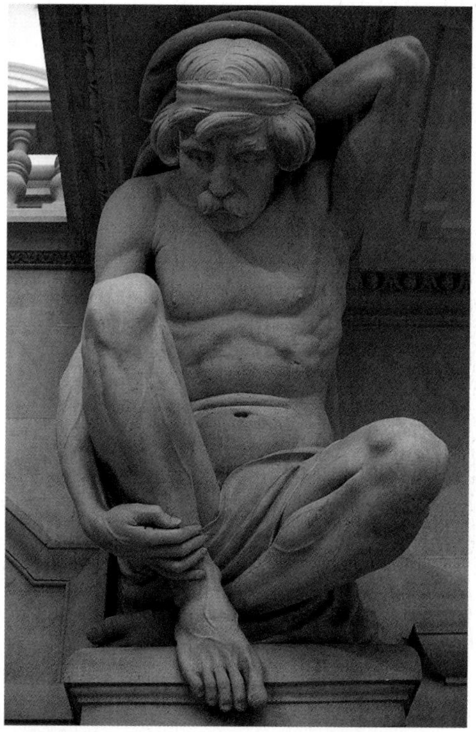

William John Smith, *One of two Atlantes* (photo. Chris Bertram)

Sir Frank Wills's façade of the Museum and Art Gallery has been described as 'hefty Roman Baroque', and these two massive figures also fit that description.[9] They complement the scale and character of the interior so well that they are rarely noticed by departing visitors.

In Bristol Museum and Art Gallery's rear hall, known as the Wills Hall, at the foot of the staircase

Lions B41

Sculptor: William John Smith

Architect: John Bertram Wills
Date: c.1929
Materials: Bath stone
Status: Grade II*
Owned by Bristol City Council
Condition: good

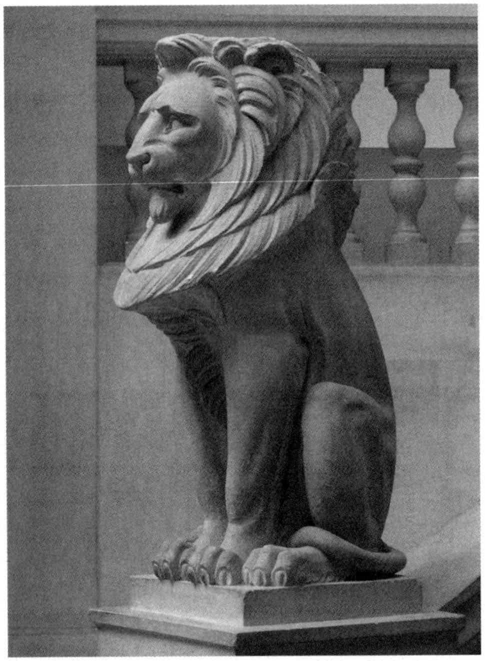

William John Smith, *Lion*

Soon after the majestic tower of the Wills Memorial Building was opened in June 1925, Sir George Arthur Wills offered to pay for a much-needed extension to Bristol Art Gallery. The rear hall of the extension became known as the Wills Hall, while the earlier front hall of the gallery came to be called the Winterstoke Hall. The architect was to be John Bertram Wills, son of Sir Frank Wills, the art gallery's architect. Both the architect and donor died before the extension was opened on 27 May 1930.[10] The building suffered bomb damage in November 1940, but the two lions were unharmed.

William John Smith (1862–1936) would have been in his later sixties when he carved these two essentially heraldic beasts. They are naturalistic and stylised; the bodies may reflect careful observation at the zoo, but the features of the heads are exaggerated and the manes have become elaborate and endearing art deco ruffs. They are almost certainly derived from or at least inspired by Alfred Stevens's much smaller iron lions on the railing posts in front of the Law Society in Chancery Lane and around the Duke of Wellington's tomb in St Paul's Cathedral.[11]

Notes

[1] K.M. Walton, *75 Years of Bristol Art Gallery*; Sir W.H. Wills, 1852–1932, later Lord Winterstoke, was then the chairman of the newly-formed Imperial Tobacco Company; the Bristol Art Gallery was officially opened by Sir Hubert von Herkomer RA (1849–1914) on 15 February 1905. [2] These details are clearly visible in a postcard presented to the Bristol Museum and Art Gallery, 2008. [3] *The Builder*, 15 April 1905, p.410. [4] Mackenzie, *Public Sculpture of Glasgow*, pp.253, 260–1, 477. [5] Bristol Magpies, *Newsletter*, T. Bradshaw, no. 97, Oct/Nov 1993. [6] E. Stonebridge, *Bristol: Heritage in Stone*, p.24. [7] As note 5; Bradshaw does not mention the Atlantes supporting the balcony at the entrance, but there is no reason to doubt the attribution. [8] Information from Roger Clarke, Bristol Museum and Art Gallery; see also Walton, as note 1, p.32. [9] Gomme et al., *An Architectural History*, p.443. [10] As note 1, pp.9, 10. [11] Ward-Jackson, *Public Sculpture of London*, pp.80, 81.

Wills Memorial Building

Architect: Sir George Herbert Oatley

Dates: 1915–25

With the crucial assistance of Henry Overton Wills III, Bristol's University College had become a university in 1909. It was in 1913, two years after his death, that his sons, George A. Wills and Henry H. Wills, announced that they wished to give the university a building in memory of their father. The building was to accommodate a great hall, reception room, council room, library and as many lecture rooms as the site could manage.

George Oatley, the appointed architect, explained that the tower was to be:

> the dominating landmark of the neighbourhood [and] its function is to compel attention to the existence of the University and, further to this end, it was designed to close the vista from the bottom of Park Street, the main artery between Bristol and Clifton.[1]

It was to fulfil its purpose triumphantly.

Building work began in 1915, stopped because of the First World War in October 1916 and resumed early in 1919. Enormous additional donations had to be made by the Wills brothers. Parts of the building were in use by 1923, but the project was not completed until 1925, when it was opened by George V, together with Queen Mary, on 25 June.

The Wills Memorial Building is a thoroughly modern construction employing reinforced concrete on the Hennibique principle. Much investigation went into the selection of the dressing stone: 'We are looking for a first class weather stone which will really stand for centuries in the atmosphere of a manufacturing city'.[2] It was Henry Herbert Wills who appears to have determined that Box ground stone, a type of Bath stone, was used, although it was Oatley who ensured that Clipsham stone from Rutland was used for architectural detailing and for the stone carving.

It is evident that Oatley believed deeply in the importance of good craftsmanship, but he was unwilling to go as far as John Ruskin, who had argued 'that all architectural ornamentation should be executed by the men who design it.'[3] Oatley alone made the final decision on subject matter. He would have agreed, however, with Ruskin that 'all art employed in decoration should be informative'.[4] This brought problems, for the great wealth of ornament on the Wills Memorial Building demanded a corresponding amount of inspiration and ideas. In 1921 Oatley wrote to his Master Builder, John Ward:

> We are for the present moment in practically an insuperable difficulty; all the ornament in this building must not be merely ornament, but something which shall express a meaning: it must be symbolical and full of interest to the enquiring mind. If those who execute the work are able to make acceptable suggestions, such suggestions would be welcomed; but at present all this devolves upon us and, whilst one is waiting for inspiration, time is passing in which the work ought to be going forward! On the other hand, we should rather have no ornament at all, than ornament which has no meaning.[5]

As the entrance doorway ornamentation makes clear, conception, design, modelling and carving could as well involve four or more separate persons as one.

Oatley was also determined upon legibility. He thought some of his designer's ideas for grotesques on the higher parts of the building were too detailed to be seen clearly from the ground, and wrote encouraging him to 'go and look at similar work at great heights on some of our celebrated cathedrals'.[6] Jean Hahn duly visited Wells, Gloucester and Worcester and reported that only Worcester had gargoyles higher than 40 feet from the ground.

On the entrance to the tower of the Wills Memorial Building, Queen's Road

Nine Muses B42

Concept: W. E. Micklewright

Modeller: E. F. Fabian

Carver: George H. Giblett

Architect: George Herbert Oatley
Date: completed 1923–5
Materials: Clipsham stone
Inscription in Gothic script beneath each figure, from left to right: CALLIOPE / THALEIA / URANIA / POLYHYMNIA / CLIO / ERATO / EUTERPE / MELPOMENE / TERSICHORE
Status: Grade II*
Owned by the University of Bristol
Condition: good; cleaned and conserved 2007

All the figures are set in Gothic niches and their names appear on short pedestals beneath the carvings. Five muses are standing, while the alternate four are presented as half-length figures. From the left the order is: Calliope, the muse of eloquence and epic poetry, holding a stylus in her right hand and a tablet in her left; Thaleia, the muse of comedy, holding a comic mask and shepherd's staff in her crossed arms; Urania, the muse of astronomy, pointing at a globe; Polyhymnia, the muse of rhetoric, pensively grasping a scroll; Clio in the centre, first of the muses and the muse of history, holding an open scroll in her left hand; Erato, the muse of lyric and amorous poetry, playing a lyre; Euterpe, muse of music and inventor of the flute, holding two pan pipes; Melpomene, muse of tragedy, holding a tragic mask and a sword; and Terpsichore, the muse of dance, also holding a lyre.

George Oatley was to alter the design of the main entrance surround several times, although the overall design of this complex building was little altered after 1914. He moved from a *porte-cochère* to an elegant ogee-arched entrance, and then to the low Tudor arch of today, but with a concave Gothic pediment above.[7]

It was one of Oatley's sculptors or stone carvers, W. E. Micklewright from Norton-sub-Hambdon, who proposed the panel of nine muses. When Mickelwright's estimate for

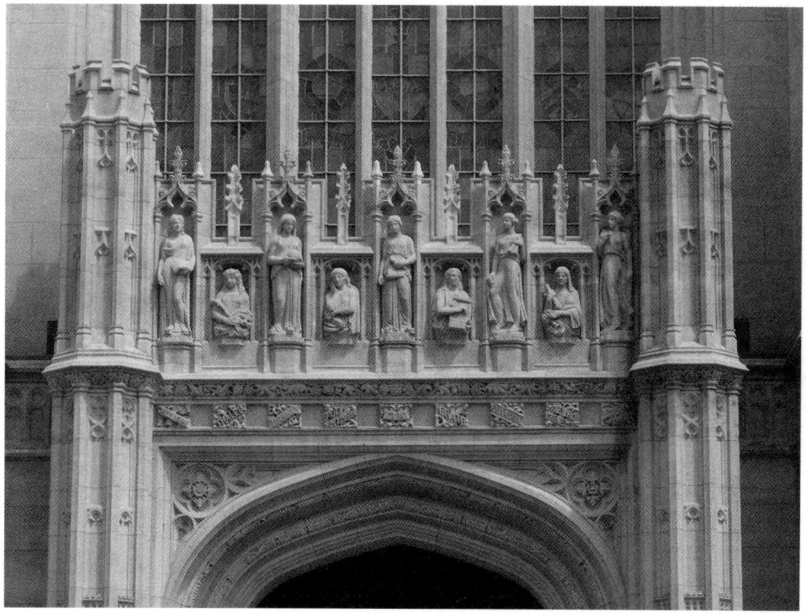

G. H. Giblett after E. F. Fabian, *Nine Muses*

carrying out the work proved too expensive, Oatley gave him £25, perhaps both as a goodwill gesture and in order to purchase the design.[8] The two attached columns of grape-laden vines that surround the entrance were carved by Mickelwright. Oatley had initially opposed this particular design, pointing out that he preferred to reserve vines for church work.[9]

How far Micklewright's proposal for the panel of muses was used is uncertain. The final appearance resulted from the cooperation of Oatley and the local sculptor Ernest F. Fabian. Their correspondence is in the University of Bristol Library's special collections, and there are references to the selection of the muses and their attributes. In a letter headed 'Figures for Main Entrance', Fabian wrote:

> I am glad to have another authority to compare with William Smith's [description], a copy of which I enclose. The design pose & symbolism must be carefully considered. I shall have suggestions to place before you later.[10]

Smith was a Bristol sculptor, and was also working on the Wills Memorial Building. His list describing the muses was checked against information and images from Keightley's *Mythology* (1852). Letters confirm that Oatley was at great pains to be correct in depicting the subjects.[11]

In June 1923 Fabian gave an estimate of £810 to include 'designing, modelling, carving and casting. I trust this will meet with your approval'.[12] He added that 'the two first full-size models are now completed in plaster. Will you kindly instruct the foreman of the Masons to see me at the School of Art, to take measurement of the stone?' Fabian identified the 'carver' who was to carry out the work and asked Oatley to deliver the stone blocks to 'Mr George H. Giblett, 18 Sydenham Road, Totterdown, Bristol'.[13] Oately accepted this estimate the following day:

> This seems reasonable and we have instructed the builders accordingly. Of course it will be Clipsham and it is very desirable that it should be as hard as possible, but it must be uniform in colour and there must be no blue patches in it, as sometimes is the case.[14]

Further evidence that Fabian completed this commission came when he wrote to ask for payment for the first half of the estimate.[15] He also reported:

> four large figures are now in Plaster & others in progress. I also have to report good progress with the carving of the first two blocks, which I am carefully watching. A pointing machine is being used to insure accuracy of proportion.[16]

The carving was still in progress in May 1924 when the four 'half-niche' figures were delayed because two Clipsham stone blocks were 'quite impossible to use, owing to the large amount of grey colour they each contain'.[17] A sketch made by Ernest F. Fabian in 1924 shows the final positions of the nine females as we see them today.[18]

Reception Room Wing, Wills Memorial Building

Figures, Decoration and Grotesques B42

Designer: Jean Hahn

Modellers: Ernest F. Fabian, Doris K. Flinn, William Smith

Carvers: Fred Jeans, W. E. Mickelwright, William Smith and others

Architect: George Herbert Oatley
Date: completed 1922–5
Material: Clipsham stone
Status: Grade II*
Owned by the University of Bristol
Condition: good

The Wills Memorial Building is perhaps England's last great secular Gothic building, a magnificent closing tribute to the Gothic Revival. Its ferro-concrete core is unseen, but its thoroughly contemporary character is represented by the heads of the fashion-conscious male and female students on either side of the entrance to the Reception Centre wing. The girl wears her plaits in buns upon her ears, rather prim and Scandinavian. It may be weathering that has narrowed and turned up her nose. Symbolic floral motifs and a lamp of learning also decorate the entrance.

Above this side entrance is the Reception Room's large oriel window on which are the four figures representing the four main faculties of the day. Medicine has a giant thigh bone and a skull; Arts has a book and scroll, quill pen and particularly long and abundant hair; Science holds a phial and a retort; and Engineering has his right hand on a cog wheel, recalling images of St Catherine.

Beneath each figure is a corbel carved with a fox's head, a hound and a hare, and a horse's head, perhaps comparing the spirit of the hunt with the pursuit of truth. In between are emblems taken from the coats of arms of the Wills family, Bristol City Council and the University of Bristol.

Higher still on the cornice below the battlements are four grotesques representing Spring, Summer, Autumn and Winter. Spring yawns and holds a staff that is bursting into leaf. Summer sniffs roses. Autumn struggles with brambles or may be pruning vines, and Winter looks old and cold, beside a sprig of holly. In between Summer and Autumn are an owl and a cockerel, representing Night and Day. Oatley's designer, Jean Hahn, wrote to the architect saying that he had included one of his ancestors, an allusion to his own name, the German for cock.[19]

Elsewhere on the building the grotesques do not have such symbolic purpose. Many are caricatures of teachers and scholars, past and present, and some are almost certainly caricatures or more straightforward portraits of the carvers' own colleagues. Oatley was to recall that the identity of most of the similar heads on Wills Hall of Residence, also by Jean Hahn, was 'obvious' and that he did remember that one of them was a caricature of John Ward, the master builder.[20]

In the centre of the eastern wing, a bay window marks the vice-chancellor's room. Above the window are four heads. Of the centre two, one holds a model of a church façade and could be a foreman who perhaps forever referred to past responsibilities. The other has the appearance of an overly animated lecturer, but he holds a ladder and could depict a workman suffering from vertigo. In contrast, to the right there is a sober contemporary portrait, possibly of Henry Herbert Wills, who oversaw every aspect of the building's plans and progress until his death in 1922.

At the southern end of the library on the short façade facing onto Park Row are portrait heads, mostly gentle caricatures, ending on the right with Field Marshall Earl Haig. He had been in Bristol in June 1922 to unveil Clifton College's memorial gateway (see College Road).

Away from the public's gaze at the back of the library, the low tower has three straightforward portrait heads among the caricatures and more extreme grotesques. Professor Conwy Lloyd Morgan, the university's first vice-chancellor, bearded and suitably dignified; Professor Ernest Francis, acting vice-chancellor, 1921–2; and James Rafter, registrar from 1921–2.[21] Rafter was carved by William Smith and it is known that Miss Doris K Flinn modelled some of the other heads.[22]

The highest grotesques on the tower are indeed often grotesque. Oatley's just demands for legibility led to especially large grimacing heads that are very deeply cut.

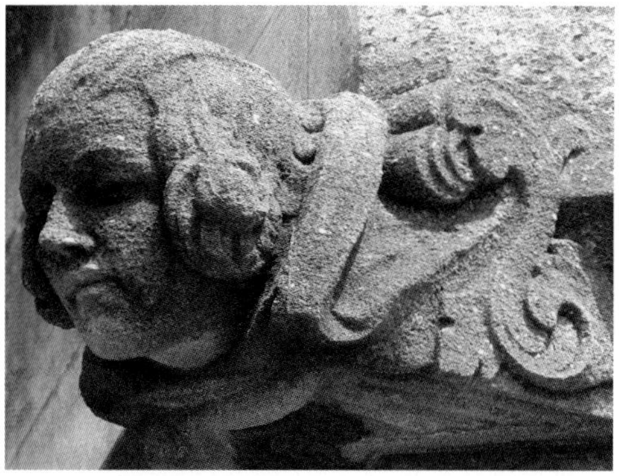

Jean Hahn, *Student's head*, left of the entrance to the Reception Room wing

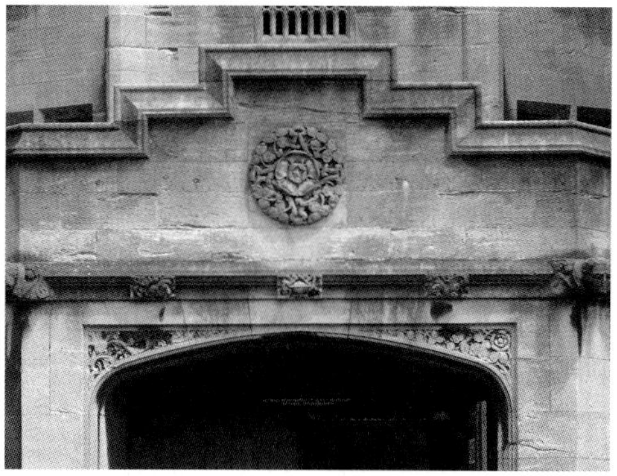

George Oatley, architect, *Entrance to the Reception Room wing*

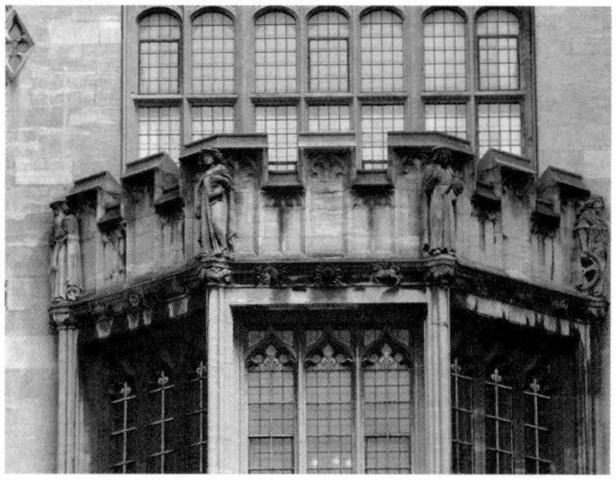

George Oatley, architect, and Jean Hahn, designer, *Medicine, Arts, Science and Engineering, above the entrance to the Reception Room wing*

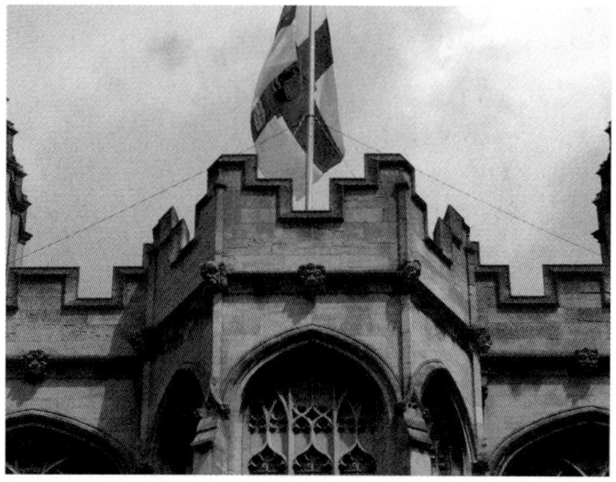

Jean Hahn, *Grotesque heads above the entrance to the Reception Room wing*

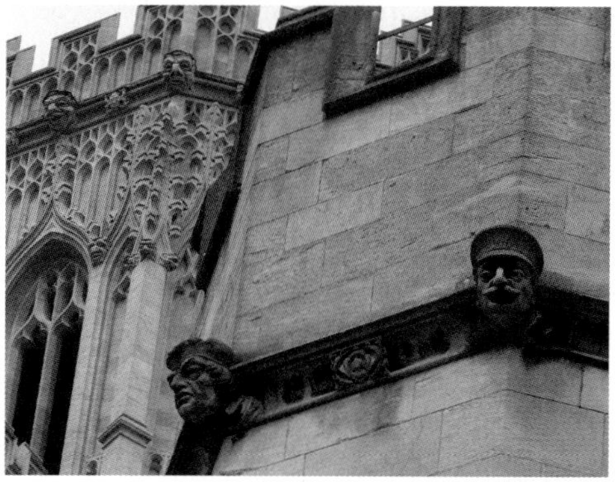

Jean Hahn, *Grotesque heads on University Tower and on the Library Wing*

Notes
[1] Quoted by S. Whittingham, *Wills Memorial Building* (Bristol, 2003), p.11, from which most of the information above is drawn. [2] Op. cit., p.18. [3] *Gentleman's Magazine*, 1858, p.53, letter from John Ruskin to Dr Acland. [4] Ibid. [5] As note 1, p.31. [6] Op. cit., p.28. [7] As note 1, pp.12, 13, 56. [8] Op. cit., p.30, and a caption from an exhibition in the Wills Building, prepared by Dr Liz Loeffer, 2003. [9] As note 1, p.30. [10] Fabian to Oatley, 4 October 1922. [11] Oatley to Fabian, 1 November 1922. [12] Fabian to Oatley, 4 June 1923. [13] Ibid. [14] Oatley to Fabian, 5 June 1923. [15] Fabian to Oatley, 7 July 1923. [16] Ibid. [17] Fabian to Oatley, 14 May 1924. [18] Drawing, dated 16 December 1924, is signed 'EFF'. [19] As note 1, p.28. [20] Quoted in Whittingham, *Sir George Herbert Oatley.* [21] Op. cit. [22] Op. cit.

Rectory Gardens, Henbury Awdlett

Leaning against the wall by the bicycle shed at the rear of Henbury Awdlett, now Woodstock School, Rectory Gardens, Henbury

Neptune A4

Sculptor: unknown

Date: c.1700
Material: stone
Dimensions: approx. 2m high
Status: not listed
Owned by Bristol City Council
Condition: poor

This battered seventeenth-century statue leans against a bicycle shed at the back of Henbury Awdlett, a house of about 1680 that is often erroneously called Henbury Manor.[1] It is now a school.

Neptune is very weathered and his forearms are missing, although it is possible that there are original fragments among the brambles at his feet. His legs have severe cracks and will certainly fracture if moved. He once held a trident with both hands. The trident was probably upright, for Neptune looks up and, thus, it may well be a friendly dolphin that is at his feet and upon which one foot rests, rather than a serpent that he would have been spearing with a downward thrust.

The statue was the centrepiece of the main courtyard fountain of a large country house nearby, once the grandest of Henbury's many substantial mansions. This was Henbury or the Great House, which Sir Samuel Astry had much enlarged around 1680. Astry also greatly extended the formal gardens and, to the south, planted a double avenue of trees that led to the top of Blaise Hill, where a small summerhouse was erected. For 'the first time the [Blaise] estate was recognisable as a pleasure park'.[2] The Neptune fountain can just be made out in Johannes Kip's spectacular bird's-eye view published in 1712.[3]

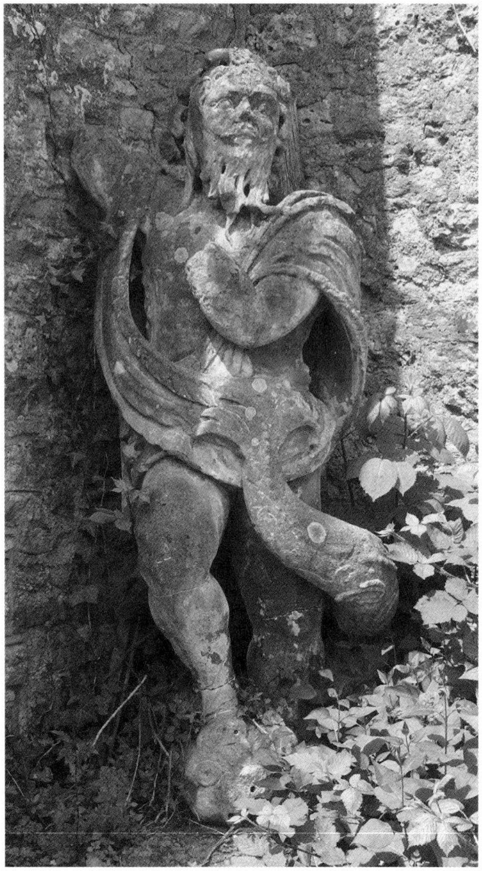

Neptune

The Henbury estate was to pass to the Smyths of Ashton Court, who sold the house separately in 1730. The entire house was demolished a hundred years later and it is possible that the statue was re-erected in the grounds of Henbury Awdlett at this time.[4] The Smyth's Henbury estate had been purchased in 1760 by Thomas Farr, who built the triangular Blaise Castle on top of the hill. J. S. Harford acquired the estate in 1789 and moved into the newly built Blaise Castle House in 1798.

Besides the lead statue of Neptune of 1721 now in the heart of Bristol (see 'The Centre', St Augustine's Parade), there is also the enormous statue of Neptune just outside the city at William Champion's former brass works and home at Warmley, South Gloucestershire. This probably dates from the mid-eighteenth century. The closest comparative statue and fountain of Neptune is the surviving stone statue at Dyrham. This is likely to date from the 1690s. It is by the elder John Harvey of Bath. The Henbury and Dyrham Neptunes are strikingly similar in their poses, but one is too worn and the other too restored to permit an attribution of the present work to Harvey.[5]

Notes

[1] Pevsner, *North Somerset*, p.466. [2] Eveleigh, *'A Popular Retreat'*, p.8. [3] Johannes Kip, Henbury, the Seat of Simon Harcourt Esq., from Atkyns, *Ancient and Present State*, 1712. [4] T. Mowl and B. Earnshaw, 'The garden ghost of the great house of Henbury', *Gloucestershire and Avon Life*, June 1981, pp.64, 5; the authors give the date of demolition as 1809 and of the sculptures move to Henbury Awdlett as 1952. [5] A. Mitchell, 'The park and garden at Dyrham', *National Trust Yearbook 1977–78*, pp.4, 8.

Redcliff Hill

In the west boundary wall, outside St Mary Redcliffe

The Redcliffe Pipe C66

Architect: attributed to Sir George Oatley

Date: 1932
Materials: semi-circular bronze panel with lion head spout
Dimensions: 160cm diameter
Inscriptions: on the circumference border, cast in raised Roman 6cm capitals – PRO SALVTE ANIMAE ROBERTI DE BERKELEIA
–: in the central semi-circular space in the same style of lettering – QVI DEDIT / DEO ET ECCLESIAE / SANCTAE MARIAE DE REDCLIVE / ET EJVS MINISTRIS / RVGEWELLE ET CONDVCTVM
–: to the left of the lion's head spout – A. D. MCXC

–: to the right of the lion's head – ERECTED /1932 / E. L. A. HERTSLET / VICAR
Status: Grade I
Owned by the vicar and churchwardens of St Mary Redcliffe
Condition: good

In about 1190, Lord Robert de Berkeley granted St Mary Redcliffe rights over his spring and well at Knowle, and in 1207 a pipe or conduit brought this water near to the church.[1] This bronze wall plaque commemorates the gift and asks us in Latin to 'Pray for the soul of Robert de Berkeley who gave to God and the church of St Mary Redcliffe and its ministers his Ruge Well and conduit AD 1190.'

The water came from a spring at Ruge (Ridge) Well in Knowle, approximately one and a half miles to the south of the church. The supply to the Redcliffe parish was later shared with St John's Hospital and the parish of St Thomas. Once a year the vicar and churchwardens of St Mary Redcliffe walk the length of the conduit to St Mary Redcliffe from Daventry Road. This annual autumn Pipe Walk is one of Bristol's oldest customs. There are two stone markers, like small tombstones, on the route, and the corporation retains the right of way along the pipe.[2] The Water Maze in Victoria Park also commemorates this ancient conduit.

In the eighteenth century, the conduit's outlet was a dipping-well below the northern end of the balustraded walkway. Today, only a low segmental arch marks the site of the original vaulted chamber, which is recorded in drawings in the Museum and Art Gallery.[3] Towards the end of the nineteenth century this fell into disuse.[4] It was the use of the water from the pipe by the masons engaged in the 1927–33 restoration of the church that led to this new memorial outlet a little further up the hill.[5]

The commemorative plaque was erected in 1932 during that major restoration programme overseen by the architect Sir George Oatley.[6] The rustication of the surrounding arch, which blends so naturally with the older balustrade above, the clear and crisp lettering and the excellent craftsmanship all point to Sir George as the designer.

A semi-circular bronze panel bearing an inscription is set into a rusticated limestone arch in the wall at the point where the fresh water was delivered. A lion's head spout that drains into a metal grille is in the centre.

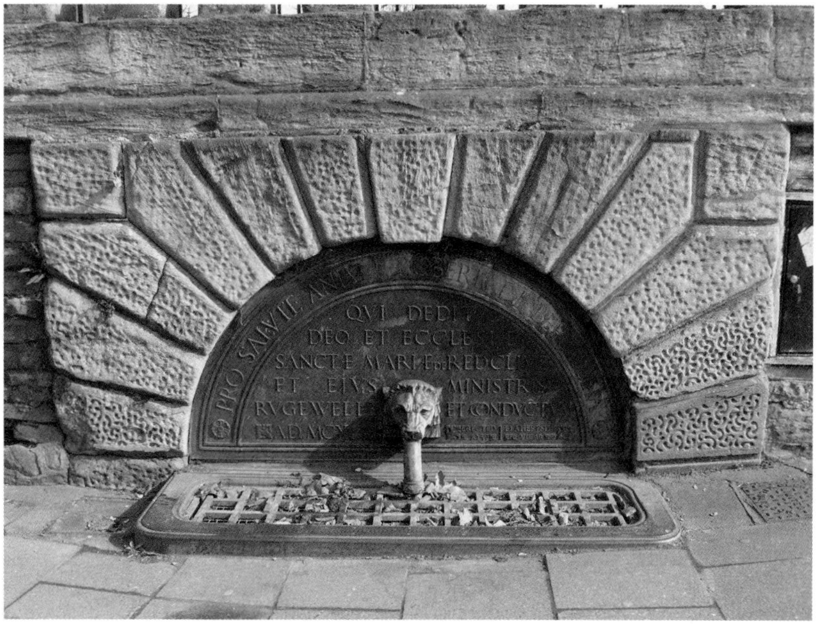

George Oatley, architect, ***Redcliffe Pipe***

Notes
[1] J. Leech, *The Pipes, Pumps, and Conduits of Bristol* (Bristol, c.1853). [2] Maurice Fells, 'The gift of water', *Bristol Evening Post*, 15 October 2002, p.2. [3] Edward Bird RA, *Redcliffe Conduit,* c.1800, K188. [4] St Mary Redcliffe Conservation Plan, 2006, p.198. [5] Cartwright, *Pictorial History of St Mary Redcliffe Bristol*, p.4. [6] M.Q. Smith, *St Mary Redcliffe,* an architectural history (Bristol, 1995), p.194.

Behind the reception desk of the Mercure Holland House Hotel, Redcliff Hill

Phoenix C67

Sculptor: Ernest Pascoe

Architects: Whicheloe Macfarlane Partnership
Date: 1974
Material: four bronze panels and stainless steel
Owned by Mercure Holland House Hotel
Condition: good

Phoenix Assurance was founded in London in 1782. In 1974 a major relocation programme, involving more than eight hundred staff, led to a move to the purpose-built Phoenix House in Bristol. The company subsequently became a part of the Royal and Sun Alliance Group and later of Canada Life. The office block was later converted to a hotel, which opened in 2007.[1]

Eighteen flame-like shapes, cut from sheet stainless steel, create a phoenix that both rises from the flames and is formed by them. The stainless steel pieces were glued into holes in the concrete wall using long thin bolts and two-part glue, Araldite epoxy resin. Thirty years later the adhesive was considered too strong to allow the work to be removed without damage.[2]

When Phoenix House was first opened, the directors of the company agreed that the main

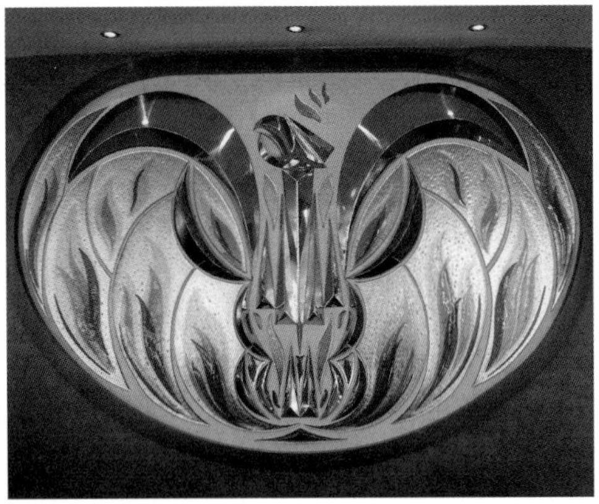

Ernest Pascoe, *Phoenix*

reception area should feature a 'phoenix statue'. Their brief was that:

> the work would embellish the building; link the historical aspects of the Phoenix Assurance Company… with the [then] modern aspects of the building; would have a symbolic value and would 'say something'; would feature the material of the day – stainless steel; and 'glow' under suitable lighting.[3]

Ernest Pascoe was commissioned to design this feature for the facing wall in the reception area. The textured concrete surface of the wall was patterned by the timber moulds in which the concrete had been poured. On conversion to a hotel, this contrasting background was covered with textured wallpaper.

There is no deliberate link between this sculpture and the last of Bristol's glasshouses, the Phoenix Glasshouse. Glasshouses once surrounded St Mary Redcliffe, but the Phoenix Glasshouse was on Portwall Lane on the opposite side of the church.[4]

Notes

[1] Graham Briscoe, Operations Support Leader, Royal & Sun Alliance, January 2001. [2] Ibid. [3] Ibid. [4] C. Witt, C. Weedon and A.P. Schwind, *Bristol Glass* (Bristol, 1984).

Redcliffe Street

In Redcliffe Quay Piazza

Exploration C63

Sculptors: Philippa Threlfall, Kennedy Collings and James Blunt

Date: 1991
Materials: obelisk, stones and ceramic surface; armillary sphere, stainless and painted steel
Dimensions: 670cm high
Inscription on a small bronze plaque in photo-engraved white enamel-filled sans serif letters, each line centred: EXPLORATION/A CELEBRATION OF/ BRISTOL'S SEAFARING HERITAGE/Obelisk – The Unknown Deep/ PHILIPPA THRELFALL & KENNEDY COLLINGS/Armillary Sphere/JAMES BLUNT/Commissioned by/THE STANDARD LIFE ASSURANCE COMPANY/MCMXCI – signed on the side facing the river, on a blue fish shape: 1991 / THRELFALL / COLLINGS / BLUNT
Status: not listed
Owned by Standard Life Assurance Company
Condition: good

'As strange a concoction of ceramic fish and copper globes as you could hope to meet.'[1] *Exploration* marked the completion of a new five-storey office development on Bristol's Floating Harbour by Standard Life Assurance. The company described the work more soberly as 'a tribute to the city's seafaring tradition and the navigators John and Sebastian Cabot'.[2]

Richard Lee of Alec French Partnership, the architects responsible for the development, has recently written:

> Philippa clad the column of the armillary sphere with images of monsters of the deep, reflecting the extraordinary journeys that sailors took into the unknown, some of whom sailed from these Bristol quays.

With some passion, he goes on to remind us that the 'little piazza created is now crying out for its footbridge from King Street, an idea that was built into the planning of the scheme way back some 20 years ago!'[3]

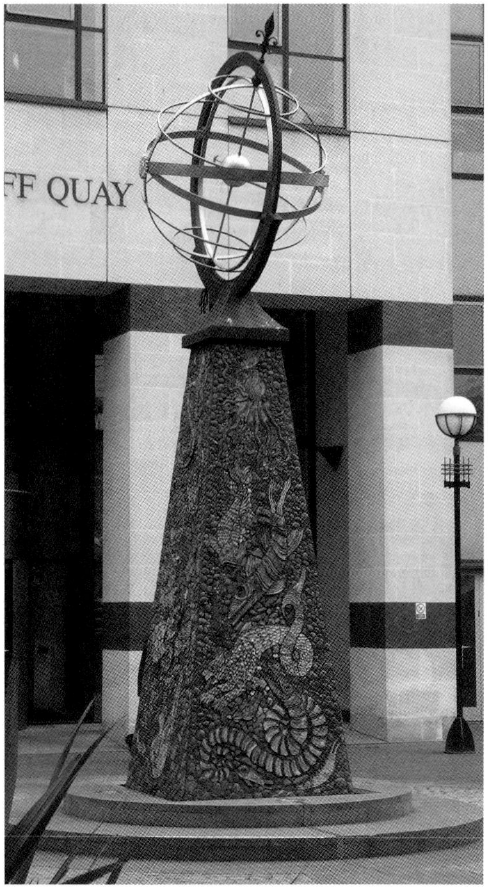

Philippa Threlfall, Kennedy Collins and James Blunt, *Exploration* and *Armillary Sphere*

The sculpture was originally intended to function both as a fountain and as a sundial. James Blunt's metal armillary sphere, made of burnished steel with gilded balls representing earth, moon and sun, surmounts a four-sided obelisk. All sides of Kennedy Collins's and Philippa Threlfall's obelisk are encrusted with stones of great variety, and there are ceramic insets forming images of sea monsters, 'believed by early mariners to be of gigantic proportions'.[4] The stones were gathered from various beaches and riverbeds in the west of England. The side facing the river depicts nine sea creatures, including the largest on the obelisk, a coiling serpent, and the smallest, a fish with wing-like gills. The circular base is made of pennant stone, inset with steel marking the main points of the compass.

The architects provided an ambitious account of the sculpture:

> It was from Bristol docks that fifteenth-century mariners set sail across the previously unexplored oceans. To aid their understanding of the globe and its position in space they turned to the armillary sphere. The rings of this [Redcliffe Quay] celestial sphere symbolise the horizon, meridians, Arctic Circles, Equator and the Tropics of Cancer and Capricorn. Across the latter passes the broad ecliptic ring depicting the passage of the sun according to the seasons and the hemisphere. On the axis relating to the latitude of Redcliffe Quay, the time is recorded by the sundial inscribed inside the Equatorial ring.[5]

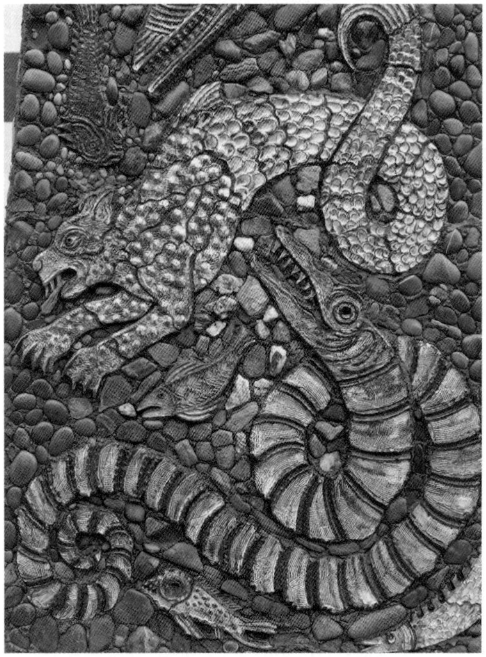

Philippa Threlfall and Kennedy Collins, *The Unknown Deep* (detail)

The complete sculpture is called *Exploration*, but the obelisk has the title *The Unknown Deep* and it was designed to have water running down the four faces.

> After three or four years, technical difficulties made this inadvisable and the source of the water was disconnected. Surfaces were painted with a sealing coat to give a 'wet' look in about 1996.[6]

The artists based their exotic creatures on ancient drawings from medieval bestiaries, some of which were found in the Chained Library of the cathedral at Wells, where Philippa Threlfall and her husband, Kennedy Collings, lived.[7]

The armillary sphere was designed and made by blacksmith James Blunt of Westbury-sub-Mendip, near Wells. It also functions as a sundial. The approximate time can be read on the inside of the equatorial ring relating to the latitude of Redcliffe Quay.[8]

The Lord Mayor of Bristol, Councillor Peter Abraham, unveiled the sculpture in December 1991. Other works in Bristol by Philippa Threlfall and Kennedy Collings include the historical reliefs on both Broad Quay House (see Broad Quay) and Colston House in Colston Street (not included).

Notes

[1] Price et al., *Castle Park*. [2] 'Harbour sculpture is all shipshape', *Western Daily Press*, 5 December 1991. [3] Undated letter to D.M., circa 2006. [4] Notes from Alec French Partnership, the architects of the office block. [5] Ibid. [6] Notes from the sculptor, Philippa Threfall, December 1998. [7] As note 2. [8] Ibid.

Redcliffe Way

In the forecourt garden of Freshford House, between the roundabout and Redcliffe Bridge

Phoenix and the Four Elements C65

Sculptor: John Doubleday

Date: 1985
Materials: patinated bronze on a pyramidal structure clad in grey marble; plinth of four courses of granite setts
Dimensions: 330cm high; approx, 250cm wide at base; panels, approx. 155cm high, 150cm wide at base
Signed on edge of one relief: J Doubleday
Status: not listed
Owned by Royal SunAlliance Life (2002)
Condition: good

When granting planning permission for the construction of Freshford House, the City of Bristol required that Phoenix Assurance 'sponsor a piece of street sculpture for the benefit of Bristol citizens in front of the building'.[1] In 1985, the directors commissioned 'the internationally known sculptor, Doubleday' to create a 'three-dimensional representational work cast in bronze'. The commission was placed soon after Doubleday's diminutive statue of Brunel had been unveiled in Bristol (now moved to Temple Way), but when his wider reputation still benefited from his earlier statue of Charlie Chaplin in Leicester Square.

The sculptor's own description of the four reliefs states:

> They represent Earth, Air, Fire and Water and form the sides of a stylised geometric mountain representing the world – on which the Phoenix alights to be reborn in flames. Earth is the pregnant figure who emerges from the clay of the relief (see hands) and who is surrounded by orchids. Air is seen against the disc of the sun – striding, borne

along by the wind which blows her hair between the fingers of her right hand. Fire is the figure emerging from flames (with stylised flames to her left). Water is the swimming figure.[2]

The bird surmounting the structure is double-sided. The mythical Phoenix, after living in the desert for 500 years, or more, would expire in flames and then rise from its own ashes.

In 1781 twelve sugar-brokers had met in a coffeehouse in Fenchurch Street, London, to form the 'New Fire Office' assurance company; the alternative name was the 'Phoenix Society'. The first policies were issued from that venue, but it was not until 1813 that an Act of Parliament formalised the title 'Phoenix Assurance Company of London'.[3] In the mid-1970s the company relocated to Bristol, first to Phoenix House and, ten years later, to a new building, then, as now, known as Freshford House. Following a merger in 1995, the building was re-named 'Royal & SunAlliance House'. The group was sold to Canada Life in 2002.

Doubleday's image of the phoenix rising from rather plump flames is strikingly similar to the phoenix depicted on the bill head and trade card for Henry Ricketts's Phoenix Glasshouse, which was built in the 1780s just two hundred yards away in Portwall Lane.[4]

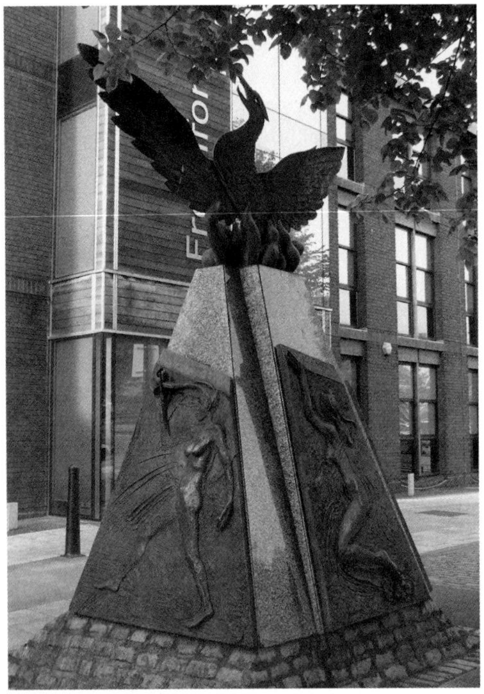

John Doubleday, *Phoenix and the Four Elements*

Notes

[1] Graham Briscoe, 'Phoenix and the Four Elements', Royal SunAlliance, August 2002. [2] John Doubleday, letter to Graham Briscoe, operations support leader, Royal SunAlliance, 21 August 2002. [3] As note 1. [4] Witt et al, *Bristol Glass*, p.58, pl. 30.

Redland Hill

In the rear garden of Queen Victoria House, now offices, opposite Swire Hospital

Memorial to Princess Charlotte A13

Architect unknown

Date: c.1818
Material: Bath stone
Dimensions: approx. 5m high; pedestal, 80cm square at the base
Inscriptions: on a square bronze plaque, with all four corners cut in a small arc – This Obelisk was erected by / JACOB WILCOX RICKETTS / to perpetuate the Memory of/HER ROYAL HIGNESS / The much lamented and beloved/PRINCESS CHARLOTTE /of WALES and SAXE COBOURG; Daughter of/HIS ROYAL HIGHNESS THE PRINCE REGENT / and Consort to his Serene Highnefs PRINCE LEOPOLD: This most illustrious Princefs, the brightnefs of whose/Character surpafses all transcript.
–: centred beneath this to the left of the depiction of a Roman oil lamp, among copperplate flourishes: WAS / BORN / Jan^{y}.6th. /1796
–: on the lamp: AND / DIED / Novr. 6th./1817/.
–: to the right of the lamp in copperplate flourishes: WAS/ MARRIED/ May 2$^{nd.}$/1816. / Thus were the Vine and Branch of true Whiggism and/Britannia's most blooming expectation, by one/ irresistible stroke, together cut off.
Status: Grade II
Owned by Estates and General
Condition: fair; at risk from the erosion of the mound upon which it stands

Had Charlotte Augusta, Princess of Wales (1796–1817) not died aged 21, she would have succeeded her father, the Prince of Wales – the future George IV – in 1831. 'Her death is one of the most serious misfortunes the country has ever met with', said the Duke of Wellington.[1] 'From the highest to the lowest, this death was felt as a calamity that demanded the intense sorrows of domestic misfortune.'[2] Not until the death of Diana, Princess of Wales, was there to be such a popular outpouring of grief.

As the only child of George, Prince of Wales, Charlotte was heir to the crown but she spent her childhood in relative obscurity. Her father, as prince regent, refused to acknowledge her as heir presumptive and, after the bitter end of his own marriage, their relationship was poor. It became still worse when Charlotte ended her engagement, which her father had promoted, to Prince William of Orange. She married instead Prince Leopold of Saxe-Coburg in 1816, and 'began to emerge from the shadows to become a significant national figure'.[3] The Whigs looked forward anxiously to the moment when she would succeed her profligate father. Princess Charlotte, they hoped, would dismiss the Tory cabinet and the Whigs would form an administration. But she died giving birth to a stillborn son on 6 November 1817, at Claremont, Esher.

Although George III had had fifteen children, there were now no legitimate grandchildren to succeed the Prince of Wales. Three of his sons were promptly encouraged to find suitable brides. The race to father a future sovereign was won by Edward, Duke of Kent.

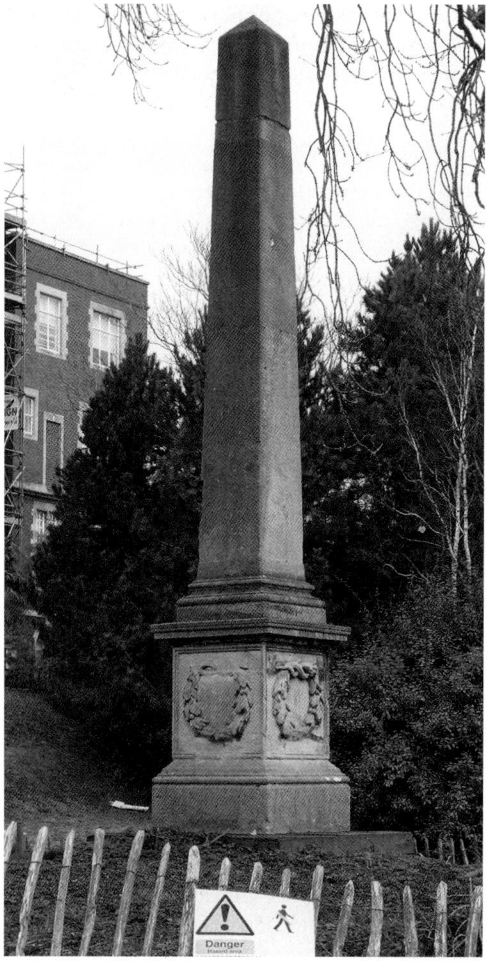

Memorial to Princess Charlotte

He married in May 1818 and the future Queen Victoria, Alexandrina Victoria, was born on 24 May 1819.[4]

Aged 80, Queen Victoria was to visit Bristol to open the Queen Victoria Jubilee Convalescent Home, in the grounds of which stood this memorial to Princess Charlotte.[5] Would she have been informed of the obelisk in the garden, dedicated to her first cousin, whose early death led to both her conception and her coronation?

The obelisk is core-filled limestone ashlar. One face of the pedestal has an engraved, sheet-copper plaque, framed by a stone moulding. Branches and vine leaves in relief on the other three sides echo the sentiment of the inscription: 'Thus were the Vine and Branch of true Whiggism… cut off.' The monument stands on an artificial hillock and the erosion of the soil at the base gives cause for concern.

There are thought to be only two other sculptural tributes to Charlotte in this country: the spectacular monument in St George's Chapel, Windsor, by Matthew Wyatt, and a later memorial to both Charlotte and Leopold now in St George's Church, Esher.[6] In Bristol, Princess Charlotte's death evidently so affected Jacob Wilcox Ricketts (1754–1839) that he erected this obelisk, with its passionate and politically inspired dedication, in the large garden of his house, Vincent Lodge, Redland. 'It is hard to believe that Ricketts was alone among his fellow party members in erecting a private monument.'[7] However, it may have been impatience as well as politics that inspired Ricketts. A national public appeal for a memorial had been launched, and by 1819 over £12,000 had been raised for 'a figure group to be erected in Hyde Park', but the prince regent stifled the proposal and appropriated the money.[8] In 1823 the announcement that a monument was finally to be placed in St George's Chapel, where the princess was buried, was greeted with hostility.

Jacob Wilcox Ricketts was 'a flamboyant character, and a man of strong views'. He was also described as 'an entrepreneur from the classic mould… [who] attracted an influential group of people around him'.[9] His major enterprises included a tobacco business, Ricketts and Wills, which he had founded in 1788 at the age of 35 with a member of the Wills family; the Bristol Porter Brewery, which became Georges Brewery, the largest in the city; and the last of the Bristol glass manufactories, the Phoenix Glasshouse. He was also a founder of Castle Bank.[10] He left

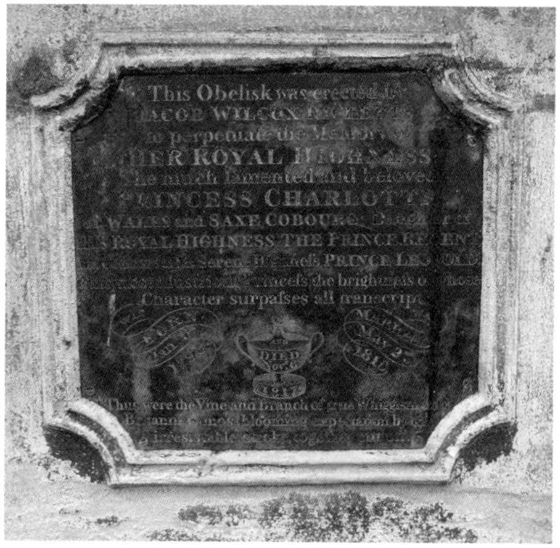

Engraved plaque on the memorial to Princess Charlotte

£250,000 and was buried at Lewins Mead Chapel.

There is one incidental link between Ricketts and the princess. He was a particular patron of the Bristol artist Edward Bird, RA, who enjoyed the title of historical painter to Princess Charlotte.

The obelisk was 'rediscovered' in 1975 among a tall and close grove of trees that have since had to be cut down. The convalescent home had become a maternity hospital, whose closure was imminent. Publicity was deliberately engineered in order to ensure the preservation of the monument in the event of the development of the site.[11] In May 1984 the plaque was reported to be missing, but it was recovered in 1991 and re-placed, after conservation, in July 1992.

Notes

[1] G. St Aubyn, *Queen Victoria: A Portrait* (London, 1991). [2] H. Martineau, *The History of England During the Thirty Years' Peace, 1816–1846* (London, 1849), p.63. [3] B. Little and M. Johns, 'So nearly a Queen', *Gloucestershire and Avon Life*, May 1984. [4] The Kents spent their honeymoon at Claremont, where Charlotte had died. [5] Opening ceremony programme, 15 November 1899. [6] Queen Victoria commissioned the memorial sculpture from Francis

John Williamson (c.1870) for Claremont House and it was subsequently moved to St George's, Esher. [7] As note 3. [8] S.C. Behrendt, *Royal Mourning and Regency Culture* (Basingstoke, 1997), p.241. The sculptor was Matthew Cotes Wyatt (1777–1862). [9] C. Weeden, 'The Ricketts family and the Phoenix Glasshouse, Bristol, 1892', *Glass Circle*, no. 4, December 1982. [10] C.H. Cave, *The Castle Bank: A History of Banking in Bristol, 1750 to 1899* (Bristol, 1899), p.158. [11] *Evening Post*, 'Mysterious memorial of a glass maker', 18 July 1975.

Royal Fort Gardens, Bristol University

In the Centenary Garden in the eastern corner of the Royal Fort Gardens, above Tankards Close

Classic Flight B32

Sculptor: John Huggins

Date: 1979
Material: bronze; base, grey slate
Dimensions: 110cm; base 93cm
Foundry: Morris Singer, Basingstoke
Plaque inscribed: JOHN HUGGINS / CLASSIC FLIGHT / Purchased by the University Appeal Fund / for the Centenary Garden / 1979
Status: not listed
Owner: University of Bristol
Condition: good, but covered in candle wax

The Centenary Garden celebrates the opening of University College, Bristol, in October 1876. It was the first college in the country to admit men and women on an equal footing and it received its royal charter as a university in May 1909.

Classic Flight is one of the earliest of a series of works reflecting John Huggins's interest in falconry. It is strikingly similar to some of the sculptor's slightly earlier bronzes inspired by the shape and power of breaking waves. One of the two upper-arching curves is now reversed and becomes concave, suggesting the upward thrust of a rising raptor. Forms that had previously expressed the force and repetitiveness of waves are subtly transformed to suggest the bird's lightness and strength.

The work was selected by a 'group from the university led by Professor Douglas Everett'.[1] It was unveiled by the university's chancellor, Dorothy Hodgkin OM, FRS.

The sculptor has recently written that the selectors:

> were very taken with the polished surfaces despite my advice that they would not stay that way outdoors. Some years ago following a comment, I agreed to refurbish the piece and did so. It was not a long-term solution and should really have been patinated all over… It would be nice to have it done for the long term and would not cost a fortune.[2]

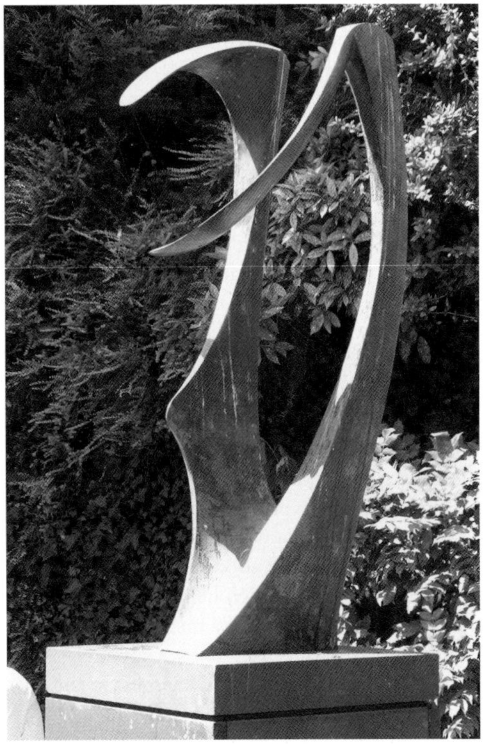

John Huggins, *Classic Flight*

A version of the work was shown at the artist's one-man exhibition, 'Flights and Slides', at the Alwin Gallery, London in 1980.[3]

Notes
[1] Letter from the sculptor, 24 June 2008. [2] Ibid. [3] P. Davies, *John Huggins Sculptor* (Somerset, 2006), illus. p. 54; the similar *Wave Forms*, also of 1979, is illustrated on p.48.

Small Street

On the Assize Courts façade in Small Street

Queen Victoria and Prince Albert C18

Sculptor: unknown

Architects: T. S. Pope and J. Bindon, 1867–70
Date: 1868
Materials: stone
Status: Grade II*
Owner: Bristol City Council
Condition: fair

The Assize Courts in Small Street were designed in 1867 by Thomas Shackleton Pope, son of the Guildhall's architect. The selection process involved much chicanery, denying Bristol a building of far superior quality by E. W. Godwin.

The sculptor of the statues of Queen Victoria and the Price Consort is as yet unknown. Prince Albert had died in December 1861 and plans for a public memorial were thought to have come to nothing.[1] T. S. Pope's winning design of 1867 has two medieval figures in the niches that were to be occupied by Victoria and Albert, and it is possible that, having raised an inadequate amount for a substantial monument to the prince, the Assize Courts provided the corporation with a way out of a predicament.[2]

Prince Albert had been granted the rank of consort in 1842 and prince consort in 1857. A great supporter of the arts and of social reform, he would have been most readily remembered in Bristol as the initiator of the Great

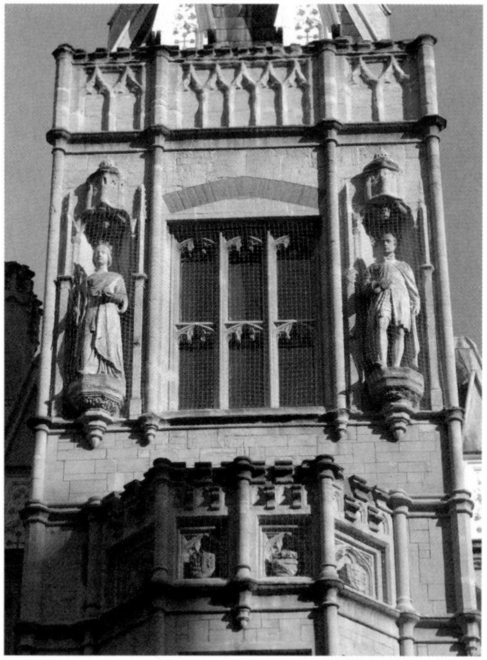

Thomas Shackleton Pope, architect, *Queen Victoria and Prince Albert*

Exhibition of 1851 and as the man who had earlier launched the SS Great Britain. The balanced pairing of these two statues concedes a rare equality between the queen and her late consort, and it seems likely that the statues were a deliberate if belated tribute to a remarkable man.

The figures of Victoria and Albert are in two separate niches on the upper part of the tower of the Assize Courts and both stand on octagonal corbels.

Notes

[1] McGrath, *The Merchant Venturers of Bristol*, p.276; the Merchant Venturers contributed £100 to the fund, but subsequently put the sum toward the purchase of portraits of the Queen and Prince Consort after Winterhalter that hang in Merchants' Hall. [2] Crick, *Victorian Buildings*, p.47, illus. pl. 48.

Somerset Square

In the centre of Somerset Square, Redcliffe, off Prewett Street

Somerset Square Fountain C68

Designer: unknown

Date: 1849
Materials: limestone; base, Pennant stone
Dimensions: approx. 6m high; 170cm wide at base
Status: Grade II
Owned by Bristol City Council
Condition: fair

Despite the recent discovery that this odd architectural conglomeration was erected in 1849, its origin remains uncertain and fanciful local explanations are still prevalent.[1]

This former fountain is near the centre of a recently re-landscaped green, surrounded on three sides by multi-storey blocks of flats. The octagonal limestone structure is on a two-layered base of Pennant stones. The first tier of eight Gothic arches supports a heavy circular cap with an acanthus band. A second tier of eight plain cylindrical columns support a plinth topped by an open urn from which a fir cone projects.

The structure survived the bombing during the Second World War, when so many of the Georgian houses on the square were destroyed. Restoration work, following efforts made by Recce Winstone through the Bristol Archaeological Committee, was carried out in 1962.[2] It was assumed at the time that the fountain had been erected in 1756, when houses were built to form two sides of Somerset Square, one of the earliest in Bristol.[3] However, it was also in 1962 that a planning department officer correctly surmised:

> My own conjecture is that… it is an assembly of unrelated pieces of stonework from other structures merely placed on top of each other. The plinth and finial are Gothic in detail while the intermediate columns are of classical design.[4]

The origin of the parts remains a mystery.

In 1996 Anthony Beeson, then fine art librarian at Bristol Central Library, noted an article in *The Builder*, aptly entitled 'A Fountain of Error – Bristol'. It was published in December 1849 and it was almost certainly written by the magazine's editor, George Godwin, then heavily engaged on his overly zealous restoration of St Mary Redcliffe. He had gone 'accidentally to Somerset Square', where he discovered that 'the old wall, which had enclosed the central area, was giving place to an iron railing and preparations were making

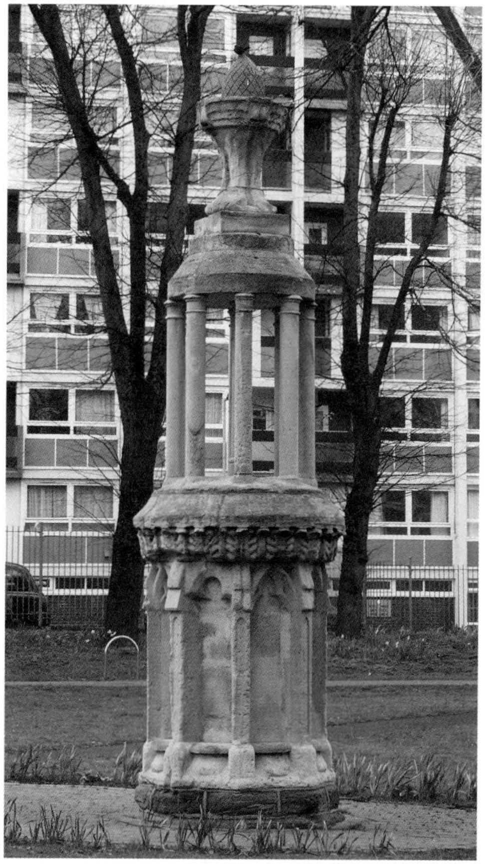

Somerset Square Fountain

for an ornamental fountain, apparently of Gothic design, in the centre'.[5] The work was being paid for by 'one spirited individual to whom many of the houses belonged'. The reporter's first reaction was 'Praise be to him!' On a second visit, probably in the late autumn of 1849, he was dismayed by the completed work.

> The basement is Gothic, with foliated panels; on this is a circular Italian peristyle of small columns, then a nondescript ornament from an indistinct recollection of that on the Tower of the Winds, and crowning all, a curiously-postured figure of Neptune with a jet-pipe out of the top of his head, leading to the conclusion that he is hereafter to be afflicted with water on the brain.

The next paragraph dismisses the design as 'good and liberal intentions… entirely thrown away… it must have cost a considerable sum of money, sufficient, under good direction, to have raised a creditable work of art.' The writer's wish was 'to prevent similar waste elsewhere, and not with the view of causing annoyance to the proprietor'. He concluded that the statue of *Neptune* 'appears to have been copied from the large statue of the god near the Temple Church in Bristol', and he pleaded for the conservation of the original *Neptune*, which today stands on The Centre. 'There are so few fountain-statues in our streets, or indeed statues of any kind, that we would suggest to the authorities the conservancy of this last-named Neptune.'[6] The small statue of Neptune on the Somerset Square fountain is no longer present and is not otherwise recorded.

The Builder's disparaging remarks would have been excellent ammunition for Councillor Graham Robertson, a future lord mayor, who objected to the £400 cost of the restoration in 1962. 'I suggest we pull it down and put up a couple of seats… It is just a chunk of stone.'[7]

A metal plaque at the entrance to the green tells us that 'Somerset Square Doorstep Green' was renovated in 2006 and is today maintained by Redcliffe Open Spaces Group. The project's supporters included the Big Lottery Fund and the European Community's Regional Development Fund. The landscape architects, AFLA, have confirmed that water supply pipes were found within the top of the structure when it was conserved by W. R. Bedford at this time.

Notes
[1] 'What is the fountain's history?', *Evening Post*, 24 April 1962; in 2008 a local resident was confident that it came from the Duke of Beaufort's estate at Stoke Gifford; English Heritage Bristol's Listed Buildings Database records the structure as a drinking fountain and conduit head from the mid- to late eighteenth century. [2] *Western Daily Press*, 8 May 1962; Winstone, *Bristol As It Was, 1950–53*, pl. 130. [3] 'Will the council buy the rest of Somerset Square?', *Bristol Evening Post*, 29 March 1956. [4] 'Oddity in the square', *Evening Post*, letter from R.A. Young, 27 April 1962. [5] *The Builder*, 15 December 1849, p.596. [6] Ibid; *Neptune* and *William III* were the only two free-standing public statues in 1849. [7] '£400 starts row over a fountain', *Western Daily Press*, 8 May 1962.

St Augustine's Parade

The pediment, panels and weathervane of E-Shed, now Watershed Media Centre

The Watershed Pediment and Weathervane C53

Architect: Edward Gabriel

Date: 1894
Materials: carved reliefs in Portland stone[1]
Dimensions: approx. 1.5m high, 7m wide
Status: Grade II
Owned by Bristol City Council
Condition: reliefs, poor; weathervane, fair, needs re-gilding

E-Shed, as the Watershed arts centre was first called, was a utilitarian dockside shed. It has been described as Edward Gabriel's most prominent surviving work, but its decorative façade and tower is also a tribute to Victorian planners.[2]

The pediment is crowded with figures and

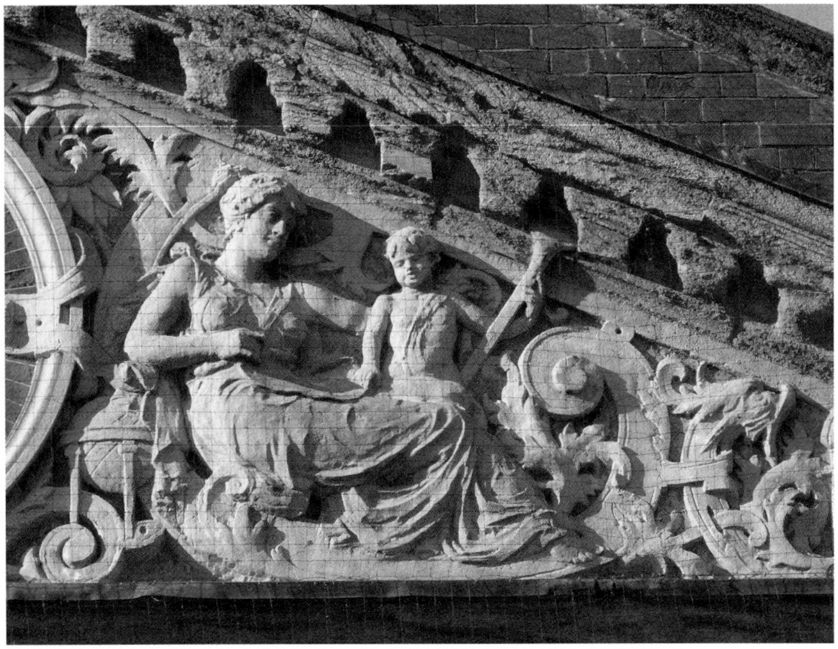

Edward Gabriel, architect, *Watershed Pediment*

flourishes of strapwork and foliage. In its centre is a brick circle, serving as a vent to the roof space. The decoration is broadly symmetrical with a recumbent female figure on each side. To the left, a woman holds a trident. She is supported by a floating putto grasping a scroll or bale. The attribute of the woman on the right is a terrestrial sphere, hinting at world trade and seafaring. Her supporter holds a long trumpet. Below the architrave are three decorative panels in the same style. A weathervane on the domed and polygonal tower to the right is a gilded two-masted galleon.

In 1894, the architect Edward Gabriel had won a competition for this building held by the Bristol Corporation's Docks Committee.[3] The committee wanted this prominently sited dockside transit-shed facing St Augustine's Parade to be 'embellished with an end façade so that the shed roof would not show above the gable'.[4] They also 'required that the building should have an attractive aspect from College Green'. There was soon appreciation for both the demands and the solution:

> The unusual architectural features… are due to its proximity to St Augustine's Parade and the approach to Clifton. Decorative treatment was adopted, it being feared that a plain design would become an eyesore.[5]

Andor Gomme has described the building as 'plain except for floridly carved pedimented and turreted north end'.[6] He also described the style as Elizabethan Arts and Crafts, and noted that the design was altered from the winning competition design. These changes can be seen in Gabriel's detailed pen and ink drawing, reproduced in Clare Crick's book.[7] The changes are few and minor and it seems likely that the general design of the sculptural decoration and of the weathervane was by the architect.

Members of the docks committee would have been very much aware that the old port of Bristol was changing rapidly. In 1892–3, the River Frome between St Augustine's Bridge (opposite Clare Street) and the Stone Bridge above St Mary on the Quay had been covered over. The statues of Edmund Burke and Edward Colston, erected in 1894 and 1895, were impressively prompt attempts to dignify this new open space (now Colston's Avenue and The Centre). Behind this highly ornamented warehouse façade of 1894 were very similar concerns that were brilliantly resolved.

The fine wrought-iron entrance gates, together with the ornate towers and lamps, are a precious and rare survival.[8] So too is the galleon weathervane, which for many years was at Underfall Yard for safekeeping. Today, it urgently needs re-gilding.

The weathervane has very recently been overshadowed by the return of the magnificent gilded galleon that was formerly on the extension to the old Bristol and West Building. That building, begun in 1980, was on the opposite side of The Centre on Broad Quay. The weathervane has now been re-erected on the new block (2009). The stylised galleon represents *The Matthew* and it is based in part upon the vessel depicted in Bristol's Admiralty Court seal.[9] It was made by Richard Quinnell, arguably the most important artist/blacksmith of the twentieth century, in about 1985. It is another example of the exemplary commissioning of sculpture by the architects, Alec French Partnership.

Notes

[1] Information from Quartz Masonry Conservation. [2] Crick, *Victorian Buildings*, p.65. [3] Ibid. [4] Ibid. [5] Stone, *Bristol As It Was*, p.62. [6] Gomme, 'Street index of buildings', p.58. [7] As note 2, p.63, pl. 64. [8] D.J. Eveleigh, *Bristol 1850–1919* (Stroud, 1980), pp.45–50. [9] Richard Lee, Alec French Partnership, 10 March 2009.

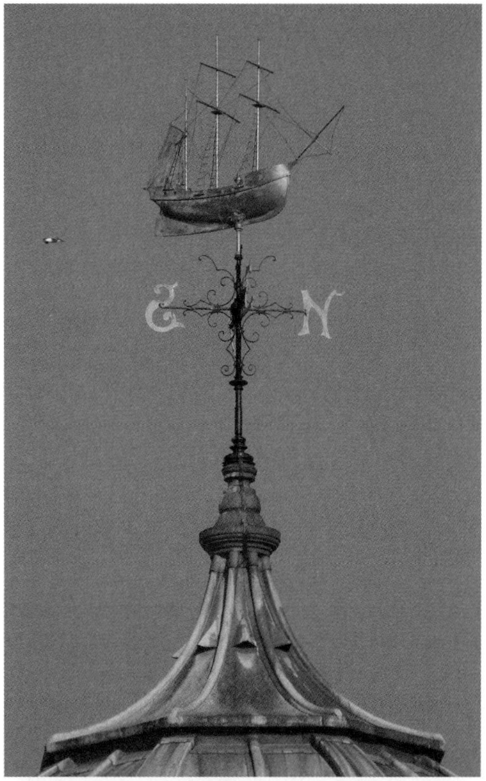

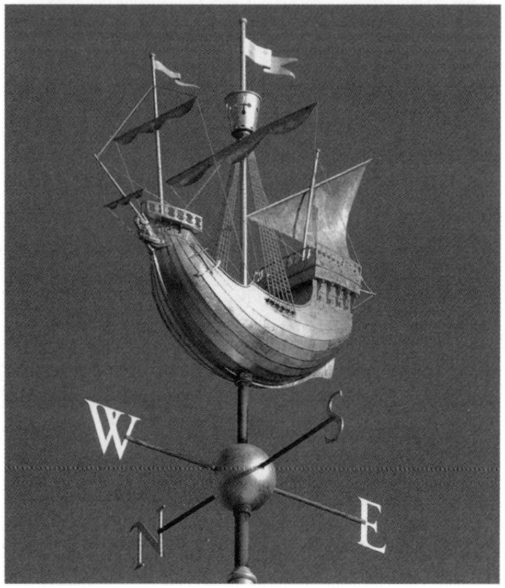

(top) Edward Gabriel, architect, *Watershed Weathervane*

(left) Richard Quinnell, *Weathervane of the Matthew*, on the Bristol and West Extension Building before demolition (photo: Stephen Morris)

Above the entrance to the Horn and Trumpet, next to Bristol Hippodrome, St Augustine's Parade

The Demerara's Figurehead C52

Sculptor: unknown

Date: post-war replica of 1851 figurehead
Material: possibly fibreglass
Status: not listed
Dimensions: approx. 2.2m high
Condition: poor

This statue is a half-size replica of the vast figurehead depicting an exotic US chief that briefly ornamented the steamship *Demerara*, launched in Bristol in 1851. That original figurehead decorated an auctioneer's premises on Quay Street at the very head of St Augustine's Reach.[1] The building, known as Demerara House, was demolished in 1937 and replaced by Electricity House by Giles Gilbert Scott. The wooden figure is said to have disintegrated on demolition, and this replica was probably erected next to the Hippodrome theatre soon after the Second World War.

William Patterson, who had constructed the steamship *Great Western* for Brunel and who had assisted with the design of the *Great Britain*, was both the designer and the builder of the *Demerara.* She was almost as big as the *Great Britain*, but more like the *Great Western* in design, being wooden-hulled and a paddle steamer. It was while being towed down the Avon Gorge with Patterson aboard, en route for Glasgow to have her engines fitted, that she struck the Gloucestershire bank just a mile down river. The ebbing tide then slewed her across the river and she was severely damaged. She was hauled back to Bristol and eventually sold in 1854. It was in the *Great Britain*'s own purpose-built dry dock that she was then converted to a sailing vessel of over 3,000 tons. The *Demerara*, renamed *British Empire*, was lost in a hurricane in the West Indies in 1867, when only two of sixty ships survived.

The wreck of the *Demerara* in the Avon Gorge had an immediate effect on shipbuilding in Bristol, and it was nearly fifty years before a ship of similar size was launched in Bristol.[2]

The *Demerara*'s original figurehead is believed to have been carved by Robert and Thomas Williams and their nephew John Robert Anderson (1828–1909) at the Mardyke.[3] Anderson is now best known as a carver of carousel animals.

Notes
[1] Winstone *Bristol As It Was*, p.8. [2] Greenacre, *From Bristol to the Sea*, p.122. [3] Transcript of A.E. Anderson's biographical notes in Bristol Industrial Museum.

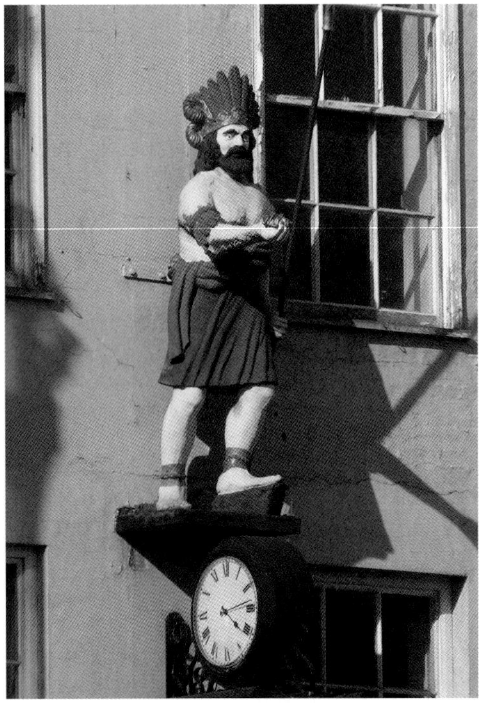

Replica of Demerara's figurehead

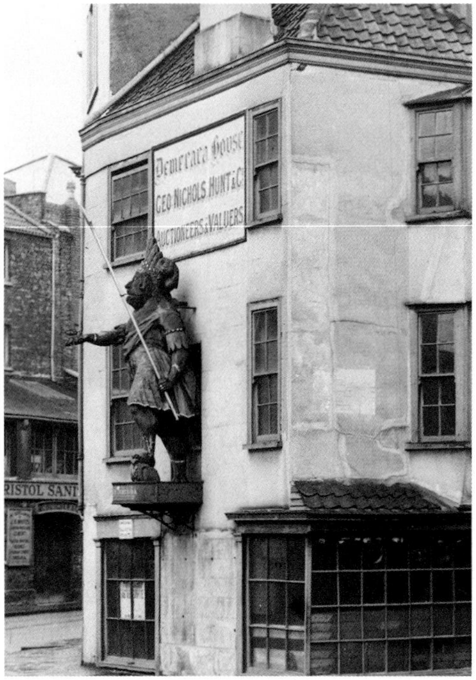

***SS Demerara's original figurehead*, Quay Street, photographed c.1910 (Bristol Industrial Museum)**

St George's Road

In the courtyard at the eastern end of Brunel House

Horse and Man B51

Sculptor: Stephen Joyce

Architects: Alec French Partnership
Date: 1984
Material: bronze, resin and fibreglass
Cast by the sculptor
Dimensions: figure, 175cm high; horse, 205cm high, 200cm long, 110cm wide
Status: not listed
Owned by Bristol City Council
Condition: fair; some damage and corrosion

Two disconnected life-size figures, freely modelled in clay with many deep crevices, have been cast in equal quantities of bronze and resin. The man has piercing eyes and a walrus moustache. He wears a peaked cloth cap and the clothes of a working man of the late nineteenth or early twentieth century. The reins by which the man leads the horse towards the entrance to the courtyard are deliberately incomplete. A cloth hangs from the harness on the right flank of the horse. *Horse and Man* stands on the floor of the courtyard on a herringbone pattern of old bricks.

The secluded setting is known to few Bristolians. The Royal Western Hotel opened in 1839. It had been designed two years earlier by the Bristol architect Richard Shackelton Pope in collaboration with Isambard Kingdom Brunel, and in anticipation of the need for accommodation for passengers travelling on both the Great Western Railway and the *Great Western* steamship.[1] To the north-east of the hotel was a large covered area, where coach passengers could alight in all weathers, called the Bazaar Ride. When Bristol's transatlantic trade foundered, the courtyard became the city's most important horse-dealing centre. It later languished as a car park.[2]

For many years the hotel was threatened with demolition. A £6 million redevelopment funded by the Co-operative Insurance Society was completed in 1984,[3] and the façade with its 'proud Ionic colonnade, attached Corinthian columns and pavilions', reflecting Brunel's courage and ambition, was retained.[4]

The sculpture was commissioned through ACCES (Avon Community Conservation Scheme funded by Avon County Council and sponsored by Manpower Services) by the development's architects, Alec French Partnership. Joyce had been employed by ACCES from 1984 to 1986 to supervise unemployed artists on various community projects. The job architect, Roger Guck, told Stephen Joyce the history of the original hotel and the later connection with the horse market, but it was the sculptor who proposed the image of a single horse-trader.[5] He rejected a mounted rider, as the sculpture would fall into the equestrian mode. The man was to represent a working man, the salt of the earth. The excellent painted pub sign for the *Horse and Groom* just a few yards down the road from Brunel House may also have played a part.

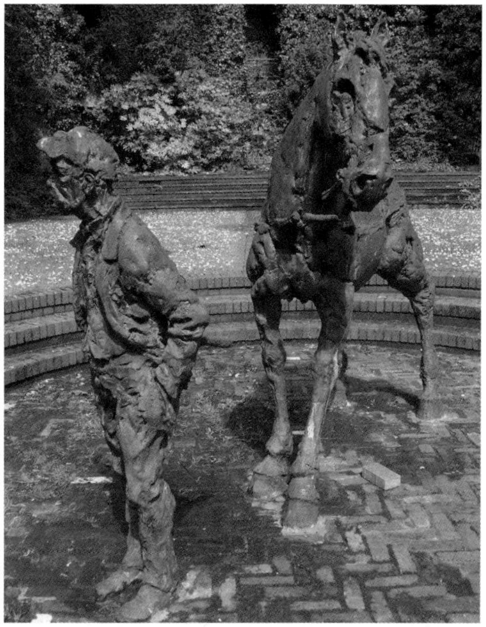

Stephen Joyce, *Horse and Man*

Joyce prepared a clay maquette, about 40cm high.[6] This was approved, and a full-sized clay version was commenced in the chapel workshop at Fishponds in Bristol. The budget was so tight that the thin steel rods used for the first armature were insufficient. The frame collapsed under nearly a ton of clay just as the modelling neared completion. All the clay had to be bagged while a metal armature was welded together and the modelling recommenced. Stephen Joyce has said that payment for the additional work on the second version was better. During the casting, and following discussions with Richard Lee of Alec French Partnership, Joyce decided to omit part of the reins to enable viewers to walk freely between the man and the horse and to minimise the possibility of damage. No specific models were used for the horse or the man, and they were based, instead, on much observation and on many drawings and photographs. The only costs were a modest £1,500 for the materials and the casting.[7]

On 21 August 1984, the Lord Mayor of Bristol, Councillor Claude Draper, unveiled the sculpture in the presence of David Wise, chairman of the Co-operative Insurance Society, Stephen Joyce and Richard Lee.[8] At this time there were plans to use the space for open-air performances in summertime, with seats for 200 people.[9]

Unfortunately this work is now weathering badly. The surface covering has worn, revealing patches of pure resin. There are breaks to the reins and it is likely that the internal metal armatures are corroding.

Notes

[1] Crick, *Victorian Buildings*, pp.14–15. [2] J. Belsey, 'The wonderful Horse Bazaar', *More Offbeat Bristol* (Bristol, 1993), p.28. [3] 'Wraps come off', *Bristol Evening Post*, 22 September 1984. [4] As note 1. [5] Stephen Joyce in conversation with D.M., 9 July 2003. [6] Notes from Stephen Joyce, 2003. [7] As note 5; Richard Lee recalls that the materials were paid for by the Co-operative Insurance Society; undated letter to D.M. [8] As note 3. [9] *Avon Report*, October 1984.

St George's Road

On the wall to left-hand side of the foyer of Brunel House

Brunel B53

Sculptor: Stephen Joyce

Architects: Alec French Partnership
Date: 1986
Material: pigmented fibreglass
Dimensions: 85cm high
Status: not listed
Owned by Bristol City Council
Condition: good

The building in which this relief is sited was originally the Royal Western Hotel. It was designed in 1837 by Richard Shackleton Pope in collaboration with Isambard Kingdom Brunel. After its conversion to offices in the mid-1980s,

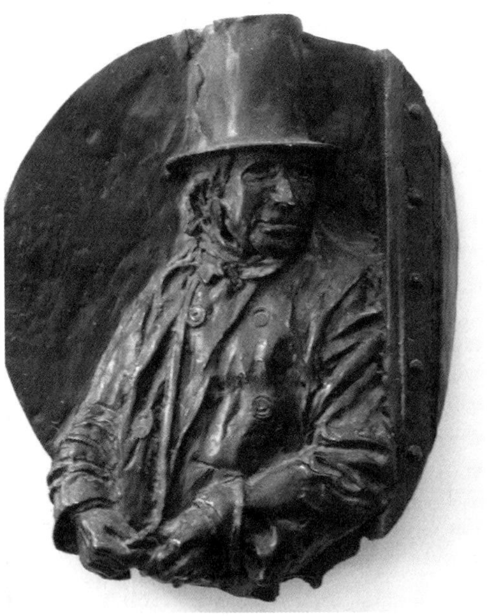

Stephen Joyce, *Isambard Kingdom Brunel*

it became the home of the city council's planning department.

This nearly life-size, half-length and high-relief image is contained in an irregular oval. Brunel wears a top hat, coat and a waistcoat. His head is half-turned to his left and he holds a pocket-watch. To his left is the strong vertical line of the edge of a railway-carriage door with rivets.

The work was commissioned while the conversion of the building was nearing completion and after the *Horse and Man* sculpture in the courtyard beside Brunel House, also by Stephen Joyce, had been finished. Joyce was approached by Roger Guck, Alec French Partnership's senior architect working on the conversion. Joyce made a clay model and this was cast in fibreglass in his studio. Stephen Joyce also designed and made the weather vane for Brunel House. This represents Halley's Comet, which was visible from Bristol in 1986.

St James's Barton

In front of St James's Barton office development, between North Street and York Street

Spirit of Bristol C2

Sculptor: Paul Mount

Date: 1968–70
Materials: stainless steel, pedestal in brick
Dimensions: 540cm high; pedestal, 550cm long, 480cm wide
Status: not listed
Ownership: unknown
Condition: fair; graffiti and some surface damage from vandalism; brick base disintergrating

The *Spirit of Bristol* is the largest free-standing sculpture to have been erected in Bristol, but the surrounding trees now hide it from public view. It has specific associations with Concorde, which first flew from Bristol in 1969 and it is already a rare echo of its time, for there is little public sculpture in Bristol from the 1960s or 1970s.

Six triangular aerodynamic shapes with straight and parabolic edges, reminiscent of ships' sails, are linked to form a single complex structure. All the stainless steel surfaces are highly polished. The very large rectangular pedestal is made of black engineering bricks. Neither the title of the work, the name of the sculptor nor the date of installation is displayed.

There was no competition for this project. *Spirit of Bristol* was commissioned by Copthall Holdings, developers of the nearby York House. Fergus Gleave, a chartered surveyor, introduced the sculptor to the developers. He had got to know Paul Mount in West Africa, where Mount was teaching in Lagos, Nigeria from 1955 to 1961. The sculptor had no brief beyond a site plan. The cost was shared with British Steel and the title, *Spirit of Bristol*, came from those dealing with the commission at Copthall Holdings.[1] The precise date of completion is unknown and there was no unveiling ceremony.[2]

Paul Mount took just over a year to design and construct the sculpture. A scale model was tested in a wind tunnel by Professor Joseph Black of the school of engineering at Bath University, and subjected to winds of up to eighty miles an hour to ensure that it would not produce whistling noises. He reported: 'the aesthetic and structural requirements match extremely well'. Professor Black had also made wind tunnel tests on Concorde. The first Concorde prototype flew from Filton in April 1969.[3]

The sculptor constructed the mild steel framework and fixed the stainless steel sheets in his Nancherrow Studio at St Just, assisted by Jim Williams, the local blacksmith. Amos Underhill of Coventry, a metal-finishing specialist who had polished the prototype engine blades developed for Concorde, gave Mount much expert advice.[4]

In order to transport the sculpture, it was made in six pieces and bolted and welded together on the site with the assistance of Christine Feiler.[5] The cost of the sculpture was £6000.[6]

In August 1971, a Bristol magazine published a large photograph of the sculpture implying that it had been very recently erected.[7] The caption read:

> A new and startlingly modern sculpture made its appearance at St James' Barton near Bristol's shopping centre [Broadmead]... a 20ft-high work in stainless steel expresses the spirit of Bristol's commercial history. On closer inspection, the artistic composition contains sails representing the city's place in maritime annals plus an aerofoil similar to that of the Concorde – two industries with which Bristol is closely linked.[8]

Later in the 1970s, a picture of the sculpture was included above the heading 'Sculpture sceptics', and the text reminded readers of the public reaction when the work was first erected:

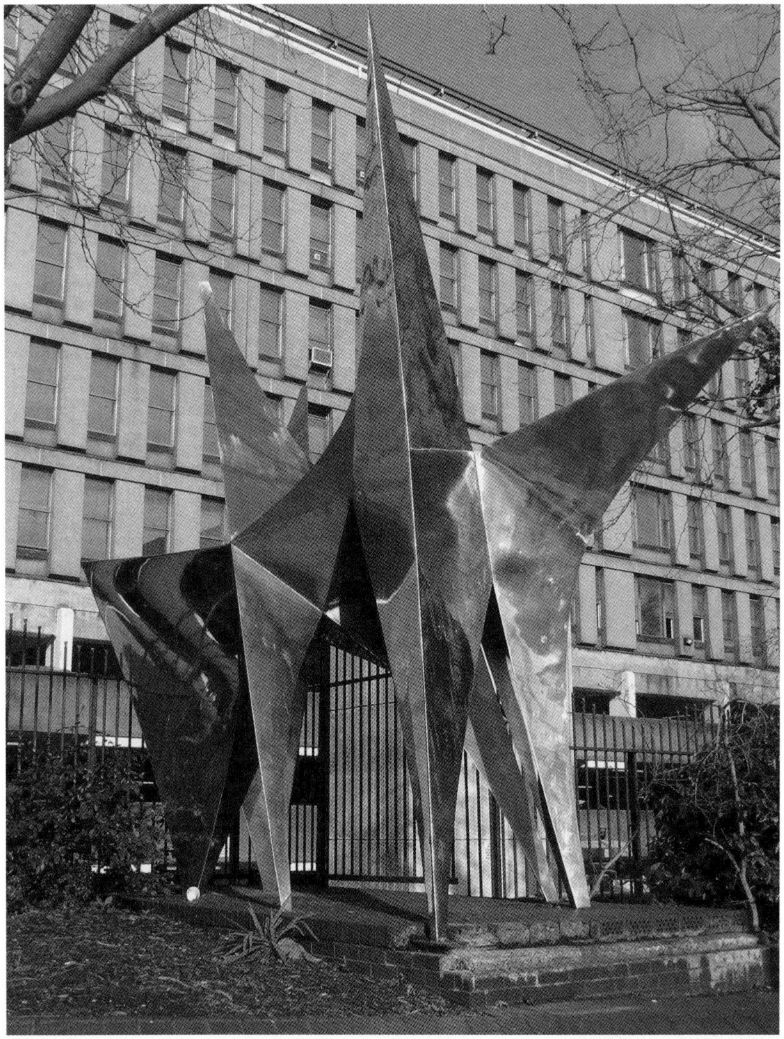

Paul Mount,
Spirit of Bristol

'There were some raised eyebrows and quite a few surprised looks when Bristolians had their first glimpse of "Spirit of Bristol", the new sculpture in St James'.[9]

By 1986, *Spirit of Bristol* was being enveloped by the trees and shrubs planted around the base. The *Evening Post* now called it the Vanishing Spirit, but showed a photograph of the sculpture 'in its former glory in 1977 – when many city people said they did not like it'.[10] 'The controversial *Spirit of Bristol* sculpture is involved in a cover up. The shiny metal sculpture has become tangled in overgrown bushes, while the organisation responsible for it remains a mystery.' The paper reported that both Avon County Council and the Bristol City Council denied that the sculpture was their responsibility. The cutting back of the foliage was not their concern. The building behind the sculpture was then occupied by National Car Parks, who also refused any responsibility. The Television Licence Records office was close to the site, but a spokesman denied liability for the upkeep but suggested the London-based agents JLW Estates might be involved.

Today, spring and summer growth almost totally conceals this tribute to the city's past achievements, and recently a tall metal fence has been erected so close to two sides of the base that the sculpture overhangs the railings.

Paul Mount presented the maquette for *Spirit of Bristol* to Professor Black in appreciation of his expert assistance. The professor's widow sold this model through the Beaux Arts Gallery in Bath in 2003, and it is now in a Bristol private collection.

In 1974, Paul Mount was commissioned to produce a substantial work for a wall on the exterior of Brigstowe House facing onto the Avon near Bristol Bridge.[11] *Skysails* remained until the mid-1990s, when the building became a hotel and the work was purchased by the University of Exeter through a gift made by Dr A. John Nunn. In 1998 it was installed on the face of the Queen's Building on the Streatham Campus amid a collection of modern sculpture, including works by Barbara Hepworth and Henry Moore.

Notes

[1] Letter from the artist, 28 June 2003. [2] Personal interview with the artist, 6 July 2003. [3] *Rolls-Royce Journal*, vol. 2, 1969, p.2. [4] As note 2. [5] Ibid; the potter Christine Feiler is the daughter of Paul Mount's wife, June Miles. [6] Ibid. [7] The date of completion of *Spirit of Bristol* was not established in conversations with the artist in 2003; Strachan, *Open Air Sculpture*, pp.96 and 268 records the dates of both 1968 and 1970; 1968 was given in recent obituary notices: *The Guardian*, 12 February 2009; *The Independent*, 16 January 2009. [8] K. Flower, *Illustrated Bristol News*, August 1971,frontispiece. [9] 'Sculpture sceptics', *Evening Post*, 31 May 1977. [10] J. Hendry, 'Vanishing spirit', *Evening Post*, 16 September 1986. [11] Welded steel wall sculpture, 540cm high; illustrated in situ; Strachan, *Open Air Sculpture*, p.96.

St Nicholas Street

Over the entrance of the former Stock Exchange, now a restaurant, 42 St Nicholas Street

Putti: Justice and Enterprise C37

Sculptor: unknown

Architect: Henry Williams
Date: 1903
Material: stone
Dimensions: approx. 1.2m high
Status: Grade II*
Condition: fair

Pevsner was brief and to the point: 'one-storeyed, of ornate debased Italian form, with black marble columns. As shockingly late as 1903'.[1] Andor Gomme later noted that the entrance design, in particular the broken pediment, niche and putti, derive from the Baroque porch of 1637 to St Mary the Virgin on the High Street, Oxford.[2] The winged angels are replaced by two putti: Justice holding scales, and Enterprise holding a model boat in one hand and a bag of money in the other. And just in case the symbolism is beyond us, the putti are named in capital letters. In the niche, the Virgin and Child are replaced by an ornate cartouche bearing the building's date, 1903.

The building was paid for by Sir George White, an important Bristol stockbroker as well as the promoter of the Bristol Tramways Company and the founder of Bristol's pioneering aircraft industry in 1910. George White had been first elected president of the Bristol Stock Exchange in 1898, and he was to present the building to the members at its opening.[3] The neighbouring building, 34 St Nicholas Street, was also developed by George White as stock exchange buildings from 1904, with W. P. Saunders as the architect.[4] It, too, has much good decorative detail.

Sir George White's artistic taste was centred upon outstanding craftsmanship. Henry Williams's superb architectural drawings and his richly ornamented façades, often in terracotta, would have appealed to him.[5] Williams was also responsible for the nearby printing works for Edward Everard, Sir George's brother-in-law (see Broad Street).

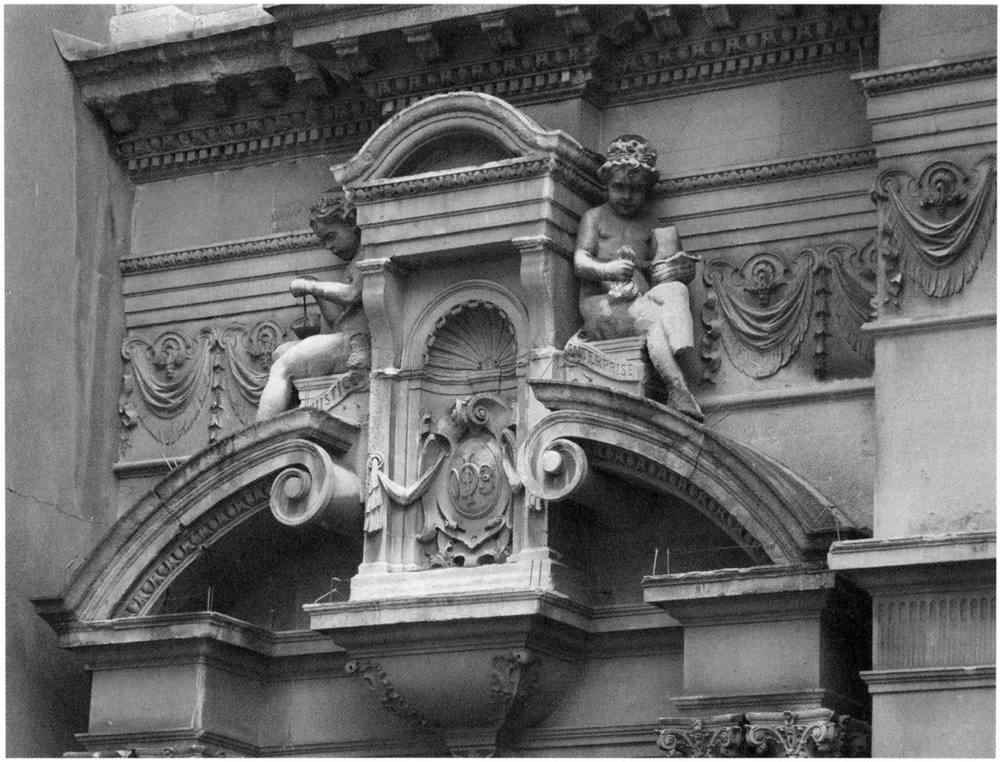

Henry Williams, architect, *Justice and Enterprise*

As well as the putti, the former Stock Exchange has a vigorously carved, if crudely painted, version of the city arms with unicorn supporters in the pediment. There is also good acanthus scroll work and art nouveau heads above the windows.

Inside the building, much of the spectacular decoration remains, including art nouveau tiles and mahogany panelling. It was 'furnished in the style of Cotham House', Sir George's home at the time.[6]

An account in the *Bristol Times and Mirror* on 30 July 1903 of the opening of the Stock Exchange names only the architect, the builders and the interior decorators. It is very possible that the architect, Henry Williams, designed the sculpture and decorative detailing of the exterior.

Within the former Stock Exchange behind the restaurant's bar, 42 St Nicholas St

The Spirit of Commerce

Sculptor: Benjamin Creswick C37

Date: 1903
Material: wood
Dimensions: 5ft 6in high by 3ft 6in wide
Condition: good

The long account in the *Bristol Times and Mirror* on 30 July 1903 of the opening of the Stock Exchange mentions at length a carved

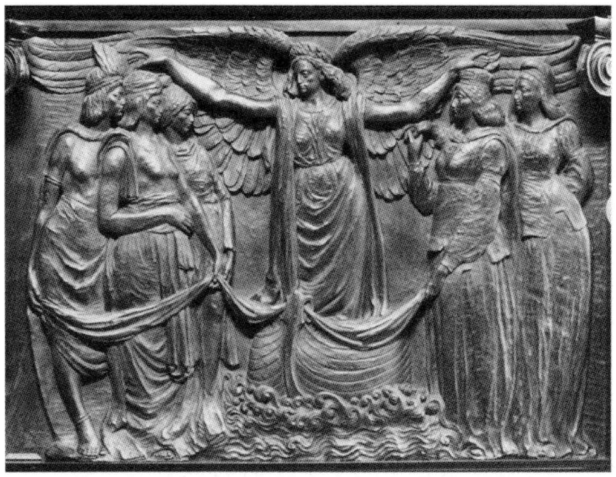

Benjamin Creswick, *The Spirit of Commerce* (photo: private collection)

wooden sculptural relief over a magnificent fireplace. It was by the Birmingham sculptor Benjamin Creswick, the master of modelling and modelled design at Birmingham Art School. It is now partially hidden behind the bar in the dining room on the ground floor of the Indian restaurant that occupies the former stock exchange. The relief's title was *Commerce Uniting the Nations*, and the description tells us that the:

> figures on the right represent Europe, and are shown more refined as befitting civilised nations. Their hands are united in friendship. The group on the left represents India, Asia and Africa, yearningly, though not without fear, receiving the message of fellowship from THE SPIRIT OF COMMERCE.

Today, the present restaurant's 'design concept' mentions Lutyens's fusion of classical and Indian architecture in New Delhi, and suggests that the restaurant's interior now enjoys a 'colonial club atmosphere', as recognisable to UK residents as to Indian princes.[7]

Notes

[1] Pevsner, *North Somerset*, p.424. [2] Gomme et al., p.355. [3] G. White, *Tramlines to the stars: George White of Bristol* (Bristol, 1995); *Bristol Times and Mirror*, 30 July 1903. [4] BRO 35810/GW/S/1-11. [5] Gomme, as note 2, p.443; Sir George White Bt. FSA has kindly pointed out that, as the main donor, Sir George White would have sanctioned the choice of Charles Holden as architect of the King Edward VII wing of the BRI 'one of the most important buildings in the history of modern architecture' (Andor Gomme). [6] As note 3. [7] www.oldindia.co.uk.

On the façade of the former Elephant public house, 20 St Nicholas Street

Elephant C38

Sculptor: 'Mr Porter'

Architect: Henry Masters
Date: 1867
Materials: relief carving in stone
Dimensions: 280cm high, 110 wide
Status: Grade II
Condition: fair

'Of the smaller taverns the Elephant in St Nicholas Street by Henry Masters (1867) with a sculpture by Mr Porter is a nice pert Victorian pub.'[1] Masters's name is on the planning application of 1866.[2] He started as a builder but 'became one of the most widely employed commercial architects in Bristol'.[3]

Nothing more has been discovered about the appropriately named Mr Porter, who may have been the sculptural decorator of the pub. In 2003 the licensee enthusiastically explained that the scrolled letter 'A' beneath the elephant was thought to be the 'signature' of the architect of the building, an American called Arnold.[4] Nothing to corroborate this has been discovered.

The former pub, once a favourite with the gay community, is now an Italian restaurant. The elephant, once pink and more recently dark grey, is now white, as is the entire façade. It is a brilliant white that entirely flattens a once delightful façade.

An inscribed panel, placed on the façade in 1981, endeavours to explain the complex history of this public house. Summarised, it says: Cock Lane appears on the James Millerd map of Bristol dated 1673. This was renamed Exchange Lane when John Wood the Elder's Exchange was erected in Corn Street in 1743. Between 1762 and 1767 a woman named Mary Thomas held the license for the Cock Tavern in St Nicholas Street. Her name later appears in a deed granted in 1787 to Samuel Worrall (1756–1821) by the dean and chapter of Bristol Cathedral for an inn called The Elephant. The writer of the inscription, Leonard Nott, suggests that this would have been the year in which the name of the inn was changed. Worrall was Bristol's town clerk from 1787 to 1819, and Worrall Road in Clifton bears his name.

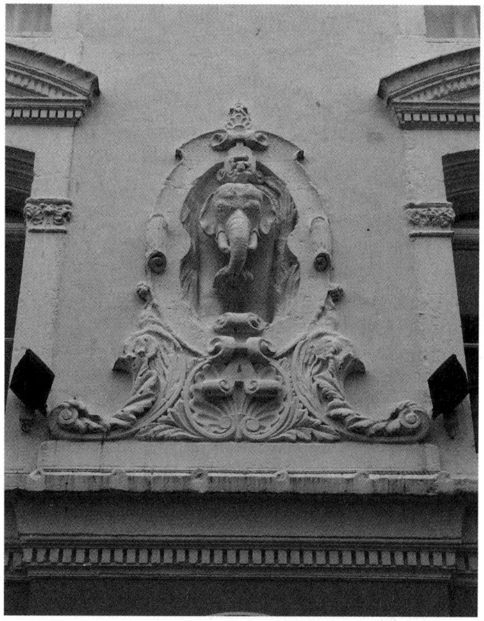

'Mr Porter', *Elephant*

Notes

[1] Gomme et al., caption p.355; the source of the attribution to Mr Porter is not given. [2] BRO plan and sectional drawing, 19 July 1866. [3] As note 1, p.438. [4] Conversation with DM, November 2003.

On the façade of Gresham Chambers, 18 St Nicholas Street

Four Busts C39

Sculptor unknown

Architects: Archibald Ponton and William Venn Gough
Date: 1868
Material: limestone
Dimensions: each roundel approximately 35cm in diameter
Status: Grade II
Condition: poor, stone crumbling worsened by impervious paint

Andor Gomme compares this building to the architects' larger design for Avon Insurance in Broad Street, and describes the façade as 'a cranky version of the same theme'. It presents a 'weird appearance... completed by four of the oddest sculptured heads in Bristol, which appear out of portholes as if caught in a pillory'.[1] The busts wear toga-like tunics and appear to have wreaths on their heads. The first two on the left are very similar and may depict handsome young men, although they have also been identified as female. The third is presumed to be a veiled female, and the fourth an old man with a very windswept beard, who has been erroneously identified as the hero of the unification of Italy, Garibaldi. They may well illustrate the seasons, or possibly the four ages of man. The stone façade is under multiple layers of paint and the faces have been repeatedly over-painted.

There is a strong similarity between the veiled head and the work of the Italian sculptor Raffaelle Monti (1818–81). Monti had come to London as a political exile in 1848, two years after the sixth Duke of Devonshire had commissioned the *Veiled Vestal.*[2] The head of that statue, now at Chatsworth, was frequently reproduced in other forms such as Parianware, and it may well have inspired the head in St Nicholas Street.

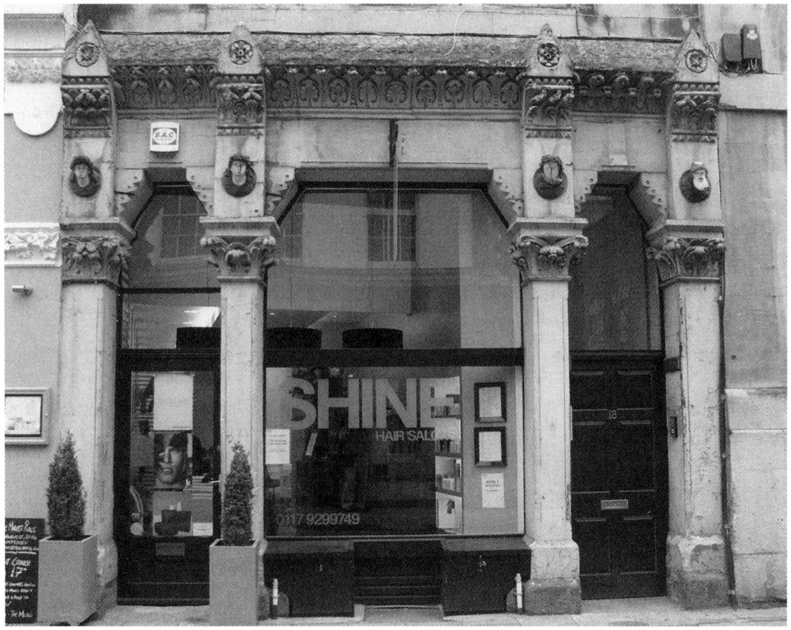

Ponton and Gough, architects, *18 St Nicholas Street*

The iconography of the sculpture on other Ponton and Gough facades suggest that the wit and whim of the carver was of paramount importance. However, the five similarly protruding heads on Ponton and Gough's lost façade to Mr Pointon's chemist shop on High Street depicted specific gods or persons associated with medicine.[3] If the original function of the shop at 18 St Nicholas Street is established, the identity of the heads may follow.

Notes
[1] Gomme et al., p.375. [2] P. Ward-Jackson, *Raffaelle Monti, ODNB.* [3] 'Apollo, Esculapius, Cesus, Minerva and so on', *The Builder* ,19 October 1867, p.757; illus. Gomme, as note 1, p.374.

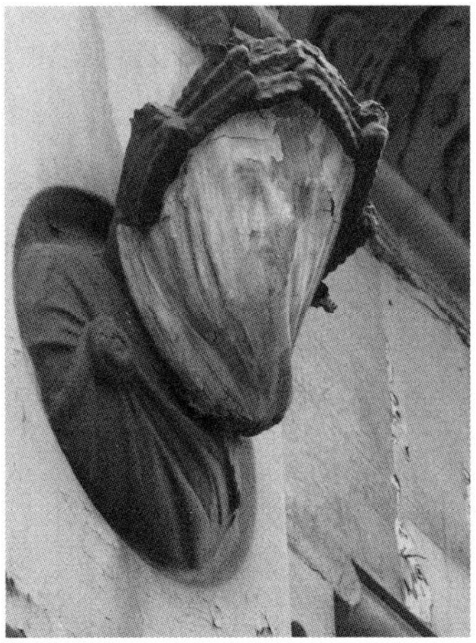

Veiled head

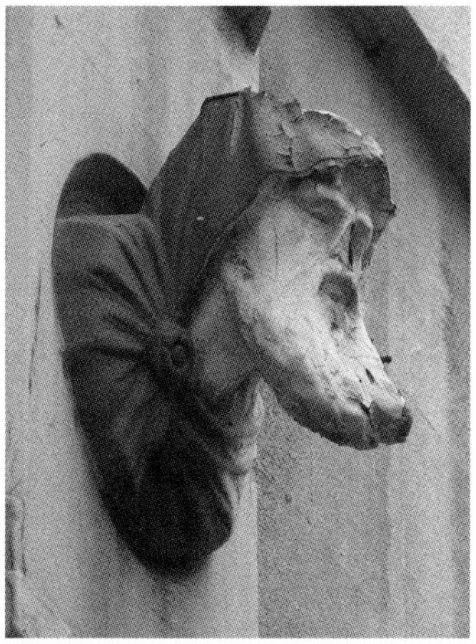

Bearded head

On the north side of the street, on the wall of the market, St Nicholas Street

Queen Victoria Drinking Fountain C40

Sculptors: W. and T. Wills

Foundry: Coalbrookdale Company
Date: 1859
Material: cast iron, painted, and marble
Dimensions: 95cm high, 95cm wide
Inscriptions: cast in the semi-circle above the niche – WILLS BROTHERS SCULP^T LONDON
–: cast in the section below the niche, now missing – GIFT OF JOHN PAYNE BUDGETT 1859
–: on the rim – CAST BY THE COALBROOKDALE C^O.
Status: Grade II
Owned by Bristol City Council
Condition: conserved and repainted 2008; water disconnected

This very early drinking fountain was installed in 1859, the year in which the Metropolitan and Free Drinking Fountain Association was formed and in which London got its first drinking fountains.[1] Liverpool, as a result of the pioneering philanthropy of Charles Pierre Melly, had already had many such fountains installed between 1854 and 1858.

Few of these reminders of Victorian life survive, and far fewer are still in working order. Vital in their day, they provided fresh water and helped to reduce outbreaks of cholera and the spread of other diseases. For the working man, they often offered the only unpolluted means of refreshment other than beer, and their proliferation was closely associated with the temperance movement.

The donor of the fountain was John Payne Budgett, a wholesale grocer and member of a prominent family in Bristol headed by Samuel Budgett, merchant and philanthropist. He attended Highbury Chapel, as did the family of H. O. Wills.[2]

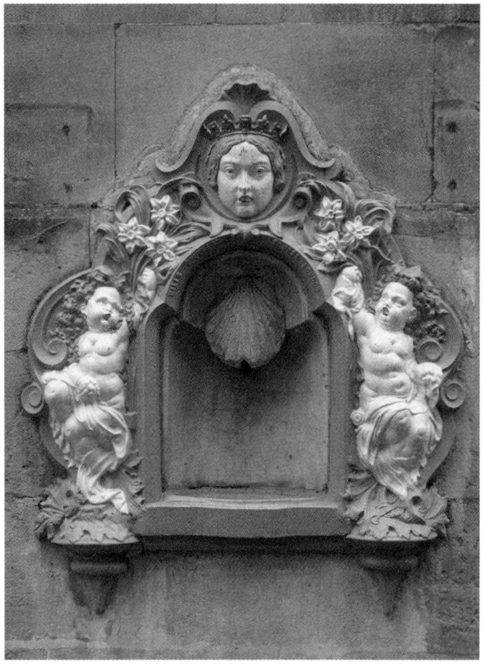

W. and T. Wills, *Queen Victoria Drinking Fountain*

The design is symmetrical. A deeply recessed marble niche has a central scalloped shell that conceals the water's source. A wood engraving in *The Art-Journal* showed an elegant chained chalice.[3] The cast iron surround has putti on either side among swirling foliage, flowers and drapery. At the apex is a full-face relief portrait of the young, crowned Queen Victoria. Centred at the base was a separately cast inscription panel. That is now missing. Previously repainted in 1981, the fountain was responsibly conserved and repainted in 2008. It continues to be obscured by the industrial rubbish bins of nearby restaurants, but not by those of the city council's market on whose land the bins stand.

The ornate cast iron surround was a stock item and one of a variety of patterns that could be selected from a large catalogue. *The Art-Journal* of 1860 praised the work:

> It is to the Messrs Wills Brothers, of Euston Road, that the promoters of drinking fountains… are eminently indebted for the ability, skill and earnestness with which they have directed their thoughts to the production of iron fountains… these gentlemen, sculptors by profession, and artists of no common ability have considered the production of iron drinking fountains to be of sufficient importance to form a distinct class of Art-manufacture. Arrangements accordingly have been made by them with the directors of the Coalbrookdale Iron Works by means of which they have secured for their designs an artistic rendering that constitutes a new era in iron castings.[4]

Arrowsmith's Dictionary of Bristol lists five other drinking fountains erected in Bristol in the same year, 1859.[5] Much the finest was the angel fountain, which was close by in High Street on the east wall of St Nicholas Church. It was erected 'by some iron merchants of this city' and was *in situ* until 1942.[6] Another was on the Triangle, Queen's Road and this was also by the 'Wills Brothers, sculptors, London' and cast by the Coalbrookdale Company. The three other drinking fountains of 1859 were at Old King Street, St Philip's Bridge and Welsh Back.

The Coalbrookdale Foundry had strong links with Bristol, originating from the Bristol Iron Company of 1708, set up by Abraham Darby, the first man to smelt iron ore with coke. His financial backers for many years, before and after he moved to Shropshire, included the Goldneys of Clifton, prosperous Bristol Quakers.

Notes

[1] W.A. Atkinson's painting, *The First Public Drinking Fountain*, 1859–60, is in the Geffrey Museum, London; the fountain depicted is in Giltspur Street in the wall of the churchyard of St Stephen Sepulchre: Ward-Jackson, *Public Sculpture of London*, p.145. [2] 'Recollections of Alfred Newell Price', paper in BRL; a biography of Samuel Budgett by William Arthur, *The Successful Merchant: Sketches of the Life of Mr Samuel Budgett, Late of Kingswood*

Hill, was first published in 1852 and went through at least 20 subsequent editions. [3] *The Art-Journal*, 1860, p.114. [4] Ibid. [5] 2nd edition, 1906, pp.149–51. [6] This cast iron (Coalbrookdale pattern 101) and marble 'angel' fountain, 3 metres tall, is said to have been 'removed to safety' to the Bristol Industrial Museum (not yet in existence in 1942), where it is, today, untraced: BCC Engineers' Department, *Memorials, Fountains and Statues*; Winstone, *Bristol in the 1940s*, pl. 9, 10. *Bristol Times*, 19 November 1859, p.8 reports on a 'champagne lunch in the vestry of St Nicholas' following the dedication; a version is on the south-eastern side of St Philip's Square, Birmingham: Lea Jones, *Bristol Curiosities*, p.72; L. Thomas, 'The Angel Fountain', *The Bristol Templar: Bristol Past Revisited* (Bristol, 1990), pp.53–5; there is a surviving marble drinking fountain, also dated 1859, on the corner wall of Trinity Hospital South at the corner of Old Market and Midland Road.

St Phillips Road

At the junction of Trinity Street and St Phillips Road, between Old Market and Lawrence Hill

Twisted Arch A20

Sculptor: Louise Vergette of Cod Steaks

Date: 2007
Material: painted steel
Dimensions: approx. 8m high
Resin plaque inscribed in relief: Twisted Arch / by Cod Steaks / to celebrate / 30 years of / Sustrans / 7-7-1977 to 7-7-2007 / and / BRISTOL & BATH / RAILWAY PATH / the first section of the / NATIONAL CYCLE / NETWORK / Sponsored by: / Aardman Animations / Arts & Business / South West / Barcan Woodward / Solicitors / Bristol City Council / Community at Heart / First Great Western Ltd / John Grimshaw / Morgan's Insurance / Temple Quay / Recruitment
Status: not listed
Owned by Bristol City Council
Condition: good

This archway was erected to celebrate the thirtieth birthday on 7 July 2007 of Sustrans, the nation's leading sustainable transport charity. It marks the beginning of the Bristol and Bath Railway Path, begun in 1979 and completed in 1986. This cycle path was the very first section of the National Cycle Network, a network that now has over a thousand sculptures and works of art along twelve thousand miles of walking and cycle paths.

The winning competition design came from Louise Vergette of Cod Steaks, a Bristol-based set design and construction company, which has worked with Aardman Animations, installed public art and worked extensively with museums and art galleries and the film and advertising industries. The work was commissioned jointly by Sustrans, Bristol City Council Parks Department and the Avon Frome Partnership, which now manages the Bristol and Bath Railway Path. The commission was supported by many local businesses and other organisations, all of which are listed on the exemplary plaque (transcribed above) set into one of the 'tree trunks'.

Twisted Arch is made of reclaimed steel, both girders and poles. It is 'a symbol of regeneration and growth',[1] an ideal gateway between city and countryside, or, more accurately at this point, between trading estate and small urban park. It is an example of Sustrans's longstanding policy of employing local artists and craftsmen, of involving local communities and businesses in the creation of the artworks and of reflecting the character and history of the locality. 'Looking more closely at the passing environment will foster greater care and responsibility for it and bring enjoyment along the way.'[2] The project was overseen by Katy Hallett, Sustrans's national art coordinator. Sustrans managed workshops with local school children who visited the future site, witnessed the fabrication process at Cod Steaks, learned about the history and importance of the route and acquired 'a sense of care and ownership of the surrounding area'.[3]

John Grimshaw is on the list of donors. The founder of Cyclebag in 1977, from which

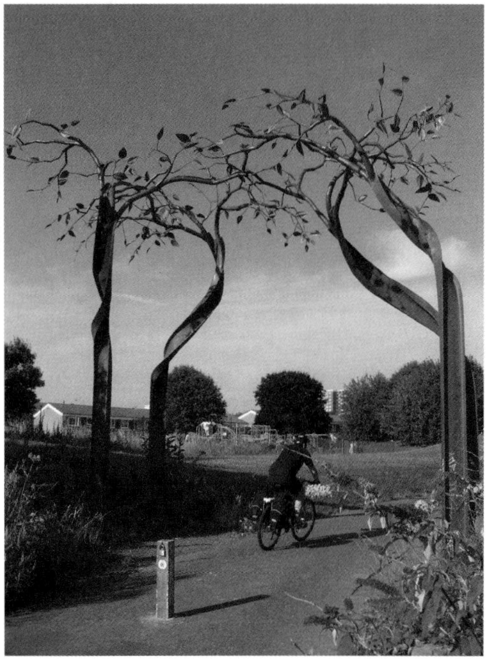

Louise Vergette of Cod Steaks, *Twisted Arch*

Sustrans grew, and chief executive for 31 years, he became Sustrans's president in 2008. His name on the plaque did not anticipate retirement; he remains very much involved. The arch is an apt and modest celebration of Sustrans's extraordinary achievement since the Bristol and Bath Railway Path was begun, near-impossible visions so often made possible by John Grimshaw's daunting optimism.

Notes
[1] www.sustrans.org.uk/; National Cycle Network, *The Bristol and Bath Railway Path: Art and the Travelling Landscape* (pamphlet, c.2006). [2] As note 1. [3] As note 1.

St Stephen's Street

13 St Stephen Street, east side

Three Portrait Roundels of John Milton, Sir Walter Raleigh and William Shakespeare C41

Sculptor and architect: unknown

Date: 1878
Material: terracotta
Dimensions: 30in diameter
Status: not listed
Owned by Bristol Backpackers
Condition: good

The heads probably depict John Milton, Sir Walter Raleigh and William Shakespeare with some uncertainty about the central bust of Raleigh.

Next to No. 13 St Stephen Street is an ornate and bombastic Italianate office block by J. H. Hirst of 1873–5. Columned and arcaded, it is faced with Bath stone. In sharp contrast, No. 13, which has been dated to 1878,[1] is faced with glazed yellow bricks with red and blue brick dressings. The façade is almost constantly in the shade and stands at the point at which the street narrows sharply. Its deliberately reflective surface, now dulled by dirt, once brought light to a dark street.[2] The decorative terracotta detailing around the windows brings relief and texture to the façade as a whole. The three roundels are an integral part of the design. They catch the light and continue to command the attention and curiosity of passers-by. These heads are of considerable sophistication, deliberately overfilling their roundels and thrust energetically forward as if through a porthole or in anticipation of the fall of a guillotine.

Neither the architect nor the owner and first occupier of the building has been established, and no satisfactory explanation for the choice of sitters has been made. Alfred, Lord Tennyson has recently been proposed for the central bust, but the costume alone makes this unlikely. Raleigh's association with tobacco could explain his presence and there is evidence within the building that it was built as a warehouse.[3]

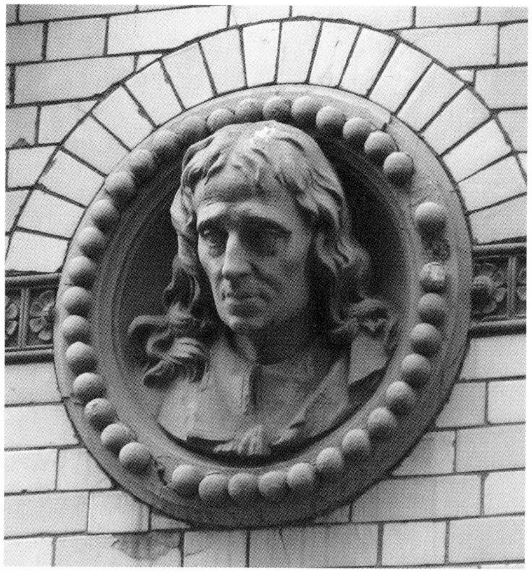

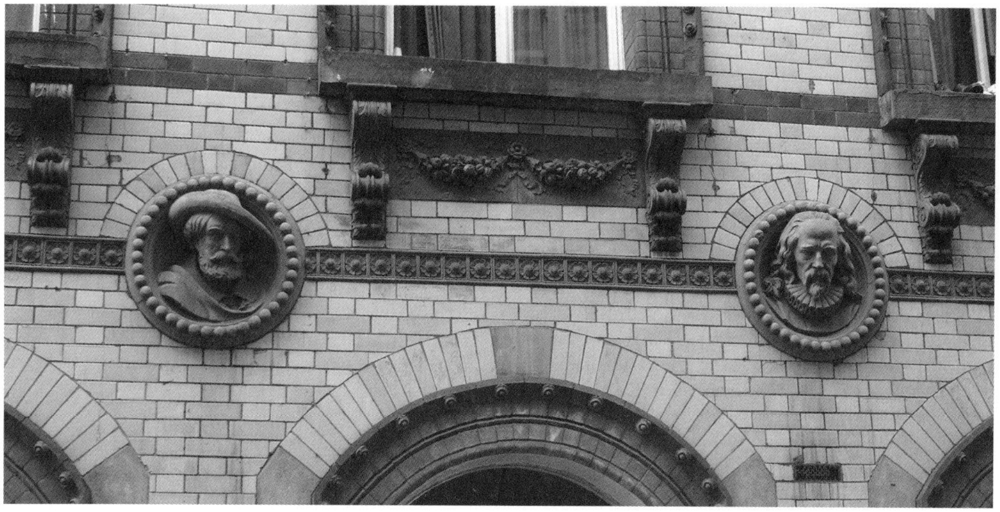

(above) ***John Milton***

(below) ***Raleigh and Shakespeare***

Notes

[1] Foyle and Cherry, *Bristol*, p.148. [2] The rear of the building is faced with glazed white tiles to similar purpose and looks on to the narrowest of all Bristol's surviving medieval streets, which once ran along the city wall. [3] Andor Gomme described the building as 'a typical round-arched warehouse of' about 1865: Gomme et al., p.354.

On the façade of No. 55 St Stephen's Street at first-floor level

Two Decorative Figures C42

Sculptor: unknown

Architect: C. F. W. Dening RWA FRIBA
Date: 1935[1]
Material: Portland stone
Dimensions: approx. 230cm high, 80cm wide
Contractor: William Cowlin and Son
Status: not listed
Owned by Land Securities
Condition: good

This five-storey office block was built as a speculative project by the Bristol builders and contractors William Cowlin and Son. At first the building was called the Tontine House. It succeeded tontine warehouses facing onto the Frome at St Augustine's Reach. Those warehouses had been completed in 1785 when 195 people invested money in the project on the tontine principle. After a specified period of

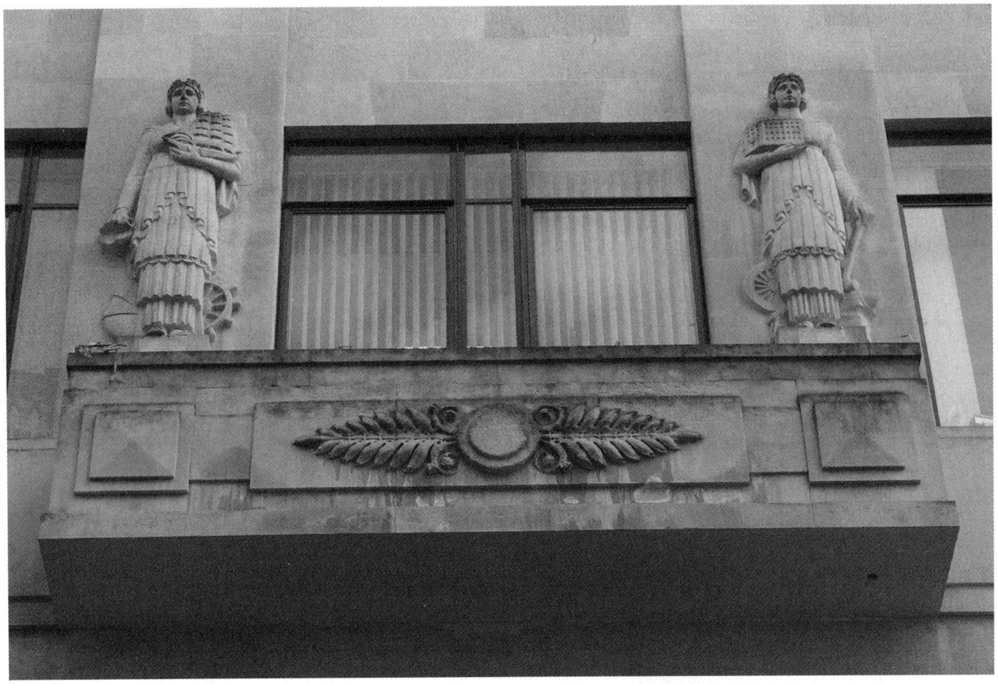

C. F. W. Dening, architect, *Figures on 55 St Stephen's Street*

time, the proceeds would have been divided among the investors or, alternatively, the last speculator left alive would have become the sole owner.[2]

The two figures in deep relief are on either side of a central second-floor window above a balcony and are directly above the original main entrance. They have laurel wreathes on their heads and wear several layers of fluted classical tunics. The left-hand figure holds a model of a three-masted sailing vessel and there is a ship's wheel at her feet and possibly also a globe. The other figure holds a model of an office block that is very similar to the one on which she stands. In her left hand a hammer rests on an anvil and to her right is a spinning wheel; these artefacts represent trade and manufacture, or perhaps enterprise and industry.

There is little sculpture of this period in Bristol. The Friends Provident building in Corn Street is one slightly earlier example, and Andrew Foyle suspects that Dening's late work may derive from Giles Gilbert Scott's façade and Hermon Cawthra's two figures.[3] However, the quality of Dening's much earlier Arts and Crafts houses in Westbury Park, the thoroughness of his pioneering book *The Eighteenth Century Architecture of Bristol* (published in 1923), and the quiet precision of this building imply considerable independence and originality.

A preparatory drawing of the St Stephen Street elevation indicates two female figures where the reliefs are sited, but neither the name of the sculptor or mason are given.[4]

Notes

[1] Foyle and Cherry, *Bristol*, p.131. [2] Greenacre, *From Bristol to the Sea*, pl. 69, p.68; see also Latimer, *Annals of Bristol*, p.151. [3] As note 1, p.137. [4] The plans are in BRO, vol. 140, folio 34.

Stapleton Road

Clifton Place Community Garden (Clifton Place Doorstep Green), beside Stapleton Road, Easton

Caterpillar and Woodlouse A19

Sculptor: Rodney Harris

Landscape architects: Reckless Orchard
Date: 2005
Materials: Staffordshire Blue Ibstock bricks with bands of yellow glaze on the caterpillar
Dimensions: caterpillar, 145cm long; woodlouse, 85cm diameter
Status: not listed
Owned by Bristol City Council
Condition: good

This small park was completed in 2005. Three years earlier, Easton had been identified as one of the first five policing priority areas in the country and it was visited by the home secretary, David Blunkett. A massive toilet block and telephone boxes on the site were being used openly for drug-dealing, and residents had for some years campaigned for their removal. A partnership between Bristol City Council and the Clifton Place Action Group, created from various local associations, was formed and a successful application to the Countryside Agency's Doorstep Greens initiative was made in May 2002. Work finally started at the end of 2004. Consultation with local residents took place, revealing substantial opposition to seating in the belief that it would encourage the return of alcoholics and drug users. This was to affect the design of the low wall surrounding the green along which Rod Harris's caterpillar crawls.

Policing priority areas (PPAs) are focused initiatives aimed at tackling high crime and anti-social behaviour, and promoting social cohesion. The style of policing delivered in PPAs is closely aligned with reassurance policing, including techniques like environmental visual audit, an emphasis on local engagement and establishing effective partnership working'.[1]

The Countryside Agency's report on the scheme, written in May 2005, 'hoped that a management plan, handing residents responsibility for the green's upkeep, will further strengthen their hold on the site'.[2] Three years on, the project has been an evident success although there may now be a problem with the continuity of commitment. There is no apparent vandalism or graffiti, but at the end of May 2008 the grass had yet to be cut for the first time that year and the flower beds, though packed and impressive, needed attention. The woodlouse could do with a gentle scrub to remove leaching, which is obscuring the detail; and it might now be discreetly raised up, so that the surrounding plants do not obscure so much of it.

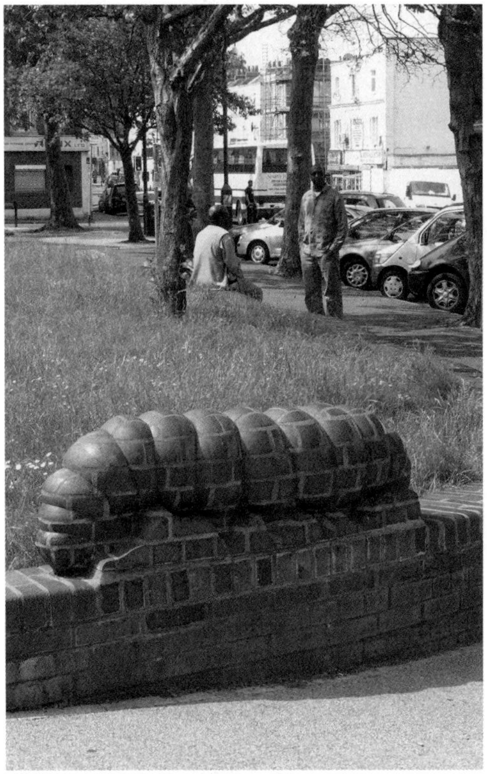

Rodney Harris, ***Caterpillar***

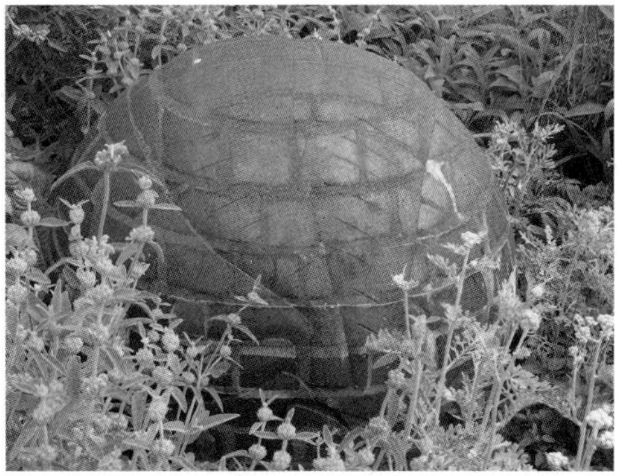

Rodney Harris, ***Woodlouse***

The caterpillar crawls along the wall at the eastern end of the green and the woodlouse rests, curled up, in the flowerbed at the opposite, western end. Both are made from Staffordshire Blue Ibstock bricks of the same colour as the surrounding wall. The Cinnabar moth's caterpillar, upon which the former work was based, is yellow and black and is often found on ragwort growing on derelict urban sites. However, the yellow glaze which has been applied to alternating segments of the caterpillar appears brown on the dark blue-grey bricks.

The sculptor has written:

> The idea of the curled up woodlouse, placed within a planting bed, came out of workshops... Symbolically its armour and form represent protection and the defensive strategies which can be seen as desirable supportive qualities in communities, families and individuals. The form and surface directly relate to the colour of woodlice and the nature of the brick walls used throughout the site... In contrast, the caterpillar idea, again the result of workshops, represents vulnerability and transformation, important themes to emerge from local people.[3]

It was the workshops that also inspired the incidentals details that can be found on the long, low surrounding wall. Fingers grip one brick as if hauling it into place from below, and there is a minaret and necklace and other personal items, encouraging that sense of ownership vital to the success of the project. On one brick is a familiar stylised female figure deliberately recalling the dreaded toilet block.

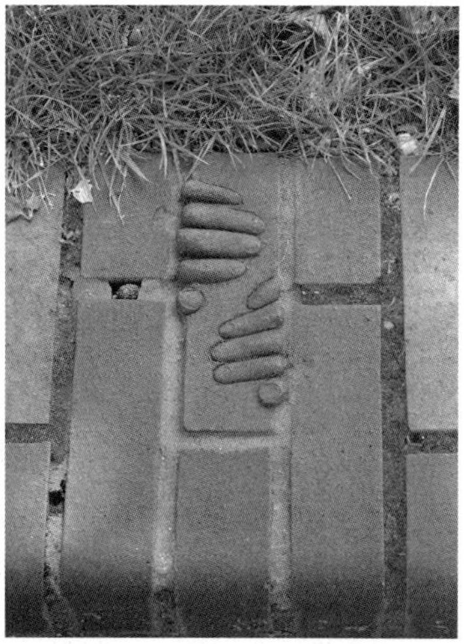

Rodney Harris, ***Brick surround*** **(detail)**

Barbara Disney's large floor mosaic at the juncture of the two halves of the green was unveiled in June 2006. Support and funding for the project as a whole came from the Countryside Agency, Big Lottery Fund, Easton and Lawrence Hill Neighbourhood Renewal, Safer Bristol, the European Union, Objective 2 Bristol and Bristol City Council.

The woodlouse was missing in August 2010.

Notes

[1] www.neighbourhoodpolicing.co.uk/faq.asp.
[2] www.countryside.gov.uk/LAR/Recreation/DG/casestudies. [3] www.jacksonharris.co.uk.

Stoke Hill

Portico to Stoke House, now Trinity College, Stoke Bishop

Entrance Portico A11

Sculptor: unknown

Date: 1669
Material: stone
Dimensions: approx. 6m high
Status: Grade II*
Owned by Trinity Theological College Bristol
Condition: good

The date of the completion of Stoke House, 1669, is recorded prominently in the pediment of the portico. The crisp detail of the numerals would suggest that they have been recut. So, too, has much of the moulding around the pediment and archway. But there is no reason to doubt the originality of the rest of this heavily sculpted entrance.

The portico is a particularly proud and flamboyant statement of the status of Sir Robert Cann (1624–85). A contemporary described him as a 'somewhat arrogant and pompous personage, fond of parading his riches'.[1] Angels with trumpets support Sir Robert's coat of arms beneath a baronet's coronet. He was a staunch royalist and a Bristol merchant with plantations in North America and the West Indies. He was high sheriff of Gloucestershire in 1651, master of the Merchant Venturers in 1658 and mayor of Bristol in 1662, when Charles II briefly visited the city while taking the waters at Bath. Cann, already a knight, accepted a baronetcy a few days later. His status evidently deeply concerned him. As a baronet he claimed precedence in council over more senior aldermen, and he foolishly petitioned the throne. He was duly reprimanded but he was to be mayor again in 1675 and MP for Bristol from 1678.

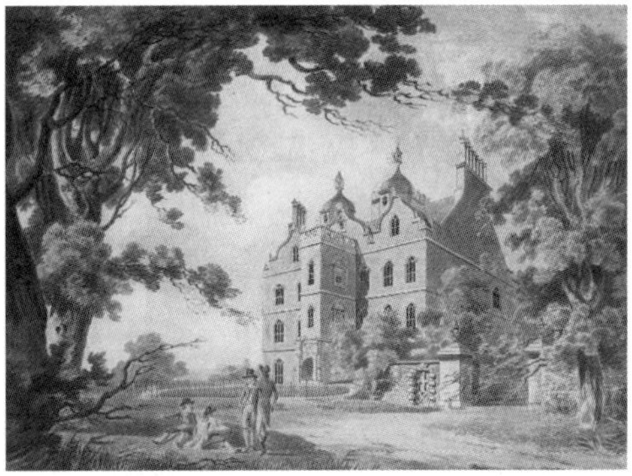

***J. M. W. Turner's watercolour of Stoke House,* 1791, private collection**

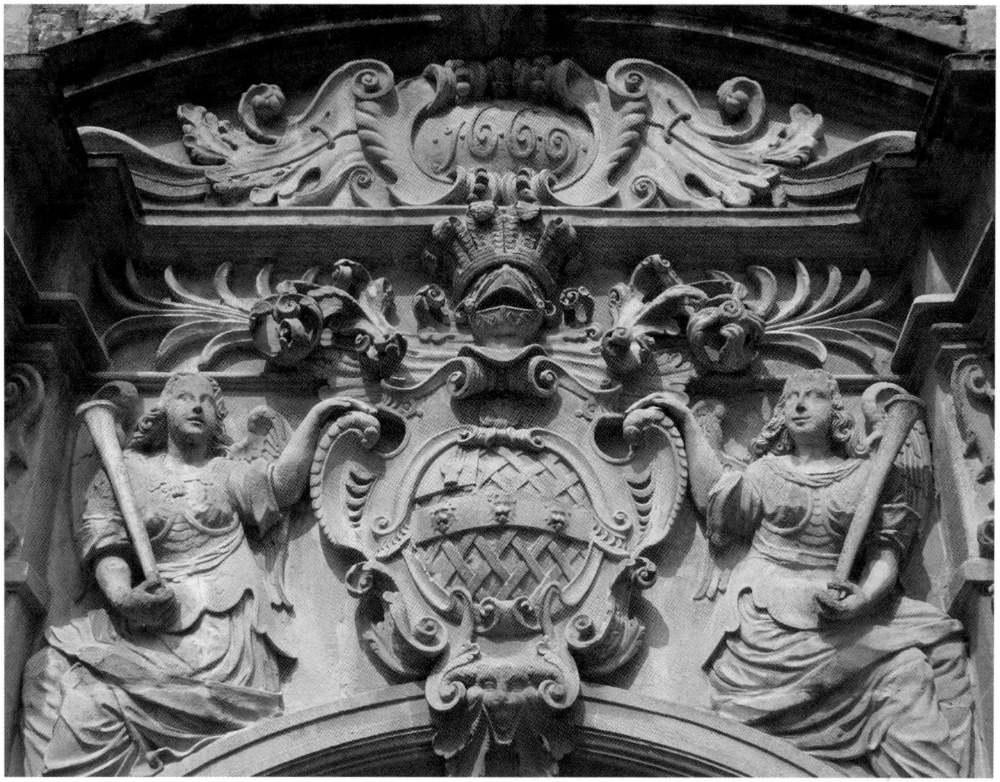

Stoke House Entrance Portico

J. M. W. Turner drew the front of Stoke House in 1791. He was then a sixteen-year-old student on holiday from the Royal Academy Schools, but he was already an exceptional architectural draughtsman.[2] His drawing is likely to be an accurate record. The portico was much as it is today, although the curved pediment may well have had a broken arch making it more obviously baroque that it now appears. It certainly lacked the lion that now presides above it. Turner's watercolour reveals that the façade was once stuccoed and had eighteenth-century Gothic windows.

Notes
[1] Nicholls and Taylor, *Bristol Past and Present*, pp.52–6; www.trinity-bris.ac.uk/index.php?id=121.
[2] *View of Stoke House, Near Bristol*, 1791, watercolour, Sotheby's, 11 11 1997 (37); Anthony Beeson, 'The genuine English tradesman', *Bristol Review of Books*, Autumn 2008, issue 7; E. Croft-Murray, 'An unpublished early watercolour by J.M.W. Turner: Cote House', *The Burlington Magazine*, vol. 90, no. 541, April 1948, pp.107–9.

At the bottom of Stoke Hill opposite the shops

Jubilee Fountain A10

Designer: unknown

Date: 1897
Materials: marble fountain and wooden surround
Dimensions: approx. 6m high
Inscribed: PRESENTED TO STOKE BISHOP IN MEMORY OF THE 60TH YEAR OF QUEEN VICTORIA'S REIGN BY FRANCIS TAGART OF OLD SNEED PARK
Status: Grade II
Owned by Bristol City Council
Condition: fair; fountain defunct

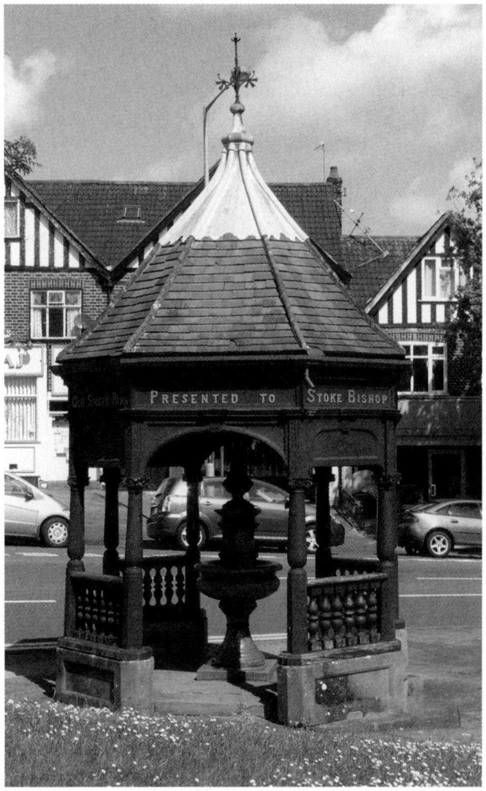

Jubilee Fountain, Stoke Hill

Francis Tagart JP, DL was the donor of this fountain and shelter, which celebrated the diamond jubilee of Queen Victoria's reign. He lived at Old Sneed Park. This seventeenth-century mansion was surrounded by a large estate that only began to diminish in size after an act of Parliament in 1853. By Francis Tagart's day, perhaps half of the estate – that part closest to Durdham Down – had been developed with substantial later Victorian houses. Much remained, however, and the gift of the fountain was the generous gesture of the lord of the manor and one of Her Majesty's deputy lord lieutenants for the county of Gloucestershire.

Sir George White, the great transport entrepreneur and founder of Bristol's aircraft industry, owned and lived at Old Sneed Park for two years before his death in 1916. The estate was to be sold in the 1920s and today only the lodges remain.[1]

Note
[1] Sneyd Park Residents' Association, *Sneyd Park: A Local Study and Guided Walk* (2001).

Stoke Park, Stoke Gifford

A motorway now carves its way through Stoke Park, 'reckon'd among the finest things in England' in the eighteenth century.[1] Rather than destroying a landscape of considerable historical significance, the motorway may yet have saved it. The spectacular situation of the mansion, with views across the park to the distant city, has become familiar to millions. Recent scholarship and archaeology have also done much to reveal the significance of the site as a whole. Its deterioration continues, however, and in July 2008 Stoke Park's position on English Heritage's Register of England's Historic Environment at Risk was confirmed.

In 1815, Matthews's *Bristol Guide* stated that Stoke Park's 'spacious Woods, Temples, and Monuments... may be justly stiled a terrestial paradise'.[2] Between 1750 and 1768, the close friendship of Norborne Berkeley, Baron Botetort, with Thomas Wright, the astronomer, landscape gardener and architect, had led to the substantial remodelling of the house and to the extensive landscaping of the park. Today, the most visible evidence of these changes are the house itself, now a print-room yellow, and the lake, known as Duchess Pond. This was drained in 1968 during the building of the M32, but subsequently reinstated as a result of local initiatives.[3]

Of Thomas Wright's many park buildings and monuments, only the obelisk and the sarcophagus survive – just. Among many lost features were a domed temple or rotunda with ten ionic columns, and an eye-catcher based on a mausoleum at Albano near Rome, known as the tomb of the Horatii and Curiatii. Both features were completed around 1756. David Lambert and Stewart Harding have drawn attention to the earnestness of this 'distinctly classical landscape', once dominated by the temple, the tomb, the obelisk and the Horatii monument, as well as to the cultivated sophistication of Norborne Berkeley himself.[4] There were also once a Gothic eye-catcher, a root house and a ruined castle, as well as tunnels and a cascade.

The Berkeley family had held the manor for four centuries until Norborne Berkeley's death, unmarried, in 1770. When his sister, the widow of the fourth Duke of Beaufort, died in 1799, the management of the estate, now part of the Beaufort estates, was overseen from Badminton. In 1907 the Stoke Park estate was first leased and then purchased by Reverend Harold Burden, who developed a pioneering hospital for the mentally handicapped at Stoke Park. The hospital and the parkland were sold by the Phoenix NHS Trust in 1985.

Bristol's county boundary passes through the obelisk, but the sarcophagus is within South Gloucestershire, which receives council tax revenues from the vast new housing estate within the park. South Gloucestershire is currently considering still further housing within the corridor between Stoke Gifford and the two motorways. On February 26 2009, Bristol City Council's cabinet agreed in principle to the acquisition of Stoke Park from the consortium of developers, including George Wimpey and Barratt Homes, that owns the land. The transfer has yet to be completed (July 2010). It is surely that authority, which is already managing substantial estates near its boundaries including Ashton Court, Kings Weston, Blaise and Oldbury Court, that should now take over the ownership and the more responsible management of the remaining parkland.

Stoke Park, near the summit of Star Hill

Obelisk Commemorating Lady Elizabeth Somerset A6

Architect: Thomas Wright

Date: c.1760 and 2004
Materials: Bath stone (white lias slabs faced with dressed slabs of oolitic limestone)
Dimensions: base, 2.53m square, 4.3m high; original total height with obelisk, 16m
Inscription on modern plaque of Irish slate: ELIZABETHA SOMERSET / CAROLL DUCIS BEAUFORT / FILIA SECUNDA HIC OBIIT VII / MAII MDCCLX / RESTITUTUM ANNO / MMIV
Status: Grade II
Owner: Stoke Park Consortium
Condition: plinth rebuilt 2004

The monument commemorates Lady Elizabeth Somerset, daughter of the fourth Duke of Beaufort. She died after a fall from her horse near this spot on 7 May 1760. Norborne Berkeley, who commissioned the monument and owned Stoke Park, was Lady Elizabeth's uncle; his sister had married the future fourth Duke of Beaufort.

In 1764, Bishop Pococke wrote a full and most valuable account of his visit to Stoke Park:

> We then proceeded to an Obelisc of Bath Stone seated on an Eminence. It is fixed on a Pedestal adorn'd with rustic Work, and ye top crown'd with a gilt Star. It was erected to ye honour of his Lordship's Neice who died here.[5]

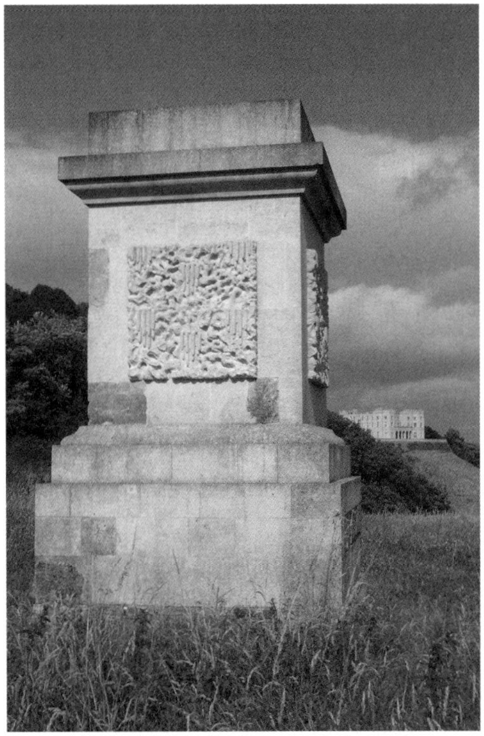

Thomas Wright, architect, *Memorial to Lady Elizabeth Somerset*

There is mention of plans for an obelisk in a notebook of Norborne Berkeley's dating from around 1750. This has led to speculation that the obelisk could have been erected before 1760, the year of Lady Elizabeth's death, and that the inscription was simply added soon afterwards.[6] Even if this did happen, it is likely that Thomas Wright was the designer. The gilded star that was once on the top of the obelisk 'seems a typical touch'.[7] Wright was a distinguished astronomer, a member of the Royal Society, and in 1750 he had published *An Original Theory of the Universe*, famous for its novel understanding of the Milky Way.

The obelisk was still intact in the 1920s, but by 1988 had been reduced to a third of its original height of approximately sixteen metres. Permission for the development of the Stoke Park estate was made conditional on the partial restoration of the house and the remaining park and monuments. Under the supervision of Simon Pugh-Jones of Barton Willmore, the reconstruction of the obelisk's plinth was excellently carried out by St Blaise of Dorchester and completed in 2004.

We know that the stonemason, Francis Grinway of nearby Mangotsfield, was the builder of the temple or rotunda at Stoke Park in 1756.[8] He would have belonged to the dynasty from which Francis Greenway, the architect of the Clifton Assembly Rooms and the so-called father of Australian architecture, was to come. We know also that Thomas Paty, the Bristol architect, builder and sculptor, was working on the house itself in 1760. A recent book on the Patys states that Thomas's elder brother, James Paty II, was actually in charge, but the evidence is not given.[9] Any of the three craftsmen could have been the builder of the obelisk or of the sarcophagus.

Stoke Park, within Barn Wood

Sarcophagus Commemorating Charles, Fourth Duke of Beaufort A7

Architect: Thomas Wright

Date: c.1756
Materials: Bath stone
Dimensions: approx. 8m high, 11m long
Recut in new and old stone, 1988: FRATERNI DIGNUS AMORIS
Status: not listed
Owner: Stoke Park Consortium
Condition: poor; at risk

It is Bishop Pococke's recently discovered account of his visit to Stoke Park in 1764 that

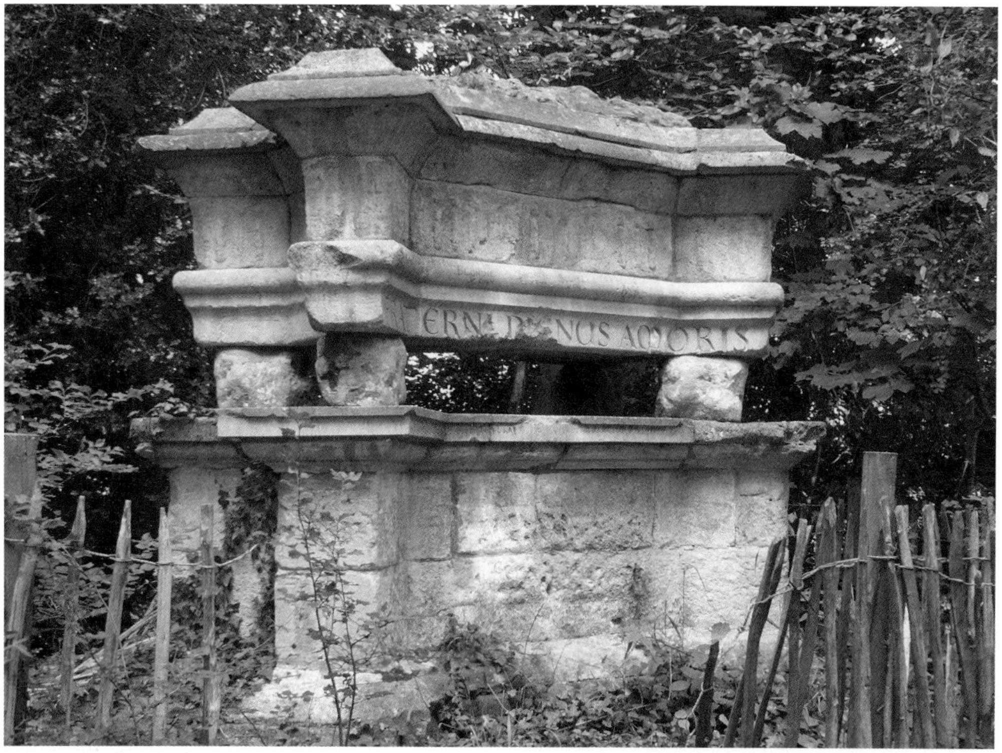

Thomas Wright, architect, *Memorial to Charles, Duke of Beaufort*

has led to the attribution of this monument to Thomas Wright and to the rediscovery of its original function.[10] Rather than celebrating an early nineteenth-century winner of the St Leger, the sarcophagus commemorates Norborne Berkeley's brother-in-law, Charles, fourth Duke of Beaufort, who died in 1756.[11]

> We then crossed over ye West Side of ye House, and crossing a Lawn came to a Wood with winding Walks – at ye Enterence of which, is a kind of sepulchral Monument on a basement, ye former being adorn'd with a frieze, of ye Doric order, and has on it this Inscription, (viz) Fraterni Dignus Amoris – being erected to ye honour of ye late Duke of Beaufort, who married Ld Botetort's only sister.[12]

The death of the fourth duke led to the realisation that the Badminton estate as a whole was very heavily in debt. The duke's substantial patronage of both Rysbrack and Canaletto would have been a minor contributing factor.[13] Norborne Berkeley was the principal trustee, and he worked very hard to reduce the Beaufort family's debts, a task continued successfully on his death by his sister, the dowager duchess. It was on her death in 1799 that Stoke Park passed to the Beauforts.

The monument was restored by the Avon Gardens Trust in 1988, a courageous move that certainly saved the structure and did much to encourage recognition of the importance and potential of the park. Alarmingly, only twenty years later, it is already seriously deteriorating and is subject to vandalism. It urgently needs to be rebuilt once again. It should also be made very much more visible, perhaps following Pococke's own description, which implies that it was close to an open 'Lawn' and at the start of a winding walk, rather than surrounded by trees and undergrowth as it is now.

Notes

[1] Bishop Pococke, 1764, quoted by S. Harding and D. Lambert, 'Thomas Wright at Stoke Park', *Garden History*, vol. 17, no. 1, 1989, pp.68–82; the information below is largely drawn from this article and from J.R. Russell, *Three Garden Buildings by Thomas Wright in Stoke Park, Bristol: Excavation and Fieldwork 1987–88* (Bristol, 1988) and Harding and Lambert, *Parks and Gardens of Avon* (Bristol, 1994). [2] Harding and Lambert, as note 1, p.68. [3] Duchess Lake Fishing Syndicate and the Stoke Park Restoration Trust. [4] Harding and Lambert, as note 1, pp.76–7. [5] quoted in full by Harding and Lambert, op. cit., fn. 9, pp.81–2; Pococke also records the inscription, confirming the mistake on the recent replacement plaque where CAROLI has become CAROLL. [6] Op. cit., p.72. [7] Ibid. [8] Russell, as note 1, p.2; Harding and Lambert, as note 1, p.75. [9] Priest, *The Paty Family*, p.34. [10] Harding and Lambert, as note 1, pp.72–3. [11] Pevsner, *Gloucestershire*, p.350. [12] Harding and Lambert, as note 1, fn. 9, p.82. [13] Eustace, *Michael Rysbrack*, pp.148–59.

Stoke Road, Durdham Down

On the right-hand side of Stoke Road in front of the water tower

Drinking Fountain A12

Architect: John Henry Hirst

Date: 1877

Materials: Bath stone with Portland stone plinth and Mansfield, pennant and granite dressings and cast iron animal heads

Dimensions: 650cm high, 420cm wide, 210cm deep

Inscription on the splash-back stone, above the basin, in light sans-serif capitals: GEO. W. EDWARDS ESQ[RE] / MAYOR / A.D.1877 / C B HARE ESQ[RE] / MASTER OF THE SOCIETY OF / MERCHANT / VENTURERS

Status: Grade II

Owned by Bristol City Council

Condition: fair

In 1874, the Bath and West of England Agricultural Society held its annual show on Durdham Down. The money taken at the gates was nearly £1,800 more than at any previous venue, and this massive fountain, erected by the Downs Committee, was a consequence of these unprecedented profits. The organising agricultural society had been founded in 1777 as the Bath Agricultural Society; today, it is the Royal Bath and West of England Agricultural Society with a permanent showground near Shepton Mallet.

This tall fountain has something of the appearance of a cenotaph or large stele. Five varieties of stone are employed.[1] Faced with Bath stone ashlar, it is rectangular in plan and elevation, with a heavy cornice and truncated pediment. The tympanum contains a much-eroded relief of the coat of arms of the city of Bristol in the same stone. Beneath the cornice is a polished red granite frieze on three sides. In keeping with the fountain's agricultural origins, this frieze is decorated with the heads of farm animals in cast iron, painted matt terracotta. The narrow west and east ends each have a single ram's head with curled horns. The main facade has three heads: from left to right, a bull, a horse and a cow. The drinking fountain in the façade is contained in an arch formed by deep semi-circular moulding of Mansfield stone that runs on three sides. Above the fountain arch is a grey keystone, carved as a scallop shell. The marble splash-back plaque displays the inscription. A semi-circular red granite basin projects from the front of the Portland stone plinth and set into both ends in semi-circular arches are water troughs for animals. None are at present in use. A door at the rear provides access, presumably to a water tank. It is surrounded by pennant stone paving.

An early minute book of the Downs Committee records that in September 1874, following the success of the agricultural show (which had covered some 38 acres of Durdham Down), the Council of the Bath and West of England Agricultural Society sent a cheque for £100 for 'improving Durdham Down as a popular Recreation Ground'.[2] Further cheques for £73.16s 4p and £104 17s 4p from the society were reported in January and December 1875, and this money was specified as intended for a drinking fountain.[3] In August 1876, the Downs Committee's surveyor, Mr Ashmead, was instructed to organise designs and estimates and the committee were soon requesting alterations to plans by J. H. Hirst, the Bristol architect of the Royal West of England Academy.[4] A legacy of £100 from Alderman Proctor was reported in December 1876, and this was also put towards the fountain. By July 1877 the work was complete, with the exception of the lettering.[5]

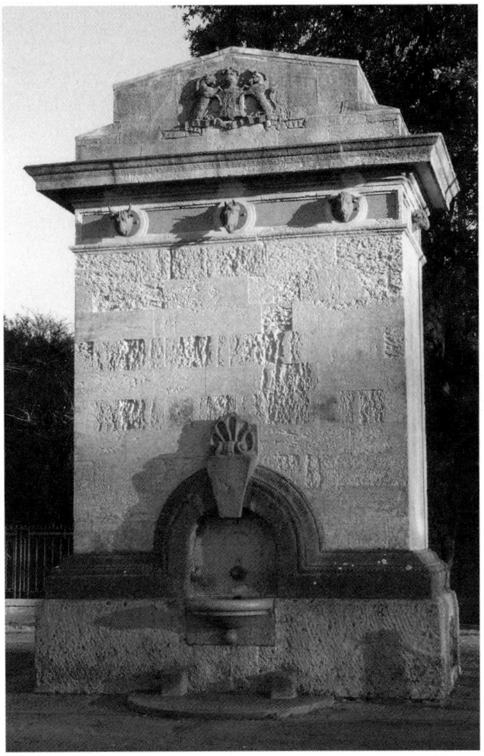

J. H. Hirst, architect, *Durdham Down Drinking Fountain*

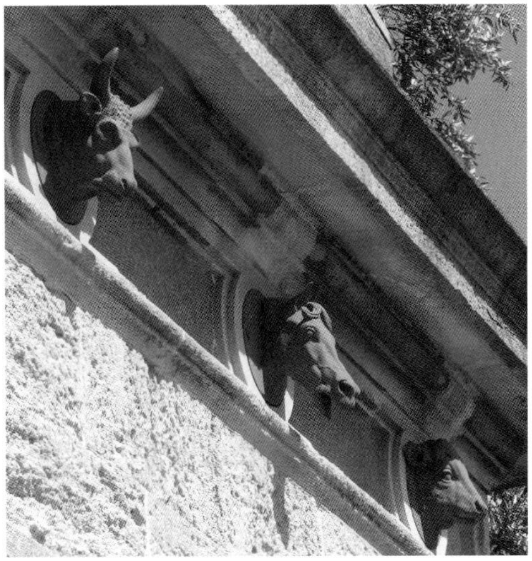

Cast-iron animal heads

The owners of Clifton Down (the Society of Merchant Venturers) and of Durdham Down (Bristol City Council) together obtained the Clifton and Durdham Downs (Bristol) Act of 1861. This ensured that the Downs 'shall evermore be kept open and unenclosed as a place of public resort'.[6] The act established the Downs Committee of councillors and merchant venturers with obligations to manage the Downs for the benefit of the citizens of Bristol. This involved, as it does today, the balancing of conflicting interests. The Bath and West of England Agricultural Society's show of 1874, whose success lead to the building of this fountain, was succeeded in 1878 by the Royal Agricultural Society's show on Durdham Down, opened in July by the Prince of Wales, the future Edward VII.[7] There were over 120,000 visitors. Delicate negotiations with the commoners of Durdham Down, who had the right to graze sheep there, had to precede all these events. It had not been forgotten that the downs had survived because they originally formed the commons of two medieval manors, and the manorial tenants had the right to turn out animals to pasture on the uncultivated commons.[8] In the 1870s there were still between 300 and 400 sheep pastured there.[9] Although the grazing of sheep was to end in 1925, the commoners still carefully maintain their rights today. This rather cumbersome fountain is a moving reminder not only of the early years of the downs as a public park, but also of its medieval origins and the reasons for the survival of this unique open space so close to a major city centre.

Conservation work on the fountain, funded by Bristol City Council, was undertaken in 1998.[10] Structural repairs were made to the upper levels of the stonework. The whole fountain was cleaned, the animal heads were secured and repainted and their stone roundels were repaired. A land drain was dug around the footings of the monument.

Notes
[1] English Heritage Bristol: Listed BuildingsDatabase, 901-1/34/1822, p.1527. [2] BRO M/BCC/DOW/1/1 Downs Committee Minute Book, p.341. [3] Op. cit., pp.353, 380. [4] Op. cit., pp.399, 400, 402. [5] Op. cit., pp.409, 425. [6] G. Nichols, *'To Keep Open and Unenclosed': The Management of Durdham Down Since 1861* (Bristol, 2005). [7] Nicholls and Taylor, *Bristol Past and Present*, vol. III, p.354. [8] E. Ralph, *The Downs, Bristol* (Bristol, 1973). [9] Nichols and Taylor, as note 7. [10] Gary Reeder, Senior Conservation Officer; letter to PMSA 14 October 1998. Reeder stated that the heads are cast iron and not terracotta, as described on the Downs notice boards and the English Heritage Listed Building citation.

Suspension Bridge Road

On the Downs, facing Sion Place

Drinking Fountain B17

Designers: Walter MacFarlane & Co

Date: 1866
Dimensions: Cast iron drinking fountain with bronze relief panels; pedestal in Hoptonwood stone; base steps, granite
Dimensions: 240cm high, 85cm square
Foundry: Walter MacFarlane & Co., Saracen Foundry, Possilpark, Glasgow.
Inscription raised in the casting, in sans-serif capitals; on the north and south-facing sides: COMING / TO THEE / THAT WE MAY DRINK, AND LIVE, AMEN. / JN. XV 26 & VII .37 – on the shield to the north: TO THE GLORY OF/GOD / IN THE USE OF/MAN & BEAST – on the shield to the south: THE / RECEIVER TO THE GIVERS / EVER SO / MAY WE GO – on the west-facing side: JESU, / LIKE STREAMS, FROM GOD THY / SPIRIT / GIVE – on the shield a three-letter monogram: M C B – on the east side the text is as on the west side, but the arms of Bristol are on the shield.
Status: Grade II
Owned by Bristol City Council
Condition: fair

This cast iron drinking fountain was erected in 1866 near the approach road to the Clifton Suspension Bridge, which had been opened just two years earlier. It was also, as it is today, next to the path up to the spectacular viewpoints by the Clifton Observatory.

The elaborate square cast iron structure has a domed canopy supported on four columns. It is decorated with biblical texts and other verses, and is presently painted a dark green. Two square, grey granite steps form the base. The fountain was a stock item with minor alterations, and the standard version was illustrated in the company's brochure as MacFarlane's Patent No. 8 Drinking Fountain, priced at £27 10s. On the standard version there was the exhortation KEEP THE PAVEMENT DRY rather than biblical texts. Eight of these standard fountains were exported from Glasgow to Sydney in 1870.[1] The main parts of the casting are the same as the much later and more ornate drinking fountain on The Green at Shirehampton, Bristol. At Shirehampton, the original basin and fountainhead, which is surmounted by a heron, have been preserved, although the structure lacks the four griffins at the top corners, which have happily survived at Clifton. The Shirehampton fountain was erected to commemorate Queen Victoria's diamond jubilee in 1897, and it bears her portrait and is topped by a crown.[2]

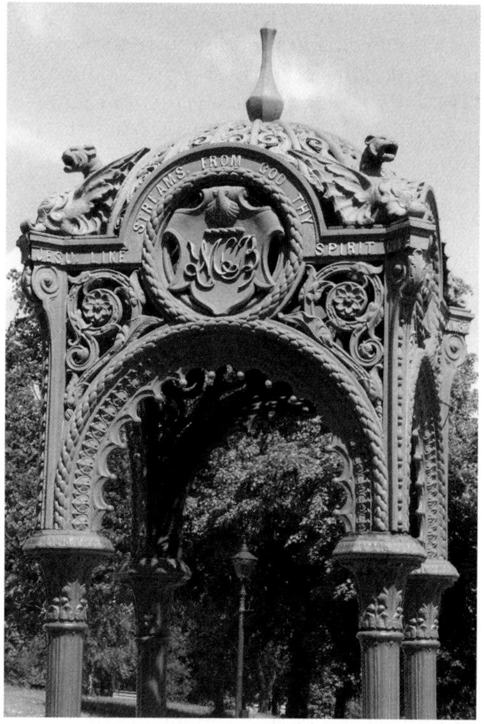

Walter MacFarlane & Co, *Suspension Bridge Road Drinking Fountain*

Walter MacFarlane & Co, *Shirehampton Drinking Fountain* (detail)

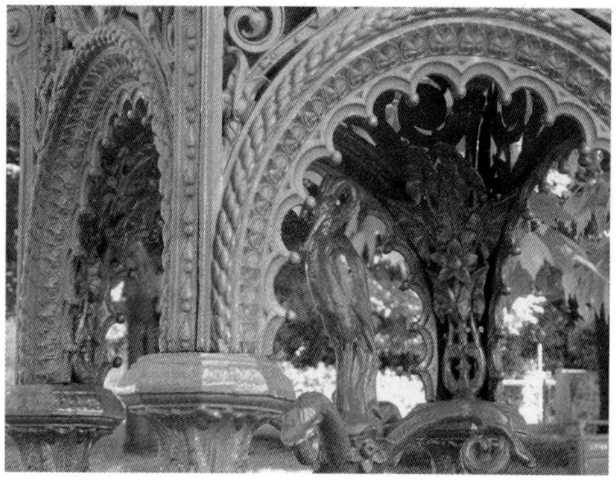

The donor of the Clifton fountain, Reverend Mourant Brock, was an 'eloquent preacher and one of the lights of the Evangelical School in the West of England', and he was the vicar of nearby Christ Church.[3] He was:

> fond of denouncing the Yellow Clay, by which term he described wealth, but he was not only one of the most persistent beggars... including some thousands of pounds for providing a tower and spire... but by no means averse to his oldest son and four of his daughters making some of the best matches available... He was very dramatic and sensational in his pulpit utterances and attitudes... He was very neat and precise in his costume, wearing quite the latest cut of low church clerical attire... he was somewhat arrogant and dictatorial and had a great sense of his own importance and position.[4]

At a meeting in July 1866, the Downs Committee agreed to the Reverend Brock's request 'to erect a fountain on the Down near the Clifton Hotel', subject to the approval of a special subcommittee and of the Society of Merchant Venturers, owners of the land.[5]

By 1982, the original fountain system had gone and the present 'modern column-type fountain with push button tap in the centre of the structure' was in place.[6] The condition was described as 'good' and the fountain was operational.[7] By 1998, all pipe work and drinking facilities had gone and there was no water supply. All the functional parts are now missing.

Notes

[1] www.cityofsydney.nsw.gov.au/waterexhibition/DrinkingPlaces/CastIronDrinkingFountains.html. [2] Illus. pls 125, 127, 8 in E. Thomas, *Shirehampton Story* (Avonmouth, 1983); Shirehampton had celebrated Queen Victoria's golden jubilee in 1887 by planting a *Wellingtonia Gigantea*, and today the fountain is in its shade. [3] A.B. Freeman, *Bristol Worthies and Notable Residents in the District*, (Bristol, 1909), pp.17–8; the Christian name of Mourant Brock's wife was Catherine, and the monogram on the fountain, MCB, implies that they were joint donors. [4] Ibid. [5] BRO M/BCC/DOW/1/1, p.140. [6] BCC Engineers' Department, *Memorials, Fountains and Statues*, p.17. [7] Ibid.

In the rock face on the north side of the road, 35 metres from the bridge's pier, Suspension Bridge Road

Brunel Centenary Plaque B18

Sculptor: A. W. Banks

Architect: Ralph Edwards
Date: 1959
Materials: bronze portrait on Westmoreland green slate
Dimensions: 150cm high, 45cm deep
Inscription in gilded Roman capitals: ISAMBARD KINGDOM BRUNEL / 9th APRIL 1806 15th SEPTEMBER 1859 / THIS TABLET WAS SET UP BY / THE CLIFTON SUSPENSION BRIDGE TRUST / 15th SEPTEMBER 1959 /
Status: Grade I (not itemised)
Owned by the Clifton Suspension Bridge Trust
Condition: good

The Clifton Suspension Bridge was finally finished in 1864, five years after Isambard Kingdom Brunel's death and 34 years after he had first designed it. It was deliberately brought to completion as a memorial to the great engineer. In 1959, one hundred years after Brunel's death, the Clifton Suspension Bridge Trust set up this additional tribute.[1]

The Westmoreland green slate tablet is incised with an inscription in well cut gold-leaf-filled lettering. On the left side of the inscription, set in an indented rectangle, is a small bronze relief by A. W. Banks. This is a full-face portrait of Isambard Kingdom Brunel in later life.

The location chosen for the Clifton Suspension Bridge Trust plaque was an outcrop of rock close to the tollgate on the Clifton side of the bridge. The wall-mounted plaque was unveiled by Brunel's granddaughter, the Dowager Lady Noble, on 15 September 1959, the exact anniversary.[2] In his opening address Edmund Poole King, the chairman of the trustees, described the bridge as 'a concept of

A. W. Banks, *Brunel Centenary Plaque*

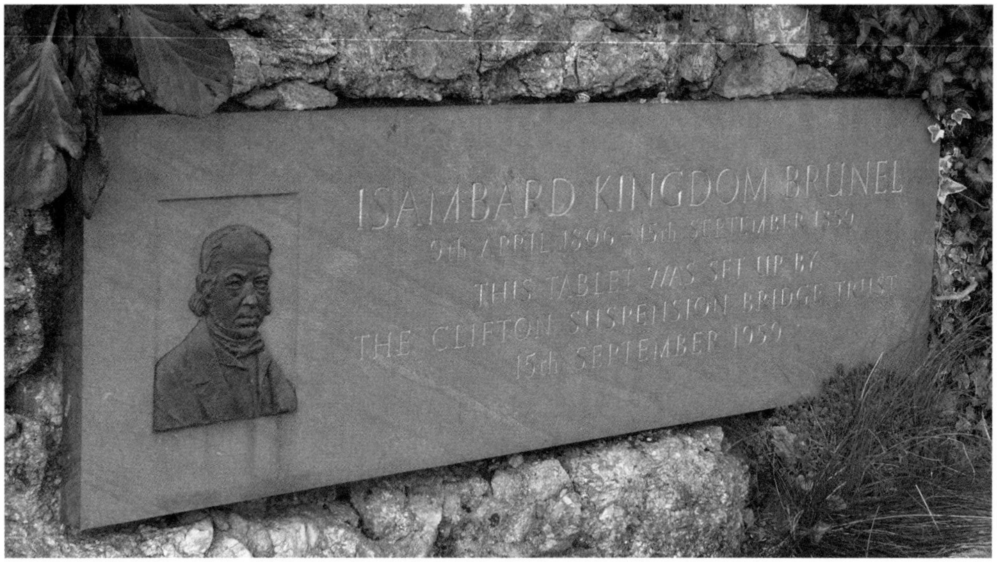

the greatest vision and in its completion it remains a very remarkable feat of engineering for all time'.[3] Professor A. J. Sutton Pippard, president of the Institution of Civil Engineers, gave the centenary address. He foresaw that Brunel would rank among the greatest of the engineering profession. Dignitaries and invited guests were later entertained at the Merchant Venturers' Hall on Clifton Down.[4] The Society of Merchant Venturers' association with the bridge dates from 1753, when William Vick, a Bristol wine merchant, left £1,000 to the care of the society with instructions that, when the sum reached £10,000 through compound interest, a bridge should be erected over the Avon from Clifton to Leigh Woods.

Today, nearly fifty years after the unveiling of the plaque and a couple of years after the bicentenary celebrations of Brunel's birth, the plaque might seem somewhat superfluous were it not now immediately above a small garden planted in 2006 with rare plants from the Avon Gorge. In July 2007, just below Brunel's relief portrait, autumn squill (*Scilla autumnalis*) was in full flower. It had been thought that the building of the Clifton pier to the bridge in the 1830s had obliterated this especially rare plant. When it was rediscovered in 1888, a tale of pioneering conservation emerged. Brunel had been warned by Mrs Glennie, the wife of his principle engineer, of the destruction he was about to cause. In response, he ordered his workmen to remove the bulb-laden turf to almost inaccessible parts of the cliff face.[5]

Notes

[1] Bristol Central Library, sculpture cuttings file, unveiling ceremony programme. [2] Ibid. [3] Text of the opening address at the unveiling. [4] As note 1. [5] Greenacre, *From Bristol to the Sea*, p.44.

Temple Back East

In front of the Osborne Clarke offices

Isambard Kingdom Brunel C73

Sculptor: John Doubleday

Date: 1982
Materials: statue, bronze; pedestal, dark grey aggregate blocks
Dimensions: 225cm high, 85cm wide by 65cm deep at base; pedestal, 40cm high, 95cm square
Foundry: The Art Bronze Foundry, Fulham, London
Inscriptions: signed – ISAMBARD / KINGDOM / BRUNEL / Doubleday sculpt / THE ART BRONZE FOUNDRY. LONDON. 1982
–: on the former plinth – ISAMBARD/KINGDOM/ BRUNEL/1806–1859
–: a bronze plaque on the pedestal read – ISAMBARD / KINGDOM / BRUNEL / 1806 – 1859 / PRESENTED TO / THE CITIZENS OF BRISTOL / BY / BRISTOL AND WEST / BUILDING SOCIETY UNVEILED / BY THE LORD MAYOR OF BRISTOL / COUNCILOR GEORGE MAGGS / 26TH MAY 1982 / SCULPTOR JOHN DOUBLEDAY
–: at the present site an anodised metal plate reads – This statue of the great engineer, Isambard Kingdom Brunel, which was/ presented to Bristol by the Bristol and West Building Society, was/created by John Doubleday, and first unveiled on 26th May 1982. It was/moved from its original site at Broad Quay in 2006, the bi-centenary of/Brunel's birth./ Not only does it now front the modern offices of Osborne Clarke, the/firm of solicitors who did much of Brunel's legal work but also/waymarks the new, additional access to Brunel's great station, created/with the development of Temple Quay. Another statue of Brunel, by the/same artist, is located at Paddington Station, the eastern end of his/great railway.
Status: not listed
Owned by Osborne Clarke
Condition: good

Isambard Kingdom Brunel (1806–59) was an engineer of international importance and renown. He worked throughout Britain, but it was in Bristol that particular advantage was taken of his genius. The Great Western Railway between London and Bristol, so vital to Bristol's continued prosperity, opened in 1841. The pioneering steam-ships *Great Western* and *Great Britain* were launched in Bristol in 1837 and 1843, and the Clifton Suspension Bridge, designed in 1831, was vital to the development of his career. This ambitious and innovative masterpiece was finally completed in 1864, five years after Brunel's death, as a memorial to him. L. T. C. Rolt, Brunel's outstanding biographer, wrote: 'more surely than any lineaments in stone or pigment, the aspiring flight of its single splendid span has immortalised the spirit of the man who conceived it'.[1]

John Doubleday's standing figure of Brunel makes reference to contemporary photographs of the engineer, in particular to those taken by Robert Howlett in 1857 depicting Brunel at Wapping, London, against the massive chains of the *Great Eastern* steam-ship. The sculptor includes links of these anchor chains, although they look more like giant pretzels. Brunel's left foot rests on a section of riveted metal and his left hand is thrust into his trouser pocket. His clothes are crumpled and he wears a stovepipe hat, with winged collar, waistcoat and frock coat. The walking stick in Brunel's right hand is not characteristic of the engineer, and this prop inadvertently recalls Doubleday's London statue of Charlie Chaplin.

Andrew Breach, the chairman of the Bristol and West Building Society – which had sponsored the statue of Charlie Chaplin in Leicester Square in 1981 – was the driving force behind the commission for the statue of Brunel. When Charles Morgan, the joint general manager of the Society, announced the decision to erect the Brunel statue in April 1981, he said:

> There is only a plaque near the Clifton Suspension Bridge, so we decided that nothing could be more suitable. Brunel was

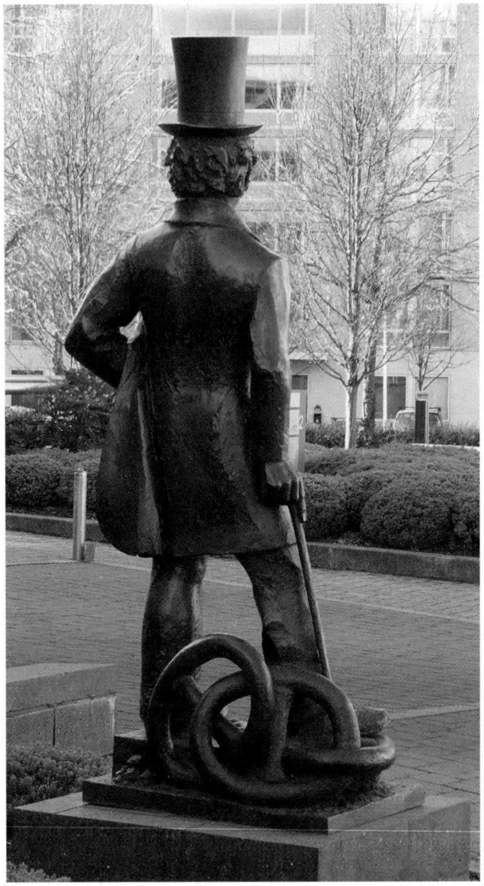

John Doubleday, *Isambard Kingdom Brunel*

> at the height of his creative powers when he worked in Bristol.[2]

The society wished to mark the completion of a new extension to its head office in 1982 by making this statue a gift to the people of Bristol.[3]

In this unusual project, the Bristol and West Building Society commissioned two statues: a standing figure for Bristol, and a companion seated figure of Brunel for Paddington railway station. Both were to be by the same sculptor. 'It will probably be the first time that two statues of the same person by the same sculptor will have been unveiled on the same day – Wednesday 26 May 1982.'[4] 'Nobody would have been more pleased than Brunel himself with the arrangement, with the ceremonies less than three hours apart.'[5] The London version, then on the concourse called the 'lawn', was unveiled at 10.45am by the Lord Mayor of Westminster, Councillor Thomas Whipham, after Andrew Breach had formally presented the work to Leslie Lloyd, general manager of the western region. Breach and Lloyd then travelled on an InterCity 125 to Bristol, where at 1.30pm the Lord Mayor, Councillor George Maggs, tugged the cord to unveil the Bristol statue.[6]

> As the figure slowly emerged, there was at first a gasp, then tentative tittering… but fortunately those who evidently found it all a bit comical pulled themselves together and the moment passed.[7]

A book on Brunel's work in Bristol was commissioned and sponsored by Bristol and West to coincide with the double unveiling.[8] The cost of the statue was said to be 'around £10,000'.[9]

Following the merger of the Bristol and West Building Society with the Bank of Ireland Group in 1997, subsequent proposals for the redevelopment of the Broad Quay site prompted a search for a new location for the statue. This reawakened some of the earlier and sharply divided opinion on the statue's artistic merit. The chairman of Bristol Civic Society was provoked into proposing 'that the statue is melted down and recast in correct human proportions… his statue from the start has been an insult'.[10]

The ultimate solution was particularly apt on two counts. Firstly, the statue was taken on by Osborne Clarke, the Bristol-based firm of solicitors, which, as Osborne Ward, had been appointed solicitors to the Great Western Railway Company in 1835. Secondly, the statue's plinth was made substantially smaller, and Brunel, now far less elevated, no longer looks so diminutive, nor quite so big-headed.

Work to demolish the Bristol and West block began in 2006, and the statue moved to Temple Quay East, outside the offices of Osborne Clarke, where a second 'unveiling' took place on 10 May 2006. Jeremiah Osborne, the last remaining relative of the Osborne family, and Lesley Perrin, the senior partner, were present. The sculptor was consulted about the decision to make the new pedestal just 40cm high, in striking contrast to the original grey brick pedestal, which was approximately 3.75m in height.

Notes

[1] L.T.C. Rolt, *Isambard Kingdom Brunel* (Harmondsworth, 1957), p.184. [2] *Evening Post*, 21 April 1981. [3] Booklet published for the 1982 unveiling ceremony: Bristol and West Building Society, *Isambard Kingdom Brunel at Broad Quay and Paddington* (Bristol, 1982), p.2. [4] *Bristol Trade and Industry*, '"Same day" unveilings for two Brunel statues', no. 2, June 1982. [5] R. Heelas, 'The Beau Brunels', *Evening Post*, 19 May 1982. [6] As note 3; the Paddington statue was later moved to the entrance hall opposite platform 1. [7] A. Kelly and M. Kelly, *Brunel, In Love with Impossible* (Bristol, 2006), p.83. [8] R.A. Buchanan and M. Williams, *Brunel's Bristol* (Bristol, 1982). [9] J. Belsey, 'Brunel shapes up for a late date in the city', *Evening Post*, 21 April 1981. [10] Alan Elkan, chairman of the Civic Society, *Evening Post*, 11 March 2004.

Temple Gate

On the façade of the former George and Railway Hotel opposite the Old Station

Queen Victoria C77

Sculptor: unknown

Architect: attributed to Henry Masters
Date: c.1870
Materials: possibly reconstituted stone
Dimensions: approx. 130cm high
Status: Grade II
Owned by Standard Commercial Property Developments
Condition: poor

By 1844, the George Inn in Temple Gate, dating from the seventeenth century, had become the George Inn and Railroad Tavern in response to the opening of Brunel's Temple Meads station in 1841.[1] Three years later, the name had been subtly updated to the George Inn and Railway Tavern. From 1867 it is listed as the George Inn and Railway Hotel, implying that the date of the present building is 1866. The rebuilding was prompted by the planning of Victoria Street, which carved a brutal swathe through medieval Bristol to link Bristol Bridge with the railway station between 1865 and 1871. A trade card from about 1875 in Blaise Castle Museum has a detailed view of the new building, now the George and Railway Hotel

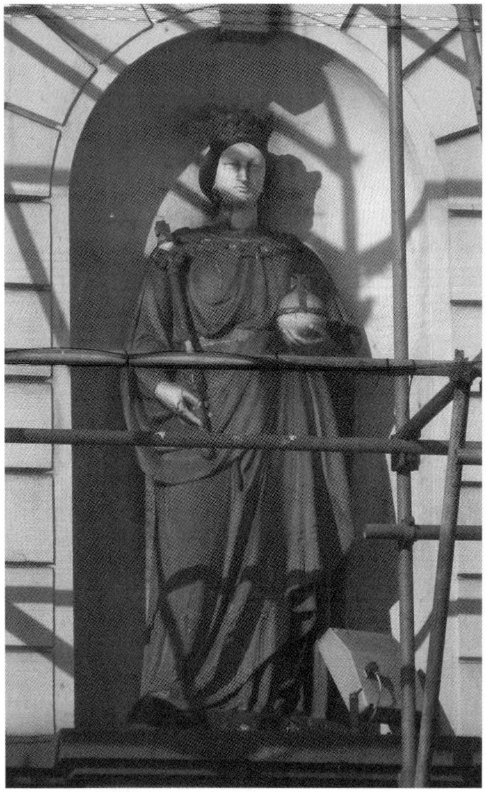

Queen Victoria

and described as a family and commercial hotel, 'Open for all Trains' and 'adjoining the station'. It shows an ornate top floor, now reduced, with complex dormer windows with ornate iron finials, a candle-snuffer spire and very tall chimneys.[2] The statue can just be seen in the niche in the centre of the first floor of the eastern Temple Way façade. The main entrance to the hotel was on the corner facing Temple Meads station.

Mike Jenner has argued that the building may well have been designed by the builder-turned-architect Henry Masters, who was responsible for the equally idiosyncratic Elephant Inn in St Nicholas Street. Masters 'had little original invention of his own', but his designs 'have a brash vigour which carries one past the insensitivities'.[3]

The building has long been derelict, but applications to develop the entire island site have once again been turned down (February 2009). The George and Railway Tavern, first listed in 1994, is to be retained.

The painted standing figure is crowned. She holds a sceptre in her right hand and an orb in her left. Her long blue cloak is tucked over her left arm. Her full-length dress is painted brown. As a whole the dress is unusual and perhaps more suited to a Byzantine empress.[4]

It is presumed that the statue depicts a young Queen Victoria, so young that it is possible that the statue had come from an earlier building. It must be remembered that, at present, the quality, material and condition of the statue are all obscured by layers of peeling paint, and by scaffolding.

Notes

[1] M. Jenner, 'The George and Railway Hotel, Temple Gate Bristol' (planning application, Bristol, 1998). [2] Op. cit., illus. p.2; also J. Winstone, *Bristol Trade Cards: Remnants of Prolific Commerce* (Bristol, c.1993), p.91 (TA5375). [3] Gomme et al., p.438. [4] Queen Victoria was not to be proclaimed Empress of India until 1 January 1877.

Temple Meads Station

On the wall, to the left of the main entrance to Temple Meads station

Memorial to Emma Saunders C78

Sculptor: E. E. Faithful

Date: 1928
Materials: white marble relief with grey slate surround
Dimensions: 90cm high, 60cm wide, 8cm deep
Inscription: BORN 1841 DIED 1927 / MISS EMMA SAUNDERS, / THE RAILWAYMEN'S FRIEND / ERECTED BY RAILWAY WORKERS AND FRIENDS / IN GRATEFUL REMEMBRANCE OF HER / FIFTY YEARS DEVOTED CHRISTIAN SERVICE
Status: Grade I
Owned by Railtrack Great Western
Condition: fair

Miss Emma Saunders was known as 'the railwaymen's friend', and these words are carved on this memorial and upon her monument in Redland Chapel's churchyard.

She was born in 1841, the year in which the first train had arrived at Temple Meads from London. In 1881 she became a pioneer member of the Railway Mission and was to devote the rest of her life to the welfare of the four thousand railway workers in the Bristol area.[1] She was then living with her widowed father, the manager of the Bristol branch of the Bank of England, in Sutton House, Clifton, diagonally opposite the Mansion House.[2]

She was assisted by devoted voluntary workers and a contemporary account tells us:

> Up and down the line, in and out of sheds, and sidings, and depots, these lady workers have gone, carrying their baskets filled with floral 'buttonholes', pausing just a moment to voice a reminder of better things and to leave their leaflet and gift of flowers.[3]

It was as a result of Miss Saunders' initiative and money that the Railway Men's Institution was opened at Bath Bridge, partly to counteract

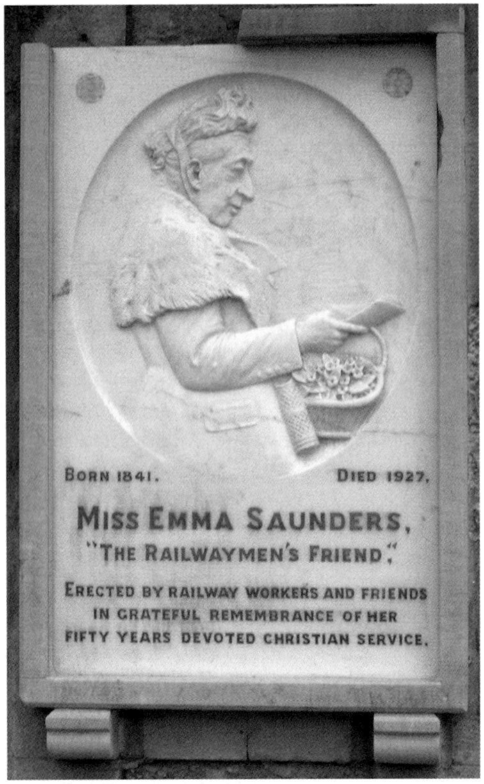

E. E. Faithful, *Memorial to Emma Saunders* (photo: Gerry Nichols, March 2006)

'the temptations of licensed premises'.[4] There was:

> a reading room and library, a hall for meetings and entertainments, billiard room, skittle alley, bagatelle room, youths' department, gymnasium, a temperance refreshment bar, and dining and tea rooms.[5]

Hundreds attended her funeral service, which took place at Christ Church, Clifton on what would have been her 86th birthday, 2 March 1927.[6] The *Western Daily Press* reported that over a thousand railwaymen at Temple Meads wore a daffodil in memory of their friend. For many years they also wore daffodils at an annual service held in her memory.[7]

The memorial, a rectangular white marble slab with a delicately cut carved bas-relief, contains a three-quarter-length profile portrait of Miss Saunders in later life. She wears a fur cape, and the paper she holds in her right hand will be one of the religious tracts that she dispensed. She holds a basket full of the flowers that she gave away, and in the background are railtracks, a bridge and station buildings.

This tribute was unveiled on 1 July 1928 by H. R. Griffiths, the divisional superintendent of the Great Western Railway.[8] A press report records that there was a service of dedication, prior to the unveiling, when the GWR Locomotive Male Voice Choir sang.[9]

'The work was executed by E. E. Faithfull, of the firm of H. Tyley, of Victoria Street.'[10] Since the end of the eighteenth century, successive generations of Tyleys had been monumental masons in Bristol and many hundreds of memorials bear their name.

The marble relief was recently glazed with perspex, causing condensation and the potentially damaging growth of mould.

Notes

[1] *Railway Magazine*, December 1985, p.590; I am grateful to Gerry Nichols for this reference and others below. [2] Joshua Saunders is listed as resident at Sutton House from 1870 to 1900; Sutton House may be the most expensive semi-detached mansion currently on the market (£3,500,000, 2009). [3] *Railway Magazine*, 1913, vol. 33, p.534. [4] *Bristol Times and Mirror*, 'Funeral of Miss Emma Saunders', 3 March 1927; for photographs of Miss Saunders distributing pamphlets and Railway Men's Institute, see R. Winstone, *Bristol's Suburbs long ago* (Bristol, 1985), pl. 369–75. [5] As note 3. [6] As note 4. [7] M. Pascoe, 'The grand old lady of a bygone age', *Bristol Observer*, 26 January 1996. [8] *GWR Magazine*, April 1927, p.148. [9] *Bristol Times and Mirror*, 2 July 1928, p.8. [10] Ibid.

By Platform 1, Temple Meads Station

Brunel Mural C79

Sculptor: Stephen Joyce, lead artist; with Peter Sutton, Shaun Keene, Joan Clews, Heather Hooper, Debbie Cross, Jonathan Barr-Lindsay, Jack Mundy and Tina Kelly

Date: 2006
Material: aluminium
Dimensions: 16m wide, 4m high
Status: not listed
Condition: good

The process of creation can be as important and rewarding as the end product itself. The charity art + power empowers disabled artists to develop their own opportunities and creative aspirations, and actively seeks to increase opportunities for disabled people to take part equally in creative life. The project group behind this mural involved eight such artists, together with the lead artist Steve Joyce, and the project coordinator Jade Wood.

The bicentenary celebrations of Isambard Kingdom Brunel's birth in 1807 were stage managed by Brunel 200, an initiative of the Bristol Cultural Development Partnership. It was through Brunel 200 that this particular project received substantial assistance from the National Lottery, the Heritage Lottery Fund, Bristol City Council and First Great Western. The site had to be one of the very few spots within the station that was both accessible to the public and not restricted by planning legislation. The selected site, the modern and plain brick wall by Platform 1, proved to be a cavity wall that could take little weight.

Severnside Community Rail Partnership backed the project, which Ove Arup expertly managed. Network Rail installed the work. Complex engineering solutions and new digital solutions were involved. M. J. Rees & Co was the surveyor, and Corus supplied the aluminium, which was laser cut by Precision Profiles. Call Print transferred the artists' drawings into digital programs, which Service Graphics printed onto the various shapes. Cerberus Engineering Services provided the invisible fixings.[1]

The artists together attended some thirty workshops to select and draw the shapes and images reflecting Brunel's life and achievements. These images range from the collapse of the Thames Tunnel to the prow of the *Great Britain*, and they are laid over the aluminium shapes, which were inspired by a variety of Brunel's designs, including a hull plate from the *Great Western* and a rudder design. The origin of the imagery and of the distinctive shapes is not easy to recognise, but displayed nearby is an exemplary explanation of each and every one. On this wall plaque are the words: 'We invite the whole community to share in our emancipation and encourage everyone to celebrate our strides towards freedom.'

The mural was unveiled by the Lord Mayor, Councillor Peter Abraham, on 16 September 2006.

Note
[1] One of two information panels by platform 1.

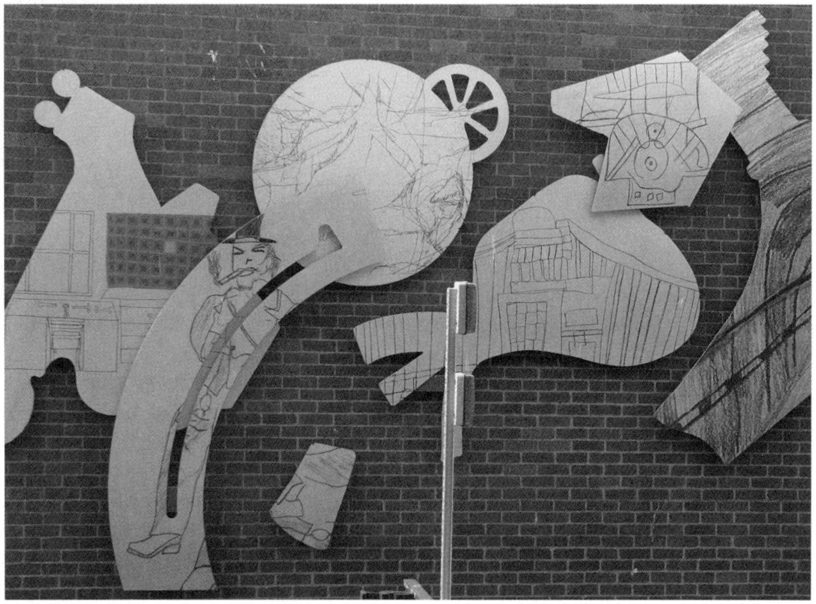

Stephen Joyce and others, *Brunel Mural*

Temple Quay

Temple Back East, in front of the Osborne Clarke offices

Templar Stone C74

Sculptor: Jane L. Rickards

Architects: Atkins Walters Webster
Date: 2004
Material: Portuguese granite
Dimensions: 280cm overall height; monolith 300cm long, 60cm wide, 80cm deep at base
Inscription on an anodised metal plate: Templar Stone / Jane L Rickards ARBS, 2004
Status: not listed
Owned by Osborne Clarke
Condition: good

Osborne Clarke, an international law firm, originated in Bristol as Osborne Ward in 1748. Its new headquarter offices were completed in 2002, as part of the Temple Quay redevelopment, on land purchased from Bristol Development Corporation. All the companies involved in the project were committed to commission some form of public sculpture in association with their building.

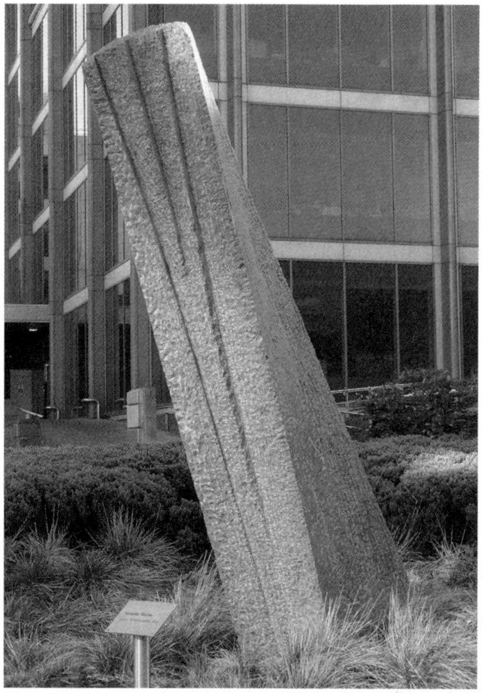

Jane L. Rickards, *Templar Stone*

The tapering shaft of grey granite rises at 60 degrees from among ornamental grasses. It is roughly cut and the surfaces are deeply scored along the shaft. The length and angle of the monolith meant that it could not be made from local stone:

> I knew of the dark grey Portuguese granite from the Alto Douro region as a stonemason friend imports it into Cornwall. We both went to José Alves' quarry where a suitable piece, 15 feet in length, was quarried and shaped roughly to my design and everyone's satisfaction. I chose the dark grey to harmonise with the new buildings of dark grey and steel and also to pay homage to the historic trade route which existed from Porto to Bristol.[1]

A commissioning team at Osborne Clarke, which included one of the architects, Mark Acker-Store from Atkins Walters Webster, chose the sculptor after a recommendation from Philip Mount of Art Search.[2] The work was commissioned by Andrew Braithwaite, one of Osborne Clarke's partners:

> Andrew's brief was for a piece of sculpture to link past, present and future referring to their own history and offices. That their new building is based on a circle was therefore a gift to me; it describes a quarter circle, and I felt that a contemporary standing stone pointing out, somehow also pointed to the future.[3]

Jane Rickards describes herself as 'a professional sculptor and healer'.[4] She writes of this sculpture:

> The 60 degree angle describes one face of a tetrahedron, which can be seen as the tip of a huge tetrahedron underground. This form is one of nature's building blocks and resonates with all cellular structure, and is deeply healing. I have named the piece *Templar Stone* with respect to the first Knights Templar historically of this area.[5]

She points out that the original Temple church was circular and that the circle encompasses the double tetrahedron in sacred geometry.[6] The sculptor lives in the Vale of Pewsey by the Wiltshire Downs and acknowledges that she has 'a feeling for the neolithic sites which abound along the Ridgeway'.[7]

Notes

[1] Letter from Jane Rickards to Douglas Merritt, 1 March 2007. [2] Letter from Andrew Braithwaite to Douglas Merritt, 26 October 2007; however Jane Rickards, see note 1, states that the contact at Art Search Ltd was Philip Herriot. [3] As note 1. [4] Artist's promotion sheet, c.2005. [5] Ibid. [6] As note 1. [7] Ibid.

On the roof of Bristol and West headquarters, 1 Temple Back East, Temple Quay

Pelorus C72

Sculptor: Pat Daw

Architects: Chapman Taylor and Stride Treglown, 1997–2000
Date: 2000
Materials: 316 grade stainless steel
Dimensions: 10m high, 3.15m wide
Metal work: Satin Stainless Fabrications, Weston-super-Mare
Status: not listed
Owned by Bristol and West
Condition: good

The sculptor chose the name *Pelorus* after consulting a sailing manual glossary and checking the definition: 'A sighting device on a ship for taking the relative bearings of a distant object, mid-nineteenth century: perhaps from *Pelorus*, said to be the name of Hannibal's pilot'.[1] The sculpture can be read as a mast, sail and pennant, and the artist herself has written that the 'name of this sculpture does not denote a visual similarity to the device, merely an associative connection'.[2] Pelorus Sound, named by Captain James Cook, is on the northern tip of the south island of New Zealand, in the Cook Strait. There is also an HMS *Pelorus*, and one of the largest private yachts in the world, that of Roman Abramovich, also bears the name.

A slatted metal construction was considered from the outset, and the design is a complex arrangement of curved tubes and flat bars. There is a 1.2m-square base plate, 32mm thick, and a central mast of 323mm diameter with a 10mm wall thickness. Welded 316 grade stainless steel was used for the entire structure for its high strength and corrosion resistance.

There was an initial design project for this commission early in 1999, conducted by Pat Daw, which involved third-year sculpture students from the University of the West of England, under the guidance of Mark Dunhill, the head of the Faculty of Fine Art, but this did not provide a conclusive design.[3] In July 1999, Pat Daw took on the commission. The brief required a maximum height of ten metres and 'a strong nautical or sailing theme'.[4] 'We wanted to add something to the city's skyline with a sculpture which reflects Bristol's maritime heritage and its reputation as a city of spires.'[5] Daw's design was examined by the consulting engineers Ove Arup, which provided

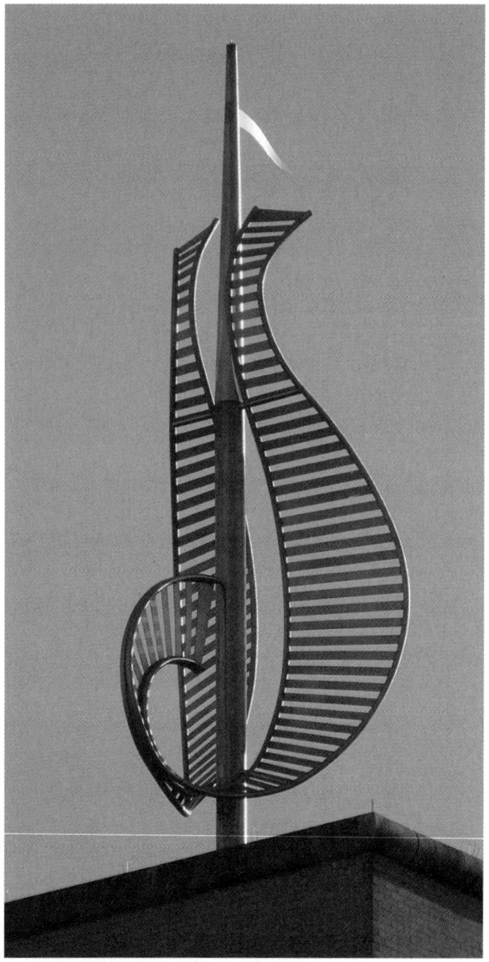

Pat Daw, *Pelorus*

calculations and steel specifications.[6] The sculpture, weighing three tonnes, had to be transported in two halves. A massive crane lifted the main section 43m above the city. The top section of the tapered mast was screwed into position like a billiard cue extension. Making and installing the structure, exclusive of all other professional fees, cost approximately £45,000.

Notes
[1] *Oxford Dictionary of English* (second edition, 2003). [2] Pat Daw, the sculptor, in a letter to SWRA, 23 October 2002. [3] Ibid. [4] RWA, *Friends Newsletter*, autumn, 2000, p.14. [5] Geoff Thomas, Bristol and West project manager. [6] Ibid.

Aligned along the Portwall, Temple Quay

Six Portwall Markers C75

Sculptor/designer: John Aiken

Date: 2004
Materials: polished black Portuguese granite and matt stainless steel
Dimensions: largest marker, 363cm by 258cm, 80cm high
Inscription on the top of the largest unit, engraved in sans-serif capitals: BELOW IS THE MEDIEVAL WATERGATE THROUGH WHICH A PASSAGE / LED FROM THE LANDS OF THE KNIGHTS TEMPLARS WITHIN TO / THE WIDE TOWN DITCH AND THE MEADOWS AND MARSHES OF THE TEMPLE MEADS BEYOND
Status: not listed
Owned by South West Regional Development Agency
Condition: good

When two lines of new office blocks in the Temple Quay development were laid out in the 1990s, the space between them was planned as a broad walkway. Its name was taken from the historic Portwall that separated medieval Bristol from the marshland and meads beyond. The Portwall marked the line of Bristol's southern defence and ran south to north to the River Avon. It was originally built around 1250 and the foundations remain. The wall had several semi-circular towers and followed the course of a ditch through open land owned by the Knights Templars. The foundations of a large round tower, known as Tower Harratz, are beneath the Bristol and West building at the edge of the Avon at the northern end of the walkway. The remains of one of the watergates that gave access from the city to the meadows can still be seen through the glass of the last and largest of the six Portwall markers.

The sculpture evolved from the desire to protect and to reveal the fragile archaeological remains of this watergate, as well as to animate the walkway itself. It was Geoff Wood, a public arts consultant, who recommended Professor Aiken – director of the Slade School of Fine Art and an artist fascinated by fortifications and by the monolithic forms of granite – as the sculptor who could best resolve the dilemma.[1]

Six polished black sculptures of varying shape and size line the centre of the walkway for over a hundred metres in two groups of three. For some they are reminiscent of catafalques. The cavernous street becomes Westminster Hall and gains a certain funereal dignity. But they are also benches and lively social meeting places for office workers, and at night the blue neon lighting, which is an integral part of the design, brings a new life to each structure and successfully animates the street as a whole.

The surfaces of the black Portuguese granite are very highly polished and have a mirror-like finish. The sides of the slabs retain evenly spaced drill marks from the quarrying process. The structures increase in size in a complex interlocking sequence, from the smallest at the southern (Temple Meads) end to the largest at the northern end. The final bench sits over a large illuminated and environmentally controlled chamber in which the archaeological remains of the watergate can be seen. The elegant inscription in the granite, recorded above, provides an explanation. Art,

John Aiken, *Portwall Marker* (one of six)

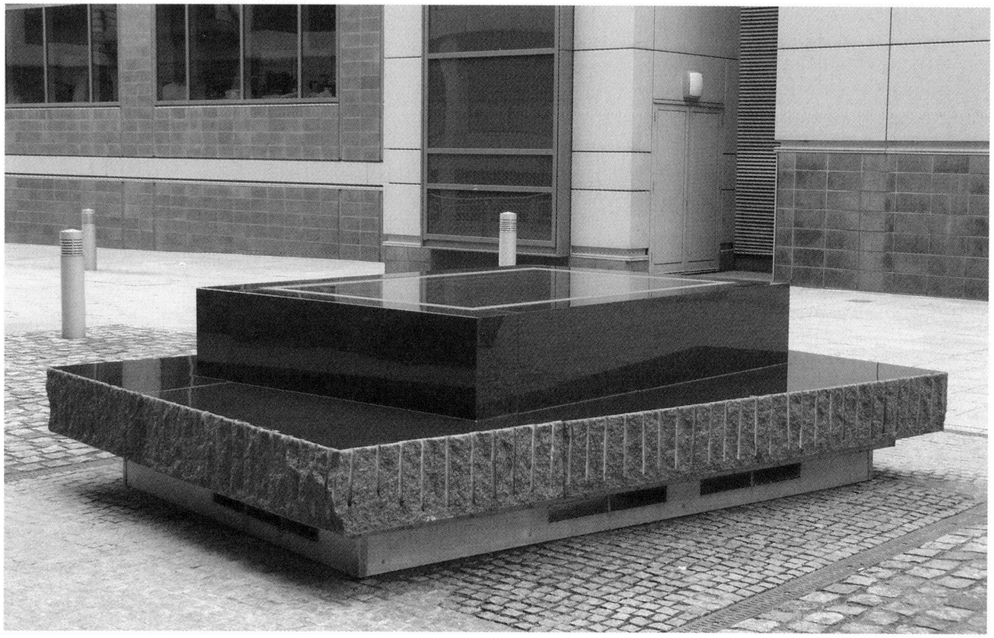

archaeology and conservation have come comfortably together.

The commission was funded by the South West Regional Development Agency and Castlemore Securities, the developers of the site. Additional bollards and approach ramps to one block at the southern end now mar the overall effect.

Note
[1] www.publicartonline.org.uk PASW regional newsletter, autumn, 2004.

Temple Way

First building north of Temple Circus on the west side of Temple Way, opposite Osborne Clarke

Rotating Columns C76

Sculptor: Walter Jack

Date: 2006–7
Materials: vitreous enamel on steel structure
Dimensions: 9m high
Fabricated by Walter Jack Studio with Springboard Design Partnership and Trico, vitreous enamellers
Status: not listed
Condition: good but not revolving

This colonnade of three tall fluted columns, coloured with a subtle variety of tones and hues of blue, has yet to function.[1] The columns should rotate. Commissioned in 2006 by the developers, Terrace Hill, the lease was sold before completion and the office block is still unoccupied.

Walter Jack's own comments confirm the importance of movement:

> When we were asked to work in this space we couldn't find much to recommend it. It is north-facing on the busy Temple Way, Bristol's inner ring road. But you're only a hundred metres from the beautiful fourteenth-century Temple Church and churchyard. Our 9m-tall classical columns are skewed to the building, to encourage people to leave Temple Way and discover the churchyard and a quiet route to the city centre. And the vitreous enamelled columns have a trick up their sleeve. They slowly rotate – one revolution every eight hours.[2]

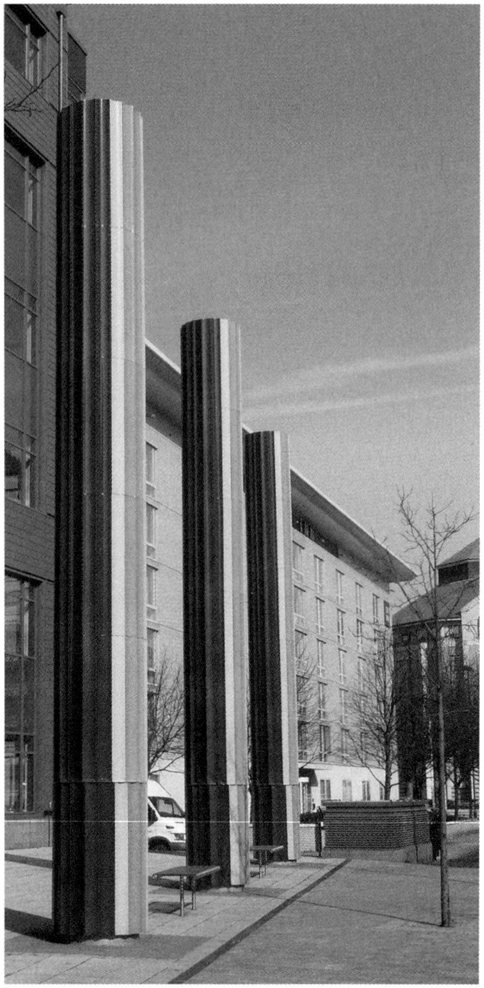

Walter Jack, *Rotating Columns*

Notes
[1] August 2008.
[2] http://www.walterjack.co.uk/Projects/P7/.

Trinity Place, Hotwells

At the junction of Hotwell Road and Merchants' Road

Memorial Fountain to Simon Short B22

Architect: Tom E. Dove

Cast iron: Hart, Son and Peard
Portrait: Jones & Willis
Date: 1902
Materials: fountain, painted cast iron; relief portrait, tin-based alloy; trough, pedestal and basin, Peterhead granite; steps, red granite
Dimensions: fountain, 190cm high, 105cm wide; pedestal, 185cm high
Bronze plaque inscription: TO COMMEMORATE THE LIFE AND WORK OF / SIMON SHORT / WHO, FOR OVER HALF A CENTURY, / AS A SEAMAN'S MISSIONARY IN THIS PORT AND SUPERINTENDANT OF / THE BETHEL SHIP, AND AS / THE PIONEER OF THE COCOA ROOMS AND / THE COFFEE TAVERN MOVEMENT, / DEVOTEDLY LABOURED FOR THE PEOPLE'S WELFARE. / THIS FOUNTAIN IS PRESENTED TO / HIS NATIVE CITY BY MANY OF HIS FELLOW / CITIZENS AND MEMBERS OF THE NATIONAL / TEMPERANCE CATERERS' ASSOCIATION.
Carved into the granite pedestal below the plaque: 1902
Status: Grade II
Owned by Bristol City Council
Condition: poor

The cocoa pods on the capitals of the cast iron columns correctly suggest that Simon Short (1826–1901) was a temperance worker. He was the most influential of the missionaries employed by Bristol's Seaman's Friend Society and Bethel Union. For over fifty years he worked for seamen in the port area of Bristol, known as Hotwells, where he was the superintendent of the 'Bethel ship', a place of rest and refuge for sailors. The inscription on

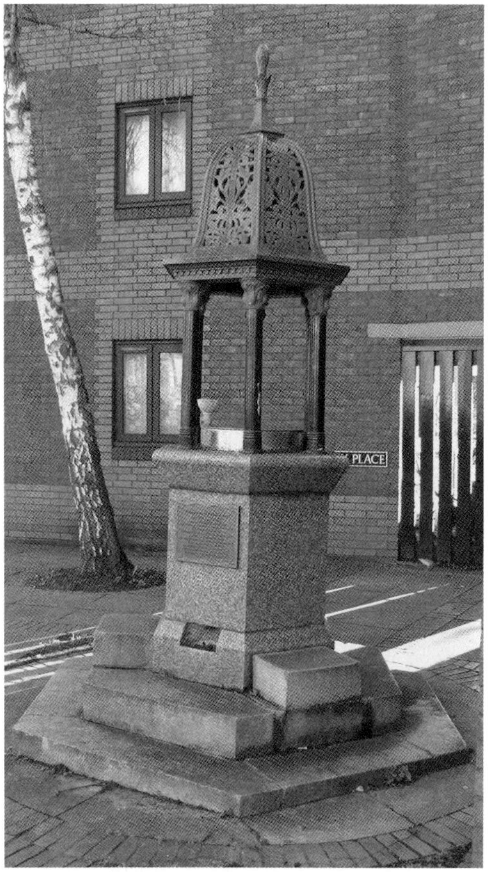

Hart, Son and Peard, ***Memorial Fountain to Simon Short***

the memorial also tells us that he was a 'pioneer of the Cocoa Rooms and the Coffee Tavern movement'.

He was one of four children born in Bristol to Solomon and Mary Short in 1826.[1] His obituary records that little was known of his early years, but that he went to sea when a young boy and experienced 'bitter treatment from drunken sailors'.[2] At the unveiling of this fountain in 1902, the lord mayor said: 'at the age of 18 he was brought to the saving knowledge of Christ and he resolved to devote his life's service to those with whom he had laboured'.[3] The 1851 census shows he was married and living in the city centre in Bell Lane.[4] In the 1850s he was appointed Seamans' Missionary to the Bethel Ship, where services were held.[5] Short was able to persuade some landlords to sell up, and their premises were turned into temperance hotels and eating houses for sailors.[6] He also promoted the coffee tavern movement in Liverpool, Newcastle-on-Tyne, Bradford and elsewhere.[7] In Bristol, with the help of associates, he purchased a ship, the *Gloriosa*, which was fitted out as a chapel in 1885. It was berthed at St Augustine's Back.[8] He died in Horfield in 1901.[9]

This free-standing drinking fountain has a six-sided cast iron foliate open-work canopy. The canopy is bell-shaped with moulded ribs, and is painted a matt blue-green and surmounted by a finial. Supporting the canopy are six cylindrical metal columns, painted black, with cocoa-pod capitals. A tin-based alloy cast metal shield, fixed to one of the rear panels of the canopy, bears a bas-relief portrait of Simon Short. In profile, facing right, Short has a full beard, long hair and spectacles. The photograph upon which this relief was based was reproduced in the *Western Daily Press* in 1925.[10] It was 'a perfect likeness', said his relatives.[11] The metal columns stand on a pink granite chamfered table that originally held a basin. Below are a pedestal, plinth and two steps, all hexagonal. Three stone blocks are positioned at alternate sides of the plinth, enabling children to reach the fountain. When restored in 1981, the old drinking system was replaced with a modern stainless steel circular fitting. This has a fixed cup-shaped mouthpiece and a stainless steel tap.

The side of the pedestal facing the Hotwell Road retained the original inscription until 2001, when it was stolen. The inscription was stamped from the reverse on to thin copper, and had become so damaged that it had been illegible for at least twenty-five years. In 2002 the original wording was found to have been recorded in a Bristol newspaper, and a year later

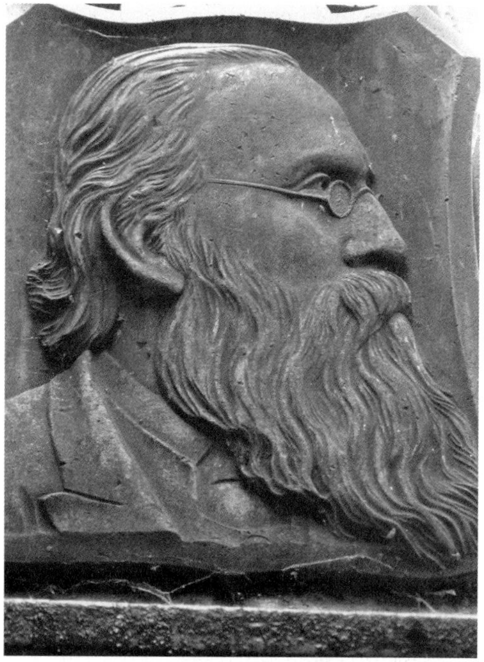

Jones & Willis, ***Portrait of Simon Short***

the full text was cast in bronze and set in place by Bristol City Council.[12] Below this plate, '1902' is cut into the granite. In the front of the plinth is a gap that forms a trough where animals can drink.

A Temperance Association conference, held in Sheffield in May 1901, resolved that a permanent memorial should be erected to commemorate 'the unique and devoted services rendered to the community by the late Mr Simon Short, of Bristol'.[13] On 13 September 1902, the Lord Mayor of Bristol, C. E. L. Gardner, unveiled the fountain on a triangle of land, planted with trees and called Sopey Park, on the Hotwell Road at the foot of Granby Hill.[14]

The fountain was designed by a Birmingham architect, Tom E. Dove, and made by Hart, Son and Peard. The relief portrait is by Jones & Willis. Both these firms were major suppliers of ecclesiastical furnishings, with outlets in both

Birmingham and London.

The portrait was originally on the same side as the plaque.[15] When the flyover system was created in the earlier 1960s, the 'charming little fountain' was dismantled and taken into store in May 1963.[16] The fountain was re-erected on the present site in July 1966.[17] During this move, the relief portrait was incorrectly fixed to the back. Planning permission granted for the flats, built on the corner of Merchant's Road in 1981, ensured that the memorial was retained.[18]

Water has penetrated the iron columns, which have corroded and split. Serious corrosion is occurring. The fountain no longer functions.

Notes

[1] I am indebted to Jane Borg of Gladstone, Queensland, Australia, a great-great-grand-daughter of Simon Short, for her paper 'Simon Short: a Seaman's Missionary', written in 2004. [2] *Western Daily Press*, Simon Short obituary, 19 March 1901. [3] 'Unveiling of Memorial Fountain', *Western Daily Press*, 15 September 1902. [4] As note 1. [5] 'Scenes on Bristol Quay 60 years ago', *Western Daily Press*, 19 October 1925. [6] As note 1. [7] M.J. Crossley Evans, 'Christian missionary work among the seamen and dockers of Bristol, 1820–1914', in J.H. Bettey, ed., *Essays in Memory of Elizabeth Ralph 1911–2000* (Bristol, 2001). [8] Ibid. [9] Ibid. [10] As note 5. [11] Ibid. [12] *Western Daily Press*, 15 September 1902; this reference was discovered by Michael Pascoe, historian and member of the Clifton and Hotwells Improvement Society. [13] As note 3. [14] As note 3; Winstone, *Bristol As It Was 1960–62*, pl. 92. [15] Ibid. [16] Dorothy Vinter, *Evening Post*, 15 October 1965; Winstone, as note 14. [17] BCC Engineers' Department, *Memorials, Fountains and Statues*, p.32. [18] Ibid.

Tyndall Avenue

On the forecourt of the University of Bristol's Centre for Sport, Exercise and Health

Flat Out B29

Sculptor: Jon Buck

Date: 2004
Material: bronze, artificially patinated to a copper-green colour; stainless steel armature
Foundry: Pangolin Editions, Chalford, Gloucestershire
Dimensions: 2m high
Status: not listed
Owned by the University of Bristol
Condition: good

The university's Centre for Sport, Exercise and Health opened in November 2002. In that month, a long list of sculptors' names was put before a panel of staff from the university and the city council. In February 2003 two artists, Jon Buck and Robert Kilvington, were selected to create design proposals for a sculpture for the façade or forecourt of the building. These were presented to the panel in May, and staff, students and the public were invited to comment. Kilvington proposed a maintenance-free abstract sculpture of ten interlocking stainless steel poles attached to the brick column to the left of the entrance. Buck's ultimately successful running figure was to be located either on the concourse in front of the brick panel or hung from the brickwork itself.

Flat Out was unveiled by Jack Russell, the former England and Gloucestershire cricketer, on 19 August 2004. It was comfortably sited on the ground against the backdrop of the red brick wall, and was provided with two discreet protective blocks of red brick that are aligned with a low wall. Unfortunately, the centre's brick wall is now regularly covered by an advertising banner of the kind that litters the façades of so many public buildings.

The centre's director, Bob Reeves, was

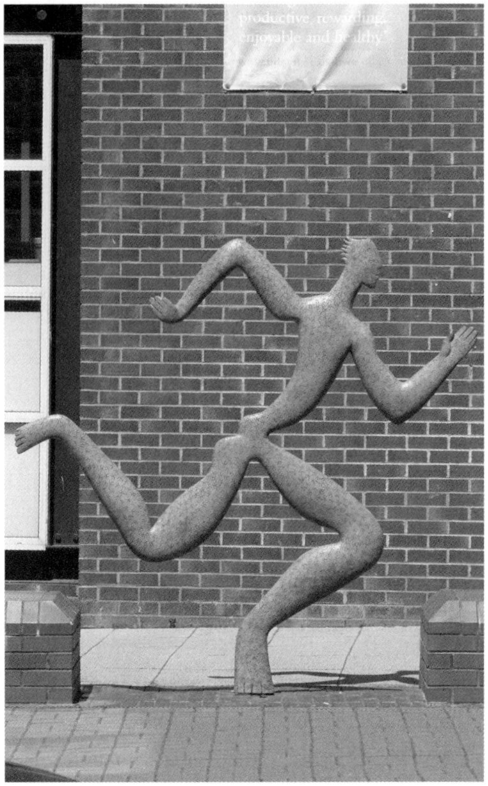

Jon Buck, *Flat Out*

quoted as saying that the 'sculpture reinforces the centre's aims: to promote the understanding of and active participation in sport, and therefore produce good health and personal well-being'.[1] Impressively, the work both supports and counteracts such earnestness of purpose. Jon Buck himself wrote in his proposal that he 'chose a running figure as it not only invokes the dynamism of human movement but also incorporates all three elements of the centre's title – sport, exercise and health'. He also stated that the symbols engraved on the figure:

> as it runs between Senate House and the centre represent the academic, fiscal and administrative areas of university life, so the

figure not only physically runs between the two centres... but also represents the individual's need to attend to both elements: body and min.[2]

Fortunately, the wit and vitality of the figure ignores such ponderous references and, presumably, once the commission was secured, the sculptor wisely limited the symbols to the recurring image of the running figure.

Jon Buck, a sculptor with a growing international reputation, was born in Bristol. Members of his family are recorded as Bristol Channel pilots based at Pill on the River Avon from 1823 to 1967.[3] They were vital to Bristol's continued success as a port.

Notes
[1] Bristol University press release, 19 August 2004.
[2] Ibid. [3] Rich, *The Bristol Pilots*, pp.140–2.

H. H. Wills Physics Laboratory, within Royal Fort Gardens, Tyndall Avenue

Entrance Surround, Lions' and Rams' Heads and Paterae B31

Sculptor: Jean Hahn, attributed to

Architect: Sir George Herbert Oatley
Date: 1921–7
Materials: Clipsham stone
Status: Grade II
Owned by the University of Bristol
Condition: good; cleaned and conserved 2008

The original main entrance to the H. H. Wills Physics Laboratory is opposite the Royal Fort and beneath the stout and immensely solid battlemented tower, with its great mullioned windows of purposeful practicality.

Dr Sarah Whittingham's forthcoming book confirms the importance of sculptural ornament to Sir George Oatley, in both its quality and its meaning.

As with the majority of Oatley's buildings, the ornament on the Physics Laboratory is expressive of its function. In the spandrels to the main entrance are carvings of early and 'modern' discoveries in experimental physics: the dispersion of sunlight by a prism by Sir Isaac Newton in 1666, and the tracks of alpha particles from radium by Charles T. R. Wilson in 1911.[1]

Dr Whittingham reveals that Oatley had originally had plans for further sculpture above the doorway. In 1928 he wrote to his nephew:

the original design included two carved Gryphons [from the Wills family coat of arms] to stand on the cornice of the columns. You will see from the [photograph] that they are features really needed to ease off the abruptness of the cornice... but I got so sick of the attempts to get an artist to model these things to my taste that I abandoned them. Better no ornament than execrable ornament![2]

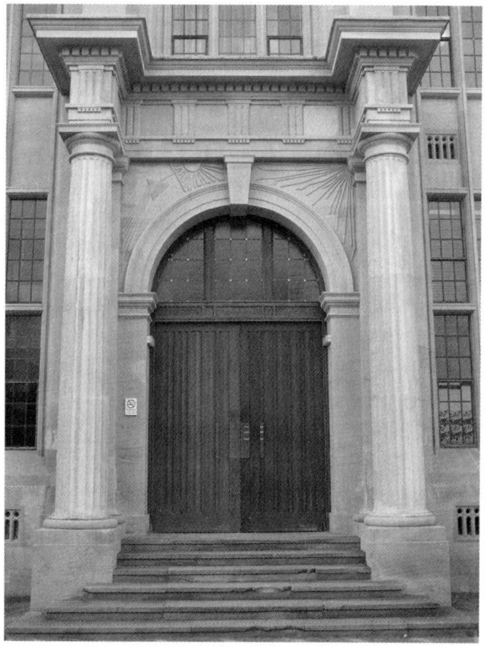

George Oatley, architect, *Entrance to H. H. Wills Physics Building*

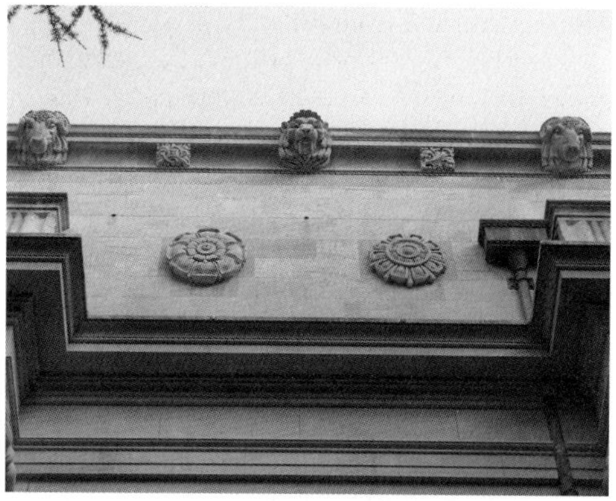

George Oatley, architect, *Lions' and Rams' Heads and Paterae*

The extensive carved decoration on the rest of the building has a scale and consistency unlike Oatley's Wills Memorial Building, the Wills Hall of Residence or St Monica Home of Rest. Instead of the strikingly various, even anarchic, grotesque heads along the cornice, there is an orderly, alternating sequence of lions' and rams' heads. Dr Whittingham outlines the Christian symbolism of much of both the internal and external decoration, in which the deep religious commitment of the architect and of Henry Herbert Wills and his wife, Dame Monica Wills, is discreetly expressed.

On the outside of the building there is more Christian symbolism in the carved paterae: twelve-petalled flowers (representing the disciples), eight-petalled roses (regeneration or resurrection), ten-petalled flowers (the ten Commandments), eight-pointed stars (again regeneration or resurrection), five-petalled flowers (the number of Jesus's wounds) and the Star of David or double Trinity Star, formed of two interlinking triangles (the six points standing for the six days of creation). Unusually placed – punctuating the cornice to the attic storey and the string courses to the building – are carved ram and lion heads. The lion represents the lion of the tribe of Judah, a symbol of Jesus. The ram is a

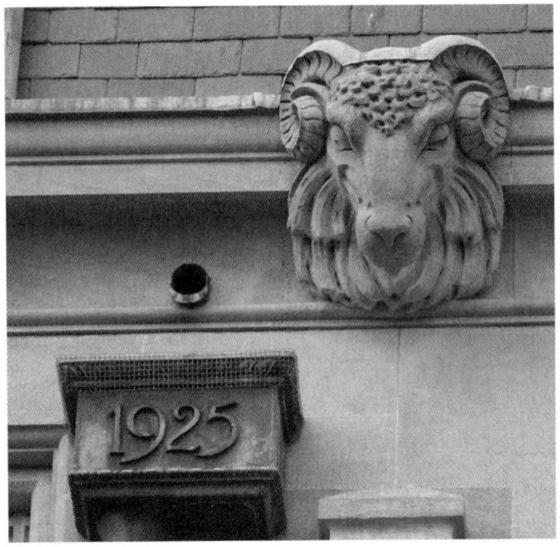

George Oatley, architect, *Ram's Head and hopper*

> Christian reference because Abraham's sacrifice of a ram instead of his son on Mount Moriah foreshadowed the ultimate sacrifice of God's own son.[3]

Henry Herbert Wills, the main benefactor of the Physics Laboratory, had himself studied engineering at Bristol University College in the years before his father had enabled its transformation into a university. He died in 1922, a year after building had begun.

Notes
[1] Whittingham, *Sir George Herbert Oatley*; the authors are especially grateful to Dr Whittingham for so readily sharing this information. [2] Ibid. [3] Ibid.

In the stairwell of the University of Bristol's H. H. Wills Physics Extension Building, Tyndall Avenue

Stretching a Point B30

Sculptor: Simon Thomas

Date: 1997
Material: stainless steel wire
Dimensions: 26m
Status: not listed
Owned by the University of Bristol
Condition: good; some outer strands missing

Stretching a Point is striking evidence of the innovative and successful series of artists' residencies in the university's physics department. They began in 1995.

Exactly 1,326 individual strands of stainless steel wire stretch from a single point just below the ceiling at the top of the stairwell. They fan out as they run down five storeys to the basement, where a spiral pattern is formed in the circular base. Each wire passes through a copper disc and into a drum, where a weight is attached and suspended. As the artist's own proposal stated, 'a kind of fibrous cone is created'.[1] The diameter of the wire is 0.24mm and the length of each strand is 24m. The literal demonstration of this exceptional difference of scale is the work's principle subject and it is also the theme, expressed symbolically, of the sculptor's tribute to the Nobel laureate and Bristol graduate, Paul Dirac (see Anchor Road).

Initiated by Professor John Steeds and Professor Sir Michael Berry,[2] the artist-in-residence scheme began with Simon Haddock, 1995–7, whose commanding painted screen is in the basement of the Physics Laboratory. Simon Thomas's subsequent residency was funded by a Wingate Fellowship. Richard Box, 2002–4, was funded by the Leverhulme Trust, and his photographs of rows of fluorescent tubes glowing from the electro-magnetic field beneath power lines have enjoyed wide publicity. Examples hang in the foyer.[3] The costs of *Stretching a Point* were met by an anonymous donation.

Notes
[1] www.simonthomas-sculpture.com/research_misc_stretching.php. [2] Ibid. [3] Explanatory caption to the residencies in the hall of the Physics Building.

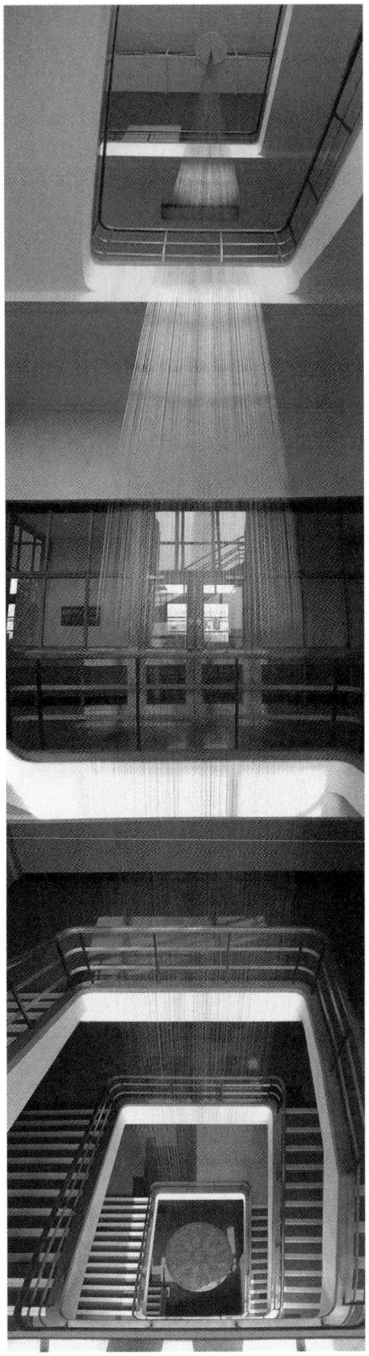

Simon Thomas, *Stretching a Point*

University Road

In the Great Hall of Bristol Grammar School, on the north wall

Dr John William Caldicott B33

Sculptor: George James Frampton

Date: 1896
Materials; bronze relief with surround of brown and green veined marble
Dimensions: 105cm high, 75cm wide
Signature top right: GEO · FRAMPTON / 1896
Inscription in raised bronze letters beneath the portrait relief: JOHN WILLIAM CALDICOTT, · D.D / JESUS COLLEGE OXFORD / HEADMASTER OF THIS SCHOOL 1860–1883 / FROM OLD PVPILS AND FRIENDS 1897
Status: Grade I
Owned by Bristol Grammar School
Condition: good

Dr John William Caldicott (1829–94) became headmaster of Bristol Grammar School in 1860 at the age of 31, perhaps paving the way for Dr John Percival's appointment to Clifton College two years later at the still younger age of 27.

> Handsome, distinguished and upright in appearance, proud and pugnacious in mind, Caldicott had been endowed by nature with the dangerous gifts of the leader, and he had imbued from his Victorian environment all its severe moral code and its shrewd worldly wisdom.[1]

He had been an exhibitioner of Pembroke College, Oxford, and a lecturer and tutor at Jesus College. He was to be headmaster for 23 years and oversaw the crucial move of the school from Unity Street to the then rural site of Tyndall's Park in 1879.[2] Big School and the Great Hall, designed by Foster and Wood, were built. Praise for the Great Hall, where the Caldicott memorial is situated, came at the official opening: 'the finest schoolroom I ever was in – so beautiful, so simple, and so commodious'.[3] Caldicott retired from the school in 1883 and became rector of Shipston-on-Stour, an appointment he held until his death in November 1894.[4] The following month, an obituary said: 'If Robert Thorne founded the school, John William Caldicott was its second founder; and it stands as his noblest monument'.[5]

The seated figure wears an academic gown and holds an open book. In the upper right-hand corner are two coats of arms. On the right are the arms of the school, based on those of Robert Thorne, the founder. The arms to the left may relate to Caldicott's family.

The proposal to erect a memorial was announced in March 1896, and the subscription list was closed at the end of the same month. The form had not been settled, but 'it will probably be a mural tablet with a portrait medallion in bronze or marble, to be placed in the Great Hall'.[6] The proposal that the memorial should be a medallion came from Herbert Thomas, clerk to the chairman of the governors.[7] A memorial committee had been formed and promises of about £200 were received. Other sculptors were invited to submit designs, but that 'of Mr Frampton [was] accepted'. Frampton, by then an associate member of the Royal Academy, was present at the unveiling on 13 June 1897. Several years later, Sir George, knighted in 1908, could have gained a more prestigious Bristol commission – the King Edward VII statue. This time he refused to enter the fray: 'I beg to say that I do not compete for commissions… as the result of competitions is very doubtful and often disappointing'.[8]

A smaller but similar relief by George Frampton of the same date, 1896, hangs in the Percival Library of Clifton College. The portrait commemorates Norman Moor, 1851–95, who became a close friend of John Addington Symonds while still a pupil at Clifton College.

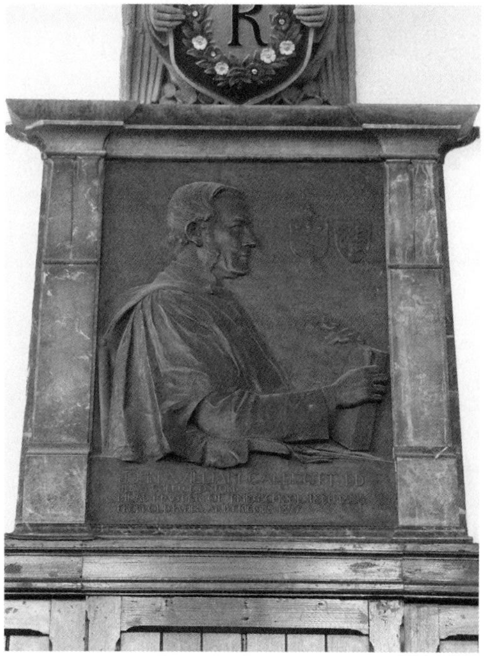

George James Frampton, *Dr John William Caldicott*

Notes
[1] Hill, *The History of Bristol Grammar School.* [2] *The Bristol Grammar School Chronicle*, no. 7, vol. VII, December 1895, p.4. [3] Ibid, p.106; the speaker was W.E. Forster, 'outstanding educational statesman of the century'. [4] As note 2. [5] As note 2, p.5. [6] As note 2, no. 8, vol. VII, March 1896, p.5. [7] As note 2, no. 12, vol.VII, July 1897, p.23. [8] BRO, Frampton to J.H. Reed, secretary to King Edward Memorial Committee, 22 February 1911.

Upper Byron Place

On the west entrance façade of St Mary's Hospital

Virgin and Child B43

Sculptor: William John Smith

Date:1933[1]
Materials: probably Bath stone
Dimensions: approx. 3m high
Status: not listed
Owned by Nuffield Hospitals
Condition: good

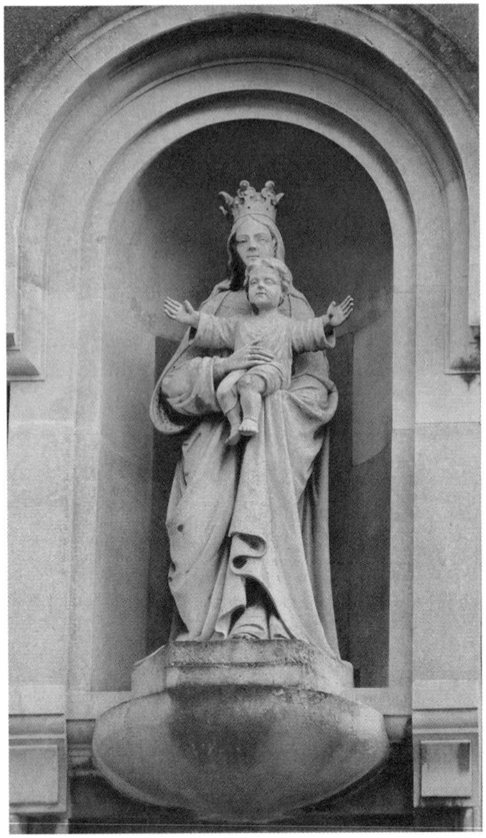

William John Smith, *Virgin and Child*

Smith's statue of the *Virgin and Child*, high up in a niche on the west façade of St Mary's Hospital, was carved when he was 71.[2] The pose is conventional, but the drapery is impressively managed. The manner in which the folds fall from the supporting hand of the Virgin is vital to the coherence and sweep of the composition. In 1986, the *Evening Post* recorded the fiftieth anniversary of Smith's death, saying: 'Bristol had mourned the death at 74 of one of the city's finest sculptors and ecclesiastical carvers – William John Smith'.[3]

Notes
[1] T. Bradshaw, *Bristol Magpies Newsletter*, no. 97, October/November 1993. [2] Ibid. [3] Ibid.

Upper Maudlin Street

In front of Bristol Royal Hospital for Children

Lollypop Be-bop C7

Sculptor: Andrew Smith

Architects: Whicheloe Macfarlane MDP
Date: 1999–2002
Materials: matt finished stainless steel and optic fibre lighting
Dimensions: 15m high
Status: not listed
Owned by United Bristol Healthcare NHS Trust
Condition: fair

> The new *Bristol Royal Hospital for Children*, opened in 2001 and dedicated to the care of children and their families across the south west of England, marks a milestone in the field of arts in healthcare.[1]

Lesley Greene was appointed in the winter of 1996–7 to develop an arts strategy for the project, ultimately managing a commissioning budget of £1.3 million and involving over

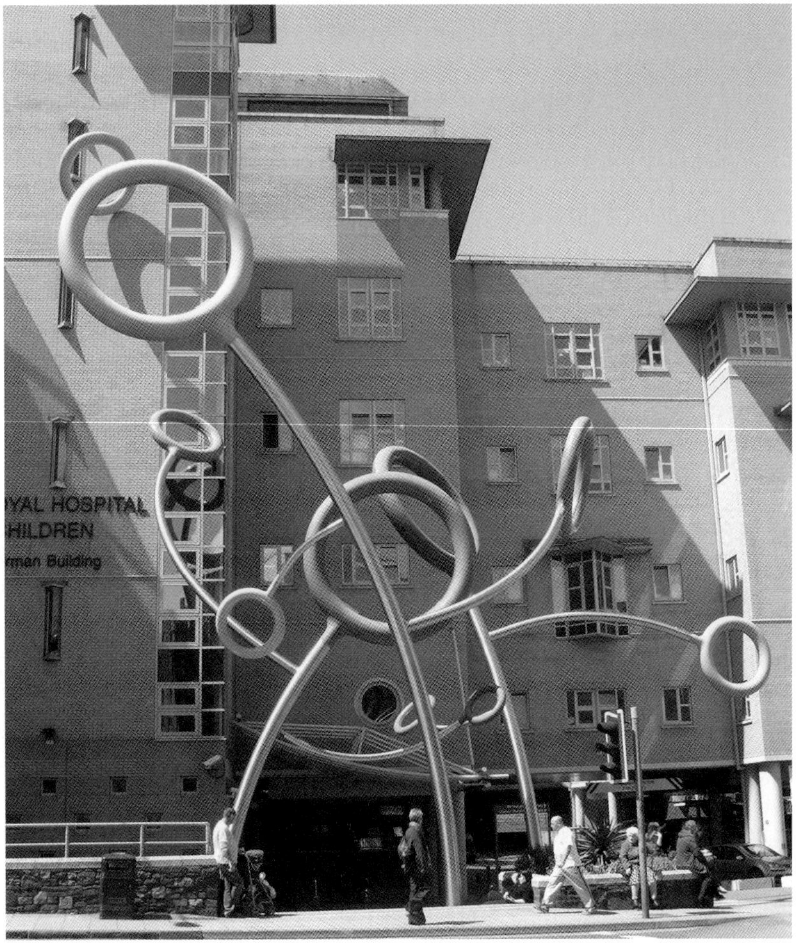

Andrew Smith, *Lollypop Be-bop*

twenty artists. Ray Smith was appointed lead artist in the spring of 1997, and together with two other artists he participated in an unprecedented amount of consultation with staff, patients and parents. The hospital was opened to patients in April 2001. Funding support was received from the Wallace and Gromit Grand Appeal, the Arts Council of England, the National Lottery, Public Art South West, Champions of Child Health and the NHS.

Lollypop Be-bop is the largest three-dimensional sculptural structure in Bristol. On top of each curved 'branch' is a coloured ring. These were originally lit from within by a fibre-optic light source to enable young patients to have the fun of interrupting the sequence of the lighting. The whole system was designed to be controlled by pressing buttons on a console on the third floor, inside the hospital. This was installed and was briefly used by the children, but the electronic system has not been maintained. A matt finish for the massive steel columns was chosen to avoid sunlight dazzling passing motorists' eyes.

Andrew Smith has said: 'I felt that the piece should convey a sense of friendliness and welcome across a range of groups.'[2] The trunks and branches were placed to give 'the whole construction a sense of growth and vitality'. He was anxious to create something in which children could actually participate, and he collaborated closely with the structural engineers, Benson-Sedwick, and with the lighting designers, Hoare Lee. Lesley Greene explained that the design was chosen because it had a strong sense of recognition and was very welcoming. The lead architect, David Radford, commented that the exuberance of the work was just what he wanted to complete the exterior. Despite the lack of interior lighting, the work succeeds in exactly these terms. Patients and hospital staff took part in the inauguration ceremony on the evening of 1 November 2001.

Notes

[1] www.publicartonline.org.uk/archive/casestudies/brch/index.php. [2] Notes by Andrew Smith, 2001.

Victoria Park

In the north-east corner of Victoria Park, Windmill Hill

St Mary Redcliffe Maze, Victoria Park A23

Designers: Peter Milner and Jane Norbury

Date: 1984
Materials: red bricks and 25 terracotta plaques
Dimensions: 9.2m diameter
Inscription: impressed into the title plaque and thereafter into 24 numbered plaques set into the brickwork of the outer wall; plaque 1 – ST. MARY / REDCLIFFE / MAZE /This maze commemorates / the recognition of the / need for clean water/1/ plaque 2 – By citizens of Bristol in / both the twelfth and twentieth centuries/2/ plaque 3 – In 1190 a pipeline was built / from Knowle to / St Mary Redcliffe church /3/ plaque 4 – This carried fresh water / from a spring to the / parish of Redcliffe /4/ plaque 5 – For many years this was / the only clean water/supply for Redcliffe /5/ plaque 6 – Cholera epidemics caused / many deaths in 1832 & / 1849. /6/ plaque 7 – Treated drinking water and / new sewers were then / provided from 1850 /7/ plaque 8 – One of these later pipe / lines also passes beneath / this park /8/ plaque 9 – This is the Southern Foul / Water interceptor sewer / built in1975-84 / 9 / plaque 10 – From St.Anne's the pipe/goes beneath Arno's Vale / Totterdown & Bedminster /10/ plaque 11 – It takes sewage from / South Bristol to / Avonmouth for treatment /11/ plaque 12 – This sewage used to / discharge directly into / the River Avon (New Cut) /12/ plaque 13 – The new pipeline will / therefore help to clear / the river of pollution /13/ plaque 14 – During work on the new / pipeline, the ancient / pipe was uncovered /14/ plaque 15 – It was still 'Ship shape / & Bristol fashion' as far / as the railway /15/ plaque 16 – Beyond there it had been / damaged by bombs near / York Road in 1941 /16/ plaque 17 – This water maze was / built over the ancient / pipeline in August 1984 /17/ plaque 18 – The spring water from that pipe now flows / through the maze /18/ plaque 19 – A special feature of the / maze is that it has / no dead ends /19/ plaque 20 – The pattern is copied / from a roof boss in / St Mary Redcliffe church /20/ plaque 21 – The new sewer and / maze were inaugurated on / Monday 22nd October 1984 /21/ plaque 22 – By the Rt. Hon. the / Lord Mayor of Bristol / Councillor Claude Draper /22/ plaque 23 – ACCESS & the Bristol / City Engineer's Dept. / designed the scheme /23/ plaque 24 – Under agency / arrangements with the / Wessex Water Authority /24
Status: not listed
Owned by Bristol City Council
Condition: fair

The unusually long and didactic inscription earnestly records that this maze commemorates a great advance in the thirteenth century in the supply of fresh water to Redcliffe and, some eight hundred years later, an important improvement in the safe disposal of south Bristol's sewage.

In 1190, Lord Robert de Berkeley granted St Mary Redcliffe rights over his spring and well at Knowle, and in 1207 a pipe or conduit brought this water near to the church.[1] In 1984 the completion of the Southern Foul-Water Interceptor sewer, which passes under Victoria Park, ensured that none of south Bristol's sewerage continued to be discharged into the Avon, but was transferred to Avonmouth for treatment.

The circular maze, 6m in diameter, is made of red Ibstock bricks. The perimeter is

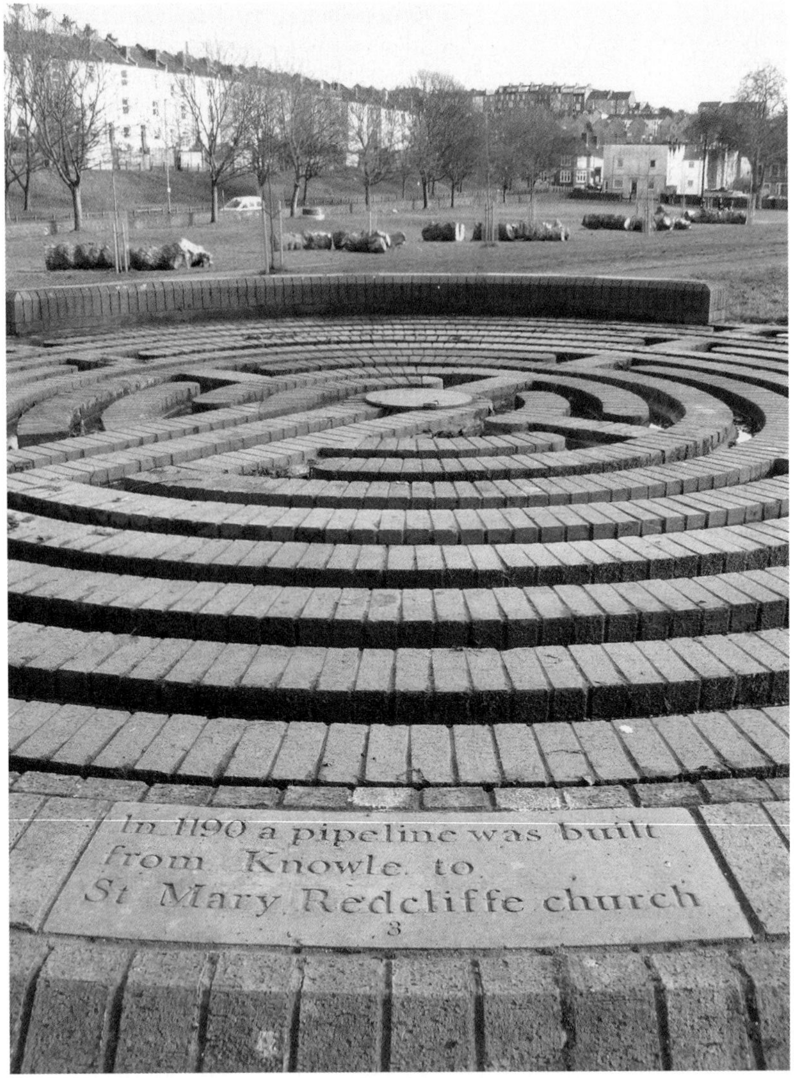

Peter Milner and Jane Norbury, *St Mary Redcliffe Maze, Victoria Park*

approximately 19m and has 25 ceramic plaques at regular intervals. These tell the history of the water supply and its effect on public health, from the benefits of the early conduit, and the deaths from the cholera epidemics in 1832 and 1849, to the new sewers in the 1850s and sewerage improvements over a hundred years later.

The Bristol architect Mike Jenner described this unusual installation as 'a delightful and brilliant idea, beautifully carried out, a constant source of pleasure to small children who float sticks around the convolutions of the channel'.[2]

Both the idea and the inspiration came from Peter Milner, an artist/designer who lived opposite Victoria Park in the 1980s. As a local resident he was aware of the inscribed stones in Victoria Park that mark the course of the medieval pipeline bringing drinking water from the spring at Knowle, through Lower Knowle and Bedminster to St Mary Redcliffe, a distance of about one and a half miles. An annual autumn Pipe Walk by the vicar, churchwardens, and parishioners of St Mary Redcliffe from the source of the spring to the church remains one of Bristol's oldest customs. The ancient pipe had been damaged by wartime bombing in Redcliffe but it was thought to be still intact as far as Victoria Park, and this was to prove correct.

Milner had first thought that it:

> would be good to have some sort of visual focus in the park that could be seen from the dramatic vantage point of St Luke's Church steps, which descend through the streets of Totterdown towards the park. The initial idea was to paint a design onto the tarmac of a playground in the park. Mazes were 'in the air' at the time.[3]

This prompted Milner to remember the roof boss in the north aisle of St Mary Redcliffe Church. Its pattern is identical to the large maze inlaid across the full width of the nave of Chartres Cathedral. This pattern is a single path design, which winds back-and-forth within a geometrical plan. The path or channel has the potential to convey a continuous stream of water from the heart of the maze. A leaf that fell

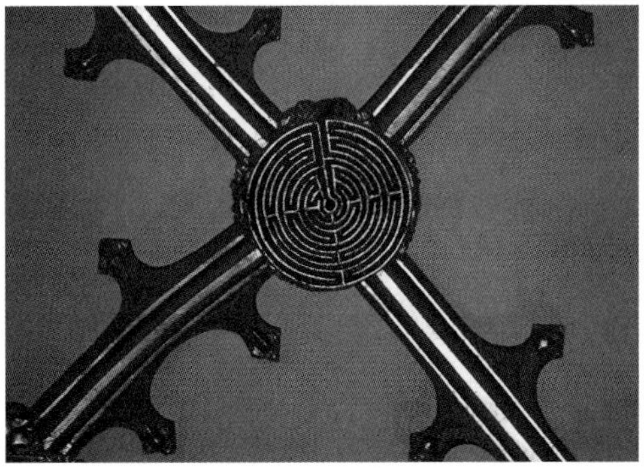

Roof boss maze in the north aisle of St Mary Redcliffe

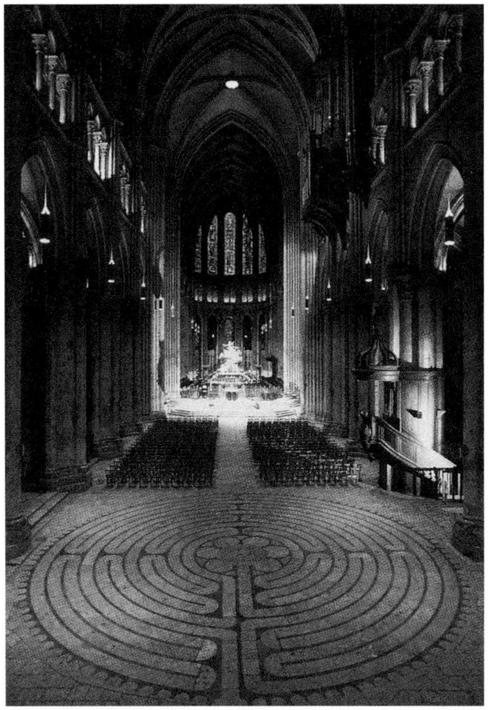

Maze in the nave of Chartres Cathedral

at the centre would float gently down every channel to the mouth at the rim. The central axis of the maze is aligned with the spire of St Mary Redcliffe, visible to the south.

Milner invited Jane Norbury, a Bristol ceramic artist with whom he had previously worked, to collaborate with him. She had already designed brick sculptures and was well aware of the long history of the famous engineering brick company at Cattybrook, near Almondsbury, north of Bristol. Now owned by Ibstock, the Cattybrook works had been founded in 1864 by Charles Richardson, the railway engineer. It had not only supplied impervious lining bricks for the Severn Tunnel, but had been the preferred brick for many major Bristol buildings, including the Imperial Tobacco Company's headquarters in Bedminster.

Milner and Norbury worked closely with Hamish Orr-Ewing, a Bristol city engineer working on the Wessex Water sewer project. During the construction of the maze, the old pipeline was uncovered and found to be in good condition as far as the railway bridge in St Luke's Road.

At the opening ceremony, St Mary Redcliffe collaborated in an event to raise funds to develop water supply in Burundi, Central Africa. This involved throwing coins into the maze as if into a fountain and a considerable amount of money was collected.

There have been recent rather crude repairs to the brickwork; the water no longer flows and the drain is blocked.

Notes

[1] Leech, *The Pipes, Pumps and Conduits of Bristol*; the outlet is marked by a lion's head tap and large semi-circular bronze surround set into the side of the churchyard wall on Redcliffe Hill (see Redcliff Hill). [2] M. Jenner, *Bristol Evening Post*, 1985. [3] Peter Milner, personal email, 3 August 2003.

Victoria Street

Transport House, Victoria Street, south side, on the corner of Mitchell Lane

Three Naked Male Figures Holding a Single Flaming Torch C69

Sculptor: unknown

Architect: White and Travis, London
Date: 1959
Material: stone
Dimensions: approx. 4m high
Inscribed: T & GWU
Status: not listed
Owned by Unite (formerly Transport and General Workers Union)
Condition: good

This impressive relief of three unusually naked men appears to have been carved in situ from the stone dressing to this corner façade. The building was opened by Frank Cousins, the

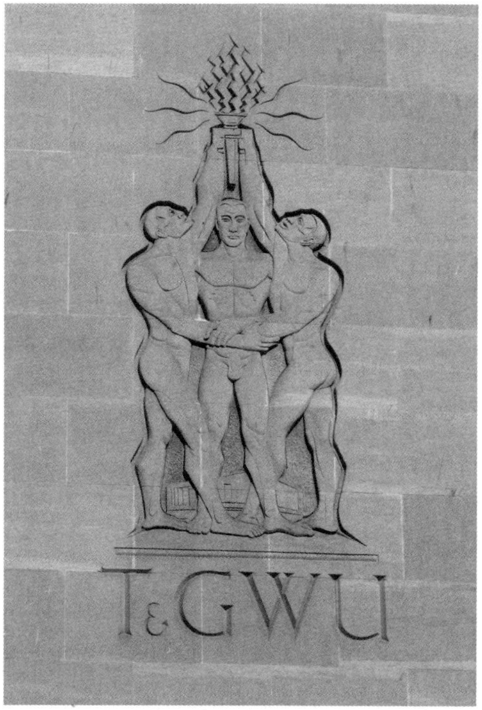

T & GWU emblem of unity

general secretary of the Transport and General Workers Union, on 30 October 1959, but newspaper accounts make no reference to the relief. In his speech he decried the term 'wildcat strike' and the tendency to suspect that communist agitators were behind every grievance. He noted that members in the west of England had proved their loyalty time and time again, and that they were proud of their close association with men like Ben Tillet and Ernest Bevin.[1]

The sculpture links the flame of truth, liberty and justice to unity of purpose and oaths of allegiance. The heroic idealism of the image may go back to Jacques Louis David's painting *The Oath of the Horatii* and his study for *The Tennis Court Oath*. The earlier painting foreshadowed the French Revolution, while the other depicted an early event within it.[2]

Bristol's regional secretary at the time of the opening of the building, Ronald Nethercott, remembers the consternation caused by the figures' nudity rather than any alarm at the image's revolutionary associations.[3]

Notes
[1] *Evening Post*, 30 October 1959. [2] Louvre and Versailles, respectively. [3] In conversation August 2008; Mr Nethercott confirms that the relief was completed before the opening, and recalls that Mr Travis was the architect.

Welsh Back

On the quayside at Welsh Back at the junction with Crow Lane

Memorial to Merchant Seafarers C62

Sculptor: David Backhouse

Date: 2001
Materials: Portland stone with a bronze collar and a bronze plaque in the paving, together with the surrounding seating and trees
Dimensions: domed column 145cm high, 110cm diameter; three circular steps, 4.5m diameter at base
Inscription: in raised Roman lettering cast in bronze on one side of the central column – Merchant Seamen / In war and peace they plied their trade / Over the angry seas / Remember them as here you stand/ Beneath these placid trees. / Capt. J. Earl / June 2000
—: inscribed on the opposite side – This memorial is a tribute to / all merchant seafarers who sailed / to and from Bristol / throughout the ages.
—: on a separate bronze plaque in the new granite setts – IN 1996 A SMALL GROUP OF LOCAL SEAFARERS FOUNDED/ THE BRISTOL BRANCH OF THE MERCANT NAVY ASSOCIATION / ONE OF ITS AIMS WAS TO CREATE A MEMORIAL AT THE HARBOUR SIDE / TO THOSE SEAFARERS WHO HELPED TO / BRING PEACE AND PROSPERITY TO THIS GREAT CITY. / IN THE YEAR 2000 DAVID BACKHOUSE FRBS RWA / WAS COMMISSIONED TO CREATE THE MEMORIAL / WHICH WAS UNVEILED BY H.R.H. THE PRINCESS ROYAL / ON 21ST MAY 2001.
—: a more recent, larger and upright memorial stone is similarly, but not identically inscribed
Status: not listed
Owned by Merchant Navy Association of Bristol
Condition: good; two of the trees, which are an integral part of the design, need replacing (2008)

A quarter of all merchant seamen died in the Second World War, 'a more grievous toll than any other service'.[1] In May 1996, the Merchant Navy Association of Bristol was formed with Harry Higgins as chairman and Derek Tedder as his deputy. By September of that year, this Bristol Branch was accepted by the national body.[2] The association's main concern was that since the 'removal from the former Seaman's Institute in Prince Street in 1981 of a plaque to commemorate the merchant seamen who lost their lives at sea, there has been no fitting tribute in Bristol to those who sailed from Bristol never to return'.[3]

Selecting and securing agreement on a suitable site was difficult. The site first proposed for a memorial comprising trees and seats was between Broad Quay and Narrow Quay. That plan involved relocating the King George V fountain on Broad Quay. As it became 'more unsatisfactory and expensive… new ideas and other sites were considered'.[4] In July 1999, members of the Memorial Committee met Steve Perry, divisional director of Central Building Control, and his associates suggested a site at Welsh Back. This was promptly accepted. By September 1999 the appeal had reached £76,866, and the city had agreed to give the site.[5] The association had earlier approached Public Arts South West and were persuaded to employ a project manager.[6] Diana Hatton was appointed. In 1998, a list of thirteen artists was compiled.[7] The appeal aimed to raise £100,000 and the budget was

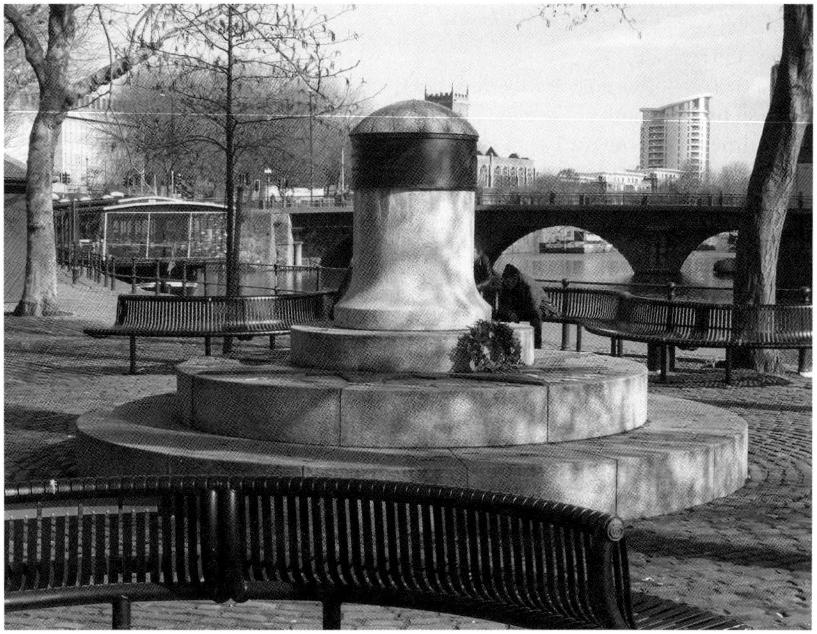

David Backhouse, *Memorial to Merchant Seafarers*

apportioned as follows: design team fees, £10,000; external works, £40,000; and artist's fees, £50,000.[8] By April 2000, a panel comprising members of the Memorial Committee, the director of the Architectural Centre and officers from Bristol City Council had shortlisted four artists and commissioned each to present designs and a model for exhibition at St Stephen's Church.[9] After gaining the views of interested people in the branch, the panel made a decision on 5 May and David Backhouse's winning design was displayed at the Architectural Centre at the end of the month.[10] For over three years Backhouse had been the preferred choice of the late Richard Hill, the driving force behind the project. The project manager helped 'with technical issues such as maintenance, artists' contracts, budgeting, planning permission and engineering issues'.[11] The design of the curved and encircling seating was also by Backhouse, and each seat bears the motif of the association.

The association had requested that the memorial 'be sufficiently dignified, appropriate for its purpose, and sensitive to the living memory of bereaved visitors'. The themes 'Navigating; Anchoring; Foundering; Harbouring' were listed.[12] Integration with the surrounding space was also an aim. After five years the resulting monument was unveiled in the summer of 2001.

With the exception of the second memorial plaque, the memorial uses Portland stone throughout. On three circular tiers, or steps, is a short, domed column, suggesting a ship's binnacle. The second tier has triangular bronze plates presenting sixteen points of the compass. A bronze collar at the top of the central column displays the inscription. The top tier comprises four stone segments, the middle eight, and the lowest tier sixteen segments.

The second plaque or memorial stone was presumably demanded by members, who may have been disappointed by the discretion of the bronze floor plaque on the far side of the monument near the water's edge. However, its obtrusiveness, scale and colouring are out of sympathy with the quiet dignity and coherence of the memorial as a whole.

Notes

[1 Merchant Navy Association, Bristol branch, *An Appeal for a Memorial Garden in Bristol Docks* (Bristol, 1998), p.1. [2] Merchant Navy Association, 'Potted history: Merchant Navy Association', BRO. [3] Ibid. [4] Ibid. Handwritten notes added to printed leaflet, p.2. [5] Ibid. [6] D. Hatton, PASW regional newsletter, autumn 2001. [7] They were: Bruce Allan, David Backhouse, Stephen Cox, Miles Davis, Roger Dean, Michael Fairfax, Neville Gabie, Richard Grasby, John Maine, Peter Randall-Page, Phillipa Threlfall, Peter Thursby and Richard Wentworth. [8] Report by the Concept Planning Group, *City Centre Promenade Harbourside Bristol Merchant Navy Association(Bristol) Memorial Project,* April 1998, p.2. [9] Diana Hatton, letter announcing exhibition of shortlisted designs, 22 April 2000. [10] As note 8. [11] As note 9. [12] As note 8.

West Street

The Palace Hotel at the corner of West Street and Lawford Street at the end of Old Market

Telamones C27

Sculptor: unknown

Architect: attributed to W. H. Hawtin
Date: 1869
Material: limestone
Dimensions: approx. 240cm high, 80cm wide
Status: Grade II
Condition: poor

The two telamones – the male version of the caryatid – dominate this curved corner-building, the Palace Hotel. They are a fully integrated part of this extensively decorated façade and are included here as a further example of the rich decorative carving on so many of Bristol's High Victorian buildings.

The two tall 'Assyrian-style' figures are rather rigid, perhaps deliberately so.[1] They are bare-chested and bearded, and on their cloth-covered heads are baskets of fruit and leaves,

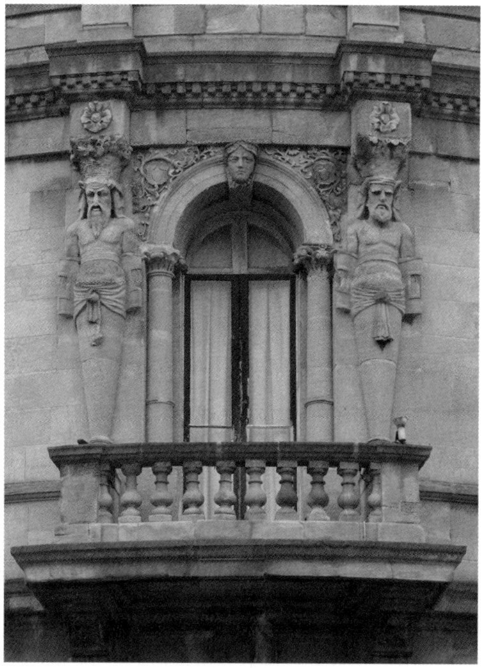

W. H. Hawtin, architect (attributed to), ***Telamones on the Palace Hotel***

which form capitals in support of the entablature. Their forearms have armour-like casing. Below their loin cloths, tied centrally, their bodies become inverted cones. The quality of the carving is unusually poor.

Andrew Foyle has recently called the Palace Hotel 'an absurdly high and pretentious gin palace, 1869–70, a speculation by Thomas Morgan to profit from a new railway station' (the Midland Railway terminus that was ultimately located half a mile away).[2] Foyle also noted the date, 1869, carved on the façade, which he attributed to the architect of the Royal Hotel, W. H. Hawtin.

Alexander Heaney, a Bristol artist, gave the façade a certain dignity in an excellent etching, *Public House*, in 1913.[3] However, in 1990 the *Bristol Evening Post* chose to ridicule the figures with the headline 'Life's not a barrel of laughs stuck up here'.[4]

The British Pub Guide recently referred to the pub's 'opulent frontage, and magnificent and unique interior', but implied that the latter was under serious threat.[5]

Notes
[1] English Heritage Listing, Bristol, 901-1/12/1659. [2] Foyle and Cherry, *Bristol*, p.265. [3] S. Stoddard, *City Impressions: Bristol Etchers 1910–1935* (Bristol, 1990), p.45. [4] *Bristol Evening Post*, 22 November 1990. [5] http://www.britishpubguide.com/cgi-bin/pubsearch.cgi?results:Bristol:353.

Whiteladies Road

1–3 Whiteladies Gate, at the junction of Whiteladies Gate and Cotham Hill

Six Statuettes of Kings and Queens B27

Architect/builder and probable sculptor: Joseph William King

Date: 1873
Material: stone, painted
Dimensions: approx. 1m high
Status: Grade II*
Condition: poor

J. W. King was an 'eccentric builder who planned extravagant schemes in various parts of the city, none of which was ever completed… There is still pleasure to be got from his fanciful decoration.'[1] The statues on this corner building announce the Royal Arcade, much of which was either not completed or was later demolished. Better known is Mr King's Royal Bazaar and Winter Gardens in Boyce's Avenue, Clifton. That was never quite finished, but it has recently become an arcade of shops once again. In Boyce's Avenue he followed the example of the wigmaker and developer, Thomas Boyce, a hundred years earlier, and named the new street that ran beside his bazaar after himself: King's Road. The statues on the Whiteladies Road arcade – Eleanor of Aquitaine and Henry II, Isabella of Angouleme and King John, Richard I, and Edward I – were

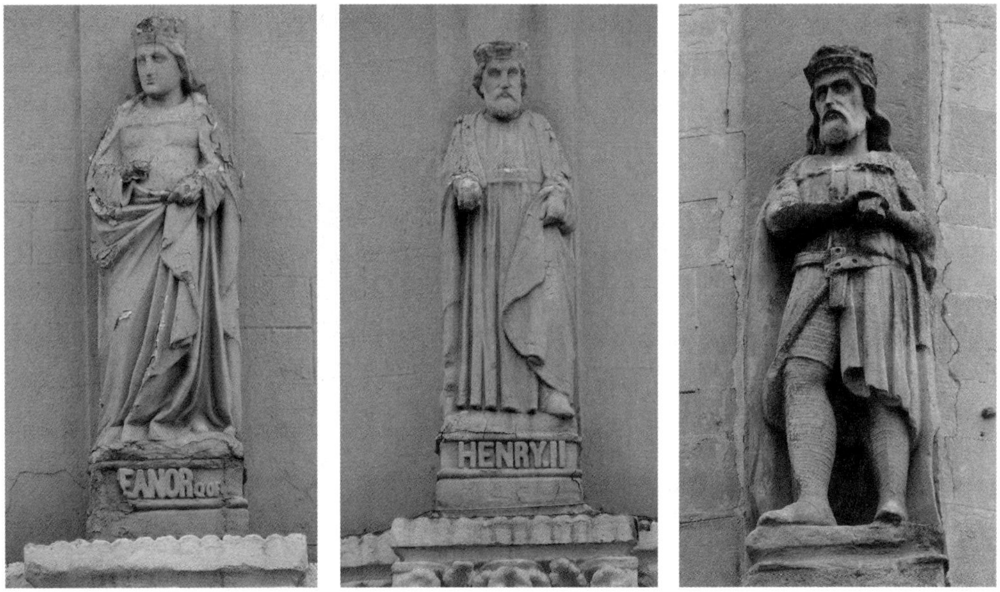

Joseph William King, from left: *Eleanor of Aquitaine*; *Henry II*; *Richard I*

presumably also intended to remind us of Mr King.

In 1855, Joseph William King was recorded as a builder and mason specialising in ornamental freestone. By 1865 he had premises in Clifton by the Artillery Ground on Whiteladies Road, and a decade later he is listed as an architect and surveyor.[2] It is very possible that he was himself the carver of the statues.

Notes
[1] Gomme, p.437. [2] S. Jones, *Whiteladies Walks: Five Town Trails in a Victorian Conservation Area* (Bristol, 1976), p.15.

2 Whiteladies Road, formerly the Royal Colonial Institute

Four Atlantes B34

Sculptor: William John Smith

Architect: Norman G. Bridgman, FRIBA, of Bridgman and Bridgman
Date: 1915
Materials: four carved figures in Bath stone
Dimensions: approx. 200cm high, 90cm wide
Inscriptions: on each globe supported by the telamon are the capitalised names of parts of the former British Empire – Australia, Canada, India and Africa
Status: Grade II
Condition: good

The premises were built for the Bristol Branch of the Royal Colonial Institute. The name was subsequently changed to Royal Empire Society and finally to the Royal Commonwealth Society, which left the building in 1964.[1] Among the purposes of the institute were the provision 'of a place of meeting for all ladies and gentlemen connected with the Colonies and British India' and the establishment 'of a Reading-room and a Library, in which recent and authentic intelligence upon Colonial and Indian subjects may be constantly available'.[2]

The architect had to deal with an irregular site, left after an old house to the east of the Victoria Rooms had been demolished.[3] There was considerable concern over the new building's proximity to the Victoria Rooms and to the King Edward VII Memorial, its statue and fountain, which were the pride of Edwardian Bristol and had been recently completed at great expense and trouble.[4] The angle of the Victoria Rooms and of the Whiteladies Road demanded that two of the adjoining facades of the new institute enjoy equal prominence without compromising the Victoria Rooms, and that the third side-façade should not conflict with the earlier building.[5] The planning application and ground plan were approved in October 1913, and Bridgman's building was opened in May 1915.[6] *The Builder* thought Norman Bridgman had succeeded with the problem of the proximity of the Victoria Rooms: 'The architect's design is less severe and monumental, [than the Victoria Rooms] but cannot be regarded as in any way disturbing or undesirable'.[7] Sensitivity about the new building was highlighted in August 1922, when there was an attempt to build an extension to the Royal Colonial Institute. Sir George Oatley advised that no land belonging to the Victoria Rooms should be sold to the Institute 'if their extension would spoil the front aspect of the Rooms'.[8]

> Emblems of the Empire have been introduced as ornaments to the column caps, cornices and leaded glass; while the names of four important possessions are carved on hemispheres, borne by figures of Atlas, surmounting panel pilasters at the principal angles.[9]

Four male figures, all in the same pose, support globes with their arms. The globes are deeply marked with lines of latitude and longitude. Minor differences in their heavily muscled torsos and faces can be seen in the carving. Australia and Canada are on the façade facing Queen's Road. India and Africa face Whiteladies Road.

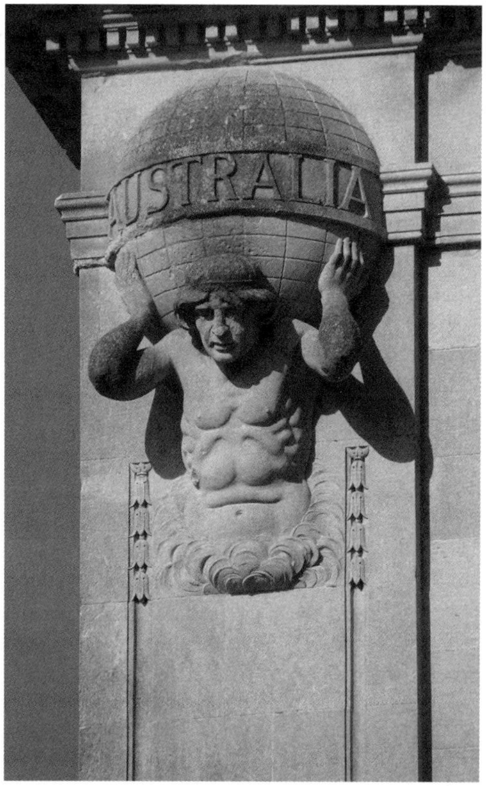

William John Smith, *Atlas, Australia*

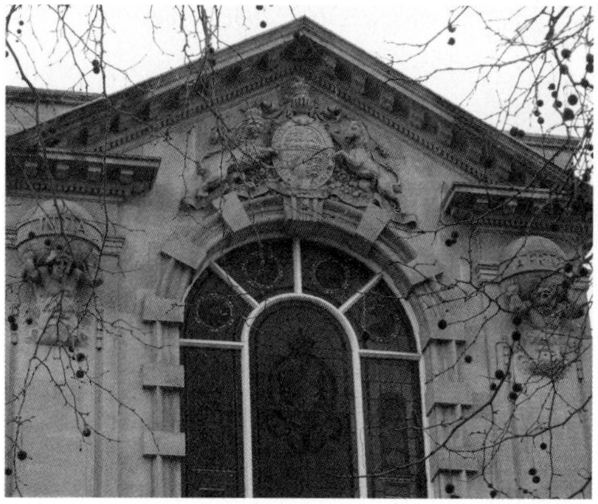

William John Smith, *Atlantes of India and Africa and the royal coat of arms*

> With its Atlantides wearily shouldering the great burden of a global empire… the elevation perfectly captures that Kiplingesque vision of an immense labour gallantly supported by an impartial master-race destined to administer peace and justice to 'the lesser breed without the Law'. [10]

William Smith, named as the sculptor in *The Builder's* review of the newly opened building in 1916, was a local man who lived in Montpelier. His largest work in Bristol is the group described as *Architecture, Painting and Sculpture* (1905) above the pediment of the Bristol Museum and Art Gallery in Queen's Road. Inside the museum, the larger Atlantes figures beside the entrance are also by him and are a decade earlier in date. Those figures are more powerful and do not have the rubbery arms that so awkwardly support the empire at the former Royal Colonial Institute. At the museum, Smith was the carver of the figures which had been modelled by a London sculptor. At the Royal Colonial Institute Smith may have been on his own.

Notes

[1] B. Little, 'The story of the Victoria Rooms', Bristol Central Library. [2] Royal Colonial Institute, Bristol branch, *Year Book 1914* (Bristol, 1915), p.6. [3] *The Builder*, 10 March 1916, p.2. [4] As note 2, p.10. [5] Ibid. [6] BRO, building plans. [7] As note 2. [8] As note 1. [9] As note 3. [10] Mowl, *Last of the Merchant Princes*, pl. 90.

Winterstoke Road

At Sainsbury's superstore, on an outside wall by the trolley bay

Four Bristol Scenes A27

Sculptor: Barbara Ash

Architects: Hoggett Lock-Necrews
Project manager: Henry Grala
Date: 1992
Materials: four Bath stone reliefs
Dimensions: approx. 60cm by 90cm
Three signed: BARBARA ASH 92
Status: not listed
Owned by J. Sainsbury plc
Condition: good

Sainsbury's have commissioned sculpture for nearly all their modern superstores. They have employed an impressive range of artists, using a wide variety of materials and approaches.

At the Winterstoke Road store, four blocks of Bath stone are set into the brick wall of the supermarket in the shopping-trolley bay, about 150cm from the ground. They have been deeply cut with identical flat-angled 'frames' and all are carved from single pieces of stone. Each portrays a different but instantly recognisable view of Bristol with an innocent childlike vision.

In the far left panel, the sculptor depicts Cabot Tower with one tree on either side. Three hot air balloons drift among the clouds as if from the annual Bristol Balloon Festival. A man sits on the ground, his back against the tree on the right. The second panel depicts the *SS Great Britain*, seen across the Floating Harbour. In the third panel an observer gazes dreamily across the steep sides of the Avon Gorge towards the Clifton Suspension Bridge. There are two ships on the river below. The fourth panel looks west across the Floating Harbour from the Industrial Museum and features the jib of the Fairbairn Steam Crane.

Barbara Ash was commissioned as the result of a limited competition. She carves her own work and these deep relief panels at Winterstoke Road were her first public commission.

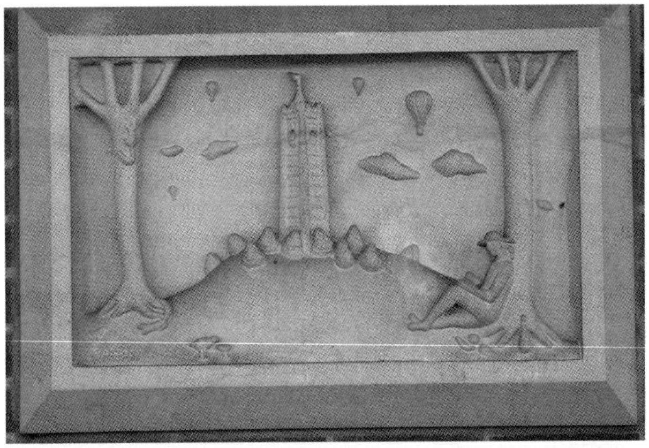

Barbara Ash, *Cabot Tower*

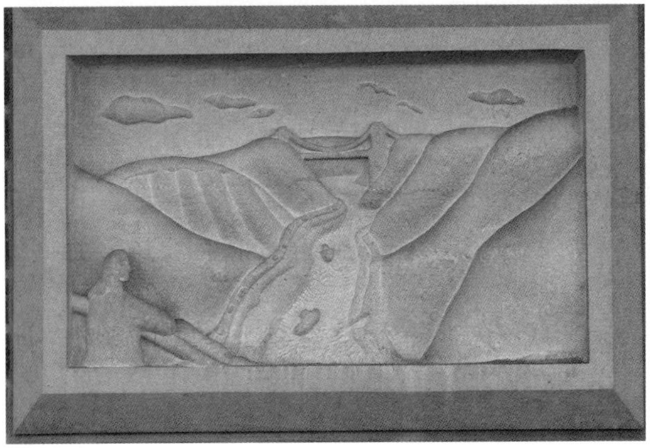

Barbara Ash, *Avon Gorge*

Worcester Road

Opposite Worcester Terrace in the grounds of the Cathedral Church of SS Peter and Paul, Clifton

Katyń Massacre Memorial B14

Sculptor: Alexander Paul Klecki

Date: 1985
Materials: fibre glass relief, mounted on an irregular piece of Cornish granite with a plinth of Portland stone
Dimensions: approx. 200cm high, 350cm wide
Inscription: in raised Roman letters – OFIAROM / KATYNIA / 1940 / IINNYCH / MEIJSC KAZNI W Z. S.S.R. / niech spoczywaja w pokoju wiecznym / TO THE MEMORY OF THOSE / MASSACRED IN KATYN 1940 / may they rest in peace
—: separately to the left-hand side – POLISH COMMUNITY / BRISTOL 1985
—: on the plinth – RZEZBA / A. P. KLECKI
Status: not listed
Condition: good

On 13 April 1943, the Germans uncovered over 4,000 corpses of Polish officers in the Katyń Forest in western Russia, now Belarus, and claimed that they had been killed by the Soviets

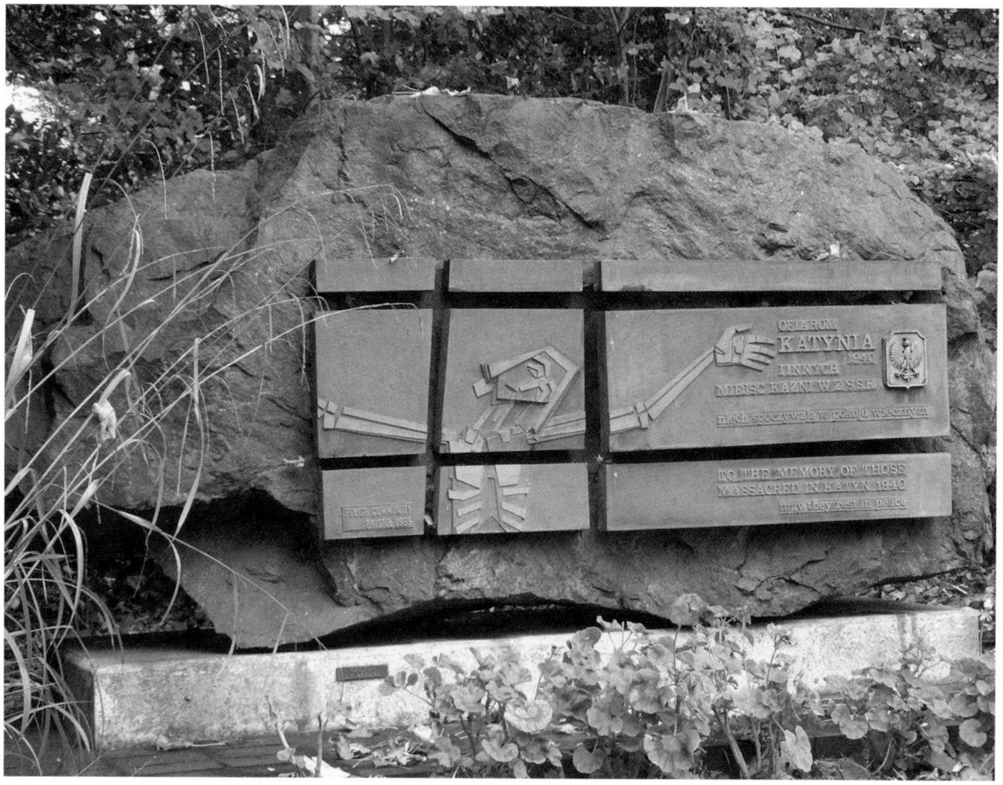

Alexander Paul Klecki, *Katyń Massacre Memorial*

in 1940. The Soviets immediately blamed the Germans and the controversy continued for over forty years. When this memorial was erected in 1985, Poland itself was still dismantling unofficial Katyń memorials in deference to the Soviet Union, which continued to deny responsibility, dating the genocide to 1941 and accusing the Germans. The Bristol memorial itself clearly dates the atrocities to 1940. In 1985, this represented a bold accusation against the Russians, for if the massacre occurred in that year, only the Soviets could have been responsible. Not until 1990 did Mikail Gorbachev finally admit the role of the Soviet secret police, the NKVD. In 1992, documents specifically implicating Joseph Stalin were released.

The Katyń massacre now refers not only to the executions in the forest itself but also to the planned massacre of over 20,000 Polish officers and men, professors, engineers, writers and others – the intelligentsia of Poland – at various locations in 1940 by the Soviets.

The memorial's nine fibreglass panels are set against a large and irregular seven-ton block of Cornish granite. The panels are separated by broad spaces, suggesting the outlines of the centre of a cross of crucifixion to which the figure of Christ is nailed. Three of the panels carry inscriptions in Polish and English, together with the Polish eagle on a shield.

The memorial was erected by the local Polish community in Bristol in 1985.[1] They are recorded as saying that the memorial commemorates:

> not only Army officers but the elite of Poland, intellectuals and priests, 4,500 in all, who were massacred in 1940. Each May Day Bank Holiday, the Polish community has a special Mass to commemorate those slaughtered at Katyń. Prayers are recited at the monument.[2]

When funds were being raised, the original intention was for the work to be placed outside the Polish church in Cheltenham Road, but the space was inadequate and Bishop Alexander accepted that the memorial should be at Bristol's Roman Catholic Cathedral in Clifton.[3]

The monument was designed and made by a Polish architect and sculptor living in London. Cornish granite was chosen for its similarity to the stone at Katyń.[4] The monolith was positioned by a Bristol resident, Alexander J. Chelmicki. It was consecrated by the Bishop of Bristol on 5 May 1985.

Bristol's memorial to Katyń predates similar tributes in Poland by several years. A cross in Kraców could not be erected until 1990. There is a war memorial at Gunnersbury Park, London, near the beginning of the M4, to Polish prisoners of war, which also makes reference to those massacred at Katyń. That memorial, a black granite obelisk, was erected after much controversy in 1976, despite representations against it from both the Soviet and Polish ambassadors.[5] Another at Cannock Chase in Staffordshire was erected in 1979.

Notes

[1] National Inventory of War Memorials, Bristol Memorial Project, April 1998. Based on 'information obtained through conversations with local Polish people'. [2] Ibid. [3] Letter from P.S.N. Boyce, National Inventory of War Memorials' researcher, 13 July 2001. [4] Ibid. [5] Byron, *London Statues*, p.367.

GLOSSARY

Italicised words indicate cross-references.

abacus: the flat slab forming the top of the *capital* of a *column*.
abutment: lateral support of an arch or bridge.
acanthus: an architectural ornament, derived from the Mediterranean plant of the same name, found mainly on *capitals, friezes* and *mouldings* of the *Corinthian order.*
acroterion (plural: **acroteria**): an ornamental block on the apex and at the lower angles of a *pediment,* bearing a statue or a carved *finial.*
aedicule: a *niche*, usually for a *statue*, framed by *columns* or *pilasters* and crowned with an *entablature* and *pediment.*
alabaster: a sulphate of lime or gypsum. It has often been used as a material for sculpture. In its natural state it has a translucency which can be enhanced by polishing, but in much early British sculpture it was painted and gilt.
allegory: a style of narrative or representation in which the events or figures symbolise another level of meaning. An allegorical figure is one which personifies a moral quality or larger concept. Such symbolic or emblematic figures and their *attributes* were frequently codified in the later medieval and renaissance periods.
aluminium: a light, silver-coloured metallic element obtained from bauxite, used for sculpture from the last years of the nineteenth century on.
Ancaster stone: an *oolitic limestone,* from Ancaster in south-west Lincolnshire, much favoured as a building stone.
apron: raised *panel* below a window or wall monument or *tablet.*
arabesque: intricate and fanciful surface decoration using symmetrical flowing lines, generally formed by the stems, leaves and tendrils of conventionalised plants, but also involving other features, such as vases, sphinxes and chimaeras.
arch: a curved structure, which may be a monument itself, e.g., a triumphal Arch, or decorative element within a monumental structure.
archivolt: a continuous moulding or series of mouldings forming the lower curve of an arch.
armillary sphere: skeleton celestial globe of metal rings representing equator, tropics etc.
art déco: a style of decorative art current in the 1920s and 30s, influenced by the rythms of jazz and cubism, essentially light and playful in character.
art nouveau: the prevalent decorative style of the years around 1900, characterised by flowing line, and artful asymmetry, sometimes associated with the arts and crafts movement, but also with literary symbolism.
atlantes (sing. **atlas**): supports in the form of full or half-length male figures, sculpted in the round or in *relief.* See also *caryatid* and *telamon.*
attic course/ attic storey: course or storey immediately above the *entablature,* less high than the lower storeys.
attribute: a symbolic object, by which an *allegorical* or sacred figure is conventionally identifiable.
banderole: ribbon-like scroll or stone band, often bearing an inscription.
basalt: dark igneous rock, commonly greenish or brownish-black, capable of being polished to a high sheen.
Bath stone: a honey-coloured *oolitic limestone* from Bath, Avon, ideal for carving, and frequently used as a building stone.
bay: division of an elevation, as defined by regular vertical features, such as pilasters, windows etc.
bell-jack: automaton, usually in the form of a man, engineered to strike the bell of a public clock.
Birmabright: the trade name of the former Birmetals Co., Clapgate Lane, Quinton, Birmingham, for various types of lightweight sheet metal in an alloy of aluminium and magnesium.
boss: knob or projection masking the junction of vaulting ribs, often elaborately carved.
brass: yellow alloy of copper and zinc.
bronze: brown alloy, most frequently of copper and tin, to which other ingredients can be added which affect its surface coloration, or *patina,* over time or in certain conditions. It has been a frequent material for sculpture since Antiquity.
bronze resin: (resin bronze, cold-cast bronze) a synthetic resin that has been coloured by means of a powdered bronze filler or alternatively coated with bronze, to provide a cheaper substitute for *cast bronze.*
caduceus: *attribute* of Hermes or Mercury, messenger of the Gods. It is a staff, around which twin snakes twine themselves, and which culminates in a pair of wings. Its symbolic significance varies, but it is most frequently associated with commerce.
Caithness stone: a grey sandstone from Caithness in north-west Scotland, whose formation from successive sedimentary deposits facilitates splitting into slabs, known as Caithness Flags. This stone is rich in fossil fish.
candelabrum: stand to support lamps or candles, consisting of a central upright and branches.
canopy: a hood or roof-like structure, projecting over a *niche,* or carried on *columns* or *piers* over a monument or sculpture, etc.
capital: the head of a *column* or pillar.
capstone: top-stone or coping.
Carrara Ware: a white matt glazed stoneware, designed to resemble marble, developed by the firm of Doulton towards the end of the nineteenth century. It was used at first for ornamental wares, and then increasingly for architectural cladding.
cartouche: an ornamental *panel* in the form of a scroll or sheet of paper with curling edges, often oval and usually bearing an emblem or inscription.
caryatid: a sculpted female figure, used in place of

a *column* or *pier* as an architectural support. See also *atlas* and *telamon*.

cast: to reproduce an object by making a negative mould of it and then pouring material (e.g. liquid plaster, molten metal) into the moulds. The principal methods of casting for metal sculpture are *lost wax* and *sand casting*.

Cattybrook brick: the Cattybrook Brick Works at Almondsbury, a few miles to the north of Bristol, was founded in 1865 by Charles Richardson, Engineer of Bristol and South Wales Railway. He realised the potential of the clay in the area for high quality engineering brick manufacture and used 30 million of them for lining the Severn Tunnel. The deep purple of these outstanding impermeable bricks is a characteristic of many later Victorian buildings in Bristol. Now owned by *Ibstock Brick* Ltd.

cavetto: a hollowed moulding with a quadrantal section.

cenotaph: a monument which commemorates a person or persons whose bodies are elsewhere.

ciborium: a fixed *canopy* over an altar, usually vaulted and supported on four columns. Also a receptacle for reservation of the sacrament.

ciment fondu: (cement fondu) a hard and quick-drying aluminous cement that can be coloured and is often used for moulded sculpture.

cipollino: banded green-and-grey marble, so called from the resemblance of its bands to the layers of an onion.

cire perdue: see *lost wax*.

classical: in its strictest sense, the art and architecture of ancient Greece and Rome, especially that of Greece in the fifth and fourth centuries BC and later Roman work copying it or deriving from it. By extension, any post-antique work that conforms to these models. See also *Neo-classicism*.

Clipsham stone: the hardest of the so-called Lincolnshire *limestones* quarried around Clipsham in Rutland. An *oolitic* limestone, usually pale cream, pale brown or buff-coloured, it contains a large number of shell fragments.

Coade stone: an artificial stone of extreme durability, and importantly, resistance to frost, manufactured and marketed by Mrs Eleanor Coade (see Biographies). It consisted of grog, flint, quartz sand, ground glass and clay, was hollow cast from piece moulds and tooled with great precision before casting.

column: a free-standing pillar, circular in section, consisting of a *shaft* and *capital*, sometimes with a *base*. An **engaged column** is one that appears to be partly embedded in a wall – also called an attached, applied, or half-column.

conduit: the structures referred to as *conduits* were the conduit heads, marking the access points to the town's piped water supply. These were frequently elaborately ornamented.

console: a decorative bracket of curved outline.

contrapposto (It. 'set against', 'opposed'): a way of representing the human body so as to suggest flexibility and a potential for movement. The weight is borne on one leg, while the other is relaxed. Consequently the weight-bearing hip is higher than the relaxed hip. This is balanced by the chest and shoulders which are twisted in the opposite direction.

corbel: projecting block, often ornamented, supporting something above.

Corinthian order: see *order*.

Cork red: a polishable carboniferous *limestone*, containing red stains and veins, quarried near Cork in Ireland. It is one of the limestones sometimes erroneously referred to as *marble*.

cornice: (i) the overhanging *moulding* which crowns a *façade;* (ii) the uppermost division of an *entablature*; (iii) the uppermost division of a *pedestal*.

cornucopia (plural **cornucopiae**): the 'horn of plenty'; a goat's horn overflowing with fruit, flowers, wheat or money.

Corsehill stone: a fine-grained, pale red-brown, slightly calcareous *sandstone* from a quarry in the vicinity of Annan in Dumfriesshire, Scotland.

Corten steel: a trade term for a type of *steel* which naturally forms a very tough protective, evenly-coloured layer of rust over its surface. Once this has formed the process stops and there is no further oxidisation and corrosion.

Craigleith stone: grey *sandstone* from the Craigleith quarry on the western outskirts of Edinburgh. This was the stone from which Edinburgh New Town was mainly built in the eighteenth and nineteenth centuries.

crocket: in Gothic architecture, an upward-pointing ornamental spur sculpted into vegetal form. Found in series on the angles of spires, pinnacles, gables, canopies etc.

cuirass: body armour, breastplate and backplate fastened together. These were often, especially in sculptural representations, given the form of idealised human torsos.

cypher (or **cipher**): interlaced initials or monogram of a person or institution.

diaper: repetitive surface decoration of lozenges or squares, flat or in relief.

direct carving: carving carried out directly in stone or wood, without use of mechanical aids for the reproduction of a preliminary model.

Dolomite stone: *limestone* which contains more than 50% carbonate minerals, of which over a half are dolomite minerals (calcium-magnesium carbonate). It resembles *marble*, but is not technically marble. When highly polished it looks like ivory.

Doric order: see *order*.

dormer: vertical-faced structure situated on a sloping roof, sometimes housing a window.

egg and dart (also called **egg and tongue**): *classical* moulding of alternating egg and arrow-head shapes.

Egyptian Cross: a T-shaped cross surmounted by an oval loop. Also called an Ankh, this is a symbol of life and rebirth.

electroplating and **electrotypes:** electroplating is the coating of base metal (generally nickel, but also copper) with silver or gold by electrolysis. The same system is used for the production of electrotypes. These are reproductions made from original models by coating moulds taken from them with metal by electrolysis. Discovered in the early nineteenth century, this technique was first used for sculpture in 1839.

emblem: typical representation, either a heraldic device, or a symbolic image of allegorical significance.

enamel: a coloured glass flux which can be combined with metal by heating. Enamel is generally applied in ground-up form, as a paste. The colours are obtained by heating silicon with metallic oxides.

entablature: in classical architecture, the superstructure carried by the *columns,* divided horizontally into the *architrave, frieze* and *cornice*.

façade: the front or face of a building or monument.

faculty: liberty to do something given by law,

authorization or licence. Needed for the modification of ecclesiastical structures.

fasces: originally a bundle of rods tied around an axe, a symbol of a Roman magistrate's authority. In architecture a decorative motif derived from this.

festoon: a sculpted ornament representing a garland of flowers, leaves, fruit, but also occasionally incorporating other symbolic objects, suspended between two points and tied with ribbons. Also called a *swag.*

fibreglass: a material made of resin embedded with fine strands or fibres of glass woven together to give it added strength. As it does not shrink or stretch, has high impact strength and can withstand high temperatures, it has become a popular material for modern sculpture.

Fibrocem: the trade name of an exceptionally hard commercially produced reinforced mortar compound, mostly used for rendering walls, notably of prison cells.

fillet: a narrow flat band running down a medieval shaft or along a roll moulding. It separates larger curved mouldings in classical cornices, fluting or bases.

finial: a terminal ornament on a spire, pinnacle etc.

fluting, flutes: concave grooves of semi-circular section, especially those running longitudinally on the shafts of *columns, pilasters,* etc.

foil: in *Gothic tracery,* an arc- or leaf-shaped decorative form which meets its neighbour at a cusp or point. The composite patterns thus created are known as trefoils, quatrefoils, cinqefoils or sexfoils, according to the number of lobes involved in them.

founder's mark: a sign or stamp on a sculpture, denoting the firm or individual responsible for its *casting.*

free-standing: of a monument or sculpture standing independently.

frieze: the middle horizontal division of a *classical entablature,* above the *architrave* and below the *cornice,* often decorated with relief sculpture. The term is also applied to any band of sculptured decoration.

gable: a triangular upper part of a wall, normally at the end of a ridged roof.

gadrooning: classical ribbed ornament like inverted fluting that flows into a lobed edge.

galvanised steel: *steel* coated with zinc as a protective barrier against atmospheric corrosion.

glass-reinforced polyester: a *polyester resin* strengthened with glass fibres.

gnomon: pillar, rod, pin or plate of sundial, showing time by its shadow on marked surface.

Gothic: descriptive of medieval art and architecture from the end of the Romanesque period to the beginning of the Renaissance. In architecture its central feature is the pointed *arch.*

granite: an extremely hard crystalline igneous rock consisting of feldspar, mica and quartz. It has a characteristically speckled appearance and may be left either in its rough state or given a high polish. It occurs in a wide variety of colours including black, red, pink and grey-green.

grotesque: a type of surface decoration in which human figures and/or animals are fancifully interwoven with plant forms. Popular in ancient Rome, the rooms thus decorated were buried for centuries. When excavated they were known in Italian as *grotte* ('caves') and so the style of their decoration became known as grotesque. By extension, this term is now applied to any fanciful decoration, which involves distortion of human or animal form.

herm: a sculpted human figure, either just the head, or the head and shoulders, or the figure down to the waist, rising from a usually square pillar. Also known as a term or terminal figure, because used in ancient times as a property boundary marker.

Hopton Wood stone: a *limestone* from Derbyshire, occurring in light cream and grey. In common with other polishable limestones it is sometimes referred to incorrectly as *marble.*

I-beam: *iron* or other metal girder whose section is in the form of an I.

Ibstock brick: the headquarters of the very large company, Ibstock Brick Ltd, which was founded in 1825 is still in the Leicestershire village of Ibstock. It specialises in facing bricks and amongst many acquisitions, acquired the *Cattybrook Brick* Co. in 1972.

iconography: illustration of subject by more or less conventionalised system of visual representation.

'ideal' sculpture: an academic definition of the higher reaches of sculptural expression. Such sculpture generally illustrated mythological, historical or literary themes, and interpreted them in a supra-naturalistic fashion, taking its cue from the traditions of classical antiquity. The expression was used most widely in the nineteenth century.

in situ: (i) of a monument or sculpture, still in the place for which it was intended; (ii) of an artist's work, executed on site.

interlace: a form of surface decoration simulating woven or entwined stems or bands.

Ionic order: see *order.*

iron: a naturally occurring metal, silver-white in its pure state, but more likely to be mixed with carbon and thus appearing dark grey. Very prone to rust (taking on characteristic reddish-brown colour), it is usually coated with several layers of paint when used for outdoor sculptures and monuments. As a sculptural material it may be either (i) cast – run into a mould in a molten state and allowed to cool to harden; or (ii) wrought – heated, made malleable, and hammered or worked into shape before being welded to other pieces. In the latter half of the twentieth century, sculptors have welded pre-cast industrial iron elements to create their own compositions.

jamb: one of the vertical sides of a door, window or archway.

Ketton stone: an *oolitic limestone* from Ketton, south-east Rutland, close to the Northamptonshire border. It is usually creamy yellow in colour and is characterised by the even size of its ooliths and the virtual absence of shells. It has long been highly valued as a material for carving.

keystone: the wedge-shaped stone at the summit of an arch, or a similar element crowning a window or doorway. Frequently this feature is made to project and to receive high or low relief carving.

lapis lazuli: sodium aluminium silicate sulphate, a bright blue hardstone containing gold specks. Ground lapis is used to create a precious form of ultramarine pigment. The material has also been much used for intaglio and inlaid work. Until the nineteenth century it could only be obtained from a region in north-eastern Afghanistan.

lead: heavy, easily fusible, and malleable base metal of a dull grey colour. Lead has occasionally been added to *bronze* alloys. Combined with tin it forms the material known as pewter. Much of the sculpture produced for open-air situations in the seventeenth and eighteenth centuries, which is described as lead sculpture, is in fact made from an alloy of this nature.

limestone: a sedimentary rock consisting wholly or chiefly of calcium carbonate formed by fossilised shell fragments and other skeletal remains. Most limestone is left with a matt finish, although certain of the harder types can take a polish after cutting and are commonly referred to as *marble.* Limestone most commonly occurs in white, grey, or tan.

loggia: a gallery, usually arcaded or colonnaded; sometimes *free-standing*.

lost wax (or ***cire perdue***)**:** metal *casting* technique used by sculptors, in which a thin layer of wax carrying all the fine modelling and details of the sculpture is laid over a fire-proof clay core and then invested within a rigidly-fixed, fire-proof, outer casing. The wax is then melted and drained away ('lost') through vents, and replaced with molten metal.

lunette: semi-circular surface on, or opening in a wall, framed by an *arch* or vault.

Mansfield stone: the town in Nottinghamshire that was the principal source of Sherwood sandstone, occurring pale yellow or pinkish-brown. It is fine grained and cuts well, but is also relatively soft and can be prone to weathering.

maquette (Fr. 'model')**:** in sculpture, a small three-dimensional preliminary sketch, usually roughly finished.

marble: in the strictest sense, *limestone* that has been recrystallized under the influence of heat, pressure, and aqueous solutions; in the broadest sense, any stone (particulraly limestone that has not undergone such a metamorphosis) that can take a polish. Although true marble occurs in a variety of colours, white has traditionally been most prized by sculptors, the most famous quarries being at **Carrara** in the Apuan Alps, Tuscany, and on the island of Paros (i.e. **Parian** marble) in the Aegean. Also prized is **Pentelic** marble, from Mount Pentelikos on the Greek mainland, characterised by its golden tone (caused by the presence of iron and mica). Other types include: **Grestela** marble, a dark-veined white marble, found in the Carrara quarries; **Sicilian** marble, a term applied to all marbles from the Apuan Alps that are white with cloudy and irregular bluish-grey veins.

mask: decorative motif representing a face or head in *relief,* of humans, gods or animals; sometimes portraits, often *grotesque*.

medallion: large medal, or panel shaped like one, often containing a portrait or symbolic image.

memento mori (L. 'remember you must die')**:** a text or image intended as a salutary reminder of the inevitability of death.

metope: in a *Doric frieze,* one of the rectangular surfaces alternating with *triglyphs,* frequently embellished with reliefs.

monogram: two or more letters interwoven to form a device, especially a person's initials interwoven (see also *cypher*).

mother of pearl: smooth, shiny and iridescent substance forming the lining of oyster and other shells, used for decorative surfaces and inlays.

motto: in heraldry, a brief text, often in Latin, inscribed on the scroll above or below the escutcheon.

moulding: a shaped ornamental strip, projecting or recessed, of continuous section.

mullion: vertical members between window lights.

mural crown: a crown in the form of a fortified wall or turret worn by the usually female figures who personify cities.

Muses: ancient Greek goddesses who preside over specific arts and sciences. They are the daughters of Zeus and the Titaness Mnemosyne ('Memory'), are nine in number, and live with Apollo on Mount Parnassus. Each has her own sphere of influence. Clio is the Muse of History, Euterpe of music and lyric poetry, Thalia of comedy and pastoral poetry, Melpomene of tragedy, Terpsichore of dancing and song, Erato of lyric and love poetry, Urania of astronomy, Calliope of epic poetry, and Polyhymnia of heroic hymns.

Neo-classicism (adj. **Neo-classical**)**:** artistic style and aesthetic movement which spread across Europe from the second half of the eighteenth century. It drew upon a renewed interest in the arts of antiquity, and was in part inspired by archaeological discoveries in and around Rome, at Pompeii and Herculaneum and elsewhere.

niche: a recess in a wall, often semi-circular in plan, usually intended to house a statue or other sculpture.

obelisk: a monumental tapering shaft, rectangular or square in section, ending pyramidally.

oculus: a circular opening or window.

onyx: a semi-precious, translucent hardstone, a type of quartz. The real onyx is generally banded black (or near black) and white. **Sardonyx,** often confused with it, is banded red, orange and white. The name **onyx marble** has been given in the trade to the much softer banded calcite alabaster.

oolitic: description of *limestones* whose structure is largely composed of ooliths, small rounded granules of carbonate of lime.

open-work: any kind of decorative work which is pierced through from one side to the other.

order: in *classical* architecture, an arrangement of *columns* and *entablatures* conforming to a certain set of rules. The Greek orders are (i) **Doric,** characterised by stout columns without *bases,* simple cushion-shaped *capitals,* and an entablature with a plain *architrave* and a *frieze* divided into *triglyphs* and *metopes*; (ii) **Ionic,** characterised by slender columns with bases, capitals decorated with volutes, and an entablature whose architrave is divided horizontally into *fasciae* and whose frieze is continuous; and (iii) **Corinthian,** characterised by relatively slender columns and bell-shaped capitals, decorated with *acanthus* leaves. The Romans added **Tuscan,** similar to the Greek Doric, but with a plain frieze and bases to the columns; **Roman Doric**, in which the columns have bases and occasionally *pedestals*, while the *echinus* is sometimes decorated with *egg and dart moulding*; and **Composite**, an enriched form of Corinthian with large volutes as well as acanthus leaves in the capital.

oriel window: a bay window cantilevered out from the wall of an upper storey, and often resting on a *corbel.*

palazzo (pl. ***palazzi***)**:** in Italian architecture, an imposing civic building or town house. The forms of Italian *palazzi* were adopted in other parts of the world, especially for clubs and commercial premises, but also for private residences.

palladium: a portable wooden image of the Greek Goddess Pallas Athena, which was supposed to have fallen from heaven, and on whose preservation the security of Troy depended.

panel: a distinct part of a surface, either framed or recessed, or projecting, which may bear a sculpted decoration or inscription.

pantheon: originally, a temple dedicated to all the gods, of which the best known example is the Pantheon in Rome, completed *c.* AD 126. By extension, the name came to be used for places or monumental complexes where national heroes, etc., were buried or commemorated (e.g., the Panthéon in Paris).

parapet: a wall bordering the edge of a high roof, or bridge etc.

passant: in heraldry, of an animal walking and looking to dexter, with three paws on the ground and right fore-paw raised.

patina: the surface colouring of, and sometimes encrustation, of metal, caused by chemical changes which may be deliberately induced in the foundry or occur naturally through exposure.

pavonazzo (from It. *pavone* = peacock)**:** white marble with mauve or purple stains and veins.

pedestal: the *base* supporting a sculpture or *column,* consisting of a *plinth,* a dado (or die) and a *cornice.*

pediment: in *classical* architecture, a low-pitched gable, framed by a *cornice* (the uppermost member of an *entablature*) and by two raking cornices. Originally triangular, pediments may also be segmental. Also, a pediment may be open at the apex (i.e. an open-topped or broken-apex pediment) or open in the middle of the horizontal cornice (an open-bed or broken-bed pediment). The ornamental surface framed by the pediment and sometimes decorated with sculpture is called the tympanum.

pendentive: a *spandrel* between adjacent arches, supporting a drum, dome or vault and consequently formed as part of a hemisphere. A pendentive may be enriched with relief sculpture.

personification: a representation of an abstract idea, moral quality or actual thing, by an imaginary person.

Phrygian bonnet: ancient conical cap with the top bent forward, worn by freed slaves, and hence identified with the cap of liberty.

pier: in architecture, a free-standing support, of rectangular, square or composite section. It may also be embedded in a wall as a buttress.

pilaster: a shallow rectangular *pier* projecting less than half its width from the wall. It may have a base and capital following the classical orders. Without these it is generally referred to as a pilaster strip.

pillar: a free-standing vertical support which, unlike a *column,* need not be circular in section.

plaque: a *panel*, fixed to a wall or *pedestal,* bearing sculpted decoration and/or an inscription.

plinth: (i) the lowest horizontal division of a *pedestal*; (ii) a low plain *base* (also called a *socle*); (iii) the projecting base of a wall.

polyester resin: a commercially produced synthetic material capable of being moulded. Its chief virtues are its tensile strength, which can be increased by the addition of *glass fibres*, and the ease with which it can be coloured.

polystyrene: polystyrene foam, which is now occasionally used by sculptors to make their preliminary models, is a packing material, made from styrene, a petroleum by-product, which has been polymerised and expanded. Polystyrene has proved a convenient material for the creation of models for sand casting, since, once the mould has been formed around it, it can be evaporated out under intense heat.

portico: a porch, consisting of a roof supported by columns.

Portland stone: a limestone from Dorset, highly durable, consistent in quality, and pure in colour, bleaching to white where exposed to the elements. It became the principal stone for grand architecture in Britain during the nineteenth century. Its suitability for such use was established in the seventeenth century, particularly by Sir Christopher Wren, whose craftsmen demonstrated how elaborately it could be carved.

predella (It. 'stool')**:** a panel with painting or relief sculpture at the foot of an altarpiece, generally of a long narrow format.

Purbeck stone: a fine-grained white *oolitic limestone*, quarried on the Isle of Purbeck in Dorset.

putto (pl. **putti**)**:** from the Italian. A representation of an idealised nude male child, used to perform a variety of allegorical and decorative functions in renaissance and later visual art.

rampant: in heraldry, especially of a lion, standing on hind legs with fore paws in the air.

relief: a sculptural composition with some or all areas projecting from a flat surface. There are several different types, graded according to the degree of their projection. The most common are (i) **bas-relief**, or low relief, in which the figures project up to half their notional depth from the surface; and (ii) **high relief**, in which the main parts of the design are almost detached from the surface. Many reliefs combine these two extremes in one design, though to do so has, at times, been considered an infringement of the classical code.

resin: the resin most frequently used in sculpture is polyester resin, a commercially produced synthetic material capable of being moulded. Its chief virtues are its tensile strength, which can be enhanced through the addition of glass fibres, and its versatility. It can either be allowed to retain its natural transparency through the addition of transparent dyes, or it can be made opaque through the addition of powder fillers or opaque pigments.

Roche Abbey stone: a white magnesian *limestone*, quarried in the vicinity of Roche Abbey in the West Riding of Yorkshire.

rotunda: a circular building, usually domed.

Rouge Royal marble: a *marble* from Philippeville, Namur, Belgium.

roundel: a circular decorative or sculpted *panel,* sometimes referred to in Italian as a 'tondo'.

sand casting: the most common technique for casting large metal sculptures. Complicated compositions have to be cast in sections. Each section of the plaster model is packed in very fine compacted sand, which forms the mould. This is then divided into parts and the model removed. These 'piece moulds' are then reassembled around a core and the molten metal is poured into the cavity. After cooling, the various sections of the sculpture are re-assembled, and rough spots and seams are removed in a finishing process.

sandstone: a sedimentary rock composed principally of particles of quartz, sometimes with small quantities of mica and feldspar, bound together in a cementing bed of silica, calcite, dolomite, oxide of iron, or clay. The nature of the bed determines the hardness of the stone, silica being the hardest.

Seravezza marble: from quarries 20 km to the southwest of *Cararra* in Tuscany.

shaft: the trunk of a *column,* between the *base* and the *capital.*

Sherwood sandstone: see *Mansfield*

slate: a metamorphic rock of sedimentary origin, its chief characteristic is the ease with which it can be cut into thin plates.

spandrel: the surface, roughly triangular in shape, formed by the outer curves of two adjoining *arches* and a horizontal line connecting their crowns. Also the surface, half this area, between the arch and a corner.

stainless steel: a chromium-*steel* alloy. The alloy is rendered stainless because its high chromium content – usually between 12 and 25% – protects its surface with a corrosion-resistant chromium oxide film.

steel: an alloy of *iron* and carbon, the chief advantages over iron being greater hardness and elasticity.

stele, stela (pl. **stelae**)**:** an upright slab of stone, originally used as a grave marker in ancient Greece. It may bear sculpted designs or inscriptions, or carry *panels* or *tablets.*

stylobate: properly speaking, a continuous base on which a row of columns stands, but sometimes used to describe the platform supporting a monument's pedestal.

supporter: in heraldry, one of a pair of figures or animals flanking the escutcheon.

swag: like a *festoon,* but may also consist of cloth or other material.

tabernacle: the biblical tabernacle was a small movable habitation. In ecclesiastical furnishing it is the word used to describe the receptacle of the sacrament, which often takes the form of a diminutive building. In monuments the word generally refers to the miniature architectural surround of an attached or relief memorial.

tablet: a small slab of stone or metal usually bearing a sculpted design or an inscription.

tau: a T-shaped cross named after the nineteenth letter in the Greek alphabet.

tazza: a saucer-shaped cup, especially one mounted on a foot.

telamon (pl. **telamones**)**:** male figure used as a pillar to support an *entablature,* named after a mythical Greek hero. See also *atlas* and *caryatid.*

term: see *herm.*

terracotta (It. 'baked earth')**:** clay that has been fired at a very high temperature and which may or may not be glazed. It is notable for its hardness and was much used for architectural ornament in the second half of the nineteenth century.

torus: a bold convex *moulding,* semi-circular in section, especially on the *base* of a *column.*

tracery: ornamental intersecting ribwork, characteristic of *Gothic* architecture, notably in the upper parts of windows, *panels,* and blind *arches,* etc.

triglyph: on a *Doric frieze,* one of the vertically-grooved blocks alternating with *metopes.*

truss: supporting structure or framework of a roof or bridge.

Tuscan order: see *order.*

tympanum: see *pediment.*

urn: vessel, generally of an ovoid form and with a circular base, used in antiquity to hold the ashes of the dead. This funerary function caused urns to be favoured images in commemorative monuments. They are also used to punctuate formal garden layouts, and to embellish *parapets.*

voussoir: wedge-shaped stones used in *arch* construction.

York stone: a carboniferous sandstone from quarries to the south of Leeds and Bradford and around Halifax, usually light brown in colour, with a fine, even grain and may be highly laminated. This latter quality renders it capable of being split into thin slabs, suitable for paving, coping, cladding etc.

MAKERS' BIOGRAPHIES

Sculptors and artists only; if we have been unable to add to the information already in the catalogue entry, the biographical entry has been omitted. Many entries take full advantage of earlier volumes in the National Recording Project series of the Public Sculpture of Britain.

Abbreviations

B1998: *Public Sculpture of Birmingham* by George T. Noszlopy, edited by Jeremy Beach
CL2003: *Public Sculpture of the City of London* by Philip Ward-Jackson
G2002: *Public Sculpture of Glasgow* by Ray McKenzie
L1997: *Public Sculpture of Liverpool* by Terry Cavanagh
M2004: *Public Sculpture of Greater Manchester* by Terry Wyke
SBC2005: *Public Sculpture of Staffordshire & the Black Country* by George T. Noszlopy and Fiona Waterhouse
WCS2003: *Public Sculpture of Warwickshire with Solihull and Coventry* by George T. Noszlopy
BRO: Bristol Record Office
Ison: *The Georgian Buildings of Bristol* by Walter Ison
Gomme, Jenner and Little: *Bristol, An Architectural History* by A. Gomme, M. Jenner and B. Little
Gunnis: *Dictionary of British Sculptors 160–1851* by Rupert Gunnis

George Gamon Adams, 1821–98, sculptor and medallist. Adams studied at the Royal Academy Schools on the recommendation of William Wyon, chief engraver at the Royal Mint, and he won the Silver Medal there in 1840. In 1846 he went to study under John Gibson, the sculptor associated with Liverpool, and in the following year Adams won the Royal Academy Gold Medal for *The Murder of the Innocents.* This was shown with two other works at the 1851 Great Exhibition. He made the death mask of the Duke of Wellington and statues of a number of distinguished public figures, among them the Duke of Wellington, Richard Cobden MP and Lord Seaton at Devonport. In his commentary, Gunnis says: 'Adams carved a number of public statues of unequal merit' and quoted the *Art Journal* (1862), which described his statue of General Napier in Trafalgar Square as being 'perhaps the worst piece of public sculpture in England'. His bust of Thomas Proctor at the Mansion House, Bristol, is undistinguished. See Clifton Down, Mansion House.

Sources: Gunnis; L1997

John Aiken, born 1950, Belfast; studied at Chelsea School of Art (1968–73) and British School at Rome (1973–5); appointed head of sculpture at Slade School of Fine Art, 1986, where he is currently professor/director. His interest in military architecture and in archaeology underpins much of his work, German fortifications in Northern France being for him 'the most impressive sculpture park in the world'. Commissions include a 40m frieze for Belfast City Hospital, 1986; works for Curzon Square and UCL Hospital, London; and monumental sculptures in Portuguese granite for the Department of the Environment, as well as the six Portwall Markers in Bristol. See Temple Quay.

Source: www.artscouncil-ni.org/collection/artists/art2.htm

Barbara Ash, born 1966, sculptor. After gaining her BA at Middlesex University, Barbara went on to a postgraduate course in Cyprus. She then spent two years at the RCA, including an exchange to Lisbon College of Art. Later she worked as an artist in residence at a special needs school in London, where she made a set of reliefs. In February 1985, she travelled to Moscow to create work for the International Ice and Snow Festival. In 1992, the year of her works at Sainsbury's in Bristol (see Winterstoke Road), she was awarded a Henry Moore Fellowship in Sculpture at Canterbury College of Art. She has had a studio/workshop at the Bristol Sculpture Shed, Spike Island Art Space.

Sources: information from the sculptor

William Aumonier, 1841–1914, architect, sculptor and carver in wood and brick. Born in London, of Huguenot stock. He exhibited at the RA and operated from premises at 1 New Inn Yard, Tottenham Court Road, London from 1880, with his sons William and Percy as assistants. Their important commissions include the New Victoria Law Courts, Birmingham (1886) and Bath Municipal Buildings (1891). They also executed wood carving for the steamships *Austral* and *Ophir*. See College Green, Bristol Central Library.

Sources: G2002

David Backhouse, born 1941. In the past twenty years, Backhouse has undertaken a number of sculptural commissions for public sites. Many of these are in London, notably *Dolphin Family* in Docklands. *Flying Figurehead* was created for Sainsbury's in Cardiff. In Bath he has a bronze statue, *The Young Mozart*, and in Bristol the *Cloaked Horseman* and the Merchant Navy Memorial (see Lewin's Mead and Welsh Back). His list of portrait commissions is long and varied. Included are the Marquess of Bath, José Carreras, Bishop Henderson of Bath and Wells and Sir Colin Davis. His largest commission to date came from the *Animals in War Memorial* competition in which forty sculptors took part. The resulting work was unveiled in Park Lane in November 2004. David Backhouse lives near Bradford-on -Avon.

Sources: information from the sculptor

Edward Hodges Baily, 1788–1867, sculptor. Born at Downend in Bristol, son of a ship's carver. After school, he worked for two years in a merchant's counting house before taking lessons in wax-modelling. Baily was converted to the 'higher aspirations' of monumental sculpture by John Bacon's monument to Mrs Draper in Bristol Cathedral. He sent work to London for inspection by John Flaxman, who then took him on as a pupil. He entered the Royal Academy Schools in 1808. In 1817, he was appointed chief modeller to the gold and silver smiths, Rundell and Bridge, and designed for the firm for the next 25 years. Baily's statue of *Eve at the Fountain* was rapturously received when shown at the Royal Academy. Executed in marble in 1821, it was purchased for the Bristol Institution (now in Bristol Museum and Art Gallery). By 1817, he had become an ARA and by 1821 an RA, the only sculptor to receive that title in the ten-year presidency of his fellow Bristol-born artist Sir Thomas Lawrence. During the 1820s, Baily executed relief sculpture for the Marble Arch and for Buckingham Palace. He had a very large practice in funerary monuments, which ranged from the routine to the theatrical and grandiose. Examples of the latter are the monuments to Sir W. Ponsonby in St Paul's Cathedral, 1820, and to Lord Holland in Westminster Abbey, 1840. Baily's public portrait statues were, however, admired for their restraint and for the uncompromising modernity of their costume. He sculpted the colossal marble figure of Nelson for Nelson's Column in Trafalgar Square, 1839–43; the monument to Sir Robert Peel for Bury, Lancs, 1852; and the deliberately prosaic portrait of George Stephenson, 1854, for the Great Hall of Euston Station (now in the National Railway Museum, York). Despite being one of the most esteemed Victorian statuaries, Baily experienced financial difficulties in the 1820s and in last years of his life. See Park Street and Corn Street, Old Council House and – for the monuments to Southey, Mrs Middleton and Dr Elwyn in Bristol Cathedral – see Katharine Eustace's essay in this volume.

Sources: Gunnis 1968; CL2003

Dail Behennah, basket-maker, took a degree in geography but also completed a City and Guilds Diploma in basketry at the London College of Furniture, which she completed in 1988. She has exhibited at major galleries throughout Britain and the USA, and her work is in many public collections, including: the Crafts Council, the Fitzwilliam Museum, and Cambridge and Birmingham Museum and Art Gallery. As well as her architectural work on the Pavilion Building at Harbourside, Bristol (see Harbourside), she also earlier designed woven rubbish bins for Castle Park. In her craft-maker interview with the V & A she said: 'I have devised most of my techniques myself and I like the structure to be visible and honest, showing a respect for the materials. My recent work is increasingly abstract and is a response to landscape and environmental concerns. I find that there is something very satisfying about pure geometric forms and I often use grids. I am interested in the effects of light and shadow as well as the visual interference as the layers of grids move into and out of view. I always try to make my work appear calm.'

Source:ww.vam.ac.uk/collections/contemporary/crafts/craft_interviews

Franta (Frantisek) Belsky, 1921–99, sculptor. Born in Brno, Czechoslovakia, son of economist Joseph Belsky. At 16 he won a prize in a sculpture competition in Prague. His family fled to England in 1938. Belsky studied at the Central School of Arts and Crafts. He joined other Czech exiles in the army to fight during the Second World War, serving in the artillery, and was decorated for his wartime service. He restarted his education, studying sculpture at the Royal College of Art. As a sculptor he was known for his portraiture but also produced abstract sculpture and architectural works. Portrait busts include Cecil Day-Lewis (National Portrait Gallery, 1952); Admiral Lord Cunningham (Trafalgar Square, 1967); Harry S. Truman (Presidential Library, Independence, Missouri, 1974); John Piper (National Portrait Gallery, 1987); and Winston Churchill (Churchill College, Cambridge). Belsky also executed many busts of members of the royal family. His public statues include Winston Churchill (Westminster College, Fulton, Missouri; British Embassy, Prague) and Lord Mountbatten of Burma (Horseguards Avenue, London, 1983). Other sculptures include *Joy Ride* (Town Square, Stevenage, 1957) and *Triga* (Callex House, Knightsbridge, 1958). The massive Shell Centre Fountain (Lambeth, 1963) is also by Belsky. He was a long-serving member and president of RSBS and a governor of St Martin's School of Art, 1967–88. He married Margaret Owen in 1964, who was to become better known as the cartoonist, Belsky. She died in 1989. In 1996 he married the Czech sculptor, Irena Sedlecka. Vaclav Havel presented Belsky with Presidential Medal of Merit in 1999. The papers of Franta Belsky – some 4,500 documents – are held by the Henry Moore Institute (2001.94) (see Narrow Plain).

Sources: Belsky, 1992; *Guardian*, 7 July 2000; Henry Moore Institute Newsletter, April/May 2006, no. 65

Philip Bews, born 1951, studied and worked in landscape architecture before taking first class BA (Hons) in fine art at Liverpool Polytechnic, 1982–6. In 1986–7 he was awarded a Sir John Moores Scholarship in fine art and was sculptor-in-residence at Birchwood Community and High School, Warrington. In 1986 he created the first of many fire sculptures. He now lives in the Forest of Dean, Gloucestershire, after moving from Cheshire in 1997. Most of his sculpture is site-specific and is often undertaken in collaboration with Diane Gorvin. He has undertaken commissions in Europe and Scandinavia, Canada, Australia, Hong Kong and Beijing. See Clifton Down, Bristol Zoo and Mall Gardens.

Source: www.bewsgorvin,co.uk

Naomi Blake, born 1924, sculptor, born in Czechoslovakia. After surviving Auschwitz, she has lived at various times in Milan, Rome and Jerusalem. On coming to London she studied for six years at Hornsey College of Art (now Middlesex University). In 1979 she was elected associate of the Royal Society of British Sculptors. Her public works include the *View II*, Hebrew University, Mount Scopus (1977); *Image*, Fitzroy Square (1979); *Sanctuary*, Waterlow Park (1985); and *Renew Our Days*, Sternberg Centre for Judaism, Finchley (1986). She has held solo exhibitions and been represented in many mixed shows in England and abroad, among them shows at the Royal West of England Academy, Bristol and Chelmsford Cathedral Festival in 1991. See College Green, Cathedral Churchyard.

Sources: information from the sculptor; CL2003; *Bristol Evening Post*, 15 December 1980

Judith Bluck, born 1936, worked as an engraver, designer and painter before finding her métier as a sculptor. She lives in North Yorkshire. Her large-scale works have taken many forms and used a variety of materials. A 24m brick relief, *The Legend of the Iron Gates*, made for the Sainsbury's site at Wilmslow, won the Otto Beit Medal of the RBS. She made the doors of the Crown Courts, Portsmouth, depicting *The Marriage of Charles II to Catherine of Braganza*. Her many animal sculptures include *Small Workhorse*, Ealing Broadway, 1985; *Sheep*, Milton Keynes; *Otter Group*, The Lanes, Carlisle; *Small Heavy Horse*, Marlow; and the Central Library in Dunedin, New Zealand. Her other works include: *The Legend of the Iron Gates*, Sainsbury's supermarket, Wilmslow, Cheshire; *Crucible Fountain*, Sheffield, 1979; *Natural Force II*, Yorkshire Building Society, Bradford; *Jimmy Dyer*, Carlisle; and *Boy on a Capstan*, Whitehaven. She is a fellow of the Art Workers' Guild. Her work has been exhibited in England, France and the USA, and she holds the Bronze and Silver Medals of the Société des Artistes Français. See Lewin's Mead.

Source: information from the sculptor

Joseph Edgar Boehm, 1834–90, sculptor. Born in Vienna, the son of Josef Daniel Böhm, an eminent Hungarian medal engraver and connoisseur. He started out as a medal engraver, and attended the Vienna Academy (1852–3), but by the late 1850s he had begun to produce statuettes of operatic celebrities. Around 1858, Boehm left Vienna for Italy. He then spent three years in Paris, where he married an English woman and converted to Protestantism. In 1862 he settled in England, where he immediately attracted attention with portrait busts and statuettes, and with his animal sculptures. In 1869 he received three commissions from Queen Victoria, and was appointed sculpture tutor to the young Princess Louise. Boehm became the queen's first sculptor in ordinary, and he was made a baronet in 1889. The lively, naturalistic modelling of his portraits, and the anatomical accuracy of his animal works – many of which were of equine subjects – struck a new note in contrast to the often bland idealism of high Victorian sculpture. Vastly prolific, Boehm created many public statues, the most celebrated being the equestrian statue of the Duke of Wellington at Hyde Park Corner, with its four attendant soldier figures, representing the four constituent nations of the United Kingdom. Boehm's assistant in his later years, and the heir to his vital modelling style, was the symbolist sculptor of *Eros*, Alfred Gilbert. See College Green.

Source: M. Stocker, *Royalist and Realist: The Life and Work of Sir Joseph Edgar Boehm*, 1988; CL2003

Richard Box, born 1969, sculptor. Completed his degree in fine art at Winchester School of Art in 1992. He moved to Bristol in 1995 to join Spike Island's Artspace and in 1992 took up a Leverhulme Residency in Bristol University's Physics Department. He was initially concerned with the specialist glass workshop but the residency culminated in the 'Field' exhibition (photographs of 1,301 fluorescent tubes powered only by the electric fields generated by overhead power lines) at the Physics Department early in 2004. He won the Bombay Sapphire Prize in the same year. An exhibition of his work was held at grvprojects, Edinburgh, in 2008. See Harbourside.

Source: www.richardbox.com

Edward George Bramwell, 1865–1944, modeller. Born in London, he studied at the City and Guilds School of Art, London, winning a silver medal for sculpture and a travelling scholarship. Working under George Frampton, W. S. Frith and T. Stirling Lee, he produced statuettes and small groups. He taught modelling at Westminster School of Art, and exhibited at the RA from 1898. See Queen's Road, Bristol Museum and Art Gallery.

Source: SBC2005

James George Bubb, 1782–1853. Bubb attended the Royal Academy Schools, winning a Silver Medal in 1805. He also worked with J. C. F. Rossi, later claiming that he had given considerable assistance in the carving of Rossi's tomb of Captain Faulkener in St Paul's Cathedral. In 1806 he won the corporation's competition for the monument to William Pitt the Younger for the Guildhall. The monument was not completed until 1813. Bubb worked for Mrs Coade's artificial stone factory, and went on to produce his own recipe for architectural terracotta. This was used very extensively on the new London Custom House, opened in 1818. Although deemed unsatisfactory, Bubb proceeded to decorate a large number of buildings in London with this material. His most inventive scheme was probably the frieze illustrating the history of music and the dance from the earliest times to the present, on the Italian Opera House in the Haymarket (1827), of which only fragments have survived. Bubb abandoned his terracotta around 1830, although he was later employed by the firm of Blashfield to model some of their architectural ornaments. At the Royal Academy, Bubb exhibited portrait busts and mythological figures. He also executed a number of church monuments. He was a prolific but not particularly talented sculptor, rather despised by the rest of the profession. See Corn Street, Commercial Rooms.

Sources: Gunnis, 1968; CL2003

Jon Buck, born 1951 in Bristol of a family of Pill pilots, Buck studied at Trent Polytechnic, Nottingham and at Manchester Polytechnic. He was a fellow in sculpture at Gloucestershire College of Arts and Technology, Cheltenham, 1980–1, and artist in residence for Thamesdown Borough Council, 1984–5. He is a senior lecturer at Southampton Solent University. He was elected a member of the RWA in 1990 and an associate of the RBS in 1994. He has had exhibitions at the Gallery Pangolin, Chalford and the Albermarle Gallery, London, and has undertaken many major public commissions. See Tyndall Avenue.

Sources: axisweb.org; RWA; University of Bristol, press release, 11 November 2005

Esmond Burton, stone- and wood-carver. Educated at Marlborough College, Burton was later articled to the carver Lawrence Turner. He was elected in 1919 as a carver to the Art Workers' Guild. He worked on the reredos of St George's Chapel in St Paul's, for the cathedral architect Mervyn Macartney, and collaborated with Goodhart-Rendel in the church of East Clandon, Surrey. His most substantial work was his contribution of figures to the screen of Ripon Cathedral, completed in 1948. His largest single work was a stone eagle on the RAF Memorial Screen at Brookwood Cemetery, designed by Edward Maufe. Burton was first and foremost a medievalist, but he also worked on occasion in a less period-specific style in stone. He was a member of the Vintners' Company, and was master from 1948–9. He was also a member and president of the Master Carvers' Association. See Denmark Street.

Sources: Sir Henry Blashfield, 'The Sculpture of Esmond Burton', *Country Life*, 27 January 1950, pp.234–5; G. T. Noszlopy and J. Beach, *Public Sculpture of Birmingham*, 1998; CL2003

Timothy Butler, born 1806. He won a silver medal from the Society of Arts in 1824, and in 1825 was admitted to the Royal Academy Schools on the recommendation of William Behnes. Two years later he was awarded the academy's silver medal. Between 1828 and 1879, Butler exhibited over 100 portrait busts at the Royal Academy. Though his first RA exhibit was entitled *Mars*, he exhibited no further ideal works. He did however produce a small number of funerary monuments. Butler's bust of Hugh Falconer (marble, 1866) is in the collection of the Royal Society, and his bust of Dr Jacob Bell (marble, 1863) is in the collection of the Pharmaceutical Society. See Colston Street, Colston Hall.

Source: Gunnis, 1968; CL2003

John Cassidy, 1860–1939, sculptor. Cassidy was born in Slane, County Meath, and left Ireland to study at the Manchester School of Art in 1892. There he won national medals and other prizes. He began to work professionally in 1887 when he was engaged to demonstrate modelling at the Manchester Jubilee Exhibition in 1882. It was from that work that commissions arose and he was able to set up as a sculptor. By 1911 he had a studio in Plymouth Grove, Manchester and wrote from there to the lord mayor of Bristol. He mentioned his Colston statue, 1895, and asked for his name to be put on the list of sculptors some months before the competition for the King Edward VII Memorial was announced. He took part but was unsuccessful. He made a statue of Queen Victoria for Belfast, and other public statues for Aberdeen, Bolton, London, and Manchester. Other works included bronze busts of Sir Charles Hallé and the Victorian painter W. P. Frith. His work was exhibited at the RA and the New Gallery. He died in Cheshire. The Slane History Society arranged an exhibition of Cassidy's life and work in 2004. See 'The Centre'.

Source: *John Cassidy: Sculptor and Painter*, 2004, Slane History Society

Hermon Cawthra, 1886–1973, sculptor. Born in London but studied at art schools in Shipley, 1904, and Leeds, 1907–9, before entering the RCA, 1909–12, and the RA Schools, 1912–6. Elected to the Royal Society of British Sculptors in 1937. He exhibited frequently at the RA and worked mostly in London. He made many memorials and monuments and architectural reliefs for cinemas and in wood, stone and bronze. E. Vincent Harris commissioned him to design *Dancing Child*, 1926, for Braintree Town Hall and he was the sculptor of the pediment of Stratton House, Piccadilly. See Corn Street.

Sources: *RA Exhibitors,1904–1950*; Waters, *Dictionary of British Artists*, 1975

Ann Christopher, born 1947, sculptor. Born in Watford, Hertfordshire, Ann Christopher first studied at Harrow School of Art. Between 1966 and 1969 she studied under Ralph Brown and Robert Clatworthy at the West of England College of Art. Among other distinctions she won the Harrison-Cowley Sculpture Award in 1968 and in 1971 the *Daily Telegraph* Young Sculptors' Competition. She is a fellow of the RBS and in 1994 gained its Silver Medal for Sculpture of Outstanding Merit. Since 1993 she has had commissions for sites in Washington DC, Plymouth, Silk Street, London, Bristol and Portishead. She is a member of the Royal Academy and the RWA. Her studio is in the West Country, near Chippenham. See Castle Park.

Sources: information from the sculptor

Thomas Clark, 1764–1829, mason and sculptor working in Bristol. An assistant to Sir Richard Westmacott at Eaton Hall. In Bristol he worked on the coats of arms on the new Council House in Corn Street, on restoration work in the Lord Mayor's Chapel and on the tomb, canopy and effigy of John Whitson in St Nicholas. See Corn Street, Council House.

Source: K. Eustace's essay, 'Bread and sermons', in this volume

Coade and Sealy, a firm that flourished between 1769 and 1843 as an artifical stone foundry. Eleanor Coade (1733–1821) came from a West

Country family and her manufactory was set up in Lambeth, beside the Thames, in 1769. The Coade factory excelled in making decorative and figurative mostly for architectural use, from material cast in moulds and then fired. Mrs Coade wisely used proficient sculptors of her day. From 1771, John Bacon the Elder acted as her chief designer. John Sealey (1749–1813) one of her cousins became a partner in 1799 when the company name was changed. When Eleanor died, the company was purchased by William Croggon, who had worked for the foundry, but it collapsed by 1833. Later reformed, the business moved from Lambeth and after 1843, when the moulds were sold, all production ceased. The largest and most prominent reminder of the endurance of her stone is the massive Coade lion on the south side of Westminster Bridge, within yards of the site of her original works. See Blaise Castle House; Corn Street, Commercial Rooms; Portland Square.

Source: A. Kelly, *Mrs Coade's Stone*, 1990

Thomas Colley, sculptor. *The Builder* records Mr T. Colley as the sculptor of two exuberant bank facades by W. B. Gingell in Corn Street: Bristol: National Provincial Bank, 33 Corn Street, 1864; and the Liverpool, London and Globe Insurance, 36 Corn Street, 1864–7. In 1870, Colley was described as of 'Stoke's-croft, Bristol, late of London', and in the same year his name appears in a Bristol directory as a 'Sculptor etc' of 10 Stokes Croft. In 1876 the directory has Thomas Colley & Son of 19 Stokes Croft. In 1880 there is also a Thomas Colley at 20 Melbourne Terrace, Newtown, Bristol; and in 1890 the business was recorded as Thomas Colley & Sons of Jamaica Street, Bristol. The only other Colley listed is Edwin Colley, sculptor, of 30 Clyde Road, Knowle. See 36 Corn Street.

Sources: *The Builder*, 19 October 1867, p.757; and 4 June 1870, pp.445, 447; *Matthews' Bristol Directory*

Stephen Cox, born 1946 in Bristol, sculptor. Cox trained at the West of England College of Art, 1964-5, Loughborough College of Art, 1965–6, and the Central School of Art, 1966–8. He then went on to teach at Coventry College of Art, 1968–72. From 1974 to 1977 he worked on minimalist 'surface works', using paint finishes on steel panels and setting them up as installations. His aim was to reclaim flatness for sculpture. In the 1980s, Cox turned his attention to stone, and sought inspiration from ancient traditions of carving. He worked in a vast variety of different stones and marbles, combining them occasionally with natural pigments. His first exhibition of stone works, at the Nigel Greenwood Gallery in 1983, consisted entirely of reliefs attached to the wall, but the following year he showed a large free-standing piece entitled *Palanzano* at the Liverpool International Garden Festival. This was named after the town in Italy where the peperino marble from which it was carved had been quarried. Italy was one of Cox's inspirational places, but in 1986 he set up a stone-carving workshop at Mahabalipuram in Southern India, and he has also worked in Egypt on locally quarried granites. In 1991, one of Cox's massive stone monoliths, entitled *Hymn*, was erected at the University of Kent, Canterbury. Although Cox has identified strongly with the religious and pantheistic qualities of Hindu temple sculpture, he has also contributed sculpture to Christian places of worship, notably the reredos, font and *Stations of the Cross* for St Peter's Church, Haringey, 1993. A substantial retrospective exhibition was held at Bristol Museum and Art Gallery in 2008 and one sculpture, owned by the artist still remains uncollected in the north churchyard of St Mary Redcliffe. See Baltic Wharf.

Sources: S. Bann and others, *The Sculpture of Stephen Cox*, London, 1995; CL2003; Tate Gallery Liverpool ,1988, *Stephen Cox; Sculpture 1977–85*, ed. Rupert Martin

Benjamin Creswick, 1853–1946, modeller. Born in Sheffield, he was apprenticed to a knife-grinder. Health problems obliged him to relinquish this profession. He was inspired after a visit to John Ruskin's Walkley Museum to emulate the drawn and modelled exhibits. He made contact with Ruskin and worked under his supervision at Coniston and Oxford. By 1884 Creswick had opened a London studio, and around this time began an association with A. H. Mackmurdo's arts and crafts organisation, the Century Guild. The Guild's magazine, *The Century Guild Hobby Horse*, in 1887 advertised his services in 'carving and modelling for terracotta or plasterwork'. In the same year, he completed his ambitious frieze of cutlers at work for Cutlers' Hall in the City of London. Raffles Davison of the magazine *British Architect*, who had already praised Creswick's work, found that the sculptor had reached new heights in this frieze. Creswick then worked briefly in Liverpool and Manchester, before taking up the post of master of modelling and modelled design at the Birmingham School of Art in 1889. Creswick produced a great deal of architectural sculpture for Birmingham buildings, and proved an inspiring teacher. He retired from his post in 1918, though he continued to accept private commissions. See St Nicholas Street.

Sources: 'An English Sculptor', *British Architect*, 22 April 1887, p.303; S. Beattie, *The New Sculpture*, New Haven and London, 1983; G. T. Noszlopy and J. Beach, *Public Sculpture of Birmingham*, Liverpool, 1998; CL2003

Patrick James Selden Daw, born 1952, sculptor. First studied at Bristol Polytechnic from 1970 until 1974, where he obtained a first class degree from the School of Sculpture. He then gained his MA in sculpture at the RCA. In 1981, a Crafts Council bursary allowed him to equip his own studio in Surrey, where he undertook architectural lettering commissions and models for film and advertising, for which he obtained two awards. Daw went to South Africa in 1992 to study wood carving, and that led to technically complex wood sculpture. *The Helix*, commissioned by the Clevedon Pier Trust, resulted from this experience. He has taught sculpture and 3D design at many institutions, among them the University of the West of England. He was elected a member of the RWA in 2003. See Temple Quay.

Source: information from the sculptor

John Doubleday, born 1947, sculptor. Born in Essex, he describes himself as 'belonging to rural Essex' and now lives at Great Totham in the house that was his parents' family home. Doubleday spent a period living in Paris and drawing in the Musée Bourdelle before he studied at Carlisle School of Art, and later Goldsmith's College. He had his first one-man exhibition at the Waterhouse Gallery in London in 1968. The majority of his output is sculpture cast in bronze. His statue of *Charles Chaplin*, 1981, is in the centre of Leicester Square, and in the south-west he has a memorial at the Royal Marine base in Lympstone, Devon, 1986. See Temple back East; Redcliffe Way.

Source: information from the sculptor

Tom E. Dove, architect. He was based in Birmingham and working at Alcester Road when he designed the Simon Short fountain in Bristol. See Trinity Place, Hotwells.

Source: *The Western Daily Press,* 15 September 1902

Susan Dring, born 1952, sculptor. Born in Bristol of a long line of stonemasons and carvers. She took up sculpting when her children went to school and was self-trained until she began working with her brother, Trevor Dring of Phidias Neoclassical in Bristol. Most of her work has been commissioned pieces for stately homes, public buildings and churches, especially in Bristol and Bath. The crest on Bristol Crown Courts and the *Mary with Christ Crucified* for the Belgian War Memorial in Kensal Green in London are her work. See Bath Road, Arnos Court Gateway.

Source: information from the sculptor

Alfred Drury, 1856–1944, sculptor. Born in London, Drury studied sculpture at the South Kensington School under the French instructors Jules Dalou and Edouard Lanteri. Between 1881 and 1885, he worked in Dalou's Paris studio as an assistant, and, on returning to London, showed *Triumph of Silenus*, which was strongly marked by the French sculptor's influence, at the Royal Academy. Work with J. E. Boehm and emulation of his contemporaries, such as Alfred Gilbert and George Frampton, helped him to form his own style. For his poetic pieces and allegories, Drury invented a characteristic female type. This proved most popular in the fanciful and dreamy busts of young girls, entitled *Griselda* and *The Age of Innocence*, both of which were frequently reproduced in bronze. Drury's many architectural commissions include the colossal allegorical groups on the War Office in Whitehall, 1904. After the First World War he executed a number of war memorials. His most successful public statues were of historical figures: Richard Hooker for Exeter, 1907; Elizabeth Fry for the Old Bailey, 1913; and Joshua Reynolds for the forecourt of Burlington House. See College Road, Clifton College.

Sources: S. Beattie, *The New Sculpture*, New Haven and London, 1983; CL2003

Edgar Thomas Earp, 1875–1955, sculptor. Edgar was the only surviving son of the prolific Victorian sculptor Thomas Earp (1828–93) by his second wife, Ellen. Thomas had been born in Nottingham, but he moved to London and set up workshops in south London. Thomas produced, almost exclusively, church monuments and statuary for many architects: Pugin, Street, Butterfield, Blomfield and the Barrys. The carvings on the *Eleanor Cross* (Charing Cross, 1863) were his work. His son, Edgar, became a partner in his father's company Earp, Son and Hobbs, but no other sculptural work, specifically by him, is known. Edgar died in Camberwell, London. See Clifton Down, Bristol Zoo.

Source: Anthony and Olive Mitchell, *Thomas Earp – Eminent Victorian Sculptor,* 2002

Ernest F. Fabian, died 1931, modeller and sculptor. Fabian is recorded as a Winchester sculptor who in 1887 prepared a model of a statue of Bishop Beaufort for the cathedral. From about 1892 he was modelling master at Bristol's Municipal School of Art, Queen's Road, retiring due to ill health in 1929. He exhibited regularly at the RWA and was an active member of the Bristol Savages, designing the president's chain of office (1910), the golf trophy and the scull and crossbones tobacco box. Some of his works are in Bristol Cathedral, and a bronze model of Ernest Board's painting of the departure of Cabot was commissioned for the Art Gallery in Halifax, Nova Scotia. In 1910 he was invited to enter Bristol's King Edward VII memorial sculpture competition. He modelled the nine muses over the entrance to the Wills Memorial Building (see Queen's Road), the figures to the bay window of the Reception Room, some of the grotesques and some of the internal carving.

Sources: *Journal of the Ecclesiastical Soc.*, 31 May, 2003, p.8; J. Hudson, *The Savage Spirit,* 2004, pp.54–5; Dr Sarah Whittingham's forthcoming book: *Sir George Herbert Oatley: Architect of Bristol*, Redcliffe Press, 2009

Ernest E. Faithful. The only reference to this monumental mason, who worked for H. Tyley of Bristol, comes from *Kelly's Directory* of 1923, which confirms that he was then living in the city at 91 St John's Lane, Totterdown. See Temple Meads Station.

Rachel Fenner, born 1939, sculptor. Born in Scarborough, Rachel Fenner first studied at Wimbledon School of Art where she concentrated on life drawing and modelling. When she moved to the RCA she became influenced by minimalism. During a period of teaching in and around London she began to exhibit her sculpture throughout the UK. In 1979 she moved to Hampshire to take up an Arts Council appointment to develop art in public places. In 1983 she became Southern Arts artist-in-residence, subsequently undertaking many site-specific commissions, including reliefs, stone carvings and brick constructions. In 1994 she was sculptor-in-residence at St David's Bishop's Palace. See Castle Park.

Source: information from the sculptor

Ian Hamilton Finlay, 1925–2006, artist. Born in Nassau, the Bahamas, he moved to Scotland, where he left school at 13. After a brief period at Glasgow School of Art, he served in the army. His earliest published work was literary: short stories and poems. His art developed through an intense preoccupation with his house and garden at Stonypath in the Pentland Hills. Poetry and sculpture were fused there, in many projects, over forty years. Spirited battles with the local government of Strathclyde enhanced his fame when his home and garden was transmuted from Stonypath to 'Little Sparta'. Now, not far south from the Athens of the North, the new place-name appears on maps. *The World Has Been Empty Since the Romans* was one of his works when he was shortlisted for the Turner Prize in 1985. His work at Little Sparta has brought him many international commissions, including France, Germany, Holland and Norway. Exhibitions were presented at the Scottish National Gallery of Modern Art (1972), the Serpentine Gallery, London (1977), and at the Tate St Ives (2003). At the age of 77 he was appointed CBE. See Great George Street.

Sources: lecture by Graeme Moore; *The Guardian*, 29 March 2006

Sir George James Frampton, 1860–1928, sculptor and medallist. Born and died in London. He was one of the most respected and influential British sculptors of his time. He studied at the London School of Art under W. S. Frith, and then at the Royal Academy Schools, before studying in Paris under A. Mercié. He became a full RA in 1902, having exhibited there from 1884. In 1910 he declined to take part in the competition for the statue for the Bristol memorial to King Edward VII, saying he did not, at that stage in his career, want to take part in competitions. He was knighted in 1908. He made statues of Queen Victoria for Calcutta, Leeds, Southport and Winnipeg. His most renowned London statues are of Edith Cavell, and the Peter Pan statue in Kensington Gardens. See University Road, Bristol Grammar School.

Sources: S. Beattie, *The New Sculpture*, New Haven and London, 1983

Andy Frost, born 1957, sculptor. Studied at Lanchester Polytechnic and Coventry and Reading Universities. Frost visited the Netherlands and the USA on scholarships from 1979 to 1982, and subsequently was Henry Moore Foundation Fellow in sculpture at the Camberwell School of Arts and Crafts. He has exhibited at the ICA Whitechapel Open, 1983, and the Welsh Sculpture Trust, 1983. He uses a wide variety of materials, including wood, steel and fibreglass. See Castle Park.

Source: information from the sculptor

Eric Gill, 1882–1940, sculptor, engraver, letter-carver and typographer. Born in Brighton, the son of a minister. In 1897 the family moved to Chichester and Gill attended the art school there for two years. In 1900 he was apprenticed to the architect W. D. Carse, but found contemporary notions of architecture not to his taste. He took lessons in masonry and lettering, the latter under Edward Johnston at the Central School of Art and Design. In 1903 Gill left the architect's office and worked as a letter-cutter. In 1904 he married, and by 1907 was living in Ditchling, Sussex. About this time he began engraving and in 1909 made his first stone figure, not following the traditional method of first producing a clay model for replication in stone, but carving directly from the stone. By now Gill had acquired influential friends, including Roger Fry and Augustus John, the latter of whom helped him set up his first solo exhibition in 1911 at the Chenil Gallery, Chelsea. Always of a deeply religious mind, in 1913 Gill converted to Roman Catholicism (becoming in 1918 a Dominican tertiary) and in the same year was commissioned to carve the Stations of the Cross for Westminster Cathedral. Following the First World War, he was commissioned to execute war memorials at Bisham, South Harting and Trumpington. He also continued working on religious commissions, including another set of Stations of the Cross, 1921–4, for St Cuthbert's Church, Bradford. In 1924 Gill moved to Capel-y-ffin, Wales, for four years. In this period he executed *Mankind*, a colossal torso in Hoptonwood stone later acquired by the Tate Gallery. In 1928 he moved to Pigotts, near High Wycombe, and over the next three years published *Art-Nonsense*, 1929, his first full-length book; including some of his finest illustrations; in 1929–32, he produced his sculptures for the exterior of Broadcasting House, including Prospero and Ariel. From 1935–8 he was engaged on his large relief, *The Creation of Adam*, for the League of Nations Palace at Geneva. In 1935 he was elected honorary ARIBA and in 1937 he was made an honorary associate of the RBS and was elected ARA (thereafter exhibiting at the RA 1938–41). He died in 1940, the year his *Autobiography* was published. See Canford Cemetery; College Road, Memorial Gateway.

Sources: M2004; Fiona MacCarthy, *Eric Gill*, 1989

Jean Hahn, 1870–1953. Born Johannes Theador Hahn in Saxony; attended art school in Paris, arriving in London in 1897. Worked on ships' figureheads in Barrow-in-Furness and Belfast, moving to Cheltenham in 1901. He is said to have helped to set up the Guild of Crafts in Birmingham, assisted by Italian craftsmen, and to have belonged to the King's Heath Guild, Birmingham. Worked at Stowe School, Hagley Hall and on Queen Mary's Dolls' House. Worked extensively for Sir George Oatley in the 1920s as designer and carver in stone and wood, producing the Wills Memorial Building, the H. H. Wills Physics Laboratory, the St Monica Home of Rest and the Wills Hall of Residence. See Queen's Road, Wills Memorial Building; Tyndall Avenue, H. H. Physics Building.

Source: Dr Sarah Whittingham's forthcoming book *Sir George Herbert Oatley: Architect of Bristol*, Redcliffe Press, 2009; indebted to Susan Moore, 'Jean Hahn: wood and stone carver', unpublished personal study, 1970

Rodney Harris, born 1966 at Weston-super-Mare, the son of a local farmer; BA (Hons) in 3D design at Bristol College School of Art and Design, leaving in 1989, and an MA at the Cardiff School of Art in ceramics. During the preparation of his thesis on 'Making public art', he contacted Walter Ritchie, whose work he admired, but whose technique of working with fired bricks is different. He also contacted Ibstock Bricks, which then had a design centre in Queen Square, Bristol, and for which he continues to undertake freelance commissions. His work is mainly site-specific public artwork, often preceded by extensive consultation exercises with local schools and community groups, encouraging adults and children to explore their creative imagination and to produce ideas for the art projects. He has worked as artist-in-residence at several schools and institutions, including the Sir John Soane Museum, London, and on many projects financed by the Arts Council of England, the Wellcome Trust and other bodies. He was sculptor-in-residence at the University of Liverpool for Capital of Culture 2008. His public art sculptures include:1991, *Basset Hounds and Basenjis*, Dogs Home, Albert Rd, Bristol; 1995, *Upholstered Brick Chesterfield Sofa* at St Werburgh's Nursery School, Bristol, with many similar subsequent commissions; 2005, *Caterpillar* and *Woodlouse*, Stapleton Road, Easton, Bristol; 2006–8, *Washing Machines*, glazed brick relief at the Shield Centre, Filton, South Gloucester. See Albert Road, Stapleton Road.

Source: information from the artist

Anne and Jerry Hicks, born 1928 and 1927, artists. Both studied at the Slade School, London and have lived in Bristol since 1951; both are members of the Royal West of England Academy. Jerry has served as artists' chairman and vice-president. They have collaborated on prize-winning stage design and designed a three-dimensional mural for the Bristol Gas Showrooms, now demolished. Anne has represented British women painters at the Musée de L'Art Moderne in Paris. Jerry was awarded the MBE for services to sport in 1994. They have both battled for the improvement of Bristol's urban design, particularly through the Bristol Civic Society. For his defence of Bristol's architectural character and for the retention of school playing fields Jerry received an honorary MA from the University of Bristol in 2004. See Myrtle Road.

Source: information from the artists and honorary MA oration, 2004

Nicola Hicks, born 1960, sculptor. Born in London and studied first at Chelsea College of Art, then at the RCA. In her subsequent career she has gained a reputation for her study of anatomy, the discipline of her drawing (often using charcoal), and for her sculpture of animals, for which she has a passion. She has had over 20 solo exhibitions since 1984 in England, Ireland, France, Canada and the USA, and has been represented in an even larger number of mixed exhibitions. In 1989 she was artist-in-residence at the Yorkshire Sculpture Park, when she worked on a project called *Out of Clay*. Her work is in many public collections, including the Tate. See Millennium Square.

Sources: information from the sculptor; At-Bristol press office

Frederick Brook Hitch, 1877–1957, sculptor. Born in London, son of the sculptor Nathaniel Hitch, he studied at the Royal Academy Schools and exhibited at the Royal Academy from 1906 to 1947. His exhibits up to 1914 were of imaginary and classical subjects. In 1917 he showed a medal commemorating the victory of Jutland Bank. Thereafter, almost all of his exhibits were portraits, with the exception of a work entitled *Grief*, shown in 1924, and the 'premiated competition sketch model for the Canadian National War Memorial for Ottawa' (RA 1926). He produced two public monuments for Adelaide, Australia: one to Captain Matthew Flinders, and the other of Sir Ross Smith (model exhibited at the RA in 1927). In 1939, Hitch's statue of the hymn-writer Charles Wesley was unveiled at Wesley's New Room, in the Horsefair, Bristol, where it joined A. G. Walker's equestrian figure of John Wesley (1932). Hitch's statue of Nelson, 1951, in Pembroke Gardens, Portsmouth, is supposed, according to its inscription, to be correct 'to the smallest detail', including the coat in which Nelson received his fatal wound. Hitch was a fellow of the Royal Society of British Sculptors. He lived in Hertford. See Horsefair.

Sources: J. Darke, *The Monument Guide to England and Wales*, London, 1991; D. Buckman, *The Dictionary of British Artists since 1945*, Bristol, 1998; CL2003

Lawrence Holofcener, born 1926, sculptor. Holofcener describes himself as a self-taught playwright, actor, librettist, composer, poet, novelist, director and sculptor. Born in Baltimore, Maryland, Holofcener was living in the Isle of Wight when he carried out the Bristol commission. He wrote songs for NBC-TV, the Broadway musical *Mr Wonderful* (with Sammy Davis Jr), and compiled a rhyming dictionary for songwriters. On Broadway he acted in *Stop the World* and *Hello Dolly*. His sculptures include *Faces of Olivier* in Chichester Theatre, 1985 (28 bas-reliefs showing Laurence Olivier in 28 roles), and a statue of Thomas Paine for Bordentown, New Jersey. See Millennium Square.

Source: information from the sculptor

Henry Richard Hope-Pinker, 1849–1927, sculptor. Studied at the RA schools and in Rome. While he was still studying, his bust of Reverend Edward Benson, the first headmaster of Wellington College, was exhibited at the RA in 1875. Until 1893 he was known as 'Pinker'. He exhibited over forty works, mostly busts, at the RA between 1875 and 1904; he lived in London throughout that period. Among his public statues are the equestrian bronze of Oliver Cromwell, 1882, for Marston Moor, Henry Fawcett in the Market Place in Salisbury, and the statue of W. E. Forster, 1890, in Victoria Embankment Gardens. See Colston Street, Colston Hall.

Sources: D. Bilbey, *British Sculpture, 1470–2000*, 2002

John Huggins, born 1938, sculptor. Born in Wiltshire, John Huggins studied at the West of England College of Art, Bristol, from 1956 to 1961. He became a part-time lecturer there in 1962, later moving to Bower Ashton, and continued his teaching career until 1976. He has exhibited extensively since 1960 with six one-man shows at London's Alwin Gallery, two at McHardy Sculpture, London, and one in 1999 at

Innocent Fine Art, Bristol. His work has been included in numerous group exhibitions in England, in venues such as the Beaux Arts Gallery, Bath, the Ashdown Gallery, Sussex, and Guernsey Sculpture Park. John is a fellow of the Royal Society of British Sculptors, and an RWA, where he has served as artists' chairman and vice-president. His work is included in the collections of the Bristol Museums and Art Gallery, the Regional Arts Council, Bristol University, Phillips Petroleum (London), Singer Friedlander Bank (London) and National Huntington Bank (Columbus, Ohio). See Royal Fort Gardens.

Source: www.uwe.ac.uk/amd/archive/huggins.htm

Graham Ibbeson, born 1951, sculptor. Ibbeson has been a professional sculptor for over 20 years, working with architects and planners to create sculpture for specific sites. He has worked in bronze, steel, stone and fibreglass. He lives and works in Barnsley and he studied at the Barnsley School of Art, Trent Polytechnic and the RCA. In 1996 he made a bronze of an early rugby hero, William Webb Ellis, for the centre of Rugby, and he has statues in Perth, Chesterfield, Middlesborough and Northampton. In 1992 he completed five relief panels for Eurotunnel at Folkestone. See Millennium Square.

Source: information from the sculptor

Walter Jack, furniture designer and sculptor. The Walter Jack Studio was set up in Bristol ten years ago and it creates furniture and architectural elements in a variety of materials for buildings and landscapes. The studio has created seating for the Bristol Museums and Art Gallery and for the Bristol Royal Hospital for Children, and (elsewhere in Bristol) the entrance feature *blueskyfence* for Callington Road Hospital, the street works in Oxford Street, The Dings, the rotating columns on Temple Way, a staircase and reception desk for the Healthy Living Centre in Barton Hill, and a major feature for the new Bristol Heart Institute (opened in 2009). The studio has also completed major commissions for Dumfries and Galloway Arts Association, St Peter's Square, Leeds, and Barnsley Civic Centre, and Abercrombie School, Derby. See Temple Way; Oxford Street.

Source: www.walterjack.co.uk

Valda Jackson, painter and sculptor. She travelled as a small child from Jamaica in 1964 to join her parents in Birmingham. Between 1984 and 1986 she took A-levels and a foundation course in art and design. She moved to Bristol to take a degree in fine art, graduating in 1989. From 1991 to 1993 she commuted to Birmingham to lecture part-time at the University of Central England. She continues to work with students in schools and colleges in Bristol and the South West. She has a studio at Spike Island, Bristol. She has had solo exhibitions at the Malcolm X Centre, Bristol, 1990, and the Morley Gallery, Westminster, 1994. Public art sculptures include: the life-size brick relief at Kingfisher House, Newmarket, of *Thoroughbred Mare and Foal*, 1995; the quarter-size relief of a castle class steam engine, *The Newport Castle*, at Station Approach, Newport, 2000–1; and *All Our Tomorrows*, St Paul's Learning and Family Centre, Bristol, 2003–5. See Grosvenor Road.

Source: information from the artist

Stephen Joyce, born 1956, sculptor. Steve Joyce lives and works in Bristol and has contributed more work to the streets of the city than any other sculptor. He studied fine art at the University of the West of England, 1976–9. He worked with Sonia Rolt and the Landmark Trust. His four major sculptures are described in this book, but he has also made 18 shop signs for three urban renewal street schemes for Bristol City Council; three viewpoint sculptures for Ashton Court; an adventure playground for St Agnes, Bristol; the large stone *Man with Fish* formerly displayed at the Riverside Garden Centre, Ashton Gate; and 35m-long sculptural railings for Ystrad Mynach, South Wales. He was made a bursary member of the Royal Society of British Architects in 1998 and has been visiting arts lecturer at Bath Spa University. He is a former chair of Spike Island Sculpture, where he has his studio. See Counterslip; Lower Maudlin Street; Narrow Quay; St George's Road; Temple Meads Station.

Source: information from the sculptor

Janice Kerbel, born 1969, Canadian artist based in London. Janice Kerbel often produces work in the form of plans and studies (for instance, wall-mounted gardens for council flats, or respiration gardens for gyms) that promise to be realisable but are never to be fulfilled. Her internationally exhibited projects include: *Underwood*, a series of love letters to the seasons; *Bank Job* and *15 Lombard St*, the meticulously detailed plan for robbing one of London's city banks; *Home Fittings*, studies of buildings that show where to step without creaking or casting shadows; and *The Bird Island Project* (www.bird-island.com), the fictitious development of a paradise island resort. See Harbourside.

Source: Artangel

Joseph William King, builder and mason, Bristol. Recorded as a builder and mason specialising in ornamental freestone in 1855, and in 1865 as an architect and surveyor on the Whiteladies Road. He was the developer of the Royal Bazaar and Winter Gardens in Boyce's Avenue, Clifton, and of the similarly unfinished Royal Arcade in Whiteladies Road. See Whiteladies Road.

Source: Gomme, Jenner and Little, p.437

Alexander Paul Klecki, born 1927, sculptor and architect. Born in Poland, he was deported by the Soviets to Siberia. From 1942 he lived and was educated in India. Since then he has lived in London. He studied architecture and worked with Sir Frederick Reed on Terminal 3 at Heathrow Airport. In 1965 he won the House of the Year Award and the Architects and Planners Award, and he has architecture in Dirab, Saudi Arabia and Abu Dhabi. He has worked in stained glass. His public sculptures include work in the St Andrew

Bobola RC church in London, and *Christ the King* in aluminium in Newcastle. See Worcester Road, Clifton Cathedral.

Source: information from the sculptor

Tim Knowles, artist. Fine art degree at Bath College of Higher Education. 1989–92. In Bristol he chaired Open City, an artists' initiative funded by South West Arts and Bristol City Council, 1993 to 1997, presenting temporary site-specific art works in the city. He was chair of Spike Island 1995–7, a vital time in the development of this successful studio and exhibition centre. He was appointed lead artist for the Harbourside regeneration development, curating and programming temporary and permanent art (due to be completed in 2009, but now delayed). His own works, especially his wind-created drawings, reflect his statement: 'The exploration of Chance and Process is core to my artistic practice.' See Harbourside.

Source: www.timknowles.co.uk

Gerald Laing, born 1936, sculptor. Laing has his own bronze foundry at Kinkell Castle in the north of Scotland, where he cast the Bristol fountain *Sabrina*. Among his other major commissions are the statue of Sherlock Holmes, 1991; a memorial to Sir Arthur Conan Doyle in Edinburgh; and *Eight Dragons*, 1994–5, for Bank underground station in London. Portrait commissions have included Pavarotti, Sam Wanamaker, Tam Dalyell and Andy Warhol. He has held visiting professorships of sculpture in New Mexico and Columbia University, New York. See Narrow Quay.

Source: information from the sculptor

Jason Lane, sculptor in recycled mechanical metal parts and of automata and kinetic sculptures. Educated at Hereford College of Art and Design and at Exeter University, 1990–3, BA in art and design. In 1995 Lane undertook research in India on regional artists working in reclaimed materials. He worked in Italy in 1996–7 and in Zimbabwe in 1997. He has done work for Crest Homes in Swindon, Portishead Marina, Sustrans, and Bristol City Council at Blaise Castle and in Ashley Road, St Paul's. He has a studio at Spike Island, Bristol and lives in Mina Road, St Werburgh's. See Blaise Castle Estate.

Source: information from the sculptor

Langlands and Bell. 'Artists Ben Langlands and Nikki Bell explore the complex web of relationships linking people and architecture and the coded systems of circulation and exchange which surround us. Based in London, Langlands and Bell have been collaborating since 1978, and exhibiting internationally since the early 1980s. The sculptures of Langlands and Bell range from architectural ground-plans presented as immaculate models or monochrome reliefs, to the full-scale architecture of the monumental steel and glass bridge recently completed at Paddington Basin in London. Their exhibition 'The House of Osama bin Laden' at the Imperial War Museum, London and IMMA Irish Museum of Modern Art, Dublin won the prize for Interactive Arts Installation at the 2004 BAFTA Awards in London.' See Harbourside.

Source; www.langlandsandbell.com

Walter MacFarlane and Co. This foundry, also known as the Saracen Foundry, made architectural and ornamental ironwork – from bandstands to commemorative busts – for over 115 years. An entry in a guide to the *Industries of Glasgow* said: 'The productions of this well-known firm are to be found in every part of the civilised world, so that it is unnecessary to enter into a detailed description of them.' They started at Saracen Lane, off Gallowgate in Glasgow, when the company was founded in 1849 by Walter Macfarlane (1817–85). More extensive works were erected in Hawthorne Street on Sir Archibald Alison's Possil Estate in 1872. By 1901 nearly 24 acres were occupied and a suburb grew to house the large workforce, estimated at over 1,200. The company was awarded medals at international exhibitions and in the years between the wars it made panels for commercial buildings, including the Union Bank in Glasgow and Selfridges in London. In 1965 the company was taken over by Allied Founders, and two years later the Possilpark works were demolished. Since then the firm's patterns have been revived and produced by Glasgow-based Heritage Engineering. See Horfield Common, Suspension Bridge Road.

Source: G2002

Kate Malone, born 1959, potter. Kate was brought up in Bristol and graduated from Bristol Polytechnic in 1982. She lives and works in London and is now one of Britain's best-known potters. She has continued to make occasional large-scale work for public places, including fish heads that rise nearly a metre out of the water on Hackney Marshes, a human-size jug and bowl fountain for Homerton Hospital, and a giant pot in Manchester City Art Galleries. Her largest public work has been installed recently in a library in Brighton. An exhibition of her pottery was held in Bristol Museum and Art Gallery in 1999. See Castle Park.

Source: information from the sculptor

David Bernard McFall, 1919–88, sculptor. Born in Scotland, he trained at Birmingham School of Art and the RCA. He was an assistant to Sir Jacob Epstein and became a close friend. The Bristol *Unicorns* was one of his earliest public commissions. Among the best-known of his portrait busts are Clement Attlee, 1965; Vaughan Williams, Royal Festival Hall, 1957; and Luciano Pavarotti. He made an over-life-size statue of Winston Churchill, 1959, at Woodford Green, Essex. McFall fought a rare form of cancer for the last seven years of his life, and he made a bronze Christ for the precinct of Canterbury Cathedral that was unveiled three months after he died. He was made ARA in 1955 and RA in 1963. See College Green, Council House.

Source: CL2003

William McMillan, 1887–1977, sculptor. Born in Aberdeen, he trained first at Gray's School of Art before going on to the Royal Academy. His career was interrupted by military service during the First World War, and his experience in the trenches is said to have marked him for life. His first Royal Academy exhibits from 1917 were of military subjects, and McMillan sculpted First World War memorials for Manchester and Aberdeen. In the later 1920s he carved much decorative garden sculpture, and experimented with unusual stones, such as green slate and *verde di Prato.* In 1931, his three-quarter-length figure *Venus* was purchased for the Tate Gallery from the Royal Academy. His public portrait statues include Earl Haig, 1932, for Clifton College; George V, 1938, for Calcutta; George VI, 1955, for Carlton Gardens, London; and Lord Trenchard, 1961, for the Embankment Gardens, London. McMillan was a designer of medals, including the Great War Medal and the Victory Medal. Immediately before the outbreak of the Second World War, he was commissioned to produce the Beatty Memorial Fountain for Trafalgar Square, in collaboration with Sir Edwin Lutyens.This was a pendant to the Jellicoe Fountain, sculpted by Charles Wheeler. After the war, Mcmillan once again worked alongside Wheeler on Sir Edward Maufe's extensions to the Royal Navy Memorials at Chatham, Plymouth and Portsmouth. In 1954, he executed the memorial to the pilots Alcock and Brown for London Airport. From 1942 onwards, he exhibited drawings and watercolours at the Royal Academy. He was elected ARA in 1925 and full RA in 1933. See College Road, Clifton College.

Source: CL2003

Peter Milner, born 1951, artist and designer. Peter Milner has lived and worked in the Bristol area since 1978. He is an artist and writer with a deep interest in the way we understand and use our environment. He has worked as a landscape designer and theatre designer, and has coordinated large environmental projects involving other artists, including the River Parret Trail in Somerset. More recently he has returned to the crafts of picture-making and writing. He collaborated with Jane Norbury on the Water Maze project. See Victoria Park.

Source: information from the artist

Victor Moreton trained at Gloucester College of Art and Design and gained his degree in sculpture and drawing. From 1973 to 1975 he studied in the USA and obtained his MA in fine arts at Dallas, Texas. He took up a fellowship at Gloucester College, and at the time of his Castle Park commission he was a member of the Artspace Studio in Bristol. See Castle Park.

Paul Mount, 1922–2009, sculptor. Born at Newton Abbot and educated at the grammar school there. He went to Paignton School of Art before entering the RCA in 1940. His studies were interrupted by war service, and he did not leave the RCA until 1948. He taught at Winchester School of Art (1948–55). Much of his sculpture has been large-scale forms integrated with architecture, using stainless steel, bronze, GRP and concrete. He taught and worked in Nigeria and had commissions for architectural sculpture in Lagos, Accra and Ibadan University. In the UK he has public work in Bristol, Exeter, St Helen's, Cardiff and London. He held one-man exhibitions at the John Whibley Gallery in Cork Street in 1968 and 1970, at the New Art Centre in Sloane Street from 1972 and with the Beaux Arts Gallery of London and Bath. ARCA, RWA. See St James's Barton.

Sources: *RWA Friends Magazine*, 2006, spring issue, p.14; obituary, *The Independent*, 16 January 2009

David Mutasa, born in Zimbabwe, 1954. An exhibition of his work was held at St David's Hall in Cardiff while he was working on the Fagon commission. His visiting scholarship to the UK was financed by the British Council. He has made several sculptures commemorating members of the Patriotic Front. These were displayed at the parliament buildings in Harare. See Ashley Road.

Source: www.aavaa.org.uk

William James Neatby, 1860–1910, sculptor, designer and painter. Born in Barnsley, trained as an architect. At 23 he went to work for Burmantofts Potteries in Leeds, designing, painting and making tiles for interior decoration. In 1899 he joined Doulton's of Lambeth, in charge of their architectural department, again designing and making ceramics. An art nouveau-style designer, he made great use of both terracotta and Carrara-ware and introduced new processes such as polychrome stoneware and Parian-ware. In 1900 or 1901 he set up a partnership with E. Hollyer Evans manufacturing furniture, metalwork and stained glass, but he continued to design for Doulton. His major commissions included painted ceramic panels for the Winter Gardens Ballroom, Blackpool (completed 1897); City Wholesale Market, Leicester (1900, later demolished; *Mermaids* panel re-erected West Bridge, Leicester, 1980); glazed terracotta frontage for the Edward Everard printing works, Broad Street, Bristol (completed 1901); City Arcade, Birmingham (1901); interior decoration of the Restaurant Frascati, Masonic Hall, Oxford Street, London (1902, demolished); and interior ceramic decoration of Harrods Meat Hall, London (1902). He was a member of the Royal Society of Miniature Painters and exhibited as a painter at the RA in 1906 and 1909. See Broad Street.

Source: M2004

Jane Norbury, born 1958, potter and sculptor. Came to Bristol in 1981 after studying ceramics at West Surrey College of Art. In her endeavour to continue making large-scale ceramics in brick clays, she made contact with Ibstock Bricks, which allowed her to fire her pieces in its tunnel kilns. Twenty-two years later she was still using that method for her larger works. She moved to France and set up a studio in Burgundy, where her work ranges from sculptural installations (such as the singing heads *Têtes Brûlées*) to hand-built garden pots and vases. She has collaborated with Peter Milner. See Victoria Park.

Source: information from the artist

John Van Nost the elder, died 1729, sculptor. An inhabitant of Mechlin, Belgium, he came to England, where he was said to have studied under Grinling Gibbons. He was employed as foreman to the sculptor Arnold Quellin until his master's death in 1686, whereupon he married Quellin's widow. Working from a yard in Haymarket, London, Van Nost had a good reputation, making lead garden figures and vases for the gardens of many houses, including Chatsworth (c.1698); Stourhead, Wiltshire; Boreham, Essex; Rousham, Oxfordshire; and Seaton Delaval, Northumberland. He made statues, vases and chimney pieces for Thomas Coke's houses in Melbourne and St James's, London; the statues on the pediment of Buckingham House; and from 1700 he made designs and a model for fountains, figures, vases, panels and pedestals for the exterior of Hampton Court, and two marble tables and chimney pieces for the interior. In 1703–10 he made lead statues for Castle Howard; in 1705–16 he made two vases and eight heads for the Duke of Kent's house at Wrest Park, Bedfordshire; and in 1723 he made a statue of Sir Robert Geffrye for the Ironmongers' Company in Shoreditch. Other statues include *William and Mary* for the Royal Exchange, London, c.1700; *Queen Mary*, University College, Oxford, 1720; and *George I*, Grosvenor Square, London, 1726. He made several important monuments, notably one for the Duke of Queensberry at Durisdeer, Dumfries, 1711, with life-size figures of the duke and duchess under a great *baldacchino* supported by four twisting Corinthian columns. Van Nost died on 26th April 1729, and his business was carried on by a nephew of the same name. See Clifton Hill, Goldney House.

Sources: K. Garlick, 'Birmingham's only "horse"', *Post*, 8 July 1952; Gunnis, 1964, pp.279–82; B1998

Eilís O'Connell, born 1953, artist. O'Connell trained at Crawford School of Art, Cork, 1970–7, with a period spent at the Massachusetts College of Art, Boston (1974-5). Two travelling fellowships followed: one awarded by the Arts Council of Northern Ireland to work at the British School in Rome, 1983–4; and the Arts Council's PS1 (New York) Fellowship, 1987–8. Her first solo exhibition was at the Hendricks Gallery, Dublin in 1981. Major prizes include the Dublin Sunday Tribune Visual Artist of the Year Award, and the Royal Society of Arts Award. While O'Connell has exhibited her work widely since the early 1970s, she has built her career largely through public commissions, some of which are on a very large scale. The distinctive sense of place that she manifests in her work may have contributed towards her success in this area. Her commissions have included *Secret Station*, 1991, for Cardiff Bay Art Trust at the Eastern Gateway, Cardiff; *The Space Between*, 1992, commissioned by the Milton Keynes Development Corporation; and *Pero's Footbridge*, Bristol. She works in a variety of materials, including stone, rubber, sheet metals, glass, plaster and bronze. In addition, she hoards found objects such as discarded agricultural tools and dairy vessels, which may eventually find their way into her sculpture. See Narrow Quay.

Sources: Buckman, D., *Dictionary of Artists in Britain since 1945*, Bristol, 1998, p.919; Elliott, A., *Sculpture at Goodwood*, Goodwood, 1999, p.118; *20th Century Painters and Sculptors*, Dictionary of British Art, volume 6, Woodbridge, Suffolk, 1990, p.343; CL2003; SBC2005

Ernest Pascoe, 1922–96, painter and sculptor. Served with the RAF during the war before attending Slade, 1945–8, where he won the Wilson Steer medal for painting and the Henry Tonks prize for drawing. He joined the West of England College of Art in 1948, becoming head of sculpture and vice-principal in 1955 and retiring as head of fine art in the 1970s, when the school had become part of the University of the West of England. Pascoe undertook commissions of great variety, from an abstract wall relief in Carwardine's restaurant (destroyed) opposite Bristol Museums and Art Gallery to a replacement head for a damaged statue within the museum, where he was also responsible for the plaster relief of the geologist William Smith and the reconstruction of the head of the Bristol Mummy. Among work for Bristol churches, he sculpted *Three Kings of Cologne* for Foster's Almshouse; a stone figure of St Stephen and a vast *Christ Ascending* for St Stephen's, Southmead; a figure of Christ over the entrance to St Mary Magdalen with St Francis, Lockleaze; and figures for a side altar in St Stephen's in the centre of the city. He involved his students in the carving of the three reliefs for the facade of Colston Hall, and in the restoration and re-erection of parts of the High Cross in Berkeley Square. He undertook the replica of the bust of Plimsoll and did many portrait bust of famous personages for Madame Tussauds. His bronze busts of several past presidents of the Royal West of England, of which he was a very active member, are in the RWA's collection. His last work may have been the re-carving of the decayed profile bust of the young Queen Victoria on the Victoria Square side of Arch House, Boyce's Avenue, Clifton, which was unveiled on 8 April 1995. See Colston Street, Redcliffe Hill.

Source: Jerry Hicks, obituary, *RWA Friends' Newsletter*, autumn 1996, p.12

James Paty I, died 1748, 'carver' of Merchant Street, Bristol (as his will states). The first of the dynasty of Paty, his earliest monument in the church at Evercreech may confirm the Somerset origins of the family. He became a burgess of Bristol in 1721, the year of his fine wall monument to Reverend Richard Sandford in St Mary Redcliffe and his iron pallisades around *Neptune*, now in 'The Centre'. He made the Quarter Jacks on Christ Church in 1728 and was paid £2 for the 'Pedestal to hold the Mayor's sword' and £5 for the font in St Stephen's in 1734, both presumed destroyed. He was the mason and builder and probably also the architect for the King Street Library, 1739–41, and assisted his nephew (or cousin) Thomas Paty with carving on the Exchange, Corn Street. He may also have worked at Redland Court and Redland Chapel. See Broad Street, Christ Church.

Sources: G. Priest, *The Paty Family, Makers of Eighteenth-Century Bristol*, 2003; Ison; Gomme, Jenner and Little; A. Beeson, *Bristol Central Library and Charles Holden*, 2006

James Paty II, 1718–79, carver and mason of 21 Horse (now Host) Street, Bristol. Younger brother of the sculptor and architect Thomas Paty, whom he sometimes assisted on major projects. Gordon Priest claims he was site architect at Stoke Park under Thomas Wright, but gives no evidence. There are signed monuments by him in *SS Philip and Jacob*, All Saints, St Thomas and Christ Church. Priest describes him as 'competent and individual but not outstanding'. On his death in 1779 his son, John Paty, 'Carver, Marble Mason, &c.', undertook to continue his father's work of 'Monuments, Chimney-Pieces, &c.'. See Clifton Down.

Sources: Ison; G. Priest, *The Paty Family, Makers of Eighteenth-Century Bristol*, 2003

Thomas Paty, 1712–89, architect and sculptor and the most successful and influential of the Paty dynasty. His earliest known contract was in September 1740 for the carving of the capitals, festoons and moors' heads for the exterior of Redland Chapel, where he also did all the superb interior carving in limewood. In 1742 he became the 'Ornament carver to the Exchange', Bristol's finest eighteenth-century building by John Wood. Among much other work in stone and wood, there is surviving sculpture at Clifton Hill House, Arno's Court, the Royal Fort and Goldney House. His monument to William Hilliard in the Lord Mayor's Chapel is the largest of the eighteenth century in Bristol. As a builder and architect he was responsible for the completion of Bristol Bridge and of St Nicholas Church, both designed by James Bridges. He was responsible for the building and design of the auditorium of the Theatre Royal, the removal and re-erection of the High Cross at Stourhead, the remodelling of the Merchants' Hall, and the design and building of many terraces and squares in Bristol. When he died, his sons John and William, calling themselves 'ARCHITECTS and STATUARIES', promised to continue their father's work. John died a month later. Thomas's son-in-law, Thomas King, was to be a prolific sculptor of monuments in Bath. See Corn Street, Clifton Down, Clifton Hill.

Sources: G. Priest, *The Paty Family, Makers of Eighteenth-Century Bristol*, 2003; Gomme, Jenner and Little; Ison; K. Eustace, 'Art and patronage in Bristol in the first half of the nineteenth century', *The British Art Journal*, vol. VII, no. 1, p.9

William Paty, 1758–1800, architect and sculptor. Son of Thomas Paty and, together with his elder brother, the first of the dynasty to be educated in London, at the Royal Academy Schools in 1775. There are many fine monuments in the south-west signed by him or bearing the name 'Paty and Son'. Christ Church, Broad Street is perhaps his architectural masterpiece, but it is for his terraces – Prince's Buildings, Royal York Crescent, Harley Place and Cornwallis Crescent – that he will always be best known. In 1801, William's yard and statuary business was sold to Henry Wood, who was to sign innumerable wall monuments.

Sources: G. Priest, *The Paty Family, Makers of Eighteenth-Century Bristol*, 2003; Gomme, Jenner and Little; Ison; Gunnis; K. Eustace, 'Bread and sermons', this volume

Charles James Pibworth, 1878–1958, sculptor. In 1910, when Pibworth was pressing to design the statue for the Edward VII Memorial in Bristol, he had moved to Cheyne Walk in London. However, he wrote to the mayor on a letter heading giving a temporary address in Bristol to draw attention to his birthplace. After studying at the Bristol School of Art in Queens Road, then at the Royal College of Art, he entered the RA Schools and was awarded prizes there in 1899, 1900 and 1902. He worked as an assistant in the studios of Professor Lanteri (of whom he made a bust), John Tweed, Albert Toft and Onslow Ford, and he also taught in London. He worked chiefly in stone, and Charles Holden commissioned him for his architectural work for some years. Among these was a large relief of *Euterpe* for the façade of the Orchestral Association, Archer Street, Westminster. Holden later used more adventurous sculptors: Jacob Epstein for the British Medical Association in the Strand, and Eric Gill and Epstein on his London Transport Headquarters at St James. Although Pibworth lived in London, his connections with Bristol remained strong. Among many portrait busts, Pibworth exhibited the bust of H. Percy Adams's wife at the Royal Academy in 1909. Pibworth was made a member of the RWA in 1903 through the influence of Lord Winterstoke when, as president, he pressed for more young artists to be elected. He was also a member of the British Society of Sculptors – proposed by F. W. Pomeroy ARA and Hamo Thorneycroft – but he never attained membership of the RA. See College Green, Library and Gatehouse.

Sources: S. Beattie, *The New Sculpture*, 1983; CL2003

Cathie Pilkington, born c.1969, sculptor. Grew up in South Manchester; did silversmithing at Edinburgh, completing an MA at the RCA in 1997. Now lives in London where she had a major exhibition at Marlborough Fine Art in 2007. See Millennium Square.

Henry Poole, 1873–1928, sculptor. Born in London, son of an architectural carver, he trained first at the South London Technical Art School and then at the Royal Academy. While attending the Academy Schools, he was also working for the sculptor Harry Bates and assisting G. F. Watts with his sculptural projects. He exhibited at the Royal Academy from 1894, but his work in the early years of the twentieth century was predominantly architectural. He established a particularly close working relationship with the architectural partners Lanchester and Rickards. Poole was associated with the neo-baroque school of architecture. He was involved with restoration and other work at St Paul's, including, after the First World War, wood-carving in the Chapel of St Michael and St George. Henry Poole's public monuments are a King Edward VII in Bristol, 1912, and Captain Ball VC in Nottingham, 1921. He also modelled the sculptural features of Sir Robert Lorimer's Royal Navy Memorials for Chatham, Plymouth and Portsmouth. In 1923–4 Poole contributed humorous sculptures to the Small Saloon Bar of H. Fuller Clark's Black Friar Public House in Queen Victoria Street, London.

Elected RA in 1927, his diploma work, *Young Pan*, combines classicism of form with *non finito* effects in marble carving. See Queen's Road, Vicroria Rooms.

Sources: S. Beattie, *The New Sculpture*, New Haven and London, 1983; H. V. Lanchester, 'Henry Poole RA 1873–1928', *Journal of the Royal Institute of British Architects*, 1928, vol.36, pp.18–23; CL2003

Niranjan Pradhan, born 1940, sculptor. Pradhan lives and works as a painter and sculptor in Calcutta. He studied at the Indian government's art college in that city, and now teaches there. He has work in Delhi, Mumbai and Calcutta. He works exclusively in the Western tradition, but much of his work in the 1990s was abstract and he is an admirer of Barbara Hepworth. See College Green; College Green, Council House.

Source: www.niranjanpradhan.com

William Prinsep, 1794–1874, amateur artist. The Prinseps were a famous English family that, for over three generations, lived and worked as administrators and merchants in India. William's father, John Prinsep, had made a fortune in India, and settled in Clifton in 1809. Several of his sons returned to India, and William was in Calcutta between 1817 and his retirement from merchant banking in 1842. A talented amateur artist, he studied in Bengal with the artist George Chinnery. His name appears as 'William Prinsep of London' in the Bristol General Cemetery Register of Burials as one of the two people who had purchased the plot 'Square L No. 4' on 26 May 1843, on behalf of themselves 'and the Committee for erecting a Monument to the Memory of the said Rajah'. See Arno's Vale Cemetery.

Source: Oxford DNB: *Henry Thoby Prinsep,* A. J. Arbuthnot, Rev. R. J. Bingle; Oxford DNB: *James Prinsep*, J. P. Losty

William Pye, b.1938, sculptor. Born in London, he studied at Wimbledon School of Art from 1958 until 1961 (where he was taught by Freda Skinner), and at the RCA from 1961 to 1965. He taught at the Central School of Art and Design from 1965 to 1970, and Goldsmith's College from 1970 until 1977, becoming a visiting professor at California State University between 1975 and 1976. His major works are primarily explorations in the qualities of water, and he has worked extensively in collaboration with architects. In 1990 he formed the William Pye Partnership, which is a sculptural and architectural practice. Making abstract metal sculptures that are often kinetic and have highly reflective surfaces, he has said that 'sculpture isn't naturally seductive but the addition of water gives it a sort of mesmeric quality to which people respond sympathetically.' His commissions include the award-winning *Balla Frois*, Glasgow Garden Festival (1988); *Slipstream and Jetstream*, passenger terminals, Gatwick Airport, 1988, for which he won an award; *Water Wall* on the British Pavilion designed by Nicholas Grimshaw and Partnership, Seville Expo, 1992; suspended water sculpture, British Embassy, Muskat, Oman, 1994; *Confluence*, water sculpture, Hertford town centre, 1994; *Cascade*, Market Square, Derby 1995; and *Water Pyramid*, Le Colisée, Paris, 1995. He has public works in the USA and Japan, and has worked on light features for Lambeth Palace, London and West India Quay for the London Docklands Development Corporation. Pye's films include *Reflections* and *Scrap to Sculpture.* See Millennium Square.

Sources: Farr, D., 'The patronage and support of sculptors' in Nairne, S. and Serota, N., *British sculpture in the twentieth century*, Whitechapel Art Gallery, London, 1991; Strachan, W.J., *Open Air Sculpture in Britain*, London, 1984; curriculum vitae provided by the artist for the WMCC Peace Sculpture Commission, 1984; Redhead, C., 'Waterworks', *Crafts,* London, vol.104, July/August 1989; 'Zen and the art of water', *Crafts*, London, vol.105, July/August 1990; Amery, C., 'Water: an art form to be tapped', *Financial Times*, 18 September 1995; Watt, J., 'Making waves', *Perspectives*, February/March 1996; letter from the artist, 19 February 1996. WCS2003

John Pym. 'John Pym's practice involves the use of installation, film and photography. The work deals specifically with how the individual relates and reacts to their own perceived environment. He builds architectural installations that can be emotionally challenging to the onlooker, forcing them to confront their own fears and neuroses. *Secret Industry* is a good example of how the work is resolved through the humorous suggestion of a smaller world that is inaccessible to everyone over six inches tall.' See Harbourside.

Source: Canons Marsh art trail leaflet

Richard Quinnell, blacksmith. 'During his career, Richard Quinnell has produced some of the most significant twentieth century ironwork in the UK and overseas, including the gates to Shakespeare's Globe in London, the coat of arms for the British Embassy in Rome and the gates to the National Ornamental Metal Museum in Memphis, Tennessee. In 1989 Quinnell was awarded an MBE for his part in the revival of what had been, for many decades, a dying craft in the United Kingdom. Richard and his late wife Jinny founded the British Artist Blacksmiths Association in 1978 and the Fire & Iron Gallery in 1982. Quinnell also founded the Quinnell School of Blacksmithing in 1996. He is a companion and freeman of the Worshipful Company of Blacksmiths of the City of London, England.' See St Augustine's Parade, Watershed.

Source: www.craftscouncil.org.uk/craft-directory

John Randall. The dates of his birth and death are not known. The only information we have is contained in a Temple parish ledger in the Bristol Record Office, which records payment 'To John Randall for the Figure *Neptune* & Peddistoll £32.10'. This suggests that he was the founder, not the sculptor, and no record of any other sculpture by him has yet been found. A Bristol newspaper dated 22 December 1787, *Sarah Farley's Bristol Journal*, says specifically: 'It [*Neptune*] was *cast* by Randall.' Confusingly, a poll book of 1734 names 'Joseph Rendall' as a founder in Bristol. That is the spelling on the present plaque. See 'The Centre'.

Source: BRO/CA27

Peter Randall-Page, born 1954, sculptor. Born in Essex but within two years his family moved to

Sussex. He studied at Bath Academy and then worked for two years with the sculptor Barry Flanagan. His work in the exhibition 'On Site' at the Arnolfini in Bristol in 1977 was the first time his sculpture was seen in public. In 1979 he worked on the conservation of thirteenth-century sculpture on Wells Cathedral, and in 1980 he won a Winstone Churchill Travelling Fellowship to study marble carving at Carrara in Italy. Since that date he has had many exhibitions throughout the UK. He became a visiting lecturer in sculpture at the RCA in 1993. He now lives and works in Devon. He works mainly in stone, and uses natural forms such as shells, fossils, fruits, eggs and pods, as well as expressive knots. See Castle Park.

Source: the artist; M2004

Georgina Redfern. Redfern commenced her foundation course at Nene College, Northampton in 1989 and then studied fine art and sculpture at Loughborough College of Art and Design, from which she graduated with a first class honours degree in 1993. She had another large scale public commission in 1992: a sculpture for Mountsorrell in Redland.

Source: National Westminster Life Insurance brochure, c. 1994

Jane Rickards, sculptor. After studying at Swindon Art School, Jane Rickards did a BA in sculpture at Cheltenham between 1975 and 1978, and later a postgraduate diploma at the City & Guilds of London Art School between 1990 and 1992. She has described herself as 'professional sculptor and healer. The intention of my work is that it be both aesthetically beautiful and geomantically balanced with its environment.' Recent major commissions are *Cipher Wave* for Alexandra Park, Wroughton near Swindon, 2005–6 (a stone monolith encircled by two shaped and perforated semi-circular steel sheets: a protective angel), and work for Kerkeri Art Centre, New Zealand. She lives near Marlborough, Wiltshire. See Temple Quay.

Sources: the artist; www.axis.org

Walter Ritchie, 1919–97, sculptor. Although Ritchie's first sculptures were modelled and cast, he soon decided that casting debased the original clay sculpture, and turned to working in stone. He learned techniques from local stonemasons, and at the age of 18 trained under Eric Gill. Ritchie thought of sculpture as part of a social and architectural scheme, and always wanted his work 'in the street' as opposed to in an art gallery. From 1947 onwards he worked primarily for local authorities, making works for schools, fire stations and other civic buildings. Due to a demand for large-scale sculptures with restricted budgets, he started experimenting with unusual techniques, including working metal by *repoussé*, carving brick walls and flame-cut steel. In 1976 he held an exhibition of his innovative works in brick at the Building Centre in London, contrasting these with Carl André's controversial pieces in the same medium, then showing at the Tate Gallery. Notable examples of his work include the Len Hutton memorial at the Oval cricket ground in London, 1988–93; and the panels for the Bristol Eye Hospital, 1986. In 1996 he held his first gallery retrospective at Ramsgate Library, and in 2000 a major retrospective exhibition of his work was held at Leamington Spa Museum and Art Gallery. See 32 Corn Street, Lower Maudlin Street.

Sources: information provided by Sally Taylor, 11 March 2000; Noszlopy, George T., *Public Sculpture of Warwickshire, Coventry and Solihull*, Liverpool, 1998, p.267f.; Ritchie, W., *Walter Ritchie: Sculpture*, Kenilworth, 1994; Ritchie, W., *Sculpture in Brick and Other Materials*, Kenilworth, 1978, pp.8-10; SBC2005

John Michael Rysbrack, 1694–1770, sculptor. Born in Antwerp where his father, Peter, was a landscape painter, he trained under the sculptor Van der Voort before he came to England in 1720. His reputation was already good. A trio of foreign sculptors – Rysbrack, Scheemakers and Roubiliac – dominated the early Georgian scene. As well as the equestrian statue of William III in Queen Square, Bristol has Rysbrack's monument to Colston in All Saints Church, 1729, and there are busts in the Lord Mayor's Chapel and Redland Chapel. Bristol Museums and Art Gallery has the terracotta bust of Edward Colston and the terracotta statue of Anthony van Dyck. Important examples of his work can also be seen at Stourhead and Badminton. See Armoury Square, Queen Square.

Source: K. Eustace, *Michael Rysbrack, Sculptor 1694–1770*, Bristol Museum and Art Gallery, 1982

Gilbert W. Seale, sculptor, modeller and plasterer. As a plasterer he worked on Battersea Town Hall, 1892–3; on the Old Bailey, 1900–7; and elsewhere in London. In Bristol he did much work for the architect George Oatley, including work at the Bristol General Hospital (fountain, south wing, chapel); Cotham House; West India House, Welsh Back; and the Frost and Reed Gallery, Clare Street. See Corn Street, Clare Street.

Sources: CL2003; A. Stuart Gray, *Edwardian Architecture: A Biographical Dictionary*, 1985; Dr Sarah Whittingham's forthcoming book *Sir George Herbert Oatley: Architect of Bristol*, Redcliffe Press, 2009

Edward Sheppard, sculptor, stone- and wood-carver. The statue *Justice* on the Old Magistrates' Court is his only known work. He is recorded in Wright & Co.'s Bristol directories from 1871 as a carver of York Street, St Paul's until 1887, when he is listed as a sculptor and stone- and wood-carver of Wilson Street, St Paul's. See Bridewell Street.

Andrew Smith, born 1962, sculptor. Smith was born in South Wales and attended art courses in South Glamorgan and then West Surrey College of Art and Design, where he gained a BA (Hons) in three-dimensional design, specialising in metals. He then spent two years at the Royal College of Art in the department of metalwork. After research travel to Berlin, Paris and Iran, he has worked as a designer of street furniture. Between 1984 and 2002 he exhibited in London, Edinburgh, Cardiff, Tokyo and Los Angeles. He has gained many commissions for public sculpture and has work in Milton Keynes, Rotherham and Kensington. He worked with Richard Quinnell and other blacksmiths, and has taught blacksmithing at West Dean College and elsewhere for 23 years. See Upper Maudlin Street.

Source: www.westdean.org.uk

Keir Smith, born 1950, sculptor. He studied fine art at the University of Newcastle upon Tyne (1969–73) and at Chelsea School of Art (1973–5). His academic interest in art of the Renaissance – painting, sculpture and architecture – is long established. Working without an agent or dealer, Smith made his way as an artist through public commissions in the 1980s, when sculpture trails and the desire for site-specific sculpture prevailed. He was appointed artist-in-residence at Grizedale Forest, Cumbria in 1979, and made a number of publicly sited sculptures, including *Towards the Open Sea* for South Hill Park in Bracknell and *Dendron* for Yorkshire Sculpture Park, both in 1983. Smith excelled in his response to such commissions, and in finding an apposite solution that referred to the history of the site and its physical nature, as with *The Iron Road* (1986) for the Forest of Dean, where carved wooden railway sleepers lie in the place of a disused track, bearing references to former lives and times particular to the forest. Long periods are devoted to drawing: not to find solutions for specific sculptures, but to develop ideas. The drawings, in pencil and watercolour, have all the intensity of his sculpture and are no less a result of concentrated activity. See Baltic Wharf.

Source: www.sculpture.org.uk/artists/KeirSmith/

William John Smith, 1862–1936, sculptor. He attended Queen Elizabeth Hospital School in Bristol, and in later life he lived in the Montpelier area of the city. Half a century after his death, the *Bristol Evening Post* noted the anniversary and described him as 'One of the city's finest sculptors and ecclesiastical carvers'. He worked on the university, the cathedral and St Mary Redcliffe church, as well as the art gallery in Queen's Road and the Royal Colonial Institute at 2 Whiteladies Road. While working in the USA he carried out carving on a house being built for the Vanderbilts. He won some national trophies for cycle racing. See Queen's Road, Bristol Museums and Art Gallery, Whiteladies Road, Upper Byron Place.

Source: T. Bradshaw, *Bristol Magpies Newsletter,* No. 97, Oct/Nov 1993

James Havard Thomas, 1854–1921, sculptor. Born in Bristol on 22 December 1854 of Welsh parents, Havard Thomas first studied at the Bristol School of Art. He then went to London as a national scholar at the National Art Training School in South Kensington from 1872 until 1875. In Paris he attended the Ecole des Beaux-Arts under J. P. Cavelier. After a brief period in London (1884–9), when he was honorary secretary to the New English Art Club, he lived and worked in Italy from 1889 until 1906. After the First World War he gained wide acclaim as a classicist. He was the first professor of sculpture at the Slade School, where he had taught from 1911. The Tate Gallery, Cardiff, Manchester, and the Bristol Museums and Art Gallery all have examples of Havard Thomas's 'ideal work'. Thomas's contribution to the new sculpture movement, in works typified by *Lycidas*, 1905, are considered to have influenced Epstein and Eric Gill. A poignant link between sculptor and subject came from Clausen, when he remembered Havard Thomas as a fellow student at the South Kensington Schools (later the Royal College of Art) in the 1870s. Sir George wrote very aptly and admiringly: 'I remember him bringing an atmosphere of the eighteenth-century classicists into the school; he would quote Burke on the Sublime and Beautiful, and would discourse on Hamilton's Greek vases… it is evident that from those early days to the end of his career, he held consistently to the same ideal to follow the classic tradition of fine sculpture.' Havard Thomas died in London on 6 June 1921. See 'The Centre', Lewins Mead.

Sources: letter, 29 July 1980 in Local Sculpture files, BRL, under Queen Victoria; Susan Beattie, The New Sculpture, Yale, 1983, p.251; Sir George Clausen, A Memoir of James Harvard Thomas, for The Leicester Galleries, reprinted in Beaux Arts Gallery catalogue, 'Commemorative exhibition of sculpture and drawings by J. Harvard Thomas', 1936; *The Grove Dictionary of Art*

John Thomas, 1813–62, sculptor. Born at Chalford, Gloucestershire, he was apprenticed to a stonemason. He later went to Birmingham, where a brother was an architect. His work came to the notice of Charles Barry, who employed him to execute the ornamental stone and wood carving on Birmingham Grammar School and to manage the production of the carving for his new Palace of Westminster. From small drawings supplied by Barry's office, Thomas and his team developed large-scale drawings that formed the basis of the full-size plasters from which the figures and architectural work were carved in stone. By the late 1840s, Thomas's skill as an architectural sculptor was widely recognised. His output was immense, and he received commissions in most of the major cities. In Manchester he provided sculptural decoration for the Free Trade Hall and the Royal Cotton Exchange. The lions on the Britannia Bridge in the Menai Straits are also his work. His church monuments include those of Dr Arnold (Rugby School Chapel, 1844) and John Brooks (Prestwich, Lancashire, 1851). The workshop continued to undertake Gothic-style carving, as shown in the series of figures connected with Bristol history for the Guildhall, Broad Street, Bristol, designed by R. S. Pope (1843–6). His workshop was equally adept at the Italian Renaissance palazzo style, then especially popular with banks. The sumptuous carving on the former West of England and South Wales District Bank in Corn Street, Bristol (1854–8) is of a very high standard throughout. His final work was a colossal statue of Shakespeare displayed at the International Exhibition of 1862. Thomas also worked as an architect, designing individual buildings in Glasgow, Oxford and Windsor; and, in the case of Somerleyton, Suffolk, a complete village. See Berkeley Square, Broad Street, Corn Street, Queen's Road.

Sources: Gunnis; B1998; M2004; T. Stevens, Oxford DNB, 2004

Simon Thomas, born 1960, sculptor. Born in Portsmouth, he attended Ravensbourne College of Art before studying sculpture at the RCA, graduating in 1988. In 1995 he was awarded a research fellowship and appointed artist-in-residence at the University of Bristol's Physics Department. He also worked closely with Hewlett Packard's European HQ in Bristol. In 2002 he returned to Bristol University as artist-in-residence at the school of mathematics. In 2005–6 he worked in the mathematics department of Portsmouth University on the geometric structure of soap bubble foam. See Anchor Road, Tyndall Avenue.

Source: www.simonthomas-sculpture.com/biography.php

Philippa Threlfall, born 1939, and **Kennedy Collings,** 1933–2002. Together they made ceramic sculpture for over thirty years for banks, airports, offices and shopping developments throughout England. As well as *Exploration* in Redcliffe Street and the twelve reliefs on Broad Quay House telling the history of Bristol, they completed other works in Bristol, including ceramic panels on the Friendly Society building in Colston Street, 1994–5; and large terracotta panels on the first floor of Froomsgate House. Philippa studied ceramics and graphic design at Cardiff College of Art and Goldsmiths' College in London, before teaching ceramics and painting at North London Collegiate College. She left London to marry Kennedy Collings in 1967, and they settled in Wells. Kennedy was born in Bristol and was educated at Clifton College before he read History and Law at Cambridge. He then worked in industry before going into partnership with his wife and forming the company Black Dog of Wells after the medieval name of their studio workshop property on Wells Cathedral land. Kennedy died in 2002 and Philippa now carries on the business with her son, Daniel. See Broad Quay, Redcliffe Street.

Source: www.philippathrelfall.com

Thomas Tyley II. The family of Tyley were active in Bristol from at least the 1790s until 1928, the date of the plaque to Emma Saunders at Temple Meads Station. Thomas Tyley the younger won a Silver Isis medal in 1811 from the Society of Arts for a group entitled *Christ Healing the Sick*. In 1830 he carved the angel on the exterior pediment of C. R. Cockerell's Holy Trinity, Hotwells, and (probably in 1839) completed the statue of Sir Charles Wetherell. Some of the best of the many monuments in Bristol Cathedral signed TYLEY BRISTOL may be by this member of the family, but 'there appear to have been two Thomases and two Jameses in two generations.' See Park Row, Red Lodge.

Sources: Gunnis; *Bristol Times and Mirror*, 2 July 1928, p.8; K.. Eustace, 'Bread and Sermons', this volume

Louise Vergette. Company director and head of model making in the props and sets department of Cod Steaks, the Bristol company that has done much work for Aardman Animation. She did much work on *Wallace and Gromit: The Curse of the Were-Rabbit*, 2005. See St Philips Road.

Paul Vincze, 1907–94, medallist. Born in Hungary, he studied at the State School of Arts and Crafts in Budapest, and later in Rome (1935–7). In 1938 he moved to England and set up a studio in London, where he became an Art Workers' Guild member and a fellow of the RBS. Vincze exhibited widely, winning a number of awards, including a silver medal at the Paris Salon (1964) and the first gold medal of the American Numismatic Association (1966). Among his output was a prize medal for the Smithsonian Institution, a series of medals for the Shakespeare Birthplace Trust, and two medals struck to commemorate the coronation of Queen Elizabeth II in 1953. See College Green, Bristol Central Library.

Source: Buckman, David, *Dictionary of Artists in Britain Since 1945*, Bristol, 1998; WCS2003

Arthur George Walker, 1861–1939, sculptor. His statuette of John Wesley was exhibited at the Royal Academy summer exhibition in 1934, two years before he was elected RA. He made public statues of the famous nineteenth-century figures Emmeline Pankhurst (in the Embankment Gardens) and Florence Nightingale (in Waterloo Place). He was born in London, the son of a shipping merchant, and he studied at the Royal Academy Schools. In his later years he lived at Parkstone, Dorset, and when he died the Bristol Wesleyans published an obituary praising him for his modesty and integrity of character. In Bristol, as well as the equestrian statue of John Wesley, he executed a *Madonna* for the chapel of St Monica Home of Rest, a *Madonna and Child* for the chapel at the Wills Hall of Residence and, at St Mary Redcliffe, a *Virgin and Child* for the south porch and an *Annunciation* for the north porch. See Horsefair, John Wesley's Chapel.

Sources: D. Merritt, *Sculpture in Bristol*, 2002; S. Whittingham, *Sir George Herbert Oatley: Architect of Bristol*, 2009

David Ward, born 1951, artist. Initially a painter, his work has developed to involve a range of media that includes photography, dance, performance, sound, light and glass. He studied at Wolverhampton and Winchester Colleges of Art. Since 1991 he has served various terms as artist-in-residence at King's College, Cambridge, the Cambridge Dark Room, Harvard University and Durham Cathedral. He gained a research fellowship at the Henry Moore Centre for the Study of Sculpture, Leeds in 1996. He has taught at Goldsmiths College, the Architectural Association and Westminster University, and has exhibited internationally. His works in relation to architecture and performance include *Chorus*, Royal Festival Hall; *Weight & Measure*, Sir John Soane's Museum; and *Bird Song*, with Siobhan Davies Dance, Linbury Studio, Royal Opera House. In 2007 his exhibition 'Orinoco', with Richard Deacon, was held in the Orangery and Artists' House at the New Art Centre. A major exhibition of his work was held at Kettle's Yard, Cambridge in 2009. See Millennium Square.

Sources: *David Ward, Slow Time*, Kettle's Yard, Cambridge, 2009; www.sculpture.uk.com/artists/david_ward/

Julian P. Warren, born 1958, sculptor. Studied law and archaeology at UCL, graduating in 1983. He left the property and construction industry in

1990, learned the rudiments of welding and became a self-taught sculptor with a special interest in the natural world. The railings of his home at 18 Burlington Road, Redland, Bristol have become a gallery of birds, insects and animals. See Clifton Down, Bristol Zoo.

Source: information from the artist

Musgrave Lewthwaite Watson, 1804–47, sculptor; born in Carlisle. On the advice of John Flaxman, Watson entered the Royal Academy Schools, and while attending classes there he became a pupil in the studio of the sculptor R. Sievier. His education and apprenticeship were extremely protracted. He spent three years in Italy; on his return in 1828, he visited Carlisle but was soon back in London, where he took a studio near the British Museum. During the ensuing decade he worked mainly for other sculptors, such as Francis Chantrey, William Behnes and E. H. Baily. By 1842 he had attained a degree of independence and was commissioned to execute a frieze for Moxhay's Hall of Commerce in Threadneedle Street. This frieze survived the demolition of the building, and can still be seen at Napier Terrace, Islington. Watson sent in two models for the competition for the pediment of William Tite's Royal Exchange in the same year, but failed to win the competition. He was recompensed with a commission for a statue of Queen Elizabeth I for the interior of the Exchange. After completing a statue of John Flaxman for UCL, Watson modelled and partially carved a double portrait statue of lords Eldon and Stowell for University College, Oxford. This work was incomplete at the time of his death. He was also selected by Sir Robert Peel to model the relief of the Battle of St Vincent for Nelson's Column. This was another commission that Watson did not live to complete. Works like the much-admired relief of the *Death of Sarpedon*, shown at the Royal Academy in 1844, inspired great hopes for Watson's future. When he died at the age of 43, it was claimed that his chances of success had been prejudiced by his unconventional lifestyle, and that British sculpture had lost one of its brightest stars. See Queen's Road, Victoria Rooms.

Sources: H. Lonsdale, *The Life and Works of Musgrave Lewthwaite Watson, Sculptor*, London, 1866; CL2003

Sue Webster, born 1967, and **Tim Noble,** born 1966, artists. Born in Leicester and Stroud, respectively, Webster and Noble 'have developed their own cult of personality as the *enfants terrible* of contemporary art. Keeping it real with their affinity to working class culture, their self-portraits have been made from garbage, dead animals, and in the form of Neanderthals. Their work also includes large electric light drawings of tattoo iconography and bling logos.' See Millennium Square.

Source: www.saatchi-gallery.co.uk/artists/noble_webster_biography.htm

Sir Charles Wheeler, 1892–1974, sculptor. Born at Codsall in Staffordshire, studied at Wolverhampton School of Art and the Royal College of Art under Professor Edouard Lantéri, where he met a fellow student, William McMillan, the sculptor of the *Haig* statue at Clifton College. He exhibited for the first time at the summer exhibition at the Royal Academy in 1914 and, from 1918, exhibited regularly there. His first commission, *Madonna and Child*, formed part of the War Memorial within the Winchester College cloisters. He was elected an associate of the Royal Academy in 1934, although he was considered at that time something of a rebel. Immediately before the outbreak of the Second World War, he was commissioned to produce his most famous work, the Jellicoe Memorial Fountain in Trafalgar Square. In 1940 he was elected a Royal Academician, and in 1956 became president of the Royal Academy for ten years (the first sculptor to hold the post). Elected a fellow of the Royal British Society of Sculptors (RBS) in 1935, he was president of the organisation from 1945 until 1949. In 1949 he received the RBS Gold Medal for distinguished services to sculpture. Later, he was instrumental in founding the Society of Portrait Sculptors (of which he became the first president in 1953). After the Second World War, he contributed sculpture to Edward Maufe's extensions to the Royal Navy War Memorials at Chatham, Plymouth and Portsmouth, and to the same architect's Mercantile Marine Memorial at Tower Hill. He was also renowned for his busts, including a marble one of the present queen. Two of Wheeler's sculptures were purchased under the Chantrey Bequest for the Tate: *Infant Christ* (bronze, purchased 1924) and *Spring* (bronze, purchased 1930). Wheeler published his autobiography, *High Relief*, in 1968. See College Green, Council House.

Sources: F. Spalding, *20th Century Painters and Sculptors*, Dictionary of British Art, vol. 6; Woodbridge, 1990, p.459; SBC2005

J. Whitehead & Sons. In 1901, the firm of Whitehead's had several London addresses, as well as branches in Aberdeen and Carrara. In 1902 Joseph Whitehead, as director of the firm, signed drawings by the architect J. F. Bentley for the marble revetments of the chapels of Westminster Cathedral. Joseph Whitehead exhibited portrait busts at the Royal Academy from 1889 to 1895. By 1906, the firm had moved to the Imperial Works, Kennington Oval, where it remained in business up to 1985. By 1909, Whitehead's had become the official contractor to the Metropolitan Drinking Fountain and Cattle Trough Association. See Blackboy Hill.

Sources: Gunnis; CL2003

Onslow Whiting, fl. 1895–1933, sculptor. A London sculptor specialising in military subjects, Whiting exhibited a representation of field guns in action at Colenso in the Boer War at the Royal Academy in 1901. In 1902 Whiting made three of the four relief panels at the base of the obelisk erected on Plymouth Hoe. This memorial was to the officers and men of the Gloucestershire, Somerset and Devon regiments who fell in the Boer War, and to HRH Prince Christian Victor of Schleswig-Holstein, one of Queen Victoria's grandsons. The Plymouth memorial's link with the Gloucestershire regiment probably led to

Whiting gaining the commission for the Bristol statue. See Queen's Road, Gloucestershire Regiment Memorial.

Wills Brothers, W. J. Wills and T. Wills, fl. 1856–84, sculptors in iron. In 1856, W. J. Wills exhibited at the Royal Academy an elaborately decorated vase with subjects taken from Milton's *Paradise Lost.* A version of this, in iron, is now in the Victoria and Albert Museum. In 1859, Wills Bros undertook to model some of the first drinking fountains provided by the Metropolitan Free Drinking Fountain Association, including the figure of *Temperance* for the fountain in front of the Royal Exchange. Without being authorised by the association, the brothers commissioned additional casts of these models from the Coalbrookdale Iron Foundry. They were much praised by the *Art Journal* and described as 'sculptors by profession'. Under the artistic supervision of the sculptors John Bell and William Theed, they continued to provide models for the association. They also executed two public statues. A model for the figure of Richard Cobden for Camden Town was exhibited at the Royal Academy in 1866, and the finished work in the following year. The monument was inaugurated on 27 June 1868. Cobden's widow had visited the Euston Road workshop to demonstrate her husband's favourite stance while speaking. The whole work cost only £320. Other commemorative statues by Wills Bros are Sir Humphry Davy in Penzance, 1872; Lord Mayo at Cockermouth, 1875; G. L. Ashworth at Rochdale, 1877; Sir Thomas White at Coventry, 1883; Henry Edwards at Weymouth, 1886; and William III for New Quay, Torbay, 1889. The statue of Henry Edwards, shown in 1884, was the brothers' last Royal Academy exhibit. They were recorded in the catalogue as resident at this time at 128 Gower Street. See St Nicholas Street).

Sources: Papers of the Metropolitan Drinking Fountain and Cattle Trough Association, held at the London Metropolitan Archive; Jean Scott Rogers, 'How Cobden came to Camden Town', *Camden History Society Review*, no. 9, 1981, pp.20–2; *The Art-Journal*, 1860, p.114; CL2003

Thomas Woolner, 1825–92, sculptor and poet. Woolner was born at Hadleigh, Suffolk. He studied under the sculptor William Behnes before joining the Royal Academy Schools in 1842. In 1844 he sent a group, *The Death of Boadicea*, to the Westminster Hall exhibition. Friendship with Rossetti led to his becoming a member of the Pre-Raphaelite Brotherhood in 1848. After failing to win the competition for a monument in Westminster Abbey to the poet Wordsworth, Woolner travelled to Australia in 1857, hoping to make a fortune in the gold fields. When the fortune failed to materialise, he set up a portrait practice in Melbourne. He returned to England in 1854, and gradually won critical acclaim, mainly with his strong, naturalistic portraits. The list of Woolner's busts reads like a roll-call of eminent Victorians: Tennyson, Newman, Gladstone, Kingsley, Carlyle, Lord Lawrence, Darwin. His public statues include Lord Palmerston in Parliament Square, 1876, and John Stuart Mill on the Embankment, 1879. Woolner was less prolific with 'ideal' sculpture. Before leaving for Australia he had executed a playfully grotesque statuette of Puck, 1847. His most ambitious imaginary work was probably *The Lord's Prayer* (1856–67), sculpted for Sir Walter Trevelyan, and still at Wallington Hall, Northumberland. Woolner also executed a number of funerary monuments, and, at Wigton, Cumbria, a Memorial Fountain with bronze reliefs of *The Seven Acts of Mercy*, 1871. Between 1877 and 1879 Woolner was professor of sculpture at the Royal Academy, though he never lectured in this capacity. See College Road, Clifton College.

Sources: A. Woolner, *Thomas Woolner RA, Sculptor and Poet: His Life in Letters*, London, 1917; B. Read and J. Barnes (eds), *Pre-Raphaelite Sculpture: Nature and Imagination in British Sculpture 1848–1914*, London, 1991; CL2003

Vincent Woropay, 1951–2002, sculptor, draughtsman and teacher. After gaining a first class degree at Brighton Polytechnic (1974–7), he studied at the Slade School of Art (1977–9), and then won a scholarship to study at the British School in Rome (1979–81). His stay in Rome was particularly influential in developing his interest in stone-carving and the classical world. Many of his sculptures are of bodily fragments, often of gigantic dimensions, some of which are juxtaposed and curiously intermingled with architectural fragments. One example is his *Hand of the River God* (1984, Bristol), in which a colossal hand originally held up a fountain, which included within it a giant who was himself holding up an obelisk. As in the paintings of De Chirico, the past is used as a source not of comfortable nostalgia, but of mystery and disquiet. His commissions include *Capo*, National Garden Festival, Stoke-on-Trent, 1986; *Hand with Chronos*, at Stoke-on-Trent Railway Station, 1988; *The Wattilisk*, Birmingham, 1988; and *Rude Block 1 and 2*, Romsey Abbey, Hampshire, 1993. From 1978 onwards, he exhibited regularly with New Contemporaries at the ICA. In 1985, he held an exhibition at Portland Clifftop Sculpture Park. His first major London exhibition was 'Supra Limum', held at the Fabian Carlsson Gallery in 1988. His work is to be found in various international collections. See Baltic Wharf.

Sources: Buckman, D., *Dictionary of Artists in Britain Since 1945*, Bristol, 1998, p.1310; Chard, C., *Vincent Woropay*, Cambridge, 1984; Crichton, F., 'Obituary: Vincent Woropay', *Independent*, 5 July 2002; Hourahane, S., *Stoneworks*, Cardiff, 1988, p.58; Lothian, M., 'Distant thunder', *Arts Review*, vol. 40, 9 September 1988, p.626; Martin, R., 'Review of Fabian Carlsson Gallery exhibition', *Flash Art* (international edition), no. 145, March/April 1989, pp.122–3; Noszlopy, George T., *Public Sculpture of Birmingham Including Sutton Coldfield*, Liverpool, 1998, p.209; Public Art Commissions Agency, *Art at the International Convention Centre*, Birmingham, 1995; Woropay, V., *Supra Limum*, London, 1988; SBC2005

David Wynne, born 1926, sculptor, best known for figurative and animal pieces. After serving in the Royal Navy (1944–7), Wynne studied at Trinity College, Cambridge, where he developed an interest in art and took up sculpture, training under Georg Ehrlich and later in Paris with Paul Landowski and Welles Bosworth. Since 1946, he has produced figures, portraits and animals. Encouraged by Epstein, he made a portrait bust of Sir Thomas Beecham in 1947, which is now in the

Royal Festival Hall. He taught art at Lanford Grove School for Girls (1953–7), but since then has focused upon producing sculpture. Wynne's work is characterised by his delight in the complex rhythms of nature. In the late 1960s, birds were his primary theme as he developed various ways of suggesting the lightness of flight. His portraits of dolphins in the early 1970s conveyed similar impressions of lightness and movement. His commissions include: *Boy with a Dolphin* (Cheyne Walk, 1974); *Five Swimmers Fountain* (Staines, 1980); *Risen Christ and Seraphim* (Wells Cathedral, 1984–5); *The Awakening Earth* (Geneva, 1988); *Gaia and Tresco Children* (Isles of Scilly, 1990); and *Goddess of the Woods* (Highgrove, 1991). Wynne designed the linked hands on the EEC 50 pence coin and the Jubilee Medal, 1977, as well as the gates onto Hyde Park made in honour of the Queen Mother's 90th birthday (1992). He was awarded the OBE in 1994. See Clifton Down, Bristol Zoo.

Sources: Buckman, D., *Dictionary of Artists in Britain Since 1945*, Bristol, 1998, p.1316; Hughes, G., *Sculpture of David Wynne 1968–74*, London, 1975; Spalding, F., *20th Century Painters and Sculptors, Dictionary of British Art*, vol. 6; Woodbridge, 1990, p.478; Stone, J. (ed.), *The Sculpture of David Wynne 1974–1992*, London, 1993; Usherwood, P., Beach, J. and Morris, C., *Public Sculpture of North-East England*, Liverpool, 2000, p.340; SBC2005

Edward William Wyon, 1811–85, sculptor. Son of Thomas Wyon, chief engraver of the seals at the Royal Mint. He joined the Royal Academy Schools in 1829, on the recommendation of E. H. Baily. In 1831 he began to exhibit wax portrait medallions and busts at the Royal Academy. Wyon worked for the Art Union, producing in 1842 its first sculpture offer, a reduction of John Flaxman's *St Michael and Satan*, described by the *Art Union Journal* as a 'glorious work'. Also for the Art Union he created a *Tazza*, 'modelled from a Greek design', which was shown at the Great Exhibition in 1851. He modelled portrait busts and reliefs of scenes from Shakespeare, for interpretation in 'statuary porcelain' by Wedgwood. Wyon's statue of *Britomart*, 1856–61, for the Mansion House marked his debut as a monumental sculptor. In 1846 he produced a bronze statue of Richard Green, shipbuilder and philanthropist, for East India Dock, London, and an extensive programme of architectural sculpture for the internal courtyard of Drapers' Hall in the city. In 1869, he produced figures of Galileo, Goethe and Laplace for the University of London building in Burlington Gardens. Wyon executed a number of characterful reliefs for funerary monuments. He was one of six sculptors invited to submit maquettes by a committee set up in 1855 after the Great Exhibition had closed. The committee's task was to commission 'modern' sculpture for the Crystal Palace on its new site at Sydenham in South London. Wyon saw this opportunity 'as a means of earning a repute for larger and nobler works'. Through bereavement and his own ill-health, he failed to deliver the two-metre marble figure, based on a subject from Edmund Spencer's *Faerie Queen*, before the imposed deadline, although he was ultimately allowed to complete the work. His desire to make 'larger and nobler' works may have been satisfied by the Bristol commission very late in his career. See Corn Street, Exchange.

Sources: Gunnis; P. Atterbury (ed.), *The Parian Phenomenon*, 1989; CL2003

BIBLIOGRAPHY

Abbreviations

BBHA: Bristol Branch of the Historical Association
BCC: Bristol City Council
BCMG: Bristol City Museums and Art Gallery
BCRL/BRL: Bristol Central Reference Library
BRO: Bristol Record Office
BRSP: *Bristol Record Society's Publications*
Church Monuments: *Journal of the Church Monuments Society*
NRP: National Recording Project
ODNB: *Oxford Dictionary of National Biography*, Harrison, B., and Matthew, C. (eds), Oxford 2004
PMSA: Public Monuments and Sculpture Association
PSBS: Public Sculpture of Britain Series
RA: Royal Academy of Arts, London
TBGAS: *Transactions of the Bristol and Gloucestershire Archaeological Society*

Books and Articles

Aesop Fables, trans. Sir Roger L'Estrange (Everyman Library), London, undated, c.1960
Alford, B.W.E., *W.D. & H.O. Wills and the Development of the UK Tobacco Industry, 1786–1965*, London 1973
Anon., *Bristol in 1898: Contemporary Biographies*, 2 vols, Brighton 1898
Anon., *Clifton and the Hotwells*, Bristol 1844
Arrowsmith's Dictionary of Bristol, Bristol 1852 (1906)
Arthur, W., *The Successful Merchant: Sketches of the Life of Mr Samuel Budgett, Late of Kingswood Hill*, London 1852
Atkyns, Sir R., *Ancient and Present State of Gloucestershire,* London 1712 (Smith, B.S., ed., Wakefield 1974)
Attwater, D., *Penguin Dictionary of Saints*, Harmondsworth c.1965 (1995)
Aubrey, J., *Brief Lives*, Barber, R. (ed.), Woodbridge 1982 (2004)
Aughton, P., *St Mary Redcliffe, the Church and its People*, Bristol 2008
Avery, C., *Bernini, Genius of the Baroque*, London 1997
Avery, J.R., *'While We Have Time', 1590–1990: Queen Elizabeth's Hospital Quarter Centenary*, Bristol 1990
Baker, M., Lieberman, I., Potts, A. and Yarrington, A., 'An edition of the ledger of Sir Francis Chantrey, R.A., at the Royal Academy, 1809–1841', *Walpole Society*, vol. LVI, 1991/1992
Baker, M., and Bindman, D., *Roubiliac and the Eighteenth-Century Monument: Sculpture as Theatre*, New Haven, CT and London 1995
Barker, K., 'The Theatre Royal Bristol, the first seventy years', in McGrath, P. (ed.), *Bristol in the Eighteenth Century*, Newton Abbot 1972
Barker, W.R, *St Mark's or the Mayor's Chapel*, Bristol 1892
Barot, R., *Bristol and the Indian Independence Movement*, BBHA no. 70, 1988
Barrett, P., *Pigou, Francis, ODNB*
Barrett, W., *History and Antiquities of the City of Bristol*, 2 vols, Bristol 1789
Bartlett, J., and Penny, J., 'Bristol's vanished Georgian armoury', Fishponds History Group, 2001
Beattie, S., *The New Sculpture*, New Haven, CT and London 1983
Beeson, A., *Bristol Central Library and Charles Holden*, Bristol 2006
—, 'The genuine English tradesman', *Bristol Review of Books*, autumn 2008
—, *Bristol in 1807*, Bristol 2009
Behrendt, S.C., *Royal Mourning and Regency Culture*, Basingstoke 1997
Belsey, J., 'Towering discoveries', *Offbeat Bristol*, Bristol 1992
—, *More Offbeat Bristol*, Bristol 1993
Bennett, A., Lanchester, H.V. and Fenn, A., *The Art of E.A. Rickards*, London 1920
Berry, M., 'Paul Dirac: The Purest Soul in Physics', *Nonesuch*, 2002
Bettey, J.H., *Bristol Observed*, Bristol 1986
—, *The Suppression of the Religious Houses in Bristol*, BBHA, no. 74, 1990
—, 'Bristol Cathedral: the rebuilding of the nave', BBHA, no. 82, 1993
—, 'St Augustine's Abbey, Bristol', BBHA, no. 88, 1996
—, *Bush, Paul, ODNB*
— (ed.), *Essays in Memory of Elizabeth Ralph 1911–2000* (*TBGAS*), Bristol 2001
— (ed.), *Records of Bristol Cathedral*, BRSP, vol. 59, 2007
Bilbey, D., with Trusted, M., *British Sculpture 1470–2000; A Concise Catalogue of the Collection at the Victoria and Albert Museum*, London 2002
Bindman, D. (ed.) (exhib. cat.), *John Flaxman R.A.*, RA, 1979
Bingham, M., *Masks and Façades: Sir John Vanbrugh, the Man in his Setting*, London 1974
Bingham, N.R. (exhib. cat.), *C.A. Busby – The Regency Architect of Brighton and Hove*, London 1991
Blacker, B.H., and Clayton, M.E., *Gray, Robert (1762–1834), ODNB*
Booker, J., *Temples of Mammon: The Architecture of Banking*, Edinburgh 1990

Borwick, F. (ed.), *Clifton College Annals and Register, 1862–1925*, Bristol 1925
Boucher, C.E., *Transactions of the Bristol and Gloucestershire Archaeological Society*, vol. 61, 1939
Bowen, F.W.E., *Queen Elizabeth's Hospital*, Bristol 1971
Bretherton, F.F., 'The Welsh Congregation at the "New Room"', *Proceedings of the Wesley Historical Society*, vol. XXIII, 1941–42
Brewer, Rev. E. Cobham, *A Dictionary of Phrase and Fable*, London, new edition, undated
Bristol Almanac and Companion, 1871
Broome, W.C., *Notes and Records of Bristol Savages 1904–1977*, Bristol 1979
Broome, J., 'Samuel Baldwin: Carver of Gloucester', *Church Monuments*, vol. X, 1995
Buchanan, B.J., *McAdam, J.L., ODNB*
Buchanan, R.A., and Williams, M., *Brunel's Bristol*, Bristol 1982
Burgess, C., *Ricart, Robert, ODNB*
Burrough, T.H.B., 'Bristol', *Studio Vista*, 1970, p.28
Butcher, E.E. (ed.), *Bristol Corporation of the Poor, 1696–1834*, Bristol Record Society, vol. III, 1932
—, *Bristol Corporation of the Poor, 1696–1898*, BBHA, no. 29, 1972
Byron, A., *London Statues: A Guide to London's Outdoor Statues and Sculpture*, London 1981
Callahan, R., *Slim, William Joseph, ODNB*
Cannan, F., 'Alabaster representation of the Holy Spirit and allegations of Lollard vandalism', *Sculpture Journal*, issue 1, 2006
Carleton, D., *The Princes of Park Row*, Bristol 1983
Carnall, G., *Southey, Robert, ODNB*
Carpenter, M., *A Life of Joseph Tuckerman*, Bristol 1848
Carter, G., *Biddulph, Thomas Tregenna, ODNB*
Cartwright, R.F., *Pictorial History of St Mary Redcliffe, Bristol*, London 1971
Cavanagh, T., *Public Sculpture of Liverpool*, Liverpool 1997
Cave, C.H., *A History of Banking in Bristol, 1750 to 1899*, Bristol 1899
Cecil, R., *Memoirs of John Bacon, Esq. RA*, London 1801
Chambers' Biographical Dictionary, ed. J.O. Thorne, London 1961
Chancellor, E.B., *Lives of the British Sculptors*, London 1911
Chilcott, J., *New Guide to Bristol, Clifton and the Hotwells*, 6th ed., Bristol 1844
Chilcott's Descriptive History of Bristol, Ancient and Modern; or a Guide to Bristol, 7th ed., Bristol 1846 -
Christie, O.F., *A History of Clifton College, 1860–1934*, Bristol 1935
Collins, J., *Eric Gill: The Sculpture*, London 1998
Collinson, P., Ramsay, N. and Sparks, M. (eds), *A History of Canterbury Cathedral*, Oxford, 1995 (2002)
Colvin, H., *Biographical Dictionary of British Architects 1600–1840*, 3rd ed., New Haven, CT and London 1995
Cook, E.H., *The Freemasons' Hall, Bristol*, Bristol 1939
Cornforth, J., and Wright, M., *The Conservation of Bristol, A Unique City*, n.d. (reprinted from *Country Life*, 27 October, 3–17 November, 8–22 December, 1983)
Costello, K., and Burley, R., *Charity on Camera in Edwardian Bristol*, Derby 1997
Cottle, B., *Thomas Chatterton*, BBHA, no. 6, 1965
Cowper, H.S., *Robert Kitchen, Mayor of Bristol;A Native of Kendal*, Kendal 1928
Coutu, J., 'Carving histories: British sculpture in the West Indies', *Church Monuments*, vol. XII, 1997
Cox-Johnson, A., *John Bacon RA 1740–1799*, St Marylebone Society, no. 4, 1961
Craske, M., *The Silent Rhetoric of the Body: A History of Monumental Sculpture and Commemorative Art in England, 1720–1770*, New Haven, CT and London 2007
Crick, C., *Victorian Buildings in Bristol*, Bristol 1975
Croft-Murray, E., 'An account book of John Flaxman, R.A.', *Walpole Society*, vol. XXVIII
—., 'An unpublished early watercolour by J.M.W. Turner: *Cote House*', *Burlington Magazine*, vol. 90, no. 541, 1948
Crossley, F.H., *English Church Monuments A.D.1150–1550*, London 1921
Crossley Evans, M.J., 'Christian Missionary work among the seamen and dockers of Bristol, 1820–1914', in Bettey (ed.), *Essays in Memory of Elizabeth Ralph 1911–2000.*
Cruden, A., *Cruden's Complete Concordance to the Bible*, London and Guildford 1933 (1977)
Curnock, N. (ed.), *The Journal of the Rev. John Wesley*, 5 vols, London 1938
Daniell, D., *William Tyndale, A Biography*, New Haven, CT and London, 1994 (2001)
—, *Tyndale, William, ODNB*
Darke, J., *The Monument Guide to England and Wales*, London and Sydney 1991
Davies, P., *John Huggins Sculptor*, Wellington, Somerset 2006
Denning, C.F.W., *The Eighteenth-Century Architecture of Bristol*, Bristol [1923] 1926
Dorment, R., 'Mourning glories', *Times Literary Supplement*, 11 November 1988
Drabble, M., *Oxford Companion to English Literature*, London 1985
Dreaper, J., *Bristol's Forgotten Victor, Lt-General Sir William Draper KB (1721–1787)*, BBHA no. 94, 1998
Edwards, M., *The New Room*, Bristol 1972
Edwards, T., *British Cities: Bristol*, London 1951
Eickelmann, C. and Small, D., *Pero, the Life of a Slave in Eighteenth-Century Bristol*, Bristol 2004
Elkin, P., *Images of Bristol*, Bristol 1995
Esdaile, K., 'Sculpture', in A.S. Turberville, *Johnson's England*, 2 vols, Oxford 1933, vol. 2, pp. 72–92

—, *English Church Monuments 1510–1840*, London 1946
Essick, R.N., and La Belle, J., *The Iliad of Homer Engraved from the Compositions of John Flaxman*, New York and London 1977
Eustace, K., 'Drawings of a neo-classical town garden in Bristol', *Connoisseur*, CCI, June 1979
— (et al.) (exhib. cat.), *Michael Rysbrack, Sculptor 1694–1770*, Bristol 1982
—, 'William III, Queen Square, Bristol 1731–1736', in Eustace et al. 1982
—, 'The post-Reformation monuments', in Collinson et al. 1995
—, *Baily, Edward Hodges, ODNB*
—, *Rysbrack, Michael, ODNB*
—, '"A place full of rich and industrious people": art and patronage in Bristol in the first half of the 18th century', *British Art Journal*, vol. VII, no. I, 2006
Evans, J., *New Guide, or Picture of Bristol with Historical and Biographical Notices* (3rd ed.), Bristol *c.*1820–3
Eveleigh, D.J., *'A Popular Retreat', Blaise Castle House and Estate*, Bristol 1987
—, *Bristol 1850–1919*, Stroud 1996
—, *Bristol 1920–1969*, Stroud 1998
—, *Bristol: The Photographic Collection*, Stroud 2003
Everard, E., *A Bristol Printing House, Spoken of in Several Fragments by Edward Everard*, London [1902]
Fedden, M., *Bristol Vignettes*, Bristol 1952
—, *Bristol Bypaths*, Bristol 1954
Fitzgerald, R., *Fry, Joseph, ODNB*
Fleming, J., *Robert Adam and his Circle in Edinburgh and Rome*, London 1962 (1978)
Fox-Davies, A.C., *A Complete Guide to Heraldry*, London 1909 (1978)
Foyle, A., and Cherry, B., *Bristol*, New Haven, CT and London 2004
Freeman, A.B., *Bristol Worthies and Notable Residents in the District*, Bristol 1909
Friedman, T.F., 'Rysbrack and Gibbs', in Eustace et al., *Michael Rysbrack*
Friedman, T.F., *James Gibbs*, New Haven, CT and London 1984
Garrard, Thomas, *E. Colston, The Philanthropist*, Bristol 1852
Gibbs, J., *A Book of Architecture*, London 1728
Gildea, J., *For Remembrance and in Honour of those who Lost their Lives in the South African War*, London 1911
Girouard, M., *The Return to Camelot: Chivalry and the English Gentleman*, New Haven, CT and London 1981
Gomme, A., Jenner, M. and Little, B., *Bristol, An Architectural History*, London 1979
Gough, P., and Morgan, S., 'Manipulating the metonymic', *Journal of Historical Geography*, 30, 2004
Graves, R., *Greek Myths*, London 1958 (1991)
Greenacre, B. (exhib. cat.), *Tim Knowles and Catherine Moorland*, Rokeby Gallery, London, 2006
Greenacre, F., and Stoddard, S. (exhib. cat.), *W.J. Muller 1812–1845*, Bristol 1991
—, *From Bristol to the Sea: Artists, the Avon Gorge and Bristol Harbour*, Bristol 2005
Grinsell, L.V., *The History and Coinage of the Bristol Mint*, Bristol 1986
Groom, N., *The Death of Chatterton*, in Heys (ed.), *From Gothic to Romantic: Thomas Chatterton's Bristol*
Gunnis, R., *Dictionary of British Sculptors, 1660–1851*, revised edition, London 1951
Hall, J., *Illustrated History of Symbolism in Eastern and Western Art*, London 1997
Harding, S., and Lambert, D., *Parks and Gardens of Avon*, Bristol 1994
—, 'Thomas Wright at Stoke Park', *Garden History*, vol. 17, no. 1, 1989
Harrison, D., *Bristol Times Revisited*, Bristol 2003
Haskell, F., and Penny, N., *Taste and the Antique: The Lure of Classical Sculpture 1500–1900*, New Haven, CT and London, 1981
Hattersley, R., *A Brand from the Burning: The Life of John Wesley*, London 2002
Herbert, A.S., *Historical Catalogue of Printed Editions of the English Bible, 1525–1961*, London 1968
Herrman, J., and Kondoleon, C., 'The poetry of water in Roman Imperial art', *Apollo*, May, 2003
Heys, A. (ed.), *From Gothic to Romantic: Thomas Chatterton's Bristol*, Bristol 2005
Higgie, J., 'Get it while you can', *Frieze Magazine*, September 2003
Hill, C.P., *History of Bristol Grammar School*, revised ed., London 1951
Holmes, R., *Coleridge: Early Visions*, London 1989
Hudson, J., *The Mansion House, Clifton*, Bristol 1993
Hulme, T.F., *John Wesley and his Horse*, London 1933
Hutchinson, S.C., 'The Royal Academy Schools, 1768–1830', *Walpole Society*, XXXVIII, 1960–62
Hutton, S., *Bristol and its Famous Associations*, Bristol 1907
Irwin, D. *John Flaxman 1755–1826 Sculptor Illustrator Designer*, London, 1979
Ison, W., *The Georgian Buildings of Bristol*, London 1952 (1978)
Jackson, L., and Malone, K., *A Book of Pots: Kate Malone*, London 2003
Jackson, T. (exhib. cat.), *Eilís O'Connell: A Decade of Sculpture*, Arnolfini, Bristol 1999–2000
Jackson-Stops, G., 'New deities for old parterres: the painting of lead statues', *Country Life*, 29 January 1987
James, D.S., *A Century of Statues: A History of the Morris Singer Foundry*, Basingstoke 1984
Janá ek, L., *Intimate Letters: Leoš Janá ek to Kamila Stösslová* (Tyrrell, J., trans. and ed.), London 1994 (2005)
Jenner, M., 'The grand finale', *Bristol Illustrated*, March 1985
—, 'The Arnos Gateway, Brislington', *Follies: International Magazine for Follies Grottoes and Garden Buildings*, Summer 1998
Jennings, S., 'Bristol High Cross', *RWA Friends' Newsletter*, Spring 2000
Jezzard, A., '"An all-round craftsman": George

Frampton's church monuments', *Church Monuments*, vol. XI, 1996
Jones, D., *Bristol's Sugar Trade and Refining Industry*, BBHA, no. 89, 2003
—, *A History of Clifton*, Chichester 1992 (2002)
—, *John Foster's Almshouse and the Chapel of the Three Kings of Cologne*, Bristol n.d.
Jones, S., *Whiteladies Walks: Five Town Trails in a Victorian Conservation Area*, Bristol 1976
Jordan, C., 'The very spirit of purity and chastity: *Eve at the Fountain*, by Edward Hodges Baily', *Sculpture Journal*, vol.15.1, 2006
Kelly, A., *Queen Square Bristol*, Bristol, 2003
—, and Kelly, M., (eds), *Brunel, In Love with the Impossible: A Celebration of the Life, Work and Legacy of Isambard Kingdom Brunel*, Bristol 2006
Kelly, Alison, 'Coade stone in Georgian gardens', *Garden History*, vol. 16, no 2, 1988
—, *Mrs Coade's Stone*, Upton-upon-Severn 1990
Kelly's Handbook to the Titled, Landed and Official Classes, London 1931
Kemp, B., *English Church Monuments,* London 1980
Kent, C., and Rev. Law, G., *Fargus, Frederick John, ODNB*
Killingley, D., *Roy, Rammohun, ODNB*
King, A., *The Centenary of the Cabot Memorial Tower 1897–1997*, Bristol 1997
King, P., 'The cadaver tomb in England', *Church Monuments*, vol. V, 1990
Knighton, C.S., *Penn, Sir William, ODNB*
Koch, A., *Sculptures from 'Academy Architecture' 1904–1908*, London 1908
Kragh, H., *Dirac, Paul Adrien Maurice, ODNB*
Lane, J., *Ann Christopher, Sculpture 1989–1994*, London 1994
Lange, A.E., *Delftware at Historic Deerfield 1600–1800*, Deerfield, MA c.2001
Langford, P., *Burke, Edmund, ODNB*
Latimer, J., *Annals of Bristol in the Nineteenth Century*, Bristol 1887
—, *Annals of Bristol 1600–1900*, 7 vols, Bristol 1893 (1906)
—, *Annals of Bristol in the Eighteenth Century*, Bristol 1893
—, *Annals of Bristol in the Seventeenth Century*, Bristol 1900
—, *Annals of Bristol in the Nineteenth Century Concluded, 1887–1900*, Bristol 1902
—, *History of the Society of Merchant Venturers of the City of Bristol*, Bristol 1903
—, *Annals of Bristol in the Sixteenth Century*, 1900 (Bath, Kingsmead reprints, 1970)
Lea-Jones, J. (ed.), 'An account of St John's Conduit, Bristol's medieval water system', *Temple Local History Group Report*, 1984, p.2
Lea-Jones, J., *Bristol Curiosities*, Edinburgh 2007
Lee, R., *Wesleyana and Methodist Pottery*, London 1988
Leech, J., *The Pipes, Pumps, and Conduits of Bristol*, Bristol, n.d
Leech, J., *Rural Rides of the Bristol Churchgoer*, Sutton, A. (ed.), Stroud, 1982 (2004)
Lees Milne, J. and Ford, D., *Images of Bath*, Richmond-upon-Thames 1982
Leighton, W., *Trinity Hospital, Bristol, TBGAS*, vol. XXXVI, 1913
Lepard, S., 'Report to the meeting, with drawings of the brazen columns at Bristol: Proceedings, 12 May 1858', *Journal of the British Archaeological Association*, 1858
Levitt, S.,*The Red Lodge*, Bristol 1986
Little, B., *The City and County of Bristol: A Study of Atlantic Civilisation*, London 1954 (1967)
—, *The Life and Work of James Gibbs*, London 1955
—, *Bristol: The Public View*, Bristol 1982
—, 'Restoring a Grecian Masterpiece', *Country Life*, 23 September 1976
—, 'So nearly a queen', *Gloucestershire and Avon Life*, May 1984
—, 'Victoriana', *Bristol Illustrated*, July 1988
Little, W.J., *John Wesley's Chapel: A Short History*, Bristol 1981
Liversidge, M., *The Bristol High Cross*, BBHA, no. 42, 1978
—, *William Hogarth's Bristol Altar-piece*, BBHA, no.46, 1980
—, 'The poetry is in the Paty', *Bristol University Newsletter*, 18 March 1982
Llewellyn, N., *The Art of Death: Visual Culture in the English Death Ritual c.1500 – c.1800*, London 1992
Lonsdale, H., *The Life and Works of Musgrave Lewthwaite Watson, Sculptor*, London 1866
Low, R., *Grant, Cary, ODNB*
MacCarthy, F., *Eric Gill*, London and Boston 1989
McConnell, A., *Plimsoll, Samuel, ODNB*
McGrath, P. (ed.), *Bristol in the Eighteenth Century*, Newton Abbot 1972
—, *The Merchant Venturers of Bristol: A History of the Society of Merchant Venturers of the City of Bristol from its Origin to the Present Day*, Bristol 1975
McIntyre, I., *Joshua Reynolds: The Life and Times of the First President of the Royal Academy*, London 2003
Mackenzie, R., *Public Sculpture of Glasgow*, Liverpool 2002
Major, S.D., *New Illustrated Handbook to Bristol, Clifton and Neighbourhood*, Bristol 1872
Manchee, T.J., *The Bristol Charities, Being the Report of the Commissioners for Enquiring Concerning Charities in England and Wales, So Far As Relates to the Charitable Institutions in Bristol*, 2 vols, Bristol 1831
Marcy, P.T., 'Eighteenth century views of Bristol and Bristolians', in McGrath (ed.), *Bristol in the Eighteenth Century*
Marmion, V.J., *The Bristol Eye Hospital: A Monograph*, Bristol 1985
Martineau, H., *The History of England during the Thirty Years' Peace: 1816–1846*, London 1849 (1850)
Matthews, W., *New History, Survey and Description of the City and Suburbs of Bristol*, Bristol 1794
Matthew's Bristol Directories (continued as J. Wright & Co.'s Directories), 1793–1900s

Matthew's Directory, 1870
Matthews, J., *Bristol Guide; by Bristoliensi*, 3rd ed., Bristol 1815
Menneer, N., and Mowl, T., *Bristol: City on the Edge*, London 2006
Merritt, D., *Sculpture in Bristol*, Bristol 2002
Middlemas, K., *The Life and Times of Edward VII*, London 1972
Milner, D., *The Royal West of England Academy Bristol, An Essay in Patronage*, Bristol 1985
Minchinton, W.E., 'The trade of Bristol in the eighteenth century', *Bristol Record Society*, vol. 20, 1957 (reprint 1966)
Mitchell, A., 'The park and garden at Dyrham', *National Trust Yearbook*, 1977–78
Mitchell, A., and Mitchell, O., *Thomas Earp: Eminent Victorian Sculptor*, Buckingham 2002
Morgan, K., *Edward Colston and Bristol*, BBHA, no. 96, 1999
—, *Colston, Edward, ODNB*
Moorcroft, D., and Campbell-Sharp, N., *Bristol in Old Photographs from the Fred Little Collection*, Gloucester 1988
Mowl, T., *John Wood, Architect of Obsession*, Bath 1988
—, *To Build the Second City: Architects and Craftsmen of Georgian Bristol*, Bristol 1991
—, *Bristol: Last Age of the Merchant Princes*, Bath 1991
Mowl, T., and Earnshaw, B., 'The garden ghost of the great house of Henbury', *Gloucestershire and Avon Life*, June 1981
Munro Smith, G., *History of the Bristol Royal Infirmary*, Bristol 1917
New, M., *Sterne, Lawrence, ODNB*
Newbould, C., and Beresford, C., *The Glosters: An Illustrated History of a County Regiment*, Stroud 1992
Nichols, G., *'To Keep Open and Unenclosed': The Management of Durdham Down Since 1861*, BBHA no. 116, 2005
Nicholls, J.F., and Taylor, J., *Bristol Past and Present*, 3 vols, Bristol 1881–1882
Oosterwijk, S., 'Food for worms, food for thought: the appearance and interpretation of the "verminous" cadaver in Britain and Europe', *Church Monuments*, vol. XX, 2005
Parry, J., *Morley, Samuel, ODNB*
Peace, D., *Eric Gill: The Inscriptions*, London 1994
Penny, J., *All the News That's Fit to Print: A Short History of Bristol's Newspapers Since 1702*, BBHA, no. 101, 2001
Penny, N., *Church Monuments in Romantic England*, New Haven, CT and London 1977
Perrier, F., *Segenta nobilium signorum et statuary*, Paris 1638
Perry, B.E., *Babrius and Phaedrus*, Cambridge, Mass. 1965
Peters, G.H., *The Plimsoll Line: The Story of Samuel Plimsoll, Member of Parliament for Derby from 1868 to 1880*, Chichester 1975
Petts, L., *The Story of 'Nipper' and the 'His Master's Voice' Picture Painted by Francis Barraud*, Bournemouth 1973
Pevsner, N., *North Somerset and Bristol, Buildings of England*, Harmondsworth 1958
— (ed.), Verey, D., *Gloucestershire, the Vale and the Forest of Dean, Buildings of England*, Harmondsworth 1970
Physick, J., *Designs for English Sculpture 1680–1860*, London 1969
Piper, D., 'The National Portrait Gallery: some recent acquisitions', *Connoisseur*, no. 54, April 1954
Pooley, C., *Notes on the Old Crosses of Gloucestershire*, London 1868
Potter, J., *Headmaster: The Life of John Percival, Radical Autocrat*, London 1998
Priest, G., and Cobb, P. (eds), *The Fight for Bristol: Planning the Growth of Public Protest*, Bristol 1980
—, *The Paty Family, Makers of Eighteenth-Century Bristol*, Bristol 2003
Prior, R., and Wilson, T., *Haig, Douglas, ODNB*
Prochaska, F., *Carpenter, Mary, ODNB*
Pryce, G., 'Communication in relation to the Bristol columns, Proceedings 9 February 1859', *Journal of the British Archaeological Association*, 1859
Quinn, D.B, *Cabot, John, ODNB*
Ralph, E., *Government of Bristol 1373–1873*, Bristol 1973
—, *The Downs, Bristol*, Bristol 1973
—, '"Nil Desperandum": Thomas Proctor 1812–1876', *Canynges Society Annual Gazette*, 1990
Read, B., *Victorian Sculpture*, New Haven, CT and London 1982
Read, L. du S., *William Powell (1735/6–1769), ODNB*
Reader, W.J., *Macadam: The McAdam Family and the Turnpike Roads, 1798–1861*, London 1980
Rich, J., *The Bristol Pilots: A Treatise on the Bristol Pilots, from their Origination, to their Amalgamation, Including a List of Pilots' Names, Dates and Some of the Boats, for almost 500 Years*, Pill c.1996
Richardson, T., *The Arcadian Friends: Inventing the English Landscape Garden*, London 2007
Ritchie, W., *Sculpture in Brick and other Materials*, Kenilworth 1978
Rogan, J. (ed.), *Bristol Cathedral, History and Architecture*, Stroud 2000
Rolt, L.T.C., *Isambard Kingdom Brunel*, Harmondsworth 1970 (1989)
Roper, I.M., *Monumental Effigies of Gloucestershire and Bristol*, Gloucester 1931
Roscoe, I., Hardy, E., and Sullivan, M.G., *A Biographical Dictionary of Sculptors in Britain 1660–1851*, New Haven, CT and London 2009
Roseveare, S., 'Sculpture in the high street', *Focus*, Whitsun 1983
Ross, J., *Cathedral Church of Bristol, Historical and Descriptive Handbook*, Gloucester 1935
Royal Academy Exhibitors, 1905–1970: A Dictionary of Artists and their Work in the Summer Exhibitions of the Royal Academy of Arts, Wakefield 1973–1982
Rudder, S., *A New History of Gloucestershire*, Cirencester 1779 (1977)
Russell, J.R., 'The "Great Court" at Kings

Weston', *Avon Gardens Trust Journal*, no. 2, Summer, 2007
—, *Three Garden Buildings by Thomas Wright in Stoke Park, Bristol: Excavation and Fieldwork 1987–88*, Bristol 1988
St Aubyn, G., *Queen Victoria: A Portrait*, London 1991
Sampson, W.A., *History of Queen Elizabeth's Hospital*, Bristol n.d.
Sansom, J. (ed.), *Public View: A Profile of the Royal West of England Academy*, Bristol 2002
Savage, R.J.G, 'Natural history of the Goldney Garden Grotto, Clifton, Bristol', *Journal of the Garden History Society*, vol. 17, no. 1 (n.d.)
Sen, A., 'Linking Bristol to Calcutta', *Nonesuch*, Spring 1998
Sherborne, J., 'William Canynges 1402–1474', BBHA no. 59, 1985
Shiercliff's Guide to Bristol and the Hotwells, Bristol 1793
Sloman, S., 'An eighteenth-century stonecarver's diary identified: eight months in the life of Thomas Parsons (1744–1813) of Bath', *British Art Journal*, vol. VII, no. 3, Winter 2006–7
Smith, M.Q., *The Harrowing of Hell Relief in Bristol Cathedral, TBGAS*, vol. 94, 1976 [Q article?]
—, *St Mary Redcliffe, An Architectural History*, Bristol 1995
Smith, N., 'Great Nassau's image, Royal George's test', *Georgian Group Journal*, vol. 6, 1996
Snodin, M., (ed.) (exhib.cat.), *Rococo: Art and Design in Hogarth's England*, London 1984
Somerville, J., *Thomas: Soapmaker of Bristol*, Bristol 1991
Southey, C.C., *The Life and Correspondence of Robert Southey*, London 1849–51, 6 vols
Southey, R., *Letters from England, 1807*, Sutton, A. (ed.), Bristol 1984
Stembridge, P.K., *Goldney, A House and a Family*, Bristol 1969
—, *Thomas Goldney's Garden: The Creation of an Eighteenth Century Garden*, Clifton 1996
Sterne, L., *A Sentimental Journey*, London 1768
Stocker, M., *Royalist and Realist: The Life and Work of Sir Joseph Edgar Boehm*, New York 1988
Stoddard, S., *Mr Braikenridge's Brislington*, Bristol 1981
—, 'George Weare Braikenridge 1775–1856: a Bristol antiquarian and his collection', M.Litt. thesis, University of Bristol, 1983
—, *City Impressions: Bristol Etchers 1910–1935*, Bristol 1990
—, *Bristol Before the Camera: The City in 1820–30: Watercolours and Drawings from the Braikenridge Collection*, Bristol 2001
—, 'The Sharples Family', in Sansom, John (ed.), *Public View* (1982).
Stone, G.F., *Bristol: As It Was and As It Is – A Record of Fifty Years of Progress*, Bristol 1909
Stonebridge, E., *Bristol: Heritage in Stone*, Bristol n.d.
Strachan, W.J., *Open Air Sculpture in Britain*, London 1984
Stuart Gray, A., *Edwardian Architecture: A Biographical Dictionary*, London 1985
Summers, J., *Remembered: The History of the Commonwealth War Graves Commission*, London and New York 2007
Swengley, N., 'Castle Park', *Crafts Magazine*, November/December 1993
Taylor, J., *A Book about Bristol, Historical, Ecclesiastical, and Biographical*, Bristol 1872
Temple, W., *Life of Bishop Percival*, London 1921
Thirsk, J., *Alternative Agriculture: A History from the Black Death to the Present Day*, Oxford 1997
Thomas, E., *Shirehampton Story*, Avonmouth 1983
Thomas, H., *The History of the Atlantic Slave Trade 1440–1870*, New York 1997
Thomas, L., 'The Angel Fountain', in *Bristol Templar: Bristol Past Revisited*, Bristol 1990
Thomas, P., *A History of Redland Park Church*, Bristol n.d.
Thrush, A., *Whitson, John, ODNB*
Turner, G., *The New Bath Guide by Christopher Anstey: An Introduction with Notes on the Text*, [Bath] 1994
Turner, K., 'Dr Viper's Monkey: Philip Thicknesse and the "Chatterton Monument"', in Heys(ed.), *From Gothic to Romantic: Thomas Chatterton's Bristol*
Turner, M., and Vaisey, D., *Art for Commerce: Illustrations and Designs in Stock at E.S.&A. Robinson, Printers*, Menston 1973
Underdown, P.T., *Bristol and Burke*, BBHA no. 2, 1961
Usherwood, N., *McMillan, William, ODNB*
Vickers, J.A., *Charles Wesley*, Peterborough 1990
Waite, C., *The Story of the Bristol Savages*, Bristol 1971
Wakefield, G.S., *John Wesley*, Peterborough 1990 (c.2003)
Wakelin, P., *Harford Family, ODNB*
Walpole, H., *Anecdotes of Painting in England*, 3 vols, London n.d.
Walton, K.M., *75 Years of Bristol Art Gallery*, Bristol 1980
—, *The Red Lodge*, Bristol 1986
Ward Jackson, P., *Public Sculpture of the City of London*, Liverpool 2003
—, *Monti, Raffaelle, ODNB*
Warin, R. and A., *Portrait of a Zoo: Bristol Zoological Gardens 1835–1985*, Bristol 1985
Warren, R.H., 'The medieval chapels of Bristol', *TBGAS*, vol. 30, 1907
Watson, S., *Secret Underground Bristol*, Bristol 1991
Weare, G.E., *Edmund Burke's Connection with Bristol, from 1774 till 1780*, Bristol 1894
Webb, M.I., *Michael Rysbrack, Sculptor*, London 1954
Weeden, C., 'The Ricketts family and the Phoenix Glasshouse, Bristol', *Glass Circle*, no. 4, 1982
Wells, C., *Grouse: The Savages' Journal*, 1929
Wheeler, C., *High Relief: The Autobiography of Sir Charles Wheeler, Sculptor*, Feltham 1968
Who Was Who, a Companion to Who's Who,

1916–1928, ed. G. Blakemore Evans, London 1934
Whinney, M., *Sculpture in Britain 1530–1830*, Harmondsworth, 1964; revised by J. Physick, London 1988
White, A., 'Biographical dictionary of London tomb sculptors, c.1560–1660', *Walpole Society*, vol. LXI, 1999
White, G., *Tramlines to the Stars: George White of Bristol*, Bristol 1995
Whittingham, S., *Wills Memorial Building*, Bristol 2003
—, *Sir George Herbert Oatley: Architect of Bristol*, Bristol 2009
Wilkins, H.J., *Edward Colston (1636–1721): A Chronological Account of his Life and Work Together with an Account of the Colston Societies and Memorials in Bristol*, Bristol 1920
Williams, M.E., *Civic Treasures of Bristol*, Bristol 1984
Wilson, C., 'The Medieval monuments', in Collinson et al. (eds), *A History of Canterbury Cathedral*
Wilson, J., 'The memorial by Nicholas Stone to Sir Thomas Bodley', *Church Monuments*, vol. VIII, 1993
Wilson, J., 'Ethics girls: the personification of moral systems on Early Modern English monuments', *Church Monuments*, vol. XIII, 1998
Winterbottom, D., *John Percival:The Great Educator*, BBHA no. 81, 1993
Winstone, J., *Bristol Trade Cards: Remnants of Prolific Commerce*, Bristol c.1993
Winstone, R., *Bristol in the 1940s*, Bristol 1961 (1970)
—, *Bristol Today*, Bristol 1963
—, *Bristol As It Was 1953–1956*, Bristol 1969 (1979)
—, *Bristol 1950–1953*, Bristol 1964 (1970)
—, *Bristol As It Was 1913–1921*, Bristol 1976
—, *Bristol in the 1880s*, Bristol 1962 (1978)
—, *Bristol in the 1850s*, Bristol 1968 (1978)
—, *Bristol in the 1920s*, Bristol 1971
—, *Bristol As It Was 1928–1933*, Bristol 1979
—, *Bristol As It Was 1950–53*, Bristol 1980
—, *Bristol As It Was, 1960–62*, Bristol 1981
—, *Bristol's Suburbs Long Ago*, Bristol 1985
—, *Bristol As It Was, 1937–1939*, Bristol 1987
Witt, C., Weedon, C., and Schwind, A.P., *Bristol Glass*, Bristol 1984
Wood, J., *A Description of the Exchange of Bristol*, Bath 1743 (1745) (facsimile, Bath 1969)
Wordsworth, W., *Poems in Two Volumes*, London 1807
Works of Horace Walpole, Earl of Oxford, ed. R. Walpole and M. Berry, 5 vols., London 1798
Wraxall, N.W., *Historical Memoirs of My Own Time*, London 1904
Wright, E., *Masterpieces of Foreign Literature Comprising Schiller's Tragedies, tr. S.T. Coleridge; Goethe's Faust; La Fontaine's Fables; Picciola by Saintine*, London 1866
Wright, S., *White, Thomas (1550–1624), ODNB*

Brochures, Leaflets and Ephemera

Anon., *David McFall Sculpture*, typescript of 1950s sculpture, PMSA (Bristol) to be deposited with BRO
Anon., description of the mural panels at Broad Quay House (BRL)
Arnolfini, 'Peter Randall-Page: sculpture & drawings 1980–1992', September 1992
Avon Report, October 1984
BCC, *The Council House Bristol*, 20 February 1930
BCC, *The Council House Bristol 1956*, 1956
BCC, *Castle Park: Public Art Programme*, c.1993
BCC, *Creative Bristol, A Sketchpad*, 2005
BCC Engineers' Department, *Memorials, Fountains and Statues*, December 1982
BCC and English Heritage, 'Aspects of the Square', *Queen Square*, 1996
Beaux Arts Gallery, *J. Havard Thomas (1854–21), Commemorative Exhibition of Sculpture and Drawings* (exhib. cat.), London 1936
Blaise Castle Estate, *Newsletter*, no. 4, 2005
Blake, N., *Sculpture by Naomi Blake*, 9 July 1981
BMAG, *Slave Trade Trail Around Central Bristol*, c.2007
Bristol Magpies, *Newsletter*, T. Bradshaw, no. 97, Oct./Nov. 1993
Bristol Naturalists' Society, *Proceedings*, 4th Series, vol. III, 1914
Bristol Trade and Industry, '"Same day" unveilings for two Brunel statues', no. 2, June 1982
Bristol and West Building Society, *Isambard Kingdom Brunel at Broad Quay and Paddington*, 1982
Bristol Zoo Book and Official Guide, 1948
Co-operative Group, Manchester, *The CWS in Bristol*, Manchester 1933
Crest Nicholson, *Harbourside's Hidden Gems: A Public Trail*, 1977
Haslemere Estates plc, 'Lewins Mead, office development prospectus', c.1984
Henry Moore Institute, *Newsletter*, no. 65, April/May, Leeds 2006
Jackson, T. and Greene, L., 'Castle Park, Bristol: a commission for Peter Randall-Page', press release, 1992
Kendall Kingscott Partnership, press release, c.1992
Lloyds Bank, *Dark Horse*, March 1957
Merchant Navy Association, Bristol branch, *An Appeal for a Memorial Garden in Bristol Docks*, Bristol 1998
Merchant Navy Association, Bristol branch, 'Potted history: Merchant Navy Association', typescript, 1998 (PMSA, Bristol, files to BRO)
National Cycle Network, *The Bristol & Bath Railway Path: Art and the Travelling Landscape*, pamphlet, c.2006
National Health Service Training Directorate, *History of St Bartholomew's Court*, c.1986
Naylor, A., 'Bridgehead Neptune', press release, 24 August 1983
Ordnance Survey Map Bristol (NW) and Clifton 1901, Alan Godfrey Maps,

Newcastle upon Tyne
Public Art South West, regional newsletter, autumn 2001
—, autumn, 2004
Royal Colonial Institute, Bristol branch, *Year Book 1914*, July 1915
Royal & Sun Alliance, *Phoenix and the Four Elements*, August 2002
RWA, *Friends Newsletter*, autumn 2000
St George's Brandon Hill, '*Girl into Reed*', press release, August 2004
Sneyd Park Residents' Association, *Sneyd Park: A Local Study and Guided Walk*, 2001
Statues, Monuments and Memorials in the Parks of the National Capital, Washington, DC, 1973
Stone, G.F., '"Bristol: As It Was and As It Is", reprinted, with additions from the Bristol Evening News 1908–1909', Bristol 1909
Stone Trades Journal, May 1903
Sustrans, information sheet, FF41
Temple Local History Group, *Newsletter*, no. 3, 1987
University of Bristol, *Convocation*, 1996
—, *Nipper*, press release, 22 January 2001
—, *Flat Out*, press release, 19 August 2004

Unpublished

Borg, J., 'Simon Short: a Seaman's Missionary', *Journal of the Bristol and Avon Family History Society*, no. 112, June 2003
Gomme, A., 'Bristol street index of buildings of architectural or historic interest', BCRL
Jenner, M., 'The George and Railway Hotel, Temple Gate Bristol', 1998, planning application 08/02566/F, 2008/9 (BRO)
Jones, D., 'The Elbridge, Woolnough, and Smyth families of Bristol in the eighteenth century, with special reference to the Spring Plantation, Jamaica', MA diss., University of Bristol, 1971; copy (BRO 34328(a))
Little, B., 'The story of the Victoria Rooms, 1836–1990', foreword to an unpublished paper in Bristol Central Library; BCL/L79.22/19
—, *Notes on the Victoria Rooms*, BCRL
Moore, G., lecture, Ian Hamilton Finlay's 80th birthday, Architecture Centre, Bristol, 28 October 2005
Naylor, A., 'Survey of Bristol's public monuments and fountains in bronze', unpublished, 1983 (BRO)
Price, A.N., 'Recollections of Alfred Newell Price', BCRL
Smith, R., 'Bristol Infirmary biographical memoirs', 3 vols, BRO
Stocker, M., 'Royalist and Realist: the life and work of Sir Joseph Edgar Boehm', PhD diss., University of Hull, 1986
Stoddard, S., 'George Weare Braikenridge 1775–1856: a Bristol antiquarian and his collection', MLitt thesis, University of Bristol, 1983
Whittingham, S., 'Sir George Herbert Oatley: a Nonconformist architect', PhD diss., University of Bristol, 2005

Newspaper, magazines and periodicals

Architects' Journal, 1 June 1933
Architectural Review, February 1959, p.192
Architectural Review, 'Sculpture in the city', April 1978, p.192
Art Journal, 1860, p.114
Art South West, 'Bristol's waterfront sculpture', September/October 1986
Bristol Evening Post, Candole, H.L., 'War memorial site approved', letter, 18 June 1930
—, 1 December 1930
—, 'Tens of thousands see Cenotaph unveiled', 27 June 1932
—, Lyne, R.F., 'How the Cenotaph came', 8 November 1946
—, 7 October 1950
—, 'Queen Victoria sets a problem', 11 October 1950
—, 25 October 1950
—, 'Statue is John Cabot', 29 August 1951
—, 'A Plimsoll memorial meeting of 1919', 14 November 1952
—, 'Bristol landmarks: 10', 3 July 1954
—, 'Thereby hangs a tale: the writer of 1,000 hymns', 22 July 1954
—, 'Will the council buy the rest of Somerset Square?', 29 March 1956
—, 30 October 1959
—, 'What is the fountain's history?', 24 April 1962
—, 'Hotwells statue is Bristol's mark for Sam Plimsoll', 12 May 1962
—, 'Bristol's bust of Plimsoll unveiled', 24 July 1962
—, Young, R.A., 'Oddity in the square', letter, 27 April 1962
—, 'A face-lift for the almshouses', 4 February 1964
—, Palmer, A., letter, 10 October 1964
—, Vinter, D., 15 October 1965
—, Morgan, Q., 'Cash in "forgotten fund" sleeps on', c.1966
—, 'Bust of Plimsoll to US', 10 September 1969
—, 3 November 1969
—, Buchanan, B., 'How Cabot got his tower', 6 September 1974
—, 30 January 1975
—, 'Mysterious memorial of a glass maker', 18 July 1975
—, 'Model statue for auction', 21 May 1977
—, 'Sculpture sceptics', 31 May 1977
—, 15 August 1980
—, Hendy, J., 'Statues are set to return', 19 September 1980
—, Belsey, J., 'Brunel shapes up for a late date in the city', 21 April 1981
—, Heelas, R., 'The Beau Brunels', 19 May 1982
—, Lee, R., letter, 10 March 1983
—, Lee, R., 'A spell of history', 15 March 1983
—, 'Two deaths at junction', 18 April 1984
—, 'Wraps come off', 22 September 1984
—, Winstone, R., letter, 24 April 1986
—, Harrison, D., 'Walter goes up the wall for his art', 31 May 1986
—, Morgan, Q., 'The whatsit on our wharf', 14 August 1986
—, Hendry, J., 'Vanishing Spirit', 16 September 1986
—, 'Tide is turning for city statue', 16 April

1987
—, 22 November 1990
—, Moss, V., 'Sculpture showpiece for park revamp', 5 September 1992
—, 'That's cool! Fountain is on stream', 17 August 1993
—, 'High profile art makes a mark on city park', 26 October 1993
—, 'A great man is remembered', 21 November 1997
—, 9 October 1998
—, 26 January 1999, p.7
—, 'Art? We'll tear it down', 9 March 1999
—, 'Thieves have carried off Jasmin', 4 May 2000
—, 'Area open again for play', 9 June 2001
—, '£5000 facelift', 31 July 2001
—, Fells, M., 'The gift of water', 15 October 2002
—, Elkan, A., letter, 11 March 2004
—, Fells, M., 'Rooms at the heart of Bristol business', 6 April 2004
—, Dymond, M., letter, 15 June 2004
—, Barrow, S., 26 October 2004
—, 'Statue of the week', 29 March 2005
—, 31 May 2005
—, 26 April 2008
—, 8 November 2008
—, 14 April 2009
Bristol Evening Times, 'City of Bristol War Memorial', 20 January 1931
Bristol Evening World, 11 October 1950
—, 'Taxi driver had a shock for the secret statue's sculptor', 31 August 1951
—, 'Queen Victoria is back in College Green', 17 March 1953
Bristol Gazette, 8 July 1843
Bristol Grammar School Chronicle, no. 7, vol. VII, December 1895
—, no. 8, vol. VII, March 1896
—, no 12, vol VII, July 1897
Bristol Magazine, August 2008
Bristol Mercury, 8 January 1810
—, 10 July 1843
Bristol Mercury and Daily Post, 'Colston Anniversary', 14 November 1895
Bristol Mirror, 28 April 1810
Bristol News, 'Millennium hat-trick', no. 32, July 1999
—, no. 48, spring 2004
Bristol Observer, 17 April 1897
—, 'Sculpture nearly finished', 15 October 1993
—, Pascoe, M., 'The grand old lady of a bygone age', 26 January 1996
Bristol Times and Mirror, 19 Nov 1859
—, Thomas Proctor obituary, 16 May 1876
—, 'The royal visit to Bristol', 26 July 1888
—, 26 November 1888
—, 30 July 1903
—, 8 February 1904
—, 'The Gloucesters in South Africa: tributes to fallen heroes', 6 March 1905
—, 'Bristol's memorial to King Edward', 5 October 1910
—, Helps, B., 11 June 1925
—, 'Funeral of Miss Emma Saunders', 3 March 1927
—, 2 July 1928
—, Earl Haig memorial, 27 June 1932
Bristol Weekly Intelligencer, 11 November 1749
Bristol and West Country Illustrated, May 1980
Builder, 15 December 1849, p.596
—, 1 July 1857, p.261
—, 19 December 1857, p.593
—, 27 December 1851, p.816
—, 15 May 1858, p.337
—, 6 August 1864, p.583
—, 8 June 1867, p.445
—, 19 October 1867, p.757
—, 4 June 1870
—, 3 August 1872, p.604
—, 24 August 1872
—, 2 May 1874
—, 22 May1886, p.762
—, 23 November 1895, p.385
—, 6 October 1898, p.308
—, 5 March 1904
—, 15 April 1905, p.410
—, 13 January 1911, p.44ff
—, 13 October 1911
—, 10 March 1916, p.2
—, 19 June 1931, pps 1092, 1100
—, 25 October 1933, pps 721, 734
—, October 1951, pps 482–6
Cliftonian, March 1903
—, June 1904
—, June 1904, p.194
—, June 1905
—, June 1922
—, July 1932, p.307
—, July 1932, p.310
Clifton Magazine, 2007
Country Life, Lavery Crook, J., letter 25 July 1963
Daily Express, 7 October 1950
—, 'Why do we let this man cast a shadow over our war dead?', 6 November 1998
Estates Times, 13 February 1975
Felix Farley's Bristol Journal, 18 July 1807
—, 28 April 1810
Financial Times, Richardson, T., 'Political hotbeds', 23 June 2007
General Evening Post, 8 July 1735
Gentleman's Magazine, S. Urban, Sir Charles Wetherell obituary, vol. XXVI, October 1846, pp. 426–30
—, John Ruskin to Dr Acland, letter, 1858, p.53
—, June 1858, p.650
—, 31 August 1716
—, 4 November 1727
—, 6 April 1733, no. 113
—, 3 November 1825
—, 3 May 1826
Gloucestershire and Avon Life, Little, B., and Johns, M., 'So nearly a queen', May 1984
GWR Magazine, April 1927, p.148
Guardian, Gibbs, G., 15 March 1999
—, Paul Mount obituary, 12 February 2009
Independent, Paul Mount obituary, 16 January 2009
Illustrated Bristol News, K. Flower, August 1971
Illustrated London News, vol. XXV, no. 703, 23 September 1854
Nonesuch, letters, University of Bristol, winter 2002
Railway Magazine, vol. 33, 1913, p.534
—, December 1985, p.590

Redland Park Recorder, vol. III, no.10, October 1903
—, 'Bristol civic memorial to the late Rev. Urijah Rees Thomas', vol. IV, no 1, 1 February 1904
Rolls-Royce Journal, no. 2, 1969
Rumsey Record, September 1957
Sarah Farley's Bristol Journal, 22 December 1787
Shipshape, 'Tideway topics', vol. 18, 1969–70
Spectator, Mark Steyn, 1 September 2001, p.43
The Times, 14 November 1895, p.10
—, 5 July 1913, p.8
—, 'Haig Memorial at Clifton', 27 June 1932
—, 'Indians asked for help to save hero's tomb', 24 November 1997
—, 7 July 2000, p.16
—, 11 August 2008, p.44
The Times Literary Supplement, Dorment, R., 'Mourning glories', 11 November 1988
Venue, 24 April–7 May 1987
—, 11–24 September 1987
West Country Life, Long, D., 18 May 1999
Western Daily Press, 'Lord Rosebery in Bristol', 31 October 1894
—, Simon Short obituary, 19 March 1901
—, 'Unveiling of memorial fountain', 15 September 1902
—, 15 November 1902
—, 'New Central & Reference Library, the sculptured panels', 21 December 1905
—, 'Scenes on Bristol Quay 60 years ago', 19 October 1925
—, 'Mr Plimsoll and Bristol', 14 February 1928
—, 'Cross heads', 14 to 22 August 1929
—, 'The Plimsoll memorial', 22 August 1929
—, 18 September 1929
—, 12 March 1930
—, 13 March 1930
—, 27 June 1932, p.8
—, 'Bust of Plimsoll', 3 July 1939
—, 7 October 1950
—, 11 October 1950
—, 28 August 1951
—, 'Statue is Cabot – sculptor says so', 29 August 1951
—, '£400 starts row over a fountain', 8 May 1962
—, 12 August 1980
—, 13 August 1980
—, 29 October 1980
—, 'Artist survived death camp', 15 December 1980
—, 'Why poor old Neptune is cracking up', 12 January 1982
—, 'Harbour sculpture is all shipshape', 5 December 1991
—, 21 November 1997

Media sources

Alfred Fagon, HTV documentary, 1987
Price, D., Rieser, M. and Swingler, S., *Castle Park: Public Art in Practice*, CD, University of the West of England, Faculty of Art, Media and Design, March 1996

Electronic sources

www.at-Bristol.org.uk/open/Aquarena.htm
www.at-
www.bristol.org.uk/open/everything.htm
www.bristolcharities.co.uk/history_almshouses_barstaple.asp
www.britishpubguide.com/cgi-bin/pubsearch.cgi?results:Bristol:353
www.cityofsydney.nsw.gov.au/waterexhibition/DrinkingPlaces/CastIronDrinkingFountains.html
www.countryside.gov.uk/LAR/Recreation/DG/casestudies
www.elpihv.co.uk/work/commissions/life-cycle
www.flowerseast.com/FE/Artists_Originals.asp?Artist=HICKS
www.jacksonharris.co.uk
www.neighbourhoodpolicing.co.uk/faq.asp
www.news.oneindia.in/2007/06/12
www.oldindia.co.uk
www.perkins-smart.com/burmacampaignsociety/archive/news_pdf/2003Mar.pdf
www.publicartonline.org.uk
www.publicartonline.org.uk/current/collaboration/craft.html
www.publicartonline.org.uk/current/collaboration/collaboration_architect.html
www.publicartonline.org.uk/archive/casestudies/atbristol/description.php
www.publicartonline.org.uk/archive/casestudies/brch/index.php
www.redlandparkchurch.co.uk
www.stpaulsunlimited.org.uk/taskgroups/documents/Minutes_April-07.doc
www.scottisharchitects.org.uk/architect_list.php?alpha=b
www.simonthomas-sculpture.com/research_misc_stretching.php
www.stridetreglown.co.uk/index.php?option=com_content&task=view&id=504&Itemid=233&limit=1&limitstart=1
www.sustrans.org
www.sustrans.org.uk/, Art and the Travelling Landscape 2007/8
www.trinitybris.ac.uk/index.php?id=121www.visiteastside.co.uk/walk/download_mp3s.html
www.ukniwm.org.uk
www.visitchurches.org.uk/content.php?nID=11&churchID=32
www.walterjack.co.uk
www.walterjack.co.uk/Projects/P7

Archives, databases, collections and surveys

Bodleian Library, Oxford
Ms Gough, Somerset

Bristol Central Reference Library, College Green
Local sculpture files, including:
Bristol Evening Post, letters, 'Why put a statue to a Hindu there … put Muller there', and 'What has Roy ever done for Bristol', undated cuttings, 1997; and Apperley, F., letter, undated cutting, 1983
Press cuttings files arranged by building, street, subject, etc.
Braikenridge Collection: originals in boxes, also

on microfilm (index available)
BCRL 24411 (BL2H) William Tyson, unnumbered ms papers: 'Notes on Bristol Bells' etc.
BCRLLC, Barney Price, postscript grandfather's recollections
BCRL B4398 *Minute Book of Cabot Celebration Committee*, W336, restricted access.
BCRL B8766-9 (1722, 1734, 1739), B8772 (1774), B10980 (1781) Bristol Poll Books
BCRL B10124, 'Milton's Drawings and Engravings', SR31, restricted access
BCRL, Gomme, A., 'Bristol street index of buildings of architectural or historic interest', unpublished, n.d., B29647, typescript
BCRL, copies of Mr Colston's settlements, 1718 (B24663) or 1839 (B11668)
BCRL, B3339 Jubilee Convalescent Home, opening ceremony programme, 15 November 1899
BCRL B34339, Bristol Ward Lists 1898–1944, typescript of councillors, mayors, sheriffs etc

Bristol's Museums, Galleries and Archives, Queen's Road, BS8
Blaise Castle Museum: trade cards
Department of Fine Art files: Blaise urns, Quarter Jacks, Malone, K.
General Register
Historical files, no.2554 (Plimsoll)
Local Artist Index
Conservation files
Correspondence
Braikenridge Collection
Topographical paintings, drawings, and prints
Sculpture, portrait busts, models etc

Bristol Record Office, 'B' Bond Warehouse, Smeaton Road
Arnolfini Archives
Municipal Buildings Committee, Minute no. 38, 16 November 1950
Municipal Buildings Committee, Minute no. 52, 18 October 1951
BCC Minutes, 'Bronze unicorns', 24 October 1950
BCC, Minute 101 'Cabot (sic) statue', 15 January 1953
BCC, 17 January 1953
BCC, Minute 90, 17 March 1955
BCC, Finance and Property Services subcommittee, 9 November 1999, no. 18

Reports
BCC Engineers' Department, 'Memorials, fountains, and statues', December 1982
BCC, *City Planning Officer's Report*, 24 March 1987
BCC, Leisure Services Committee, Randall-Page, P., 'Castle Park Project: a strategy for arts and crafts', July 1990
BCC, Director of Leisure Services, 'Public Art Development Plan', October 1995
BCC, Planning Department, Clivedon Conservation Workshop Ltd, Report [Plimsoll], November 2005
BCC, Bristol Creative Neighbourhoods; Neighbourhood Arts Strategy, 2005

Avon Report, October 1984
City Centre Promenade Harbourside, Bristol Merchant Navy Association (Bristol) Memorial Project, Concept Planning Group, April 1998
St Mary Redcliffe Conservation Plan, 2006

Bristol Corporation of the Poor
Bristol Institution, book of letters from honorary members
Bristol Institution, proceedings of the subcommittee for the regulation of the exhibition rooms, 31 August 1825
Bristol Institution, special subcommittee book, 1824–1826
Bristol Institution, 'Committee Book for General Purposes', 1822–27
Merchants' Hall, 'Books of Proceedings: Book 4' (microfilm)
Newspapers: *Bristol Evening Post, Western Daily Press*
Bristol General Cemetery Company Records, 'Register of Burials'
BRO/071199
BRO 01125, Exchange
BRO 02179(1–5)
BRO 02919, *Gloucestershire Regimental Memorial*, Queen's Road, 1904–1911; correspondence
BRO 03801
BRO 03919, *King Edward VII Memorial*, Queen's Road; correspondence
BRO 04221, 1/C30, Exchange
BRO 04312(29), two drawings by Gough
BRO 04223, Exchange
BRO 08767
BRO 28049 (102a–f), Bristol High Cross
BRO 30631 (14 a–b)
BRO 33746, *Vanburgh Album*, vol. 131, 1996
BRO 34328(a), Jones, D., 'Elbridge, Woolnough, and Smyth families of Bristol…', MA Diss., University of Bristol, 1971
BRO 35810/GW/S/1–11, relating to Stock Exchange, Corn Street
BRO 38544/1
BRO Common Council Proceedings (CCP) 1704-22
BRO CCP Voucher box 37/38
BRO CCP Voucher box 36, 1750
BRO CCP Voucher box 110
BRO AC/AS 70/2 87
BRO Audit 1733

BRO F/AC/Box/47/1 1739–1740, Bristol Corporation payments
BRO AC/WO/10(14) a–d
BRO Audits 04026 (99), no. 22 and no. 82
City of Bristol, 'Abstract of Accounts (1894–1895) General Disbursements'
BRO M/BCC/DOW/1/1 Downs Committee Minute Book
BRO/CA27, St Paul's Fair, parish records, Temple District
BRO StJ, Parish Accounts 1710–1752
BRO P/StJ/V/4, December 29 1746.
BRO P/StJ/ChW/Ic), Accounts

BRO P/St JB, Vestry Minutes 1676–1726
St John's Parish Accounts 1710–1752
BRO P/AS/ChW/3(b), Vestry Committee of All Saints
BRO P/RG/R/3b, 18 October 1754

BRO: Building plans etc.
BRO John Foster and John Wood, Elevation for Foster's Almshouse, Colston Street
BRO, scale drawing by F.E.L. Harris, 1902
BRO Vol. III, f.27–8, plans and the façade elevation by A.W. Roques and Giles Gilbert Scott
BRO, documents relating to Wills Memorial Building, Queen's Road, 1915–1925
BRO, vol. 140, folio 34, plans for 55 St Stephen's Street
BRO Drawing 1477/57, April 1950, Chantry Court, Denmark Street
BRO III/68 typescript, Tolzey inscriptions
BRO, Childs and Sulzmann, Architects, proposal, Public Art at Building 12a
BCC, Blaise Castle Dairy Garden design brief, August 2002

PMSA (Bristol) to be deposited with BRO
Photographs
Acanthus Ferguson Mann Architects, correspondence, 2001
Alec French Partnership, correspondence and notes
Christopher, Ann, notes, July 1996
Contractor, Carla, correspondence and notes, 1998
Doubleday, John, and Briscoe, Graham, correspondence, 2001–2
Greed, Geoffrey, correspondence, 2009
Greene, Lesley, List of proposed commissions/sites of Castle Park, 20 November 1991
Huggins, John, correspondence, 2008
Joyce, Stephen, notes, 2003
Milner, Peter, correspondence 2000–3
Mount, Paul, correspondence and interview, 2003
Newspaper cuttings, including *Bristol Evening Post*, Jenner, M., 'Works of art that reveal waste', undated cutting, inscribed '1985'
Public Art Development Trust, correspondence and papers relating to the Baltic Wharf Competition; artists' proposals. etc. (Cox, Smith, Woropay), 1983–6
Reeder, Garry, Senior Surveyor, Bristol City Council, correspondence, 1998–2000
Rice, Rene, correspondence
Smith, Andrew, notes, 2001
Threfall, Philippa, notes, December 1998

Bristol Urban Archaeological Database Monument Record
No. 517M

British Library
British Library, ADD. 38678, cat.no. 19-1911-1915, Riddell, R., collections concerning E.H.Baily RA

Courtauld Institute of Art, London
Conway Library Photographic Archive

English Heritage Bristol: Listed Buildings Database
PRN: 901-1/15/70, Central Reference Library
PRN: 901-1/15/72
PRN: 901-1/2/83, p.436
PRN: 901-1/11/86, Colston Hall
PRN: 901-1/34/1822, p.1527
PRN: 901-1/16/563, 36 Corn Street, p.472
PRN: 901-1/41/18, p.130
PRN: 901-1/56/428, Arnos Court
PRN: 901-1/9/957, Royal West of England Academy
PRN: 901-1/12/1659, Palace Hotel
PRN: 901-1/14/785, Goldney

Henry Moore Institute, Leeds
Belsky archive (2001.94)
Wood's Album of Monumental Masonry, HMI (Woo 13)

Lloyds Bank Group Archives

National Inventory of War Memorials
Bristol Memorial Project, April 1998, no. 7324

National Portrait Gallery, London
Alexander Bassano, Jubilee Cabinet Album (X8753)

National Register of Archives
Marquess of Linlithgow Archives, Hopetoun House, Edinburgh
NRA(S) 888 Bundle 630, estimate from John Nost I, 1709
Bundle 2694, contract 1718
Duke of Northumberland MS 121/177, Alnwick Castle, transcript supplied by Miss Stembridge [PMSA Bristol, deposit BRO]

National Trust
Blaise Hamlet files

New Room Library, The New Room, John Wesley's Chapel, 36 The Horsefair, Bristol
Correspondence between E.S. Lamplough and Sir George Oatley, 1930–8

Royal Academy of Arts, London
R.A. Library 8516/51A (Thomas Paty drawings)

University of Bristol Library Special Collections:
Paty Wood Collection, DM1874
Goldney family papers 1603-1933, DM1398, DM1466

William Andrews Clark Memorial Library, University of California, Los Angeles
Eric Gill papers, MS Gill (photocopies, PMSA Bristol deposit BRO)

INDEX

Note: page numbers in **bold** represent photographs.